DIAGNOSIS OF DISEASES OF THE CHEST

An Integrated Study Based on the
Abnormal Roentgenogram

VOLUME I

ROBERT G. FRASER, M.D., F.R.C.P. (C)

Professor of Diagnostic Radiology,
McGill University, and
Diagnostic Radiologist-in-Chief,
Royal Victoria Hospital, Montreal

J. A. PETER PARÉ, M.D.

Associate Professor of Medicine,
McGill University,
Joint Cardiorespiratory Service,
Royal Victoria Hospital, Montreal

W. B. SAUNDERS COMPANY

Philadelphia   London   Toronto

W. B. Saunders Company: West Washington Square
Philadelphia, Pa. 19105

12 Dyott Street
London, WC1A   1DB

833 Oxford Street
Toronto 18, Ontario

Diagnosis of Diseases of the Chest

ISBN 0-7216-3850-3

Print No.:   9   8   7   6

*This book is dedicated
to the memory of*

DR. FELIX G. FLEISCHNER

Pioneer, Inspired Teacher,
Dedicated Physician and Radiologist,
A Humble and Compassionate Human Being

PREFACE

This book was written with the aim of defining an approach to the diagnosis of diseases of the chest based on the abnormal roentgenogram. Experience over the years has led the authors to the conclusion that the chest roentgenogram represents the focal point or sheet anchor in the diagnosis of the majority of pulmonary diseases, many patients presenting with either no symptoms and signs or entirely nonspecific ones. This emphasis on the roentgenogram as the first step in reaching a diagnosis does not represent an attempt to relegate history and physical examination to a position of no importance, but merely to place them in proper perspective. In no other medical field is diagnosis so dependent upon the intelligent integration of information from roentgenologic, clinical, laboratory, and pathologic sources as in diseases of the chest. We submit that the roentgenogram is the starting point in this investigation; the knowledge of structural change thus obtained, when integrated with pertinent clinical findings and results of pulmonary function tests and other ancillary diagnostic procedures, enables one to arrive at a confident diagnosis. Some patients manifest symptoms and signs that themselves are virtually diagnostic of some chest disorders, but even in such cases the confirmation of diagnosis requires the presence of an appropriate roentgenographic pattern.

A glance through the pages will reveal an abundance of roentgenographic illustrations that might create the illusion that this book is written primarily for the roentgenologist, but this is not our intention. In fact, the clinical, morphologic, and laboratory aspects of many diseases are described at greater length than the roentgenologic, a fact that points up the broad interest we hope the book will engender among internists, surgeons, and family practitioners interested in chest disease. The numerous illustrations reflect the aim of the book—to emphasize the value of the roentgenogram as the *first* rather than the *major* step in diagnosis.

During the writing of the book, our original plan was considerably modified as the format unfolded and we became even more aware of the complexities of design and organization. Originally, our approach to differential diagnosis suggested a division of chapters on the basis of specific roentgenographic patterns. It soon became apparent, however, that since many diseases give rise to various different roentgenographic patterns, this method of presentation would require tedious repetition of clinical and laboratory details in several chapters. To obviate this, we planned tables of differential diagnosis, listing etiologic classifications of diseases which produce specific roentgenographic patterns and describing briefly the clinical and laboratory characteristics of each disease, thus facilitating recognition of disease states.

v

The tables are designed to be used with the text in the following manner. When a specific pattern of disease is recognized, the appropriate table should be scanned and those conditions selected which correspond most closely with the clinical picture presented by the patient. Additional information about the likeliest diagnostic possibilities can be obtained by referring to the detailed discussions in the relevant sections of the text (page numbers are cited after each diagnosis). The tables relate to 17 basic patterns of broncho-pulmonary, pleural, and mediastinal disease; they are grouped together in Chapter Five in Volume I and may be located with ease from the black marks which stain the upper corners of their pages. Each table is preceded by a detailed description and representative illustrations of the specific roentgeno-graphic pattern. An attempt has been made to indicate the relative incidence of the diseases.

Although our original plan called for a one volume presentation, it soon became apparent that the length of the text and the number and size of illus-trations necessary for full coverage of the subject required two volumes. Volume I includes descriptions of the normal chest, methods and techniques of investigation, clinical features, and roentgenologic signs of chest diseases, the tables of differential diagnosis, and chapters devoted to diseases of develop-mental origin and the infectious diseases; in Volume II appear detailed dis-cussions of the morphologic, roentgenologic, and clinical aspects of all other diseases of the thorax arranged in chapters according to etiology.

The roentgenograms have been reproduced by two different techniques, the majority in Volume I by the logEtronic method and those in Volume II by direct photography. The publishers have been generous in allotting sufficient space for the reproduction of the roentgenograms in a size adequate for good detail recognition.

Much of the material in the book has been based on our personal experi-ence gained during the past almost two decades we have had a predominant interest in pulmonary disease. Obviously, this experience has been greatly enhanced by the extensive literature that has accumulated during these years, and we are mindful of the tremendous help we have received from the con-tributions of others. Our free use of the literature is reflected in the extensive bibliography.

Certain differences from the contents of other books on respiratory dis-ease will be noted. First, this text contains no reference to treatment: since drug therapies and surgical techniques are constantly changing, any attempt to include them would make the book out of date almost before it was published. Second, we have intentionally made only passing reference to pulmonary disease peculiar to children, a full description of which would require a complete separate text.

The relative incidence of respiratory diseases has changed considerably over the last quarter century. In some, such as tuberculosis and bron-chiectasis, a decreased frequency reflects improved public health measures and therapeutic innovations; in others, man's therapeutic triumphs have proved a mixed blessing, enabling patients with disabling chronic respiratory disease to live longer despite formerly fatal pneumonias. Perhaps even more important, man himself is responsible for varying the spectrum of respiratory disease as a result of his irresponsible insistence upon increasing the amount and variety of atmospheric pollutants. Inhaled contaminated air not only is regarded as the major etiologic factor in chronic obstructive pulmonary dis-ease and the inorganic-dust pneumoconioses but also has been incriminated in the etiology of several hypersensitivity diseases of the lungs. This last group comprises the "extrinsic" form of allergic alveolitis, and the number of conditions involved, when added to the better-known "intrinsic" counterpart —the collagen diseases—is largely responsible for the length of the chapter devoted to immunologic diseases. Other changes that have contributed to the "new face" of pulmonary disease include increasing knowledge of the hormonal effects of neoplasms, the discovery that various immunologic defects may reduce host resistance to infection, and finally the appearance in the Western world of parasitic infestations and bacterial infections formerly considered so rare in those areas as to warrant little consideration in differential diagnosis but now of some importance because of the modern-day ease of intercontinental travel. Although the novelty of these recent changes may have led the authors to consider them in greater detail and length than is their due, the emphasis may serve to bring them into proper perspective.

Finally, we recognize our fallibility. It is inevitable that some observations in a text of this magnitude will prove erroneous in time or will find disagreement among our knowledgeable readers. This we expect and accept. We sincerely hope that such differences of opinion will be made known to us, so that they may be weighed and, where appropriate, introduced into subsequent editions or revisions. It is only through such interchange of information and opinion that we can hope to establish on a firm basis the knowledge necessary to a full understanding of respiratory disease.

R. G. F.

J. A. P. P.

ACKNOWLEDGMENTS

It is difficult, even in retrospect, to appreciate the complexities involved in the production of a book of this magnitude. Although the writing of manuscript and the choice and preparation of illustrations proved the most formidable part of the undertaking, the many steps necessary to the final product required the unselfish and enthusiastic contributions of many hands and minds, and the support and encouragement we received from many of our friends who urged us forward in our task is greatly appreciated. To acknowledge all separately would make tedious reading, and therefore we say "Thank you" to everyone who helped us and restrict individual acknowledgment to those who have contributed time and effort.

It is not possible to overstate our gratitude to our secretaries, Miss Coni Reed and Miss Elizabeth McKee, who handled magnificently the tedious and necessarily precise task of transcribing manuscript from tape, typed the several drafts up to and including final manuscript, and cheerfully coped with all of the innumerable problems encountered. Their patience and devotion in accomplishing this thorny chore has been exemplary. During the final period their task was somewhat lightened by the able assistance of Mrs. Jean Riti and Miss Madeleine Miller, who also maintained the same cheerful acceptance of heavy workloads.

At the inception of the book, Miss Ursula Matthews accepted the awesome task of editing manuscript, and we are deeply grateful to her for seeing the job through to completion, despite a move to another city before the book was finished. She reduced the literary ineptness of the authors to a minimum without altering the meaning of the written word, and we are most grateful for her talent. The tedious job of recording, filing, checking, and final validation of the almost 4500 references was carried out with meticulous accuracy by Miss Catherine Mayhew and Mr. Richard Fraser, often in extremely frustrating circumstances. The devotion and diligence with which they carried out this task is deeply appreciated.

Dr. W. M. Thurlbeck deserves special mention for his invaluable contributions, specifically the descriptions of morphology in Chapters 1 and 2 and the legends for the majority of the pathology illustrations throughout the book. In addition, he critically reviewed Chapters 8 and 12, and his many helpful suggestions resulted in modification of these and other sections. His substantial contributions are most gratefully acknowledged. Several of our medical colleagues were kind enough to review sections of the manuscript and to offer advice for their improvement. Special thanks are due to Drs. Peter Macklem, John Henderson, and Margot Becklake for their valued counsel and discerning criticism.

The majority of case histories and roentgenograms reproduced here are of patients of members of the Attending Staff of the Royal Victoria Hospital. Our indebtedness to these friends and colleagues cannot be overemphasized, not only for their generosity in permitting us to publish these case reports but also for the benefit of their experience and guidance over the years. We wish to acknowledge particularly the assistance given by certain physicians who devoted time and effort to providing roentgenograms and case reports: Dr. George Genereux of the University of Saskatchewan, Saskatoon; Dr. David Berger and Dr. D. D. Munro of the Royal Edward Chest Hospital, Montreal; and Drs. J. F. Meakins, R. E. Donevan, and R. E. Dollfuss of the Royal Victoria Hospital.

During the period of writing, it was inevitable that the time expended by the authors on teaching and clinical responsibilities within the Departments of Diagnostic Radiology and Medicine was reduced significantly. These additional responsibilities were added to the already overburdened shoulders of our colleagues in these two Departments, who accepted them without objection. Their contributions to the book, although indirect, are sincerely appreciated.

The superb art work throughout these volumes was the accomplishment of J. Gebhardt Smith, medical artist of the Royal Victoria Hospital, whose craftsmanship and rich experience in medical illustration is readily apparent in these pages. We are indebted to her for the expertise with which she culled from our vague descriptions the true sense of what we wished to depict. The majority of the diagrams were charted by Mr. Lionel Bartlett, chief respiratory technician of the Royal Victoria Hospital, with his usual excellent draftsmanship.

We are indebted to Dr. J. Gilbert Turner, former Executive Director of the Royal Victoria Hospital, for arranging financial assistance, particularly toward the cost of illustrations. And, throughout, we have received tremendous support and cooperation from the publishers, notably Mr. John Dusseau, Mr. Michael Jackson, and Mr. Sam Mink, who effectively and sympathetically minimized the many obstacles we encountered.

Finally, and with immense gratitude, we recall the patience and understanding displayed by our wives and children throughout our labors. Without their continuous encouragement, this book surely would not have been completed, and we acknowledge their many virtues with much love.

R.G.F.

J. A. P. P.

CONTENTS

VOLUME I

1

THE NORMAL CHEST 1

Introduction.. 1
The Lung Unit.. 2
The Airways and Pulmonary Ventilation 8
The Pulmonary Vascular System 36
Development of the Lung 58
The Nervous System.. 58
The Pleura 59
The Lymphatic System 66
The Mediastinum... 72
The Diaphragm.. 80
The Chest Wall.. 82
The Normal Chest Roentgenogram.. 85
Perception in Chest Roentgenology....................................... 99

2

METHODS OF ROENTGENOLOGIC AND PATHOLOGIC INVESTIGATION..... 103

Roentgenologic Examination 104
Method for Pathologic Examination....................................... 134

3

METHODS IN CLINICAL, LABORATORY, AND FUNCTIONAL
INVESTIGATION 139

Clinical History 140
Physical Examination.. 148
Special Diagnostic Procedures 156

4

ROENTGENOLOGIC SIGNS IN THE DIAGNOSIS OF CHEST DISEASE......... 187

Diseases of the Lung Which Cause an Increase in
    Roentgenographic Density 189
Diseases of the Lung Which Cause a Decrease in
    Roentgenographic Density.. 315
Roentgenologic Signs of Diseases of the Pleura 341

5

TABLES OF DIFFERENTIAL DIAGNOSIS 377

General Comments 377
How to Use the Tables 378
Table 5-1. Homogeneous Shadows Without Recognizable
    Segmental Distribution 379
Table 5-2. Homogeneous Shadows of Recognizable Segmental
    Distribution 393
Table 5-3. Inhomogeneous Shadows Without Recognizable
    Segmental Distribution 407
Table 5-4. Inhomogeneous Shadows of Recognizable Segmental
    Distribution 413
Table 5-5. Cystic and Cavitary Disease 421
Table 5-6. Solitary Pulmonary Nodules Less Than 6 cm in
    Diameter ("Coin" Lesions) 435
Table 5-7. Solitary Pulmonary Masses 6 cm or More
    in Diameter 448
Table 5-8. Multiple Pulmonary Nodules, With or
    Without Cavitation 456
Table 5-9. Diffuse Pulmonary Disease With a Predominantly
    Acinar Pattern 465
Table 5-10. Diffuse Pulmonary Disease With a Predominantly
    Nodular, Reticular, or Reticulonodular Pattern 475
Table 5-11. Diffuse Pulmonary Disease With a Mixed Acinar
    and Reticulonodular Pattern 492
Table 5-12. Generalized Pulmonary Oligemia 499
Table 5-13. Unilateral, Lobar, or Segmental
    Pulmonary Oligemia 509
Table 5-14. Pleural Effusion Unassociated With Other
    Roentgenographic Evidence of Disease in the Thorax 518
Table 5-15. Pleural Effusion Associated With Other
    Roentgenographic Evidence of Disease in the Thorax 527
Table 5-16. Hilar and Mediastinal Lymph-node Enlargement 543
Table 5-17. Mediastinal Widening 555

6

PULMONARY ABNORMALITIES OF DEVELOPMENTAL ORIGIN 568

Agenesis, Aplasia, and Hypoplasia of the Lungs 568
Anomalies of the Pulmonary Vasculature 569
Bronchopulmonary Sequestration 577
Congenital Bronchial Cysts 581
Congenital Bronchial Atresia 583
Congenital Cystic Adenomatoid Malformation of the Lung 588

7

INFECTIOUS DISEASES OF THE LUNGS 589

Pneumonia Due to Gram-positive Aerobic Bacteria 592
Pneumonia Due to Gram-negative Aerobic Bacteria 600
Pneumonia Due to Anaerobic Organisms 611
Mycobacterial Infections of the Lungs 614
Mycobacterium Tuberculosis 614

Anonymous Mycobacteria... 640
Mycotic Infections of the Lung................................... 642
Infections of the Lungs Due to the Viruses, Mycoplasma
    Pneumoniae, and the Rickettsiae 674
Respiratory Syndromes... 675
Respiratory Infections Due to Viruses 681
Respiratory Infections Due to Rickettsiae 697
Renal-Transplantation Pneumonia 700
Parasitic Infestation of the Lung............................. 700
Protozoan Infestation 701
Metazoan Infestation.. 705

VOLUME II

8

NEOPLASTIC DISEASES OF THE LUNGS 723
    Benign Neoplasms... 723
    Malignant Neoplasms... 736
        Bronchogenic Carcinoma 736
        The Solitary Pulmonary Nodule....................... 765
        Bronchiolar (Alveolar-Cell) Carcinoma.............. 770
        Hodgkin's Disease 771
        The Lymphosarcoma Group 784
        Leukemia... 785
        Multiple Myeloma (Plasmacytoma)..................... 790
        Metastatic Neoplasms 792

9

EMBOLIC AND THROMBOTIC DISEASES OF THE LUNGS 804

10

PULMONARY HYPERTENSION AND PULMONARY DISEASE OF
CARDIAC ORIGIN 832
    Pulmonary Hypertension.................................... 832
    Pulmonary Edema.. 853

11

DISEASES OF ALTERED IMMUNOLOGIC ACTIVITY 866
    Collagen or Connective-tissue Diseases of the Lung ... 866
    Immunologic Deficiency Syndromes....................... 897

12

INHALATION DISEASES OF THE LUNG............................. 906
    Inhalation Diseases Due to Organic Dust (Organic-dust
        Pneumoconiosis) 907
    Inhalation Diseases Due to Inorganic Dust (Inorganic-dust
        Pneumoconiosis) 918

Inhalation Diseases Caused by Noxious Gases and
   Soluble Aerosols... 948
Inhalation Diseases Unrelated to Dusts or Fumes...................... 956

13

DISEASES OF THE AIRWAYS... 966

Asthma.. 969
Chronic Bronchitis 982
Pulmonary Emphysema 993
Clinical and Physiologic Manifestations of Chronic
   Bronchitis and Emphysema... 1015
Bullous Disease of the Lungs 1023
Local Emphysema.. 1032
Bronchiectasis... 1039
Other Forms of Obstructive Pulmonary Disease 1051

14

PLEUROPULMONARY DISEASE CAUSED BY EXTERNAL
PHYSICAL AGENTS 1068

Pleuropulmonary Changes in Nonpenetrating Trauma.............. 1069
Penetrating Trauma 1085

15

DISEASES OF THE LUNG OF UNKNOWN ORIGIN.................................. 1086

16

DISEASES OF THE PLEURA 1144

Pleural Effusion 1144
Pneumothorax... 1159
Pleural Thickening.. 1161

17

DISEASES OF THE MEDIASTINUM 1165

18

DISEASES OF THE DIAPHRAGM AND CHEST WALL.............................. 1217

The Diaphragm.. 1217
The Chest Wall 1235

19

RESPIRATORY DISEASE ASSOCIATED WITH A NORMAL
CHEST ROENTGENOGRAM... 1250

REFERENCES.. 1271

INDEX OF FIRST AUTHORS OF CITED LITERATURE............................ i

SUBJECT INDEX xxix

1

THE NORMAL CHEST

INTRODUCTION
THE LUNG UNIT
    THE ACINUS AS AN ANATOMIC UNIT
        The Lobule
        Canals of Lambert
        Alveolar Pores
        Direct Airway Anastomoses
    THE ACINUS AS A ROENTGENOLOGIC UNIT
    THE ACINUS AS A FUNCTIONAL UNIT
THE AIRWAYS AND PULMONARY VENTILATION
    MORPHOLOGY
        The Bronchi and Bronchioles
        The Limiting Membrane
    ROENTGENOLOGY
        The Trachea and Main Bronchi
        The Lobar Bronchial Segments
        Tracheobronchial Anomalies
    FUNCTION
        The Composition of Gas in Alveoli
        Mechanics of Acinar Ventilation
THE PULMONARY VASCULAR SYSTEM
    MORPHOLOGY
        Arteriovenous Anastomoses
    ROENTGENOLOGY
    FUNCTION
        Perfusion of the Acinar Unit
        Factors Which Influence Pulmonary Circulation
        Diffusion of Gas from Acinar Units to Red Blood Cells
        The Matching of Capillary Blood Flow with Ventilation in the Acinus
        Blood Gases and H-ion Concentration (pH)
DEVELOPMENT OF THE LUNG
THE NERVOUS SYSTEM
THE PLEURA
    MORPHOLOGY
    ROENTGENOLOGY
        Fissures
    PHYSIOLOGY
        Pressures
        Fluid Formation and Absorption

THE LYMPHATIC SYSTEM
    LYMPHATICS OF THE LUNGS AND PLEURA
    LYMPHATICS OF THE MEDIASTINUM
        The Anterior Mediastinal Compartment
        The Posterior Mediastinal Compartment
        The Middle Mediastinal Compartment
    PATTERNS OF LYMPH DRAINAGE OF THE LUNGS
        On the Right Side
        On the Left Side
THE MEDIASTINUM
    THE MEDIASTINAL COMPARTMENTS
        The Anterior Mediastinal Compartment
        The Middle Mediastinal Compartment
        The Posterior Mediastinal Compartment
    THE HEART
        Position
        Size and Contour
    OTHER ASPECTS OF MEDIASTINAL CONFIGURATION
        The Azygos Vein
THE DIAPHRAGM
        Roentgenographic Height of the Normal Diaphragm
        Relationship Between the Height of the Right and Left Hemidiaphragms
        Range of Diaphragmatic Excursion on Respiration
        Physiologic Variations in Diaphragmatic Contour
THE CHEST WALL
    The Soft Tissues
    The Bones
THE NORMAL CHEST ROENTGENOGRAM
    Normal Lung Density
    Alteration in Lung Density
    The Pulmonary Markings
PERCEPTION IN CHEST ROENTGENOLOGY
    Observer Error
    Threshold Visibility
    Psychologic Aspects of Roentgenologic Interpretation

INTRODUCTION

Descriptions of the anatomy of the normal chest as viewed roentgenographically usually are concerned with gross morphology in relation to roentgenology, with emphasis on such details as the spatial distribution of the bronchial and arterial trees, the location of bronchopulmonary segments, and the configuration of the dia-

1

phragm. Although such information is essential to a thorough understanding of roentgen pathology, it fails to take into consideration the minute structure of the lung, which is generally relegated to the province of the histopathologist. We are of the opinion that this lack of emphasis on peripheral anatomy is erroneous: since the majority of pulmonary diseases that produce alteration in roentgenographic density involve the lung parenchyma, we feel that our attention should be directed first toward knowledge of peripheral lung structure and the roentgenographic appearance of involvement of individual parenchymal units.

Since the prime purpose of this book is to describe roentgenographic patterns and to discuss their differential diagnosis, little purpose would be served by reviewing in great detail the physiology of respiration, which has been done so well by others.[1-3] Nevertheless, a truly proficient interpretation of the roentgenogram requires not only familiarity with the anatomy of the lung but also a knowledge of pulmonary physiology, a requirement that is even more necessary in view of the ever-increasing number of dynamic roentgenographic procedures that are being performed.

With these points in mind, this chapter begins with a concise account of the minute structure of the lung, dealing in turn with its morphology, its roentgenology, and its function.

THE LUNG UNIT

THE ACINUS AS AN ANATOMIC UNIT

In the bronchial pathway to the periphery of the lungs, the last purely conducting structure is the terminal bronchiole. The portion of the lung distal to the terminal bronchiole is the *acinus*, which comprises respiratory bronchioles, alveolar ducts, alveolar sacs, and alveoli (Figure 1–1). It is in this region that gas exchange takes place. The precise arrangement and exact number of structures that form the acinus are not known, since reconstruction is extremely difficult and tedious. However, it is known that respiratory bronchioles have some alveoli in their walls and that cuboidal epithelium lines the lumen between alveoli. Progressively more alveoli are present in succeeding generations of respiratory bronchioles. Respiratory bronchioles are succeeded by alveolar ducts whose walls are formed by a musculoelastic mesh through which alveoli protrude outward. Alveolar ducts lead to the terminal, blind structures of the respiratory tree—alveolar sacs, which also are lined entirely by alveoli but in which there is no smooth muscle.

A variety of terms has been used for the same structures in the acinus, and the reader is referred to the excellent review by Pump.[8] It seems likely that divisions within the acinus follow a pattern of ir-

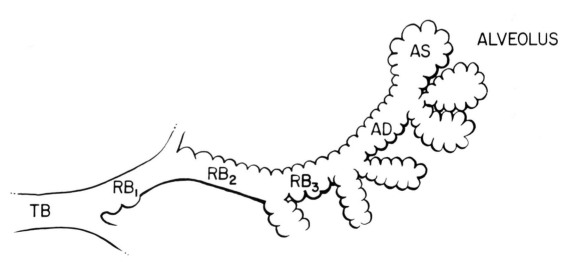

Figure 1–1. **Component Parts of the Acinus.** TB-terminal bronchiole. RB-respiratory bronchiole. AD-alveolar duct. AS-alveolar sac. (Thurlbeck, W. M.: Chronic obstructive lung disease. In: Sommers, S. C. (ed.), *Pathology Annual: Nineteen Sixty-eight*. Appleton-Century-Crofts, 1968, p. 377.)

regular dichotomy with axial and lateral pathways, as in the conducting system (*see* page 8). Thus, there may be from two to nine generations of respiratory bronchioles. The last respiratory bronchiole gives rise to a complex terminal spray of alveolar ducts and sacs in which dichotomous, trichotomous, or even quadrivial division occurs in irregular fashion. It can be estimated that there are about 400 alveolar ducts and sacs in an acinus and 18 last-order respiratory bronchioles arising from one terminal bronchiole. There are altogether about 14 million alveolar ducts and sacs, which contain the greater portion of the lungs' 300 million alveoli, each of which has a diameter of 250 to 300μ when fully inflated.[9] Alveoli are polygonal and have a continuous lining formed of flattened epithelial cells. In the sharp angles of the alveoli are plumper cells, with oval nuclei and granular cytoplasm. These corner cells, which are known also as type-II or septal cells, have many mitochondria, are metabolically highly active, and contain characteristic osmophilic inclusions which are thought to be the origin of the surface-active material that lines the alveolar surface.[10, 11] The total alveolar surface area is some 40 to 100 sq m, depending upon body size.[12] This area, in which gas transfer takes place, is extremely thin, and Schulz[97] has calculated that the thickness of the pathway from alveolar gas to the plasma layer of blood is 0.36 to 2.5μ—a small distance in terms of the diameter of a normal red blood cell.

The Lobule

The lobule is usually defined as the smallest discrete portion of the lung that is surrounded by connective-tissue septa, and corresponds to the "secondary lobule" described by Miller.[4] Since the septa are variable in size and extent, the size of the lobule is variable. It should not be confused with Miller's "primary lobule," which consists of an alveolar duct, its vessels, and the structures arising from them. The secondary lobule rarely is recognizable roentgenographically as a unit of structure; only when edema fluid or other pathologic tissue within the interlobular septa renders these structures visible as septal lines (B lines of Kerley; *see* Figure 4–52, page 242)

can the volume of lung between two lines be recognized as a secondary lobule. It is obvious that such a limitation negates the usefulness of Miller's definition for purposes of pathologic-roentgenologic correlation.

To overcome this limitation, Reid and Simon[158] proposed an alternate definition, based on a subdivision of peripheral lung structure that is more constant and is recognizable both morphologically and roentgenographically. These authors pointed out that if one follows a bronchial pathway to the periphery of the lung in a well-filled bronchogram (Figure 1–2), a stage is reached at which branching of the parallel-walled pathway occurs every 0.5 to 1.0 cm. After three or four such branchings, an abrupt transition takes place in which the branching patterns occur at 2- to 3-mm intervals. These have been termed the "centimeter" and "millimeter" patterns, respectively. The centimeter pattern of branching represents small bronchi and bronchioles and the millimeter pattern relates to terminal bronchioles. Reid and Simon[158] proposed that the lobule be redefined as the cluster of three to five terminal bronchioles which form the millimeter pattern of branching at the end of a bronchial pathway (either axial or side branch), together with the respiratory tissue it supplies. As opposed to the conventional definition, theirs relates to a structure which is constant. We feel that this proposal possesses considerable merit: It designates a unit of lung tissue which is not only recognizable morphologically but also can be easily identified *in vivo* bronchographically.

Since each terminal bronchiole gives origin to a single acinus, and the Reid lobule comprises a cluster of three to five terminal bronchioles, the lobule is made up of three to five acini. Although variable in size, it measures approximately 1 cm in diameter in the adult.[158] If one divides a sphere 1 cm in diameter into three to five roughly equal parts, each part measures approximately 5 to 7 mm in diameter. Stated another way, division of a sphere 1 cm in diameter into units measuring 6 mm in diameter yields four to six units. These calculations agree with the original description by Loeshcke[7] in 1921, that the acinus measures approximately 6 mm in diameter, and with Reid's statement that the lobule

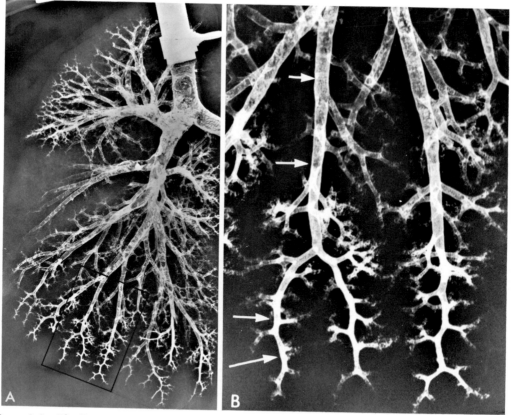

Figure 1–2. **The Pattern of Bronchial and Bronchiolar Branching.** *A,* Roentgenogram of an excised right lung following insufflation of particulate lead into the tracheobronchial tree. *B,* Magnified view of the peripheral airways of the lateral basal segment; upper arrows point to the "centimeter pattern" of branching, lower arrows to the "millimeter pattern." (Roentgenogram through the courtesy of Dr. James Hogg, Department of Pathology, McGill University.)

measures 1 cm in diameter and contains three to five acini, each approximately 6 mm in diameter.

Canals of Lambert

The distal portions of the bronchiolar tree, particularly the preterminal bronchioles, contain a number of epithelium-lined tubular communications with surrounding alveoli.[14] The physiologic significance of these structures is not known, but obviously they provide an accessory route for the passage of air directly from the bronchioles into alveoli.

Alveolar Pores

Although these are often called the pores of Kohn, von Hayek[15] attributes their original description to Henle. It is thought that they are present in the lungs of all mammals, though they may be relatively more common in some species. In the human lung, they are openings, or discontinuities, of the alveolar wall, about 10 to 15μ in diameter. The lung distal to an obstructed bronchus or bronchiole may be ventilated via an adjacent airway. This process, known as collateral air drift, is brought about, at least in part, by the pores of Kohn. The lung of the dog has no interlobular septa and, therefore, the lobar tissue is continuously interconnected.

Direct Airway Anastomoses

Martin[16] recently showed direct communications between "respiratory bronchioles" in the dog, measuring up to 120μ in diameter, which appeared to cross intersegmental planes. Although termed "respiratory bronchioles" by the author, the figures illustrate communications between what appear to be alveolar ducts. They were found relatively frequently and, because of their large size, may contribute significantly to collateral ventilation.

THE ACINUS AS A ROENTGENOLOGIC UNIT

Since the acinus represents the portion of the lung parenchyma distal to the terminal bronchiole, the millimeter pattern of bronchiolar branching is an anatomic landmark for the bronchographic recognition of peripheral lung structure. In addi-

tion, it is reasonable to assume that since an acinus is a macroscopic structure, it might be visible roentgenologically when completely or partially filled with contrast material or with inflammatory exudate. In 1924 Aschoff[5] suggested that consolidation of a single acinus by tuberculous inflammatory exudate or granulation tissue results in a rosette-like appearance, which he termed the "acino-nodose" lesion (Figure 1–3). Identical shadows were created by Twining[18] in 1931 by overfilling with Lipiodol the bronchial tree of lungs removed at autopsy (Figure 1–4). Although neither Aschoff[5] nor Twining[18] proved conclusively

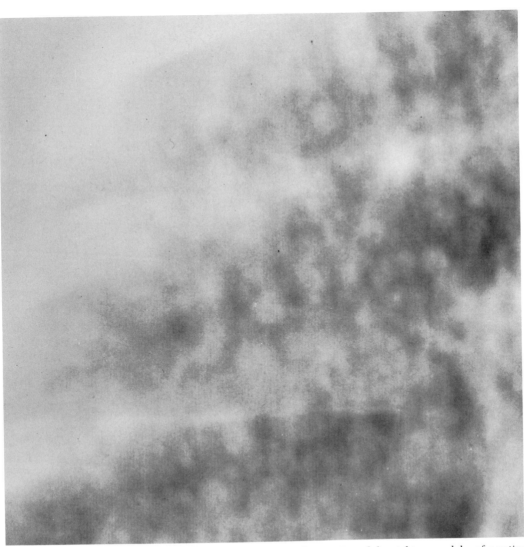

Figure 1–3. **Acinar Shadows.** Magnified view of a tomographic section of the right upper lobe of a patient with bronchogenic spread of tuberculosis from a cavity in the right lower lobe (not illustrated). On the original roentgenogram, individual acinar shadows measured 4 to 5 mm in diameter.

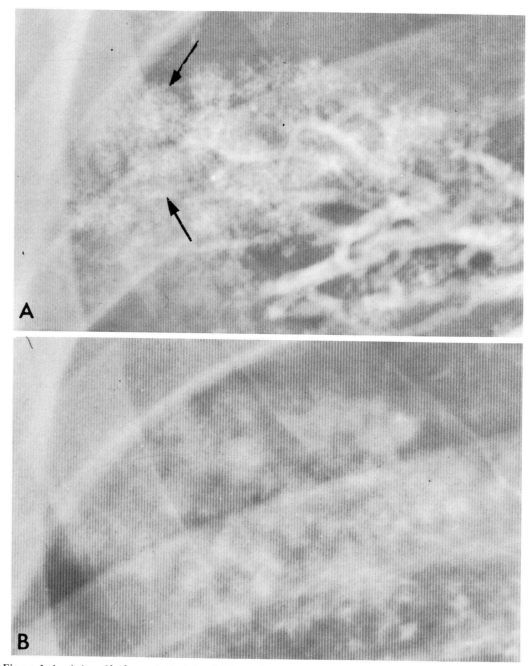

Figure 1–4. **Acinar Shadows.** *A,* Peripheral filling of respiratory bronchioles during bronchography (arrows). *B,* 24 hours later the contrast agent has absorbed but has incited an acute air-space edema resulting in the "rosette" shadows of acinar consolidation.

that the "acino-nodose" shadow represented a single acinus morphologically (nor in fact has anyone since, to our knowledge), it is clear that the similarity of the two structures in size and configuration is more than circumstantial. Thus while recognizing the possibility of semantic error, we intend to use the designation *acinar*

throughout this book to describe these units of peripheral airspace consolidation.

In recent years, Ziskind and his associates[19, 20] and Felson[21] have revived a deserved interest in this structure. These authors should be credited with bringing into proper perspective the importance of the recognition of "alveolar-filling" diseases that produce the roentgenographically visible rosette shadows or acinar pattern. In conditions such as pulmonary edema, acute alveolar pneumonia, and idiopathic pulmonary hemorrhage, recognition of this distinctive pattern enables the roentgenologist to narrow the differential diagnosis down to the relatively few diseases capable of consolidating parenchymal air spaces (Figure 1–5). This important aspect of roentgen pathology is referred to repeatedly in the relevant sections of this book.

THE ACINUS AS A FUNCTIONAL UNIT

As defined, the lung unit, which is analogous to the nephron of the kidney, is that portion of the lung parenchyma distal to the terminal bronchiole. This definition is highly acceptable to both anatomists and roentgenologists, but is there evidence that this portion of lung is also a functional unit? Most physiologists describe the alveolus as the unit of the lung. However, in so doing, they do not equate this with the anatomic alveolus but rather with a hypothetical unit which, because of our lack of knowledge of correlation between physiology and anatomy, cannot be defined morphologically. In fact, it would be unrealistic to consider the structural alveolus a physiologic unit. Each alveolus is one of a family of 20 or thereabouts, arising from a common alveolar duct and receiving from a common arteriole capillaries which connect the alveoli with one another.[22, 23] It is

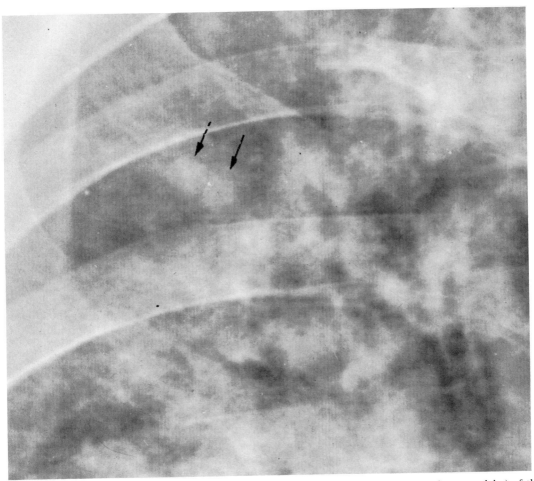

Figure 1–5. **Air-space Consolidation in Acute Pulmonary Edema.** Magnified view (right upper lobe) of the roentgenogram of a patient with diffuse pulmonary edema resulting from aspiration of liquid gastric contents. Air-space consolidation is largely confluent but two relatively discrete acinar shadows can be seen near the center of the field (arrows).

unlikely that, in normal circumstances, the behavior of any one alveolus differs from that of its "siblings." Thus, it seems likely that Miller's primary lobule,[4] comprising the alveolar duct and its ramifications that arise from a third-order respiratory bronchiole, is the smallest portion of lung that can be considered in the concept of a physiologic unit of lung function. Farther up the bronchial tree at the level of the terminal bronchiole, a greater portion of lung is included as a unit of function, since distal to this point there are some 400 alveolar-duct units. Do the 8000 alveoli that make up this acinus behave similarly? This question cannot be answered yet, although accumulating evidence on grounds of both structure and physiology suggest that they do (as will be discussed in relation to ventilation/perfusion ratios). For this reason, and in order to envisage a physiologic counterpart of the morphologic and roentgenologic unit, the basic functioning unit of the lung is taken to be the acinus, *i.e.*, all of that portion of the lung parenchyma distal to the terminal bronchiole.

THE AIRWAYS AND PULMONARY VENTILATION

MORPHOLOGY

The function of the bronchial tree is to conduct air to the alveolar surface, where gas transfer takes place between respired air and gas dissolved in the blood of the alveolar capillaries. The inspired air should be evenly distributed to the alveolar capillary bed, with minimal resistance to flow. In addition, the bronchi and lungs must be able to protect themselves against noxious external agents, whether these be physical, chemical, or biological. The greater part of the length and the smaller part of the volume of the respiratory tract is concerned only with the conduction of air; this part comprises bronchi and bronchioles, which differ in that there is cartilage in the walls of the former. The remaining part of the tract is the acinus, which is concerned with both conduction and gas exchange, the latter function assuming greater importance distally.

Bronchi and Bronchioles

Bronchial and bronchiolar division generally is dichotomous, but the divisions from the parent bronchus often are unequal and the distance between bronchial divisions quite variable, producing a pattern of irregular branching. When the two branches are of approximately equal size, their cross-sectional area is about 20 per cent greater than that of the parent branch and their angles of branching are equal. When they are of unequal size the smaller branch deviates more from the line of direct continuation of the parent bronchus. When the distance from the main bronchus to the periphery of the lung is small, as in the lung substance at the hilum, small branches from the parent bronchus form a spiral; these are called lateral pathways. When the distance is great, the branches are of about equal size, producing approximately linear (axial) pathways. The number of bronchi in the pathways varies considerably, depending upon the distance from hilum to periphery; thus, there may be as few as six generations of bronchi and bronchioles in a lateral pathway and as many as 15 in an axial one. These extreme variations are illustrated in Table 1–1.

The cartilages of the main-stem bronchi are horseshoe-shaped, as in the trachea (Figure 1–6). In lobar and segmental bronchi they consist of irregularly shaped plates which form much of the wall. As the pathway proceeds distally, the cartilages become progressively smaller and less complete until finally, in bronchi about 1 to 2 mm in diameter, they surround only the origins of the bronchioles arising from them. The bronchial muscle lies between the open ends of the horseshoe-shaped cartilages in the major bronchi, where it is attached to the inner perichondrium about 1 mm from their ends. As the cartilages diminish in size and become irregular, the attachments extend further along the cartilages until, finally, the bronchi are encircled by muscle. In the smaller bronchi and the bronchioles, the muscle bundles form a crisscrossed, spiral, geodesic network.

The epithelium of the bronchi is of pseudostratified ciliated type and contains numerous goblet cells. As the pathway proceeds distally the epithelium becomes progressively thinner, to become single-layered in the bronchioles, and the number of goblet cells decreases. In the terminal bronchioles, the goblet cells and cilia have disappeared and the epithelium has become flattened. The origin of mucus found

Table 1-1. Bronchial and Bronchiolar Division

| | GENERATION FROM | | | | | |
STRUCTURE	TRACHEA	SEGMENTAL BRONCHUS	TERMINAL BRONCHIOLE	NUMBER	DIAMETER	CROSS-SECTIONAL AREA	
Trachea	0			1	2.5 cm	5 sq cm	
Main bronchi	1			2	11-19 mm	3.2 sq cm	
Lobar bronchi	2/3			5	4.5-13.5 mm	2.7 sq cm	Cartilaginous
Segmental bronchi	3/6	0		19	4.5-6.5 mm	3.2 sq cm	conducting
Subsegmental bronchi	4/7	1		38	3-6 mm	6.6 sq cm	structures
Bronchi		2-6		various	various	various	
Terminal bronchi		3-7		1000	1.0 mm	7.9 sq cm	
Bronchioles		5-14		various	various	various	
Terminal bronchiole		6-15	0	35,000	0.65 mm	116 sq cm	
Respiratory bronchioles			1-8	various	various	various	No cartilage
Terminal respiratory bronchiole			2-9	630,000	0.45 mm	1000 sq cm	in their walls
Alveolar ducts and sacs			4-12	14×10^6	0.40 mm	1.71 sq m	
Alveoli				300×10^6	0.25-0.30 mm	70 sq m (surface area)	

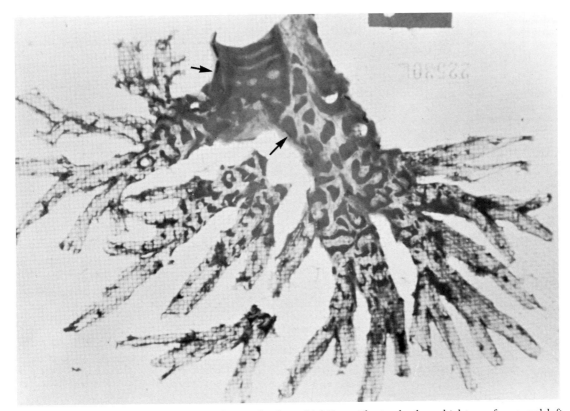

Figure 1-6. Cartilage Distribution in the Tracheobronchial Tree. The tracheobronchial tree of a normal left lung removed at necropsy has been dissected free, laid out on a wire mesh and stained for cartilage. Note that the horseshoe-shaped cartilages in the trachea (upper arrow) extend for a short distance into the upper-lobe bronchus but that the cartilage in the lower-lobe bronchus (lower arrow) and peripheral bronchi form discrete islands.

in these bronchioles is not known, though it has been shown not to originate from mucous glands of the bronchi; von Hayek[24] believes it to be a special secretion of cells that bulge into the lumen of the bronchiole (Clara cells[25]). There is some evidence that the excessive mucous secretion rich in eosinophils that occurs in asthma may be the product of these cells.

Underneath the epithelium is the basement membrane, and deep to this is the membrana propria, which is composed of loose fibrous tissue with a rich capillary network. The bronchial mucous glands belong to the membrana propria but frequently extend externally to the cartilage or muscle wall. The glands are mixed tubuloacinar in type and usually are termed mixed serous and mucous glands; in fact, the gland acini are more appropriately designated distended or nondistended (by mucus).[26] It seems likely that cyclic production of mucus converts one to the other, since mucopolysaccharides are present in "serous" acini also. Mucous glands extend to the small bronchi, roughly paralleling the distribution of cartilage. The volume of bronchial mucous glands is much greater than that of goblet cells, and it is likely that bronchial glands secrete most of the mucus contained in the tracheobronchial tree. Bands of longitudinal elastic fibers form dense bundles in the membrana propria, causing a ridging of the bronchi that becomes less conspicuous distally. These longitudinal elastic fibers connect with circularly arranged elastic fibers that are in relation to the muscular layer and, in the small bronchioles, through the circular elastic fibers to the surrounding alveolar and septal elastic tissue, thus forming a continuum through the lungs. It is believed that this radial tethering mechanism plays a major part in maintaining patency of the bronchioles. The peribronchial connective tissue surrounds the bronchi to the point where the bronchiolar walls become continuous with lung parenchyma. It is continuous with the periarterial connective tissue and, near the hilum, with the perivenous connective tissue. At the hilum and at the periphery of lobules there is continuity between the interlobular (septal) connective tissue and the subpleural connective tissue.

The Limiting Membrane

The true lung parenchyma (alveoli) is sharply delineated from surrounding connective tissue by a limiting membrane which is composed of dense elastic tissue and collagen and which merges into the elastic fibers of alveolar walls.[15] The membrane forms a boundary between alveolar parenchyma and the loose connective tissue of the bronchovascular tree, the interlobar septa, and the pleura; the loose connective tissue at the latter site constitutes the subpleural connective tissue or vascular layer of the pleura (see page 59). Blood vessels, nerves, and lymphatics lie in these compartments of loose connective tissue, which together form the interstitial space. Pressure may be more negative in this space than in the pleural cavity, and air and fluid readily accumulate there.

ROENTGENOLOGY

It is of obvious importance for physicians interested in diseases of the chest to be familiar with the terminology and general spatial distribution of the bronchi and of the bronchopulmonary segments they supply. However, the number of variations from the norm of subdivision of the bronchial tree precludes detailed consideration of the subject in this book.* In addition, we feel that a thorough understanding of pulmonary disease requires more a familiarity with the anatomy of bronchopulmonary segments, the zones or regions of the lung supplied by the segmental bronchi, than with detailed knowledge of bronchial branching, since the former is only roughly dependent upon the latter.

Knowledge of segmental bronchial terminology and the mode of bronchial branching is important for two main reasons. (1) Surgical resection for localized disease, notably bronchiectasis, often can be limited to segments: it is desirable to remove no more pulmonary tissue than is necessary

---

*Bronchial anatomy has been described in detail in several articles by Boyden, Scannell, and their associates,[27-33] and in the monographs by Boyden[34] and by Bloomer and associates,[35] and the interested reader is directed to those sources for detailed information.

for cure. (2) The bronchoscopist may need assistance from bronchographic findings to determine which segment is affected; intrabronchial conditions such as a small peripheral bronchogenic carcinoma or a small foreign body may be situated sufficiently far in the periphery of the lung as to remain undetected during standard bronchoscopic examination.

In this section, therefore, it will suffice to present a standard nomenclature of bronchopulmonary anatomy and to describe the prevailing pattern of segmental bronchial branching; minor variations in the pattern that occur fairly frequently will be indicated.

In 1943 Jackson and Huber[36] published a nomenclature of the bronchial segments which was widely adopted and which remains the generally accepted terminology in North America (see Table 1–2). The terminologies recommended by the Thoracic Society of Great Britain in 1949 introduced minor variations of the Jackson and Huber nomenclature.[37] In 1955 Boyden[34] introduced a numerical system for identification of bronchial segments which also is widely used. Although these three variations are included in the table, the Jackson-Huber nomenclature is used exclusively throughout this book.

It is interesting that no official nomenclature exists for the major bronchi interposed between the trachea and the segmental bronchi of the five pulmonary lobes. Through common usage, the designation "main bronchi" is applied to the major bronchi arising from the bifurcation of the trachea down to the origin of the upper-lobe bronchus on each side, and "intermediate bronchus" to the segment between the right upper-lobe bronchus and the origins of the right middle- and lower-lobe bronchi.

The Trachea and Main Bronchi

The trachea is, to all intents and purposes, a midline structure; a slight deviation to the right after entering the thorax is a normal finding and should not be misinterpreted as evidence of displacement (Figure 1–7A). Its walls are parallel except on the left side

Table 1–2. *Nomenclature of Bronchopulmonary Anatomy**

JACKSON-HUBER	BOYDEN	BROCK	THORACIC SOCIETY OF GREAT BRITAIN
UPPER LOBE			
Apical	B^1	Apical	Apical
Anterior	B^2	Pectoral	Anterior
Posterior	B^3	Subapical	Posterior
RIGHT MIDDLE LOBE			
Lateral	B^4	Lateral	Lateral
Medial	B^5	Medial	Medial
RIGHT LOWER LOBE			
Superior	B^6	Apical	Apical
Medial Basal	B^7	Cardiac	Medial basal
Anterior Basal	B^8	Anterior basal	Anterior basal
Lateral Basal	B^9	Middle basal	Lateral basal
Posterior Basal	B^{10}	Posterior basal	Posterior basal
LEFT UPPER LOBE			
Upper Division			Upper division
Apical-Posterior	$B^{1\,\&\,3}$	Apical and subapical	Apicoposterior or apical and posterior
Anterior	B^2	Pectoral	Anterior
Lower (Lingular) Division			Lingular (lower) division
Superior Lingular	B^4	Superior lingular	Superior lingular
Inferior Lingular	B^5	Inferior lingular	Inferior lingular
LEFT LOWER LOBE			
Superior	B^6	Apical	Apical
Anteromedial	$B^{7\,\&\,8}$	Anterior	Anterior basal
Lateral Basal	B^9	Middle basal	Lateral basal
Posterior Basal	B^{10}	Posterior basal	Posterior basal

*Modified slightly from Hinshaw, H. C., and Garland, L. H.: Diseases of the Chest, W. B. Saunders Co., Philadelphia, 1963, with permission of the authors and publisher.

just above the bifurcation, where a smooth indentation caused by aortic impression commonly exists; rarely a smaller indentation is present at the tracheobronchial angle on the right side, due to the azygos vein. Bronchographically, the trachea, main bronchi, and intermediate bronchus have a smoothly serrated contour, created by the indentations of the horseshoe-shaped cartilage rings positioned at regular intervals along these structures. A deficiency of the cartilage rings (the open end of the horseshoe) is closed by a pliable membranous sheath which produces a flat contour posteriorly.

The trachea divides into the two major bronchi at the carina. The angle of bifurcation is variable and is most acute in asthenic subjects. The course of the right main bronchus distally is more direct than the left—a fact of considerable importance in relation to aspiration; Weingärtner, quoted by von Hayek,[15] has stated that the carinal angle may vary from 50 to 100 degrees, the angles which the right and left major bronchi make with the median plane in these two extremes being 20°/30° to 45°/55°. The transverse diameter of the right main bronchus at total lung capacity is greater than that of the left (15.3 mm, compared with 13.0 mm[38]), although its length before the origin of the upper-lobe bronchus as measured at necropsy is shorter (average, 2.2 cm, compared with 5 cm on the left[39, 40]).

The air column of the trachea, both major bronchi and the intermediate bronchus should be plainly visible on well-exposed standard roentgenograms of the chest in frontal projection (see Figure 1–67, page 92); due to a more horizontal position, the air column of the left main-stem bronchus may appear in lateral projection as a circular or oval radiolucency, whereas the right main-stem bronchus appears to be tubular (see Figure 1–68, page 94).

The Lobar Bronchial Segments

On this and the following pages, the anatomic distribution of the bronchial segments is described and illustrated. Each segmental bronchus is considered separately, preceded by reproductions of a right bronchogram and corresponding drawings in posteroanterior (Figure 1–7) and lateral (Figure 1–8) projections, and of a left bronchogram similarly depicted (Figures 1–19 and 1–20).

RIGHT UPPER LOBE. The bronchus to the right upper lobe arises from the lateral aspect of the main-stem bronchus approximately 3 cm from the carina. The upper-lobe bronchus divides at slightly more than 1 cm from its origin, most commonly, into three branches.[28, 30, 35] (Figures 1–9 to 1–11). The pattern of branching in the right upper lobe is variable, particularly in relation to the supply of the axillary portion of the lobe, and reference to the aforementioned literature is recommended to those who desire more detailed information on this subject. Of some interest, although of no definite significance, is the relatively infrequent origin of the upper-lobe bronchus or of one of its branches (usually the apical bronchus) from the lateral wall of the trachea (the "tracheal bronchus").

RIGHT MIDDLE LOBE. The intermediate bronchus continues distally for 3 to 4 cm from the take-off of the right upper-lobe bronchus and then bifurcates to become the bronchi to the middle and lower lobes. The middle-lobe bronchus arises from the anterolateral wall of the intermediate bronchus, almost opposite the origin of the superior segmental bronchus of the lower lobe; 1 to 2 cm beyond its origin it bifurcates into lateral and medial segments (Figures 1–12 and 1–13).

RIGHT LOWER LOBE. The first segment to originate in the lower lobe, the superior segmental bronchus (Figure 1–14), arises from the posterior aspect of the lower-lobe bronchus immediately beyond its origin; thus, it is almost opposite the take-off of the middle-lobe bronchus. The four basal segments of the lower lobe may be identified with ease roentgenologically by applying a few basic principles of anatomy. Reference to Figures 1–15 to 1–18 will show that in the frontal projection of a well-filled bronchogram, the order of the basal bronchi from the lateral to the medial aspect of the hemithorax is *anterior/lateral/posterior/medial*. As the patient is rotated into 45-degree oblique and lateral projections, the relationship anterior/lateral/posterior is maintained; hence the mnemonic "A.L.P.," which has been employed advantageously by Nelson.[41] As pointed out by him, the relationship of one basal bronchus to another is easily recognized by use of the A.L.P. designation, the medial basal segment being projected between the lateral and posterior segments in the 45-degree oblique projection and between the anterior and lateral segments in the lateral projection.

LEFT UPPER LOBE. The left main bronchus is somewhat longer than the right, measuring approximately 5 cm in length. About 1 cm beyond its origin from the anterolateral aspect of the main bronchus, the bronchus to the left upper lobe either bifurcates or trifurcates, usually the former. In the bifurcation pattern, the upper division almost immediately divides again into two segmental branches, the apical posterior and anterior (Figures 1–21 and 1–22). The lower division is the lingular bronchus, which is roughly analogous to the middle-lobe bronchus of the right lung. When trifurcation of the left upper-lobe bronchus occurs, the apical posterior, anterior, and lingular bronchi originate simultaneously. As in the right upper lobe, the bronchial supply to regions of the left upper lobe is variable.[27, 29]

The lingular bronchus extends antero-inferiorly for 2 to 3 cm before bifurcating into superior and inferior divisions (Figures 1–23 and 1–24).

LEFT LOWER LOBE. With one exception, the divisions of the left lower-lobe bronchus are identical in name and anatomic distribution to those of the right lower lobe (Figures 1–25 to 1–28). The exception lies in the absence of a separate medial basal bronchus, the anterior and medial portions of the lobe being supplied by a single anteromedial bronchus — although Boyden[34] prefers to designate two separate basal bronchi, the anterior and medial, as on the right side. The mnemonic A.L.P. applies as well to the left lower lobe as to the right for identification of the order of basilar bronchi and their relationship to one another in frontal, oblique, and lateral projections.

Tracheobronchial Anomalies

It may be difficult to decide whether deviation from the prevailing pattern of bronchial branching should be classified as truly anomalous or as a minor variation in the norm. Obviously, any such deviation may be important to the surgeon in determining his approach to pulmonary resection. For example, the tracheal bronchus, and "mirror-image" bronchial trees (bronchial isomerism), may be associated with cardiovascular anomalies or situs inversus, and their presence should be brought to the attention of the surgeon when operative intervention is planned. Many bronchial anomalies, *e.g.*, bronchial atresia or agenesis, produce alteration in lung density, and, therefore, are discussed in relevant chapters of this book.

FUNCTION

The purpose of respiration is to supply oxygen for the metabolic needs of cells and to remove carbon dioxide, one of the waste products of cellular metabolism. In the unicellular organism this is accomplished simply by diffusion of these gases across the cell membrane. In man, although the basic purpose is the same, a complex mechanism is required to accomplish it. To bring oxygen from the atmosphere into contact with the cell membrane requires not only passage of the air down a long system of branching tubes, but also an additional means of transport to convey oxygen to even the most distant cells. This process utilizes two areas of diffusion, one in which oxygen is taken up by blood in pulmonary capillaries, and the other where oxygen arrives at the tissue membrane. The elimination of carbon dioxide is accomplished by the same procedure, but in reverse: diffusion from tissues into blood, and then conveyance to lung capillaries, where the gas diffuses from liquid to gas phase and moves up the tubular conducting system and is exhaled.

Normal lung function requires the provision at the alveoli of sufficient oxygen to satisfy the demands of the tissues and sufficient movement of gas in the tracheobronchial tree to eliminate carbon dioxide brought to the alveoli. The needs of the tissues for oxygen — and consequently, the quantity of carbon dioxide eliminated — vary considerably, owing mainly to muscle activity. At rest, the oxygen requirement may be 200 to 250 ml/min, whereas during maximal exercise it may increase to 20 times this amount. To satisfy this variation in oxygen need in normal circumstances, a similar increase in volume of ventilation is necessary. This is accomplished by stimuli from various sources, the origin depending upon the circumstances of the need: Oxygen lack, carbon dioxide excess in the

(Text continues on page 30.)

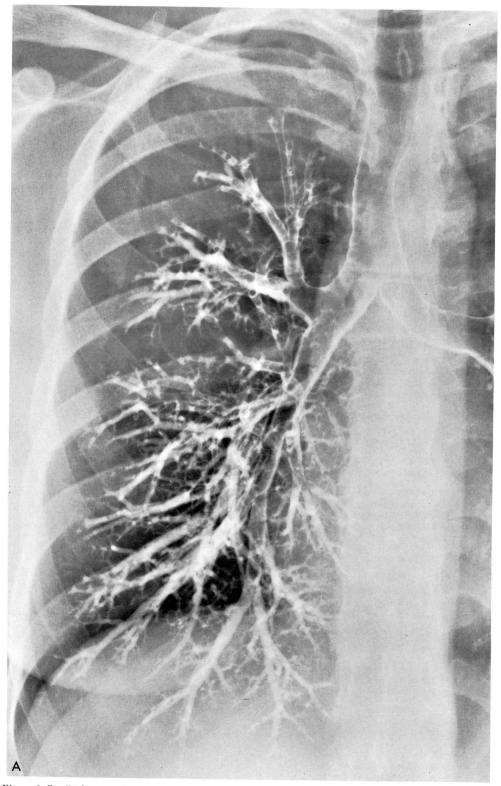

Figure 1–7. **Right Bronchial Tree (Frontal Projection).** *A,* Normal bronchogram of a 39-year-old woman.

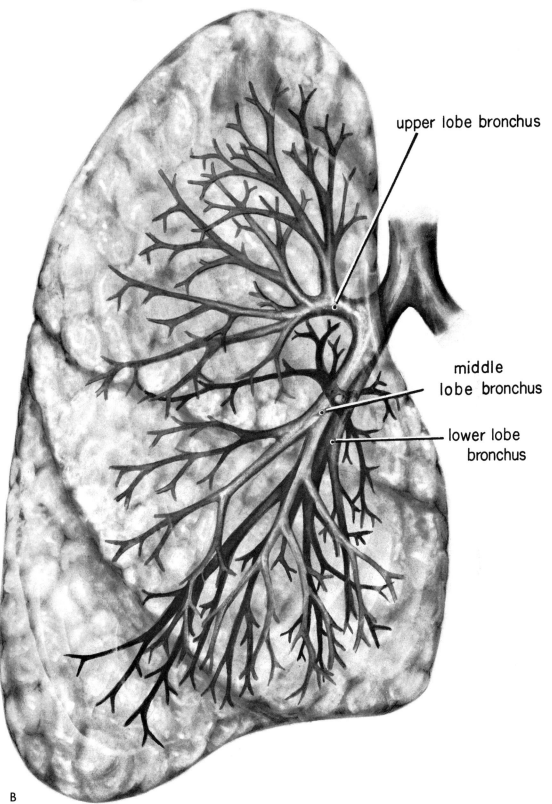

upper lobe bronchus

middle
lobe bronchus

lower lobe
bronchus

B

Figure 1-7. *Continued.* *B,* Semidiagrammatic drawing. *See* Figures 1–8 to 1–18, inclusive, for anatomic distribution of individual segmental bronchi.

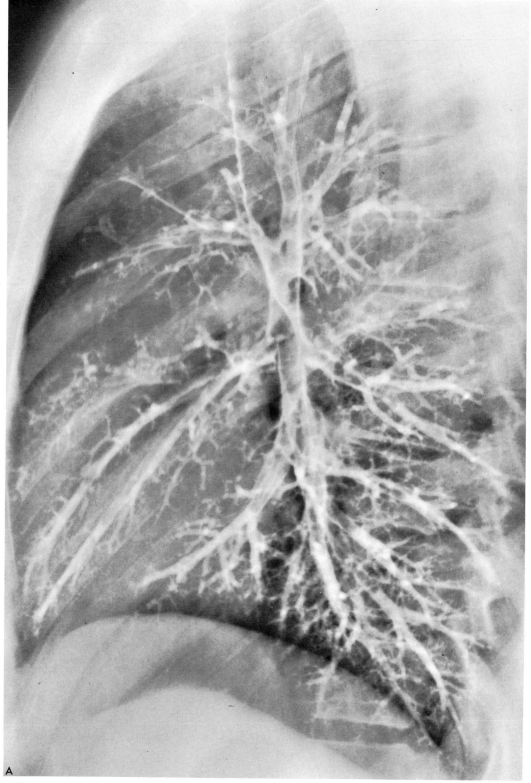

Figure 1–8.   **Right Bronchial Tree (Lateral Projection).** *A,* Normal bronchogram of a 39-year-old woman.

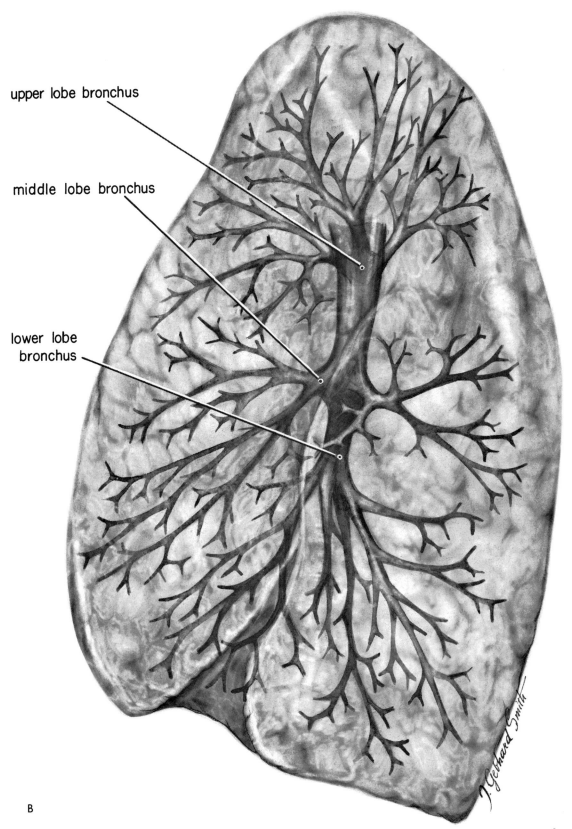

upper lobe bronchus

middle lobe bronchus

lower lobe
bronchus

B

Figure 1-8. Continued. B, Semidiagrammatic drawing. *See* Figures 1–8 to 1–18, inclusive, for anatomic distribution of individual segmental bronchi.

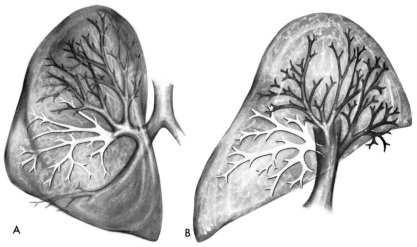

Figure 1–9. **Anterior Segmental Bronchus, Right Upper Lobe.** *A,* Frontal projection; *B,* lateral projection. This segment is directed anteriorly and laterally to supply that portion of the upper lobe contiguous to the minor fissure.

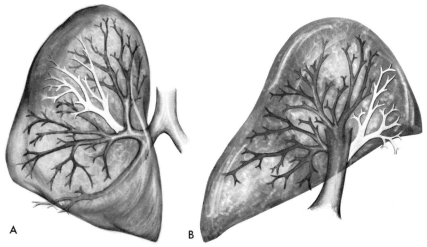

Figure 1–10. **Posterior Segmental Bronchus, Right Upper Lobe.** *A,* Frontal projection; *B,* lateral projection. This bronchus extends posteriorly, laterally, and somewhat superiorly to supply the posterolateral portion of the lobe.

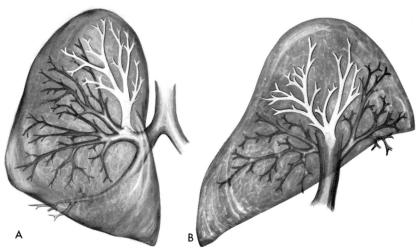

Figure 1–11. **Apical Segmental Bronchus, Right Upper Lobe.** *A,* Frontal projection; *B,* lateral projection. This bronchus supplies the superior paramediastinal zone, including the lung apex.

18

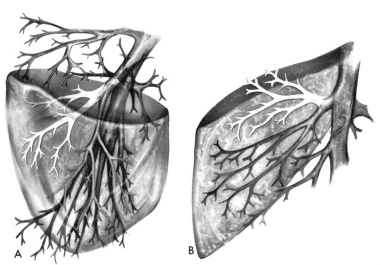

Figure 1–12. **Lateral Segmental Bronchus, Right Middle Lobe.** *A,* Frontal projection; *B,* lateral projection. This segment extends anterolaterally to supply that portion of the middle lobe which lies contiguous to the minor fissure and the anterior segment of the right upper lobe; its extreme lateral portion abuts against the chief fissure.

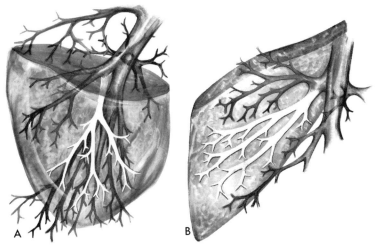

Figure 1–13. **Medial Segmental Bronchus, Right Middle Lobe.** *A,* Frontal projection; *B,* lateral projection. This bronchus extends anteromedially to supply the portion of the middle lobe which is contiguous to the heart and to the lower portion of the chief fissure.

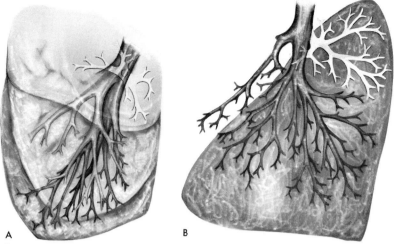

Figure 1–14. **Superior Segmental Bronchus, Right Lower Lobe.** *A,* Frontal projection; *B,* lateral projection. Usually this bronchus has three subsegments which extend superiorly, laterally, and inferiorly to supply the apical region of the lower lobe.

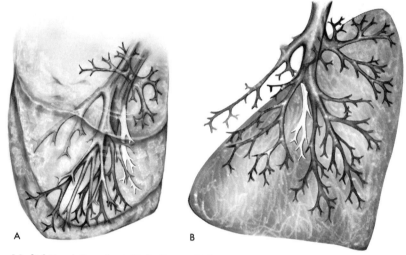

Figure 1–15. **Medial Basal Bronchus, Right Lower Lobe.** *A,* Frontal projection; *B,* lateral projection. This is the first branch of the lower-lobe bronchus beyond the superior segmental bronchus; it is the smallest of the basal segments and the most medial in frontal projection. It arises from the medial aspect of the lower-lobe bronchus to supply the anteromedial portion of the lower lobe contiguous to the posterior portion of the heart and the lower end of the chief fissure.

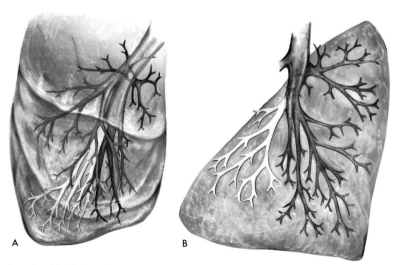

Figure 1–16. **Anterior Basal Bronchus, Right Lower Lobe.** *A,* Frontal projection; *B,* lateral projection. This bronchus is the most lateral of the basal bronchi, extending anterolaterally into the costophrenic sulcus.

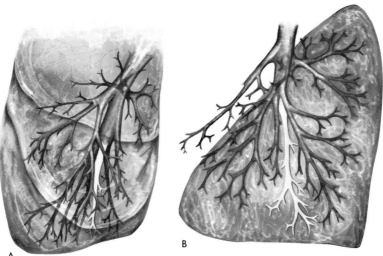

Figure 1–17. **Lateral Basal Bronchus, Right Lower Lobe.** *A*, Frontal projection; *B*, lateral projection. In frontal projection, this bronchus is projected just medial to the anterior basal bronchus; it extends laterally and slightly posteriorly to supply the portion of the lower lobe that lies behind the anterior basal bronchopulmonary segment. Neither the anterior nor the lateral bronchopulmonary segments relate to the major fissure, being separated from it by the medial segment.

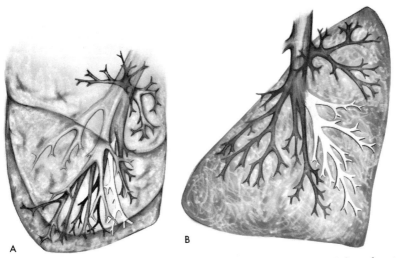

Figure 1–18. **Posterior Basal Bronchus, Right Lower Lobe.** *A*, Frontal projection; *B*, lateral projection. In frontal projection this bronchus appears between the lateral and medial basal bronchi; it supplies the posteroinferior portion of the lower lobe and extends into the posterior costophrenic gutter.

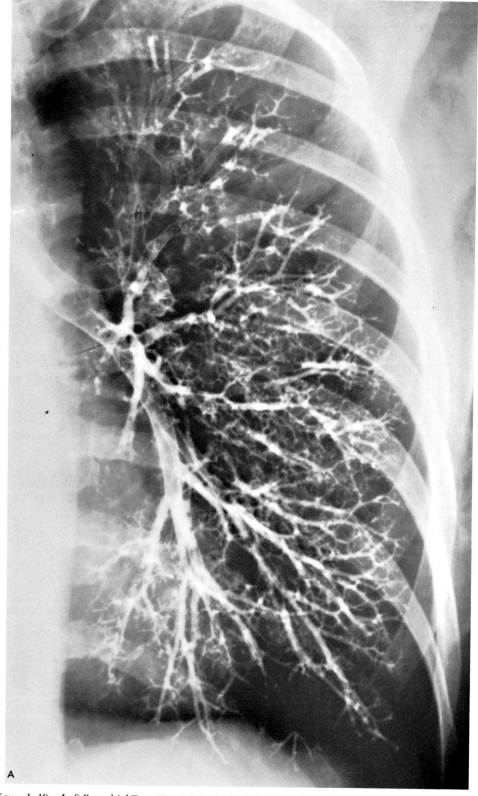

Figure 1–19.   **Left Bronchial Tree (Frontal Projection).** *A,* Normal bronchogram of a 39-year-old woman.

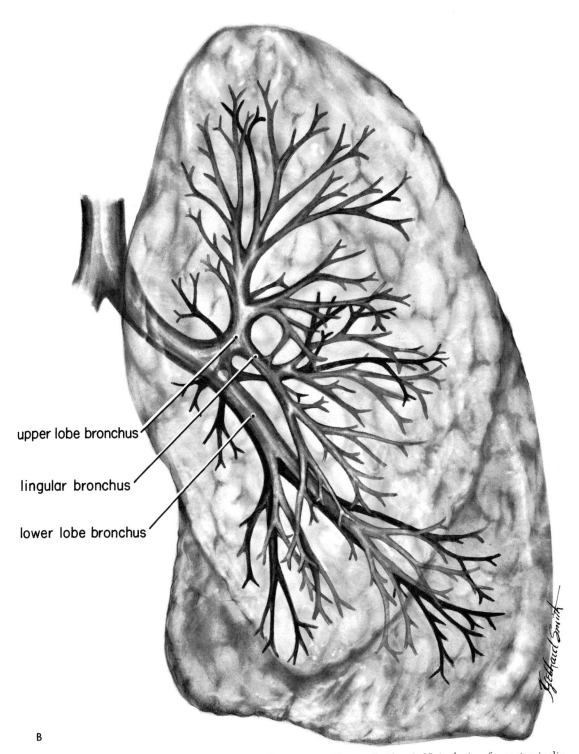

upper lobe bronchus

lingular bronchus

lower lobe bronchus

B

Figure 1–19. Continued. B, Semidiagrammatic drawing. *See* Figures 1–20 to 1–28, inclusive, for anatomic distribution of individual segmental bronchi.

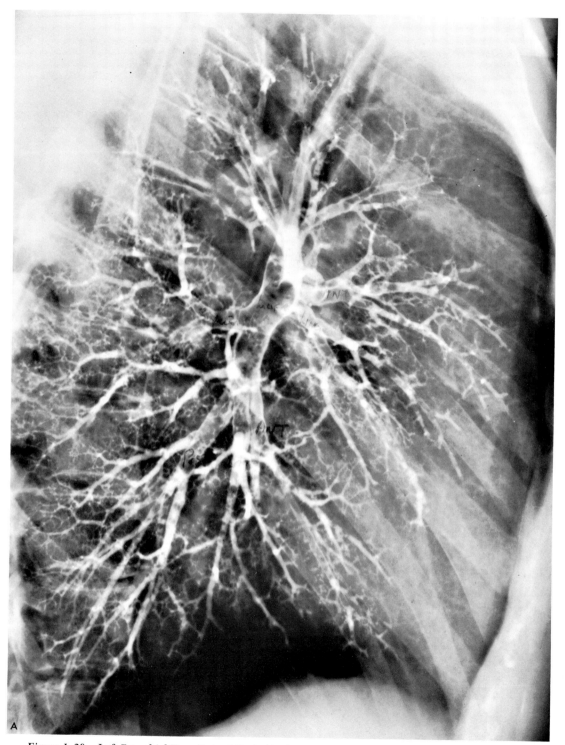

Figure 1–20. **Left Bronchial Tree (Lateral Projection).** *A,* Normal bronchogram of a 39-year-old woman.

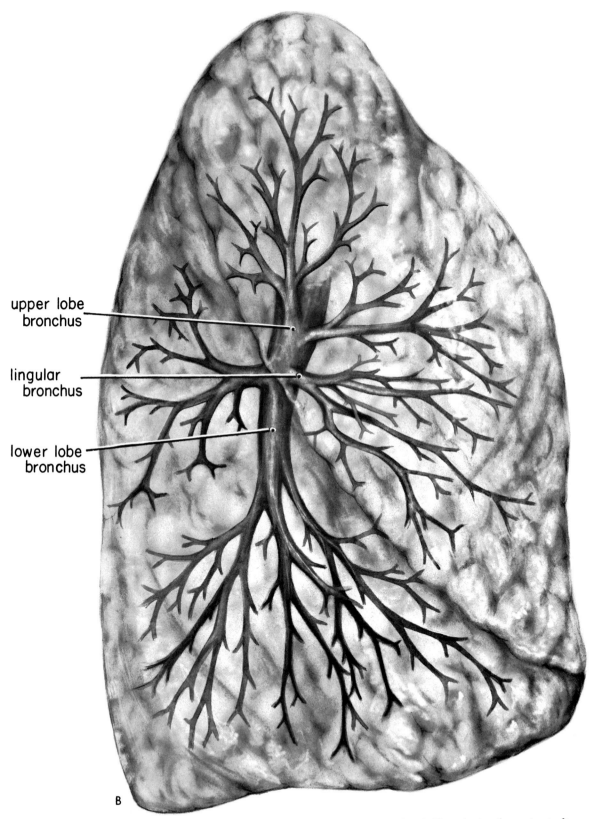

upper lobe
bronchus

lingular
bronchus

lower lobe
bronchus

B

Figure 1–20. Continued.   *B*, Semidiagrammatic drawing. *See* Figures 1–20 to 1–28, inclusive, for anatomic distribution of individual segmental bronchi.

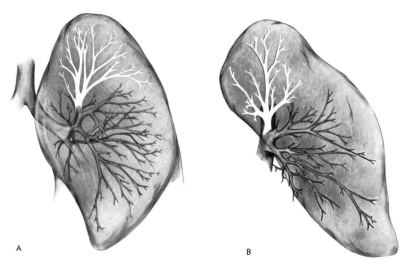

Figure 1-21. **Apical Posterior Bronchus, Left Upper Lobe.** *A,* Frontal projection; *B,* lateral projection. This bronchus bifurcates into apical and posterior segments which supply areas of the left upper lobe in a pattern similar to that of corresponding bronchi in the right upper lobe.

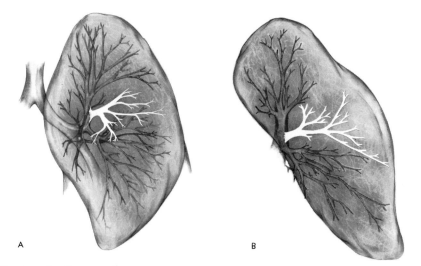

Figure 1-22. **Anterior Segmental Bronchus, Left Upper Lobe.** *A,* Frontal projection; *B,* lateral projection. The distribution is the same as in the right upper lobe.

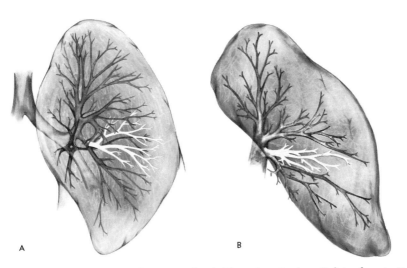

Figure 1–23. **Superior Segmental Bronchus, Lingula.** *A*, Frontal projection; *B*, lateral projection. This bronchus supplies the anterolateral portion of the lingula.

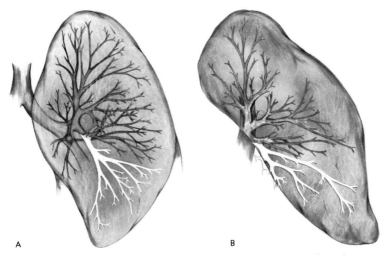

Figure 1–24. **Inferior Segmental Bronchus, Lingula.** *A*, Frontal projection; *B*, lateral projection. This segment supplies the inferomedial portion of the lingula contiguous to the left border of the heart. The lingula is somewhat larger in volume than the middle lobe of the right lung.

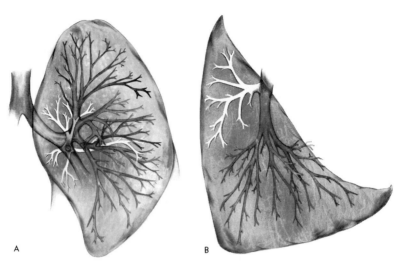

Figure 1–25. **Superior Segmental Bronchus, Left Lower Lobe.** *A,* Frontal projection; *B,* lateral projection. The distribution of this segment is similar to the corresponding segment of the right lower lobe.

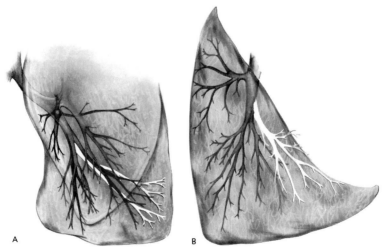

Figure 1–26. **Anterior Basal Bronchus, Left Lower Lobe.** *A,* Frontal projection; *B,* lateral projection. Distribution is similar to the corresponding segment of the right lower lobe. *See* text regarding medial basal bronchus.

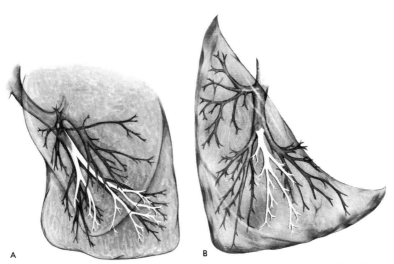

Figure 1-27. **Lateral Basal Bronchus, Left Lower Lobe.** *A,* Frontal projection; *B,* lateral projection. Distribution is similar to the corresponding segment of the right lower lobe.

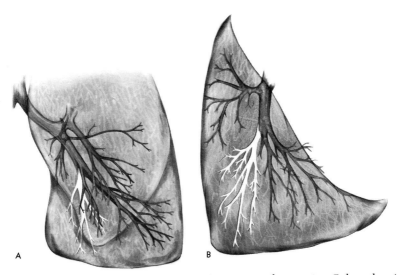

Figure 1-28. **Posterior Basal Bronchus, Left Lower Lobe.** *A,* Frontal projection, *B,* lateral projection. Distribution is similar to the corresponding segment of the right lower lobe.

blood, nervous reflexes from the lungs themselves, chemoreceptors in blood vessels, and other reflexes from somatic and visceral tissues, including the cerebral cortex, act directly or indirectly on the respiratory center to produce movement of the diaphragm and intercostal muscles and, thus, an appropriate increase in ventilation. It follows that this increase in ventilation to satisfy the need for oxygen will be of no avail if there is not a parallel increase in circulating blood through the lungs to carry oxygen to the tissues. Accordingly, rate and stroke volume increase and, during exercise, for example, raise the cardiac output from, say, 5 liters/min to 25 to 30 liters/min.

Keeping in mind the chemical, nervous, and mechanical stimuli that act directly or indirectly on the respiratory center, cardiac muscle, airways, and pulmonary vessels and that vary the quantity of ventilation and perfusion of blood to the acinar unit, let us focus our attention on this unit, since it is here that the lung fulfills its role in the process of respiration. To do this we shall consider (1) alveolar gas and its composition, (2) the mechanism by which this gas is moved in and out of the acinus, (3) perfusion of the acinus, (4) the process of diffusion of gas in the acinar unit and across the alveolocapillary membrane to red blood cells, (5) the matching of blood flow with ventilation in the acinar unit, and the end result of these processes, (6) blood gases and H-ion concentration.

The Composition of Gas in Alveoli

The composition of this gas depends upon the rate and amount of oxygen removed and of carbon dioxide added by capillary blood (which, in turn, depends upon aerobic metabolism of tissues) and the quantity and quality of the gas which reaches the acinus through the tracheobronchial tree.

VENTILATION OF THE ACINUS. At sea level, air contains approximately 21 per cent oxygen and 79 per cent nitrogen and has an atmospheric pressure of 760 mm Hg; the amount of carbon dioxide and other gases is negligible and can be disregarded. The partial pressures of these gases are approximately 159 mm Hg for oxygen ($Po_2 = 21/100 \times 760$) and 601 mm Hg for nitrogen ($PN_2 = 79/100 \times 760$). As air is inhaled into the tracheobronchial tree, the body temperature fully saturates it with water vapor at a partial pressure of 47 mm Hg, so that the partial pressure of oxygen drops to 149 mm Hg (($760 - 47) \times 21/100$). At sea level, therefore, the ventilation of alveoli depends upon the quantity of gas-containing oxygen, at a Po_2 of 149 mm Hg, that the thoracic "bellows" moves per minute into the acinus. Assuming that the conducting system is unobstructed, the quantity of gas reaching the alveoli depends upon the depth of respiration (tidal volume), the volume of the conducting system (dead-space gas which does not reach the alveoli), and the number of breaths per minute. If a subject moves 450 ml with each breath, has a respiratory dead space of 150 ml, and a respiratory rate of 15 per minute, his total minute ventilation is 6750 ml (450 ml × 15); since each breath contributes 300 ml of fresh air to the alveolar spaces, total alveolar ventilation is 300 × 15, or 4.5 liters/min. However, it must be realized that at the end of the previous expiration the dead space was filled not with atmospheric air but with expired air having a composition equivalent to that in the acinus. This means, therefore, that with each inspiration the first 150 ml reaching the alveoli has the composition of alveolar gas and the next 300 ml is inspired air saturated with water vapor; these two differently composed gas volumes probably mix instantly in the acini. The remaining 150 ml of the tidal volume of 450 ml is in the conducting system at the end of the inspiration (Figure 1–29).

ALVEOLAR-CAPILLARY GAS EXCHANGE. In addition to the contribution of ventilation to the composition of gas in the acinus, blood flow in the pulmonary capillaries varies the composition by the continuous removal of oxygen and addition of carbon dioxide. Obviously, as a result of these two dynamic processes, the composition of alveolar gas fluctuates, not only throughout the respiratory cycle but also from breath to breath and even from acinus to acinus (*see* page 50).

The quantity of oxygen removed from and carbon dioxide added to alveolar gas depends largely upon the metabolism of tissues. However, in man at rest—assuming that perfusion of blood and ventilation of acinar units are well matched—every 100 ml of blood allows approximately 5.6 ml of carbon dioxide to diffuse into the alveolar

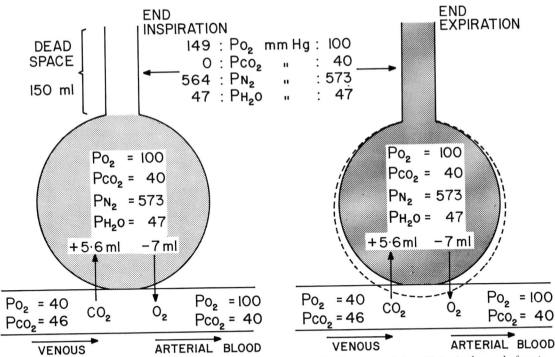

Figure 1–29. **A Diagram Portraying the Conducting System Leading to an Acinar Unit.** At the end of an inspiration of 450 ml of air, 150 ml of fresh air (saturated with water vapor) are situated within the conducting system and the remaining 300 ml have entered and mixed with alveolar gas. At end-expiration the conducting system (dead space) is filled with alveolar air. Carbon dioxide moves from the capillary blood to the alveolus and oxygen from the alveolus to the capillary blood so that the gas composition of alveolar gas and blood are altered. *See* text.

spaces. At the same time, 7 ml of oxygen leaves the acinar units and is carried away by each 100 ml of blood going to the tissues. The partial pressure of carbon dioxide (P_{CO_2}) in the acinus then is 40 mm Hg (713 × 5.6/100). The removal of oxygen, decreasing it from approximately 21 per cent to 14 per cent, gives a partial pressure of oxygen (P_{O_2}) of 100 mm Hg (713 × 14/100) (Figure 1–29).

SUMMARY. The composition of acinar gas varies with the metabolism of the tissues and the total alveolar ventilation. Increasing activity of tissues results in greater oxygen consumption and carbon dioxide production, which in turn lower the P_{O_2} and raise the P_{CO_2} of the mixed venous blood returning to the lungs. The total alveolar ventilation depends upon tidal volume and respiratory rate.

Mechanics of Acinar Ventilation

Movement of atmospheric air down the conducting system to the acinar unit requires a certain force or pressure to overcome the "elastic" recoil of the lungs and the thoracic cage, the frictional resistance of pulmonary tissue and chest wall, and the resistance of the airways themselves. This pressure is produced by contraction of the muscles of inspiration, mainly the diaphragm, to a lesser extent the external intercostal muscles, and, in circumstance requiring greatly increased ventilation, the accessory respiratory muscles in the neck. At the end of inspiratory effort the inspiratory muscles relax; expiration usually occurs passively as the "elastic" parenchyma recoils to its resting state. If elastic recoil is defective, or if the conducting system is obstructed, expiratory muscles, particularly the abdominal mucles, come into play. This occurs also when large quantities of air are moved rapidly in and out of the chest.

Thus, air is brought to the acinus by the contraction of respiratory muscles, which exert a force or pressure to overcome the elastic recoil and frictional resistance of lung and thoracic cage, as well as the airway resistance of the tracheobronchial tree.

"ELASTIC" RECOIL OF LUNG PAREN-CHYMA AND THE THORACIC CAGE. The pressure in the pleural space normally is subatmospheric, *i.e.*, 4 to 5 cm H_2O below that of the atmosphere. If air is introduced into this "space" and the visceral and parietal layers of pleura are allowed to separate, the lungs and the thoracic cage assume new positions, the former collapsing and the latter enlarging (Figure 1–30). This is the "elastic" recoil which is overcome by contraction of the respiratory muscles and expansion of the thoracic cage and which represents the main mechanical impedance during quiet breathing.

On inspiration, the respiratory muscles act *initially* to overcome the "elastic" recoil of the lungs only; the thoracic cage, with an elastic recoil which allows a more expanded state, actually aids pulmonary inflation. As inspiration continues, the chest wall goes beyond its resting position and the force of muscular contraction then is exerted against the recoil of both lung and thoracic cage. As the cage expands, the intrapleural pressure becomes more subatmospheric, the acini and conducting tubes enlarge, gaseous pressure in the alveoli decreases in relation to atmospheric pressure at the mouth, and air moves down the conducting system. The force or pressure exerted on the lungs by muscle contraction overcomes both elastic recoil and flow resistance; this pressure is measurable since it is reflected in the degree of change in intrapleural pressure. Measurement is made directly or, more conveniently, by use of an intraesophageal balloon which reflects changes in intrapleural pressure. The relationship of the change in intrapleural pressure to the volume of gas which moves into the lungs is expressed as liters/cm H_2O and is known as lung compliance. To distinguish the force or pressure needed to overcome "elastic" recoil from that required to overcome resistance in the air-

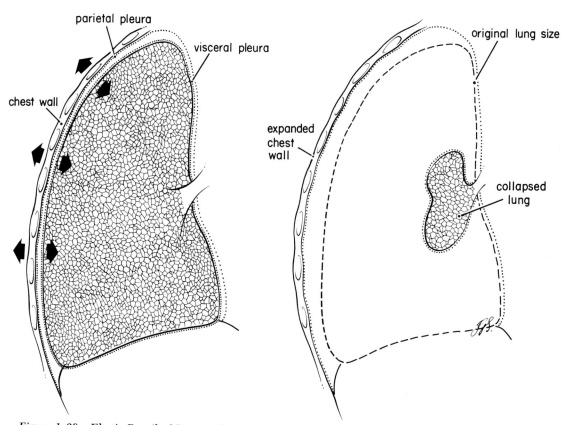

Figure 1–30. **Elastic Recoil of Lung and Cage.** Arrows indicate the elastic recoil of lung and thoracic cage. Introduction of air into the pleural cavity causes lung and thoracic cage to assume "resting" positions.

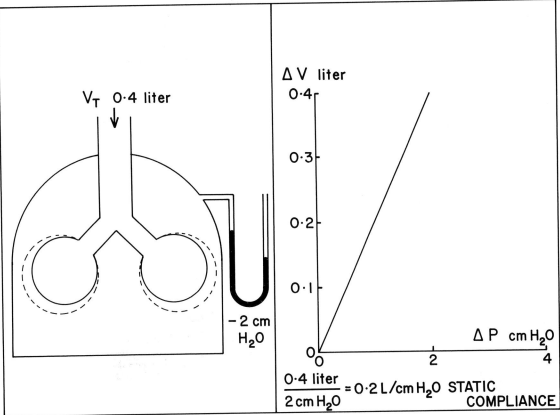

Figure 1–31. **Pressure–Volume Relationships.** A change of 2 cm H_2O in pleural pressure (ΔP) results in a volume change (ΔV) of 0.4 L of tidal air (V_T) in two hypothetical acini. The diagram on the right depicts the change in volume of 0.4 L and the change in pressure of 2 cm H_2O. The static compliance in this example is 0.2 L/cm H_2O.

ways and lung tissue, measurement is made with breathing suspended, when flow in the bronchi ceases and flow resistance is eliminated. Under these conditions, only the pressure required to overcome elasticity is measured. The resulting volume change affected by the pressure change is the static compliance (Figure 1–31). As the normal lung becomes more inflated it becomes less compliant; for this reason it is more informative to express compliance as the change in intrapleural pressure required to produce a volume change at a specific degree of lung inflation, generally functional residual capacity (FRC). Edema and fibrotic or granulomatous infiltration render the lungs stiffer and less compliant, so that more pressure is required to move a given volume of gas; or, to put it differently, a given pressure moves a smaller volume. When the elastic architecture of the lung is faulty, as in emphysema, a given pressure may actually produce a greater volume change than in

the normal lung, and in such a case compliance is increased.

"Elastic" recoil of the lung has been attributed in part to the peculiar arrangement of collagenous and elastic fibers.[42, 43] The helical structure of this fibrous network gives the lungs an elastic behavior similar to that of a coil spring. However, tissue elasticity is not the only component of the elastic recoil of the lungs. This was first indicated by the work of von Neergaard[44] in 1929, who measured the pressure-volume relationships of a fluid-distended lung and an air-distended lung and found less elastic recoil in the former: less pressure change was required to fully distend the fluid-filled lung than the air-filled lung. Von Neergaard deduced that a surface tension, a force which tended to contract alveolar spaces and to resist expansion, existed in each alveolus between its lining and its gas content. He suggested that this surface tension accounted for most of the lung's elastic recoil and that it was eliminated when gas was replaced by liquid.

SURFACE TENSION AND SURFACTANT. Subsequent work indicates that the surface tension at the air-liquid interface of the alveolar wall is variable, depending upon whether the lungs are inflating or deflating. The layer lining the alveoli contains a substance which can lower surface tension as alveolar spaces decrease in size during expiration.[45-49] Perhaps surface tension is best exemplified by a child's bubble pipe: the bubble on the mouth of the bowl tends to retract into the pipe and a distending force is necessary to counteract this effect.[50] A soap bubble, however, has a constant surface tension. An analogous but somewhat different situation exists in relation to the acinus on the end of the terminal bronchiole or the alveoli on the end of the alveolar duct. As distending pressure decreases and the alveoli become smaller in expiration, the collapse that occurred in the child's bubble pipe is prevented by the presence in the lining membrane of a surface-active substance, or surfactant, which can lower surface tension almost to zero.

It is believed that deep breaths are required from time to time to replenish the surface-active substance and that continued shallow breathing may eventually lead to collapse.[51] The implications of the effect of surface tension and surfactant on the capillary circulation are considerable; they are discussed in a subsequent section (*see* page 46). Surfactant is generally considered to be secreted by alveolar corner cells. A recent report indicates that surfactant originates in Clara cells in the distal bronchioles, and that subsequently it is taken up from the alveoli by alveolar corner cells.[184] It probably is a lipoprotein whose chief lipid is alpha dipalmitoyl-lecithin, a substance which may be in osmophilic lamellar inclusions in certain alveolar epithelial cells.[52]

Under experimental conditions it has been shown that occlusion of blood supply to a lung, occlusion of a main bronchus, or the prolonged inhalation of high concentrations of oxygen or carbon dioxide results in a loss of surfactant and the development of atelectasis. In addition, there are at least three clinical conditions in which loss of surfactant appears to be responsible for lung collapse: (1) hyaline membrane disease of the newborn;[53] (2) atelectasis in patients who have died after use of an artificial heart-lung system during open-heart surgery;[54] and (3) after hyperbaric oxygen therapy.[818] Experimental evidence indicates that this substance becomes inactivated whenever circulation to the acinus is inadequate or when plasma proteins escape into the alveoli. Several reviews of this subject have been published recently.[50, 55-57]

RESISTANCE OF THE AIRWAYS. During quiet breathing, most of the work of the respiratory muscles is required to overcome elastic recoil; when ventilation becomes more rapid, flow increases and increased work is necessary to overcome resistance in the conducting airways. Resistance increases in direct proportion to the length of a tubular conducting system, so that twice as much pressure is required to maintain the same flow in a tube doubled in length. However, reduction in the radius of a tube by one-half requires a 16-fold increase in pressure to maintain the same flow. These principles of laminar flow pertain to rigid, smooth tubes. Bronchial flow and airway resistance are more complicated: not only are the bronchial tubes irregular but they branch frequently and vary in caliber throughout the respiratory cycle. These additional features create turbulence which adds to resistance. Resistance is different during inspiration and expiration and varies with both lung volume and flow rate. Because of the nature of the branching of the bronchial tree, the total cross-sectional area becomes markedly increased with each new generation beyond the segmental bronchi, with the result that resistance is much less in the bronchioles than in the bronchi (*see* Table 1-1, page 9).

Anatomic differences between the larger cartilaginous bronchi and the smaller membranous bronchioles suggest a difference in function of these two portions of the conducting system which is supported by certain physiologic studies.[58, 59] Bronchi which contain cartilage remain patent after removal from the body; bronchioles, however, because of their content of elastic and muscle tissue, collapse in similar circumstances.[60] During life these cartilages not only maintain patency of the larger airways during expiration but also prevent overdistention during maximal inspiration.[58] These two portions of the conducting system differ not only in the construction of their walls but also in the fact that they occupy different thoracic-cage "compartments," which are separated by a strong elastic limiting membrane.[15] The cartilage-containing airways appear to have a potential space around them[22] and are affected more by changes in transpulmonary pressure (the difference between pressure at the mouth and intrapleural pressure) than by changes in the lung volume.[38, 59, 61] The bronchioles, on the other hand, lie on the other side of a limiting membrane which fuses with the bronchial walls at the point where the cartilage disappears.[15] They lie within the lobule, tightly connected to the pulmonary parenchyma, and the patency of their lumina is influenced by changes in lung volume.

During expiration, as lung volume becomes smaller and intrapleural pressure becomes less subatmospheric, resistance in both bronchi and bronchioles increases. Most of the increase in resistance, however, is in the bronchi and is due to their bronchomotor tone. In the absence of bronchomotor tone, there is very little increase in resistance as lung volume decreases until the lung volume becomes very small.[62]

In addition to these passive forces acting on the conducting system and causing increase or decrease in resistance, there are active stimuli to both bronchodilatation and bronchoconstriction. These are mediated through nervous pathways or by the action of chemicals, either on the receptor sites for postganglionic fibers or through direct action on smooth muscle. The action of histamine is of particular interest: injection of this substance into the pulmonary artery causes constriction of alveolar-duct sphincters and, thus, expulsion of air from acinar units. It is thought that microemboli act by the release of histamine, which causes closure of the alveolar ducts. This selective response to histamine when injected into the pulmonary artery reflects the fact that the blood supply to the acinus is from pulmonary arterioles, whereas the remainder of the airways is supplied by bronchial arterioles.[63]

Reflex local bronchoconstriction occurs when adjacent major pulmonary arteries are obstructed, constituting what appears to be a compensatory mechanism to divert ventilation to perfused areas.[64, 65] The operation of this mechanism may be prevented by the inhalation of 3 to 5 per cent carbon dioxide and it is thought that bronchoconstriction occurring in these circumstances is due to the reduced PCO_2.[153]

A sudden increase in resistance, as during attacks of asthma, prolongs expiration and thereby prevents complete emptying of the acinar unit; the next inspiration enlarges the unit and thus increases the functional residual capacity. This increase in lung volume augments elastic recoil to supply greater expiratory force.

Obstruction in the airways is not always the result of constriction of smooth muscle, and may be due to mucus in the bronchi or bronchioles or, as in emphysema, to "weak" walls. In this condition airway resistance is increased both because of loss of elastic tissue to hold open the smaller bronchi or bronchioles and because of the development of a high intrapleural pressure in an attempt to force air out of the alveolar spaces.

TISSUE RESISTANCE. During movement of the chest, in addition to airway resistance, tissue resistance is present; this is caused by displacement of lung tissue itself, the rib cage, the diaphragm, and the abdominal contents. It is generally thought that in a healthy person, tissue resistance accounts for about 20 per cent and airway resistance 80 per cent of total pulmonary resistance. This, however, may be an overestimate.[185] Tissue resistance is increased when the lung is infiltrated by granulomatous, fibrotic, or malignant tissue. During expiration some of the elastic force is used to overcome this additional frictional resistance, and, since there is less force available to overcome resistance in the conducting system, expiration is slowed.

SUMMARY. The force required to overcome the "elastic recoil" and the resistance of lungs, bronchial tubes, and thoracic cage is measured as a pressure in centimeters of water. The relationship of pressure to volume of gas moved in and out of the lungs is known as compliance and is expressed as liters/cm H_2O. Compliance is decreased when the lung is made stiffer by fibrotic or granulomatous infiltration; it is increased when pulmonary elastic recoil is reduced, as in emphysema. Elastic recoil is only partially due to the elasticity of lung parenchyma. A major component is dependent upon alveolar surface tension, which increases with inspiration and decreases with expiration; this tension is modified by a substance known as surfactant, which is present in the alveoli.

During quiet breathing most of the work of the respiratory muscles is required to overcome elastic recoil. During rapid respirations the increase in flow, the irregularity of the bronchi (which produces turbulence), and the bronchomotor tone add a significant impedance to ventilation. Bronchospasm or mucus in the airways add to this resistance. Loss of elastic support to the smaller bronchi and bronchioles and development of a high intrapleural pressure during expiration are responsible for the severe degree of airway resistance which develops in emphysema. Parenchymal and thoracic-wall tissues also create a resistance to respiration and this may be considerable when diseased lungs are diffusely infiltrated.

THE PULMONARY VASCULAR SYSTEM

MORPHOLOGY

The pulmonary arterial system accompanies the bronchial tree and divides with it, a branch always accompanying the appropriate bronchial division; these have been termed "conventional" branches. However, it was shown recently that many accessory branches of the pulmonary artery arise at points other than corresponding bronchial divisions.[66] These accessory branches outnumber the conventional ones; they originate throughout the length of the arterial tree and are most frequent peripherally.

The pulmonary arterial system may be conveniently divided into three types—elastic, transitional, and muscular. The arteries that accompany bronchi are elastic, and those that run with nonrespiratory bronchioles are muscular: the former vessels have a well-defined internal and external elastic lamina, with seven or more elastic laminae between, and the latter have an internal and an external elastic lamina with less than four elastic laminae between. Vessels that have intermediate amounts of elastic tissue are termed "transitional" arteries. The number of generations of the types of artery differs in various pathways. In the anterior basal segmental artery (Figure 1–32), elastic arteries stop at about the sixth order, followed by two orders of tran-

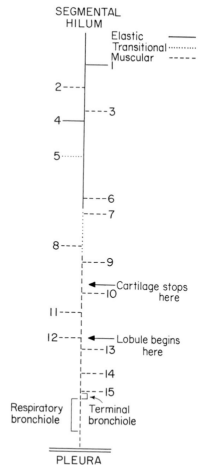

Figure 1–32. **Structure of the Pulmonary Arteries.** Diagrammatic representation (drawn to scale) of the full length of an anterior basal segmental artery. The structure of the artery is related to bronchial generations, and only conventional branches are included— those which accompany airways. (Reproduced with the permission of the Editor of *Clinical Radiology* and of the authors—Elliott, F. M., and Reid, Lynne: Some new facts about the pulmonary artery and its branching pattern. Clin. Radiol., *16*:193-198, 1965.)

sitional arteries coinciding with the end of the cartilage in the bronchi. Beyond this the vessels are muscular in type. Many muscular vessels arise proximally from elastic vessels which correspond to side branches along lateral pathways of the bronchial tree. The muscular arteries measure about 2000μ in diameter at their point of origin and diminish to about 100μ at the level of the terminal bronchiole. The walls become progressively thinner, with loss of elastic lamina and muscle. Beyond the level of the terminal bronchioles the arteries lose their continuous muscle coat and become arterioles, with a single elastic lamina. Within the acinus, arterioles continue to divide and accompany their respective branches of the respiratory tree to the level of the alveolar sacs. Many accessory branches are given off to supply the walls of the acinar pathways and the alveoli. These branches, as well as those which terminate around the alveolar sacs, are sometimes called precapillary arterioles; they break up to form the capillary network of the alveoli themselves. The capillary network of the alveoli is the densest in the body, and the area of capillary surface is only slightly less than that of the alveolar surface.

The *bronchial arteries*, usually three in number (sometimes more), are inconstant in origin; they may arise from the aorta or from any of the first three intercostal, subclavian, or internal mammary arteries. They supply the bronchial wall as far as the terminal bronchioles, forming one arterial plexus in the peribronchium and another in the tunica propria. The bronchial arteries also supply the tracheobronchial lymph nodes, the midesophagus, and the mediastinal pleura. Distal branches anastomose with one another and with the systemic arterial supply of the pericardium. In some forms of bronchiectasis the bronchial artery system is greatly hypertrophied and may carry significant quantities of blood.

The *pulmonary venous radicles* arise from capillaries distal to the alveolar meshwork and from the capillary network of the pleura. Histologically, venules are indistinguishable from arterioles other than by their position. The venous system drains via the interlobular septa, and thus does not accompany the corresponding bronchial or arterial tree. A bronchial vein plexus, which corresponds to the bronchial artery plexus, extends proximally from the level of the respiratory bronchioles and connects at intervals with the pulmonary veins; most of the veins of the intrapulmonary bronchi drain into the pulmonary veins. The venous drainage of the large bronchi and the tracheal bifurcation form a few small trunks (bronchial veins) that drain into the azygos system and receive branches from the mediastinum. Connections exist between these veins and the intrabronchial venous plexus.

Arteriovenous Anastomoses

Precapillary anastomoses between pulmonary arteries and veins, and between bronchial and pulmonary arteries, may be found in disease; it is not certain whether they occur in the normal lung. Data concerning pulmonary arteriovenous anastomoses are conflicting; some authors claim to have found connections up to 420μ in diameter, whereas others have seen none. Liebow[67] recently reviewed this controversial subject. Turner-Warwick[68] found no anastomoses between systemic and pulmonary arteries in normal lung, but in diseased lungs she observed subpleural and intrapleural anastomoses that appeared to represent enlargement of pre-existing channels.

ROENTGENOLOGY

The *main pulmonary artery* curves upward from the pulmonic valve to form a segment of the left border of the heart. At the level of the carina and slightly to the left of the midline it bifurcates into right and left branches (Figure 1–33). The right branch is almost horizontal in position, and divides into two main branches while still within the mediastinum and before reaching the hilum; the left curves sharply *upward* and backward as it passes into the left hilum, which, therefore, is situated slightly higher and more posterior than the right. In a series of 500 normal subjects in whom the relative levels of the hila were assessed, the left hilum was higher than the right in 97 per cent, the majority (80.4 per cent) showing a difference in level of 0.75 to 2.25 cm.[69] In 3 per cent the hila were at the same level and in none was the right higher than the left. The right hilum usually is projected in the plane of the sixth interspace posteriorly.

The *right pulmonary artery* lies posterior to the aorta and the superior vena cava and anterior to the right main bronchus (Figures 1–33 and 1–34). Its superior branch, the truncus anterior, supplies most of the upper lobe. It curves superiorly and anteriorly over the upper-lobe bronchus and then divides into three branches which follow the anterior, apical, and posterior segmental bronchi. Jefferson[70] found that in 90 per cent of patients a portion of the posterior bronchopulmonary segment is supplied by a separate arterial branch which arises from the descending artery distal to the take-off of the truncus anterior.

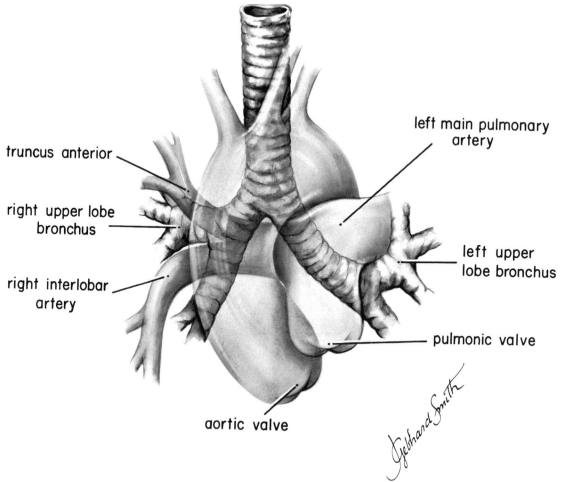

truncus anterior

right upper lobe
bronchus

right interlobar
artery

left main pulmonary
artery

left upper
lobe bronchus

pulmonic valve

aortic valve

Figure 1–33. **Anatomic Relationship between the Central Pulmonary Arteries, the Tracheobronchial Tree, and the Aorta.** The *right pulmonary artery* lies posterior to the ascending aorta and anterior to the right main bronchus. Its superior branch (the truncus anterior) curves superiorly and anteriorly over the upper-lobe bronchus; its inferior branch (the interlobar artery) passes in front of the intermediate bronchus and curves abruptly downward along the lateral aspect of this bronchus. The *left pulmonary artery* passes immediately anterior and lateral to the lower portion of the left main bronchus; the lower of its two main branches in the hilum (the interlobar artery) curves slightly posteriorly over the top of the upper-lobe bronchus and descends abruptly along the lateral aspect of the lower-lobe bronchus (*see* Figure 1–38, page 43).

The inferior of the two pulmonary arteries in the right hilum (the interlobar artery) is much larger than the truncus anterior (Figure 1–34); it passes in front of the intermediate bronchus and on the lateral aspect of this bronchus descends abruptly into the major fissure. It supplies one branch (in 50 per cent of cases, two branches) to the middle lobe, one to the superior segment of the lower lobe, and, in random order, four branches which accompany the basal bronchi of the lower lobe. As in the bronchial tree, the anterior basilar artery, which extends into the lateral costo-

phrenic sulcus, is the most laterally situated basilar artery.

The *left pulmonary artery* splits into two branches within the left hilum after passing immediately anterior and lateral to the lower portion of the left main bronchus (which thus is hyparterial in position, in contrast to the right main bronchus, which is eparterial) (Figure 1–34). The left pulmonary artery is on a more posterior plane than the right, a difference which usually allows of distinction between the two vessels on lateral roentgenograms. The upper (and smaller) of the two divisions of the

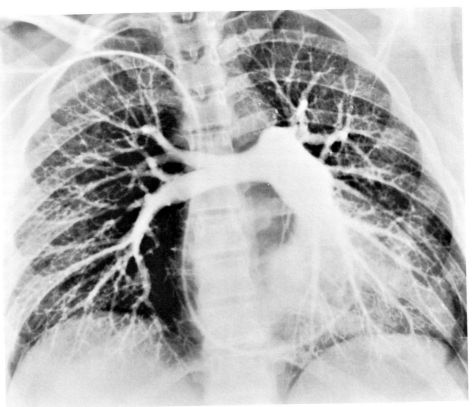

Figure 1–34. **Pulmonary Angiogram.** Arterial phase. *See* text for description.

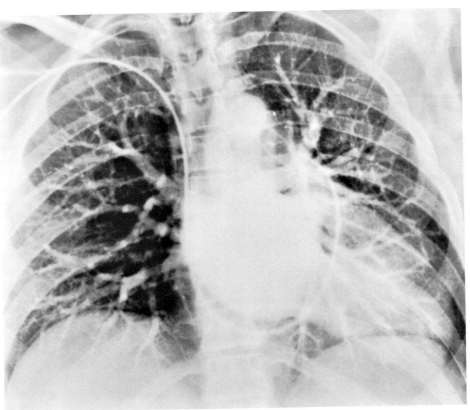

Figure 1–35. **Pulmonary Angiogram.** Venous phase. *See* text for description.

left pulmonary artery sends two or more branches to the apical posterior segments and one to the anterior segment of the upper lobe, following closely the anatomic distribution of the segmental bronchi. Thus, no major vessel to the left upper lobe is analogous to the truncus anterior to the right. The lower of the two main vessels in the hilum (the interlobar artery) curves sharply over the top of the upper-lobe bronchus and descends abruptly, along the lateral aspect of the lower-lobe bronchus, into the major fissure (*see* Figure 1–68, page 94). The lingular artery, with its two branches, arises from the anterior aspect of this vessel. The superior segmental artery of the lower lobe arises from the posterior aspect of the descending artery, just proximal to the origin of the lingular artery. The arterial ramifications to the remainder of the lower lobe

are similar in name and number to the basal bronchi they accompany.

The spatial distribution of pulmonary veins is even more variable than that of the arteries (Figures 1–35 and 1–36). The prevailing pattern comprises two large veins on each side which enter the mediastinum at a level slightly below the pulmonary arteries and anterior to them. On the right side, the superior pulmonary veins drain the upper lobe and usually the middle lobe, although in some cases a separate vein from the middle lobe drains directly into the left atrium or joins with the inferior pulmonary vein; the inferior vein drains the whole of the lower lobe. On the left side, the superior and inferior pulmonary veins drain the upper and lower lobes, respectively, although occasionally lingular drainage is into the inferior vein.

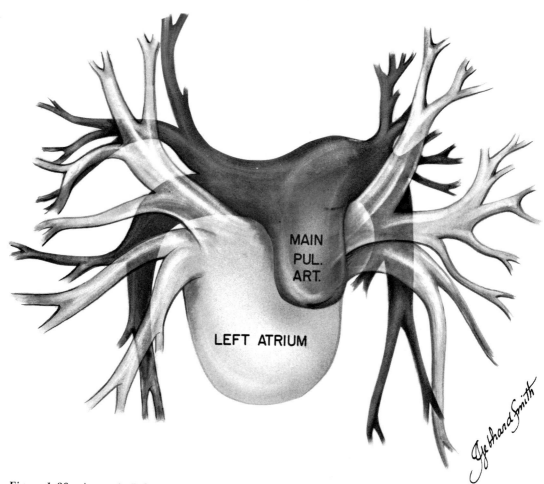

Figure 1–36. **Anatomic Relationship between Pulmonary Arteries and Veins.** In the upper portions of the lungs, the veins (light shading) run lateral to their respective arteries (dark shading); in the mid- and lower-lung zones, the veins lie inferior to the arteries (*see also* Figure 1–37).

Distinction between arterial and venous trunks within the lung fields often can be made without difficulty if certain anatomic relationships are borne in mind (Figure 1–36). The course of the veins within the lungs is remote from the bronchoarterial bundles. This remoteness begins in the periphery of the lungs, where the arterial system is in the center of the lobules and the venous system is within the interlobular septa. This relationship persists, so that in all areas the arteries and their corresponding veins are separated by air-containing lung parenchyma and, thus, should be distinguishable (Figure 1–37). In the upper lobes, the veins run either lateral or inferior to their respective arteries; for example, in the apical segment the vein lies lateral to its artery, whereas in the anterior and posterior segments the relatively horizontal position of the vascular channels is such that the veins lie inferior to the arteries. This inferior relationship of vein to artery usually exists in the right middle lobe and lingula also. Distinction between arteries and veins usually is easier in the lower lobes because of the general vascular topography: the relatively horizontal position of the venous channels contrasts with the almost vertical course of the arteries, a relationship which is particularly well demonstrated in the right lower lobe on a frontal roentgenogram. In the lateral projection, confluence of the pulmonary veins is on a plane slightly anterior to the course of the pulmonary arteries; in this position, the inferior pulmonary vein on the left side often is visualized as a well-circumscribed, round or oval density at its entry into the left atrium—an appearance that should not be mistaken for a mass lesion. As might be expected, throughout the lung fields the caliber and density of the veins are roughly equal to those of their companion arteries.

Although with experience it is often possible to distinguish arteries from veins on standard roentgenograms of the chest in various projections, the confusion of linear shadows may cause some difficulty in identification. The improvement in visualization of vascular shadows to be gained from tomography has been stressed by numerous authors,[71-74] and this technique is strongly recommended when it is important to assess spatial distribution and caliber of the vascular tree (Figure 1–37). In the region of the hila, particularly, tomography may be the only method by which the confusion of vascular shadows may be sorted out; in this situation, the lateral projection often is more revealing than the anteroposterior, as emphasized by Simon[75] (Figure 1–38).

The importance in roentgenographic diagnosis of a proper assessment of the caliber of the hilar pulmonary arteries is considerable. There is little doubt that the most significant sign is a change in the caliber from one examination to another, particularly in relation to the diagnosis of pulmonary embolism; when comparison is not possible or when evidence of pulmonary arterial hypertension is sought, appreciation of the rapidity of tapering of the arteries as they proceed distally is more reliable than mensuration. Roentgenographic measurement of segments of the pulmonary vascular tree appears to us to be of limited value, particularly since it is difficult to establish reproducible reference points for measurement. The figures supplied by Chang,[76] who measured the right descending pulmonary artery in more than 1000 normal adult subjects, appear to be the most accurate available. This author found the normal upper limit of the transverse diameter of the right descending pulmonary artery during inspiration to be 16 mm in males and 15 mm in females; caliber on inspiration was consistently greater than on expiration, the difference varying from 1 to 3 mm.

Perhaps a more useful method of estimating increase or decrease in pulmonary artery caliber is the artery/bronchus index described by Wójtowicz.[74] In a study of 1200 tomograms of 250 normal subjects, this author showed that the ratio of the transverse diameter of a pulmonary artery to that of the bronchus contiguous to it was independent of age, sex, and type of body-build and that it represents a less subjective and more accurate method of assessing disturbances in the pressure and flow in the pulmonary circulation than is possible with direct measurement of the caliber of the artery itself. We have had no experience with this method but think it useful, especially when pulmonary angiography is not feasible. (Examples of the normal mean values of the artery/bronchus indices are 1.03 immediately distal to the take-off of the right upper-lobe bronchus and 1.40 immediately beyond the origin of the left upper-lobe bronchus.)

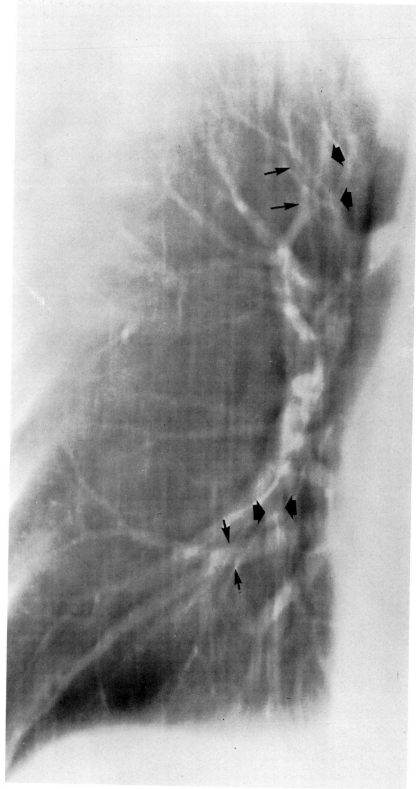

Figure 1–37. **Anatomic Relationship between Pulmonary Arteries and Veins.** Tomographic section of the right lung in AP projection, supine position. Note the lateral relationship of veins (thin arrows) to arteries (thick arrows) in the upper-lung zone. In the lower zone, the relatively horizontal position of the venous channels (thin arrows) contrasts with the almost vertical course of the arteries (thick arrows).

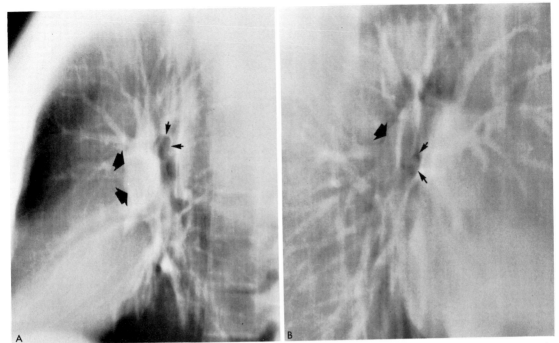

Figure 1-38. **The Hila in Lateral Projection.** *A,* In a lateral tomographic section through the *right* hilum, the tracheal air column is well seen. The oval shadow of the right main pulmonary artery (thick arrows) lies immediately anterior to the air column of the main-stem and intermediate bronchi; immediately above and slightly posterior to this vessel is the circular air column of the right upper-lobe bronchus cut across (thin arrows); the lower-lobe vessels can be seen descending in a slightly posterior direction. *B,* A tomographic section of the *left* hilum reveals certain differences from the right which permits their distinction; the left pulmonary artery is superimposed on the air column of the left main bronchus and immediately above the circular air column of the left upper-lobe bronchus (thin arrows); the interlobar artery (thick arrow) curves posteriorly and inferiorly across the aortic window, giving origin from its posterior surface to the branch of the superior segment of the left lower lobe. The lower-lobe veins can be seen to cross the arteries at a sharp angle.

FUNCTION

Perfusion of the Acinar Unit

Perfusion of acinar units is accomplished through a vast network of thin-walled capillaries which measures 70 to 100 sq m in surface area. The amount of blood in these vessels is estimated to be 60 to 100 ml in the resting subject, increasing to 150 to 250 ml during exercise.[22, 77-80] It is of interest that these figures, which were calculated by measuring uptake of carbon monoxide by red blood cells flowing through capillaries, agree closely with estimates made by anatomic techniques.[81, 82] This may be interpreted as indicating that the capillary vascular bed is maximally distended during peak exercise.[80]

Various pressures modify the flow of blood through the capillaries. (1) *The intravascular pressure* has a mean value of only 14 mm Hg in the pulmonary artery, despite the fact that it handles the same cardiac output as the systemic circulation. (2) *The transmural vascular pressure* is the intravascular pressure minus intrapleural pressure in larger vessels lying outside the lobular limiting membrane. In smaller vessels and capillaries lying within the membrane it is best expressed as the difference between intravascular hydrostatic pressure and alveolar pressure. (3) *The driving pressure* in the pulmonary circulation is the difference between arterial and pulmonary venous or left atrial pressures in the lower part of the lung and the difference between arterial and alveolar pressures in the upper part of the lung, in upright subjects at rest (Figure 1-39). The pressure in capillaries cannot be measured directly; it must be more than 5 mm Hg (left atrial pressure) for blood to move, and has been estimated to be about 9 mm Hg

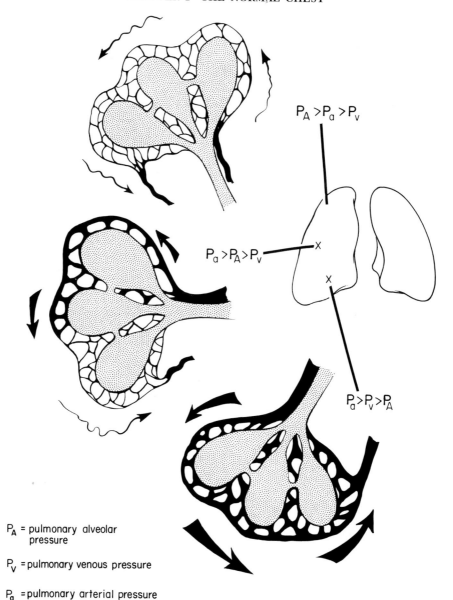

$$P_A > P_a > P_v$$

$$P_a > P_A > P_v$$

$$P_a > P_v > P_A$$

P_A = pulmonary alveolar
      pressure

P_v = pulmonary venous pressure

P_a = pulmonary arterial pressure

Figure 1–39. **Diagram Depicting the Influence of Gravity on Perfusion of Acinar Units in Upright Man.** *In the upper unit,* alveolar pressure (P_A) is higher than pulmonary artery pressure (P_a) so that the capillaries are virtually empty. *In the mid lung,* alveolar pressure (P_A) is lower than arterial pressure (P_a) but higher than venous pressure (P_v) so that blood flow occurs through the arterial end of the capillaries but is impeded on the venous end. *The unit at the base of the lung* shows dilated capillaries throughout since both arterial (P_a) and venous (P_v) pressures are greater than alveolar pressure (P_A).

at the arterial end and 6 mm Hg at the venous end. Since the colloidal osmotic pressure is thought to be 25 to 30 mm Hg, under normal resting conditions a considerable force keeps the alveoli dry; and even during maximal exercise, when the cardiac output increases to 25 to 30 liters/min, in a healthy man, the hydrostatic pressure does not exceed osmotic pressure.

The hemodynamics of the pulmonary circulation cannot be deduced on the basis of laws that relate to a rigid tubular system. Like the conducting system, the circulatory system is distensible; it branches and bends; it is subject to changing pressure on its walls and has a pressure at each end, either or both of which may vary in degree in certain circumstances. Flow is pulsatile but probably always laminar in small vessels and sometimes turbulent in larger ones. Viscosity is greater in the main vessels, but overall resistance to flow is mainly from arterioles and capillaries. When the left atrial pressure and transpleural (alveolar minus intrapleural) pressure are constant, an increase in pulmonary artery pressure causes vessels to distend (transmural pressure increase). As with the conducting system, doubling or halving the radius causes a 16-fold change in resistance; in this case, as cardiac output increases, vessels widen, and closed capillaries open, leading to a fall in resistance.[83]

SUMMARY. Both physiologic and anatomic measurements indicate that the amount of blood in the capillaries in a resting subject is 60 to 100 ml, increasing to 150 to 250 ml during exercise.

Various pressures influence the flow of blood through pulmonary capillaries. The hydrostatic intravascular pressure in the pulmonary artery has a mean value of only 14 mm Hg. The transmural vascular pressure is the intravascular pressure minus the intrapleural pressure in the larger vessels, and in smaller vessels and capillaries it is believed to be the difference between the intravascular hydrostatic and alveolar pressures. The driving pressure in the pulmonary circulation is greatly influenced by gravity. In erect subjects the driving pressure in the upper lung, where alveolar pressure is greater than pulmonary venous pressure, is the difference between arterial and alveolar pressures. In the lower lung the driving pressure is the difference between arterial and venous pressures.

The intravascular pressure in the capillaries is considered to be in the range of 6 to 9 mm Hg, and the great distensibility of these vessels prevents a significant rise even during severe exertion. The colloidal osmotic pressure is 25 to 30 mm Hg, which serves to keep the alveoli dry even with a five-fold increase in cardiac output.

Factors Which Influence Pulmonary Circulation

GRAVITY. The lung measures approximately 30 cm from apex to base, and the hilum is positioned at about the midline. The pulmonary artery enters the lung at the hilum. Since a column of blood 15 cm high is equivalent to a column of mercury 11 mm

high, in the erect subject gravity affects the intravascular pressure to the extent that systolic, diastolic, and mean pressures are reduced by 11 mm Hg at the apex and are increased by 11 mm Hg at the base. If pulmonary arterial pressure in the hilar vessels is taken as 20/9 mm Hg, it follows that pressure at the extreme apex will be 9/ −2, and that no perfusion will occur in the apical zone during diastole; at the base, the pressure will be 31/20, which will cause increase in the capillary pressure in this area and will render the lung base more susceptible to transudation of fluid into the alveoli. Since the pulmonary veins enter the left atrium at approximately the same level, there will be a similar and proportional variation in venous pressure also (Figure 1–39).

The effect of gravity largely governs the distribution of blood flow in the lungs. At the extreme apex in upright man at rest there is no flow simply because the pulmonary arterial pressure is insufficient to overcome the effect of gravity. Farther down the lung, pressure on the arterial side rises but is opposed by alveolar pressure, which readily compresses the thin-walled capillaries. Therefore, the driving pressure in the upper part of the lung is the difference between arterial and alveolar pressures. Since alveolar pressure is not influenced by gravity, and arterial pressure gradually increases down the lung, the driving pressure and, therefore, blood flow also increase. However, because intravascular pressure decreases in the passage of blood from arteriole to venule, alveolar pressure is greater than venous pressure in the upper lung, and the venous end of the capillary is constricted; the degree of constriction decreases gradually as the increasing effect of gravity causes a rise in venous pressure and allows a greater flow of blood as the lung base is approached (Figure 1–39). At one point, venous pressure rises above alveolar pressure, and below that point the driving pressure of blood through the lung is the difference between arterial and venous pressures. Despite the fact that the driving pressure does not increase, because arterial and venous pressures are influenced equally by gravity, blood flow continues to increase as the base of the lung is approached; this is due to the increasing intravascular pressure or transmural pressure on both arterial and venous ends, which dilates the vessels and thereby reduces pulmonary vascular resistance to flow.

Summary. The effect of gravity is to reduce the pulmonary circulation in the upper lung and to increase it in the lower lung. There is no circulation in the capillaries at the extreme apex in erect resting subjects. The pulmonary artery pressure increases from apex to base, and circulation in the capillaries occurs as soon as the pulmonary intravascular pressure is greater than the alveolar pressure. The driving pressure of blood through the lungs becomes the difference between arterial and venous pressures as soon as the effect of gravity causes the pulmonary venous pressure to exceed the alveolar pressure. As the base of the lung is approached, pulmonary circulation continues to increase, not because of an increase in driving pressure—which cannot occur, because arterial and venous pressures are equally affected by gravity—but through the increased transmural pressure, which dilates the pulmonary vasculature and reduces resistance.

INTRAPLEURAL PRESSURE AND LUNG VOLUME.   We have seen that the conducting system to the acinar unit runs in two separate "lung compartments." Similarly, larger arteries and veins are outside the lobular limiting membrane and are influenced by their own transmural pressures, the vessels dilating during inspiration as the pressure difference between the lumen and intrapleural "spaces" increases and constricting during expiration as the pressure difference decreases. Vessels within the limiting membrane, like the membranous airways, are affected by changes in lung volume. The small muscular arteries and arterioles lie beside the airways, whereas the veins are between the lobules at the periphery. During inspiration, the increase in lung volume results in dilatation of the vessels, which are closely interconnected with alveolar tissue within the compartment. During expiration, as the lung assumes a position of rest, the vessels narrow and their blood volume decreases.

It is not known what effect changes in lung volume exert on the pulmonary capillaries. Some believe that dilatation of the capillaries causes pulmonary vascular resistance to decrease during lung inflation.[84] The majority, however, consider that these thin-walled vessels are compressed during inspiration, with a resultant increase in

vascular resistance.[85-87] There is reason to believe that the compression of the pulmonary capillary bed, with its consequent decrease in blood volume, is offset by the rise in volume in the larger vessels during inspiration.[88] Still an unknown quantity in this regard is the part played by surface tension, which is thought to increase as alveoli distend (*see* page 34) and, consequently, would be expected to counteract the effect of compression by pulling away from capillary walls. This concept is not supported by studies of quickly frozen, living lung tissues, which show the alveolus not as a globular or hemispherical structure but as a polygonal figure with mostly flat septa. However, the possibility remains that surface tension of considerable degree exerts an influence on the vessels at the angles of the septa, where curvature is pronounced.[22, 89]

SUMMARY.   The larger pulmonary arteries and veins dilate during inspiration as the difference between intravascular and intrapleural pressures (transmural pressure) increases and constrict during expiration as the pressure difference decreases. The smaller arteries and arterioles, closely interconnected with alveolar tissue, dilate as lung volume increases during inspiration and narrow during expiration. The capillaries probably are compressed during inspiration, leading to an increase in resistance. Surface tension in the alveoli, which increases during inspiration, may counteract the compressing effect of alveolar distention.

NEUROGENIC AND CHEMICAL EFFECTS.   In addition to the pressure and volume changes which passively influence the pulmonary vasculature, some active stimuli can modify capillary circulation to acinar units. Hypoxemia and acidosis appear to be the most potent of these. Such stimuli have not only a vasomotor effect but also a direct action on the myocardium (and, hence, on cardiac output) as well as an indirect effect on both myocardium and vessels via the sympathicoadrenal system; thus, their influence on the hemodynamics of the pulmonary circulation is complex.[90] Systemic hypoxemia acts on the carotid body and triggers a reflex mechanism that gives rise to arteriolar vasoconstriction. Local hypoxia is reported to produce vasoconstriction locally,[91] probably by acting on the arteriole that accompanies the terminal bronchiole, *i.e.*, in the circulation which supplies the acinar unit—an ideal area in which to reduce circulation when ventilation is inadequate.[92] Acidosis, whether metabolic (diabetic ketosis, renal failure, or lactic acidosis) or resulting from an increase in the P_{CO_2}, also causes local vasoconstriction and in poorly ventilated acini acts synergistically with the hypoxemic effect. An increased left atrial or pulmonary venous pressure is thought to be the stimulus for production of arteriolar constriction, which protects capillaries from excessive hydrostatic pressure in such conditions as mitral stenosis.[93, 94, 1367]

Both the arterial and the venous circulation are sensitive to various drugs (*e.g.*, epinephrine, isoproterenol, serotonin, and histamine) under experimental conditions, but the significance of these findings in relation to the human lung in health or in disease is not known.

The effects of precapillary and postcapillary hypertension on pulmonary hemodynamics are considered in more detail in later sections in relation to the diseases which produce these conditions. The existence of precapillary anastomotic channels between bronchial and pulmonary vessels in the normal lung is controversial, but it is known that they are present in certain disease states. Several types have been found in association with congenital pulmonary artery stenosis, bronchiectasis, and pulmonary diseases that give rise to interstitial fibrosis,[68] and their functioning has been demonstrated by use of angiographic techniques and by analysis of oxygen saturation during catheterization of lobar arteries.[95, 819] Since systemic arterial pressure is six to eight times greater than pulmonary artery pressure, flow is from bronchial to pulmonary vessels; as Liebow[96] has pointed out, vascular resistance is increased in these diseased areas, thus allowing blood in the pulmonary circulation to be diverted to better functioning lung units.

SUMMARY. Hypoxemia and acidosis appear to be potent vasomotor stimuli to the pulmonary vasculature. A local vasoconstrictive effect, possibly at the level of the arteriole accompanying the terminal bronchiole, is considered to be responsible for preventing circulation of poorly ventilated acinar units. In certain disease states, bronchial—pulmonary artery anastomoses may increase the vascular resistance in damaged and underventilated areas, thereby diverting pulmonary blood flow to functioning units.

Diffusion of Gas from Acinar Units to Red Blood Cells

DIFFUSION IN THE ACINAR UNIT. Diffusion of a gas occurs passively from an area of higher partial pressure of the gas to one of lower partial pressure. In a gaseous medium, a light gas diffuses faster than a heavier one. In a liquid or in tissue the rate of diffusion is largely dependent upon the solubility of the particular gas in that medium. Oxygen is slightly lighter than carbon dioxide and, therefore, diffuses more rapidly in acinar gas. In water and tissue, carbon dioxide is more soluble than oxygen, and diffuses through these media 20 times faster than does oxygen. Since both are able to diffuse many thousands of times more rapidly in a gaseous medium than in water or tissue, diffusion out of acini consists largely in getting through the alveolocapillary membrane and plasma and in and out of the red cell. Because diffusion through these structures is accomplished much more readily by carbon dioxide than by oxygen, outward diffusion of carbon dioxide never is a clinical problem, and further discussion need concern only the diffusion of oxygen.

Assuming a tidal volume of 450 ml and a dead space of 150 ml, 300 ml of fresh air and 150 ml of dead-space alveolar air from the previous expiration enters the acinar units during each inspiration (Figure 1–29, page 31). Since the units already contain seven or eight times this volume (functional residual capacity), the "fresh" air which enters last may fill only the respiratory bronchioles and main ducts. In the normal lung, however, because of the rapid diffusion of oxygen in a gaseous medium, complete mixing of this fresh air with intra-acinar gas is probably instantaneous. In obstructive emphysema, with the breakdown of alveolar septa and the creation of much larger air spaces, mixing may be delayed, and in these circumstances gaseous diffusion may limit the diffusing capacity.[820]

DIFFUSION ACROSS THE ALVEOLOCAPILLARY MEMBRANE. The membrane through which oxygen diffuses to reach plasma in capillaries comprises (1) a surface-active liquid which lines the intra-alveolar membrane, (2) alveolar epithelial cells with attenuated cytoplasm, (3) basement membrane to the epithelial layer, (4) loose connective tissue, (5) basement membrane to the capillary endothelium, and (6) capillary endothelium. Schulz[97] considers that diffusion takes place only through the lateral cytoplasmic extensions of the alveolar epithelial cells, and states that the "blood-air pathway" in a normal lung is 0.36 to 2.5μ thick. Through this thin membrane, with a driving pressure of approximately 60 mm Hg (PO_2 of alveolar gas minus PO_2 of mixed venous blood [100 − 40 = 60 mm Hg]), under resting conditions oxygen almost fully saturates the blood in one-third of the time taken by blood to traverse the pulmonary capillaries. During exercise, with increased cardiac output and pulmonary capillary blood, the transit time is reduced: nevertheless, aided by the slightly higher PO_2 due to increased ventilation, the blood is virtually saturated by oxygen by the time it reaches the end of the capillary. With decreased alveolar PO_2 (e.g., due to atmospheric conditions at high altitude, respiratory-center depression, or neuromuscular disease), the driving pressure of oxygen is reduced; exercise under these conditions results in a shortened transit time which, together with the reduced driving pressure, may limit diffusion, so that the end-capillary blood may be only partly oxygenated. Although the transit time is thought of in relation to capillaries only, it is probable that the process of diffusion starts in the arterioles which are the origin of capillaries, since their walls are in direct contact with alveolar air.[22, 24, 186]

In addition to the aforementioned factors which affect diffusion, the total area in which flowing blood comes in contact with ventilated acinar units influences the capacity for diffusion. This is exemplified by the decrease in diffusion which occurs after pneumonectomy[1] and may be responsible in part for the decrease in diffusing capacity which occurs in emphysema—in which disease a considerable amount of the alveolocapillary membrane often is destroyed. The amount of effective alveolocapillary membrane often is reduced because of mismatching of capillary circulation with acinar ventilation (see page 52); since this may be an inevitable accompaniment of diseases which cause thickening of the alveolocapillary membrane, assessment of responsibility for diffusion impairment may be difficult.[98, 99]

Many diseases may involve the acinar unit in such a way as to interfere with diffusion (Figure 1–40). In such cases the arterial oxygen saturation may be normal in patients at rest, despite significant reduction in diffusing capacity; however, exercise elicits hypoxemia because the transit time through capillaries is decreased.

INTRAVASCULAR DIFFUSION. The crossing of the alveolocapillary membrane by oxygen does not complete the process of diffusion, and it is probable that resistance to gas movement into red cells often is greater than that to gas movement from the alveoli into the blood.[100] This is due not to the distance to be traversed through plasma to the red cell but to the rate of reaction of oxygen molecules with red-cell contents. Differences in the rate of gas exchange in the red cell, the final phase of diffusion, are not important in relation to normal lungs breathing air, but they play a significant role in diffusion impairment in states of low alveolar oxygen tension and in anemia.

MEASUREMENT OF DIFFUSING CAPACITY. Measurement of the capacity for diffusion of oxygen is a very complicated and perhaps unreliable procedure. It is necessary to know the mixed venous PO_2, in order to determine the driving pressure of oxygen; and the rate of diffusion varies along the capillary as the driving pressure decreases while the PO_2 in capillary blood increases. Because of these problems, carbon monoxide generally is used to measure diffusion; it has a great affinity for hemoglobin and, therefore, only a minute quantity of a low concentration (0.3 per cent) is required. The diffusing capacity for carbon monoxide is the amount of this gas taken up per minute, divided by the difference between partial pressures of carbon monoxide in the alveolus and in capillary blood. Since there is no carbon monoxide in mixed venous blood, the amount of gas taken up is the difference between the carbon monoxide content of inspired and expired gas. The denominator of the equation is equal to the mean alveolar PCO_2, which can be calculated from an end-tidal sample; the mean capillary PCO is so small that it can be ignored. Several techniques have been developed for using this gas; the advantages of particular methods were discussed in detail by Bates and Christie.[1]

SUMMARY. The diffusion of oxygen from alveolus to red blood cell is influenced by the difference between alveolar and mixed venous PO_2, the total area and thickness of alveolocapillary membrane, and the number of red blood cells and their transit time in the pulmonary capillaries. For technical reasons the diffusing capacity is measured most conveniently and accurately with minute quantities of a low concentration of carbon monoxide.

The Matching of Capillary Blood Flow with Ventilation in the Acinus

Ideally, alveolar ventilation and alveolar perfusion should be uniform; *i.e.*, each acinus should receive just the right amount of air to oxygenate the hemoglobin completely and to remove the carbon dioxide

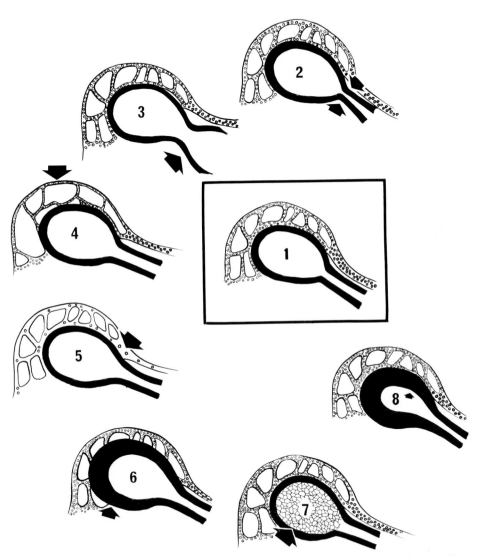

Figure 1–40. **Pathophysiology of Diffusion Defect.** The structure in the center of the diagram (1) is a normal air-containing acinar unit in which are depicted a conducting system, an alveolar cell lining, a normal amount of tissue between air space and capillary endothelium, and a capillary network containing a normal number of red blood cells. The acinar units around the periphery depict various mechanisms of diffusion defect:

(2) Obstruction to air entry.
(3) Dilatation and confluence of respiratory bronchioles (resulting in an increased pathway for diffusion, as in centrilobular emphysema).
(4) Loss of capillaries.
(5) Anemia.
(6) Increase in tissue between air space and capillary endothelium.
(7) Replacement of air in air space by edema, exudate, or blood.
(8) Increase in alveolar lining cells.

given off during gas exchange. This would mean that each of the 33,000 acini, with its 400 alveolar ducts and 8000 alveoli, would receive equal portions of the alveolar ventilation (V̇A), which is estimated to average 4.5 liters/min, and of the alveolar perfusion (Q̇), which averages 5 liters/min. In other words, not only would the ratio of ventilation to perfusion (V̇A/Q̇) be 4.5:5.0 liters, or 0.9 for each lung, but each acinar unit would have an identical ratio. Despite the fact that this is not true even for the normal lung, the concept of an "ideal" V̇A/Q̇ ratio is useful as a point of reference in judging relationships between ventilation and perfusion within the acini.

When the V̇A/Q̇ ratio is not ideal, i.e., other than 0.9, it is either because perfusion is reduced relative to ventilation or because ventilation is decreased relative to blood flow.

The effect of gravity is to increase blood flow to the most dependent portion of lung. In upright man this is the lung base. As stated (see page 45), the increase in blood flow in the middle part of the lung is due to a rising hydrostatic pressure in the arteries and arterioles; since intra-alveolar pressure does not change, the rise in hydrostatic pressure causes an increase in driving pressure. In the lower lung, where pulmonary venous pressure exceeds alveolar, the driving pressure of blood through the lung is the difference between pressure on the arterial end and that on the venous end of the capillary. Since gravity affects the intravascular pressure on the venous end to the same extent as on the arterial end, the driving pressure does not change as the base of the lung is approached. However, vessel distention caused by the increase in intramural pressure reduces resistance in this part of the pulmonary circulation and thus permits ever-increasing blood flow down to the lung base.

Ventilation of the lung is modified by gravity also.[101] The effect of gravity is to increase intrapleural pressure down the lung, i.e., make it less subatmospheric, and thus decrease transpulmonary pressure. Therefore, at the end of a quiet expiration, the acinar units are less distended and their volume is smaller in the lower than in the upper lung regions. During the next inspiration, any change in transpulmonary pressure results in relatively more regional ventilation of lower than of upper lung zones. In other words, since functional residual capacity is proportionally less in lower than in upper lung regions, the lower regions receive a larger percentage of inspired air. If this increase in ventilation from apex to base were directly proportional to the increase in blood flow, the V̇A/Q̇ ratio would not vary throughout the lung. However, this is not the case, and since the effect of gravity is greater on perfusion than on ventilation, blood and gas are slightly mismatched; i.e., the V̇A/Q̇ ratio changes down the lung.

For many years various methods which use inert gases, such as helium, nitrogen, and argon, have been used to determine the distribution of inspired gas to the alveoli (see Chapter 3). These tests detect the presence of poorly ventilated areas but do not locate them and yield normal values when ventilation is uniform, even when perfusion is uneven.

Areas with reduced and absent perfusion contribute little or no carbon dioxide to the expired air; if their volume of ventilation is large enough they cause significant dilution of the carbon dioxide to the total expired gas, since inspired gas going to unperfused areas contains insignificant amounts of carbon dioxide and the gas is expired virtually unchanged. In such circumstances, comparison of the PCO_2 of arterial blood and that of expired gas coming from the alveoli shows that the normal gradient of 2 mm Hg is increased to 6 mm Hg, or more. As with methods using inert gases for the detection of abnormal distribution of ventilation, this demonstration of abnormal distribution of perfusion indicates only that this mismatching of blood and gas exists and does not locate it.

More recently, radioactive gases have been used to determine regional ventilation and perfusion.[102-104] These techniques detect the presence of inequality of perfusion and ventilation at various levels in the lungs of normal subjects. The counters, which measure the radioactivity, "look" at many hundreds of acinar units at one time and obviously reflect the sum total of their V̇A/Q̇ ratios. In contrast to other methods of assessing ventilation and perfusion distribution, they record the ratios which obtain regionally. These methods are useful in studies of the normal lung and are proving their worth in measurement of lung function in various diseases.[105, 106]

At least three groups using radioactive gases have shown beyond question that gravity changes the $\dot{V}A/\dot{Q}$ ratio from "ideal" values in the normal subject.[102-104] The $\dot{V}A/\dot{Q}$ ratio varies between 2 and 3 at the apex of the lung and between 0.5 and 1.0 at the base. The top-to-bottom gravity effect is absent when the subject is supine and is reversed in the head-down position; it is exaggerated at the apices when pulmonary arterial pressure falls and at both top and bottom during acceleration of the body. This last maneuver not only deprives the upper lung of blood but also diverts flow to the lower lung, which may be unventilated because of closure of the conducting system due to the increase in intrapleural pressure.[107]

INCREASED VENTILATION/PERFUSION RATIOS. Increase in the $\dot{V}A/\dot{Q}$ ratio indicates too much ventilation in relation to the amount of blood flowing through that area. Under normal conditions the highest ratios are at the extreme apices of the lungs, where it is believed there are acini which are not perfused in man standing at rest. Therefore, the ratio in such an acinus which is still ventilated can be expressed as infinity. The existence of such units is predicted from knowledge of the effect of gravity on intravascular pressure, which indicates that alveolar pressure is higher than capillary in this region. There is some evidence, however, that perfusion of the lung occurs even when capillary pressure is slightly less than alveolar pressure;[108, 109] intra-alveolar surface tension, pulling away from the capillary wall and thus keeping the capillary open, has been credited with responsibility for this phenomenon,[108] but results of Staub's studies of frozen lung tissue do not support this explanation.[22]

Ventilation of totally underperfused acinar units serves no purpose; neither does a portion of that to units which are overventilated relative to their perfusion. It is possible to determine the disproportion in ventilation in relation to blood flow; this volume is referred to as "wasted ventilation" or "alveolar dead space." When it is added to the volume of the conducting system, *i.e.*, the anatomic dead space, the total is expressed as the "physiologic" dead space. This may be greatly increased in certain disease states, such as embolism to large pulmonary arteries, in which ventilation persists despite little or no circulation, or when large bullous or cystic areas communicate with the conducting system. In such conditions a decreased number of acinar units is available for gas exchange, and, if cardiac output remains unchanged, it follows that ventilation has to increase to expel the usual amount of carbon dioxide and to maintain the usual level of oxygenation. The P_{CO_2} of arterial blood can be kept within normal limits by this adjustment (*see* page 52), but the P_{CO_2} of the end-tidal gas (the expired gas, after subtracting the volume from the anatomic dead space) is reduced because of the contribution from the alveolar dead space. This alveolar-arterial gradient for P_{CO_2} can result only from overventilation relative to perfusion, *i.e.*, a predominance of acinar units with high $\dot{V}A/\dot{Q}$ ratios.

DECREASED VENTILATION/PERFUSION RATIOS. Conversely—and this applies to the base of the lung in normal upright man —there may be too little ventilation in relation to the amount of pulmonary blood flow. In such circumstances, an acinar unit, which is totally unventilated but is perfused, has a $\dot{V}A/\dot{Q}$ ratio of zero. An underventilated unit does not raise the P_{O_2} or lower the P_{CO_2} of the end-capillary blood to the same degree as does a unit with uniform ventilation and perfusion. Therefore blood leaving acinar units with low $\dot{V}A/\dot{Q}$ ratios and going to the left side of the heart and to the systemic circulation decreases the P_{O_2} of arterial blood and increases the P_{CO_2}. This is equivalent to saying that there is some "wasted blood flow" from these units, analogous to the wasted ventilation, which contributes to the expired gas from units that are overventilated relative to their blood flow. This blood adds to the venous admixture caused by "absolute shunts," which exist even in normal lungs. Absolute shunting, *i.e.*, the passage of venous blood through the lungs, without any contact with alveolar gas, occurs in the normal state because bronchial blood flow is partially taken up in the pulmonary venules. In diseased lungs, absolute shunts may develop between pulmonary arterioles and venules, by-passing acinar units, and may contribute significant amounts of blood to the venous admixture. The relative amounts of blood contributed to the venous admixture by absolute shunts and by acini with low $\dot{V}A/\dot{Q}$ ratios can be calculated while the subject breathes 100 per cent oxygen.

Poorly ventilated acini may result from a loss of distensibility (compliance) of the lung units, from the presence of obstruction to flow (resistance) in the conducting system, which prevents satisfactory ventilation in the time taken for a respiratory cycle, or from an abnormally long distance for gas diffusion to the alveolar wall. Regardless of cause, the inhalation of 100 per cent oxygen results in gradual replacement of nitrogen by oxygen, even in the most poorly ventilated unit, so that blood leaving the unit becomes fully saturated. On the other hand, this inspired gas with a high PO_2 (670 mm Hg) does not come in contact with blood flowing through absolute shunts. It follows that any hypoxemia of arterial blood that remains during the inspiration of 100 per cent oxygen is due to absolute shunting. However, because 100 per cent oxygen not only saturates hemoglobin completely but also dissolves 2 ml oxygen per 100 ml blood, as against 0.3 ml when room air is breathed, an absolute shunt of 20 per cent or less may be undetected if measurement is made of only oxygen saturation of arterial blood and not of PO_2. This is because oxygen dissolved in plasma attaches to and fully saturates hemoglobin when blood coming from the lungs, which are exposed to a partial pressure of 100 per cent oxygen, mixes with shunted blood on the left side of the heart. The venous admixture from a shunt of 20 per cent or less can be detected, however, by determining the PO_2 of arterial blood—which, in the absence of an absolute shunt, should be approximately 600 mm Hg.

Since both a lowered PO_2 (indirectly) and a raised PCO_2 (directly) stimulate the respiratory center and augment ventilation, it follows that, if some acinar units are underventilated and thus create hypoxemia and hypercarbia, total alveolar ventilation is increased. This affects well-ventilated acinar units in that carbon dioxide is washed out and their alveolar PCO_2 is reduced, which allows for a higher PCO_2 gradient and, therefore, a greater driving pressure for diffusion between blood and gas. Consequently, excess carbon dioxide retained by blood circulating through poorly ventilated units is balanced by an output larger than normal from units that are perfused and well ventilated. Comparison of the dissociation curves for carbon dioxide and oxygen (Figure 1–41) shows that, although

this compensation can be readily accomplished for carbon dioxide, the shape of the oxygen curve prevents further significant oxygenation at high levels of PO_2. Even if the ventilation of an acinar unit is doubled, raising the PO_2 from 100 to 125 mm Hg, the curve is so nearly horizontal in this range that arterial oxygen saturation increases from 97.5 per cent to only 98.5 per cent. In other words, ventilation/perfusion inequality leading to hypoxemia is not associated with carbon dioxide retention so long as sufficient numbers of acinar units are well ventilated.

SIGNIFICANCE OF VENTILATION/PERFUSION INEQUALITY. Although gravity effects considerable changes in perfusion and in $\dot{V}A/\dot{Q}$ ratios from top to bottom of the lung, the overall effect on gas exchange in normal upright man is small. It has been estimated that the PO_2 of arterial blood would be only 3 mm Hg higher if perfusion matched ventilation exactly.[107] Increased flow to the lungs, as occurs during exercise or in the presence of left-to-right cardiac shunts, produces a more even distribution of blood, as does pulmonary arterial or venous hypertension.

Unevenness of ventilation and perfusion is the major cause of cyanosis in patients with respiratory disease. However, it is remarkable how severely the lung may be diseased without deviation of the arterial oxygen saturation from the normal range of 95 to 100 per cent: it may remain so when a lobe or even an entire lung has been destroyed by bronchiectasis or emphysema. In many cases this may be explained by the simultaneous destruction by disease of vessels and airways. In such circumstances, despite the fact that both ventilation and perfusion are uneven, they are matched, and the $\dot{V}A/\dot{Q}$ ratios approach "ideal." In addition to these fortuitous "pathologic occurrences," compensatory physiologic mechanisms attempt to maintain $\dot{V}A/\dot{Q}$ ratio and arterial oxygen saturation within normal limits. Since, as pointed out by Staub,[22] the pulmonary microcirculation lacks sphincters and innervation, it appears that blood distribution in capillaries is purely random and is influenced by such minor factors as blocked capillaries (by microembolism and leukocytes) and, perhaps, even the angle of a capillary as it comes off the arteriole. If such is the case, it seems almost essential that some regional

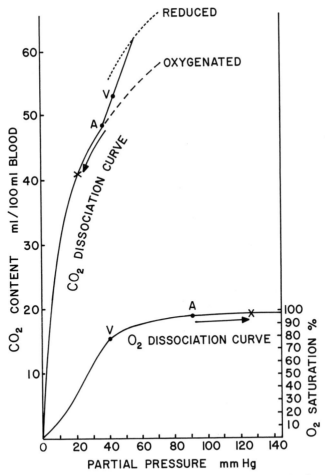

Figure 1-41. **The Carbon Dioxide and Oxygen Dissociation Curves of Blood.** The arrows (A → X) indicate the effect of doubling the ventilation on both CO_2 content and O_2 content (arterial oxygen saturation). The normal values for both arterial (A) and venous (V) oxygen and carbon dioxide are noted. It can be seen that, at any given PCO_2, reduced blood can carry more carbon dioxide than oxygenated blood. *See* text.

control to match ventilation and perfusion should exist at entry to the lung unit. For this reason it seems logical to assume that the very close association of terminal bronchiole and arteriole in the same connective-tissue sheath is more than a chance occurrence. This would be an ideal site to shut off perfusion when ventilation was inadequate or to reduce ventilation when blood flow was lacking. A low PO_2 in the gas approaching the acinus may act at this site:[92] by producing a constriction of the pulmonary arteriole it may divert blood to areas which are better ventilated. Studies with an electrode inserted into pulmonary arteries 2 mm in diameter clearly show that inspired gas diffuses into the lumen of such vessels.[186] There is also a mechanism for reducing ventilation in areas with little or no perfusion. The stimulus to this bron-

chiolar or bronchial constriction is a low PCO_2, but the exact site of action has not been determined.[64, 65, 153]

SUMMARY. Even in the normal lung there is mismatching of ventilation and perfusion. Both are affected by gravity but perfusion to a greater extent than ventilation and, therefore, the upper lung is overventilated and the lower underventilated relative to circulation. The distribution of inspired gas can be detected with the use of inert gases. The distribution of blood can be measured by comparing the PCO_2 of arterial blood with the PCO_2 of mixed alveolar expired gas. These methods of determining distribution indicate the likelihood of gross mismatching of blood and gas but do not indicate which areas of the lung are responsible. Radioactive gases can be inhaled and can be injected into a systemic vein, and by use of scintillation counters over the chest wall, regional ventilation and perfusion can be estimated. Each counter will measure the sum total of $\dot{V}A/\dot{Q}$ ratios of large numbers of acini.

An *increased* ventilation/perfusion ratio (greater than 0.9) indicates too much ventilation relative to perfusion; such a situation exists normally in the upper lungs. The surplus of ventilation can be calculated and is known as "wasted ventilation." This, together with the anatomic dead space, represents the "physiologic" dead space. In certain disease states, such as pulmonary embolism or large bullae, which communicate with the bronchial tree, the physiologic dead space may be considerable and is reflected in an increase in the arterial–alveolar PCO_2 gradient.

A *decreased* ventilation/perfusion ratio (less than 0.9) indicates too little ventilation relative to perfusion. Such a situation exists normally in the lower lung zones. The surplus of perfusion ("waste blood flow") is indicated by the degree of reduction in arterial blood PO_2.

Hypoxemia due to underventilated alveoli can be distinguished from that due to absolute shunts in the lung when the patient breathes 100 per cent oxygen: this raises the PO_2 to the normal level of 600 mm Hg, or more, in cases of hypoventilation resulting from any cause. Some degree of absolute shunt is present if this level is not reached.

Pulmonary capillary blood leaving underventilated areas is not fully saturated with oxygen and has a raised PCO_2. When there is sufficient healthy lung remaining, an increase in ventilation allows maintenance of the PCO_2 at a normal level in the arterial blood, but, because of the shape of the oxygen-dissociation curve, usually hypoxemia is not corrected.

The effect of gravity in normal upright man is to decrease the PO_2 to 3 mm Hg less than it would be in "ideal" circumstances. Even when the pulmonary parenchyma is largely destroyed there may be very little mismatching of perfusion and ventilation. Simultaneous destruction of circulation and air spaces account for this in part, but there are physiologic mechanisms also which prevent circulation to poorly ventilated areas and ventilation to poorly perfused areas.

Blood Gases and H-ion Concentration (pH)

The ability of the lung to perform its prime function—the exchange of oxygen and carbon dioxide—is readily determined from analysis of a sample of arterial blood. The oxygen carried can be measured as arterial oxygen saturation or as PO_2. Arterial oxygen saturation = O_2 content/O_2 capacity (per cent). Since each 1.0 g of hemoglobin can combine with 1.34 ml O_2, the oxygen capacity of a subject with 15 g hemoglobin per 100 ml blood is approximately 20 ml/ 100 ml blood. The content is the amount of oxygen that the blood actually contains; this can be determined in a sample by extracting under anaerobic conditions. In a subject with normal lungs breathing air at sea level this amounts to 19 ml (or slightly more) and, therefore, oxygen saturation is $19/20 \times 100$, or 95 per cent.

The PO_2 may be determined from the oxygen-dissociation curve, using arterial oxygen saturation, but this is not truly reliable, because of the almost horizontal slope of the upper part of the curve (*see* Figure 1–41). The PO_2 can be measured directly, by use of an electrode—which, as we have seen, is the only way of determining total oxygen carried by hemoglobin and plasma during the inhalation of 100 per cent oxygen.

In contrast to oxygen, which is carried almost entirely by hemoglobin, approximately 75 per cent of carbon dioxide is contained in plasma. In the resting subject, whereas mixed venous blood holds about 15 ml O_2/100 ml blood at a PO_2 of 40 mm Hg and an oxygen saturation of 75 per cent, its carbon dioxide content is about 52 ml/100 ml blood at a PCO_2 of 45 mm Hg. Although the red blood cell carries only 25 per cent of the carbon dioxide it plays an essential role in the transport of this gas to the lungs; it contains the enzyme carbonic anhydrase, which rapidly hydrates the carbon dioxide passing through the erythrocyte membrane and converts it into carbonic acid, H-ions, and bicarbonate ions. The bicarbonate ions (HCO_3) quickly permeate the cell membrane and enter the plasma in exchange for chloride ions; in this manner, as bicarbonate, most of the carbon dioxide from the tissues is carried by the blood. Since blood which contains reduced hemoglobin can carry more carbon dioxide than can fully oxygenated blood at the same PCO_2, the circumstances are ideal for the uptake of carbon dioxide in the tissues and its unloading in the pulmonary capillaries when the hemoglobin has been reoxygenated (*see* Figure 1–41).

In anemia, no matter how severe, the PO_2 is normal and the hemoglobin is fully saturated, oxygen content and capacity being reduced. However, the small amount of oxygen taken up by the blood indicates the presence of the anemia and the resultant reduction in total oxygen transport to the tissues. When normal hemoglobin is replaced by methemoglobin, sulfhemoglobin, or carboxyhemoglobin, the PO_2 remains normal, although spectrophotometric analysis of the sample reveals reduction in oxygen saturation.

Arterial hypoxemia may be due to one or more of four mechanisms — diffusion defect, true shunt, ventilation/perfusion inequality, or hypoventilation.

A reduction in diffusing capacity is most commonly seen in emphysema, in which it is due to ventilation/perfusion inequality and loss of alveolocapillary membrane, and in those diseases that give rise to thickening of the alveolocapillary membrane from granulomatous, fibrotic, or neoplastic infiltration. As already mentioned (*see* page 48), this latter group may have VA/Q inequality also, which in some undoubtedly plays a major part in reducing the capacity for diffusion. Hypoxemia may be absent at rest, but during exercise, when the intracapillary transit time is reduced, arterial oxygen saturation and PO_2 are decreased. The PCO_2 is normal or may even be reduced, because carbon dioxide diffuses through a tissue membrane 20 times as readily as oxygen; also, these subjects tend to hyperventilate and thereby produce a decrease in carbon dioxide with a secondary decrease in bicarbonate, to compensate for the respiratory alkalosis.

A true shunt of venous blood to systemic circulation may be due to congenital cardiac disease, arteriovenous aneurysm of the lung, or, in some diseases which affect the parenchyma, precapillary anastomosis of the pulmonary arteriole and venule. The shunted blood never comes in contact with acinar units, whether or not these are ventilated, and for this reason the PO_2 of the arterial blood cannot be raised to a normal value (approximately 600 mm Hg) during inhalation of 100 per cent oxygen. In fact, when the shunt handles 10 per cent or more of the cardiac output, the arterial PO_2 will not rise above 400 mm Hg when 100 per cent oxygen is inhaled. All other mechanisms which produce hypoxemia can be fully corrected by the inspiration of 100 per cent oxygen, which replaces nitrogen in even the poorest ventilated acini. In true shunt, no matter how large, the PCO_2 always is normal or low, since additional ventilation effects removal of more carbon dioxide from acini which are perfused and ventilated. The inability of this compensatory hyperventilation to significantly improve uptake of oxygen is apparent on study of the oxygen- and carbon dioxide-dissociation curves (*see* Figure 1–41). Double the ventilation results in a decrease in PCO_2 from 40 to 20 mm Hg, with elimination of considerable amounts of carbon dioxide, whereas the increase in PO_2 that results from increase in ventilation produces an almost insignificant increase in arterial-blood oxygen content and saturation.

In most cases the hypoxemia and cyanosis that accompany pulmonary disease are due to VA/Q inequality. Chronic bronchitis and emphysema are the clinical conditions most commonly associated with this physiologic disturbance. The capillary blood that flows by underventilated acinar units is not fully saturated and does not release a normal amount of carbon dioxide, since the gradient between the PCO_2 of blood and of the acinus is reduced. However, again because of the difference in the dissociation curves, hyperventilation of well-ventilated acini, with consequent reduction in PCO_2 in such areas, increases the blood-to-acinus gradient and effects greater elimination of carbon dioxide from these areas. Consequently, patients with VA/Q inequality may have low, normal, or increased PCO_2. The PCO_2 increases as the disease advances and the work of breathing results in greater production of carbon dioxide by the muscles of respiration than can be eliminated by the fewer normally functioning acini; or, perhaps more correctly, the PCO_2 rises when the patient, exposed to the discomfort of excessive respiratory effort, settles subconsciously for a higher arterial-blood PCO_2 — which, incidentally, is a compensatory mechanism, since it increases the PCO_2 gradient between blood and acinus. Patients with diseases that give rise to $\dot{V}A/\dot{Q}$ inequality can correct their hypoxemia and cyanosis by breathing 100 per cent oxygen, as oxygen replaces nitrogen in even the poorest ventilated areas. When carbon dioxide retention also is present, prolonged inhalation of oxygen increases the concentration of carbon dioxide in arterial blood, and confusion and coma may result. This further retention of carbon dioxide during oxygen breathing is due to removal of the carotid body's hypoxemic stimulus to ventilation.

Hypoxemia and carbon dioxide retention associated with hypoventilation is, in fact, only a gross example of $\dot{V}A/\dot{Q}$ abnormality. In diseases of the respiratory center itself and in neuromuscular disease affecting the thoracic cage, the overall decrease in ventilation may be generalized, resulting in underventilation despite normal perfusion, i.e., the $\dot{V}A/\dot{Q}$ ratio may be reduced in every acinus in both lungs. When obesity is associated with hypoventilation, with resultant polycythemia, hypoxemia, and carbon dioxide retention, the $\dot{V}A/\dot{Q}$ inequality may be localized to the lung bases.[111] This form of hypoxemia may be readily corrected by the patient's taking a few deep breaths of even room air; this finding, together with good function-test values of bronchial flow, differentiates this condition from obstructive lung disease. The inhalation of 100 per cent oxygen by patients with general hypoventilation causes them to respond with further decrease in ventilation and its consequences, as occurs in other diseases which cause $\dot{V}A/\dot{Q}$ inequality.

Together with the analysis of arterial blood to determine oxygen saturation (or PO_2)—which indicates the abnormal physiologic process and, when combined with clinical information, aids in diagnosis—determination of the H^+ concentration (pH) of the blood is of the utmost importance. When carbon dioxide retention is present, the H^+ concentration indicates whether this represents acute respiratory failure or whether it is due to chronic failure in which the kidneys have had time and possess the ability to compensate by increasing bicarbonate. When the H^+ concentration is reduced and the PCO_2 also is below the accepted range, acute respiratory alkalosis is present. A normal concentration of H^+ with a decreased PCO_2 indicates chronic hyperventilation and a lapse of time

sufficient for the development of compensation by the kidneys.

In addition to the respiratory causes of variation in PCO_2, H^+ concentration, and bicarbonate, some nonrespiratory (metabolic) processes produce acidosis and alkalosis and require secondary or compensatory under- or overventilation to return the acid-base balance to normal. A respiratory and nonrespiratory condition may act simultaneously; this occurs most commonly in cases of concurrent respiratory and cardiac arrest, when carbon dioxide accumulates and tissue hypoxia leads to an increase in formation of lactic acid.

Another somewhat confusing variation in acid-base balance is due to sudden improvement in ventilation in patients with chronic carbon dioxide retention. These subjects usually have emphysema and are in respiratory failure, their carbon dioxide retention being compensated by a secondary increase in bicarbonate. Artificial ventilation with a respirator produces a sudden fall in PCO_2, and, since the kidneys cannot adjust immediately, nonrespiratory alkalosis ensues. The same effect may be seen in cases of hypoventilation syndrome when arterial blood is drawn for gas analysis: the procedure induces sudden increase in ventilation, leading to a fall in PCO_2 but little change in the elevated level of bicarbonate.

Various changes in acid-base balance seen in our pulmonary function laboratory over a period of six months are illustrated by the short case histories depicted in Table 1–3.

SUMMARY. The amount of oxygen carried by the arterial blood can be measured by determining its content per 100 ml blood and dividing this by the total amount of oxygen the same blood can carry when exposed to oxygen (oxygen capacity): this ratio is known as the arterial oxygen saturation. A more reliable method is to measure the PO_2 of arterial blood with an electrode.

Most of the carbon dioxide is carried in the plasma as bicarbonate. The red blood cell, however, contains carbonic anhydrase, an enzyme which converts carbon dioxide into carbonic acid, H ions, and bicarbonate, the last of which crosses the cell membrane in exchange for chloride ions. Blood which contains reduced hemoglobin can carry more carbon dioxide, a circumstance which is ideal for assimilating carbon dioxide in the tissues and releasing it in the lungs.

Table 1-3. *Disturbances in Acid-Base Balance*

TESTS AND NORMAL VALUES / DIAGNOSIS	Age	Sex	H⁺ 35 to 45 mEq/l	pH 7.35 to 7.45	PCO₂ 35 to 45 mm Hg	HCO₃⁻ 22 to 28 mM/l	Po₂ 80 to 100 mm Hg	O₂Hb 95 to 100 %	CLINICAL HISTORY
Chronic Bronchitis and Emphysema	74	M	83	7.08	79	16.5		44	The patient was cyanotic and comatose when the first blood was drawn. A severe combined respiratory and nonrespiratory acidosis was found. Over the next 48 hours bicarbonate therapy slowly corrected the acidosis and oxygen the hypoxemia but the patient remained comatose with raised PCO₂ (bloods 2 and 3). An endotracheal tube was inserted and artificial ventilation was given by respirator. The fourth blood was taken 24 hours later while breathing room air. The PCO₂ was reduced considerably and the patient was left in mild nonrespiratory alkalosis.
			69	7.16	90	28		100	
			48	7.32	85	38		96	
			32	7.49	57	40		82	
Status Asthmaticus	45	F	36	7.44	51	32		83	The first and second blood were drawn at 48 hour intervals in a patient with an unusually prolonged attack of asthma. A compensated respiratory acidosis was found (both PCO₂ and bicarbonate raised). With intensive bronchodilator therapy the bronchospasm largely cleared and the patient was left with a mild nonrespiratory alkalosis. All bloods were taken while breathing room air.
			42	7.38	60	32		68	
			30	7.52	44	33.5	70	92	
Middle Cerebral Artery Thrombosis	58	F	31	7.51	29.2	22		90	The first blood was drawn following a sudden onset of coma and hemiplegia. The patient had aspirated. Respiratory alkalosis with mild hypoxemia was shown. The second blood was taken just before death with the patient breathing O₂. Hyperventilation persisted but a nonrespiratory acidosis had caused a fall in bicarbonate and the H⁺ concentration was just above normal limits.
			46	7.34	16	9		100	
Liver Cirrhosis Terminal Renal Failure	62	M	50	7.30	29	14			This patient who was in a terminal state and died two days later showed a nonrespiratory acidosis (bicarbonate down and H⁺ concentration up) partially compensated by hyperventilation (PCO₂ down).
Nephrolithiasis and Pyonephrosis Bronchopneumonia	72	M	53	7.28	38.5	16.8		92	A blood urea nitrogen of 205 mg per 100 ml indicated that this nonrespiratory acidosis (bicarbonate down, H⁺ concentration up) was due to renal failure. Autopsy showed in addition bilateral bronchopneumonia which may account for his failure to produce a compensatory hyperventilation (PCO₂ unchanged).
Kidney Transplant	40	F	41	7.39	30	17.5			Since this blood was taken in a patient who had a recent kidney transplant and who showed slight nitrogen retention, it presumably represents a mild nonrespiratory acidosis with secondary hyperventilation. This picture is also quite compatible with a primary respiratory alkalosis with secondary renal compensation.
Pyloric Peptic Ulcer with Obstruction. Schizophrenia	49	F	30	7.52	59	43			This schizophrenic patient was admitted with persistent vomiting. A nonrespiratory alkalosis (bicarbonate up, H⁺ concentration down) partially compensated by hypoventilation (PCO₂ up) was found. The vomiting was corrected and the acid-base balance was returned to normal (bloods not shown). Ten days later she was readmitted in a similar state and the attempt to compensate for the nonrespiratory alkalosis was reflected both in the lowered Po₂ and the raised PCO₂ (second blood). A pyloric ulcer was found and a subtotal gastrectomy was done. The final blood taken a few days after the operation showed a return of acid-base values to normal.
			26	7.58	60	54	61	87	
			38	7.42	34.5	21			

In diffuse infiltrative disease of the alveolar septa, arterial hypoxemia is due partly to $\dot{V}A/\dot{Q}$ inequality and partly to diffusion defect and may be manifest only during exercise. Since carbon dioxide diffuses 20 times as readily as oxygen, in these diseases the diffusion defect is for oxygen only, and the P_{CO_2} is normal or low.

A true or absolute shunt results in hypoxemia without carbon dioxide retention. Patients with this condition hyperventilate and maintain low or normal levels of carbon dioxide. In chronic bronchitis and emphysema, hypoxemia is due mainly to $\dot{V}A/\dot{Q}$ abnormality; the P_{CO_2} is low, normal, or high depending upon the patient's ability to hyperventilate and the presence of sufficient remaining functioning lung to compensate. Disease of the neuromuscular system or the respiratory center causes general hypoventilation and, therefore, hypoxemia and carbon dioxide retention. In the hypoventilation associated with obesity the $\dot{V}A/\dot{Q}$ ratio at the lung bases appears to be grossly decreased; the unsaturation and carbon dioxide retention are readily corrected by the patients' taking a few deep breaths of even room air.

Measurement of the H^+ concentration of the arterial blood is an essential part of blood-gas analysis. Acute carbon dioxide retention is manifested by a rise in P_{CO_2} and a normal level of bicarbonate and, therefore, increase in H^+ concentration. Chronic carbon dioxide retention is accompanied by raised bicarbonate and normal H^+ concentration. Similarly, a low P_{CO_2} with decreased H^+ indicates acute hyperventilation and, with normal H^+ concentration, chronic hyperventilation. Secondary hyperventilation and hypoventilation may be initiated by nonrespiratory acidosis or alkalosis. Respiratory and nonrespiratory acid-base disturbances may occur simultaneously and can be interpreted only in full knowledge of the clinical situation.

DEVELOPMENT OF THE LUNG

The lung develops as a ventral outpouching of the foregut at 24 days of embryonic life. Intrauterine development is conveniently, if somewhat arbitrarily, divided into three periods: glandular, canalicular, and alveolar. The first, or *glandular phase*, lasts until the sixteenth week; during this time the primitive lung bud divides and redivides dichotomously and grows into the surrounding mesenchyme. At the end of this period bronchial divisions are nearly complete, but cartilage and bronchial glands continue to develop until the twenty-fourth week. The *canalicular period* is characterized by growth of the peripheral portion of the bronchial tree, producing the areas destined to become the acinus; during this period, capillaries grow into the lung, separating the epithelial cells into groups. The *alveolar phase* begins at about 24 weeks and is characterized by the development of evaginations of the terminal epithelium-lined tubes to form alveoli. At about 28 weeks, continuation of alveolar growth, attenuation of the lining epithelium, and capillary ingrowth produce an adequate area for gas exchange. Alveoli continue to develop through the remaining period of intrauterine life, until, at birth, there are approximately 24 million alveoli. For a long time it has been known that the lungs continue to grow after birth, but it is only recently that this has been determined quantitatively.[148] Alveoli continue to increase in number until the age of 8 years, when the full adult complement is reached. The alveolar surface area increases from 2.8 sq m at the time of birth to 32 sq m at age 8 years and continues to increase until the subject is 18 to 20 years of age. Alveolar surface area is linearly related to body surface area. The site and mode of alveolar development between birth and maturity are not known for certain. The adult complement of conducting airways is present at birth, and the alveolated structures (alveolar ducts and sacs) increase from 2 million at birth to 14 million at age 8 years (and maturity). This increase may be brought about by new growth of alveolar ducts and sacs, or by conversion of previously nonalveolated bronchioles to alveolar ducts and sacs, or a combination of the two.

THE NERVOUS SYSTEM

Sensory fibers from the lung run in the vagus and are derived from various sources. The bronchial epithelium contains nerve endings which are sensitive to tactile stimulation and which continue as far as respiratory bronchioles. Stretch receptors are present in the lamina propria, muscle, and cartilage of the bronchi. The pulmonary veins are particularly well supplied, and the terminals of the subendothelial nerves probably are chemoreceptors. Branches associated with venules lie in septa in the periphery of lobules, and it is likely that these are sensitive to stretch. Pressor receptors are present in the muscle of pulmonary arteries and veins.

The motor supply is derived from both sympathetic and parasympathetic systems. The sympathetic supply is from the second, third, and fourth thoracic sympathetic ganglia, and the parasympathetic, through the vagus, forms peribronchial and perivenous ganglia. Motor supply in the bronchial tree extends as far as the terminal bronchioles, and in the pulmonary artery and vein to the limit of muscle. The bronchial arteries also have a rich nerve supply.

THE PLEURA

MORPHOLOGY

The lung is encased by the visceral pleura, a stable membrane which is separated from the limiting membrane of the lung by a layer of loose connective tissue. The pleura is only loosely attached to the limiting membrane—the two are readily separated in the plane of the subpleural connective tissue, and fluid or air may collect in this layer. Expansion of the lung is restricted to some extent by the limiting membrane and the pleura, as evidenced by the close correlation between total lung volume at full inspiration during life and lung volume after death, even with high transpulmonary pressures. Further, impressions caused by the heart and great vessels remain after death, despite inflation to high transpulmonary pressure.

The pleura consists of a thin superficial layer or endopleura and a denser, deeper layer known as the chief layer. The superficial layer consists of a delicate sheet of elastic and collagenous fibers, in no particular pattern, underlying a sheet of mesothelial cells. These cells are thin and flattened, a few microns thick and about 30μ in diameter; they may swell to become cuboidal and can multiply rapidly. The chief layer of the pleura, which is responsible for its mechanical stability, consists of dense collagenous and elastic tissue. The chief layer crosses intralobar fissures with the superficial layer.

The subpleural connective tissue consists of loose connective tissue which is a continuation of the pulmonary interstitial tissue. Lymphatic channels, veins, arteries, and a rich capillary network are present in this layer, which is also referred to as the vascular layer of the pleura. Irregularly placed bands of collagenous and elastic fibers extend perpendicularly or obliquely from the chief layer to the limiting membrane, although, as mentioned previously, these two layers are but loosely bound together.

ROENTGENOLOGY

The combined thickness of the parietal and visceral pleural layers over the convexity of the lungs and over the diaphragmatic and mediastinal surfaces is insufficient to render these layers roentgenographically visible in the normal human subject. The diaphragmatic and mediastinal pleura, even if uniformly thickened to a moderate degree, is never visible, since its water density precludes roentgenographic separation from the contiguous diaphragm and mediastinum. Over the convexity of the lungs, however, thickening of only slight degree (1 to 2 mm, for example) can be appreciated because of the greater density of contiguous ribs. Such an appearance is evidence of either current pleural disease or residual thickening from past disease.

In the interlobar regions, contiguous layers of visceral pleura are roentgenographically visible because of the presence of air-containing lung on both sides. Interlobar fissures become visible when the x-ray beam passes tangentially along their surfaces; when visualized, these constitute a valuable aid to the assessment of disease of the pulmonary lobes which form them. Much of our knowledge of the incidence of roentgenographic visualization of normal and accessory fissures was supplied by Felson,[69, 119] whose review of the chest roentgenograms of large numbers of normal human subjects provided accurate statistics on this and other aspects of normal roentgen anatomy.

Fissures

NORMAL INTERLOBAR FISSURES. Fissures form the contact surfaces between pulmonary lobes. They vary greatly in depth from complete separation of lobes to no more than a superficial slit not more than 1 to 2 cm deep in the surface of the lung. The depth of interlobar fissures is important: The less complete a fissure line the larger the bridge of lung parenchyma connecting two contiguous lobes; such parenchymal bridges provide a ready pathway for collateral air-drift or for the spread of disease from one lobe to another, thereby creating roentgenographic signs that may give rise to erroneous conclusions. Therefore, in assessing certain diseases, due consideration should be given the depth of interlobar fissures.

Interlobar surfaces seldom appear flat when viewed anatomically. For example, major fissures face forward and slightly outward in their upper half, whereas in their lower half they face forward and slightly medially (similar to an airplane propeller) (Figure 1–42). Similarly, the minor fissure, although in a generally horizontal plane, may make a double curve, the medial portion being convex upward and the lateral half convex downward, thus creating a shallow S configuration. These curvatures explain the relative infrequency with which fissures are visualized along their entire length; however, should complete roentgenographic visualization be desired, it is necessary only to rotate the patient slightly into different obliquities to bring all portions of the fissures into profile. In some cases the configuration of the entire fissure can be extrapolated or interpolated quite accurately from the appearance of short segments.

THE OBLIQUE (MAJOR) FISSURE. This fissure (Figure 1–43), which separates the upper (and middle) lobe from the lower lobe, begins at or about the level of the fifth thoracic vertebral body and extends obliquely downward and forward, roughly paralleling the sixth rib, ending at the diaphragm a few centimeters behind the anterior pleural gutter. The major fissures are incomplete at the mediastinal surface of the lungs much more frequently than is generally realized; Schall and Hoffman are said by Shanks and Kerley[120] to have found failure of the main fissure to reach the mediastinal surface above or below the hilum in 50 per cent of lungs. In lateral roentgenographic projection, if portions of both major fissures are visualized, the laterality

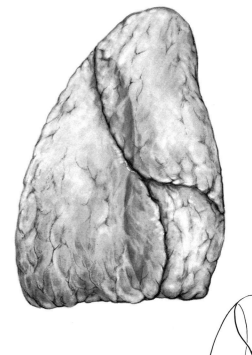

Figure 1–42. **Interlobar Fissures, Right Lung.** A drawing of the right lung from its lateral aspect reveals the major fissure to be shaped like an airplane propeller, its upper half facing forward and slightly laterally and its lower half forward and slightly medially.

of each can be determined from the junction of the right fissure with the horizontal fissure or by the relationship of both to the hemidiaphragms (the left hemidiaphragm being identifiable by its relationship to the gastric air bubble).

THE HORIZONTAL (MINOR) FISSURE. This fissure (Figure 1–43), which separates the anterior segment of the right upper lobe from the right middle lobe, lies in a roughly horizontal plane at about the level of the fourth rib anteriorly. As has been indicated, its contour is variable—to a point, in fact, at which Felson concluded on the basis of a study of 1000 normal subjects that significance cannot be attached to displacement of the fissure unless it is of major degree.[69] Anatomically the minor fissure rarely reaches the mediastinum, and then only in its anterior portion; despite this, one of the more constant relationships of the minor fissure noted by Felson roentgenograph-

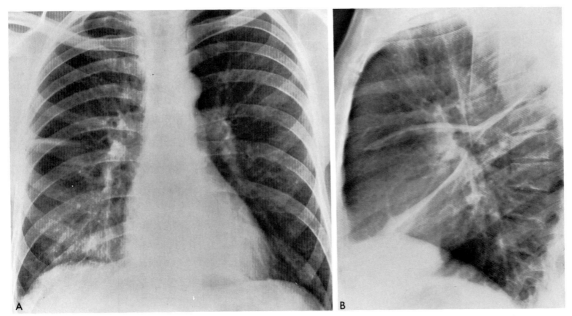

Figure 1–43. **Interlobar Fissures, Right Lung.** The presence of minimal interlobar effusion renders the fissures clearly visible in posteroanterior (A) and lateral (B) roentgenograms.

ically was its medial termination at the lateral margin of the inferior pulmonary artery, about 1 cm distal to the origin of the artery. Reports of the roentgenographic visualization of the minor fissure in normal subjects vary considerably: Felson[69] saw it in 56 per cent, Ritter and Eyband[121] in 70 per cent, and Simon[122] in over 80 per cent.

ACCESSORY (SUPERNUMERARY) FISSURES. It is important to realize that any segment of lung may be partially or completely separated from its adjacent segments by an accessory pleural fissure. The incidence anatomically is much higher than is generally appreciated, amounting to about 50 per cent of lungs, according to von Hayek.[15] These fissures vary in their degree of development from superficial slits in the lung surface not more than 1 to 2 cm deep to complete fissures which extend all the way to the hilum. More often than not these accessory fissures are of little more than academic interest roentgenologically; when well developed, however, their recognition is important for two reasons: (1) the segment they subtend may be the only site of disease whose spread is prevented by the presence of a fissure and (2) when a fissure is present in a specific anatomic location, such as between the superior and basal segments of the right lower lobe, it may be mistaken for

the minor fissure between upper and middle lobes and thus create confusion in interpretation.

Perhaps the best known of the accessory fissures, although of no known pathologic significance, is the *azygos fissure* (the mesoazygos), which is created by downward invagination of the azygos vein through the apical portion of the right upper lobe (Figures 1–44 and 1–45). The familiar curvilinear shadow which extends obliquely across the upper portion of the right lung is formed by four pleural layers (two parietal and two visceral), since the azygos vein is anatomically external to the parietal pleura and thus invaginates four layers in its downward course. The fissure terminates in the "tear-drop" shadow caused by the vein itself at a variable distance above the right hilum. Felson states that this fissure is visible in 0.4 per cent of chest roentgenograms.[119]

According to Boyden,[821] the bronchial supply of the azygos lobe is somewhat variable: either the apical (B[1]a) or the anterior (B[1]b) subsegmental branch of the apical bronchus is always present; in larger lobes, both these subsegments or the apical subsegments of the apical (B[1]a) and posterior (B[3]a) segmental bronchi may be present. The importance of the anomaly roentgenologically (in addition to the reasons previously stated) lies in the fact that the apical pleural surfaces fail to separate in the presence of pneumothorax.

A fissure line, traditionally referred to as "the inferior accessory fissure of the right lower lobe," is present rather frequently anatomically; von Hayek[15] found it in 30 per cent of lungs, and Schaffner is said to have seen it in 45 per cent of 210 lungs studied at necropsy.[123] This accessory fissure is of variable depth, from a superficial slit to a complete fissure extending all the way to the hilum; when complete, it isolates the medial basal segment of the lower lobe which thus becomes the inferior accessory or retrocardiac lobe. Roentgenographically, a fissure line extending su-

periorly and slightly medially from the inner third of the right hemidiaphragm is visible in approximately one-third of subjects, according to Felson,[119] but whether this line represents the anatomic inferior accessory fissure is open to some question. Although Felson feels that they are the same, Simon[124] regards the roentgenographic shadow as the medial reflection of the normal chief fissure between the middle and lower lobes visualized in profile. We have no personal evidence to support either contention, but on the strength of the evidence presented, we are inclined to favor the latter interpretation.

Another accessory fissure with which the roentgenologist should be familiar is that which separates the superior segment from

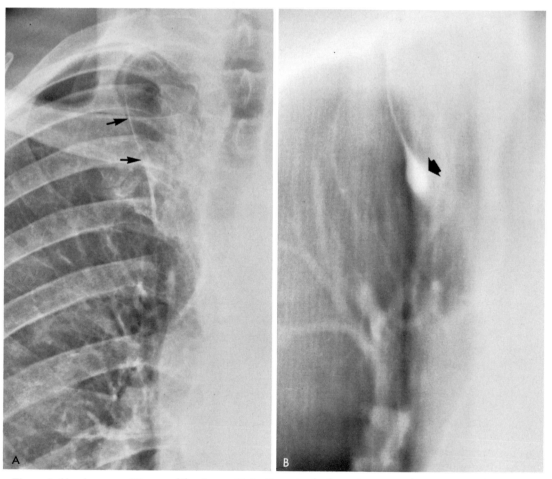

Figure 1–44.   **Accessory Fissure of the Azygos Vein.** On a standard roentgenogram in posteroanterior projection (*A*), the fissure can be identified as a curvilinear shadow (arrows) extending obliquely across the upper portion of the right lung, its lower end some distance above the right hilum. A tomographic section with the patient in the supine position (*B*) permits better visualization of the tear-drop shadow of the vein (arrow) because of distension.

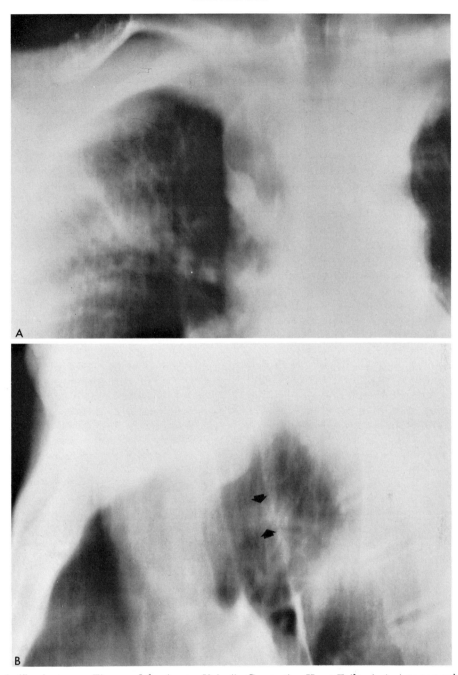

Figure 1–45. **Accessory Fissure of the Azygos Vein (in Congestive Heart Failure).** *A,* A tomographic section of the upper thorax in anteroposterior projection, supine position, reveals a slightly distended azygos vein at the lower end of a thickened fissure. The patient was in cardiac decompensation. *B,* In lateral projection, the shadow of the vein (arrows) can be seen lying in a horizontal plane extending anteriorly to the shadow of the brachiocephalic vessels.

the basal segments of the lower lobes, more commonly on the right (Figure 1–46). Since this fissure commonly lies in a horizontal plane at the same level as the minor fissure, the two may be confused in a frontal roentgenogram, although their separate anatomic positions may be clearly established on lateral or oblique roentgenography. Boyden[125] states that another accessory fissure, which separates the lingula from the remainder of the left upper lobe, occurs in 8 per cent of cases; when this is present the arrangement of fissures is a mirror image on the two sides.

In recent years a line shadow has been described which lies in a vertical plane in the lower portion of the chest of some infants and children; this is termed the "vertical fissure line."[126-128] The line is visible on frontal projections of the thorax and extends from the lateral portion of the diaphragmatic dome upward and slightly medially, roughly parallel to the thoracic wall, terminating at the level of the horizontal fissure. It has been identified in both lungs but more often in the right. Several theories have been postulated to explain this fissure line; most of the evidence indicates that it represents the lower portion of the major fissure which has been thrown into profile because of alteration in position of the middle and lower lobes. Precisely how or why this positional change occurs is not clear, but the major importance of the line lies in its recognition as such and in its differentiation from the visceral pleural line in pneumothorax. It seems likely that, ultimately, this will prove to be similar to the phenomenon seen in the chest roentgenograms of adults, when partial collapse of the lower lobe has caused downward and medial displacement of the major fissure,

thus rendering it visible in profile in frontal projection.

PHYSIOLOGY

The visceral and parietal pleura form smooth membranes which facilitate the movement of the lungs within the pleural space. The membranes secrete and absorb pleural fluid which renders movement easy.

Pressures

Pressure within the pleural cavity represents the difference between the elastic forces of the chest wall and of the lungs. Lung tissue has a natural tendency to recoil and will continue to do so even after the lungs have been removed from the body. Thus, even at the end of a maximal expiration (residual volume) the lungs tend to collapse. By contrast, the chest wall rests at about 55 per cent of vital capacity; below this volume it has a natural tendency to expand, and above this it tends to recoil inward toward the resting position. At resting lung volume (at the end of a quiet expiration, or functional residual capacity) the chest wall is still below its resting position of 55 per cent of the vital capacity. Thus, the chest wall's tendency to expand

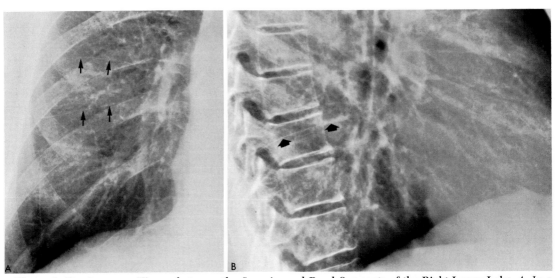

Figure 1–46. **Accessory Fissure between the Superior and Basal Segments of the Right Lower Lobe.** *A,* In a posteroanterior projection of the lower half of the right lung two horizontal fissures can be identified, the superior (upper arrows) representing the normal minor fissure and the inferior (lower arrows) representing an accessory fissure between the superior and basal bronchopulmonary segments of the right lower lobe. *B,* In lateral projection, only the accessory fissure is visualized (arrows).

outward is opposed by an equal and opposite force from the lungs. At this point
pleural pressure is about −5 cm H_2O. However, pleural pressure is not uniform
throughout the pleural cavity, although its
precise variation and its cause and effects
are not certain.[101] Pleural pressure is more
negative at the apex of the pleural cavity
than at the base, and the gradient probably
is about 0.2 cm H_2O per centimeter vertical
height—although a steeper pressure gradient has been suggested recently.[129] The
gradient is not uniform and is greater over
the upper than the lower zones of the lung.
It is gravity-dependent, since it is reversed
in subjects in the head-down position.

The effects of this gradient have been
demonstrated by Milic-Emili and others,[101]
who have shown that the upper lung zones
are more expanded than the lower in subjects in the upright position at all lung
volumes other than total lung capacity. The
lower lung zones expand more than the
upper during inspiration, and this is reflected by the greater ventilation of the
lower zones in healthy, young, erect subjects. Regional volume behavior of the lung
has been compared to that of an easily ex-
tensible coiled spring.[101] If the spring is
held at its upper end so that it is acted upon
only by the force of gravity, the coils will
be further apart at the upper than at the
lower end of the spring: this is analogous
to the greater alveolar volume in upper than
in lower lung zones. If the spring is length-
ened by applying a weight at the botton,
the distances between coils will increase
until they are equal: The change in distance
between the coils is greater at the lower
end, corresponding to the greater change
in volume at the bottom of the lung.

Fluid Formation and Absorption

In normal man, transudation and absorption of fluid within the pleural cavity follow
the Starling equation and depend upon a
combination of hydrostatic pressures, colloid osmotic pressures, and tissue pressures.
The latter are not known, but knowledge
of the first two forces suggest that, in health,
fluid is formed at the parietal pleura and
absorbed at the visceral pleura (Figure
1–47). The net hydrostatic pressure which
forces fluid out of the parietal pleura results
from the hydrostatic pressure in the systemic capillaries that supply the parietal
pleura (30 cm H_2O) and the pleural pres-

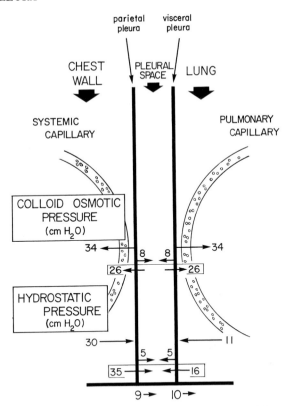

Figure 1–47. Diagrammatic Representation of the
Pressures Involved in the Formation and Absorption
of Pleural Fluid. *See* text for description.

sure (−5 cm H_2O at functional residual
capacity). Thus, the net hydrostatic drive
is 35 cm H_2O pressure. The colloid osmotic
pressure in the systemic capillaries is 34
cm H_2O, and that of the pleura[130] approximately 8 cm H_2O, which yield a net drive
of 26 cm colloid osmotic pressure from the
pleural space to the capillaries of the parietal pleura. The balance of these forces (35
− 26 cm = 9 cm H_2O) is directed from the
parietal pleura to the pleural cavity. The
visceral pleura, other than over the mediastinal surfaces, is supplied by pulmonary
artery capillaries, whose hydrostatic pressure is approximately 11 cm H_2O. Other
pressures remain roughly constant. Thus,
the net hydrostatic pressure from visceral
pleura toward pleural cavity is 16 cm H_2O
(11 cm less −5). The osmotic colloid pressures remain constant, with a pressure of
26 cm away from the pleural cavity. The
net effect of these forces is a drive of 10 cm
H_2O (26 − 16 cm) toward the visceral pleural capillaries. The preceding is an oversimplification since it ignores tissue pressures, the permeability of the mesothelial

layer, and pressures within the lymphatics through which excess fluid will be absorbed. However, this estimate of the forces that act on pleural fluid is supported by the findings of Agostoni and associates[131] that the visceral pleura of the dog absorbs saline at a pressure related to these forces.

It should be appreciated that, in health, pleural fluid is of low protein content, amounting to approximately 100 mg per 100 ml;[809, 810] such a low concentration permits formation of fluid by the parietal pleural capillaries and its absorption by the visceral pleural capillaries according to Starling's principles. When protein concentration rises sufficiently, to a figure in excess of approximately 1.0 g per 100 ml, the effect of colloid osmotic pressure of the visceral pleural capillaries is reduced to negligible proportions, and the only route of absorption of pleural fluid will be via the lymphatics by bulk flow.[811, 812] Since parietal pleural lymphatic vessels pass through the diaphragm and intercostal muscles, it might be thought that movement of the chest wall might increase lymphatic flow and speed of absorption from the pleural space; Burgen and Stewart[812] have shown that such occur in unanesthetized dogs. Stewart[809] has found that the rate of absorption of protein-high fluid in humans falls significantly during the night; he has postulated that a decrease in rate and depth of respiration during sleep might account for this phenomenon.

It is apparent that abnormal amounts of fluid may accumulate when there is an increase in hydrostatic pressure, a decrease in colloid osmotic pressure, or an increase in capillary permeability. Increased hydrostatic pressure causes the pleural effusion that occurs in heart failure; increased capillary permeability is responsible in inflammatory and neoplastic disease of the pleura. The *site* of accumulation of fluid is dependent upon hydrostatic forces and, to some extent, upon capillary attraction between the lung and the thoracic wall (*see* Chapter 4).

THE LYMPHATIC SYSTEM

LYMPHATICS OF THE LUNGS AND PLEURA

Although the entire cardiac output passes through the lungs and the lung has a rich lymphatic supply, lymphatic flow from the lungs is small compared with that which drains the systemic circulation. The pleural lymphatics are of variable size and number and occur much more frequently over the lower than the upper lobes (Figure 1–48A). Lymph flows in them for a variable distance on the surface of the lung and then passes centrally to the hilum, via the septal, perivenous, and peribronchial lymphatics. Alveoli and alveolar sacs have no lymphatic ducts, which start in the region of the alveolar ducts and respiratory bronchioles and flow centripetally in the bronchovascular sheath toward the hilum (Figure 1–48B). Lymphatic channels also drain the periphery of the lung lobules, where they run in the lobular septa along with the pulmonary veins (the site of Kerley "B" lines). The lymph flow in these also is toward the hilum, except in the subpleural region, where pleural lymphatics occasionally dip into the lung and then return to the surface to become pleural again.[677] Anastomotic channels exist between the perivenous lymphatics and those in the bronchovascular sheath; they measure up to 4 cm in length and usually lie approximately midway between the hilum and the periphery of the lung (it is distention of these communicating lymphatics that results in Kerley "A" lines). Numerous valves, 1 to 2 mm apart, direct the flow of lymph in both pleural and intrapulmonary lymphatics.

Normal lymph nodes may be found in the substance of the lung, far from the hilum: Trapnell[112] found intrapulmonary lymph nodes in five of 28 lungs in which he could outline the deep lymphatic channels. Occasionally, a peripheral lymph node may present as a coin lesion.[113]

LYMPHATICS OF THE MEDIASTINUM

Although our major concern is with lymphatic drainage of the lungs and pleura, involvement of the mediastinal lymph nodes occurs not infrequently in diseases arising in the breast, the chest wall, the diaphragm, or intra-abdominal or retroperitoneal structures; therefore, a thorough understanding of all afferent and efferent drainage pathways and of nodal anatomy is imperative. Individual patterns of lymph node enlargement may supply an important clue to the origin or nature of a disease process arising inside or outside the thorax.

Intrathoracic lymph nodes usually are divided into two main anatomic groups, the parietal and visceral mediastinal nodes. The former drain the thoracic wall and certain extrathoracic tissues, and the latter are concerned almost entirely with intrathoracic structures. For purposes of roentgenographic description, however, such a classification is less useful than one based on subdivision of groups of nodes in relation to the three mediastinal compartments. Since extensive communications exist not only between the parietal and visceral groups of nodes but also within the visceral group itself, an anatomic description based on mediastinal zones possesses considerable merit.

The Anterior Mediastinal Compartment

Two chains of lymph nodes are present in the anterior compartment, the sternal and the anterior mediastinal (visceral) groups (Figure 1–49).

THE STERNAL (ANTERIOR PARIETAL OR INTERNAL MAMMARY) GROUP. This group is situated extrapleurally. The nodes are scattered along the internal mammary arteries and behind the anterior intercostal spaces and costal cartilages bilaterally. Two or three may be directly retrosternal. These nodes are variable in number but occur more consistently superiorly. Their afferent channels drain the upper anterior abdominal wall, the anterior thoracic wall, the anterior portion of the diaphragm, and the medial portions of the breast. They communicate with the visceral group of anterior mediastinal nodes and the cervical nodes, and their main efferent channels are the right lymphatic duct or bronchomediastinal duct on the right and the thoracic duct on the left.

THE ANTERIOR MEDIASTINAL (PREVASCULAR) GROUP. This group comprises

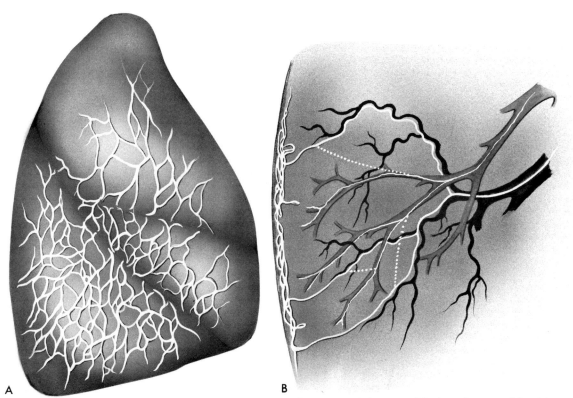

A   B

Figure 1–48. **The Lymphatic Drainage of the Pleura and Lungs.** *A,* A drawing of the lateral aspect of the right lung shows the pleural lymphatics to be much more numerous over the lower half of the lung than over the upper. *B,* In a coronal section through the midportion of the lung, lymphatic channels from the pleura enter the lung at the interlobular septa and extend medially to the hilum along venous radicals (dark shaded vessels); lymphatic channels originating in the peripheral parenchyma extend medially in the bronchovascular bundles (light shaded vessels). Communicating lymphatics (dotted lines) extend between the peribronchial and perivenous lymphatics.

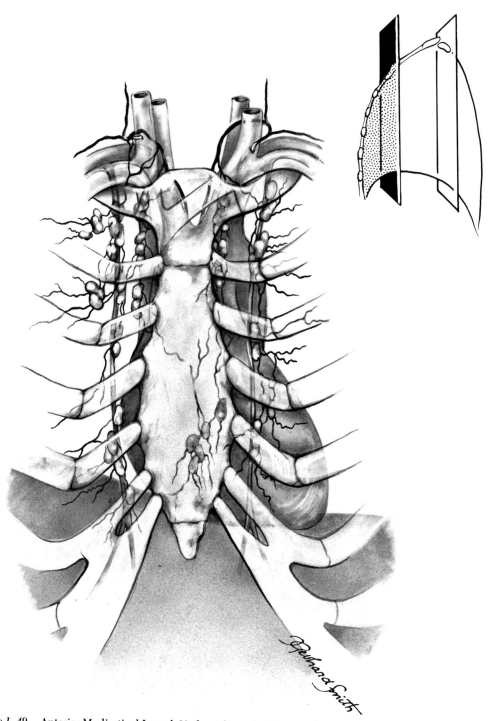

Figure 1-49. **Anterior Mediastinal Lymph Nodes.** The nodes illustrated are chiefly those of the anterior parietal group scattered along the internal mammary arteries and behind the anterior intercostal spaces and costal cartilages bilaterally. The prevascular (visceral) group relate to the superior vena cava and innominate vein on the right and to the aorta and carotid artery on the left.

the second group of nodes in the anterior mediastinal compartment; they belong to the visceral collection. A few nodes are situated posterior to the sternum in the lower thorax, but the majority are grouped in the prevascular areas bilaterally, along the superior vena cava and innominate vein on the right and in front of the aorta and carotid artery on the left side. A few lie anterior to the thymus behind the manubrium. These nodes drain most of the structures situated in the anterior mediastinum, including the pericardium, part of the heart, the thymus, the thyroid, the diaphragmatic and mediastinal pleura, and the anterior portions of the hila bilaterally. Their efferent channels drain via the bronchomediastinal trunk or thoracic duct.

The Posterior Mediastinal Compartment

Groups of nodes belonging to both the parietal and the visceral chains lie in the posterior mediastinum (Figure 1–50).

THE INTERCOSTAL (POSTERIOR PARIETAL) GROUP. This group lies laterally, in the intercostal spaces, and medially, in the paravertebral areas adjacent to the heads of the ribs. Both groups drain the intercostal spaces, the parietal pleura, and the vertebral column. They communicate with the posterior mediastinal group of visceral nodes and possess efferent channels which drain to the thoracic duct from the upper portions of the thorax and to the cisterna chyli from the lower thoracic area.

THE POSTERIOR MEDIASTINAL GROUP. This group of visceral nodes is situated along the lower esophagus and descending aorta. They possess afferent channels from the posterior portion of the diaphragm, the pericardium, the esophagus, and directly from the lower lobes of the lungs. They communicate with the bifurcation group of tracheobronchial nodes and drain mainly via the thoracic duct.

The Middle Mediastinal Compartment

This compartment also includes parietal and visceral components.

THE PARIETAL GROUP. This group is of little importance roentgenologically.

The nodes are situated mainly around the pericardial attachment to the diaphragm and drain the diaphragm itself and portions of the liver. Efferent pathways pass anteriorly to the sternal or anterior mediastinal nodes and posteriorly to the posterior mediastinal nodes.

From the roentgenologic point of view the other lymph nodes in the middle mediastinal compartment undoubtedly constitute the most important group in the thorax: the *tracheobronchial, carinal,* and *bronchopulmonary* nodes (Figure 1–51). Although these groups freely communicate with one another, in many cases involvement is predominantly in one group.

THE TRACHEOBRONCHIAL NODES. These nodes are scattered along the lateral aspects of the trachea and in the tracheobronchial angles and are more numerous on the right than on the left. One node which is fairly constant in position is situated in the right tracheobronchial angle contiguous to the azygos vein; this is commonly referred to as the azygos node. Afferent channels arise from the bronchopulmonary and bifurcation nodes, from the trachea and esophagus, and from the right or left lung directly without diversion via the bronchopulmonary or bifurcation nodes. Direct communication exists with the anterior and posterior groups of visceral mediastinal nodes. The efferent channels are the bronchomediastinal trunk on the right and the thoracic duct on the left.

THE BIFURCATION (CARINAL) NODES. These nodes are situated along the anterior and inferior aspects of the carina and extend downward along the medial aspects of the main bronchi to the origin of the lower-lobe bronchi bilaterally. They receive afferent drainage from the bronchopulmonary nodes, the anterior and posterior mediastinal nodes, the heart, pericardium, and esophagus, and directly from both lungs. Efferent drainage is to the right tracheobronchial group.

THE BRONCHOPULMONARY NODES. These nodes are numerous bilaterally but variable in number. They lie in the angles between the bronchial bifurcations in the hilar regions and are closely related to the arteries and veins. Their afferent supply is from all pulmonary lobes, and efferent drainage is to the bifurcation and tracheobronchial nodes.

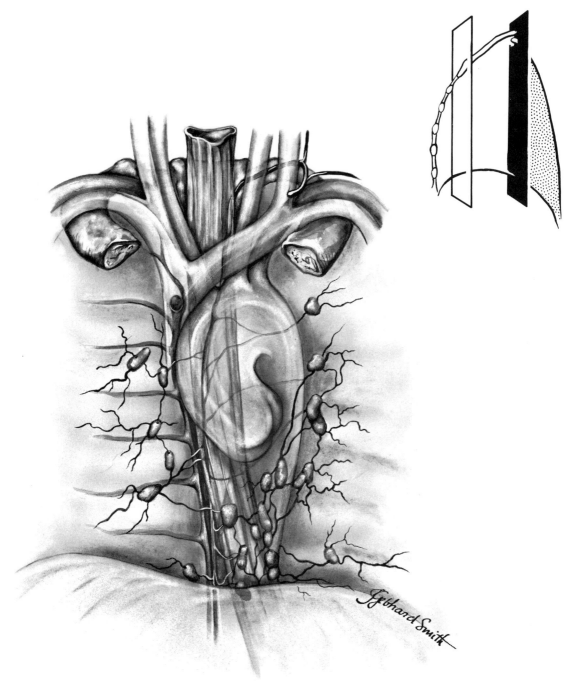

Figure 1–50. **Posterior Mediastinal Lymph Nodes.** The intercostal (posterior parietal) group lies laterally, in the intercostal spaces, and medially, in the paravertebral areas adjacent to the heads of the ribs. The visceral group of posterior mediastinal nodes is situated along the lower esophagus and descending aorta.

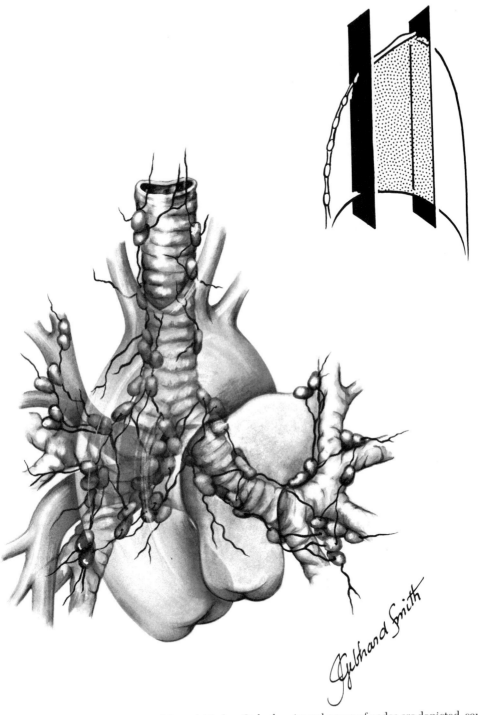

Figure 1–51. **The Middle Mediastinal Lymph Nodes.** Only the visceral group of nodes are depicted, consisting of the tracheobronchial, carinal and bronchopulmonary nodes. *See* text for description.

PATTERNS OF LYMPHATIC DRAINAGE OF THE LUNGS

The location of enlarged lymph nodes within the mediastinum may be of importance in determining the site of origin within the lungs of an infectious or neoplastic process. Much of our knowledge of patterns of regional lymph node drainage from the lung derives from Rouvière's treatise[114] on the anatomy of the human lymphatic system, published in 1938, which was based on necropsy studies of 200 fetuses, neonates, and children. Many of his observations were subsequently confirmed by McCort and Robbins[115] and by Nohl.[116] Rouvière subdivided the lungs into three main drainage areas, the superior, middle, and inferior, without correspondence to pulmonary lobes.

On the Right Side

On the right side, in the superior area, lymph drains directly into the paratracheal and upper bronchopulmonary nodes. The middle zone drains directly into the paratracheal nodes, the bifurcation nodes, and the central group of bronchopulmonary nodes. The inferior zone drains into the inferior bronchopulmonary and bifurcation nodes and the posterior mediastinal chain. Thus, on the right side, all the lymph drains eventually via the right lymphatic duct.

On the Left Side

On the left side, Rouvière[114] stated that, in the superior area, lymph drains into both the prevascular group of anterior mediastinal nodes and directly into the left paratracheal nodes. The middle zone drains mainly via the bifurcation and central group of bronchopulmonary nodes and partly directly into the left paratracheal group. The inferior zone drains into the bifurcation and inferior bronchopulmonary nodes and into the posterior mediastinal chain. Thus, according to Rouvière,[114] the superior portion and part of the middle zone drain via the left paratracheal nodes into the thoracic duct, and lymph drainage from the remainder of the left lung empties eventually into the right lymphatic duct.

The "crossover" phenomenon was long thought to be of diagnostic and therapeutic importance in diseases which originated in the middle or lower portion of the left lung. However, recent investigations have cast some doubt on the validity of the phenomenon in adult patients. For example, in a study of 1000 consecutive necropsies, Klingenberg[117] found 17 cases of primary carcinoma of the left lung, only one of which had heterolateral prescalene-node metastases; unfortunately, the sites of origin in the left lung were not stated. Similarly, Baird[118] performed bilateral prescalene-node biopsies in 218 patients of whom 110 had bronchogenic carcinoma; the direction of lymphatic spread within the mediastinum was cephalad and usually ipsilateral, irrespective of the location of the primary growth. Contralateral spread occurred uncommonly and with about equal frequency from the two lungs.

On the strength of these observations, it is reasonable to conclude that prescalene-node biopsies should always be performed first on the same side as the pulmonary disease; should this prove negative, contralateral biopsy may *occasionally* be productive.

THE MEDIASTINUM

The mediastinum constitutes a compartmented septum or partition which divides the thorax vertically (Figures 1–52 and 1–53). For descriptive purposes, it is traditionally divided into two major compartments, the superior and the inferior, the latter being subdivided into anterior, middle, and posterior compartments. Since each compartment contains anatomic structures which are almost unique to it, many of the affections to which the mediastinum is subject tend to occur *predominantly* in one or other compartment; thus, this anatomic subdivision has considerable merit. However, of the four compartments, the superior possesses little practical importance as a separate division; defined as that area bounded superiorly by the thoracic inlet and inferiorly by a line drawn from the angle of Louis (the manubriosternal angle) to the intervertebral disc between the fourth and fifth thoracic vertebrae, it not only contains structures which extend across this imaginary line into the inferior mediastinum but also some which extend into it from below. In this book, therefore, the entire mediastinum from the thoracic inlet to the diaphragm is considered to possess three major compartments, the an-

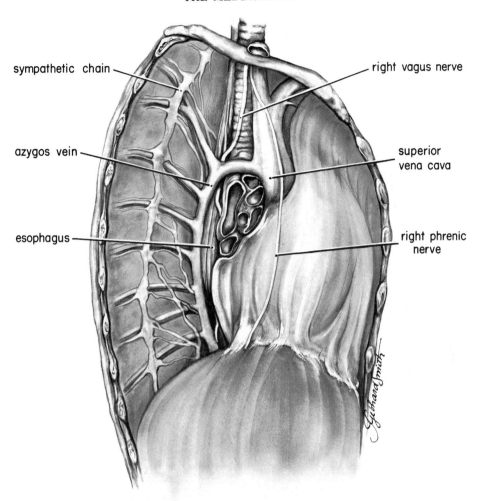

sympathetic chain

right vagus nerve

azygos vein

superior vena cava

esophagus

right phrenic nerve

Figure 1–52. **The Mediastinum—Right Lateral Aspect.** In the anterior mediastinum, the thymus gland is not depicted. In the middle mediastinal compartment can be identified the pericardium overlying the heart, the superior vena cava, the phrenic nerve, the upper half of the vagus nerve, a cross section of the bronchi and vessels in the hilum, and the horizontal portion of the azygos vein. In the posterior compartment are depicted the esophagus and the azygos vein with its intercostal tributaries. The sympathetic chain lies along the lateral aspect of the vertebral column (and therefore not truly mediastinal).

terior, middle, and posterior, without reference to a separate superior compartment.

The anatomic boundaries of the mediastinum are as follows: *lateral,* the parietal pleural reflections along the medial aspects of both lungs; *superior,* the thoracic inlet; *inferior,* the diaphragm; *anterior,* the sternum; and *posterior,* the anterior surfaces of the thoracic vertebral bodies.

THE MEDIASTINAL COMPARTMENTS

The Anterior Mediastinal Compartment

The anterior mediastinal compartment (Figures 1–52 and 1–53) is bounded an-

teriorly by the sternum and posteriorly by the pericardium, aorta, and brachiocephalic vessels. It contains the thymus gland and the anterior mediastinal lymph nodes, including both parietal and visceral groups. It is relatively narrow, particularly inferiorly, where the pericardium overlying the right ventricle is in contact with the lower portion of the sternum.

The Middle Mediastinal Compartment

The middle mediastinal compartment (Figures 1–52 and 1–53) contains the pericardium and heart, the ascending and transverse arch of the aorta, the superior and

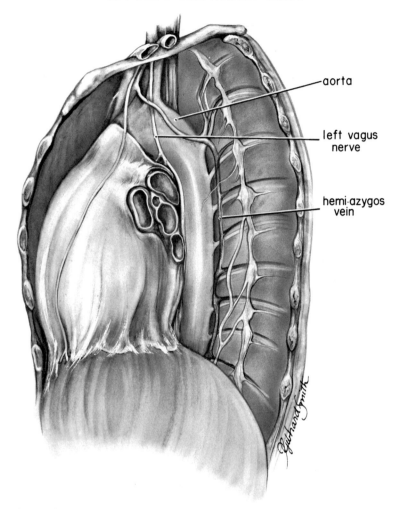

aorta

left vagus
nerve

hemi·azygos
vein

Figure 1–53.   The Mediastinum—Left Lateral Aspect. No anatomic structures are depicted in the anterior mediastinum. In the middle mediastinal compartment, in addition to the structures already described in Figure 1–52, are the ascending and transverse arch of the aorta and the brachiocephalic arteries. Most of the vagus nerve can be identified. In the posterior mediastinal compartment, the descending thoracic aorta and hemiazygos veins can be seen.

inferior vena cavae, the brachiocephalic arteries and veins, the phrenic nerves and upper portion of the vagus nerves, the trachea and main bronchi and their contiguous lymph nodes, and the pulmonary arteries and veins.

The Posterior Mediastinal Compartment

The posterior mediastinal compartment (Figures 1–52 and 1–53) lies between the pericardium and the anterior aspect of the vertebral column. It contains the descending thoracic aorta, the esophagus, the thoracic duct, the azygos and hemiazygos

veins, the sympathetic chains and the lower portion of the vagus nerves, and the posterior group of mediastinal lymph nodes. Since the posterior limit of the mediastinum is formed by the anterior surface of the vertebral column, the paravertebral zones and posterior gutters are not included in the mediastinum.

It is important to recognize certain lines which are visible within the mediastinal contour on well-exposed frontal roentgenograms of the chest, since deviations in their pattern may supply important clues to the presence of disease. The reflection of the pleura from the posterior thoracic wall onto the *right* side of the mediastinum is smooth and uninterrupted by protruding structures except for the right atrium, the superior vena cava above, and the inferior vena cava below. It is invisible, therefore, on frontal roentgenograms of the chest. By contrast, on the left side, the descending thoracic aorta protrudes slightly laterally in the posterior mediastinal compartment, causing lateral displacement of the mediastinal pleura posterior to it. This creates *the paraspinal line* (Figure 1–54), a shadow first described by Brailsford,[132] consisting of a longitudinal density projected about midway between the outer border of the descending thoracic aorta and the vertebral column, extending from the aortic arch above to the diaphragm below.[133] In cases of right-sided aorta, when the descending aorta passes downward on the right, the paraspinal line appears on the right side. As might be expected, elongation of the thoracic aorta displaces the paraspinal line laterally; similarly, deformity of the line may be an important indication of disease of various structures in the posterior mediastinum and vertebral column, subjects which are discussed in detail in Chapter 17.

Three other contour lines are visible sometimes on frontal roentgenograms of the chest, particularly when high kilovoltage or tomographic techniques are employed. *The anterior mediastinal line*[134] is a thin linear density measuring no more than 1 to 2 mm in diameter, projected over the air column of the trachea for a distance of a few centimeters distal to the plane of the junction of the manubrium and the body of the sternum (Figure 1–55). This line, which represents the anterior mediastinal septum, is produced by the combined shadows of the visceral and parietal pleura of the two contiguous upper lobes, possibly with a small amount of areolar tissue interposed between. It may be confused with a somewhat similar density, the *posterior mediastinal line* (Figure 1–56A), which is slightly higher and is formed by apposition of the pleural surfaces of the two lungs in the supra-aortic triangle of the posterior mediastinal compartment.[135] This linear density also projects over the air column of the trachea and usually is situated at a higher level than the anterior mediastinal line, its center being in the plane of the upper surface of the manubrium. Its right side generally is slightly concave. Since the esophagus descends through the supra-

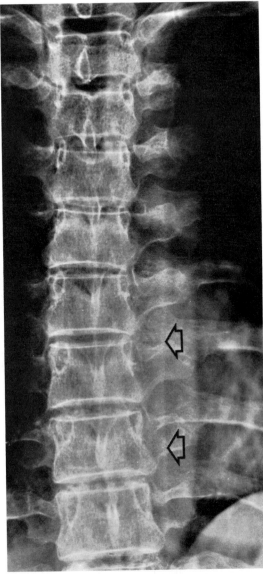

Figure 1–54. **The Paraspinal Line.** A roentgenogram of the mediastinum in anteroposterior projection, supine position; normal 42-year-old male. A longitudinal shadow (arrows) extending from the arch of the aorta to the diaphragm is projected about midway between the lateral border of the descending aorta and the vertebral column; this shadow is caused by the paravertebral mediastinal pleura being displaced laterally by the descending aorta.

aortic triangle, it is probable that this organ contributes to the formation of the posterior mediastinal line (Figure 1–56B and C)—a concept emphasized by Cimmino, who designated the line the "esophageal-pleural stripe";[136-138] he saw it in 25 of 200 consecutive chest roentgenograms.

The lower lobes may come into close apposition in the inferior portion of the pos-

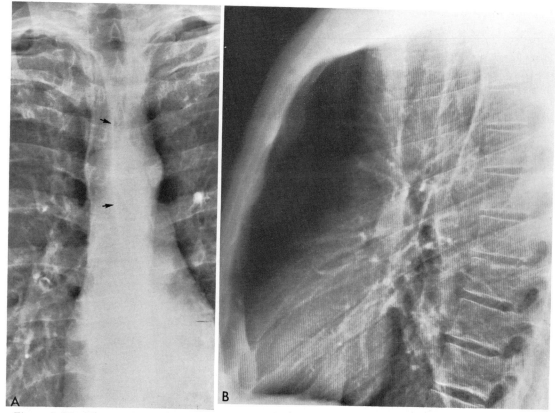

Figure 1–55. **The Anterior Mediastinal Line.** *A,* A roentgenogram of the chest in posteroanterior projection reveals a thin line shadow projected over the air column of the trachea (arrows). It is caused by the combined shadows of the visceral and parietal pleura in the anterior mediastinal septum. *B,* In the lateral projection, note the deep retrosternal air space.

terior mediastinal compartment, in a triangular area of the mediastinum posterior to the heart and anterior to the spine, which is known as the retrocardiac space or the space of Holzknecht. In this region, the mediastinum deviates slightly to the left of midline; the esophagus, lying in the central portion of this mediastinal septum, is related intimately to the adjacent pleural surface covering the right lower lobe, thus creating what Cimmino refers to as the *inferior esophageal-pleural stripe*[137, 138] (Figure 1–56A). In normal subjects this measures 3 to 5 mm in width with the esophagus distended;[138] greater widths than this may indicate the presence of esophageal disease.

Detailed definition of the anterior mediastinal line and the superior and inferior esophageal-pleural stripes has been obtained by Lodin[139] through the use of axial transverse tomography.

THE HEART

It is clearly beyond the scope of this book to discuss the heart in any detail. However, it is important to recognize that certain deviations in the normal roentgen anatomy of the cardiovascular silhouette may give rise to confusion.

Position

In a frontal roentgenogram of the normal chest (*see* Figure 1–67, page 92), the position of the heart in relation to the midline of the thorax depends greatly upon the build of the patient. As has been pointed out by Simon,[122] the heart shadow of an asthenic patient is almost exactly midline in position, projecting only slightly more to the left than to the right of the midline. In those of more sthenic build, the heart lies more to the left than to the right (in the range of three-quarters to one-quarter).

These statements assume, of course, that the roentgenograms are exposed with the lungs fully inflated.

Size and Contour

Due chiefly to the influence of systole and diastole, both size and contour may vary in any one patient from one examination to another, even when all examinations are made with an identical degree of lung inflation. In a series of 200 normal subjects studied by Simon,[122] the maximal difference in transverse cardiac diameter on successive examinations was 2 cm (in one patient only), and the average variation was 0.5 cm for the whole group.

When the influence of systole and diastole is controlled (which may be accomplished easily by exposures of one second or longer), the major influences on cardiac size and contour are three-fold. (1) *The height of the diaphragm*, which, in turn, is influenced by the degree of pulmonary inflation: obviously, the lower the position of the diaphragm, the longer and, therefore, narrower, the cardiovascular contour will become. (2) *Intrathoracic pressure*: this factor influences not only cardiac size but also the appearance of the pulmonary vascular pattern. (3) *Body position*: assuming equality of all other factors, the heart is broader when the subject is recumbent than when he is erect. The physiologic and

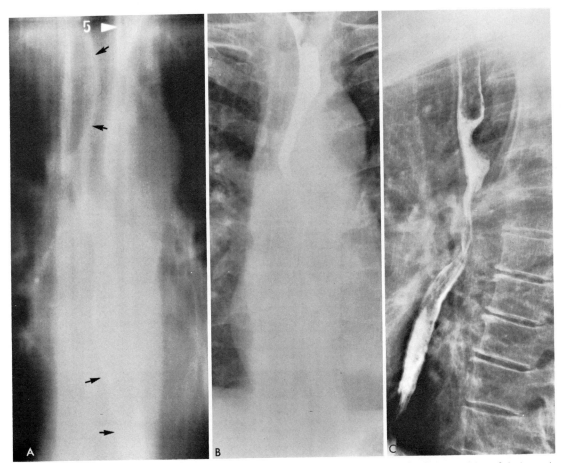

Figure 1–56. **The Posterior Mediastinal Line and the Superior and Inferior Esophageal—Pleural Stripes.** *A*, A tomographic section of the posterior mediastinum reveals a longitudinal curvilinear shadow (upper arrows) projected over the air column of the trachea; this line is formed by apposition of the pleural surfaces of the two lungs posteriorly in the supra-aortic triangle. It is probable that the esophagus contributes to the formation of this line as revealed in the posteroanterior and lateral roentgenograms of the chest (*B* and *C*) with barium in the esophagus—thus the designation superior esophageal—pleural stripe. The inferior esophageal—pleural stripe seen in *A* (lower arrows), is situated in the retrocardiac space of Holzknecht and is formed by the right mediastinal pleura; the esophagus is intimately related to this pleural surface.

roentgenographic effects of variation in intrathoracic pressure and body position are discussed in detail later in this chapter.

It is to be emphasized that standardization of all these influences is essential to accurate comparison of heart size on films taken at different times. Methods of standardization may vary but could well include the following criteria. The patient should be in the erect position in posteroanterior projection, at a standard 6-ft focus-film distance, with the lungs inflated to total lung capacity (or some other easily reproducible level of lung inflation, measured by spirometry), at a known intrathoracic pressure (preferably atmospheric pressure, which is attained by suspending respiration with glottis open and specifically without a Valsalva maneuver), and with a radiation exposure of one second or longer. It is clear that the time required to perform such an examination renders it impracticable for routine use: These parameters are outlined only to stress the importance of their control if comparisons of heart size on successive examinations are to be accurate.

OTHER ASPECTS OF MEDIASTINAL CONFIGURATION

Physiologic accumulations of fatty tissue commonly occur bilaterally in the cardiophrenic recesses, producing an obtuse angular configuration of the inferior mediastinum at its junction with the diaphragm (Figure 1–57). Usually their density is slightly less than that of the heart, allowing identification of cardiac borders through them. These pleuropericardial fat shadows should not be misinterpreted as cardiac enlargement or as mediastinal or diaphragmatic masses of possible importance.

In a posteroanterior roentgenogram of the chest (see Figure 1–67, page 92), the right mediastinal border from the right atrium to the lung apex is formed by the superior vena cava and the innominate vein. In the normal subject, providing the chest is correctly centered, the ascending aorta contributes nothing to the mediastinal contour. The extreme superomedial portion of the right hemithorax in the plane of the second and third posterior interspaces may be formed by the right subclavian artery. On the left side, the silhouette of the superior mediastinum above the arch of the aorta is formed mostly by the subclavian artery.[140]

The Azygos Vein

The azygos vein usually is visible in frontal chest roentgenograms of normal subjects as a slightly flattened elliptical shadow in the right tracheobronchial angle (Figure 1–58A). Fleischner and Udis[141] measured the vein from its outer border to the contiguous tracheal air column on teleroentgenograms of erect subjects and recorded a maximum normal transverse diameter of 6.0 mm. Evidence accumulated since this first report suggests that this figure may be a trifle low; for example, Felson[822] states that a transverse diameter of 10 mm may be normal, and we have personally observed several normal subjects whose vein measured 9 mm. Perhaps the definitive work on the subject, however, is the recent report of Keats and his associates[823] who measured the diameter of the arch of the azygos vein of 100 men and 100 nonpregnant women and recorded the following results: in men, minimum size 3 mm, maximum size 7 mm, average size 4.91 mm; in nonpregnant women, minimum size 3 mm, maximum size 7 mm, average size 4.87 mm. It seems reasonable to conclude that while normal subjects may occasionally have an azygos vein measuring up to 9 or 10 mm in diameter, the vast majority will be 7 mm or less; if a patient has a vein of more than 7 mm in diameter, one should exercise caution in labeling it as normal before excluding all causes of azygos enlargement.

Of considerable interest in this last report[823] was the wide range of measurements and increased average size of the azygos arch observed in 100 pregnant women: the minimum size was unchanged at 3 mm, but the maximum size was 15 mm and the average 7.14 mm. This normal effect of pregnancy should be borne in mind when considering the differential diagnosis of azygos vein enlargement.

Doyle and his associates,[142] who used a tomographic technique with a shorter focus-film distance and with the patient supine, (Figure 1–58B) measured the maximum diameter of the azygos vein in 48 normal subjects and plotted this against several parameters, including age, sex, weight, height, and body surface area. The only significant correlation was between body weight and azygos vein diameter. Standardization of all measurements to a body

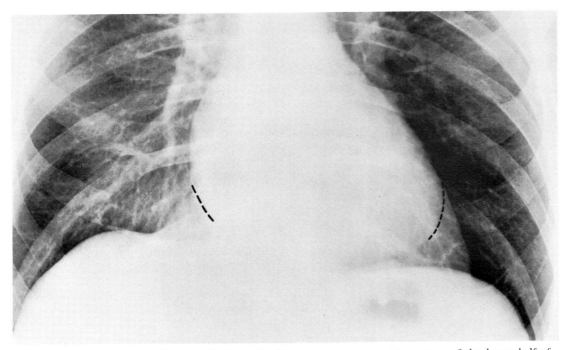

Figure 1–57. **Pleuropericardial Fat Shadows.** In this posteroanterior roentgenogram of the lower half of the thorax, physiologic accumulations of fatty tissue can be identified in the cardiophrenic recesses bilaterally. The borders of the heart are indicated by dotted lines.

Figure 1–58. **The Azygos Vein Shadow.** *A,* A roentgenogram in the erect position shows the azygos vein as an elliptical-shaped shadow projected in the right tracheobronchial angle (arrows). *B,* In the same subject, a tomographic section of the mid-mediastinum in the supine position demonstrates a much larger vein shadow (arrows) owing to distension brought about by the supine body position.

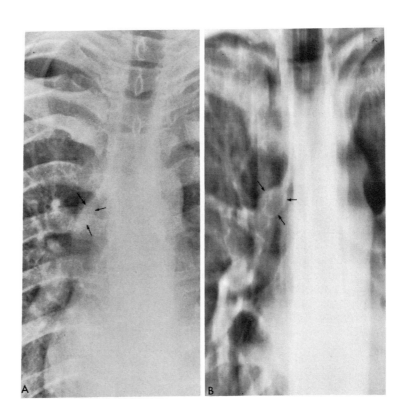

weight of 140 lb yielded a mean azygos-vein diameter of 14.2 mm; in only eight subjects was the weight-standardized vein diameter greater than 16 mm.

Visualization of this vein assumes considerable importance in some diseases, notably portal hypertension, obstruction of the superior vena cava, and congestive heart failure; familiarity with its normal roentgenographic appearance is important.

THE DIAPHRAGM

The diaphragm is a musculotendinous sheet which separates the thoracic cavity from the abdominal cavity (see Figure 18–1). The central tendon is a broad sheet of decussating tendon fibers, in shape similar to a broad-bladed Australian boomerang; the point of the "boomerang" is directed toward the sternum and the concavity toward the spine. The muscle fibers arise anteriorly from the xiphoid process, around the convexity of the thorax from ribs seven to 12, posteriorly from the lateral margins of the first, second, and third lumbar vertebrae on the right side, and from the first and second lumbar vertebrae on the left. These fibers converge toward the central tendon and are inserted into it nearly perpendicular to its margin. The muscle fibers are of variable length, from 5 cm anteriorly at the sternal origin to 14 cm posterolaterally where they originate from the ninth, tenth, and eleventh ribs.[15] Von Hayek[15] points out that it is the posterolateral portion of the hemidiaphragms, where the muscle fibers are longest, that undergoes the greatest excursion on respiration. The muscle fibers which comprise the sternal attachment and those that arise from the seventh rib are separated bilaterally by triangular spaces poor in muscular and tendinous tissue. These triangular spaces, called the foramina of Morgagni, constitute weak areas in the diaphragm. Deficiencies in the origins of the muscle bundles from the posterolateral rib cage, called the foramina of Bochdalek, similarly create areas of potential weakness.

Roentgenographic Height of the Normal Diaphragm

Definitive study of the height of the hemidiaphragms on roentgenograms of normal adults was reported by Lennon and Simon[143] in 1965. These authors assessed frontal roentgenograms of the chest of 500 normal adults, 250 of each sex, all over 21 years of age. In 94 per cent, the level of the cupola of the right hemidiaphragm was projected in a plane ranging from the anterior end of the fifth rib to the sixth anterior interspace; 41 per cent were at the level of the sixth rib anteriorly; and only 4 per cent were at or below the level of the seventh rib. Generally speaking, the height of the right dome was higher in women, in subjects of heavy build, and in those over the age of 40.

Relationship Between the Height of the Right and Left Hemidiaphragms

The tendency for the right diaphragmatic dome to be on a plane approximately one-half an interspace higher than the left is well recognized, but of 500 normal subjects examined by Felson[69] the left hemidiaphragm was at the same height or was higher than the right in 9 per cent. Half the subjects comprising the 9 per cent had gaseous distension of the stomach or colon, a finding also mentioned by Simon[122] as being a common cause of left hemidiaphragmatic elevation. In 2 per cent of Felson's 500 cases the right hemidiaphragm was higher than the left by more than 3 cm.

It is a common error for students of roentgenology to ascribe elevation of the right hemidiaphragm to the presence of the mass of the liver beneath it. To these and other interested readers we recommend Wittenborg and Aviad's report[144] of their investigation of organ influence on normal diaphragmatic posture. These workers studied the chest roentgenograms of 60 children with anomalous organ positions. They found that the apex of the heart normally lies on the same side as the lower hemidiaphragm and that this relationship is maintained in the majority of cases of congenital malpositions of thoracic and abdominal viscera; further, they observed that the greater the degree of normality in development of the heart into a right and left side, the more often was the disparity in the height of the hemidiaphragms clearly defined and constant. The relationship of diaphragmatic height to cardiac anomalies is stated as follows: "In the presence of clear-cut inequalities in height of the hemidiaphragms (and absence of complicating pulmonary or neuromuscular disease) the odd-shaped cardiac silhouette may take on more meaning with the knowledge that, in all probability, the apex of the systemic or functional left ventricle is projected over the lower hemidiaphragm, irrespective of whether it be right or left and irrespective of the presence of anomalous positions of other organs."[144]

Thus it is clear that the lower position of one hemidiaphragmatic dome is intimately related to the presence of the contiguous mass of the left side of the heart.

Range of Diaphragmatic Excursion on Respiration

In a series of 204 patients studied by Simon,[161] the range of excursion of the two hemidiaphragms from full inspiration to full expiration was compared. In 23 per cent excursion was equal and symmetrical, in 50 per cent the right hemidiaphragm made a greater excursion than the left (mean difference, 0.75 cm), and the reverse occurred in 27 per cent (mean difference, 0.94 cm). In 188 patients, the mean excursion measured 3 to 6 cm in 140 (74 per cent), less than 3 cm in 44 (23 per cent), and greater than 6 cm in only four patients.

Physiologic Variations in Diaphragmatic Contour

Scalloping of the diaphragm, in which the normally smooth contour is replaced by a series of smooth arcuate elevations, is relatively uncommon (Figure 1–59); Felson[69] observed it in only 5.5 per cent of 500 normal subjects. In the majority it was confined to the right side and in only a small percentage was it bilateral. The significance of this pattern is not known.

In some subjects, muscle slips originating from the lateral and posterolateral ribs may be visualized as short meniscus-shaped shadows along the lateral half of the hemidiaphragms bilaterally. These are produced by exceptionally low descent of the diaphragm during inspiration. Although such appearances are more common in association with severe pulmonary overinflation (Figure 1–60), as in asthma or emphysema, they may occur in the normal state, particularly in healthy young men; in the absence of supportive evidence they should not be interpreted as a sign of air-trapping.

Local "eventration" may occur anywhere in the diaphragm but is seen most commonly in the anteromedial quadrant on the right. This finding possesses no known

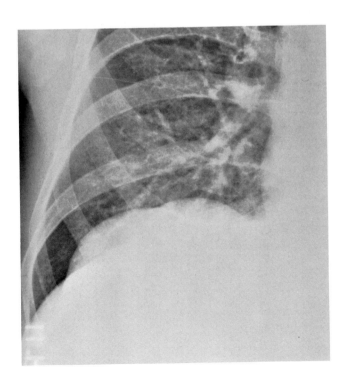

Figure 1–59. **Scalloping of the Diaphragm.** A roentgenogram of the right hemidiaphragm reveals two smooth arcuate elevations disturbing the normally smooth contour of the dome, a finding of no known significance.

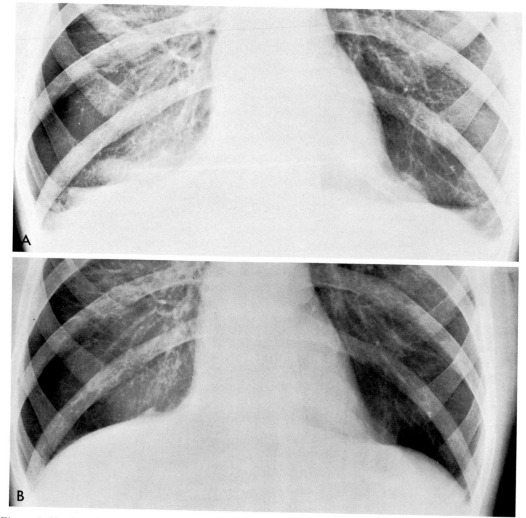

Figure 1-60. **Diaphragmatic Muscle Slips.** Inspiratory (*A*) and expiratory (*B*) roentgenograms of the lower half of the thorax of a patient with severe emphysema reveal short meniscus-shaped shadows extending laterally from each hemidiaphragm. These muscle slips are prominent on full inspiration and disappear on expiration.

significance; since it is reasonable to include this with other forms of eventration, it will be discussed further in Chapter 18.

THE CHEST WALL

The structures of the thoracic wall, both soft-tissue and osseous, form a complex of shadows on roentgenograms of the chest which may be important to roentgenographic analysis, and a working knowledge of their normal anatomy and variations is indispensable.

The Soft Tissues

On frontal roentgenograms of the thorax (*see* Figure 1-67, page 92) the soft tissues, consisting of the skin, subcutaneous fat, and muscles, usually are distinguishable along the upper shoulders and lateral thoracic wall, and on successive examinations may constitute a valuable sign of loss or gain in weight. The pectoral muscles form the anterior axillary fold, a structure which normally is visible in both male and female patients, curving smoothly downward and medially from the axilla to the rib cage. In men, particularly those with heavy muscular development, the inferior border of the pectoralis major muscle may be seen as a downward extension of the anterior axillary fold, passing obliquely across the middle portion of the lung fields bilaterally. In women, this shadow is obscured by the breasts, whose presence and size must be taken into consideration in assessment of density of the lower lung fields. Congenital absence of the pectoralis muscle occurs but is rare.[824]

In many cases the shadow of the sternomastoid muscle is visible as a density whose lateral margin parallels the spine in the medial third of the lung apices; it curves downward and laterally to blend with the companion shadow on the superior aspect of each clavicle. The latter shadow, which is 2 to 3 mm thick, parallels the superior aspect of the clavicle; it is formed by the skin and subcutaneous tissue overlying the clavicles and is rendered visible roentgenologically by the presence of the supraclavicular fossae and the tangential direction in which the x-ray beam strikes the clavicles.

Situated immediately behind the sternum is a structure to which little attention has been paid in the roentgenologic literature — the internal thoracic muscle.[146, 907] This muscle arises from the sternum, along the posteroinferior surface of the body and xiphoid, and extends upward and laterally to insert on the inner surfaces of the second through the sixth costal cartilages and adjacent ribs. In a series of 120 consecutive lateral chest roentgenograms, the muscle was identified as an obliquely placed density lying more or less parallel to the sternum in 37 patients, 26 male and 11 female.[146] In a more extensive roentgenographic study of 500 patients carried out by Shopfner and his colleagues,[907] the muscle was visualized in 390 (78 per cent).

The Bones

In the absence of pulmonary or pleural disease, deformity of the spine, or congenital anomalies of the ribs themselves, the rib cage should be perfectly symmetrical on the two sides. Both the upper and lower borders of the ribs should be sharply defined except in the middle and lower thoracic regions; here the thin flanges created by the vascular sulci on the inferior aspects of the ribs posteriorly are visualized *en face*, thus creating a less distinct inferior margin. In some cases the inferior aspects of the ribs posteriorly within 2 or 3 cm of their tubercles may show local superficial indentations; these should not be mistaken for pathologic rib notching, which is situated more laterally near the midclavicular line

in cases of increased collateral circulation through the intercostal vessels.

Calcification of the rib cartilages occurs commonly, and probably is never of pathologic significance. The first-rib cartilage usually is the first to calcify, frequently shortly after the age of 20. In a roentgenographic study of 100 adults, 60 of whom were male and 40 female, Sanders[908] observed fairly consistent differences in the pattern of costal calcification in the two sexes: in the male, the upper and lower borders of the cartilage become calcified first, extending in continuity with the end of the rib; calcification of the central area follows. In contrast, calcification in women tends to occur first in a central location, in the form of either a solid tongue or as two parallel lines extending into the cartilage from the end of the rib. All of the five women who showed a "male pattern" of calcification had had previous pelvic surgery, and the author suggests that the pattern of costal cartilage calcification is under hormonal control.

Thin smooth shadows of water-density which parallel the ribs and measure 1 to 2 mm in diameter project adjacent to the inferior and inferolateral margins of the first and second ribs and to the axillary portions of the lower ribs. These "companion shadows" (Figure 1–61) are caused by visualization in tangential projection of a combination of parietal pleura and the soft tissues immediately external to the pleura; care must be taken not to misinterpret them as local pleural thickening. In 300 normal subjects in whom the companion shadows were specifically sought by Felson,[69] they were seen adjacent to the first rib in 35 per cent and the second rib in 31 per cent. In approximately half of the cases the shadows were bilateral; when unilateral, they were more commonly on the right side. Companion shadows adjacent to the axillary portions of the lower ribs were seen more often (in 75 per cent of 700 normal subjects).

Congenital anomalies of the ribs are relatively uncommon; supernumerary ribs (Figure 1–62) arising from the seventh cervical vertebra were identified in 1.5 per cent of 350 normal subjects examined by Felson;[69] nearly all were bilateral but many had developed asymmetrically. Other anomalies, such as hypoplasia of the first rib (observed by Felson in 1.2 per cent of 350 normal subjects[69]), bifid or splayed anterior ribs, and, rarely, local fusion of ribs

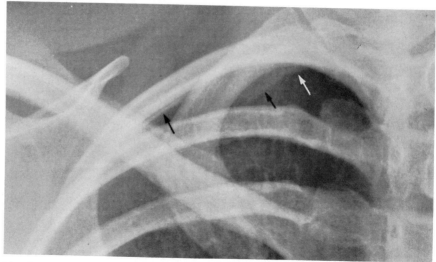

Figure 1–61. **Companion Shadows of the Ribs.** A magnified view of the apex of the right hemithorax reveals thin smooth shadows of water density lying roughly parallel to the inferior surfaces of the first and second ribs (arrows). These companion shadows are caused by visualization in tangential projection of a combination of parietal pleura and the soft tissues immediately external to the pleura.

usually are important only in that they may result in an erroneous interpretation of abnormal lung density.

Occasionally the inferior aspect of the clavicles has an irregular notch or indentation 2 to 3 cm from the sternal articulation; this is of variable size and shape, from a superficial saucer-shaped defect to a deep notch 2 cm wide by 1.0 to 1.5 cm deep.

These *rhomboid fossae* (Figure 1–63) give origin to the costoclavicular or rhomboid ligaments which radiate downward to bind the clavicle to the first rib.[145, 824] The incidence varies from 10 per cent of clavicles studied anatomically[825] to 0.59 per cent of 10,000 photofluorograms reported by Shauffer and Collins.[826] Of the latter cases, 39 were unilateral and 20 bilateral.

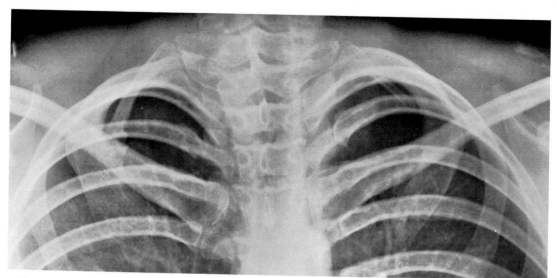

Figure 1–62. **Cervical Ribs.** Bilateral supernumerary ribs arise from the seventh cervical vertebra. The right rib is longer than the left and shows a synchondrosis with the medial aspect of the first rib.

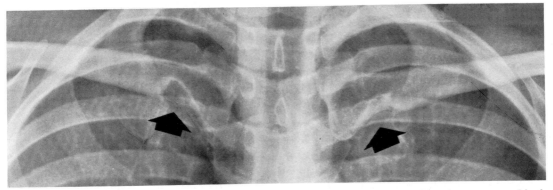

Figure 1–63. **Rhomboid Fossae.** An irregular notch or indentation is present in the inferior aspect of both clavicles approximately 2 cm from their sternal end (arrows). These fossae give origin to the costoclavicular or rhomboid ligaments.

A tiny foramen may be seen occasionally near the superior aspect of the center of the clavicle, either unilaterally or bilaterally; this foramen transmits the middle supraclavicular nerve and is said to be present in 6 per cent of dry skeletal specimens.[824]

The normal *thoracic spine* is perfectly straight in frontal projection and gently concave anteriorly in lateral projection. Its roentgenographic density in lateral projection decreases uniformly and progressively from above downward, and any deviation from this should arouse suspicion of intrathoracic disease.

The lateral and superior borders of the *manubrium* are the only portions of the sternum visible on frontal projections of the thorax, although the whole of the sternum should be well visualized tangentially in lateral roentgenograms. Brief mention may be made of the intrathoracic rib, a rare congenital anomaly of which only ten examples had been reported by 1965.[147] This unusual anomaly consists of an accessory rib which arises within the bony thorax, more commonly on the right than the left, either from the anterior surface of a rib or from the contiguous vertebral body; it extends downward and slightly laterally to end at the diaphragm. Its only importance lies in its recognition as an innocuous intrathoracic structure.

THE NORMAL CHEST ROENTGENOGRAM

As the preceding sections have shown, the lungs are composed of an almost incredible complex of tissues, each of which separately performs a unique function but all of which, when integrated, perform the act of respiration. The morphologist can examine each tissue and pronounce on its normal or abnormal characteristics; in many ways, through the application of special techniques such as bronchography and angiography, the roentgenologist may similarly assess individual components of the lungs, although his methods are necessarily more gross in scope. However, the bulk of roentgenograms of the chest which the diagnostician must interpret are plain films, with no help from contrast media, and here he is dealing with a summation of relatively low-contrast objects forming a complex group of roentgenographic shadows of varying definition and density. The composition of the lungs in relation to their "density"* and to their roentgenographic pattern is a facet of chest roentgenology which has received insufficient attention in the literature, and in this section an attempt is made to clarify some of these issues.

---

*In this context, the word "density" applies to the *weight of tissue per volume*, or specific gravity (for comparative purposes, the figures for lung tissue may be related to the density of soft tissue as equivalent to water at 1.0 g per ml and to the density of air as zero). It should not be confused with "roentgenographic density," which is a measure of the blackening of film caused by a reduction in silver emulsion by the incident roentgen beam. The greater the amount of radiation which passes through the body, the greater will be the blackening of the roentgenogram; thus, since the tissue density of bone is greater than that of lung, transmission of roentgen rays through bone is less, so that on chest roentgenograms bones appear relatively white in comparison with the blackness of lung. Therefore, *roentgenographic density is dependent upon "tissue" density*, at least in adequately exposed chest roentgenograms.

Normal Lung Density

It is readily apparent that the "roentgenographic density" of the lungs is the result of the absorptive powers of each of its component parts — gas, blood, and tissue. Although precise figures for the relative contributions of blood and tissue vary somewhat depending upon whether results are obtained by anatomic or physiologic methods, data have been compiled which allow a reasonable approximation (*see* Table 1–4).

If we apply the *average* figures for total maximal tissue volume, derived from anatomic and physiologic estimates, and the predicted total lung capacity (6500 ml)[152] of a 20-year-old man, 170 cm in height, the *average density* of lung is 740 g: 7240 ml,* or 0.10 g per ml.

This figure, of course, represents the density of a structure whose composite parts are uniformly distributed throughout it, a situation which hardly pertains in the lung. Some of the roentgenographic density of lung is contributed to by the major blood vessels, which are visible as homogeneous tapering structures having a density of 1.0 g per ml. Since the average density of lung is only 0.10, a considerable portion of lung tissue must possess a density *less* than this, to compensate for the relatively high density of the visible blood vessels; obviously a high proportion of air must be contained in such tissue — logically, the lung parenchyma or respiratory portion of the lung.

Weibel[81] estimated that the lung parenchyma comprises 90 per cent of total lung volume. By use of a point-counting technique, the same investigator measured the volumetric proportion of the three components of lung parenchyma: *air* accounted for 92 per cent, and *tissue and capillary blood*, 8.0 per cent (including interstitium, endothelial, and epithelial cells, vessel walls, and blood). On the basis of Weibel's figures and again assuming a total lung volume of 7240 ml, the parenchymal component is approximately 6500 ml (90 per cent of 7240 ml), of which 500 ml consists of tissue and blood (8 per cent of 6500 ml). Thus, *the density of lung parenchyma at total lung capacity is 0.08* (500 g: 6500 ml). *It follows that in a chest roentgenogram*

---

*The ratio of total weight (740 g, with a volume of 740 ml) to total volume (6500 ml + 740 ml).

***Table 1–4.** *Pulmonary Tissue and Blood Volumes in ml*

	EXTRAVASCULAR TISSUE VOLUME	PULMONARY BLOOD VOLUME	TOTAL MAXIMAL TISSUE VOLUME
Staub,[22] 1963°	275	350	625
Loyd, *et al.*,[149] 1966†	420	430	850
Average	350	390	740

°Estimate of the lungs of a 70 kg man, based on anatomic studies of five healthy men.

†Estimate of the lungs of a 70 kg man, 70 inches in height, derived from a nomogram constructed by Loyd and his associates[149] from physiologic data (based on the determination of pulmonary tissue volume described by Sackner and his co-workers[150] and of pulmonary blood volume described by McGaff and his associates[151]).

all the tissue visible in the peripheral 2 cm of the lung or between vascular shadows has a density of 0.08 g per ml.

If the extravascular tissue volume is assumed to be constant, the overall roentgenographic density of lung (average, 0.1 g/ml) is the result of the ratio of its blood and gas content. The blood content may be further subdivided into a capillary component, which creates the *background density* of the lung parenchyma (0.08 g/ml), and a larger vessel component, which creates the *visible lung markings* (density, 1.0 g/ml). Figures for *total capillary blood volume* vary according to the technique used for measurement. Physiologic techniques have yielded estimates, in the resting subject, of 60 to 100 ml,[22, 77-79] whereas anatomic studies have indicated a volume of 150 to 200 ml.[81, 82] Piiper[187] subdivided total pulmonary blood volume in the dog into its three vascular components and estimated 27 per cent to be in the arteries, 38 per cent in capillaries, and 35 per cent in veins. If these percentages can be extended to the human lung, the average of 390 ml for total pulmonary blood volume (*see* Table 1–4) may be broken down to indicate a *capillary volume of 150 ml and a larger-vessel volume of 240 ml.* A capillary blood volume of 150 ml probably represents an acceptable average of the figures obtained by anatomic and physiologic techniques of measurement, although it is somewhat higher than the figures quoted earlier in this chapter in the discussion on physiology of acinar perfusion.

It is important to appreciate the distinction between capillary and visible vessel components of the lung, in their separate contributions to lung density. For example, variation in total *capillary* blood volume probably is difficult, if not impossible, to appreciate subjectively on plain roentgenograms of the chest (although this may be accomplished objectively by roentgen densitometry; *see* Chapter 2). Although an increase in capillary blood volume is known to occur in ventricular septal defect[154] and in atrial septal defect,[155] without concomitant alteration in lung volumes,[156] it is doubtful whether the increase in lung density which must result from this increased capillary volume can be appreciated roentgenographically, except by densitometric means. In such situations, roentgenologic assessment of vascular plethora (pleonemia) must be based on an increase in the size and number of visible pulmonary vessels, both arterial and venous.

It is emphasized that these statements apply only to conditions in which *uniform* alteration in perfusion exists throughout the lungs—for example, in the pleonemia that accompanies intracardiac left-to-right shunt (Figure 1–64*A*) or in the oligemia of diffuse emphysema (Figure 1–64*B*). When reduction in blood flow is local, as with lobar emphysema (Figure 1–64*C*) or occasionally with massive pulmonary embolism (Westermark's sign[157]), alteration in density in the involved area of lung is the result of a reduction in *both* capillary blood volume (background density) and visible vascular shadows. Such alteration of background lung density is an exceedingly valuable roentgenologic sign and is referred to repeatedly throughout this book.

Alteration in Lung Density

In any clinical situation, alteration in roentgenographic lung density may be due to one of three mechanisms or a combination thereof.

PHYSIOLOGIC MECHANISMS. A frequently observed physiologic variation in lung density with which every roentgenologist is familiar is the change that may occur from one examination to another on the same subject, depending upon depth of inspiration. Such variation is readily explained by comparing the contributions of the three components of the lung to its den-

sity. For example, again consider a 20-year-old man, 170 cm in height, and assume that pulmonary blood volume and tissue volume are reasonably constant at different degrees of lung inflation; according to the tables of normal values constructed by Goldman and Becklake,[152] predicted lung volumes for such a subject will be: total lung capacity, 6.5 liters; functional residual capacity, 3.4 liters; and residual volume, 1.5 liters. Assuming a total maximal tissue volume of 740 ml, average lung density at total lung capacity is 0.10; at functional residual capacity, density is almost double (0.18), and at residual volume it is more than treble (0.33) (Figure 1–65). Thus, it is clear that, assuming total pulmonary blood volume to be constant at different degrees of lung inflation, *lung density is inversely proportional to the amount of contained gas.*

PHYSICAL (OR TECHNICAL) MECHANISMS. Symmetry of roentgenographic density of the two lungs in a normal subject is dependent upon proper positioning of the patient for roentgenography. If the patient is rotated as little as 2 to 3 degrees, the density of the lung closer to the film will be uniformly *greater* than the density of the other lung (Figure 1–66). This effect is produced by the greater thickness of thoracic-wall musculature through which the x-ray beam must pass when a patient is rotated either to the right or to the left. A similar effect may be produced by scoliosis or by incorrect centering of the x-ray beam. Since comparison of the density of the two lungs plays such an important part in the assessment of chest roentgenograms, correct positioning of the patient and centering of the x-ray beam are crucial.

PATHOLOGIC MECHANISMS. Excluding from consideration the contribution to roentgenographic density from the soft tissues of the thoracic wall and providing that physiologic and physical causes can be excluded, variation in lung density always is due to an increase or decrease in one or more of the three elements, air, blood, and tissue. As discussed in the Introduction, a change in density is seldom produced by alteration in one component to the exclusion of the others: examples of such "pure" alteration are the reduction in density (increased translucency) produced by pulmonary embolism without infarction (Westermark's sign), in which there is reduction in blood volume but little change in gas or

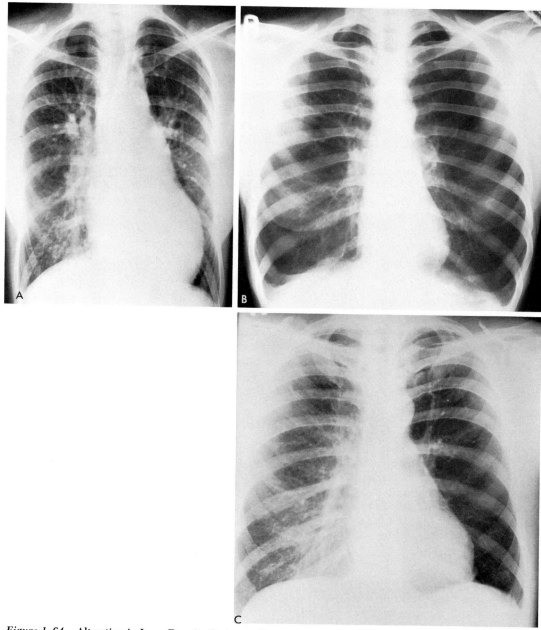

Figure 1–64.   **Alteration in Lung Density Owing to Abnormalities of Perfusion.** Generalized pleonemia as seen in patent ductus arteriosus (A) and diffuse oligemia as in generalized emphysema (B) are evidenced by an increase or decrease, respectively, in the size of the major pulmonary vessels rather than by discernible alteration in background lung density. When alteration in blood flow is local as in unilateral emphysema (Swyer-James syndrome) (C), reduction in density is apparent because of a decrease in *both* capillary blood volume (background density) and visible vascular shadows.

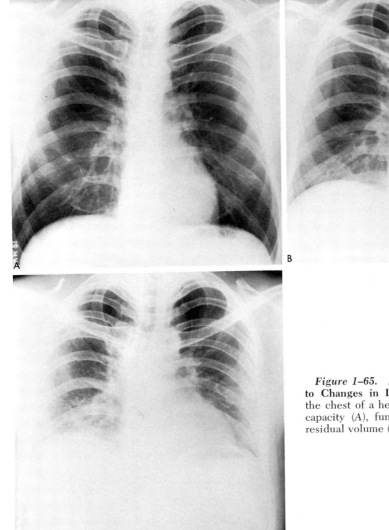

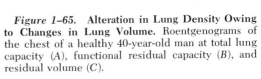

Figure 1–65. **Alteration in Lung Density Owing to Changes in Lung Volume.** Roentgenograms of the chest of a healthy 40-year-old man at total lung capacity (*A*), functional residual capacity (*B*), and residual volume (*C*).

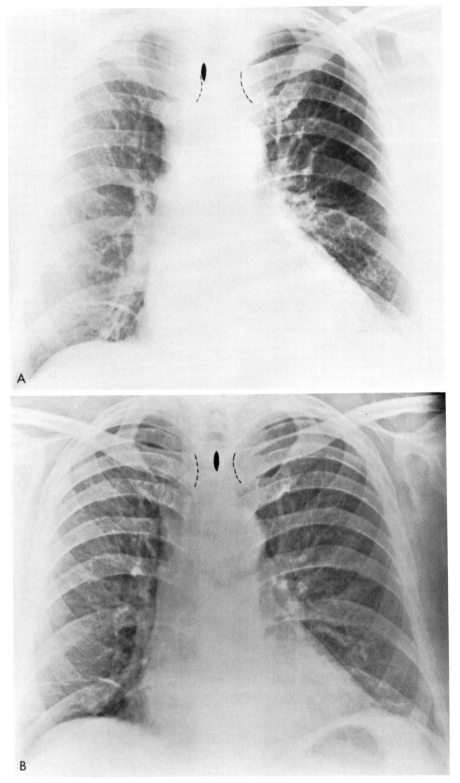

Figure 1–66. **Alteration in Lung Density Owing to Improper Positioning.** *A,* A roentgenogram of the chest in posteroanterior projection was exposed with the patient rotated slightly into the right anterior oblique position, producing an overall increase in density of the right lung compared to the left (the solid elliptical shadow and dotted lines represent a vertebral spinous process and the medial ends of the clavicles respectively). In *B,* positioning has been corrected and the asymmetry has disappeared.

Table 1–5. *The Composition and Density of Normal Lung*

LUNG VOLUME

Arterial blood volume[*]	105 ml
Capillary blood volume[*]	150 ml
Venous blood volume[*]	135 ml
Total pulmonary blood volume	390 ml[†]
Extravascular tissue volume	350 ml[†]
Total blood and tissue volume	740 ml
Total lung capacity[‡]	6500 ml
Total lung volume	7240 ml

LUNG DENSITY

Average density at TLC (6500 ml) = 7240/740	0.10 g/ml
Average density at FRC (3400 ml) = 4140/740	0.18 g/ml
Average density at RV (1500 ml) = 2240/740	0.33 g/ml

PARENCHYMAL VOLUME

Lung parenchyma = 90% total lung volume[§] (90% 7240 ml)	6500 ml
Tissue and capillary blood (8% of parenchyma[§])	500 ml
Air (92% of parenchyma[§])	6000 ml

PARENCHYMAL DENSITY

Density at TLC = 6500/500	0.08 g/ml

[*]Piiper[187]
[†]See Table 1–4 (page 86)
[‡]20-year-old man 170 cm in height[152]
[§]Weibel,[81] 1962

tissue volume; or diffuse pulmonary infiltration, such as sarcoidosis, in which there is increase in extravascular tissue volume but little change in gas or blood volume. In the majority of clinical situations, change in density, whether increased or decreased, local or diffuse, is the result of a change in all three components. The relative contribution of each component is discussed in detail in the appropriate sections.

In Table 1–5 is summarized the contributions to the total volume of the lungs of their component parts, together with the average density of lung at different volumes, and the composition and density of lung parenchyma.

The Pulmonary Markings

It is of the utmost importance for the roentgenologist to have a thorough knowledge of the pattern of linear markings throughout the normal lung. Unfortunately, such knowledge cannot be gained through didactic teaching; it requires exposure to thousands of normal chest roentgenograms to acquire the experience—perhaps, more, the art—to be able to distinguish normal from abnormal. It requires not only familiarity with the distribution and pattern of branching of these markings (which are described in the section on roentgen anatomy), but also an awareness of normal caliber, extent of normal roentgenologic visibility, and changes that may occur in different phases of respiration and in various body positions. There are two main reasons for the need of such knowledge: (1) a change in the caliber of arteries and veins constitutes one of the most valuable roentgenologic signs of pulmonary venous and pulmonary arterial hypertension and (2) a redistribution of vessels, with consequent modification of the number of roentgenologically visible markings, may constitute the major evidence for pulmonary collapse or previous pulmonary resection.

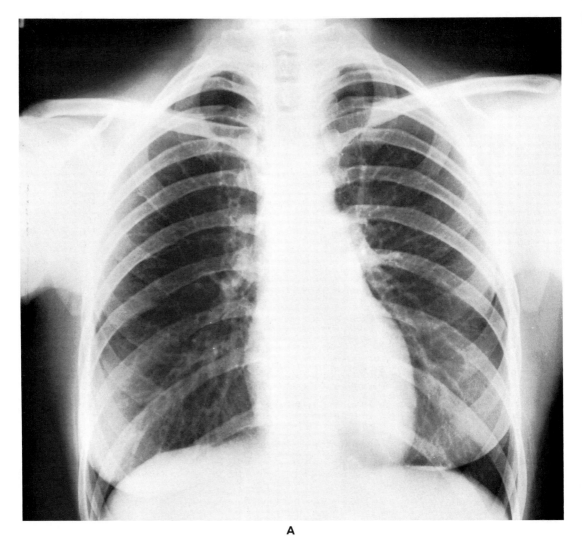

A

Figure 1–67. **Normal Chest Roentgenogram, Posteroanterior Projection.** *A,* A roentgenogram of the chest in the erect position of an asymptomatic 26-year-old woman.

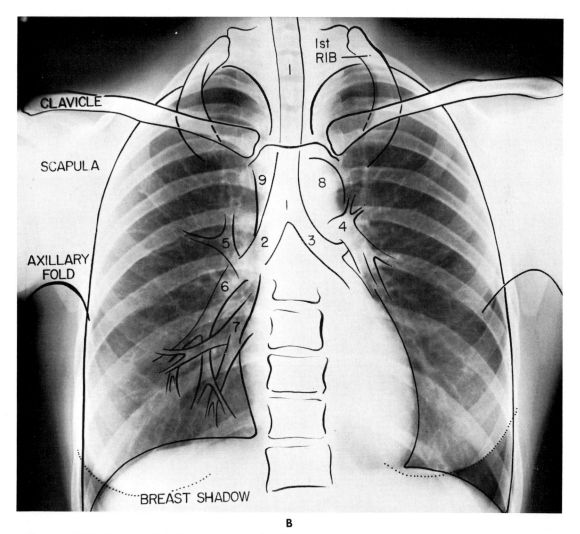

B

Figure 1–67. Continued. B, A diagrammatic overlay shows the normal anatomic structures numbered or labeled: (1) trachea; (2) right main bronchus; (3) left main bronchus; (4) left pulmonary artery; (5) right upper lobe pulmonary artery; (6) right interlobar artery; (7) right lower and middle lobe vein; (8) aortic knob; (9) superior vena cava.

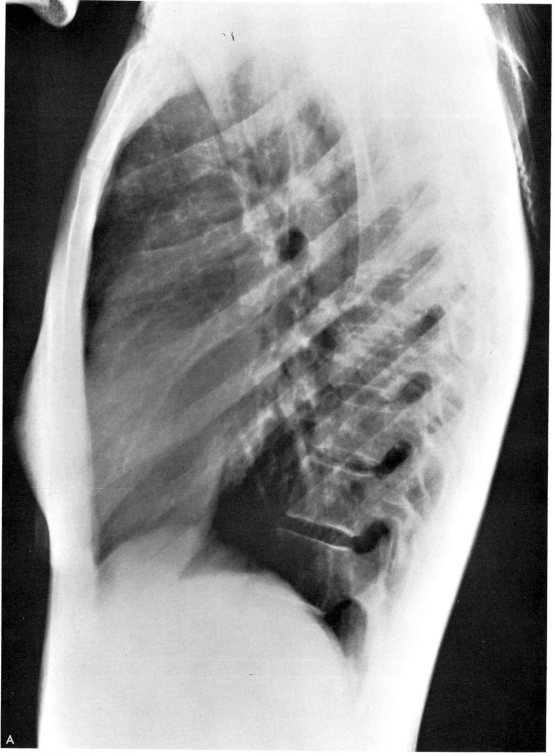

Figure 1-68. **Normal Chest Roentgenogram, Lateral Projection.** *A,* A roentgenogram of the chest in the erect position of an asymptomatic 26-year-old woman.

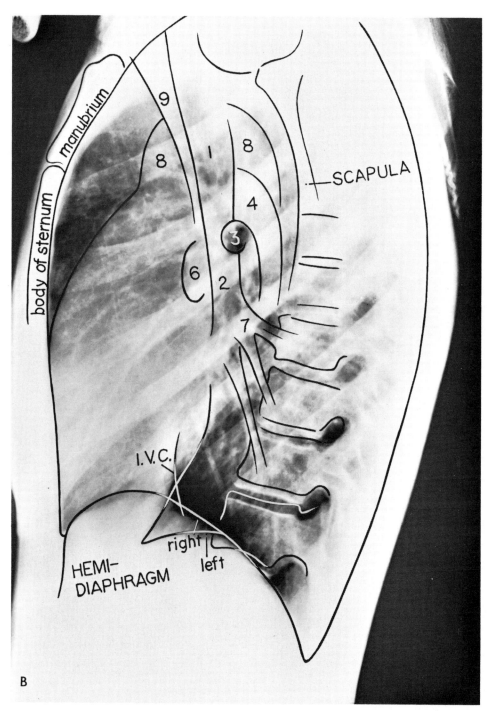

Figure 1–68. Continued. B, A diagrammatic overlay shows the normal anatomic structures numbered or labeled: (1) trachea; (2) right main bronchus; (3) left main bronchus; (4) left interlobar artery; (6) right main pulmonary artery; (7) confluence of pulmonary veins; (8) aortic arch; (9) brachiocephalic vessels.

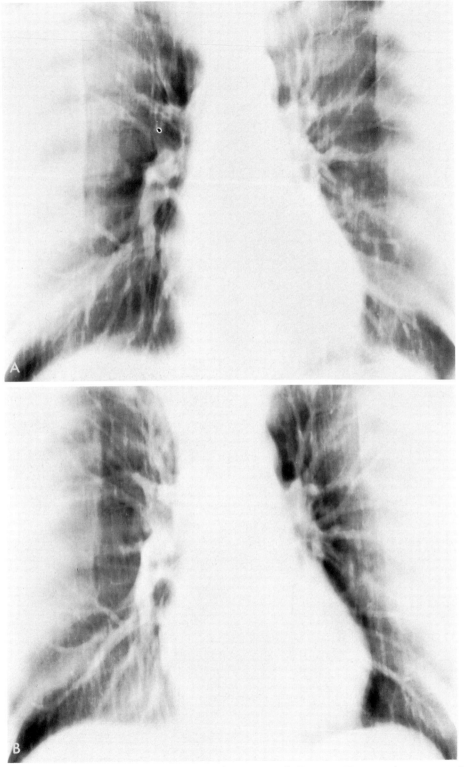

Figure 1–69. **Effect on Pulmonary Vasculature of Change in Body Position.** Tomographic sections through the midportion of both lungs in the erect (*A*) and supine (*B*) positions reveal a significant difference in the size of vascular channels. In the supine roentgenogram, not only are the upper lobe arteries and veins more prominent than in the erect study but the overall "grayness" of the upper zones is greater, indicating increased capillary perfusion. Note the difference in the size of the azygos vein in the two studies.

The linear markings are created by a complex bundle of structures which are intimately related to one another in their passage through the lungs (Figures 1–67 and 1–68). These structures are the pulmonary arteries, the bronchial arteries, the bronchi, the nerves, and the lymphatic channels and lymphoid collections; all of these structures are connected, at least proximal to the arterioles, by a cuff of loose areolar tissue. The arterial bundles fan outward from both hila, tapering gradually as they proceed distally. In the normal state they are visible to about 1 to 2 cm from the visceral pleural surface over the convexity of the lung, at which point lung structure becomes totally acinar in type and the lung markings invisible (the lung parenchyma). Jefferson[70] pointed out that on arteriograms a centimeter and millimeter pattern of branching vessels can be identified in the periphery of the lung, analogous to the pattern on bronchograms described by Reid and Simon;[158] only rarely, however, can such a pattern be distinguished on plain roentgenograms.

As is indicated in a previous section dealing with the pulmonary vascular tree, the anatomic remoteness of the pulmonary veins from the arteries often renders their distinction possible roentgenographically (see Figure 1–37, page 42). In the region of the pulmonary ligaments, especially, no difficulty should be encountered in distinguishing these vessels, since the pulmonary veins in the lower lung zones lie almost horizontally and on a lower plane than the arteries (see Figure 1–36, page 40). Simon[162] pointed out that a horizontal line drawn across a posteroanterior roentgenogram of the chest at a midpoint between the apex and diaphragm separates the pulmonary artery complex in the hila (at or above this line) and the veins (below the line). The veins which drain the upper lobes are lateral to their respective arteries, not only in the hilar regions but in the lung fields also. This relationship is particularly valuable in the right hilar region, where the superior pulmonary vein forms the lateral aspect of the hilum superiorly and thus produces the upper limb of its concave configuration (see Figure 1–37). Flattening of this concavity provides good evidence for collapse of the right upper lobe, or, in the presence of pulmonary venous hypertension, indicates engorgement of the upper-lobe vein.[159]

In a roentgenogram of the chest of an erect subject there is usually some discrepancy between the size of the linear markings in the upper lung fields compared with those in the lower, due largely to lesser perfusion of the upper zones. Because of hydrostatic pressure, when the subject is erect, pulmonary blood flow increases progressively from apex to base, a unit volume of lung at the base of the thorax having four to eight times the blood flow of a similar volume at the apex.[104] When roentgenography is carried out with the patient in the horizontal position, this discrepancy in vascular size largely disappears, due to removal of the influence of gravity. The caliber of the upper-lobe vessels in such circumstances is influenced also by the increase in pulmonary blood volume which occurs when the patient is supine and which, according to Daley and his associates, amounts to approximately 30 per cent.[160] Thus, the gravitational advantage enjoyed by the upper lobes in the supine position may result in the upper-lobe vasculature appearing quite different in such films compared with films made in the erect position, a discrepancy which must not be misinterpreted as evidence of disease (Figure 1–69).

Roentgenograms of the chest in many normal erect subjects show more prominent linear markings in the left upper zone than in the corresponding region of the right lung. This asymmetry is understandable in the light of the findings of Dollery and his associates[163] in studies employing lung-scanning techniques with [15]oxygen-labeled carbon dioxide; they found significantly greater blood flow through the left than the right upper zone in normal subjects.

Complex interrelationships between transthoracic pressure and pulmonary blood flow occur during inspiration and expiration and during the Valsalva or Mueller maneuver.* It has been established that during inspiration the blood volume increases in the pulmonary arteries and veins and decreases in the capillaries.[164] This

---

*The Valsalva maneuver consists of forced expiration against a closed glottis, and the Mueller maneuver consists of inspiration against a closed glottis. For proper hemodynamic effect, pressures of plus and minus 40 to 50 cm H$_2$O, respectively, should be maintained for seven to ten seconds. For roentgenograms to be comparable, both maneuvers should be performed at the same degree of lung inflation, preferably at the end of a quiet inspiration.

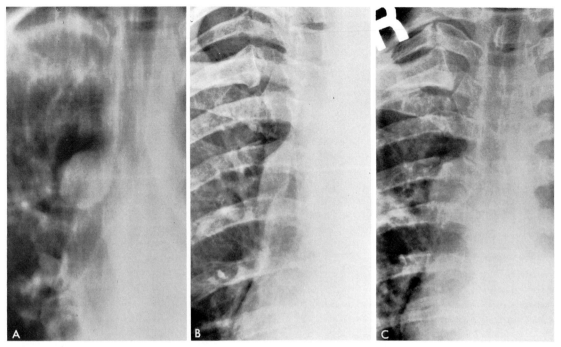

Figure 1-70. Value of Valsalva and Mueller Procedures in Distinguishing the Vascular or Solid Nature of Intrathoracic Lesions. *A,* A tomographic section of the mid-mediastinum reveals a well-defined circular shadow situated in the right tracheobronchial angle; differential diagnosis includes an enlarged azygos lymph node or a markedly dilated azygos vein. *B,* A roentgenogram of the same area in the erect position during the Valsalva procedure reveals a marked reduction in the size of the shadow. *C,* A similar projection during the Mueller procedure shows a considerable increase in the size of the shadow compared to *B.* Subsequent angiographic studies proved the shadow to be a markedly dilated azygos vein associated with infradiaphragmatic interruption of the inferior vena cava.

change in volume has been documented roentgenographically by Chang,[76] who measured the right descending pulmonary artery in more than 1000 patients and found the caliber consistently larger during inspiration than during expiration in normal subjects, the range of difference being 1 to 3 mm. He found these measurements particularly helpful in the assessment of pulmonary hypertension, in which the inspiratory/expiratory ratio was reversed; this point has been emphasized by Rigler also.[165]

Use of the Valsalva and Mueller maneuvers to produce increase and decrease, respectively, in intra-alveolar pressure has important but limited application in roentgen diagnosis.[166] In 1944 Westermark[167] suggested that increasing the intra-alveolar pressure might prove valuable in differentiating certain diseases of the lungs roentgenographically. He considered that increasing the intra-alveolar pressure re

duced the size of congested vessels in pulmonary venous engorgement and "pushed" edema fluid from the airspaces and interstitium back into the vascular tree, thus allowing differentiation of congestion from an infectious process in which this phenomenon did not occur. Although it possesses interesting theoretic possibilities, this technique has proved of little practical value in our experience, partly because congestion and inflammation seldom are confusing entities. However, the Valsalva maneuver may be used to advantage in another context — differentiation of vascular and solid lesions within the thorax:[165, 166] Vascular structures are reduced in size when intra-alveolar pressure is increased, whereas solid lesions remain unchanged. The method is of particular value in the differentiation of an azygos vein from an enlarged azygos lymph node (Figure 1-70), or a pulmonary arteriovenous fistula from a solid mass lesion. Tomography may be employed to considerable advantage during these maneuvers, as pointed out by Amundsen.[168]

These examples of the use of the Valsalva and Mueller maneuvers indicate a trend which has been increasingly emphasized in recent years—the application of physiologic principles to roentgen diagnosis. Knowledge of pathophysiology has played a major role in the roentgenologic study of the cardiovascular system for many years, but it probably has not received the attention in pulmonary diseases that it deserves. A major stimulus to its more frequent application was given by Rigler[165] in 1959, in his classic paper entitled "Functional Roentgen Diagnosis: Anatomical Image—Physiological Interpretation," to which the reader is referred for a concise dissertation on this important topic. Repeated reference is made throughout this book to the ways in which physiologic events may be used to aid in roentgenologic diagnosis of pulmonary disease.

PERCEPTION IN CHEST ROENTGENOLOGY

Observer Error

The roentgenologic diagnosis of chest disease begins with *identification* of an abnormality on a roentgenogram: that which is not *seen* cannot be appreciated. These statements may appear self-evident, but in fact they express an observation which deserves constant re-emphasis. The confidence which a roentgenologist gains in his ability to *interpret* changes which are apparent roentgenographically must not be mistaken for an improvement in the accuracy with which he sees them in the first place. Many studies of the accuracy of diagnostic procedures, notably those by Garland[169, 170] and by Garland and Cochrane,[171] have revealed an astonishingly high incidence of both intraobserver* and interobserver† error among experienced roentgenologists. For example, in one series

---

*Inconsistent observations made by one roentgenologist on two separate readings of the same roentgenograms.

†Inconsistent observations made by two or more roentgenologists on the same roentgenograms.

quoted by Garland,[169] the interpreters missed almost one-third of roentgenologically positive minifilms and overread about 1 per cent of negative films; in another series reported by the same author,[170] based only on positive roentgenograms, interobserver error varied by 9 to 24 per cent and intraobserver error by 3 to 31 per cent. Since these figures are derived from studies by competent, experienced observers, it is clear that no roentgenologist should be lulled into a false sense of security concerning his competence to "see" a lesion: confidence should be continually modified by studied scientific reserve.

The reasons for observer error are both subjective and objective and are highly complex; every physician who is concerned in interpretation of chest roentgenograms must make himself familiar with the physical and physiologic principles of perception, so that errors may be kept to a minimum. Some of the more important of these principles are outlined here, but the reader is urged to review more extensive works on the subject, particularly those by Tuddenham[172-175] and by Garland.[169] The discussion by Riebel[176] on the use of the eyes in roentgenologic diagnosis is also commended.

A roentgenogram may be inspected in two ways, each of which may be usefully employed in different situations. Directed search is a method whereby a specific pattern of inspection is carried out, commonly along such lines as thoracic and extrathoracic soft tissues, bony thorax, mediastinum, diaphragm, pleura, and, finally, the lung fields, the last-named usually by individual inspection and comparison of the zones of the two lungs from apex to base. Such a method *must* be employed by roentgenologists-in-training, for it is only through the exercise of this routine during thousands of examinations that the *pattern* of the normal chest may be recognized. The alternative method of inspection is *free search*, in which the roentgenogram is scanned without a preconceived orderly pattern. This technique is recommended by Tuddenham,[172] who found some objective evidence of its being the scanning method employed by the majority of expert roentgenologists; our experience supports this. However, we consider that discovery of an abnormality during free-search scanning must be followed by an orderly pattern of inspection, so that other, less obvious, abnormalities are not overlooked.

It is important to view every chest roentgenogram from a distance of at least six to eight feet, or alternatively through diminishing lenses. The reasons are twofold: (1) the slight nuances of density variation between similar zones of the two lungs may be better appreciated at a distance than at the traditional position of viewing and (2) the visibility of shadows with ill-defined margins is significantly improved by minification. The physiologic mechanisms underlying this improved visibility have been explained by Tuddenham:[172] The perception of a roentgenologic shadow in the lungs is dependent in large measure upon the gradation of density at the border of the lesion or on its sharpness of definition. At standard viewing distance, a lesion whose borders are sharply defined is more readily appreciated on the retina than is a lesion whose borders are indistinct. Since such appreciation is dependent upon the visual angle which the border of the lesion subtends at the observer's retina, increase in viewing distance (or, alternatively, the use of a diminishing lens), by reducing this visual angle, improves appreciation of a lesion whose borders are indistinct. A practical demonstration of this principle was provided by Newell and Garneau[177] through roentgenography of multiple lucite discs whose borders had been bevelled at increasing angles from the perpendicular; the discs whose margins were perpendicular to the x-ray beam showed no variation in degree of perceptibility with distance of viewing, whereas perception of the bevelled discs improved significantly with minification. The practical application of this basic physiologic principle of viewing to every-day roentgenography cannot be overstressed.[172]

Since perception of a roentgen image depends upon the rate of change in illumination across the retina corresponding to the border of the roentgen shadow (the retinal illumination gradient[172]), magnification logically should reduce perception by increasing the distance across the retina over which a given change in illumination occurs. Although this is true for many intrapulmonary lesions whose borders are indistinct, magnification may aid in the perception of small shadows of relatively high contrast, in much the same manner as it improves the visibility of trabeculae in bone. We find magnification of value in the assessment of diffuse diseases of the lung in which numerous densities of relatively high contrast are crowded so closely together as to be almost indistinguishable with standard viewing; a classic example is provided by the tiny calcific shadows of alveolar microlithiasis (see Figure 2–2, page 107).

In general, therefore, it may be said that minification, either by distance viewing or through the use of diminishing lenses, should be employed at some time in every roentgenographic examination of the chest; magnification is of value only when small shadows of relatively high contrast and sharp definition are difficult to separate visually at a standard viewing distance.

As a further means of reducing the frequency of "missing" lesions roentgenologically, the mechanism of double viewing has been advocated by several authors, notably Tuddenham[172] and Garland.[169] The latter considers that dual interpretation, either by the same observer on two different occasions or by two different observers, decreases by at least a third the number of positive films missed. (It is important, of course, that the interpretation given on the first reading should not be known at the second.) We cannot dispute the improvement in diagnostic accuracy to be expected from dual interpretation of every roentgenographic examination of the chest, but the practicality of employing the method as a routine in large departments of radiology rather staggers the imagination. Two compromise solutions are suggested: (1) a second reading of all films first interpreted as negative; and (2) a more universal adoption of the practice of referring physicians personally viewing the roentgenograms of their patients. Many chest physicians and surgeons become highly competent in roentgen interpretation as a result of many years of personal viewing; if this is carried out in consultation with the roentgenologist, the "second look" inevitably reveals a significant number of abnormalities that were missed on the first interpretation.

In a survey conducted by Berkson and his associates[178] at the Mayo Clinic, diagnostic accuracy improved with the use of stereoscopic roentgenograms. Of 500 chest examinations (98 positive and 402 negative) reviewed by nine "readers" (five roentgenologists and four chest specialists), the incidence of "false negatives" was 18.5 per cent and of "false positives" 3.4 per cent when single posteroanterior roentgenograms were viewed. When stereoscopic roentgenograms were reviewed at a second interpretation, the average for false negatives was reduced to 14.9 per cent and for false positives to 2.5 per cent. This report originated from an institution in which stereoscopy is an advanced art; what amounts to a relatively low gain in diagnostic accuracy in experienced hands would undoubtedly be even less in centers in which stereoscopy is little used.

Threshold Visibility

In a study reported by Newell and Garneau[177] in 1951 in which lucite discs were employed as test objects, it was found that a structure of unit density must be at least 3 mm in thickness to be roentgenographically visible. Further, it was observed that this *threshold visibility* applied only if the margins of the lucite discs were parallel to the plane of the roentgen beam—visibility diminished progressively as the margins were increasingly bevelled. In 1963, Spratt and his associates[179] found that roentgenologists were able to locate the shadows of lucite balls regularly only if they measured 1.0 to 2.0 cm in diameter; lucite balls of 0.6 cm in diameter could be located only when projected over intercostal spaces, and those as small as 0.3 cm could be identified only in retrospect. The difference between the 3 mm measurement of Newell and Garneau[177] and the larger figures reached by Spratt and his colleagues[179] lies in the character of the *border* of the shadow; the 3 mm measurement applies only to lesions whose borders are sharply defined; it is apparent that a lesion with indistinctly defined or bevelled margins (such as a sphere) must be greater than 3 mm in diameter to be roentgenologically visible. Some support is lent these observations by roentgenologic-pathologic correlative studies which have shown that most solitary tumors are not diagnosed roentgenologically until their diameter exceeds 6 mm[179] and that a cancer less than 1.0 cm in diameter cannot be diagnosed roentgenologically with standard roentgenographic methods.[180]

These limits of visibility apply, of course, to individual shadows within the lung, rather than to multiple diffuse nodular densities produced, for example, by miliary tuberculosis. In the latter instance, the question of summation of images is raised, and, although we are not able to enter into a discussion of the pros and cons of summation as a roentgenographic effect, we consider that the proposals put forward by Resink[181] possess considerable merit. This author suggests that wide distribution of a large number of small lesions throughout the lungs allows visibility of individual deposits only when they are *not* summated and that when summation does occur the appreciation of individual deposits is lost through blurring. (It should be noted that concepts of the effects of summation are conflicting; for example, Newell and Garneau[177] state that objects of subliminal absorption may be brought above threshold by summation of their shadows, an opinion which is directly contrary to that of Resink.)

Certain objective reasons for missing lesions during roentgenologic interpretation have been clarified by studies in which postmortem roentgenography of the chest has been correlated with subsequent study of the lungs morphologically.[182, 183] In a study of more than 300 cadavers, Greening and Pendergrass[182] found that the lesions most often missed roentgenographically were small calcified or uncalcified nodules 3 mm or slightly more in diameter, situated in the region of the pleura or subpleural parenchyma. Many metastatic nodules which measured up to 1 cm in diameter were not visualized. In four of the 300 cases, lesions measuring 2 to 5 cm in diameter which were discovered on roentgenography of the removed lungs were not visible even in retrospect in the roentgenographs made with the lungs *in situ*. These authors describe two areas within the thorax in which it is difficult to project a lesion so that it is related to air-containing parenchyma without a superimposed confusion of overlying bones and major blood vessels—over the convexity of the lungs in close proximity to the pleura and rib cage, and in the paramediastinal regions, where the shadows of the aorta, heart, and spine are quite dense. Lesions in close proximity to the diaphragm probably come within the same category. Clearly, it is important to be aware of these relatively "blind" areas in the thorax and to pay particular attention to them in the development of a scanning routine.

Another area to which appropriate attention should be directed in roentgenographic interpretation comprises all the structures outside the limits of the thorax. The importance to diagnosis of such abnormalities as hepatomegaly or splenomegaly, calcification in these organs, displacement or alteration in the contour of the gastric air bubble, and calcification within the thoracic soft tissues, cannot be overstressed. Finally, we have been impressed repeatedly by the information to be gained from thorough inspection of the "corners and borders" of roentgenographs; in most departments the name and age of the patient is inscribed thereon by photographic imprinting, and these particulars should be noted for definite identification. Similarly, an appreciation of the presence of dextrocardia or transposition of the thoracic and abdominal viscera may depend upon the position of the "right" or "left" marker.

Psychologic Aspects of Roentgenologic Interpretation

This subject is all too often neglected. Three aspects will be considered briefly, and the reader is referred to more complete discussions of this important topic.[169, 172, 176]

READER FATIGUE. The recent enormous increase in the use of roentgenologic services, together with the dearth of roentgenologists, has resulted in a significant increase in the number of examinations each roentgenologist may be required to report. The inevitable result has been "reader fatigue." No experienced roentgenologist denies the diminution in visual and mental acuity that develops during the day when the workload necessitates a heavy reporting schedule. The degree of susceptibility varies, but fatigue eventually affects all to a degree at which lack of efficiency accrues to the detriment of the patient. Each individual must set his own standards, but two mechanisms may be employed to reduce reader fatigue to a minimum: frequent "rest periods" away from the viewbox and the establishment of a reasonable maximal number of examinations to be reported each day.

PHYSICAL ASPECTS. The atmosphere in which reporting is carried out deserves more attention than it is often given. Quiet surroundings, away from distracting influences, are a prime requisite for necessary thought and reflection. Viewing facilities should be optimal; Garland[169] points out that the illuminator probably is the least expensive and yet one of the most important pieces of apparatus in any department of roentgenology; yet, all too often, insufficient attention is paid to such aspects as light intensity and background illumination. Riebel's work[176] on the use of the eyes in roentgenology deserves attention in this regard. The necessity for comfort and convenience of viewing and dictation requires no comment.

INTANGIBLE FACTORS. Intimately linked with the complex causes of observer error are several abstract phenomena which inevitably confront all roentgenologists and which defy adequate explanation. A typical example is the variation with which the same examination may be reported from one day to another: a roentgenogram of the chest (often in the troublesome borderland between normal and abnormal) may be pronounced normal on Monday morning and be interpreted by the same observer as showing "diffuse reticular disease" on Friday afternoon! It is a moot point whether fatigue is the dominant influence in these intraobserver disagreements; rather, they may be more realistically ascribed to a "state of mind," which is continually fluctuating and which represents an intangible influence on one's approach to a problem. It is important to recognize that intraobserver disagreements are bound to occur, but it is of even greater importance to continually strive to reduce their incidence by effecting the most efficient system of roentgenographic perception of which one is capable.

2

METHODS OF ROENTGENOLOGIC AND PATHOLOGIC INVESTIGATION

ROENTGENOLOGIC EXAMINATION
  STANDARD ROENTGENOGRAPHY
    Routine Projections
    Roentgenographic Technique
    Inspiratory-Expiratory Roentgenography
    Valsalva and Mueller Maneuvers
    Roentgenography in the Supine Position
    Roentgenography in the Lateral Decubitus
      Position
    Roentgenography in the Oblique Position
  ROENTGENOLOGIC PROCEDURES FOR THE
    EVALUATION OF INTRATHORACIC DYNAMICS
    Fluoroscopy
    Cinefluorography
    Roentgen Kymography
    Roentgen Densitometry
  TOMOGRAPHY
    Technique
    Indications
  BRONCHOGRAPHY
    Indications
    Contraindications
    Techniques of Examination
    Cinefluorographic Studies of Bronchial
      Dynamics
    Bronchographic Contrast Media
  ANGIOGRAPHY
    Pulmonary Angiography
    Angiocardiography
    Aortography

    Bronchial Arteriography
    Superior-vena-cava Angiography
    Azygography
  CONTRAST STUDIES BY GAS INSUFFLATION
    Mediastinal Pneumography
    Diagnostic Pneumothorax
    Diagnostic Pneumoperitoneum
    Diagnostic Pneumopericardium
  ROENTGENOLOGIC METHODS IN THE ASSESSMENT
    OF LUNG FUNCTION
    Determination of Lung Volumes
    Studies of Ventilation
    Studies of Perfusion
  LUNG SCANNING
    Gaseous Radionuclides
METHODS FOR PATHOLOGIC EXAMINATION
  POSTMORTEM INFLATION OF THE LUNG
    Inflation to an Arbitrary Degree
    Inflation to an Arbitrary Pressure
    Inflation to Total Lung Capacity
    Inflation to Estimated Volume
    Defects of Lung Inflation Techniques
  THE DISTENDING MEDIUM AND FIXATION
    Gaseous Fixatives
    Liquid Fixatives
  EXAMINATION OF THE LUNG
  RECORDING AND STORAGE
  SPECIAL POSTMORTEM TECHNIQUES
  SURGICAL SPECIMENS
    Biopsy

ROENTGENOLOGIC EXAMINATION

In this book, the approach to the diagnosis of chest disease involves two basic steps in a logical sequence of events: first, *identification* of a pathologic process roentgenologically and second, through *correlation* of these preliminary roentgenographic findings *with the clinical picture*, arrival at a diagnosis which takes into account the results of special roentgenologic procedures, laboratory tests, pulmonary function tests, scintillation scanning, and surgical procedures, such as bronchoscopy and biopsy. In this chapter the roentgenographic and pathologic methods we employ are described. Emphasis is placed on the techniques that have proved most valuable in our experience; however, procedures which others have employed to advantage but which we have found unrewarding will be described briefly together with our reasons for regarding them as unprofitable.

The cornerstone of roentgen diagnosis is the plain roentgenograph. This statement cannot be overemphasized—all other roentgen procedures, such as fluoroscopy, tomography, and special contrast studies, are strictly ancillary. With a few exceptions, to which reference is made, establishing the *presence* of a disease process by plain roentgenography of the chest should constitute the first step; if this first examination does not show clearly the nature and extent of the lesion, additional studies can be carried out to *complement* the plain roentgenograph. We specifically challenge the attitude of authors who advocate fluoroscopy as a preliminary procedure in diagnosis, to be followed by roentgenography *where indicated by fluoroscopic findings*.[188] Such an approach inevitably results in nondetection of an appreciable number of lesions, and, in addition, could constitute a radiation hazard to both roentgenologist and patient which might prove intolerable (although such a danger is reduced to almost negligible proportions by image amplification). When it is realized that visual perception of a fluoroscopic image is greatly inferior to that of a roentgenographic image, and when this is compounded by the fact that, even with roentgenograms, experienced interpreters may miss as many as 30 per cent of positive findings in observer-error experiments,[169-172, 178] the futility of employing fluoroscopy as even a rough screening procedure is obvious. Also, unless spot films are exposed, fluoroscopy possesses the additional disadvantage of being a purely subjective examination with no permanent record. It should be emphasized, therefore, that, whereas in certain circumstances fluoroscopy enjoys certain advantages over roentgenography, it should never be used except to *complement* roentgenography.

STANDARD ROENTGENOGRAPHY

Routine Projections

Roentgenologists vary in their appreciation of which projections of the thorax constitute the most satisfactory basic or "routine" views for preliminary evaluation. Many, including the authors, prefer posteroanterior and lateral projections but recognize that stereoscopic films in posteroanterior projection may be equally informative to those experienced in stereoscopy. Both techniques are satisfactory, since both allow a three-dimensional view of the thorax. No pathologist is satisfied with examination of a specimen from only one aspect; he must not only turn it over and view all aspects but also must incise it and view its inner structure; no less should the roentgenologist—himself a gross morphologist—be satisfied to examine as complex a structure as the thorax in one direction only, despite the fact that he possesses the ability to "look through" the structure he is examining.

Thus, any combination of projections which allows a three-dimensional view of the thorax constitutes a satisfactory basic examination. Variations on this "routine" may be numerous, depending upon economic circumstances and the whims of the roentgenologist. For example, roentgenography of the chest as a screening procedure (as in mass surveys) is carried out on such a colossal scale that it has become economically unsound to take more than a single posteroanterior view; one cannot be overly critical of this development, since the subjects are ostensibly asymptomatic. At the other end of the scale are those roentgenologists who are not satisfied with only two views of the thorax and whose routine includes a third projection, such as an overpenetrated view in posteroanterior projection. There is little doubt that such a routine allows a more thorough assessment of the thoracic contents than is possible with only two views, but it is problematic whether the diagnostic yield justifies the additional time and expense. If money and facilities were unlimited and the radiation hazard negligible, we would have no hesitation in employing the following combination of views as a routine for all patients suspected of having chest disease: stereoscopic views in posteroanterior projection at total lung capacity, a single posteroanterior view at residual volume, lateral views at TLC and at RV, right and left lateral decubitus projections, and an overpenetrated view in posteroanterior or anteroposterior projection. Economics being what they are, however, we regard the compromise of two views in posteroanterior and lateral projection as reasonably acceptable.

Roentgenographic Technique

The basic principles of roentgenographic technique are as follows. (1) Positioning must be such that the x-ray beam is properly centered, that the patient's body is not rotated, and that the scapulae are rotated sufficiently anteriorly as to be projected free of the lung fields. (2) Respiration must be fully suspended, preferably at a position of total lung capacity (as discussed in Chapter 1, probably it is unimportant whether or not the patient unknowingly performs a Valsalva maneuver, unless information is specifically sought about heart size). (3) Exposure factors should be such that the resultant roentgenograph permits faint visualization of the thoracic spine *and* the intervertebral discs so that lung markings behind the heart are clearly visible; the time of exposure should be as short as possible, consistent with the production of adequate contrast. (4) In heavy subjects, in whom high kilovoltage is necessary for adequate penetration, appropriate grids must be employed to reduce scatter radiation to a minimum (if stationary grids are used, these should be of extremely fine line if visualization of fine lung detail is to be preserved). Unfortunately, all too frequently technical factors are such that optimal roentgenographic density is achieved over the lung fields generally but without adequate penetration of the mediastinum or the left side of the heart (Fig-

ure 2–1); this tendency results in serious limitation of roentgen interpretation. As has been stressed by Tuddenham,[172] moderate overexposure can be easily compensated for by bright illumination; underexposure, on the other hand, cannot be compensated for by any viewing technique and, since it prevents visualization of vital areas of the thorax, should not be tolerated in any circumstances. With perseverance, it is always possible to develop roentgenographic techniques which obviate problems of underexposure.

From time to time special roentgenographic procedures are developed which employ variations in technique to accomplish a particular purpose. Among these are two methods which have been used to considerable advantage by some roentgenologists. The *high-kilovoltage technique*[189, 190] employs kilovoltages above the 125 kv range. Since the coefficient of x-ray absorption of bone and soft tissue approaches equality at and above this kilovoltage, roentgenographic visibility of the bony thorax is reduced with only slight change in the overall visibility of lung structure; thus, although visualization of the mediastinal contents is greatly improved, the roentgenograph possesses a very broad gray scale contrast which many roentgenologists, ourselves included, find objectionable. Excessive penetration of the apices may be obviated to some extent by use of wedge filters, as advocated by Lynch,[190] and perhaps such an approach deserves further application. The second roentgenographic variation which has received some attention in recent years is the *air-gap technique* described by Jackson[191] in which an air gap of six inches is interposed between the patient and the x-ray film. A high-kv technique and a ten-foot focus-film distance are employed; since the air gap acts as a filter, no grid is required. The resultant roentgenograph is said to yield a clearer visualization of the pulmonary vasculature but unfortunately suffers from deterioration in visibility of small parenchymal shadows. At the time of writing, we have had little experience with this method but view it as a technique of potential merit.

Magnification roentgenography is achieved by altering the position of the object such that the object-film distance is increased and the target-object distance decreased. A ratio of 1:1 magnifies the ob-

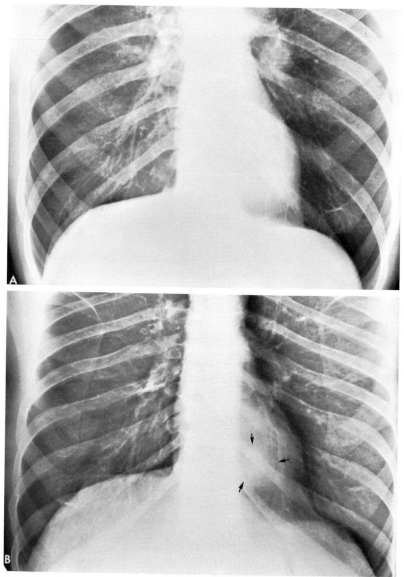

Figure 2–1.   **The Hazard of Roentgenographic Underexposure.** *A,* A roentgenogram of the lower half of the thorax in posteroanterior projection reveals no obvious abnormalities. The mediastinum and left side of the heart are underpenetrated. *B,* A more heavily penetrated view (in slight lordotic projection) demonstrates a somewhat poorly defined nodular mass situated in the lung behind the left heart (*arrows*). Even in retrospect, this lesion is not visible in *A.*

ject to twice normal size. Disregarding other important factors that affect image sharpness (such as intensifying screens), the smaller the focal spot of the anode the sharper will be the definition. It is to be stressed that with the usual target-film distances employed in clinical roentgenography, anatomic structures of approximately the same size as or smaller than the focal spot of the x-ray tube cannot be reproduced with sharp definition[813] (at the

time of writing, the smallest practical focal spot size is 0.3 mm); this limitation is based on the geometric unsharpness created by penumbra and obviously is increased the greater the object-film distance. As pointed out by Tuddenham,[172] magnification is helpful only in resolving high-contrast shadows so closely approximated as to be distinguished with difficulty on standard roentgenograms (Figure 2–2); such a situation pertains, for example, when the myriads of tiny vessels in the periphery of the lung are opacified during angiography. With rather limited experience to date, we have found magnification roentgenography of the chest without concomitant contrast studies to be confusing rather than clarifying.

The *lordotic projection* may be made in either anteroposterior projection or in a modified posteroanterior projection as recommended by Simon;[122] a modification of the anteroposterior view suggested by Jacobson and Sargent[942] seems to possess some merit—instead of assuming the rather uncomfortable lordotic pose, the patient stands erect and the x-ray tube is angled 15 degrees cephalad; the chief advantage of this modification lies in its reproducibility.

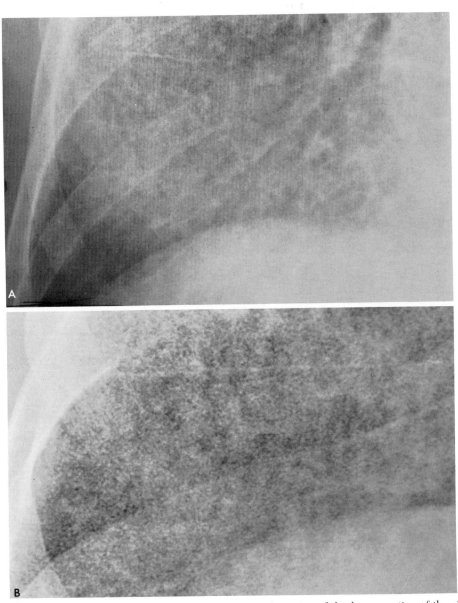

Figure 2–2. **Value of Roentgenographic Magnification.** *A*, A section of the lower portion of the right lung of a posteroanterior roentgenogram (photographically magnified) of a patient with pulmonary alveolar microlithiasis. The tiny calcispherytes can be visualized but tend to be confluent and thus indistinct. *B*, The same area of a roentgenogram made at 1:1 roentgenographic magnification using a 0.3 mm focus tube. Significant improvement in visibility of the individual calcispherytes has been obtained.

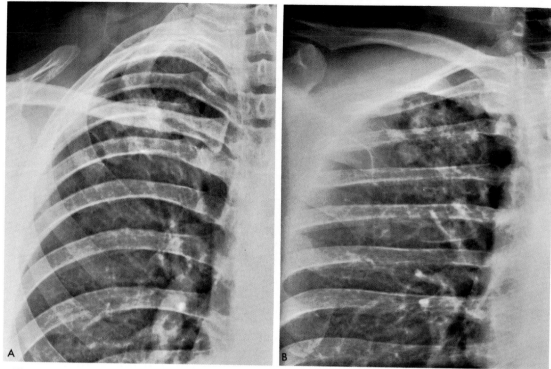

Figure 2–3.   **Value of Lordotic Projection.** *A,* A view of the upper half of the right lung from a standard roentgenogram in posteroanterior projection. Parenchymal disease is apparent but is poorly visualized because of superimposition of clavicle and ribs. *B,* In anteroposterior lordotic projection, the disease is better visualized (although tomographic examination would have been more profitable in clarifying the precise nature of the disease).

The lordotic projection is frequently advocated as a means of better visualizing the lung apices (Figure 2–3), superior mediastinum, and thoracic inlet, of establishing the location of a lesion by parallax, and of allowing visualization of the minor fissure in suspected cases of atelectasis of the right middle lobe[192, 193] (*see* Figure 4–41C, page 230). We are not particularly impressed by the value of this projection. If an apical lesion is suspected from a standard posteroanterior roentgenogram, its *presence* may be confirmed by stereoscopic lordotic films, but it is probable that, in any event, additional studies such as tomography will be required to elucidate its *nature*. We are frequently impressed by the waste of time and money in performing examinations in lordotic projection when a direct approach by tomography would yield more information.

Inspiratory-Expiratory Roentgenography

Roentgenograms exposed in full inspiration (total lung capacity) and maximal expiration (residual volume) may supply useful information about diaphragmatic excursion, although fluoroscopy is preferable for assessment of restriction of motion or paradoxical motion of one hemidiaphragm relative to the other. Undoubtedly, the main indication for inspiration/expiration studies lies in the investigation of air-trapping, either general or local: when air-trapping is widespread, as in spasmodic asthma or emphysema, diaphragmatic excursion is reduced symmetrically and lung density undergoes little change; when air-trapping is local, as results from a check-valve bronchial obstruction or from lobar emphysema, the expiratory roentgenogram reveals restriction of ipsilateral diaphragmatic elevation, a shift of the mediastinum toward the contralateral hemithorax, and relative absence of density change in involved bronchopulmonary segments (Figure 2–4). The need for full expiration to residual volume cannot be overemphasized; in these circumstances we find it useful sometimes to supervise roentgenography personally and frequently use a spirometer

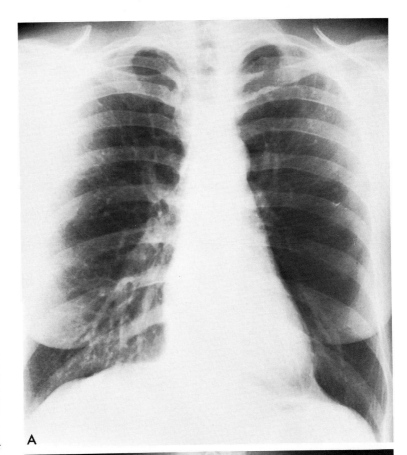

Figure 2–4. Value of Inspiratory/Expiratory Roentgenography in the Assessment of Air Trapping. *A,* A roentgenogram in full inspiration (TLC) of a 31-year-old woman who had unilateral emphysema (Swyer-James syndrome). *B,* In full expiration (RV), the presence of left-sided air trapping is evidenced by a shift of the mediastinum to the right, reduction in left hemidiaphragmatic excursion, and a marked discrepancy in overall density of the two lungs. (*See also* Figure 2–7, page 114.)

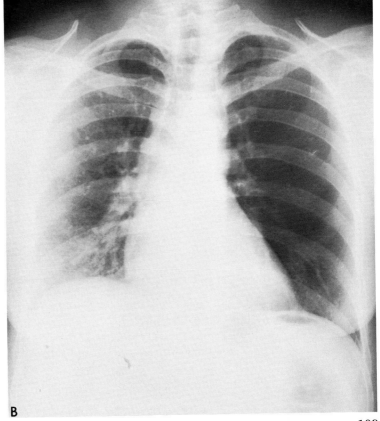

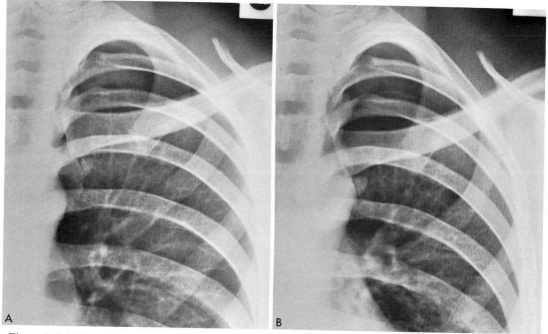

Figure 2–5. The Value of Inspiratory/Expiratory Roentgenography in the Diagnosis of Pneumothorax. *A,* A view of the upper half of the left lung from a roentgenogram exposed at full inspiration (TLC) of a 39-year-old man who complained of abrupt onset of left chest pain. The clinical suspicion of pneumothorax was not confirmed on this study because of the lack of clear-cut visualization of a visceral pleural line. *B,* In full expiration (RV), the visceral pleural line is clearly visualized.

to ensure precision of volume at the moment of roentgenographic exposure.

In cases of suspected pneumothorax in which no visceral pleural line is visible on a standard roentgenogram exposed in full inspiration or in which findings are equivocal, a film taken in full expiration may show the pleural line to better advantage (Figure 2–5): the rationale lies in the fact that, at full expiration, the volume of air in the pleural space is relatively greater in relation to the volume of lung, so that separation of pleural surfaces renders the visceral pleural line more clearly visible; in addition, a change in the relationship of the pleural line to overlying ribs may permit clearer visibility on expiration.

Valsalva and Mueller Maneuvers

As discussed in Chapter 1, these may provide useful information in determining the vascular or solid nature of intrathoracic masses (*see* Figure 1–70, page 98). Since for accurate comparison lung volumes must be roughly the same on the two roentgenograms, use of a spirometer is advisable to control the degree of lung inflation; the end of quiet inspiration probably is the most

satisfactory position from which to institute both maneuvers. Pressures may be measured on a simple water manometer, plus 40 to 50 cm water for the Valsalva and minus 40 to 50 cm water for the Mueller. Pressures should be sustained for a minimum of 10 seconds before exposure. Either the erect or horizontal position may be employed, depending upon the information sought.

Roentgenography in the Supine Position

The majority of chest roentgenography is performed with the patient in the erect position, but occasionally circumstances demand that the patient be supine, usually postoperatively or in cases of severe illness. Because of the shorter focus-film distance usually required and the anteroposterior direction of the x-ray beam, magnification of the heart and superior mediastinum often amounts to 15 to 20 per cent, compared with 5 per cent in conventional posteroanterior teleroentgenography. Care must be taken not to misinterpret the magnification as organic enlargement. Roentgenography in supine patients is liable to result

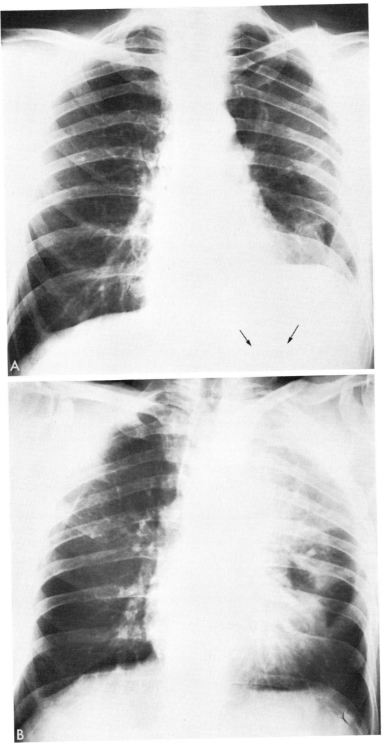

Figure 2–6. **Value of Supine Roentgenography in the Assessment of Pleural Effusion.** *A,* A chest roentgenogram in the erect position reveals what appears to be a marked elevation of the left hemidiaphragm, although the shape of the dome and the distance between the dome and the gastric air bubble (*arrows*) suggest the presence of an infrapulmonary effusion. *B,* A roentgenogram exposed in the recumbent position (actually slightly Trendelenberg) shows the left hemidiaphragm to be in normal position and the pleural fluid to be displaced to the upper portion of the hemithorax. Roentgenography in the lateral decubitus position would have been equally informative.

in diagnostic error in relation to the pulmonary vascular shadows also. As discussed in Chapter 1, pulmonary blood flow is approximately 30 per cent greater in supine than in erect subjects, and, therefore, the pulmonary vascular shadows may appear larger; in the upper lungs, this dilatation is enhanced by the removal of the effects of gravity and the consequent increase in flow to upper lung zones (see Figure 1–69, page 96). Compounding of these effects by the magnification factor results in an apparently alarming degree of "engorgement" which, unless care is exercised, can be falsely interpreted as evidence of disease. Errors in diagnosis usually are obviated if attention is paid to the definition of the vascular shadows: Sharpness of definition is maintained in the presence of simple increase in flow and is lost in the presence of bronchopneumonia or pulmonary venous engorgement and interstitial edema.

Certain other situations necessitate studies in the supine position to clarify questions which have arisen with conventional roentgenograms in the erect position; examples include the differentiation of pleural fluid from thickening and distinction between an elevated hemidiaphragm and a large infrapulmonary accumulation of fluid (Figure 2–6) (in this last situation, free fluid extends over the posterior pleural surface, thereby revealing the true position of the hemidiaphragm). It is probable, however, that in these two situations, roentgenograms exposed with the patient in the lateral decubitus position are of greater diagnostic value than studies in the supine position, since it is usually easier to identify fluid accumulation along the lateral thoracic wall than to appreciate the overall change in density of a hemithorax caused by extension of fluid over the posterior pleural surface.

Roentgenography in the Lateral Decubitus Position

In this technique, the patient lies on one side, with the x-ray beam oriented in a horizontal plane. Since in the majority of instances the dependent hemithorax is the side being specifically examined, it is desirable to elevate the thorax on a nonabsorbing support such as a foam cushion or mattress. The technique is invaluable for the identification of small pleural effusions.

Less than 100 ml of fluid may be identified on well-exposed roentgenograms in this position, whereas those taken with the patient erect seldom reveal convincing evidence of pleural effusions of less than 300 ml.[194] Roentgenography in lateral decubitus position is useful also to demonstrate a change in position of an air-fluid level in a cavity or to ascertain whether a structure which forms part of a cavity represents a freely moving intracavitary foreign body (e.g., a fungus ball or mycetoma).

A modification of the standard lateral decubitus projection was introduced by Müller and Löfstedt[785] as a means of more precisely identifying small amounts of fluid in the pleural space. They placed a pillow under the patient's hip so that the trunk sloped downward at an angle of about 20 degrees; the lower arm was extended above the head and the trunk rotated dorsally so that the scapula paralleled the horizontal table (to prevent the scapula from obscuring the lower thoracic margin). Roentgenography was carried out at a position of expiration, the rationale being that the reduction in the volume of the thoracic cavity would raise the fluid to a maximal level (while such rationale is undoubtedly correct, we feel that the technique would suffer from the lack of contrast between the relatively deflated lung and the layer of pleural fluid adjacent to it; exposure at a position of moderate inspiration is probably preferable). In his superb treatise on the roentgen examination of pleural fluid, Hessén[786] confirmed the superiority of the Müller and Löfstedt technique in identifying small amounts of pleural fluid.

Roentgenography in the Oblique Position

Occasionally, oblique studies are useful in locating a disease process, with or without prior fluoroscopy, but they seldom produce information which is not more reliably gained by more searching techniques, such as tomography.

ROENTGENOLOGIC PROCEDURES FOR THE EVALUATION OF INTRATHORACIC DYNAMICS

Fluoroscopy

The fluoroscopic screen registers a constant image of the object being examined and thus allows appreciation of the dynamic activity of roentgenographically visible intrathoracic structures. *With few exceptions, fluoroscopy should be restricted to this purpose.* Although image amplification and television techniques have eliminated the major disadvantages of conventional fluoroscopy (poor image sharpness, high radiation dosage, and the necessity for dark adaptation), the appreciation of small pulmonary lesions by this means is significantly less than with roentgenographic films. For example, it has been stated that even an amplified fluoroscopic image will not ordinarily reveal a noncalcified lesion of less than 1 cm in diameter in the midlung field.[195]

As mentioned earlier, the size and shape of vascular and cystic lesions within the thorax may vary when the patient changes from the erect to the recumbent position or performs the Valsalva or Mueller maneuver. Such changes may be appreciated fluoroscopically when the lesion is large enough, but seldom with the same accuracy as can be achieved roentgenographically. Of similar character is the effect of variation in body position on the relationship of intrathoracic masses to fixed structures such as the spine or ribs; Felson[69] has stressed the value of this sign as a method of establishing whether a mass originates from the thoracic cage or from relatively mobile intrathoracic structures. Since this procedure entails assessment of movement of one structure relative to another, rather than motion *within* a structure, the superiority of roentgenography over fluoroscopy is readily apparent.

Fluoroscopy may supply useful information concerning movement of the diaphragm and thoracic wall during respiration. Particularly in acute subphrenic disease and occasionally in acute pulmonary or pleural disease, restriction of excursion of one hemidiaphragm may constitute an important clue to their presence. Similarly, when local air-trapping is present, as in lobar or unilateral emphysema or soon after impaction of a foreign body (Figure 2-7), restriction of diaphragmatic excursion and rib approximation on the affected side during forced expiration may be the sole evidence of an abnormality which may give rise to only very subtle changes on roentgenograms exposed in full inspiration. Mediastinal swing during deep breathing sometimes is better appreciated through observation of dynamic movement than through study of roentgenograms made in inspiration and expiration.

Fluoroscopy and cinefluorography may indicate the presence or absence of pulsation in an intrapulmonary mass, thus allowing differentiation between its vascular or solid nature. Similarly, the amplitude and regularity of pulsation of the cardiac chambers, aorta, and pulmonary arteries can be readily appreciated fluoroscopically, as may the presence of calcifications in a cardiac valve, the pericardium, and the major vessels. Such findings may be of major importance in the assessment of pulmonary diseases of cardiovascular origin. A thin layer of epicardial fat sometimes is visible as a line of reduced density paralleling the margins of the heart and representing the approximate position of the visceral pericardium; since pericardial effusion accumulates outside this line, separation of the line from the outer contour of the cardiac silhouette is reliable evidence for the presence of this condition. Visualization of the line is improved substantially by the use of cinefluorography.

Identification of abnormalities of esophageal position or contour can play an important role in roentgenologic diagnosis. Displacement due to enlargement of the thyroid gland or left atrium may indicate an origin of pulmonary disease whose cause otherwise might not be evident (*e.g.*, thyroid metastases or pulmonary hemosiderosis secondary to mitral stenosis). As has been emphasized by Fleischner[196] and Middlemass,[197] deformity caused by enlarged mediastinal lymph nodes may constitute a cardinal sign in the diagnosis of bronchogenic cancer or in the assessment of operability once the diagnosis has been established. Disturbance in esophageal dynamics, as in achalasia or scleroderma, may be the chief indication of the origin of the patchy consolidation seen in aspiration pneumonitis or the diffuse reticular pattern of interstitial fibrosis. Fluoroscopy always should precede roentgenography in the investigation of esophageal disease: Not only is fluoroscopy the only method for revealing abnormalities of dynamics (*e.g.*, aperistalsis), it also allows appreciation of minimal but persistent irregularities of contour which might appear insignificant

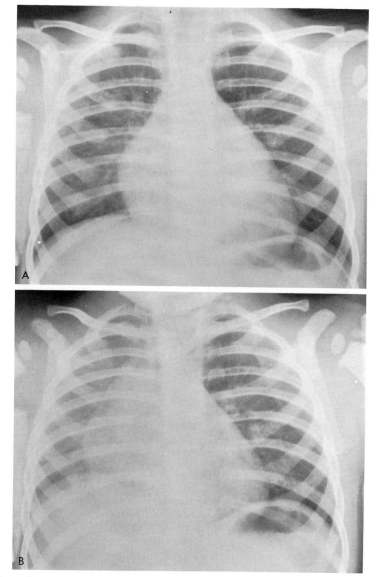

Figure 2–7. **Value of Inspiratory/Expiratory Roentgenography in the Assessment of Bronchial Obstruction.** *A*, A roentgenogram in full inspiration (TLC) of an 11-month-old girl with sudden onset of dyspnea. No abnormalities are apparent. *B*, At full expiration (RV), the volume of the left hemithorax has changed little from the inspiratory roentgenogram and the mediastinum has shifted markedly to the right. The findings are those of a check-value obstruction of the left main bronchus (a crayon was removed bronchoscopically). Fluoroscopy would have shown the mediastinal swing to excellent advantage but would provide no more information than can be gleaned from these static roentgenograms.

on roentgenograms of the barium-filled esophagus. When attention is directed toward a specific area, spot films or cinefluorographic studies may be obtained for permanent record. Since deformity may be small and local, as when due to a single enlarged lymph node, fluoroscopic inspection always should be carried out in several different projections. Hypoperistalsis or aperistalsis often is better appreciated cinefluorographically.

Finally, as a rough screening procedure, fluoroscopy may supply useful information about the pulmonary ventilatory capacity, a subject which is considered in more detail in the section dealing with the application of roentgenologic methods to the assessment of lung function.

Cinefluorography

Cinefluorographic recording of rapidly occurring events within the thorax supplies an important adjunct to fluoroscopy, since it allows leisurely study and restudy of these movements without imposing upon the patient or the roentgenologist the hazard of high radiation dosage inherent in prolonged fluoroscopy. With modern apparatus, contrast and detail are remarkably good and are superior to visual perception of the fluoroscopic screen or television monitor. However, cinefluorography cannot achieve the sharpness of definition of the larger roentgenographic images obtainable with large film changers. These changers employ film sizes up to 14×14 inches and thus can include the whole of both lung fields of most patients. In general, up to four to six exposures per second can be taken, which is adequate for study of the pulmonary vascular bed angiographically. It is probable that the application of magnification techniques will be of considerable value in this field.

Roentgen Kymography

Although fluoroscopy can provide qualitative evaluation of diaphragmatic movement, at best it gives only a very rough quantitative indication of disturbances in motion. In 1958, Goldenthal and his associates[198] described a specially designed kymographic technique for assessment of diaphragmatic movement. The kymographic grid consists of a series of lead strips 30 mm wide, 1 mm apart. The grid is stationary at the level of the diaphragm, with the lead strips parallel to the body; a prolonged x-ray exposure is made while the roentgenographic film moves at right angles from left to right at a fixed speed controlled by a motor-driven timer. As the patient performs a particular respiratory maneuver, such as a single forced expiration, the excursions of 1-mm segments of each hemidiaphragm are recorded. Usually it is possible to record three such segments of each hemidiaphragm on a $14'' \times 17''$ roentgenogram. Since the lower ribs also are shown on the roentgenogram, costal excursion of ribs 7 to 10 may be assessed as well. In a series of 20 normal subjects investigated by Goldenthal and associates,[198] the range of diaphragmatic excursion from total lung capacity to residual volume on a single forced expiration averaged 6.6 cm on the right and 7.7 cm on the left. Elevation of the diaphragm during forced expiration was rapid, being 89 per cent complete within the first second. In addition to its application to the study of lung function, about which more is said in a later section, this technique has been used to study various intrathoracic and intra-abdominal abnormalities, including acute pulmonary disease[199] and abdominal conditions,[200] obstructive airway disease,[198, 201] postoperative pulmonary complications,[202] and silicosis.[203]

Roentgen Densitometry*

This technique has received considerable attention in recent years as a roentgenologic method for studying pulmonary ventilation and perfusion.[204–215, 936, 937] It involves measurement of the flux of x-rays or gamma-rays penetrating selected zones of the lungs during the respiratory cycle. Photomultiplier tubes pick up the radiation and transform it into an electric signal, which is amplified and fed into an appropriate recorder. Thus, a continuous record is obtained of variations in density occurring during quiet respiration, forced expiration, and cough, providing a comparison of the ventilatory capacity of different portions of the lung. Vascular pulsation can be recorded when the breath is held, and ventilation and pulsation can be related to simultaneous spirometric and electrocardiographic tracings. This technique possesses attractive possibilities and apparently is capable of providing much the same information as the radioactive-xenon method of estimating regional ventilation and perfusion. Further reference to the application of roentgen densitometry is made in the section dealing with roentgenologic methods of assessing lung function.

TOMOGRAPHY†

Technique

Tomography allows selective visualization of a predetermined layer of tissue to

---

*Synonyms: fluorodensimetry, fluoroscopic densography, statidensigraphy, and cinedensigraphy.

†Synonyms: body-section roentgenography, planigraphy, laminagraphy, stratigraphy, sectional roentgenography.

the exclusion of structures lying superficial or deep to it. Regardless of the type of motion employed, the technique involves reciprocal movement of the x-ray tube and film at proportional velocity. The reciprocal motion causes blurring of all structures not continuously "in focus" during excursions of the tube and film, so that the image of only a thin "slice" is recorded in detail on the roentgenogram. The level of tomographic "cut" is controlled by the ratio of the tube-object distance to the object-film distance, so that this level may be altered by varying the ratio. The thickness of the "cut" is governed by the length of tube-film travel—the shorter the excursion, the thicker the layer recorded (zonography).

Various reciprocal movements of tube and film have been developed, including rectilinear, circular, elliptical, and hypocycloidal; transverse tomography "cuts" the body in cross section rather than longitudinally and involves reciprocal movement of patient and film, the x-ray tube remaining stationary. Each movement possesses certain advantages in specific circumstances, and the reader is directed to the pertinent literature, particularly the monograph by Kane[216] and the more recent reviews by Carter and associates[217] and Greenwell and Wright.[218] Rectilinear tomography probably is the simplest to perform and the most widely available and generally is adequate for most studies of the thorax; however, it possesses certain disadvantages which should be borne in mind, the most troublesome being its failure to obscure shadows of linear structures which lie in the same direction as the tube-film excursion. For example, a longitudinal tomographic section of the mediastinal structures shows the density of the mediastinum itself, an unfortunate circumstance which may lead to confusion. This disadvantage may be obviated by rotating the long axis of the patient on the x-ray table so that the direction of tube excursion is oblique in relation to the mediastinum. Any of the other reciprocal movements, such as circular, elliptical, or hypocycloidal, similarly prevents this occasionally troublesome feature.

The polycassette provides roentgenographs of multiple tomographic sections with one exposure, with a resultant reduction in time and radiation exposure and only negligible deterioration in roentgenographic definition.

Certain other special tomographic procedures deserve mention, although we profess little practical experience with them. Axial transverse tomography,[219] in which the section is in the transverse rather than the longitudinal plane, is said to provide clearer definition of the size and anatomic relationships of intrathoracic masses, particularly in the mediastinum,[220, 221] in the evaluation of thoracic deformities,[222] and in the estimation of mediastinal herniation and displacement.[139] Tomography has been employed in conjunction with procedures which require injection of contrast media, (e.g., with bronchography[223-225, 346] and angiography[226, 227, 814]); since the contrast media themselves should produce high contrast—and, therefore, sharp roentgenographic definition—the advantages of these combined procedures are not entirely clear to us.

Indications

Two main indications exist for tomography of the thorax. (1) Precise knowledge of the morphologic characteristics of lesions which are visible on plain roentgenograms but whose nature is obscured by superimposition of images lying superficial and deep to them: perhaps the best example of this indication lies in the detection of pulmonary cavitation (Figure 2–8). In a study of 271 tomograms of 172 patients with pulmonary tuberculosis, Favis[228] showed that in 10.7 per cent tomography revealed cavitation of which no suggestion appeared on conventional roentgenograms; in an additional 8.8 per cent, cavitation which was only suspected on plain roentgenograms was conclusively demonstrated tomographically; conversely, in 18.8 per cent tomography failed to show cavities which were suspected from plain roentgenograms. In general, these findings have been confirmed by others[229] and illustrate the substantial improvement in detection of changes in roentgenographic density afforded by tomography. When searching for cavities, it is preferable to examine the patient in the erect position, since only then will air-fluid levels be demonstrable.

Other examples of this indication include identification of calcium in pulmonary nodules, separation of the confusing shadows of the hila,[75] and clarification of sharpness of definition and smoothness or nodularity

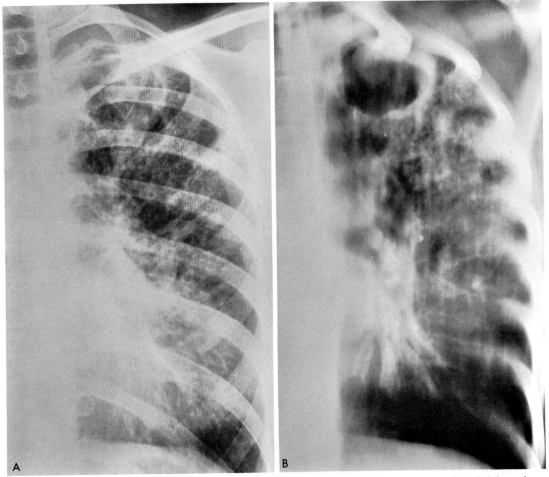

Figure 2–8. **Value of Tomography in the Assessment of Pulmonary Cavities.** *A,* A view of the left hemithorax from a standard roentgenogram in posteroanterior projection reveals extensive disease throughout much of the left lung. A curvilinear shadow in the plane of the first interspace anteriorly suggests the possibility of a cavity. *B,* A tomographic section through the midportion of the left lung reveals a large, well-defined cavity in the apex. Pulmonary tuberculosis.

of outline of pulmonary or mediastinal lesions (Figure 2–9).

(2) Clearer visualization of shadows which on plain roentgenograms are poorly defined and indistinct because of summation of images: undoubtedly the prime example of this indication lies in the study of the bronchi and the pulmonary vasculature (*see* Figure 1–37, page 42). It has been shown conclusively that visualization of the arterial and venous pattern of the lungs in such conditions as emphysema, pulmonary hypertension, and congenital anomalies of venous communication can be greatly improved by use of full lung tomography.[71-74, 230] Similarly, visualization of the trachea and proximal large bronchi

is very clear tomographically, particularly with the use of rotational techniques[217, 218] or with the "inclined sagittal tomography" described by Sommer and Laubenberger.[231] Pajewski[232] stressed the value of tomography in the lateral oblique projection for evaluation of the segmental bronchovascular tree, on the basis that branching occurs in a plane posteromedially to anterolaterally; positioning involves rotation of the patient 15 to 25 degrees from lateral projection.

In many cases the presence and character of bronchial deformity may be assessed accurately—to a degree, in fact, at which the necessity for bronchography, a more time-consuming and hazardous procedure,

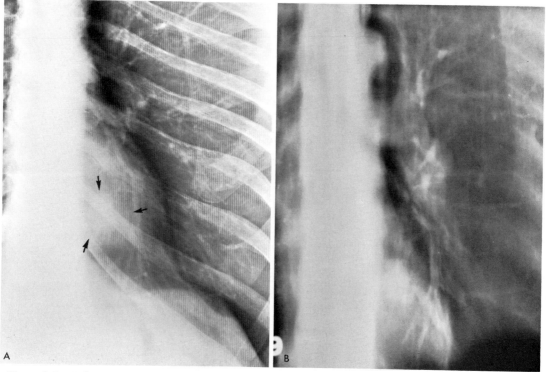

Figure 2–9.   **Value of Tomography in the Assessment of Pulmonary Masses.** *A,* A view of the lower half of the left hemithorax from a roentgenogram in slight lordotic projection reveals a poorly defined mass behind the heart (*arrows*). *B,* A tomographic section through the left lower lobe reveals the mass to much better advantage; its margin is seen to be lobulated and no calcium is identified. Bronchogenic carcinoma.

frequently is obviated. Visibility of small bronchi coursing through a peripheral parenchymal consolidation may supply an important clue to the nature of the disease process.

Tomographic sections made for some other purpose often reveal lesions not suspected from plain roentgenograms. This is not surprising when one considers the previously cited important observations of Newell and Garneau,[177] concerning threshold visibility of pulmonary shadows, and of Greening and Pendergrass,[182] who showed that a pulmonary carcinoma as large as 5 cm in diameter can be missed roentgenographically when it is situated in certain "blind" areas of the thorax. Of particular clinical interest in this regard is the detection of metastatic lesions: Providing the primary lesion has been eradicated, the removal of a single metastasis from the lungs may be curative; thus, when a single metastatic lesion is visualized in a lung

roentgenographically, the importance of thorough tomographic study of the lungs generally for the identification of other metastatic foci possesses obvious therapeutic and prognostic importance.

BRONCHOGRAPHY

Since the first description of bronchography by Sicard and Forestier[233] in 1922, many techniques for its performance and a multitude of agents as contrast media have been described. It is clearly outside the scope of this work and would serve little useful purpose to describe the advantages and disadvantages of all techniques and media in detail; it will suffice to describe the techniques which over the years, and with trial of other methods, we have found to be the most efficient in our circumstances. Brief reference is made to other methods, about which the reader may gain further information from the literature.

Despite its ease of performance, bronchography should not be carried out without due consideration of its potential hazards. Apart from the very real danger of its causing allergic reaction to both the topical anesthesia and the bronchographic medium itself (ranging from bronchospasm through iodism to frank anaphylaxis and death), bronchography gives rise to a temporary impairment of ventilation and diffusion[234, 938] which should not be disregarded, especially in patients with respiratory insufficiency. Similarly, it is apparent that the injection of 10 to 15 ml of a foreign material into a lung must give rise to a foreign-body reaction, of however small degree.[235-241] For these reasons, bronchography should never be performed without due consideration and ample justification. Since bilateral bronchography may be expected to produce double the disturbances in pulmonary function produced by a unilateral study, it is preferable to examine only one lung in the first place, the other lung being examined separately, two or three days later, if this is indicated. Bilateral bronchography possesses the additional disadvantage of producing superimposition of the bronchi of both lungs in lateral projection, leading to potential confusion in identification.

Indications

As with most specialized diagnostic procedures, the indications for bronchography vary widely in different institutions. Our personal experience over the years has led us to adopt a conservative approach to this procedure for two reasons: (a) more direct diagnostic procedures, such as bronchoscopy, are more informative and less hazardous and (b) in some conditions, *e.g.*, in cases of hemoptysis in association with a normal chest roentgenogram, bronchography possesses a low discovery rate. On the basis of this experience we have adopted four general indications for bronchography (the assessment of activity in pulmonary cavitary disease by barium installation and the "wall sign" [see later discussion][265, 815] might be considered a fifth indication).

1. Investigation of chronic productive cough, particularly in young patients or those in whom the clinical history and physical examination suggest that chronic bronchitis is not the cause. Bronchography is indicated in these patients irrespective of a normal chest roentgenogram: in one study,[242] the plain chest roentgenogram was normal, even in retrospect, in 7 per cent of patients with significant bronchiectasis.

2. Investigation of patients with clinically established bronchiectasis, to assess severity and establish precisely the distribution of disease. Bronchographic study as a guide to surgical treatment of pulmonary tuberculosis[243] might be included in the same category.

3. Investigation of segmental bronchial obstructions, when the nature of the obstructive process cannot be established by bronchoscopy or tomography.

4. Determination of bronchial patency or deformity in relation to space-occupying lesions situated in the midzones or in the periphery. As has been stressed by Molnar and Riebel,[244] differentiation of benign and malignant consolidation in the periphery of the lungs may be aided by knowledge of the presence and nature of deformity of the bronchial tree in relation to the mass.

Contraindications

The major contraindication to the performance of bronchography undoubtedly is respiratory insufficiency; in some patients with severe emphysema, for instance, the resultant exacerbation of dyspnea and cyanosis may require vigorous therapeutic measures for their relief. Great care should be exercised in performing bronchography in patients with spasmodic asthma, particularly when this is in active phase; both the topical anesthesia and the contrast medium may induce additional bronchospasm of intolerable severity. When bronchography appears warranted despite inherent hazards, oxygen, antispasmodic agents, and cortisone must be readily available in case of symptomatic deterioration.

Iodism no longer constitutes an absolute contraindication to bronchography, since barium-carboxymethylcellulose preparations are iodine-free and are eminently satisfactory media for bronchial opacification.

Techniques of Examination

The bronchographic techniques most widely used include supraglottic injection, the transglottic catheter method (in which a catheter is inserted through the glottis via the nose or mouth), and the percutaneous cricothyroid technique (administration either directly through a needle[245] or by a modified Seldinger technique[239, 246, 939]). We prefer the transglottic technique, in which a soft, rubber, urethral catheter is inserted through the larynx via a naris and into a selected site in the bronchial tree. Briefly, our technique is as follows. Premedication consists of 50 mg. of meperidine hydrochloride (Demerol) and 1/100 to 1/150 grain of atropine sulfate 30 to 45 minutes before the examination. The catheter is inserted through the naris until its tip lies in the hypopharynx; with the patient's tongue fully extended, approximately 6 ml of 4 per cent lidocaine hydrochloride (Xylocaine) is injected slowly through the catheter onto the surface of the larynx; this rapidly produces topical anesthesia. Under fluoroscopic control, the catheter is inserted through the larynx and its tip is positioned in the main bronchus of the lung to be examined. Respiration is suspended in full expiration while 6 ml of 2 per cent lidocaine hydrochloride (Xylocaine) is injected rapidly, and then the patient is instructed to take a deep breath, which distributes the anesthetic throughout the bronchial tree.[247] Injection is carried out with the patient lying on the side to be examined, 45 degrees from vertical. In most cases this aspiration technique results in a satisfactory degree of anesthesia of the dependent bronchial tree within three to four minutes.

The injection of 12 to 15 ml of contrast medium is carried out under fluoroscopic control, with the patient lying at the same angle and rotated so that the side to be examined is lowermost. He is instructed to respire deeply, and 2 to 3 ml of medium is injected during the expiratory phase of each respiration. The rotation of the patient and the tilt of the table are varied to produce opacification of the desired segments. Spot films may be made during the filling procedure. When adequate filling has been obtained, roentgenograms of the chest are exposed with the patient upright at a distance of six feet, in posteroanterior, oblique, and lateral projections. Then he is instructed to cough and to breathe deeply for about five minutes, and roentgenography in posteroanterior and oblique projections

is repeated. It is useful to obtain a cine-fluorographic record of the dynamics of the tracheobronchial tree during the interim period of deep breathing and coughing.

We are firmly of the opinion that this period of coughing and deep breathing is essential to the proper performance of all bronchographic studies. Providing that the contrast medium is of the proper viscosity and temperature (body temperature) and that an excessive amount has not been injected (not more than 20 ml), no difficulty should arise because of excessive peripheral filling or "alveolarization": this word is in quotation marks to emphasize the fact that it is a misnomer and should be deleted from the vocabulary. As demonstrated by the excellent experimental investigation carried out by Weber[248] in 1951, the pattern of overfilling is produced by opacification of terminal bronchioles and not alveoli, a fact which also was emphasized by Reid and Simon[158] in 1958 in their pathologic-roentgenologic correlative study. Only when a water-soluble contrast medium of low viscosity was injected could Weber show that true alveolar filling occurred. Although the term "alveolarization" is in such common usage that eradication will be very difficult, it creates such a wrong impression in relation to peripheral-lung anatomy that we feel it essential to substitute the more accurate descriptive phrase *bronchiolar filling*.

The importance of the centimeter and millimeter pattern of bronchiolar branching as a guide to the concept of the acinus was stressed in the descriptions of normal anatomy in Chapter 1. Bronchography is the only method by which these structures may be visualized roentgenologically and it behooves us to grasp every advantage offered. Patients should be *encouraged* to cough, therefore—not cautioned to restrict it. Filling of the peripheral bronchiolar tree is not the only benefit to be gained by this maneuver. In the study of bronchiectasis, coughing may produce filling of bronchiectatic segments not visualized at the time of instillation of contrast medium; conversely, it may produce filling of normal segments of bronchial tree peripheral to one which earlier appeared dilated (Figure 2–10). Similarly, the incidence of such false-negative and false-positive bronchograms in bronchiectasis may be reduced

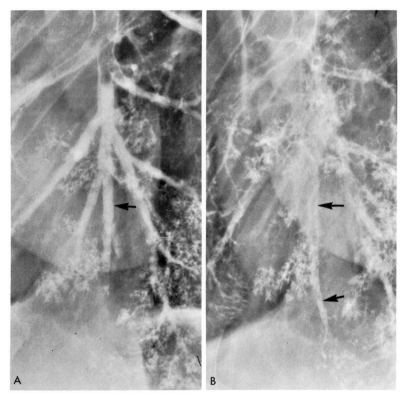

Figure 2–10. Value of Post-tussic (or Delayed) Bronchography in the Assessment of Bronchiectasis. *A*, A view of the basilar segments of the right lower lobe immediately following injection of contrast medium. One of the branches of the lateral basal segment (arrows) appears slightly dilated and is incompletely filled peripherally. Query bronchiectasis. *B*, A similar view five minutes after vigorous coughing reveals good filling of the periphery of this segment (*arrows*), thus excluding bronchiectasis.

by the use of *delayed films*, as recommended by Abrams and his associates.[249] In a study of 100 consecutive bronchograms of 75 patients in which delayed roentgenograms were obtained 30 to 60 minutes after bronchography, these investigators found the delayed films of diagnostic value in at least 22 cases: The presence of bronchiectasis which was not evident during the original study was revealed in ten cases, and the possibility of bronchiectasis suggested on the original films was proved erroneous in 12.

The mechanism by which peripheral filling occurs during coughing is sometimes misunderstood. In well over 200 cinefluorographic studies following bronchography, we have never seen peripheral dissemination of contrast medium result from the expulsive wave of a cough; rather, it is the deep inspiration before a cough which propels medium distally.[250]

The aspiration technique of bronchography, which was described independ-ently by Nordenström[247] and Priviteri[251] in the same year, efficiently and rapidly provides bronchial filling in most patients. When the tip of the catheter is positioned in the region of the take off of the upper-lobe bronchus, the patient is tilted 40 to 60 degrees from vertical and rotated so that the side to be examined is lowermost, and the whole bolus of contrast medium is injected rapidly during suspension of respiration in full expiration. The patient is instructed to inspire fully, with resultant dissemination of contrast medium throughout all segments of the bronchial tree. Since the success of this maneuver depends largely upon the preservation of vital capacity (or, to put it colloquially, peripheral "suck"), we have found it ineffective in the presence of obstructive airway disease, such as chronic bronchitis or emphysema.

Selective bronchography, in which a specific bronchial segment is catheterized for special study, may be of value when routine methods fail to delineate some segments or when definitive local bronchial pathology is sought before surgery. It may be of particular value for the investigation of patients whose pulmonary reserve is reduced and in whom opacification of the whole bronchial tree could cause significant symptomatic deterioration through its deleterious effect on pulmonary function. Preshaped Metras catheters[252-254] or Odman arterial catheters[255] are clearly superior to soft, rubber, urethral catheters for the study of selected bronchial segments.

The technique recently described by Nordenström and Carlens,[256] in which *bronchial biopsy* is performed in association with bronchography, may prove to be of great value. When a suspicious area is located bronchographically, the tip of the catheter is placed adjacent to the lesion under fluoroscopic control and biopsy forceps are inserted directly down the bronchographic catheter. Further development and application of this technique may demonstrate its value when location of a lesion is difficult or impossible bronchoscopically.

Cinefluorographic Studies of Bronchial Dynamics

The important contributions of Di-Rienzo[59, 257, 258] and Fleischner[259] to knowledge of the bronchial tree included not only purely morphologic findings but also observations of functional characteristics during respiration and coughing. Conclusions concerning dynamic activity were drawn from appearances of static roentgenograms exposed during these respiratory maneuvers, so that timing of specific events was understandably lacking. However, these authors' pioneering studies stimulated further investigation which, in recent years, has had the benefit of cinefluorographic techniques for the accurate recording and timing of specific dynamic events.[38, 61, 250, 260-262]

Cinebronchography yields an accurate record of the rapid events which occur in the bronchial tree during forced expiration and cough, events that formerly could be only roughly appreciated fluoroscopically or on static roentgenograms. During the expulsive wave of a cough, bronchial caliber reduces from maximum to minimum in 40 milliseconds or less—a rapidity that necessitates use of cine-frame speeds of at least 30 frames/sec for clear appreciation without image blurring. Studies of several segments of the bronchial tree during forced expiration and cough have revealed significant differences in the response of the bronchial tree in different diseases. In a large percentage of patients with chronic bronchitis and emphysema, for example, a disproportionate collapse of the main bronchi to the lower lobes occurs during forced expiration which is not seen in normal lungs.[38] A similar phenomenon occurs in most cases of severe bronchiectasis.[261] In many of these patients, simultaneous cinebronchography and manometric recording of pleural pressure, intrabronchial pressure, and air flow at the mouth have shown that premature lower-lobe bronchial collapse is associated with air-flow obstruction at this site, thus yielding convincing evidence that the larger airways play a significant role in the pathogenesis of air-trapping in diseases characterized by over-inflation.[61]

It is clear that cinebronchography can reveal useful information about the dynamic behavior of the bronchial tree—although the present state of our knowledge renders much of this information of theoretical rather than practical value.

Bronchographic Contrast Media

The advantages and disadvantages of the many contrast media available for bronchography will not be discussed in detail. However, we think it important to list the media that we consider should not be recommended. Iodized oil: because of its long retention within the lung; iodized oil with sulfonamide: because of a high incidence of reaction in the lung parenchyma;[236] water-soluble media: because of their irritation of the bronchial mucosa and, therefore, the requirement for an excessive degree of topical anesthesia and because of their tendency to produce excessive peripheral filling; diiodopyridone (Hytrast): our experience with Hytrast in more than 60 cases[263] as well as that of others[816] indicated an intolerable incidence of clinical and pathologic side effects, and despite its high density and excellent coating ability we feel that it should be employed only with great caution.

The remaining commonly employed media (oily and aqueous propyliodone

[Dionosil] and barium-carboxymethylcell-ulose mixtures) probably differ but little in their contrast or toxicity.[240] We employ aqueous propyliodone almost exclusively, more because we have found it entirely satisfactory than for any known superiority over the oily medium. The enthusiasm of Nelson and his associates[264] for barium-carboxymethylcellulose suspensions may result in more extensive use of this contrast medium; it not only produces a high degree of contrast but is purportedly associated with a very low incidence of clinical and pathologic side effects; also, it may be used with impunity in patients with known hypersensitivity to iodine. The development of an efficient method for nebulizing barium and carboxymethylcellulose will be welcomed.

A dividend to be derived from the use of barium-carboxymethylcellulose suspensions not available from iodine compounds is the tendency for barium particles to outline the walls of some pulmonary cavities through a process of phagocytosis.[265, 815] Of 27 patients, described by Christoforidis and his associates,[265] in whom barium suspension entered a cavity or cavities during bronchography, in 18 the wall of a cavity remained outlined for several weeks or months; in the remaining nine, the contrast medium disappeared within two days. Of the 43 patients, described by Andrews and colleagues,[815] in whom barium suspension entered a cavity, a positive "wall sign" was observed in 32 (75 per cent). Pathologically, this "wall sign" was found to be associated in all cases with infection and ulceration of the cavity wall which allowed free access of the barium to phagocytes in the wall; in those cases with a negative "wall sign" the cavities were either noninfected bronchogenic cysts or open, healed, epithelialized tuberculous cavities.

Of considerable interest is the recent development by Nadel and his associates[817] of a practical method of bronchography using powdered tantalum. The extremely high density and negligible toxicity of this metal clearly make it a very desirable contrast material. Although its application at the time of writing has been largely restricted to the experimental animal, this substance appears to have great potential as a superior bronchographic medium in humans.

ANGIOGRAPHY

Included under this heading are those procedures in which injection of contrast media into the vascular structures of the thorax may be useful in the investigation and diagnosis of thoracic disease; they include pulmonary angiography, angiocardiography, aortography, bronchial arteriography, superior-vena-cava angiography, and azygography. Only the general indications for these procedures are considered here; detailed discussion is presented in other chapters in relation to specific diseases.

It is necessary to state that we have developed an attitude toward thoracic angiography which clearly is more conservative than that of many others. In several situations in which others successfully employ angiography, as in assessment of the operability of lung cancer, we rely more heavily on traditional methods of roentgenologic investigation. It is inevitable that the contents of this book reflect this attitude. However, to disregard the experience of others would be negligent; therefore, in this section and wherever these procedures are mentioned in other chapters, our discussion of angiographic techniques and findings is based largely on the observations of others.

Pulmonary Angiography

TECHNIQUE. Depending upon individual circumstances, pulmonary angiography may be performed by various routes: (a) by venous injection into one arm or into both arms simultaneously, through a needle or, preferably, a catheter; (b) via a catheter into the superior vena cava, right atrium, right ventricle, or main pulmonary artery; or (c) by selective injection into either the right or left pulmonary artery or one of its branches. In pulmonary angiography, as in all other special angiographic procedures, it is essential to determine individual requirements for each examination in relation to the specific circumstances. For example, when there is a pulmonary neoplasm arising in the paramediastinal zone and the integrity of the superior vena cava is in doubt, substantially more information can be gained if the pulmonary angiogram is performed via an arm vein rather than by intracardiac or pulmonary artery injection.

Generally speaking, however, there is no doubt that direct injection into the main pulmonary artery or one of its branches invariably produces clearer opacification of the pulmonary vascular tree than does venous or intracardiac injection; the superior visualization usually outweighs any disadvantage inherent in the catheterization procedure. An additional benefit of selective injection has been described by Cicero and Del Castillo.[266] These authors performed 146 examinations on 137 patients, each of whom was subjected to two procedures—filling of the entire pulmonary arterial tree by injection into the right side of the heart and segmental arteriography by placement of the catheter in the artery of the segment being studied—and reported superior results with the second method. This finding relates to the fact that the presence of disease in a segment of the arterial tree causes blood to be shunted away from that segment; thus, whereas a flood injection tends to opacify comparatively normal branches remote from the disease, medium injected selectively into an abnormal segment opacifies that area. Similarly, wedge arteriography[267] and magnification techniques[268, 976] provide improved visibility of small peripheral arterial branches. The erect position is preferred for pulmonary angiography[269] because most patients can achieve a much lower position of the diaphragm when they are standing than when supine.

INDICATIONS. (a) Detection of congenital abnormalities of the pulmonary vascular tree: these include agenesis or hypoplasia of a pulmonary artery, coarctation of one or more pulmonary arteries (peripheral pulmonic stenosis), idiopathic dilatation of a pulmonary artery, and arteriovenous malformation of the lung.

(b) Detection of congenital anomalies of the pulmonary venous circulation: anomalous pulmonary venous drainage, pulmonary venous varix.

(c) Investigation of acquired disease of the pulmonary arterial and venous circulation (Figure 2–11): primary pulmonary

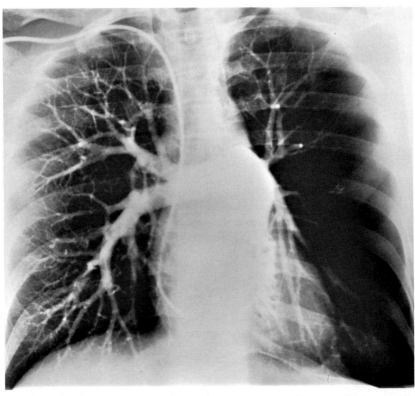

Figure 2–11. **Value of Pulmonary Angiography in the Investigation of Acquired Disease of the Pulmonary Vascular Tree.** A pulmonary angiogram exposed immediately after the rapid injection of contrast material into the main pulmonary artery reveals a sparse circulation throughout the whole of the left lung and a normal arterial tree on the right. Although diminutive, the left pulmonary artery is present and intact. Unilateral pulmonary emphysema (Swyer-James syndrome).

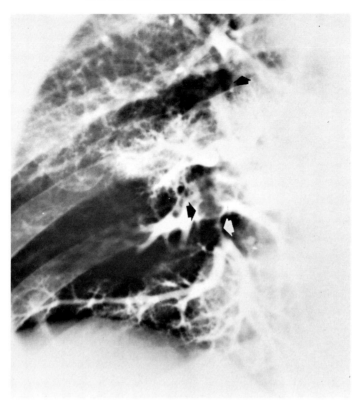

Figure 2–12. **Value of Pulmonary Angiography in the Investigation of Thromboembolic Disease.** A view of the lower half of the right lung following the rapid injection of contrast medium into the right main pulmonary artery. Numerous defects (*arrows*) can be identified within several of the branches of the right pulmonary arterial tree.

arterial hypertension, secondary pulmonary arterial and venous hypertension, emphysema, and conditions of obscure origin leading to pulmonary venous obstruction (*e.g.*, mediastinitis).

(d) Investigation of the resectability of bronchogenic cancer.[269-275]

(e) Investigation of peripheral pulmonary lesions.[276]

(f) Thromboembolic disease of the lungs (Figure 2–12). The important role that pulmonary angiography can play in the investigation of thromboembolic disease is no longer in dispute; in selected cases it may be of great diagnostic importance.[277-283]

Angiocardiography

TECHNIQUE. The technique depends in some measure on the information sought. For intracardiac abnormalities such as left atrial myxoma, direct intracardiac injection via a catheter usually produces better opacification than venous injection in the arm, either unilaterally or bilaterally. Gen-

erally, however, either procedure yields satisfactory results, particularly when venous injection is made in both arms simultaneously.

INDICATIONS. (a) Identification of intrathoracic abnormalities that may produce secondary effects on the pulmonary vasculature.

(b) In the differential diagnosis of space-occupying lesions within the mediastinum when it is not known whether the lesion originates within the pericardium or from tissues outside it.[284]

(c) In the diagnosis of pericardial effusion: Carbon dioxide has been employed as a safe and efficient contrast agent for the investigation of pericardial disease.[285]

Aortography

TECHNIQUE. The preferred technique is direct catheterization of the thoracic aorta percutaneously,[286] with either flooding of the aorta or selective catheterization of a particular vessel. An alternate method

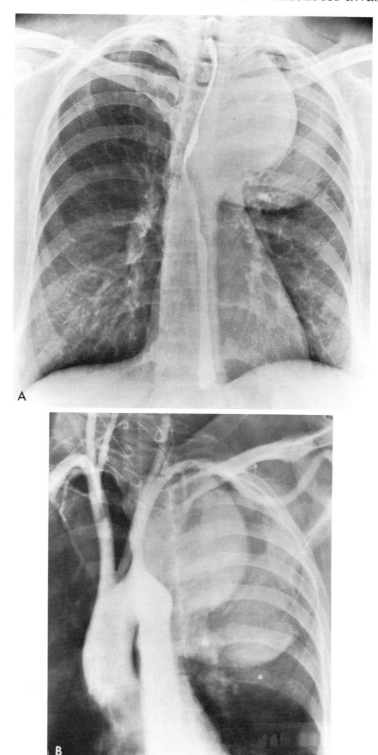

Figure 2–13. **Value of Aortography in the Assessment of Space-Occupying Lesions in the Mediastinum.** *A,* A chest roentgenogram in posteroanterior projection reveals a huge mass projected over the upper half of the left hemithorax contiguous to the mediastinum, obscuring the shadow of the aortic arch and displacing the midportion of the barium-filled esophagus to the right. An aortic aneurysm could not be excluded. *B,* An aortogram performed by percutaneous catheterization (Seldinger technique) shows the aorta to be intact although displaced slightly downward and to the right by the mass. Mesothelioma arising from the mediastinal pleura.

is the late, "levogram" phase of angiocardiography following simultaneous injection into the arm veins bilaterally; this technique provides satisfactory opacification in selected cases when direct catheterization of the aorta is contraindicated.

INDICATIONS. (a) In the differential diagnosis of space-occupying lesions in the mediastinum, e.g., to distinguish aneurysms of the aorta from other mediastinal mass lesions contiguous to the aorta[284] (Figure 2-13). Selective angiography of the subclavian and internal mammary arteries has been successfully employed in the evaluation and differentiation of anterior mediastinal masses.[287]

(b) Precise identification of aortic anomalies, such as patent ductus arteriosus or aortic coarctation.

(c) Identification of anomalous vessels, such as an artery supplying a sequestered lobe.[288, 289]

Bronchial Arteriography

TECHNIQUE. Optimal opacification can be achieved only by selective catheterization.[290, 291, 940] When the bronchial arteries are markedly hypertrophied and tortuous, they may be visualized in some cases by an aortic flood technique or even in the levogram phase of angiocardiography.

INDICATIONS. It is questionable whether bronchial arteriography can aid in the diagnosis or management of pulmonary disease, although as a research procedure it has provided much useful information about the pathophysiology and pathology of several pulmonary abnormalities associated with increased bronchial collateral circulation (chronic suppurative disease and chronic pulmonary oligemia).[68, 96, 269, 290, 292, 293] The procedure is of limited value in the investigation of peripheral pulmonary lesions, since both primary and metastatic neoplasms may receive their blood supply from the bronchial arteries,[290] and even some benign neoplasms show a "tumor blush."[294]

Superior-vena-cava Angiography

TECHNIQUE. This procedure may be carried out by unilateral or simultaneous bilateral arm-vein injection or via a catheter inserted into the superior vena cava or into one of its large tributary veins.

INDICATIONS. (a) In the investigation of obstruction of the superior vena cava (the superior-vena-cava syndrome).

(b) In the investigation of space-occupying lesions, either within the mediastinum or within the lung contiguous to the superior mediastinum, in which involvement of the great vein may indicate inoperability. Selective injection of the thymic vein[978] by retrograde catheter technique has been reported to be superior to other roentgenologic methods in the investigation of thymic masses in myasthenia gravis.

Azygography

TECHNIQUE. Since the major tributaries of the azygos and hemiazygos veins in the thorax are the intercostal veins, the first approach to the opacification of the azygos system was via the ribs. The technique involved needle puncture of an inferior rib posterolaterally and the rapid intraosseous injection of 10 to 20 ml of contrast medium.[295-298] A technique possessing certain advantages over the intraosseous method was described by Wilder and Lindgren[943] in 1962 and has been employed with success by other investigators.[944, 945] In this method, a catheter is introduced directly into the azygos via the femoral vein, right atrium, and superior vena cava; in addition to the superior opacification it provides, the technique permits recording of intravascular pressures.

INDICATIONS. (a) In the investigation of operability of lung cancer.[295-300] It is important to note that, although an abnormal azygogram is a strong indication of inoperability, a normal azygogram is of little positive value. Combined superior-vena-cava and azygos angiography has been reported to possess certain advantages over either method alone in the investigation of patient with suspected lung cancer.[301] We concur with Wolfel and his associates[299] that in the majority of cases azygography adds little information about the mediastinum that cannot be found by other, simpler, roentgenologic means.

(b) In the investigation of an enlarged azygos vein. Severe cirrhosis of the liver,[142] obstruction of the superior vena cava, congestive heart failure,[302, 303] or anomalous pulmonary venous drainage[304] may cause enlargement of the azygos vein in the right tracheobronchial angle. Idiopathic aneurysmal dilatation has been reported as an isolated anomaly.[305, 306] When the inferior vena cava is congenitally absent (infrahepatic interruption with azygos continuation[307]), the azygos system becomes the main route for the return of systemic blood from beneath the diaphragm; azygography may aid in the investigation, but the true nature of this anomaly is better elucidated by injection of contrast medium into the femoral vein below. Although this anomaly is harmless *per se*, its association with other congenital cardiovascular anomalies must be recognized.[308, 307]

CONTRAST STUDIES BY GAS INSUFFLATION

Insufflation of gas into thoracic or abdominal compartments has been employed for diagnostic purposes with various degrees of success. To our knowledge it has not received the enthusiastic endorsement of most diagnosticians, probably because other, simpler, and less time-consuming techniques accurately yield the information required in most situations. There is no doubt, however, that in some cases gas insufflation may provide information not available from other techniques; therefore, a brief description of the techniques and indications for these procedures appears worthwhile.

Mediastinal Pneumography

TECHNIQUE. Gas injected into the mediastinum follows the pathways of least resistance in the loose areolar tissue along the fascial planes, particularly in the anterior mediastinum. There are many methods for the introduction of gas, with little to recommend one rather than another; all are accomplished relatively easily, and none is associated with significant complications or side effects. Routes which have been recommended include the *transtracheal*, in which the needle is inserted into the retrotracheal space in the neck,[309] the *suprasternal*,[310, 311] the *transsternal*, in which the needle is inserted through the manubriosternal joint,[312] the *subxiphoid* approach, and the indirect method of *presacral* retroperitoneal insufflation, in which 1500 ml of gas is injected and the patient walks about for 15 min. to allow diffusion of gas into the mediastinum.[313] An interesting technique

has been developed by Berne and his associates in which pneumomediastinography is performed via a catheter which is placed in the mediastinum after scalene-node biopsy;[315, 316] this technique appears to be eminently suitable for patients with bronchogenic carcinoma in whom both procedures may reveal useful information.

The type of gas used depends to some extent on the time element; carbon dioxide and nitrous oxide undoubtedly are the safest from the point of view of inadvertent injection into the blood stream, but both are absorbed rapidly within the mediastinum and, therefore, require prompt roentgenographic study. A technique in which two types of gas are used[309, 316] seems to us to possess considerable merit; the needle is inserted—in this technique, via the transtracheal route—and a preliminary injection of 100 ml nitrous oxide or carbon dioxide is made, followed by fluoroscopic and roentgenographic study to determine whether there has been adequate dissemination of gas; this is followed by the injection of sufficient oxygen to adequately delineate the mediastinal compartments under study. The relatively slow absorption of oxygen permits leisurely roentgenographic study.

INDICATIONS. Pneumomediastinography is most successfully applied in the differential diagnosis of space-occupying lesions in the anterior mediastinal compartment. Indications include identification of thymic enlargement in patients with myasthenia gravis,[310, 311, 314] evaluation of resectability of bronchogenic carcinoma,[311, 315, 316] differentiation between pulmonary and mediastinal origin of a space-occupying mass,[314] and assessment of the extent and nature of lymph-node enlargement, particularly in the anterior mediastinum.[311] Posen and his associates[317] described a patient in whom a parathyroid adenoma was demonstrated by pneumomediastinography after angiography of the inferior thyroid artery had failed to show the lesion, and it may be that this technique will prove useful in locating these elusive tumors.

Diagnostic Pneumothorax

Artificial pneumothorax may aid in the diagnosis of space-occupying lesions which relate to the pleura. Separation of the parietal and visceral layers of pleura permits identification of the anatomic origin of a lesion from the chest wall, diaphragm, or mediastinum and distinguishes between these and lesions which originate from the visceral pleura or lung. Care is necessary to ensure that the lesion is viewed in profile, and the degree of rotation that produces precise tangential projection should be determined fluoroscopically. The amount of gas injected varies with the position of the lesion: If this is on the convexity of the thorax, 100 to 200 ml may produce sufficient separation of the pleural surfaces; when the lesion relates to the diaphragm or mediastinum, almost total pneumothorax may be necessary to adequately separate the pleural surfaces; roentgenography with the patient in the lateral decubitus or Trendelenburg position may accomplish the same end with smaller amounts of gas. Abnormalities which relate to the diaphragm sometimes are better delineated by induction of pneumoperitoneum, particularly when their roentgenographic appearance suggests that they may be diaphragmatic hernia or local diaphragmatic eventration.[318]

When it has been established by pneumothorax that a lesion arises from the pleura, thoracoscopy (*see* page 157) may aid in further elucidating its character, although it is probable that thoracotomy should be performed at once.

Diagnostic Pneumoperitoneum

Artificial pneumoperitoneum may be of great value in determining the nature of a mass that arises in or contiguous to the diaphragm. It is particularly useful in studying cardiophrenic densities whose significance cannot be established by simpler techniques; for example, local diaphragmatic eventration, with or without "herniation" of a portion of the liver, may be accurately identified in this manner[318] (Figure 2-14). Asch[319] emphasizes the value of pneumoperitoneum in locating inflammatory disease which has arisen above or below the diaphragm; since basal pulmonary disease and pleural effusion are common in both situations, the injection of a small amount of gas into the peritoneum generally allows identification of the primary site of disease, by demonstrating obliteration of the subphrenic space in acute subphrenic disease and its freedom from obliteration when the disease is primarily intrathoracic.

In a case described by Hill and his associates,[320] an interesting by-product of the application of this technique was the demonstration of an anomalous artery which passed upward across the subphrenic space, from the aorta to the diaphragm, to supply a pulmonary sequestration.

Diagnostic Pneumopericardium

The injection of gas into the pericardial space seldom is indicated in the roentgenographic diagnosis of chest disease. It may be of use occasionally in the differentiation of mass lesions which arise in or adjacent to the pericardium.[321]

ROENTGENOLOGIC METHODS IN THE ASSESSMENT OF LUNG FUNCTION

It is inevitable that over the years roentgenographic techniques have been devised to estimate parameters of lung function.[322, 323] Some of these, notably the determination of lung volume, possess a high degree of accuracy when compared with physiologic methods of measurement; the majority, however, either lack sufficient precision to be of much value or necessitate the use of highly complex apparatus not generally available. While it is clear that the refined techniques of pulmonary function testing described in Chapter 3 will serve as the sheet anchor of physiologic investigation in the majority of cases, certain roentgenologic procedures may yield useful information either as rough screening methods or when physiologic techniques are not available.

Determination of Lung Volumes

Many ingenious roentgenographic methods have been devised for the determination of lung volume;[324] unfortunately, most of these are so inaccurate as to be unacceptable except as a rough gauge. This lack of accuracy is due largely to the awkward shape of the thorax and to the difficulty in estimating the volumetric contributions of the diaphragmatic domes, heart, pulmonary blood volume, and tissue volume. However, in 1960 an ingenious method was described by Barnhard and his associates[1023] in which the lungs were pictured as a stack of five horizontal elliptical cylindroids. The volume of each of these

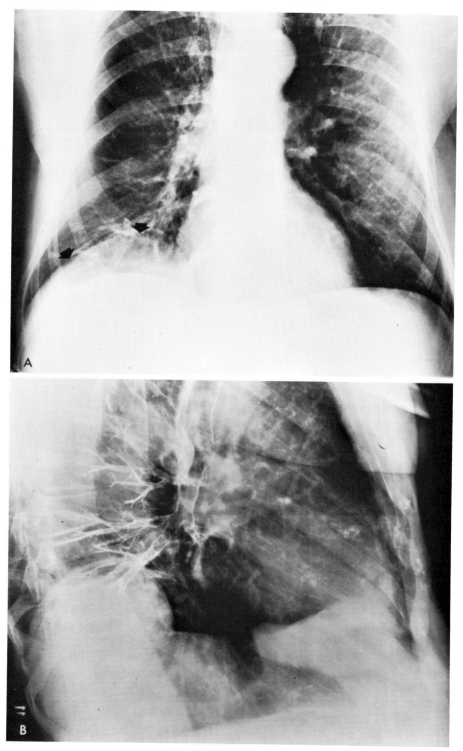

Figure 2–14.   *See legend on opposite page.*

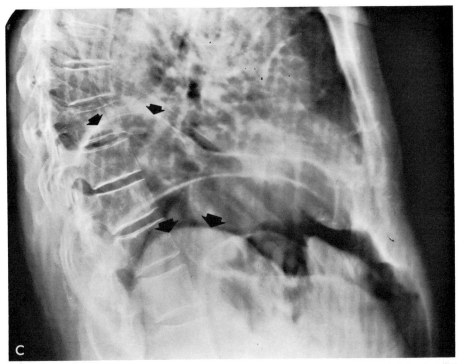

Figure 2–14. **Value of Diagnostic Pneumoperitoneum in the Assessment of Masses Arising in or Contiguous to the Diaphragm.** *A,* A chest roentgenogram in posteroanterior projection reveals a smooth, well-defined mass related to the right hemidiaphragm (*arrows*). In *B,* the mass is seen to be situated posteriorly and to be associated with deformity and apparent obstruction of one of the basal segmental bronchi of the right lower lobe. *C,* Following injection of gas into the peritoneal space, a roentgenogram exposed in the erect position, lateral projection, reveals gas outlining a smooth, well-defined elevation in the posterior portion of the right hemidiaphragm (*upper arrows*). A portion of liver which occupied this space can be seen outlined by gas inferiorly (*lower arrows*). Localized eventration of the posterior portion of right hemidiaphragm.

five segments was measured and their total was the capacity of the thorax. The volumes of the heart, the right and left hemidiaphragms, the intrathoracic extracardiac blood, and the lung tissue were totaled and subtracted from the thoracic capacity, to yield the total volume of gas in the lungs. Measurements obtained with this technique agreed well with those obtained by conventional means in healthy subjects and in patients with congestive heart failure, but were significantly greater in patients with emphysema when compared with figures obtained by gas-dilution methods for measurement of TLC. Barnhard's technique was subsequently modified by Loyd and his associates[149] in the light of new physiologic data concerning pulmonary tissue and blood volume. These investigators compared their roentgenographic method with plethysmographically determined TLC in normal subjects and in patients with pulmonary fibrosis, emphysema, sarcoidosis, or pulmonary neoplasm and showed a high degree of agreement in all. In emphysema, as might be anticipated, the roentgenographic method was more accurate than gas-dilution techniques in the assessment of total long capacity. When TLC was known, RV was readily obtained by subtracting the spirometrically obtained vital capacity. An experienced observer could make the measurements in less than 30 minutes and the technique had a high degree of reproducibility. Despite its accuracy, it seems unlikely that this method will be widely applied, particularly in institutions where physiologic tests of pulmonary function are readily available; where such facilities are not available, however, its provision of rapid, accurate measurement of TLC and RV can be of value in selected patients.

Studies of Ventilation

Fluoroscopy and roentgenography may be useful as rough screening measures in the investigation of pulmonary ventilation. Estimates of diaphragmatic and costal excursion during quiet and forced respiration may indicate the presence of restricted ventilation, either bilaterally symmetrical, as in diffuse bronchospasm or emphysema, or asymmetrical, as may occur in association with obstructive overinflation resulting from bronchial neoplasm or foreign body. As indicated in a previous section, *roentgen kymography* produces more quantitative information concerning diaphragmatic and costal excursion than does simple fluoroscopy.[198-203] In a study of 20 normal subjects and 47 patients with ventilatory dysfunction, Goldenthal and his co-workers[198] recorded roentgen-kymographic tracings of diaphragmatic and costal excursion during forced expiration that correlated well with bronchospirometric ratings of each lung. Similarly, a correlative kymographic spirometric study carried out by Lasser[201] in 300 cases showed good correspondence with measurements of both timed vital capacity and expiratory flow rate.

Roentgen densitometry, the technique of which was described in a previous section (*see* page 115), provides a method for studying regional pulmonary ventilation by recording variation in roentgenographic density of the lung during respiration.[204-215, 937, 977] Simultaneous densitometric and spirometric records obtained by Laws and Steiner[213] showed close correlation in normal subjects and in patients with general airway obstruction. Similarly, in 32 patients with local obstructive disease, Karwowski[210] showed excellent correlation between densitometric and bronchospirometric values; he stressed the superiority of densitometry in the investigation of local disturbances in ventilation, compared with the inconvenience and discomfort of bronchospirometry.

Studies of Perfusion

Since it is reasonable to assume that the volume of extravascular interstitial tissue is constant, the roentgenographic density of lung is dependent upon the ratio of the amount of blood in the vascular tree to the amount of gas in the airways. At any one time, therefore, at a given degree of lung inflation, the density of the lung should reflect the absolute amount of blood present within the vascular tree, including the capillaries. The presence of oligemia or pleonemia, if of sufficient degree, may be appreciated on standard roentgenograms of the chest through assessment of decrease or increase, respectively, in the size of pulmonary vascular markings. Alteration in pulmonary capillary volume seldom can be appreciated by subjective evaluation of background lung density; that such can be revealed by roentgen densitometry, however, has been shown by Kourilsky and his co-workers[212] and by Standertskjöld-Nordenstam.[214] Working independently, these authors compared densitometric recordings of the periphery of the lung with electrocardiographic tracings made simultaneously and showed that the densitometric record allows identification of the various phases of the pulmonary pulse and that it is a true record of pulmonary pulsation-perfusion. Similarly, Laws and Steiner[213] found good correlation between densitometric records and pulmonary artery pressures obtained simultaneously during cardiac catheterization: They consider that density variations must be related to changes in the volume of blood in the lungs.

The recent development of the technique of tetrapolar electrical impedance detection by Nyboer and his associates[326] may well replace other methods as a convenient tool for the study of central as well as peripheral pulmonary circulation.

LUNG SCANNING

Although still in its infancy, nuclear medicine has made a substantial contribution to diagnosis in chest disease, and there is every reason to believe that the development and refinement of new techniques will result in a great expansion in our knowledge of pulmonary function and morphology in health and in disease. Fundamental research is proceeding rapidly along many fronts, notably in the refinement of recording devices and the development of newer radiopharmaceuticals. To date, clinical application of lung-scanning techniques has been restricted to two relatively narrow fields of interest—in thromboembolic disease, with tagged macroaggregates of albumin (MMA) as the chief vehicle, and ventilation/perfusion studies of lung function, using radioactive xenon and other gaseous radionuclides. Since appropriate sections of this book contain reference to the application of these methods in investigation, only a brief consideration of the techniques employed is given here.

Generally speaking, the use of radioactive isotopes in the lung involves the recording on sensitive devices of the gamma radiation produced by radionuclides injected intravenously into the blood stream or inhaled into the airspaces. The pick-up devices are scintillation counters, which may be in the form of multiple stationary probes such as have been employed with radioactive xenon, scintillation scanners which cover the field of interest in "strips," or the scintillation camera which records the flux of gamma radiation emanating from the lungs in a single exposure, much like a roentgenograph.

For studies of the pulmonary circulation, the most commonly used vehicle for the radionuclide is MAA, which is prepared by heating human serum albumin to 100° C. The resultant particle sizes range from 10 to 100μ in diameter and depend to a great extent upon a constant pH of 5.4 to 5.5.[327-330] The albumin may be labeled with [131]iodine,[327] [51]chromium,[329] or [99M]technitium.[331] [113M]Indium-tagged iron hydroxide, a short-lived isotope, is said to possess certain advantages over MAA for lung scanning.[332]

Since the basis of the procedure is the trapping within the small vessels of the lung of the macroaggregates of albumin, particle size is critical. The majority of particles less than 10μ in diameter pass through the lung "sieve" and are picked up by the reticuloendothelial system, largely in the liver and spleen,[329, 330, 333] whereas particles larger than 70 to 100μ in diameter may obstruct larger vessels, with resultant deleterious effects; an optimal particle size of 10 to 50μ in diameter has been found to produce consistently satisfactory results. Disappearance time from the lungs is nearly exponential, biological half-life ranging from five to ten hours;[329] in 24 hours, radioactivity disappears from the lung when ^{131}I is the radionuclide and decreases to 25 per cent with [51]Cr.[329] With rare exceptions,[334] the extensive clinical experience of several investigators[327-330] has revealed no significant toxicity or mobidity associated with the injection of human serum albumin. Radiation

dosage rates are well within tolerable limits.

The technique involves the intravenous injection of a standard quantity of tagged MAA, graded to body weight, containing a specified quantity of radionuclide (for example, 300 microcuries of ^{131}I or 1000 microcuries of ^{51}Cr); most of the particles are trapped in the first capillary bed they encounter, which is in the lung, and counting is begun immediately by scintillation scanning or by scintiphotography with the scintillation camera. Reproducibility of scans is reported to be excellent.[979]

The major *indication* for this technique lies in the field of thromboembolic disease,[335q, 941] and this application is discussed in detail in Chapter 9. Suffice to say here that studies with tagged MAA may be expected to be of diagnostic value only when the scan image is compared with the chest roentgenogram. Many physiologic and pathologic conditions such as the posture of the patient during tracer injection, obesity, cardiomegaly, and cardiac decompensation alter lung images and must be recognized and taken into account to enable correct interpretations.[980] Since any disease that may lead to consolidation or atelectasis, or both, may be associated with reduced or absent pulmonary artery perfusion, reduced or absent radioactivity on scanning does not necessarily indicate the presence of embolism. When the clinical picture is suggestive of embolism, however, and when the chest roentgenograph shows neither consolidation nor atelectasis, scintillation studies may be pathognomonic. Since modern medical and surgical techniques in the treatment of pulmonary embolism may be curative, it is essential that the diagnosis be made by whatever means the physician has at his disposal; in a significant number of cases, isotope studies may be the only definitive diagnostic procedure. It cannot be overemphasized, however that in the majority of cases of pulmonary embolism a positive diagnosis can be made only by integrating information gained from all methods of investigation.[981]

Gaseous Radionuclides

The application of radioactive xenon (^{133}Xe), oxygen-labeled carbon dioxide, and other gaseous radionuclides in the investigation of pulmonary function, particularly ventilation/perfusion relationships, is discussed briefly in the section on physiologic aspects of the acinar unit and is referred to in greater detail in the section of pulmonary function tests in Chapter 3.

METHODS FOR PATHOLOGIC EXAMINATION

The lungs collapse after removal from the body and thus must be reinflated post mortem if emphysema is to be recognized. Further, reinflation is useful in diagnosing many other disorders. The lung is a large organ of complex arrangement and few diseases affect it uniformly throughout, making a random section technique of examination inadequate. There are some special techniques that may be extremely valuable in the assessment of the general patterns of the bronchi and pulmonary vasculature and these will be described briefly.

Postmortem Inflation of the Lung

Postmortem inflation can be an exceptionally simple procedure but often is not performed because pathologists fear that they will produce artefacts. In general, any special method should avoid artefacts so far as possible and should overcome those caused by removal and handling of the lung after death. It is also important that some attempts be made to re-expand lungs to a standard degree, although, as will be apparent later, this is perhaps not so critical as it appears at first sight. Many methods have been described and these may differ in principle, as well as detail. The ultimate choice is likely to be dictated by such practical considerations as cost, time involved, and the purpose for which the lung is inflated.

The degree of expansion that a lung will reach depends upon the transpulmonary pressure and the compliance of the lung, (i.e., change in volume per unit change of pressure). The first of these has been the subject of much attention, whereas little notice has been taken of the latter. Each lung has an individual compliance during life, and its compliance after death may be affected by coincidental terminal pneumonia, congestion, edema, or thrombosis, as well as by the previous history of inflation and deflation of the lung.[336] Distending the lung by

fluid rather than air produces another complication. When air is excluded from the system, the pressure-volume relationship undergoes complete change because of alterations in tension at the alveolar surface: in these circumstances, compliance is approximately doubled. However, the described methods of distending with fluid do not entirely exclude air from the system, and the pressure-volume characteristics of such air-fluid systems are not known. The situation becomes even more complicated when a fixative, either gaseous or liquid, is used, since lung compliance alters as tissue fixation proceeds. Finally, compliance may differ from one region to another, particularly when the lung is emphysematous, so that various degrees of inflation may be produced within one lung.

The degree of expansion is not so critical as might appear at first. When the increase in volume is distributed evenly throughout the lung, the diameter of an airspace varies with the cube root of the change in volume. Thus, a 50 per cent increase in lung volume gives rise to only a 15 per cent increase in the diameter of the airspaces. Intersubject variation in air-space diameter has been only briefly investigated,[12] but it is known that this may be up to 50 per cent—which is greater than any variation produced by variations in inflation. It should be noted that an absolutely controlled and known degree of expansion is necessary only for making absolute measurements within the lung; changes in lung tissue corresponding to the clinical syndrome of emphysema are essentially those of widespread destruction, and there is no evidence that simple hyperinflation produces this syndrome. There is no fear that inflation techniques will produce emphysema as is sometimes supposed. It also follows that none but the most skilled observer, using a meticulous inflation technique and making extensive measurements, could recognize the so-called "compensatory emphysema" that occurs, for example, after pneumonectomy.

Inflation of the Lung to an Arbitrary Degree, Ignoring the Pressure

The most practical end-point for assessment is apparent full inflation, and most often expansion to this degree is attempted. The easiest way to accomplish this is to distend the lung with formalin introduced into the bronchi under positive pressure. The lung is left overnight in a large vat of formalin and can be examined the next morning. A maximal pressure head of 50 to 100 cm of formalin is suitable; a smaller pressure head can be obtained by raising the lung in relation to the fluid level in the bottle from which it is inflated. A full head of pressure may be required for lungs from patients who die in status asthmaticus, and lower pressures (10 to 20 cm H_2O) should be used to inflate lungs from older patients and those thought to have emphysema. Alternatively, expansion to apparent full inflation can be accomplished with air (with gaseous fixative, if necessary) from a positive-pressure air line or from a cylinder of compressed air. Flow within the system is maintained by leaks through the pleura. The lung is kept distended until dry and rigid, which takes four to seven days. Full inflation may be achieved also by exerting a negative pressure around the lung with a plethysmograph.

Expansion to apparent full inflation is the easiest method, but carries with it certain problems. (a) It is not certain how much artefact may be produced by overinflation. After its removal from the body, the lung's expansion is no longer limited by the chest cage, so that inflation to maximal capacity may produce volumes much larger than during life. However, it was established recently that lung volumes at apparent full inflation are similar to predicted TLC values.[337] Thus, the lung size is limited to some extent by the pleura. (b) The tissue may rupture if too great a pressure is applied. This occurs, but interstitial accumulation of fixative or gas results, not true destructive emphysema. (c) When a lung is distended with liquid fixative and left without a constant head of pressure it diminishes 22 to 30 per cent in volume, even when the bronchus is closed. The greater part of this decrease in volume occurs in the first few hours after inflation, and the change is complete within 12 hours. Much of it is the result of leakage through pleural tears, but it occurs in airtight lungs also, and this, presumably, is due to solution and diffusion of gas and fixative and to tissue shrinkage.

Despite the difficulties, this remains the simplest method of distending lungs and, in the case of formalin distention, requires no special apparatus and represents the minimal requirement for inflating lungs. This technique has provided the descriptions of the pathology in emphysema that are in use today, and there is seldom a reason why it should not be used as a routine procedure on one lung in all necropsies.

Instead of being distended to apparent full inflation, lungs have been expanded to the size of the pleural cavity after death. This is no more satisfactory, since the amount of air expelled is variable, depending greatly upon the length of time elapsing between death and necropsy.

Inflation of the Lung to an Unknown Degree at an Arbitrarily Selected Pressure

Because each lung has its own degree of compliance, the application of the same arbitrarily elected pressure to different lungs may produce a variable, rather than an identical, degree of expansion. For example, the pressure frequently chosen to inflate lungs after death is 20 cm H_2O. In life, this figure represents the dividing line of maximal attainable negative intrapleural pressure between normal subjects and those with emphysema. In postmortem studies, inflation at this pressure should overinflate lungs with emphysema and underinflate normal lungs. However, when fluid fixatives are used at this pressure, postmortem lung volumes are close to those predicted or found during life. This occurs because of the increased compliance of the lung due to the abolition of the surface-active forces at the alveolar surface, and all lungs are thus maximally inflated.

Distention at the Known Pressure Necessary to Produce Total Lung Capacity of that Particular Lung

To determine the pressure required to inflate fully one particular lung, it is necessary to perform postmortem pressure-volume studies on that lung. This is time-consuming, requires extra apparatus, and is neither necessary nor suitable for *routine* diagnostic procedures. Further, there is some question as to the accuracy of such pressure-volume curves—with the lungs outside the thorax, their maximal volumes are unlikely to be precisely those that existed during life.

Inflation of the Lung to an Estimated Volume

Hartung[338] inflated lungs to their volume at two-thirds vital capacity, by introducing fixative into the bronchus in a volume calculated from standard prediction formulas of lung volumes and knowledge of the average amount of air in the lungs at time of autopsy. Martin, quoted by Weibel and Vidone,[339] suggested a formula for calculating the apparent degree of expansion of a lung, but this is only an approximation and not likely to be more accurate than inflating to estimated full expansion.

It is apparent from consideration of these four methods of inflation that reinflation of the lung can be standardized only in exceptional circumstances, if at all. One major effect of reinflation, however, is to abolish distortion produced by handling the lung. Most pathologists are aware of the so-called "alternating" emphysema and atelectasis seen in histologic slides of an ill-prepared lung; this can be overcome by the use of any inflation method, provided that the tissue is subsequently handled with care and not compressed in preparation for histologic study.

Defects of Lung Inflation Techniques

It is difficult to distinguish antemortem from postmortem thrombi in the fixed inflated lung, and dissection of pulmonary arteries and bronchi is difficult in sliced specimens. Bacteriologic culture also is made more difficult, but bronchial swabs can be taken, and, if culture is essential, the lung may be cut into while fresh and a swab taken, the incision sutured or clamped, and the lung inflated. Pulmonary edema also may be less easy to recognize, but this is due in part to the use of dilute formalin or to air-drying and fixing.

THE DISTENDING MEDIUM AND FIXATION

Experts disagree about the relative merits of gaseous and fluid fixative, and, indeed, each has its merits; either may be combined with the various methods of inflation.

Gaseous Fixatives

These often produce wrinkled specimens, poorly suited for histologic examination, but the rigid lungs are easy to handle and are excellent for teaching purposes. Boiling formalin produces steam as well as formalin gas, and, therefore, does not dehydrate lungs as rapidly as gas alone, and the resultant preservation for histologic study is usually adequate.

Liquid Fixatives

Liquid formalin has the advantage of producing better histologic preparations, but without prolonged fixation the lungs are not so rigid or easy to handle as dried specimens. Fixation with Zenker's solution is excellent, producing a fairly rigid lung within 24 hours, but this method requires care and attention. A combination of gas and fluid fixatives may be used by partially fixing and air-drying with formalin steam and completing fixation with Zenker's solution. This method requires special apparatus, and the degree of fixation is no better than with Zenker's solution alone.

Inflation of the lung is required most frequently as a simple diagnostic aid. As such, the procedure should be simple, inexpensive, and quick; the inflated lung should be available for conference next day. Only simple fluid fixation fulfills these criteria, and formalin is the best and cheapest fixing fluid.

EXAMINATION OF THE LUNG

As most diseases, and emphysema in particular, are irregularly distributed in the lung, it is important to examine as much of the organ as possible. Careful naked-eye appraisal of an entire vertical section of lung is the minimal acceptable examination, but even under these conditions a significant degree of emphysema, particularly panlobular emphysema, can easily be missed. Lungs are best sectioned on a commercial meat-slicer, but formalin-fixed specimens can be cut with a sharp knife. Examination of a slice (floated under water after barium impregnation, if the lung has been fluid-fixed) with a dissecting microscope is, by far, the best method of making an accurate assessment of emphysema. The three-dimensional effect is very pleasing, and pneumonia, fibrosis, and other lesions can be recognized readily. Photographs of good quality can be taken through all standard dissecting microscopes, which may also have attachments for three-dimensional pictures. Representative histologic sections should be taken in all cases, since structures cannot be identified with certainty with a dissecting microscope. We also believe that the topography of lesions is much better appreciated in distended, sliced lungs than in the distorted, limp tissue of sliced, undistended, unfixed lungs. The advantages far outweigh the disadvantages: There seems to be no reason why simple distention by liquid formalin should not be a routine procedure for the examination of all lungs, whether necropsy or surgical specimens.

RECORDING AND STORAGE

The paper-mounted, whole-lung-section technique developed by Gough and Wentworth[340] has proved to be the method of choice for the recording and storage of observations, as well as providing suitable material for other observers. It is a simple and easy technique and its use is essential in any laboratory interested in lung disease: We believe that it should be practiced in all major pathology departments. Photographs of wet lung slices, enlarged, if necessary, to life size, form an adequate, though not perfect, method of storage and record at about one-fifth the cost of whole-lung sections.

SPECIAL POSTMORTEM TECHNIQUES

Many injection masses have been used for postmortem *angiography*. The most satisfactory is the Schlesinger mass,[341] which is fluid at room temperature and solidifies when formalin is added. Distention and fixation of the lung with formalin introduced into the bronchi solidifies the gelatin in the vessels. *Bronchography* can be performed, using either Schlesinger mass or finely particulate barium or lead insufflated into the bronchial tree. The cheapest and easiest material to use for making *corrosion casts* is vinylite, but this material contracts when it solidifies, so that measurements made then are valueless. Thompsett's technique[342] produces the best casts, but the material used is not readily available in North America. Cinephotography of serial sections records the maximal amount of information with the least effort. A photographic method of reconstructing serial sections has been described,[343] but appears to be expensive and

time-consuming. The mechanical properties of the lung may be assessed by *postmortem function studies*, which provide valuable information.

LUNG MORPHOMETRY. The concept of morphometry of the lung pioneered by Weibel[9] has been applied but little to abnormal lungs, although interest in these techniques has been stimulated by their use in measurement of emphysema.[345] At least 12 different subjective measurements of emphysema have been described;[337] the methods differ in many respects, and it seems likely that there is a wide variation of interobserver interpretation, even among experts. Objective measurements of emphysema are still in their infancy and there is no simple, objective measurement of emphysema readily available at present. Hypertrophy of the mucous glands may be quantitated, using the Reid index to assess chronic bronchitis (*see* Chapter 13), but has well-defined limitations in this respect.

These methods of lung morphometry have been used in research rather than routine investigation—as have the "special techniques" described previously. It is a sad commentary on the practice of pathology that this should be so. Diagnostic medicine has made numerous advances in the last decades—research techniques of the 1950's are standard diagnostic tests today—but morphologic diagnostic techniques have remained essentially unchanged over the past 100 years. Many of these special techniques, and morphometry in particular, should be used in diagnosis, and this is a likely development.

SURGICAL SPECIMENS

Surgical specimens differ from necropsy specimens in that the urgency of diagnosis is greater and bacteriologic diagnosis assumes greater importance. We advocate routine inflation of surgically resected lung specimens, provided that this does not conflict with these two conditions. In many instances, cancer is diagnosed preoperatively; in these cases, the lung can be inflated and can be examined the next day. In most other instances sections of tissue should be examined immediately, by quick frozen section or rapid paraffin processing. Similarly, specimens through the resection margin should be submitted at this time. When infection is suspected or possible, a piece of the lesion removed under aseptic conditions should be routinely submitted to microbiology. We also recommend as a routine that a swab be taken from the bronchial tree and submitted for microbiologic examination. Material for microscopic investigation should be prepared in the operating room, where conditions are sterile and contamination of the specimen is avoided. When an incision in the lung is necessary to obtain material, this can be clamped or sutured before inflation.

Specimens are best examined by probing the major and segmental bronchi and cutting the lung along the plane of the bronchi into the major lesion, using a large, sharp, flat knife. With care, the major bronchi leading into the lesion are clearly shown; when slices are not made through the entire lung, the organ can be preserved as one specimen. Thin sagittal slices can then be made, starting from the lateral surface, to reveal incidental peripheral lesions. It goes without saying that lymph nodes should be identified, dissected out, and submitted for section. Vascular invasion has prognostic significance; its presence or absence should be recorded in every case of tumor.

Organisms may be recognized by use of special stains, particularly Gomori's stain for fungi and fluorescent and acid-fast stains for tubercle bacilli; these have the advantage of speed over microbiologic investigation but are not as definitive.

The information gleaned by the pathologist is greatly advanced by his knowledge of the clinical history and roentgenographic findings. Ideally, examination of the specimens should be conducted with a roentgenologist and a clinician: such a situation yields maximal information for patient care, teaching, and, in some instances, research.

Biopsy

LUNG. Interpretation of lung biopsies is not easy. Co-operation between clinician, roentgenologist, and pathologist produces a vastly greater precision of diagnosis, and it is important that the surgeon contribute his share by biopsying representative areas and recording fully the gross appearances at operation. Opinions as to the efficacy of lung biopsy as a diagnostic procedure depend upon whether idiopathic pulmonary fibrosis is considered a proper diagnosis. If so, a positive diagnosis is made in most biopsies on patients with roentgenographically diffuse lung disease. Because of the wide variation in situation and severity of emphysema, the pathologist or clinician who extrapolates findings in biopsy specimens to the remainder of the lung is foolhardy indeed.

PLEURA. Needle biopsy of the pleura has proved a rewarding diagnostic procedure since its introduction in 1955. From the pathologists's point of view, the Cope and Harefield[347] (Abrams) needle yields the most satisfactory specimens; in only about 2 per cent of cases is the tissue sample inadequate, as opposed to the Vim-Silverman needle, with which about a quarter of tissue samples are inadequate. Care should be taken in embedding and cutting tissue to ensure that pleura and not only muscle is sectioned. Provided that the technical staff know that the tissue is pleura, there is little difficulty in this regard; haphazard cutting of the tissue may result in sections showing muscle only, in which case the block should be further sectioned at several levels.

SCALENE NODES. There are no technical problems so far as the pathologist is concerned. The fat pad should be carefully dissected out and all lymph nodes, no matter how small, submitted for section. Malignant tumors may be seen microscopically in small and apparently normal lymph nodes. The value and diagnostic yield of these biopsy techniques is discussed in detail in Chapter 3.

3

METHODS IN CLINICAL, LABORATORY, AND FUNCTIONAL INVESTIGATION

CLINICAL HISTORY
    SYMPTOMS OF RESPIRATORY DISEASE
        Cough and Expectoration
        Hoarseness
        Shortness of Breath
        Chest Pain
        Hemoptysis
    PAST ILLNESSES AND PERSONAL HISTORY
        Family History
        Occupational and Residential History
        System Enquiry
PHYSICAL EXAMINATION
    METHOD OF EXAMINATION AND SIGNIFICANT
        CHEST SIGNS
        Inspection
        Palpation
        Percussion
        Auscultation
    EXTRATHORACIC MANIFESTATIONS OF
        PULMONARY DISEASE
        Clubbing and Hypertrophic Pulmonary
          Osteoarthropathy
        Cyanosis
    THE DEPENDABILITY OF PHYSICAL FINDINGS
SPECIAL DIAGNOSTIC PROCEDURES
    ENDOSCOPIC EXAMINATION
        Laryngoscopy
        Bronchoscopy
        Mediastinoscopy
        Thoracoscopy
        Esophagoscopy
    BIOPSY PROCEDURES

        Bronchoscopic Biopsy
        Pulmonary Parenchymal Biopsy
        Pleural Biopsy
        Lymph Node Biopsy
    BACTERIOLOGY IN PULMONARY DISEASE
        Collection of Material
        Smears and Cultures
        Animal Inoculation
SKIN TESTS
BIOCHEMICAL TESTS
    Sputum
    Pleural Fluid
    Blood Serum
CYTOLOGY
    Nonmalignant Cells in Pulmonary Secretions
    Nonmalignant Cells in Pleural Fluid
    Malignant Cells in Pulmonary Secretions
    Malignant Cells in Pleural Fluid
HEMATOLOGIC PROCEDURES IN LUNG DISEASE
ELECTROCARDIOGRAPHY
PULMONARY FUNCTION TESTS
    Lung Volumes
    Measurement of Composition of Alveolar Gas
    Measurement of Mechanics of Acinar
        Ventilation
    Measurement of Perfusion of Acinar Units
    Measurement of the Diffusion of Gas in Acinar
        Units
    Measurement of Matching of Blood Flow and
        Ventilation
    Measurement of Blood Gases and H^+-ion
        Concentration

CLINICAL HISTORY

The fundamental importance of precise history-taking in arriving at the correct diagnosis becomes evident in subsequent chapters, in which the multifarious clinical conditions that can give rise to similar roentgenographic patterns are considered. With any abnormality seen roentgenographically, a logical diagnosis may be made on the information elicited by careful history-taking, findings during meticulous physical examination, and intelligently directed laboratory or pulmonary function tests. In pulmonary disease the key to solution of abnormal roentgenographic shadows most often lies in thorough awareness of the patient's complaints. In some cases, despite the presence of symptoms indicating advanced and disabling disease, the chest roentgenogram may be normal, a finding which, in itself, limits the diagnostic possibilities and excludes diseases invariably associated with an abnormal roentgenogram. The differential diagnosis of respiratory disorders with normal roentgenograms is discussed in Chapter 19.

Good history-taking is an art. It requires that the patient be at ease, confident in the doctor's ability, and prepared to divulge all pertinent details that will enable his physician to identify the cause of his malady. Of particular importance is the avoidance of an atmosphere of hurry, although often the physician must patiently return a digressing patient to a discussion of pertinent information. After the patient has given an account of his complaints the physician should elicit further details. For example, the significance of dyspnea requires more information as to its onset: was it sudden, or gradual? Its severity: does it occur when he is walking slowly in the street, or only when he runs upstairs? Does it require exertion or develop even at rest? At what time of day is it particularly obvious? Is it made worse when he lies flat? The patient's answers to these questions, and to others intended to clarify other major symptoms, frequently give the physician a good idea of the diagnosis by the time he has completed taking the history of the illness. Then he should elicit any pertinent information concerning past illnesses and personal habits. Of fundamental importance in lung disease is such information as the patient's tobacco consumption, in what form and what quantity. Areas of residence and travel should be ascertained; even a brief exposure elsewhere can result in an infection or infestation which might otherwise be overlooked. Similarly, a complete and chronologic occupational history may indicate that the patient's complaints are due to exposure to a specific substance known to be an occupational hazard, or may identify a nonspecific dust or fume to which chronic cough and expectoration may be attributable. Finally, since lung disease frequently is only one manifestation of a more general process, or secondary to a disease involving other organs, an account of the function of other body systems is essential.

The symptoms of respiratory disease are cough and expectoration, shortness of breath, chest pain, and hemoptysis. These will be considered individually and in greater detail, after which further consideration will be given to the pertinence of personal, occupational, and residential history and to disease of other organ systems commonly associated with respiratory disorders.

SYMPTOMS OF RESPIRATORY DISEASE

Cough and Expectoration

Cough is a defensive mechanism designed to rid the conducting passages of mucus and foreign material. The afferent pathways of the cough reflex are in the trigeminal, glossopharyngeal, superior laryngeal, and vagus nerves. The nerve endings in the upper respiratory tract are sensitive to contact with foreign material and to volume change in their vicinity and respond to sulfur dioxide and, presumably, other noxious chemical agents (chemoreceptors) in the smaller bronchi.[238, 348] The acinar units have no nerve supply, and, therefore, for acinar disease to initiate coughing, it is necessary that material from these areas move up into larger airways, into the presence of nerve endings. The efferent pathways of the cough-reflex arc lie in the recurrent laryngeal nerve, which causes closure of the glottis, and in the phrenic and spinal nerves, which effect contraction of the diaphragm and other respiratory muscles against a closed glottis. The most sensitive areas of the conducting system are in the larynx and epicarina and at the bifurcation of the major bronchi.

In addition to its being precipitated by foreign material irritating nerve endings in airway passages, a cough may occur sometimes as a result of stimulation of the parietal pleura and even of afferent pathways originating in other viscera.

The character of a cough is rarely useful in indicating the disease process responsible. However, frequently patients describe a cough that originates from a need to "clear the throat" and that both physician and patient visualize as coming from the upper respiratory tract. These patients usually have a chronic postnasal drip and the cough is often described as "hacking"—a short, dry, oft-repeated cough, different from the deep "loose" cough heard in patients with disease of more peripheral regions, in the bronchi or lung parenchyma. Patients with tracheal lesions sometimes have a "brassy" cough, whereas a "bovine" sound has been described in association with laryngeal paralysis.

Cough may be dry or productive. An acute dry cough often develops in the early stages of virus infections involving both upper and lower respiratory tracts. A dry cough may occur in association with bronchogenic carcinoma, although the majority of these patients smoke many cigarettes and, therefore, have bronchitis and produce some mucoid expectoration. A dry, very irritating cough, often occurring in spasms, may be an early symptom of left-sided heart failure. A short, dry cough may be a nervous habit: this is usually recognized as such by the patient or his family and he rarely seeks medical advice for this complaint.

Most dry coughs, if sufficiently prolonged, eventually become productive. The expectorated material is clear and mucoid when the stimulus to cough and to hypersecretion by bronchial mucous glands is viral in origin or due to foreign substances, such as smoke or atmospheric pollution, but otherwise becomes colored and purulent, with secondary bacterial infection.

The time of occurrence of the cough may be useful in determining its origin. Most people with chronic cough complain that it is worse when they lie down at night; this is particularly true of those who have bronchiectasis or a postnasal drip from chronic sinusitis. The patient with chronic bronchitis or bronchiectasis also expectorates when he gets up in the morning. Spasms of coughing due to bronchial asthma or left-sided heart failure frequently occur at night and may wake the patient. A cough occurring in association with, or shortly after, ingestion of food may indicate aspiration into the tracheobronchial tree.

The character and quantity of expectorated material may suggest the diagnosis. The patient with chronic bronchitis expectorates daily in small quantities, usually mucoid material, but with "colds" this may become yellow or green and sometimes slightly blood-streaked. Saccular bronchiectasis gives rise to copious, purulent, and often blood-streaked expectoration every day. The gelatinous and rusty expectoration formerly associated with pneumococcal pneumonia has rarely been seen since the advent of antibiotics, and bacterial pneumonia is now more commonly associated with thick yellow or greenish sputum. A foul or fetid odor indicates infection from fusospirochetal or anaerobic organisms and usually develops in cases of lung abscess. Casts of the bronchial tree indicate inspissated mucus and are seen in bronchitis and bronchial asthma. A few patients with alveolar-cell carcinoma expectorate copious amounts of mucoid or milky secretions; in such cases the very quantity of material establishes the diagnosis.

Although a cough itself may not indicate the underlying disease process, its combination with other symptoms may be highly suggestive. If it occurs suddenly during an acute febrile episode and is associated with hoarseness, viral laryngotracheobronchitis is very likely the cause. When associated with stridor, some intrinsic or extrinsic obstruction to the upper respiratory passages is present. An associated generalized wheeze usually is indicative of acute bronchospasm, although very rarely an endotracheal or mediastinal lesion in the region of the carina may be responsible. A persistent local wheeze during expiration often indicates the presence of an intrinsic bronchogenic lesion, such as carcinoma.

An alarming, although rare, symptom following a spasm of coughing is syncope; the patients usually are of stocky build and smoke and drink heavily. Although commonly attributed to cerebral ischemia from decreased cardiac output due to a sudden rise in intrathoracic pressure, syncope can occur before a decline in peripheral blood pressure and after a single cough.[349] The electroencephalogram shows a pattern similar to that obtained after cerebral concussion, and it was suggested that the loss of consciousness may be caused by a concussion-like effect of rapid pressure increase in the cerebrospinal fluid.[349] In some cases, cough syncope is associated with neoplastic or vascular cerebral lesions.[350]

Frequently, the onset of cough is so insidious that the patient is unaware of the symptom; this is a particularly common finding among heavy smokers, who at first may deny this symptom and then make light of it, fearful that the doctor may suggest their giving up the habit. The association of cigarette smoking and bronchitis is discussed at greater length in the sections on chronic bronchitis and emphysema (see page 982), but it may be well to emphasize here that any change in the character of a cough may indicate bronchogenic malignancy, just as a change in bowel habit may be indicative of carcinoma of the lower bowel.

Hoarseness

As mentioned previously, when this symptom occurs acutely and is associated with symptoms of infection of the upper respiratory tract, it is indicative of viral laryngitis. Patients who from habit or in their occupation talk a lot may regain their normal voice only with difficulty. If the symptom persists for more than a month, the vocal cords should be examined for evidence of an intrinsic neoplasm or granulomatous process or unilateral abductor palsy. The common pulmonary cause of persistent hoarseness is a mediastinal lesion, usually bronchogenic carcinoma involving the recurrent laryngeal nerve. Secondary laryngeal lesions may develop in cases of pulmonary tuberculosis with cavitation.

Shortness of Breath

The symptom of dyspnea or awareness of breathing is due to an increase in the stiffness of the lung, in airway resistance, in exercise ventilation, or, most commonly, to a combination of these.[1] The actual mechanism, whereby dyspnea is signaled, is unknown, but Campbell and Howell[351] formulated an ingenious explanation on the basis of proprioceptive mechanisms in the respiratory muscles and thoracic cage which create an awareness of disproportion between muscular effort and the level of ventilation produced.

This symptom probably includes several sensations. In normal subjects made hyperpneic, the sensation experienced differed from one subject to another but remained the same in a particular individual, whether produced by breathing 7 per cent carbon dioxide, exercise, or the intravenous infusion of vanillic acid diethylamide.[352] The anxious patient "unable to take a deep breath," the patient with emphysema having difficulty in tying his shoelaces, and the athlete who has just run 100 yards in under 9.5 seconds are almost certainly enduring different types of discomfort; nevertheless, all will agree that they are short of breath. Thus, in determining the diagnosis, the physician must obtain not only a thorough description of the sensation perceived but also an account of the circumstances that tend to precipitate this sensation and its association with other symptoms.

A detailed description is most useful in differentiating organic causes of shortness of breath from functional or psychoneurotic dyspnea. The latter variety, which is related to tension or anxiety, is the most common cause of shortness of breath and is said to occur in 10 per cent of patients attending offices of specialists in internal medicine.[353] Frequently it is associated with various other symptoms but can occur independently. Usually it is described as an inability to take a deep breath or to get air "down to the bottom of the lungs," and the patient often spontaneously demonstrates by taking a deep breath. If he does not, it is helpful to ask him to breathe as he does when he is short of breath. He will respond by taking a deep breath, and, as history-taking continues, may subconsciously repeat the sighing respirations from time to time. In dyspnea of organic cause, on the other hand, the sensation is more difficult to describe; the patient may say he is "short-winded" or that he "puffs" and on request will demonstrate hyperpnea, breathing more deeply and perhaps more rapidly than normal.

The circumstances in which this sensation occurs should be elucidated. Patients who are short of breath at rest and not on exercise almost invariably have functional dyspnea; they may say that shortness of breath occurs when they are at home after a busy day, or while they are "sitting around doing nothing." An exception to this rule is the patient with spasmodic asthma, who may be able to indulge in strenuous exercise without shortness of breath in the intervals between periodic attacks of extreme dyspnea. On direct questioning the patient with functional dyspnea may give a history of chronic tension or of episodes of acute nervous tension precipitating his complaint, but just as frequently he denies such an association.

Inability to lie flat because of a feeling of suffocation, or of waking during the night with shortness of breath, strongly suggests the presence of organic disease; since attacks of asthma often occur during the night, this symptom does not necessarily indicate failure of the left side of the heart, but it should arouse suspicion and a careful physical examination should be directed toward exclusion of this. Although the desire for three or four pillows under the head while in bed commonly relates to mitral stenosis or left-sided ventricular failure, many patients with chronic bronchitis and emphysema are more comfortable in this position, particularly when the disease is advanced or when coughing and expectoration are severe.

Shortness of breath only on exertion is strong evidence for organic disease and renders functional dyspnea unlikely. The degree of exertion necessary to provoke it and whether this sensation occurs invariably in the same circumstances should be ascertained. Most patients with established emphysema perceive little difference in the amount of exertion that produces shortness of breath from day to day; significant daily variation, invariably due to changes in the degree of spasm or bronchial secretions, is a diagnostic indication of asthma or an asthmatic form of chronic bronchitis. All varieties of chronic obstructive lung disease may deteriorate suddenly, with increasing dyspnea, in an atmosphere of smog. Some patients do not complain of undue dyspnea during exertion but state that it develops afterwards, while they are at rest. Usually this indicates some form of left-sided heart failure, but in our experience it is due sometimes to a variant of chronic bronchitis or asthma in which bronchospasm or increase in bronchial secretions is precipitated by exercise.

In contrast to the patients with chronic bronchitis and emphysema, who gradually and almost imperceptibly experience more severe shortness of breath with lesser degrees of exertion, the person who has been in good health and in whom this symptom develops suddenly usually has pneumothorax. More rarely, it may represent the initial episode of bronchospasm due to allergic asthma or the first indication of heart disease due to mitral stenosis or acute myocardial infarction. Acute dyspnea may occur also with pneumonia or diffuse bronchiolitis, but in these conditions there are usually premonitory symptoms of fever and cough, with or without infection of the upper respiratory tract, which readily differentiate them. The sudden onset of dyspnea, often with obvious hyperpnea and tachycardia, in an ill patient or a postoperative patient may denote pulmonary embolism.

Of equal importance to the event which precipitates it is the relationship of dyspnea to other symptoms. In bronchitis or emphysema dyspnea which develops during exertion almost invariably is preceded by a long history of cough and expectoration; dyspnea is perceived and gradually increases in severity, occurring with less and less exertion. In angina pectoris, shortness of breath may be so closely linked to "tightness" in the chest that the patients with coronary insufficiency may have difficulty in determining which symptom limits their activity and even may be unable to differentiate one sensation from the other. In such patients this combination of symptoms usually is associated with exertion and characteristically requires immediate complete cessation of activity — in contrast to dyspnea during exertion by patients with emphysema, which may allow continuance at a slower pace. Patients with heart disease who cannot increase their cardiac output to meet the tissues' demand for extra oxygen during exercise may experience not only shortness of breath but also weakness. Dyspnea of functional or psychoneurotic origin may be associated with a great variety of symptoms. The dyspnea may be confused with weakness and fatigue, and many of these patients describe these sensations as if they were identical; some symptoms may relate to resultant hyperventilation, and other probably are directly due to tension or anxiety. Normal subjects rendered hypocapneic and alkalotic through hyperventilation experienced a feeling of unreality and lightheadedness, as well as some alteration in awareness;[354] they also noted tingling and numbness of the hands, feet, and circumoral area, sensations presumably due to hypocapnea, but were not bothered by precordial discomfort or sweating, symptoms not uncommonly described by chronically anxious patients who complain of shortness of breath and are considered to have hyperventilation syndrome. Shortness of breath due to bronchospasm may be difficult to diagnose when patients are seen in the interval between episodes with no signs of the disease; a diagnosis of bronchial asthma is suggested by a history of coughing, and particularly wheezing, during or after episodes of dyspnea, since these symptoms are not associated with functional disorders.

Chest Pain

PLEURAL PAIN. Although disease involving the thoracic cage and its contents can give rise to multifarious pains, disease of the lung itself may progress to an advanced stage and result in death without producing even minor chest pain: this is because the lung tissue and visceral pleura lack a sensory apparatus to detect pain. The parietal pleura, on the other hand, is richly supplied with sensory nerves which come from the intercostal nerves and the nerves to the diaphragm. The nerve endings are stimulated by inflammation and stretching of the membrane, and not, as was thought in the past, by the friction of visceral pleura against parietal pleura. Pleural pain may vary in degree, from lancinating discomfort during slight inspiratory effort to a less severe, but still sharp, pain that may "catch" the patient at the end of a maximal inspiration. Pleural pain often disappears or is reduced to a dull ache during expiration or breath-holding. Pressure over the intercostal muscles in the area of pain may not elicit discomfort, and when it does, the pain is mild in comparison with the subjective sensation. This is in contrast to chest-wall pain, which is associated with a palpable zone of extreme tenderness, often localized to a very small area of muscle. Except when it involves the diaphragm, the diseased area of pleura, which often is secondary to a pulmonary parenchymal lesion, typically underlies the area where pain is perceived. The central part of the diaphragm is innervated by the phrenic nerve, and the sensory afferent fibers enter the cervical cord mainly in the third and fourth cervical posterior nerve roots; hence, irritation of the central portion of the diaphragmatic pleura is referred to the neck and the upper part of the shoulder. The outer parts of the diaphragmatic pleura are supplied by lower intercostal nerves, which enter the thoracic cord in the seventh to twelfth dorsal posterior nerve roots; irritation of this portion of the pleura causes referral of pain to the lower thorax, the lumbar area, and the upper abdominal region. Pleural pain usually signifies inflammatory or malignant disease but also may accompany pneumothorax. The mechanism by which the parietal pleura is irritated in pneumothorax is not known; the pain may be made worse by deep inspiration, may have an aching quality, or may be felt simply as a tightness in the chest.

MEDIASTINAL PAIN. In contrast to pleural pain, which is fairly characteristic and originates in the parietal pleura, pain from the mediastinal area may vary in quality and is due to a variety of diseases. The trachea, esophagus, pericardium, aorta, thymus gland, and many lymph nodes are situated in the mediastinum, and disease involving any of these organs or tissues may cause pain in that region; it should be borne in mind that inflammation or neoplastic infiltration of the mediastinal compartment itself may cause discomfort locally. The quality, intensity, and radiation of the pain, and the factors that precipitate it, are of importance in determining from which organ or tissue the sensation arises. It may be felt in the retrosternal or precordial area and may radiate to the neck or arms or through to the back. The most common retrosternal pain is that due to myocardial ischemia; this is described as "squeezing," "pressing," or "choking," and may extend to the neck or down the left arm or both arms; the onset is abrupt and the pain is associated with circulatory collapse. The severe pain due to myocardial infarction may be closely simulated in other entities; these include massive pulmonary embolism, in which the mechanism of the pain is not completely understood but is thought to result from acute pulmonary hypertension. A "squeezing" or "pressing" pain identical to that of angina pectoris may be experienced by patients with severe chronic pulmonary hypertension due to mitral stenosis or multiple small pulmonary emboli. Acute pericarditis may cause pain confusingly similar to that of myocardial disease; the pain often has a precordial distribution and may be made worse by breathing or swallowing. Dissecting aneurysm of the aorta also may give rise to similar pain and should be suspected when pain is severe from the outset, instead of gradually increasing, and when it radiates to the back and down the abdomen into the lower limbs. A local aneurysm of the aorta may cause "boring" retrosternal or back pain when it erodes sternum, ribs, or vertebrae. Esophageal disease may give rise to "burning" pain and usually is clearly associated with the ingestion of food. Those who have regurgitation of acid gastric juice complain that the pain is worse when they recline and may be relieved when they stand. A common retrosternal sensation, which presumably originates in sensory nerve endings of the tracheal mucosa, is the painful rawness under the sternum experienced by patients with infection of the upper respiratory tract and dry, hacking cough.

CHEST-WALL PAIN. Pain originating in, or referred to, the chest wall, not due to parietal pleural irritation, is a common complaint. When this pain appears to originate in intercostal muscle fibers there may be a history of trauma which produced strain or even tearing, but more often there is no obvious precipitating cause and the condition is labeled as myositis or fibrositis. In our experience, local pain and tenderness in chest muscle frequently is associated with infection of the upper respiratory tract, with residual dry cough, often paroxysmal. In such cases tenderness may be elicited by pressure over the painful area, usually in the anterolateral lower intercostal muscles. This pain can be differentiated from true "pleural pain," since it increases little or not at all during deep inspiration but may be aggravated by coughing or trunk movement, and usually does not disappear between paroxysms of coughing. Muscle pain unassociated with the dry cough of an upper respiratory infection or with direct trauma to the intercostal muscles requires careful investigation to exclude other conditions that may cause referral of pain.

Another chest-wall pain is that due to pressure or inflammation irritating the posterior nerve root. This is known as radicular pain; it follows the specific intercostal nerve distribution and radiates around the chest from behind or, in some cases, is localized to one area. Usually it is described as dull and aching and is made worse by movement, particularly coughing. It may be due to a protruded intervertebral disc, rheumatoid spondylitis, malignant disease involving the vertebrae, or inflammatory or malignant disease within the spinal canal. A variety of intercostal nerve-root pain whose origin may be difficult to identify in the early stages, before the appearance of the typical rash, is that due to herpes zoster. The pain usually is described as "burning" and frequently is felt over a wide area unilaterally along the pathway of one or more intercostal nerves.

Pain confined to vertebral and paravertebral areas may originate in inflammatory or neoplastic disease of the vertebrae, and percussion over the vertebral spines may elicit local tenderness due to disease in the underlying vertebral body. An unusual form of pain, usually in bone, is that experienced by patients with Hodgkin's disease or other neoplasms; this lasts for an hour or more after the ingestion of even small amounts of alcohol.[355]

Pain in the chest wall may be due to disease of the ribs. In addition to those of known traumatic origin, rib fractures may result from prolonged episodes of severe coughing. The costochondral junctions of the ribs may be the site of perichondritis which often is associated with tenderness and swelling (Tietze's syndrome); usually the pain is persistent and described as "gnawing" or "aching." The ribs may be involved in a metastatic process or multiple myeloma and rarely by a primary tumor, such as fibrosarcoma; the pain is generally appreciated before the mass develops, at first poorly localized but later as a dull, boring ache over the area of invasion.

"PRECORDIAL CATCH." A benign transitory pain of undetermined origin has been described under the title "precordial catch."[356] Probably this syndrome of anterior chest pain is familiar to most practicing physicians, because of personal experience of the sensation.[357] It is a severe, sharp pain, occurring at rest or during mild activity, located over the left side of the chest, usually at the cardiac apex, and lasting from 30 seconds to five minutes. It comes on suddenly during inspiration and the invariable reaction is a brief suspension of respiration; then breathing is maintained at a shallow level while the pain disappears gradually. Its onset is often associated with poor posture, improvement in which sometimes relieves the pain. The mechanism is unknown, the condition is very common, and its importance lies solely in the fact that it must be differentiated from other chest pain of more serious consequence.

Hemoptysis

This is often a presenting complaint in an otherwise asymptomatic patient: the patient is alarmed and regards this finding as indicative of serious disease. The physician should do likewise and should never reassure the patient and send him on his way, since every patient who complains of an initial episode of hemoptysis should have at least a chest roentgenogram and many require more extensive investigation.

The source of bleeding may be from the upper respiratory tract. The patient may have a nosebleed, with some blood trickling into the pharynx and causing him to cough and expectorate. The pharynx itself may bleed because of its involvement in an ulcerative process. Bleeding from these sites usually can be distinguished from hemoptysis, originating in the lower respiratory tract, by clinical examination. When there is doubt as to the source of bleeding the patient should be assumed to have lung disease and should be investigated accordingly. Patients with a history of acute or chronic bronchitis sometimes expectorate blood-streaked sputum, but it must not be forgotten that even a trace of blood in the sputum may be the first indication of the presence of bronchogenic carcinoma. Bleeding is a common complaint of patients with bronchial adenoma. In bronchiectasis, bloody expectoration may be the only symptom; usually it is abundant and originates in granulation tissue. Less frequent causes of bleeding from the bronchial tree are the erosion of broncholiths through the wall of the bronchus and dilatation of bronchial veins in association with mitral stenosis. Rarely, a dramatic, exsanguinating hemoptysis results from rupture of an aortic aneurysm into a bronchus.

Bleeding from the lung itself may be due to a local lesion, including pulmonary infarction, pneumonia, lung abscesses and cysts, and various granulomata of the lung, including tuberculosis, mycotic infections, and Wegener's granuloma. Although systemic disorders with a bleeding tendency rarely, if ever, are manifested by isolated bleeding from the lower respiratory tract, they may give rise to severe hemoptysis accompanied by bleeding into other viscera and the skin. The possibility of pulmonary or bronchial lesions as a source of bleeding should be investigated when patients on anticoagulant therapy cough up blood. A few patients who complain of blood "welling up" in the throat have hematemesis from esophageal varices, and this possibility should not be overlooked, particularly when bleeding is brisk and the blood is dark.

Although the amount of hemoptysis is of little value in establishing the diagnosis, the character of the bloody sputum may suggest the underlying disease process. As already mentioned, simple streaking of mucoid material can occur in bronchitis, but may denote a more serious condition, such as tuberculosis or bronchogenic carcinoma. When the sputum is frankly bloody and does not contain mucoid or purulent material it is more likely due to pulmonary infarction than to pneumonia, particularly if it persists unchanged for several days. Bloody material mixed with pus should suggest pneumonia or lung abscess in acute illness, and bronchiectasis in chronic disease. When the blood is diluted, giving it a pink and sometimes frothy appearance, pulmonary edema from left-sided heart failure should be suspected.

Hemoptysis is referred to throughout this book in relation to the various conditions with which it is associated, and statistical analyses of the frequent causes are considered here. Since there is disagreement as to exactly what this symptom entails, reported series of patients exhibiting blood in the sputum reflect the authors' concepts of hemoptysis. If patients with chronic bronchitis with blood-streaked sputum are included, bronchitis and bronchiectasis are the most common causes when a specific diagnosis can be made;[358-360] this applies in western countries, in which a specific diagnosis is made in approximately 50 per cent of patients with hemoptysis. Obviously, the major causes of hemoptysis depend to a great extent on the degree of control of pulmonary tuberculosis and, in certain areas, of the lung fluke *Paragonimus westermani*. In Western Europe and North America, bronchogenic carcinoma is said to be responsible for hemoptysis in 5 to 10 per cent of cases.[358-360] Bronchiectasis associated with inactive tuberculosis of the upper lobes was reported to be more common than active tuberculosis as a cause for hemoptysis,[359] and this is our experience. The percentage of patients with normal roentgenograms in whom no definite diagnosis can be made varies from 15 per cent[361] to 58 per cent.[359] The elucidation of hemoptysis in association with a normal chest roentgenogram is discussed in greater detail on page 757; in summary, we consider that such patients require not only a thorough initial investigation but also, if such an investigation proves unrewarding, close follow-up with repeated chest roentgenograms.

PAST ILLNESSES AND PERSONAL HISTORY

Establishment of the correct diagnosis may depend upon a knowledge of the patient's past medical history or his personal habits: The respiratory symptoms or abnormal chest roentgenogram may simply represent previous active lung disease which has left its imprint on the pulmonary parenchyma, or a lung lesion may be a belated metastasis from a primary malignancy elsewhere which was removed many years earlier. A patient's memory should be jogged for recall of dates and places of previous chest roentgenograms, and these should be obtained for comparison with the present one. Patients should be questioned about medication: Many acute and chronic bacterial and mycotic infections occur in patients on long-term antibiotic and corticosteroid therapy, and lipoid pneumonia may follow the use of nose drops or laxatives containing mineral oil. Respiratory failure may be wholly or partly attributable to recent sedation. The number of cigarettes a patient smokes each day may be of significance in suspected cases of bronchogenic carcinoma or bronchitis and emphysema. As with corticosteroid therapy, poor diet and a heavy consumption of alcohol may play a major part in lowering resistance to infection; this statement is supported by clinical evidence, and recent experimental work[362] indicates that all three of these factors, as well as hypoxia, appear to inhibit clearing of bacteria from the normally sterile lower respiratory tract. The personal history is not complete without enquiry about contact with animals, domestic and wild. This pertains not only to the patient with allergies, whose bronchospasm may be due to his household pet, but also, for example, to the patient with an acute pneumonic lesion who may have contracted ornithosis from a sick bird in his home, tularemia from skinning a wild rabbit, or Q-fever from inhalation of dust contaminated by sheep or cattle.

Family History

In pulmonary disease, the importance of this aspect lies particularly in the discovery of a potential source of infection. Tuberculosis remains the most serious of the pulmonary diseases that spread in the home, but many acute virus infections may be disseminated throughout a household and such an occurrence recently may be significant in the investigation of patients with acute pneumonitis.

Some pulmonary diseases have a familial incidence, presumably on a genetic basis. They include some cases of pulmonary emphysema,[363, 365, 366] a hereditary form of Hamman-Rich syndrome (familial fibrocystic pulmonary dysplasia), hereditary telangiectasia, mucoviscidosis, Kartagener's syndrome, pulmonary myomatosis, and alveolar microlithiasis. These diseases are rare and may be recognized only when a familial incidence is revealed. All of these conditions are considered in greater detail in other chapters.

Occupational and Residential History

A complete history of occupation from the time of first employment is essential in patients whose chest roentgenograms show the pattern of diffuse pulmonary disease. Although silicosis remains the most common of the pneumoconioses, an ever-growing list of pulmonary diseases due to occupational exposure must be kept in mind; these diseases are considered in Chapter 12 and were reviewed recently.[367, 368] In addition to the pneumoconioses that cause diffuse granulomatous and fibrotic parenchymal disease, exposure to various chemical fumes, such as high concentrations of sulphur dioxide, may result in severe bronchial damage, and fumes and dust represent a hazard in many occupations which may elicit severe, although presumably reversible, bronchitis and bronchospasm. Farmers appear to be particularly liable to occupational lung disease; exposure to mouldy hay may cause severe bronchospasm and result in diffuse pulmonary granulomata, a disease known as "farmer's lung." Droppings from wild[369, 370] and domestic birds provide a favorable nitrogenous substrate for the growth of fungi, particularly *Histoplasma capsulatum*, to which workers on poultry farms may be heavily exposed. High concentrations of the nitrogen dioxide in fresh silage may cause severe bronchiolitis, pulmonary edema, and bronchiolitis fibrosa obliterans; this condition is known as "silo-filler's disease." Residence in an area of heavy atmospheric pollution may lead to the development of lung disease. Pollution, mainly from industry, may not only have a nonspecific irritating effect on patients with chronic bronchitis or chronic obstructive disease, but also may contain more specific hazards, such as asbestos and beryllium, which are known to cause granuloma and fibrosis, and even mesothelioma in patients who live in the vicinity of mines and plants where these substances are used.

A history of residence in, and even of travel through, an area where coccidioidomycosis or histoplasmosis is endemic may be pertinent, and parasitic diseases should be suspected in emigrants from areas in which they are endemic. Patients who have resided recently in India and who have bronchospasm, severe leukocytosis, and eosinophilia very likely have tropical eosinophilia, caused by a filarial parasite. A mass pulmonary lesion in a young farmer from Greece or Italy may well be a hydatid cyst. Chronic cor pulmonale in an Egyptian suggests the possibility of schistosomiasis. The patient from Central China who has chronic hemoptysis may have paragonimiasis, and not tuberculosis.

System Enquiry

Since lung involvement may be only one manifestation of a general disease process, enquiry concerning all body systems may prove revealing. In some instances, the mere fact that certain organs or tissues are involved in combination with the lung may suggest the diagnosis; for instance, the patient with diffuse lung disease who has Raynaud's phenomenon and difficulty in swallowing almost certainly has scleroderma, and multiple lung cavities in association

with severe nasal trouble and hematuria undoubtedly represent Wegener's disease. System enquiry may reveal symptoms indicating a primary site for multiple discrete coin lesions in the lung which had been suspected of being metastatic deposits. Bronchogenic oat-cell carcinoma may be associated with abnormality in almost any organ or tissue in the body (*see* Chapter 8), and symptoms of the extrapulmonary manifestations of this unusual tumor can be elicited by system enquiry. Similarly, a diagnosis of chronic pulmonary insufficiency and respiratory failure may be made after eliciting a history of headache, confusion, tremor, twitching or somnolence,[371, 372] and can be confirmed by determination of the arterial-blood P_{CO_2}.

PHYSICAL EXAMINATION

The diagnosis of chest disease requires competence in examination of the chest. The physician who does not become proficient in this art and who makes his judgment of underlying pathology purely on the basis of roentgenographic findings inevitably is guilty of diagnostic errors and sloppy management. The chest roentgenogram has not replaced the physician's eyes, ears, and hands; rather, it represents an additional, valuable diagnostic method which is complementary to the technique of physical examination, providing information which the latter cannot give.

The present-day student is fortunate in having roentgenography and pulmonary function tests as indispensable aids in perfecting his technique in physical examination. Only when he has become skilled in this method can he judge how thorough the examination of any specific patient should be. Circumstances will arise in which he will have to depend upon his senses in making decisions concerning therapy which may fundamentally affect the life of the patient; this may occur in the home, where roentgenography is unavailable, or even in the hospital when the patient is too sick to be moved or circumstances dictate an immediate decision such as the removal of air in the case of tension pneumothorax.

Physical signs are judged to be abnormal on the basis of deviation from norms determined through the examination of many patients with healthy lungs, and the quality of the changes indicates the underlying pathologic process. Roentgenology also attempts to define pathology by a variation from accepted normal standards, through interpretation of patterns of decreased or increased density. The chest roentgenogram may be interpreted as being normal when there is serious and advanced pulmonary disease detectable only by physical examination; conversely, often gross abnormality is revealed by roentgenography when physical findings are normal.

METHOD OF EXAMINATION AND SIGNIFICANT CHEST SIGNS

The front of the thorax is best examined with the patient supine, and the back when he is sitting or standing; patients who are too weak to sit upright unaided should be supported by someone standing at the foot of the bed and holding their hands. When this is impossible, because of extreme weakness or serious illness, the patient should lie on his right side and then roll over on to his left side, the upper-most hemithorax being examined in turn. It is important to keep in mind always that the examination of the chest is a comparative exercise, any single region of one side being compared with the similar area of the other side; this rule applies equally for inspection, palpation, percussion, and auscultation.

Inspection

Inspection of the patient is well under way by the time the physical examination has begun. Throughout history-taking the physician has had ample opportunity to note the character of cough, the presence or absence of hyperpnea, sighing respirations, or grimaces of pain accompanying cough or respiration. In the examining room the thoracic cage is inspected for evidence of deformity, and the skin for its color and evidence of collateral venous circulation. Chest movement is observed and the rate of respiration is noted. Estimating the depth of respiration is a notoriously difficult clinical judgment, particularly in patients who have predominantly diaphragmatic breathing. A local lag during inspiration may not be obvious during quiet breathing, and for this reason the patient should be asked to take a deep breath and the movement of the chest cage on the two sides should be compared.

A lag during inspiration, or an area of diminished movement seen or felt and involving all or part of a hemithorax, may be the only physical sign indicating disease of the lung or pleura. It indicates loss of elasticity of the underlying tissues, or compensatory spasm of intercostal and diaphragmatic musculature in the vicinity, to avoid pain on movement. This sign is present in acute disease such as atelectasis, pneumonia, or pleurisy; or it may indicate a longstanding chronic or inactive fibrotic process of the lung or pleura, and then is often associated with scoliosis of the dorsal spine, with the concavity to the diseased side. When the loss of volume is considerable, whether due to an acute or chronic lesion, there may be a shift of the mediastinum; this is detectable as displacement of the apical cardiac impulse and the trachea toward the involved side. With fibrosis, and particularly with atelectasis, the lower intercostal spaces may be abnormally sucked in during inspiration.

Palpation

A suspected lag detected on inspection of the chest may be confirmed when a hand is placed on each hemithorax while the patient breathes deeply. The apical cardiac impulse and the trachea should be palpated, since any shift from normal position is indicative of loss of volume or a relative increase in volume of one hemithorax in comparison with the other. The left parasternal region should be palpated to determine whether a heave is present, denoting right ventricular hypertrophy. The intercostal spaces and ribs should be palpated in order to find tumor masses and in an attempt to elicit tenderness to pressure. The axillae and the cervical region should be carefully explored to detect lymph nodes.

Percussion

The chest wall is then percussed, once again comparing identical areas on the two sides. Since the degree of resonance is influenced by the thickness of the chest wall and the volume of lung underlying the percussion finger, "normal" percussion differs not only from patient to patient but also from area to area in the same patient. The percussion note in disease and in health may vary from tympanitic (over the stomach gas bubble) to flat (over the liver) sounds which are readily detectable by even the inexperienced; between these extremes are degrees of hyperresonance and dullness whose significance can be evaluated only with experience. The percussion note is produced by vibration of the percussed finger and sympathetic vibrations of the chest wall and underlying tissues and organs. The quality of the note is composed of its loudness, pitch, and timbre. The amplitude of vibrations (loudness) is much less over solid organs, such as the heart and liver, than over healthy lung, which, because of its elasticity, vibrates more. The loudness also depends upon the force of the stroke and the thickness of the chest wall. An accumulation of fluid between the percussed finger and the underlying lung reduces the intensity or loudness. Resonance elicited by percussion over healthy aerated lung is distinguishable from the dull note obtained over a solid organ by the rapidity of vibrations (pitch) and by the presence of overtones superimposed on the basic note (timbre); the resonant note has a lower pitch and more overtones. The difference between the normal, resonant note and the tympanitic note—such as is heard on percussion over gas in the stomach—is due largely to difference in timbre. In the presence of lung disease, the percussion note varies from the impaired resonance heard over an area of pneumonia which is partially consolidated, to the dullness over a completely consolidated or collapsed segment or lobe, and the extreme dullness or flatness which indicates a large accumulation of pleural fluid. At the other end of the scale, the note is hyperresonant in cases of emphysema and pneumothorax and sometimes is tympanitic over large superficial cavities or pneumothorax. An unusual form, known as "skodaic resonance," is heard sometimes over a partly compressed upper lung region when the lower portion is collapsed by pleural effusion; the note has a "boxy" quality and the mechanism of its production is unknown.

Before turning from percussion to a consideration of auscultatory findings it should be stressed that the lung tissue assessed by the percussing finger is only the superficial 5 cm: no matter how much force is used in this method of examination, the central portion of the lung remains "silent." Also, the differences in note are perceived not only by the ears but also by the sense of touch; over solid tissue the examining fingers appreciate a difference in vibration, as well as a sensation of resistance which can be distinguished from the sense of elasticity felt over air-containing areas.

Auscultation

Auscultation of the lungs is best performed with a stethoscope with small internal volume and small endpiece-skin contact.[110] The quality and intensity of the breath sounds, as well as the presence or absence of adventitious noises, are ascertained by listening while the patient breathes quietly and then deeply, with the bell or diaphragm held firmly against his chest. The quality of breath sounds varies from region to region, even in normal subjects, depending upon the proximity of larger bronchi to the chest wall. In the axillae or at the lung bases a vesicular sound is heard during inspiration, and often early in expiration, which has been likened to the rustle of wind in the trees. The sound of air flow has a somewhat different quality over the trachea and upper retrosternal area; the pitch is higher, and expiration is clearly audible and lasts longer than the inspiratory phase. Between the scapulae and anteriorly under the clavicles, particularly on the right side, the breath sounds assume characteristics of both vesicular and bronchial air flow and are described as bronchovesicular.

The intensity of "air entry" of breath sounds should be appraised. Again, this depends upon the thickness of the chest wall and the region of the lung examined, as well as upon the depth of respiration.

Finally, and this applies particularly when other findings indicate consolidation of the lung, vocal resonance should be determined. The patient is asked to whisper the words "ninety-nine," which normally results in a soft, barely audible, somewhat confused murmur reaching the ears through the stethoscope, but which is heard clearly when the lung is consolidated and the bronchus patent.

The mechanism of production of breath sounds is not completely known. It is thought that the original sound comes from the passage of air to and fro through the narrowed aperture of the glottis. A high-pitched inspiratory noise is heard, followed by a pause and then by the higher-pitched, louder and longer expiration. This sound, which is heard very well over the trachea, is modified slightly in the bronchial tubes, in which expiration becomes even more high-pitched. However, at the periphery of the lung the character of the sound is radically changed: inspiration is louder than expiration, which is short and may not even be heard. There is no pause between inspiration and expiration, and the sound has a soft rustling quality; it is known as "vesicular breathing." This alteration in the original "glottic" noise is believed to be due to a dampening effect of the spongy lung tissue and also to the entry of air from thousands of narrow terminal bronchioles into acinar units. Coope[373] compared the added effect of all these tiny murmurs to "the murmuring of innumerable bees" when a single bee at a distance may not be heard.

Many factors may contribute to reduction or complete abolition of vesicular breathing. It may be difficult to hear breath sounds during shallow breathing due to weakness or neuromuscular disease. Diminished air entry, due to complete obstruction of a lobar or segmental bronchus or reduction in compliance resultant upon edema or fibrosis of interstitial tissue, respectively, may eliminate or diminish the vesicular murmur. Complete destruction of acinar units, as in chronic obstructive emphysema, may result in very faint air entry. The transmission of breath sounds may be interrupted by an excess of subcutaneous fat, or may be completely suppressed by fluid or air in the pleural cavity.

The quality of breath sounds changes from vesicular to bronchovesicular or bronchial when underlying parenchyma partly or completely loses its air content; this occurs in pneumonia and in "nonobstructive" atelectasis. Consolidated or airless lung tissue is an excellent conductor of high-pitched, prolonged expiratory sounds which emanate from adjacent bronchi. Occasionally, when it occurs in consolidated lung, a cavity serves as a resonating chamber, and breathing assumes a hollow, reverberating, low-pitched quality known as "cavernous." Another modification of the noise of bronchial air flow is "amphoric" breathing, which results from the presence of a tense pneumothorax over a collapsed lung, usually with an open bronchopleural fistula; this sound is high-pitched and metallic in quality.

The voice sounds may assist in indicating pathologic changes. Normally, a soft, confused, barely audible sound is heard over lung distant from large bronchi. In the presence of consolidation or nonobstructive atelectasis, voice sounds become more distinct and produce a noise known as "bronchophony"; in many cases of consolidation the words are distinctly audible over the involved area when the patient whispers "ninety-nine"; this is known as "whispering pectoriloquy" and is a useful sign to confirm suspected pneumonic consolidation. In some cases, when large accumulations of fluid compress the lower portion of the lung the voice sounds have a nasal quality over the upper lung (analogous to skodaic resonance on percussion).

Unfortunately, the terminology of adventitious sounds is not standard and it almost appears that every doctor has his own classification. The student is further confused by the imaginative physician who introduces subjective and fanciful terms which have no benefit in teaching the art of physical examination. The word "râle" is derived from "death-rattle," a coarse, discontinuous, bubbling sound which emanates from the trachea and large bronchi of dying patients who are too weak to cough. Laennec[374] considered the words "rale" and "rhonchus" to be synonymous; the lack of distinction has resulted in considerable confusion since the Latin word "rhonchus" translates, in English to "wheeze," a descriptive term more appropriate to the continuous noise caused by partial obstruction of bronchial tubes. Subsequent writers attempted to resolve this confusion by subdividing the adventitious sounds of air passing in and out of the bronchi and alveoli into rhonchi (continuous noises) and crepitations (discontinuous noises).[679] This has not met with general acceptance, and most physicians reserve the term crepitations for the very fine, discontinuous noises believed to represent the separation of sticky, moist surfaces as air enters the acinar unit or by the actual penetration of air into alveolar spaces which contain edema or exudate. Particularly confusing is the term "dry rales," which may be used synonymously with rhonchi (continuous noises), in contradistinction to "moist rales" (discontinuous noises). We use a terminology which is descriptive and simple and which probably is the most widely accepted by present-day physicians (see Table 3–1).

Table 3–1. *A Classification of Adventitious Sounds Which Has the Virtues of Being Simple and Most Widely Used*

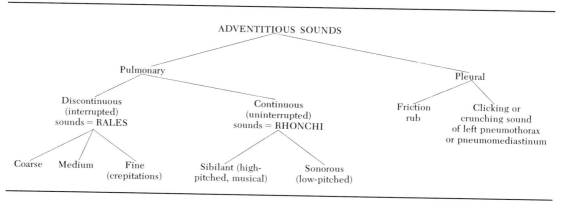

Adventitious sounds are divided into those having their origin in the bronchopulmonary tree and those indicating disease of the pleura. *Rales* are discontinuous noises, which may be fine (usually at the end of inspiration, as air enters the acinar unit), medium (often during both inspiration and expiration, as air flows by an excess of fluid in the smaller bronchi), and coarse (the low-pitched, bubbling sounds which result from the accumulation of secretions in larger bronchi and the trachea). Rales are present more often during inspiration than expiration, because then the flow of air is faster. They may be elicited during a rapid, deep breath, or—and this is particularly applicable to the fine variety—a deep breath after a maximal expiration ended by a cough (posttussive rales). Fine rales are sometimes detected at the end of a deep inspiration, and usually at the lung bases, even in normal subjects; they are thought to represent the opening of atelectatic acinar units after shallow breathing, a consequence of a lack of deep inspirations to replenish the alveolar surface-active substance. Fine rales, however, usually are persistent and multiple and often occur in showers; they are indicative of pulmonary edema or the alveolar exudate of pneumonia. They may be modified in the proximity of a cavity or pneumothorax, which act as resonating chambers and alter the timbre. They have a high-pitched superficial quality in cases of diffuse pulmonary infiltration with general loss of lung volume; to our knowledge, no one has ventured an explanation for the occurrence of rales in these latter patients, many of whom do not have a productive cough. These rales do not disappear on coughing; they may represent the passage of air into innumerable atelectatic units, the resulting sound being intensified by adjacent airless pulmonary parenchyma. Medium and coarse rales are heard as edema fluid or exudate moves up the bronchial tree and may be audible in patients with bronchopneumonia, bronchiectasis, or chronic granulomatous diseases such as tuberculosis or the mycoses.

Other adventitious sounds which originate in the bronchopulmonary tree are the high-pitched (sibilant) and low-pitched (sonorous) continuous noises which should be called *rhonchi*. These indicate partial obstruction by thick mucus in the bronchial lumen, edema, spasm, or a local lesion of the bronchial wall. They are louder during expiration, when the bronchial passages are narrower, but may be heard in both the inspiratory and expiratory phases in many patients. A wheeze is the sound of a rhonchus heard at a distance without the aid of a stethoscope, or which the patient himself may detect. Local wheezing, appreciated as such by the patient, or a local rhonchus, heard with the stethoscope, which does not disappear with coughing, may indicate organic obstruction by neoplasm. The term "wheezing respirations" is used sometimes to denote the persistent inspiratory and expiratory rhonchi, generally of the musical, sibilant variety, which are heard all over the chest during bronchospasm. Rhonchi not appreciated during quiet breathing may become audible when the rate of air flow is increased during fast, deep breathing or when the bronchial tubes are narrowed during maximal expiration.

The other group of adventitious sounds

represents manifestations of pleural disease, in which inflammation of the pleura roughens these membranes and covers them with sticky, fibrinous exudate. During both inspiration and expiration, and particularly in areas in which excursion of the thoracic cage is greatest, a rubbing, rasping, or leathery sound may be heard as the visceral lining moves against the parietal lining. This noise usually is associated with pain. Its disappearance during breath-holding, but not with coughing, renders it unlike rhonchi due to partial obstruction by mucus, which can closely resemble pleural friction rub. This sound indicates primary pleural disease due to trauma, neoplasm, or inflammation or that secondary to an underlying pulmonary neoplasm, infarction, or pneumonia and disappears when fluid forms and separates the two membranes.

Several sounds relate to the presence of air or air and fluid in the pleural cavity. Most of these, such as the Hippocratic succussion splash and the bell sound described by Hilton Fagge,[375] which is produced by tapping one coin against another placed on the chest wall, are of historic rather than diagnostic interest. More recently Hamman[376] described a crunching or clicking sound over the lower retrosternal area, synchronous with the heart beat, which he thought was pathognomonic of air in the mediastinum. Scadding and Wood[377] commented that this sound is often audible with the stethoscope and noticed by the patient only when he is lying on his left side, and they found it more commonly associated with a small left pneumothorax, an opinion held by most now. In a recent report of 24 patients in whom this sound was heard, 22 had left-sided pneumothorax and only two had pneumomediastinum.[378] This sign is of diagnostic importance in that it may indicate the presence of small, roentgenologically undetectable collections of air in the mediastinum. It was heard in some patients with left-sided pneumothorax whose standard posteroanterior chest roentgenogram in full inspiration was reported as normal but whose roentgenogram during expiration showed air in the pleural cavity.[378]

EXTRATHORACIC MANIFESTATIONS OF PULMONARY DISEASE

A complete physical examination is essential in every case of lung disease. In some patients the diagnosis may be suggested by the discovery of a mass or an enlarged abdominal organ. The skin and endocrine and central nervous systems are those most commonly involved in association with lung disease. Many pulmonary lesions have cutaneous manifestations; this subject was reviewed by Beerman and Kirshbaum[379] and is discussed in detail in relation to differential diagnosis in other chapters in this book. Endocrinopathies and many other extrapulmonary manifestations have been linked to oat-cell carcinoma of the lung and are considered on page 757. The neurologic symptoms of respiratory failure have been referred to; the signs are of equal importance[380] and are discussed on page 1017 in reference to advanced emphysema. Peripheral neuropathies are seen occasionally in association with bronchogenic carcinoma and are discussed more fully in the section relating to this disease (*see* page 759). Recent studies of electromyograms and nerve biopsies suggest that the muscular wasting seen in some cases of chronic obstructive lung disease may be due to abnormal metabolism of Schwann cells.[738] The present section is concerned with clubbing and cyanosis: one or both of these signs are found in many, and must be sought in all, cases of pulmonary or pleural disease.

Clubbing and Hypertrophic Pulmonary Osteoarthropathy

These two signs are not synonymous, since clubbing frequently is found in the absence of the full-blown picture of osteoarthropathy, and "pulmonary osteoarthropathy" occasionally occurs without clubbing. Confusion of simple clubbing with pulmonary osteoarthropathy probably is responsible for the great variation in the reported incidence of the two conditions in association with bronchogenic carcinoma, which varies from 2 per cent to 48 per cent. The diagnosis of pulmonary osteoarthropathy requires joint symptoms, namely, arthralgia with swelling and stiffness affecting mainly the fingers, wrists, ankles, and knees, or deep-seated bone pain. The roentgenogram usually shows subperiosteal new bone formation in the long bones of the lower limbs, and some consider this finding a prerequisite for the diagnosis.[381] Except in the very rare case of the familial idiopathic form, which may present a picture identical to that of pulmonary osteoarthropathy, the presence of clubbing or osteoarthropathy is highly significant of visceral disease, particularly intrathoracic. Malignant chest tumors account for 90 per cent of typical pulmonary osteoarthropathy; the majority of these are primary[382] but a few are metastatic.[383] This picture of periostitis is not seen in tuberculosis: Of 309 patients admitted consecutively to a tuberculosis sanatorium, none of the three patients with pulmonary osteoarthropathy had pulmonary tuberculosis of any grade; two had cancer and one a pyogenic abscess.[384] The pathogenetic mechanism of this unusual picture is not fully understood, but it is agreed that the earliest anatomic change in the limbs is an overgrowth of highly vascular connective tissue, followed by subperiosteal new bone formation.[385] This appears to be secondary to a reflex mechanism in which the vagus nerve serves as the afferent pathway; an efferent autonomic pathway has not been described. The stimulus presumably comes directly from abnormal intrathoracic "masses"[386] or indirectly from ischemia in tissue distal to areas containing masses.[387] Procedures, such as the removal of a primary lung lesion, exploratory thoracotomy, or unilateral vagotomy, are followed by a prompt reduction in the increased rate of blood flow, then by resolution of soft-tissue overgrowth, and some weeks later by regression of the bony changes, although the clubbing itself may not disappear completely.[788] Cross-circulation experiments in dogs did not significantly affect the blood flow in the limbs of either dog, and this, together with the fact that some of these patients have normal arterial oxygen saturation,[385] tends to exclude a "hormonal" mechanism such as has been postulated by Turner-Warwick.[68] The finding of increased estrogen excretion in patients with pulmonary osteoarthropathy due to various causes[388] is of interest but does not necessarily indicate an etiologic role. The primary, often familial, idiopathic form, which is known as pachydermoperiostosis, presumably is on the same basis of increased blood flow, but it is not known whether the primary form also is attributable to an autonomic reflex.[386]

Cyanosis

In many patients with lung disease the skin and mucous membranes are blue or bluish-gray; this is most obvious in the nail beds or buccal mucosa and usually represents severe hypoxemia of arterial blood, due to ventilation-perfusion inequality. Cyanosis is best appreciated in adequate sunlight and is virtually impossible to recognize under fluorescent lamp.[791] It is estimated that 5 g hemoglobin/100 ml blood has to be reduced before cyanosis is visible, and, therefore, this sign is never present in patients with severe anemia.[389] It may be due to inadequate saturation of arterial blood leaving the left side of the heart, to excessive slowing in the peripheral capillaries, or to both.

The central or hypoxemic variety associated with lung disease is seen most commonly in patients with chronic obstructive emphysema and then indicates that many acinar units have low alveolar ventilation/perfusion ratios ($\dot{V}A/\dot{Q}$); in other words, a large part of lung that is not fully ventilated is still perfused with venous blood. Another, rarer, variety of central hypoxemia which may lead to cyanosis in lung disease is that due to pulmonary arteriovenous aneurysm. In this condition a true shunt takes place—a complete by-pass of the acinar unit—in which venous blood passes into the arterial circulation without an opportunity to collect oxygen in the lungs. In other lung diseases, such as severe acute alveolar pneumonia with circulatory collapse, both central and peripheral factors undoubtedly play a part: The venous blood in the pulmonary capillaries encounters airless acini, and the same blood stagnates in systemic capillaries and allows excessive removal of oxygen by the tissues. Probably both factors are responsible for the cyanosis so commonly seen in patients who have diffuse pulmonary infiltration with clubbing; even when they have only a mild degree of arterial oxygen unsaturation the nail beds are definitely dusky blue. Cardiac conditions with a right-to-left shunt may engender a central form of cyanosis, but are differentiated from pulmonary conditions by the clinical findings and the results of pulmonary function tests. Arterial oxygen unsaturation due to shunting also occurs in association with cirrhosis of the liver, but then is rarely if ever severe enough to incur cyanosis.

Peripheral cyanosis is either paroxysmal and precipitated by cold, as in Raynaud's disease, or general and prolonged, in the latter case often with systemic hypotension and indications of circulatory collapse. The former type occurs in scleroderma, which not uncommonly involves the lung; the latter is more common in primary heart disease, such as myocardial infarction, than in lung conditions, but may occur in association with cor pulmonale and hypoxemia and then indicates a very poor prognosis.

When cyanosis is central in origin the nail beds usually are deep blue or blue-gray and the skin is warm, whereas peripheral cyanosis usually is associated with cold, clammy skin and dusky, livid nail beds. Frequently it is not possible on appearance alone to differentiate with certainty between central and peripheral cyanosis, and other clinical findings may not indicate the cause. However, the degree of oxygen saturation of arterial blood will give the answer.

When the pathogenesis of cyanosis appears obscure, methemoglobinemia or sulphemoglobinemia should be considered. Rarely, methemoglobinemia is primary and congenital. More commonly, the coffee-colored pigment results from the administration of drugs, including nitrates, chlorates, quinones, aniline dyes, sulfonamide derivatives, acetanilid, and phenacetin. Sulphemoglobinemia and methemoglobinemia may occur simultaneously, usually as the result of ingestion of the same drugs, and then the cyanosis is leaden-hued. When either of these conditions is present, the venous blood is brownish even after being shaken in air for 15 minutes; the diagnosis can be confirmed by spectroscopic analysis to identify the absorption bands.

THE DEPENDABILITY OF PHYSICAL FINDINGS

Although physical examination of the chest may reveal information that cannot be obtained from roentgenography, it is inexcusable to rely upon physical findings alone and ignore the latter method of diagnosis when these facilities are available. This error in judgment usually occurs when the patient is treated at home for symptoms and signs suggestive of the early stages of pneumonia. When his condition improves with therapy the physician may neglect to arrange a follow-up roentgenogram and may realize his mistake only when the patient again complains of symptoms referable to his lungs and roentgenography shows a central bronchogenic carcinoma which was undoubtedly responsible for the previous obstructive pneumonitis. Similarly, hospital patients with pneumonia should not be lost sight of until the chest roentgenogram has cleared completely.

The dependability of physical findings should be considered from the viewpoint of error also. It is disturbing to note the disagreement in detecting abnormal physical signs:[390, 391] Smyllie and associates[390] concluded that it was difficult to visualize how observer error could be reduced, since it appeared to reflect neither experience nor the method of clinical teaching. It is perhaps time to reassess the validity of many physical signs of lung diseases, using as yardsticks factual knowledge of roentgenography and pulmonary physiology. This has been done in cardiology, and, although it is questionable whether physical signs of pulmonary disease would ever reach the diagnostic importance of those of heart disease, some conception of the accuracy of individual signs is desirable. In one study,[391] in which various findings on examination of the chest were correlated with the degree of emphysema as judged by physiologic measurement of flow rates in the bronchial tubes ($FEV_{1.0}$) the results were only barely statistically significant; however, it is surprising that a clinical equivalent of the measured FEV was not used as a sign of chronic obstructive disease. The length of a forced expiration after the patient has inspired can be appreciated with the stethoscope, or even measured with a stop-watch.[392] In our opinion, an even better test for the assessment of obstructive disease is to have the patient breathe in and out as rapidly as possible for 10 to 15 seconds while listening with the stethoscope. This is the clinical counterpart of the maximal breathing capacity (MBC) which, with a little experience, can be closely predicted on the basis of this simple procedure. Regional lung ventilation, as assessed by radioactive-gas techniques (see pulmonary function tests), may be correlated with clinical findings and provide a useful, objective index of the intensity of breath sounds. We are impressed by the correlation between local intensity of breath sounds detected by the stethoscope and the vascular pattern seen on the roentgenogram in patients with emphysema. In many cases the breath sounds and the pulmonary vasculature to that area of lung are similarly decreased indicating either coincidental destruction of pulmonary parenchyma and vessels or a compensatory mechanism by which pulmonary blood supply is diverted from poorly ventilated to better ventilated units. A comprehensive objective assessment of contemporary clinical methods of examining the chest can be made, and the results of such a study might serve to revitalize the art of physical diagnosis.

Difference of opinion among observers is not confined to chest signs and is apparent in the recognition of such extrapulmonary signs as cyanosis and clubbing. In Comroe and Botelho's study,[393] observers could not detect cyanosis until the arterial oxygen saturation had fallen to 80 per cent, and one-quarter failed to appreciate this sign when saturation was 70 to 75 per cent. Thus, even when cyanosis is not detected, analysis of the arterial blood Po_2 or oxygen saturation may reveal hypoxemia of severe degree.

Although advanced clubbing is unlikely to lead to any difference of opinion among observers, early clubbing is frequently the source of controversy,[982] and, in one study,[394] discrepancies in its detection were equally divided between experienced examiners and medical students.

SPECIAL DIAGNOSTIC PROCEDURES

ENDOSCOPIC EXAMINATION

Laryngoscopy

The larynx may be examined indirectly, by use of a mirror, or directly; the latter may be combined with bronchoscopy.

Laryngoscopy should be performed in any patient who complains of a persistent, dry, hacking or brassy cough and particularly when this is associated with hoarseness of the voice. The vocal cords should be well visualized, not only to exclude a local lesion but also to detect paralysis—which would account for the hoarseness. In the latter instance, roentgenography may reveal a mediastinal lesion involving a recurrent laryngeal nerve. When the larynx appears healthy and the vocal cords move freely, bronchoscopy is indicated to rule out an endotracheal or endobronchial origin for the patient's symptoms.

Bronchoscopy

This procedure, which formerly was the prerogative of the otolaryngologist, is being adopted by the internist and surgeon specializing in lung disease. This is right, for in most cases the results must be considered in the light of other findings and a general knowledge of lung disease. In our hospital, bronchoscopy is done almost exclusively by chest surgeons, except for the removal of a foreign body from the tracheobronchial tree. Since the most common indication for this procedure is suspicion of endobronchial neoplasm, the obvious person to look down the bronchoscope should be the surgeon, who requires a clear picture of the extent of the lesion and its position in the bronchial tree so as to assess resectability and to determine how much lung should be removed. The experienced bronchoscopist may recognize fixation of the mediastinum or loss of the normal "sharpness" of the carina, indicating compression of bronchi by involved lymph nodes.

Satisfactory bronchoscopy requires the patient's confidence in the bronchoscopist, and explanation of the procedure and reassurance of the patient take but a few minutes and may greatly facilitate examination. If at all possible, bronchoscopy should be done under local anesthesia. The patient's cooperation is required to obtain a satisfactory specimen of bronchial lavage, and his loss of cough reflex while under general anesthesia usually results in an inadequate specimen. With reassurance and premedication with sedatives the patient is able to relax and need not be restrained. The local anesthetic is used, first with a nebulizer and subsequently by spraying of the vocal cords and trachea under direct view by the bronchoscopist. Since an essential feature of most bronchoscopies is bronchial lavage to obtain secretions from the bronchial tree, it should be kept in mind that some local anesthetics have antibacterial action. Tetracaine (Pontocaine) has a particularly significant inhibitory effect on the cultural growth of *Mycobacterium tuberculosis*,[395, 396] and lidocaine (Xylocaine) is said to be inhibitory to fungi and nontuberculous bacteria. Examination of the bronchial tree requires the use of right-angle and oblique telescopes for direct vision of the orifices of the segmental bronchi on each side.

The major indication for bronchoscopy is

roentgenographic evidence of bronchial obstruction, usually manifested by loss of volume of a lung, a lobe, or a segment, and occasionally by roentgenographic appearances of local overinflation due to a check-valve mechanism by an obstructing lesion which allows the passage of air during inspiration. Bronchoscopy is indicated when carcinoma of the lung is suspected: Approximately 50 per cent of such tumors are visible by this means, and lesions in the lung periphery can be diagnosed by cytologic examination of aspirated bronchial secretions. A new technique incorporates a minute brush at the end of a flexible wire which is introduced through the bronchoscope, under fluoroscopic visualization, to the area of peripherally situated tumors; brisk brushing with subsequent lavage and aspiration yielded specimens which were found to be malignant tissue in 11 of 12 cases in one series.[397]

Another indication for bronchoscopic examination is hemoptysis. Despite the danger inherent in bronchoscopy during active bleeding, sometimes it is necessary to perform this when bleeding is copious and the roentgenogram does not indicate the source. Knowledge of the site of bleeding is helpful to the performance of resectional surgery if exsanguination appears imminent. Segarra[398] reported that lesions which gave rise to hemoptysis were identified roentgenographically or bronchoscopically in 498 (73 per cent) of 675 patients; bleeding was due to bronchial cancer in 39 per cent, bronchitis in 25 per cent, and endobronchial lesions produced by peribronchial lymph-node calcification in 15 per cent. The lesion that caused the hemoptysis was identified during bronchoscopy in approximately 50 per cent of those whose roentgenograms were normal. The importance of bronchoscopy in the diagnosis of bronchogenic carcinoma when hemoptysis occurs but the chest roentgenogram is normal was demonstrated in two reports each of five patients.[399, 400]

Bronchoscopy is useful for therapeutic purposes also, such as the removal of a foreign body or secretions which cause obstruction postoperatively or in bronchial asthma.

The risk inherent in bronchoscopic examination appears to be slight, although cardiac arrhythmias are not unusual. Tachycardia appears to be mainly reflex in origin, since it occurs when the bronchoscope touches the trachea,[401] but may also follow absorption of local anesthetics and premedication with atropine. Bronchoscopic examination without biopsy is unlikely to cause a serious degree of bleeding, although extreme care should be exercised when an aortic aneurysm may be present.

Mediastinoscopy

This endoscopic examination is used diagnostically to see and biopsy lymph nodes within the mediastinum. As originally described by Carlens,[402] this procedure is carried out through an incision in the suprasternal notch; the soft areolar tissues are dissected along the whole length of the trachea, and biopsy material is removed under direct vision through an instrument similar to that used for esophagoscopy in children. Mediastinoscopy is used chiefly to assess the resectability of bronchogenic carcinoma. In one study of 122 cases in which node tissue was removed by this means[403] tumor was present in 28, in 19 of which other methods indicated that the neoplasm was unresectable; the other nine patients underwent thoracotomy, but the lesion was found to be unresectable in seven. Of the 94 patients in whom mediastinoscopy showed no evidence of involvement in that area, 72 were operated on and resectable lesions were found in 67.

For more complete assessment of the mediastinum this procedure can be combined with carbon dioxide or oxygen insufflation through a small catheter into the mediastinal cavity followed by appropriate roentgenography (mediastinography).[983]

Complications to mediastinoscopy are said to be unusual or insignificant, although Van Der Schaar[403] reported injury to the recurrent laryngeal nerve and azygos vein, as well as implantation of tumor at the operative site; similarly Bridgman and associates[984] reported severe venous hemorrhage and phrenic paralysis.

Thoracoscopy

After the induction of pneumothorax an endoscope is inserted through an incision in the intercostal space to give a direct view of the lung surface. Formerly, thoracoscopy was used to locate pleural adhesions that prevented satisfactory collapse of the lung after artificial pneumothorax; then an instrument was inserted through a separate incision in an intercostal space and the adhesions were cut under direct vision. Lung[404] or pleural[405] biopsy under thoracoscopic view is advocated by some; however, since pulmonary disease reduces the respiratory reserve and pneumothorax enhances this defect, probably it is safer to biopsy the lung through a standard or limited thoracotomy incision in an area where the roentgenogram shows disease (*see* page 159).

Esophagoscopy

Pulmonary disease may occur in association with esophageal lesions and diagnosis may be facilitated by direct endoscopic examination of the esophagus. The procedure should be preceded by fluoroscopy and roentgenography.

Aspiration pneumonia may be secondary to diverticula, achalasia, or stenosis, or as a result of peptic ulceration or neoplasm of the esophagus. When the origin of expectorated blood is not known, direct view of the lower esophagus may be indicated to detect bleeding varices. Diffuse pulmonary lesions can occur in association with dysphagia in patients with scleroderma, in which case esophagoscopy, fluoroscopy and cinefluorography may be required to confirm the diagnosis.

BIOPSY PROCEDURES

Bronchoscopic Biopsy

Bronchoscopy itself is unlikely to lead to any serious complications, although allergic reactions to the anesthetic agents do occur rarely. Despite the sparsity of reports of serious consequences of biopsy of endobronchial lesions,[985] experienced bronchoscopists are reluctant to take specimens from very vascular tumors, and we know of several cases of near or actual exsanguination when this was done. There seems little reason for biopsy of lesions shown bronchoscopically to require resectional surgery.

Positive biopsy of the bronchial wall as a diagnostic procedure in sarcoidosis[406] and other diffuse interstitial diseases[460] has been reported when the bronchial mucosa appeared normal on naked-eye examina-

tion. Even though bleeding was not severe in the reported cases, we are hesitant to recommend such a procedure because of the possibility of fatal hemorrhage. Although it might be thought that the risk of severe hemorrhage would lessen the more peripheral the biopsy is taken, this has not been the experience of Gaensler.[407]

Nordenström and Carlens[256] described an ingenious method of biopsying endobronchial tumors, with forceps inserted down a catheter after locating the lesion by bronchography; tissue may be taken from areas nearer the lung periphery than is possible by other methods.

Another promising procedure is the use of a fluorescent hematoporphyrin derivative which accumulates preferentially in neoplastic tissue. The substance is injected intravenously three hours before bronchoscopy, and the bronchoscope is modified to detect fluorescence. A report from the Mayo Clinic[408] describes results obtained with this method in 50 patients; a significant degree of fluorescence was detected in the neoplasm in nearly all of the 20 patients with bronchogenic carcinoma. In one patient in whom standard bronchoscopy and chest roentgenography showed nothing abnormal, fluorescence was detected in apparently normal mucosa at the orifice of the right upper lobe and biopsy of this area revealed malignancy. The authors state that this form of diagnosis could not be applied to upper-lobe bronchi beyond the reach of biopsy forceps and stress the danger of photosensitivity reactions if patients are exposed to direct sunlight less than 48 hours after the test.

Whatever procedure is used to biopsy lung, pleura, or lymph nodes, it is essential that some of the tissue should be sent to bacteriology and mycology laboratories — or, better still, the material should be inoculated on culture media in the operating room itself.

Pulmonary Parenchymal Biopsy

This method of obtaining material is particularly useful in cases of diffuse parenchymal disease of the lung in which the condition often cannot be diagnosed on clinical and roentgenographic findings alone. Tissue may be obtained by direct biopsy through an incision in the intercostal space, by blind, needle biopsy into the parenchyma of the lung, or through a broncho-scope introduced into a peripheral bronchus in the lower or middle lung regions.

OPEN LUNG BIOPSY. The chest is opened through a standard thoracotomy incision or a limited incision large enough to allow removal of a cube of tissue measuring about 4 c cm. Like Gaensler and his associates,[558] we prefer general rather than local anesthetic for this operation, in case extension of the incision is necessary. Some tissue is ballooned out through the small incision by exerting positive pressure in the lung, a clamp is applied, and the tissue is removed. This direct lung biopsy through a limited incision, which was originally proposed by Andrews and Klassen,[409] applies particularly when the disease process is so diffuse that any portion of tissue is likely to reveal the diagnosis. When disease is more confined, a full thoracotomy incision is recommended; the lungs can be examined and the site of biopsy chosen. The larger incision is not associated with greater morbidity or mortality rates than the limited incision but usually necessitates a longer hospital stay.

PERCUTANEOUS LUNG BIOPSY. This procedure includes aspiration into a syringe with an ordinary needle and the nonaspiration type of biopsy with specially designed needles. Lauby and associates,[410] who use the former procedure, reported their experience with 648 biopsies in 21 years, originally with an ordinary beveled needle and later with the Franseen needle.[411] They considered the procedure to be contraindicated in cases of diffuse parenchymal disease and concentrated their attention on lesions thought to be bronchogenic carcinoma in which all other methods of diagnosis had failed. Nordenström has advocated percutaneous biopsy of focal pulmonary lesions using television-monitored image amplified fluoroscopy to facilitate accurate positioning of long needles of 0.9 to 1.1 mm external diameter in the lesions.[986, 988] This is an aspiration type of biopsy which, in Nordenström's hands, has been successful in 90 per cent of approximately 2000 cases.[988] Other investigators have shown a similar success rate[989, 990] and have claimed a low incidence of minor complications including pneumothorax and minimal hemoptysis. (Rabinov and associates[990] reported a 35 per cent incidence of minimal pneumothorax following 43 biopsies of 39 patients.) This

procedure appears promising, particularly in patients in whom the diagnosis of suspected pulmonary neoplasm cannot be made from more conventional procedures.

In 1938 Silverman[412] introduced a cutting needle, a modification of which (the Vim-Silverman needle) has been used since for pleural as well as lung biopsy. This consists of an inner, split, cutting needle which is driven into the lung and an outer needle which is pushed over and compresses the cutting blades; both needles are rotated 180 degrees and are removed with a thin sliver of tissue between the blades. This needle is particularly useful for biopsying solid lesions and much less so in diffuse parenchymal disease. Using this needle, Smith[413] failed to obtain satisfactory pieces of tissue in seven of 24 patients and subsequently had his instrument-maker design a new needle (Jack needle), with which he obtained diagnostic material in 16 of 17 cases of diffuse disease. Manfredi and Krumholz[991] found percutaneous biopsy to provide diagnostically useful tissue in 77 per cent of cases, the majority being solid lesions. Since 15 to 30 seconds of breath-holding are required for this procedure, patients who are either dyspneic at rest or are coughing incessantly are unlikely candidates. Pulmonary hypertension and cysts or bullae in the proposed area for biopsy are also contraindications.[992]

A high speed air-drill, not requiring prolonged breath-holding, has been used successfully in both solid and diffuse lung lesions.[993]

TRANSBRONCHIAL PULMONARY BIOPSY. This is done with very fine, flexible forceps inserted through the bronchoscope to the periphery of the lung; tissue may be obtained from lower and middle lobes but not from upper lobes. Transbronchial peripheral parenchymal biopsy is useful when thoracotomy is not justified in poor-risk patients; using this method, Smart[418] obtained pathologic tissue in only 33 per cent of cases, whereas Andersen and his colleagues at the Mayo Clinic obtained diagnostic material in 11 of 13 patients.[460] Another series of 30 cases proved technically successful but hardly fruitful from a diagnostic point of view.[984] Fluoroscopically controlled transbronchial biopsy combined with bronchial brushing has been reported: Fennessy[994] uses a forceps on the Vim-Silverman needle principle for this procedure and is able to reach lesions in the very periphery of the lung. Leoncini and Palatresi[995] have also had success with transbronchial biopsy under fluoroscopic control in the diagnosis of diffuse lung disease.

INDICATIONS AND CHOICE OF METHOD. It is difficult to state dogmatically the indications for lung biopsy. The chest roentgenograms of most patients who are considered for this procedure show diffuse, bilateral, nodular, reticular or acinar patterns. We consider it justifiable that patients who have diffuse pulmonary disease *but who are asymptomatic* should be followed closely without resort to lung biopsy. Many cases of sarcoidosis can be diagnosed from the roentgenogram and the clinical picture, and, in these, lung biopsy probably is not indicated. There remains the large percentage of cases in which the disease has produced symptoms and is progressive and in which the roentgenogram and the clinical picture show nothing specific to indicate the diagnosis. In these cases, unless the patient is too old or too ill to warrant the slight risk, biopsy is mandatory: like others,[558] we have seen such patients in whom biopsy led to the diagnosis of a condition amenable to treatment. Also, we have faced the dilemma of seeing patients become more dyspneic until they were so disabled that we were hesitant to recommend this diagnostic procedure. In some cases, for purposes of compensation, a tissue diagnosis is useful, although it is of interest that Andrews and Klassen[409] reported only ten cases of proved pneumoconiosis among 23 patients with diffuse parenchymal disease who gave a history compatible with such a diagnosis, the other cases proving to be sarcoid, cancer, nonspecific infections, and fibrosis.

Opinions differ as to the relative merits of biopsy procedures in diffuse pulmonary disease, particularly in reference to their morbidity and mortality rates. In their excellent review Gaensler and colleagues[558] stated that needle biopsy has a higher mortality rate, incurs more complications, and yields many fewer positive results than direct lung biopsy; they estimated the average mortality rate in association with open lung biopsy to be 1.8 per cent and reported one death in their own series of 105 cases. Lauby and associates[410] recorded only three deaths in 520 cases of needle biopsy and thought that only one was directly attributable to the procedure. No mortality was reported in a series of 48 needle biopsies[415] and in one of 126 cases of percutaneous needle biopsy.[416]

It has been stated that no deaths or serious complications due to percutaneous lung biopsy with a cutting needle have appeared in the literature;[991, 992] nevertheless, the workers responsible for this statement alluded to a complicating hemoptysis of 750 ml in one of their patients. Smith[996] described one death following use of a Jack needle, and we are aware of one fatal hemorrhage following percutaneous lung biopsy with a Vim-Silverman needle.[1] Morbidity can occur with both the direct and the percutaneous procedures, and tension pneumothorax, intercostal neuralgia, and bleeding appear to be the most serious common complications.

From a review of the literature it seems that both methods have their proponents, and the variation in reported complications may relate to the inclusion or exclusion of poor-risk patients. There is no doubt, however, that the tissue obtained by direct lung biopsy is of greater diagnostic value than that obtained by percutaneous needle biopsy. Although Krumholz and colleagues[416] stressed the fact that Gaensler and associates[558] had one death in their series of open biopsy, whereas their own series of percutaneous biopsy was without mortality, 34 per cent of Krumholz's cases were still undiagnosed after biopsy, compared with 4.8 per cent of Gaensler's.[558] In fact, most series of needle biopsies show only 50 to 60 per cent success in obtaining tissue for diagnosis,[410, 415] whereas open lung biopsy yielded pathologic tissue in 95 per cent of Gaensler's cases, and in 75 per cent of Delarue and Strangway's.[417]

Whatever the method used, the tissue should be subjected to thorough examination, including not only pathologic and bacteriologic studies but also chemical analyses and, in certain cases, electron microscopy. Advances in our knowledge of the many nonspecific diffuse granulomata and fibroses are dependent not only upon reports of the inhalation of some substance hitherto unrecognized as toxic but, more importantly, upon the thorough analysis of morphologic and chemical changes in tissue.

Although like others,[414] we have tended in the past to restrict the use of biopsy in local lesions to patients with presumed unresectable bronchogenic carcinoma, we are impressed with recently described biopsy procedures for such lesions. The large series reported by Nordenström[988] using percutaneous aspiration biopsy and that by

Fennessy[994] using the transbronchial method, both without serious complications, are particularly encouraging. These techniques are proving useful in differentiating malignant and benign local lesions and thus avoiding the necessity of thoracotomy. It should not be forgotten, however, that like operative intervention these procedures very likely lead to blood-stream seeding of neoplastic cells.

Pleural Biopsy

NEEDLE BIOPSY. This diagnostic procedure, which is rarely associated with troublesome complications, should be carried out in every case of pleural effusion when thoracentesis is indicated. It was introduced by DeFrancis and co-workers in 1955 for diagnosing tuberculous pleural effusion.[419] The three needles commonly used are the Vim-Silverman, the Cope, and the Abrams or Harefield needle. Although the literature abounds with reports of the use of these biopsy needles, it is difficult to determine which gives the best results; success depends largely upon the ability of the operator, the number of attempts he makes in any one case, and the selection of the patients. Leggat[420] who used both Vim-Silverman and Abrams needles, considered that the latter gave much better results. His experience was limited, however, and others have had considerable success with the Vim-Silverman needle, ranging from 60 per cent positive biopsies[421] to as high as 75 per cent.[422] Rao and associates[423] recorded 64 per cent positive diagnoses; however, because nine of 32 patients whose biopsy specimens were interpreted as showing nonspecific inflammatory reactions were proved subsequently to have tuberculosis or malignancy, these authors concluded that the Vim-Silverman needle was not efficient. The Cope needle[347] yielded pathologic tissue in 83 per cent of patients with tuberculous effusions and 75 per cent of those with carcinomatous effusion in one series[424] and in approximately 70 per cent of subsequently proved malignant or tuberculous effusions in another.[425] It was used equally successfully, without the development of even one pneumothorax, in 17 patients without effusion.[425] A recent report by Cope and Bernhardt[426] indicates that this needle yields positive biopsy material in approximately 50 per cent of patients with cancer and 80 per cent of those with tuberculosis. The diagnosis of tuberculous pleurisy with effusion usually is made pathologically on the findings of a granuloma, and only rarely are acid-fast organisms seen in the section or grown on culture.[427, 428] The cutting portion of the Cope needle has been known to bend and break off in the pleural space.[997] Cope has recently instructed the manufacturers to strengthen this portion of his needle.[998]

Pleural fluid should be aspirated at the time of biopsy, no matter which biopsy needle is used. Sison and Weiss reported 87 per cent accurate diagnosis with combined examination of needle biopsy and cell block from pleural fluid in cases of neoplasm.[421] Cultures may be positive in cases of tuberculous effusion despite negative biopsy results.

We have had considerable success with the Harefield needle, which is particularly useful because fluid may be aspirated through it before the biopsy is taken. Although Abrams, at Harefield Hospital, first described and presumably designed this needle,[430] its clinical use was first described by Mestitz and colleagues[429] who reported a positive diagnostic yield in 80 per cent of cases of tuberculous pleurisy and in 60 per cent of malignant pleurisy. The procedure used during biopsy with this needle was described in detail by a Mayo Clinic group[431] who, like us, restrict its use to patients with pleural effusion. Published reports indicate that needle biopsy of the pleura should be carried out whenever thoracentesis is performed and that invariably it should precede treatment for tuberculous effusion. In common with others,[432, 433] we remove fluid for cytology, culture, and biochemical studies and then take several pieces of tissue by needle biopsy; when this yields no diagnostic material, direct pleural biopsy is advised through a limited thoracotomy incision.

OPEN PLEURAL BIOPSY. Some physicians prefer to biopsy the pleura directly, since they consider it no more difficult and the tissue specimens superior to those obtained by needle biopsy.[434] However, because of the added risk of a general anesthetic—which we consider should be given for direct pleural biopsy, even with a limited thoracotomy incision[431]—and since, in competent hands, needle biopsy does not add to the risk of the thoracentesis that would be done in any case, we recommend restriction of direct pleural biopsy to those cases of pleural effusion in which needle biopsy does not give a specific diagnosis. The major problem in pleural effusion of undetermined etiology is the decision to treat or not to treat the patient for tuberculosis. Although it may be too early to state dogmatically that treatment for tuberculosis is not required for patients in whom percutaneous or direct pleural biopsy does not reveal granuloma and whose pleural fluid is negative on culture, this may be so.[435, 436]

In some cases of pleural effusion it may be necessary to make a full thoracotomy incision for diagnostic purposes; when primary tumor of the pleura is suspected, this procedure should be carried out and it may be advantageous to precede it by induction of pneumothorax and a chest roentgenogram which may aid in outlining the tumor and the area to biopsy.

Lymph Node Biopsy

SCALENE NODE BIOPSY. This operation, which was first described by Daniels,[437] consists in removal of tissue lying on the scalene group of muscles, including the fat pad which lies medially in the supraclavicular fossae. In cases of proved or suspected bronchogenic carcinoma it is used mainly to ascertain whether the neoplasm has spread beyond the thorax. It has been used also as a diagnostic procedure in cases of diffuse pulmonary disease, with or without hilar adenopathy, and when mediastinal, hilar or paratracheal adenopathy is seen roentgenographically in association with clear pulmonary parenchyma. The percentage of positive results varies according to the extent of the operation and the selection of patients. In one series,[438] pathologic tissue was obtained in only 14 per cent of patients in whom only the scalene fat pad was removed but in 55 per cent when the right thoracic-duct lymph node also was removed. Obviously, the positive yield will be higher when cases are selected on the basis of enlarged lymph nodes in the mediastinum, than when those with diffuse parenchymal diseases without lymph-node enlargement are included. After Rouviére[114] described the lymph drainage from the right lung to be to the lymph nodes in the right supraclavicular area and drainage from the lower half of

the left lung to be to the same area, it was customary for surgeons to biopsy the right scalene area whenever the disease process involved the right lung or the lower half of the left. Nohl,[439] who reported 58 scalenenode biopsies, stated that right-sided lung lesions are associated with pathologic changes in the supraclavicular nodes on the right side only, and that disease in the left lung or both lungs, or bilateral hilar enlargement, more frequently spreads to scalene nodes on the right side than the left. He concluded that the left supraclavicular nodes should be removed only when they are palpable and that bilateral exploration is justifiable only when biopsy of the scalene nodes on the right side is negative. By contrast, Klingenberg[117] in a postmortem study of prescalene metastases, found no evidence of spread from left lung to right scalene nodes. In 110 cases of bilateral prescalene-node operation in patients with bronchogenic carcinoma, Baird[118] demonstrated conclusively that Rouviére's findings in infants and fetuses do not apply to adults; he concluded that spread is principally ipsilateral and uncommonly contralateral, and the latter may occur just as often from right to left as from left to right. The findings of several other workers[440, 999, 1000] also have cast doubt on Rouviére's description of lymphatic drainage in relation to adults.

Lal and Poole[441] reported 112 scalenenode biopsies in patients who had solitary or multiple local lung lesions or diffuse pulmonary disease but in whom carcinoma was not obviously present; the biopsy yielded pathologic tissue in 30 per cent of cases, including all 15 patients who had palpable lymph nodes but only 18 of 96 without palpable lymph nodes. Leckie and colleagues[442] diagnosed carcinoma on biopsy findings in only one of 81 patients without palpable nodes, whereas Wilson and associates[443] recorded 20 per cent positive diagnoses under similar circumstances. There is no doubt that there is a much higher positive yield if the supraclavicular nodes are palpable—probably 85 per cent or higher compared to little more than 15 per cent when nodes are not palpable.[999, 1001] The percentage of positive findings in nodes increases in proportion to the number of sarcoid cases included: Even when supraclavicular nodes are not palpable, 70 to 80 per cent of patients with clinically apparent sarcoidosis have granulomata in the pre-scalene lymph nodes.[444-447]

The risk of the operation varies with the extent of resection of tissue and the competence of the surgeon. Although this procedure is commonly considered to be straightforward and without significant risk, and usually is relegated to members of the house staff, complications do occur and deaths have been reported. Major complications include injuries to the large vessels in the area, production of lymphatic fistulae or Horner's syndrome, and infection which extends into the mediastinum. Berger and colleagues[448] reported one near-fatal injury to the subclavian artery and two cases in which incision of major veins resulted in air emboli. Skinner,[449] who reported 186 biopsies of scalene lymph nodes at the Massachusetts General Hospital, recorded two deaths and a total of 6 per cent serious complications. Thomas and associates[999] reported two fatalities from pneumothorax and one case of lymphatic fistula.

The indications for this operation are not clearly defined. When the diagnosis is unknown and supraclavicular nodes are palpable, they should be removed. When bronchogenic carcinoma is suspected, or even when its presence has been proved by bronchoscopic or cytologic procedures, probably the scalene-node region should not be explored unless there is roentgenologic evidence of paratracheal or tracheobronchial lymph node involvement. We agree with Skinner's statement[449] that in cases of potentially resectable bronchogenic carcinoma without palpable supraclavicular lymph nodes the risk of death or major complications approximately equals the 6 to 7 per cent positive results that can be expected. When sarcoidosis is suspected the yield of positive results, which is much higher (70 to 80 per cent), may justify performance of this procedure for diagnostic purposes.

BIOPSY OF MEDIASTINAL LYMPH NODES. The approach to the mediastinum is direct, by thoracotomy, by mediastinoscopy,[402] by catheterization through a transjugular or paraxiphoid approach,[1002, 1003] or by bronchoscopic needle puncture of lymph nodes through the bronchial wall.

Direct approach to the mediastinum is made through the usual thoracotomy incision or a limited incision over the mediastinal area.[450] The open technique has the advantage of permitting more extensive exploration of the mediastinum. Mediastinoscopy[451] revealed mediastinal metastases in 30 per cent of cases of bronchogenic cancer and, when combined with biopsy, yielded evidence of sarcoidosis in 87 per cent of patients in whom this had been diagnosed clinically—slightly more than the highest reported with prescalene lymph-node biopsy in this disease. In another series,[452] mediastinoscopy revealed mediastinal lymph-node involvement in 43 (31 per cent) of 140 patients with bronchogenic carcinoma. Perhaps it is premature to estimate the value of mediastinoscopy or to determine indications for its performance; also, even though its proponents consider this a benign procedure, many physicians are hesitant to open a passage to the mediastinum for fear of major complications, not the least of which might be infection.

Two rather ingenious techniques of mediastinal lymph node biopsy have been described by Nordenström,[1002, 1003] one through the jugular fossa into the superior mediastinum and the other from the region of the xiphoid process into the inferior mediastinum. Either a blunt cannula (with an external diameter of approximately 2 mm) or a catheter is inserted into the mediastinum under televised fluoroscopic control, and a biopsy instrument introduced through it under direct vision to the enlarged lymph nodes. In Nordenström's hands, no serious complications were encountered in a relatively small number of cases examined.

Biopsy of mediastinal lymph nodes may also be carried out with a needle inserted through the bronchial wall under direct vision with a bronchoscope. In one series[453] this procedure established the diagnosis in 26 of 69 cases of bronchogenic carcinoma, and it yielded pathologic tissue in 50 per cent of 613 biopsies in a series reported by Šimeček,[454] who combines this procedure with pneumomediastinography and believes it should be included as a diagnostic step when mediastinoscopy and biopsy of the mediastinal and prescalene nodes prove negative. Bridgman and associates[984] have also employed this technique with success and without serious complications. They make the point that the carina may look completely normal through the bronchoscope and yet biopsy can be positive for malignancy.

PARASTERNAL OR INTERNAL-MAMMARY NODE BIOPSY. This form of biopsy has been advocated for the establishment of the etiology of pleural effusions. In one series the internal mammary lymph nodes were involved in 12 of 16 patients with tuberculosis and in two of nine patients with neoplasm of the lung.[455] Of 17 patients with pleural effusion studied by Burke and Wilson,[456] in whom the tuberculin test was positive and culture of the effusion was negative, the parasternal lymph nodes were found to contain granulomata in 11, with tubercle bacilli in some. It may be that this operation should be performed in patients with primary pleural effusion who have negative cultures and negative needle biopsies. Should it also fail to yield diagnostic material a direct pleural biopsy should follow.

BACTERIOLOGY IN PULMONARY DISEASE

Collection of Material

SPUTUM. A most important aid to the definitive diagnosis of lung disease lies in the proper collection of sputum and the diagnostic methods used in its examination. Unfortunately, the chest physician and the bacteriologist appear to live in different worlds in most hospitals and their talents are seldom combined to full advantage. Frequently a specimen of "sputum" arrives in the bacteriology laboratory as a faint, rapidly-drying stain at the bottom of the sputum box. Almost every clinical situation in chest disease requires that the bacteriology laboratory receive a fresh specimen of sputum, preferably from well down in the lungs and at least from the posterior pharynx. The physician whose patient has acute pneumonia accomplishes two purposes by watching the patient cough and spit into the sputum box: Gross examination of the material may indicate an important clue to diagnosis and he can ensure that some dependable person (in many cases, preferably himself) immediately conveys the expectorated material to the bacteriology laboratory. If he himself goes, the physician can discuss the clinical problem with the bacteriologist, who often may advise a bacteriologic diagnostic method appropriate to the clinical picture. In the case of out-patients, the expectorated material should be collected in a screw-capped glass jar which has been thoroughly cleaned and placed in boiling water for at least three minutes. The patient should be instructed to cough up material from deep in his lungs on arising in the morning and to arrange for its immediate transport to the hospital where it should be inoculated immediately on culture medium.

Fresh specimens are required in bacterial, mycotic, and viral diseases, and the only indications for collecting expectorated material over a prolonged period are the determination of its quantity and quality and to obtain material for acid-fast culture, which is positive most often when sputum is collected for 24 to 72 hours. However, since acid-fast bacilli often are detectable on film smears of freshly expectorated material, the longer period of collection may not be necessary in many cases of cavitary disease or lobar consolidation suspected to be due to tuberculosis.

Unfortunately, many patients who are admitted to hospital with pneumonia have been given antibiotics before admission, with the result that significant pathogens fail to grow on culture. When this occurs, it is wise to repeat the culture, bearing in mind that immediate inoculation of a fresh specimen is essential. When a patient fails to respond to antibiotic therapy appropriate to the pathogen originally detected, further cultures should be made, since another pathogenic agent, perhaps acquired in hospital, may be responsible for the lack of clinical improvement.

Use of an aerosol solution of propylene glycol with 10 per cent normal saline to induce production of sputum was originally suggested by Bickerman and associates[457] who administered this to 180 subjects without sputum or cough and obtained material in 86 per cent. The same authors subsequently described an apparatus to be used for this method of stimulating secretions in which the solution is warmed to a temperature of 115 to 125° F.[458] A solution of sulphur dioxide was similarly successful[408, 459] in patients unable to produce sputum.

The value of this method in obtaining sputum and positive smears in patients with tuberculosis was reported.[461] A variety of solutions have been used by Yue and Cohen[1004] to induce expectoration in suspected cases of tuberculosis. Superheated nebulized 10 per cent sodium chloride or acetyl cysteine administered by DeVilbiss nebulizer over a 15-minute period would appear to be the method of choice. At least six studies[462-466, 1004] show sputum induction to be superior to gastric lavage in revealing active tuberculosis, although in three of these[463, 465, 466] comparison of results obtained with the two methods showed that in a few cases acid-fast bacilli were found in gastric washings but not in aerosol-induced sputum.

GASTRIC LAVAGE. A plastic tube is passed down into the patient's stomach when he wakes in the morning and swallowed pulmonary secretions are siphoned out; the material should be cultured immediately for acid-fast organisms. Although, as stated previously, sputum induction appears to give a higher yield of positive results, these two methods are complementary and both are indicated in cases of suspected pulmonary tuberculosis. Some patients, such as small children, the mentally retarded, and the acutely ill, may be unable to cooperate in performing sputum induction and gastric lavage alone may be the only method feasible. Malignant cells from bronchial secretions were found in gastric washings in ten cases reported by Bernhardt and colleagues[467] which may indicate that this diagnostic method could be regarded as complementary to the more common means of obtaining material for cytologic examination.

TRACHEAL ASPIRATION AND LAVAGE. In the past, saline solution was squirted into the region of the vocal cords or via a catheter through the larynx into the trachea, to produce coughing and to permit aspiration of tracheal secretions. With the advent of newer techniques, including the use of aerosols, it is unnecessary to subject patients to the discomfort inherent in the older procedures. Pecora[468] threads a catheter through a needle inserted percutaneously into the trachea and obtains secretions from the lower respiratory tract, a procedure that could prove useful in cases of acute fulminating pneumonia when the patient cannot raise sputum. Enzymes could be added to liquefy the material so that it could be aspirated through the narrow catheter.

SWABS OF UPPER RESPIRATORY TRACT. Obtaining laryngeal swabs as a screening procedure for activity in tuberculosis is simple and often they yield organisms. The use of superheated solutions to induce sputum, although more time-consuming, should prove more fruitful, although to our knowledge no comparative study has been made. Swabs of the pharynx or naso-pharynx, which frequently are taken in suspected virus disease, should be placed immediately in a liquid solution containing salt and either gelatin or bovine serum albumin, with or without antibiotics.[469] This material should be delivered immediately to the laboratory for inoculation; when preparation is delayed for a few hours the specimen should be kept at $-40°$ C or, if the delay is to be longer, at $-70°$ C.

EXAMINATION OF STOOL. As can be appreciated from Table 3–2, microscopic examination of slides (with cover slip) of fecal material is indicated in many parasitic diseases of the lungs; also, viruses can often be isolated in stools. Centrifugation filtration methods may be used to concentrate parasites or eggs.[470]

BLOOD. A culture should be made at the height of fever, using an aseptic technique, in every case of acute fulminating pneumonia. In cases of lung disease thought to be viral the blood should be drawn early in the disease; part of the aliquot should be used for culture and part for the identification of antibodies (see later discussion) due to pathogens.

PLEURAL EFFUSION. The presence of pleural effusion is determined by the roentgenographic appearance and physical signs. The area of maximal accumulation is judged from posteroanterior and lateral roentgenograms and is confirmed by percussion of the chest wall; others[1005] have used reflected ultrasound for this purpose. In most cases thoracentesis is performed through the interspace at the site of maximal dullness, usually posteriorly or posterolaterally. However, in many cases of pleural effusion apparent roentgenographically the history or physical examination, or both, may arouse suspicion of an underlying parenchymal lesion. In such cases as much fluid as possible should be removed, to give a clearer view of underlying lung parenchyma that may be hidden by the opacification of a large accumulation of effusion. In these circumstances the needle should be inserted low in the thoracic cage.

The patient sits on the bed, either with the bed-head raised at a right angle or with his legs over the side of the bed and his feet on a chair, with his arms resting on a pillow on a bedside stand. The hand on the side of the proposed thoracentesis should be placed on the opposite shoulder, to widen the intercostal space. This procedure should not cause a significant degree of pain, and it is wise to reassure the patient be-

Table 3–2. *Parasitic Pulmonary Infestations*

ORGANISM	ISOLATION AND IDENTIFICATION			
	MICROSCOPIC AND CULTURAL CHARACTERISTICS	SEROLOGIC TESTS	SKIN TESTS	LEUKOCYTE COUNT°
Endamoeba histolytica	Amebae in sputum or stool; cysts in stool.	Complement fixation test of limited value.	Nil	Moderate, sometimes with eosinophilia.
Toxoplasma gondii	Mice inoculation of suspected material and demonstration of intracellular crescent-shaped protozoan.	Sabin-Feldman dye test. Complement fixation test.	Yes	Normal with some lymphocytosis.
Pneumocystis carinii	1 to 3 μ irregular organism may be found in sputum or in lung biopsy.	Complement fixation test.	Nil	Mild to considerable with neutrophilia.
Ascaris lumbricoides	Adult worms or typical mammilated outer shell ova in stools.	Nil	Nil	Mild to moderate with eosinophilia.
Strongyloides stercoralis	Larvae in stools and rarely in sputum.	Nil	Nil	Mild to considerable with eosinophilia.
Ancylostoma duodenale Necator americanus	Ova or mature worms in stools.	Nil	Nil	Eosinophilia; leukopenia to moderate leukocytosis usually normal.
Trichinella spiralis	Larvae seen in muscle biopsy specimens ten days post infection.	Precipitin complement fixation and flocculation tests.	Yes	Mild to considerable with eosinophilia.
Filaria species (tropical eosinophilia)	Lung biopsy or microfilariae in nocturnal blood rarely.	Complement fixation test.	Yes	Considerable with extreme degree of eosinophilia.
Toxocara species (Visceral larva migrans)	Larvae seen in eosinophilic granuloma in liver biopsy.	Of limited value.	Nil	Considerable with extreme eosinophilia.
Echinococcus granulosus	Scolices found in sputum.	Complement fixation test.	Yes	Normal to moderate in 20 to 25 per cent. Slight eosinophilia.
Cysticercus cellulosae	Ova or mature worms in stools. Biopsy of subcutaneous lesion.	Complement fixation test of limited value.	Yes	Normal to mild, no eosinophilia.
Paragonimus westermani	Typical operculated eggs in sputum or stool.	Complement fixation test.	Yes	Usually normal without eosinophilia.
Schistosoma mansoni S. japonicum S. haematobium	Typical ova of each variety in stool, urine and rarely in sputum. Lung biopsy.	Specific precipitin tests.	Yes	Moderate leukocytosis and eosinophilia.

°Leukocyte count– <5,000 = Leukopenia
5,000–10,000 = Normal
10,000–12,000 = Mild
12,000–15,000 = Moderate
>15,000 = Considerable

forehand and to make sure he is comfortably positioned. The skin should be sterilized over an area of at least three interspaces and the patient should be draped. In our experience, the key to a successful thoracentesis and a comfortable patient is the use of plenty of local anesthetic—at least 5 ml of 1 per cent or 2 per cent lidocaine hydrochloride (Xylocaine) or a similar anesthetic and, for the patient with a very thick chest wall, as much as 10 ml. When the skin is frozen the needle is introduced gradually through the chest wall, allowing some anesthetic to infiltrate intercostal muscle. The patient usually complains of a twinge of pain when the parietal pleura is touched. In this area anesthetic should be liberally injected, with the needle withdrawn and reinserted at different angles until a satisfactorily large area of parietal pleura in that interspace is anesthetized. The No. 25 needle used for anesthetizing the skin surface only is replaced by a

No. 22 needle for infiltrating the muscle down to the parietal pleura and to penetrate the pleura and remove fluid. Usually, 20 ml of fluid is sufficient when thoracentesis is carried out solely for diagnostic purposes. A 5 to 10 ml syringe is used during induction of anesthesia and is replaced by a 20 ml syringe for collection of fluid. If large amounts of fluid are to be withdrawn the replacement of the needle by an intravenous catheter is useful.[1006]

It is our opinion that in the majority of cases initial thoracentesis should be combined with biopsy of the parietal pleura. When the diagnosis is "certain" and the effusion is considered to be secondary to pneumonia, heart failure, or kidney disease, pleural biopsy may not be required; nevertheless, even in these cases the etiology of an effusion often is doubtful, and pleural biopsy does not result in serious complications and often provides information of diagnostic importance.

We prefer the Harefield needle for pleural biopsy. When the anesthetic has been infiltrated and the No. 22 needle is in the effusion, a clamp is applied on the needle, flush with the skin; 20 ml pleural fluid is drawn into the syringe, and the syringe and needle are withdrawn. A clamp is applied on the Harefield biopsy needle the same distance from the sharp trocar tip as from the point of the No. 22 needle to its clamp. A small incision is made with a scalpel through anesthetized skin and the needle, with its inner (cutting) cylinder in the closed position and with a three-way stop-cock and 50 ml syringe attached to the needle adapter, is introduced through the anesthetized muscle and pleura until the clamp reaches the thoracic wall. Then the inner cutting cylinder is rotated, allowing fluid to pass through the side opening in the needle and into the syringe. Often the fluid is slightly blood-tinged, from trauma of the trocar, which is why specimens for diagnostic purposes should be taken before the pleural-biopsy needle is introduced. When most of the fluid has been removed, the biopsy needle is withdrawn slowly, with some pressure on the needle toward the side containing the biopsy notch; the notch is placed laterally to avoid intercostal vessels, and, when parietal pleura slips into the notch, the needle's withdrawal is suddenly interrupted. When this happens, the cutting cylinder is rotated and the biopsy needle is withdrawn containing the specimen. It is wise to take several specimens, even when the first appears satisfactory, for bacteriologic culture as well as pathologic examination. Inability to obtain fluid by routine means may indicate the presence of empyema, in which case the material is too thick to pass through a No. 22 needle. When the clinical circumstances suggest this, a No. 16 needle should be inserted after production of a satisfactory degree and extent of anesthesia. Empyema can be diagnosed on gross examination of aspirated fluid. In cases of loculated effusion the exploring needle should be withdrawn and reinserted at different angles: it is in these circumstances that adequate infiltration of anesthetic in the parietal pleura is so important. When no fluid is withdrawn at the first attempt, despite strong evidence of its presence, thoracentesis should be repeated in higher or lower interspaces, after further anesthesia.

Complications with thoracentesis are rare. When there is only a small amount of fluid between the parietal and visceral pleura, the needle may penetrate the lung; this mistake, which is readily recognizable by the aspiration of frothy blood, is not uncommon and does not appear to cause serious bleeding or lead to pneumothorax. It may be avoided by continuous pull on the barrel of the syringe as it is slowly introduced through the parietal pleura; this enables the operator to find even a thin film of pleural fluid between the membranes. The amount of fluid withdrawn depends upon the circumstances; the chief indication for complete removal is to obtain a clearer view of the underlying lung or because the fluid is making the patient dyspneic. It is unwise to remove fluid too rapidly from patients who are in heart failure or who have severe anemia, since acute pulmonary edema is likely to develop in these circumstances; therefore, only a limited amount should be removed at any one time, and the use of a vacuum bottle is not recommended.

Smears and Cultures

All patients acutely ill with pneumonia when admitted to hospital should be encouraged to cough and spit into a sputum box as soon as possible. The fresh sputum should be smeared on a slide, Gram-stained, and inoculated on culture medium. The choice of antibiotic should be made on the basis of the Gram stain and before obtaining culture and sensitivity results from the bacteriology laboratory. Patients whose smears show organisms predominantly Gram-negative or with the morphologic appearance of staphylococci should be diagnosed as having these forms of pneumonia, and the appropriate antibiotics should be given. This does not mean that one can diagnose the etiologic agent of pneumonia by the smear alone; subsequent culture may reveal a pathogen different from that suspected from preliminary smear. However, since patients with severe acute pneumonia may die before the results of culture are forthcoming, this smear represents the most dependable method of making a tentative diagnosis and instituting appropriate therapy. Although the normal person without bronchopulmonary disease has sterile bronchi,[471] his upper respiratory tract contains nonpathogenic cocci and bacilli which are apparent on routine smears. For this reason, in cases of fulminating pneumonia, it is important to get a specimen which originates in the lower respiratory tract; if such a specimen is not produced by spontaneous cough, transtracheal aspiration may be necessary.[468]

Furthermore, even positive sputum cultures of a pathogenic bacterium do not necessarily signify that a pneumonic process is due to the cultured organism. When the growth is heavy or pure, more reliance may be placed on this finding, but decisions concerning therapy and management must be based on clinical features as well. Hemolytic coagulase-positive *Staphylococcus aureus* is usually not pathogenic for a healthy adult but may well cause pneumonia if the patient has had influenza recently or is suffering from a debilitating disease, particularly if the organism was acquired in hospital and is penicillin-resistant. Most patients admitted to hospital with bronchopulmonary infection have had some antibiotic therapy before admission, and the finding of only nonpathogenic Gram-negative organisms on admission may be due simply to antibiotic suppression of more sensitive bacteria; also, the causal pathogen may be a virus, whose identity may (or may not) be disclosed by subsequent serologic studies. Clinical clues, such as the gross appearance of the sputum, increased numbers of polymorphonuclear leukocytes in the peripheral blood, and roentgenographic evidence of alveolar pneumonia, may indicate that the pneumococcus cultured is in fact the cause of the disease. If the patient shows satisfactory clinical response, changing the antibiotic or adding another as successive cultures grow different potential pathogens represents an irresponsible and often dangerous approach to the care of the patient with pneumonia.

Mycobacterium tuberculosis and other mycobacteria may be apparent in sputum smears stained by the Ziehl-Neelsen method. A presumptive diagnosis of tuberculosis can be made on this evidence but definitive diagnosis can be made only when culture reports are received. Homogenization of the sputum with 2 per cent sodium hydroxide and acetyl cysteine prior to inoculation of culture media is advocated.[1007, 1008] At least two media of the many available should be used for culture of these organisms, since some strains grow better on one type than on another. The organism is identifiable by the colony appearance and rate of growth.

Diagnosis may be made quickly by use of fluorescent microscopy.[559] The fluorescent dye localizes in acid-fast bacilli and renders them visible on the dark background.

Table 3–3 summarizes the bacteriologic features of the many bacterial and viral diseases that may affect the lungs.

Positive cultures for various "saprophytic" fungi are often obtained after the administration of antibiotics, and evaluation of their pathogenicity requires careful appraisal of the clinical picture. Little significance attaches to the finding of species of candidae, including *Candida albicans*, even in heavy growth; this organism can be considered to be pathogenic only when it is grown on culture and is seen histologically in lung biopsy.[472, 560] Other potentially pathogenic fungi, such as geotrichum, mucor, and aspergillus, are commonly saprophytic, and the clinical findings rarely lead to a suspicion of pathogenicity.[473]

Isolation of the organism, whether it be bacterium, virus, rickettsia, or fungus, undoubtedly is the only conclusive means of diagnosing infectious disease, but the culture of some pathogens is fraught with danger and may lead to laboratory-acquired disease. The etiologic agents of tularemia[474] and Q-fever[475] fall into this category, and great care should be taken in handling material in cases of suspected or known disease of this type. It may even be wise to settle for a presumptive diagnosis based on the results of serologic and skin tests. Fungus disease also has been reported to originate in the laboratory, due to *Coccidioides immitis*[476] and *Histoplasma capsulatum*.[477]

Animal Inoculation

Although the use of animals for the isolation of bacteria has been largely abandoned because of improvements in culture techniques, guinea pig inoculation is still used in tuberculosis and may prove complementary to other diagnostic tests. The pathogens of Q-fever and psittacosis can be isolated by intraperitoneal inoculation of guinea pigs or mice, but extreme care must be exercised to avoid laboratory-acquired infection. Goodwin and associates[478] stated recently that the early stage of chronic pulmonary histoplasmosis, before the development of cavitary disease, is not readily diagnosed by the usual methods; in the majority of their 28 cases a positive culture was obtained only after passage through mice. The use of animal inoculation in various infectious diseases is summarized in Tables 3–3 and 3–4.

SEROLOGIC AND SKIN TESTS. These methods are particularly useful in the diagnosis of pulmonary viral or mycotic infections. They portray the antigen-antibody reactions that take place in the skin and the test tube, usually as a result of the development of antibodies in the patient; therefore, in the more acute viral diseases the findings may not indicate the etiologic agent until the convalescent state of the disease is reached. These tests are widely used in diagnosing a number of chronic pulmonary disorders and, in the field of epidemiology, to establish the prevalence of diseases of infectious origin in specific geographic areas. Since the patient has usually recovered by the time the antibody titer rises and, thereby, indicates the diagnosis, these tests are not often of direct diagnostic value in individual cases, but they are useful in identifying the etiologic agents of various diseases in population groups.[479-486]

Serologic Testing. Serologic testing has its greatest use in determining the causative pathogens in various bacterial, viral, mycotic, and parasitic diseases (*see* Tables 3–2, 3–3, and 3–4). In the great majority of instances the test is dependent upon the development in the patient's serum of antibodies that cause agglutination, precipitation, or complement-fixation when exposed to specific antigens. Although very high titers on one occasion may strongly suggest the specific etiologic agent, rising or falling titers in serial or paired serologic tests some time apart constitute much stronger evidence. In those diseases in which the antigen is a bacterium in the sputum, the diagnostic test can be carried out, after the organism has been cultured, within a few days of onset of the illness. This applies to pneumococcal, Friedländer's, or Klebsiella pneumonia, for which specific antisera are available and can be used to determine the type or strain of the organism.

Serologic testing is of most practical value in relation to chronic pulmonary disease, and this is well exemplified in fungal infections. The two mycoses in which serologic tests play a distinct role in diagnosis are coccidioidomycosis and histoplasmosis. Salvin[487] and Rickert and Campbell[488] summarized the usefulness of these tests in various mycoses; the latter authors correlated positive skin tests and positive serologic tests with the finding of *Histoplasma capsulatum* in pathologic material from 123 patients: The skin test was positive in 117, whereas serologic testing gave a positive response in only 73 (48 per cent), with a titer of 1:32 or greater in but 16, presumably indicating that the disease was inactive in most cases at that time.[488] In coccidioidomycosis the complement-fixation test is used primarily to determine whether the disease is disseminated. This is accomplished by serial serum testing: A rising titer suggests dissemination of the disease and the need for treatment. Cross-reactions occur between mycotic diseases and are so prevalent in blastomycosis that serologic testing is of limited diagnostic value in this disease. Precipitins to an antigenic extract of *Aspergillus fumigatus* have been identified; they appear to be fairly specific[489] and can be used to determine whether cavitary disease is due to this organism[490] and whether patients with bronchial asthma are sensitive to the fungus.[491]

Serologic testing of patients with byssinosis, with an antigen prepared from dried cotton plant, revealed high titers of antibodies in cardroom workers.[492] Since this diagnosis is readily made by the typical clinical picture and a history of exposure to cotton dust, this finding is of greater academic interest than practical value.

In addition to the more-or-less specific antibodies, nonspecific cold-agglutination antibodies and antibodies to streptococcus MG are found in approximately 50 per cent of patients with *Mycoplasma pneumoniae* infections and constitute strong evidence

(*Text continues on page 174.*)

Table 3–3. Bacterial, Rickettsial, and Viral Pulmonary Infections

ORGANISM	ISOLATION AND IDENTIFICATION			LEUKOCYTE COUNT°
	MICROSCOPIC AND CULTURAL CHARACTERISTICS	SEROLOGIC TESTS	SKIN TESTS	
Diplococcus pneumoniae	Tentative identification on smear. Culture on blood agar. Mouse inoculation.	Specific antiserum to identify type.	Nil	Considerable with neutrophilia.
Staphylococcus aureus	Tentative on smear. Colonies hemolyze blood agar. Organism is coagulase positive.	Nil	Nil	Considerable with neutrophilia.
Streptococcus pyogenes	Tentative on smear. Lancefield Group A on culture. Beta hemolysis on blood agar.	Nil	Nil	Considerable with neutrophilia.
Bacillus anthracis	Tentative on smear, culture on peptone agar.	Nil	Nil	Normal to considerable with neutrophilia.
Listeria monocytogenes	Motile organism showing hemolysis on blood agar.	Nil	Nil	Moderate with lymphocytosis.
Pseudomonas aeruginosa	Tentative on smear. Heavy growth on artificial medium required for pathogenicity.	Nil	Nil	Leukopenia to moderate.
Pseudomonas pseudomallei (Malleomyces pseudomallei)	Aerobic or anaerobic standard culture media. Motile pleomorphic with one or two flagellae at one pole.	Agglutination test.	Nil	Normal to moderate.
Klebsiella aerogenes	Tentative on smear. Mucoid gelatinous colonies on agar. Biochemical tests and type specific capsule.	Specific antiserum to identify type.	Nil	Leukopenia to moderate.
Escherichia coli	Tentative on smear. Heavy growth on artificial medium required for pathogenicity.	Nil	Nil	Normal to moderate.
Proteus species	Tentative on smear. Heavy growth on artificial medium required for pathogenicity.	Nil	Nil	Normal to considerable.
Salmonella species	Tentative on smear. S. *typhosa* or S. *choleraesuis* usually. Differentiation on basis of biochemical and agglutination tests.	Agglutination	Nil	Leukopenia to moderate.
Hemophilus influenzae	Encapsulated organism with capsular swelling in appropriate biologic fluid. Nasopharyngeal swab culture on blood agar in children.	Nil	Nil	Normal to moderate.
Bordetella pertussis	Smear nasopharyngeal swab on Bordet-Gengou agar. Fluorescent antibody technique.	Nil	Nil	Moderate to considerable with lymphocytosis.
Pasteurella tularensis (brucella tularensis)	Tentative on smear. Body fluids cultured on blood agar directly or after passage through mouse or guinea pig.	Agglutination	Yes	Normal to considerable.
Pasteurella pestis	Tentative on smear. Body fluids cultured on blood agar directly or after passage through mouse or guinea pig.	Agglutination. Complement fixation.	Nil	Mild to moderate.

°Leukocyte count– <5,000 = Leukopenia   5,000–10,000 = Normal   10,000–12,000 = Mild
12,000–15,000 = Moderate   >15,000 = Considerable

| ORGANISM | ISOLATION AND IDENTIFICATION | | | |
	MICROSCOPIC AND CULTURAL CHARACTERISTICS	SEROLOGIC TESTS	SKIN TESTS	LEUKOCYTE COUNT°
Bacteria anitratum	Large white or mucoid colony on agar. Inability to reduce nitrates.	Nil	Nil	Mild to moderate.
Brucella species	10 per cent CO_2 needed for *B. abortus* culture on tryptose phosphate. Differentiate species on basis of biochemical and serologic tests.	Agglutination	Yes	Leukopenia to normal.
Malleomyces mallei	Species differentiated antigenically. Culture on enriched agar. Guinea pig inoculation.	Agglutination. Complement fixation.	Yes	Leukopenia to normal.
Bacteroides species	Anaerobic culture required. Frequently combined with anaerobic streptococci and fusospirochetal organisms.	Nil	Nil	Normal to moderate.
Mycobacterium tuberculosis and unclassified	Tentative identification on smear. Colony appearance identifies strain. Animal inoculation.	Agar double diffusion test and hemagglutination tests of limited value.	Yes	Normal to mild with mild monocytosis.
Mycoplasma pneumoniae	Growth of pleuropneumonia-like organism on enriched agar or beef broth. Cultivation in simian cell tissue culture and chorioallantoic membrane.	Cold agglutination. Specific complement fixation. Fluorescent stainable antibody.	Nil	Usually normal; rarely from mild to considerable.
Influenza virus	Human and simian cell tissue culture. Inoculation of chick embryos.	Complement fixation. Hemagglutination. Neutralization. Fluorescent antibody staining.	Nil	In primary virus pneumonia mild to severe with neutrophilia.
Parainfluenza virus	Human and simian cell tissue culture.	Neutralization. Complement fixation. Hemabsorption with guinea pig erythrocytes.	Nil	Usually normal. Rarely mild to moderate leukocytosis.
Respiratory syncytial virus	Human, simian, and bovine cell tissue culture from nasal or pharyngeal secretions.	Neutralization. Complement fixation.	Nil	Usually normal.
Rubeola virus	Human and simian cell tissue culture. Inoculation of chick embryos. Giant cells in urine or throat washings.	Nil	Nil	Normal
Coxsackie virus	Culture in human amnion or rhesus monkey kidney.	Neutralization	Nil	Leukopenia to moderate.
ECHO viruses	Human and simian cell tissue culture.	Neutralization. Complement fixation.	Nil	Normal to moderate.
Adenoviruses	Human and simian cell tissue culture.	Complement fixation.	Nil	Normal to mild.
Varicella-zoster	Human cell tissue culture. Intranuclear inclusion bodies in sputum cells of patients with pneumonia.	Complement fixation. Neutralization. Fluorescent stainable antibody.	Nil	Normal to considerable.
Cytomegalovirus	Human cell tissue culture.	Complement fixation. Agglutination.	Nil	Normal or perhaps abnormal due to underlying primary disease.
Lymphocytic choriomeningitis	Simian cell tissue culture. Inoculation of chick embryos.	Complement fixation.	Nil	Leukopenia to moderate.

(Table continues on following page.)

Table 3–3. *Bacterial, Rickettsial, and Viral Pulmonary Infections (Continued)*

ORGANISM	ISOLATION AND IDENTIFICATION			
	MICROSCOPIC AND CULTURAL CHARACTERISTICS	SEROLOGIC TESTS	SKIN TESTS	LEUKOCYTE COUNT°
Infectious mononucleosis	Causative agent not isolated.	Heterophile antibody agglutination.	Nil	Leukocytosis early. Leukopenia with mononucleosis later.
Cat scratch fever	Causative agent not isolated.	Nil	Intradermal test with cat scratch antigen.	Normal
Psittacosis (ornithosis)	Inoculation of mice or chick embryos with sputum or blood.	Complement fixation. Wassermann and Kahn positive in 26 per cent.	Nil	Usually normal; rarely leukopenia or mild to moderate leukocytosis.
Lymphogranuloma venereum	Tissue culture. Inoculation of chick embryos.	Complement fixation.	Yes	Mild to moderate.
Coxiella burnetti	Culture of body fluids in chick embryos. Guinea pig inoculation.	Complement fixation. Agglutination.	Nil	Normal in 60 per cent. Mild to moderate.
Rickettsia tsutsugamushi	Peritoneal inoculation of mice with blood.	Agglutinins to proteus OX-K antigen.	Nil	Leukopenia to normal.

Table 3–4. *Mycotic Pulmonary Infections*

ORGANISM	ISOLATION AND IDENTIFICATION			
	MICROSCOPIC AND CULTURAL CHARACTERISTICS	SEROLOGIC TESTS	SKIN TESTS	LEUKOCYTE COUNT°
Histoplasma capsulatum	On glucose agar at 30°C mycelial growth with tuberculate spores; on cysteine blood agar at 37°C or in tissues stained with silver nitrate $2\mu \times 4\mu$ yeast cells occur. Mice inoculation useful.	Agglutination, precipitation, and complement fixation. Mycelial and yeast antigens should both be used.	Yes	Normal to mild. Rarely considerable in cavitary disease. Leukopenia in disseminated cases.
Coccidioides immitis	On glucose agar at 30°C mycelial growth with arthrospores; in human body fluids or tissues or after inoculation into mice or guinea pig 20 to 80μ spherules are seen.	Agglutination and complement fixation tests.	Yes	Normal to moderate. Eosinophilia usually with erythema nodosum.
Blastomyces dermatitidis	On glucose agar grows slowly as mycelia with conidia. On blood agar grows as single budding doubly refractile walled yeast organisms.	Yeast phase complement fixation test of limited value.	Yes	Normal to moderate; rarely considerable.

°Leukocyte count– <5,000 = Leukopenia
5,000–10,000 = Normal
10,000–12,000 = Mild
12,000–15,000 = Moderate
>15,000 = Considerable

Table 3–4. Mycotic Pulmonary Infections (Continued)

ORGANISM	MICROSCOPIC AND CULTURAL CHARACTERISTICS	SEROLOGIC TESTS	SKIN TESTS	LEUKOCYTE COUNT°
	ISOLATION AND IDENTIFICATION			
Cryptococcus neoformans	On glucose agar and on blood agar at 37°C 4 to 20μ yeast cells; these spherical organisms with a thick capsule may be identified in body fluids with india ink stain.	Precipitation tests both for antibody and antigen.	Nil	Normal to moderate.
Actinomyces israelii	On enriched agar under anaerobic conditions delicate gram-positive hyphae; in tissues or body fluids; mycelial clumps (sulfur granules) may be identified.	Nil	Nil	Normal to moderate.
Nocardia species	On glucose agar and on blood agar under aerobic conditions delicate branching filamentous hyphae; organism is gram-positive and some strains are acid-fast.	Nil	Nil	Moderate, usually neutrophilia. Occasionally lymphocytosis or leukopenia.
Aspergillus species	On glucose agar broad septate hyphae with characteristic conidiophores expanding into large vesicles form.	Precipitation	Yes	Normal to moderate, sometimes eosinophilia.
Candida species	On corn-meal agar thick-walled chlamydospores; in body fluids and tissues 2 to 4μ thin-walled oval budding yeast are seen.	Agglutination	Yes	Normal to moderate.
Phycomycetes (mucormycosis)	On glucose agar wide non-septate hyphae bearing large (100μ) globular sporangia develop.	Nil	Nil	
Geotrichum species	On glucose agar oval or spherical arthrospores separated from hyphae; in sputum there may be large rectangular arthrospores with rounded ends.	Agglutination	Yes	Eosinophilia in bronchial form.
Sporotrichum schenckii	On glucose agar at 30°C delicate hyphae supporting conidiophores; on enriched media at 37°C cigar-shaped gram-positive yeasts are found.	Agglutination and complement fixation.	Yes	Normal to moderate.
Blastomyces brasiliensis	On glucose agar mycelial growth with branching hyphae and conidia; in tissues or on culture at 37°C multiple budding yeast organisms are seen.	Complement fixation.	Yes	
Allescheria boydii	On glucose agar thin hyphae with stalks bearing single conidium; large (50 to 200μ) flask shaped ascospores are also seen.	Nil	Nil	
Torulopsis glabrata	On glucose agar reproduces by budding but fails to produce septate hyphae.	Nil	Nil	Normal

for the presence of this disease. However, cold agglutinins sometimes develop in other infectious diseases involving the lungs.

The mixing of specific serum with an antigen from the patient comprises a different form of antigen-antibody reaction which is not strictly a serologic test; this technique has thrown new light on the early immunologic diagnosis of infectious diseases.[493, 1009] The process requires the mixing of antigen with specific antibody either one of which is labeled with fluorescent dye. An antigen-antibody reaction is shown by fluorescent areas in histologic sections after thorough washing to remove unbound reagent. In most instances antiserum to the suspected organism is mixed with tracheobronchial secretions or cultures of this material. This is the direct method which requires labeling of the specific antibody to the suspected antigen. An indirect method which does not require fluorescent dye-tagging of specific antibody is of even greater practical value: This consists of an anti-immunoglobulin to one species of animal prepared in another species. This antiglobulin fluorescent conjugate can then be overlaid on the histologic preparation and in this way a number of specific antibodies to suspected antigenic organisms can be looked for at the same time.[1010] This procedure allows for diagnosis in the acute phase of various infections and its use in *Mycoplasma pneumoniae*,[494, 495] *H. capsulatum*,[496, 497] and *respiratory syncytial virus* infections[1011] has been reported.

SKIN TESTS

These tests may be divided into those used to detect hypersensitivity to allergens which produce immediate reactions and those used in the diagnosis of bacterial, fungal, and parasitic diseases which usually give rise to delayed reactions.

IMMEDIATE REACTIVITY. Scratch or intradermal tests are used to detect atopy, seasonal and perennial rhinitis, and asthma using common inhalants such as pollens, moulds, dusts, and danders; foods and drugs are used when the patient's history indicates specific sensitivity. Application of the allergens provokes more-or-less specific reactions. Some have a nonspecific irritating quality. Pollen extracts are almost always specific and usually of clinical significance. This is true also for mould-spore extracts and for many danders and some foods, but not for house dust, feathers, wool, kapok, and silk. Skin tests are particularly useful when they confirm a history indicating specific allergy and form the basis of a desensitization program.

SKIN TESTS FOR BACTERIA, FUNGI, AND PARASITES. Tables 3-2, 3-3, and 3-4 summarize the use of these reactions for diagnostic purposes. The only valuable skin tests for bacterial infections are those used in suspected mycobacterial disease and in the diagnosis of tularemia.

The tuberculin test is a delayed-reaction test, using old tuberculin (OT) produced by heat sterilization of cultures of tubercle bacilli or purified protein derivative (PPD) of various mycobacteria. An intradermal injection of 0.1 ml of intermediate-strength PPD or 1:1000 OT is usually recommended, but first-strength PPD or 1:10,000 OT should be used when active disease is strongly suspected. Development of induration at least 5 mm in diameter within 48 to 72 hours constitutes a positive reaction. Reactions of 10 mm or more in diameter are indicative of tuberculosis, active or arrested. Reactions of more than 5 mm and less than 10 mm in diameter to old tuberculin or to purified protein derivative of *M. tuberculosis* suggest the possibility of atypical mycobacterial infection and indicate the need for differential Mantoux testing.[1012, 1013] This is particularly true for children with cervical adenitis.[1012] False negative reactions are rare, and false positive reactions in mycotic or other infections do not occur.[1014] This test is most useful as a method of eliminating *M. tuberculosis* or other mycobacteria in the differential diagnosis of pulmonary disease.

The skin test for tularemia consists in the intradermal injection of antibody which causes a reaction within five days of the onset of disease. Skin tests using brucellin or brucellergen in the diagnosis of infections due to *B. melitensis* do not reflect the degree of activity of the infection and may stimulate the formation of agglutinins. Such a test is of limited value in the rare case of pulmonary disease suspected of being due to this organism; if it is to be used, the agglutination test should be performed first. Skin tests for fungus infections aid in the diagnosis of histoplasmosis and coccidioidomycosis but not blastomycosis.[498] When histoplasmin is used for intradermal skin testing, blood should be drawn then or at least within four days, since the injected material can produce circulating antibodies;[499, 500] however, this does not occur when the yeast-phase antigen is used.[501]

Skin tests in the presence of parasitic infestation give rise to variable reactions. In trichinosis, the injection of an antigen prepared from extracts of ground dry trichinae produces an immediate reaction. Both immediate and delayed reactions occur when the Casoni test is performed in cases of hydatid disease. Skin tests are of value in filariasis and toxoplasmosis, although positive results may not be obtained in the latter until several months after the onset of the disease.

BIOCHEMICAL TESTS

Sputum

The biochemical determination of the composition of bronchopulmonary secretions has not as yet received much attention as a diagnostic procedure. Burgi and colleagues[1015] have advocated the lactic dehydrogenase activity (LDH) and the semiquantitative estimate of deoxyribonucleic acid (DNA) by fluorescent microscopy as indicators of an active flare-up of infection in chronic bronchitis.

Pleural Fluid

Pleural fluid should be examined for cellular content, and aliquots should be sent to bacteriology, pathology, and biochemistry laboratories. The cytology, both malignant and benign, is considered later.

PROTEIN CONTENT. The terms "transudate" and "exudate" are still used in relation to pleural effusion, but the present tendency is to group effusions according to protein content rather than specific gravity. Carr and Power[502] summarized experiences at the Mayo Clinic over a four-year period and concluded that the concentration of protein almost always differentiates transudates of congestive heart failure from exudates due to cancer or tuberculosis: Eighty-four per cent of 43 specimens of pleural fluid attributable to congestive heart failure contained less than 3.0 g of protein per 100 ml of fluid, whereas 92.8 per cent of 167 effusions due to cancer and all 20 tuberculous effusions had more than 3.0 g/100 ml. In most cases, pleural fluid associated with cirrhosis of the liver was low in protein, whereas that due to pulmonary infarction, pneumonia, and lupus erythematosus had the higher protein concentration of an exudate.

Simultaneous electrophoretic analysis of serous pleural effusions and blood serum is of little diagnostic value, although correlation of the globulin pattern appears to be closer in tuberculous effusion than in other forms.[503]

GLUCOSE CONTENT. Opinions differ as to the significance of the concentration of glucose in pleural fluid. Glenert,[504] who examined 50 pleural effusions, concluded that the glucose content does not reflect the diagnosis and is no lower in tuberculosis than in other conditions. However, true values are obtained only when the pleural fluid and peripheral blood are taken simultaneously from fasting patients[505] — conditions not observed in Glenert's study.[504] There may be some value in determining the glucose content of a further specimen of pleural fluid after giving a glucose meal, since it is said that ingested glucose increases the very low values often found in tuberculosis[505] but not those associated with rheumatoid arthritis.[506] Extremely low concentrations of glucose in pleural fluid have been reported in tuberculosis[507] and rheumatoid arthritis[508-510] and it seems that values below 26 mg per 100 ml almost always indicate these diseases, whereas those of 80 mg per 100 ml or more are commonly associated with other causes, particularly neoplasm.

FAT CONTENT. Chylothorax should be suspected when the gross appearance of the effusion is cloudy or milky. In such cases the fat content will be greater than 400 mg per 100 ml and the protein content almost invariably greater than 3 g per 100 ml.[1016] Effusions in tuberculosis and in rheumatoid disease occasionally have a high cholesterol content and may closely resemble chylothorax.[1017]

HYALURONIC ACID. Two reports indicate that this substance may be present in pleural effusion due to pleural mesothelioma and not in those of different pathogenesis.[511, 512]

ENZYMES IN THE PLEURAL EFFUSION. A higher amylase content in pleural effusion than in blood serum indicates that the effusion is due to pancreatitis; the effusion usually is on the left side and may be hemorrhagic.[513–515] Early reports[516, 517] suggested that the concentration of lactic acid dehydrogenase was higher in effusions associated with malignant disease than in others. This was not borne out by subsequent studies which reported similar activity in inflammatory conditions, including tuberculosis.[518–520] A high level of alkaline phosphatase was found in the pleural fluid in one case of alveolar-cell carcinoma, suggesting that the enzyme may have been produced by the tumor.[521]

Blood Serum

Since pulmonary involvement may be only part of a generalized disease, and since chronic processes in the lung are often secondary to some other illness, many varied biochemistry procedures may prove useful in determining the etiology of abnormal shadows seen roentgenographically. One specific biochemical test of pulmonary parenchymal damage is the determination of lactic dehydrogenase (LDH) in the serum in pulmonary infarction. Wacker and associates[522, 523] described a triad of findings diagnostic of pulmonary infarction, although not present in every case: increase in the serum LDH, normal levels of serum glutamic oxaloacetic transaminase (SGOT), and elevated serum bilirubin values. Several of our cases have shown a major increase in LDH, reaching a peak within two to three days and associated with normal SGOT values, after an acute episode of pain compatible with pulmonary infarct, and later, very rapidly decreasing to within normal range.

CYTOLOGY

Nonmalignant Cells in Pulmonary Secretions

Reference has been made to the diagnostic significance of polymorphonuclear leukocytes in material expectorated by patients with bacterial pneumonia. In bronchial asthma, eosinophils may be found in association with octahedral Charcot-Leyden crystals and spiral casts from small bronchi (Curschmann's spirals); however, this finding aids little, if at all, in establishing the diagnosis, which will have been made on the basis of a history of bronchospasm and the physical examination. The only other nonmalignant cells that may be of diagnostic value when found in sputum are macrophages. Patients who give a history of potential aspiration of mineral oil should have their sputum examined for the presence of macrophages containing oil, and hemosiderin-laden macrophages may be found in the sputum of patients who have hemoptysis and whose roentgenograms show the acinar pattern of pulmonary hemosiderosis.

Nonmalignant Cells in Pleural Fluid

The relative numbers of red blood cells, polymorphonuclear granulocytes, eosinophils, and lymphocytes in pleural fluid may indicate the etiology of the effusion.

When erythrocytes predominate, even when the effusion is not pink or obviously bloody, the conditions leading to hemorrhagic effusion should be kept in mind. These include neoplasm, pulmonary infarction, trauma, spontaneous pneumothorax, and, rarely, tuberculosis and Meigs' syndrome. When the effusion is grossly bloody, a "bloody tap" has to be ruled out; when this has occurred the red-cell content is higher in the first part of the aspirated effusion.

A large number of neutrophils in the pleural fluid indicates bacterial pneumonia. Polymorphonuclear leukocytes may predominate during the early stages of tuberculous effusion, but this type of effusion is more commonly associated with a lymphocytic response: it is a fairly safe rule to consider an effusion with a cellular content of over 50 per cent polymorphonuclears not due to tuberculosis, whereas an effusion with more than 70 per cent lymphocytes and associated with a positive tuberculin reaction should be considered tuberculous unless another cause is strongly evident.[524] Lymphocytic pleural effusions (over 50 per cent of cells being lymphocytes) are much more commonly associated with positive pleural biopsy: in Yam's series,[1018] 50 per cent of cases with lymphocytic effusion had a positive pleural biopsy compared to only 10 per cent of those with nonlymphocytic effusion. An effusion which contains predominantly erythrocytes is more likely to be neoplastic than tuberculous, but the relative proportions of the various white blood cells do not differentiate these two most common causes of chronic pleural effusion.

Eosinophilic effusion may occur in a great variety of conditions and is not necessarily associated with blood eosinophilia. Eosinophils rarely occur in tuberculous or neoplastic pleural effusions,[525, 526] and this may be the most important inference that can be drawn from this finding. In one series the diagnosis could be established in only six of 11 patients whose fluid contained more than 25 per cent eosinophils.[527] Pulmonary infarction is said to be a relatively frequent cause,[528] and histoplasmosis and coccidioidomycosis sometimes give rise to eosinophilic pleural effusion.[525, 528] Pleural biopsy in six cases of eosinophilic effusion showed nonspecific pleuritis in five and rheumatoid granuloma in one.[525]

Malignant Cells in Pulmonary Secretions

Cytologic examination of pulmonary secretions by the Papanicolaou technique is the most accurate method for diagnosing bronchogenic carcinoma: Three authors have reported positive cytologic findings in 90 per cent or more of histologically proved cases.[459, 529, 531] This method of diagnosis of pulmonary malignancy is far superior to bronchoscopy or to biopsy of prescalene lymph nodes, although these procedures may prove complementary.[532]

The use of heated aerosol solutions of propylene glycol and sulfur dioxide to obtain secretions from more peripheral areas of the respiratory tract most likely is responsible for the ever-increasing success with the Papanicolaou technique.[529, 533-538] An even greater degree of diagnostic accuracy is reported with repeated specimens,[529, 531] and Umiker had 96 per cent positive findings when more than five specimens were examined in proved cases of carcinoma.[529] However, Lerner and associates almost invariably obtained positive results with the first specimen.[539] Kuper and associates [1019] have described two techniques for concentrating neoplastic cells: (a) soluble swabs used at bronchoscopy and (b) differential centrifugation of sputum after liquefaction by ultrasonic energy. The former may even surpass direct lung biopsy in reliability, and the latter has proved useful not only for the detection of malignant cells[1020] but also in nonmalignant sputum cytology.[1021] Although comparative studies have not been made of the relative cytologic merits of sputum specimens and bronchial washings, one group of authors stated that every one of their cases of bronchogenic carcinoma diagnosed by examination of bronchial washings had had positive sputum previously.[539]

Diagnostic material may be obtained in an even greater percentage of cases with the use of a 50 per cent solution (instead of the usual 10 to 15 per cent) of propylene glycol as an aerosol; part of the secretory material is smeared and examined by the Papanicolaou technique, and part is prepared and stained as cell blocks.[533, 534]

Peripheral lesions which cannot be biopsied and which remain undiagnosed despite repeated cytologic examination of aerosol-induced sputum may yield pathologic material during bronchial brushing. A microbrush is introduced, under fluoroscopic control, through a catheter in the segmental bronchus to the site of the lesion; the bronchial lumen is brushed, irrigated, and suctioned.[255, 397, 540, 541, 543] Malignant cells from bronchial secretions are found sometimes in gastric washings.[467]

In some patients whose bronchial secretions repeatedly show positive cytology the roentgenogram is normal.[534, 539, 544] Even after bronchoscopy and bronchography the source of the malignant cells may not be identified, and, since secretions may spill over from one side to the other, selective bronchial aspiration from a lung or lobe may not identify the site of the lesion.[539] The management of this perplexing situation is discussed on page 764.

The Papanicolaou technique is useful in detecting malignant cells from metastatic pulmonary lesions also; in two reported series they were present in 38 per cent[545] and 44 per cent[538] of cases.

"False positives," showing class V cells by the Papanicolaou technique do occur but are rare; they are reported to represent 1 to 3 per cent in most series.[531, 539, 546] "False negatives" are thought to be due to a lack of communication between the tumor and the bronchial lumen, to bronchial stenosis, or to the misinterpretation of smears.[459, 547]

Fluorescence microscopy has been used in exfoliative cytology as a means of screening for cancer of the lung.[548] The average examination time of the specimen is about one-half that taken with the Papanicolaou method, but the positive yield is only 83 per cent of that obtained by the latter method.

Malignant Cells in Pleural Fluid

These are found in about 50 to 60 per cent of cases of effusion due to malignant disease.[550, 551] The fact that some of these effusions are secondary to pneumonitis distal to an obstructing bronchogenic carcinoma probably accounts for this small positive yield. False positives occur commonly because of the difficulty of distinguishing malignant from mesothelial cells. The Millipore-filter technique and cell block are considered in one report[552] to be more productive than the Papanicolaou method; and certainly, as discussed in the section on pleural biopsy, positive results are obtained more often with a Cope or Harefield needle.

HEMATOLOGIC PROCEDURES IN LUNG DISEASE

Polycythemia frequently but not invariably occurs in association with chronic hypoxemia in pulmonary disease. In some patients who have endured long periods of hypoxemia and whose blood shows normal values for hematocrit and hemoglobin, the red-cell mass is actually increased but is not recognized as such because of simultaneous increase in plasma volume. In such circumstances determination of the blood volume reveals an absolute polycythemia.

Anemia does not commonly occur in lung disease. It may develop in relation to a chronic infectious process or widespread malignancy, and in some cases of pulmonary hemosiderosis anemia may be noted even before the patient expectorates blood; in this latter condition the appearance of anemia in a patient whose roentgenogram shows a diffuse acinar pattern may constitute an important diagnostic pointer.

Variations in the total and differential leu-kocyte count may play a major role in the differential diagnosis of lung disease (*see* Tables 3–2, 3–3, and 3–4. A leukocytosis of over 15,000 white cells per c mm, with a predominance of polymorphonuclear cells, is strong evidence for bacterial rather than viral pneumonia. It must be remembered, however, that fulminating bacterial pneumonia may be associated with normal or even low white-cell counts. In volunteers inoculated with several different viruses, Douglas and associates[1022] found a leukocyte response only in those who developed symptoms. This response consisted of an early increase in neutrophils and decrease in lymphocytes, with a reversal of these findings later in the illness. When the differential leukocyte count shows eosinophilia, the diagnostic possibilities are limited: bronchial asthma, drug reactions, parasitic infestations, collagen diseases, and rarer causes, such as Hodgkin's disease, sarcoidosis, and mycotic infections, should be considered.

The culture of bone-marrow aspirate sometimes aids in the diagnosis of chronic infections, and the detection of malignant cells in the bone marrow may establish the nature of pulmonary lesions seen on the chest roentgenogram.

ELECTROCARDIOGRAPHY

An electrocardiogram is of fundamental importance in differentiating myocardial infarction from acute massive pulmonary embolism. It is also useful in indicating lung disease as a cause of heart failure in patients who might otherwise be considered to be suffering from coronary artery insufficiency or myocardial disease. The electrocardiographic abnormalities of diffuse lung disease[553] must be familiar to the physician specializing in this field and are reviewed in relation to cor pulmonale and pulmonary hytertension.

PULMONARY FUNCTION TESTS

Lung Volumes

The volumes and capacities of the lung can be appreciated from a study of the diagram depicted in Figure 3–1. There are

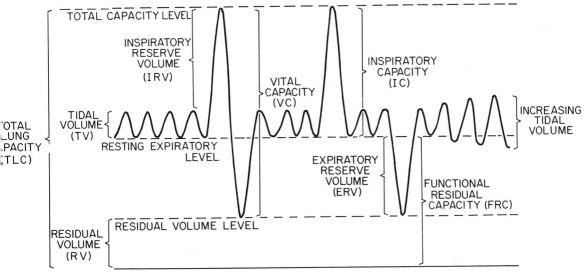

Figure 3–1. Lung Volumes and Capacities. *See* text for description.

four volumes: (1) the tidal volume (TV), which is the amount of gas moving in and out of the lung with each respiratory cycle; (2) the residual volume (RV), which is the amount remaining in the lung after a maximal expiration and is the only lung volume that cannot be measured directly by spirometry; (3) the inspiratory reserve volume (IRV), the additional gas that can be inspired from the end of a quiet inspiration; and (4) the expiratory reserve volume (ERV), the additional amount of gas that can be expired from the resting or end-expiratory level.

There are also four capacities, each of which contains two or more volumes: (a) total lung capacity (TLC), which is the gas contained in the lung at the end of a maximal inspiration; (b) vital capacity (VC), which is the amount that can be expired after a maximal inspiration; (c) inspiratory capacity (IC), which is the amount of gas that can be inspired from the end of a quiet expiration; and (d) functional residual capacity (FRC), which is the volume of gas remaining in the lungs at the end of a quiet expiration.

VITAL CAPACITY (VC) AND ITS SUBDIVISIONS. Although this volume of gas can be measured from the end of a maximal expiration to full inspiration, it is usually expressed as the amount of air expelled from the lungs after a maximal inspiration. In obstructive lung disease, because air is

trapped in the lungs, the VC is less when maximal inspiration is followed by maximal expiration than when it is determined from the end of maximal expiration to maximal inspiration. The VC usually is measured with a spirometer; predicted normal values have been calculated based on age, sex, and height.[152] Since there is considerable variation even among normal subjects, no significance should be attached to a measured value that varies 20 per cent or less from the predicted value. The VC also varies depending upon the position of the patient when the volume is recorded; it is less when he is supine than when he is erect.

The VC serves little purpose as an independent measurement of pulmonary function but can be of significant value when considered in conjunction with the results of other tests of pulmonary function. It is a useful index of day-to-day changes in the clinical state of patients with neuromuscular disease. The subdivisions of VC, particularly the inspiratory capacity and inspiratory reserve volume, are rarely useful in assessing pulmonary function. The ERV is greatly reduced in patients with obesity and hypoventilation syndrome, in which state the $\dot{V}_A/\dot{Q}$ ratios are low at the lung bases.[111] The TV varies greatly in normal subjects, and the measurement of this by itself usually is not informative; however, multiplication of TV by the respiratory rate per minute yields the minute volume, and in some cases alveolar hypoventilation can be assessed on these two indices alone.

The ratio of measured as a percentage of predicted normal VC to measured as a percentage of predicted normal forced expiratory flow rates (EFR) indicates whether insufficiency is "restrictive" or "obstructive." In obstructive disease the VC is relatively well maintained in comparison with forced EFR, whereas in restrictive disease the EFR may be close to normal and the VC very definitely decreased.

FUNCTIONAL RESIDUAL CAPACITY (FRC) AND RESIDUAL VOLUME (RV). Inert gases are used to measure these compartments. Two methods are commonly used—the open-circuit method, using nitrogen, and the closed-circuit method, using helium. With the open-circuit method the patient breathes 100 per cent oxygen for seven minutes and all expired gas is collected. FRC is calculated by multiplying the amount of gas expired during this period by the percentage of nitrogen in the expired gas. RV is determined by subtracting ERV, as measured on a spirometer, from FRC. With the closed-circuit method the patient breathes from a spirometer containing a known concentration of helium. At the beginning of the experiment the helium concentration in the lungs is zero; as the patient breathes in and out of the spirometer, the gas mixes between spirometer and lungs until the concentration of helium is the same in both. FRC is calculated from the concentration of helium before and at the end of the experiment and the volume in the spirometer. When the lung contains poorly ventilated areas it may be necessary to continue the test for upward of 20 minutes before equilibrium is attained.

The RV is readily obtained by subtracting from FRC the ERV as measured on the spirometer.

When the thorax contains volumes of gas which barely communicate with the conducting tubes, equilibrium between patient and spirometer may appear to be reached while gas is still entering these areas so slowly as to go undetected. To measure the true thoracic gas volume in these circumstances it is necessary to place the patient in a body box (plethysmograph). With this apparatus the thoracic volume can be calculated by applying Boyle's law, which states the relationship between changes in pressure and volume of a gas at constant temperature. The figure obtained, minus FRC determined by the open- or closed-circuit method, is the volume of lung in poor communication with the conducting system.

RV increases with age and in such circumstances does not significantly interfere with function. A marked increase in FRC and RV may occur in the presence of obstructive lung disease; in such cases the volume measured by the body plethysmograph may be higher than that obtained by the open- or closed-circuit method.

In common with VC values, measurements of lung volumes by themselves are of little use in the assessment of lung function, but they may be most informative when considered with the results of other pulmonary function tests.

TOTAL LUNG CAPACITY (TLC). The TLC is calculated simply by the addition of RV and VC. This measurement in itself can be misleading, since TLC may be normal in the presence of serious disease—and, in fact, may be much greater than normal in patients with emphysema, because of increase in the FRC. In "restrictive" disease of the lungs or thoracic cage, the TLC is decreased because of decrease in VC or RV or both.

As with RV and FRC, the TLC may be falsely low when measured by helium and nitrogen methods. Volumetric determination based on posteroanterior and lateral roentgenograms of the chest has been shown to correlate better with values obtained by body plethysmograph in emphysematous patients and may be accomplished by experienced workers in 15 to 20 minutes.[149, 1023, 1024]

Measurement of Composition of Alveolar Gas

As stated in Chapter 1, the composition of gas in the acinar unit is dependent upon alveolar ventilation and mixed venous P_{O_2} and P_{CO_2} of the blood in the pulmonary capillaries. The mixed venous blood gases can be determined by analysis of samples obtained through a catheter in the right side of the heart, but this procedure is not suitable for routine use. Mixed venous P_{CO_2} has been measured by a rebreathing method[555, 556] which yields accurate values. The arterial blood P_{CO_2} can be calculated from these results by assuming a constant arterial–venous P_{CO_2} difference of 6 mm.

Ventilation of the acinar unit can be estimated with dependable accuracy in subjects with normal lungs. For this, the total minute ventilation is measured with a spirometer or by collecting expired air in a rubber or plastic bag and determining its volume during passage through a meter. The end-tidal sample accurately reflects the alveolar gas composition in normal lungs; this sample is obtained toward the end of expiration, when the dead space has been washed out. The alveolar ventilation of the normal subject can be calculated from the end-tidal sample of carbon dioxide or oxygen, the volume of expired gas, and the volume and gas content inspired. When the lungs are diseased, however, the situation is not so simple, since there may be many acinar units which are not uniformly ventilated and which empty late in expiration. In such circumstances it is difficult, if not impossible, to obtain a true alveolar (or acinar) sample, and a reliable estimate of alveolar ventilation requires measurement of the total minute ventilation and subtraction from this of an assumed volume of anatomic dead space, based on several factors, including age, sex, FRC, and tidal volume. The volume of alveolar ventilation per minute of a patient with diseased lungs may equal that of a subject with healthy lungs of the same age, sex, and build. Despite the fact that the patient has some units which are barely ventilated, he has others that are overventilated, and, therefore, total ventilation may be normal.

There is no doubt, however, that the most accurate index of alveolar ventilation is analysis of an arterial blood sample, which gives values for P_{CO_2} and P_{O_2}. This is considered in greater detail later, but it can be said here that a P_{CO_2} value above the normal range indicates that many acinar units are poorly ventilated.

Measurement of Mechanics of Acinar Ventilation

MEASUREMENT OF COMPLIANCE. As discussed in Chapter 1, compliance is the relationship between the pressure required to overcome "elastic recoil" and the volume of air that moves into the lung as a result of this pressure change. To avoid the effect of resistance, and to measure compliance alone, the test is done in a "static" position, that is, while the breath is held with the glottis open. As the normal lung becomes more inflated it becomes less compliant and the pressure-volume curve becomes more horizontal (*see* Figure 3–2). Compliance is expressed in liters/cm H_2O. Pressure is measured by a manometer at-

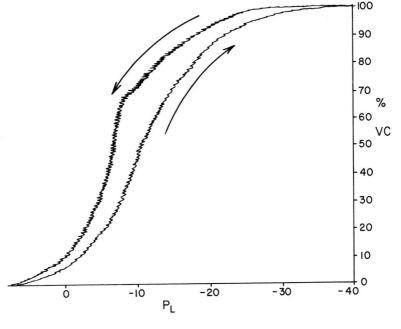

Figure 3–2. **Pressure–Volume Curve.** A pressure–volume tracing of a young male adult measured in both inspiration and expiration from residual volume to total lung capacity and back to residual volume. The upper curve represents the expiratory tracing. Notice the more horizontal appearance (decrease in compliance) as total lung capacity is reached.

tached to a tube leading to a thin-walled balloon which is swallowed to the mid-esophagus. The volume is measured either by use of a pneumotachograph at the mouth, with integration of the pneumotachogram signal, or while the patient breathes from a spirometer. This pressure-volume curve includes measurement of the "elastic" properties of the elastic and collagen tissues of the lungs and those of the thoracic cage and the force required to overcome the surface-tension effect of the alveoli. The surface-active properties of removed lung tissue can be measured, but no technique has been devised to determine the surface-lining tension *in vivo.*

MEASUREMENT OF RESISTANCE

Spirometry. These are indirect methods for determining the resistance of the airways and lung tissue. A single forced inspiratory or expiratory curve is measured on a revolving drum or a bellows-type apparatus and is expressed as liters/min moved in or out of the lung. In patients with obstructive lung disease a simple spirogram during deep breathing often shows the longer expiration than inspiration and the air-trapping that occurs after maximal inspiration. The "timed vital capacity" may be used to quantify expiration; after an inspiration, the patient exhales as rapidly as he can all of the air in his lungs. This is the forced expiratory volume (FEV); the amount expired during the first 0.75 second, the first 1.0 second,

and the first 3.0 seconds, are expressed $FEV_{0.75}$, $FEV_{1.0}$, and $FEV_{3.0}$. Normal persons exhale approximately 83 per cent of VC in 1.0 second and approximately 97 per cent in 3.0 seconds, whereas expiratory flow curves of patients with obstructive lung disease are prolonged. On the other hand, although patients with a restrictive lung condition such as fibrosis may have a substantially reduced VC, they can have almost normal $FEV_{1.0}$ and $FEV_{3.0}$ values, since there is no bronchial obstruction.

Many ways of expressing the forced-expiration curve have been devised. In our laboratory we measure FEV on a rapidly revolving drum and from this curve determine $FEV_{0.75}$ (the volume expired in the first three-quarters of a second), which is multiplied by 40 and is expressed in liters/min. This is sometimes referred to as the indirect maximal breathing capacity (MBC) or maximal voluntary ventilation (MVV) (*see the following discussion*), since it has been shown that, in normal subjects, $FEV_{0.75} \times 40$ closely correlates with direct measurement of the MBC or MVV. In addition, we measure the middle half of the FEV curve and express this volume in liters/sec (Figure 3–3).

In place of the single forced expiratory curve recorded on a spirometer, measurement of the maximal volume of gas that can be breathed per minute is used in some laboratories; this also is known as the MBC or

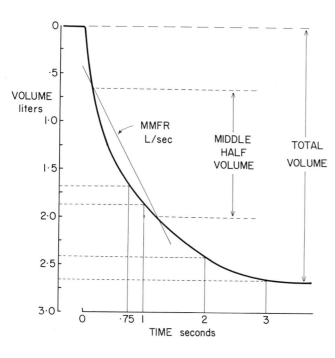

Figure 3–3. **Measurement of Ventilatory Volumes.** This graph depicts the curve of a forced vital capacity (FVC) in which a total volume of 2.6 liters has been expired in 3 seconds ($FEV_{3.0}$). Volumes expired during the ¾ second ($FEV_{0.75}$), 1 second ($FEV_{1.0}$), and 2 second ($FEV_{2.0}$) intervals are also indicated. The maximal midexpiratory flow rate (MMFR) can be calculated at 1.3 liters/sec.

MVV. It can be calculated from a tracing made while the patient breathes in and out of a spirometer as rapidly as possible for 15 seconds, or by collecting the expired gas in a bag for the same length of time. The value is multiplied by four to give the volume in liters/min. Since this test is very tiring, particularly for patients with abnormal lungs, it is used less and less.

Although these indirect methods for assessing resistance in the lungs are simple to perform and are widely used, they must be interpreted with caution: (1) the test requires the co-operation of the patient, and falsely low values may be recorded and (2) it does not indicate specific mechanical abnormalities, since patients with decreased compliance have reduced flow rates, and, therefore, direct measurements of resistance are preferable.

Use of Body Plethysmograph. Since resistance equals the pressure difference divided by the volume flow, resistance in the airways can be determined only with knowledge of the instantaneous air flow and the difference between atmospheric and alveolar pressures. Air flow can be determined with a pneumotachograph, but the measurement of alveolar pressure requires a more elaborate procedure. The patient breathes in and out in an airtight box and the pressure around him is measured and recorded by a very sensitive manometer. The alveolar pressure can be calculated from the change in pressure in the box during the respiratory cycle.

Use of Mouth Pressure For Determining Airway Resistance. Alveolar pressure can be determined indirectly by using an electrically controlled shutter; while this device momentarily shuts off flow during inspiration, the mouth pressure (which, presumably, is equal to the alveolar pressure immediately before interruption) is recorded. The apparatus is cheaper but yields less accurate values than the body plethysmograph.

Normal values as determined by the body plethysmograph during rapid, shallow breathing range from 0.6 to 2.4 cm H_2O/liter/sec, with flow rates of 0.5 liter/sec in adults.

Measurement of Perfusion of Acinar Units

MEASUREMENT OF VOLUME, FLOW, AND PRESSURE. Although volume, pressure, and flow of blood in individual acinar units cannot be determined, their values in the lungs as a whole can be measured during catheterization of the right side of the heart. Cardiac output can be measured while the patient is resting or exercising, using the Fick method or dye-dilution curves. Instantaneous pulmonary capillary flow (VC) can be measured by two methods. In the first, the patient inhales a mixture of 80 per cent nitrous oxide and 20 per cent oxygen while seated in a body plethysmograph; the sensitive manometer which records the pressure around the patient shows an abrupt fall as nitrous oxide leaves the acini to dissolve in the blood. Carbon monoxide is used in the second method to measure diffusion; the membrane component can be separated from that due to the blood, and VC can be estimated.[77, 78]

MEASUREMENT OF THE DISTRIBUTION OF CAPILLARY BLOOD. The relative VC to each lung can be determined from the oxygen uptake recorded during bronchospirometry, in which a special catheter is introduced through the trachea, separating the conducting system to each lung. The oxygen uptake of individual lobes can be measured, but this technique is not suitable for routine use in even the most sophisticated laboratories. Newer methods for determining the distribution of pulmonary capillary blood make use of a radioactive gas, such as xenon; this is injected and its regional distribution throughout the lungs is measured by scintillation counters placed over the chest wall. Radioactive carbon dioxide, which is inhaled, can be used similarly. These methods are still gross and do not detect the distribution of blood to the barely macroscopic acinar unit. Further reference is made to this technique in the discussion of ventilation/perfusion ratios.

Measurement of the Diffusion of Gas in Acinar Units

As stated in Chapter 1, the diffusing capacity formerly was calculated directly from the diffusion of oxygen; carbon monoxide has largely replaced this gas, for technical reasons. The diffusing capacity for carbon monoxide (DL_{CO}) is computed as follows:

$$DL_{CO} = \frac{\text{ml of CO taken up by capillary blood}}{\text{mean alveolar PCO} - \text{mean capillary PCO}}.$$

The amount of carbon monoxide taken up by capillary blood is calculated by subtracting volume × CO concentration of expired gas from volume × CO concentration of inspired gas. Determination of the denominator of this equation is more subject to error in cases of lung diseases. In normal subjects, a sample of gas expired at the end of tidal volume reflects accurately the mean alveolar Pco, and, since the normal mean capillary Pco is so small that it can be ignored, the diffusing capacity can be calculated reliably. However, in diseased lungs which have relatively underventilated areas that empty late, the normal sharp division between dead-space gas and alveolar gas is lost and the end-tidal sample does not necessarily represent the mean alveolar Pco.

Several techniques for use with carbon monoxide have been devised for measuring the diffusing capacity. The main differences between these techniques are the length of time the carbon monoxide is kept in the lungs and the methods of determining the mean alveolar Pco. The single-breath method entails the inhalation of a gas which contains minute quantities of carbon monoxide and breath-holding for ten seconds. The steady-state technique requires the inhalation of the carbon monoxide gas mixture for several breaths, until alveolar Pco remains constant. We use the steady-state method and determine mean alveolar Pco from an end-tidal sample under resting conditions. In addition to the diffusing capacity, the fractional removal of carbon monoxide is calculated from the end-tidal sample; this confirms the accuracy of the diffusing-capacity value, since both decrease simultaneously in the majority of cases.[557]

The fractional uptake of carbon monoxide is the amount removed divided by the amount inspired; thus:

$$\text{CO uptake (\%)} = \frac{\text{CO inspired} - \text{CO expired}}{\text{CO inspired}}.$$

During hyperventilation, fractional carbon dioxide uptake may decrease but the diffusing capacity is unchanged. During hypoventilation, however, the diffusing capacity may be reduced due to a very low tidal volume, whereas fractional carbon monoxide uptake decreases to a lesser extent. Diffusing capacity during exercise can be determined by the steady-state method; however, an end-tidal sample obtained in these circumstances is not reliable, and since the numerator of the equation for calculating

the diffusing capacity for carbon monoxide becomes the chief determinant, in such instances it is valid to calculate alveolar Pco from the inspired and expired carbon monoxide concentrations, assuming a value for the respiratory dead space.

The diffusing capacity reflects not only the thickness of the alveolocapillary membrane but also the total area of this membrane and the hemoglobin content of the pulmonary capillary blood. Removal of a lobe or an entire lung reduces the overall diffusing area. Inequality in the ventilation/perfusion ratio results in a decrease in the diffusing capacity, because less carbon monoxide is taken up by poorly ventilated or poorly perfused areas than by areas with normal perfusion and ventilation. Since the uptake of carbon monoxide by capillary blood is due mainly to its great affinity for hemoglobin, in cases of anemia the diffusing capacity may be reduced because of hemoglobin lack. During exercise, the increased size of the pulmonary vascular bed and increased cardiac output cause increase in the diffusing capacity.

Measurement of Matching of Blood Flow and Ventilation

MEASUREMENTS OF DISTRIBUTION OF INSPIRED AIR. Poorly ventilated acinar units receive less oxygen from a single deep breath of 100 per cent oxygen and empty later during the next expiration than well-ventilated acini. This is the rationale of the single-breath 100 per cent oxygen test with continuous analysis by nitrogen meter of the expired air. After a single inspiration of 100 per cent oxygen, the first part of the expiration contains 100 per cent oxygen, which comes from the dead space. Next, the expired gas comes from the acini; if these empty synchronously and are equally ventilated the nitrogen meter curve shows a horizontal line throughout the rest of the expiration. Poorly ventilated acini receive smaller amounts of oxygen and empty late so that during the next complete expiration the nitrogen curve slopes upward as it records their contribution.

The percentage of nitrogen expired can be calculated in a multiple-breath method during which the patient breathes 100 per cent oxygen for seven minutes. When the distribution of inspired air is uniform the nitrogen content of an "alveolar" sample at the end of the seven minutes is 2.5 per cent or less. In patients with impaired distribution, 10 to 20 minutes may elapse before the nitrogen content of poorly ventilated areas has been replaced by oxygen, and the nitrogen content of an "alveolar" sample taken at the end of seven minutes may greatly exceed the normal figure of 2.5 per cent.

The third method for determining the distribution of inspired gas makes use of the helium closed-circuit apparatus and is expressed as the mixing efficiency (ME). This apparatus can be used to calculate lung volumes also, including RV. The patient is connected to the circuit and breathes from a spirometer containing helium,[557] and the concentration of expired gas is measured by a katharometer; the distribution is determined by recording the number of breaths taken before the helium concentration remains steady.

MEASUREMENT OF DISTRIBUTION OF PULMONARY CAPILLARY BLOOD. Uneven distribution of pulmonary capillary blood in the presence of relatively uniform ventilation can be detected when the areas of unperfused lung are large. The alveolar PCO_2 is determined by analysis of a sample of expired gas taken at the end of tidal volume (end-tidal) or at the end of maximal expiration (end-expiratory) and is compared with the arterial PCO_2. A PCO_2 difference of greater than 6 mm Hg indicates the presence of large numbers of unperfused acini; the expired gas from these areas contains no carbon dioxide and, therefore, decreases the PCO_2 of the total sample of gas. This measurement becomes less accurate with the development of compensatory mechanisms which decrease ventilation to unperfused areas and divert inspired air to those that are well perfused.

MEASUREMENT OF INEQUALITY OF VENTILATION/PERFUSION RATIOS. Unlike the single-breath method, which utilizes an inert gas that measures the distribution of inspired air only, continuous analysis of a single expiration by means of a carbon dioxide analyzer gives information pertaining to both ventilation and perfusion and their uniformity. A rise in the carbon dioxide concentration throughout expiration indicates perfusion of poorly ventilated areas which empty late in the expiratory phase.

An increase in the "physiologic" dead space, which can be calculated with the Bohr equation,[1] is another method for assessing inequality of ventilation/perfusion. Inequality when there is overperfusion relative to ventilation is manifested by an increase in the alveolar-arterial difference for nitrogen (A–a N_2). In poorly ventilated areas which are perfused the PO_2 is decreased, whereas the PCO_2 and PN_2 are increased. The arterial blood PN_2 is reflected in the PN_2 of the urine, and the A–a N_2 can be determined by gas chromatography without the necessity for arterial puncture. Since nitrogen is an inert gas, the venous blood and arterial blood PN_2 are identical. Thus, a true or "absolute" shunt of venous to arterial blood effects no change in the alveolo-arterial nitrogen difference, and, since there appears to be no alveolar-end-capillary difference for nitrogen, this test can be used to rule out blood-shunt and diffusion defect to confirm whether hypoxemia is due to ventilation/perfusion inequality. In other words, a difference in nitrogen values in arterial blood (or urine) and alveolar gas can result only from inequality of ventilation/perfusion ratios, due to the perfusion of poorly ventilated areas.

Bronchospirometry is used to detect differences in ventilation and perfusion in the two lungs. When oxygen uptake is decreased and ventilation to one lung is normal or nearly so, perfusion is abnormal.

In recent years, tests have been devised which not only detect the presence of ventilation/perfusion inequality in the lung but also its location. These methods are still in their infancy and necessitate expensive equipment, but results obtained so far are so spectacular that undoubtedly these techniques will be widely used in routine pulmonary function assessment in the future. This use of radioactive oxygen and carbon dioxide was summarized in a recent monograph by West,[107] and the inhalation and intravenous injection of radioactive xenon to show the distribution of inspired gas and the perfusion of pulmonary capillaries has been used by workers in the Cardio-respiratory Service of the Royal Victoria Hospital.[102, 909–914]

Measurement of Blood Gases and H⁺ ion Concentration

Arterial blood can be obtained almost as easily as venous blood. Brachial or radial arteries should be used in preference to femoral arteries, which should be punctured only as a last resort. Since arteries are deeper than veins they are more evasive; therefore, the area should be infiltrated with local anesthetic, which serves the double purpose of reducing pain and vasospasm. It is no longer necessary to use a Cournand or Riley needle for routine arterial puncture; we use very sharp disposable needles which fit tightly on to the adapter of a 10 or 20 ml syringe. A heparin solution is drawn through the needle and allowed to coat the sides of the syringe, and then all of the air and heparin is expelled. The needle is introduced at an angle of 45 to 90 degrees at the site of maximal pulsation; a pulsatile flow into the syringe is seen when the lumen of the vessel is entered. It is wise to maintain pressure on the site of puncture for five to ten minutes after withdrawal of the needle. The orifice of the needle is immediately sealed with a rubber stopper; any air which gets into the barrel of the syringe should be expelled before the needle is stopped. Results are most accurate when the sample is analyzed immediately; when this is not possible the sample should be placed in a refrigerator.

The Van Slyke method of measuring oxygen content and oxygen capacity of arterial blood is used still in the modern pulmonary function laboratory as a yardstick for checking the accuracy of newer methods. In our routine laboratory we use a spectrophotometric method (Beckman Instruments, Inc., Fullerton, California) to determine the arterial oxygen saturation, and we simultaneously measure the P_{O_2} of the arterial blood with an electrode (Instrument Laboratories, Inc., Watertown, Mass.). This assessment of arterial blood oxygen by two methods is useful for detecting technical errors, since the accuracy of values can be ascertained by reference to the oxygen dissociation curve.

P_{CO_2} and H^+ ion concentration also can be measured with electrodes (Instrument Laboratories, Inc., Watertown, Mass.). It is essential that the accuracy of these delicate instruments be checked from time to time, using an Astrup apparatus to make duplicate measurements.

In infants or young children arterialized capillary blood samples may be obtained from the finger or heel with a heparinized capillary tube and the results compare favorably with simultaneously obtained arterial blood.[1025]

4

ROENTGENOLOGIC SIGNS IN THE DIAGNOSIS OF CHEST DISEASE

DISEASES OF THE LUNG WHICH CAUSE
 INCREASE IN ROENTGENOGRAPHIC
 DENSITY
 PREDOMINANT AIR-SPACE DISEASE
  Parenchymal Consolidation
  Parenchymal Atelectasis
 PREDOMINANT INTERSTITIAL DISEASE
  Concepts of Roentgenologic Anatomy
  Roentgenographic Patterns of Diffuse
   Interstitial Diseases
 COMBINED AIR-SPACE AND INTERSTITIAL
  DISEASE
  Combined Air-Space Consolidation and
   Interstitial Disease
  Combined Air-Space Consolidation, Air-
   Space Atelectasis, and Interstitial Disease
 GENERAL SIGNS IN DISEASES WHICH CAUSE
  INCREASE IN ROENTGENOGRAPHIC DENSITY
  The Character of the Border of a Pulmonary
   Lesion
  Change in Position of Interlobar Fissures
  Cavitation
  Calcification
  Bulla Formation
  Change in Size or Position of Intrathoracic
   Lesions
  Distribution of Disease within the Lungs
   (Anatomic Bias)

  Roentgenologic Localization of Pulmonary
   Disease (the "Silhouette" Sign)
  The Time Factor in Roentgenologic Diagnosis
 LINE SHADOWS
  Line Shadows of Parenchymal Origin
  Line Shadows of Interstitial and
   Bronchovascular Origin
  Line Shadows of Pleural Origin
DISEASES OF THE LUNG WHICH CAUSE
 DECREASE IN ROENTGENOGRAPHIC
 DENSITY
 ROENTGENOLOGIC SIGNS
  Alteration in Lung Volume
  Alteration in Vasculature
  Pulmonary Air Cysts
ROENTGENOLOGIC SIGNS OF DISEASES OF
 THE PLEURA
 ROENTGENOLOGIC SIGNS OF PLEURAL EFFUSION
  Typical Arrangement of Free Pleural Fluid
  Atypical Arrangement of Free Pleural Fluid
  Loculation of Pleural Fluid
 ROENTGENOLOGIC SIGNS OF PLEURAL
  THICKENING AND CALCIFICATION
  Pleural Thickening
  Pleural Calcification
  Pleural Neoplasms
 ROENTGENOLOGIC SIGNS OF PNEUMOTHORAX
  Tension Pneumothorax (and Hydrothorax)

The integration of information obtained from a systematic interpretation of the chest roentgenogram and a careful analysis of the clinical status of the patient yields a high degree of diagnostic accuracy in most diseases of the chest. However, although the final assessment must take into account the patient's history, physical examination, laboratory tests, and pulmonary function studies, it behoves the roentgenologist to glean as much information as possible from an objective assessment of the roentgenogram *before* attempting clinical correlation. A roentgenographic pattern of disease may be sufficiently distinctive that an etiologic diagnosis can be made with reason-

187

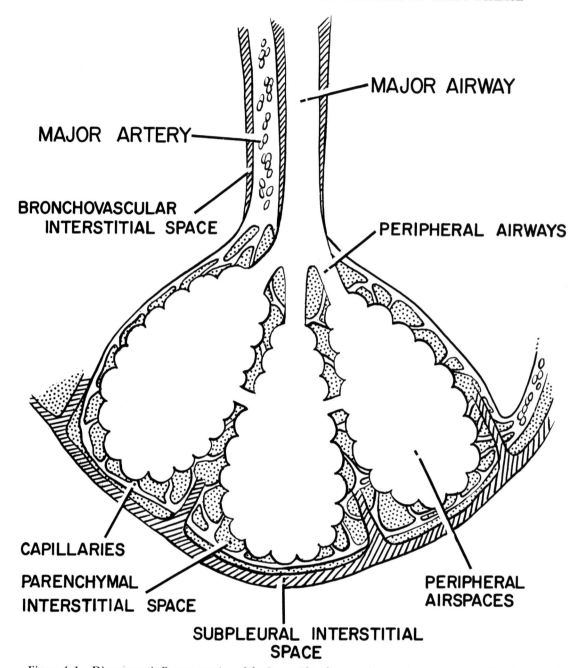

MAJOR AIRWAY

MAJOR ARTERY

**BRONCHOVASCULAR
INTERSTITIAL SPACE**

PERIPHERAL AIRWAYS

CAPILLARIES

**PARENCHYMAL
INTERSTITIAL SPACE**

**PERIPHERAL
AIRSPACES**

**SUBPLEURAL INTERSTITIAL
SPACE**

Figure 4–1.   **Diagrammatic Representation of the Lung.** This diagram depicts the components of the lung which are involved in the majority of pulmonary diseases — the large and small airways, the peripheral air spaces (including communicating channels), the arteries, veins, and capillaries, and the bronchovascular, subpleural, and parenchymal interstitial space. Throughout the chapter this diagrammatic representation of the normal lung is reproduced alongside diagrams depicting disturbances in morphology.

able certainty on that evidence alone; and then confirmation will depend upon whether the roentgenologic conclusions and the clinical picture can be reconciled. Thus, a systematic approach to roentgenologic interpretation is of cardinal importance:

Appreciation of such signs as the size of pulmonary lesions, their number and density, homogeneity and sharpness of definition, their anatomic location and distribution, and the presence or absence of cavitation or calcification is necessary to an understanding of the pathogenesis of the disease and inevitably leads to a reasonable differential diagnosis.

The roentgenographic characteristics of specific disease entities are given in their relevant chapters. This chapter is devoted to a description of *basic roentgen signs* as they indicate the *fundamental nature* of disease. It is subdivided into three major sections — increase in roentgenographic density, decrease in roentgenographic density, and diseases of the pleura.

Since a knowledge of the pathogenesis and pathology of a disease process is necessary to an understanding of the roentgenographic images it creates, wherever possible the signs are related to their gross and microscopic morphologic characteristics and to the mechanisms by which these changes took place (Figure 4–1).

DISEASES OF THE LUNG WHICH CAUSE AN INCREASE IN ROENTGENOGRAPHIC DENSITY

In essence, the lung consists of two main functioning tissues — that for *conduction* (the bronchi, blood vessels, and lymphatics) and that for *gaseous exchange* (the acini, or lung parenchyma, consisting of peripheral

air spaces, extravascular interstitial tissue, and capillaries). Excluding the vascular system, it is obvious that all pulmonary disease causing increase in density in the periphery of the lung involves a change in one or both of two components, the air spaces and extravascular interstitial tissue. Although most diseases which affect the acinus so as to produce an increase in roentgenographic density involve *both* the air spaces and interstitial tissue to a variable extent, it is helpful to divide these diseases into three general groups, *depending upon which component is predominantly affected:*

1. *Air spaces.* The air may be either (a) replaced by tissue or fluid (consolidation) or (b) absorbed and not replaced (atelectasis).

2. *Interstitial tissues.*

3. *Total acinus* (combined air spaces and interstitial tissues).

PREDOMINANT AIR-SPACE DISEASE

Parenchymal Consolidation

In this situation the air within the acinus is *replaced* by fluid, tissue, or exudate, and the result is *consolidation* of the parenchyma (Figure 4–2). Typically, many contiguous acini are involved with the production of uniform shadows of increased density

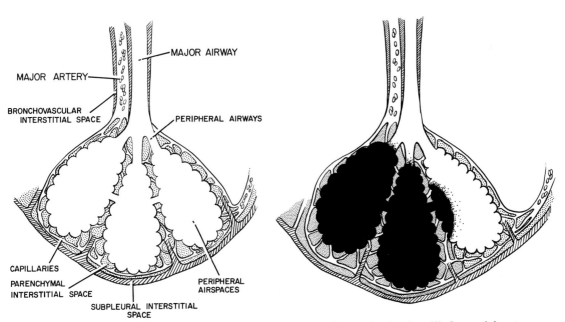

Figure 4–2. **The Lung Diagram: Peripheral Air-space Consolidation.** Exudate has filled two of the air spaces and is flowing into the third via pores of Kohn. Volume is unaffected, and the airways are patent. The parenchymal interstitial tissue is increased in amount around the consolidated air spaces.

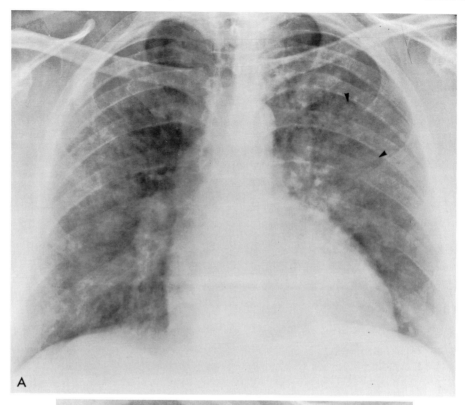

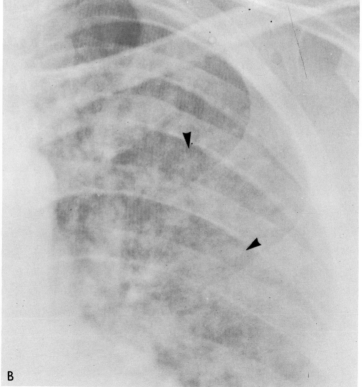

Figure 4–3.   **Idiopathic Pulmonary Hemorrhage.** A posteroanterior roentgenogram of the chest (A) reveals extensive air-space consolidation throughout both lungs, confluent in many areas but patchy in others, permitting identification of acinar shadows (B, *arrows*).

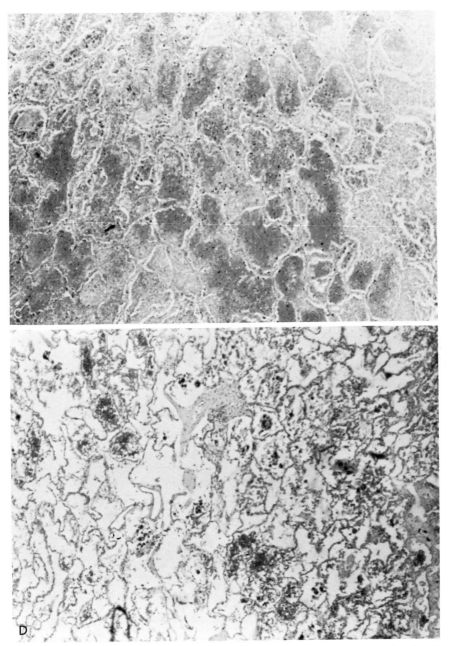

Figure 4–3. Continued. Photomicrographs from a biopsy specimen (*C* and *D*) show the alveoli to be filled with blood, uniformly in *C* and focally in *D*.

varying in size from a few centimeters to a whole lobe. Sometimes, however, *individual shadows,* 4 to 6 mm in diameter, can be identified which coincide roughly with the size and configuration of single acini and are a distinctive feature of air-space consolidation.

THE "ACINAR" SHADOW. In 1924 Aschoff[5] first drew attention to a distinctive roentgenographic appearance of what he interpreted as a single acinus consolidated by tuberculous inflammatory exudate and granulation tissue; he likened it to a rosette and termed it the "acino-nodose" lesion. Since the acinus is a unit of parenchymal structure measuring approximately 6 mm in diameter, it is reasonable perhaps to *assume* that replacing its air with fluid or tissue of unit density would result in a roentgenographic shadow, approximately 6 mm in diameter, fairly well circumscribed, and with a slightly irregular contour (*see* Figure 1–3, page 5, Figure 1–4, page 6, and Figure 1–5, page 7). In fact, such shadows are identified frequently in diseases known to be associated with parenchymal consolidation. *We wish to emphasize, however, that neither Aschoff,[5] nor to our knowledge anyone else, has provided convincing evidence by roentgenologic-histologic correlation that such a shadow actually represents consolidation of a single acinus.* Despite this lack of proof it is useful to recognize these shadows as a sign of *air-space consolidation*, and although aware of a potential semantic error, we use the term "acinar shadow" throughout this book to designate these important densities. In recent years, Ziskind and his associates[19, 20] and others[6, 21] have emphasized the importance of recognition of the "acinar pattern" in diffuse pulmonary disease, and this emphasis has led to a major improvement in roentgenologic diagnostic accuracy.

In diffuse diseases of the lung characterized by air-space consolidation (*e.g.,* acute pulmonary edema and idiopathic pulmonary hemorrhage [Figure 4–3]), in many cases one or more discrete acinar shadows can be seen, although confluence of the densities precludes visualization of individual acini in most areas of the lungs (*see* Figure 1–5). Groups of confluent acinar shadows often are separated by normal air-containing parenchyma, creating a pattern of numerous "fluffy," rather poorly defined densities throughout the lung fields. The overall picture may suggest a heterogeneous nonuniform consolidation, and it is important to recognize that *each individual group* of acinar lesions is homogeneous — an observation which establishes the true nature of the underlying pathology. In localized diseases, such as acute pneumococcal pneumonia or exudative tuberculosis, acinar shadows are confluent, so that the density is more or less homogeneous throughout but may have, at its borders, occasional acinar shadows whose margins are either completely surrounded by air-containing lung or only partly obscured by the consolidation.

Obviously, identification of an acinar shadow establishes the *anatomic location* of a disease process, *not* its mechanism of production, and extends the differential diagnosis to a multitude of diseases of varying pathogenesis which characteristically produce acinar consolidation.

1. Acute alveolar edema — the inflammatory exudate of an acute infection; or the edema associated with acute left-ventricular failure, or with increased capillary permeability due to inhalation of noxious gases or the aspiration of acid gastric contents.

2. Bleeding into the acini — idiopathic pulmonary hemorrhage.

3. Aspiration of blood or lipid.

4. Certain primary lung neoplasms — alveolar-cell carcinoma or locally invasive lymphoma; and rarely metastatic neoplasms.

5. Idiopathic conditions such as alveolar proteinosis (and rarely sarcoidosis).

Each of these is capable of producing acinar shadows; once the anatomic location has been established, analysis of the pattern and distribution of the roentgenographic changes should reduce the number of differential diagnostic possibilities to relatively few entities and occasionally will allow of confident diagnosis; where such is not possible from objective evidence alone, correlation with clinical information usually leads to a positive diagnosis.

NONSEGMENTAL DISTRIBUTION. A characteristic feature of diseases associated with air-space consolidation is failure to respect segmental boundaries. In widely disseminated disease, such as acute pulmonary edema, a lack of segmental distribution is not unexpected. Even in localized disease, however, intersegmental spread occurs; for example, in acute pneumococcal pneumonia, infection is propagated centrifugally via the pores of Kohn[364, 549, 554, 561–564, 566] (Figure 4–4). Since segment boundaries do not impede the passage of air or fluid via the pores of Kohn, the exudate of acute alveolar pneumonia can spread throughout the lung periphery (Figure 4–5). Consequently, such diseases are nonsegmental in distribution, an observation which is of major importance in establishing the pathogenesis of the disease process and thereby in arriving at an etiologic diagnosis.[567, 568]

In acute alveolar pneumonia, because the infection is propagated by centrifugal spread, the advancing margin of consolidation frequently is fairly smooth and sharply

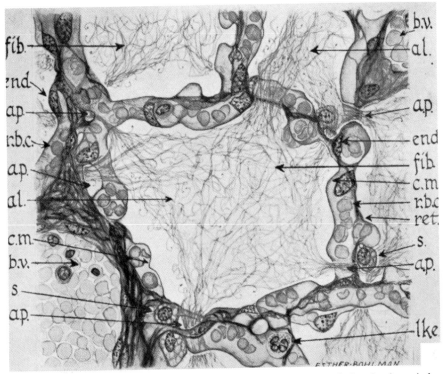

Figure 4–4. **Interalveolar Communications.** Camera lucida drawing of several alveoli of a rat's lung following injection of sterile heparinized plasma into the bronchial tree. Fibrin threads can be seen to be passing through several pores of Kohn. Key to labels: *al.*, alveolar space; *a.p.*, alveolar pore; *a.ph.*, alveolar phagocyte; *b.v.*, blood vessel; *cap.*, blood capillary; *c.m.*, capillary membrane; *end.*, endothelial cell of capillary; *fib.*, fibrin network; *L.*, lymphocyte; *lke.*, granular leukocyte; *r.b.c.*, red blood cell; *ret.*, reticulum; *s.*, septal cell. (From Loosli, C. G., A.M.A. Arch. Path., *24*:743, 1937.)

circumscribed (Figure 4–6).[568] This sharp definition has been remarked upon in acute Friedländer's pneumonia also.[69, 569]

THE AIR BRONCHOGRAM. Consolidation of the lung parenchyma, with little or no involvement of conducting airways, creates another unique roentgenographic sign. In acute alveolar pneumonia, for example, consolidation generally begins in the subpleural parenchyma (Figure 4–7), the exudate spreading rapidly centrifugally so as to surround bronchi and bronchioles as it advances toward the hilum. Since the consolidation is entirely parenchymal, the air in the bronchi is not displaced. Thus, contrast is produced between the air within the bronchial tree and the surrounding, airless parenchyma, so that the normally invisible bronchial air column becomes roentgenographically visible (Figure 4–8). This invaluable sign was described originally by Fleischner[259, 570] in 1927 and was aptly named the "air-bronchogram" sign by Fel-

son.[69] *Regardless of etiology, any pathologic process associated with an air bronchogram must be anatomically situated within the lung parenchyma.* The majority of diseases associated with air-space consolidation show the sign to some degree, although in some—for example, pulmonary infarction—it may be only temporary because of filling of the airways by blood or exudate. Alveolar filling need not be complete; an air bronchogram almost always is apparent and frequently is well defined in diseases in which air-space consolidation occurs but in which alveolar filling is incomplete (e.g., hyaline membrane disease[571–573] and pulmonary alveolar microlithiasis[574]).

ABSENCE OF COLLAPSE. In acinar consolidation, the absence of loss of volume is not difficult to understand when one considers the pathogenesis of these processes. In the first place, air in the acini is replaced by an equal or almost equal quantity of fluid or tissue. Second, since the process is pre-

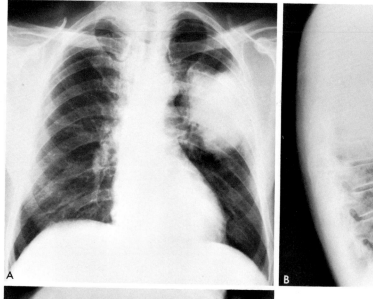

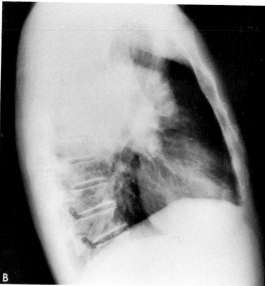

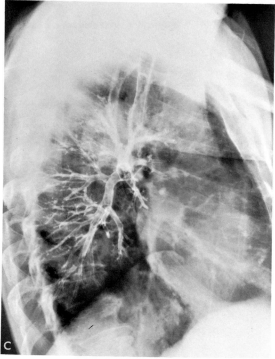

Figure 4–5. **Acute Air-space Pneumonia.** Postero-anterior (*A*) and lateral (*B*) roentgenograms of the chest show consolidation of the axillary zone of the left upper lobe (heavy growth of *D. pneumoniae* from the sputum). The consolidation is homogeneous except for an indistinctly visualized air bronchogram; the spreading margin is fairly sharply circumscribed. A lateral projection of a left bronchogram (*C*) shows that the consolidation observed in *A* and *B* overlapped the axillary branches of both the anterior and apicoposterior segmental bronchi of the left upper lobe, indicating the nonsegmental distribution of the disease. (From Fraser, R. G., and Wortzman, G., J. Canad. Ass. Radiol., *10*:37, 1959.)

dominantly parenchymal, the airways leading to the involved portions of lung remain patent; thus there is no reason for collapse to occur before exudate fills the air spaces. Again there are occasional exceptions to this rule — for example, pulmonary infarction, in which loss of volume may occur as a result of influences other than airway obstruction.

In summary, therefore, the roentgeno-logic signs associated with air-space (acinar) consolidation are as follows.

1. The acinar shadow.
2. Relatively homogeneous density where acinar consolidation is confluent.
3. The air bronchogram.
4. Nonsegmental distribution.
5. Negligible degree of collapse.

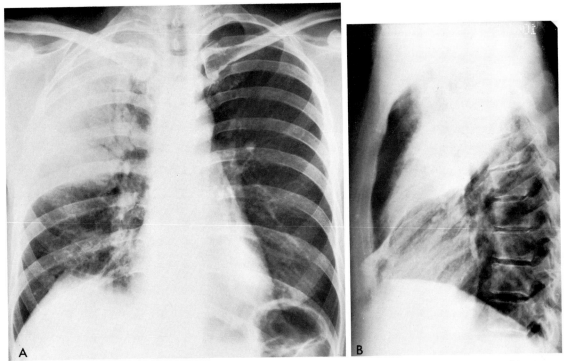

Figure 4–6. **Acute Air-space Pneumonia.** Posteroanterior (*A*) and lateral (*B*) roentgenograms reveal homogeneous consolidation of the right upper lobe (heavy growth of *D. pneumoniae* from the sputum); a well-defined air bronchogram is present. There is no loss of volume and, in fact, the upper half of the chief fissure is bulged slightly posteriorly. The anterior (retrosternal) portion of the lobe is unaffected, in keeping with the nonsegmental character of acute air-space pneumonia. (From Fraser, R. G., and Wortzman, G., J. Canad. Ass. Radiol., *10*:37, 1959.)

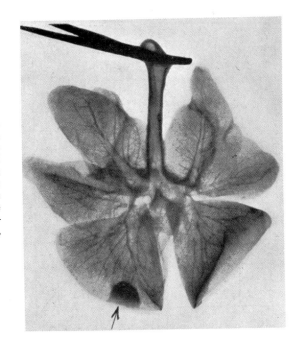

Figure 4–7. **Early Experimental Pneumococcal Pneumonia.** Roentgenogram of the excised lungs of a dog removed one hour after intrabronchial injection of 0.5 ml Type I *D. pneumoniae* culture. The consolidation is subpleural in location (*arrow*) and is still situated within the confines of the segment into which the culture was injected. Its rounded margin indicates centrifugal spread, however, and suggests that the inflammatory exudate soon will extend beyond the segmental boundary. (From Robertson, O. H., Coggeshall, L. T., and Terrell, E. E., J. Clin. Invest., *12*:467, 1933.)

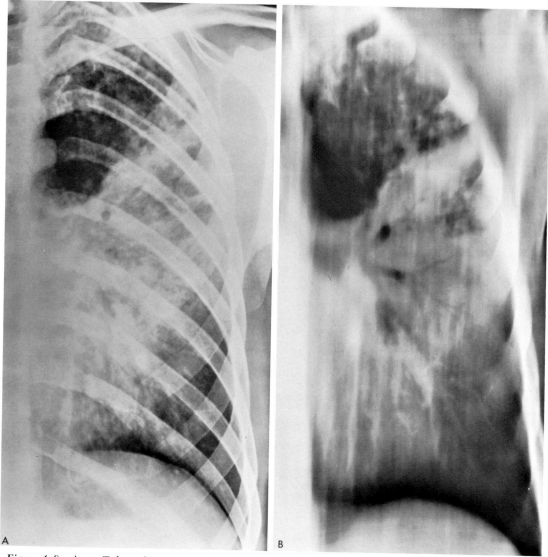

Figure 4–8. **Acute Tuberculous Pneumonia.** There is extensive consolidation of the axillary and lingular zones of the left upper lobe (*A*). The consolidation is largely homogeneous except for a well-defined air bronchogram, particularly well-illustrated in an anteroposterior tomogram (*B*). Acinar shadows can be identified in the upper portion of the left lung, suggesting bronchogenic spread of *Mycobacterium tuberculosis.*

Parenchymal Atelectasis

In its pure form atelectasis may be regarded conceptually as the antithesis of consolidation: In the former, air is absorbed and not replaced, and, in the latter, it is replaced by fluid or tissue of approximately equal volume. In both, the involved lung is airless and of unit density. Thus, from a roentgenologic point of view, the major difference is one of volume: in consolidation, volume is normal; in atelectasis, it is reduced.

The terminology of pulmonary atelectasis is controversial. Etymologically, the word is derived from the Greek *ateles* (incomplete) and *ektasis* (stretching); the interpretation placed on this by the semantic purist is that "incomplete stretching" is necessarily neonatal and cannot be applied to a state which develops after full inflation has occurred. We prefer to use the word in its broad sense—to denote diminished air within the lung, associated with reduced lung volume—and, therefore, including not only failure of lung expansion in the neonatal period and collapse due to resorption of air, but also shrinkage due to pulmonary fibrosis.

Since we have described atelectasis essentially in terms of lung volume, it is important to consider the mechanisms which keep the lung expanded. Alterations in these mechanisms provide a suitable basis for classifying atelectasis. However, the resultant lesions are variable and depend upon the circumstances existent at the time. These will be considered, and the roentgenographic abnormalities will be described in the light of these principles.

MAINTENANCE OF LUNG VOLUME. As described in Chapter 1 (see page 64), the lung has a natural tendency to collapse and does so when removed from the chest. While the lungs are in the thoracic cavity, this tendency is opposed by the chest wall; and at the resting respiratory position (FRC) the tendency of the lung to collapse and the tendency for the chest wall to expand are equal and opposite. When the chest wall is interfered with (e.g., thoracoplasty) or there is a space-occupying process within the thorax (e.g., pneumothorax), the lung retracts and its volume decreases; this is *passive atelectasis*. A similar mechanism exists at the edge of an expanding lesion within the lung; when adjacent lung parenchyma is compressed by a tumor mass, *compression atelectasis* results.

In a static system, the volume that the lung attains depends upon the applied force and the opposing elastic forces, the sum of which is generally termed compliance, or change in volume per unit change in pressure. It follows that, when the lung is stiffer than normal, i.e., when compliance is decreased, lung volume is decreased. This classically occurs when there is pulmonary fibrosis, and this is *cicatrization atelectasis*. The pressure-volume behavior is dependent also upon the forces acting at the air-tissue interface of the alveolar wall (see Chapter 1). As alveoli diminish in volume, the surface tension of the interface diminishes, owing to the effect of the "alveolar lining fluid," or surfactant. When the action of surfactant is interfered with, as may occur in the respiratory-distress syndrome or after by-pass surgery, there may be widespread collapse of alveoli. This type of atelectasis has been referred to as microatelectasis or nonobstructive atelectasis, but we shall refer to it as *adhesive atelectasis*.

The most common form of atelectasis, and the most complex, is due to the resorption of gas from the alveoli, such as may occur in acute bronchial obstruction. Since we have classified other forms of atelectasis on the basis of mechanism rather than etiology, this type of atelectasis is best termed *resorption atelectasis*.

RESORPTION ATELECTASIS. Resorption atelectasis occurs when communications between alveoli and trachea are obstructed (Figure 4–9). The mechanism of resorption is simple: The partial pressure of gases in the mixed venous blood is lower than in the alveolar air; as blood passes through the alveolar capillaries, the partial pressures of its gases equilibrate with alveolar pressure. The alveoli diminish in volume corresponding to the quantity of oxygen absorbed, and their pressure remains atmospheric. As a consequence, the partial pressures of carbon dioxide and nitrogen in the alveoli rise relative to capillary blood, and both gases diffuse into blood to maintain equilibrium. Thus a further reduction of alveolar volume occurs with a consequent rise of alveolar-capillary blood Po_2 gradient; oxygen diffuses into capillary blood, and this cycle is repeated until all alveolar gas is absorbed. In a previously healthy lobe, all air will have disappeared after 18 to 24 hours.[575] Since oxygen is selectively absorbed much more rapidly than nitrogen, when a lobe is filled with oxygen at the moment occlusion occurs (a situation which might pertain during anesthesia), collapse occurs much more rapidly and should show roentgenographic signs in less than an hour.[576] In fact, Rahn[917] has shown that the rate of lung collapse after blocking an airway is 60 times faster when oxygen is breathed than when air is breathed. Collapse may occur very rapidly when a one-way valve allows air to escape from a lobe but prevents its entrance: Coulter[575] produced total lobar collapse in 49 minutes after insertion of such a valve in a dog's bronchus, and Henry and Miscall[577] observed complete lobar atelectasis in a human subject within a few minutes of his assuming the supine position, due to a mobile bronchial tumor's impacting in a bronchus and acting as a one-way valve.

It is important to realize that *resorption atelectasis is not the inevitable or only accompaniment of bronchial obstruction, nor is obstruction of a major bronchus the only cause of resorption atelectasis*. The effect of obstruction of the airways depends upon

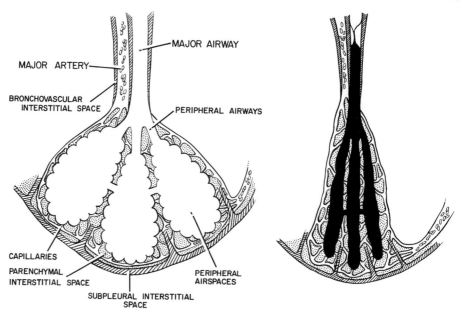

Figure 4–9. **The Lung Diagram: Resorption Atelectasis.** The major airway is obstructed, and the peripheral airways and air spaces are airless and collapsed.

the site and extent of bronchial or bronchiolar obstruction, the pre-existing condition of the lung tissue, and collateral drift. This last feature is so important, and generally so little emphasized, that it deserves special mention.

COLLATERAL AIR DRIFT. Collateral ventilation or collateral air drift are the terms used to describe ventilation of alveoli other than by the direct airway connections to these alveoli. There are three routes of collateral ventilation (*see* Chapter 1, page 4). (1) *The pores of Kohn*, which are circular or oval discontinuities in alveolar walls (Figure 4–10). (2) *The canals of Lambert*, which are epithelium-lined tubules between preterminal bronchioles and the alveoli surrounding them; they not only supply alveoli in the normal pathway distal to the particular preterminal bronchiole, but also alveoli subtended by other preterminal bronchioles. (3) *Direct airway anastomoses*, about 120μ in diameter, which were described recently in the dog by Martin.[16] It is not known which of these routes is the most important in man, but it is quite clear that considerable collateral ventilation can occur, even from upper to lower lobes (Figure 4–11). Of particular importance is the fact that air may be trapped in collaterally ventilated lung (Figure 4–12). The analysis by

Brown and his associates[578] of 160 children with foreign bodies in the tracheobronchial tree supplied useful information in this regard; obstructive overinflation was by far the most common roentgenographic finding, being present in 109 patients (68.1 per cent); collapse was the presenting roentgenographic finding in only 22 (13.8 per cent). Although it is not possible to ascertain from their data whether the operative mechanism in production of the overinflation was a "check valve" or collateral air drift, if the latter were responsible this would explain the large discrepancy between the number of cases of overinflation and those with atelectasis. The observations of Culiner and Reich[579] that overinflation occurs distal to bronchial atresia suggests that collateral ventilation may be as important as the check-valve mechanism. In fact, it has been implicated in the pathogenesis of emphysema,[579, 580, 3232, 3251] in which case the airway obstruction is situated in distal bronchioles.

If collateral air drift is such a potent force in preventing parenchymal collapse, in what circumstances does collapse occur? This depends chiefly upon the site of bronchial obstruction—if in a lobar bronchus, the development of atelectasis is readily explained by the absence of a parenchymal

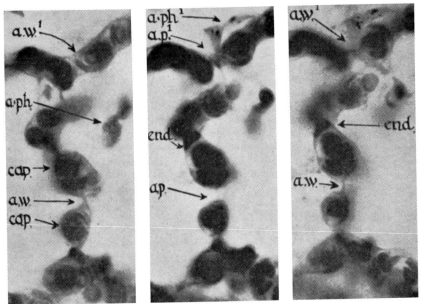

Figure 4–10. **Pores of Kohn.** Photomicrographs of a normal alveolar wall of a dog's lung taken at three different planes of focus. In numbers 1 and 3, the alveolar wall is intact at *a.w.* In number 2, the middle plane, a complete interruption in the alveolar wall is seen at *a.p.* This is an interalveolar communication, or pore of Kohn. Key to labels: *a.p.*, alveolar pore; *a.ph.*, alveolar phagocytes; *a.w.*, alveolar wall; *cap.*, capillary filled with red blood cells; *end.*, endothelial cell of capillary wall. (From Loosli, C. G., A.M.A. Arch. Path., 24:743, 1937.)

bridge from the involved lobe to a contiguous lobe; if the obstruction is in a segmental or subsegmental bronchus, the development of collapse must be due to some influence *preventing* collateral air drift[579] — probably inflammatory exudate. Fleischner[581] confirmed the presence of alveolar exudate in cases of "plate-like" atelectasis.

Even excluding the effect of collateral air drift, the end result of bronchial obstruction is not necessarily a collapsed, airless lobe. For example, pre-existing intralobar infection may lead to pneumonic consolidation of sufficient severity to prevent any great loss of volume (Figure 4–13). Infection occurs frequently in association with such slowly progressive, obstructive processes as bronchogenic carcinoma or bronchial adenoma, so that the loss of volume may be only slight or moderate (Figure 4–14). Pneumonitis, bronchiectasis, and abscesses which develop behind the obstruction generally are of sufficient degree to counteract, at least partly, collapse induced by air absorption. The resultant roentgenographic picture of "obstructive pneumonitis" is characteristic and should immediately alert the physician to the presence of an obstructing endobronchial lesion.

Another variable is the formation of intra-alveolar edema. Since intrapleural pressure represents the balance of forces between inward recoil of the lung and the position of the chest wall, it becomes more negative when air is resorbed and collapse results. This negative pressure is transmitted to the interstitial space of the lungs, and when of sufficient magnitude, results in an increased hydrostatic pressure, which pulls fluid from the vascular bed. Such fluid exudation occurs to some extent in all cases of acute obstruction atelectasis. Although assessment of volumetric reduction necessarily is rough, it might reasonably be estimated that 24 to 48 hours after complete bronchial occlusion the volume of a pulmonary lobe is seldom reduced more than 50 per cent. Since a fully collapsed lung (as in total pneumothorax, for example) occupies a volume no larger than a man's fist, it is not difficult to appreciate the large amount of fluid which must exude into the substance of a lobe so that its volume is reduced by only 50 per cent. This accumulation of sterile edema fluid behind a bronchial obstruction is appropriately termed "drowned lung." Should the obstruction persist and the obstructed lobe remain sterile, volumet-

(Text continues on page 203.)

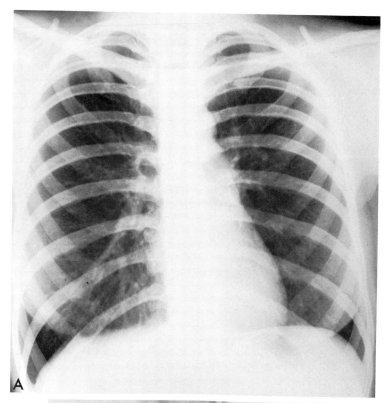

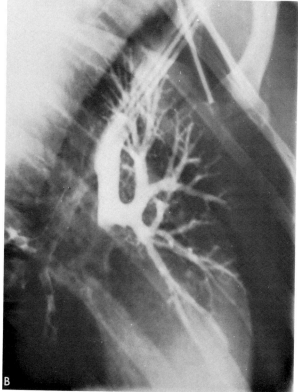

Figure 4–11. **Interlobar Collateral Air-drift.** In the postero-anterior roentgenogram (*A*), the left hemidiaphragm is elevated and the heart displaced to the left, both to slight degree. The vascular markings to the lower half of the left lung are diminutive compared to those on the right. Despite the signs indicating loss of volume, no shadows are present to indicate gross parenchymal collapse. A left bronchogram (*B*) shows the left lower-lobe bronchus to be totally obstructed at its origin by an intraluminal mass. The only way in which air could enter the lower lobe was by collateral air-drift from the normally ventilated upper lobe. The oligemia presumably resulted from reflex vasoconstriction secondary to alveolar hypoventilation. Proved bronchial adenoma.

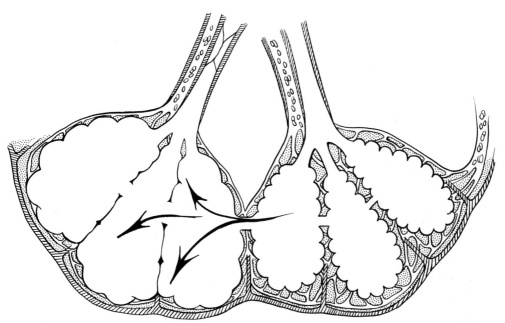

Figure 4–12. **The Lung Diagram: Collateral Ventilation Associated with Air-trapping.** The airway on the left is obstructed, that on the right patent; the parenchyma distal to the obstructed airway is being ventilated by collateral air-drift. The diagram depicts a situation in which air enters the obstructed segment more easily than it leaves, thus resulting in air-trapping.

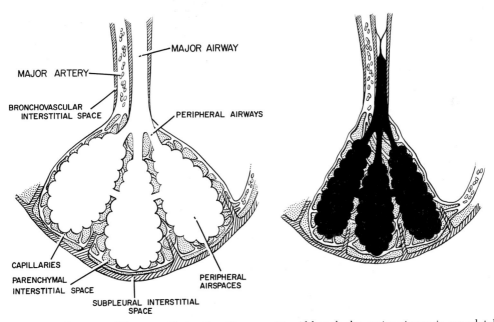

Figure 4–13. **The Lung Diagram: Obstructive Pneumonitis.** Although the major airway is completely obstructed, loss of volume of the peripheral air spaces is only moderate; outpouring of edema fluid (or inflammatory exudate) has prevented the complete collapse depicted in Figure 4–9.

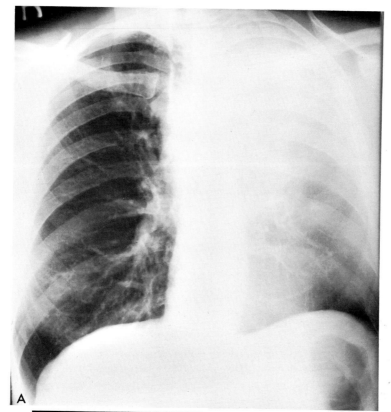

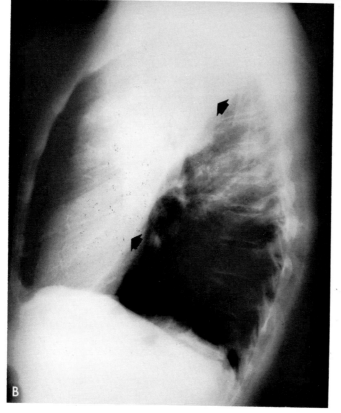

Figure 4–14. **Obstructive Pneumonitis—Left Upper Lobe.** Posteroanterior (*A*) and lateral (*B*) roentgenograms reveal homogeneous opacification of the left upper lobe; there is no air bronchogram. The chief fissure (*arrows*) is not displaced forward, and the only signs indicating loss of volume are slight mediastinal shift and hemidiaphragmatic elevation. Collapse was prevented by the development of severe pneumonia distal to a completely obstructed left upper-lobe bronchus—the "drowned lung." Proved bronchogenic carcinoma.

ric readjustment takes place within the hemithorax whereby other compensatory processes attempt to restore the normal volume of the hemithorax. As these other mechanisms play an increasingly important role in restoring pleural pressure to normal levels, the excess fluid within the "drowned lobe" is gradually reabsorbed, and eventually the lobe occupies the smallest possible volume. The result is chronic uncomplicated atelectasis. The collapsed lobe may be so small that it is almost invisible roentgenographically and then the diagnostician must rely heavily on evidence provided by signs of compensatory phenomena.

Resorption atelectasis may occur in the absence of occlusion of a major bronchus but cannot develop unless there is interruption of communication between alveoli and a major airway. Perhaps the best example is lower-lobe bronchiectasis consequent upon childhood bronchopulmonary infection. Sufficent obliterative and stenosing bronchitis and bronchiolitis results, so that ventilation through normal channels is inadequate. Collateral ventilation may be interfered with in two ways: the pathways leading to the channels for collateral ventilation may be obliterated or narrowed, and the

parenchymal disease may be sufficiently extensive to interfere with the collateral channels themselves. In this situation permanent atelectasis ensues and, together with bronchial infection, results in bronchiectasis. This is, of course, an oversimplification; the results of bronchial and bronchiolar obliteration vary, and, at the other extreme, air-trapping, overinflation, and emphysema may result, and pulmonary fibrosis of varying degree and severity may be produced. Thus, a wide variety of lesions may be present in resorption atelectasis owing to peripheral airway obstruction (Figure 4–15), and roentgenographic density generally is less uniform than when a major airway is obstructed. Another difference is apparent between resorption atelectasis produced by central obstruction and that produced by peripheral obstruction. In the latter, an air bronchogram will be seen if there is sufficient parenchymal collapse, since the obstruction is peripheral to the major bronchial tree (Figure 4–16). Resorption atelectasis due to peripheral airway disease sometimes is referred to as "nonobstructive atelectasis" because the major airways are not occluded; this term is both confusing and incorrect and is best avoided.

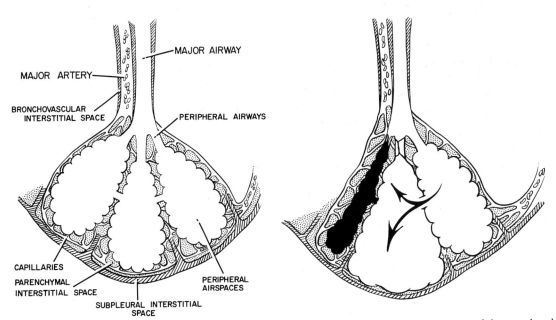

Figure 4–15. **The Lung Diagram: Effects of Peripheral Airway Obstruction.** The major airway and the peripheral airway on the right are patent, but the two peripheral airways on the left are totally obstructed. The central air space is air-containing as a result of collateral air-drift from the right air space through patent collateral channels. Since the communicating channels between the central and left-sided air spaces are filled with exudate, air-drift is prevented and the left air space has collapsed.

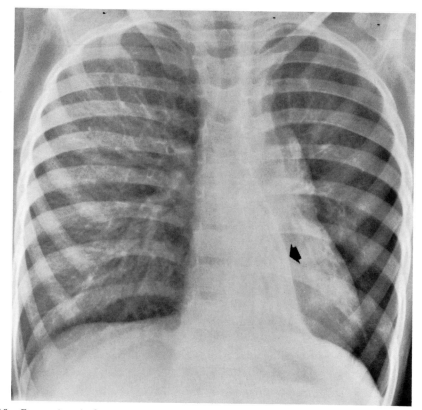

Figure 4-16. **Resorption Atelectasis Due to Peripheral Airway Obstruction.** The left lower lobe is almost completely collapsed (*arrow* points to the interface between the displaced major fissure and the overinflated upper lobe). Despite the severe atelectasis, a well-defined air bronchogram can be clearly identified out to the periphery. Bronchoscopy showed no evidence of bronchial obstruction. Note compensatory signs of atelectasis — marked overinflation of the left upper lobe, mediastinal shift to the left, and less hemidiaphragmatic elevation. Three-and-one-half year old girl approximately two years following acute adenoviral pneumonia of the left lung; the lobe eventually re-expanded spontaneously. (Courtesy Dr. R. I. MacPherson, Winnipeg Children's Hospital.)

Resorption atelectasis may result from reversible bronchial obstruction; in such cases, when the obstruction is removed the lung reinflates — a situation illustrated by postoperative resorption atelectasis due to bronchial obstruction by a mucous plug (*see* Figure 4–30, page 216).

In summary, it is important to recognize that *parenchymal atelectasis may be present without major bronchial obstruction:* In cases of chronic atelectasis, as in bronchiectasis, the pathogenetic mechanisms are fairly well understood; when collapse is acute and temporary, as in the postoperative state, a complex group of forces appears to operate whose precise nature we do not fully comprehend.

PASSIVE ATELECTASIS. This term (*synonym:* relaxation atelectasis) denotes pulmonary collapse that occurs in the presence of pneumothorax or hydrothorax (Figure 4-17). Providing the pleural space is free (that is, without adhesions), collapse of any portion of the lung is proportional to the amount of air or fluid in the adjacent pleural space. In upright man, the tendency for air to pass to the upper portion of the pleural space results in a relatively greater degree of collapse of upper-lobe tissue than of lower. This fact is of particular importance when diagnostic pneumothorax is employed to differentiate the intrapulmonary or extrapulmonary location of a lesion in the base of the hemithorax; separation of the base of the lung from the diaphragm requires induction of a very large pneumothorax when the patient is erect, but is easily achieved when he is recumbent or preferably in the Trendelenburg position. For the same reason, identification of tiny pneumothorax, particularly in infants, is easier with the patient in the lateral decubitus position, using a horizontal roentgen beam.

It might be thought logical that shrinkage

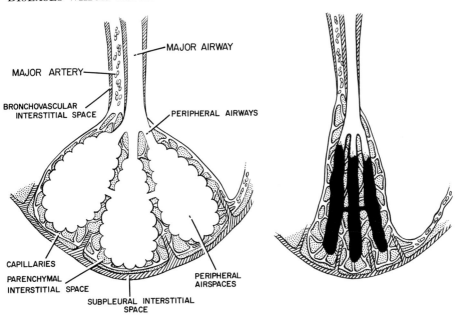

MAJOR AIRWAY

MAJOR ARTERY

BRONCHOVASCULAR
INTERSTITIAL SPACE

PERIPHERAL AIRWAYS

CAPILLARIES

PARENCHYMAL
INTERSTITIAL SPACE

PERIPHERAL
AIRSPACES

SUBPLEURAL INTERSTITIAL
SPACE

Figure 4–17. **The Lung Diagram: Passive Atelectasis.** The peripheral air spaces are collapsed and airless but in contrast to the situation in resorption atelectasis (*see* Figure 4–9), the airways are patent.

of a lung to half its normal projected area would result in doubled roentgenologic density. That this is not so is evidenced by the difficulty commonly experienced in visualizing the lung edge in any case of spontaneous pneumothorax, even of moderate degree (Figure 4–18). As pointed out by Dornhorst and Pierce,[567] as a lung shrinks

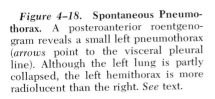

Figure 4–18. **Spontaneous Pneumothorax.** A posteroanterior roentgenogram reveals a small left pneumothorax (*arrows* point to the visceral pleural line). Although the left lung is partly collapsed, the left hemithorax is more radiolucent than the right. *See* text.

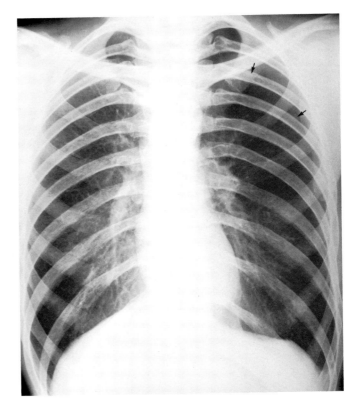

under pneumothorax, its density does not notably increase until its projected area is reduced to about one-tenth its normal area at total lung capacity. The probable explanation for this anomalous situation is twofold: first, the reduction in lung volume is approximately balanced by a reduction in its blood content, the net roentgenologic density being altered only slightly; and second, air in the pleural space both anteriorly and posteriorly serves as a nonabsorbing medium, thus contributing to the overall radiolucency of the roentgenographic image. It is important that the physician be aware of this unusual facet of density change in the passive atelectasis of pneumothorax; it constitutes a likely diagnostic pitfall for the unwary.

The total pulmonary collapse that occurs in association with tension pneumothorax presents a unique opportunity for appreciating how small a volume the lung may occupy when its parenchyma is totally airless. A lung whose volume at total lung capacity may be of the order of 3½ liters may shrink to no larger than a man's fist (Figure 4-19).

It must be emphasized that even when pneumothorax-induced collapse is total, the lung mass is not completely airless—the lobar and larger segmental bronchi are sufficiently stable structurally to resist collapse; therefore, they remain air-filled and, although reduced in caliber, should be apparent as an air bronchogram (Figure 4-19). For obvious reasons, it is essential that this sign be sought carefully in any case of total or almost total pneumothorax; the absence of an air bronchogram should immediately arouse suspicion of the possibility of endobronchial obstruction.[530] It is clear that, in such circumstances, the lung will not re-expand no matter how rigorous the therapeutic maneuvers to reduce the pneumothorax; the onus is on the roentgenologist to recognize this sign so that remedial steps can be taken to remove the bronchial obstruction bronchoscopically.

COMPRESSION ATELECTASIS. Compression atelectasis (*synonym:* "mantle" atelectasis) differs little from passive atelectasis. The process is localized, however, and designates that form of parenchymal collapse

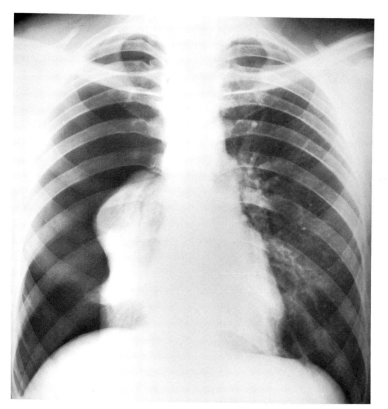

Figure 4–19. **Pneumothorax with Total Pulmonary Collapse.** A posteroanterior roentgenogram following spontaneous pneumothorax reveals the small volume occupied by a whole lung when totally collapsed. The well-defined air bronchogram indicates airway patency.

which occurs contiguous to a space-occupying mass within the thorax (Figure 4–20). Any process which occupies space within the thorax—for example, pleural effusion, peripheral bronchogenic carcinoma, lung abscess, or a markedly enlarged heart—will "compress" the contiguous lung and result in airlessness of a thin layer of parenchyma. The pathologist is accustomed to seeing a thin zone of collapsed lung adjacent to a pulmonary mass; however, in the majority of instances such airless lung is contiguous to tissue of identical density, and the roentgenographic differentiation of the basic lesion and compressed lung adjacent to it often is impossible. It is only when such compression occurs contiguous to a zone of relative radiolucency, such as a bulla or bleb, that the compressed lung can be recognized as a distinct shadow of increased density; even in such circumstances, however, the wall of even a large bulla may be no more than a hair-line shadow, indicating the extremely small volume which lung parenchyma may occupy when it is completely collapsed.

Generally speaking, therefore, compression atelectasis is seldom of roentgenologic significance as a cause of increased density.

ADHESIVE ATELECTASIS. This term describes alveolar collapse in the presence of patent airway connections and, thus, is true "nonobstructive" atelectasis (Figure 4–21). The subject is controversial and poorly understood. The best examples are the respiratory-distress syndrome of newborn infants and acute radiation pneumonitis (Figure 4–22). In both conditions atelectasis may be a prominent feature, and may be related, at least in part, to an inactivation of surfactant. Clements[874] has shown that surfactants are important in reducing the surface tension of an alveolus as its surface area or volume decreases. In other words, they protect against collapse in that the critical closing pressure of alveoli occurs at a lower volume and distending pressure. Surfactant has been found to be absent in pneumonic lungs with associated atelectasis,[927] as well as in purely atelectatic human lung.[879] It is thought that in many conditions in which hyaline membranes form within the alveoli—for example, acute radiation pneumonitis, influenza, rheumatic fever, and uremia—some interference takes place in the conversion of plasminogen into the fibrinolytic enzyme plasmin; similarly, inhibition of plasminogen activator is presumed to be the cause for atelectasis in hyaline membrane disease of infants.[932]

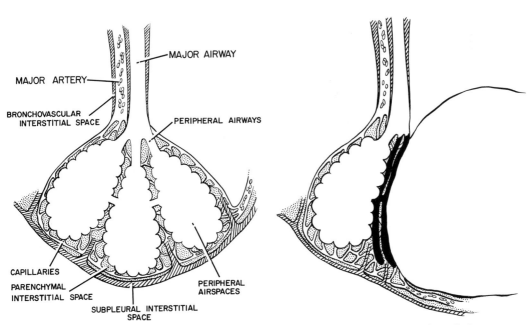

MAJOR AIRWAY

MAJOR ARTERY

BRONCHOVASCULAR INTERSTITIAL SPACE

PERIPHERAL AIRWAYS

CAPILLARIES

PARENCHYMAL INTERSTITIAL SPACE

PERIPHERAL AIRSPACES

SUBPLEURAL INTERSTITIAL SPACE

Figure 4–20. **The Lung Diagram: Compression Atelectasis.** A large "bulla" situated on the right has compressed contiguous parenchyma resulting in total air-space collapse.

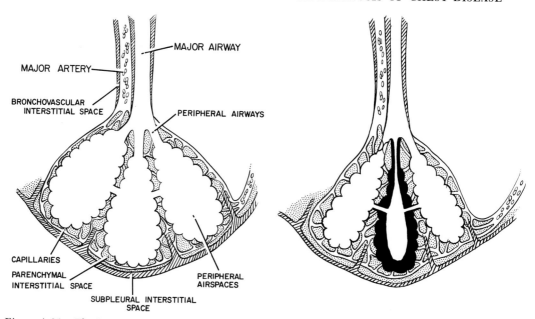

Figure 4–21.   **The Lung Diagram: Adhesive Atelectasis.** Three situations are depicted: the air space on the right has lost considerable volume due to inactivation of surfactant; the central air space is lined with edema fluid (hyaline membrane); the peripheral airway leading to the left-sided air space is obstructed. Note that the small airways in the center and on the right are patent.

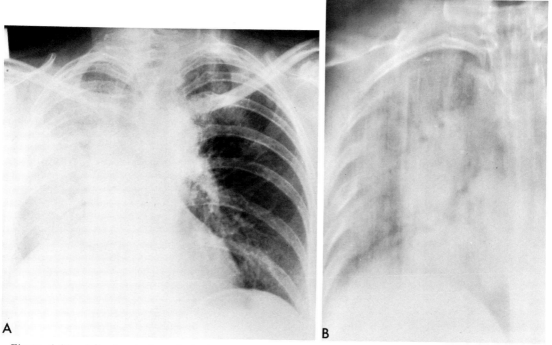

Figure 4–22.   **Adhesive Atelectasis in Acute Radiation Pneumonitis.** A posteroanterior roentgenogram (*A*) reveals severe loss of volume of the right lung associated with marked mediastinal shift and hemidiaphragmatic elevation; the density is rather granular (the oblique shadow across the left upper lung is an artefact). A well-defined air bronchogram (seen to better advantage on the anteroposterior tomogram—*B*) indicates major airway patency.

It is likely that adhesive ("nonobstructive") atelectasis plays a part also in loss of volume occurring postoperatively, and probably accounts for the marked arteriovenous shunting that may occur even when chest roentgenograms are relatively normal.

Various other disease processes occur concomitantly with adhesive atelectasis. These may be related to the causal agent, such as congestion, edema, or hemorrhage, or the hyaline membrane that forms in cases of radiation pneumonitis. Edema sometimes is a prominent feature of the respiratory-distress syndrome. Thus, the roentgenographic density of affected lung may be greater than anticipated from reduction in lung volume alone. Since the process is peripheral, an air bronchogram will be present (Figure 4–16).

CICATRIZATION ATELECTASIS. Some may object to the inclusion of loss of lung volume due to fibrosis as a type of atelectasis, but we believe this entity is best described here. Further, diffuse idiopathic pulmonary fibrosis (Hamman-Rich disease) is best considered as a diffuse collapse of air spaces with proximal bronchiolectasis. Thus, cicatrization is a useful concept, although we readily admit that multifarious factors affect lung volume in most examples of this condition. The pathologic process is one of fibrosis with resultant cicatrization; the fibrosis may or may not be associated with parenchymal destruction, but in either event results in loss of volume of the affected portion of lung. Not only is air per unit lung volume decreased, but, also, tissue per unit lung volume is increased, thus increasing roentgenographic density. The roentgenologic signs depend upon whether the process is local or general.

Localized disease is best exemplified by chronic infection, often granulomatous in nature, and epitomized by long-standing productive pulmonary tuberculosis. In essence, it is a chronic "nonobstructive" atelectasis in which the destruction of lung parenchyma is followed by fibrosis and progressive loss of volume through cicatrization (Figure 4–23). The peripheral bronchi and bronchioles are generally destroyed along with the parenchyma, so that resorption atelectasis also occurs; the more proximal bronchi become dilated, so that the morphologic picture is one of chronic bronchiectasis and parenchymal scarring. The roentgenologic signs are as might be expected (Figure 4–24): a segment or lobe occupying a volume smaller than normal, with a density which is nonhomogeneous due to dilated air-containing bronchi (often better demonstrated by tomography), and

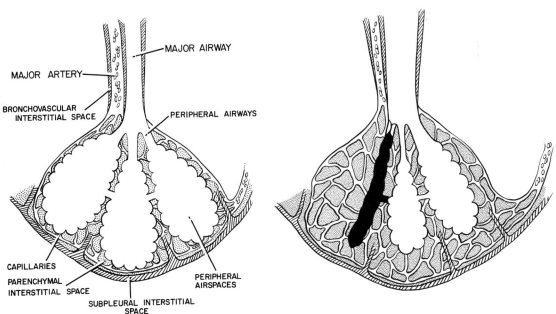

MAJOR AIRWAY

MAJOR ARTERY

BRONCHOVASCULAR INTERSTITIAL SPACE

PERIPHERAL AIRWAYS

CAPILLARIES

PARENCHYMAL INTERSTITIAL SPACE

PERIPHERAL AIRSPACES

SUBPLEURAL INTERSTITIAL SPACE

Figure 4–23. **The Lung Diagram: Local Cicatrization Atelectasis.** The interstitial space is increased in amount and density (fibrosis). The left air space is totally obliterated while those to the right show different degrees of loss of volume. The major airway is dilated (bronchiectasis) as is the peripheral airway on the right (bronchiolectasis).

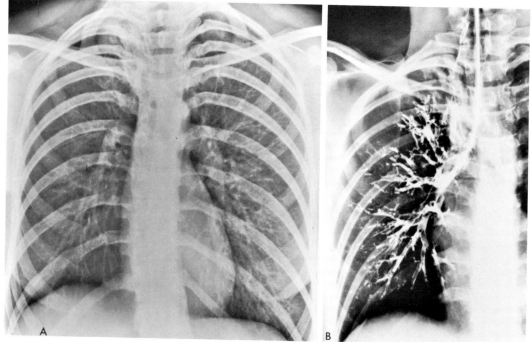

Figure 4-24.   **Local Cicatrization Atelectasis, Right Upper Lobe.** A posteroanterior roentgenogram (*A*) shows a poorly defined shadow lying in the right superior paramediastinal zone. Marked loss of volume of the right upper lobe is indicated by elevation of the right hilum and displacement of the trachea to the right. In a right bronchogram (*B*), displacement of the trachea is well shown as is dilatation and distortion of the upper lobe segmental bronchi, particularly the apical segment. Chronic fibroproductive tuberculosis with tuberculous bronchiectasis.

with irregular thickened strands extending from the collapsed segment to the hilum. The compensatory signs of chronic loss of volume are usually evident—local mediastinal shift, frequently manifested by a sharp deviation of the trachea when segments of the upper lobe are involved, displacement of the hilum (which may be severe in upper-lobe disease), and compensatory overinflation of the remainder of the affected lung. The loss of volume may be so severe as to render the collapsed lung almost invisible on standard posteroanterior chest roentgenograms, particularly if involvement of apical or apical-posterior segments of an upper lobe results in incorporation of the shadow of the collapsed lung into that of the mediastinum (Figure 4-24); in such circumstances, the diagnostician must rely on evidence of compensatory signs of pulmonary collapse.

Generalized fibrotic disease of the lungs also may be associated with loss of volume (Figure 4-25). In chronic interstitial pulmonary fibrosis, for example, involvement of the parenchymal interstitial space results in

widespread reduction in the volume of air-containing parenchyma (Figure 4-26); this may be evident roentgenologically through the presence of elevation of the diaphragm and overall reduction in lung size. In our experience, this gradual reduction in thoracic volume in cases of diffuse interstitial disease is a useful indicator of the fibrotic nature of the pathologic process.

It is to be emphasized that other diseases associated with pulmonary fibrosis may produce an entirely different roentgenographic pattern (Figure 4-27). For example, the fibrotic stage of pulmonary sarcoidosis may be associated with marked compensatory overinflation or even emphysema, so that the fibrotic component tends to become compressed into relatively small areas of the lung; in silicosis, conglomerate mass shadows in the upper portions of the lungs, due to the coalescence of individual fibrotic lesions, is an excellent example of this type of phenomenon; the lower portions of the lungs respond to the reaction with a severe degree of overinflation (Figure 4-28).

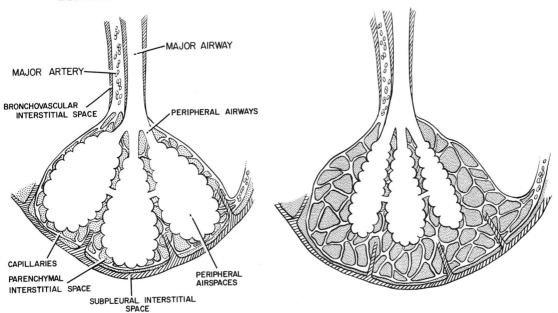

Figure 4-25. **The Lung Diagram: General Cicatrization Atelectasis.** There is a marked increase in interstitial tissue with uniform reduction in the volume of all air spaces as a result of cicatrization. The dilatation of the major airway seen in local cicatrization atelectasis is not a prominent part of the picture although peripheral airway dilatation may occur.

In summary, atelectasis may occur through five mechanisms which in any given situation may operate independently or in combination.

1. *Resorption atelectasis* occurs when communications between the trachea and alveoli are obstructed; the obstruction may be in a major bronchus or in multiple small bronchi or bronchioles.

2. *Passive atelectasis* (relaxation atelectasis) denotes the loss of volume which accompanies a space-occupying process in the thorax, particularly pneumothorax or hydrothorax.

3. *Compression atelectasis* differs little from passive atelectasis, and designates the localized form of parenchymal collapse which occurs contiguous to a space-occupying process such as a pulmonary mass or bulla.

4. *Adhesive atelectasis* (nonobstructive or microatelectasis) denotes air-space collapse in the presence of patent airway communications; it is related to a complex group of forces among which abnormality of the surface-active agent is probably predominant.

5. *Cicatrization atelectasis* designates the loss of volume which results from pulmonary fibrosis, either localized or generalized.

ROENTGENOLOGIC SIGNS OF ATELECTASIS. The roentgenologic signs of atelectasis may be both *direct* and *indirect,* the latter consisting of the compensatory phenomena referred to previously.

Direct roentgenologic signs (Figure 4-29):

1. *Local increase in density.* As discussed previously, the volume of an airless lobe or segment depends not only upon which order of bronchus is obstructed but also upon the amount of edema fluid, either sterile or infected, within the obstructed lung. In the absence of pneumothorax, *a collapsed lobe is always peripheral in position.*[582] The reasonable inference can be made that the visceral pleura covering the collapsed lobe continues to maintain an intimate relationship to the parietal pleura *no matter how complete the collapse.*

2. *Displacement of interlobar fissures.* Displacement of the fissures which form the boundary of a collapsed lobe forms one of the most dependable and easily recognized signs of atelectasis (Figure 4-29). For each lobe, the position and configuration of the displaced fissure is predictable for a given loss of volume; these factors are considered later in relation to patterns of lobar and segmental collapse.

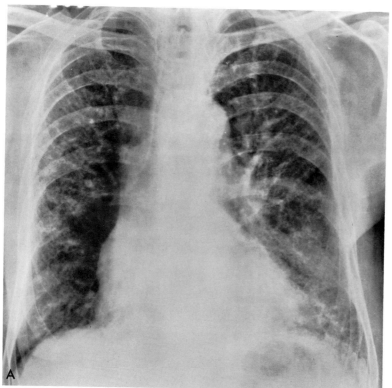

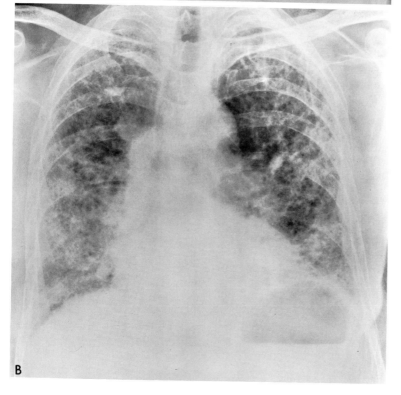

Figure 4-26. Cicatrization Atelectasis in Idiopathic Interstitial Pulmonary Fibrosis. A posteroanterior roentgenogram (A) reveals a coarse reticular pattern throughout both lungs. Two years later (B), not only is the reticulation much more marked but there has occurred considerable loss of lung volume. Both roentgenograms exposed at total lung capacity. (Roentgenogram reproduced in A courtesy Dr. W. B. Ayre, Montreal.)

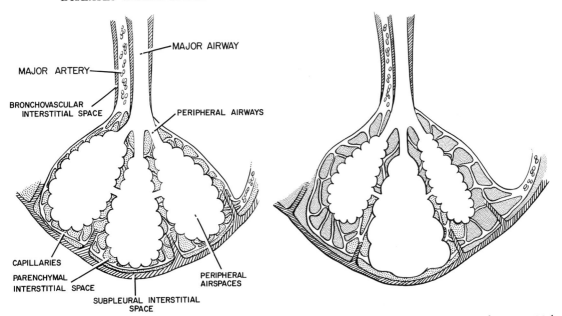

Figure 4–27. **The Lung Diagram: Cicatricial Atelectasis with Compensatory Overinflation.** The interstitial tissue around the left and right air spaces is increased in amount and density, resulting in loss of volume of the air spaces. The central air space is surrounded by normal interstitial tissue and has overinflated to compensate for adjacent loss of volume.

Indirect roentgenologic signs:

These include the phenomena which develop to compensate for the reduction in intrapleural pressure—diaphragmatic elevation, mediastinal shift, approximation of ribs, and overinflation of the remainder of the lung (Figures 4–29 and 4–30). The part which each compensatory mechanism plays in any given situation is somewhat unpredictable, although predominance is governed in large measure by the anatomic position of the collapsed lobe; all four mechanisms may be operative to a roughly equal degree, or one or two may predominate to the exclusion of others. Two general rules deserve emphasis. (1) Displacement of the diaphragm and mediastinum is maximal contiguous to the major collapse; for example, lower-lobe collapse tends to elevate the posterior more than the anterior portion of the hemidiaphragm and to displace the inferior more than the superior mediastinum; conversely, upper-lobe collapse is associated with upper mediastinal displacement, often with little hemidiaphragmatic elevation. (2) The shorter the duration of the atelectasis, the greater the predominance of diaphragmatic and mediastinal displacement (Figure 4–30); the more chronic the collapse, the more will compensatory overinflation predominate (Figure 4–29).

(a) *Elevation of the hemidiaphragm.* As already stated, hemidiaphragmatic elevation always is a more prominent feature of lower than of upper-lobe collapse (compare Figure 4–30A and C). In the lower lung zones, elevation tends to occur in the area contiguous to the lobe involved—posterior elevation in lower-lobe collapse and anterior elevation in middle-lobe or lingular collapse (although, in the latter situation, diaphragmatic displacement seldom occurs to a significant degree). When assessing diaphragmatic elevation one should take into consideration possible variations in the relationship of the two hemidiaphragms: Although the right dome normally is approximately half an interspace higher than the left, Felson,[69] who reviewed the chest roentgenograms of 500 normal subjects, recorded a deviation from the normal relationship in 11 per cent: in 9 per cent, the two were level or the left was higher than the right, and in 2 per cent the right hemidiaphragm was more than 3 cm higher than the left. When attaching significance to diaphragmatic elevation, the influence of subphrenic disease must not be disregarded; although atelectasis secondary to airway obstruction is a common complication of the postoperative period after laparotomy, it should be borne in mind that

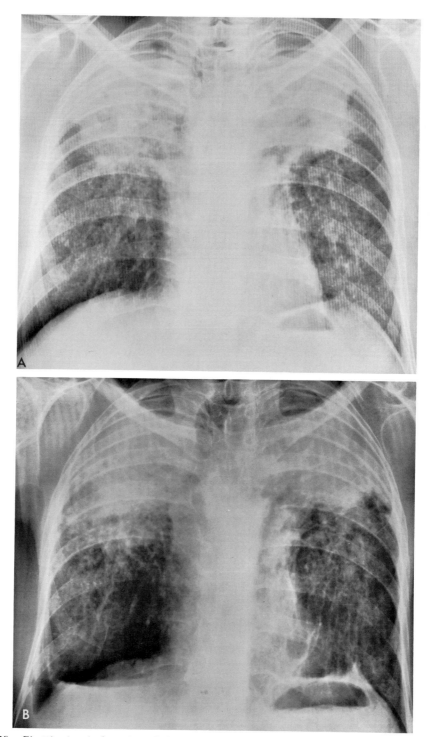

Figure 4–28. **Cicatrization Atelectasis with Compensatory Overinflation.** A posteroanterior roentgenogram (*A*) shows massive consolidation of both upper lobes associated with a diffuse nodular pattern throughout the lower half of both lungs. Proven silicosis with advanced conglomeration (progressive massive fibrosis). Two years later (*B*), the conglomerate shadows have increased in size while the nodular pattern in the lower lungs has diminished markedly in extent and in some areas has virtually disappeared. The silicotic nodules have become incorporated into the conglomerate shadows, leaving behind markedly overinflated parenchyma.

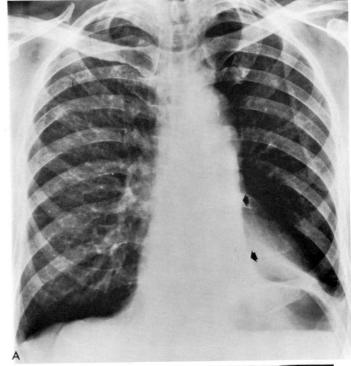

Figure 4–29. **Atelectasis of the Left Lower Lobe.** A posteroanterior roentgenogram (*A*) shows a triangular shadow of homogeneous density situated in the inferomedial portion of the left hemithorax. Its lateral margin (*arrows*) represents the interface between the collapsed left lower lobe and the overinflated left upper lobe. Indirect signs of atelectasis include increased radiolucency of the left upper lobe compared to the right, redistribution of vascular markings, and elevation of the left hemidiaphragm. The mediastinum shows little if any shift. In lateral projection (*B*), the shadow is barely visible as an area of increased density situated in the posterior costophrenic sulcus, but its presence is indicated by the loss of visibility of the posterior portion of the left hemidiaphragm (the silhouette sign).

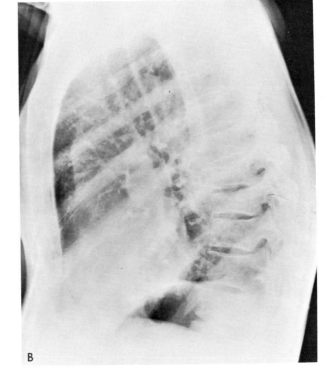

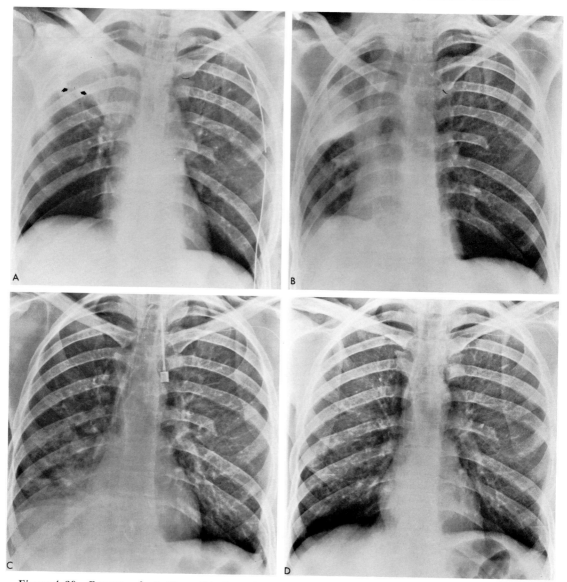

Figure 4–30.   **Roentgenologic Signs of Atelectasis.** A roentgenogram of the chest in anteroposterior projection, supine position (*A*) reveals a homogeneous shadow in the upper portion of the right hemithorax; its concave lower margin (*arrows*) is formed by the upward displaced horizontal fissure; the right hemidiaphragm is slightly elevated. Atelectasis of the right upper lobe (24 hours postoperative thoracoabdominal repair of hiatus hernia). Twenty-four hours later (*B*), the right upper lobe collapse is clearing, but the diaphragmatic elevation has increased and the mediastinum has shifted markedly to the right; note the approximation of ribs. These signs indicate acute obstruction of the lower-lobe bronchus with progressing collapse. Twenty-four hours later (*C*), the right lower lobe is almost airless; the right upper lobe has re-expanded. Note that diaphragmatic elevation is greater with lower-lobe than with upper-lobe collapse (compare *A* and *C*). Twenty-four hours later (*D*), all signs have disappeared; the lungs are now normal roentgenographically.

diaphragmatic elevation may result directly from "splinting" secondary to abdominal pain or subphrenic infection.

(b) *Mediastinal displacement.* The normal mediastinum is a surprisingly mobile

structure and reacts promptly to differences in pressure between the two halves of the thorax (Figure 4–30). The anterior and middle mediastinal compartments are less stable than the posterior and, therefore, shift to a greater extent. The degree of shift usually is greatest in the region of major pulmonary collapse; thus, tracheal and upper mediastinal displacement is a feature of upper-lobe collapse and may be negligible when the lower lobes are involved; in the latter instance, the inferior mediastinum undergoes the greatest displacement. As with the diaphragm, normal variations in configuration of the mediastinum should be recognized; this is less of a problem with the trachea and upper mediastinum than with the heart, since the trachea is consistently a midline structure; the amount of cardiac silhouette which projects to the right of the spine varies in normal subjects, however, and care must be taken not to misinterpret a central position of the heart as necessarily evidence of displacement.

(c) *Compensatory overinflation.* Overinflation of the remainder of the ipsilateral lung is one of the most important and reliable indirect signs of atelectasis (Figure 4–29). It seldom occurs rapidly and, in the early stages of lobar collapse, usually is of less diagnostic help than the other compensatory phenomena, such as diaphragmatic elevation and mediastinal displacement. As the period of collapse lengthens, however, overinflation becomes more prominent and the diaphragmatic and mediastinal changes regress. The degree to which the lung can be overinflated, while not significantly affecting its functional capabilities, is truly remarkable: In one of our patients, a young woman whose whole left lung and right lower and right middle lobes were removed because of severe bronchiectasis, the remaining right upper lobe has overinflated and fills the whole thorax (Figure 4–31); her pulmonary function, while obviously impaired, is approximately what might be predicted for one-fifth the normal complement of pulmonary tissue.

Roentgenologic evidence of compensatory overinflation may be extremely subtle. It may be difficult to estimate the increase in lung translucency which results from the greater air:blood ratio, but appreciation may be enhanced by viewing the roentgenograph from a distance of several feet or through minification lenses. Clearly, more reliable evidence for overinflation is supplied by the *alteration in vascular markings* which occurs as a result of the larger volume occupied by the lung (Figure 4–29);[583] the vessels are more widely spaced and are sparser than in the normal contralateral lung. As emphasized by Simon,[122] appreciation of vascular redistribution may be facilitated by full lung tomography.

When only a segment of one lung is collapsed, compensatory overinflation usually is restricted to the remainder of that lung, at least insofar as is apparent roentgenographically. When greater amounts of one lung become atelectatic, the tendency is greater for overinflation to involve the contralateral lung; this may progress to the stage where the opposite lung herniates across the mediastinal septum. These herniations occur in the three weakest areas of the mediastinum where the two lungs are separated only by loose connective tissue:[139] (1) the anterior mediastinal compartment, at the level of the first three or four costal cartilages, limited anteriorly by the sternum and posteriorly by the great vessels; (2) the posterosuperior mediastinum, at the level of the third to fifth thoracic vertebrae, limited anteriorly by the esophagus, trachea, and great vessels and posteriorly by the vertebral column (the supra-aortic triangle); and (3) the posteroinferior mediastinum, limited anteriorly by the heart and posteriorly by the vertebral column and aorta (the retrocardiac space, or space of Holzknecht). Roentgenologic appreciation of anterior mediastinal herniation generally is not difficult, through visualization of the displaced anterior mediastinal line (*see* Figure 1–55, page 76); the curvilinear density caused by the apposed pleural surfaces usually is visible, on a posteroanterior roentgenogram, protruding into the involved hemithorax; in lateral projections the anterior mediastinum appears exceptionally radiolucent and increased in depth. Appreciation of herniation through the posterior mediastinal weak areas may be more difficult; these portions of the mediastinal septum normally form the superior and inferior pleuroesophageal stripes (*see* Figure 1–56, page 77), and recognition of their displacement to one side may be facilitated by overpenetrated sagittal projections, by tomography, or by opacification of the esophagus with barium.

The importance of differentiating mediastinal "herniation" and mediastinal "displacement" was stressed by Lodin.[139] Although the distinction is valid, we feel that it is largely semantic: "herniation" indicates that a portion of the mediastinal pleura on one side has penetrated *through* the me-

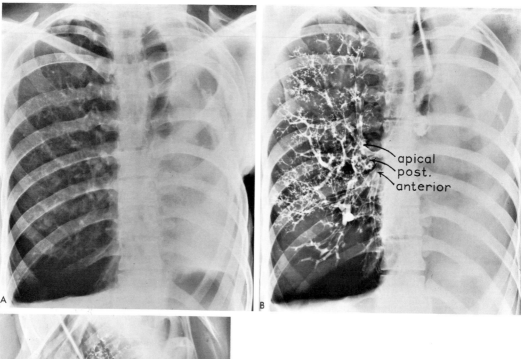

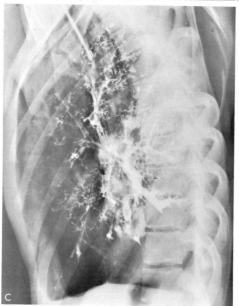

Figure 4-31. **Compensatory Overinflation: The One-lobe Thorax.** Over a span of several years, thoracotomy was performed on this 28-year-old woman on three different occasions for advanced incapacitating bronchiectasis: on the first, the left lower lobe and lingula were removed, on the second, the left upper lobe, and on the third, the right middle and lower lobes. At the time of each thoracotomy, the bronchial tree was found to be normal bronchographically in those areas subsequently affected. A right bronchogram (*B* and *C*) reveals only three segmental bronchi of the right upper lobe, at least one of which shows moderately advanced bronchiectasis. *See* text.

diastinal septum and has invaginated a portion of the opposite pleural cavity, whereas "displacement" technically implies a shift of the whole mediastinum without selective herniation.

When a whole lung becomes atelectatic subsequent to obstruction of a main bronchus, the resultant loss of volume of the hemithorax must be largely compensated for by overinflation of the contralateral lung (similar to the situation after pneumonectomy) (Figure 4–31). The mediastinal shift may be large and necessarily is associated with overinflation of the contralateral lung; since the mediastinum is less stable anteriorly than elsewhere, the anterior septum is rotated laterally and posteriorly, the normal lung overinflating to such an extent that it occupies the whole anterior portion of the thorax. Thus, the heart and the collapsed lung are displaced into the posterior portion of the ipsilateral hemithorax. In such circumstances, the roentgenologic appearance in lateral projection is distinctive:[584] Depth and radiolucency of the retrosternal air space are increased, the heart and great vessels are displaced posteriorly, and there is a general increase in density posteroinferiorly (Figure 4–31); the margin of the collapsed lung may be sharply delineated where it comes in contact with the opposite, overinflated lung. As emphasized by Lubert and Krause,[584] such an appearance allows easy differentiation of massive collapse from massive unilateral pneumonic consolidation or pleural effusion (Figure 4–32).

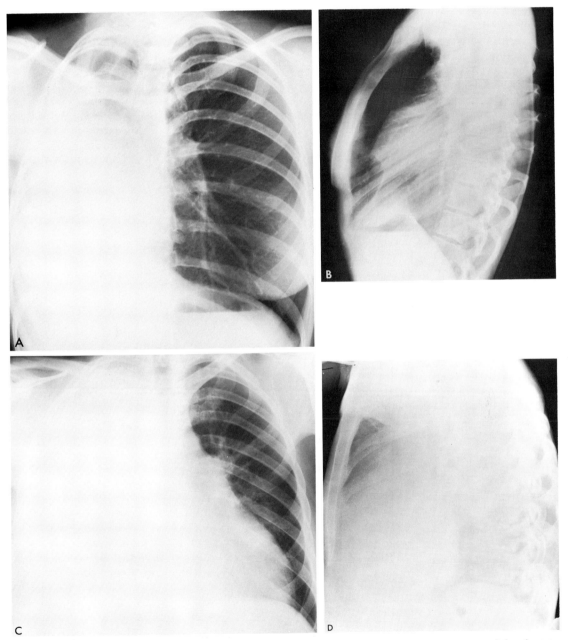

Figure 4–32. **Comparison of Massive Collapse and Massive Pleural Effusion.** Roentgenograms of the chest in posteroanterior and lateral projections (*A* and *B*) of a patient whose right lung has been removed (analogous to total right pulmonary collapse) reveals marked shift of the mediastinum into the posterior portion of the right hemithorax, with herniation of the overinflated left lung across the midline into the anterior right chest (note the clear retrosternal space). In *C* and *D* (roentgenograms of another patient), a massive right pleural effusion has resulted in a shift of the mediastinum to the left; in lateral projection opacity of the thorax is more or less homogeneous (the uniform filter effect). Compare the appearance of the retrosternal space in the two patients.

(d) *Displacement of the hila.* The hila frequently are involved in the redistribution of anatomic structures within the thorax in the presence of atelectasis, and such displacement constitutes an invaluable sign of collapse. It occurs more predictably in collapse of the upper than of the lower lobes and generally is more marked the more chronic the atelectasis (for example, chronic scarring of the upper lobes as a result of tuberculosis commonly is associated with severe upward displacement of the ipsilateral hilum (Figure 4–24). Downward displacement of the hila in lower-lobe collapse generally is more difficult to appreciate with the same degree of conviction as upward displacement; downward displacement of the left hilum, however, may result in the two hila being level in the thorax, a finding which is almost always significant since it occurs in only 3 per cent of normal subjects.[69]

Of equal importance to displacement of the hila as a sign of atelectasis is the *redistribution* of vascular shadows which form these structures. The right hilum normally possesses a concave lateral aspect formed by the superior pulmonary vein above and the descending pulmonary artery below. Simon[122] showed that when the right upper lobe is collapsed the superior pulmonary vein rotates medially so as to flatten the right hilar concavity. In collapse of other lobes, the pattern of change in relationship between hilar vascular shadows is much the same as that of redistribution of vascular shadows throughout the lungs as described previously.

(e) *Changes in the chest wall.* Approximation of the ribs is, in our experience, the least dependable of all compensatory signs of atelectasis. Even a slight degree of rotation of the patient at the time of roentgenography may produce a degree of asymmetry of the two sides of the rib cage that renders assessment of abnormal approximation difficult or even hazardous. The difficulty may be further compounded by alterations in rib angulation produced by even minor degrees of scoliosis. Whereas approximation of ribs as a sign of smallness of a hemithorax may be of some value in cases of chronic loss of volume, as from cicatrization, we feel that it should not be relied upon too heavily as an accurate indicator of reduction in hemithoracic volume in cases of acute lobar collapse.

(f) *Absence of an air bronchogram.* With the exception of atelectasis of the so-called "nonobstructive" variety, pulmonary atelectasis cannot be associated with visible air in the bronchial tree. If bronchial obstruction is of sufficient degree to cause absorption of air from the parenchyma of the involved lobe or segment, it must also cause absorption of gas from the bronchial tree. Particularly in situations where pneumonitis behind the obstruction is sufficiently severe that consolidation predominates over atelectasis, the absence of an air bronchogram is a roentgenologic sign of vital importance, since it may be the only sign that allows differentiation between an obstructive process produced by a bronchogenic carcinoma and a consolidative process such as simple bacterial pneumonia.

In summary, the roentgenologic signs of atelectasis are:

A. *Direct:*
   1. Local increase in density.
   2. Displacement of interlobar fissures.
B. *Indirect:*
   1. Elevation of the hemidiaphragm.
   2. Displacement of the mediastinum.
   3. Compensatory overinflation.
   4. Displacement of hila.
   5. Approximation of ribs.
   6. Absence of an air bronchogram (usually).

PATTERNS OF LOBAR AND SEGMENTAL ATELECTASIS. Roentgenologists are indebted to Robbins and Hale[585, 629–634] for clarifying for the first time the varied roentgenographic patterns of lobar and total pulmonary collapse. More recently, Lubert and Krause[582, 586, 587] depicted patterns of collapse in a most lucid manner in line drawings and by three-dimensional models. In the descriptions to follow we have borrowed freely from the publications of these authors; our findings have not differed fundamentally from their original observations.

As discussed earlier in this section, the roentgenographic pattern of atelectasis may be influenced by several variables: for example, pre-existing disease within the involved lobe or elsewhere in the lungs, a relatively fixed thoracic cage or mediastinum, pleural adhesions, pleural fluid, or pneumothorax, alone or in various combinations, alter the "typical" roentgenographic pattern. These variables are not discussed here; the patterns described are those which typically occur in collapse of previously normal lung tissue.

Since the degree of collapse of a lobe is governed largely by the amount of exudation into it, the resultant roentgenographic image varies from a consolidated lobe in which there is only minimal loss of volume to a state of total lobar collapse; therefore, the anatomicospatial relationships in each lobe are described from a state of full inflation through all stages to total atelectasis.

Providing the pleural space is intact (*i.e.*, no pneumothorax or hydrothorax), certain fundamental characteristics are common to all forms of collapse within the lung, regardless of the lobe involved or whether the collapse is of a whole lung or of a subsegment. It is important to realize that, regardless of the severity of collapse, the *visceral pleural surface of the involved lobe or segment continues to relate intimately to the parietal pleura;* in other words, the visceral pleural surface never retracts inward so as to lose contact with the parietal pleura over the convex or mediastinal surfaces of the hemithorax. Since movement is thus restricted hilarward, and since the medial aspect of the lobe is relatively fixed at the hilum, the form which the collapsed lobe must eventually adopt is limited. The resultant shape is also partly affected by the semirigid components of the lung (the bronchi, arteries, and veins), which can be crowded together in very close apposition in one plane but whose capacity for shortening is limited. As depicted by Lubert and Krause,[586] any pulmonary lobe in its fully inflated state may be likened to a pyramid with its apex at the hilum and its base contiguous to the parietal pleura; as the lobe progressively loses volume, two of the surfaces of the pyramid approximate, so that the end result of total collapse is a flattened triangle, or triangular "pancake," whose apex and base maintain contiguity with the hilum and parietal pleura, respectively.

Lubert and Krause[582] emphasized that the roentgenologist must not be misled by lack of correlation between what he recognizes as spatial readjustment roentgenographically and what the surgeon or pathologist finds at thoracotomy or necropsy — in the latter situations, pneumothorax dissipates all anatomicospatial relationships in the intact thorax: this is a rare aspect of roentgenologic-pathologic correlation which is notoriously inaccurate.

Total Pulmonary Atelectasis. When a complete lung collapses because of obstruction of a main bronchus, the compensatory phenomena which evolve are identical in character to those which develop with lesser degrees of pulmonary collapse but obviously are greater in degree and in some respects are less readily apparent. Elevation of the ipsilateral hemidiaphragm is recognizable only on the left side, where the stomach bubble indicates its position. The hemithorax usually shows evidence of retraction. It is on the mediastinum, however, where by far the most important effect is exerted by the net difference in pressure between the two halves of the thorax. As the normal contralateral lung overinflates, the whole mediastinum moves to the involved side, the greatest shift occurring anteriorly, where the mediastinum is weakest. As the overinflated lung moves across the midline it displaces the heart, aorta, and collapsed lung posteriorly. The resultant roentgenologic signs in lateral projection were clearly defined by Lubert and Krause:[584] Depth and radiolucency of the retrosternal air space are increased, with a general increase in roentgenographic density in the posterior portion of the thorax (Figure 4-32); if the overinflated normal lung has rotated sufficiently so as to come in contact with the collapsed lung, the interface between the two may appear delineated by the silhouette sign (*see* page 291). In posteroanterior projection, the uniform opacity caused by the superimposed cardiovascular structures and collapsed lung are interrupted by the radiolucency of the overinflated contralateral lung which has passed across the midline of the thorax. The margin of the overinflated lung usually is visualized extending a variable distance into the involved hemithorax.

Lubert and Krause[584] have emphasized the importance of assessing the retrosternal space in lateral projection in the differentiation of total pulmonary collapse from massive pulmonary consolidation or massive pleural effusion (Figure 4-32). In the latter two conditions the anterior mediastinum is little altered in appearance although its density may be increased; in total unilateral collapse the anterior mediastinum is increased not only in depth but also in radiolucency. These authors refer to the "uniform filter effect" observed in total pulmonary consolidation and massive pleural effusion, in which the absorption of x-rays passing through the thorax in lateral projection is uniform, thereby preventing identification of a specific roentgenographic shadow. In total unilateral pulmonary collapse, if rotation of the lung has not occurred posteriorly, the "uniform filter effect" may be apparent, but such an event must be most unusual in practice.

Lobar Atelectasis.   The patterns created by atelectasis of the right and left upper lobes differ and, therefore, are described separately; the lower lobes have almost identical patterns and are considered together.

Right upper lobe—The minor fissure and the upper half of the major fissure approximate by shifting upward (Figure 4–33). Both fissures become gently curved, with their convexity upward in lateral projection; the minor fissure shows roughly the same curvature in posteroanterior projection (Figure 4–34). As volume loss increases, the visceral pleural surface sweeps upward over the apex of the hemithorax, so that the lobe

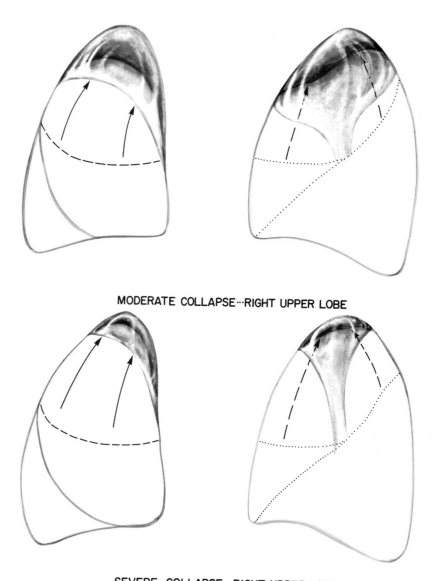

MODERATE COLLAPSE···RIGHT UPPER LOBE

SEVERE COLLAPSE···RIGHT UPPER LOBE

Figure 4-33.   Patterns of Lobar Collapse: Right Upper Lobe. *See* text for description.

comes to occupy a flattened position contiguous to the superior mediastinum (Figure 4–35). When completely collapsed, its volume is so small that in posteroanterior projection its shadow creates no more than a slight widening of the superior mediastin-um — to a point, in fact, where Simon[588] stressed the pitfall of misinterpreting this shadow as apical pleural thickening. In lateral projection, the collapsed lobe may appear as an indistinctly defined triangular shadow with its apex at the hilum and its

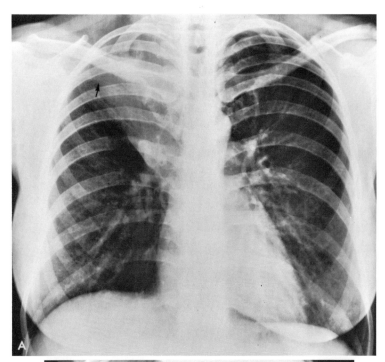

Figure 4–34. Atelectasis of the **Right Upper Lobe (Moderate).** Roentgenograms in posteroanterior (A) and lateral (B) projection show a homogeneous shadow in the upper portion of the right hemithorax. In posteroanterior projection the lower border of the shadow is formed by the upward displaced minor fissure (*arrow*), also identifiable in lateral projection as a rather indistinctly defined shadow anteriorly. The upward displaced major fissure is seen clearly in lateral projection (*arrow*). Bronchial adenoma totally obstructing the right upper-lobe bronchus.

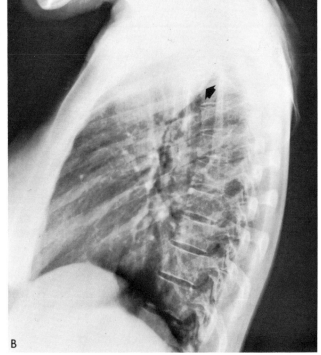

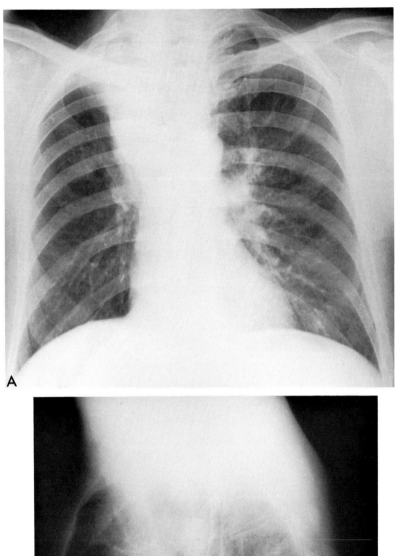

Figure 4–35.   **Atelectasis of the Right Upper Lobe (Severe).** The collapse is more severe than in Figure 4–34, the whole upper lobe presenting as a homogeneous shadow in the superior paramediastinal zone (*A*). The lateral border is sharply defined. A distinct shadow cannot be identified in lateral projection (*B*). Carcinoma of the right upper-lobe bronchus.

base contiguous to the parietal pleura just posterior to the extreme apex of the hemithorax (the "mediastinal wedge"). Usually the collapsed lobe is immediately contiguous to the mediastinum, so that no air shadow separates the two; in a reported case of right upper-lobe collapse,[589] however, what appeared roentgenologically as a sickle-shaped paramediastinal air space was shown at necropsy to be interposed overinflated lower lobe.

Left upper lobe — The major difference between collapse of the left and of the right upper lobes relates to the absence of a mi-

nor fissure on the left, on which side all lung tissue anterior to the major fissure is involved (Figure 4–36). This fissure, which is slightly more vertical than the chief fissure on the right, is displaced forward in a plane roughly parallel to the anterior chest wall, a relationship which is depicted particularly well on lateral roentgenograms (Figure 4–37). As volume loss increases, the fissure moves further anteriorly and slightly medially, until on lateral projection the shadow of the lobe is no more than a broad linear opacity contiguous and parallel to the anterior chest wall (Figure 4–38). The conti-

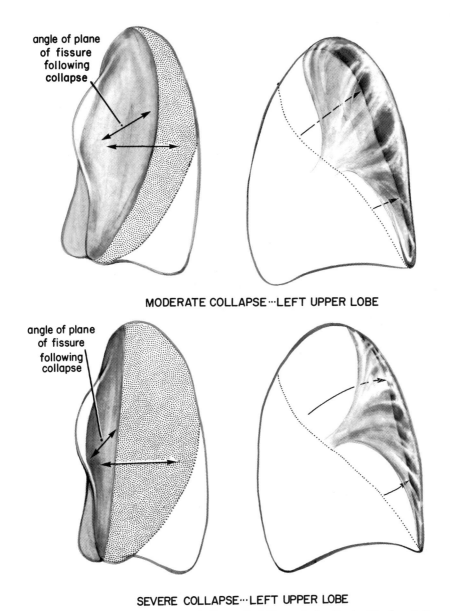

MODERATE COLLAPSE···LEFT UPPER LOBE

SEVERE COLLAPSE···LEFT UPPER LOBE

Figure 4–36. Patterns of Lobar Collapse: Left Upper Lobe. *See* text for description.

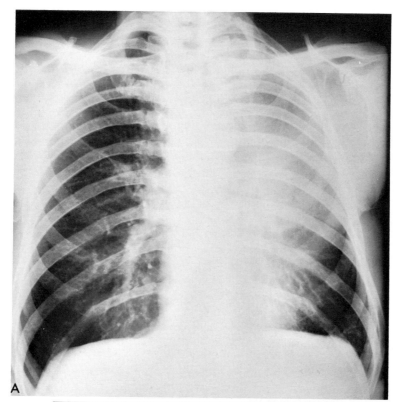

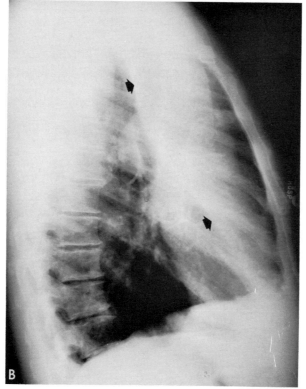

Figure 4–37. **Atelectasis of the Left Upper Lobe (Moderate).** In posteroanterior projection (*A*), the entire left border of the heart is obscured by a homogeneous shadow projected over the upper two thirds of the left hemithorax. In lateral projection (*B*), the chief fissure is displaced anteriorly (*arrows*). Note the absence of an air bronchogram, indicating bronchial obstruction. The left hemidiaphragm is moderately elevated. Bronchogenic carcinoma left upper-lobe bronchus, with obstructive pneumonitis.

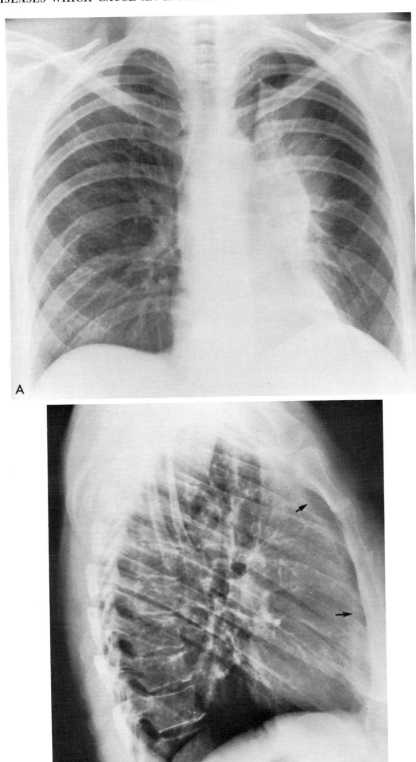

Figure 4–38. **Atelectasis of the Left Upper Lobe (Severe).** The homogeneous shadow created by the almost complete collapse of the left upper lobe occupies the anteromedial portion of the left hemithorax contiguous to the mediastinum. In posteroanterior projection (A), the apex of the hemithorax is occupied by the overinflated lower lobe. In lateral projection (B), the chief fissure has swept far anteriorly and can be identified as a rather indistinctly defined shadow of increased density paralleling the anterior chest wall (*arrows*). The "mediastinal wedge" can be only vaguely distinguished.

guity of the collapsed lobe with the anterior mediastinum obliterates the left cardiac border in frontal projection (the "silhouette sign"—*see* page 291). The apical segment tends to retract downward, the space it vacates being occupied by the overinflated superior bronchopulmonary segment of the lower lobe; the apex of the hemithorax thus contains aerated lung (Figure 4–38).[590] The "mediastinal wedge" produced by the triangular density extending from the collapsed parenchyma to the hilum often is difficult to visualize but may be seen on a lateral tomogram. Should atelectasis become complete (an uncommon occurrence), the lower end of the chief fissure swings upward anteriorly to produce the final result of a triangular density with its apex at the hilum and its base contiguous to the parietal pleura at the apex of the hemithorax (in a position somewhat more anterior than is seen in total right upper-lobe collapse).

Shift of the superior mediastinum as a compensatory phenomenon generally is more marked in left than in right upper-lobe collapse, probably because of the larger volume of the former. Herniation of the right lung across the anterior mediastinal septum (Figure 4–37) may separate the collapsed left upper lobe from the anterior chest wall and produce an exceptionally radiolucent retrosternal space as viewed in lateral projection, with a sharp line of definition between the herniated right lung and the collapsed left upper lobe.

Right middle lobe—Atelectasis of the right middle lobe provides the anomalous situation of being one of the easiest diagnoses to make on lateral roentgenography and one of the most difficult on posteroanterior projection. With progressive loss of volume, the minor fissure and the lower half of the major fissure approximate and are almost in contact when collapse is complete (Figure 4–39). The resultant triangular "pancake" of tissue has its apex at the hilum and its base contiguous to the parietal pleura over the anterolateral convexity of the thorax. In lateral projection it appears as a linear shadow of increased density, no more than 2 or 3 mm wide; in posteroanterior projection, there may be no discernible increase in density—the only evidence for disease may be obliteration of a portion of the right cardiac border (the "silhouette sign"), due to contiguity of the right atrium and the medial bronchopulmonary segment of the collapsed lobe (Figure 4–40). This lack of density on posteroanterior projection is caused by the obliquity of the collapsed lobe in a superoinferior plane: at any point its thickness is insufficient to cast a discernible roentgenographic shadow. When the patient is placed in a lordotic position, the downward-displaced minor fissure becomes oriented in a

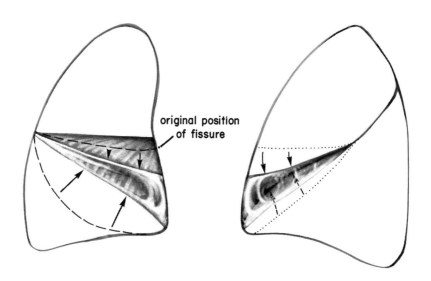

COLLAPSE ∙∙∙ RIGHT MIDDLE LOBE

Figure 4–39. Patterns of Lobar Collapse: Right Middle Lobe. *See* text for description.

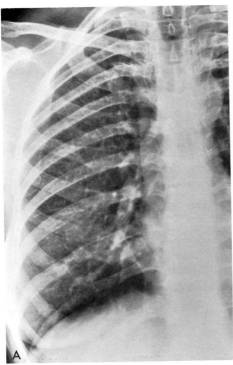

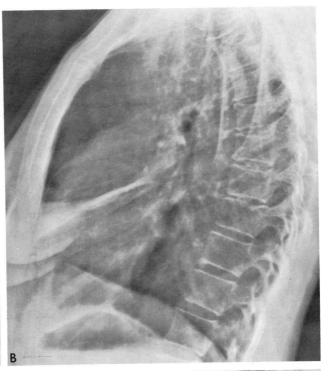

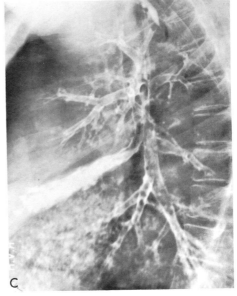

Figure 4-40. **Atelectasis of the Right Middle Lobe.** A view of the right lung from a posteroanterior roentgenogram (*A*) shows no convincing evidence of a shadow of increased density. Evidence of disease is provided by obliteration of the right border of the heart by airlessness of the right middle lobe (the silhouette sign). In lateral projection (*B*), a thin triangular shadow representing airless right middle lobe between approximated fissures can be identified extending anteroinferiorly from the region of the hilum. A right bronchogram (*C*) shows severe crowding of bronchiectatic middle-lobe segmental bronchi; the middle-lobe bronchus is widely patent. Chronic "right middle-lobe syndrome."

plane parallel to the roentgen beam, so that the collapsed lobe is visualized as a thin "sail-like" shadow extending from the lateral chest wall medially and slightly inferiorly along the right cardiac border (Figure 4-41).

Lower lobes—The fissures approximate in such a manner that the upper half of the chief fissure swings downward and the lower half backward (Figure 4-42). This displacement is best appreciated in lateral projection, but during its downward displacement the upper half of the fissure may become clearly evident in posteroanterior projection as a density with a sharply defined upper surface extending obliquely downward and laterally from the region of the hilum (Figures 4-43 and 4-46). As collapse progresses, the lobe moves posteromedially to occupy a position in the posterior costophrenic gutter and medial costovertebral angle. Since the flat surface of the

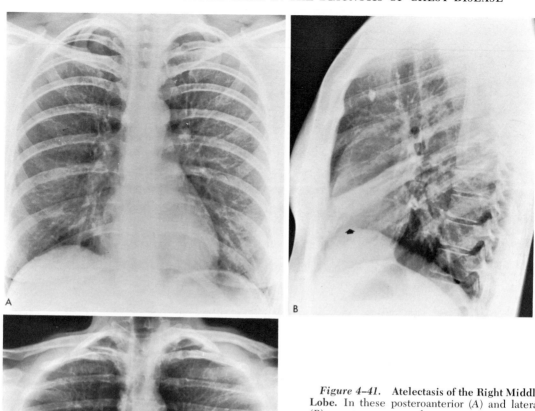

Figure 4–41. **Atelectasis of the Right Middle Lobe.** In these posteroanterior (A) and lateral (B) roentgenograms, the pattern is similar to that seen in Figure 4–40: the sole evidence of disease in frontal projection is loss of visibility of the right border of the heart. In lordotic projection (C), however, the collapsed right middle lobe is clearly visualized as a sail-like shadow since the plane of the x-ray beam parallels the downward displaced horizontal fissure. Envisage B in lordotic projection. Note the local elevation of the right hemidiaphragm anteriorly (*arrows* in B and C). Chronic "right middle-lobe syndrome."

triangular "pancake" lies against the mediastinum, the thickness of tissue traversed by the roentgen beam in lateral projection may be insufficient to cast a shadow in this projection. However, the "mediastinal wedge" (consisting of the conducting tissues) should be apparent as a narrow triangular band of increased density extending downward and posteriorly from the hilum (Figure 4–44). In frontal projection, providing exposure factors ensure adequate penetration of the heart, the collapsed lobe should be plainly visible as a diminutive

triangular density in the costovertebral angle (Figure 4–45).

Combined Lobar Atelectasis. Since involvement of the two lobes of the left lung results in total pulmonary collapse, only in the right lung can atelectasis of two lobes simultaneously produce a distinctive roentgenographic pattern.

Combined right middle-lobe and right lower-lobe atelectasis (Figure 4–46)—The major and minor fissures are displaced downward and backward so that the resultant density occupies the posteroinferior portion of the hemithorax. Lubert and Krause[582] state that on a posteroanterior roentgenogram the density created by the collapsed lobes completely obliterates the shadow of the right dome of the diaphragm and may possess an upper surface which is either concave or convex upward. Thus, this condition may easily be confused with pleural effusion (either "typical" or infrapulmonary in configuration).

Combined right upper-lobe and right middle-lobe atelectasis (Figure 4–47) — Be-cause of the independent and even remote origin of the lobar bronchi of these lobes, such an occurrence must be uncommon, although Lubert and Krause[582] state that they have seen it "more frequently than might be anticipated": because of the independent bronchial origins, either multiple etiologies or a single etiology operating at two anatomic locations must be invoked to explain coincidental involvement. Although these authors claim to have seen combined lesions in carcinoma, adenoma, metastatic

(Text continues on page 236.)

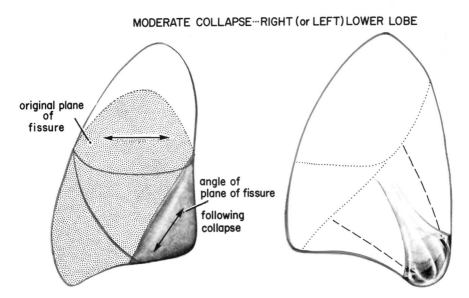

MODERATE COLLAPSE···RIGHT (or LEFT) LOWER LOBE

SEVERE COLLAPSE···RIGHT (or LEFT) LOWER LOBE

Figure 4–42. Patterns of Lobar Collapse: Right (or Left) Lower Lobe. *See* text for description.

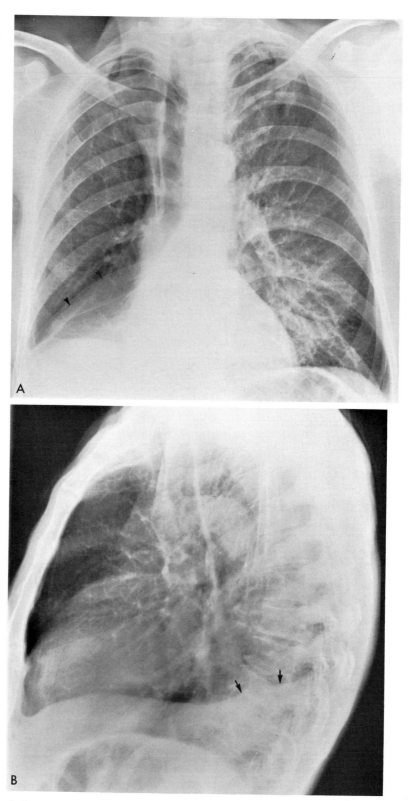

Figure 4-43. **Atelectasis of the Right Lower Lobe.** In posteroanterior projection (*A*), a triangular shadow of homogeneous density is projected in the plane of the right cardiophrenic angle. Its upper border is fairly sharply circumscribed (*arrows*) and is produced by the interface between the downward displaced chief fissure and contiguous aerated lung. The right upper and middle lobes are overinflated to compensate. In lateral projection (*B*), a poorly defined shadow can be identified posteroinferiorly, obliterating the posterior costophrenic gutter and the posterior portion of the right hemidiaphragm (*arrows*). A mediastinal wedge cannot be identified.

232

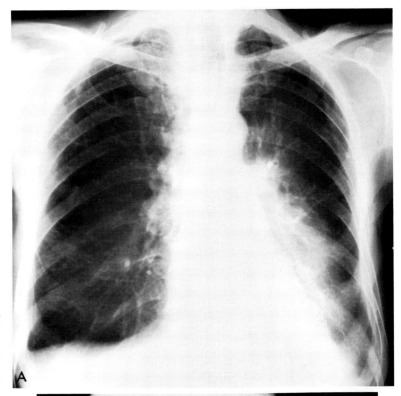

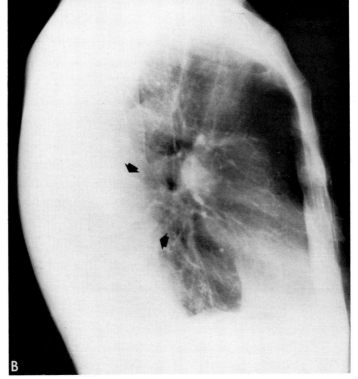

Figure 4-44. **Atelectasis of the Left Lower Lobe (Moderate).** There is more obstructive pneumonitis and less collapse in this lower lobe than was present in the patient illustrated in Figure 4-43. In lateral projection (*B*), a mediastinal wedge can be identified (*arrows*) situated somewhat higher than is usually the case with lower-lobe collapse.

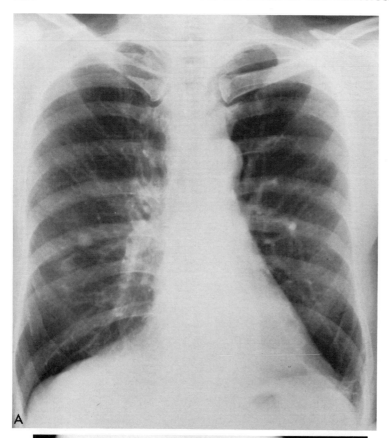

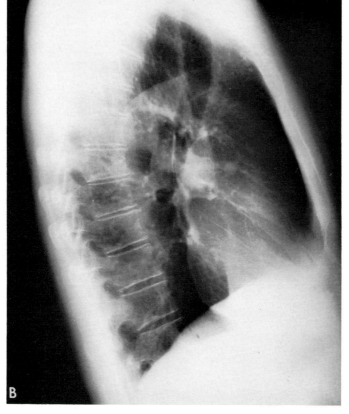

Figure 4–45. **Atelectasis of the Left Lower Lobe (Severe).** In posteroanterior projection (*A*), the collapsed left lower lobe is represented by a broad shadow of homogeneous density projected behind the heart and adjacent to the vertebral column. Its lateral border is formed by the interface between the downward displaced chief fissure and contiguous overinflated upper lobe. No abnormal shadows can be identified in lateral projection (*B*). In frontal projection, note the increased translucency of the left hemithorax compared to the right due to compensatory overinflation. The solitary nodule in the right mid-lung was a histoplasmoma. The left lower-lobe atelectasis was related to longstanding varicose bronchiectasis.

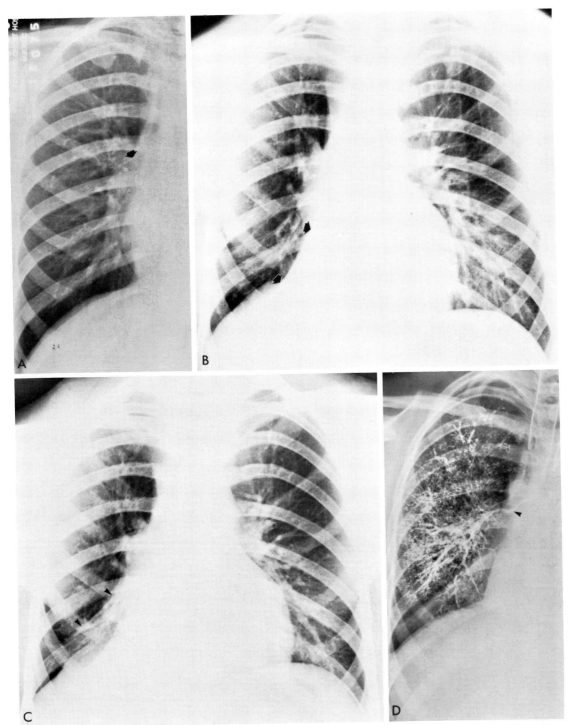

Figure 4–46. **Atelectasis of the Right Middle and Lower Lobes Combined.** A view of the right hemithorax from a posteroanterior roentgenogram (A) shows a thin line shadow (*arrow*) extending obliquely downward from the right side of the mediastinum across the hilum. This line represents the chief fissure which has been displaced downward as a result of loss of volume of the right lower lobe. Note the absence of any shadow representing airless lung parenchyma. One month later (B), the right lower lobe has become totally atelectatic and consists of a triangular shadow of homogeneous density projected in the plane of the right cardiophrenic angle (*thick arrows*); the collapsed lobe is situated posteriorly (the lack of visualization of the right border of the heart is due to roentgenographic underpenetration rather than to the silhouette sign). The horizontal fissure is displaced downward. One month later (C), the shadow of the lower-lobe collapse is unchanged but there has occurred further medial displacement of the horizontal fissure (*arrows*) due to greater loss of volume of the middle lobe. A bronchogram performed at this time (D) reveals total obstruction of the intermediate-stem bronchus just beyond the upper-lobe take-off (*arrow*). Only the upper-lobe bronchial tree is opacified. At thoracotomy, a hard mass 8 × 3 cm was found posteriorly, compressing the esophagus and lower-lobe bronchi; chronic caseating granulomatous inflammation of lung and lymph nodes of undetermined etiology. (Courtesy Dr. David Berger, Royal Edward Chest Hospital, Montreal.)

tumor, and inflammatory disease, they feel that mucous plugs probably were a direct, contributing etiologic factor in most cases. The only example that we have seen was caused by mucous impaction. The roentgenographic pattern pro-

duced by this combined lesion is identical to that seen in collapse of the left upper lobe.

Segmental Atelectasis. The roentgenographic patterns of segmental atelectasis do not differ fundamentally from those of lobar

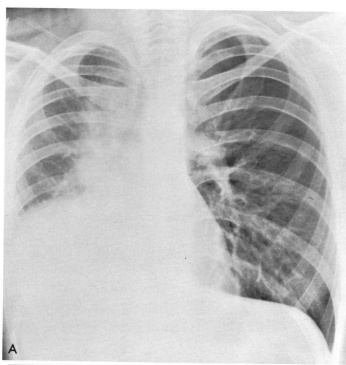

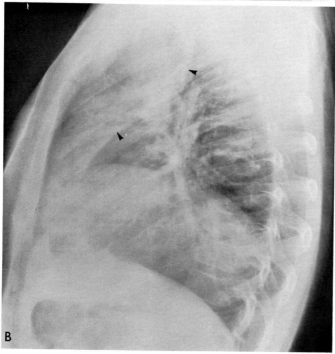

Figure 4–47. **Atelectasis of the Right Upper and Middle Lobes Combined.** Posteroanterior (*A*) and lateral (*B*) roentgenograms reveal a pattern of collapse which is virtually identical to that seen in the left upper lobe (compare Figure 4–37). The collapsed lobes relate to the anteromedial aspect of the hemithorax; thus, in lateral projection (*B*) the major fissure is seen to be displaced forward (*arrows*). The apex of the right hemithorax is occupied by the overdistended lower lobe. Compensatory signs of diaphragmatic elevation and mediastinal shift are readily apparent. Twelve-year-old boy with spasmodic asthma; a mucous plug impacted in the right upper-lobe bronchus was coughed up spontaneously; the right middle-lobe collapse was chronic and irreversible (chronic "right middle-lobe syndrome").

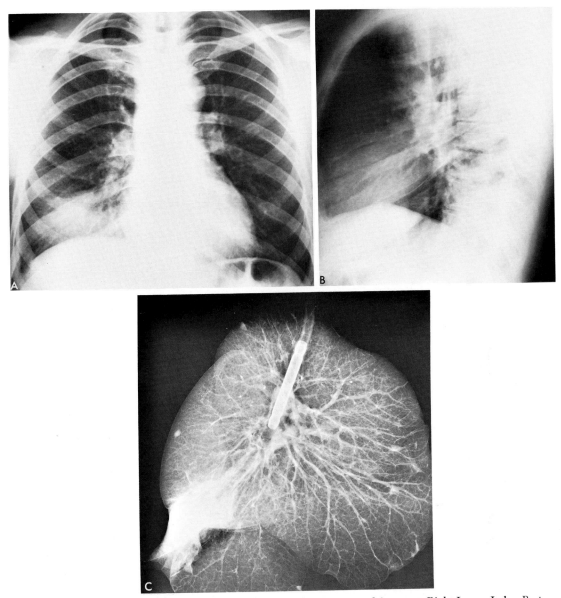

Figure 4–48.   **Segmental Atelectasis and Consolidation, Posterior Basal Segment, Right Lower Lobe.** Postero-anterior (*A*) and lateral (*B*) roentgenograms reveal a homogeneous opacity localized to the posterior broncho-pulmonary segment of the right lower lobe; no air bronchogram is present. The process is both consolidative and atelectatic, the latter evidenced by posterior displacement of the major fissure. A lateral roentgenogram of the resected lung (*C*) shows the precise segmental nature of the disease; as a result of preoperative chemo-therapy, the bronchial obstruction had been partly relieved so that the operative specimen shows a well-defined air bronchogram. Squamous cell carcinoma of the posterior basal bronchus.

collapse, except in regard to the volume of lung involved. In all cases, a triangular den-sity is created whose apex is directed to-ward the hilum and whose base is contig-uous to the parietal pleura (Figures 4–48 and 4–49). As might be anticipated, the resultant density depends not only upon the original

volume of the obstructed segment but also upon the amount of exudation into it. In un-complicated atelectasis, the roentgeno-graphic shadow may be no more than linear (Figure 4–50) and may be visible only if the x-ray beam happens to fall along its flat plane.

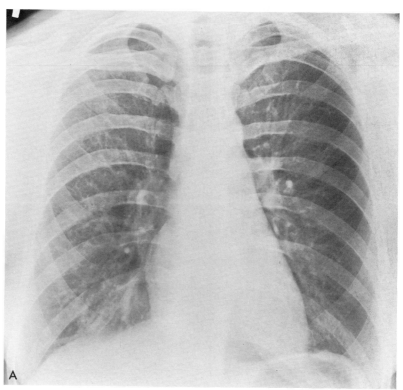

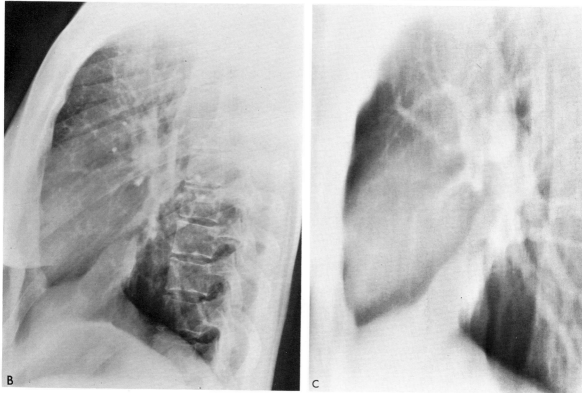

Figure 4–49. **Segmental Atelectasis and Consolidation, Anterior Basal Segment, Right Lower Lobe.** A triangular shadow of homogeneous density conforming to the anatomic distribution of the anterior basal bronchus is situated in the inferior portion of the right lower lobe, its base contiguous to the right hemidiaphragm and its apex pointing toward the hilum; there is moderate loss of volume; the absence of an air bronchogram indicates bronchial obstruction. The shadow is rather indistinctly defined in posteroanterior projection (A) but well-circumscribed in lateral projection (standard roentgenogram (B) and tomogram (C)). Bronchostenosis secondary to endobronchial tuberculosis.

238

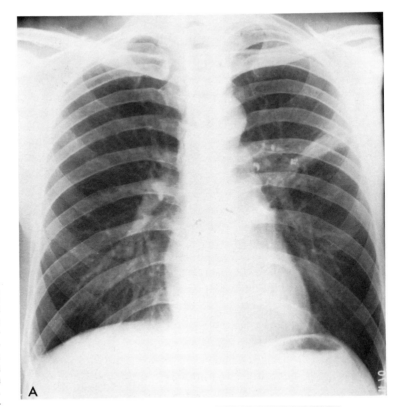

Figure 4–50. **Subsegmental Atelectasis, Left Upper Lobe.** A broad, band shadow can be seen in both the posteroanterior roentgenogram (*A*) and the anteroposterior tomogram (*B*) extending in a roughly horizontal plane from the lateral aspect of the left hilum to the axillary visceral pleura. The shadow is of varigated density, suggesting the presence of air within dilated airways. The calcific density at the medial aspect of the shadow is a broncholith which is partially obstructing the affected bronchus. Presumed histoplasmosis.

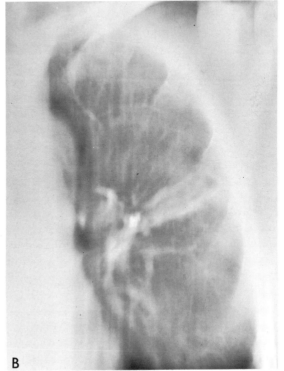

PREDOMINANT INTERSTITIAL DISEASE

This heading covers the multitude of pulmonary diseases characterized by predominant involvement of the interstitial tissues of the lung. Conceptually, these diseases are the antithesis of the alveolar consolidative processes, in that *alveolar air is largely preserved and it is the tissues surrounding the air spaces that are increased in volume.* The number of diseases capable of producing a predominantly interstitial involvement of the lungs is enormous. Occasionally the roentgenographic pattern is sufficiently distinctive to allow of a confident diagnosis on the basis of roentgenologic appearances alone. In some, the diagnosis may be strongly suggested when roentgenographic changes are considered with the history or with evidence supplied by special roentgenographic procedures, laboratory findings, or pulmonary function values. In the majority, however, architectural disturbance is so similar that a definitive diagnosis cannot be made without resource to histologic examination of tissue removed at biopsy.[591, 592]

Concepts of Roentgenologic Anatomy

It will be recalled that the lung parenchyma is sharply demarcated from the connective tissues of the bronchovascular tree, the interlobular septa, and the pleura by a limiting membrane[15] which is composed of dense elastic tissue and collagen and which merges into the elastic fibers of alveolar walls (*see* page 10). The blood vessels, nerves, and lymphatics lie in this compartment of loose connective tissue which we term the *perivascular interstitial space.* In addition, there is a small interstitial space in the walls of the alveoli themselves; this is referred to as the *parenchymal (or acinar) interstitial space,* in keeping with our use of the term "parenchyma" to denote the gas-exchanging part of the lung (*see* Figure 4–1, page 188).

The *perivascular interstitial space* consists of the sheath of loose connective tissue situated around the bronchovascular bundles which form the visible lung markings. This interstitial sheath extends out as far as the peripheral bronchioles, beyond which the airways are intimately related to the parenchyma. A similar sheath exists around the venous radicals within the lung, and this interstitial space is continuous with the peripheral interlobular septa which contain the veins and lymphatics that drain the peripheral parenchyma; it is also continuous with the subpleural interstitial space. The *parenchymal (acinar) interstitial space* lies between the alveolar epithelium and the capillary basement membrane. This space is small and is made up of elastic and collagen fibers.

Since interstitial diseases of the lung will generally, if not always, affect both "compartments" to some degree, it might be argued that their subdivision is arbitrary and of little practical importance. From a roentgenologic point of view, however, we have found their distinction of some value, chiefly because their individual involvement usually produces distinguishable roentgenographic patterns. For example, one of the common abnormalities affecting the interstitial tissues of the lung is pulmonary edema, particularly when of a "subacute" nature due to transient pulmonary venous hypertension.[593] This edema fluid is deposited chiefly within the perivascular sheath and interlobular septa (Figure 4–51), although it accumulates to some degree in the parenchymal interstitial tissues also. It is this anatomic localization which produces the typical roentgenographic pattern of a loss of the normal sharp definition of the pulmonary vascular markings, a haziness and loss of demarcation of the hilar shadows, and thickening of the interlobular septa (B lines of Kerley) (Figure 4–52). Edema fluid which accumulates in the *parenchymal* interstitial tissues in these circumstances generally produces little or no discernible roentgenographic changes. The pattern of roentgenologic abnormality in such instances is predominantly one of perivascular interstitial-tissue involvement. A similar distribution of disease occurs in lymphangitic spread of carcinoma,[681] pneumoconiosis,[594] and interstitial lymphoma (Figure 4–53).[595] Although these diseases generally are diffuse in their anatomic distribution, involvement of the perivascular tissue space may show the same type of change roentgenographically in certain localized diseases such as bronchopneumonia.

Contrast this picture of predominantly perivascular interstitial-space involvement with the appearances of involvement primarily of the acinar (parenchymal) interstitial space (Figure 4–54). The usual connotation of the expression "interstitial disease of the lungs" is a diffuse alteration in lung ar-

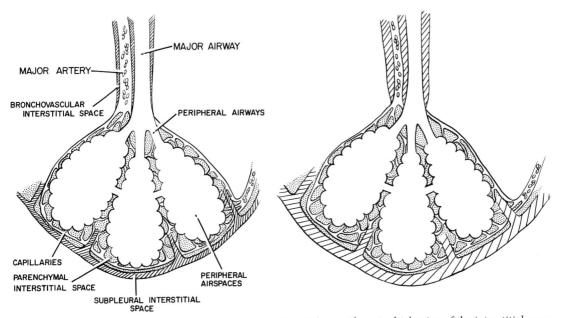

MAJOR AIRWAY

MAJOR ARTERY

BRONCHOVASCULAR
INTERSTITIAL SPACE

PERIPHERAL AIRWAYS

CAPILLARIES
PARENCHYMAL
INTERSTITIAL SPACE

PERIPHERAL
AIRSPACES

SUBPLEURAL INTERSTITIAL
SPACE

Figure 4–51. **The Lung Diagram: Perivascular Interstitial Edema.** There is thickening of the interstitial space around the airways and major vessels, as well as of the subpleural connective tissue and interlobular septa. The parenchymal interstitial tissues are relatively unaffected.

chitecture, characterized by the *reticulonodular pattern* (Figure 4–55). This pattern is caused by an abnormal accumulation of tissue in the parenchymal interstitial space of the lungs. Anatomically, the disease may be more or less confined to the *interalveolar septa* or may be diffuse throughout the interstitial tissues of the lung, including the vascular sheath, but it is the increase in parenchymal interstitial tissue that creates the basic change in architecture.

The roentgenographic pattern of interstitial disease varies not only according to its predominant anatomic location, as discussed previously, but also according to its etiology. For example, *local diseases* in which parenchymal interstitial involvement is predominant generally are of infective etiology (for example, acute *Mycoplasma* or virus pneumonia); in such circumstances, it is exceptional for the inflammatory reaction to be confined to the interstitial space; extension of the inflammation into parenchymal air spaces and smaller airways modifies the roentgenographic pattern of pure interstitial involvement in predictable fashion (Figure 4–56); in cases of air-space consolidation, partial or complete, the rosette or stippled shadows of the acinar

lesion are superimposed upon the basic reticular pattern of the interstitial disease (Figure 4–57); inflammation of small airways leads to obstruction to air flow and peripheral subsegmental collapse. Thus, depending upon the severity of air-space or bronchiolar involvement, the interstitial pattern may be wholly or partly obscured. Similarly, *generalized interstitial diseases,* either subacute or chronic, may affect all parenchymal elements in varying degree, although involvement of the interstitium is predominant. For example, one of the most common examples is now often termed "fibrosing alveolitis" (Hamman-Rich disease) (Figure 4–58). This term indicates the extent of distortion of the parenchyma which results. The morphologic picture is not one of simple thickening of alveolar walls with retention of pulmonary architecture; in its advanced stages the disease obliterates the alveoli and dilates the bronchioles proximal to obliterated acini. The lesions in the early stages are not well documented, but may predominantly involve the parenchymal interstitial space with a mononuclear infiltrate, with only slight air-space involvement.

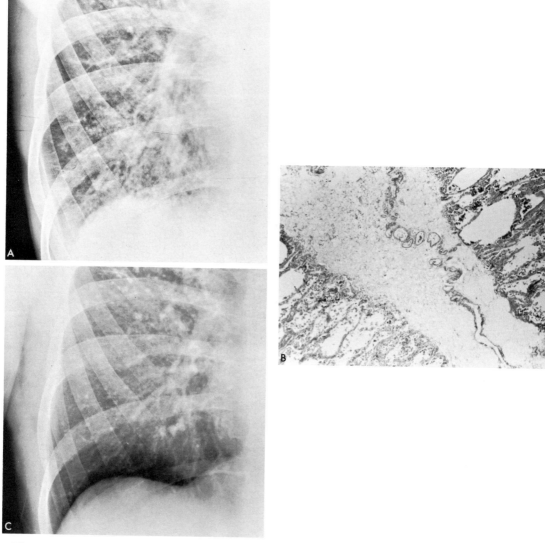

Figure 4–52.   **Pulmonary Interstitial Edema.** A magnified view of the lower half of the right lung (*A*) shows the vascular markings to be hazy and indistinct due to the accumulation of fluid in the perivascular interstitial space. Thin horizontal lines of increased density measuring approximately a centimeter in length can be identified along the axillary lung margin inferiorly; these are due to an accumulation of edema fluid in the interlobular septa (Kerley B lines). A photomicrograph (*B*) of an identical shadow of another patient studied at necropsy reveals a markedly thickened edematous interlobular septum extending across the field, the parenchyma above and below showing congestion and hemosiderosis; a lymphatic channel can be seen passing through the center of the edematous septum. The line shadow observed roentgenographically thus is due to edema of the septum rather than to distention of the lymphatic. A magnified view of the lower half of the right lung of the same patient illustrated in *A*, but some days later (*C*), shows the vascular shadows to have regained their sharp definition; the Kerley lines have disappeared.

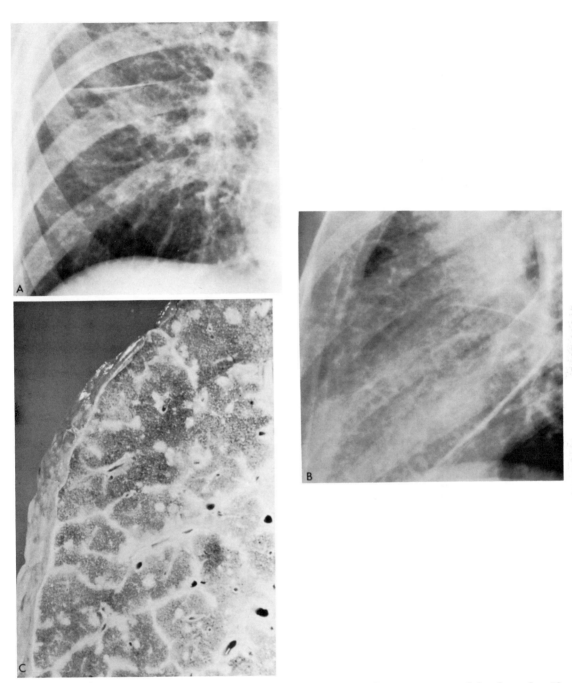

Figure 4–53. **Interstitial Reticulum Cell Sarcoma.** Magnified views of roentgenograms of the chest of an 18-year-old man with proven reticulum cell sarcoma. In frontal projection, the lower half of the right lung (A) shows rather poor definition of the lung markings; in lateral projection (B), a coarse network of line shadows can be identified in the retrosternal area running roughly perpendicular to the plane of the sternum. A photograph of the anterior portion of the lung removed at necropsy (C) reveals extensive thickening of the interlobular septa and perivascular interstitial tissues with reticulum cell sarcoma.

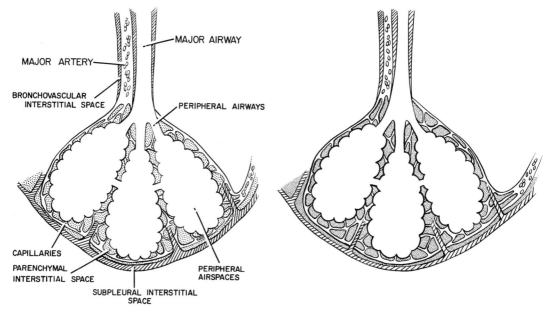

Figure 4–54. **The Lung Diagram: Parenchymal Interstitial Disease.** There is an increase in the amount of parenchymal interstitial tissue. The airways and air spaces are largely unaffected.

Roentgenographic Patterns of Diffuse Interstitial Disease

Confusion in the interpretation of diffuse interstitial lung disease is not surprising—not only are the patterns numerous and extremely varied but our knowledge of their precise nature suffers from a lack of accurate roentgenologic-pathologic correlation. We cannot yet predict accurately the pathologic anatomy in a significant number of these diffuse diseases. Further, even the broadest correlations, such as the morphologic basis for so-called reticular, nodular, or granular patterns (*vide infra*) are not known. A knowledge of roentgenologic pathology cannot be firmly established without accurate morphologic correlation, and the evidence that this can be obtained in many of these diffuse lung diseases is conflicting. For example, in coal-workers' pneumoconiosis, Gough and his associates[2872] found good correspondence between the number and size of opacities observed roentgenographically and those found in paper-mounted full-lung sections. Conversely, Oosthuizen and Theron,[596] using the same pathologic methods as Gough and his associates,[2872] emphasized the lack of

correlation between roentgenographic findings and post-mortem appearances of whole-lung sections in patients with silicosis. However, although it is evident that the roentgenologic interpretation of diffuse disease cannot yet be based on a solid pathologic foundation, in the majority of situations abnormal interstitial patterns can be described and classified precisely enough to allow of reasonable conclusions concerning their morphologic characteristics.

Much of the confusion concerning diffuse interstitial lung disease has arisen because of doubt over precisely what we see and what we are able to see on a chest roentgenogram. For example, it might be logical to assume that a network of densities forming a reticular pattern should be produced by linear accumulations of tissue within the lung; or, conversely, that a nodular pattern should be produced by multiple nodular lesions throughout the lungs. Clearly, such an assumption is only partly valid; the roentgenographic effect of *superimposition* of many layers of densities within the lungs is poorly understood, but there is little doubt that superimposition creates variations in pattern which are in large measure unpredictable. This raises

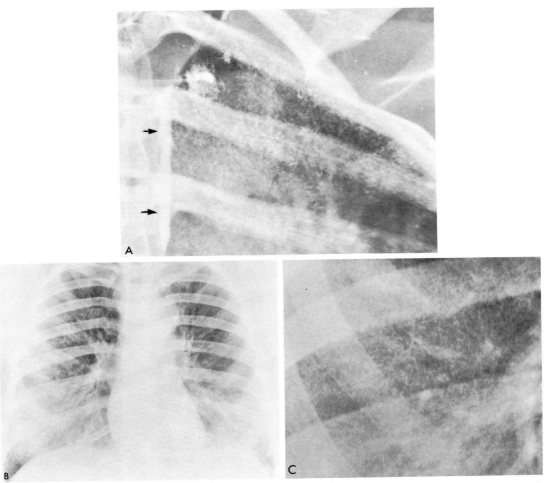

Figure 4–55.   The Reticulonodular Pattern. A magnified view of the apex of the left upper lobe approximately one and one-half hours following the injection of 7 ml of Lipiodol into the lymphatics of each leg (A) reveals a fine network of shadows of high density. This network is caused by the presence of contrast medium in the microvascular circulation of the lung. The thoracic duct can be identified on the left (*arrows*). A posteroanterior roentgenogram (B) exposed 24 hours later reveals a fine stippled pattern throughout both lungs, distributed diffusely and evenly; this pattern is so fine that it is barely visible on a standard roentgenogram but with primary and secondary magnification (C) reveals itself as a fine reticular pattern (the nodular component is thought to be due to visualization of line shadows on end).

one of the most fascinating issues of the interpretation of diffuse lung disease — the controversial question of summation of images (precise superimposition of identical shadows in the direction of the roentgen beam). The principle of summation has been invoked by many to explain the roentgenographic visibility of multiple shadows which, individually, would be of insufficient size to cast a roentgenographic shadow — for example, the lesions of miliary tuberculosis. However, studies carried out by Resink[181] strongly suggest that summation of shadows is not the method by which multiple subliminal densities (below the limit of roentgenologic visi-

bility) become supraliminal (roentgenologically visible); in fact, Resink believes that in such circumstances individual shadows become visible *only when they are not summated*. Although with our present knowledge we are inclined to support Resink's thesis, unfortunately this theory leaves unanswered the question of visibility of tiny nodules such as those of miliary tuberculosis which by all standards of threshold visibility should be subliminal. This remains a roentgenologic enigma.

One other facet of this problem deserves mention. The four basic roentgenographic patterns of interstitial disease are ground-glass (granular), reticular, nodular, and

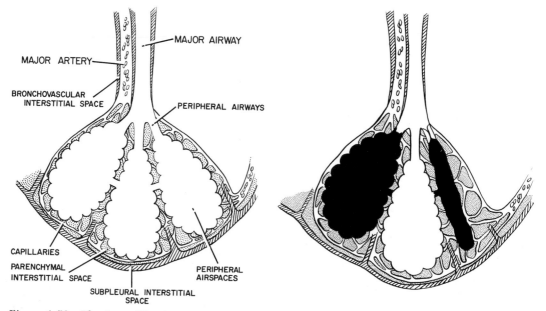

Figure 4–56. **The Lung Diagram: Combined Interstitial and Air-space Disease.** The interstitial tissues are increased in quantity as in Figure 4–54, but in addition, the air space on the left is consolidated and that on the right collapsed (due to bronchiolar obstruction). The central air space is normal.

mixed reticulonodular. Although reticular and nodular patterns exist in pure forms, it is probable that most interstitial diseases possess a mixed reticulonodular architecture. In some, the pattern may begin as reticular and be transformed into a relatively pure nodular pattern as the disease progresses; such a transformation has been emphasized by Wholey and associates in Hamman-Rich disease.[591] Similarly, it is logical that in a reticular network, particularly if it is coarse, many linear densities will be seen *en face* and thus appear as a reticular pattern roentgenographically, but many must be seen on end and thus simulate nodules. This dual roentgenographic pattern produced by purely reticular disease was emphasized by Stolberg and his co-workers, who studied it in pulmonary Hodgkin's disease.[595] Because of this obvious visual effect, it might appear logical to designate all of these diseases "reticulonodular"; however, as is shown later, the distinction between reticular and nodular diseases not only possesses certain morphologic significance but also may be important in relation to the effects each may exert on pulmonary function.

While recognizing these several imponderables in the field of diffuse interstitial lung disease, it is nevertheless tempting to devise a classification based on recognizable roentgenographic patterns of disease. The following does not consist of a detailed description of specific disease processes but rather a presentation of *patterns* of disease, in the form of a descriptive classification; in each instance an attempt is made to relate the roentgenographic pattern with morphology.

Before discussing specific roentgenographic manifestations of diffuse interstitial lung diseases, it might be worthwhile to indicate the roentgenologic changes which are common to all and without which the purely interstitial site of involvement should be held in some doubt. Since the disease is anatomically interstitial, the acini remain air-containing (although their volume may be reduced by such effects as cicatrization). It is self-evident, therefore, that diffuse *interstitial disease must be of inhomogeneous roentgenographic density;* by this feature alone it should be possible in the majority of cases to distinguish interstitial from air-space disease. Secondly, and for the same reason, the airways generally are not involved to a significant degree, so that, by and large, there is nothing to prevent air

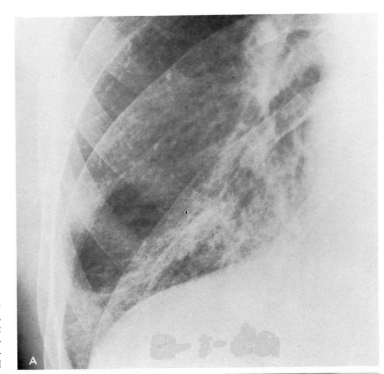

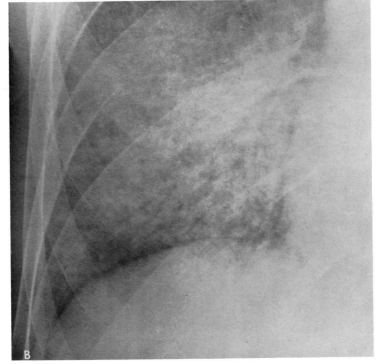

Figure 4–57. Combined Interstitial and Air-space Disease. A view of the lower half of the right lung from a posteroanterior roentgenogram (A) reveals a fine reticular pattern indicative of interstitial disease. Two weeks later (B), the disease has shown considerable extension, and an acinar pattern has been superimposed upon the reticulation indicating air-space involvement. Acute *Mycoplasma* pneumonia.

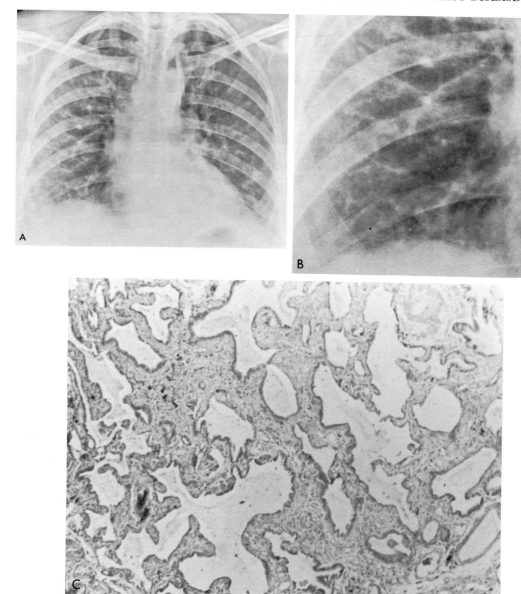

Figure 4–58. **Hamman-Rich Disease.** Coarse irregular linear strands form a random pattern throughout the lungs which is not characteristically reticular. There is considerable loss of lung volume generally. A magnified view of the lower portion of the right lung (*B*) shows the pattern to better advantage. A representative histologic section of lung removed at necropsy (*C*) shows severe disorganization of lung architecture; irregular cystic spaces lined by bronchiolar epithelium contain much mucoid material and are separated from each other by thick fibrous tissue bands which also contain smooth muscle and chronic inflammatory cells.

from reaching the lung parenchyma: therefore, *volume reduction due to airway obstruction is not a feature of interstitial disease* (although it is emphasized that volume may decrease when interstitial fibrosis leads to cicatrization).

Four basic patterns of interstitial disease may be recognized: (1) ground-glass, or granular, (2) nodular, (3) reticular, and (4) reticulonodular.

THE GROUND-GLASS PATTERN. This pattern (*synonym:* granular stippling, reticulogranular, granular) is produced when interstitial tissue has increased to such an extent that density is increased, but the deposits are individually invisible. The roentgenographic appearance is one of relatively homogeneous "clouding" or haze over the lung fields. When the roentgenographic technique allows visibility of extremely fine detail, it is sometimes possible with a magnifying glass to identify tiny nodular densities (such as might be present in early miliary tuberculosis) or an extremely fine reticulation (such as might be visualized in early asbestosis[597]). This roentgenographic pattern is often seen in chest roentgenograms of patients who have undergone lymphangiography (Figure 4–55A).[598, 599]

The ground-glass appearance has been described as being quite typical of the early stages of asbestosis[597] and berylliosis,[600] and in these two diseases may be reasonably attributed to minimal fibrosis or granulomatous inflammation affecting the parenchymal interstitial space. It is logical to assume that this ground-glass opacification or granular stippling might be observed at some stage in the majority of interstitial lung diseases, providing the roentgenograms were made early in their course.

THE NODULAR PATTERN. The purely nodular interstitial diseases of the lungs are perhaps best epitomized by hematogenous affections such as miliary tuberculosis (Figure 4–59). Since the infecting organism arrives in the lungs via the circulation and is trapped in the capillary sieve, it *must* be purely interstitial in location (at least early in its course—as the infection spreads, it may involve the acinar air spaces). As the tubercles grow, they create a ground-glass pattern and eventually reach sufficient size to be roentgenographically visible as tiny, discrete punctate densities. Early disseminated hematogenous carcinomatosis might have an identical appearance. The interstitial location of these hematogenous diseases is clearly established by their pathogenesis, but many other diseases of widely differing pathogeneses exert their earliest morphologic changes in the interstitial space. For example, certain inhalation diseases such as silicosis[340] are characterized by the formation of discrete nodular lesions within the interstitial space (Figure 4–60). Similarly, sarcoidosis may be associated with multiple well-defined nodular shadows throughout the interstitial tissues, varying in size from granular

(so small that they are individually invisible, so that the basic pattern is ground-glass) to 10 mm in diameter.[601]

It is to be stressed that a nodular pattern of diffuse lung disease does not positively indicate an interstitial location. For example, alveolar microlithiasis[574] is characterized roentgenographically by tiny discrete nodular opacities, widely distributed throughout the lungs (*see* Figure 2–2, page 107), caused by minute "calcispherites" situated entirely *within* the alveoli (although Greenspan[1681] recently produced evidence that calcispherites may originate and grow in the interstitial space, to be extruded into the alveoli when they reach a certain size). Similarly, a diffuse nodular pattern is not unusual in silo-fillers' disease, due to a nodular inflammatory process in the bronchioles and surrounding tissue (bronchiolitis fibrosa obliterans).[602]

THE RETICULAR PATTERN. This consists of a network of linear densities which may be conceived as a series of "rings" surrounding spaces of air density (Figure 4–61). This pattern contrasts with the roentgenographic pattern of such diseases as alveolar microlithiasis, in which pinpoint opacities are surrounded by rings of air density, or with the "stippled pattern" of incomplete acinar filling, in which small punctate deposits are surrounded by rings of air density.

The precise pattern of the reticulation depends upon several variables, the two most important of which are the degree of thickening of the interstitial space and the effects which the interstitial involvement exerts on parenchymal air spaces. It is useful to describe a reticular pattern according to the size of the "net"; the terms fine, medium, and coarse, although arbitrary, are in wide use and appear generally acceptable. The descriptive term "honeycombing" has gained greatly in popularity in recent years and is applied to a great variety of roentgenographic patterns that bees would recognize only with great difficulty! The term is widely used by pathologists as an overall description of all types of widespread pulmonary fibrosis. We are of the opinion that the term honeycombing should be reserved for those roentgenographic patterns in which a honeycomb is *reasonably* represented—a coarse reticular pattern in which the air

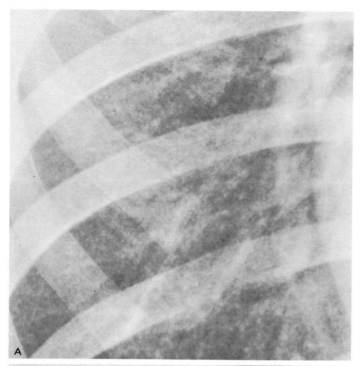

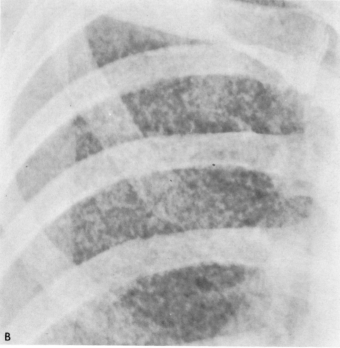

Figure 4–59. **Patterns of Interstitial Disease: Nodular.** Magnified views of posteroanterior roentgenograms of two different patients with proven miliary tuberculosis; in both cases, the pattern is purely nodular. In *A*, the nodules are tiny and very discrete; in *B*—a later stage of the disease—the nodules are larger in size but are still fairly discrete. (Courtesy Dr. Romeo Ethier, Montreal Neurological Hospital.)

spaces measure not less than 5 or 6 mm in diameter. More is said later about the pathogenesis of this unusual roentgenographic pattern.

The reticular pattern in its "pure" form results from increase in the amount of tissue in the interstitial space of the lung;

when this is in the lung parenchyma, it represents a thickening of the alveolar septa. An excellent example of roentgenologic-morphologic correlation was provided by studies of the reaction which occurred in the interstitial tissues of the lungs after lymphangiography: Fraimow

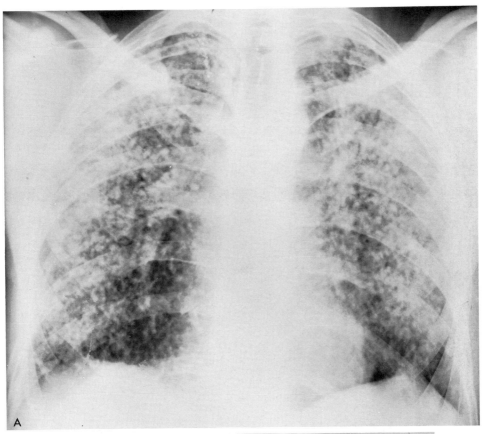

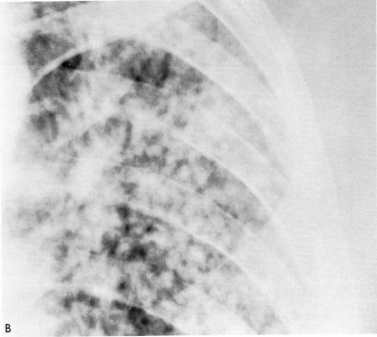

Figure 4–60. **Patterns of Interstitial Disease: Nodular.** A purely nodular pattern is present in this patient with stage III uncomplicated silicosis (proved by biopsy). The nodules are so large and of such great density that they appear confluent in some areas, thus suggesting conglomeration. *B* is a magnified view of the upper left lung seen in *A*.

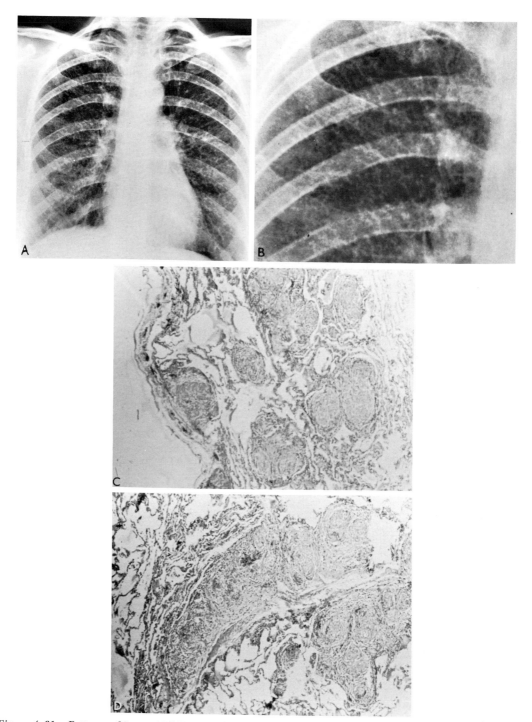

Figure 4–61.   **Patterns of Interstitial Disease: Reticular.** A posteroanterior roentgenogram (A) and a magnified view of the right upper lung (B) reveal a fine network pattern characteristic of reticulation. Photomicrographs of lung removed at biopsy (C and D) reveal typical sarcoid granulomas. In C, the granulomas appear to be nodular in character, whereas in D they appear to be oriented in a longitudinal plane. It is postulated that the majority of the deposits are in fact longitudinally oriented, the nodular appearance being created by the fact that these are cut in cross section.

and colleagues[599] obtained pulmonary tissue by biopsy within 12 hours after the lymphatic injection of Ethiodol (iodinated ethyl ester of the fatty acid of poppy-seed oil) and found lipid droplets widely distributed throughout the pulmonary capillary bed, corresponding to a fine granular stippling observed throughout both lungs roentgenographically. Biopsy specimens obtained the day after lymphangiography revealed a smaller but still appreciable amount of lipid material in the parenchymal interstitial space but no longer exclusively in the capillary bed, much of it having passed into the extravascular interstitial tissues and, to a lesser extent, into the alveoli. In our experience, roentgenograms at this stage usually show a fine reticular pattern (Figure 4–55), an appearance which has been observed by Bron and his colleagues also.[598] It is noteworthy that in the 20 patients studied by Fraimow and his associates[599] the average diffusing capacity had decreased from 21.2 to 15.9 two hours after the injection, at a time when capillaries were blocked by oil embolism; gradual but incomplete improvement in diffusing capacity occurred during the next 24 hours, an effect which these authors interpret as secondary, due probably to the membrane component of diffusion. Thus, in these studies, the morphologic, roentgenologic, and functional abnormalities resultant upon lymphangiography showed good correlation.

The observation that different roentgenographic patterns of reticulation merely indicate different degrees of severity of interstitial replacement is lent some support by numerous reports describing transition from a fine reticular pattern (even beginning with a ground-glass pattern), through all stages of fine, medium, and coarse reticulation, to honeycombing. This progression of changes has been described in many varied disease processes, including idiopathic interstitial fibrosis,[591] "rheumatoid lung,"[603] asbestosis,[597] and pulmonary myomatosis.[604, 605] It is probable that the majority of diffuse interstitial diseases of the lung would be found to follow the same pattern of progression if they could be observed throughout their course (which is seldom possible—the early stages usually are asymptomatic and, therefore, are discovered fortuitously, and the end stage of honeycombing often has no chance to develop before the patients die of the disease).

THE HONEYCOMB PATTERN. As mentioned earlier, honeycombing is a descriptive term which probably is overused. To the best of our knowledge, the term was coined originally to describe the roentgenographic pattern seen in the late stages of histiocytosis-X, in which air-containing cystic spaces measuring 5 to 10 mm in diameter are separated by a very coarse reticular network (Figure 4–62).

The morphologic counterpart of honeycomb lung, as we have defined it, has three characteristic features (Figure 4–62C): (1) formation of cysts 5 mm or more in diameter, which are lined by bronchiolar epithelium; (2) the cysts have thickened fibrous walls; and (3) intervening lung parenchyma is grossly distorted and often obliterated. The distinction between "honeycomb lung" and fibrosing alveolitis (Hamman-Rich disease) depends upon the size of the cysts. In the latter condition the majority of cysts are "microcysts" up to 3 mm in diameter; however, in this condition and the allied disorders scleroderma and rheumatoid lung, large cysts may develop. Honeycomb lung differs from the large cysts of centrilobular emphysema and pulmonary myomatosis also in that the cysts in these two diseases are not entirely lined by bronchiolar epithelium, fibrosis of the wall is slight or absent, and intervening lung parenchyma is not collapsed or fibrotic.

Thus, although the roentgenographic pattern of honeycombing is highly suggestive of histiocytosis-X,[591] it may be produced by other diseases, including tuberous sclerosis,[606] rheumatoid lung,[603] pulmonary muscular hyperplasia or pulmonary myomatosis,[604, 605, 607] and chronic interstitial fungal infections.[1]

THE RETICULONODULAR PATTERN. Although a linear network throughout the interstitial tissue may present roentgenographically as a purely reticular pattern, the orientation of some of the linear densities parallel to the x-ray beam frequently suggests a nodular component in addition to the reticular. Although in any given situation, it is conceivable that a reticulonodular pattern may be produced by this mechanism, it may be produced also by an *admixture* of nodular deposits and diffuse linear thickening throughout the intersti-

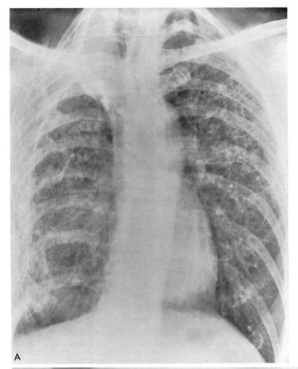

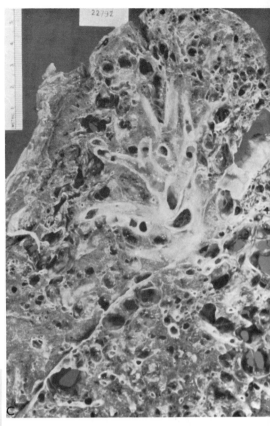

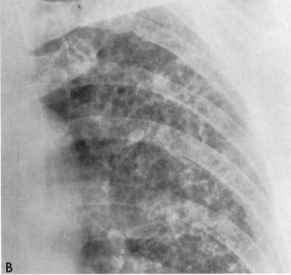

Figure 4-62. **Patterns of Interstitial Disease: Honeycomb.** A posteroanterior roentgenogram (A) reveals a diffuse alteration in roentgenographic pattern which is more apparent in the upper than the lower portions of the lungs (the extensive thickening and calcification of the pleura on the right resulted from a remote traumatic hemothorax). In the magnified view of the left upper lung (B), irregular cystic spaces can be identified ranging in size from 3 to 10 mm and possessing fairly thick walls. This is the characteristic appearance of the honeycomb pattern. A photograph of a cross section of the whole lung removed at necropsy (C) shows gross disorganization of lung architecture with small and large cystic spaces scattered widely throughout the lung.

tial space (Figure 4-63)—as, for example, in pulmonary sarcoidosis or lymphangitic carcinomatosis.

MODIFYING INFLUENCES. Certain secondary effects that may be produced by diffuse interstitial disease may modify the basic roentgenographic pattern to a considerable extent. For example, emphysema, either secondary to bronchiolar obstruction or compensatory to pulmonary fibrosis, may distort the pulmonary architecture and render the original disease pattern unrecognizable: the combination

of conglomerate shadows and compensatory emphysema in advanced silicosis exemplifies this situation. Similarly, the cicatrization produced by diffuse interstitial fibrosis may severely reduce lung volume, with resultant crowding of the reticular markings. Such modifying influences usually occur in relation to fairly definite etiologic and pathogenetic circumstances and, therefore, may aid considerably in differentiation of the many diseases in which diffuse alteration occurs in the interstitial pattern.

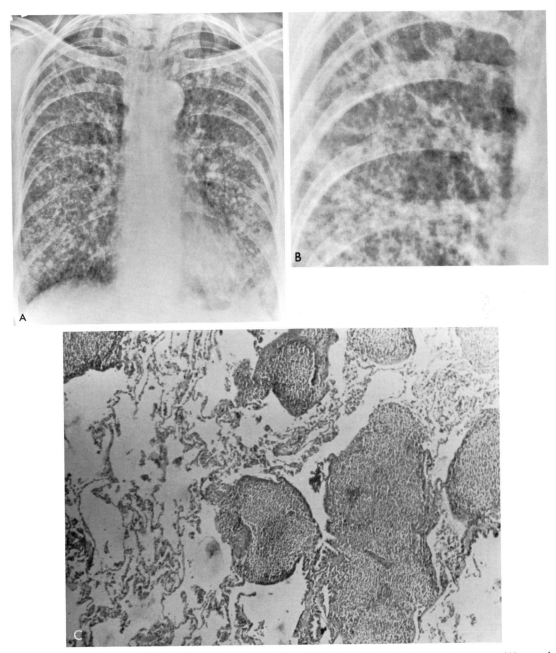

Figure 4–63. **Patterns of Interstitial Disease: Reticulonodular.** A posteroanterior roentgenogram (*A*) reveals diffuse disease throughout both lungs, more or less uniformly distributed. In the magnified view of the right upper lung (*B*), the pattern can be seen to be composed of an admixture of a coarse network (representing the reticular component) and irregular nodules ranging in size from 2 to 4 mm. A photomicrograph of lung removed at biopsy reveals well-defined nodular lesions some of which appear to be longitudinally oriented. Giant follicular lymphoma.

COMBINED AIR-SPACE AND INTERSTITIAL DISEASE

So far we have discussed the three fundamental changes that occur within the lung to cause increase in density: (1) replacement of air in the parenchymal air spaces (consolidation); (2) absorption of air from the parenchymal air spaces (atelectasis); and (3) increase in interstitial tissue. Although "pure" involvement of the lung by any one of these mechanisms perhaps is the exception rather than the rule, this descriptive subdivision serves the useful purpose of directing attention to the basic alteration in lung architecture that allows interpretation of the underlying pathologic abnormality. Thus, regardless of the etiology, when an acinar shadow is identified, it is *known* that at least part of the disease process is associated with air-space consolidation; similarly, a reticulonodular pattern necessarily implies involvement of the interstitial space of the lung; and, with few exceptions, loss of volume implies bronchial or bronchiolar obstruction. With these facts in mind we can base roentgen interpretation on a firm analytic foundation.

In many pulmonary diseases, perhaps the majority, the roentgenologic and pathologic changes include a *combination* of the three fundamental abnormalities. No matter how complex the admixture of changes may be, however, identification of the *individual* changes generally allows of a composite picture of the whole.

In considering the diseases characterized by a combination of the three basic changes, it is useful to subdivide them into two broad groups—those in which interstitial disease and air-space consolidation are combined, and those in which all three are combined (consolidation, atelectasis, and interstitial disease).

Combined Air-Space Consolidation and Interstitial Disease

The pattern created by this combination is best exemplified by pulmonary edema secondary to pulmonary venous hypertension (Figure 4-64). The roentgenographic manifestations of *interstitial involvement* are largely those of a change in the perivascular interstitial sheath (Figure 4-65A): edema fluid within the sheath increases

the size and reduces the definition of lung markings in a distinctive pattern. The roentgenographic manifestations of *parenchymal air-space consolidation* which are produced by edema fluid within the acini, consist of a few discrete and several confluent "fluffy" densities characteristic of acinar-filling processes (Figure 4-65B): this combination of interstitial and acinar patterns is virtually pathognomonic of pulmonary edema of cardiac origin. Obviously, if the air-space consolidation is produced by edema *other* than of cardiac origin, the roentgen pattern will be different: the acinar pattern may be identical but changes due to perivascular interstitial edema will be lacking. It must be emphasized that when alveolar edema is extensive and is distributed in a "butterfly" pattern, this *itself* may obscure the lung markings and thereby, regardless of etiology, destroy the contribution which interstitial involvement might make to the differential diagnosis.

Another example of combined involvement of this type is acute pneumonitis of *Mycoplasma* or viral etiology (Figure 4-57). This infection characteristically causes acute interstitial inflammation, creating a pattern early in its course of fine-to-medium reticulation in segmental distribution. This "pure" interstitial involvement often is of short duration, the inflammatory reaction soon extending into the parenchymal air spaces and resulting in consolidation. Air-space involvement frequently is patchy in distribution, so that individual acinar shadows usually can be identified. Since involvement of the conducting airways is relatively insignificant, loss of volume is negligible in the acute stage of the disease.

Combined Air-Space Consolidation, Air-Space Atelectasis, and Interstitial Disease

This type of involvement perhaps is best exemplified by acute bronchopneumonia, for example, of streptococcal origin (Figure 4-66). The inflammation involves bronchial and bronchiolar walls and produces acute bronchitis and bronchiolitis; the bronchovascular interstitial sheath is inflamed and edematous; dissemination of the infection peripherally leads to patchy air-space consolidation; and the bronchiolitis leads to irregular bronchiolar ob-

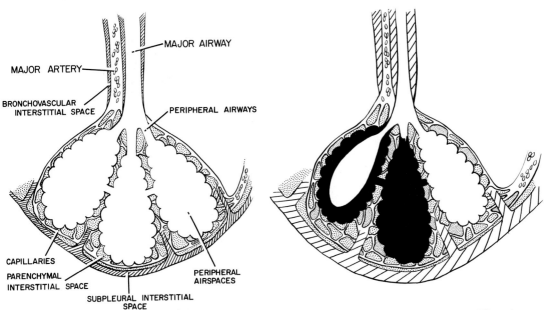

Figure 4-64. The Lung Diagram: Combined Air-space Consolidation and Interstitial Disease. There is a considerable increase in the interstitial tissues in all of its perivascular, subpleural, and parenchymal components. In addition, the central air space is totally consolidated and the left air space shows a deposition of tissue on its inner lining (for example, a hyaline membrane). The right air space is normal.

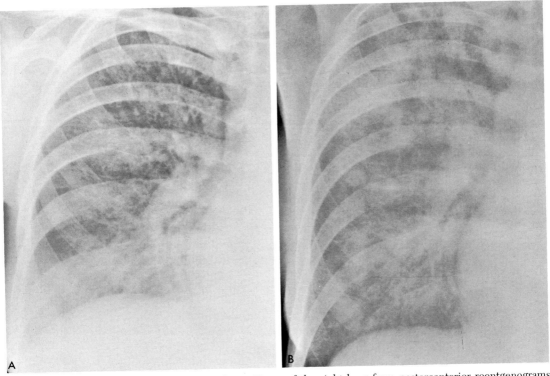

Figure 4-65. Interstitial and Air-space Edema. Views of the right lung from posteroanterior roentgenograms of the same patient on two different occasions. In A, the vascular markings are indistinct and hazy due to accumulation of edema fluid in the perivascular interstitial space. In the lower lung particularly, poorly defined shadows of increased density are due to air-space edema. No septal lines are present. Somewhat later (B), the pulmonary edema is much more severe and is characteristically air-space in type. An air bronchogram is present. A few septal lines (Kerley B lines) can be identified above the left costophrenic sulcus, indicating the presence of interstitial as well as air-space edema.

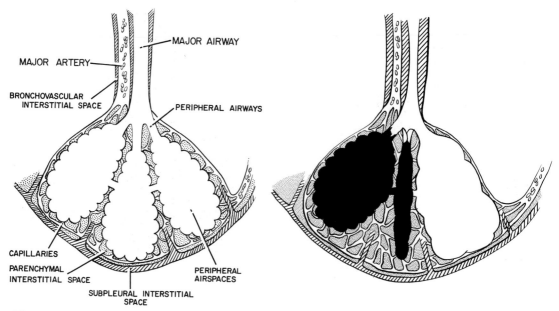

Figure 4–66. **The Lung Diagram: Combined Air-space Consolidation, Air-space Atelectasis, and Interstitial Disease.** Multiple abnormalities are depicted: the interstitial tissues are increased in volume in each of their perivascular, subpleural, and parenchymal components. The left air space is consolidated; the central air space is totally collapsed from bronchiolar obstruction; the right air space is overdistended in compensation for the atelectasis.

struction, resulting in focal areas of air-space collapse (Figure 4–67). Patchy areas of lung parenchyma may show no abnormality or may overinflate to compensate for the focal atelectasis. Because of the mechanism of spread the involvement is necessarily segmental. The resultant roentgenographic pattern of changes depicts the interstitial involvement, irregular zones of peripheral air-space consolidation, peripheral air-space collapse, and normal or over-inflated parenchyma. Because of this admixture, individual acinar shadows are seldom recognizable. Depending upon the degree of consolidation volume loss in the segment may be slight or moderate; because of the focal areas of normal or over-inflated parenchyma, the overall density is inhomogeneous.

There are infrequent exceptions to this typical roentgenographic pattern. For example, when the organism is highly virulent, involvement of the parenchymal air spaces may be so extensive that consolidation is confluent. If such consolidation occurs so rapidly that loss of volume is negligible, it may be impossible to distinguish between this form of pneumonia and pri-

mary acute alveolar pneumonia, such as that caused by *Diplococcus pneumoniae* (although an air bronchogram should be absent in the former and present in the latter).

Several other influences also, such as abscess formation and bulla or bleb formation, may modify the typical roentgenographic pattern; these are considered in detail in the next section.

Other diseases which may be expected to produce a similar pattern of combined involvement are numerous. Examples include chronic bronchiectasis (which on purely roentgenologic grounds may be indistinguishable from acute bronchopneumonia) and chronic aspiration pneumonia (such as might result from esophageal stenosis).

GENERAL SIGNS IN DISEASES WHICH CAUSE INCREASE IN ROENTGENOGRAPHIC DENSITY

In addition to the basic signs already described, there are several roentgen signs that may aid in determining the nature of

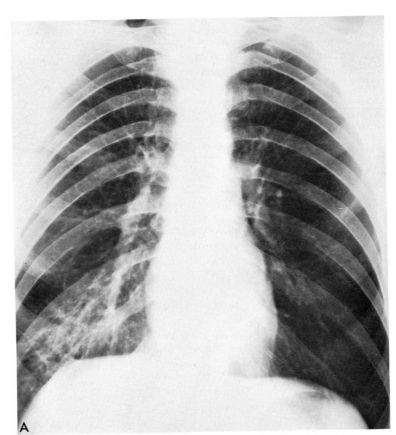

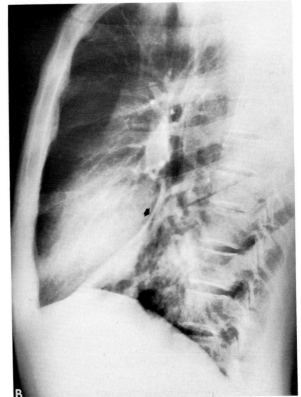

Figure 4–67. **Bronchopneumonia, Right Lower Lobe.** Posteroanterior (*A*) and lateral (*B*)
roentgenograms reveal patchy
consolidation of the anterior
and lateral basal segments of the
right lower lobe. Posterior bowing of the chief fissure (*arrow*)
indicates some degree of loss of
volume. The inhomogeneous
nature of the disease suggests
combined air-space consolidation, focal atelectasis, and focal
compensatory overinflation.

a pathologic process within the lungs. The signs to follow will be described in general terms only, the intention being to indicate the *mechanisms* by which they are produced and the significance which each possesses in roentgen interpretation.

The Character of the Border of a Pulmonary Lesion

The sharpness of definition of a consolidative process within the lungs gives some indication as to the nature of its marginal tissues. Acute air-space pneumonia (*e.g.*, from *Diplococcus pneumoniae*) which has extended to an interlobar pleural surface has a sharply defined contour along that border; where it does not abut against a fissure its margin will be less distinct (Figure 4–68), since it is formed by a spreading zone of confluent acinar lesions. Regardless of the etiology and extent of acinar consolidation, the margin between consolidated lung and contiguous air-containing parenchyma has the same definitive character, whether the lesion be, for example, a small focus of exudative tuberculosis or massive consolidation due to *Klebsiella pneumoniae*. The margin of a well-organized fibrotic granulomatous lesion may be expected to be sharply defined, whereas the margin of an infiltrative cancer logically will be indistinctly defined and fuzzy.

As statement of fact, these observations stand up to fairly close scrutiny; roentgenographic assessment of the margin of a pulmonary lesion coincides reasonably accurately with the morphologic appearance of the junction of consolidated tissue and normal lung parenchyma. Unfortunately, what is seen is an anatomic border, not the nature of the cells forming the border. In an analysis of 155 solitary lung lesions, Bateson[608] found that 58 of 80 primary carcinomas (73.5 per cent) had indistinctly defined margins and the remaining 22 were well defined; of 20 inflammatory lesions 15 had ill-defined margins and five were well defined; only the 40 mixed tumors and other benign lesions had sharply defined margins in all cases. It may be concluded, therefore, that although the sharpness of definition of a pulmonary density gives *some* indication of its nature (Figures 4–69 and 4–70), it cannot be a sign of *absolute* value in establishing a diagnosis (Figure 4–71).

The *smoothness of contour* (as distinct from nodularity or lobulation) possesses a significance which in many respects is similar to that of sharpness of definition. *In general*, smoothness of contour suggests benignity (Figure 4–69), and nodularity or lobulation indicates malignancy (Figures 4–72 and 4–73). Of 100 solitary circumscribed bronchogenic carcinomas studied by Bateson,[609] 29 had well-defined margins and *all* of these were lobulated. Probably the "umbilication" or notching of the border of a solitary pulmonary nodule described by Rigler[610] as a sign of malignancy is merely a manifestation of lobulation. Unfortunately, umbilication is not an infallible sign of malignancy, since in our experience and that of others[611] it is present in a significant number of inflammatory nodules; for example, Drevvatne and Frimann-Dahl[611] found umbilication in 16 of 22 cases of tuberculoma.

"Satellite lesions" might be included here since these are closely related to the margins of a pulmonary lesion. They are small punctate areas of increased density in close proximity to a larger lesion, generally a solitary peripheral "coin lesion," and usually are thought to suggest an inflammatory nature of a parenchymal lesion, particularly of tuberculous etiology (Figure 4–74). Satellite lesions were observed in 9.8 per cent of 52 cases of tuberculoma described by Bleyer and Marks[612] and in ten of 122 patients with tuberculosis described by Steele.[613] However, in the latter series, satellite lesions were found in three of 280 cases of primary carcinoma, an incidence which is admittedly very low but which, nevertheless, belies the validity of assuming an inflammatory origin for a peripheral lesion on the strength of these lesions.

Change in Position of Interlobar Fissures

It has been established that displacement of fissures toward a zone of increased density constitutes one of the most valuable signs of lobar or segmental collapse. Equally as valuable a sign but much less frequent in occurrence is displacement of interlobar fissures in the opposite direction from the involved lobe – in other words, bulging of the fissures. Clearly, this is evidence of expansion of the involved lobe; since diseases of increased density

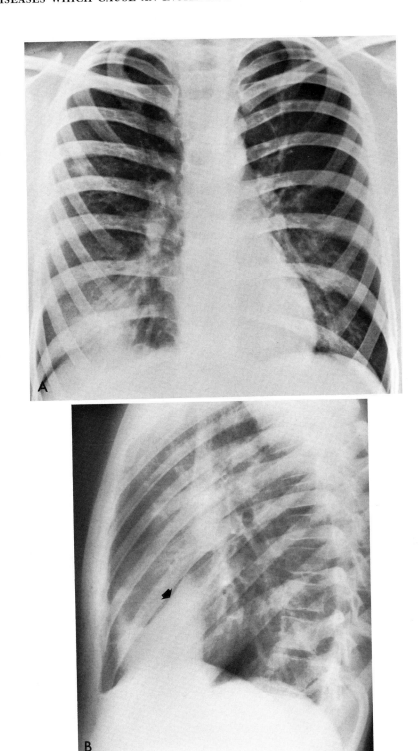

Figure 4-68. **Acute Air-space Pneumonia.** Posteroanterior (*A*) and lateral (*B*) roentgenograms reveal consolidation of the anterior basal zone of the right lower lobe; the shadow is homogeneous except for an air bronchogram (visualized in *A*). Where the consolidation abuts against the chief fissure (*arrow*), it is sharply defined, but its definition posteriorly, medially, and laterally is less sharp due to the spreading nature of the inflammatory reaction.

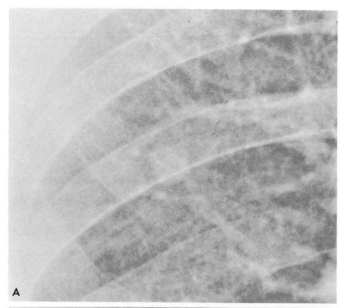

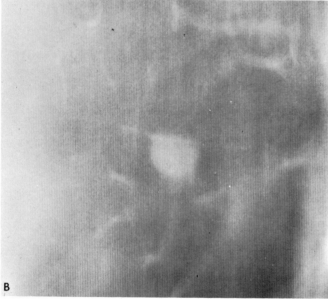

Figure 4–69. **Histoplasmoma.** Magnified views of the midportion of the right lung from a posteroanterior roentgenogram (*A*) and an anteroposterior tomogram (*B*). This chronic granulomatous lesion is sharply circumscribed around its whole periphery.

capable of increasing the volume of a lobe are relatively few, recognition of such displacement frequently allows of specific etiologic diagnosis.

Bulging of fissures occurs most commonly in acute exudative infections of the lung in which the virulence of the organism produces an abundant exudate; the most common of these are pneumonia caused by *Klebsiella pneumoniae* (Friedländer's pneumonia),[569] *Diplococcus pneumoniae, Mycobacterium tuberculosis,* and *Bacillus pestis* (plague pneumonia). Acute

lung abscess frequently causes increased volume of a lobe particularly when a check-valve mechanism in the communicating airway leads to distension of the abscess cavity with trapped air (a causative mechanism which may be in force early in the course of acute Friedländer's pneumonia) (Figure 4–75).

In addition to the acute pneumonias, any space-occupying mass within a lobe may displace a fissure if the lesion occupies significant volume or if it is contiguous to the fissure: peripheral bron-

(Text continues on page 266.)

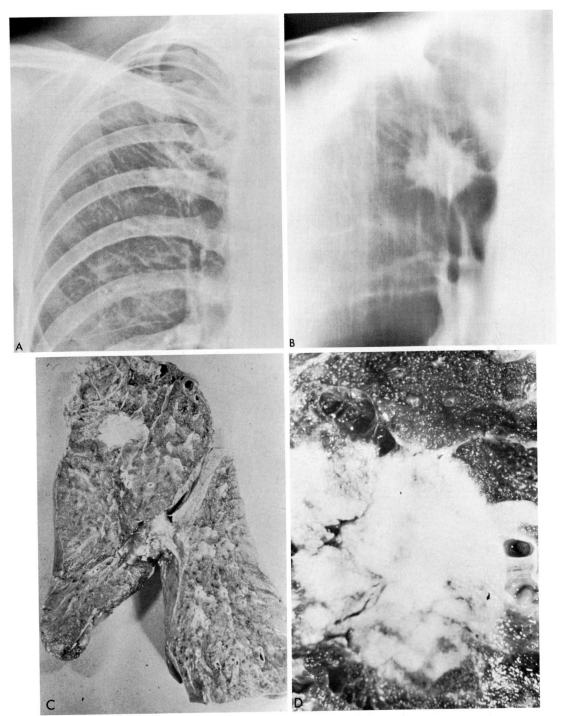

Figure 4–70.   **Peripheral Adenocarcinoma.** Views of the right upper lung from a posteroanterior roentgenogram (*A*) and an anteroposterior tomogram (*B*) reveal a very irregular shadow of homogeneous density possessing a shaggy indistinct outline. Linear strands extend from the lesion to the axillary pleural surface and to the mediastinum. This type of outline is strongly suggestive of bronchogenic carcinoma. Photographs of the cut section of the lung removed surgically (*C* and *D*) show the markedly irregular border of the lesion. Bronchogenic carcinoma.

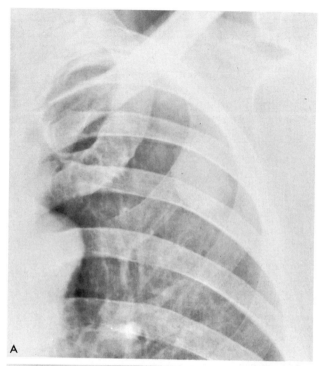

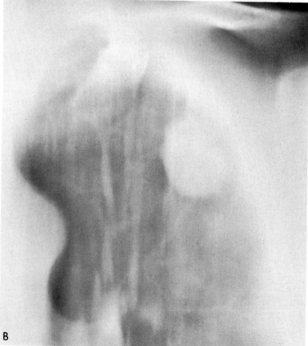

Figure 4–71. **Peripheral Adenocarcinoma.** Views of the upper half of the left lung of a posteroanterior roentgenogram (A) and an anteroposterior tomogram (B) reveal a slightly nodular although sharply circumscribed mass of homogeneous density. The sharp definition of this adenocarcinoma is in contrast to the lesion seen in Figure 4–70 and indicates the pitfall of using sharpness of definition as a sign of absolute value in establishing the benignancy or malignancy of a peripheral lesion.

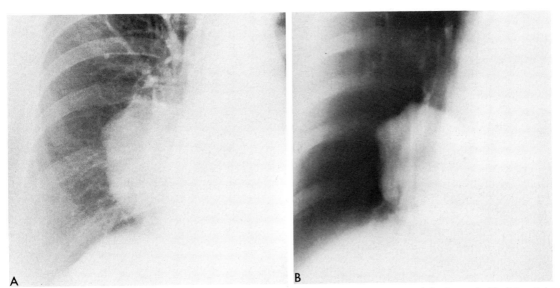

Figure 4–72. **Solitary Metastasis from Primary Carcinoma of the Colon.** Views of the lower half of the right lung from a posteroanterior roentgenogram (*A*) and an anteroposterior tomogram (*B*) show a large mass of homogeneous density possessing a sharply demarcated but lobulated contour. The lobulation is highly suggestive but not conclusive evidence of malignancy. Compare Figure 4–73.

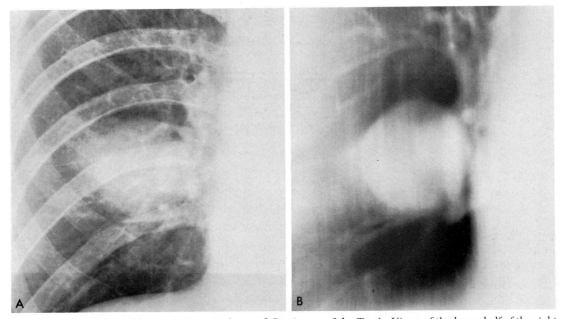

Figure 4–73. **Solitary Metastasis from Embryomal Carcinoma of the Testis.** Views of the lower half of the right lung from a posteroanterior roentgenogram (*A*) and an anteroposterior tomogram (*B*) reveal a solitary mass of homogeneous density possessing a sharply demarcated and perfectly smooth margin. Such an appearance is fairly common in large metastatic deposits in the lung. Compare Figure 4–72.

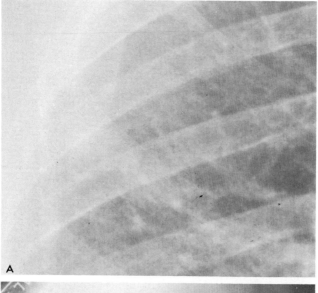

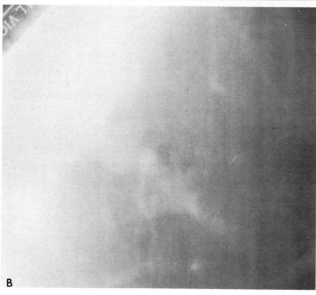

Figure 4–74. **Satellite Lesions in Histoplasmosis.** Magnified views of a small portion of the right upper lung from a posteroanterior roentgenogram (*A*) and an anteroposterior tomogram (*B*) show a sharply circumscribed solitary nodule 12 mm in diameter adjacent to the visceral pleura. It contains no calcium. Several smaller nodular shadows ranging in diameter from 2 to 6 mm can be identified in the lung medial to the main lesion. These satellite lesions provide highly suggestive, but not conclusive, evidence of an infectious etiology of a solitary peripheral nodule. Proved histoplasmosis.

chogenic carcinoma is perhaps the most common of these masses (Figure 4–76).

The interlobar fissures ordinarily act as an efficient barrier to the passage of parenchymal disease from one lobe to another. A few diseases, however, show a propensity for crossing pleural boundaries, thus creating a sign invaluable to differential diagnosis. Undoubtedly the most common cause of pleural transgression is mycotic infection of the lungs, particularly actinomycosis: These organisms not only pass across interlobar fissures but also across the visceral and parietal pleural layers over the convexity of the lung, and they may incite abscesses and osteomyelitis

in the chest wall. Pulmonary tuberculosis, particularly in children, may transgress pleural boundaries; bronchogenic carcinoma does so rarely.

Cavitation

The word "cavity" implies a focus of increased density whose central portion has been expelled and replaced by air. The presence of an air-fluid level is not necessary to the definition, nor are size of the cavity or thickness of its wall. The terms "cavity" and "abscess" are not synonymous; an intrapulmonary abscess without communication with the bronchial

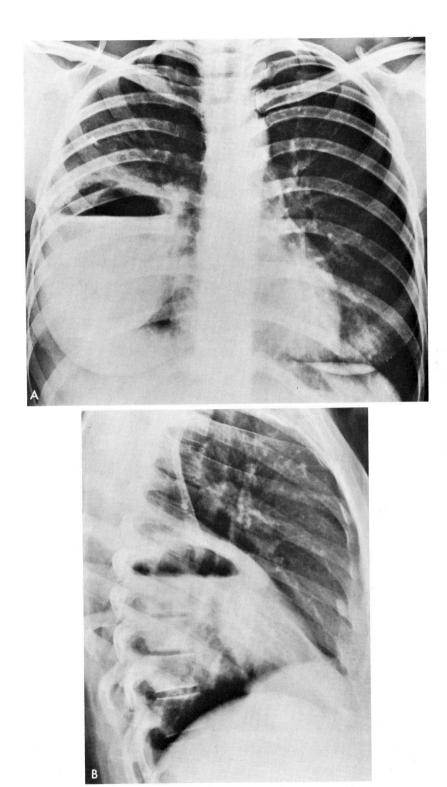

Figure 4–75. **Bulging of Interlobar Fissures: Acute Staphylococcal Lung Abscess.** Roentgenograms in postero-anterior (*A*) and lateral (*B*) projection reveal a large abscess in the right lower lobe producing upward bulging of the major fissure.

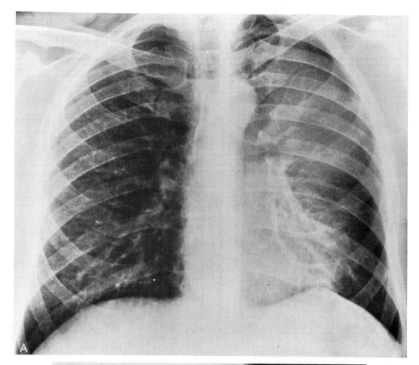

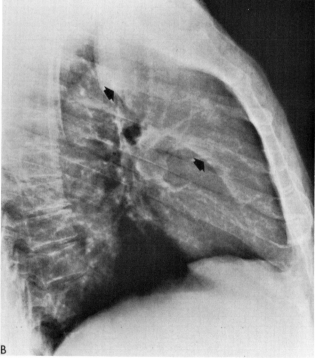

Figure 4–76. **Bulging of Interlobar Fissures: Bronchogenic Carcinoma.** Roentgenograms in posteroanterior (A) and lateral (B) projection reveal obliteration of much of the left border of the heart by a shadow whose homogeneity is undisturbed by an air bronchogram. Anterior displacement of the chief fissure (*arrows*) and elevation of the left hemidiaphragm indicate considerable loss of volume. The lower half of the chief fissure is concave anteriorly, the upper half concave posteriorly. This bulging of the upper portion of the fissure is due to a large peripheral bronchogenic carcinoma. Metastatic lymph nodes from this tumor produced upper lobe bronchial obstruction and atelectasis.

tree is roentgenographically homogeneous; only when the abscess cavity communicates with the bronchial tree, thereby allowing air to replace necrotic material, should the term "cavity" be applied (Figure 4–77).

The great majority of pulmonary cavities are caused by necrosis of tissue and by the expulsion of necrotic material into the bronchial tree. Exceptions to this are uncommon; for example, the rupture of a bronchogenic cyst or an echinococcus cyst whose natural contents were originally fluid rather than necrotic tissue; or the infection of an already existing cystic space, such as a bulla. The mechanism by which necrosis occurs varies, according to the underlying disease: In infectious processes such as acute staphylococcal pneumonia, the virulence of the infection leads to tissue death; the necrosis of neoplasms probably is related to deficient blood supply;[614] in septic emboli it is likely that there is a combination of both vascular deficiency and inflammatory necrosis.

The roentgenographic demonstration of pulmonary cavitation may be simple or exceedingly difficult. If the cavity contains fluid, as is frequently the case, the identification of an air-fluid level is clearly pathognomonic; should there be doubt as to the presence of an air-fluid level on standard roentgenograms exposed with the patient erect, lateral decubitus projection with a horizontal x-ray beam may be helpful in demonstrating alteration in the position of the fluid. A major difficulty in diagnosis may occur when cavities are small or are situated either among an inhomogeneous group of densities or in anatomic regions ordinarily difficult to visualize (such as the paramediastinal zones). In these latter cir-

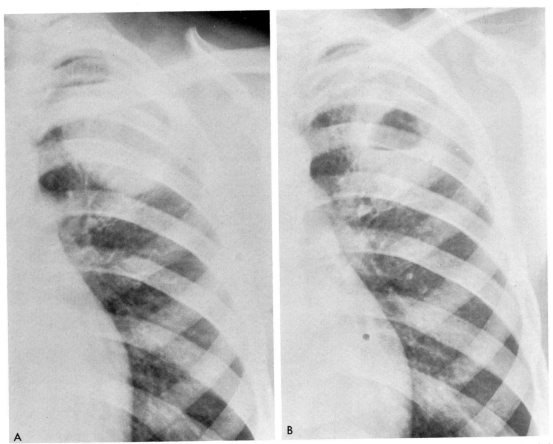

Figure 4–77. **Acute Staphylococcal Lung Abscess and Cavity.** A posteroanterior roentgenogram of the left lung (*A*) reveals a rather sharply circumscribed mass of homogeneous density in the left apical zone. Three days later (*B*), there has appeared a central air-containing cavity possessing an air-fluid level. An abscess is present on both roentgenographic studies but only on the second is there a cavity. Fourteen-year-old boy; pure growth of *Staphylococcus aureus* from the sputum.

cumstances, tomography may be essential to confirmation of diagnosis (*see* Figure 2–8, page 117) or, perhaps more commonly, to identification of cavitary disease which was not even remotely suspected on plain roentgenography.

Although the nature of cavity formation within specific disease groups varies considerably, in most cases the general patterns give some indication of the underlying etiology (Figure 4–78). The roentgenographic features which should be noted in any case of cavitary lung disease include the thickness of the cavity wall, the smoothness or irregularity of its inner lining, the presence and character of its contents, whether lesions are solitary or multiple, and, where multiple, the number which have cavitated. The following examples are given to indicate prevailing patterns; in each category, exceptions to the general rule occur occasionally.

The cavity wall usually is thick in acute lung abscess (Figure 4–79), primary (Figure 4–80) and metastatic carcinoma, and Wegener's granulomatosis (Figure 4–84)[615] and usually is thin in infected bullae and posttraumatic cysts (Figure 4–81).

Character of Inner Lining. This usually is irregular and nodular in carcinoma (Figure 4–80), shaggy in acute lung abscess (Figures 4–75 and 4–79), and smooth in most other cavitary lesions.

Nature of Contents. In the majority of cases the contents are fluid and offer no distinctive characteristics. In certain diseases, however, the contents may be so typical as to be pathognomonic—for example, the intracavitary fungus ball (mycetoma; aspergilloma) (Figure 4–82) or intracavitary thrombus or fibrin ball, both of which form an intracavitary mass which is freely movable; or the collapsed mem-

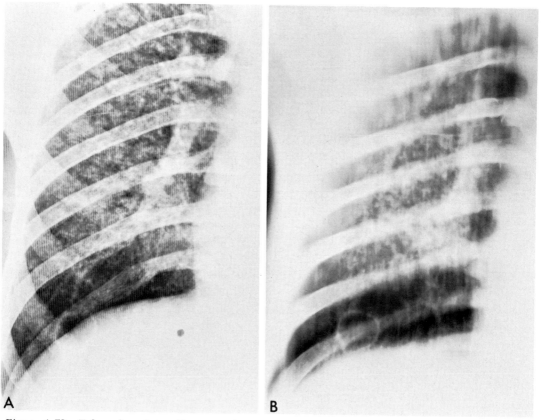

A   **B**

Figure 4–78. **Tuberculous Lung Abscess with Bronchogenic Spread.** A posteroanterior roentgenogram (*A*) and anteroposterior tomogram (*B*) of the right lung reveal a well-defined thin-walled cavity in the base of the right lower lobe. As expected, only the erect study (*A*) shows an air-fluid level (the tomogram was performed in the supine position). Multiple poorly defined shadows possessing the typical characteristics of acinar lesions can be identified throughout much of the right lung, representing bronchogenic spread from the tuberculous cavity. This combination of changes comprises almost certain evidence of a tuberculous etiology. (Courtesy Dr. David Berger, Royal Edward Chest Hospital, Montreal.)

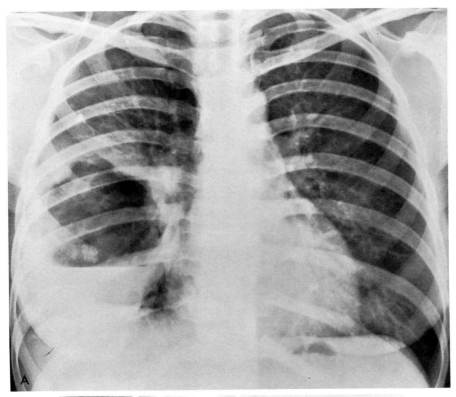

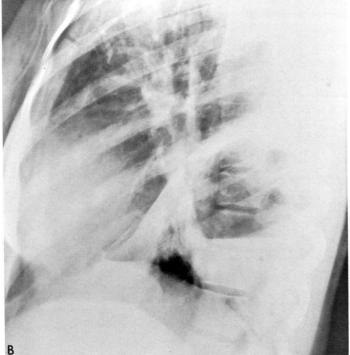

Figure 4–79. **Acute Staphylococcal Lung Abscess.** Roentgenograms in posteroanterior (A) and lateral (B) projection reveal a huge cavity in the right lower lobe. The thickness of its wall and shaggy irregular nature of its inner lining suggests an acute lung abscess.

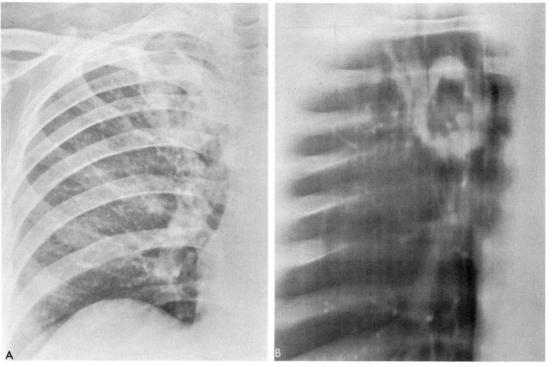

Figure 4-80. **Cavitating Bronchogenic Carcinoma.** Views of the upper half of the right lung from a postero-anterior roentgenogram (*A*) and an anteroposterior tomogram (*B*) reveal a rather poorly defined cavitating mass. The thickness of the wall and irregular nodular character of the inner lining are highly suggestive of bronchogenic carcinoma. Proven highly differentiated squamous cell cancer.

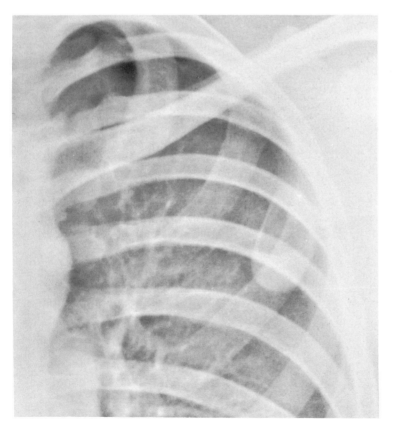

Figure 4-81. **Posttraumatic Lung Cyst (Pulmonary Laceration).** A view of the upper half of the left lung from a postero-anterior roentgenogram reveals a sharply circumscribed oval shadow just deep to the visceral pleura. A central radiolucency and air-fluid level indicate communication with the bronchial tree. A small pneumothorax is present. The thinness and smoothness of the wall, as well as the anatomic location of the lesion, are consistent with the diagnosis. Nineteen-year-old man 12 days after a car accident. The lesion gradually resorbed over a period of three months. (Courtesy Dr. J. G. Monks, Saskatoon.)

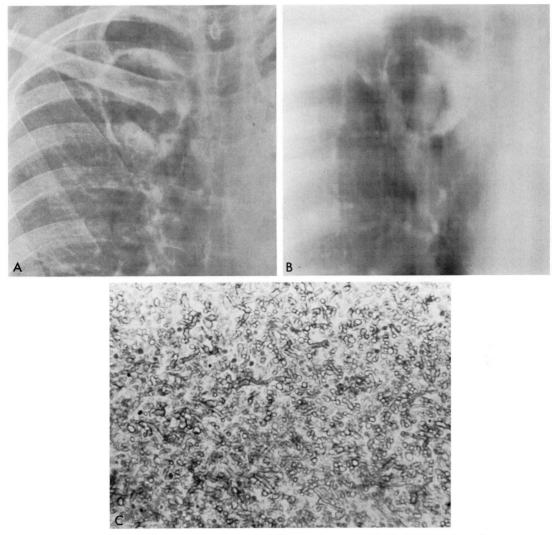

Figure 4–82.   **Intracavitary Fungus Ball (Mycetoma).** Views of the upper half of the right lung from a postero-anterior roentgenogram (A) and an anteroposterior tomogram (B) reveal a rather thin-walled but irregular cavity in the paramediastinal zone. Situated within it is a smooth oblong shadow of homogeneous density whose relationships to the wall of the cavity change from the erect (A) to the supine (B) positions. A photomicrograph of the intracavitary mass (C) reveals multiple mycelial threads characteristic of *Aspergillus*. The cavity was of tuberculous etiology.

branes of a ruptured echinococcus cyst which float on top of the fluid within the cyst and create the characteristic "water-lily" sign[616] or the "sign of the camalote" (a water plant found in South American rivers).[1682]

A rare but characteristic intracavitary mass is that associated with massive pulmonary gangrene in which extensive necrosis of lung tissue occurs in cases of acute Friedländer's or pneumococcal pneumonia; irregular pieces of sloughed lung parenchyma float like icebergs in the cavity fluid.[963]

Multiplicity of Lesions. Some cavitary disease is characteristically solitary—for example, primary bronchogenic carcinoma, acute lung abscess, and posttraumatic lung cyst (Figures 4–79, 4–80, and 4–81); others are characteristically multiple—for example, metastatic neoplasm (Figure 4–83), Wegener's granulomatosis (Figure 4–84), acute coccidioidomycosis,[617] and acute pyemic abscesses.

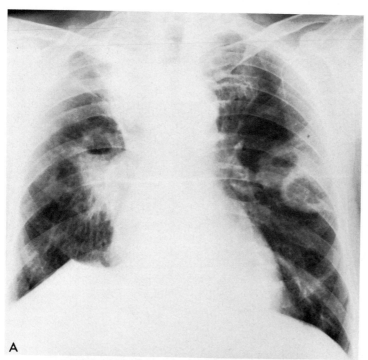

A

B

Figure 4–83. **Multiple Cavities in Metastatic Bronchogenic Carcinoma.** A posteroanterior roentgenogram reveals severe atelectasis of the right upper lobe which proved to be due to bronchogenic carcinoma of the lobar bronchus. Three excavating masses possessing thick walls but smooth inner linings can be identified in the lungs. A sagittal slice of the right lung removed at necropsy (B) shows a large cavitating mass in the superior segment of the lower lobe; massive tumor involvement of the upper lobe and paratracheal nodes is present; the metastatic lesions possessed the same histologic characteristics as the primary upper lobe lesion.

Brief mention is made of simulation of cavities—an uncommon occurrence. Some cavitary lesions visible on premortem roentgenograms are found at necropsy to contain no air and to show no communication with the bronchial tree. Histologically, the center of such lesions is necrotic, and it is assumed that some histochemical change has occurred in this necrotic material whereby its lipid content is sufficiently high to cause a relatively radiolucent shadow roentgenographically, thus simulating cavitation (Figure 4–85). This phenomenon has been described in pulmonary tuberculosis, where the center of the lesion was caseous,[618] and in multiple pulmonary metastases.[619]

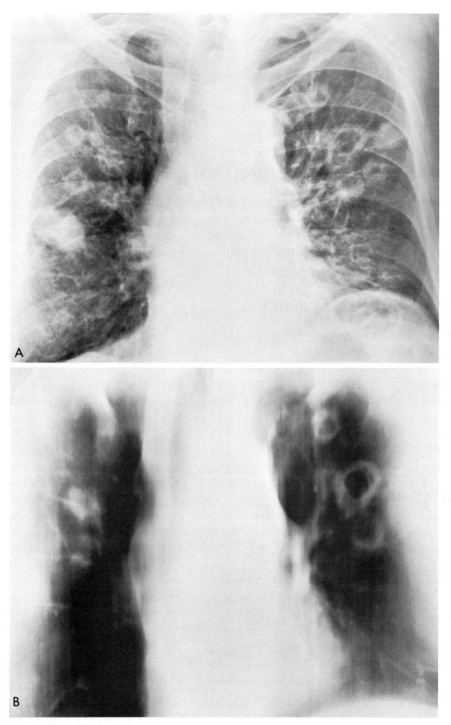

Figure 4–84. **Multiple Cavities in Wegener's Granulomatosis.** A posteroanterior roentgenogram (A) and an anteroposterior tomogram (B) show multiple thick-walled cavities scattered throughout both lungs but predominantly in the upper zones. The lesions range from 1.5 to 3 cm and are rather thick-walled. At least three lesions show no evidence of cavitation.

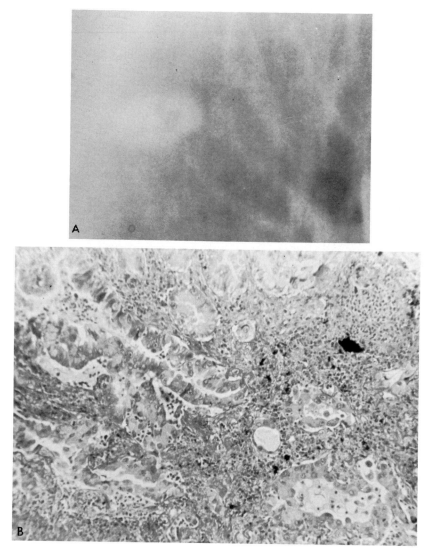

Figure 4–85.   **Pseudocavitation.** A magnified view of a tomographic section of the upper half of the right lung (*A*) reveals a solitary, sharply-circumscribed nodule whose homogeneity is interrupted by three central zones of lesser density. A photomicrograph of a portion of the lesion removed surgically (*B*) shows a glandular pattern of neoplastic cells separated by a fibrous stroma containing a chronic inflammatory cell infiltrate. This bronchiolo-alveolar cancer arose at the periphery of a fibrocaseous granuloma in which no organisms were identified. It is thought that the central radiolucencies observed roentgenographically were caused by the zones of caseous necrosis; although the roentgenographic density of the radiolucencies is slightly greater than one might anticipate if they were gaseous, distinction from true cavitation in such cases is not always possible. Combined bronchiolo-alveolar carcinoma and fibrocaseous granulomas.

Calcification

Calcification within the thorax is important to the assessment of pulmonary disease. In the majority of cases, it is dystrophic, generally occurring in tissue which for some reason has degenerated or become necrotic. Although metastatic calcification occurs occasionally, presumably as the result of the low pH of lung tissue,

it is seldom if ever roentgenographically visible, being discovered by the pathologist during histologic examination.

Both the distribution and character of calcification should be noted since each possesses diagnostic significance. Broadly speaking, calcification occurs in three general forms within the thorax.

1. The single, often densely calcified focus, situated anywhere in the lungs

and representing calcification of a healed primary granulomatous lesion, most frequently is due to either tuberculosis or histoplasmosis (Figure 4–86). This "Ghon lesion" usually is part of a complex, of which calcification of a drainage lymph node in the hilum or mediastinum is the other part (the Ranke complex). Calcification usually is homogeneous in the pulmonary lesion, whereas the lymph node generally shows punctate deposits scattered throughout it. Identification of the Ghon complex fairly conclusively establishes previous infection by one of these two major causative organisms; the decision as to which organism was responsible may be aided roentgenologically by identification of multiple punctate calcifications within the spleen, which are almost always due to histoplasmosis.[620]

2. The presence and character of calcifications within solitary pulmonary nodules supplies information useful to the differential diagnosis of these perplexing lesions. First, and most important, it is the most reliable single piece of evidence that a lesion is benign.[621] (A notable exception is the solitary metastasis from osteogenic sarcoma or chondrosarcoma which frequently undergoes calcification or ossification [Figure 4–87].) Second, the character of the calcification may be a reliable indication as to the etiology of the lesion—for example, a *small central nidus* almost always suggests a granulomatous lesion (Figure 4–88), although it occasionally occurs in hamartoma; *lamination* is almost pathognomonic of a granuloma and is the most reliable sign of benignancy; "popcorn ball" calcification is characteristic of hamartoma; and *multiple punctate foci* may be seen in either granulomas or hamartomas (Figures 4–89 and 4–90).[621]

Tomography is strongly recommended in the investigation of solitary peripheral nodules, not only for the identification of calcification which is not visible on plain roentgenograms, but also for its better visibility when its presence is suggested on plain-film study.

Calcification developing in organized pulmonary artery thrombus is an uncommon manifestation of thromboembolic disease, seldom recognized or reported.

3. Diffuse calcification may be caused by several conditions but in each usually

(Text continues on page 283.)

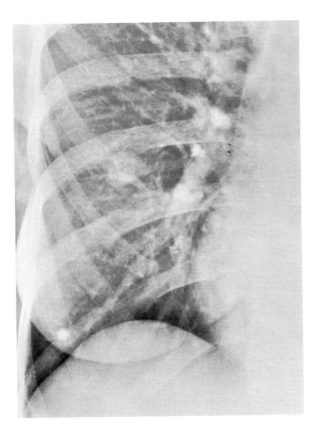

Figure 4–86. **The Ranke Complex.** A view of the lower half of the right lung from a posteroanterior roentgenogram reveals a solitary densely calcified nodule just above the right costophrenic sulcus (the Ghon lesion); the calcification is homogeneous although irregular. Situated in the right hilum are three or four lymph nodes containing scattered punctate calcium deposits. The solitary nodule in the right mid-lung proved to be metastatic adenoacanthoma of the uterus.

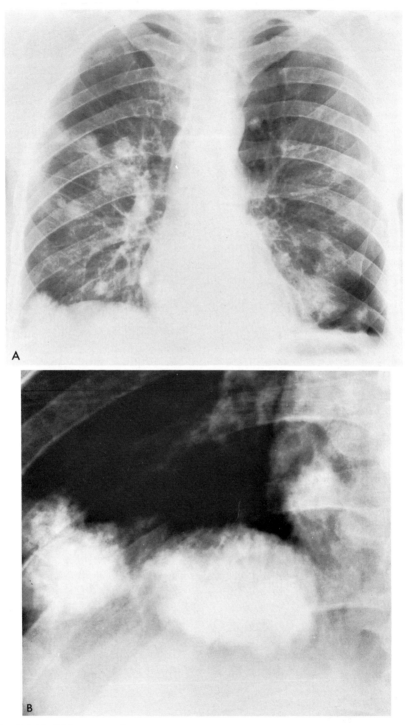

Figure 4–87.   **Calcified Metastases from Osteogenic Sarcoma.** A posteroanterior roentgenogram (*A*) reveals multiple nodular shadows throughout both lungs, varying considerably in size. A spontaneous pneumothorax is present on the left, a remarkably frequent complication of metastatic osteogenic sarcoma. A detailed view of the lower right lung from an overexposed roentgenogram (*B*) reveals extensive calcification (? ossification) of the two largest metastatic lesions. (Courtesy Dr. George Genereux, University Hospital, Saskatoon.)

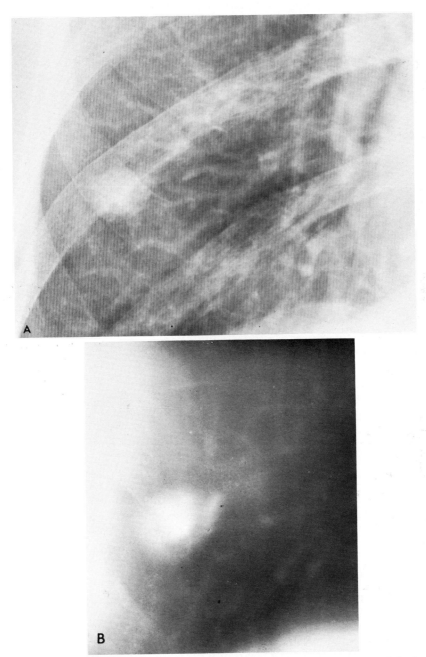

Figure 4–88. **Calcification of Solitary Peripheral Nodules: The Central Nidus.** Views of the lower portion of the right lung from a posteroanterior roentgenogram (*A*) and an anteroposterior tomogram (*B*) reveal a solitary, well-defined peripheral nodule containing a central nidus of calcium. Such an appearance is highly suggestive (if not diagnostic) of chronic granulomatous disease. Proved histoplasmoma.

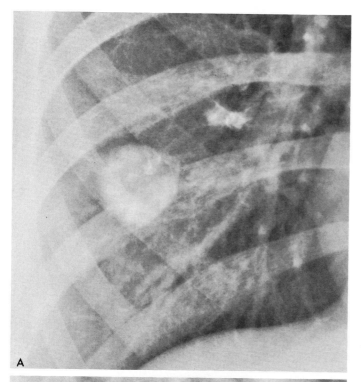

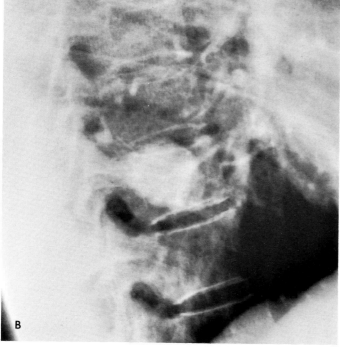

Figure 4–89.   **Calcification in Solitary Peripheral Nodules: Chronic Granuloma.** Views of the inferior portion of the right lung from posteroanterior (*A*) and lateral (*B*) roentgenograms reveal a slightly irregular but well-circumscribed solitary nodule measuring 2.5 cm in diameter; several irregular deposits of calcium are scattered randomly throughout the mass. Chronic granulomatous inflammation of unknown etiology (stains for acid-fast bacilli and fungi were negative). (Courtesy Dr. Gerald Maguire, Montreal General Hospital.)

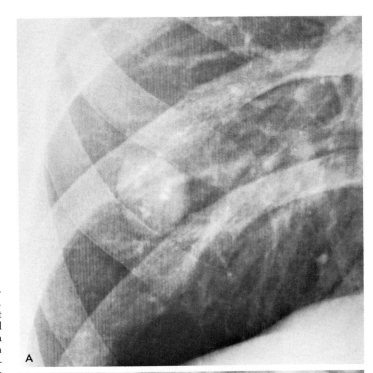

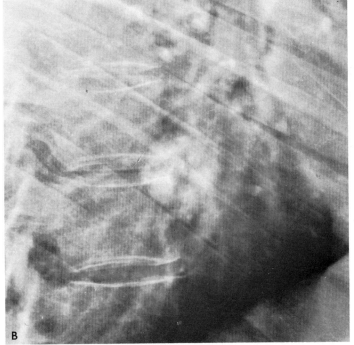

Figure 4–90. **Calcification in Solitary Peripheral Nodules: Hamartoma.** Views of the lower portion of the right lung from posteroanterior (A) and lateral (B) roentgenograms show a solitary nodule almost identical in appearance and position to that illustrated in Figure 4–89; the calcium deposits are somewhat larger, however, and are more suggestive of the descriptive designation "popcorn." Proved hamartoma. (Courtesy Dr. David Berger, Royal Edward Chest Hospital, Montreal.)

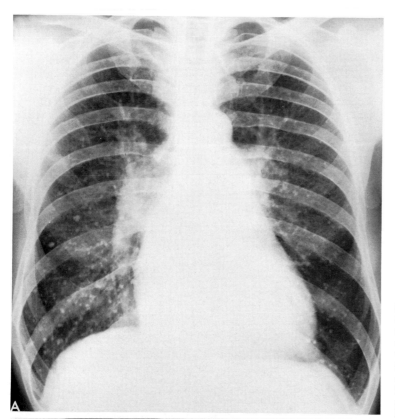

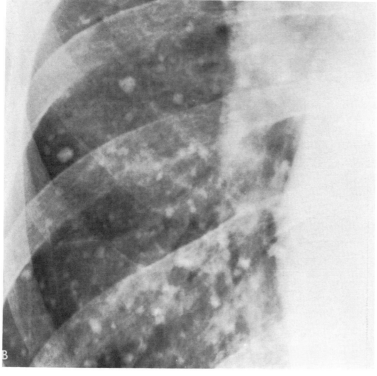

Figure 4–91. **Pulmonary Ossification in Mitral Stenosis.** A posteroanterior roentgenogram (*A*) of a 46-year-old man with longstanding mitral stenosis and severe pulmonary arterial hypertension reveals multiple densely calcified nodular shadows ranging in diameter from 1 to 5 mm situated predominantly in the lower half of each lung. The shadows are seen to better advantage in a magnified view of the lower half of the right lung (*B*). Lesions of this type and localization are highly suggestive (if not diagnostic) of longstanding mitral stenosis. They should not be confused with hemosiderosis.

is distinctive. For example, the tiny punctate "calcispherytes" of alveolar microlithiasis present a roentgenographic image which is unique and can hardly be mistaken for anything else (*see* Figure 2–2, page 107). Multiple nodular calcifications or ossifications occur in a variety of conditions, including mitral stenosis (Figure 4–91)[622, 623] and certain healed disseminated infectious diseases such as tuberculosis,[624] histoplasmosis, and varicella pneumonitis (Figure 4–92).[625, 626] The multiple ossifications of mitral stenosis usually can be differentiated from the calcifications of healed infectious disease by their size (the ossifications of mitral stenosis measure up to 8 mm in diameter, whereas calcifications are generally no more than 2 to 3 mm) and occasionally by the identification of trabeculae of bone. Pulmonary interstitial ossification is a rare disease in which the roentgenographic pattern is one of branching calcific densities extending along the bronchovascular distribution of the interstitial space.[627]

4. Lymph-node calcification usually is amorphus and irregularly distributed throughout the involved node (Figure 4–86). It results most commonly from healed granulomatous infection. *"Eggshell" calcification* is uncommon and consists of a ring calcification of the periphery of lymph nodes. It occurs most typically in silicosis (Figure 4–93); although the bronchopulmonary nodes are most frequently affected, involvement of the mediastinal nodes and even retroperitoneal nodes has been described.[628] Since we have seen at least three cases of proved sarcoidosis with eggshell calcification of lymph nodes, this sign cannot be regarded as pathognomonic of silicosis.

The monograph by Salzman[1683] on lung calcifications in roentgen diagnosis is recommended as additional reading on this important topic.

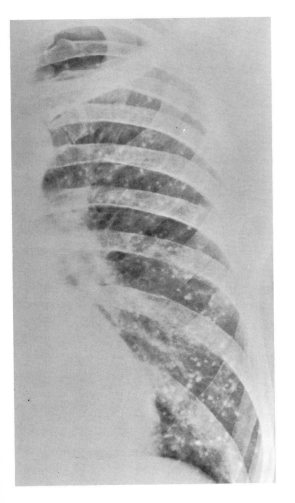

Figure 4–92. **Multiple Nodular Pulmonary Calcifications.** A posteroanterior roentgenogram of the left lung reveals small punctate calcifications scattered widely from apex to base, fairly uniform in size and measuring 2 to 3 mm in diameter; the appearance of the right lung was identical. The distribution and size of the deposits is suggestive of healed granulomatous infection (particularly histoplasmosis) or remote varicella pneumonitis. The etiology in this patient was not established.

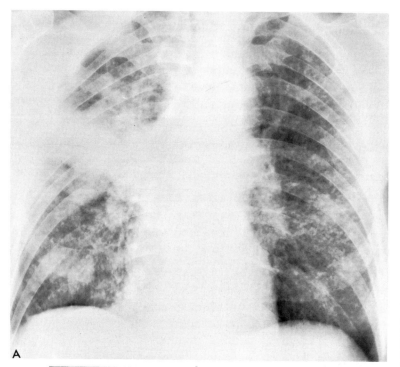

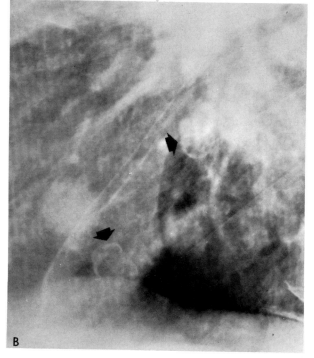

Figure 4–93. Eggshell Calcification of Lymph Nodes. A posteroanterior roentgenogram (A) reveals diffuse reticulonodular disease throughout both lungs. The mass in the right mid-lung and parahilar region proved to be primary bronchogenic carcinoma and the large nodules in the right lower lung field metastases. A view of the lower half of the chest in lateral projection (B) reveals two ring calcifications (*arrows*) characteristic of eggshell calcification of lymph nodes. The solitary nodule anterior to the chief fissure was a metastasis. Proved silicosis and primary bronchogenic carcinoma.

Bulla Formation

Bullae are cystic air-containing spaces within the lung parenchyma measuring more than 1 cm in diameter in the distended state. Since they occur occasionally as a complication of consolidative diseases of the lung, they may be expected to modify the roentgenographic appearances to a considerable extent.

Apart from their common occurrence in emphysema (a subject which is discussed in a later section in this chapter), bullae undoubtedly occur with greatest frequency as a complication of acute staphylococcal pneumonia, particularly in infants and children (Figure 4–94). Their pathogenesis is believed to be related to a check-valve obstruction of a small bronchus or bronchiole, with distension of the lung

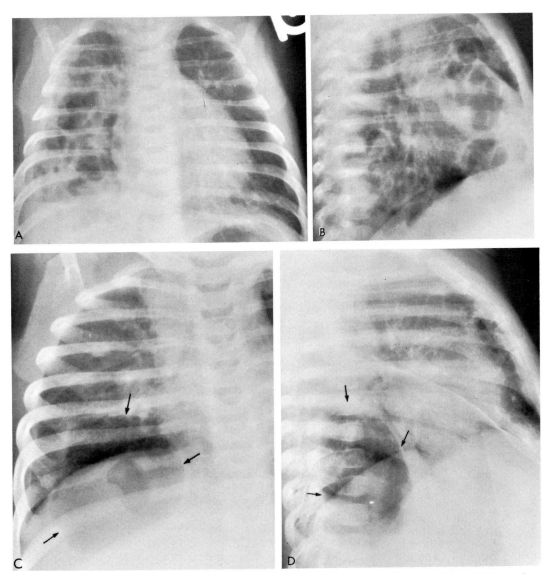

Figure 4–94. **Pneumatocele Formation in Acute Staphylococcal Pneumonia.** Views of the right hemithorax from anteroposterior (A) and lateral (B) roentgenograms reveal marked variegation of density throughout the right lung produced by irregular zones of consolidation separated by numerous cystic spaces (the left lung was normal). A small pleural effusion is present. Two days later (C and D), considerable resolution has occurred in the consolidation but there has developed a large well-defined air-containing space in the lower lobe (*arrows*) characteristic of a pneumatocele. One-and-one-half month old infant with proved staphylococcal pneumonia. (Courtesy Dr. J. Scott Dunbar, Montreal Children's Hospital.)

distal to the obstruction in the form of a coalescent cystic space or pneumatocele. Such a lesion in a child with acute pneumonia is virtually pathognomonic of staphylococcic etiology; it occurs frequently, having been found in 34 of 75 cases of staphylococcal pneumonia described by Hendren and Haggerty.[635] In adults, bulla formation is uncommon in pneumonia but may occur in other diseases, both local and general (apart from emphysema); for example, traumatic lung cyst may develop after nonpenetrating chest injury (Figure 4–81),[636, 637] and bullae may be a complication of certain diffuse diseases, such as tuberous sclerosis.[638]

The roentgenographic manifestations of bullae and blebs are considered in more detail in a later section of this chapter (*see* page 336).

Change in Size or Position of Intrathoracic Lesions

The effects produced by a change in intrathoracic pressure on the size and configuration of vascular lesions within the lungs has been alluded to and constitutes an invaluable sign in the diagnosis of these lesions (*see* Figure 1–70, page 98).[168, 639–641] Application of the Valsalva and Mueller maneuvers not only aids in the differentiation of vascular and solid lesions of the parenchyma of the lung and of an azygos vein from an enlarged azygos lymph node but also may help in sorting out the confusing shadows which form the hila of the lungs. Tomography facilitates these assessments in the majority of cases.[168]

The decision as to whether an intrathoracic mass in the periphery of the thorax is intrapulmonary or extrapulmonary is of obvious importance to diagnosis. Although such differentiation may be made readily by the induction of diagnostic pneumothorax (Figure 4–95), useful information may be gained by the application of simpler roentgenographic techniques. Consider, for example, a mass situated in the posterior thoracic gutter

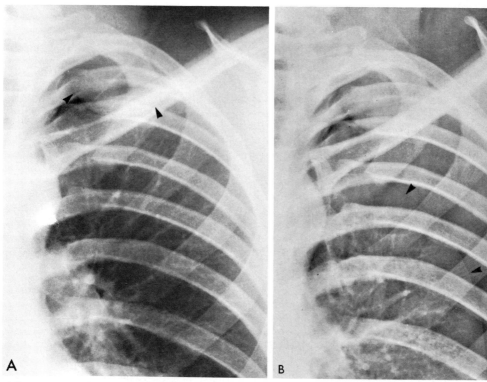

Figure 4–95. **The Value of Diagnostic Pneumothorax in Establishing the Origin of a Peripheral Mass.** A view of the upper half of the left lung from a posteroanterior roentgenogram (*A*) reveals a sharply circumscribed mass of homogeneous density situated in the immediate apex contiguous to the rib cage (*arrows*). A similar view following institution of pneumothorax (*B*) (*see* collapsed lung at *arrows*) shows no change in the position of the mass, thereby establishing its origin from the pleura or chest wall. Lipoma attached to the second rib.

contiguous to the visceral pleura. On roentgenograms of the chest exposed in full inspiration and in full expiration, one of two possibilities exists: (1) if the mass shows no change in its relationship to contiguous ribs, it must arise from the tissues of the thoracic wall; and (2) if the relationship alters, the mass must be intrapulmonary in location (Simon[122] employs this technique to advantage in differentiating a nipple shadow from an intrapulmonary nodule). The same information may be gained by roentgenography in different body positions—an intrapulmonary mass frequently alters its relationship to contiguous ribs or vertebrae on roentgenograms exposed in the erect, supine, and lateral decubitus positions (Figure 4–96); the relationship does not alter when the lesion arises in the thoracic wall or paravertebral tissues (Figure 4–97).

The *change in shape* of an intrathoracic mass with variations in intrathoracic pressure and body position may indicate a fluid rather than a solid nature of its contents. For example, a "spring-water" cyst in the anterior mediastinum may undergo a change in contour from inspiration to expiration or from erect to supine position, whereas a solid teratoid tumor undergoes no change. This sign has been used to advantage by Gramiak and Koerner[642] in the identification of the fluid nature of subpleural lipomas.

Distribution of Disease Within the Lungs (Anatomic Bias)

For several reasons, some known and others obscure, many diseases of the lungs tend to develop in certain anatomic locations and not in others. Knowledge of such

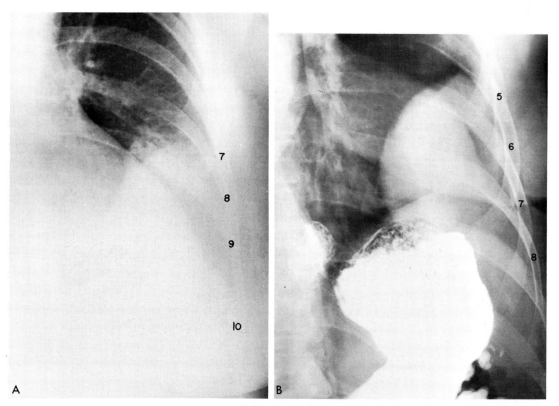

Figure 4–96. **Change in Position of Intrathoracic Masses.** A view of the lower half of the left hemithorax from a posteroanterior roentgenogram exposed in the erect position (*A*) reveals a rather poorly defined homogeneous mass lying in the posterior portion of the thorax contiguous to the diaphragm and lateral chest wall; in this body position, it relates to the axillary portion of ribs seven to ten. A view of the same area with the patient in the prone position (*B*) shows the mass to relate to the axillary portion of ribs five to eight. Such movement establishes the fact that the mass is not attached to the rib cage. At thoracotomy, the mass was found to arise from the costal surface of the visceral pleura to which it was attached by a long pedicle. Pathologic diagnosis—fibroma.

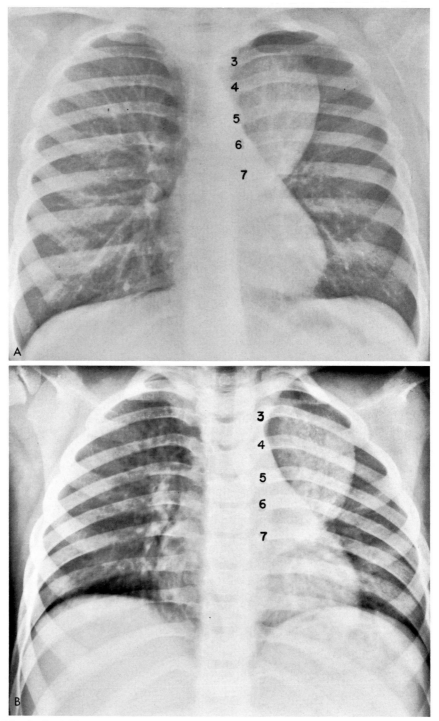

Figure 4–97. **Lack of Change in Position of Intrathoracic Lesions.** On both a posteroanterior roentgenogram exposed in the erect position (*A*) and an anteroposterior roentgenogram exposed in the supine position (*B*), a large, smooth, partly calcified mass can be identified in the posterior paravertebral gutter; in both body positions, it bears a constant relationship to ribs three to seven, indicating fixation to the bony thorax or contiguous tissues.

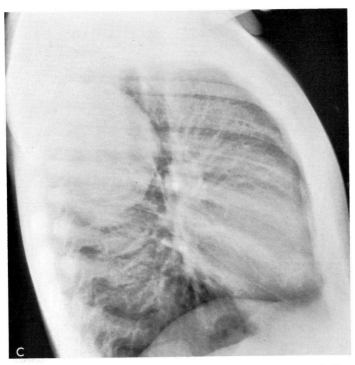

Figure 4–97. *Continued.* In lateral projection (C), the position of the mass is well illustrated. Asymptomatic five-year-old boy. Pathologic diagnosis—well-differentiated juvenile ganglioneuroma. (Courtesy Dr. J. Scott Dunbar, Montreal Children's Hospital.)

anatomic bias is of obvious diagnostic importance; the following examples are not meant to be complete but should serve to indicate how this sign may be used to advantage in differential diagnosis.

Aspiration pneumonia is a typical example of a disease in which the influence of gravity largely establishes the anatomic distribution of disease (Figure 4–98). Should aspiration occur when the patient is supine (during the postoperative period, for instance), the upper lobes are involved more often than the lower[643] and their posterior portions more frequently than their anterior; conversely, should aspiration occur with the patient erect, involvement of the lower lobes predominates.[578] Whether the patient is supine or erect, aspiration occurs more readily into the right than into the left lung, due to the more direct origin of the right main bronchus from the trachea.

Gravity also plays a significant role in the pathogenesis of acute pneumococcal pneumonia. In an ingenious series of experiments on dogs, Robertson and Hamburger[563] showed that the anatomic site in which pneumonia developed could be controlled by altering the position of a dog's thorax so that bacteria-laden exudate flowed into specific segments under the influence of gravity. That this effect is operative in humans is lent support by the tendency of acute alveolar pneumonia to occur predominantly in the posterior portions of pulmonary lobes.[567, 568]

The important influence exerted by gravity on the hemodynamics of the pulmonary circulation has received much attention in recent years, and is dealt with in detail in the section concerning the pulmonary vasculature (*see* Chapter 10).

Pulmonary infarction occurs much more frequently in lower than in upper lobes. Fleischner[644] reported an incidence of 10 per cent infarcts in the upper lobes, but stated that whereas this figure may accurately reflect postmortem incidence it probably is higher than in those who survive infarction. This anatomic bias probably is related to the more direct flow pattern of blood from the main pulmonary arteries

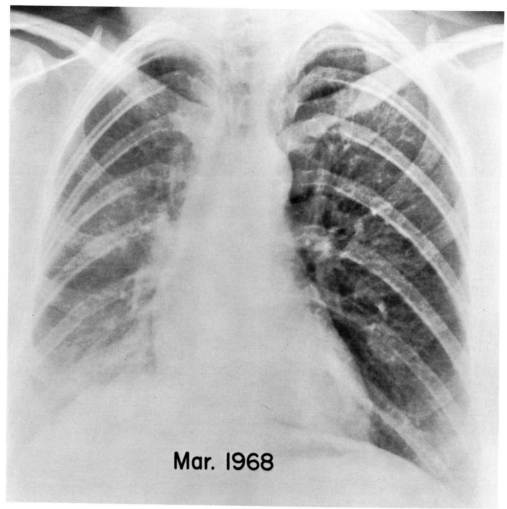

Mar. 1968

Figure 4–98. **Anatomic Bias in Disease: Aspiration Lipid Pneumonitis.** A posteroanterior roentgenogram reveals diffuse increase in opacity and loss of volume of the right lung; the pattern suggests combined air-space and interstitial disease of some form. On biopsy, the lung proved to harbor much lipid material within both air spaces and interstitial tissues. This 29-year-old mentally retarded and epileptic woman was asymptomatic except for rather severe constipation for which she took one and one-half to 2 oz of mineral oil per day; close questioning revealed the fact that she lay predominantly on her right side while sleeping.

into lower than into upper lobes. For the same reason, metastatic lesions occur more frequently in lower lobes; a solitary mass in an upper lobe is unlikely to be metastatic.

This preponderance of metastatic neoplastic involvement in lower than in upper lobes is reversed in the case of primary bronchogenic carcinoma, for as yet unexplained reasons; in 250 cases analyzed by Garland,[645] the ratio of upper-to-lower lobe origin was approximately 2½ to 1. Such predilection shown by primary and metastatic neoplasms for a specific anatomic zone can be of obvious value in

their differentiation. Cavitary carcinoma similarly shows a strong anatomic bias to the upper lobes; of 80 cases of bronchogenic carcinoma described by Rutishauser,[646] eight showed cavitation roentgenographically; of these, seven were in the upper lobes and one in the apex of a lower lobe. Clearly, such anatomic distribution does not assist in differentiation from cavitary tuberculosis.

Pulmonary tuberculosis provides a singular opportunity to employ anatomic bias in differential diagnosis. In reinfection tuberculosis of adults, the susceptibility of the apical and posterior bronchopulmonary segments of the upper lobes and the superior segment of the lower lobes is well recognized: these three segments were involved in *all* of 100 cases described by Lentino and associates,[647] and in whole (93 per cent) or in part (3.4 per cent) of 500 patients with cavitary tuberculosis described by Poppius and Thomander.[648] These segments of lung, termed "the upper lung" by the former[647] and "the vulnerable portions" of lung by the latter,[648] are characterized by poor perfusion, diminished respiratory ventilation, and a distribution of bronchi favoring bronchogenic spread.[647] The rarity with which the anterior bronchopulmonary segment of an upper lobe is affected *to the exclusion* of other segments is sufficient to make the diagnosis of reinfection tuberculosis in this area extremely unlikely (only one case was reported by Lentino and his colleagues[647]).

Tuberculosis of the lower lung zones of which 94 examples were reported by Segarra and associates,[649] is said to be present in 0.5 to 4.0 per cent of patients admitted to sanatoria in the U.S.A.; the majority of these cases (72 per cent in the series reported by Segarra and associates[649]) occurred in young women.

In contrast, *primary tuberculosis* shows an anatomic bias which is the antithesis of that in reinfection tuberculosis; in 90 children studied by Frostad,[650] there was remarkable predominance of involvement of the anterior segments of the right lung, both in the upper and middle lobes. The reasons underlying this notable difference in anatomic distribution in primary and reinfection tuberculosis are not entirely clear.

Pulmonary sequestration occurs almost exclusively in the lower lobes, most commonly in the posterior basilar bronchopulmonary segment and more commonly on the left side than on the right.[651, 652] According to Witten and associates,[653] only three cases of intralobar bronchopulmonary sequestration involving the upper lobes had been reported in the literature by 1962 (they reported three additional cases). Intrapulmonary bronchogenic cysts had a similar but less-marked predilection for the lower lobes, two-thirds of 32 cases reported by Rogers and Osmer[654] being so located.

Diffuse lung disease not infrequently shows an anatomic bias which may be important to differential diagnosis. For example, the "ground-glass" density and reticulation of asbestosis typically is of basal distribution.[597, 655] Chronic idiopathic interstitial fibrosis and interstitial fibrosis of scleroderma frequently are predominantly basal in distribution, particularly in their early stages. Conversely, pulmonary involvement in diatomite pneumoconiosis is characteristically upper lobe in distribution,[656] as is the upper-lobe predilection for the conglomerate shadows of complicated silicosis and coal-workers' pneumoconiosis.

Roentgenologic Localization of Pulmonary Disease (the "Silhouette" Sign)

The anatomic location of the great majority of pulmonary diseases which cause local increase in density may be precisely established from posteroanterior and lateral roentgenograms. When doubt exists, fluoroscopic examination, oblique or stereoscopic roentgenography, or tomography, may be employed as additional localizing procedures. Two situations exist however, in which the precise location of disease may be difficult to establish — when multiple segments of both lungs are involved, with resultant confusion of superimposed shadows in lateral projection; and when only an anteroposterior projection of the chest is available for evaluation (for example, in the immediate postoperative period or when a patient is otherwise too ill for standard roentgenography). In these circumstances, the "silhouette sign"[657] may be employed with great benefit. Felson and Felson[657] gave credit to Dunham for having made the first reference to this invaluable roentgenographic sign in the mid 1930's. Since that time many authors have emphasized its value in localizing pulmonary disease.[585, 586, 629–634, 657–660] Roentgenographic visualization of the mediastinal and diaphragmatic contours is obtained because of contrast with the air-containing lung contiguous to them. When consolidation or atelectasis affects any portion of lung adjacent to a border of the mediastinum or diaphragm, that border no longer can be visualized roentgenologically (Figure 4–99). The corollary is that a density within the lungs which does *not* obliterate the mediastinal or diaphragmatic contour cannot be situated within lung contiguous to these structures (Figure 4–100). Clearly, such a sign can be of

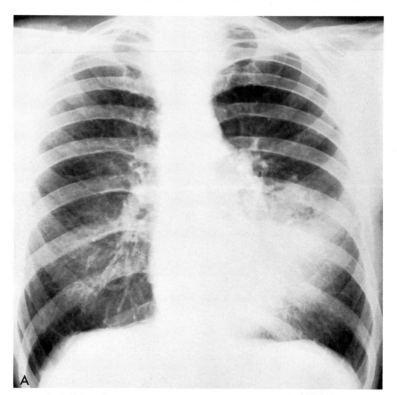

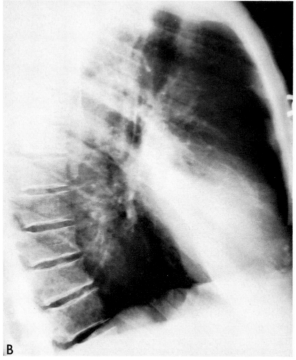

Figure 4-99. **The Silhouette Sign.** Posteroanterior (*A*) and lateral (*B*) roentgenograms reveal obliteration of the left heart border by a shadow of homogeneous density situated within the lingula; such obliteration inevitably indicates lingular disease (providing there is adequate roentgenographic exposure). Squamous cell carcinoma of the lingular bronchus with distal obstructive pneumonitis.

value only when structures have been adequately penetrated; for example, in an underpenetrated roentgenogram, a massive

consolidation of the right lower lobe prevents visualization of the right border of the heart, merely because the flux of roentgen rays is of insufficient penetration to reproduce the shadow of the heart through the massive lower-lobe density—despite the fact that there is air-containing lung contiguous to the heart. The "silhouette sign" is perhaps of greatest use in the differentiation of middle-lobe and lingular disease from lower-lobe disease, but in many other sites it may allow precise anatomic localization—for example, obliteration of the aortic knuckle on the left side by airlessness of the apical-posterior segment of the left upper lobe (Figures 4-101, 4-102, 4-103; *see also* Figure 4-14,

(*Text continues on page 297.*)

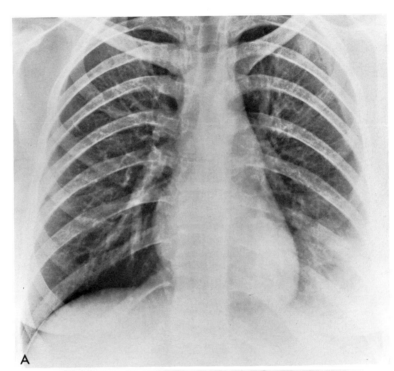

Figure 4-100. The Silhouette Sign. In posteroanterior projection (*A*), homogeneous consolidation obscures the dome of the left hemidiaphragm from the heart border to the costophrenic sulcus. The left heart border is clearly defined and distinct. This combination of changes implies that the consolidation must lie in a plane behind the heart but contiguous to the left hemidiaphragm in a position tangential to the x-ray beam—that is, the anterior bronchopulmonary segment. Were the consolidation situated more posteriorly, the diaphragmatic dome tangential to the plane of the beam would be contiguous to air-containing lung and thus would be visible. In lateral projection (*B*), note the precise anatomic localization to the anterior bronchopulmonary segment. In *A*, the segment of the left hemidiaphragm from the heart border medially is obscured by contiguity with the heart—an additional example of the silhouette sign.

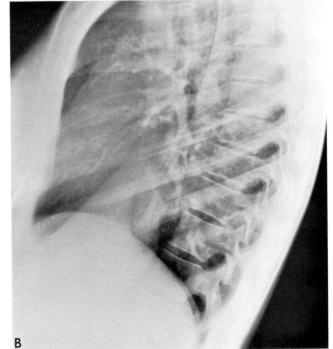

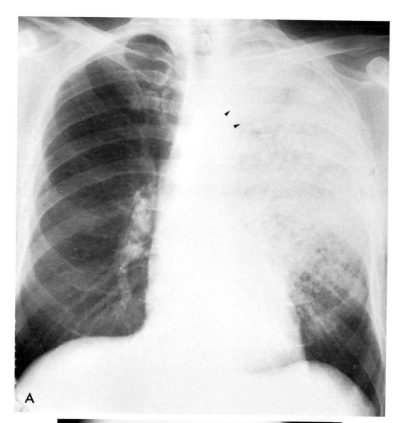

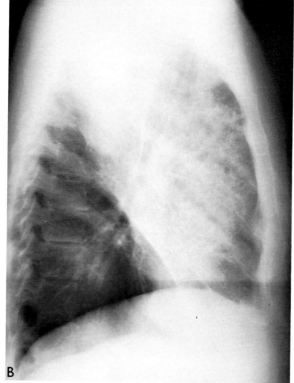

Figure 4–101. The Silhouette Sign: Left Upper Lobe Consolidation. In posteroanterior projection (*A*), a somewhat inhomogeneous consolidation of the upper half of the left lung obliterates the aortic knob (approximate position indicated by *arrows*), the left hilum, and the upper half of the left heart border. To obliterate the aortic knob there must be airless lung in the apical-posterior segment of the left upper lobe; to obliterate the left heart border there must be disease in the lingula; thus the consolidation must occupy the entire left upper lobe. In lateral projection (*B*), the consolidation is truly restricted to the left upper lobe; note the relationship of the consolidation to the transverse arch of the aorta. Acute *Klebsiella* pneumonia.

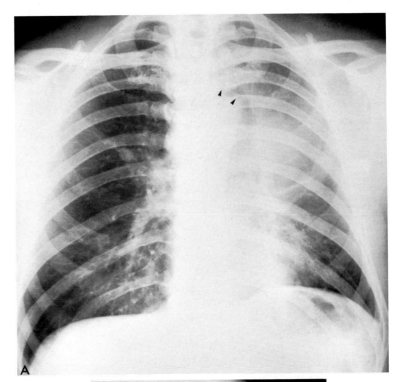

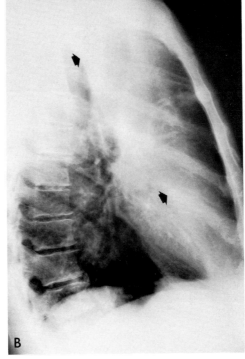

Figure 4–102. The Silhouette Sign: Combined Consolidation and Atelectasis of the Left Upper Lobe. In posteroanterior projection (*A*), a homogeneous opacity in the upper two thirds of the left lung obscures the left hilum and the left heart border but only the upper portion of the aortic knob (approximate position indicated by *arrows*). Since part of the aortic knob can be identified, it is clear that the consolidation must be situated more anteriorly than was the case in Figure 4–101. In lateral projection (*B*), the major fissure can be seen to be displaced sufficiently anteriorly (*arrows*) to permit air-containing lung to relate to the transverse arch of the aorta. Squamous cell carcinoma of the left upper lobe bronchus with obstructive pneumonitis.

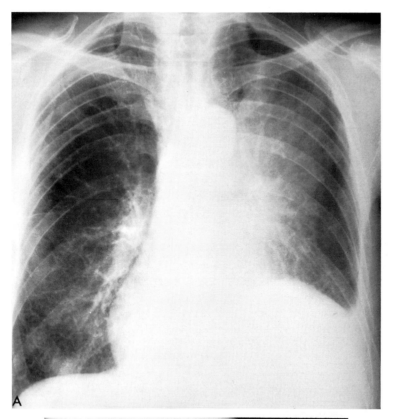

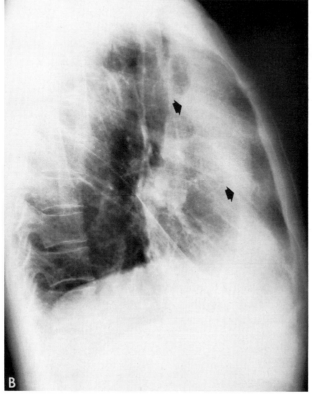

Figure 4–103. **The Silhouette Sign: Atelectasis of the Left Upper Lobe.** In posteroanterior projection (*A*), both the aortic knob and left hilum are clearly visualized indicating that there must be air-containing lung contiguous to them; the left heart border is obscured, however. This combination localizes the airless lung to the left upper lobe but on a more anterior plane than was observed in Figures 4–101 and 4–102. In lateral projection (*B*), the major fissure is displaced far anteriorly (*arrows*), indicating severe atelectasis of the upper lobe.

page 202), obliteration of the ascending arch of the aorta and of the superior vena cava by consolidation of the anterior bronchopulmonary segment of the right upper lobe, or obliteration of the posterior paraspinal line by airlessness of the lung contiguous to this structure in the left posterior gutter.

Although this sign has had its greatest application in the localization of pulmonary disease, we have found it to be almost as useful in actual identification of a disease process. For example, on a posteroanterior roentgenogram the increase in density produced by total collapse of the right middle lobe may be negligible, and in fact impossible to appreciate subjectively; however, the silhouette sign is an invariable accompaniment of such collapse (apparent as loss of sharp definition of the right heart border) and should permit the categorical statement that there is disease in the right middle lobe (a lateral or lordotic projection will be confirmatory [Figure 4-104]); similarly, a minor degree of consolidation or atelectasis in a posterior basal segment of a lower lobe may be extremely difficult to identify as a shadow of absolute increase in density, but the loss of visibility of the posterior portion of the hemidiaphragm as seen in lateral projection allows positive identification of disease in that segment (Figure 4-105).

The physical basis underlying production of the silhouette sign was questioned recently by Tuddenham,[172] who stated that obliteration of a portion of the mediastinal or diaphragmatic contour is produced *not* by the contiguity of the disease process to the involved border but because the shape and configuration of airless lung is identical to that of the obliterated structure. Thus, if one could envisage a volume of lung in the right lower lobe whose medial surface was identical in all respects to the contour of the right border of the heart, consolidation of this volume would cause obliteration of the right heart border— providing the two were exactly superimposed in posteroanterior projection. Tuddenham feels that such does not occur in the human thorax because the distribution of bronchopulmonary segments prevents such volumetric consolidation. Our attempts to validate Tuddenham's thesis by the use of wax models were unsuccessful.

To recapitulate, the *silhouette sign* is an extremely valuable roentgenologic sign in both localizing and identifying local pulmonary disease. It can be defined in no better words than those of Felson and Felson,[657] who should be commended for emphasizing its importance in roentgenologic diagnosis: *"An intrathoracic lesion touching a border of the heart or aorta will obliterate that border on the roentgenogram; an intrathoracic lesion not anatomically contiguous with a border of the heart or aorta will not obliterate that border."*

Mention should be made of two other roentgen signs recently described by Felson[1684]—the "hilus overlay sign" and the "hilus bifurcation sign." The former permits differentiation of true cardiomegaly from large anterior mediastinal masses which mimic cardiac enlargement; in the presence of an anterior mediastinal mass, the hilum is projected medial to the lateral border of the mass, and in cardiomegaly the hilum is displaced laterally. The "hilus bifurcation sign" is meant to differentiate hilar masses from vascular structures in cases of hilar enlargement: if vessels are seen to arise directly from the hilar shadow, the enlargement is vascular; if vessels appear to arise medial to the lateral aspect of the hilar shadow, the enlargement is caused by an extravascular mass.

The Time Factor in Roentgenologic Diagnosis

In clinical practice, situations occur relatively frequently in which a lack of specificity of roentgenologic signs precludes positive diagnosis. In both acute and chronic diseases of the lung, roentgenographic signs may overlap so that only differential diagnostic possibilities can be suggested at the time of the first examination; if a positive diagnosis cannot be established by integration of clinical and laboratory evidence and pulmonary function tests, changes in the roentgenographic picture over the subsequent days, weeks, or months often are of great diagnostic value. A few examples will illustrate the importance of the assessment of time relationships in roentgenologic diagnosis.

Acute pneumonia due to *Diplococcus pneumoniae* or *Mycoplasma pneumoniae* organisms usually can be differentiated on

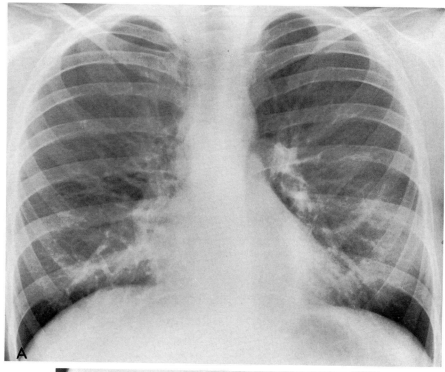

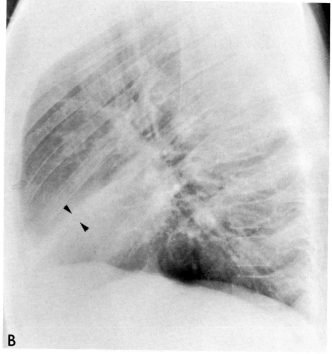

Figure 4-104. **The Silhouette Sign: Atelectasis of the Right Middle Lobe.** In posteroanterior projection (*A*), there is little evidence of local increase in density but the right heart border is indistinct; on this basis alone, the conclusion may be reached that there is disease in contiguous lung, almost certainly the right middle lobe. In lateral projection (*B*), a broad line shadow can be seen to extend anteroinferiorly from the hilum to the anterior costophrenic sulcus (*arrows*). This represents the collapsed right middle lobe between approximated minor and major fissures. Chronic "right middle-lobe syndrome."

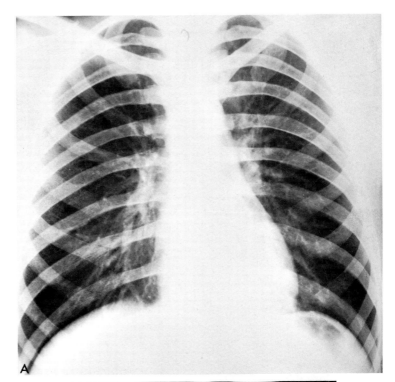

Figure 4–105. **The Silhouette Sign: Identification of Disease.** In posteroanterior projection (*A*), no definite abnormality is identifiable (admittedly the roentgenogram is underpenetrated). In lateral projection (*B*), the shadow of the right hemidiaphragm is clearly visualized from front to back (*thick arrows*); in contrast, the left hemidiaphragm (*thin arrows*) can be identified only to a point even with the plane of the vertebral column; posterior to this point it is obscured. This represents absolute evidence of disease in the bronchopulmonary segment contiguous to this portion of the hemidiaphragm—the posterior basal segment. The silhouette sign in such a case may be usefully employed to *identify* disease which may not be otherwise apparent. Acute bronchopneumonia.

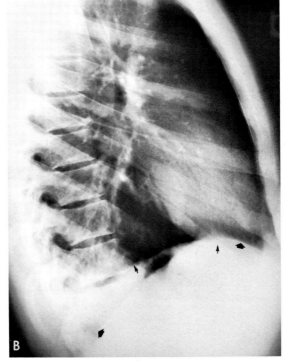

the basis of characteristic roentgeno-graphic patterns. Should this not be possible immediately, the evolution of changes in roentgenograms over the next few days sometimes allows distinction, even without antibiotic therapy (the progression of changes despite penicillin therapy might suggest a *Mycoplasma* etiology (*see* Figure 4-57, page 247), thereby suggesting administration of a more efficacious antibiotic). The progress of changes after pulmonary embolism allows of significant deductions concerning the underlying pathologic process: A consolidative process which undergoes relatively rapid clearing within seven to ten days indicates pulmonary hemorrhage without necrosis; should the density persist and undergo progressive retraction and loss of volume, true infarction and tissue death may be assumed to have occurred. The rapidity with which diffuse interstitial pulmonary edema may appear and disappear (often within hours) allows immediate differentiation from irreversible interstitial disease, which it may closely mimic.

Finally, it is surprising how frequently a small area of parenchymal consolidation in an upper lobe, presenting the typical roentgenographic appearance of exudative tuberculosis, disappears in about seven to ten days, thereby indicating a less-significant etiology (Figure 4-106).

It is clear that, in all of these examples, it would be preferable to be able to suggest the correct diagnosis at the time of the first roentgenogram, so that treatment might be instituted immediately. However, when this is impossible, and when clinical and laboratory evidence is inconclusive, the observation of progressive changes in roentgenograms over a period of time draws attention to the need for not only the discontinuation of useless therapy in the face of an erroneous diagnosis, but also the institution of a suitable therapeutic regime when the true nature of the process becomes known.

It is not only in the field of acute pulmonary disease that the time relationship is important. Growth characteristics of peripheral pulmonary nodules have been

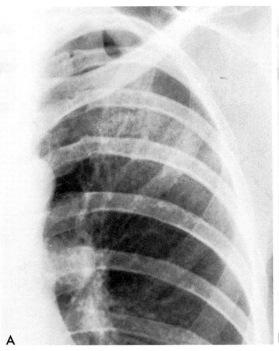 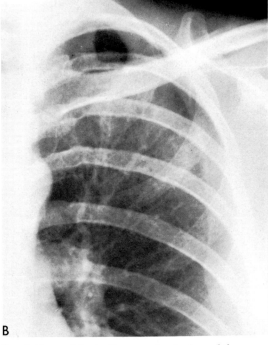

A   B

Figure 4-106. **The Time Factor in Diagnosis: Rapid Resolutions of Acute Pneumonia.** A view of the upper half of the left lung from a posteroanterior roentgenogram (A) reveals a poorly defined area of consolidation whose appearance strongly suggests a tuberculous etiology. Five days later (B), the disease has almost completely disappeared; such rapidity of resolution almost certainly excludes *Mycobacterium tuberculosis* as the causative agent. Heavy growth of *D. pneumoniae* from the sputum.

the subject of much attention in recent years. The "doubling-time"* hypothesis developed by Collins and associates[661] and extended by Nathan and his colleagues,[662] and by others,[663-667] has supplied us with useful information about the natural history of bronchogenic carcinoma. For example, Nathan and his colleagues[662] concluded from a study of 177 cases of malignant lesions of the lung (previously investigated by Collins and associates[661]) that any solitary pulmonary nodule which has a doubling time of 280 days or less is almost certainly malignant, conversely, pulmonary nodules whose rate of growth falls outside this "malignant zone" in almost all cases are benign.

Clearly, the "doubling-time" hypothesis yields a more accurate assessment of the underlying nature of disease than does simple increase in size. Since benign lesions such as hamartoma,[668, 669] histoplasmoma, and certain others also may undergo slow growth, increase in size *per se* should not be the sole consideration in governing the therapeutic approach to a pulmonary nodule.

The conclusions reached from these and other similar studies are of great diagnostic importance and are considered in detail in Chapter 8. It suffices here to stress the value of applying the growth-rate principle to the roentgenologic assessment of peripheral pulmonary nodules.

LINE SHADOWS

The normal substratum of all chest roentgenograms is formed by line shadows—the vascular markings and interlobar fissures; the roentgenologic appearance of these was described in Chapter 1. The present section describes the many line shadows of varied etiology which are seen from time to time in roentgenograms of the chest and which can be grouped most appropriately under this descriptive umbrella. Primary and secondary abnormalities of the pulmonary vasculature of

the lungs comprise a comprehensive topic in their own right and are considered in detail in Chapter 10.

Some useful purpose is served by classifying abnormal line shadows on the basis of their origin from the anatomic "compartments"—the *lung parenchyma*, the *interstitial space* and *bronchovascular bundles*, and the *pleura*. It is recognized that considerable overlap may occur between these subdivisions, particularly the first two, but from a conceptual point of view their anatomic distinction permits an easier understanding of their pathogenesis and morphology.

Line Shadows of Parenchymal Origin

PLATE-LIKE ATELECTASIS. Plate-like atelectasis (*synonyms*: platter atelectasis, discoid atelectasis) was originally described by Fleischner[670] in 1936 and appropriately has come to bear the eponymous designation "Fleischner's lines." Despite their frequency as a sign of pulmonary disease and the numerous studies which have been carried out to investigate their nature,[122, 581, 670, 671, 673, 674] their precise pathogenesis remains shrouded in a veil of mystery. They consist of linear shadows of increased density, almost always situated in the lung bases 1 to 3 cm above the diaphragm (Figure 4-107); only occasionally are they identified in the upper lobes. Although usually oriented in a roughly horizontal plane, they may be slightly obliquely placed, depending upon the zone of lung affected and thus on the relationship to the hemidiaphragm (Figure 4-108). They vary in thickness from 1 to 3 mm and commonly are several centimeters in length. They may be single or multiple, unilateral or bilateral. Studies of the thorax in various degrees of obliquity, either roentgenographically or fluoroscopically, invariably show the lines to extend to a pleural surface, although in the posteroanterior projection such a relationship may not be evident; the pleural surface may be either mediastinal or over the convexity of the lung. Several lines may be grouped in close proximity to one another, although, as pointed out by Fleischner and his associates,[671] a single zone of atelectasis may be visualized as several lines, owing to a variation in its plane of orientation to the roentgen beam. The intrapulmonary location of the lines

---

*"Doubling" refers to *volume*, not to diameter. Assuming a nodule to be spherical, multiply its radius by 1.25 to obtain the radius of a sphere whose volume is double, *e.g.*, the volume of a nodule 2 cm in diameter (1.0 cm radius) is doubled by the time its diameter reaches 2.5 cm.

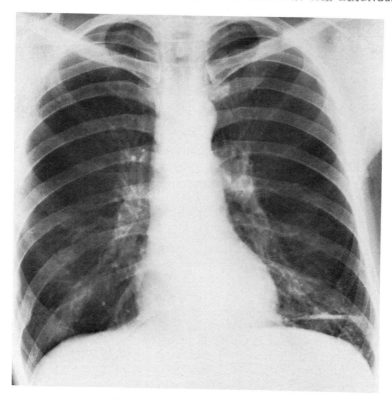

Figure 4–107. Line Shadows: Plate-like Atelectasis. A postero-anterior roentgenogram reveals a line shadow measuring 3 mm in width and 9 cm in length situated in a plane just above the left hemidiaphragm and roughly horizontal in position; the left hemidiaphragm is slightly elevated. The shadow was barely visible in lateral projection. Two days postoperative laparotomy; the line had disappeared four days later.

may be readily established by demonstrating their movement independent of the chest wall during respiration.

As with many other line shadows observed roentgenologically, it is difficult to determine the precise morphologic nature of plate-like atelectasis, chiefly because the pathologist frequently is unaware of its presence. Fleischner and his colleagues[671, 675] described the typical gross appearance as a grayish-blue linear band of collapsed lung, slightly depressed below the pleural surface. When the lung is inflated the atelectatic zone does not expand, so that the depression below the pleural surface is accentuated. Histologically, the collapsed lung is sharply circumscribed from the adjacent air-containing parenchyma, the latter showing varying degrees of overinflation. The small bronchi and bronchioles leading to the collapsed zone show inflammatory changes of varying degrees of severity, and often contain mucous plugs. Fleischner[675] stated that the alveoli not only are collapsed but commonly show an "alveolitis," with inflammatory exudate lying within the alveoli and the interalveolar septa. It is probable that the latter change is intimately involved in the pathogenesis of the process.

Pathogenetically, plate-like atelectasis almost invariably is associated with diseases leading to diminished diaphragmatic excursion, but it is doubtful whether this factor *per se* produces focal atelectasis without the presence of other influences—for example, plate-like atelectasis is uncommon in cases of uncomplicated diaphragmatic elevation such as eventration or phrenic paralysis. A frequent contributing factor is intra-abdominal disease, usually inflammatory. After abdominal surgery, for example, it is probable that a complex group of changes combine to produce plate-like atelectasis: the restriction of diaphragmatic excursion leads to diminished ventilation of the lungs, most marked in the bases; coughing is inhibited, due to the pain and discomfort it engenders; as a result bronchial secretions accumulate in the dependent portions of the lungs and lead to obstruction in the small airways. It is questionable whether airway obstruction by itself results in focal atelectasis, however, since collateral air drift ostensibly constitutes a potent force in preventing parenchymal collapse. Collateral air drift depends upon the integrity of the pores of Kohn and, as Fleischner[581] and others[579] pointed out,

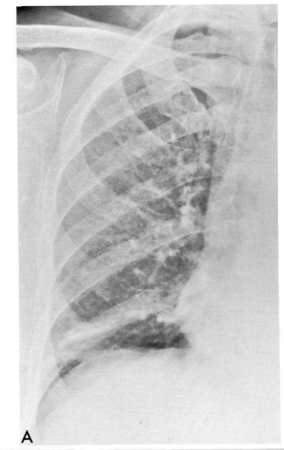

Figure 4–108. Line Shadows: **Plate-like Atelectasis.** In posteroanterior projection (*A*), a rather broad line shadow can be identified lying in a plane just above the right hemidiaphragm. In lateral projection (*B*), the shadow can be seen to be situated within the right middle lobe with its anterior extremity abutting against the visceral pleura. Twenty-four hours postoperative cholecystectomy; the line had disappeared two days later.

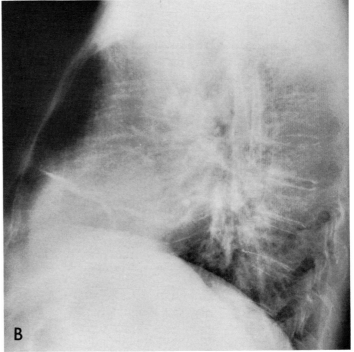

the presence of exudate within the collapsed alveoli and interalveolar septa should effectively block alveolar pores. The combination which might effectively lead to plate atelectasis, therefore, is (a) restricted diaphragmatic excursion, (b) small-airway obstruction due to stagnant secretion, and (c) absence of collateral air drift, due to alveolitis.

The influence of postoperative pneumoperitoneum on the development of pulmonary complications was studied by Bevan.[674] This author observed considerable reduction in the incidence of atelectasis postoperatively when measures were taken to avoid leaving large amounts of gas within the peritoneum at the time of laparotomy. We feel that the evidence that this reduction in complications is related to the reduction in diaphragmatic elevation is not entirely convincing.

The role played by surfactant in the pathogenesis of plate atelectasis is not entirely clear and is controversial, but it is probable that abnormalities of the surface-active agent are operative in some degree. Also, the influence of diminished perfusion as a consequence of reduced ventilation may be implicated in decreased surfactant production.[50, 55-57]

Plate-like atelectasis almost invariably is a temporary process; well-marked lines present on one examination may be absent on roentgenograms obtained only a few hours later. Their importance lies not so much in the functional derangement they themselves are capable of producing—since the volume of lung involved is diminutive—but in the disturbance of the general state of pulmonary ventilation and perfusion which contributes to their development and which indicates in a broad sense the overall effect on the physiology of respiration. It is important to recognize them, therefore, not as insignificant line shadows in the lung bases but as a sign of pathophysiology whose influence in the postoperative period may be of moment.

SEGMENTAL PULMONARY COLLAPSE. When unassociated with obstructive pneumonitis, atelectasis of a subsegment, a segment, or even a total pulmonary lobe may cause a line shadow roentgenographically. From the descriptions of the patterns of lobar and segmental atelectasis earlier in this chapter it will be recalled that parenchymal collapse produces a flattened triangular segment of lung, with its base at the parietal pleural surface and its apex directed toward the hilum. Such a flattened segment when visualized *en face* may cast a hardly discernible roentgenographic shadow; when the roentgen beam is parallel to its flat axis, however, the roentgenographic shadow is linear, the width of the line being roughly proportional to the amount of lung involved. For example, when viewed in lateral projection, total collapse of the right middle lobe creates a broad linear shadow 2 to 3 mm thick situated between the approximated horizontal and chief fissures (*see* Figure 4-40, page 229) (none of the other pulmonary lobes is capable of producing such a line shadow). Segmental or subsegmental atelectasis elsewhere in the lungs is similarly capable of producing line shadows. Depending upon the anatomic location, the linear configuration may be most evident in a particular projection—for example, atelectasis of a lateral subsegment of an upper lobe presents as a linear shadow in posteroanterior projection, whereas collapse of an anterior subsegment is best appreciated in lateral projection.

PARENCHYMAL SCARRING. A segment of lung which was the site of infectious disease and which has undergone healing through fibrosis and scar formation may present as a line density. Again, the width of the linear shadow depends in large measure upon the amount of lung originally involved. Healed upper-lobe reinfection tuberculosis is a common example of this type of line shadow (Figure 4-109). Several such linear shadows may be grouped fairly closely together, commonly extending from the hilum to the visceral pleural surface and diverging slightly toward the periphery. In many cases compensatory overinflation of the adjacent lung parenchyma is present.

The line shadow created by healed pulmonary infarction represents fibrous scarring secondary to lung necrosis. Since the scarring of both healed infarction and healed infection is segmental in distribution, it might be anticipated that the resultant line shadows would be roughly similar in distribution, but such is not the case. For some reason as yet incompletely understood, the dense linear shadows of healed infarction, commonly situated in a

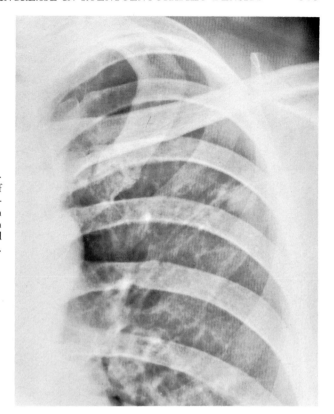

Figure 4–109. **Line Shadows: Healed Pulmonary Tuberculosis.** A view of the upper half of the left lung of a posteroanterior roentgenogram reveals a well-defined nodular shadow in the axillary lung zone. Line shadows of uneven width can be seen to extend both centrally and peripherally from the lesion. Presumed scarring.

lower lobe, may be oriented in any plane and may run in almost any direction, apparently displaying little respect for the "rules" of segmental distribution. This lack of conformity to the general pattern of bronchovascular distribution has been a source of much diagnostic confusion but is of such frequent occurrence as to be the rule rather than the exception. Simon and Reid[1685] have recently postulated that line shadows associated with thromboembolic disease may be due to thrombosed pulmonary veins, an explanation which we find rather attractive since it explains the unusual anatomic "nonconformity" to the bronchovascular distribution typical of these shadows. In several cases we have observed recently, line shadows associated with apparent thromboembolic incidents have been shown to relate to the left atrium (Figure 4–110), thus supporting the Simon and Reid thesis. The linear shadows of healed infarction always extend to a pleural surface, similar to plate atelectasis; according to Fleischner and his colleagues[671] these densities often terminate in a nodular rounded extremity at the

pleural surface, a finding not observed in atelectasis. Other points which may allow differentiation of healed pulmonary infarcts from plate-like atelectasis include the following:[671] Although healed infarcts may measure up to 10 cm long, they are commonly much shorter than this and generally are shorter than the shadows of plate-like atelectasis. Infarcts may be oriented in any plane, whereas plate-like atelectasis is almost always horizontal and lies in a plane roughly parallel to the diaphragm (Figure 4–110). Diaphragmatic excursion is almost always restricted in plate-like atelectasis and is seldom abnormal in healed infarction. The shadows of atelectasis are temporary and usually disappear within a few days, whereas the line shadows of healed infarction are permanent.

THE WALLS OF BULLAE AND BLEBS. These lesions are air sacs within the lung or visceral pleura, respectively, and measure at least 1 cm in diameter when distended. The walls of bullae are formed by compressed lung and of blebs by a thin layer of fibrous tissue, but in both cases

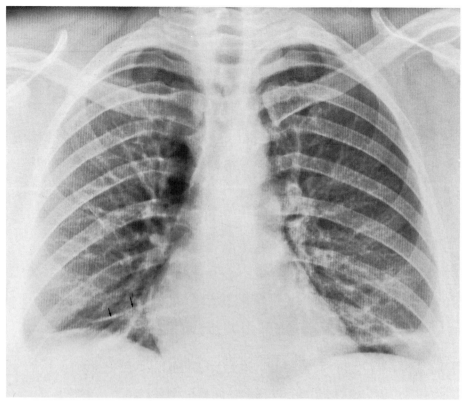

Figure 4-110. **Line Shadows: Healed Infarction.** A posteroanterior roentgenogram reveals two distinct line shadows in the right base. The inferior of the two is running in a plane corresponding to the bronchovascular distribution; the other (*arrows*) is oriented in a roughly horizontal plane and its medial extremity points toward the left atrium. Right lower lobe infarction two weeks previously. The broad line shadow in the left lung base is plate-like atelectasis.

the roentgenographic shadow they create is linear; their contour usually is gently curved in conformity with the distended nature of the air space (Figure 4-111). Both may be single or multiple, so that the number of line shadows is highly variable. Their size varies from 1 cm in diameter up to a single, huge air space occupying the whole of a hemithorax. The thickness of the lines depends partly upon the size of the air sac (the larger its size, the greater the thickness of compressed lung forming the wall) and partly upon whether an inflammatory reaction is or has been present in contiguous parenchyma.

These structures are considered in greater detail in the section, in this chapter, dealing with diseases of decreased density.

Line Shadows of Interstitial and Bronchovascular Origin

SEPTAL OR LYMPHATIC LINES. In 1933 Kerley[676] described certain linear shadows

in the chest roentgenogram which he ascribed to engorged lymphatics. In 1951 he further categorized three different patterns of linear change which he designated "A" lines, "B" lines, and "C" lines.[948] Our knowledge of the pathogenesis and morphology of these lines has increased tremendously in recent years, but Kerley's valuable contribution in first drawing attention to their importance as a roentgenologic sign has continued to be recognized by the eponymous designation "Kerley A," "Kerley B," and "Kerley C" lines.

Kerley "A" lines are straight or almost straight linear densities, not more than 1 mm thick and 2 to 4 cm long, within the substance of the lung; their course bears no definite relationship to the anatomic distribution of the bronchovascular bundles (Figure 4-112). In a postmortem study of the lymphatics of the human lung, Trapnell[677] demonstrated anastomotic lymph channels crossing from perivenous to peribronchial locations, most being

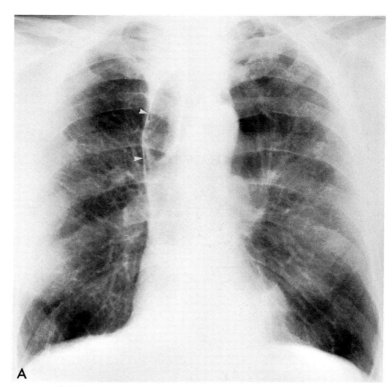

Figure 4–111. Line Shadows: The Wall of a Bulla. Posteroanterior (A) and lateral (B) roentgenograms reveal a large bulla lying in the retrosternal area. The right side of the bulla forms a hairline shadow (*arrows*). Shorter, vertically oriented line shadows situated in the right base represent the walls of smaller bullae.

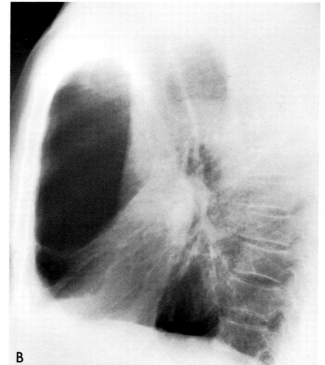

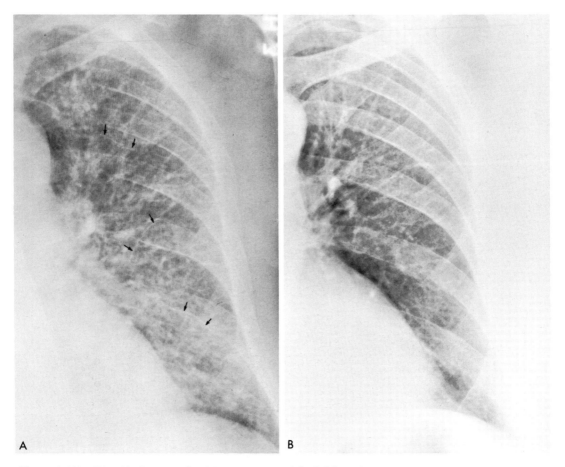

Figure 4–112. **Line Shadows: Kerley A Lines.** A view of the left lung from a posteroanterior roentgenogram (*A*) reveals a coarse network of linear strands widely distributed throughout the lung. Several long line shadows measuring up to 4 cm in length can be identified in the central zone approximately midway between the axillary lung margin and the heart (*arrows*); the orientation of these lines does not conform to the distribution of bronchovascular bundles. These are Kerley A lines and represent engorgement of communicating lymphatics. A roentgenogram made several days later (*B*) shows complete clearing. Cardiac decompensation.

situated approximately midway between hilum and pleura and none more peripherally. The weight of evidence indicates that "A" lines are due to an increase in the amount of fluid or tissue within these anastomotic or communicating lymphatics and in the connective tissues surrounding them.[677] Depending upon the disease process which causes them, they may be reversible (as in pulmonary edema) or irreversible (as in pneumoconiosis or lymphangitic carcinoma).

Kerley "B" lines are less than 2 cm long (shorter than "A" lines). In contrast to "A" lines, which lie in the substance of the lungs, "B" lines are situated in the periphery; they form short straight lines, no more than 1 mm thick, and lie roughly perpendicular to the pleural surface (Figure 4–113). Their outer ends invariably abut against the visceral pleura. Care must be taken not to mistake small vascular shadows in the periphery of the lung for Kerley "B" lines; the former branch, a characteristic never seen with "B" lines. "B" lines are caused by an increased amount of fluid or tissue in the interlobular septa of the lungs, chiefly in the perilymphatic interstitial tissue (*see* Figure 4–52*C*, page 242).[678] (It is unlikely that lymphatic engorgement *per se* can produce a roentgenographically visible shadow.) Because of their anatomic location they are sometimes referred to as "septal lines." Their pathogenesis varies widely: one of the most common causes is intersti-

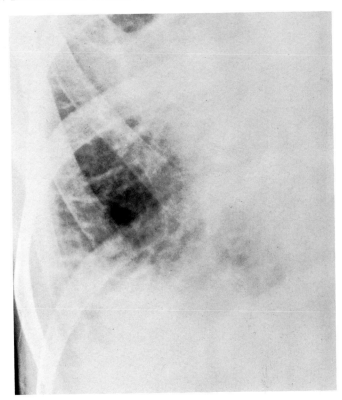

Figure 4-113. **Line Shadows: Kerley B Lines.** A magnified view of the lower portion of the right lung of a posteroanterior roentgenogram reveals several line shadows measuring approximately 1 cm in length and oriented in a horizontal plane perpendicular to the axillary pleura (there is a small pleural effusion as well). These are Kerley B lines, caused by edema of the interlobular septa. With therapy, some but not all of these lines disappeared, although those that remained became somewhat thinner; such incomplete clearing is due to irreversible fibrosis and hemosiderosis of the septa secondary to repeated episodes of edema.

tial pulmonary edema secondary to pulmonary venous hypertension (as in mitral stenosis or left ventricular failure); in such circumstances the influence of gravity on pulmonary hemodynamics leads to the development of interlobular septal edema in the lower portions of the lungs and not in the upper; thus, line shadows are seen to best advantage just above the costophrenic angles on posteroanterior and oblique roentgenograms. When the edema is transient, septal lines appear and disappear sporadically with each episode of decompensation; with repeated insults of this character, or in the presence of chronic and severe pulmonary venous hypertension, fibrosis and hemosiderin deposits within the interlobular septa lead to the development of permanent, irreversible "B" lines. In those diseases in which the pathogenesis is other than edema, the anatomic distribution of "B" lines may be entirely different. For example, in pneumoconiosis,[594, 948] sarcoidosis,[680] lymphangitic carcinomatosis,[681] lipid pneumonia,[682] lymphoma (*see* Figure 4-53, page 243),[595] and diffuse interstitial edema of amniotic

or trophoblastic embolism, in which the influence of gravity on hemodynamics is absent, septal lines may be visible anywhere in the periphery of the lungs where septa normally occur anatomically— along most of the axillary portion of the lung up to the apex and in the retrosternal space.[672]

Kerley "C" lines are, in our opinion, a roentgenologic nonentity. They are reputed to be due to engorgement of pleural lymphatics, but we do not believe that a single layer of lymphatics projected *en face* could conceivably cast a roentgenographic shadow, an opinion to which Trapnell[677] subscribes. Rather, it is likely that the fine network of interlacing linear shadows sometimes seen in cases of interstitial pulmonary edema is due to the superimposition of many Kerley "B" lines in the anterior and posterior portions of the lungs (Figure 4-114), an explanation which has been lent much support in a recent roentgenologic-pathologic correlative study carried out by Heitzman and associates.[683] It is probable that such a network of shadows is a manifestation of severity

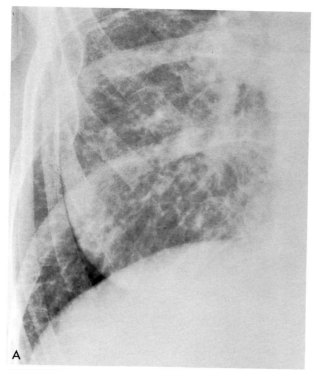

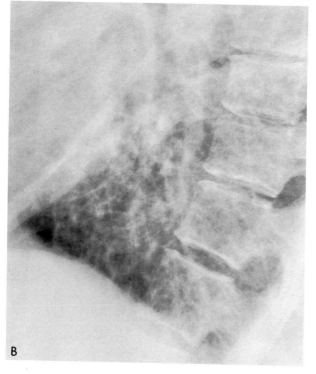

Figure 4–114. **Line Shadows: Kerley C Lines** view of the lower half of the right lung from a post anterior roentgenogram (A) shows several Kerley lines in the axillary lung zone inferiorly. In addit a coarse network of line shadows can be seen in medial half of the lung, revealed to better advant in the section of lateral roentgenogram shown in This coarse reticulation is caused by so-called C li which we regard as no more than a multitude of ede tous interlobular septa visualized *en face.*

of interlobular edema rather than of a separate and distinct anatomic involvement of lymphatic channels.

The morphologic character and significance of Kerley "A" and "B" lines are emphasized appropriately in relation to the diseases in which they form a significant part of the roentgenologic picture.

LINEAR COMMUNICATIONS BETWEEN PERIPHERAL PARENCHYMAL LESIONS AND THE HILA. Not infrequently line shadows of varying width are visible extending from a peripheral parenchymal density to the hilum (Figure 4–115). Usually they are uneven in width and their course may be interrupted for varying distances. Their conformity to the pattern of vascular distribution establishes their anatomic location within bronchovascular bundles. Such communicating strands have been described in both infectious[122] and neoplastic[684] processes, and in the former may be seen in either the active or healed stages of the disease. For example, Simon[122] stated that in cavitary tuberculosis

the connecting line shadows are due to an admixture of tubercles, fibrous tissue, thickened lymphatics, and thickened bronchial walls; when the tuberculosis becomes chronic and productive, fibrosis is a more predominant process histologically, with the result that the line shadows become more dense and more clearly visible. Peripheral mass or "coin" lesions may be associated occasionally with line shadows extending to the hilum (Figure 4–115); since the sign may be present in both infectious and neoplastic lesions it is of no value in differential diagnosis. In a study of 165 cases of peripheral-lung cancer, Marmorshtain[684] reported seeing a track from the tumor shadow to the hilum in 122 cases (73.9 per cent); histologically, these tracks consisted of an admixture of peribronchial and perivascular fibrosis and infiltration by tumor elements. Our experience does not coincide with Marmorshtain's astonishingly high figures, and it is our impression that such communicating tracks are rather uncommon in cases

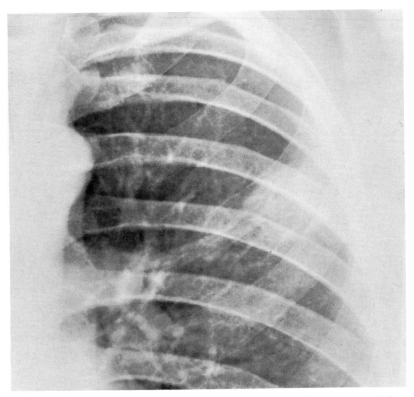

Figure 4–115. **Line Shadows: Communication Between a Parenchymal Mass and the Hilum.** A view of the upper half of the left lung from a posteroanterior roentgenogram reveals a rather poorly defined homogeneous mass situated in the axillary portion of the lung. Extending from the medial aspect of the mass to the hilum are a group of line shadows which were proved on resection to be caused by neoplasm extending along the bronchovascular bundles, predominantly in the lymphatics. Bronchogenic carcinoma.

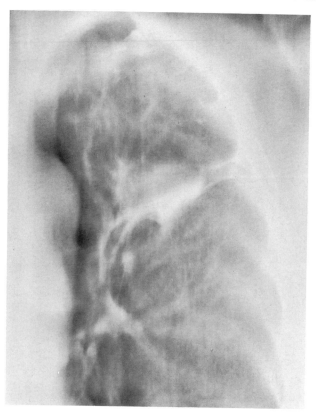

Figure 4-116. Line Shadows: Communication Between a Peripheral Mass and the Visceral Pleura. A view of the upper half of the left lung from an anteroposterior tomogram reveals a rather indistinctly defined homogeneous mass lying in the mid-lung zone. A prominent line shadow extends from the lateral margin of the mass to the pleura, resulting in a V-shaped deformity of the pleura due to indrawing. Proved exudative histoplasmosis.

of peripheral carcinoma; the reasons for the discrepancy of these points of view are not clear.

When a parenchymal mass of almost any etiology is situated near the periphery of the lung, a line shadow occasionally can be identified extending from the mass to the visceral pleura, commonly associated with a local indrawing of the pleura (Figure 4-116). Simon[122] ascribed these line shadows to various causes, including a tag of pleura drawn in by fibrous scarring, a fibrous scar subsequent to previous infectious disease, or a zone of subsegmental atelectasis produced by bronchiolar obstruction secondary to the lesion itself. Rigler[685] observed this sign in 20 of 25 cases of alveolar-cell carcinoma and feels that its presence is highly suggestive evidence for the diagnosis; he states further that, although such lines may occur occasionally in cases of peripheral adenocarcinoma, he has not observed it in squamous-cell cancer.

TUBULAR SHADOWS (BRONCHIAL WALL SHADOWS). The air column of the trachea, main bronchi, the intermediate bronchus on the right, and the lower-lobe bronchus on the left normally is visible on well-exposed roentgenograms. Where these structures are in contact with air-containing parenchyma, their walls also are visible, since their thickness is sufficient to cast a roentgenographic shadow. Beyond the immediate confines of the hilar shadows, however, neither the bronchial walls nor their air columns should be visible normally; thus, when tubular shadows are identified outside the hilar limits they constitute a definite sign of disease. Tubular shadows are double-line shadows which may be parallel or slightly tapered as they proceed distally and always follow the bronchovascular distribution; they may branch in a manner typical of the bronchial tree. When one of the paired lines is contiguous to a vessel it casts no roentgenographic shadow, but visualization of the single line paralleling the vessel has the same significance as a tubular shadow.

Undoubtedly the most common cause of tubular shadows is bronchiectasis (Figure 4-117). In this condition the line shadows are roughly parallel and measure 1 mm or slightly more in width. The width of the

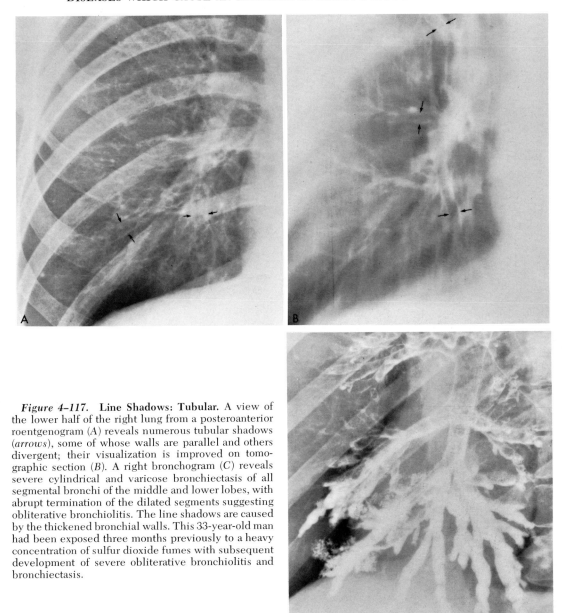

Figure 4–117. **Line Shadows: Tubular.** A view of the lower half of the right lung from a posteroanterior roentgenogram (*A*) reveals numerous tubular shadows (*arrows*), some of whose walls are parallel and others divergent; their visualization is improved on tomographic section (*B*). A right bronchogram (*C*) reveals severe cylindrical and varicose bronchiectasis of all segmental bronchi of the middle and lower lobes, with abrupt termination of the dilated segments suggesting obliterative bronchiolitis. The line shadows are caused by the thickened bronchial walls. This 33-year-old man had been exposed three months previously to a heavy concentration of sulfur dioxide fumes with subsequent development of severe obliterative bronchiolitis and bronchiectasis.

air column separating them depends upon the severity of the bronchial dilatation. Since chronic bronchiectasis frequently is associated with atelectasis, multiple tubular shadows may be crowded together with little air-containing parenchyma separating them. Morphologically these line shadows are caused by a combination of thickened bronchial walls and peribronchial fibrosis and alveolar collapse. When bronchiectatic segments become filled with retained mucus or pus their tubular appearance is transformed into homogeneous band-like densities which Simon[122] terms the "gloved-finger" shadow (Figure 4–118).

In 1960, Hodson and Trickey[686] drew attention to the frequency with which tubular shadows are seen in the lungs of children who have bronchial asthma, being identified in 121 (64 per cent) of 190 such patients. They divided the patients into three groups: chronic infectious

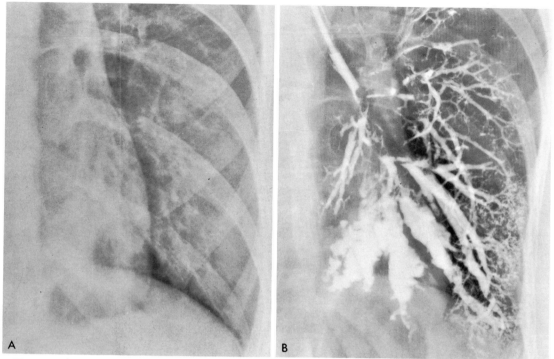

Figure 4–118. **Line Shadows: The "Gloved-Finger" Shadow.** A view of the lower half of the left lung from a posteroanterior roentgenogram (*A*) shows several broad, slightly divergent line shadows situated in the bronchovascular distribution of the left lower lobe; the appearance resembles gloved fingers. A bronchogram (*B*) shows severe varicose bronchiectasis of several of the basal bronchi of the left lower lobe; the appearance in *A* is produced by these dilated bronchi filled with mucus and pus.

asthma (26), purely allergic asthma (58), and asthma of mixed etiology (106). They identified bronchial walls in 88 per cent of those with infectious or mixed-etiology asthma and in only 9 per cent of those with the allergic type and therefore related bronchial wall thickening in asthma to the presence of chronic infection. In a series of 22 patients who died in status asthmaticus, Cardell[687] described the histologic changes in the bronchi of those in whom there was an infective factor as consisting of infiltration of the walls with eosinophils, lymphocytes, plasma cells, and a thick peribronchial cuff of fibrous tissue containing many abnormal capillaries; in those in whom the asthma was purely allergic in type, there was little or no peribronchial fibrosis and the cellular infiltrate was almost entirely eosinophilic. From the reproductions in Cardell's article it is not clear whether the airways whose histologic changes he describes are of the same order as those which create tubular shadows roentgenographically; they ap-

pear to be much more peripherally situated and probably are bronchioles.

There is one other group of patients in whom the tubular shadows are of undetermined nature and pathogenesis. Most commonly they are seen as isolated shadows in the right lower lobe of adult patients of any age; their walls may be parallel as in bronchiectasis or may taper in much the same fashion as a normal bronchus. Colloquially referred to by the British as "tram lines," they seem to occur most frequently in cases of chronic bronchitis; Bates[688] and his colleagues reported their presence in 45 per cent of 185 patients with chronic bronchitis. In describing the roentgenologic changes of chronic bronchitis, Simon[689] attributed such isolated tubular shadows to an accompanying bronchiectasis, but his evidence was not entirely convincing. There is no doubt that tubular shadows may be visualized in the roentgenograms of patients who have never complained of chronic cough and who have no respiratory symptoms; for instance, we see them in a surprising number of annual roent-genograms of young, asymptomatic nurses. The suggestion that these line shadows are due to thickened bronchial walls secondary to chronic bronchitis probably is untenable; Reid[542] showed that the thickness of a bronchial wall from its epithelium to its cartilage plates increases by about a third in chronic bronchitis, due to an increase in mucous gland elements, and we consider that such an increase is hardly likely to render a normally invisible structure roentgenographically visible. Our attempts to solve this roentgenologic enigma by correlating postmortem roentgenograms of inflated lungs with subsequent histologic examination of visible tubular shadows have been unsuccessful. For the moment at least, "tram lines" must remain a descriptive term for roentgenographic shadows whose significance is not known.

LINE SHADOWS DUE TO THROMBOTIC ARTERIES. Simon[690] described line shadows usually oriented in a horizontal plane in the lung bases, occurring in middle-aged or elderly subjects whose history did not suggest a previous thromboembolic episode and who had shown no other abnormalities that might suggest a cause for plate-like atelectasis. Although the pathologic basis of many of these lines is elusive, some have been shown to be due to a thrombosed artery, in some cases associated with fibrosis in contiguous lung parenchyma. In some of these cases, simultaneous bronchography and tomography failed to show any relationship between the lines and the bronchial tree. We wonder whether these are not in fact thrombosed veins rather than arteries, in keeping with the thesis recently put forward by Simon and Reid.[1685]

Line Shadows of Pleural Origin

In addition to the normal interlobar fissure lines and those which occur sporadically in anomalous locations such as the azygos fissure, some line shadows which originate in the pleura are important direct or indirect signs of disease. Thickening of the interlobar fissures, even of minimal degree, may be the only sign indicative of a pleural effusion. Particularly in children, such thickening may occur long before the

usual signs of effusion into the free pleural space appear. In patients who are acutely ill, thickening of the interlobar fissures generally indicates effusion, although when a history of acute illness is absent or previous films are not available for comparison, it may be impossible to differentiate a small effusion from pleural fibrosis secondary to earlier infectious disease. In such circumstances a subsequent examination should establish the true nature of the pleural change.

Fibrous pleural thickening over the anterior or posterior lung surfaces occasionally gives rise to rather broad linear densities usually situated near the lung bases (Figure 4–119). These line shadows tend to be rather "stringy" in appearance and commonly are oriented in a horizontal or oblique plane—not unlike the scars of old pulmonary infarction. Their true nature usually is evidenced by their association with other signs of old pleural thickening (such as obliteration of the costophrenic angle) or by the fact that their relationship to contiguous ribs changes little during respiration.

Another important pointer of disease is the visceral pleural line in pneumothorax, whose recognition is of paramount importance in the diagnosis of that condition. Of a similar nature is the "double" pleural line seen along either side of the mediastinum in cases of mediastinal emphysema (Figure 4–120); the line shadow is created by the combined thicknesses of parietal and visceral pleura, dislocated laterally by mediastinal gas. Herniation of one lung across the anterior mediastinal septum may be evident only in the curvilinear pleural line caused by the combined thicknesses of the two visceral and parietal pleural surfaces; as was pointed out in the section on atelectasis, this may constitute an important sign of compensatory overinflation in the presence of atelectasis.

DISEASES OF THE LUNG WHICH CAUSE A DECREASE IN ROENTGENOGRAPHIC DENSITY

The diseases of the lung that cause a decrease in roentgenographic density (increase in translucency) can be considered appropriately in the same manner as

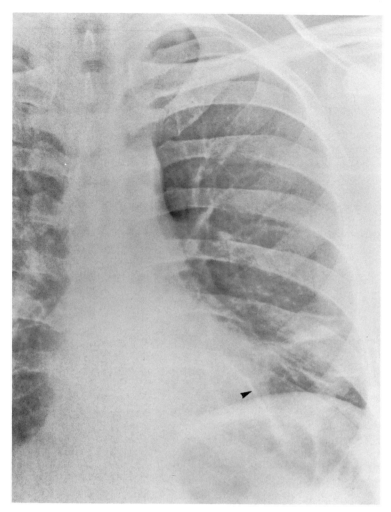

Figure 4-119. Line Shadows: Pleural Thickening. Several irregular line shadows of varying thickness and length are present over the lower portion of the left lung; the left hemidiaphragm is moderately elevated and the costophrenic angle blunted. Most of these line shadows are caused by irregular thickening of the pleura over the posterior portion of the left lower lobe (one line shadow indicated by an *arrow* follows the bronchovascular distribution and is caused by parenchymal scarring).

diseases causing an increased density, but as their antithesis. Just as an increase in density may be caused by a combination of changes in the relative amounts of air, blood, and interstitial tissue, so may a decrease in density result from an alteration in these three elements, but in the opposite direction. In both groups of diseases, seldom is one component altered to the exclusion of the others, but it is useful to subdivide the diseases on the basis of predominant modification of each component, individually and in combination.

It is emphasized that here we are dealing with the diseases of the *lung* that cause reduced roentgenographic density and not of the thorax as a whole. Any assessment of chest roentgenograms must take into consideration the contribution which abnormalities of *extrapulmonary tissue* might make to reduced density. For example, certain pleural diseases

(*e.g.,* pneumothorax) and some congenital and acquired abnormalities of the chest wall (*e.g.,* congenital absence of the pectoral muscles [Figure 4-121], mastectomy [Figure 4-122], poliomyelitis, and other neuromuscular disorders which affect one side of the thorax) produce unilateral radiolucency which easily might be mistaken for pulmonary disease unless their possibility is borne in mind continuously.

In the discussion on lung density in Chapter 1, it was pointed out that, for all practical purposes, assessment of changes in lung density must be purely subjective, except when roentgen densitometry is employed. In diseases of increased density, assessment may be relatively simple, since the variation in density from normal lung to consolidated lung approximates a factor of 10—from the average density of lung parenchyma (0.08 g/ml) to the density of consolidated lung (1.0 g/ml). By contrast, the reduction from normal lung density in diseases associated with increased translucency may be very slight, and probably amounts to no more than 0.01 or 0.02 g/ml. Thus we are faced with the apparent paradox of attempting to classify a group of diseases on the basis of a roentgenologic sign which is at best extremely subtle. The reasons by which this approach may be justified are two-fold:

1. In *generalized* diseases of the lung characterized by diffuse pulmonary overinflation (for example, spasmodic asthma or diffuse obstructive emphysema) general reduction in density or "increased translucency" traditionally is cited as a reliable roentgenologic sign of these diseases. In fact, however, the validity of this sign is questionable. For many reasons, of which the most cogent is the wide variation in exposure factors which characterizes much chest roentgenography, the impression of "increased translucency" is not only unreliable as a sign of overinflation but may be false, particularly in healthy young males with a large total lung capacity. In such situations, reliance must be placed on the *secondary signs* which are an integral part of these diseases; then recognition of the overall pattern of roentgenographic change permits the *inference* that lung density must be reduced, thus allowing inclusion in this broad category of disease. Such reasoning appears somewhat artificial but serves to focus attention on those signs which are of greatest diagnostic reliability rather than on one we have found undependable.

2. In *localized* diseases associated with reduced roentgenographic density (for example, lobar emphysema or a large bulla) the story is entirely different. These conditions provide a region of lung in which change in density can be compared with the remainder of the same lung or the opposite lung, thus supplying the dependable criterion of contrast. Thus, this group of local diseases can be classified according to absolute change in density, an advantage lacking in generalized disease. This is not to imply that secondary signs are not as valuable in local as in general disease; as is shown, signs of overinflation and of alteration in vasculature play an integral role in the diagnosis and differential diagnosis of all diseases characterized by reduction in density.

Accepting that diseases of reduced den-

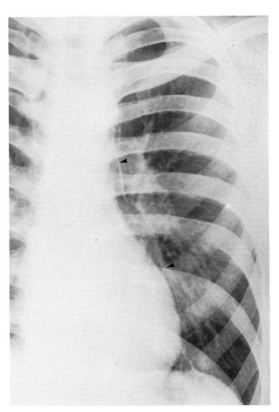

Figure 4–120. **Line Shadows: The Pleural Line in Mediastinal Emphysema.** A thin, continuous line shadow is present along the left border of the cardiovascular silhouette extending from just above the aortic knob to the left hemidiaphragm (*arrows*). This represents the combined thickness of the visceral and parietal pleural membranes separated off the mediastinum by an accumulation of mediastinal gas. Spontaneous pneumomediastinum of unknown etiology; uneventful recovery.

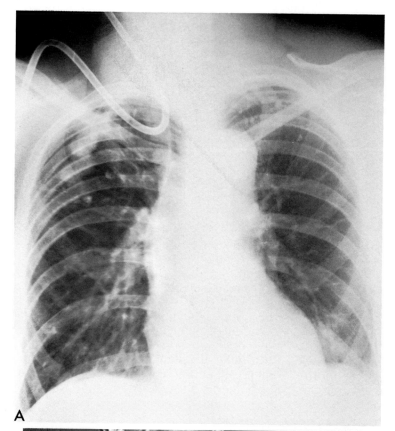

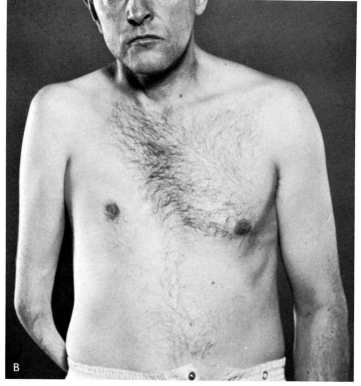

Figure 4–121. Unilateral Hyperlucency: Congenital Absence of the Musculature of the Right Shoulder Girdle. A posteroanterior roentgenogram (*A*) reveals a marked asymmetry of radiolucency of the two lungs. Fairly extensive nodular scarring of the right upper lobe is associated with moderate upward displacement of the right hilum indicating considerable loss of volume of the right upper lobe. However, the loss of volume was considered insufficient to account for compensatory overinflation of the middle and lower lobes of a degree which would explain the difference in radiolucency. A considerable disparity in thickness of the supraclavicular soft tissues (and of the axillary folds) suggested an anomaly of the thoracic wall. A photograph of the patient (*B*) shows marked underdevelopment of the musculature of the right shoulder and chest wall, associated with phocomelia of the right arm.

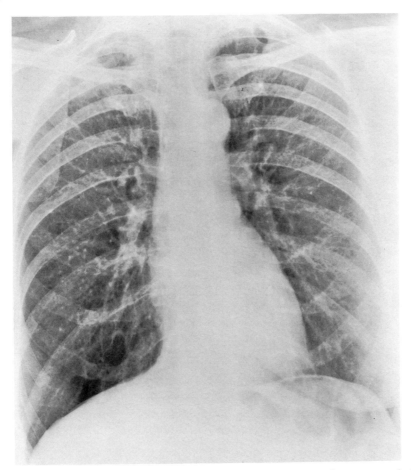

Figure 4–122.   **Unilateral Hyperlucency: Radical Mastectomy.** In this case, the greater radiolucency of the right hemithorax is the result of previous radical mastectomy (breast plus pectoralis muscles).

sity are characterized by an alteration in the ratio of the three components—air, blood, and interstitial tissue—four combinations of changes can effect reduced lung density.

INCREASE IN THE AMOUNT OF AIR, WITH BLOOD AND TISSUE REMAINING UNCHANGED (FIGURE 4–123). This group of diseases is exemplified by obstructive overinflation without lung destruction. It may be either *local* (*e.g.,* check-valve bronchial obstruction due to a foreign body or neoplasm, compensatory overinflation secondary to pulmonary resection or to atelectasis) or *general* (*e.g.,* spasmodic asthma, acute bronchiolitis in infants).

INCREASE IN THE AMOUNT OF AIR WITH CONCURRENT REDUCTION IN BLOOD AND TISSUE (FIGURE 4–124). This group is epitomized by diffuse obstructive emphy-sema; not only are the lungs overdistended but also the capillary bed is reduced and the alveolar walls are dissipated. Bullae and thin-walled cysts may be included as examples of local diseases within this category.

NORMAL AMOUNT OF AIR BUT DE-CREASE IN BLOOD (AND TISSUE) (FIGURE 4–125). This group is characterized by lack of pulmonary overinflation and reduc-tion in the quantity of blood and tissue. *Local* diseases include lobar or unilateral emphysema and pulmonary embolism without infarction. The generalized abnor-malities include diseases characterized by diminished pulmonary artery flow (*e.g.,* tetralogy of Fallot) and diseases affecting the peripheral vascular system (*e.g.,* pri-mary pulmonary hypertension and mul-tiple peripheral pulmonary emboli).

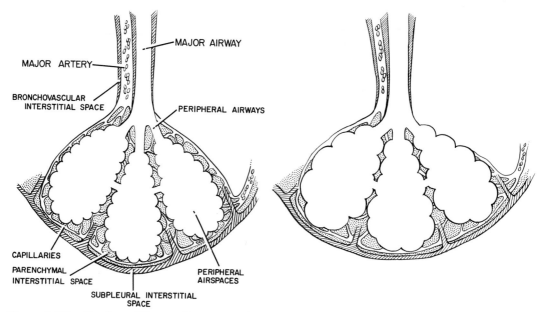

Figure 4–123. **The Lung Diagram: Increase in the Amount of Air, Blood, and Tissue Being Unchanged.** The only abnormality depicted is an increase in the size of the peripheral air spaces.

REDUCTION IN ALL THREE COMPO-NENTS (FIGURE 4–126). This condition occurs rarely and probably relates to only one abnormality—unilateral pulmonary-artery agenesis. Usually the lung is reduced in volume and derives its vascular supply solely from the systemic circulation; the resultant density usually but not always is reduced.[17]

On the basis of this conceptual representation, and using the roentgenologic signs to be described, it is possible to make a reasonably confident diagnosis in most cases of pulmonary disease that

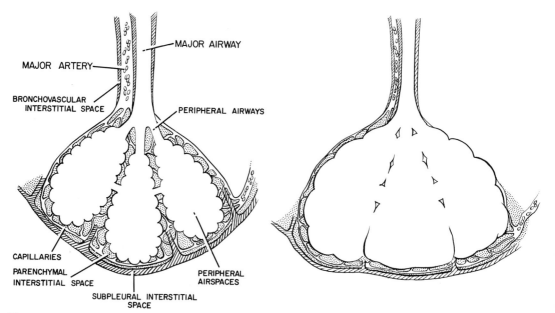

Figure 4–124. **The Lung Diagram: Increase in Air with Concomitant Reduction in Blood and Tissue.** The peripheral air spaces are markedly dilated, with dissolution of their walls. The major artery and vein are reduced in caliber and the capillaries greatly diminished in number.

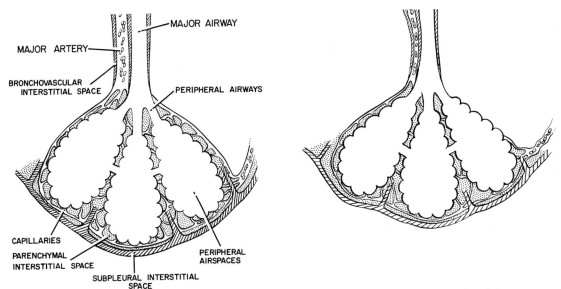

Figure 4–125. **The Lung Diagram: Normal Air, Diminished Blood and Tissue.** The peripheral air spaces are normal in size but the major artery and vein are reduced in caliber and the capillaries diminished in number.

cause a decrease in density. In the following description, no attempt is made to describe roentgenologic characteristics of individual disease entities; specific affections will be cited only to exemplify points under discussion.

ROENTGENOLOGIC SIGNS

Alteration in Lung Volume

With the single exception of the rare reduction in lung volume that occurs in unilateral pulmonary-artery agenesis, all diseases of the lung resulting in reduced density *in which lung volume is altered*

are characterized by *overinflation*. The roentgenologic signs of overinflation depend upon whether the process is general or local.

GENERAL EXCESS OF AIR IN THE LUNGS. Signs to be observed include changes in the diaphragm, the retrosternal space, and the cardiovascular silhouette (Figure 4–127). At total lung capacity, the diaphragm is depressed, often to the level of the seventh rib anteriorly and the eleventh interspace or twelfth rib posteriorly in the severe overinflation of diffuse emphysema, and the normal "dome" configuration is flattened, particularly as viewed in lateral projection. The severity of flattening may be of value in differential diag-

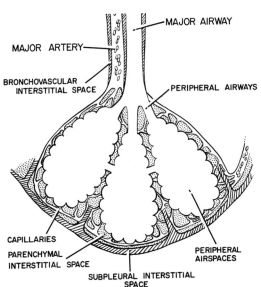

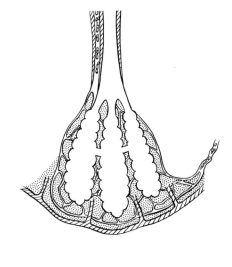

Figure 4–126. **The Lung Diagram: Decrease in Air, Blood, and Tissue.** All elements of the lung are diminished.

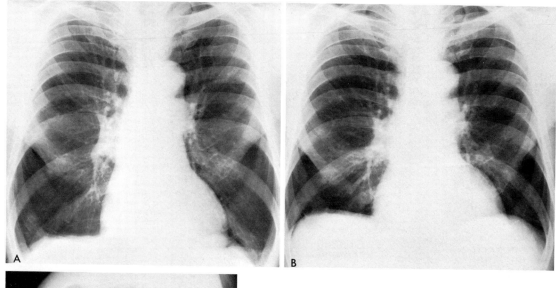

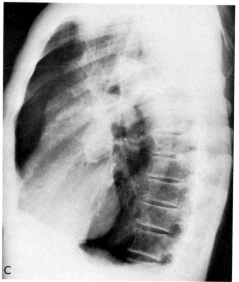

Figure 4-127. **Diffuse Emphysema.** Posteroanterior roentgenograms of the chest in inspiration (*A*) and expiration (*B*) reveal a low position and somewhat flattened contour of both hemidiaphragms; excursion of the diaphragm from TLC to RV is reduced. In lateral projection (*C*), the superior aspect of the diaphragm is concave rather than convex and the retrosternal air space somewhat deepened. The lungs are generally oligemic.

nosis, invariably being most marked in emphysema; the overinflation of emphysema may cause the diaphragmatic contour to be actually concave rather than convex upward (Figure 4-127), a sign which we have not seen in other than destructive lung disease; in asthma the upper surface is nearly always convex (an observation which applies to adults only—severe air-trapping in infants and children may be associated with remarkable depression of diaphragmatic domes [Figure 4-128]). The low position of the diaphragm increases the angle of the costophrenic sinuses, sometimes to almost a right angle. Costophrenic muscle slips, extending from the diaphragm to the posterior and posterolateral ribs, may

be prominent, but these are seen occasionally in normal adults who have taken an exceptionally deep breath and, therefore, should not be regarded as a sign of great importance (*see* Figure 1-60, page 82).

Limitation of diaphragmatic excursion during respiration is a reliable sign of air-trapping and pulmonary overinflation, particularly but not exclusively in emphysema. Whereas the normal range of diaphragmatic excursion is between 5 and 10 cm, the range in emphysema, for example, may be no more than 1 to 2 cm (Figure 4-127).[122]

In lateral projection, separation of the cardiovascular structures from the sternum indicates an increase in the depth of the

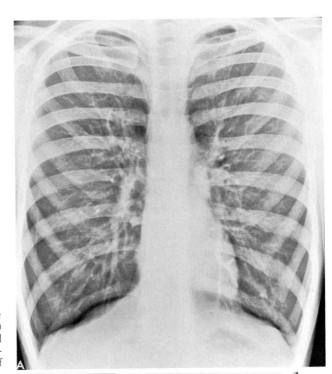

Figure 4–128. **Air-trapping in Spasmodic Asthma.** Posteroanterior (*A*) and lateral (*B*) roentgenograms of the chest of a 14-year-old boy with longstanding spasmodic asthma reveal a low position and flattened contour of both hemidiaphragms. In lateral projection, one hemidiaphragm can be seen to possess a concave superior surface (*arrows*). The retrosternal air space is markedly deepened and the sternum bowed anteriorly.

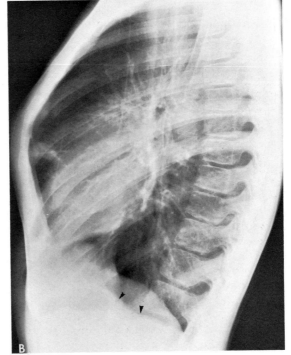

retrosternal air space; in one study of asymptomatic patients with pulmonary emphysema[691] the distance between the sternum and the anterior surface of the ascending aorta measured 2.5 cm or more. A lateral roentgenogram exposed at full expiration usually shows obliteration of the retrosternal air space in normal subjects, whereas the depth and radiolucency of the retrosternal space are similar during full inspiration and expiration in patients with emphysema or other diseases characterized by a general excess of air in the lungs.[692] Simon[693] emphasized the value of assessing the distance from the diaphragm at which the anterior surface of the heart becomes separated from the anterior thoracic wall, this distance being reduced when overinflation is general (Figure 4–127C).

Alteration in the size and contour of the thoracic cage is a variable and usually undependable sign of an excess of air in the lungs. Although the barrel-shaped chest is commonly regarded as indicative of emphysema, often its roentgenologic expression as an increase in the anteroposterior diameter of the chest is inconspicuous; both anterior bowing of the sternum and increased thoracic kyphosis are totally unreliable as significant roentgenologic signs in the assessment of excess air in the lungs.[694]

When the diaphragm is depressed the heart tends to be elongated and narrow and central in position. This long vertical configuration of the cardiovascular contour is of little value as a roentgenologic sign, but it creates difficulty in the assessment of cardiac enlargement when pulmonary hypertension has given rise to right ventricular hypertrophy and cor pulmonale. An interesting paradox concerns the variation in cardiac diameter from inspiration to expiration in certain diseases characterized by severe air trapping and general overinflation. In normal subjects the cardiovascular shadow narrows during inspiration and widens during expiration; in acute spasmodic asthma, acute bronchiolitis of infants,[695] and diffuse obstructive emphysema,[69] paradoxical enlargement during inspiration and diminution during expiration are said to occur.

LOCAL EXCESS OF AIR. Overinflation of a segment or of one or more lobes, the remainder of the lungs being normal, oc-

curs under two quite different sets of circumstances—with and without air-trapping; distinction between the two is of major diagnostic importance. Overinflation *with air-trapping* results from obstruction to the egress of air from the involved lung parenchyma; it occurs from many causes, in all of which the common pathogenetic denominator is airway obstruction—for example, foreign bodies in the tracheobronchial tree,[578] lobar emphysema in infants (Figure 4–129),[696–698] congenital atresia of the left upper-lobe bronchus (Figure 4–130),[699, 700] and perhaps most commonly with bronchial neoplasms. Overinflation *without air-trapping* occurs as a compensatory phenomenon: parts of the lung assume a larger volume than normal in response to a loss of volume elsewhere in the thorax. This may occur after surgical removal of lung tissue (Figure 4–131) or as a result of atelectasis (Figure 4–132) or parenchymal scarring, but in any event the remaining lung contains more than its normal complement of air. Since there is no airway obstruction, the roentgenologic signs are different from those of conditions in which air-trapping plays a significant role. Thus, it is important to consider the roentgenologic signs of local excess of air under two headings—static and dynamic—according to the presence or absence of airway obstruction.

Static Signs. By "static" is implied the changes apparent on standard roentgenograms exposed at total lung capacity.

A. Alteration in lung density. The fact that the excess of air is local permits comparison with normal density in the remainder of the ipsilateral lung or in the contralateral lung; thus, in contrast to those diseases in which air is generally excessive, alteration in density is a significant and reliable sign. The increased translucency is due chiefly to an increase in air in relation to blood content; blood flow to the affected lung is either normal or reduced, the only difference being that, in the latter circumstances, the increase in translucency is even greater.

B. Alteration in volume. The volume of the affected lung depends entirely upon whether the excess of air is compensatory (secondary to resection or atelectasis) or due to airway obstruction. Since compensatory overinflation is the expansion of lung tissue beyond its normal volume to

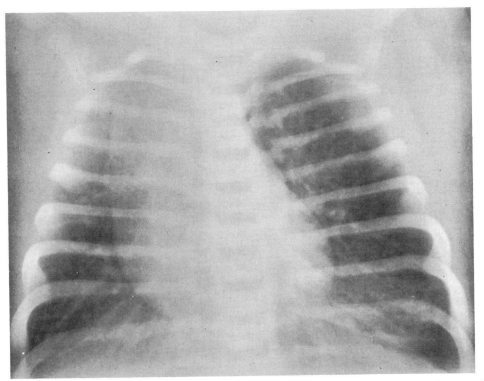

Figure 4-129.   **Local Excess of Air: Congenital Lobar Emphysema.** An anteroposterior roentgenogram of a two-day-old infant reveals considerable shift of the mediastinum to the right due to overinflation of the left upper lobe. Circumoral cyanosis was present during crying, but there was no evidence of respiratory distress. Left upper lobectomy with uncomplicated recovery. (Courtesy Dr. J. Scott Dunbar, Montreal Children's Hospital.)

fill a limited space, the volume which the expanded lung tissue occupies cannot be greater than the original volume for which it compensates. When the excess of air is due to a check-valve bronchial obstruction, however, the volume of affected lung often is greater than normal (Figure 4-129) (an effect which may be related, in some cases at least, to collateral air drift, as stressed by Culiner[701]). The main roentgenologic sign of increased volume is displacement of structures contiguous to overinflated lung, the degree varying with the amount of lung involved and its location: if a lower lobe, the hemidiaphragm may be depressed and the mediastinum shifted to the contralateral side; if an upper lobe, the mediastinum may be displaced and the thoracic cage expanded (Figure 4-129); if a whole lung is involved, the hemithorax in general is enlarged, with depression of the diaphragm, shift of the mediastinum, and enlargement of the thoracic cage. One of the more reliable signs of *lobar* overinflation is outward bulging of the interlobar fissure.

C. Alteration in vascular pattern. The linear markings throughout the affected lung are splayed out in a distribution consistent with the extent of overinflation, and their angles of bifurcation are increased. Providing blood flow is maintained at normal or almost normal levels, the caliber of the vessels is not significantly altered.

Dynamic Signs. By "dynamic" is implied changes that occur during respiration; they are most readily apparent on fluoroscopy although many of the signs may be seen equally clearly on roentgenographs exposed during full inspiration and maximal expiration.

When local increase in translucency is caused by *compensatory overinflation,* during expiration the volume of the overinflated lobe decreases proportionately with the normal lung tissue: since airway obstruction is not a force to be contended with, the affected lung parenchyma deflates normally. Since the overinflated

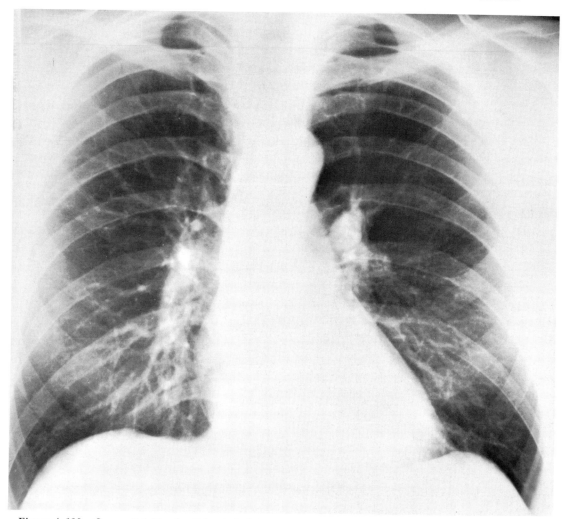

Figure 4–130. **Congenital Atresia of the Apical Segment, Left Upper-lobe Bronchus.** A posteroanterior roentgenogram reveals increased radiolucency of the upper half of the left lung due to both excess of air and diminished blood. The oval mass related to the upper border of the left hilum represents inspissated mucus within the lumen of the affected bronchus distal to the atresia. The affected bronchopulmonary segment is air-containing due to collateral air-drift from contiguous, normally ventilated segments. Oligemia presumably is the result of vasospasm secondary to diminished ventilation. (Courtesy Dr. George Genereux, University Hospital, Saskatoon.)

lung tissue contains more air than normal at total lung capacity, it still contains a greater than normal complement of air at residual volume and, therefore, still is relatively more translucent.

When *airway obstruction* is the major pathogenetic mechanism of local overinflation, the roentgenologic signs are vastly different. When the patient expires, air is trapped within the affected lung parenchyma and there is little change in volume, whereas the remainder of the lung deflates normally. The roentgenologic signs depend upon both the vol-

ume of lung affected and its anatomic location: since during expiration there is negligible change in the amount of air within the obstructed lung parenchyma, density is little altered and the contrast between affected areas and normally deflated lung is maximally accentuated at residual volume (*see* Figure 2–7, page 114). Since the overinflated parenchyma occupies space within the hemithorax, contiguous structures are displaced away from the affected lobe during expiration: the mediastinum shifts toward the contralateral side, elevation of the hemi-

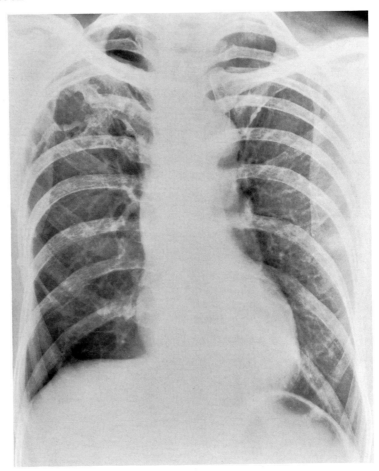

Figure 4-131. Overinflation without Air-trapping: Compensatory to Lobectomy. The right hemithorax is more radiolucent than the left due to overinflation of the right upper and middle lobes following resection of the lower lobe for bronchogenic carcinoma. Note the redistribution of vascular markings. The nodule in the left lung is a metastasis.

diaphragm is restricted, and the thoracic cage maintains its position of inflation; distribution of the vascular pattern throughout the overinflated lobe changes little, and the major fissure remains bulged outward. These dynamic changes are particularly impressive when viewed fluoroscopically: when the patient breathes deeply and rapidly, the mediastinum swings like a pendulum, away from the lesion during expiration and back to the midline during inspiration; the extent of diaphragmatic excursion and the extent of reduction in size of the thoracic cage are diminished on the ipsilateral side.

It cannot be overemphasized that evidence of local excess of air may be extremely subtle on roentgenograms exposed at full inspiration (*see* Figure 2-7, page 114); where such changes are even remotely suspected, studies of dynamics should be carried out. Since it is probable that the majority of endobronchial lesions manifest signs of obstructive overinflation

at some stage in their course, a high index of suspicion is of paramount importance to early diagnosis.

Alteration in Vasculature

Just as overinflation may reflect abnormality of the conducting airways of the lung, so may alteration in the vascular pattern indicate abnormality of perfusion. To carry the analogy further, overinflation may result from abnormality of either the proximal large airways (check-valve obstruction due to an endobronchial lesion) or of the peripheral small airways or bronchioles (acute bronchiolitis or emphysema); similarly, vascular loss may be central or peripheral, due in the former to vascular obstruction (for example, pulmonary artery thrombosis) and in the latter to peripheral vascular obliteration (for example, emphysema or multiple peripheral pulmonary emboli).

As with overinflation, alteration in lung vasculature may be either general or local;

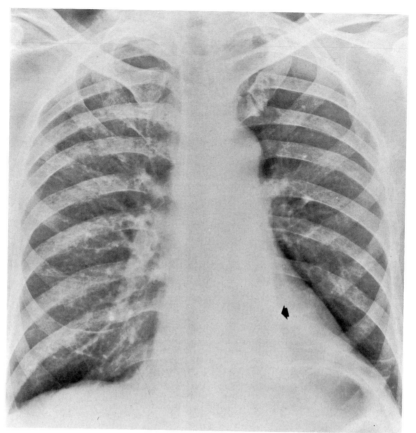

Figure 4–132. **Overinflation without Air-trapping: Compensatory to Atelectasis.** The left lower lobe is totally atelectatic (*arrow*); the left upper lobe has overinflated to compensate for the loss of volume and consequently contains more than its normal complement of air.

since the roentgenologic signs differ somewhat, it is desirable to describe them separately.

GENERAL REDUCTION IN VASCULATURE. The sheet anchor in the diagnosis of diffuse pulmonary oligemia is a reduction in caliber of the pulmonary arterial tree throughout the lungs. As pointed out in Chapter 1, appreciation of such vascular change is a subjective process based on a thorough familiarity with the normal; although such an assessment admittedly is subject to intraobserver error, it has not been replaced to our knowledge by any method which permits accurate evaluation by objective means, with the possible exception of roentgen densitometry. In an observer-error study of proved pulmonary overvascularity and undervascularity[702] the former was detected with significantly greater accuracy than the latter; this experiment dealt with children only, but it is probable that similar results would obtain

in adult patients. As previously emphasized, undervascularity is more readily appreciated on full-lung tomograms than on plain roentgenograms.[72–74]

Since reduction in the size of peripheral vessels constitutes the main criterion in the diagnosis of all diseases in this category, reliance must be placed on secondary signs for their differentiation. There are two ancillary signs of major importance: *the size and configuration of the central hilar vessels* and *the presence or absence of general pulmonary overinflation*. The following examples serve to indicate how these signs may be usefully employed in differential diagnosis. Three combinations of changes are possible.

1. *Small peripheral vessels; no overinflation; normal or small hila.* This combination indicates a reduction in pulmonary blood flow from central causes and is virtually pathognomonic of cardiac disease, usually congenital (Figure 4–133). Such

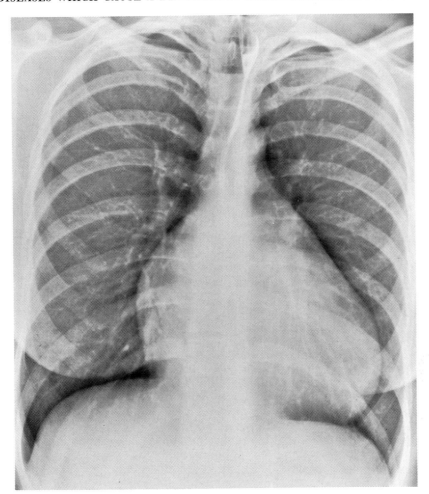

Figure 4–133. **Diffuse Oligemia without Overinflation: Ebstein's Anomaly.** The peripheral pulmonary markings are diminished in caliber, and the hila are diminutive; the lungs are not overinflated. The contour of the markedly enlarged heart is consistent with Ebstein's anomaly. Proved case.

anomalies as the tetralogy of Fallot, Ebstein's anomaly, and, occasionally, isolated pulmonic stenosis are associated with a reduced pulmonary artery blood flow manifested roentgenographically by small peripheral vessels and hila.

2. *Small peripheral vessels; no overinflation; enlarged hilar pulmonary arteries.* This combination may result from peripheral or central causes. The *peripheral* conditions include primary pulmonary arterial hypertension,[703] multiple peripheral emboli, and pulmonary hypertension secondary to chronic schistosomiasis;[704] in each of these the major changes apparent roentgenographically are the consequence of pulmonary arterial hypertension and consist in enlargement of the hilar pulmonary arteries and diminution of the peripheral vessels (Figure 4–134). The most common cause of *central* origin is massive pulmonary-artery thrombosis without infarction;[705, 706] in this situation the reduction in peripheral pulmonary-artery flow results from mechanical obstruction in the large hilar pulmonary vessels, the latter being ballooned out by thrombus within them; severe cardiac enlargement usually is present, due to acute cor pulmonale (Figure 4–135).

3. *Small peripheral vessels; general pulmonary overinflation; normal or enlarged hilar pulmonary arteries.* This combination is virtually pathognomonic of diffuse destructive lung disease, usually emphysema (Figure 4–136).[707–709] Since diffuse overinflation is characteristic of spasmodic asthma also, recognition of peripheral vas-

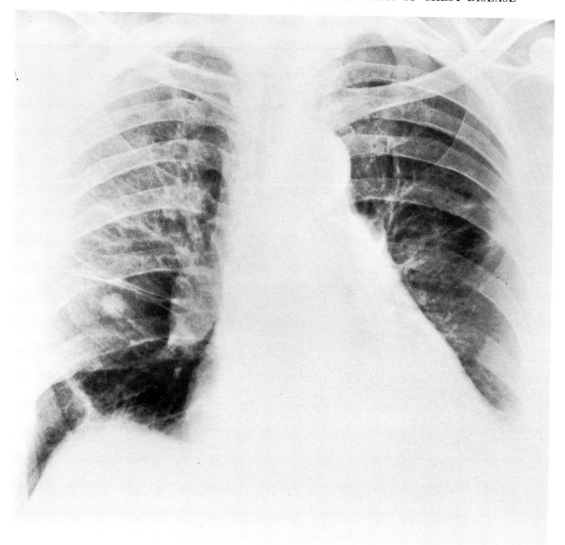

Figure 4–134. **Diffuse Oligemia without Overinflation: Multiple Peripheral Pulmonary Embolization.** The peripheral lung markings are markedly reduced in caliber and the lungs generally oligemic. The hila are grossly enlarged as a result of pulmonary arterial hypertension. The lungs are not overinflated.

culature deficiency is of paramount importance in the differentiation of these two conditions (Figure 4–137). (Roentgenographic differentiation may be facilitated by the use of full-lung tomography.[72]) Enlargement of the hilar pulmonary arteries may occur but is not essential to the diagnosis; it indicates the presence of pulmonary arterial hypertension resulting from chronic increase in vascular resistance and usually is seen only in the late stages of chronic obstructive emphysema. In such circumstances, the rapid tapering of pulmonary vessels distally is accentuated by the hilar enlargement.

LOCAL REDUCTION IN VASCULATURE. The same three combinations of changes apply as in general reduction in vasculature; the major difference lies in their effects on pulmonary hemodynamics. In the following examples the affected portion of lung may be segmental, lobar, or multilobar.

1. *Small peripheral vessels; no overinflation; normal or small hilum.* This combination is epitomized by lobar or unilateral hyperlucent lung, variously known by the eponyms Swyer-James syndrome[710] and MacLeod's syndrome (Figure 4–138).[711] This unique abnormality is

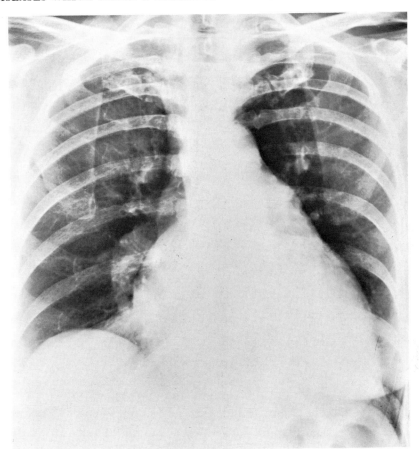

Figure 4–135. **Diffuse Oligemia without Overinflation: Massive Pulmonary Artery Thromboembolism without Infarction.** Marked oligemia of both lungs is associated with moderate enlargement of both hila and rapid tapering of the pulmonary arteries as they proceed distally. The cardiac contour is typical of cor pulmonale. There is no overinflation.

characterized by normal or slightly reduced lung volume at total lung capacity, severe airway obstruction during expiration, greatly reduced circulation (oligemia), and a diminutive hilum;[712, 713] the increased vascular resistance in affected areas results in a shunt of blood to the contralateral lung or unaffected lobes, with resultant pleonemia. Pathogenetically it is believed to be related to acute bronchiolitis during infancy,[711, 713] since the volume of the lung in adulthood is related, at least in part, to the age at which bronchiolar damage occurred. Although this combination of roentgenologic changes is virtually pathognomonic of Swyer-James syndrome, a similar picture may be produced by unilateral pulmonary-artery agenesis (*see* Figure 5–42, page 510), in which the pul-

monary artery is interrupted in the region of the hilum so that the lung is devoid of pulmonary-artery perfusion.[17, 714–716] On plain roentgenographic study, the two may be distinguished by the virtual absence of a hilar shadow in pulmonary-artery agenesis and a diminutive hilar shadow in MacLeod's syndrome; also, in the former the volume of affected lung is nearly always less and the airways are not obstructed. In pulmonary-artery agenesis the linear markings through the affected lung are caused by the greatly increased bronchial arterial circulation; those through the contralateral lung often are increased in size—pulmonary plethora or pleonemia—as a result of associated intracardiac left-to-right shunts. Pulmonary arteriography will accurately differentiate

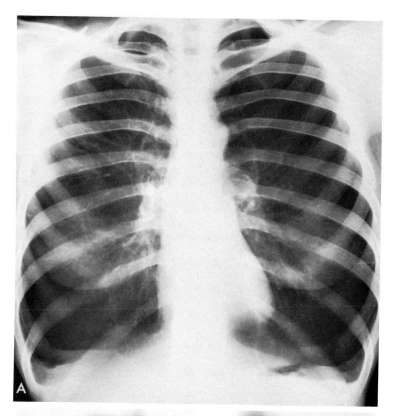

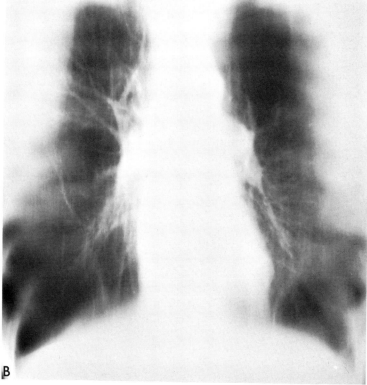

Figure 4–136. **Diffuse Oligemia with Generalized Overinflation: Emphysema.** The peripheral vasculature of the lungs is markedly diminished as revealed in both the posteroanterior roentgenogram (*A*) and the anteroposterior tomogram (*B*). Despite the severe oligemia, the hilar pulmonary arteries are not enlarged. The lungs are severely overinflated.

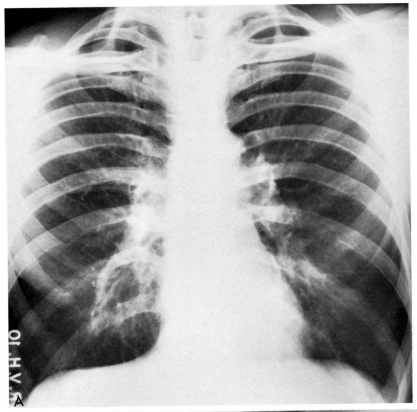

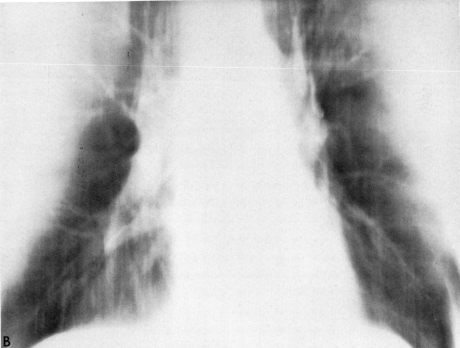

Figure 4–137. **Generalized Overinflation with Normal Peripheral Vasculature: Spasmodic Asthma.** Although the degree of overinflation is almost as great as was seen in Figure 4–136, the peripheral vasculature is perfectly normal in caliber. Assessment of peripheral vasculature is facilitated by full-lung tomography (*B*).

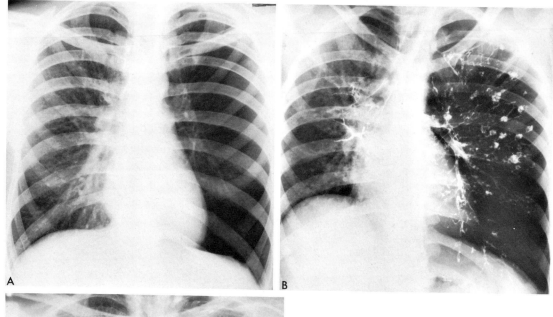

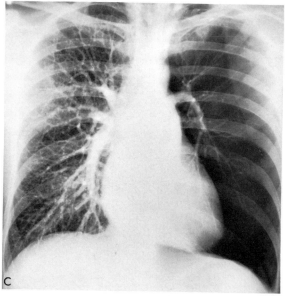

Figure 4–138. **Unilateral Hyperlucent Lung: Swyer-James or MacLeod's Syndrome.** A postero-anterior roentgenogram exposed at TLC (A) reveals a marked discrepancy in the radiolucency of the two lungs, the left showing severe oligemia. The left hilar shadow is diminutive. The left lung appears to be of approximately normal volume compared to the right. An anteroposterior roentgenogram at RV following bronchography (B) demonstrates severe air-trapping in the left lung, little change in volume having occurred from TLC. Since deflation of the right lung is normal, the mediastinum has swung sharply to the right. The bronchial tree shows less bronchiectasis than is generally the case, although there is filling of numerous large spaces typical of emphysema. In the pulmonary angiogram (C), the discrepancy of blood flow to the two lungs is readily apparent; note that the left pulmonary artery is present although diminutive (differentiation from congenital absence of the left pulmonary artery).

the two should standard roentgenographic techniques leave the diagnosis in doubt.

Fouché and D'Silva[717] induced unilateral miliary emboli of pulmonary arteries in animals and produced a roentgenographic effect similar to that of Swyer-James syndrome; however, airway obstruction was absent, a sign which differentiates these two conditions. A similar combination of roentgenographic changes occurs sometimes in humans when pulmonary arterial flow is reduced as a result of compression or obstruction of a pulmonary artery by a contiguous compressive or invasive process (Figure 4–139). Generally speaking, however, such a process results in either en-largement or increase in density of the involved hilum.

2. *Small peripheral vessels; no overinfla-tion; enlarged hilar pulmonary arteries (or an enlarged hilum).* This combination almost always is due to unilateral pulmo-nary-artery embolism without infarction (Figure 4–140). The occluding embolus or thrombus almost invariably leads to en-largement of the involved artery.[718] Since bronchial obstruction is not a feature, there is no overinflation—on the contrary, lung volume may be reduced. As with Swyer-James syndrome, the remainder of the ipsilateral lung and the contralateral lung may be proportionately pleonemic as

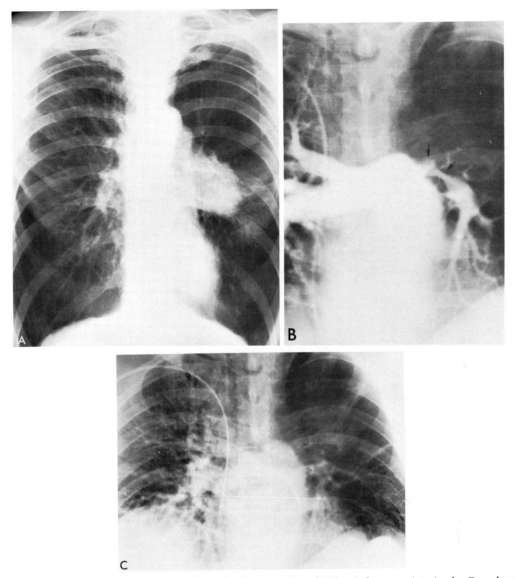

Figure 4–139.   Unilateral Pulmonary Oligemia: Compression of Hilar Pulmonary Arteries by Bronchogenic Carcinoma. A posteroanterior roentgenogram (A) reveals discrepancy in the radiolucency of the two lungs, the left being oligemic and comparatively more radiolucent. The large hilar mass proved to be primary squamous cell carcinoma. This patient did not have a pulmonary angiogram, but an angiogram on another patient showing a similar hilar mass (but less reproducible changes on standard roentgenography) reveals the effects on the pulmonary circulation to be anticipated in such a situation: in the arterial phase (B), there is marked narrowing and distortion of the main pulmonary artery and its interlobar branch (*arrows*); the upper lobe arteries are completely occluded. In the late capillary and early venous phase (C), opacification of the vasculature of the left lung is markedly reduced compared to the right and there is delayed flow through the lower lobe arteries.

a result of redistribution of blood flow, although this may not be readily apparent on standard roentgenograms. A similar roentgenographic picture may be produced by obstruction of a pulmonary artery by invasive neoplasm; in these circumstances the hilar enlargement is due to the original lesion rather than to the vessel, although the overall roentgenographic appearance may be the same. Jacques and Barclay[719] described identical roentgenographic changes in sarcomatous replacement of the lumen of the pulmonary artery.

3. *Small peripheral vessels; overinfla-*

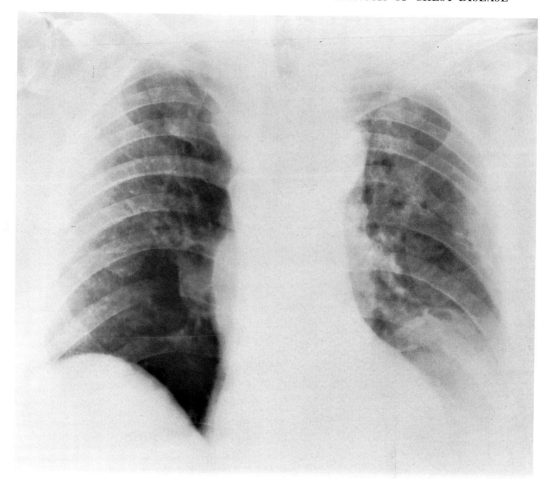

Figure 4–140.   **Lobar Oligemia without Overinflation: Thromboembolism without Infarction.** An anteroposterior roentgenogram exposed in the supine position demonstrates marked increase in the radiolucency of the lower half of the right lung. The vascular markings are diminished in caliber and the descending branch of the right pulmonary artery is dilated and sharply defined; this vessel tapers rapidly as it proceeds distally. Lobar oligemia as a result of thromboembolism without infarction constitutes Westermark's sign.

tion; normal hilar pulmonary arteries. This combination is distinctive of obstructive emphysema. The roentgenographic appearance of the vascular deficiency of emphysema often is local rather than general; in one study, 13 of 26 patients with established emphysema had predominantly local involvement:[72] the lower or upper lobes or almost any combination of individual lobes may be predominantly affected (Figure 4–141). The involved portions of lung show a combination of overinflation and severe diminution in peripheral vasculature; less involved areas tend to be pleonemic, presumably due to a redistribution of blood to them caused by the increased resistance to pulmonary blood

flow in emphysematous areas. Since the lack of increase in vascular resistance in uninvolved lung prevents the development of pulmonary artery hypertension, the hilar pulmonary arteries do not enlarge.

Pulmonary Air Cysts

This term is used for all thin-walled air-containing intrapulmonary spaces which are roentgenologically visible, regardless of their pathogenesis. Although their clinical significances vary widely, it is useful to include these lesions under one heading for purposes of roentgenologic description. One of the most important

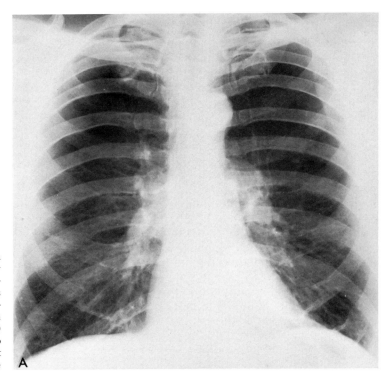

Figure 4–141. Lobar Oligemia with Overinflation: Pulmonary Emphysema (Local). A postero-anterior roentgenogram (A) reveals a marked reduction in the vascularity of both upper lung zones. An anteroposterior tomogram (B) shows the upper lobe oligemia to excellent advantage; note that "grayness" of the lower half of the left lung is greater than the corresponding area of the right lung, indicating greater microvascular perfusion of the left lower lobe than of the right. Since vascular resistance in the lower lung zones is normal, blood has been redistributed from the upper to the lower lobes so that pulmonary arterial hypertension has not developed.

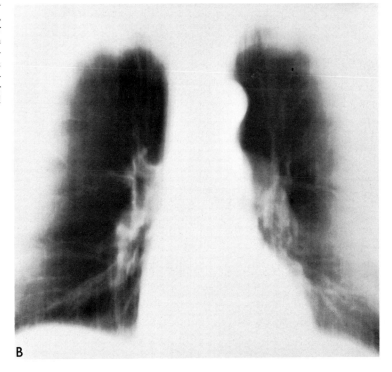

distinctions to be made is to whether an air cyst is a solitary abnormality in otherwise healthy lung or part of generalized pulmonary disease: the implications in regard to the effects on pulmonary function are of obvious importance and were covered in detail by Bates and Christie.[1]

A pulmonary air cyst (bulla or bleb) is an air-containing space varying in size from 1 cm in diameter to the volume of a whole hemithorax and possessing a smooth wall of minimal thickness (from a hairline to 2 to 3 mm); the space may be unilocular or separated into several compartments by thin septa (Figure 4–142); it may arise *de novo*, when the surrounding lung is normal, or may occur secondary to other disease, usually infectious and commonly associated with much parenchymal scarring (Figure 4–143); in the latter circumstances the cyst is associated with a variable amount of disease in adjacent parenchyma. Secondary signs may or may not be present, depending upon the size of the cyst; for example, when a huge bulla occupies most of the volume of one hemithorax (Figure 4–144), signs of air

trapping are apparent during deep breathing—the mediastinum is displaced to the side of the normal lung during expiration, and ipsilateral hemidiaphragmatic excursion and movements of the thoracic wall are restricted. When an air cyst occupies most of one lobe, lobar expansion may be apparent, with outward bulging of the interlobar fissure. Cysts characteristically are avascular, an observation which may be facilitated by tomographic examination, particularly in small lesions; although seldom indicated, angiography[720] and bronchography are useful in showing displacement of pulmonary vessels and the bronchial tree around the cyst. These roentgenologic signs conform to the physiologic observations that pulmonary air cysts are poorly ventilated and unperfused.[720] Studies of the mechanical properties of pulmonary cysts and bullae[4318] showed that, during expiration, the cysts inflate while the rest of the lung deflates (Figure 4–143), a paradox attributed to airflow restriction by small deficiencies in the walls of the bullae occasioned by loss of alveolar tissue: when the air cyst is

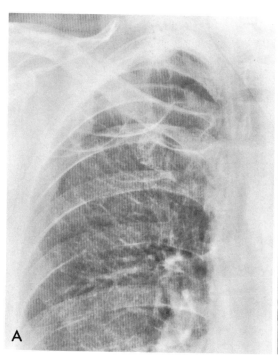
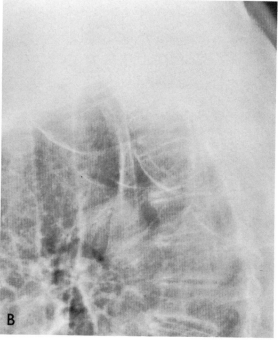

A   B

Figure 4–142.   **Bullae or Blebs.** Views of the upper half of the right lung in posteroanterior (A) and lateral (B) projections reveal several cystic spaces in the lung apex sharply separated from contiguous lung by curvilinear, hairline shadows. The appearance suggests multiple blebs or bullae rather than a single space separated into compartments by thin septa.

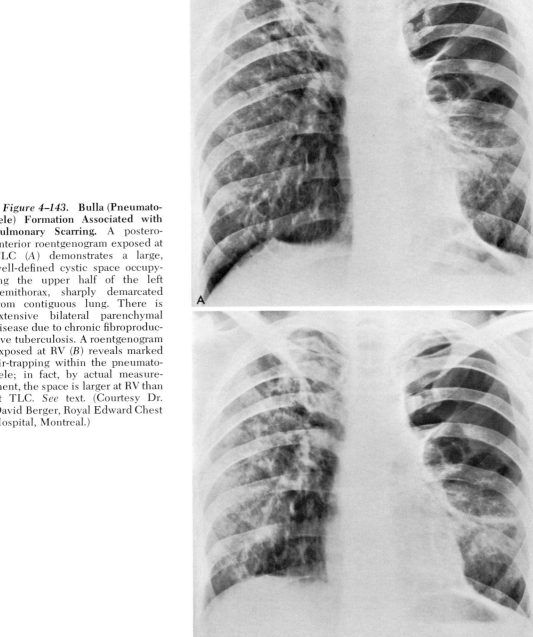

Figure 4–143. Bulla (Pneumatocele) Formation Associated with Pulmonary Scarring. A posteroanterior roentgenogram exposed at TLC (A) demonstrates a large, well-defined cystic space occupying the upper half of the left hemithorax, sharply demarcated from contiguous lung. There is extensive bilateral parenchymal disease due to chronic fibroproductive tuberculosis. A roentgenogram exposed at RV (B) reveals marked air-trapping within the pneumatocele; in fact, by actual measurement, the space is larger at RV than at TLC. *See* text. (Courtesy Dr. David Berger, Royal Edward Chest Hospital, Montreal.)

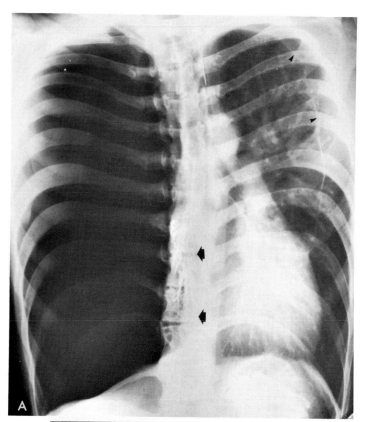

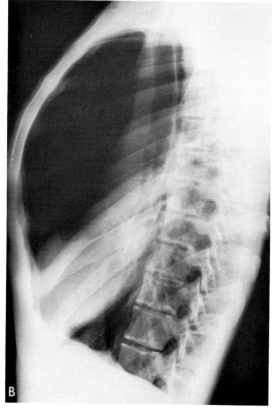

Figure 4–144. **Pneumatocele.** An anteroposterior roentgenogram of the chest following bronchography reveals a huge air sac completely filling and overdistending the right hemithorax and extending across the anterior mediastinal septum almost as far as the left axillary pleura (the line shadow indicated by thin *arrows* is formed by four layers of pleura). The right lung is compressed into a small nubbin of tissue situated in the midline; note the markedly crowded right bronchial tree (*thick arrows*). In lateral projection (*B*), herniation of the pneumatocele across the anterior mediastinal septum has resulted in marked increase in depth of the retrosternal air space and posterior displacement of the heart and major vessels.

filled these communications are compressed, resulting in a state of permanent inflation. This mechanism appears analogous to the obstructive overinflation which has been attributed to collateral air drift in cases of bronchial obstruction.

The specific characteristics of individual forms of pulmonary air cyst are discussed in detail in Chapter 13. A brief outline of the nomenclature to be used and of the general characteristics of each lesion are presented here.

Pulmonary air cysts may be *congenital* or *acquired*. The congenital type includes bronchogenic cysts whose fluid contents have been expelled, and "congenital cystic disease" of the lung;[722] air cysts as part of intralobar pulmonary sequestration also should qualify as disease of congenital origin. Acquired disease includes the two common types of pulmonary air cysts, *blebs* and *bullae*. Blebs are usually small, seldom exceeding 1 or 2 cm in diameter; they are immediately subpleural and most frequently develop over the apices of the lungs. The mechanism of their development generally is attributed to the dissection of air from a ruptured alveolus through interstitial tissue into the thin fibrous layer of visceral pleura, where it accumulates in the form of a cyst.[723, 724] These lesions usually are regarded as the major cause of spontaneous pneumothorax. *Bullae* are intrapulmonary structures and generally are attributed to excessive rupture of alveolar walls; their walls consist of compressed parenchymal tissue.[723] The role played by bronchial or bronchiolar obstruction in the pathogenesis of these structures is not clear, although probably check-valve obstruction is operative in at least some cases; for example, the development of bullae in decompression workers has been repeatedly attributed to bronchiolar obstruction.[725, 726, 728] There is no doubt that some bullae develop as a sequel of lung abscess, of either tuberculous or staphylococcal etiology; resolution of acute pneumonia surrounding the abscess leaves a thin-walled cystic space which presents no distinguishing features from a bulla arising *de novo* in otherwise healthy lung (Figure 4-145). (It has been suggested that direct communication between postabscess bullae and the bronchial tree allows these structures to be opacified with bronchographic contrast media,

whereas bullae of other origins do not communicate;[729] we have observed this communication after acute lung abscess in two cases [Figure 4-146].) Posttraumatic pneumatoceles which result from lung-tissue laceration associated with nonpenetrating chest trauma may present as typical thin-walled air cysts,[637] with or without an air-fluid level (*see* Figure 4-81, page 272). Although rare, bronchial carcinoma which mimics a thin-walled cyst[731] points up the hazard in dismissing every cystic pulmonary lesion as inconsequential.

Finally, bullae frequently occur as a manifestation of diffuse pulmonary emphysema. In such circumstances the cysts are characteristically very thin-walled, frequently are small, and usually are distributed widely throughout the subpleural zone.

ROENTGENOLOGIC SIGNS OF DISEASES OF THE PLEURA

Since by far the most common and most important abnormality affecting the pleura is effusion, it is worth while reviewing briefly the forces that govern the formation and absorption of fluid in the normal pleural space (*see* Chapter 1, page 65, for more detailed discussion of the normal physiology of the pleura). It will be recalled that, in health, fluid is formed at the parietal pleura and absorbed at the visceral pleura (*see* Figure 1-47, page 65). Transudation and absorption depend primarily upon a balance between hydrostatic pressure, which forces fluid out of the capillaries, and osmotic pressure of blood, which draws tissue fluid into capillaries. Since colloid osmotic pressure and pleural pressure exert an equal effect on both pleural surfaces, the only difference in the forces acting on the parietal and visceral pleura is that hydrostatic pressure is systemic in the parietal pleural capillaries (approximately 30 cm H_2O) and pulmonary in the visceral pleural capillaries (approximately 11 cm H_2O). The net effect is a driving pressure from the parietal pleural capillaries to the pleura of 9 cm H_2O. Thus, normal pleural dynamics ensure that the accumulation of pleural fluid is effectively prevented by an osmotic-hydrostatic pressure gradient.[130]

Despite this usually effective combina-

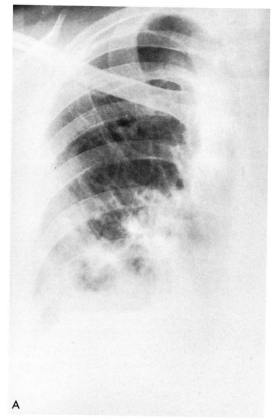

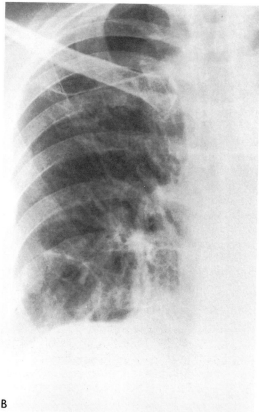

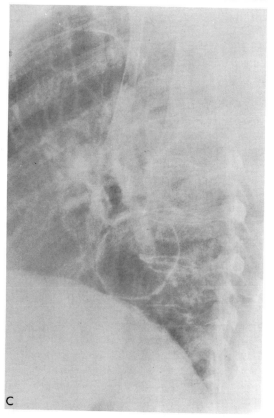

Figure 4–145. **Solitary Bulla Resulting from Healing of a Tuberculous Cavity.** A view of the right hemithorax from a posteroanterior roentgenogram (*A*) reveals a thick-walled cavity in the lung base, possessing a prominent air-fluid level (*Mycobacterium tuberculosis* was cultured from the sputum). Two months later, posteroanterior (*B*) and lateral (*C*) roentgenograms reveal a solitary bulla as a residuum of the previous cavity; this bulla underwent no change on subsequent roentgenologic examinations.

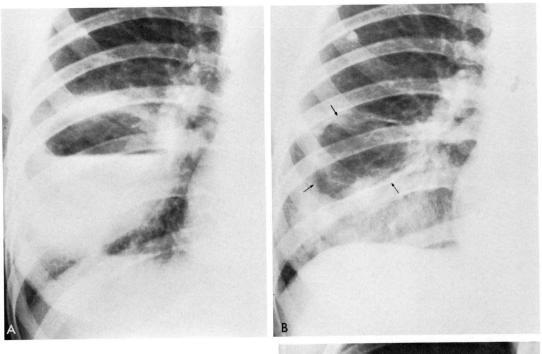

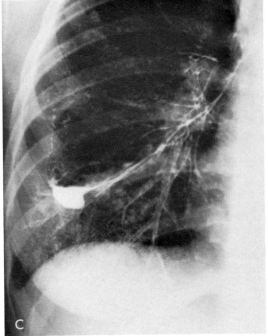

Figure 4–146. **Communication with the Bronchial Tree of a Solitary Postinflammatory Bulla.** A view of the lower portion of the right lung from a postero-anterior roentgenogram (A) reveals a large thick-walled abscess containing a prominent air-fluid level (heavy growth of *Staphylococcus aureus* from the sputum). One month later (B), most of the pneumonia had re-solved leaving a thin-walled bulla as a residuum (*arrows*). A bronchogram performed at this time (C) shows contrast medium forming an air-fluid level within the bulla.

tion of forces, there is convincing evidence that physiologically occurring pleural fluid can be visualized roentgeno-graphically in a significant percentage of normal healthy humans. Using their modification of the lateral decubitus pro-jection with a horizontal x-ray beam (Figure 4–147), Mueller and Lofstedt[785] visualized pleural fluid in 15 of 120

healthy subjects (12.5 per cent). They per-formed thoracentesis on some of these subjects and concluded that the smallest amount of fluid that could be identified by this technique was 3 to 5 ml; the largest amount found in a healthy subject was 15 ml. In a subsequent study carried out on 300 healthy subjects (163 women, 137 men), Hessen,[786] who used a similar tech-

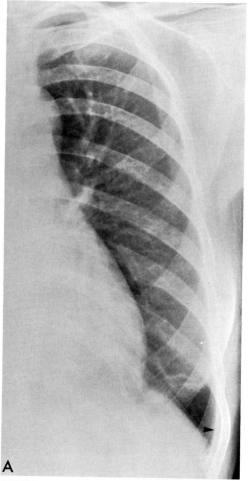

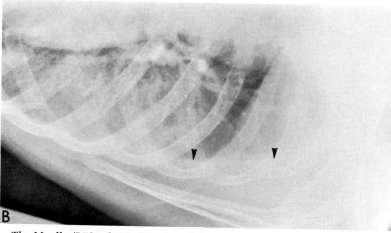

Figure 4–147.   **The Mueller/Löfstedt Modification of the Lateral Decubitus Position for the Demonstration of Small Pleural Effusions.** A view of the left lung from a posteroanterior roentgenogram exposed in the erect position (A) reveals slight thickening of the pleural line just above the costophrenic sulcus (*arrow*): *probable* small pleural effusion. In the Mueller/Löfstedt modification of the lateral decubitus position (B), the pelvis is elevated so that the most concave portion of the upper thorax is dependent; the scapula is rotated so that its shadow does not interfere with visualization of the subcostal pleura. An accumulation of fluid measuring almost a centimeter in thickness is clearly demonstrated (*arrows*).

nique, found conclusive evidence of roentgenologically demonstrable fluid in 12 subjects (4.0 per cent) and suggestive evidence in an additional 19 (6.3 per cent). The thickness of the fluid layer varied from 1 mm to 10 mm and averaged 5 mm. Fluid was identified unilaterally in some subjects and bilaterally in others, and in some the amount varied from one examination to another. Fluid was often observed during repeated examinations of the same subjects, suggesting to Hessen that such a fluid accumulation was an inherent feature of the individual's physiologic status. It is of interest that in 92 women examined by the same technique within a few days post partum, Hessen demonstrated convincing evidence of pleural fluid in 21 (22.8 per cent) and the possibility of fluid in a further 14 (15 per cent).

These studies are of obvious practical importance insofar as they indicate that small amounts of pleural fluid may be demonstrated roentgenographically in the absence of disease; thus, they point up a potential source of error in the diagnosis of clinically significant pleural effusion.

Reported figures for the amount of pleural fluid required for roentgenographic demonstration in the erect subject vary from 250 to 600 ml.[787, 789, 790] Rigler[194] was the first to suggest that smaller quantities—as little as 100 ml—could be shown by roentgenography in the lateral decubitus position, and there is no doubt that his development led to improved accuracy in the roentgenologic diagnosis of pleural effusion. The subsequent studies of Mueller and Lofstedt[785] and of Hessen[786] reduced this figure still further—to 10 to 15 ml—and it appears reasonable to accept the latter figures as the amount of fluid demonstrable when special roentgenographic techniques are employed.

ROENTGENOLOGIC SIGNS OF PLEURAL EFFUSION

Typical Arrangement of Free Pleural Fluid

It will be recalled from the discussion on the physiology of the pleura in Chapter 1 (*see* page 64), that the negative pressure within the pleural cavity represents the difference between the elastic forces of the chest wall and of the lungs. Lung tissue has a natural tendency to recoil but is prevented from doing so beyond a certain maximal point by the inherent tendency of the chest wall to expand outward with an equal, opposite force. Thus, intimate contact between the visceral and parietal pleural surfaces is maintained in the normal subject. When a buffer medium (*e.g.*, fluid or gas) is introduced into the pleural space, the lung can recoil inward toward its fixed moorings at the hilum, the amount of retraction depending upon the quantity of buffer. The site of retraction depends upon the position of the buffer medium within the pleural space, as illustrated by the different effects of hydrothorax and pneumothorax: in the upright subject, the effect of gravity causes gas to rise and fluid to fall in the pleural space. The difference in manner in which the lung responds to these two buffer media is purely a matter of anatomic location—in the former instance the upper portions of the lung retract, and in the latter the lower portions. The different roentgenographic appearances of the two media is due solely to the fact that one is radiopaque and the other radiolucent; for example, if a patient with a pleural effusion of 1 liter were roentgenographed in a 90-degree head-down position, the form of the lung would be *roughly* the same as if 1 liter of gas were present with the patient erect (Figure 4–148). There exists a tendency for the lung to maintain its traditional shape at all stages of collapse, a characteristic termed by Fleischner[792] the "form elasticity" of the lung. In the presence of pneumothorax, or when the thoracic cage is opened (thoracotomy or necropsy), the shape of the lung in its completely collapsed state is to all intents and purposes a miniature replica of its shape in the fully distended form (*see* Figure 4–19, page 206). The same effect occurs when pleural effusion or pneumothorax is present, except that the collapse may be local rather than general.

These two influences—gravity and elastic recoil—are the major forces that control the arrangement of free fluid in the pleural space.[786, 792] Fluid gravitates first to the base of the hemithorax, where it comes to lie between the inferior surface of the lung and the hemidiaphragm (Figure 4–149)—particularly posteriorly, where the

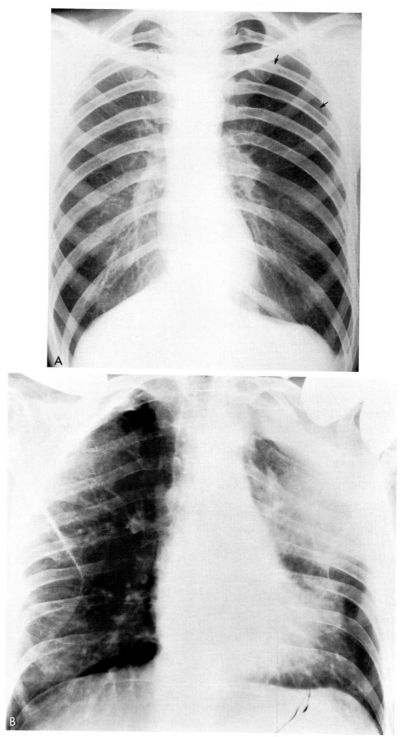

Figure 4-148.   **Similarity in the Effects on the Lung of Pneumothorax and Hydrothorax.** A posteroanterior roentgenogram of the chest (erect position) of a patient with a small pneumothorax (A) reveals partial collapse of the upper and mid-portions of the lung (visceral pleural line at *arrows*). In *B* is illustrated the roentgenogram of another patient with a moderate pleural effusion on whom roentgenography was carried out in a 45-degree Trendelenburg position. The effects on the lung in these two situations are almost identical.

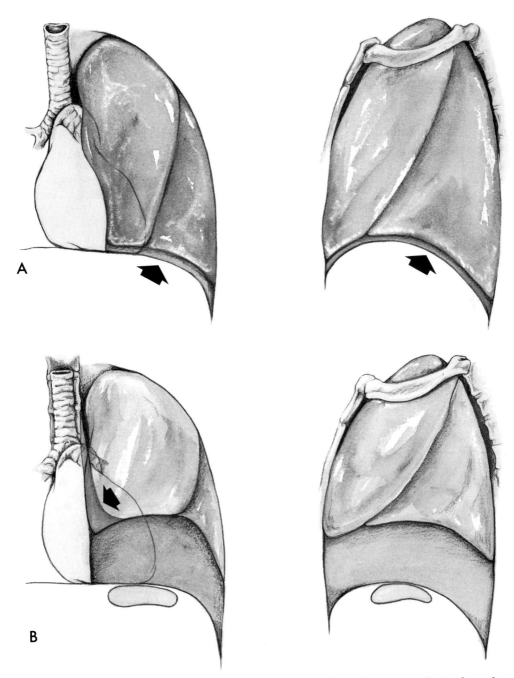

Figure 4–149. **Infrapulmonary Accumulation of Pleural Fluid.** In these drawings are depicted two degrees of infrapulmonary effusion: in *A*, the situation is "typical" in that it represents the *usual* anatomic location of small amounts of fluid (up to 500 ml); in *B*, the amount of fluid is large (*e.g.*, 1500 ml) and the local infrapulmonary accumulation thus "atypical." *See* text.

pleural sinus is deepest; with increasing amount, the fluid spills out into the costophrenic sinuses posteriorly, laterally, and, eventually, anteriorly; with further accumulation, it spreads upward in mantle-like fashion around the convexity of the lung, tapering gradually as it assumes a higher position in the thorax. As the thickness of the fluid layer becomes less superiorly, the influence of *capillary attraction* between pleural surfaces comes into force, this constituting the third force affecting the characteristic arrangement of free pleural fluid.

On the basis of this description, the typical roentgenographic appearance of pleural effusion is not difficult to construct. Consider the hypothetical situation of a "moderate" pleural effusion (1000 ml) (Figure 4-150): such an amount of fluid will completely obscure the hemidiaphragm and the costophrenic sinuses and will extend upward around the anterior, lateral and posterior thoracic wall, to about the midportion of the hemithorax. Since the mediastinal surface of the lung possesses relatively less elastic recoil, due to its fixation at the hilum and pulmonary ligament, less fluid accumulates along this surface than around the convexity. Thus, in posteroanterior projection, the density of the fluid will be high laterally and will curve gently downward and medially, with a smooth meniscus-shaped upper border, to terminate along the mid-cardiac border. In lateral projection, since the fluid has ascended along the anterior and posterior thoracic wall to roughly an equal extent, the upper surface of the fluid density will be semicircular, being high anteriorly and posteriorly and curving smoothly downward to its lowest point in the mid-axillary line. Comparison of the maximal height of the fluid density in the posteroanterior and lateral projections will show that this height is identical posteriorly, laterally, and anteriorly (Figure 4-150); the meniscus shape is caused by the fact that the layer of fluid is of insufficient depth to cast a discernible shadow when viewed *en face*. This typical configuration was excellently reproduced roentgenographically by Fleischner,[792] who constructed paraffin-wax models in the shape of half a hollow truncated cone. An ingenious experiment with a plexiglass phantom designed by Khomiakov and Fedorova[793] accomplished

identical roentgenographic results, as did the studies of Davis and his colleagues with plaster;[1686] the interested reader is directed to these three articles for lucid illustrations of the roentgenographic appearance of pleural effusion.

Since the distribution of fluid within the free pleural space tends to obey the law of gravity, and since the lung tends to maintain its shape when compressed, the first place fluid accumulates in the erect patient is between the inferior surface of the lower lobe and the diaphragm: in effect, the lung is "floating" on a layer of fluid (Figure 4-149). If the amount of fluid is small it may occupy this position solely without spilling over into the costophrenic sinuses, even the most dependent sinus posteriorly (Figure 4-151). In such circumstances the configuration of the hemidiaphragm is maintained and the appearance on posteroanterior and lateral roentgenograms suggests no more than a slight elevation of that hemidiaphragm. Bearing in mind that there is individual variation in the height of the diaphragm in normal subjects, it is readily apparent that small accumulations of fluid in the pleural space can be easily missed roentgenologically. It is only if the physician possesses a high index of suspicion of the possibility of a small pleural effusion that the diagnosis may be confirmed by roentgenography in the lateral decubitus position with a horizontal x-ray beam (or preferably, the "inclined" side position of Müller and Löfstedt[785]). Thus, as Hessén[786] emphasized, "infrapulmonary" localization is the *usual* mode of distribution in the free pleural space, not atypical (although the accumulation of large amounts of fluid in an infrapulmonary location may be reasonably considered paradoxical or atypical; this subject is dealt with in the section on atypical arrangement of pleural fluid).

When the amount of fluid in the infrapulmonary pleural spaces reaches a "critical" level, it spills over into the posterior costophrenic sinus and obliterates that sinus as viewed in lateral roentgenographic projection. The normally sharp costophrenic angle is obliterated by a shallow homogeneous shadow whose upper surface is meniscus-shaped. Due to pleural capillarity, the shadow inevitably is associated with increase in the width of the

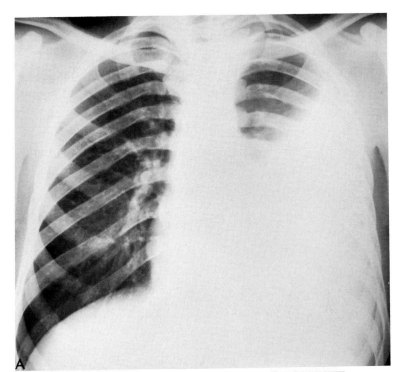

Figure 4–150. **Large Pleural Effusion: Typical Arrangement.** Posteroanterior (*A*) and lateral (*B*) roentgenograms exposed in the erect position demonstrate uniform opacification of the lower two thirds of the left hemithorax. The upper level of the fluid is meniscus-shaped in both PA and lateral projection (*arrows on B*). Note that only the right hemidiaphragm is visualized in lateral projection, the left being obscured by fluid (the silhouette sign).

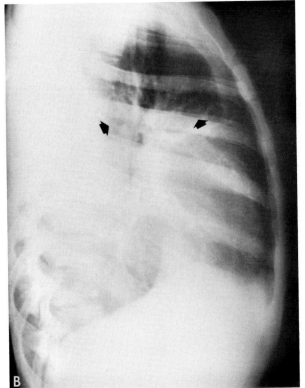

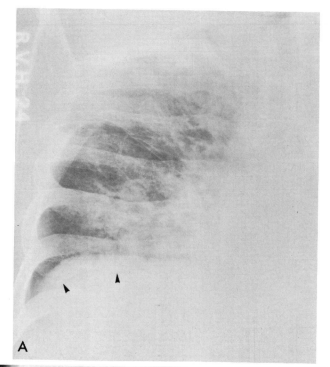

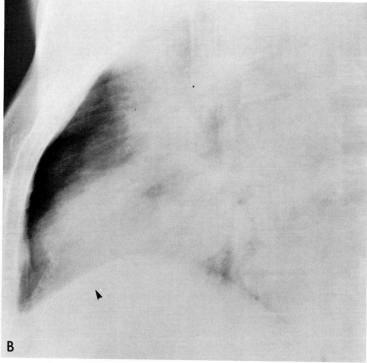

Figure 4–151. **Infrapulmonary Pleural Effusion Associated with Pneumoperitoneum.** Views of the right hemithorax from postero-anterior (*A*) and lateral (*B*) roentgenograms (exposed in the erect position post mortem) demonstrate a thin line of air density (*arrows*) situated approximately 1 cm below the base of the right lung, roughly parallel to the right hemidiaphragm. Since this gas is situated within the peritoneal space, it outlines the undersurface of the right hemidiaphragm, indicating the presence of a layer of fluid approximately 1 cm in thickness between the diaphragm and the undersurface of the right lung. By multiplying the anteroposterior and lateral dimensions of the right hemidiaphragm by the thickness of fluid (1 cm), it was estimated that the amount of fluid in the pleural space was approximately 400 ml. At necropsy, the right pleural space was found to contain 450 ml. This study demonstrates the large quantity of fluid which may accumulate in an infrapulmonary location without producing convincing roentgenologic evidence of its presence.

pleural line extending up the posterior thoracic wall: this represents the earliest roentgenologic manifestation of the typical mantle distribution. It is emphasized that such a roentgen appearance—pseudodia-

phragmatic elevation due to infrapulmonary localization, with or without obliteration of the posterior costophrenic sulcus—may be present without other discernible evidence of pleural effusion; for example, a posteroanterior roentgenogram may reveal a normally sharp lateral costophrenic angle. Since the evidence supplied by blunting of the posterior costophrenic sinus may be subtle, the need for lateral roentgenograms of excellent technical quality is obvious.

With increasing amounts of fluid, the roentgenologic signs develop in predictable fashion—obliteration of the lateral and eventually anterior costophrenic sulci, and extension of fluid up the chest wall in its usual mantle distribution.

Occasionally, the only roentgenologic evidence of pleural effusion is a slight general thickening of the interlobar pleural septa. Interlobar fissures which may appear perfectly normal on one examination may show a slight but definite increase in width on a subsequent examination, still without any other evidence of free effusion (see Figure 1-43, page 61). This change, occasionally referred to as "wet pleura," usually is a manifestation of congestive heart failure rather than a direct effect on the pleura by infection or neoplasm, for example.

The effects on the thorax as a whole of the accumulation of large amounts of fluid in the pleural space depend largely upon the condition of the ipsilateral lung. Even small amounts of fluid produce "compression" atelectasis of contiguous lung, in much the same manner as when air is the buffer medium in pneumothorax. When pleural effusion is massive, collapse of the ipsilateral lung may be almost complete. Despite the presence of severe compression atelectasis, however, the overall effect of a massive effusion almost invariably is that of a space-occupying process, with enlargement of the ipsilateral hemithorax, displacement of the mediastinum to the contralateral side, and severe depression and flattening of the ipsilateral hemidiaphragm; in fact, the hemidiaphragm may be depressed so severely as to be concave superiorly (Figure 4-152).[794] When one hemithorax is totally opacified, appreciation of the balance of forces between the two sides of the thorax is of obvious importance: If the mediastinum shows no shift and the hemidiaphragm is but little depressed, the presence of disease within the ipsilateral lung may be stated with absolute certainty (Figure 4-153); the conclusion that *must* be reached is that the balance of forces between effusion (a space-occupying process) and parenchymal disease (which reduces volume) ensures that the volume of the hemithorax is not greater than normal. The possibility that an obstructing endobronchial lesion (*e.g.*, bronchogenic carcinoma with pleural metastases) is present is obvious: in fact, total opacification of one hemithorax without mediastinal or diaphragmatic displacement is highly suggestive of bronchogenic cancer with pleural metastases. (Exceptions are uncommon—for example, extensive mesothelioma.)

Atypical Arrangement of Free Pleural Fluid

The typical arrangement of fluid in the free pleural space requires that the underlying lung be free of disease and thus capable of preserving its shape even while recoiling from the chest wall—that is, it maintains its "form elasticity." An alteration in this uniform recoiling tendency is the influence by which most if not all atypical arrangements of pleural fluid may be explained. It has been suggested[786, 792] that the presence of parenchymal disease in any portion of the lung and of any type—consolidation, atelectasis, fibrosis—modifies the retractility of that portion of the lung locally so that pleural fluid is attracted to it. An alternative explanation proposed by Setnikar and Agostoni[1687] is that when the retraction force of the lung is not uniform, fluid is attracted to those areas of the thorax where the retraction force is greatest; since elastic recoil decreases with reduction in lung volume, the retraction force in the region of lobar or segmental collapse will be *less* than in areas where lung tissue is normal. In such circumstances, the upper border of a pleural effusion will be *higher* where the attraction force is greatest and *lower* where elastic recoil is least (that is, in the region of parenchymal disease).

Although the mechanism whereby this local attraction occurs is not known precisely, there is little doubt that it is related in the majority of cases to underlying pulmonary disease. Thus, the major roentgenologic significance of atypical pleural effusion is that it *alerts the physician to the presence of parenchymal as well as pleural disease.*

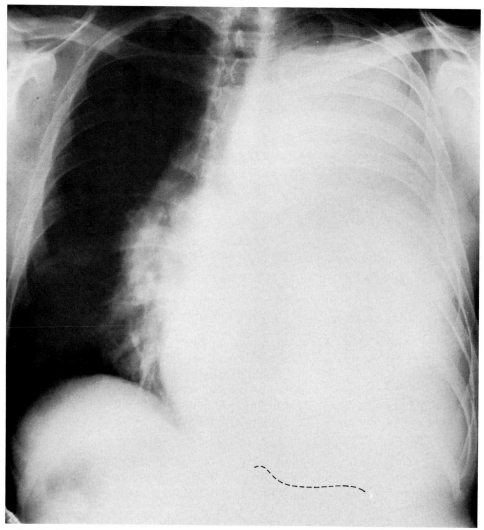

Figure 4–152. **Massive Effusion, Underlying Lung Normal.** A posteroanterior roentgenogram reveals total opacification of the left hemithorax by a massive pleural effusion. The mediastinum is displaced to the right. The stomach bubble (*dotted line*) is displaced far inferiorly and its upper surface is concave rather than convex, suggesting that the hemidiaphragm possesses the same contour. A faint air bronchogram can be visualized through the fluid in the medial portion of the left lung; the underlying lung was normal. Pleural metastases from carcinoma of the maxillary antrum.

The roentgenographic appearance of atypical pleural-fluid accumulation in disease affecting individual lobes has been described in detail.[786, 792] Two examples will illustrate the variations produced. In *lower-lobe disease*, fluid tends to accumulate posteromedially; in posteroanterior projection, the density tends to be higher on the mediastinal than on the axillary border, its upper surface curving downward and laterally toward the lateral costophrenic sulcus (simulating the shadow of combined atelectasis and consolidation of the right middle and lower lobes); in lateral projection, the upper border of the density roughly parallels the major fissure, beginning high in the thorax posteriorly and curving downward and anteriorly, toward the anterior costophrenic gutter (which may be clear and sharp) (Figure 4–154). We have seen one patient in whom lower lobe parenchymal consolidation was associated with an effusion whose upper level was disproportionately high in the axilla and the meniscus unusually low (Figure 4–155)—a distribution which co-

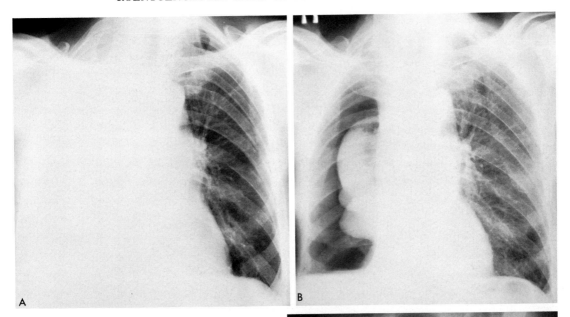

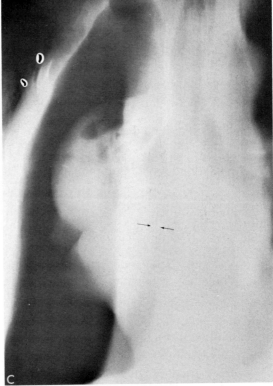

Figure 4–153. **Massive Pleural Effusion Associated with Obstructive Atelectasis of the Underlying Lung.** A posteroanterior roentgenogram (*A*) shows total opacification of the right hemithorax; in contrast to the situation in Figure 4–152, the mediastinum is central in position. Following removal of almost all the fluid and replacement with an equal quantity of air (without air replacement, the patient became severely dyspneic), the right lung (*B*) can be seen to be totally collapsed and airless (with the exception of small quantities of air in the upper lobe); the configuration of the collapsed lung resembles the profile of a face whose nose is the right middle lobe and chin the right lower lobe. In such a situation, the absence of an air bronchogram constitutes absolute evidence of endobronchial obstruction. An anteroposterior tomogram (*C*) confirms the airlessness of the right middle and lower lobes and reveals the intermediate-stem bronchus to be obstructed at its distal end (*arrows*). At thoracotomy, stenosis of the intermediate-stem bronchus was found to be due to compression by enlarged lymph nodes replaced by adenocarcinoma.

incides with the postulate of Setnikar and Agostoni.[1687] In some patients with disease of the *right middle lobe,* a posteroanterior roentgenogram reveals disruption of the typical smooth contour of pleural fluid along the lateral chest wall at the level of the horizontal fissure (Figure 4–156); at this point, the thickness of the fluid layer increases abruptly and appears as a density whose upper margin is sharply defined, coinciding with the precise location and configuration of the horizontal fissure (picturesquely described by Fleischner[792] as the "middle-lobe step"). Although we have seen this "middle-lobe step" a number of times, we have never been able to

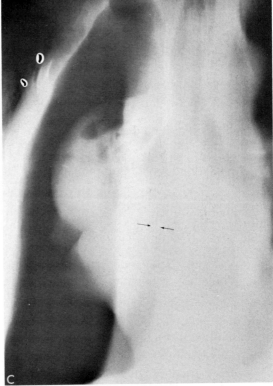

(Text continues on page 357.)

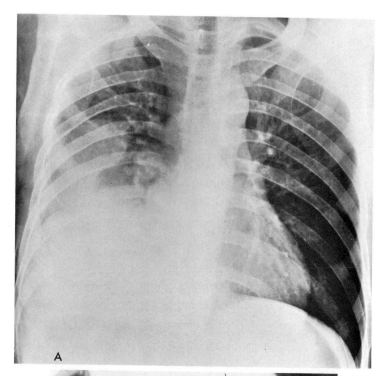

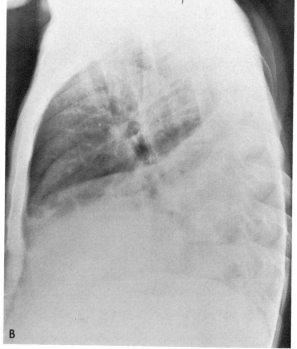

Figure 4–154. **Right Pleural Effusion, Atypical Accumulation.** A moderate-sized right pleural effusion identified on postero-anterior (*A*) and lateral (*B*) roentgenograms does not possess the typical meniscus-shaped upper border in either projection; it is high posteriorly and low anteriorly so as to simulate consolidation of the middle and lower lobes (particularly as visualized in lateral projection). Right lower lobe pneumonia with effusion.

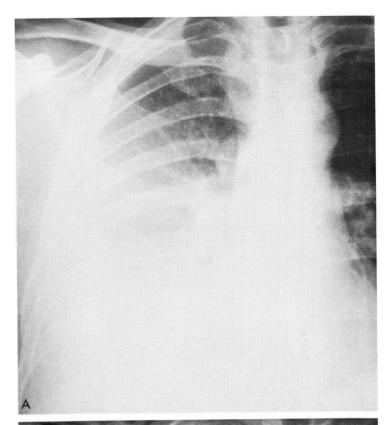

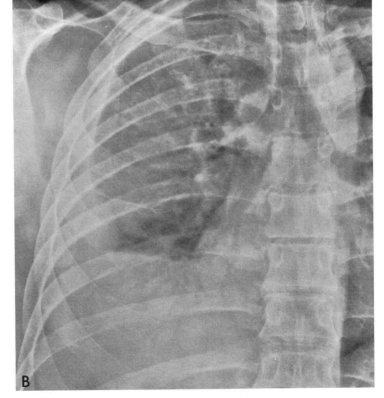

Figure 4–155. **Atypical Accumulation of Pleural Fluid.** A view of the right hemithorax from a postero-anterior roentgenogram (A) reveals a right pleural effusion whose upper border lacks the typical meniscus-shaped contour. Accumulation along the axilla is much higher than is usually the case and the pleural border descends abruptly to the diaphragm. With heavier exposure (B), the configuration of the fluid is seen to better advantage; in addition, a well-defined air bronchogram can be identified in the distribution of the basal segments of the right lower lobe. Acute air-space pneumonia of the right lower lobe with pleural effusion.

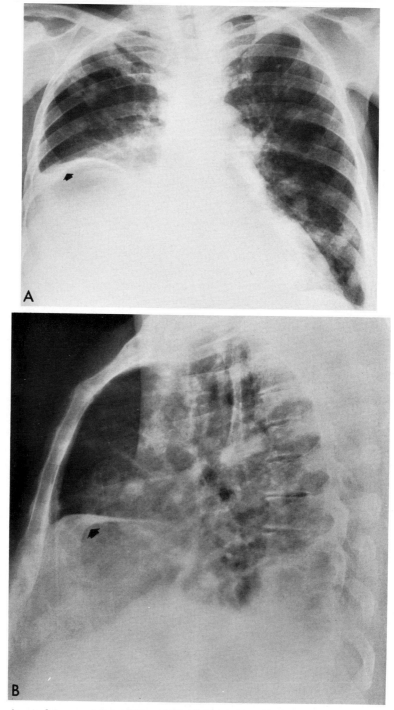

Figure 4–156.   **Atypical Accumulation of Pleural Fluid: The "Right Middle-lobe Step."** Posteroanterior (*A*) and lateral (*B*) roentgenograms exposed in the erect position show a right pleural effusion whose upper border lacks the typical meniscus-shaped contour. The fluid appears to ascend along the lateral and anterior chest wall to the region of the horizontal fissure into which it extends in considerable amount (*arrows*). The reasons underlying this unusual accumulation are not clear. Multiple nodules are present throughout both lungs; both the nodules and the effusion are the result of metastases from carcinoma of the breast.

prove convincingly that there was selective middle-lobe disease.

Since roentgenography in other than the erect position will detect any change in distribution of *free* pleural fluid, examination in the supine or, preferably, lateral decubitus position will show displacement of the fluid over the posterior or lateral pleural space, respectively. In this way, the nature of these unusual densities may be clarified in questionable cases (*e.g.*, an effusion simulating lower-lobe consolidation). In addition, these procedures permit clearer visualization and more accurate assessment of the underlying parenchymal disease.

Some physicians hold the notion that the removal of fluid by thoracentesis in cases of combined parenchymal and pleural disease permits better visualization of the diseased lung underlying the pleural effusion. In fact, this procedure is seldom productive from a roentgenologic point of view (although obviously advantageous in providing fluid for pathologic and biochemical examination). The reasons for this lack should be obvious in the light of the foregoing discussions: since atelectasis usually is present, the removal of fluid accentuates the forces which are trying to compensate for the parenchymal collapse; thus the mediastinum and diaphragm are shifted further toward the affected side, so that fluid remaining in the pleural space will still accumulate around and obscure the underlying diseased parenchyma. Thus, supine and lateral decubitus roentgenography is clearly superior for the assessment of underlying parenchymal disease.

There is disagreement as to whether *infrapulmonary pleural effusion* (*synonyms*: subpulmonary, diaphragmatic) should be considered atypical, since, as already discussed, this is the site where effusion first accumulates "normally." Usually, increasing amounts of fluid spill over into the costophrenic sulci and produce the roentgenologic signs already described. However, for reasons as yet incompletely understood, sometimes fluid continues to accumulate in an infrapulmonary location without spilling into the costophrenic sulci or extending up the chest wall, producing a roentgenographic configuration in the erect subject which closely simulates diaphragmatic elevation (thus the designation "pseudodiaphragmatic contour") (Figure 4–149). Infrapulmonary pleural effusion occurs in such multifarious conditions of varied etiology (inflammatory, cardiovascular, traumatic, neoplastic, and renal[786, 792, 795–797]) that it is difficult to cite a specific pathogenetic mechanism. Similarly, the nature and specific gravity of the fluid seem to possess no real significance, since the effusion may be either an exudate or a transudate. "Encapsulation" secondary to fibrous pleural adhesions plays no part in the pathogenesis, since appropriate positioning of the patient invariably shows the fluid spread over the free pleural space. Perhaps the explanation offered by Fleischner[792] comes closest to explaining the phenomenon on a logical basis, although his theory may not apply in all cases. He proposed that infrapulmonary effusion develops in precisely the same manner as atypical accumulation of fluid elsewhere in the pleural space—as a result of local changes in contiguous lung which modify its recoil tendency. Fleischner's theory was supported recently by a report of three cases of pneumothorax in which the gas seemed to localize in the infrapulmonary area;[798] in all three patients, local parenchymal disease ("infection and atelectasis") was said to be present in the lower lobes.

Some roentgenologic characteristics are common to most cases of infrapulmonary effusion[786, 792, 796–800] and any combination of these warrants further confirmatory roentgenographic study in supine or lateral decubitus position. All of these signs refer to changes observed on posteroanterior and lateral roentgenograms of the erect patient.

1. Infrapulmonary accumulation may be unilateral or bilateral; when unilateral, it occurs more commonly on the right.[796]

2. In posteroanterior projection (Figure 4–157) the peak of the pseudodiaphragmatic configuration is lateral to that of the normal hemidiaphragm, being situated near the junction of the middle and lateral thirds rather than near the center, and slopes down sharply toward the lateral costophrenic recess.

3. On the left side, the pseudodiaphragmatic contour is separated further than normal from the gastric air bubble (Figure 4–157); the diaphragm and the bubble nor-

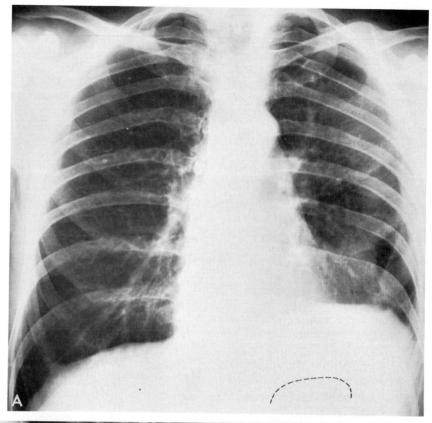

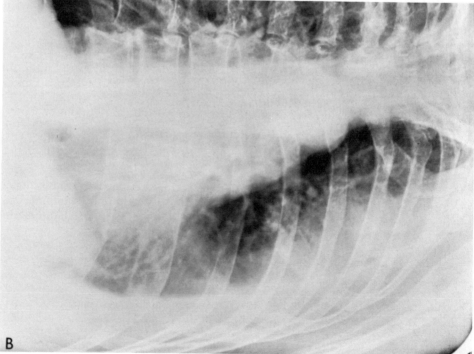

Figure 4–157.   **Infrapulmonary Pleural Effusion.** A posteroanterior roentgenogram exposed in the erect position (A) shows a high left pseudo-diaphragm whose peak is more laterally situated than that of a normal hemidiaphragm. It is situated several centimeters from the stomach bubble (*dotted line*). The costophrenic sulcus is sharp. A roentgenogram exposed in the left lateral decubitus position with a horizontal x-ray beam (B) shows the fluid to have extended along the axillary lung zone.

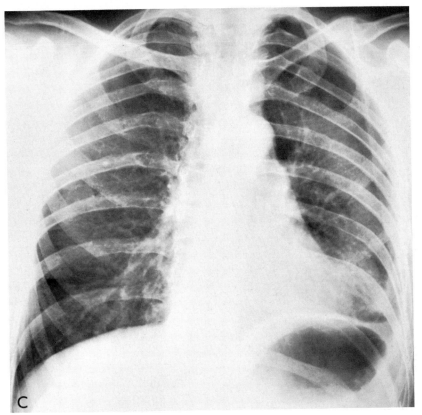

Figure 4-157. *Continued.* Following removal of approximately 1000 ml of fluid, a posteroanterior roentgenogram in the erect position (C) shows normal apposition of the gastric air bubble to the left hemidiaphragm.

mally are in contact, although care is needed to detect cases in which the spleen or the left lobe of the liver is interposed.

4. Both the lateral and the posterior costophrenic sulci may be sharp and clear (Figure 4-158), although not uncommonly the posterior gutter appears blunted because fluid has spilled over into it. (Petersen[796] states that the posterior gutter is obliterated *without exception.*) The anterior costophrenic gutter is invariably clear.

5. In lateral projection (Figure 4-158), a characteristic configuration is frequently seen anteriorly where the convex upper margin of the fluid meets the major fissure. The contour anterior to the fissure often is flattened, this segment descending abruptly to the costophrenic angle. A small amount of fluid usually is apparent in the lower end of the chief fissure at its junction with the infrapulmonary collection.

6. In posteroanterior projection, a thin triangular density may be observed in the left paramediastinal zone, with its apex approximately half-way up the mediastinum and its base contiguous to the pseudodiaphragmatic contour inferiorly (Figure 4-159). This shadow represents mediastinal extension of the infrapulmonary fluid collection and was observed in eight of 39 patients in one study;[795] since it is posterior in position, it obliterates (or widens) the left paravertebral pleural line.[801]

7. *Fluoroscopic examination* usually reveals no impairment of diaphragmatic excursion during respiration. The pseudodiaphragmatic contour may pulsate synchronously with cardiac pulsation, fluid waves being propagated from the heart toward the lateral chest wall; Fleischner[792] demonstrated this phenomenon electrokymographically.

Finally, both fluoroscopy and roentgenography in frontal projection with the patient tilted to one side usually show the infrapulmonary fluid spilling over into the lateral costophrenic sulcus. This maneuver, originally described by Hessen,[786] is

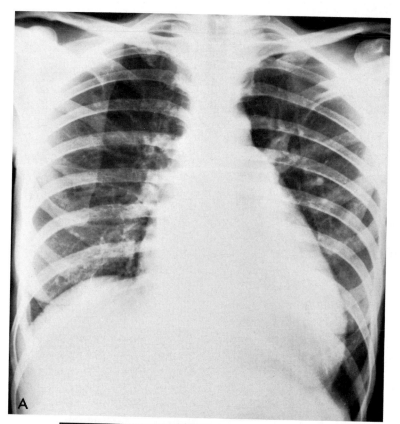

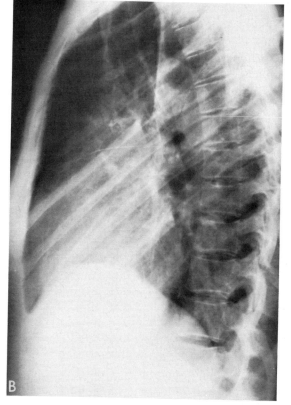

Figure 4-158. **Infrapulmonary Pleural Effusion.** Postero-anterior (*A*) and lateral (*B*) roentgenograms show what appears to be a high right hemidiaphragm; both the lateral and posterior costophrenic sulci are sharp although minimal thickening of the pleural line immediately above the lateral sulcus suggests that the shadow may be due to an infrapulmonary effusion. This suspicion is heightened by the characteristic configuration of the shadow in lateral projection: its anterior portion ascends abruptly and in almost a straight line to the region of the chief fissure; a "dome" configuration is present posterior to this point. The major fissure is slightly thickened by fluid.

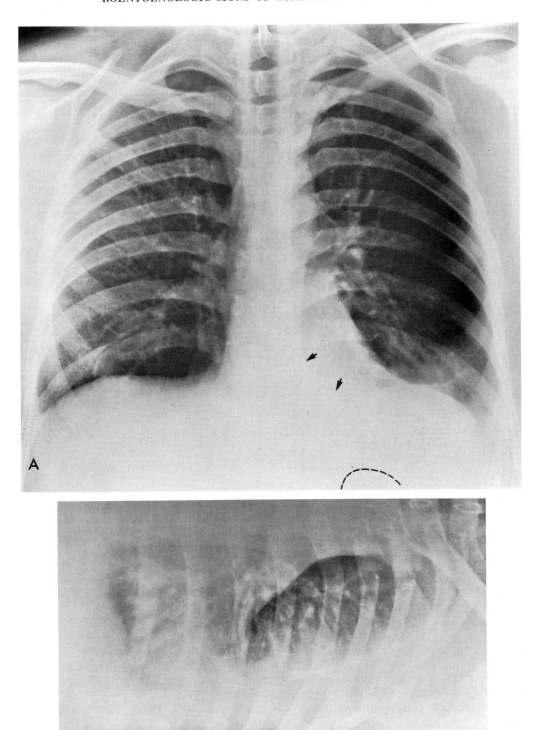

Figure 4–159. **Bilateral Infrapulmonary Pleural Effusion.** In posteroanterior projection (A), the "hemi-diaphragms" are at the same level. This roentgenogram conceivably could be interpreted as normal except for three changes which suggest that there is bilateral infrapulmonary effusion: (1) the cardiac shadow is too short, suggesting that its lower portion may be enveloped by fluid; (2) the stomach bubble (*dotted line*) is situated several centimeters from the left "hemidiaphragm"; (3) a triangular shadow of homogeneous density can be identified in the posterior costovertebral angle (*arrows*), suggesting upward extension of fluid along the posterior mediastinal septum. Confirmation of bilateral infrapulmonary effusion was obtained by roentgenography in the lateral decubitus position with a horizontal x-ray beam (the left side is illustrated in *B*).

confirmatory when other roentgenographic findings are inconclusive. In any event, lateral decubitus roentgenography with a horizontal beam should be performed in all cases (Figures 4–157 and 4–159), both to confirm the diagnosis and to permit assessment of the quantity of fluid more accurately than is possible with the patient erect.

Loculation of Pleural Fluid

Loculated or encysted pleural effusions may occur anywhere in the pleural space, either between parietal and visceral pleura over the periphery of the lung or between visceral layers in the interlobar septa. Encapsulation is caused by the presence of adhesions between contiguous pleural surfaces and, therefore, tends to occur during or following episodes of pleuritis – often pyothorax or hemothorax. Over the convexity of the thorax the loculated effusion appears as a smooth sharply demarcated, homogeneous density protruding into the hemithorax and compressing contiguous lung (Figure 4–160). Fluoroscopic examination with subsequent roentgenography in tangential projection helps to establish their precise location for subsequent diagnostic or therapeutic thoracentesis. Mediastinal encysted effusions are uncommon in our experience; they may be situated anteriorly or posteriorly in various locations.[120]

Interlobar encysted effusions are typically elliptical when viewed tangentially, and their extremities blend imperceptibly with the interlobar fissure. In some conditions, particularly congestive heart failure, the effusion may simulate a mass roentgenographically and be misdiagnosed as a bronchogenic neoplasm (Figure 4–161);[802, 803] however, their distinctive configuration in either posteroanterior or lateral projection should establish the diagnosis. These fluid accumulations tend to absorb spontaneously when the heart failure is relieved and, therefore, have acquired the designation "vanishing tumor" (synonyms: "phantom tumor," "pseudo-tumor").[804] In one series[804] the effusion was localized to the right horizontal fissure in 78 per cent of the 41 cases.

It is sometimes difficult to differentiate encapsulated fluid in the lower half of the major fissure from atelectasis or combined atelectasis and consolidation of the right middle lobe. Three points should be borne in mind in this differentiation. (1) Should the minor fissure be visible as a separate shadow, the diagnosis of encapsulated fluid becomes certain. (2) Encapsulated fluid tends not to obscure the right heart border, whereas middle-lobe atelectasis almost invariably does (silhouette sign). (3) In lateral projection, encysted effusion usually is shown to have a bulging surface on one or both sides, but when the right middle lobe is diseased the borders of the shadow tend to be straight or slightly concave.

ROENTGENOLOGIC SIGNS OF PLEURAL THICKENING AND CALCIFICATION

Pleural Thickening

Thickening of the pleural line over the convexity of the thorax and occasionally in the interlobar fissures occurs fairly commonly and is familiar to all roentgenologists. Although Felson identified it in only 1.2 per cent of 500 army recruits,[69] undoubtedly it is present in a higher percentage of general hospital populations. The thickness of the pleural line may increase to 1 to 10 mm, generally after an episode of pleuritis and almost exclusively as a result of thickening of the visceral pleural surface. Severe degrees of thickening may markedly restrict pulmonary expansion, in which case surgical removal by "peeling" may be curative. Although sometimes local, pleural thickening more often is uniform over the whole lung surface, presenting as a thin line of unit density separating the air-containing lung from contiguous ribs (Figure 4–162). The costophrenic recesses often are partly or completely obliterated, particularly laterally, and roentgenography in lateral decubitus position may be necessary to differentiate such old fibrous thickening from a small pleural effusion; in cases of pleural thickening, however, the blunted costophrenic angle usually is sharply angulated rather than meniscus-shaped, and often the two can be distinguished on this evidence alone.

Although thickening of the apical pleura in the form of a "pleural cap" frequently is seen roentgenologically its etiology is ob-

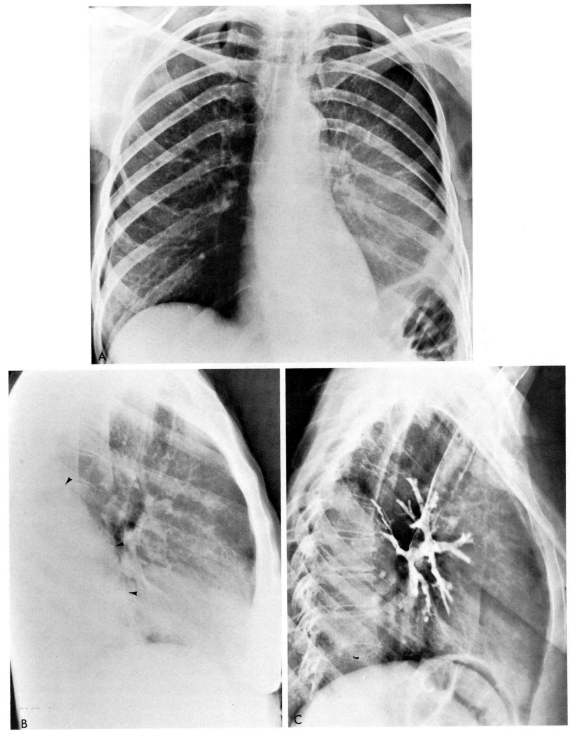

Figure 4–160. **Loculated Empyema.** Posteroanterior (A) and lateral (B) roentgenograms reveal a sharply demarcated, homogeneous opacity in the posterior portion of the left hemithorax possessing a border in lateral projection which is concave posteriorly (*arrows*); the shadow conforms to no segmental distribution. A lateral roentgenogram following bronchography (C) shows displacement by the mass of the basal bronchi of the lower lobe, suggesting an extrapulmonary origin. Loculated empyema following thoracoabdominal resection of the esophagus for carcinoma; *Aerobacter aerogenes* in pure culture.

scure (Figure 4–163); it is usually attributed to prior tuberculosis. Care should be taken not to confuse this shadow with the companion shadows of the first and second ribs (*see* Figure 1–61, page 84), nor to fail to recognize that what appears to be apical pleural thickening may be an early manifestation of a more serious condition—apical pulmonary cancer, or Pancoast tumor.

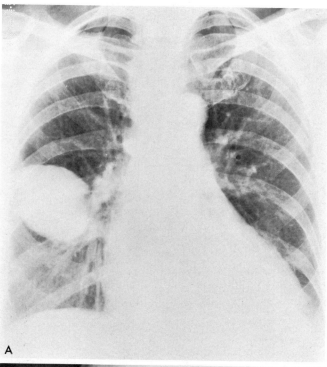

A

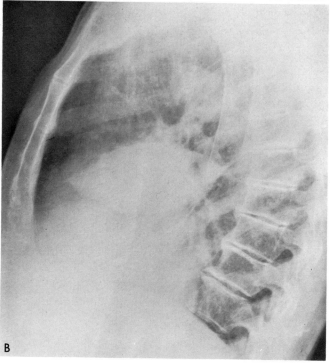

B

Figure 4–161. **Loculated Effusion in the Minor Fissure.** A posteroanterior roentgenogram (A) reveals a sharply circumscribed shadow of homogeneous density in the right mid-lung zone. In lateral projection (B), the true nature of the shadow can be appreciated: the mass is elliptical in shape, its pointed extremities being situated anteriorly and posteriorly in keeping with the position of minor fissure. This loculated effusion developed during a recent episode of cardiac decompensation; it disappeared completely within three weeks.

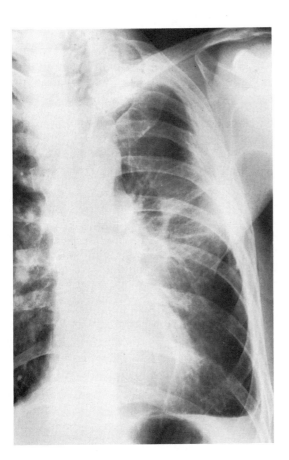

Figure 4–162. **Pleural Thickening.** A view of the left hemithorax from a posteroanterior roentgenogram reveals generalized thickening of the pleural line around the axillary border of the left lung. The left costophrenic sulcus is obliterated. The volume of the lung is reduced as evidenced by shift of the mediastinum to the left. Remote hemothorax.

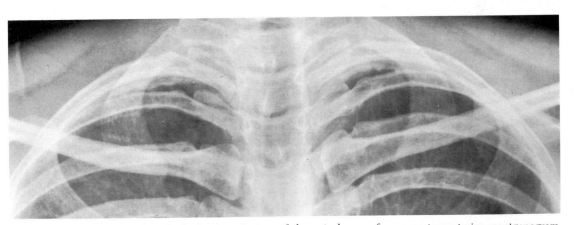

Figure 4–163. **Apical Pleural Thickening.** A view of the apical zones from a posteroanterior roentgenogram reveals irregular symmetrical thickening of the apical pleura. The irregularity serves to differentiate this thickening from companion shadows of the ribs.

Pleural Calcification

This is most often the result of a remote hemothorax, pyothorax, or tuberculous effusion and is commonly associated with thickening of the pleura over the whole surface of the lung. The calcification may be in the form of a broad continuous sheet (Figure 4–164) or as multiple discrete plaques, and usually extends from about the level of the mid-thorax posteriorly, around the lateral lung margin in a generally inferior direction, in roughly the same line as the chief fissure (Figure 4–165). The calcium usually is deposited on the inner surface of the thickened visceral pleura, resulting in a thick layer of tissue of unit density interposed between the calcium and the thoracic wall (Figure 4–164). In contrast to the next described form of pleural calcification, that secondary to em-

pyema or hemothorax is nearly always unilateral.

Pleural calcification of an entirely different form is now recognized to be a frequent occurrence in silicatosis[805, 806] (including asbestosis and talcosis). Working in central Finland, Kiviluoto[807] found 126 cases of pleural thickening of unusual type in 39,000 chest roentgenograms. Although none of these patients had a history of occupational exposure to dust, all but eight did live or had lived in an area close to two open anthophyllite-asbestos mines. Similarly, in 59 of 166 cases (35 per cent) of uncomplicated asbestosis studied by Oosthuizen and Theron in South Africa,[596] roentgenography showed calcific pleural plaques without detectable changes in the lungs. The roentgenologic characteristics of calcification in silicatosis are sufficiently different from that secondary to empyema

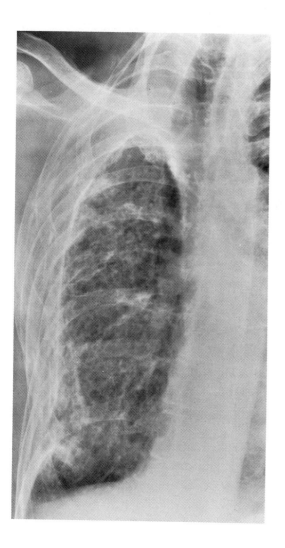

Figure 4–164. **Pleural Thickening and Calcification.** A view of the right hemithorax from a postero-anterior roentgenogram reveals extensive thickening of the pleura over the convexity of the right lung, of greatest degree at the apex and tapering off toward the base. A continuous sheet of calcium can be identified on its inner aspect. Moderate loss of volume is evidenced by shift of the trachea. These changes are the result of a remote hemothorax in a patient with pulmonary histiocytosis-X.

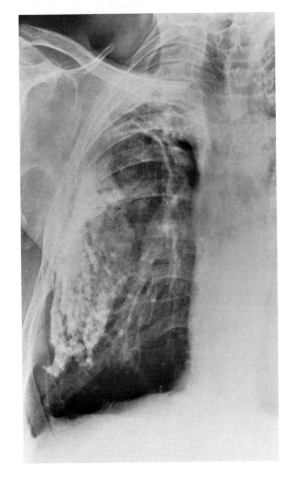

Figure 4-165. **Pleural Calcification.** A view of the right hemithorax from a posteroanterior roentgenogram reveals a heavy, broad sheet of calcium situated over the convexity of the lung and oriented in a position roughly corresponding to the axillary line of the chief fissure. There is considerable loss of volume of the right upper lobe as evidenced by elevation of the right hilum and displacement of the trachea. Old fibrotic upper lobe tuberculosis; the pleural calcification resulted from tuberculous empyema.

or hemothorax that no difficulty should arise in differentiation (Figure 4-166). The calcification usually forms in plaques, is commonly diaphragmatic in position, and sometimes is associated with extensive thickening of the pleura; it occurs invariably in the parietal pleura, in contrast to its situation in the visceral pleura when secondary to pyothorax or hemothorax. It is commonly bilateral but may be unilateral. The mediastinum may be involved, but calcification of the interlobar pleura has not been observed.[807] It is of interest that in Kiviluoto's series there was a very low incidence of pulmonary fibrosis and no cases of bronchogenic carcinoma. (Asbestosis is one of the few pneumoconioses in which the incidence of bronchogenic and pleural neoplasm is known to be increased.)

Kiviluoto[807] postulated that the mechanism of production of calcification in asbestosis consists in mechanical irritation of the parietal pleura: he suggests that, during respiration, protruding ends of

asbestos fibers implanted near the visceral pleura move against the parietal pleura and scratch it, resulting in small hemorrhages which subsequently calcify.

Pleural Neoplasms

These are discussed in detail in Chapter 16, and the present section is concerned only with two roentgenologic signs which may be of considerable value in distinguishing between diseases which arise in the lung and in the pleura. *Local mesothelial neoplasms* may arise from either the parietal or visceral pleural surface, over the convexity of the lung, or from an interlobar fissure. Neoplasms which arise from a fissure may simulate an intrapulmonary "coin" lesion or an encapsulated interlobar effusion; in either case, diagnostic pneumothorax should help to establish the true nature of the lesion (Figure 4-167). When they arise from the convexity of the

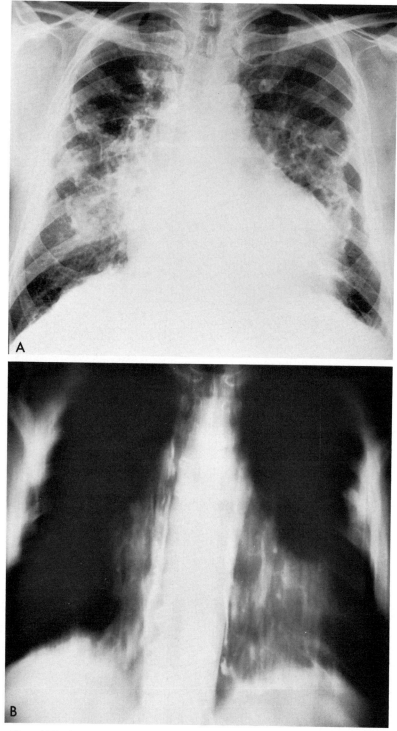

Figure 4–166.   **Pleural Thickening and Calcification in Silicatosis.** A posteroanterior roentgenogram (A) reveals multiple irregular plaques of calcium scattered in a random fashion over the lower two thirds of both lungs. The pleura is generally thickened over both lungs. The lungs are not grossly abnormal. An anteroposterior tomogram (B) shows extensive plaque formation over both hemidiaphragms and along the posterior mediastinal septum bilaterally. A 70-year-old man with a history of talc exposure; presumptive diagnosis—talcosis.

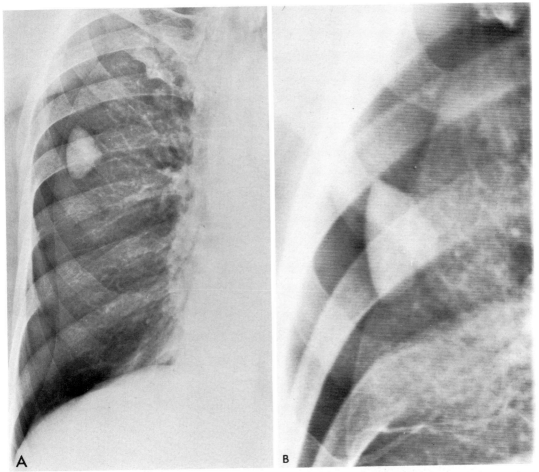

Figure 4–167. **Local Pleural Mesothelioma.** A view of the right hemithorax from a posteroanterior roentgeno-gram reveals a sharply circumscribed shadow of homogeneous density situated in the periphery of the right lung; diagnostic pneumothorax had been induced, but the roentgenographic appearance before this procedure was that of a peripheral nodule of undetermined type. Fluoroscopic examination showed the mass to be attached to the lung rather than to the parietal pleura; a spot film (B) in an oblique projection shows the mass to be extrapulmonary. Proved benign mesothelioma.

lung these solitary tumors may be either sessile or pedunculated,[314, 808] but in either event they almost invariably form an obtuse angle with the chest wall when viewed in profile. It is important to recognize this obtuse angle, since it distinguishes these lesions from those which arise within the lung parenchyma which tend to form an acute angle with the chest wall. Again, diagnostic pneumothorax yields confirmatory evidence. *Diffuse mesothelial neoplasms,* which usually are highly malignant, commonly are accompanied by pleural effusion. Even when the effusion is massive, however, there tends

to be little displacement of the mediastinum and diaphragm away from the involved hemithorax (Figure 4–168).[808] The reasons for this are not clear, except when neoplastic invasion of the mediastinal surface of the lung has caused bronchial occlusion and resulted in atelectasis. Regardless of mechanism, however, the lack of displacement is important to the roentgenologic diagnosis of this highly malignant lesion—although it should be borne in mind that a similar picture may be produced by primary bronchogenic carcinoma with obstructive atelectasis and metastatic pleural effusion.

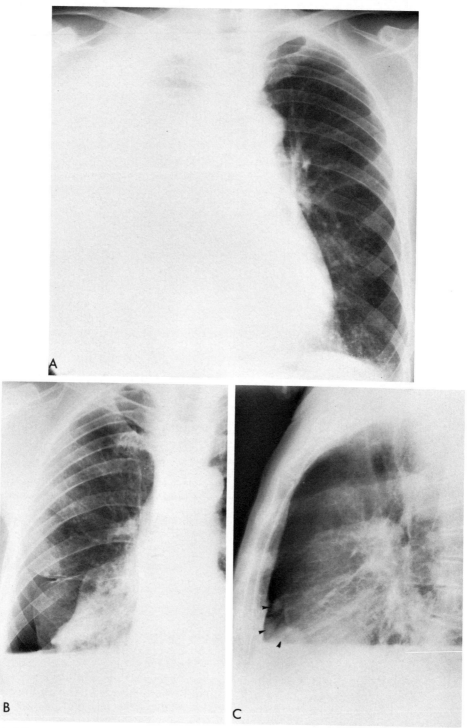

Figure 4–168.   **Diffuse Malignant Mesothelioma.** Despite the presence of a massive right pleural effusion on the posteroanterior roentgenogram (*A*), the mediastinum shows little if any displacement, suggesting the presence of an endobronchial obstructing lesion in the right lung. Following thoracentesis (*B*), the right upper lobe has almost completely reinflated and the right middle lobe partly, but the right lower lobe is almost completely collapsed. In lateral projection (*C*) three nodules of moderate size can be identified in the anteroinferior portion of the right hemithorax (*arrows*). At thoracotomy, these nodules proved to be masses of malignant mesothelioma; multiple nodules were scattered over the visceral and parietal pleura, and the right lung was generally "constricted" by tumor; there was invasion of the lung at the hilum of the right lower lobe with compression of the right lower-lobe bronchus—thus the roentgenographic effects observed.

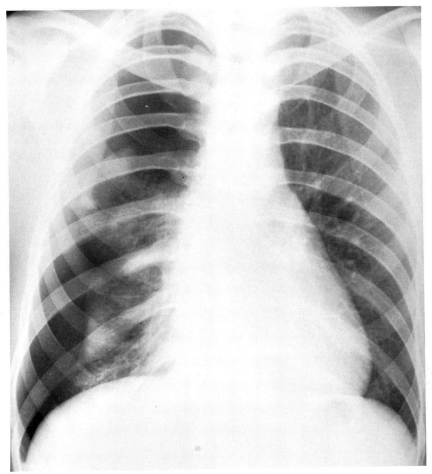

Figure 4–169. **Effect of Pneumothorax on Lung Density.** A posteroanterior roentgenogram reveals a moderate right pneumothorax; despite the fact that the right lung has been reduced in volume by approximately 50 per cent, its density (except in local areas) is little different from that of the left lung. *See* text.

ROENTGENOLOGIC SIGNS OF PNEUMOTHORAX

The discussion earlier in this section on the influence on the underlying lung of a buffer medium within the pleural space applies as well to pneumothorax as to hydrothorax. The only difference is in the manner by which gravity affects the media: air rises to the apex of the hemithorax and causes early collapse of the upper portion of the lung; fluid falls to the bottom of the hemithorax and compresses the lower lobe. When pneumothorax is present, the weight of the lung in its gaseous surroundings causes it to drop to its most dependent position, slung by its fixed attachment at the pulmonary ligament. For this reason, a large pneumothorax is necessary to produce complete collapse of the lung including its lower lobe. This fact is of practical importance when it is desired to clarify the nature of a process within the thorax situated contiguous to the diaphragm: it is necessary either to introduce a large amount of gas into the pleural space, or to employ the influence of gravity by positioning the patient head-down, to permit gas to pass into the infrapulmonary space.

A positive roentgenologic diagnosis of pneumothorax can only be made on identification of the visceral pleural line (*see* Figure 4–18, page 205). Since the lung is partly collapsed by the pneumothorax it might be anticipated that its density would be increased and that this altered density compared with that of the normal lung should be sufficient to suggest the diagnosis; in fact, this is not so. Dornhorst and Pierce[567] were the first to point out that, as the lung progressively collapses with increase in the size of the pneumothorax, blood flow through it diminishes; therefore the ratio of air and blood is not materially altered and the overall density of the collapsing lung is not changed (Figure 4–169). Undoubtedly the gas in

371

the pleural space anterior and posterior to the collapsed lung makes an important contribution to overall density, but, regardless of the mechanism involved, the empirical observation made by Dornhorst and Pierce is valid: roentgenographic density of a collapsing lung changes little until volume is greatly reduced.

Identification of the visceral pleural line usually is not difficult even on roentgenograms exposed at total lung capacity. When pneumothorax is strongly suspected clinically but a pleural line is not visualized (possibly obscured by an overlying rib), gas in the pleural space can be readily identified by either of two procedures. (1) Roentgenography in the erect position in full expiration (the rationale being that lung volume is reduced although the volume of gas in the pleural space is constant, thereby providing a smaller surface of visceral pleura in contact with air) (*see* Figure 2–5, page 110); the same maneuver may be used to reveal small amounts of pleural fluid. (2) Roentgenography in the

lateral decubitus position with a horizontal x-ray beam; the rationale here is obvious—air rises to the highest point in the hemithorax and is more clearly visible over the lateral chest wall than over the apex, where confluence of overlying bony shadows may obscure fine linear shadows.

Sometimes a small pneumothorax may resemble an apical bleb or bulla, particularly when the pneumothorax is encapsulated. When the air in the pleural space is free, distinction usually is possible by roentgenography in the lateral decubitus position. However, small fibrous strands across the air-shadow of an encapsulated pneumothorax may render differentiation impossible (Figure 4–170). Small pleural blebs, which undoubtedly are the most common cause of spontaneous pneumothorax, may be more easily identified by tomography, especially when the lung is partially collapsed; in such circumstances the blebs tend to undergo less collapse than the normal surrounding parenchyma. Fibrous adhesions between the visceral and

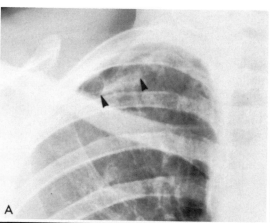
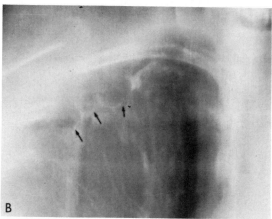
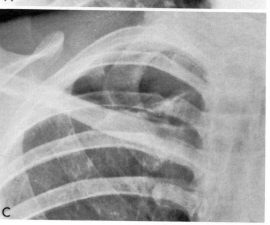

Figure 4–170. **Combined Apical Blebs and Pneumothorax.** A view of the apical portion of the right hemithorax from a posteroanterior roentgenogram (*A*) reveals at least two well-defined blebs measuring approximately 1 cm in diameter (*arrows*). It is difficult to be certain whether or not a pneumothorax is present. A tomographic section (*B*) shows at least three blebs (*arrows*), apparently separated from the parietal pleura by a small pneumothorax. In such circumstances, the presence or absence of pneumothorax may be difficult to establish. Three weeks earlier (*C*), a roentgenogram had shown evidence of a moderate right pneumothorax; the blebs cannot be positively identified on this study.

parietal pleural layers in the region of blebs constitute a sign of prognostic significance, since they tend to "hold the communication open" and thereby prevent spontaneous re-expansion (Figure 4–171).

Hydropneumothorax should be immediately apparent on roentgenograms exposed in the erect position, by dint of the air-fluid level inevitably produced (Figure 4–172). Encapsulated hydropneumothorax may occur as single or multiple encysted collections, some of which may contain air-fluid levels and others not (Figure 4–173). Fluoroscopy or roentgenography of a patient in various body positions sometimes shows fluid pass from one apparently loculated space into another, thereby establishing the fact that they communicate.

Tension Pneumothorax and Hydrothorax

On the evidence supplied by roentgenograms of the chest at total lung capacity, the detection of increased pressure in a pneumothorax may be exceedingly difficult, especially if the pneumothorax is complete and collapse of the ipsilateral lung total (Figure 4–171). Since the pressure in the contralateral hemithorax is negative, inevitably the mediastinum shifts away from the side of the pneumothorax;

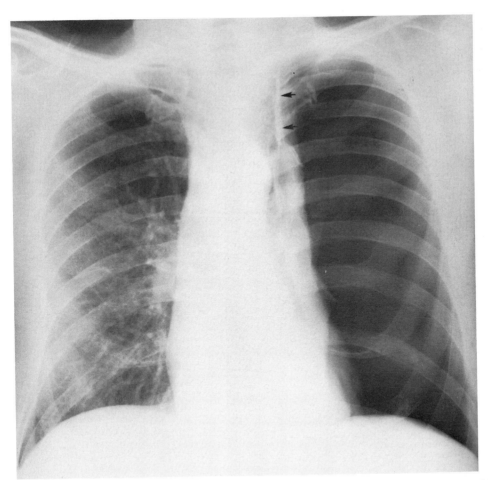

Figure 4–171. **Tension Pneumothorax.** A posteroanterior roentgenogram reveals complete collapse of the left lung due to spontaneous pneumothorax. A prominent line shadow extending from the apex of the collapsed lung to the apex of the hemithorax (*arrows*) represents a pleural tag extending from an apical bleb to the parietal pleura (proved at thoracotomy); the pleural tag held the bleb open and prevented re-expansion of the lung. Before thoracotomy, the pneumothorax proved to be under considerable tension; note that the roentgenographic signs of tension are by no means convincing.

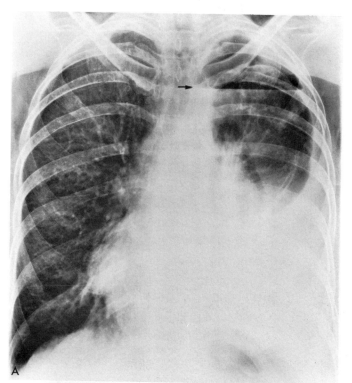

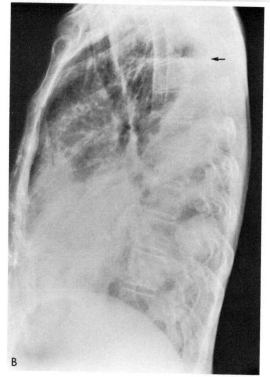

Figure 4–172.   **Hydropneumothorax.**
Posteroanterior (*A*) and lateral (*B*) roentgenograms reveal a prominent air-fluid level in the upper portion of the left hemithorax (*arrows*). The partly collapsed lung is protruding slightly above the air-fluid level; the fact that the fluid below this level possesses a meniscus-shaped upper contour indicates that the lung below the level is well inflated. Metastatic carcinoma of the breast (note the large metastatic nodule in the lower portion of the right lung).

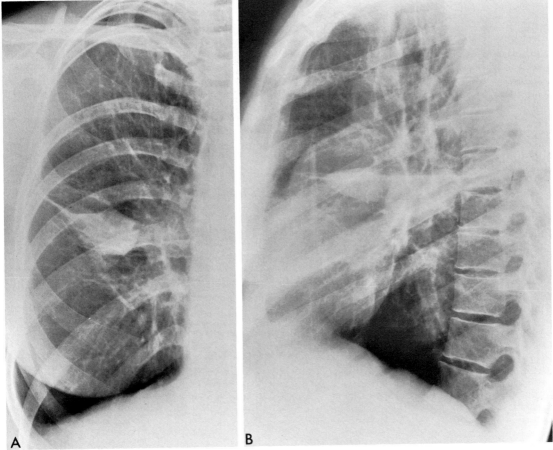

Figure 4–173.   Encapsulated Hydropneumothorax. Views of the right hemithorax from posteroanterior (A) and lateral (B) roentgenograms reveal a sharply circumscribed shadow in the region of the minor fissure; an air-fluid level is situated within the shadow. This encapsulated hydropneumothorax developed within the minor fissure following an exclusion operation for emphysema.

such a shift must not be mistaken for evidence of tension pneumothorax. As air is absorbed from the pleural space, ipsilateral pleural pressure becomes negative and the mediastinum moves back to the midline (although mediastinal swing is still apparent fluoroscopically—toward the side of the pneumothorax during inspiration and away from it during expiration). Should a check-valve mechanism exist which allows air to enter the pleural space during inspiration, but prevents its exit during expiration, the roentgenologic findings may be identical to those previously described except that the contralateral mediastinal shift and the ipsilateral hemidiaphragmatic depression may be more marked. On fluoroscopic examination, however, the situation should be

clear: the increased tension prevents mediastinal shift toward the side of the pneumothorax on inspiration and may thereby severely restrict inflation of the normal lung, constituting what may be the major cause of respiratory difficulty. For the same reason, movement of the ipsilateral diaphragm is markedly restricted during respiration. This combination of changes, *when viewed fluoroscopically*, should prompt the diagnosis of tension pneumothorax, but the unreliability of assessing the presence or absence of tension on plain roentgenograms deserves emphasis.

Tension hydrothorax, although rare, constitutes as much of a danger as tension pneumothorax, perhaps more so, since the possibility of its occurrence is not generally recognized. Rabinov and his colleagues[1690] reported a case of a 23-year-old woman with metastatic undifferentiated carcinoma in whom massive pleural effusion increased greatly over a brief period of time and caused severe dyspnea and eventual collapse. At thoracotomy, serosanguinous fluid spurted to a height of about 25 cm; several liters were removed. The explanation suggested by the authors for this unusual circumstance seems reasonable: serum albumin was severely diminished, amounting to 1.4 g per 100 ml, and the protein content of the pleural fluid was 4.8 g per 100 ml; thus, colloid osmotic pressure difference between blood and pleural space was reversed, creating an alteration of pleural-space dynamics which favored a massive accumulation of fluid. Although such a set of circumstances must be rare indeed, it is well to bear in mind the possibility of such in any patient with a massive pleural effusion, disproportionately increasing symptoms, and progressive deterioration in condition.

5

TABLES OF DIFFERENTIAL DIAGNOSIS

GENERAL COMMENTS
HOW TO USE THE TABLES
    TABLE 5–1. HOMOGENEOUS SHADOWS WITHOUT
        RECOGNIZABLE SEGMENTAL DISTRIBUTION
    TABLE 5–2. HOMOGENEOUS SHADOWS OF
        RECOGNIZABLE SEGMENTAL DISTRIBUTION
    TABLE 5–3. INHOMOGENEOUS SHADOWS
        WITHOUT RECOGNIZABLE SEGMENTAL
        DISTRIBUTION
    TABLE 5–4. INHOMOGENEOUS SHADOWS OF
        RECOGNIZABLE SEGMENTAL DISTRIBUTION
    TABLE 5–5. CYSTIC AND CAVITARY DISEASE
    TABLE 5–6. SOLITARY PULMONARY NODULES
        LESS THAN 6 CM IN DIAMETER ("COIN"
        LESIONS)
    TABLE 5–7. SOLITARY PULMONARY MASSES 6
        CM OR MORE IN DIAMETER
    TABLE 5–8. MULTIPLE PULMONARY NODULES,
        WITH OR WITHOUT CAVITATION
    TABLE 5–9. DIFFUSE PULMONARY DISEASE
        WITH A PREDOMINANTLY ACINAR PATTERN

TABLE 5–10. DIFFUSE PULMONARY DISEASE
    WITH A PREDOMINANTLY NODULAR,
    RETICULAR, OR RETICULONODULAR PATTERN
TABLE 5–11. DIFFUSE PULMONARY DISEASE
    WITH A MIXED ACINAR AND RETICULO-
    NODULAR PATTERN
TABLE 5–12. GENERALIZED PULMONARY
    OLIGEMIA
TABLE 5–13. UNILATERAL, LOBAR, OR
    SEGMENTAL PULMONARY OLIGEMIA
TABLE 5–14. PLEURAL EFFUSION
    UNASSOCIATED WITH OTHER
    ROENTGENOGRAPHIC EVIDENCE OF DISEASE
    IN THE THORAX
TABLE 5–15. PLEURAL EFFUSION ASSOCIATED
    WITH OTHER ROENTGENOGRAPHIC EVIDENCE
    OF DISEASE IN THE THORAX
TABLE 5–16. HILAR AND MEDIASTINAL LYMPH-
    NODE ENLARGEMENT
TABLE 5–17. MEDIASTINAL WIDENING

GENERAL COMMENTS

This book is based on the premise that the logical first step in the diagnosis of diseases of the chest is an assessment of the pattern of changes revealed on a chest roentgenogram and that correlation of these findings with the clinical history and with abnormalities revealed by physical examination, laboratory investigation, pulmonary function testing, and special investigations will yield a positive diagnosis in the majority of cases. If this proposition is accepted, clearly it is necessary to evaluate the chest roentgenogram on a basis of pattern recognition in which individual patterns can be related to pathogenesis and thence to etiology. To describe a roentgenographic shadow as an "infiltrate" says no more than that the lung is abnormal; to describe the *pattern* that the shadow possesses — homogeneous or inhomogeneous, segmental or nonsegmental, air-space or interstitial — constitutes an attempt to assess the *mechanism* by which the disease developed and thus to suggest its cause.

With these sequences in mind we compiled 17 tables which list all the basic roentgenographic patterns of chest disease, each table providing a nosologic approach to the differential diagnosis of disease of that pattern. Within the tables the classification of disease is on an etiologic basis, categories being arranged in the same order as the chapters in the book — developmental, infectious, neoplastic, and so forth.

Each table includes *all* common diseases and the *majority* of uncommon diseases which produce that particular pattern. **Because of the large number of diseases listed and to facilitate appreciation of the likeliest possibilities in any given case, in these tables the diseases which are the most frequent cause of each pattern are printed in boldface type.** The search for rare conditions in order to achieve completeness has not been exhaustive, since we feared that the tables would become too cumbersome to be of practical use. Even with careful selection, however, it was found necessary to include a vast number of diseases in some tables (*e.g.,* Table 5-10), with the result that their length may prove awesome. In addition, our desire to reduce length to practical proportions is hindered by the necessity for repetition. Considerable overlap of patterns is inevitable, necessitating the inclusion of the same diseases in several tables: for example, bronchogenic carcinoma arising in and obstructing a segmental bronchus characteristically produces homogeneous opacification in precise seg-

mental distribution; antibiotic therapy may partly relieve the obstruction and result in air entry into the involved segment, producing an inhomogeneous segmental pattern.

Descriptions of the characteristics of the specific pattern precede each table, and roentgenograms which manifest the typical pattern are shown.

HOW TO USE THE TABLES

The tables are designed to be used in the following manner. When a specific roentgenographic pattern is recognized, the appropriate table is consulted and reviewed. The headings in each table are intended to provide a brief review of the characteristics of each disease that might aid differentiation from others which cause the same pattern. Thus, the most likely diagnostic possibilities are selected. Page references on the right-hand side of each table indicate the section in the text in which the disease is discussed in detail.

Table 5-1

HOMOGENEOUS SHADOWS WITHOUT RECOGNIZABLE SEGMENTAL DISTRIBUTION

This pattern is epitomized by acute air-space pneumonia caused by *Diplococcus pneumoniae.* Typically the inflammation begins in the subpleural parenchyma and spreads centripetally through pores of Kohn; since segmental boundaries do not impede such spread, consolidation tends to be nonsegmental. An air bronchogram is almost invariable and should not be misinterpreted as evidence of inhomogeneity. If the distribution of the disease is roughly segmental (for example, when acute air-space pneumonia fills a whole lobe), the presence of an air bronchogram should take precedence over apparent segmental distribution in establishing the pathogenesis and therefore the etiology of the disease.

The nonsegmental character of parenchymal consolidation relates largely to its pathogenesis. For example, the volume of lung affected by acute irradiation pneumonitis corresponds roughly to the area irradiated, with little tendency to segmental or lobar distribution.

In addition to the cases illustrated on the following pages, the following figures appearing elsewhere in the book may be referred to as representative of this pattern:

Figure	Page
4- 5	194
4- 6	195
4- 7	195
4- 8	196
4-22	208
4-28	214
4-68	261
6- 5	580
7- 1	594
7- 3	603
7- 4	618
7-39	699

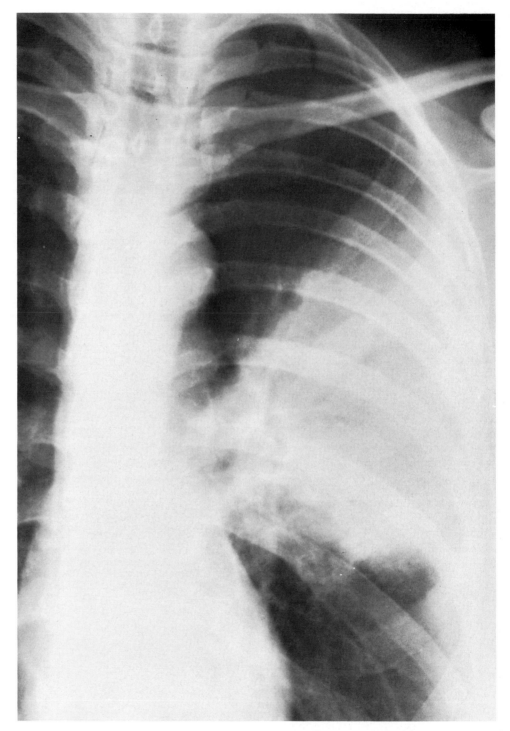

Figure 5–1. **Homogeneous Nonsegmental Consolidation: Acute Pneumococcal Pneumonia.** A view of the left hemithorax from a posteroanterior roentgenogram reveals consolidation of the axillary zone of the left upper lobe; the consolidation is homogeneous except for a well-defined air bronchogram. There is no loss of volume. The spreading margins are fairly sharply circumscribed despite the fact that they do not abut against a fissure. This pattern is virtually pathognomonic of acute air-space pneumonia, most commonly due to *Diplococcus pneumoniae.*

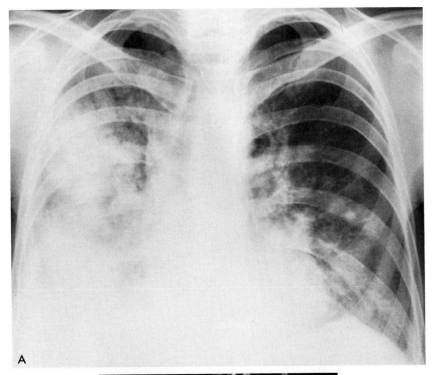

Figure 5–2. **Homogeneous Nonsegmental Consolidation: Hodgkin's Disease.** A posteroanterior roentgenogram (A) reveals extensive consolidation of much of the right lung, particularly its lower two-thirds; the consolidation possesses no clear-cut segmental distribution. An air bronchogram is present. There is little, if any, loss of volume. Patchy shadows of a similar nature can be identified in the lower portion of the lungs. A photograph of a cut section of the right lung removed at necropsy (B) shows extensive replacement of the lower and middle lobes by Hodgkin's tissue; the nonsegmental distribution is indicated by the lack of involvement of portions of the superior and anterior segments of the lower lobe. Twenty-seven-year-old woman; Hodgkin's granuloma.

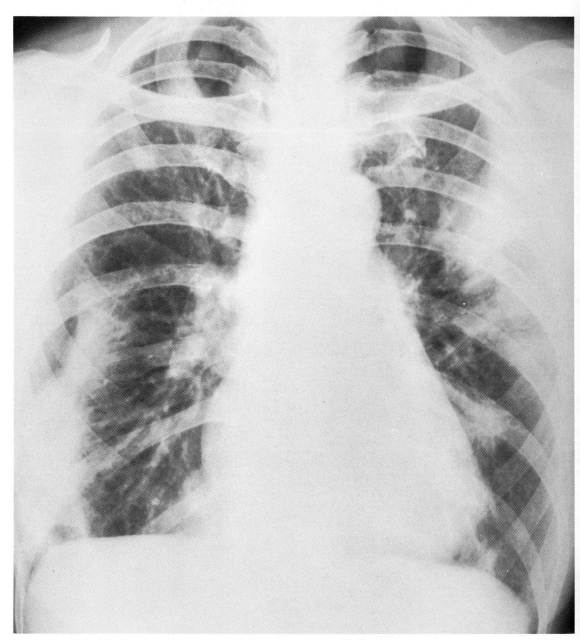

Figure 5–3. **Homogeneous Nonsegmental Consolidation: Loeffler's Syndrome.** A posteroanterior roentgenogram reveals rather poorly-defined shadows of homogeneous density situated in the axillary zones of both lungs. Although the consolidations are peripheral in location, a few small air-containing airways can be identified within them, representing an air bronchogram. There is no communication on either side between the hila and the consolidated lung. Serial roentgenograms revealed rapid change in the size and configuration of the shadows, these areas resolving and new areas of consolidation appearing in other areas of the lungs. This "fleeting" nature of peripherally-situated homogeneous nonsegmental consolidations represents the characteristic feature of Loeffler's syndrome (transient pulmonary shadows with eosinophilia).

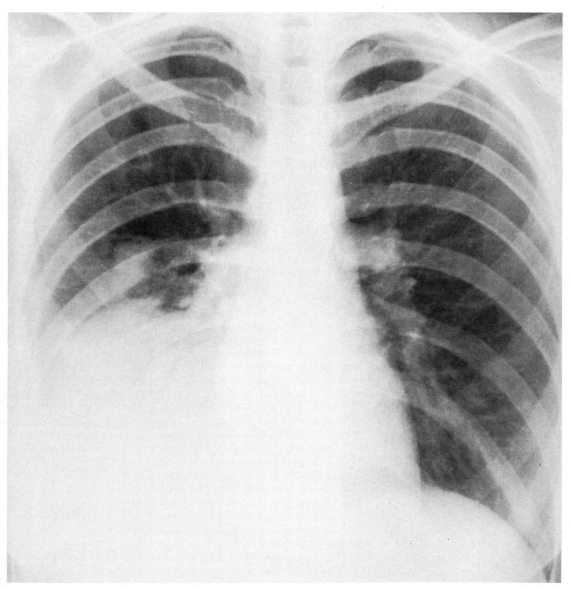

Figure 5–4. **Homogeneous Nonsegmental Consolidation: Traumatic Pulmonary Contusion.** A posteroanterior roentgenogram of a 15-year-old girl approximately seven days following a car accident reveals homogeneous consolidation of the lower half of the right lung, possessing rather indistinctly defined margins; the consolidation is restricted to the lower lobe but possesses no clear-cut segmental distribution. There is no loss of volume; in contrast to the previous three cases, an air bronchogram cannot be identified. This shadow represents severe pulmonary contusion which resolved completely during the next three weeks. Traumatic pulmonary contusion characteristically occurs deep to the region of maximum trauma and shows no clear-cut segmental distribution. (Courtesy Dr. J. G. Monks, Saskatoon.)

Table 5-1. *Homogeneous Shadows Without Recognizable Segmental Distribution*

	ETIOLOGY	LOSS OF VOLUME	ANATOMIC DISTRIBUTION
DEVELOPMENTAL	Pulmonary arteriovenous fistula	0	Lower lobe predilection.
INFECTIOUS	**Bacteria** *Diplococcus pneumoniae*	0 to +	Influence of gravity; therefore dependent portions of upper and lower lobes.
	Klebsiella-aerobacter species (Friedlander's bacillus)	Tendency to expansion of involved lung, although volume may be normal or even reduced.	Upper lobe predilection; often multilobar.
	Mycobacterium tuberculosis (primary)	0 to +	Slightly more frequent in upper lobes; no predilection for either anterior or posterior segments.
	Mycobacterium tuberculosis (reinfection)	0 to +	Upper lobe predilection, predominantly posterior (influence of gravity on endobronchial spread).
	Pasteurella tularensis (tularemia)	0	No lobar predilection; may be multilobar.
	Bacteroides species	0	Predominantly lower lobes.
	Pseudomonas aeruginosa	0	Generalized or nonspecific.
	Pseudomonas pseudomallei	0	Single or multiple lobes.
	Bacterium anitratum	0	No lobar predilection.
	Proteus species	0	Upper lobe predilection.

Table 5–1. *Homogeneous Shadows Without Recognizable Segmental Distribution*
(Continued)

ADDITIONAL FINDINGS	COMMENTS
Fairly extensive racemose opacity, ill-defined but homogeneous, occupying much of one broncho-pulmonary segment (but not truly segmental).	Represents a complex angiomatous mass possessing a number of feeding and draining vessels (*see* also Table 5–6). (*See* page 573.)
Air bronchogram almost invariable; fairly sharply circumscribed margins, even where not abutting against fissure; cavitation rare.	Confluent air space consolidation begins in subpleural parenchyma and spreads centripetally via pores of Kohn; therefore no tendency to segmental involvement. (*See* page 592.)
Cavitation common; air bronchogram almost invariable; pleural effusion may be present.	**Differs from pneumococcal pneumonia in propensity to cavitation and tendency to expand involved lung. (*See* page 604.)**
Ipsilateral hilar or paratracheal lymph node enlargement almost invariable in children but in only about 50 per cent of adults. Pleural effusion in 10 per cent of affected children (almost always associated with parenchymal disease) and in approximately one third of adults (often as the sole manifestation). Cavitation and miliary spread rare.	(*See* page 616.)
Cavitation common. Individual acinar shadows frequently identifiable elsewhere in lungs due to endobronchial spread. Air bronchogram invariable.	**Acute tuberculous pneumonia. Infection may transgress interlobar fissures from one lobe to another or occasionally may extend into chest wall and form abscesses (empyema necessitatis). (*See* page 621.)**
Hilar lymph-node enlargement and pleural effusion common; cavitation rare.	**May be extensive involvement of both lungs; oval or spherical homogeneous consolidation. (*See* page 608.)**
Cavitation common in those cases believed to be due to septic infarcts. Empyema almost invariable, sometimes with sufficient gas production to be visible roentgenographically.	Commonly associated with microaerophilic streptococci. (*See* page 612.)
Pleural effusion common.	Less common method of presentation than homogeneous segmental consolidation (Table 5–2). (*See* page 600.)
———	Homogeneous consolidation due to confluence of multiple areas of air space consolidation. Involvement may be extensive, resembling pulmonary edema. (*See* page 601.)
Empyema frequent, sometimes without underlying pulmonary disease.	(*See* page 610.)
Abscess formation frequent.	(*See* page 606.)

Table continues

385

Table 5–1. *Homogeneous Shadows Without Recognizable Segmental Distribution*
(Continued)

	ETIOLOGY	LOSS OF VOLUME	ANATOMIC DISTRIBUTION
	Hemophilus influenza	0	No lobar predilection.
	Pasteurella pestis (the Black Plague)	0	No lobar predilection.
	Fusiform bacilli and *Spirochaeta*	0	Posterior portions of upper or lower lobes.
	Fungi **Actinomyces israelii** (actinomycosis) **Nocardia** species (nocardiosis)	**0**	Lower lobe predilection, often bilateral.
	Blastomyces dermatitidis (blastomycosis)	**0**	Upper lobe predilection in ratio of 3:2.
	Histoplasma capsulatum (histoplasmosis)	0	No predilection.
INFECTIOUS *(Cont.)*	*Coccidioides immitis* (coccidioidomycosis)	0	Lower lobe predilection.
	Candida albicans (candidiasis)	0	No predilection.
	Geotrichum species (geotrichosis)	0	Upper lobe predilection.
	Aspergillus species (primary aspergillosis)	0	No predilection.
	Parasites **Entamoeba histolytica** (amebiasis)	**0**	**Right lower lobe almost exclusively.**
	Paragonimus westermani (paragonimiasis)	**0**	**No predilection.**
	Ascaris lumbricoides (ascariasis)	0	Multilobar.
	Strongyloides stercoralis	0	Multilobar.
	Ancylostoma duodenale and *Necator americanus*	0	Multilobar.

Table 5–1. *Homogeneous Shadows Without Recognizable Segmental Distribution*
(Continued)

Additional Findings	Comments
Effusion common.	Uncommon presentation (*see* Table 5–4). (*See* page 607.)
Pleural effusion in some cases.	May be overwhelming infection, with multilobar involvement and pulmonary edema pattern. (*See* page 609.)
Tends to progress to acute lung abscess.	Acute air space pneumonia tends to occur when aspirate is of watery consistency (*see* also Table 5–4). (*See* page 613.)
Cavitation common; pleural effusion and extension into chest wall characteristic (with or without rib destruction). Similarly may transgress interlobar fissures from one lobe to another.	Roentgenographic patterns of these organisms are indistinguishable. (*See* pages 662 and 663.)
Cavitation uncommon (15 per cent); pleural effusion and lymph-node enlargement rare, as is chest wall involvement.	Contrast with actinomycosis and nocardiosis in frequency of cavitation, pleural effusion and chest wall involvement. (*See* page 656.)
Hilar lymph node enlargement common; cavitation may occur.	This pneumonic type is considerably less common than inhomogeneous primary histoplasmosis (*see* Table 5–3). (*See* page 643.)
Hilar and paratracheal lymph node enlargement may be present; cavitation common.	(*See* page 652.)
May cavitate.	Less common presentation than inhomogeneous segmental pattern (*see* Table 5–4). (*See* page 668.)
Cavitation common, usually thin-walled.	(*See* page 672.)
Cavitation uncommon.	Much less common presentation than as opportunistic invader (fungus ball or mucoid impaction). (*See* page 664.)
Right pleural effusion very common. Cavitation occurs in minority of cases.	Organisms enter thorax via diaphragm from liver abscesses. (*See* page 701.)
Isolated nodular shadows, usually cavitary; may be pleural effusion.	Organisms enter thorax via diaphragm; spread via bronchial tree. (*See* page 716.)
———	Löffler-type pattern suggested by fleeting nature of consolidation. (*See* page 705.)
———	Löffler-type pattern. (*See* page 707.)
———	Löffler-type pattern. (*See* page 708.)

Table continues

Table 5-1. *Homogeneous Shadows Without Recognizable Segmental Distribution*
(Continued)

	ETIOLOGY	LOSS OF VOLUME	ANATOMIC DISTRIBUTION
NEOPLASTIC	Hodgkin's disease	0	No predilection.
	Lymphosarcoma group	0	No predilection.
	Primary pulmonary pseudolymphoma	0	No predilection.
	Bronchioloalveolar carcinoma	0	No predilection.
IMMUNOLOGIC	Löffler's syndrome	0	Peripherally situated without lobar predilection.
	Polyarteritis nodosa	0	Peripheral lung zones, without lobar predilection.
INHALATIONAL	Silicosis-complicated (P.M.F.)	+ to +++ (cicatrization atelectasis).	Characteristically conglomerate shadows develop in the periphery of the mid or upper lung zones and in time tend to migrate toward the hilum.
	Coal workers' pneumoconiosis-complicated (P.M.F.)	0 to ++ in areas of conglomeration (cicatrization atelectasis).	Marked predilection for upper lobes; tends to originate in the periphery of the lung, migrating toward the hilum over a period of years.

Table 5–1. *Homogeneous Shadows Without Recognizable Segmental Distribution (Continued)*

ADDITIONAL FINDINGS	COMMENTS
Almost invariably associated with hilar or mediastinal lymph-node enlargement. Pleural effusion in 30 per cent of cases. Air bronchogram almost invariable.	Individual lesions may coalesce to form larger areas of homogeneous consolidation. (*See* page 771.)
Often without associated hilar and mediastinal node enlargement. Pleural effusion in one third. Air bronchogram invariable.	(*See* page 784.)
Lymph nodes characteristically are *not* involved. Air bronchogram invariable.	Consolidation may appear segmental but in the majority of reported cases has failed to reach the visceral pleura over the convexity. (*See* page 735.)
Air bronchogram invariable.	Malignant cells may be found in sputum which is usually mucoid and sometimes copious. (*See* page 770.)
Consolidation may be single or multiple, generally ill-defined and transitory or migratory in character. Cavitation, pleural effusion, lymph-node enlargement, and cardiomegaly do not occur.	Invariable eosinophilia. Main differential diagnosis from hypersensitivity aspergillosis. (*See* page 870.)
Consolidation tends to be patchy and fleeting in nature and thus indistinguishable from Löffler's syndrome. Cavitation may occur.	Other roentgenographic manifestations of *polyarteritis nodosa* include pulmonary venous engorgement, pulmonary edema, accentuated markings, and "miliary" nodulation. (*See* page 875.)
The background pattern of diffuse silicosis may be quite apparent, but the more extensive the progressive massive fibrosis, the less the nodularity apparent in the remainder of the lungs (due to incorporation of nodular lesions into the massive consolidation). Because of cicatrization atelectasis, compensatory overinflation or overt emphysema of remainder of lung is common. Cavitation may occur in conglomerate lesions. Hilar lymph node enlargement is usual and in an occasional case may be associated with "egg-shell" calcification.	Conglomerate shadows represent confluence of individual silicotic nodules, usually but not always associated with superimposed tuberculosis. Their margins are usually irregular and somewhat ill-defined so that they tend to simulate peripheral bronchogenic carcinoma. (*See* page 919.)
The background of diffuse nodular or reticulonodular shadows is usually evident although incorporation of the individual foci into the conglomerate consolidation may render the nodular pattern inconspicuous. Compensatory overinflation or emphysema develops in lower lobes in response to cicatrization atelectasis.	Conglomerate shadows tend to be rather indistinctly defined but are homogeneous unless cavitation has developed (which occurs occasionally due either to ischemic necrosis or more commonly to superimposed tuberculosis). (*See* page 939.)

Table continues

Table 5–1. *Homogeneous Shadows Without Recognizable Segmental Distribution* (*Continued*)

	ETIOLOGY	LOSS OF VOLUME	ANATOMIC DISTRIBUTION
TRAUMATIC	Pulmonary parenchymal contusion	0 to +	Usually in lung directly deep to area traumatized although it may develop as well or even predominantly on the side opposite from the trauma due to contracoup affect. No conformity to lobes or segments.
	Acute irradiation pneumonitis	++ to ++++	The volume of lung affected generally but not always corresponds to the area irradiated; no tendency to segmental or lobar distribution.
	Lung torsion	0 to +	A whole lung.
IDIOPATHIC	Eosinophilic granuloma	0	Peripherally situated without lobar predilection.

Table 5–1. *Homogeneous Shadows Without Recognizable Segmental Distribution (Continued)*

ADDITIONAL FINDINGS	COMMENTS
Roentgenographic changes develop soon after trauma, almost invariably within six hours. Increase in size and loss of definition of vascular markings extending out from the hila indicates hemorrhage and edema in the major interstitial space.	The most common pulmonary complication of blunt chest trauma. The roentgenographic pattern varies from irregular patchy areas of air-space consolidation to diffuse and extensive homogeneous consolidation. Consolidation results from exudation of edema fluid and blood into the parenchyma of the lung in both its air-space and interstitial components. (*See* page 1069.)
Despite severe loss of volume, segmental bronchi tend to be unaffected so that an air bronchogram is almost invariable. Roentgenographically demonstrable pleural effusion is very uncommon although there may be fairly extensive thickening of the pleura.	The reaction of the lung to irradiation is affected by a number of variables including the dosage of radiation administered, the time over which it is given, the site to which the radiation is directed and the condition of the lung prior to irradiation. (*See* page 1076.)
Torsion occurs through 180 degrees so that the base of the lung comes to lie at the apex of the hemithorax and the apex at the base: the pattern of pulmonary vascular markings is thus altered in a predictable manner.	If torsion is not relieved, vascular supply is compromised and the lung becomes opaque due to exudation of blood into the air spaces and interstitial tissues. (*See* page 1076.)
———	A rare manifestation of the disease, usually occurring in individuals with a background of allergy; blood eosinophilia common. Histologically identical to the diffuse disease. (*See* page 1110.)

Table 5-2

HOMOGENEOUS SHADOWS OF RECOGNIZABLE SEGMENTAL DISTRIBUTION

This pattern is characterized by the effects of endobronchial obstructing lesions — segmental atelectasis with or without obstructive pneumonitis. Since the pathogenesis involves bronchial obstruction, the resultant shadow necessarily is of specific bronchopulmonary segmental distribution. An air bronchogram should be absent except when the atelectasis is "adhesive" or "nonobstructive" in type or when therapy has relieved the obstruction, thereby permitting the entry of air in the involved segmental bronchi.

Acute confluent bronchopneumonia also, commonly of staphylococcal etiology, produces this pattern. The pathogenesis of bronchopneumonia implies a segmental distribution; the virulence of the infection results in confluence of consolidation and consequent homogeneity. As in obstructive pneumonitis, an air bronchogram seldom is present.

In addition to the cases illustrated on the following pages, the following figures appearing elsewhere in the book may be referred to as representative of this pattern:

Figure	Page
4–14	202
4–29	215
4–35	224
4–47	236
4–76	268
4–99	292
7–33	678
8– 1	726

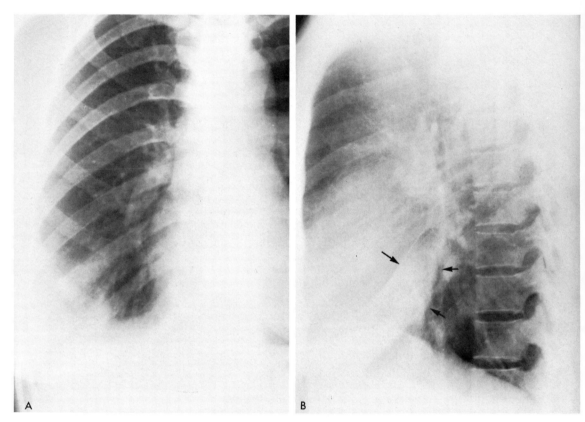

Figure 5–5.   **Homogeneous Segmental Consolidation: Acute Confluent Bronchopneumonia.** Views of the right hemithorax from posteroanterior (A) and lateral (B) roentgenograms reveal homogeneous consolidation confined to the precise anatomic distribution of the anterior basal bronchopulmonary segment of the right lower lobe. The consolidation occupies a triangular segment of lung with its apex at the hilum and its base at the visceral pleura (*arrows* in B). There is no evidence of an air bronchogram. Heavy growth of *Staphylococcus aureus* from the sputum; complete roentgenologic resolution in ten days.

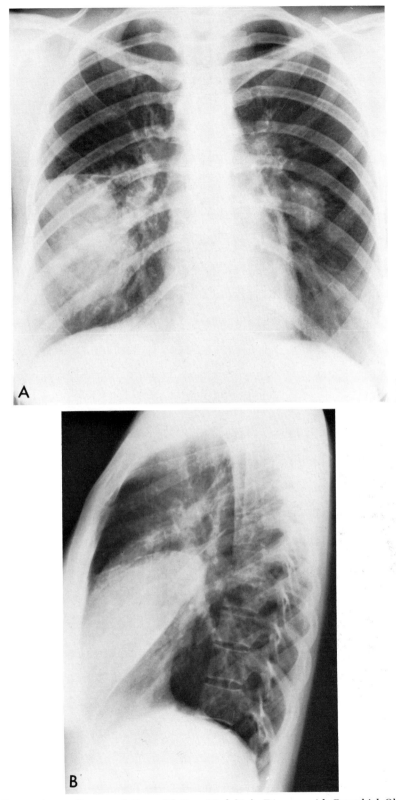

Figure 5–6. **Homogeneous Segmental Consolidation: Hodgkin's Disease with Bronchial Obstruction.** Posteroanterior (*A*) and lateral (*B*) roentgenograms show consolidation of the whole of the right middle lobe; the shadow is homogeneous and does not contain an air bronchogram. A well-circumscribed mass is present in the left lung contiguous to the hilum. The right middle lobe shadow is produced by a *combination* of consolidation of lung parenchyma by Hodgkin's tissue and obstruction of the bronchus by endobronchial Hodgkin's (if no bronchial obstruction were present, an air bronchogram should be present). The left parahilar mass is due to parenchymal Hodgkin's granuloma. *See also* Figure 8–28, page 781, which shows roentgenograms of the same patient several months later at a time when the right middle lobe showed considerably more atelectasis.

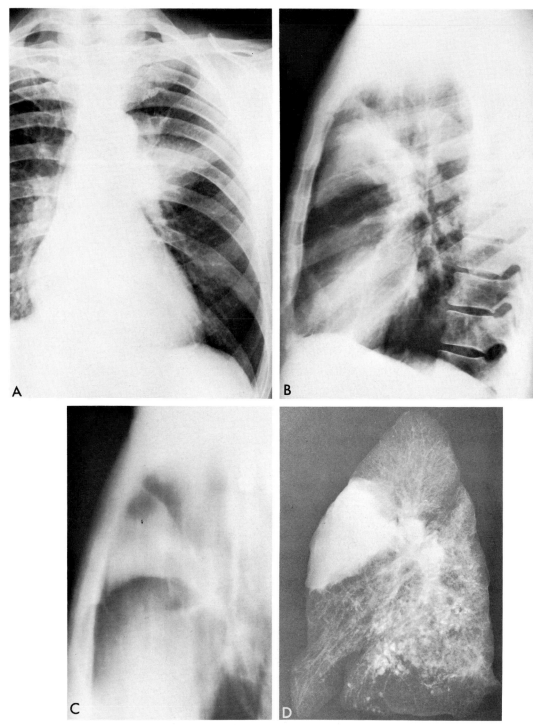

Figure 5–7. **Homogeneous Segmental Consolidation/Atelectasis: Bronchogenic Carcinoma.** A triangular shadow of homogeneous density is situated in the anterior portion of the left upper lobe, its base contiguous to the retrosternal pleura and its apex at the left hilum. The shadow is seen *en face* in posteroanterior projection (A) and in profile in lateral projection (standard roentgenogram [B] and tomogram [C]). The absence of an air bronchogram indicates bronchial obstruction; the relatively minor degree of loss of volume denotes obstructive pneumonitis. Squamous cell carcinoma of the anterior segmental bronchus of the left upper lobe. A lateral roentgenogram of the resected lung (D) shows the sharp definition and precise segmental distribution of the shadow to excellent advantage. (Courtesy Dr. D. D. Munro, Royal Edward Chest Hospital, Montreal.)

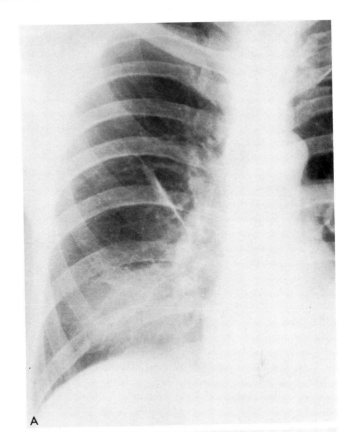

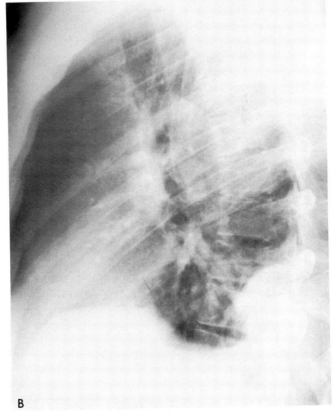

Figure 5–8. **Homogeneous Segmental Consolidation: Pulmonary Infarction.** Views of the right hemithorax from posteroanterior (A) and lateral (B) roentgenograms reveal a shadow of homogeneous density situated in the base of the right lung. The definition of the shadow is indistinct in posteroanterior projection but sharp in lateral projection where it presents a convex surface pointing toward the left hilum. This configuration is characteristic of a "Hampton hump" and strongly suggests the diagnosis of pulmonary infarction; the association of a small pleural effusion (see only in lateral projection) increases the likelihood of this diagnosis. The consolidation is localized to the posterior basal segment of the right lower lobe; there is no air bronchogram. Forty-four-year-old man with compatible history; the diagnosis was supported by positive enzyme changes but was not confirmed by angiography.

Table 5-2. *Homogeneous Shadows of Recognizable Segmental Distribution*

	ETIOLOGY	LOSS OF VOLUME	ANATOMIC DISTRIBUTION
DEVELOPMENTAL	Pulmonary arterio-venous fistula	+ to ++++	Predilection for lower lobes.
INFECTIOUS	**Bacteria** *Staphylococcus aureus*	0 to ++	No lobar predilection.
	Mycobacterium tuberculosis (primary)	0 to ++++	2:1 predominance of right lung over left; predilection for anterior segment of upper lobe or medial segment of middle lobe.
	Diplococcus pneumoniae	0 to +	Influence of gravity; therefore dependent portions of upper and lower lobes.
	Streptococcus pyogenes	0 to ++	Predominantly lower lobes.
	Pseudomonas aeruginosa	0 to ++	Predominantly lower lobes.
	Hemophilus pertussis (whooping cough pneumonia)	+ to ++	Predominantly lower lobes.
	All other bacteria listed in Table 5–4	0 to ++	Predominantly lower lobes.
	Fungi *Histoplasma capsulatum*	+ to ++++	Predilection for right middle lobe.
	Phycomycetes class	0 to +	No predilection.

Table 5–2. *Homogeneous Shadows of Recognizable Segmental Distribution (Continued)*

ADDITIONAL FINDINGS	COMMENTS
The feeding artery and draining vein may be partly or completely obscured by the shadow of the collapsed segment.	Bronchial compression with resultant atelectasis or obstructive pneumonitis is a rare complication. (*See* page 573.)
Abscess formation common; pleural effusion (empyema) common, particularly in children, with or without bronchopleural fistula (pyopneumothorax).	This is confluent bronchopneumonia; air bronchogram exceptional. (*See* page 595.)
Associated paratracheal or hilar lymph node enlargement in two thirds of patients.	Atelectasis results from either compression from enlarged lymph nodes or from endobronchial tuberculosis; atelectasis occasionally is preceded by obstructive "emphysema." In adults, tuberculous bronchostenosis tends to show a female sex predominance and a lower lobe predilection. (*See* page 616.)
Air bronchogram almost invariable; cavitation rare.	True segmental distribution very uncommon, and only when whole lobe involved. (*See* page 592.)
Pleural effusion almost invariable.	As confluent bronchopneumonia, this is a more common method of presentation than inhomogeneous involvement (*see* Table 5–4). (*See* page 598.)
Abscess formation with empyema common, with or without bronchopleural fistula (pyopneumothorax).	Confluent bronchopneumonia; a less common method of presentation than inhomogeneous involvement (*see* Table 5–4). (*See* page 600.)
"Shaggy heart" sign.	Confluent bronchopneumonia, associated with some degree of atelectasis in at least 50 per cent of cases; in pertussis, pneumonia may be caused by secondary invader or by *Hemophilus pertussis* itself. (*See* page 608.)
———	These bacteria characteristically produce an inhomogeneous consolidation, but on occasion the densities may be confluent thus leading to homogeneous consolidation. (*See* page 416.)
Enlargement of bronchopulmonary lymph nodes an invariable accompaniment.	Compression from enlarged nodes results in obstructive pneumonitis or atelectasis. Calcification of compressing lymph nodes may be associated with erosion into the bronchial lumen and the production of broncholithiasis. (*See* page 643.)
———	Segmental consolidation may occur either from primary invasion of the organism (confluent bronchopneumonia) or less commonly from pulmonary infarction secondary to pulmonary arterial invasion. (*See* page 671.)

Table continues

Table 5–2. *Homogeneous Shadows of Recognizable Segmental Distribution (Continued)*

	ETIOLOGY	LOSS OF VOLUME	ANATOMIC DISTRIBUTION
INFECTIOUS *(Cont.)*	Other fungi listed in Tables 5–1 and 5–4	0 to +	Predominantly lower lobes.
	Viruses and Rickettsia Q fever	0	Predominantly lower lobes.
	All viruses listed in Table 5–4 (including Mycoplasma)	0 to +++	Lower lobe predilection.
NEOPLASTIC	**Bronchial adenoma**	+ to ++++	Tends to arise from large or segmental bronchi. May occur in any lobe without clear-cut lobar predilection.
	Papilloma	+ to ++++	No predilection.
	Hamartoma Leiomyoma Fibroma Lipoma Myoblastoma Neurogenic tumors Chondroma Endometriosis	+ to ++++	No definite predilection.
	Bronchogenic carcinoma (squamous cell, oat cell, or undifferentiated)	+ to ++++	The ratio of right to left lung is 6:4 and a similar ratio exists from upper to lower lobes. The neoplasm arises from the main or lobar bronchi in 20 to 40 per cent of cases and from segmental bronchi in 60 to 80 per cent.
	Hodgkin's disease	+ to ++++	No known predilection.

Table 5–2. *Homogeneous Shadows of Recognizable Segmental Distribution (Continued)*

ADDITIONAL FINDINGS	COMMENTS
————	These fungi characteristically produce an inhomogeneous consolidation (bronchopneumonia), but on occasion the densities may be confluent thus leading to homogeneous consolidation. (*See* page 386 and 416.)
Pleural effusion is occasionally seen. Hilar lymphnode enlargement rare.	**Extent of consolidation may range from one segment to a complete lobe. (*See* page 697.)**
Pleural effusion and hilar node enlargement very uncommon.	These organisms characteristically cause inhomogeneous segmental consolidation, but on occasion the densities may be confluent. During the stage of resolution of adenoviral pneumonia, particularly in children, there may occur severe adhesive ("nonobstructive") atelectasis; despite the marked loss of volume, an air-bronchogram usually is present. (*See* page 416.)
Typical findings are those of "obstructive pneumonitis" or "drowned lung." The adenoma may be identified on the plain roentgenograms or by tomography or bronchography. Metastatic lymph nodes may occasionally be identified in the hilum or elsewhere.	**In 75 per cent of cases this is the method of presentation of bronchial adenoma. (*See* page 724.)**
Endobronchial papillomas are commonly multiple and are associated with similar lesions in the larynx and trachea. Tomography of the larynx, trachea, and lungs may be diagnostic. Bronchiectasis and abscess formation distal to the endobronchial lesions is frequent. Excavation of the lesions may occur.	(*See* page 731.)
————	Rarely any of these neoplasms may arise from the bronchial wall and obstruct the bronchial lumen leading to obstructive pneumonitis. The more common method of presentation is as a solitary nodule or "coin lesion" (chondromas are perhaps the exception to this statement, these tumours commonly being endobronchial). (*See* pages 730-736.)
The neoplasm may be identified as a mass distinct from the obstructive pneumonitis. Enlarged metastatic lymph nodes may be present in the hilum and elsewhere. Pleural effusion in 10 to 15 per cent of cases.	**Air trapping distal to bronchial obstruction is a rare manifestation. (*See* page 736.)**
Hilar and/or mediastinal lymph node enlargement commonly associated. Other patterns of lung involvement may also be associated, particularly parenchymal consolidation presenting as a homogeneous density possessing no recognizable segmental distribution (*see* Table 5–1).	Atelectasis (with or without obstructive pneumonitis) results from bronchial obstruction, almost always due to endobronchial involvement by Hodgkin's tissue; rarely may be caused by compression from enlarged lymph nodes. Absence of air bronchogram of differential value. (*See* page 771.)

Table continues

Table 5–2. Homogeneous Shadows of Recognizable Segmental Distribution *(Continued)*

	ETIOLOGY	LOSS OF VOLUME	ANATOMIC DISTRIBUTION
NEOPLASTIC *(Cont.)*	Lymphosarcoma group	+ to ++++	No known lobar predilection.
THROMBOEMBOLIC	Thromboembolism with infarction or hemorrhage	0 to ++	Lower lobes, usually posteriorly but often nestled in the costophrenic sinus; less than 10 per cent in upper lobes. May be multiple.
INHALATIONAL	Aspiration of solid foreign bodies	+ to ++++	Lower lobes almost exclusively, ratio of right to left being 2:1.
	Lipoid pneumonia	0 to +	Generally dependent portions of lower and upper lobes (occasionally right middle lobe or lingula).
AIRWAYS DISEASE	Mucoid impaction	+ to +++	Predilection for upper lobes.
	Mucoviscidosis	There is local segmental loss of volume but the total lung volume is increased.	No predilection.
	Familial dysautonomia (Riley-Day syndrome)	Some loss of volume in local areas of segmental disease but lung volume generally increased.	Local atelectatic areas predominantly in right upper lobe, less frequently the right middle and left lower lobes.

Table 5–2. *Homogeneous Shadows of Recognizable Segmental Distribution (Continued)*

ADDITIONAL FINDINGS	COMMENTS
Hilar and/or mediastinal lymph node enlargement commonly associated. Other patterns of lung involvement may also be associated, particularly parenchymal consolidation presenting as a homogeneous density possessing no recognizable segmental distribution (*see* Table 5-1).	Lymphosarcoma rarely presents as an endobronchial deposit leading to segmental atelectasis and pneumonitis, but only in the secondary form of the disease. (*See* page 784.)
Ipsilateral hemidiaphragm frequently raised; increase in size and abrupt tapering of feeder artery is characteristic; pleural effusion may be present. Signs of postcapillary hypertension due to associated cardiac disease may be present.	The size of the infarcted area is generally 3 to 5 cm in diameter but ranges from barely visible to 10 cm in diameter; occasionally shows truncated cone appearance ("Hampton's Hump"). The homogeneity may not always be obvious, particularly in the stage of resolution. (*See* page 804.)
The foreign body is opaque (*e.g.* a tooth) in approximately 10 per cent of patients.	Segmental collapse or consolidation occurs in only 25 per cent of cases, the remainder being categorized by "obstructive overinflation." (*See* page 956.)
None	The characteristic roentgenographic pattern is alveolar consolidation, commonly homogeneous but sometimes associated with isolated acinar shadows, particularly in the early stages of the disease. The segmental nature of the consolidation may be quite precise. (*See* page 964.)
Round, oval, or elliptical masses or "coin lesions" seen in proximal bronchi. The pulmonary parenchyma distal to the mucous plug may be collapsed or show varying degrees of obstructive pneumonitis but commonly is air-containing due to collateral airdrift from contiguous segments.	This condition is identical to hypersensitivity aspergillosis with respect to roentgenographic pattern and pathology, if not etiology. (*See* page 1055.)
Local segmental shadow seen on a background of diffuse coarse reticulation and patchy overinflation.	More commonly this disease shows a generalized coarse reticular pattern without associated changes due to bronchial obstruction. (*See* page 1062.)
Local areas of increased density on background or diffuse reticulation and hyperinflation.	More commonly the picture is one of diffuse reticulation only. (*See* page 905.)

Table continues

Table 5–2. *Homogeneous Shadows of Recognizable Segmental Distribution (Continued)*

	ETIOLOGY	LOSS OF VOLUME	ANATOMIC DISTRIBUTION
TRAUMATIC	Bronchial fracture	++ to ++++	One or more lobes or an entire lung.
	Postoperative adhesive atelectasis	+ to +++	Lower lobe predilection.
IDIOPATHIC	Sarcoidosis	+ to ++++	No predilection.
	Amyloidosis	+ to +++	Atelectasis or obstructive pneumonitis may involve a segment, a whole lobe, or a whole lung, but there is no predilection for anatomic site.

Table 5–2. *Homogeneous Shadows of Recognizable Segmental Distribution (Continued)*

ADDITIONAL FINDINGS	COMMENTS
Pneumothorax, pneumomediastinum, and subcutaneous emphysema. Fractures of the first three ribs frequently associated, particularly in adults (53 per cent of cases).	Atelectasis develops as a result of displacement of fracture ends and is commonly a late development. The occurrence of atelectasis sometime after an accident should strongly suggest the diagnosis (additional confirmatory evidence provided by fractures of one or more of the first three ribs). (*See* page 1075.)
The usual findings associated with postoperative thoracotomy—pleural effusion, diaphragmatic elevation, and so forth.	Occurs predominantly following cardiac surgery, particularly with use of extracorporeal circulation. The degree of collapse varies considerably. Since the mechanism of atelectasis operates peripherally, an air bronchogram is invariable. (*See* page 207.)
Almost invariably associated with more characteristic changes such as hilar and mediastinal lymphadenopathy and a diffuse reticulonodular pattern.	A rare complication of endobronchial sarcoidosis which may be suspected from other roentgenographic findings and can only be confirmed by bronchoscopy and bronchial biopsy. (*See* page 1087.)
Occasionally associated with peripheral parenchymal consolidation with amyloid tissue.	This is a very rare cause of tracheobronchial obstruction. (*See* page 1121.)

Table 5-3

INHOMOGENEOUS SHADOWS WITHOUT RECOGNIZABLE SEGMENTAL DISTRIBUTION

Reinfection tuberculosis undoubtedly is the most common producer of this pattern—focal areas of parenchymal consolidation separated by zones of air-containing lung. Although tuberculosis commonly is localized to the apical and posterior *regions* of an upper lobe, it seldom is truly segmental; in other words, it does not tend to affect a pyramidal section of lung whose apex is at the hilum and base at the visceral pleura. It must be emphasized that the presence of cavitation *in itself* should not be interpreted as a cause of inhomogeneity. For example, acute confluent bronchopneumonia, which typically produces homogeneous segmental consolida-

tion, may cavitate and thus create a shadow of relative inhomogeneity; such disease clearly is different pathogenetically from reinfection tuberculosis, in which cavitation accentuates an already inhomogeneous pattern.

In addition to the cases illustrated on the following pages, the following figures appearing elsewhere in the book may be referred to as representative of this pattern:

Figure	*Page*
7– 5	619
7– 6	625
7– 7	626
7–46	719
8–27	780
8–41	800

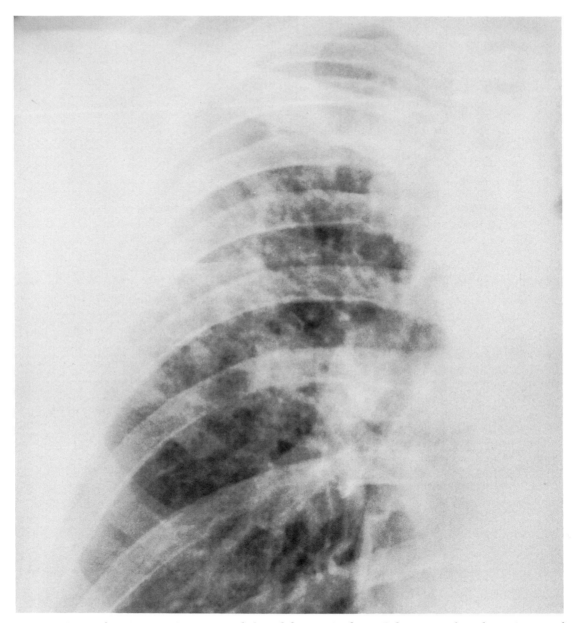

Figure 5–9. **Inhomogeneous Nonsegmental Consolidation: Exudative Pulmonary Tuberculosis.** A view of the upper half of the right lung from a posteroanterior roentgenogram demonstrates patchy areas of homogeneous density separated by zones of air-containing lung. Both the posterior portion of the upper lobe and the superior portion of the lower lobe are affected but involvement is not truly segmental. A moderate-sized cavity accentuates the inhomogeneity. Forty-year-old male; *Mycobacterium tuberculosis* cultured from the sputum. (Courtesy Dr. J. F. Meakins, Montreal.)

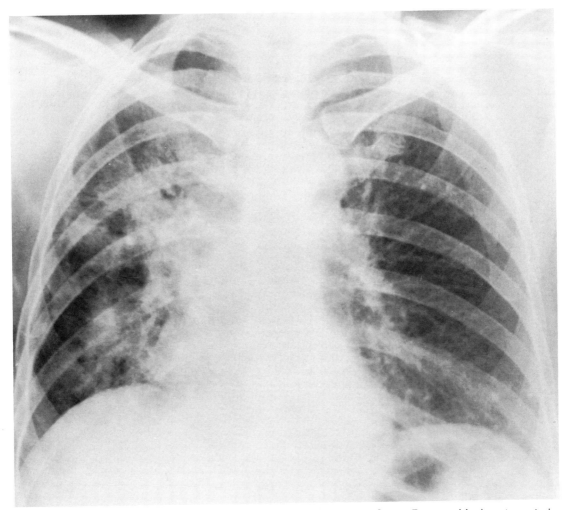

Figure 5–10. **Inhomogeneous Nonsegmental Consolidation: Acute Irradiation Pneumonitis.** A posteroanterior roentgenogram reveals extensive disease throughout the right lung, possessing random distribution without confinement to specific segments; the central and mid lung zones are affected more than the peripheral. An air bronchogram indicates that the process is chiefly one of air-space consolidation although there is moderate loss of lung volume as evidenced by mediastinal shift and right hemidiaphragmatic elevation. Sixty-eight-year-old woman approximately two months following a course of cobalt therapy to anterior mediastinal lymph nodes for metastatic carcinoma of the breast; complete roentgenologic resolution occurred in six months.

Table 5–3. *Inhomogeneous Shadows Without Recognizable Segmental Distribution*

	ETIOLOGY	LOSS OF VOLUME	ANATOMIC DISTRIBUTION
DEVELOPMENTAL	Congenital cystic ade-nomatoid malformation	None (the lesion is expanding).	———
INFECTIOUS	**Bacteria** *Mycobacterium* species	0	Apical and posterior por-tion of upper lobes (rarely anterior alone); superior portion of lower lobes.
	Pseudomonas pseudomallei	+ to +++	Predominantly upper lobes.
	Klebsiella-aerobacter species	+ to +++	Predominantly upper lobes.
	Bacillus anthracis	0	No known predilection.
	Bacteroides species	0	Predominantly lower lobes.
	Fungi *Histoplasma capsulatum*		Primary infection com-monly in lower lobes; postprimary disease usu-ally in upper lobes.
	Coccidioides immitis		Upper lobes.
	Blastomyces dermatitidis	0	Upper lobe predomi-nance in ratio of 3:2.
	Aspergillus species		No predilection.
	Viruses and Mycoplasma All viruses listed in Table 5–4	0	Predominantly lower lobes.
TRAUMATIC	Chronic irradiation fibrosis; irradiation pneumonitis.	+++ to ++++	Generally corresponds to the area irradiated.

Table 5-3. *Inhomogeneous Shadows Without Recognizable Segmental Distribution*
(Continued)

ADDITIONAL FINDINGS	COMMENTS
Tends to expand involved hemithorax. Mass contains numerous irregular air-containing cysts.	Appears to be seen only in infants; mass communicates with bronchial tree and is supplied by the pulmonary circulation. (*See* page 588.)
Cavitation not infrequent; effusion and lymph-node enlargement rare.	**Reinfection tuberculosis. (*See* pages 621 and 640.)**
Frequently associated with cavitation.	Resembles reinfection tuberculosis. Has been described as "unresolved pneumonia." (*See* page 601.)
May be associated with cavitation.	The chronic phase of the disease; closely simulates pulmonary tuberculosis. (*See* page 604.)
Mediastinal lymph node enlargement predominant finding.	Shadows due to pulmonary hemorrhage, not to pneumonia. (*See* page 599.)
Empyema and cavitation.	(*See* page 612.)
In primary disease, hilar lymph-node enlargement frequent; pleural effusion may be present but is not common. In reinfection disease, cavitation may be present, but as with reinfection tuberculosis, hilar lymph-node enlargement uncommon. In reinfection disease, a calcified focus elsewhere in the lungs is frequently present, similar to the Ranke complex of primary tuberculosis.	**There are no clear-cut distinguishing roentgenographic features from primary or reinfection tuberculosis. (*See* page 643.)**
Densities may be "fleeting" in character and may leave behind thin-walled cavities.	This is the so-called benign form of the disease and is generally asymptomatic. (*See* page 652.)
Cavitation in 15 per cent of cases; bone involvement in 25 per cent, either by direct extension across pleura or by blood stream. Pleural effusion and lymph-node enlargement rare.	(*See* page 656.)
None	A rare method of presentation. (*See* page 664.)
None	A specific segmental distribution may not be recognizable at certain stages of these acute pneumonias. (*See* page 416.)
Characteristically there is obliteration of all architectural markings due to replacement with fibrous tissue. Dense fibrotic strands frequently extend from the hilum to the periphery.	Differentiation from lymphangitic spread of carcinoma may be difficult if changes are bilateral although lack of progression over a period of time should permit differentiation. Acute irradiation pneumonitis characteristically produces a homogeneous nonsegmental pattern (*See* Table 5-1) but in some cases is inhomogeneous. (*See* page 1076.)

Table 5–4

INHOMOGENEOUS SHADOWS OF RECOGNIZABLE SEGMENTAL DISTRIBUTION

This pattern characterizes bronchopneumonia or "lobular" pneumonia. The infection is propagated distally in the bronchovascular bundles and thus invariably is of segmental distribution. The parenchymal changes consist in a combination of focal consolidation, atelectasis, and overinflation, resulting in an inhomogeneous roentgenographic pattern. Bronchiectasis produces the same type of pattern.

In addition to the cases illustrated on the following pages, the following figures appearing elsewhere in the book may be referred to as representative of this pattern:

Figure	Page
4– 16	204
4– 24	210
4– 57	247
4– 67	259
4–105	299
4–118	314
7– 29	667
8– 6	744

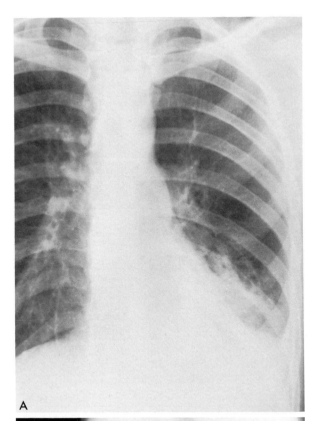

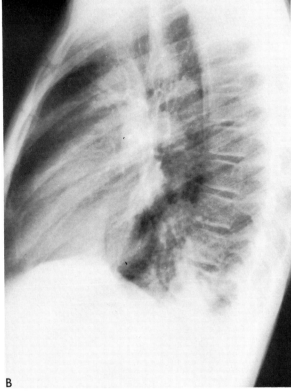

Figure 5–11. Inhomogeneous Segmental Consolidation: Acute Bronchopneumonia. Views of the left hemithorax from posteroanterior (A) and lateral (B) roentgenograms show patchy inhomogeneous consolidation of the posterior and lateral bronchopulmonary segments of the left lower lobe. The affected lung is roughly conical in shape with its apex at the hilum and its base at the diaphragmatic visceral pleura. There is some loss of volume as evidenced by elevation of the left hemidiaphragm and shift of the mediastinum. Heavy growth of *Hemophilus influenzae* from the sputum.

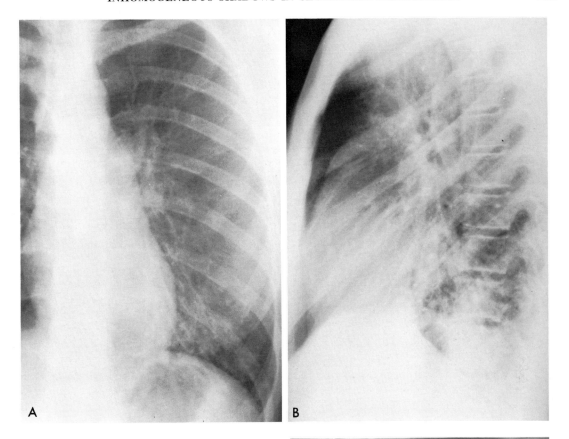

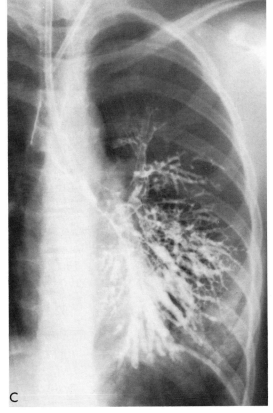

Figure 5-12. **Inhomogeneous Segmental Consolidation: Cylindrical Bronchiectasis.** Views of the left lung from posteroanterior (*A*) and lateral (*B*) roentgenograms demonstrate patchy shadows of increased density occupying all basal bronchopulmonary segments of the left lower lobe; in posteroanterior projection particularly, the shadows are oriented in the distribution of the bronchovascular bundles. There is little loss of volume. A bronchogram (*C*) shows cylindrical dilatation of all basal bronchi of the left lower lobe. The affected bronchi terminate abruptly and there is no peripheral bronchiolar filling. Fourteen-year-old girl.

Table 5–4. *Inhomogeneous Shadows of Recognizable Segmental Distribution*

	ETIOLOGY	LOSS OF VOLUME	ANATOMIC DISTRIBUTION
INFECTIOUS	**Bacteria** *Hemophilus influenzae*	+ to ++	Predominantly lower lobes.
	Escherichia coli	+ to ++	Predominantly lower lobes.
	Pseudomonas aeruginosa	+ to ++	Predominantly lower lobes.
	Mycobacterium species	+ to +++	Apical and posterior segments upper lobes; superior segment lower lobes.
	Fusiform bacilli and *Spirochaeta*	+ to ++	Posterior portions of upper and lower lobes.
	Salmonella species *Brucella* species *Staphylococcus aureus* *Streptococcus pyogenes* *Hemophilus pertussis* *Diplococcus pneumoniae* *Klebsiella-aerobacter* species	+ to ++	Predominantly lower lobes.
	Fungi *Histoplasma capsulatum*	+ to +++	Upper lobes.
	Candida albicans	+ to ++	No predilection.
	Phycomycetes group (including mucor species) *Sporotrichum schenckii*	+ to ++	No known predilection.
	All other fungi listed in Table 5–1	+ to ++	Variable
	Viruses *Mycoplasma pneumoniae* (Eaton agent)	0	Predominantly lower lobes.
	Influenza Adenoviruses Psittacosis (ornithosis) Parainfluenza Coxsackie	0	Predominantly lower lobes.

Table 5–4. *Inhomogeneous Shadows of Recognizable Segmental Distribution (Continued)*

ADDITIONAL FINDINGS	COMMENTS
Pleural effusion common. ⎫ ⎬ ⎭	Typical roentgenographic pattern of broncho-pneumonia. (*See* pages 607, 606, and 600.)
Frequently associated with tuberculous bron-chiectasis and sometimes with cavitation.	Chronic stage of the disease, usually fibrotic (but not necessarily inactive). (*See* pages 621 and 640.)
Commonly results in chronic bronchiectasis.	Aspiration pneumonia; tends to occur when aspirate is bulky in consistency. (*See* page 613.)
Variable with specific organism.	On rare occasions, any of these organisms may give rise to an inhomogeneous segmental pattern (bronchopneumonia). *See* pages 607, 611, 595, 598, 608, 592, and 604.
———	Appearance indistinguishable from chronic reinfection tuberculosis. (*See* page 643.)
May be associated with cavitation.	This pattern of bronchopneumonia is the usual method of presentation. (*See* page 668.)
———	Bronchopneumonia. (*See* pages 671 and 672.)
Variable with specific organism.	The chronic stage of the disease—usually fibrotic. (*See* page 386.)
Pleural effusion and lymph node enlargement rare in adults. Hilar lymph-node enlargement found in 25 per cent of children.	Characteristic reticular pattern with superimposed patchy areas of air space consolidation. Generally indistinguishable from virus pneumonitis. (*See* page 678.)
Hilar lymph-node enlargement is seen in some patients with ornithosis.	Roentgenographic pattern indistinguishable within the group and indistinguishable from *Mycoplasma pneumonia*. (*See* pages 682, 688, 695, 685, and 687.)

Table continues

Table 5–4. *Inhomogeneous Shadows of Recognizable Segmental Distribution (Continued)*

	ETIOLOGY	LOSS OF VOLUME	ANATOMIC DISTRIBUTION
INFECTIOUS *(Cont.)*	**ECHO** Rubeola	0	Predominantly lower lobes.
	Respiratory syncytial	0	Predominantly lower lobes.
	Parasites *Toxoplasma gondii*	0	No predilection.
NEOPLASTIC	**Hodgkin's disease**	**0**	**No predilection.**
	All endobronchial neoplasms either benign or malignant	0 to ++++	As with individual lesion.
IMMUNOLOGIC	Systemic lupus erythematosus	Progressive loss of lung volume may be characteristic but is unrelated to roentgenographic evidence of localized pulmonary disease.	Commonly peripherally situated in the lung bases.
INHALATIONAL	Chronic aspiration pneumonia	+ to +++	**Posterior segments of lower or upper lobes; on serial roentgenographic examinations, anatomic distribution may vary considerably.**
	Aspiration of solid foreign bodies	+ to ++	Almost exclusively lower lobes, the ratio of right to left being 2:1.
	Lipoid pneumonia	0 to +	Dependent portions of upper and lower lobes (occasionally right middle lobe or lingula).
AIRWAYS DISEASE	Bronchiectasis	+ to +++	**More frequent in lower lobes and right middle lobe. Multiple segments or lobes may be involved.**

Table 5-4. *Inhomogeneous Shadows of Recognizable Segmental Distribution (Continued)*

ADDITIONAL FINDINGS	COMMENTS
Hilar lymph node enlargement frequent.	In measles this pattern is probably due to superimposed bacterial bronchopneumonia. (*See* pages 688 and 686.)
Diffuse overinflation secondary to bronchitis and bronchiolitis.	Characteristically a disease of infants and young children, but may occur in adults. (*See* page 685.)
Hilar lymph node enlargement common.	(*See* page 703.)
Mediastinal and hilar lymph node enlargement almost invariable. Kerley lines in some cases. Pleural effusion in 30 per cent of cases.	**The most common form of pulmonary parenchymal involvement. Results from direct extension from mediastinal and hilar nodes along lymphatics or interstitial tissues.** (*See* page 771.)
———	In any situation where a neoplasm has resulted in obstructive pneumonitis, the partial relief of the obstruction while under therapy may permit visualization of air-containing distorted channels within the obstructed segment.
Cardiac enlargement in 35 to 50 per cent of patients, commonly due to pericardial effusion. Bilateral pleural effusion common.	Pulmonary change is nonspecific, generally in form of basal pneumonitis or focal atelectasis. (*See* page 867.)
Almost always associated with underlying condition such as Zenker's diverticulum, esophageal stenosis, achalasia, or disturbances in swallowing of neuromuscular origin.	**The roentgenographic picture suggests typical "bronchopneumonia." Multiple segments may be involved. Bronchiectasis may develop in involved segments.** (*See* page 959.)
The foreign body is radiopaque in approximately 10 per cent of cases.	The pattern is purely segmental and is produced by a combination of atelectasis and pneumonitis secondary to bronchial obstruction. May be associated with bronchiectasis. (*See* page 956.)
None	A reticular pattern may develop as a result of the movement of oil (in macrophages) from the air spaces into the interstitial tissues. (*See* page 964.)
Saccular bronchiectasis may show fluid levels. Compensatory overinflation may be present in unaffected lung.	(*See* page 1039.)

Table 5–5

CYSTIC AND CAVITARY DISEASE

This table includes all forms of pulmonary disease characterized by circumscribed air-containing spaces with distinct walls. This broad definition includes such entities as blebs, bullae, and cystic bronchiectasis. Air-fluid levels may be present or absent. Cavities may be single or multiple.

In addition to the cases illustrated on the following pages, the following figures appearing elsewhere in the book may be referred to as representative of this pattern:

Figure	Page
2– 8	117
4– 75	267
4– 78	270
4– 80	272
4– 81	272
4– 82	273
4– 94	285
4–143	339
4–145	342
6– 4	579
7– 44	717
8– 29	782

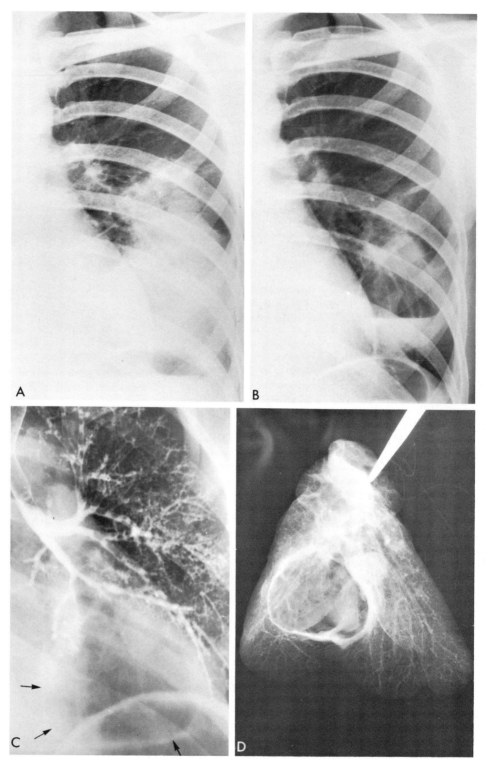

Figure 5-13. **Cavitary Disease: Intralobar Pulmonary Sequestration.** A view of the left hemithorax from a posteroanterior roentgenogram (*A*) shows a sharply-circumscribed shadow of homogeneous density situated in the lower half of the left lung; it does not conform to a bronchopulmonary segment and in fact its configuration suggests a peripheral mass. In lateral projection, it was seen to be situated posteriorly. Approximately one month later (*B*), the mass has diminished considerably in size and now presents as a cavity containing a prominant air-fluid level; note the contiguity with the left hemidiaphragm. A bronchogram (*C*) performed about three months after the examination illustrated in (*B*) reveals the basal bronchi to be festooned around a large cystic space (*arrows*). At thoracotomy, the mass was found to be supplied by a systemic artery passing into the lower lobe from the diaphragm. A roentgenogram of the resected lobe (*D*) shows the cyst to excellent advantage. Twenty-six-year-old woman who had been asymptomatic until the onset of acute pneumonia approximately one week before the roentgenogram illustrated in *A*.

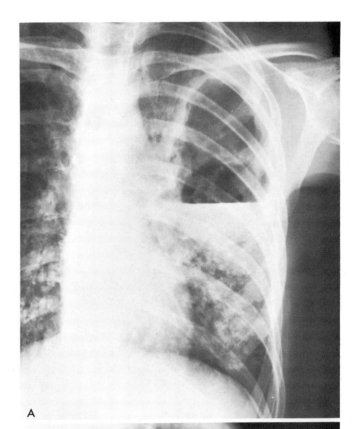

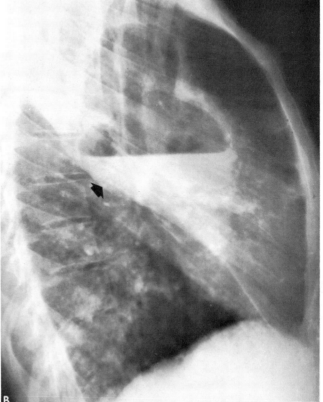

Figure 5–14. **Cavitary Disease: Acute Lung Abscess.** Posteroanterior (A) and lateral (B) roentgenograms show a large cavity in the posterior portion of the left upper lobe, possessing a prominent air-fluid level. The cavity wall is of moderate thickness and possesses an irregular, shaggy inner lining. The major fissure is bowed posteriorly (*arrow* in B). The patchy shadows in both lungs represent contrast medium from previous bronchography. Twenty-four-year-old woman with long-standing history of spasmodic asthma. Heavy growth of *Staphylococcus aureus* from the sputum.

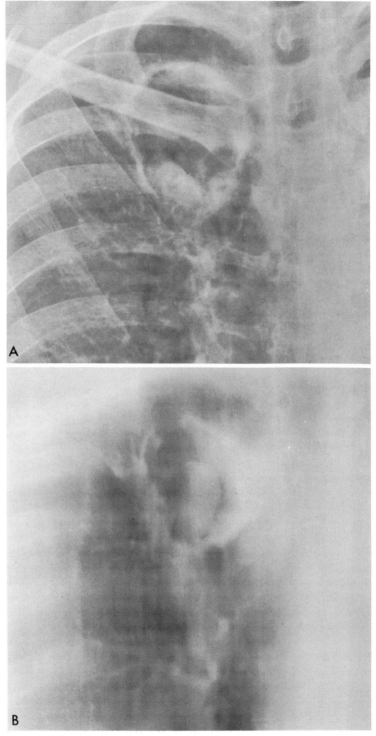

Figure 5–15. **Cavitary Disease: Chronic Tuberculous Cavity Containing a Mycetoma.** Views of the upper half of the right lung from a posteroanterior roentgenogram (*A*) and an anteroposterior tomogram (*B*) reveal a thin-walled, irregular cavity in the paramediastinal zone. Situated within it is a smooth, oblong shadow of homogeneous density whose relationships to the wall of the cavity change from the erect (*A*) to the supine (*B*) positions. A photomicrograph of the intracavitary mass (*see* figure 4–82, page 273) revealed multiple mycelial threads characteristic of *Aspergillus*. The cavity was of tuberculous etiology.

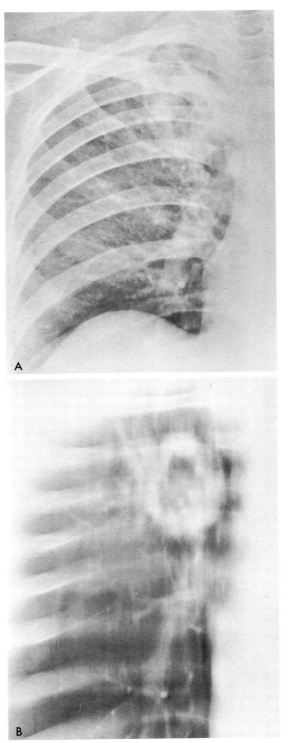

Figure 5–16. **Cavitary Disease: Cavitating Bronchogenic Carcinoma.** Views of the upper half of the right lung from a posteroanterior roentgenogram (*A*) and an anteroposterior tomogram (*B*) reveal a rather ill-defined cavitating mass. The thickness of the wall and irregular nodular character of the inner lining are highly suggestive of bronchogenic carcinoma. Proved highly differentiated squamous cell cancer.

Table 5–5. *Cystic and Cavitary Disease*

		ETIOLOGY	ANATOMIC DISTRIBUTION	CHARACTER OF WALL
DEVELOPMENTAL		Intralobar bronchopulmonary sequestration	Two-thirds of cases left lower lobe, one-third right lower lobe. Almost invariably contiguous to diaphragm.	May be thin- or thick-walled.
		Bronchogenic cyst	Medial third of lower lobes.	Thin-walled.
INFECTIOUS	Bacteria	*Staphylococcus aureus*	No lobar predilection.	Tends to be thick with ragged inner lining.
		Klebsiella-aerobacter group (Friedlander's)	Upper lobes predominate.	Tends to be thick with ragged inner lining.
		Mycobacterium species	Apical and posterior regions of upper lobes and apical region of lower lobes.	Tends to be of moderate thickness. Inner lining generally smooth.
		Pseudomonas aeruginosa *Escherichia coli* *Bacteroides* species	Predominantly lower lobes.	Highly variable.
		Bacillus proteus	Predominantly upper lobe.	Tends to be thick, with ragged inner lining.
		Salmonella species	——	——
		Diplococcus pneumoniae	Upper lobe predilection.	Thick, with ragged inner lining.
		Pseudomonas pseudomallei	Upper lobes predominate.	Moderately thick.
		Malleomyces mallei	No lobar predilection.	Highly variable.

Table 5–5. *Cystic and Cavitary Disease (Continued)*

ADDITIONAL FINDINGS	COMMENTS
Air-fluid levels may be present. The cyst volume may change on serial roentgenographic examination. Cyst may be masked by pneumonia in surrounding parenchyma.	Cyst may be solitary but more commonly multi-locular or multiple. (*See* page 578.)
Air-fluid levels may be present. When pneumonitis leads to communication between cyst and the bronchial tree, the cavity may be masked by the surrounding pneumonia.	Seventy-five per cent of bronchogenic cysts eventually become air-containing as a result of communication with contiguous lung. (*See* page 582.)
Pleural effusion (empyema) with or without bronchopleural fistula (pyopneumothorax) almost invariable in children and may occur in adults.	In adults, cavities result from tissue necrosis; in children, air-containing spaces commonly due to pneumatocele formation. Staphylococcal pyemia may lead to multiple small abscesses widely distributed throughout both lungs. (*See* page 595.)
Pleural effusion (empyema) may be present. Cavity rarely contains large masses of necrotic lung.	Abscess formation in acute pneumonia. Cavities are usually single but tend to be multi-locular. Multiple cavities may be present if pneumonia multilobar. (*See* page 604.)
Cavities may be multiple.	Cavitation tends to be a more prominent feature of atypical mycobacterial disease than of mycobacterium tuberculosis. (*See* pages 621 and 640.)
Empyema frequent.	Often the result of bacteremia from an extra-thoracic focus (G-U tract). Tends to occur in debilitated states (alcoholism or diabetes). (*See* pages 600 and 612.)
May be associated with loss of volume of affected lobe. Pleural effusion uncommon.	(*See* page 606.)
Frequently associated with empyema.	(*See* page 607.)
The cavity may contain large irregular masses of necrotic lung.	A rare complication of fulminating pneumococcal pneumonia. (*See* page 592.)
Effusions rare.	(*See* page 601.)
Empyema	(*See* page 611.)

Table continues

Table 5–5. *Cystic and Cavitary Disease (Continued)*

	ETIOLOGY	ANATOMIC DISTRIBUTION	CHARACTER OF WALL
	All other bacteria listed in Tables 5–1 to 5–4	——	——
	Fungi *Actinomyces israelii* *Nocardia* species	Lower lobe predilection, often bilateral.	Generally thick-walled.
	Histoplasma capsulatum	Predominantly upper lobes.	Variable.
	Coccidioides immitis	Predominantly upper lobes.	Tend to be very thin-walled.
	Blastomyces dermatitidis	No predilection.	Variable, but generally thick-walled.
	Cryptococcus neoformans	Predominantly lower lobes.	Variable, but generally thick-walled.
INFECTIOUS *(Cont.)*	*Sporotrichum schenckii* *Geotrichum* species	Upper lobe predilection.	Characteristically thin-walled.
	Phycomycetes group	Not distinctive.	——
	Aspergillus species *Candida albicans*	——	——
	Parasites *Entamoeba histolytica* (amebiasis)	Almost restricted to right lower lobe.	Generally thick-walled with irregular ragged inner lining.
	Paragonimus westermani	No predilection.	Characteristically thin-walled, with local elevation or hump on inner lining.
	Echinococcus granulosus (hydatid cyst)	Lower lobe predilection.	Air may dissect between ectocyst and endocyst creating a halo; or contents of cyst may be expelled into bronchial tree leaving a thin-walled cystic space.

Table 5–5. Cystic and Cavitary Disease (Continued)

ADDITIONAL FINDINGS	COMMENTS
———	*Rarely* any bacterium may lead to abscess or cavity formation, particularly in debilitated patients with lowered resistance.
Pleural effusion (empyema) is common as is extension into the chest wall with or without rib destruction.	Roentgenographic patterns of these two organisms are indistinguishable. (*See* pages 662 and 663.)
Cavities may be multiple.	No clear-cut distinguishing roentgenographic features from reinfection tuberculosis. (*See* page 643.)
These thin-walled cavities tend to occur in the asymptomatic form of the disease following "fleeting" pneumonitis.	Not to be confused with cavitating coin lesions which tend to be somewhat thicker-walled and frequently multiple (*see* Table 5–8). (*See* page 652.)
Cavitation occurs in about 15 per cent of cases. Pleural effusion and hilar lymph node enlargement very uncommon.	(*See* page 656.)
Cavitation occurs in about 15 per cent of cases. Pleural effusion and hilar lymph-node enlargement very uncommon.	(*See* page 657.)
———	(*See* page 672.)
———	(*See* page 671.)
———	Primary disease of the lungs rarely cavitates; characteristically these organisms are opportunistic invaders in the form of fungus balls (mycetoma) in chronic debilitating disease with cavitating pneumonic lesions of other etiology. (*See* pages 664 and 668.)
Right pleural effusion almost invariable.	Organisms enter thorax via right hemidiaphragm from liver abscess. (*See* page 701.)
In addition to cavities, there may be isolated nodular shadows containing vacuoles. Pleural effusion rarely.	Organisms enter thorax via diaphragm from peritoneal space. (*See* page 716.)
Irregularities of fluid layer caused by collapsed membranes (water-lily sign or sign of the camalote). Hydropneumothorax occasionally.	(*See* page 712.)

Table continues

Table 5–5. Cystic and Cavitary Disease (Continued)

	ETIOLOGY	ANATOMIC DISTRIBUTION	CHARACTER OF WALL
NEOPLASTIC	Bronchogenic carcinoma	Clear-cut predilection for upper lobes, both lungs being affected equally.	Tends to be thick, with an irregular, nodular inner lining (mural nodules). Thin-walled cavities simulating bronchogenic cysts occur occasionally.
	Hematogeneous metastases	Cavitation occurs more frequently in upper than in lower lobe lesions.	May be thin- or thick-walled.
	Hodgkin's disease	Lower lobe predilection.	Thin- or thick-walled.
THROMBOEMBOLIC	Thromboembolism with infarction	Lower lobe predilection predominantly posterior and lateral segments.	May be thick, with shaggy inner lining.
IMMUNOLOGIC	Wegener's granulomatosis	Widely distributed and bilateral, with no predilection for upper or lower lung zones.	Usually thick, with irregular inner lining. In time, cavities may become thin-walled cystic spaces.
	Rheumatoid necrobiotic nodule	Peripheral subpleural parenchyma, commonly in lower lobes.	Thick with smooth inner lining. With remission of the arthritis, cavities may become thin-walled and gradually disappear.
INHALATIONAL	Silicosis—complicated (P.M.F.)	Strong predilection for upper lobes.	Tends to be thick with irregular inner lining.
	Coal workers' pneumoconiosis—complicated (P.M.F.)	Strong predilection for upper lobes.	Tends to be thick with irregular inner lining.

Table 5–5. Cystic and Cavitary Disease (Continued)

ADDITIONAL FINDINGS	COMMENTS
Chunks of necrotic cancer occasionally may become detached and lie free within the cavity, simulating fungus ball.	Cavitation occurs in 2 to 10 per cent of bronchogenic carcinomas, most commonly in lesions peripherally located. The majority are squamous cell in type (adenocarcinomas and large cell undifferentiated carcinomas cavitate occasionally, small cell carcinomas rarely if ever). (*See* page 736.)
Cavitation may involve only a few of multiple nodules throughout the lungs, such nodules characteristically showing considerable variation in size.	Cavitation in metastatic neoplasms less common (4 per cent) than in primary neoplasms (9 per cent). Occurs more frequently in squamous cell neoplasms but also in adenocarcinoma (particularly from the large bowel) and sarcoma. (*See* page 794.)
Cavities are frequently multiple. Commonly associated with mediastinal and hilar lymph-node enlargement.	Cavitation occurs characteristically in peripheral parenchymal consolidation. (*See* page 771.)
Prominent feeding artery, associated pleural effusion, raised diaphragm, or multiple lesions may suggest the diagnosis. A mass of necrotic lung may separate and lie within the cavity, simulating intracavitary fungus ball.	Usually associated with septic infarction. An extremely rare manifestation which may be misdiagnosed unless clinical picture and associated roentgenographic findings suggest the possibility. (*See* page 804.)
Cavities commonly multiple but all masses do not necessarily cavitate.	Cavitation occurs eventually in from one third to one half of patients. With treatment, cavitary lesions may disappear or heal with scar formation. (*See* page 873.)
Pleural effusion or spontaneous pneumothorax.	Well circumscribed masses are more frequently multiple than solitary and range in size from 3 mm to 7 cm. Cavitary nodules wax and wane in concert with frequently associated subcutaneous nodules. (*See* page 883.)
Background of nodular or reticulonodular disease is inevitable although serial examinations may reveal diminution in the number of nodules due to incorporation into the massive consolidation. Hilar lymph-node enlargement is the rule, with or without egg-shell calcification.	Cavitation in conglomerate lesions is usually the result of superimposed tuberculosis but sometimes is due simply to ischemic necrosis. (*See* page 919.)
Background of simple coal workers' pneumoconiosis throughout the remainder of the lungs.	Cavitation in conglomerate shadows is due either to superimposed tuberculosis or to ischemic necrosis. (*See* page 939.)

Table continues

Table 5–5. Cystic and Cavitary Disease (Continued)

	ETIOLOGY	ANATOMIC DISTRIBUTION	CHARACTER OF WALL
AIRWAYS DISEASE	**Blebs or bullae**	**Predilection for upper lobes, particularly extreme apex.**	Thin-walled.
	Cystic bronchiectasis	Predilection for lower lobes.	Thin-walled.
TRAUMATIC	Pulmonary parenchymal laceration (traumatic lung cyst)	Characteristically in the peripheral subpleural parenchyma immediately underlying the point of maximum injury.	Typically thin-walled.

Table 5–5. *Cystic and Cavitary Disease (Continued)*

ADDITIONAL FINDINGS	COMMENTS
With infection, fluid levels may develop. In some cases, roentgenologic evidence of diffuse emphysema will be present.	The thinness of the wall is the main differentiating feature from true cavitation. (*See* page 1023.)
Usually considerable loss of volume of affected segment or segments.	"Cavities" represent severely dilated segmental bronchi. Usually multiple and commonly with air-fluid levels. (*See* page 1044.)
The presence of laceration may be masked by surrounding pulmonary contusion. In some cases of bullet or knife wounds of the lung, a central radiolucency may be observed along the course of the bullet track, simulating a cavity when viewed in the same direction as the wound.	Approximately half these lesions present as thin-walled air-filled cavities (with or without air-fluid levels) and the remainder as pulmonary hematomas. They may be single or multiple, unilocular or multilocular; they are oval or spherical in shape and range from 2 to 14 cm in diameter. (*See* page 1069.)

Table 5–6

Solitary Pulmonary Nodules Less than 6 cm in Diameter ("Coin" Lesions)

For the purposes of this table, the criteria for inclusion in this category are as follows:

1. The presence of a solitary roentgenographic shadow not exceeding 6 cm in its largest diameter.

2. The lesion is fairly discrete but not necessarily sharply circumscribed.

3. It may have any contour (smooth, lobulated, or umbilicated) or shape.

4. It may be calcified or cavitated.

5. Satellite lesions may be present.

6. The lesion is surrounded by air-containing lung; *or* if it is adjacent to the visceral pleural surface over the convexity of the thorax, at least two thirds of its circumference is contiguous to air-containing lung.

7. Symptoms may be present.

In addition to the cases illustrated on the following pages, the following figures appearing elsewhere in the book may be referred to as representative of this pattern:

Figure	*Page*
4–69	262
4–70	263
4–71	264
4–74	266
4–88	279
4–89	280
6– 3	575
6– 7	584
6–10	587
7–16	635
7–19	647
8– 4	729

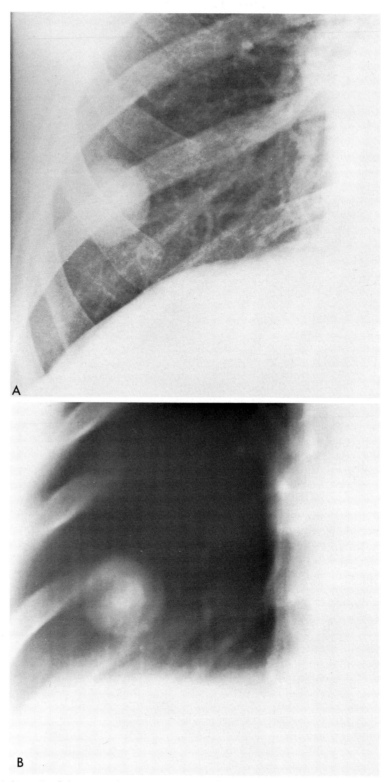

Figure 5–17. **Solitary Nodule: Histoplasmoma.** Views of the lower portion of the right lung from a postero-anterior roentgenogram (*A*) and an anteroposterior tomogram (*B*) reveal a solitary, sharply-circumscribed nodule measuring 3.0 cm in diameter. The lesion is spherical and is homogeneous in density except for a central nidus of calcification seen to best advantage on the tomogram. Pathologically, the lesion was characterized by chronic granulomatous inflammation, probably due to histoplasmosis. This roentgenographic appearance is typical of histoplasmoma, particularly the central calcific focus which produces the so-called "target" appearance. (Courtesy Dr. Max Palayew, Jewish General Hospital, Montreal.)

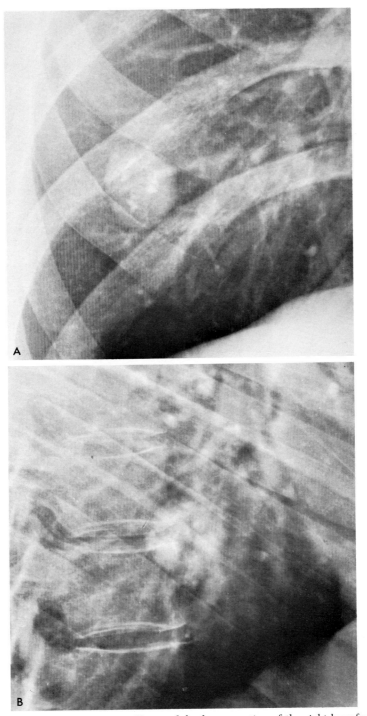

Figure 5–18. **Solitary Nodule: Hamartoma.** Views of the lower portion of the right lung from posteroanterior (*A*) and lateral (*B*) roentgenograms show a solitary, sharply-circumscribed nodule measuring 3 cm in diameter. Irregular calcium deposits throughout the lesion are suggestive of the descriptive designation "popcorn." Proved hamartoma. (Courtesy Dr. David Berger, Royal Edward Chest Hospital, Montreal.)

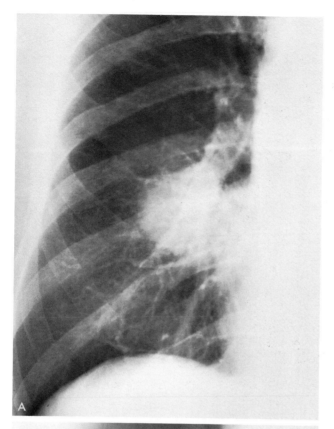

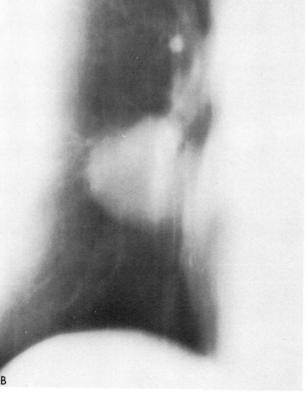

Figure 5–19. **Solitary Nodule: Squamous Cell Bronchogenic Carcinoma.** Views of the lower half of the right lung from a postero-anterior roentgenogram (A) and an antero-posterior tomogram (B) demonstrate a solitary mass which measures 5 cm in its greatest diameter. The mass is situated within the right middle lobe (note the silhouette sign). Its margins are fairly sharply circumscribed although somewhat irregular. The mass is perfectly homogeneous and shows no evidence of calcification. The size of the mass and its nodular contour suggest primary bronchogenic cancer. Sixty-year-old asymptomatic male.

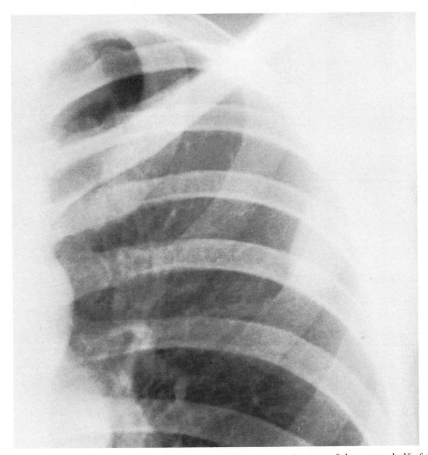

Figure 5-20. **Solitary Nodule: Posttraumatic Pulmonary Hematoma.** A view of the upper half of the left lung from a posteroanterior roentgenogram reveals a smooth, sharply-circumscribed, oval mass projected in the plane of the anterior portion of the third rib, immediately subpleural in location. Its density is homogeneous. Nineteen-year-old man with a history of severe trauma to the chest in a car accident six weeks previously; this roentgenogram was made three weeks after the study illustrated in Figure 4–81, page 272, at which time an air-fluid level was present within the mass. Over the following weeks the shadow gradually diminished in size and disappeared completely without residua four months later. (Courtesy Dr. J. G. Monks, Saskatoon.)

Table 5–6. *Solitary Pulmonary Nodules Less Than 6 cm in Diameter ("Coin" Lesions)*

	ETIOLOGY	INCIDENCE	LOCATION
DEVELOPMENTAL	Bronchogenic cyst	Peak incidence third decade; predilection for males and Yemenite Jews.	Lower lobe predilection, most commonly medial third.
	Bronchopulmonary sequestration (intralobar and extralobar)	Rare in this size range.	Almost invariably lower lobe, related to diaphragm.
	Pulmonary arteriovenous fistula	0.6 per cent of Bateson's series. In two thirds of cases, lesions are single.	More common in lower lobes.
	Varicosity of a pulmonary vein	Very rare (20 cases reported by 1966).	Medial third of lung (lingular vein on left or medial basal pulmonary vein on right).
	Congenital bronchial atresia	Very rare.	Strong predilection for the apicoposterior bronchus of the left upper lobe.
INFECTIOUS	Bacteria *Mycobacterium tuberculosis* (tuberculoma)	Common	Predilection for upper lobes, the right more often than the left.

Table 5–6. *Solitary Pulmonary Nodules Less Than 6 cm in Diameter ("Coin" Lesions) (Continued)*

SIZE AND SHAPE	CALCIFICATION	CAVITATION	COMMENTS
Usually several cms; round or oval, smooth, well-defined.	Rarely in wall; calcium has been reported in cyst contents.	Yes, when communication occurs with bronchial tree.	Two thirds of bronchial cysts are pulmonary, one third mediastinal. Cysts are homogeneous until communication established with contiguous lung, usually because of infection (occurs eventually in **75** per cent of cases). (*See* page **582**.)
Commonly measure over 6 cm in diameter (*See* Table 5–7).	No	Common	(*See* page 577.)
Up to 6 cm; round or oval, slightly lobulated, sharply defined.	Occasionally, probably due to phleboliths.	No	Diagnosis by identification of feeding artery and draining vein. Angiography of *both lungs* imperative if surgery contemplated in order to identify multiple fistulae not visible on plain roentgenograms. 40 to 65 per cent of cases have hereditary hemorrhagic telangiectasia. (*See* page 573.)
Several cms; round or oval, lobulated, well-defined.	No	No	Change in size with Valsalva and Mueller procedures. Differential diagnosis from arteriovenous fistula by late filling and slow drainage on pulmonary angiography. (*See* page 576.)
Oval; approximately 2×5 cm; smooth, sharply defined.	No	No	The mass consists of inspissated mucus which accumulates within the bronchus immediately distal to the point of obliteration; the lung parenchyma distal to the occlusion is overinflated due to collateral air drift. (*See* page 583.)
0.5 to 4 cm; round or oval; 25 per cent are lobulated.	Frequent	Uncommon	"Satellite" lesions in **80** per cent; the draining bronchus may show irregular thickening of its wall or occasionally bronchostenosis. (*See* page 633.)

Table continues

Table 5–6. *Solitary Pulmonary Nodules Less Than 6 cm in Diameter ("Coin" Lesions) (Continued)*

	ETIOLOGY	INCIDENCE	LOCATION
	Fungi *Histoplasma capsulatum* (histoplasmoma)	Common	More frequently in the lower than in the upper lobes.
	Coccidioides (coccidi- oidomycoma)	Rare	Upper lobe predilec- tion.
	Aspergillus fumigatus (mucoid impaction)	Very uncommon; largely restricted to patients with bron- chospasm.	Upper lobe predilec- tion.
INFECTIOUS *(Cont.)*	**Parasites** *Echinococcus* (Hydatid cyst)	Common in endemic areas.	Lower lobe predilec- tion, right more often than left.
	Dirofilaria immitus	Rare	No known predilection.
NEOPLASTIC	Bronchial adenoma	Incidence com- pared to broncho- genic carcinoma 1 to 50. 20 to 25 per cent of all bronchial adenomas present as solitary nodules.	Predilection for right upper and middle lobes and lingula.

Table 5–6. *Solitary Pulmonary Nodules Less Than 6 cm in Diameter ("Coin" Lesions) (Continued)*

SIZE AND SHAPE	CALCIFICATION	CAVITATION	COMMENTS
Seldom more than 3 cm in diameter; round or oval; typically sharply circumscribed.	Common, often central in location, thus producing the "target" appearance.	Rare	"Satellite" lesions fairly common. Histoplasmomas may be multiple, ranging considerably in size. Associated hilar lymph node calcification is common. (*See* page 645.)
0.5 to 3.0 cm; round or oval; typically sharply circumscribed.	In some cases.	Common; may be thin- or thick-walled.	(*See* page 654.)
Two to 6 cm (rarely up to 8 cm in diameter); tends to be finger-like but may be Y-shaped or V-shaped in conformity with bronchial subdivision.	No	True cavitation occurs rarely as a result of lung necrosis, although air-fluid levels may be visible within the markedly dilated bronchus.	The mass is caused by mucoid impaction within a proximal segmental bronchus. It tends to be transient in nature, although it may persist unchanged for weeks or even months, or may increase in size while under observation. When the lesion clears, it leaves as a residuum cylindrical or saccular dilatation of the affected bronchi. The impacted bronchus may or may not cause atelectasis of the involved segment; atelectasis frequently prevented by collateral airdrift. (*See* page 666.)
Up to 6 cm (*see* Table 5–7). Almost always well circumscribed. Tendency to bizarre irregular shape.	Very rare.	Common	(*See* page 712.)
Well-circumscribed.	No	Sometimes	Involvement of larger pulmonary arteries may result in a shadow simulating pulmonary infarction. (*See* page 711.)
Average 4 cm (range 1 to 10 cm) round or oval, sharply circumscribed, slightly lobulated.	Rare	Rare	The remaining 75 per cent of bronchial adenomas relate to a bronchial lumen and lead to segmental atelectasis or obstructive pneumonitis. (*See* page 724.)

Table continues

Table 5–6. *Solitary Pulmonary Nodules Less Than 6 cm in Diameter ("Coin" Lesions) (Continued)*

	ETIOLOGY	INCIDENCE	LOCATION
	Hamartoma	Comprise approximately 5 per cent of solitary peripheral nodules.	No lobar predilection.
	Leiomyoma Fibroma Lipoma Hemangioma Hemangioendothelioma Hemangiopericytoma Chemodectoma Granular-cell myoblastoma Neurogenic neoplasms Chrondroma Endometriosis	Very rare.	No definite predilection.
	Fibrin body	Rare	Most commonly in the posterior pleural gutter.
NEOPLASTIC *(Cont.)*	Bronchogenic carcinoma	Varies widely; in patients referred for resection, approximately 40 per cent of solitary nodules will be malignant.	Predominantly upper lobes.
	Hematogenous metastasis	3 to 5 per cent of asymptomatic nodules.	Predominantly lower lobes.
	Bronchioloalveolar carcinoma	The most common method of presentation of local bronchioloalveolar carcinoma.	No predilection.

Table 5–6. *Solitary Pulmonary Nodules Less Than 6 cm in Diameter ("Coin" Lesions) (Continued)*

SIZE AND SHAPE	CALCIFICATION	CAVITATION	COMMENTS
The majority are less than 4 cm in diameter; well-circumscribed; more often lobulated than smooth in a ratio of 2:1.	Incidence varies widely in reported series, but certainly occurs in a minority of cases. "Popcorn" configuration virtually diagnostic.	No	Ten per cent arise endobronchially and then may cause bronchial obstruction, atelectasis, or obstructive pneumonitis. Serial examination may reveal slow growth. (*See* page 730.)
Up to 6 cm; usually well defined.	Rarely.	No	Rarely these neoplasms may arise within a bronchial wall and thus be manifested roentgenographically by bronchial obstruction and peripheral atelectasis or obstructive pneumonitis (*see* Table 5–2). (*See* pages 723-736.)
Size variable. Round, oval or irregular.	No	No	Consists of a conglomerate mass of fibrin which develops in serofibrinous pleural effusion or in a pre-existing pulmonary cavity in which hemorrhage has occurred. Pleural fibrin bodies have been related by some to the condition "Zuckerguss." (*See* page 735.)
Commonly over 2 cm. Margins tend to be ill-defined, lobulated, or umbilicated.	Very rare.	2 to 10 per cent.	Satellite lesions very uncommon. (*See* page 736.)
Three mm to 6 cm; smooth or slightly lobulated. Tend to be well-circumscribed.	Rarely and only in osteogenic sarcoma or chondrosarcoma.	Occasionally	In 25 per cent of cases, metastatic lesions to the lungs are solitary. (*See* page 794.)
Range 1 to 6 cm; round, smooth, or lobulated; may be sharply circumscribed or ill-defined.	No	Rarely.	An air bronchogram or air bronchiologram is a common roentgenographic feature, except in the smaller lesions. Tends to be very slow growing. (*See* page 770.)

Table continues

Table 5-6. *Solitary Pulmonary Nodules Less Than 6 cm in Diameter ("Coin" Lesions) (Continued)*

	ETIOLOGY	INCIDENCE	LOCATION
NEOPLASTIC *(Cont.)*	The lympho-sarcoma group	Rare	No predilection.
	Multiple myeloma (plasmacytoma)	Rare	No predilection.
IMMUNOLOGIC	Rheumatoid necrobiotic nodule	Rare	In the peripheral sub-pleural zone, usually lower lobes.
INHALATIONAL	Lipoid pneumonia	Rare	Usually dependent portions of upper and lower lobes, but sometimes right middle lobe or lingula.
TRAUMATIC	Pulmonary hematoma	Uncommon	Usually in a peripheral subpleural location.
IDIOPATHIC	Amyloidosis	Extremely rare cause of solitary nodules.	No predilection.

Table 5–6. *Solitary Pulmonary Nodules Less Than 6 cm in Diameter ("Coin" Lesions) (Continued)*

SIZE AND SHAPE	CALCIFICATION	CAVITATION	COMMENTS
Three mm to 6 cm; round, ovoid, triangular or polyhedral; tends to have fuzzy outline.	No	In reticulum cell sarcoma, "cyst-like" lesions may occur which resemble cavitation.	May be a manifestation of either primary or secondary disease. (*See* page 784.)
Up to 6 cm; lobulated.	No	No	No distinguishing features from peripheral bronchogenic carcinoma. (*See* page 790.)
Three mm to 7 cm; well-circumscribed, smooth.	No	Common. Cavities possess thick walls and smooth inner lining.	More commonly multiple than solitary. Pleural effusion may be present. Eosinophilia in some patients. Nodules wax and wane in concert with the frequently associated subcutaneous nodules and in proportion to the activity of the rheumatoid arthritis. (*See* page 883.)
Five mm to 6 cm; sharply circumscribed, smooth or lobulated.	No	No	(*See* page 964.)
Size highly variable —commonly 2 cm to 6 cm but may be very large (*see* Table 5–7); oval or round, sharply circumscribed, smooth.	No	A hematoma occurs as a result of hemorrhage into a pulmonary parenchymal laceration or traumatic lung cyst—thus an air fluid level may be present as a result of communication with the bronchial tree.	Generally undergo slow but progressive decrease in size, although they may persist for long periods of time, sometimes up to four months. May be multiple. Not uncommonly result from segmental or wedge resection of lung parenchyma. The presence of a hematoma may be masked by surrounding pulmonary contusion. (*See* page 1069.)
Up to 5 cm in diameter.	Occasionally in the periphery.	Occasionally	This peripheral form of amyloidosis may also occur in the form of multiple parenchymal masses. Rarely may be associated with deposits in a bronchial wall leading to atelectasis or obstructive pneumonitis. (*See* page 1121.)

Table 5–7

SOLITARY PULMONARY MASSES 6 CM OR MORE IN DIAMETER

The general characteristics of lesions included in this table are the same as for solitary "coin" lesions. The separation of a group of entities into this category on the basis of size alone perhaps is arbitrary but appeared necessary in view of the restriction on size imposed by most authorities for inclusion of solitary nodules as so-called "coin" lesions.

In addition to the cases illustrated on the following pages, the following figures appearing elsewhere in the book may be referred to as representative of this pattern:

Figure	Page
4–72	265
4–73	265
4–96	287
7–26	660

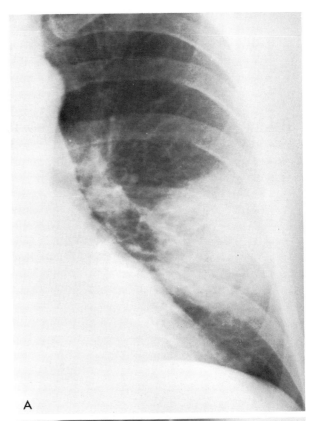

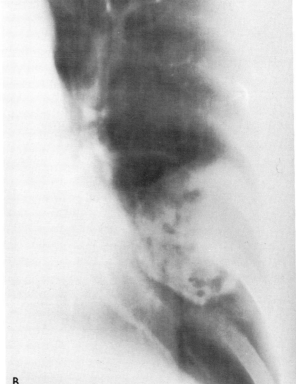

Figure 5–21. **Masses Over 6 cm in Diameter: Cryptococcosis.** Views of the lower two thirds of the left lung from a posteroanterior roentgenogram (A) and an anteroposterior tomogram (B) reveal a roughly circular mass measuring 7 cm in diameter. Its margins are sharply circumscribed although somewhat irregular. In the center of the mass are several irregular air-containing spaces ranging in size from a few millimeters to 2 cm; these represent multiple cavities within the consolidated parenchyma. This pattern is suggestive of pulmonary infection due to *Cryptococcus neoformans*; the organism was recovered from the sputum.

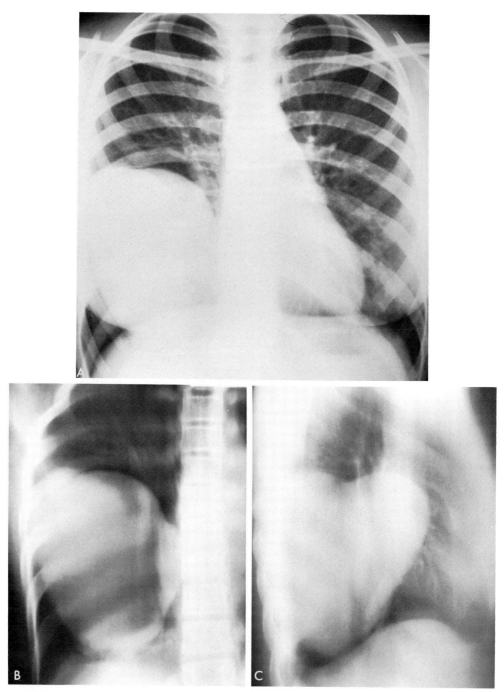

Figure 5–22.   **Masses Over 6 cm in Diameter: Echinococcus (Hydatid) Cyst.** A posteroanterior roentgenogram of the chest of an 11-year-old girl (A) reveals a large, sharply-defined mass situated in the lower portion of the right lung. Tomographic sections in anteroposterior (B) and lateral (C) projections show the mass to be located within the right lower lobe; it is homogeneous in density and contains no calcium. Its superior border shows a sharp indentation which gives the mass a rather bizarre shape reminiscent in lateral projection of a valentine heart. Such bizarre shapes are common in hydatid cyst and result from impingement by the soft, fluid-filled mass on comparatively rigid pulmonary structures such as bronchovascular bundles. The child was asymptomatic; an abnormality was known to have been present on her chest roentgenogram two years previously. At thoracotomy, the cyst was readily enucleated from the surrounding lung and was removed intact without the necessity for removal of normal lung tissue.

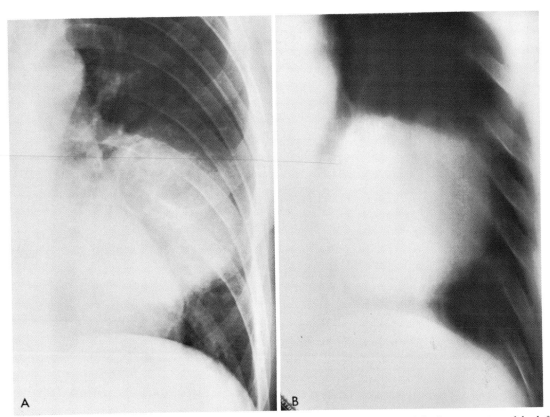

Figure 5–23. **Masses Over 6 cm in Diameter: Bronchogenic Carcinoma.** Views of the lower portion of the left lung from a posteroanterior roentgenogram (*A*) and an anteroposterior tomogram (*B*) reveal a large, roughly circular mass measuring 8 cm in diameter. Its margins are indistinct and somewhat lobulated; it is homogeneous in density and contains no demonstrable calcium. Both the lobulation and indistinct definition suggest primary bronchogenic cancer. This 50-year-old male was well until four months prior to admission when he developed a dry, hacking cough which worsened progressively to the time of admission. The lower lobe was resected; histologically, the neoplasm was somewhat atypical, being designated "clear-cell adenocarcinoma."

Table 5–7. *Solitary Pulmonary Masses 6 cm or More in Diameter*

	ETIOLOGY	LOCATION
DEVELOPMENTAL	Intralobar broncho-pulmonary sequestration	Two-thirds of cases left lower lobe; one third of cases right lower lobe; rare elsewhere. Almost invariably contiguous to diaphragm in posterior bronchopulmonary segment.
	Extralobar broncho-pulmonary sequestration	Related to left hemidiaphragm in 90 per cent of cases, lying immediately above, below, or within it.
INFECTIOUS	Acute lung abscess	Predilection for posterior portions of upper or lower lobes.
	Cryptococcus neoformans (cryptococcosis)	Lower lobe predominance, usually in the periphery.
	Echinococcus (Hydatid cyst)	Predilection for lower lobes, right more often than left.
NEOPLASTIC	All benign neoplasms listed in Table 5–6.	No definite predilection.
	Bronchogenic carcinoma	Predominantly upper lobes.
	Hematogenous metastasis	Predominantly lower lobes.

Table 5-7. *Solitary Pulmonary Masses 6 cm or More in Diameter (Continued)*

SHAPE	CALCIFICATION	CAVITATION	COMMENTS
Round, oval, or tri-angular in shape and typically well-cir-cumscribed.	No	Frequent	Enclosed within visceral pleura of af-fected lung. Although cystic in nature, mass remains homogeneous until com-munication established with contiguous lung as a result of infection. Supplied by systemic artery and drains via pulmonary veins. (*See* page 578.)
Well-defined homo-geneous mass.	No	Seldom	Frequently associated with other ano-malies and sometimes with diaphrag-matic eventration. Enclosed within its own visceral pleural layer—therefore seldom infected or air-containing (*cf.* intralobar). Supplied by systemic artery (usually from abdominal aorta) and drains via systemic rather than pulmon-ary veins (IVC or azygos system). (*See* page 581.)
Tends to be round; somewhat ill-defined when acute but sharply circum-scribed when chronic.	No	Almost inevitable.	Usually of staphylococcal etiology. The mass may remain unchanged for many weeks without perforation into bron-chial tree. (*See* page 613.)
Tends to be well cir-cumscribed, homo-geneous in density and solitary.	No	Reported in 16 per cent of cases.	(*See* page 657.)
Sharply circum-scribed; tends to possess bizarre, ir-regular shape.	Extremely rare.	Common	Communication with bronchial tree may produce the "meniscus" sign or "sign of the camalote." (*See* page 712.)
Well-circumscribed, smooth.	Rarely	No	Any of these neoplasms may reach a large size, particularly chemodectoma, neurogenic tumors, and leiomyoma (*See* page 444.)
Margins tend to be ill-defined, lobulated, or umbilicated.	No	Fairly common.	Most common method of presentation of large cell carcinoma, somewhat less common in adenocarcinoma and squamous cell carcinoma and very un-common in small cell carcinoma. (*See* page 736.)
Tend to be sharply circum-scribed, somewhat lobulated.	Rare—re-stricted to metastatic osteogenic sarcoma or chondro-sarcoma.	Predominantly in upper lobe lesions but is uncommon.	(*See* page 794.)

Table continues

453

Table 5–7. *Solitary Pulmonary Masses 6 cm or More in Diameter (Continued)*

	ETIOLOGY	LOCATION
NEOPLASTIC *(Cont.)*	Bronchioloalveolar carcinoma	No predilection.
	The lymphosarcoma group	No clear-cut lobar predilection; tends to be more centrally than peripherally located.
	Multiple myeloma (plasmacytoma)	Over the convexity of thorax contiguous to chest wall.
INHALATIONAL	Lipoid pneumonia	Dependent portions of upper and lower lobes (occasionally right middle lobe or lingula).

Table 5–7. *Solitary Pulmonary Masses 6 cm or More in Diameter (Continued)*

SHAPE	CALCIFICATION	CAVITATION	COMMENTS
Tends to be ill-defined.	No	No	Tend to be very slow growing; may occupy most of the volume of a lobe, but there is no tendency to cross interlobar fissures. Air bronchogram frequent. (*See* page 770.)
Smooth and fairly sharply circum-scribed.	No	Rare	May be a manifestation of either primary or secondary lymphosarcoma. Often without associated hilar or mediastinal lymph node enlargement. Tends to grow slowly. Rarely obstructs the bronchial tree so that an air bronchogram is almost invariable. (*See* page 784.)
Sharply circum-scribed, possessing an obtuse angle with the chest wall.	No	No	Due to protrusion into the thorax of a primary lesion originating in a rib—thus almost invariably associated with a destructive lesion of one or more ribs. May reach a very large size. (*See* page 790.)
Well-circumscribed, smooth or lobulated.	No	No	Usually homogeneous in density. Closely simulates peripheral broncho-genic carcinoma. (*See* page 964.)

Table 5–8

MULTIPLE PULMONARY NODULES, WITH OR WITHOUT CAVITATION

The individual lesions generally possess the same characteristics as those described in Table 5-6.

Cavitation or calcification may be present or absent in some or all of the lesions.

In addition to the cases illustrated on the following pages, the following figures appearing elsewhere in the book may be referred to as representative of this pattern:

Figure	Page
4–83	274
4–84	275
4–87	278
7–20	648
8–32	787
8–39	798

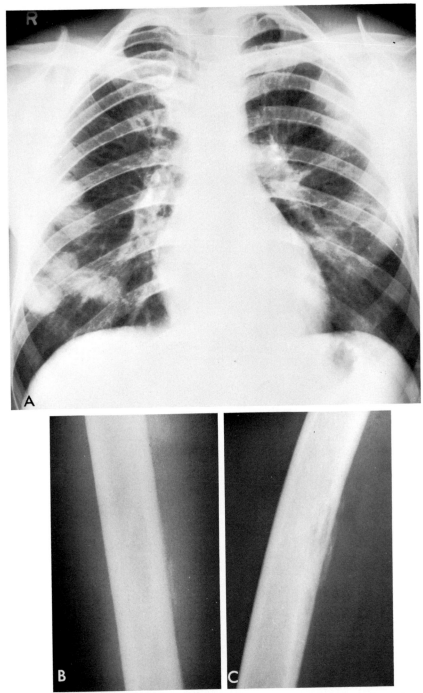

Figure 5-24. **Multiple Nodules: Pyemic Abscesses.** A posteroanterior roentgenogram (A) reveals several, sharply-circumscribed nodules ranging from 2 to 3 cm in diameter situated predominantly in the right lower lobe and the left upper lobe. The masses are homogeneous in density and show no evidence of cavitation (although cavitation eventually occurred in the majority). Anteroposterior (B) and lateral (C) views of the mid-shaft of the right femur show an irregular area of rarefaction in the cortex, associated with subperiosteal new bone formation along the posterior and medial aspects of the bone. This 24-year-old man first developed symptoms referable to his chest, consisting of a severe "chest cold" with retrosternal and bilateral axillary pain and cough productive of moderate quantities of yellow-brown sputum; approximately ten days later swelling and throbbing pain developed in the thigh. The possibility of Ewing's sarcoma was entertained until the patient developed severe constitutional symptoms consisting of night sweats, chills, and high fever. *Staphylococcus aureus* was cultured from the sputum and from pus obtained from the thigh at incision and drainage. Acute osteomyelitis and metastatic pyemic abscesses.

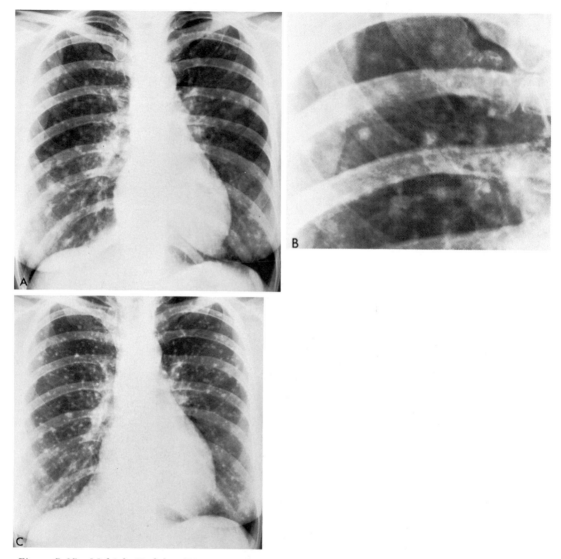

Figure 5–25. **Multiple Nodules: Disseminated Histoplasmosis.** A posteroanterior roentgenogram (A) reveals a multitude of nodules widely disseminated throughout both lungs, ranging from 3 to 10 mm in diameter. Several of the nodules contain a tiny central nidus of calcium (as seen in a magnified view of the right upper lung [B]). Open lung biopsy showed the nodules to consist of chronic granulomatous inflammation containing *Histoplasma capsulatum* organisms. Three years later, a posteroanterior roentgenogram (C) shows all lesions to have diminished markedly in size and to have undergone uniform calcification. This sequence of changes from well-defined nodules to multiple tiny calcifications is characteristic of disseminated histoplasmosis, although the calcifications could also represent the end result of chicken pox (varicella-zoster) pneumonia. (Courtesy Dr. David Berger, Royal Edward Chest Hospital, Montreal.)

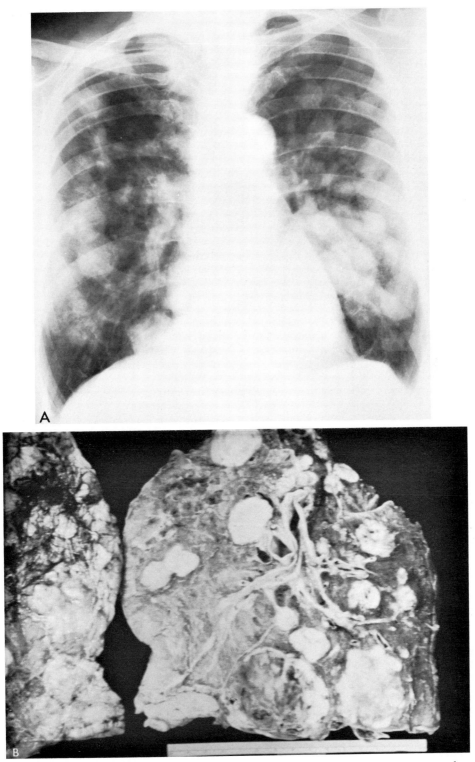

Figure 5–26. **Multiple Nodules: Hematogenous Metastases.** A posteroanterior roentgenogram reveals multiple, sharply circumscribed nodules scattered widely throughout both lungs; they range in diameter from 1 to 6 cm and are homogeneous in density and roughly spherical. A photograph of a cross section of the lung removed at necropsy (*B*) shows the sharp definition and marked variation in size of the metastatic nodules; the large mass in the left lower lobe has undergone hemorrhagic necrosis. Primary fibrosarcoma of the ilium with hematogenous metastases; 72-year-old male.

Table 5–8. *Multiple Pulmonary Nodules, With or Without Cavitation*

	ETIOLOGY	LOCATION	SIZE AND SHAPE
DEVELOPMENTAL	Pulmonary arteriovenous fistula	Lower lobe predilection.	One to several cm; round or oval, lobulated, well-circumscribed.
INFECTIOUS	**Pyemic abscesses**	**Generalized but more numerous in lower lobes.**	**Range from 0.5 to 4 cm; usually round and well-circumscribed.**
	Coccidioides immitis	Upper lobe predilection.	0.5 to 3.0 cm; round or oval, well-circumscribed.
	Paragonimus westermani	Lower lobe predilection, usually in the periphery.	3 to 4 cm; well-circumscribed.
NEOPLASTIC	Papilloma	No predilection.	Up to several cm; round, sharply circumscribed.
	Hematogenous metastases	**Predilection for lower lobes.**	**Three mm to 6 cm or more; typically round and sharply circumscribed.**
	The lymphosarcoma group	More numerous in lower lung zones.	Three mm to 7 cm; round, ovoid, triangular, or polyhedral, usually with fuzzy outlines.
	Multiple myeloma (plasmacytoma)	No known predilection.	Lobulated.

Table 5–8. *Multiple Pulmonary Nodules, With or Without Cavitation (Continued)*

CALCIFICATION	CAVITATION	GENERAL COMMENTS
No	No	Multiple in one third of all cases. Diagnosis by identification of feeding artery and draining vein; lesions may change in size between Valsalva and Mueller procedures; angiography necessary to identify all fistulae. 40 to 65 per cent of cases associated with hereditary hemorrhagic telangiectasia. (*See* page 573.)
No	Common, usually thick-walled.	(*See* page 597.)
Sometimes	Common; may be thin- or thick-walled.	In approximately 2 per cent of affected patients, multiple cavities may be associated with pneumothorax and empyema. In contrast to tuberculosis, cavitary disease may occur in anterior segment of an upper lobe. (*See* page 652.)
Occasionally	Common	Multiple ring shadows or thin-walled cysts are characteristic. (*See* page 716.)
No	Frequent	Obstruction of airways leads to peripheral atelectasis and obstructive pneumonitis. Diagnosis is suggested by a combination of multiple solid or cavitary lesions throughout the lungs associated with laryngeal or tracheal papillomas. (*See* page 731.)
Rare, but if present, virtually diagnostic of osteogenic sarcoma or chondrosarcoma.	In approximately 4 per cent of cases, more frequently in upper lobes.	**Wide range in size of multiple nodules is highly suggestive of the diagnosis. Seldom associated with mediastinal or bronchopulmonary lymph-node enlargement. (*See* page 795.)**
No	"Cyst-like" lesions may occur in reticulum cell sarcoma, simulating cavitation.	A manifestation of *secondary* lymphosarcoma. Mediastinal and bronchopulmonary lymph-node enlargement is associated in some cases. (*See* page 784.)
No	No	(*See* page 790.)

Table continues

Table 5–8. *Multiple Pulmonary Nodules, With or Without Cavitation (Continued)*

	ETIOLOGY	LOCATION	SIZE AND SHAPE
IMMUNOLOGIC	Wegener's granulomatosis	Widely distributed, bilateral, no predilection for upper or lower lung zones.	Five mm to 9 cm; round, sharply circumscribed.
	Rheumatoid necrobiotic nodules	Peripheral sub-pleural parenchyma, more commonly lower lobes.	Three mm to 7 cm; round, well-circumscribed, smooth.
IDIOPATHIC	Amyloidosis	No predilection.	Up to 5 cm in diameter.

Table 5–8. *Multiple Pulmonary Nodules, With or Without Cavitation (Continued)*

CALCIFICATION	CAVITATION	GENERAL COMMENTS
No	In a third to a half of patients; characteristically thick-walled.	May be associated with focal areas of pneumonitis. Typically occurs in patients who manifest no allergic background. Note related but somewhat different condition "allergic granulomatosis." (*See* page 873.)
No	Common, usually with thick walls and smooth inner lining.	Nodules tend to wax and wane in concert with subcutaneous nodules and in proportion to the activity of the rheumatoid arthritis. With remission of arthritis, cavities may become thin walled and gradually disappear. In Caplan's syndrome, nodules tend to develop rapidly and appear in crops; both cavitation and calcification may occur in this variety of rheumatoid nodule. (*See* page 883.)
The periphery of the lesion may calcify.	Sometimes	May also occur as solitary lesions. Rarely associated with atelectasis or obstructive pneumonitis from bronchial deposits. (*See* page 1121.)

Table 5–9

DIFFUSE PULMONARY DISEASE WITH A PREDOMINANTLY ACINAR PATTERN

"Diffuse" implies involvement of all lobes of both lungs. Thus, although the disease necessarily is widespread, it need not affect all lung regions uniformly. For example, the lower lung zones may be involved to a greater or lesser degree than the upper, or the central and midportions of the lungs may be more severely affected than the peripheral ("bat's wing" distribution).

The term "acinar pattern" implies airspace consolidation, which may be confluent and thereby render individual acinar shadows unidentifiable.

Other abnormalities such as pleural effusion and cardiac enlargement may be present.

In addition to the cases illustrated on the following pages, the following figures appearing elsewhere in the book may be referred to as representative of this pattern:

Figure	Page
1– 5	7
4– 3	191
7–23	652
7–31	670
7–32	671
7–34	684
7–35	691
8–40	799

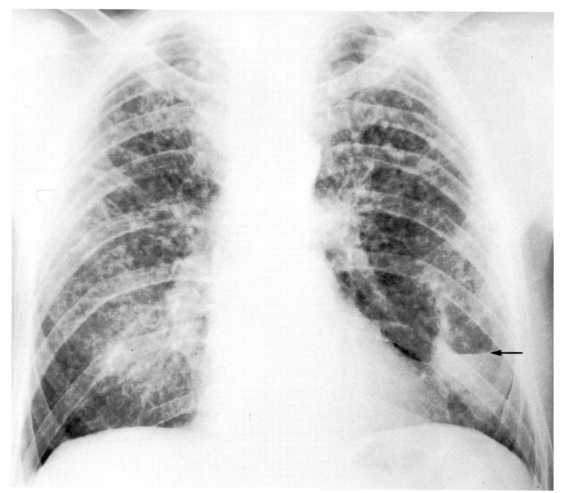

Figure 5–27. **Diffuse Disease (Acinar): Bronchogenic Spread of *Mycobacterium tuberculosis.*** A posteroanterior roentgenogram reveals a prominent air-fluid level in the lower portion of the left lung (*arrow*); the wall of the abscess cavity is rather poorly visualized in this projection. Throughout the remainder of both lungs are multiple rather ill-defined shadows ranging from 4 to 6 mm in diameter; several of these densities are discrete and can be identified as individual acinar shadows; the upper two thirds of the lungs are involved to a greater extent than the lower. This is a characteristic picture of bronchogenic spread of *Mycobacterium tuberculosis*; the source of the organisms was the left lower lobe abscess.

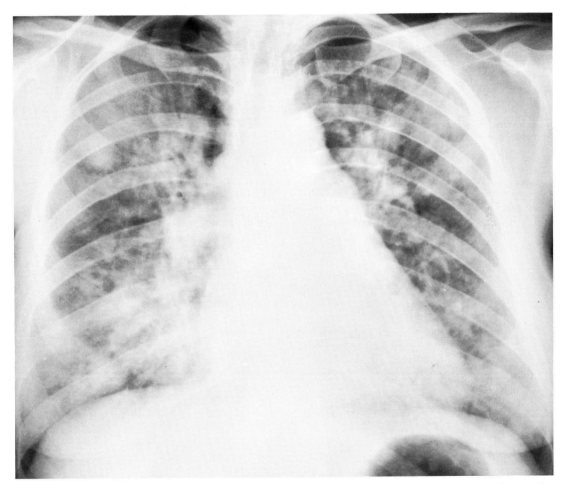

Figure 5–28. **Diffuse Disease (Acinar): Pulmonary Edema.** A posteroanterior roentgenogram reveals extensive involvement of both lungs by shadows possessing the typical characteristics of air-space consolidation. In most areas, the shadows are confluent so as to produce homogeneous density; in other areas, individual acinar shadows can be identified. An air bronchogram is readily visualized, particularly in the right lung. This diffuse air-space edema had completely resolved roentgenologically 48 hours later. Pulmonary edema secondary to mitral stenosis.

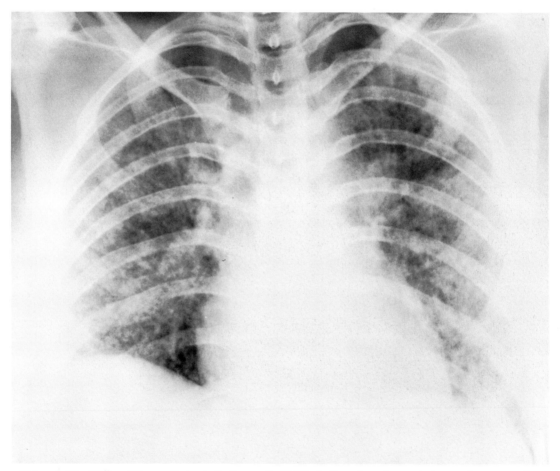

Figure 5–29. **Diffuse Disease (Acinar): Posttraumatic Fat Embolism.** An anteroposterior roentgenogram shows diffuse involvement of both lungs by patchy shadows of increased density ranging up to 5 mm in diameter. The shadows are confluent in some areas (*e.g.,* left mid lung) but throughout most of the lungs are discrete, permitting identification of individual acinar shadows. Seventeen-year-old girl four days following fracture of pelvis.

Table 5-9. *Diffuse Pulmonary Disease With a Predominantly Acinar Pattern (Continued)*

ADDITIONAL FINDINGS	COMMENTS
Hilar lymph-node enlargement frequent.	Acute widely disseminated histoplasmosis; symptoms may be disproportionately mild. Over a period of years, healing may result in multiple small calcific foci. (*See* page 643.)
Hilar lymph-node enlargement in some cases.	Over a period of many years, healing may result in multiple small calcific foci throughout the lungs. (*See* page 689.)
"Mitral configuration" of the heart may be present.	This pattern in acute influenza virus pneumonia occurs particularly in patients who have mitral stenosis or are pregnant. (*See* page 682.)
Pleural effusion in 8 to 10 per cent. Mediastinal lymph-node enlargement uncommon.	Diffuse disease occurs more often in a mixed pattern (*see* Table 5-11). (*See* page 770.)
————	A rare manifestation of hematogenous metastases. (*See* page 795.)
Fracture of extremities, pelvis, or axial skeleton usually present. Heart size normal.	Lesions appear within one to two days after trauma and resolve within one to four weeks. Absence of cardiac enlargement and of signs of postcapillary hypertension aid in differentiation from pulmonary edema of cardiac origin. (*See* page 828.)
Associated findings depend largely on the etiology of the edema—for example, signs of interstitial pulmonary edema (septal lines and so forth) in edema of cardiac origin.	(*See* page 853.)
————	Changes are those of intra-alveolar hemorrhage. Commonly associated with nephritis. This entity may be situated somewhere between Goodpasture's syndrome and polyarteritis nodosa. Sensitivity to penicillin has been incriminated. (*See* page 879.)
To be noted are the normal cardiac size and the absence of signs of pulmonary venous hypertension.	Roentgenographic pattern is one of diffuse patchy air-space consolidation typical of pulmonary edema. May occur with aspiration of sea water (in near-drowning), ethyl alcohol, kerosene, and by far the most common, acid gastric juice (Mendelson's syndrome). (*See* page 958.)
A pneumatocele may develop in an occasional patient as a consequence of bronchial or bronchiolar obstruction.	The roentgenographic pattern is characteristic of patchy air-space consolidation due to edema. The hila tend to be indistinct and hazy due to edema. (*See* page 952.)

Table continues

Table 5–9. *Diffuse Pulmonary Disease With a Predominantly Acinar Pattern (Continued)*

	ETIOLOGY	ANATOMIC DISTRIBUTION	VOLUME OF THORAX
INHALATIONAL *(Cont.)*	**Noxious gases** Silo-filler's disease (NO$_2$ toxicity)—acute phase Sulphur dioxide Phosgene Acute cadmium poisoning Secondary to burns	Diffuse	Unaffected
	Acute berylliosis (fulminating variety)	Diffuse	Unaffected
	Acute berylliosis (insidious variety)	Diffuse	Unaffected
IDIOPATHIC	Pulmonary hemosiderosis Goodpasture's syndrome Diffuse pulmonary hemorrhage in hemorrhagic diathesis	Widespread but more prominent in perihilar areas and in mid and lower lung zones.	Unchanged
	Alveolar proteinosis	Bilateral and symmetrical, commonly in a "butterfly" distribution. Resolution tends to occur asymmetrically.	Unchanged
	Hyaline membrane disease of the newborn.	Widespread	Tends to be slightly increased in early stages and reduced in later stages.
	Alveolar microlithiasis	Widespread, although the lower lobes show greater opacification due to larger volume of parenchyma.	Unchanged
	Sarcoidosis	Diffuse	Unchanged

Table 5–9. *Diffuse Pulmonary Disease With a Predominantly Acinar Pattern (Continued)*

ADDITIONAL FINDINGS	COMMENTS
None.	The widespread acinar pattern is due to acute pulmonary edema which develops within several hours of exposure and which usually clears completely if the patient survives. (*See* page 948.)
———	Morphologic changes consist of severe proteinaceous edema of the lungs. Roentgenologic changes characteristically develop rapidly following an overwhelming exposure. (*See* page 946.)
None.	Roentgenographic changes consist of diffuse bilateral "haziness" with subsequent development of irregular patchy densities scattered widely throughout the lungs; develop one to four weeks after the onset of symptoms. Roentgenographic clearing may take two to three months. (*See* page 946.)
Confluence of opacities may occur—in which circumstances an air bronchogram will be seen. Lymph-node enlargement may be recognized occasionally.	An acinar pattern is seen in relatively pure form in the early stages of these diseases but with passage of the alveolar hemorrhage into the interstitial space, the pattern becomes reticular. (*See* page 1122.)
None.	Differentiated from subacute pulmonary edema on the basis of absence of cardiac enlargement and of signs of pulmonary venous hypertension; Kerley "B" lines have been reported however. (*See* page 1128.)
Well-defined air bronchogram. Minute radiolucencies in the lung periphery probably represent air bronchiologram.	Although characteristically this disease is one of acinar involvement, a diffuse reticular pattern suggesting fibrosis may be present in the late stages and in a small percentage of those who recover. (*See* page 1135.)
Spontaneous pneumothorax is a rare complication.	The roentgenographic pattern is pathognomonic. Superimposition of thousands of microliths will cause an almost uniformly white appearance to the lower lungs, often with total obliteration of the mediastinal and diaphragmatic contours. (*See* page 1131.)
Hilar and mediastinal lymph node enlargement in many cases.	An uncommon pattern in this disease. (*See* page 1087.)

Table 5–10

DIFFUSE PULMONARY DISEASE WITH A
PREDOMINANTLY NODULAR, RETICULAR,
OR RETICULONODULAR PATTERN

The large number of diseases capable of producing an "interstitial" pattern within the lungs has made this table the longest in the group. As with diseases characterized by an acinar pattern, "diffuse" involvement connotes affection of all lobes of both lungs, although the pattern may be more marked in some areas. Other abnormalities may be present, such as pleural effusion, hilar and mediastinal lymph-node enlargement, and cardiac enlargement. The individual patterns may be described as follows.

NODULAR. The purely nodular interstitial diseases of the lungs perhaps are best epitomized by hematogenous infections such as miliary tuberculosis. Since the infecting organism arrives via the circulation and is trapped in the capillary sieve, it must be purely interstitial in location, at least early in its course. The pattern consists of discrete punctate shadows which range from tiny nodules 1 mm in diameter (barely visible roentgenographically) to 5 mm.

RETICULAR. This pattern consists of a network of linear shadows which may be conceived as a series of "rings" surrounding spaces of air density. It is useful to describe a reticular pattern according to the size of the "mesh": the terms fine, medium, and coarse are widely used and appear generally acceptable.

RETICULONODULAR. This pattern may be produced by a mixture of nodular deposits and diffuse linear thickening throughout the interstitial space. In addition, although a linear network throughout the interstitial tissue may appear roentgenographically as a purely reticular pattern, the orientation of some of the linear densities parallel to the x-ray beam may suggest a nodular component.

THE HONEYCOMB PATTERN. In this book, the term "honeycomb pattern" is restricted to a very coarse reticulation in which the air spaces in the "mesh" measure not less than 5 to 6 mm in diameter.

In addition to the cases illustrated on the following pages, the following figures appearing elsewhere in the book may be referred to as representative of this pattern:

Figure	Page
2– 2	107
4–26	212
4–53	243
4–55	245
4–58	248
4–60	251
4–61	252
4–62	254
4–63	255
7–42	710
8–33	788
8–38	797

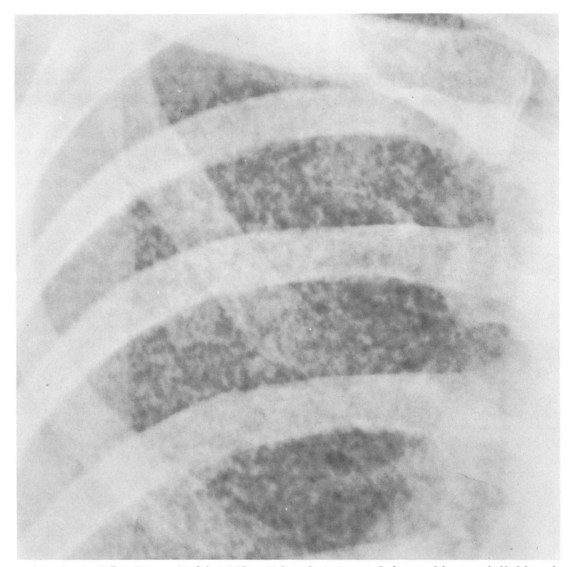

Figure 5–31. **Diffuse Disease (Nodular): Miliary Tuberculosis.** A magnified view of the upper half of the right lung from a posteroanterior roentgenogram shows multiple nodules of uniform size measuring approximately 2 mm in diameter. The shadows are quite discrete. Proved miliary tuberculosis. (Courtesy Dr. Romeo Ethier, Montreal Neurological Hospital.)

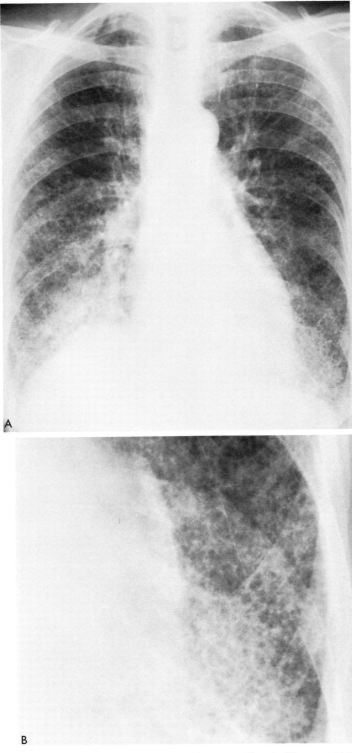

Figure 5–32. **Diffuse Disease (Reticular): Interstitial Pulmonary Fibrosis (Rheumatoid Lung Disease).** A posteroanterior roentgenogram (*A*) reveals a diffuse reticular pattern throughout both lungs, more marked in the bases than elsewhere. The reticulation is "fine" in character. No other roentgenographic abnormalities are apparent. A magnified view of the lower portion of the left lung (*B*) reveals the pattern to better advantage. From a purely objective point of view, this pattern is not in any way diagnostic. Sixty-eight-year-old woman with established rheumatoid arthritis.

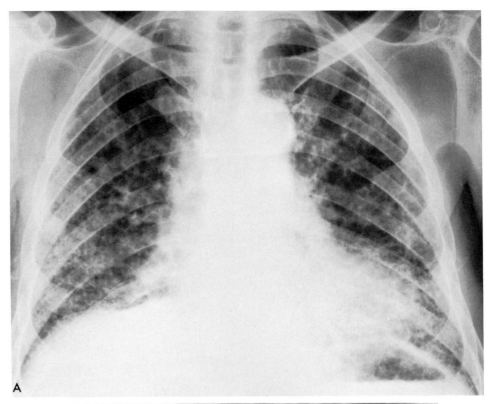

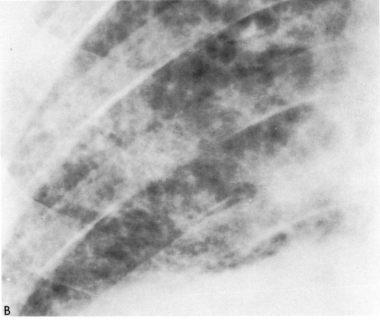

Figure 5–33. **Diffuse Disease (Reticular): Idiopathic Interstitial Pulmonary Fibrosis (Hamman-Rich).** A posteroanterior roentgenogram (*A*) reveals a diffuse reticular pattern throughout both lungs, more evident in the bases than elsewhere. The pattern is much coarser than was observed in Figure 5–32 but is still predominantly reticular. The volume of the lungs is generally reduced, indicating diffuse cicatrization; such loss of volume in diffuse interstitial disease is highly suggestive of either Hamman-Rich disease or diffuse systemic sclerosis (scleroderma). A magnified view of the lower portion of the right lung (*B*) shows the pattern to better advantage.

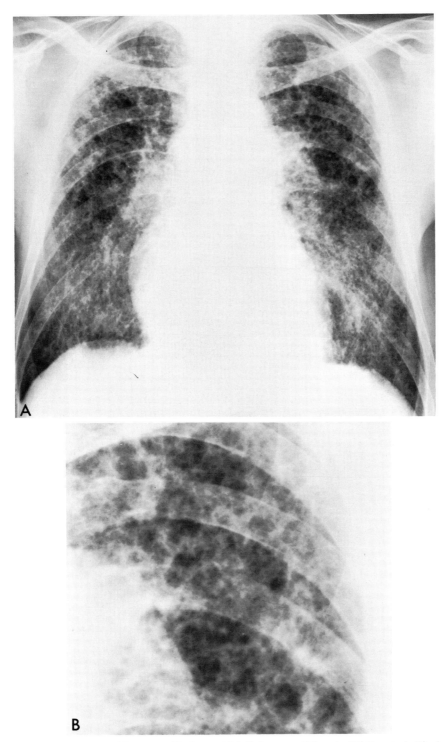

Figure 5-34. **Diffuse Disease (Honeycomb): Interstitial Pulmonary Fibrosis (Histiocytosis-X).** A posteroanterior roentgenogram (A) reveals extensive involvement of both lungs by a very coarse reticulonodular pattern, shown to better advantage in a magnified view of the upper portion of the left lung (B). In the upper lung zones particularly, the coarse reticular network is separated by air-containing spaces of moderate size, creating the honeycomb pattern. Enlargement of the pulmonary arteries indicates the presence of pulmonary arterial hypertension. Proved eosinophilic granuloma (Histiocytosis-X).

Table 5–10. *Diffuse Pulmonary Disease With a Predominantly Nodular, Reticular, or Reticulonodular Pattern*

	ETIOLOGY	ANATOMIC DISTRIBUTION	VOLUME OF THORAX
INFECTIOUS	**Bacteria** *Mycobacterium tuberculosis*	Generalized, uniform.	Unaffected
	Staphylococcus aureus	Generalized, uniform.	Unaffected
	Salmonella species	Generalized, uniform.	Unaffected
	Fungi *Coccidiodes immitis*	Generalized, uniform.	Unaffected
	Cryptococcus neoformans	Generalized, uniform.	Unaffected
	Blastomyces brasiliensis	Generalized, uniform.	Unaffected
	Blastomyces dermatitidis	Generalized, uniform.	Unaffected
	All other fungi listed in Tables 5–1 to 5–4	Generalized, uniform.	Unaffected
	Viruses Rubeola	Generalized, uniform.	Unaffected
	Parasites *Schistosoma* species (schistosomiasis)	Generalized, uniform.	Unaffected
	Filaria species (filariasis)	Generalized, uniform.	Unaffected
	Pneumocystis carinii	Generalized, uniform.	Unaffected
NEOPLASTIC	**Bronchioloalveolar carcinoma**	Diffuse	Unaffected
	Lymphangitic carcinomatosis	Commonly generalized but more prominent in the lower lung zones.	Serial roentgenographic studies may reveal generalized reduction in volume.

480

Table 5–10. *Diffuse Pulmonary Disease With a Predominantly Nodular, Reticular, or Reticulonodular Pattern (Continued)*

ADDITIONAL FINDINGS	COMMENTS
None.	Characteristic miliary pattern resulting from hematogenous dissemination. (*See* page 629.)
When of sufficient size, lesions may excavate to produce microabscesses.	Miliary pattern (hematogenous dissemination). (*See* page 595.)
There may be disseminated destructive lesions of bone.	Miliary pattern (hematogenous dissemination). (*See* page 607.)
Generalized hematogenous spread may lead to destructive lesions of bone.	Miliary pattern (hematogenous dissemination). (*See* page 652.)
None	Miliary pattern (hematogenous dissemination). (*See* page 657.)
None	Hematogenous dissemination with production of miliary pattern is the only pulmonary manifestation of the disease. Seen only in South America. (*See* page 673.)
Thoracic or remote bone involvement.	Miliary pattern (hematogenous dissemination). (*See* page 656.)
None	Rarely any of the fungi may produce disseminated miliary disease.
Lymph node enlargement is common.	Reticulonodular. Primary measles infection of lungs may be associated with secondary bacterial pneumonia. (*See* page 686.)
The central pulmonary arteries may be dilated secondary to vascular obstruction.	Hematogenous dissemination with production of a reticulonodular pattern. (*See* page 719.)
Hilar lymph-node enlargement in some cases.	Tropical pulmonary eosinophilia. Hematogenous dissemination with production of very fine reticulonodular pattern of low density. (*See* page 709.)
No lymph-node enlargement or pleural effusion.	Early stage manifestation. (*See* page 704.)
Pleural effusion in 8 to 10 per cent, always in association with pulmonary involvement.	The roentgenographic pattern is basically nodular; less common than a mixed pattern (*see* Table 5–11). Metastatic carcinoma of the pancreas may produce a pattern indistinguishable roentgenologically or morphologically. (*See* page 770.)
Hilar or mediastinal lymph-node enlargement is frequent but is not necessary to the diagnosis. Kerley B lines frequent.	Although the basic change is linear or reticular, there may be a coarse nodular component as well. (*See* page 798.)

Table continues

Table 5-10. *Diffuse Pulmonary Disease With a Predominantly Nodular, Reticular, or Reticulonodular Pattern (Continued)*

	ETIOLOGY	ANATOMIC DISTRIBUTION	VOLUME OF THORAX
NEOPLASTIC *(Cont.)*	Hodgkin's disease	Generalized	Unaffected
	Lymphosarcoma group	Diffuse	Unaffected
	Leukemia	Diffuse	Unaffected
THROMBOEMBOLIC	Embolism from oily contrast media	Diffuse, uniform.	Unaffected
CARDIOVASCULAR	Interstitial pulmonary edema	Diffuse but predominantly lower lung zone.	Usually unaffected
	Pulmonary fibrosis secondary to chronic postcapillary hypertension	Predominantly mid and lower lung zones.	Unaffected
	Hemosiderosis secondary to chronic postcapillary hypertension	Predominantly mid and lower lung zones.	Unaffected
IMMUNOLOGIC	Scleroderma (diffuse systemic sclerosis)	Generalized but more prominent in lung bases.	Serial roentgenographic studies may reveal progressive loss of lung volume.
	Rheumatoid disease	Generalized but more prominent in lung bases.	Serial roentgenographic studies may reveal progressive loss of lung volume

Table 5–10. *Diffuse Pulmonary Disease With a Predominantly Nodular, Reticular, or Reticulonodular Pattern (Continued)*

ADDITIONAL FINDINGS	COMMENTS
Mediastinal and hilar lymph-node enlargement almost invariably associated.	Differentiation from sarcoidosis or lymphangitic carcinoma may be difficult or impossible on purely roentgenologic grounds. (*See* page 771.)
Pleural effusion in about one third of cases. Mediastinal and hilar lymph-node enlargement may be inconspicuous or absent.	In some cases of reticulum cell sarcoma, this diffuse pattern may be due to Sjögren's syndrome. The roentgenographic pattern may simulate lymphangitic carcinoma. (*See* page 784.)
Mediastinal and hilar lymph-node enlargement may be present but not necessarily. Pleural effusion in some cases.	This is the usual pattern of pulmonary parenchymal involvement, but tends to occur only in the terminal stages of the disease. Resembles lymphangitic carcinoma. (*See* page 785.)
None	The typical pattern is finely reticular; complete clearing usually occurs within 48 to 72 hours although an abnormal pattern may persist for up to 11 days. In the early stages an arborizing pattern may be apparent due to filling of arterioles with contrast medium (similar to that seen on pulmonary arteriography). This complication usually occurs following lymphangiography with ultrafluid Lipiodol. (*See* page 830.)
Varies with the etiology of the edema, but usually those associated with pulmonary venous hypertension.	Roentgenographic pattern consists of loss of normal sharp definition of pulmonary vascular markings, haziness of the hilar shadows, and thickening of the interlobular septa (Kerley B lines). (*See* page 853.)
Typical cardiac configuration of chronic mitral valve disease. Almost invariably associated with signs of severe pulmonary venous and arterial hypertension. Ossific nodules may be present.	Roentgenographic pattern consists of a rather coarse but poorly defined reticulation. Probably related to recurrent episodes of air space and interstitial edema and hemorrhage. (*See* page 843.)
Typical cardiac configuration of chronic mitral valve disease. Almost invariably associated with signs of severe pulmonary venous and arterial hypertension. Ossific nodules may be present.	Pattern consists of tiny punctate shadows of low density. The incidence morphologically (25 per cent of cases of mitral stenosis) is much higher than roentgenographically. Usually associated with high levels of pulmonary arterial pressure. (*See* page 843.)
Associated findings include esophageal dysperistalsis, terminal pulp calcinosis, absorption of distal phalanges, and widening of the periodontal membrane. Pleural effusion uncommon.	The roentgenographic pattern in the early stages consists of a fine reticulation which tends to coarsen and become reticulonodular as the disease progresses. Small cysts measuring up to 1 cm in diameter may be identified in the lung periphery, particularly in the bases. (*See* page 889.)
Incidence of coexisting pleural effusion and pulmonary disease not clear, but the two are probably independent. Roentgenographic evidence of rheumatoid arthritis in most patients.	In the early stages, the roentgenographic pattern is punctate or nodular in character; in the later or fibrotic stage, the pattern consists of medium-to-coarse reticulation. (*See* page 882.)

Table continues

Table 5–10. *Diffuse Pulmonary Disease With a Predominantly Nodular, Reticular, or Reticulonodular Pattern (Continued)*

	ETIOLOGY	ANATOMIC DISTRIBUTION	VOLUME OF THORAX
IMMUNOLOGIC *(Cont.)*	Dermatomyositis and polymyositis	Generalized but more prominent in lung bases.	Serial studies may reveal progressive loss of lung volume, particularly if polymyositis involves the muscles of respiration.
	Sjögren's syndrome	Generalized but more prominent in lung bases.	Unaffected
	Waldenstrom's macroglobulinemia	Generalized	Unaffected
	Nitrofurantoin-induced pulmonary disease	Generalized but more prominent in lung bases.	Unaffected
INHALATIONAL	**Organic dust pneumoconiosis** **Diseases of alveolar hypersensitivity (extrinsic allergic alveolitis)** Farmers' lung Pigeon breeders' lung Mushroom workers' lung Bagassosis Suberosis Maple bark disease Pituitary snuff disease Smallpox handlers' lung Sisal workers' disease Malt workers' lung Sequiosis Thatched roofs and chronic lung disease Grain-weevil hypersensitivity Hen-litter sensitivity Lycoperdonosis	Generalized	Unaffected
	Inorganic dust pneumoconiosis Silicosis (simple)	Generalized but often predominantly mid and upper lung zones.	Little affected.

Table 5–10. *Diffuse Pulmonary Disease With a Predominantly Nodular, Reticular, or Reticulonodular Pattern (Continued)·*

ADDITIONAL FINDINGS	COMMENTS
Additional findings may be those associated with scleroderma or rheumatoid arthritis.	In patients with diffuse lung involvement, the roentgenographic pattern is reticular or reticulonodular and may be indistinguishable from the changes of scleroderma or rheumatoid disease. These diseases often occur in conjunction with primary malignancy elsewhere. (*See* page 894.)
This syndrome consists of a triad of keratoconjunctivitis sicca, xerostomia, and recurrent swelling of the parotid gland. Occasionally appears in association with any of the collagen diseases.	One third of patients show a diffuse reticulonodular pattern similar to that of other collagen diseases characterized by vascular involvement. Joint changes resemble rheumatoid or psoriatic arthritis. Remarkable female sex predominance. (*See* page 896.)
May be associated with localized homogeneous consolidation.	Diffuse reticulonodular pattern is produced by infiltration of interstitium by lymphoid and plasmacytoid cells. (*See* page 897.)
Pleural effusion in some cases.	Pattern consists of a diffuse fine reticulation. Almost invariably associated with peripheral blood eosinophilia. A similar roentgenographic pattern associated with eosinophilia may occur in the absence of known exciting cause. (*See* page 873.)
Vary somewhat depending on specific disease entity, chiefly regarding hilar and mediastinal lymph-node enlargement.	Considerable similarity exists in the roentgenographic pattern observed in all these diseases, ranging from a diffuse nodular pattern through coarse reticulation characteristic of diffuse interstitial fibrosis. While the pattern is generally "interstitial" in type, involvement of air spaces in the form of acinar shadows may be observed in most if not all during the acute stage of the disease. Irreversible changes of fibrosis tend to occur with continuous or repeated exposure. (*See* pages 908-919.)
Hilar lymph-node enlargement frequent, uncommonly associated with "egg-shell" calcification (5 per cent). Pleural thickening in late stages. Kerley A and B lines are common and may be present without visible nodules.	The roentgenographic pattern ranges from well-circumscribed nodular shadows of uniform density varying from 1 to 10 mm in diameter to a reticular or reticulonodular appearance. (*See* page 919.)

Table continues

Table 5-10. *Diffuse Pulmonary Disease With a Predominantly Nodular, Reticular, or Reticulonodular Pattern (Continued)*

	ETIOLOGY	ANATOMIC DISTRIBUTION	VOLUME OF THORAX
	Coal workers' pneumoconiosis (simple)	Generalized	Unaffected
	Asbestosis	In the early stages, predominantly lower lung zones; later generalized.	Normal or slightly reduced.
	Talcosis	Identical to asbestosis.	As with asbestosis.
	Siderosis	Widely disseminated.	Unaffected
INHALATIONAL (Cont.)	Kaolin (china-clay) pneumoconiosis	Generalized	Unaffected
	Chronic berylliosis	Diffuse	In advanced cases there may be marked loss of lung volume.
	Aluminum pneumoconiosis (aluminosis, bauxitosis, Shaver's disease)	Diffuse	Considerable loss of lung volume may occur.
	Pneumoconiosis due to radiopaque dusts Stannosis (tin oxide) Barytosis (barium sulfate) Rare earth pneumoconiosis (cerium, etc.)	Generalized	Unaffected

Table 5–10. *Diffuse Pulmonary Disease With a Predominantly Nodular, Reticular, or Reticulonodular Pattern (Continued)*

ADDITIONAL FINDINGS	COMMENTS
Enlargement of hilar lymph nodes is present in some cases but is seldom a predominant feature.	The roentgenographic pattern is typically nodular but may be predominantly reticular in the early stages. Nodules vary from 1 to 10 mm in size and tend to be somewhat less well defined than in silicosis. (*See* page 939.)
The pleural manifestations dominate the picture roentgenographically and consist of thickening with or without calcification. Hilar lymph-node enlargement is seldom if ever a notable feature.	The roentgenographic pattern may be divided into three stages: a fine reticulation occupying predominantly the lower lung zones and creating a ground-glass appearance of the lungs—the early changes; a stage in which the interstitial reticulation becomes more marked, producing the "shaggy heart" sign; and a late stage in which reticulation is generalized throughout the lungs. Note high incidence of associated neoplasia. (*See* page 933.)
The sheet anchor in the roentgenologic diagnosis of talcosis is pleural plaque formation—often diaphragmatic in position and massive. Progressive massive fibrosis may develop identical to that seen in silicosis and coal workers' pneumoconiosis.	Pulmonary involvement similar to asbestosis. (*See* page 937.)
None	The roentgenographic pattern is reticulonodular in type, the deposits being of rather low density compared to the silicotic nodule. In the siderosis of silver polishers, a fine stippled pattern is created. If the free silica content of dust is high (siderosilicosis), the pattern is indistinguishable from silicosis. (*See* page 943.)
Progressive massive fibrosis may occur as a late manifestation as in silicosis and coal workers' pneumoconiosis.	The roentgenographic pattern ranges from no more than a generalized increase in lung markings to a diffuse nodular or "miliary" mottling. (*See* page 939.)
Focal areas of emphysema may be identified in advanced cases, usually in the upper lobes. Spontaneous pneumothorax occurs in over 10 per cent of patients.	The roentgenographic pattern varies with degree of exposure: if minor, there is a diffuse granular "haziness"; with moderate exposure, the pattern is nodular, the nodules being ill-defined and of moderate size (calcification of nodules has been observed); in advanced cases, the pattern may be chiefly reticular. (*See* page 946.)
Pleural thickening occasionally. Emphysematous bullae develop commonly and are associated with a high incidence of pneumothorax.	The roentgenographic pattern consists of a fine to coarse reticular pattern, sometimes with a nodular component. (*See* page 947.)
Lymph node enlargement is not a feature.	The roentgenographic pattern is basically nodular, the nodules being of very high density. A reticular or reticulonodular pattern may be observed in barytosis. None of these dusts is fibrogenic. (*See* page 945.)

Table continues

Table 5–10. *Diffuse Pulmonary Disease With a Predominantly Nodular, Reticular, or Reticulonodular Pattern (Continued)*

	ETIOLOGY	ANATOMIC DISTRIBUTION	VOLUME OF THORAX
INHALATIONAL *(Cont.)*	Silo-filler's disease (nitrogen dioxide)— third phase	Diffuse	Unaffected
AIRWAYS DISEASE	Chronic obstructive emphysema (predominantly centrilobular in type)	Generalized, uniform.	Slight to moderate increase.
	Mucoviscidosis	Generalized, uniform.	Considerable over-inflation.
	"Small airways disease"	Generalized	Unaffected or slight overinflation.
	Acute bronchiolitis	Generalized but predominantly lower lobes.	Overinflation, characteristically severe and generalized.
	Familial dysautonomia (Riley-Day syndrome)	Generalized	Increased
IDIOPATHIC	Sarcoidosis	Usually generalized but in stages of development or resolution may show some lack of uniformity.	Usually unaffected although fibrosis may be associated with emphysema and overinflation.
	Interstitial pulmonary fibrosis (Hamman-Rich syndrome)	There is a predilection for the lower lung zones in the early stages, but becoming more generalized and uniform as the disease progresses.	Sequential studies will show progressive loss of lung volume.
	Histiocytosis-X (eosinophilic granuloma)	Diffuse but with a tendency for predominance of lesions in the upper lung zones.	Usually normal.

Table 5–10. Diffuse Pulmonary Disease With a Predominantly Nodular, Reticular, or Reticulonodular Pattern (Continued)

ADDITIONAL FINDINGS	COMMENTS
None	This phase is characterized roentgenographically by miliary nodulation whose appearance tends to lag behind the recurrence of symptoms. The multiple discrete nodular shadows of varying size tend to become confluent in the more severe cases. The nodulation may disappear in time although it commonly persists for a considerable period after acute symptoms have subsided. (*See* page 950.)
Signs of pulmonary arterial hypertension are inevitable, often associated with cor pulmonale.	The pattern is better described as a coarse increase in lung markings rather than reticular or reticulonodular. May be referred to as "increased marking (I.M.)" emphysema. (*See* page 1008.)
May be associated with segmental areas of consolidation or atelectasis due to broncho-pneumonia or bronchiectasis.	The pattern is one of accentuation of the linear markings throughout the lungs giving a coarse reticular appearance. (*See* page 1062.)
Signs of pulmonary arterial hypertension and cor pulmonale in chronic advanced disease.	The roentgenographic pattern is reticulonodular and simulates sarcoidosis (but without hilar lymph node enlargement). Diagnosis should be suggested when the pulmonary function pattern is obstructive rather than restrictive. (*See* page 1052.)
Multiple focal areas of pneumonia or atelectasis may be present.	A reticulonodular pattern is present in some cases, particularly in patients with underlying spasmodic asthma. Acute bronchiolitis more commonly causes simple overinflation alone. (*See* page 1051.)
Local areas of segmental consolidation and atelectasis may be present, particularly in the right upper lobe and less frequently the right middle and left lower lobes.	The roentgenographic pattern is identical to that of mucoviscidosis. (*See* page 905.)
Hilar and mediastinal lymph-node enlargement often comprise the earliest roentgenologic finding, with diffuse lung involvement developing subsequently (with or without disappearance of the node enlargement). In approximately 25 per cent of cases, the pulmonary changes exist alone.	The pattern is usually reticulonodular in type, although ranging from purely nodular to purely reticular. In the approximately 20 per cent of cases which progress to fibrosis the pattern is coarsely reticular, somewhat uneven in distribution and associated with bulla formation and generalized overinflation. (*See* page 1087.)
Hilar lymph-node enlargement and pleural effusion do not occur.	In the early stages the pattern is one of fine reticulation predominantly in the lung bases; the later stage is characterized by a generalized coarse reticular or reticulonodular pattern with "honeycombing" in some cases. (*See* page 1104.)
Hilar and mediastinal lymph-node enlargement is exceedingly rare as is pleural effusion. Spontaneous pneumothorax in some cases.	The roentgenographic pattern varies with the stage of the disease, beginning with nodular and progressing to reticulonodular and finally to a typical honeycomb pattern. Probably the most common cause of a honeycomb pattern. (*See* page 1110.)

Table continues

Table 5–10. *Diffuse Pulmonary Disease With a Predominantly Nodular, Reticular, or Reticulonodular Pattern (Continued)*

	ETIOLOGY	ANATOMIC DISTRIBUTION	VOLUME OF THORAX
IDIOPATHIC *(Cont.)*	Idiopathic pulmonary hemosiderosis Goodpasture's syndrome	Usually widespread but may be more prominent in the perihilar areas and the mid and lower lung zones.	May be a slight decrease in late stages of the disease.
	Desquamative interstitial pneumonitis	Generalized but showing a distinct predominance for the lower lung zones.	Progressive loss of lung volume in the later stages of the disease.
	Pulmonary myomatosis	Usually generalized but predominantly basal.	May be decreased but seldom to the extent seen in Hamman-Rich disease.
	Amyloidosis	Variable	Overinflation in the tracheobronchial form of the disease.
	Wilson-Mikity syndrome	Widely disseminated.	Increased
	Lymphocytic (lymphoid) interstitial pneumonia	Generalized	Unaffected
	Oxygen toxicity	Generalized, uniform	Increased
OTHER	Spider angiomas in cirrhosis of the liver	Predominantly basal.	Unaffected

Table 5–10. *Diffuse Pulmonary Disease With a Predominantly Nodular, Reticular, or Reticulonodular Pattern (Continued)*

ADDITIONAL FINDINGS	COMMENTS
———	A reticular pattern in these diseases indicates hemosiderin deposition and fibrosis in the interstitial tissues. Early in the disease, the pattern represents a transition stage from acute hemorrhage into the air spaces to complete resolution, but in the later stages, interstitial fibrosis is permanent. (*See* page 1122.)
Occasionally spontaneous pneumothorax, pleural effusion and cor pulmonale; rarely segmental atelectasis.	This disease is felt by some to represent an early stage of diffuse interstitial pulmonary fibrosis. (*See* page 1109.)
Pleural effusion and pneumothorax are common.	The basic pattern is coarse reticulonodular in type and may progress to a typical "honeycomb" appearance. (*See* page 1118.)
Hilar lymph nodes may be enlarged.	Pulmonary disease usually occurs in primary rather than secondary amyloidosis. The pattern may be nodular (simulating miliary tuberculosis) in the parenchymal form of the disease or may consist in an increase in bronchovascular markings in the tracheobronchial form. Associated with evidence of involvement of other organ systems. (*See* page 1121.)
———	Pattern consists of very coarse reticulation separated by air-containing cyst-like foci. (*See* page 1136.)
———	This is diffuse pseudolymphoma. (*See* page 736.)
Those of the underlying disease for which oxygen therapy is administered.	Infants in respiratory distress who are placed on oxygen for long periods of time develop a "spongy" lung with fibrosis, atelectasis and focal areas of emphysema. This may represent the late stages of hyaline membrane disease or the effects of long-term oxygen inhalation. Has also been described in adults. (*See* page 1137.)
None	Pattern consists of ill-defined nodules of small size. Associated with hypoxemia due to arteriovenous shunting. (*See* page 1264.)

Table 5–11

DIFFUSE PULMONARY DISEASE WITH A MIXED ACINAR AND RETICULONODULAR PATTERN

The pattern created by combined air-space consolidation and interstitial disease is best exemplified by pulmonary edema secondary to pulmonary venous hypertension. The roentgenographic manifestations of interstitial involvement consist in increased size and loss of definition of lung markings, due to the presence of edema fluid within the sheath; air-space consolidation is manifested by discrete and confluent "fluffy" densities characteristic of acinar-filling processes.

Another example of the mixed pattern is that produced by generalized bronchiolo-alveolar carcinoma: nodular and acinar components reflect the replacement of air spaces by malignant cells, and the linear or reticular component is due to the extension of carcinoma along the bronchovascular bundles, chiefly within lymphatics (lymphangitic carcinoma).

In addition to the cases illustrated on the following pages, the following figures appearing elsewhere in the book may be referred to as representative of this pattern:

Figure	Page
4–65	257
7–40	701
7–41	706
8–21	774
8–22	775

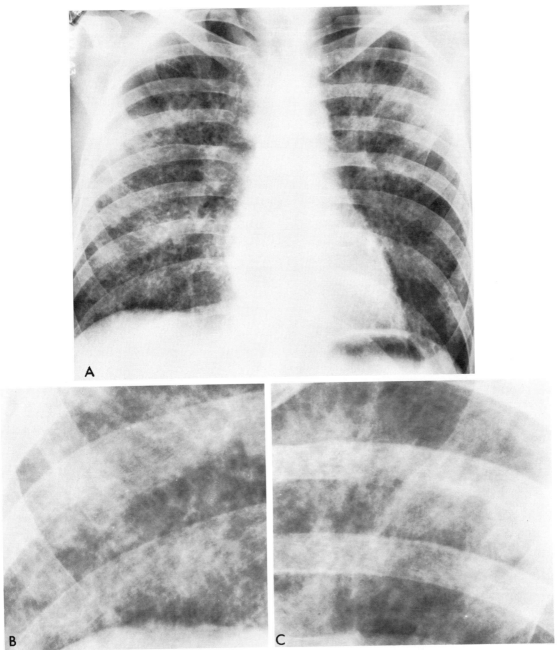

Figure 5–35. **Diffuse Disease (Mixed):** *Pneumocystis carinii* **Pneumonia.** A posteroanterior roentgenogram (*A*) demonstrates generalized involvement of both lungs by a process whose pattern is coarsely reticulonodular (seen to better advantage in a magnified view of the right lower lung [*B*]). Superimposed upon this pattern in the upper lung zones are confluent acinar shadows representing air-space consolidation (magnified view of left upper lung [*C*]). *Pneumocystis carinii* organisms were identified premortem in material obtained by needle aspiration and at necropsy throughout both lungs. This 32-year-old male had been the recipient of a renal transplant two-and-a-half years previously and was receiving maintenance doses of corticosteroids and immunosuppressive drugs.

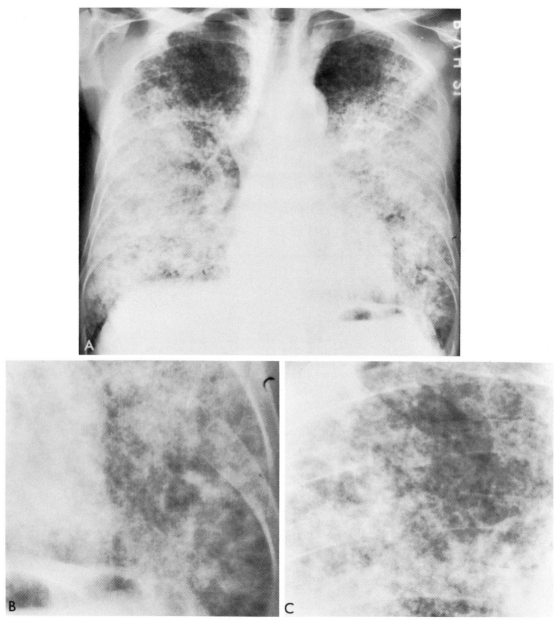

Figure 5–36. **Diffuse Disease (Mixed): Generalized Bronchioloalveolar Carcinoma.** A posteroanterior roentgenogram (*A*) reveals extensive involvement of both lungs by mixed air-space and interstitial disease. In the mid
and lower lung zones, consolidation is largely confluent although acinar shadows can be identified in a magnified
view of the left base (*B*). The reticulonodular pattern is most evident in the upper lung zones (*C*).

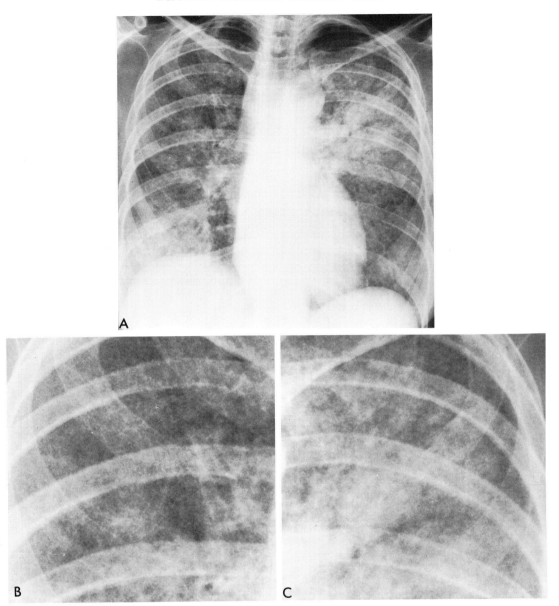

Figure 5-37. **Diffuse Disease (Mixed): Idiopathic Pulmonary Hemosiderosis.** A posteroanterior roentgenogram (*A*) shows extensive bilateral parenchymal disease, only the lung apices being spared. The patterns of disease are different in the two lungs, that on the right being finely reticulonodular (as revealed in a magnified view of the upper portion of the right lung [*B*]) and that in the left lung being chiefly acinar in type (magnified view of left upper lung [*C*]). Serial roentgenographic studies of this patient over the past several years had shown repeated episodes of acute pulmonary hemorrhage which, for some unknown reason, had affected chiefly the right lung; as a consequence, this lung had shown progressive deposition of hemosiderin in the interstitial space with a resultant reticular pattern; these changes had become irreversible. Just prior to this roentgenogram, the patient had suffered a fresh pulmonary hemorrhage which involved chiefly the left lung—thus the typical pattern of diffuse air-space consolidation on this side. While predominantly unilateral involvement is most unusual in this disease, IPH characteristically produces a mixed roentgenographic pattern—a predominant acinar pattern due to intra-alveolar hemorrhage followed by a reticular pattern due to passage of blood constituents into the interstitial space. In *A*, the longitudinal shadow visualized on the right side of the mediastinum is due to a markedly dilated esophagus secondary to achalasia.

Table 5–11. Diffuse Pulmonary Disease With a Mixed Acinar and Reticulonodular Pattern

	ETIOLOGY	ANATOMIC DISTRIBUTION	VOLUME OF THORAX
INFECTIOUS	Cytomegalovirus (cytomegalic inclusion disease)	Generalized, uniform.	Usually unaffected.
	Pneumocystis carinii	"Butterfly" or diffuse distribution.	Unaffected
	Mycoplasma pneumoniae and all viruses listed in Table 5–4	Generalized, uniform.	Unaffected or slightly decreased.
NEOPLASTIC	Bronchioloalveolar carcinoma	Generalized	Unaffected
INHALATIONAL	Alveolar hypersensivity diseases (extrinsic allergic alveolitis) (*see* Table 5–10)	Generalized	Unaffected
IDIOPATHIC	Pulmonary hemo-siderosis Goodpasture's syndrome	Usually widespread but may be more prominent in the perihilar areas and the mid and lower lung zones.	Usually unaffected.
	Hexamethonium lung	Generalized	Unaffected
	Busulfan lung	Generalized	Unaffected

Table 5–11. Diffuse Pulmonary Disease With a Mixed Acinar and Reticulonodular Pattern (Continued)

ADDITIONAL FINDINGS	COMMENTS
None	Combined interstitial and air-space disease with production of mixed reticulonodular and acinar patterns. (*See* page 693.)
None	Dissemination probably by inhalation. Pattern is combined reticulonodular and acinar. Frequently occurs in combination with cytomegalovirus infection. (*See* page 704.)
None	Diffuse reticular pattern early, with superimposition of patchy air-space consolidation. (*See* page 678.)
Prominent line shadows extending along the bronchovascular bundles towards the hila usually represent lymphatic permeation. Pleural effusion in 8 to 10 per cent. Mediastinal lymph nodes uncommon.	The mixed pattern consists of acinar, nodular, and reticulonodular components. (*See* page 770.)
Vary somewhat depending on specific disease entity, chiefly regarding hilar and mediastinal lymph-node enlargement.	The majority of these diseases produce a relatively pure "interstitial" pattern which is either nodular or reticulonodular. However, in some cases acinar shadows representing air-space involvement are superimposed on the reticular pattern during the acute stage of the disease. (*See* page 484.)
Rarely hilar lymph-node enlargement. Coalescence of lesions may permit visualization of an air bronchogram.	The mixed pattern is caused by a combination of patchy air-space consolidation from hemorrhage and the presence of hemosiderin and fibrous tissue in the interstitium. It may clear completely or may leave a residuum of reticulation due to irreversible interstitial fibrosis. (*See* page 1122.)
None	The pattern is believed to result from the organization of recurrent pulmonary edema secondary to left heart failure. Develops in patients receiving this drug in the treatment of hypertension. (*See* page 1121.)
The chest roentgenogram may clear partly or completely on discontinuation of the drug.	Deposition of fibrin, fibrous tissue, and mononuclear cells within the alveoli and interstitial tissues has been demonstrated morphologically. (*See* page 1119.)

Table 5-12

GENERALIZED PULMONARY OLIGEMIA

This table includes all diseases in which there is reduction in the caliber of the pulmonary arterial tree throughout the lungs. As stressed previously, appreciation of such vascular change is a subjective process based on a thorough familiarity with the normal. Since reduction in the size of peripheral vessels constitutes the main criterion of diagnosis of all diseases in this category, differentiation depends upon secondary signs. The two ancillary signs of major importance are the size and configuration of the central hilar vessels and the presence or absence of general pulmonary overinflation. Three combinations of changes are possible.

1. Small peripheral vessels; no overinflation; normal or small hila. This combination indicates reduction in pulmonary blood flow from central causes and is virtually pathognomonic of cardiac disease, usually congenital.

2. Small peripheral vessels; no overinflation; enlarged hilar pulmonary arteries. This combination may result from peripheral or central causes (respectively, primary pulmonary arterial hypertension or massive pulmonary-artery thrombosis without infarction).

3. Small peripheral vessels; general pulmonary overinflation; normal or enlarged hilar pulmonary arteries. This combination is virtually pathognomonic of pulmonary emphysema.

In addition to the cases illustrated on the following pages, the following figures appearing elsewhere in the book may be referred to as representative of this pattern:

Figure	Page
4-127	322
4-133	329
4-134	330
4-135	331
4-136	332

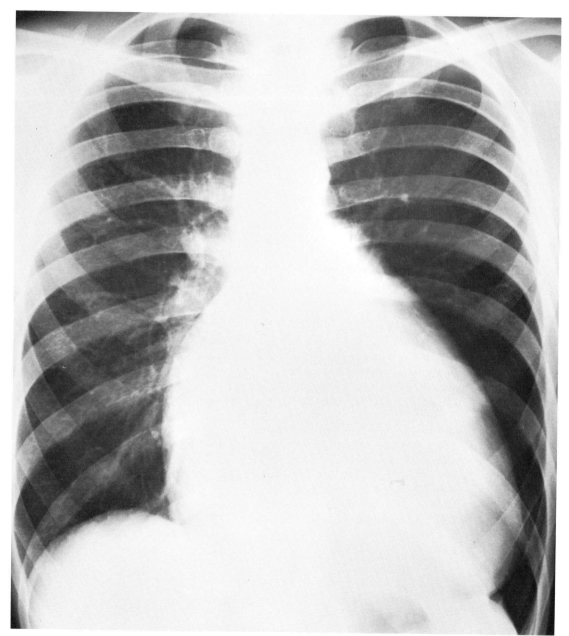

Figure 5–38. **General Pulmonary Oligemia: Ebstein's Anomaly.** A posteroanterior roentgenogram reveals a markedly enlarged heart whose right border strongly suggests dilatation of the right atrium. The hila are diminutive and the peripheral vessels narrow and attenuated. Pulmonary oligemia is uniform throughout both lungs. This 20-year-old man was relatively asymptomatic and was able to take part in sports; there was no cyanosis. The anomaly was surgically corrected.

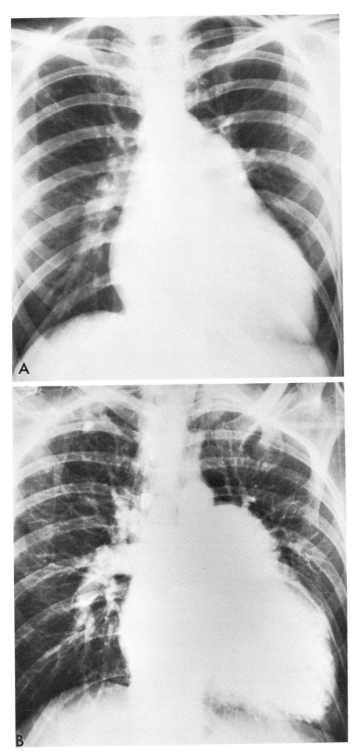

Figure 5–39. **General Pulmonary Oligemia: Primary Pulmonary Hypertension.** A posteroanterior roentgeno-gram (*A*) reveals moderate enlargement of the heart with a contour suggesting right ventricular dilatation. The hilar pulmonary arteries are enlarged and taper more rapidly than normal as they proceed distally. The lungs are not overinflated. Apart from the oligemia, the lungs show no evidence of abnormality. A pulmonary angiogram (*B*) exposed 11 seconds after the rapid injection of contrast medium into an antecubital vein demonstrates opacifica-tion of the right chambers of the heart and of the pulmonary arterial tree at a time when all contrast should have passed through the lungs into the left heart and systemic circulation; this indicates a tremendous increase in re-sistance in the pulmonary arterial circulation (at catheterization, the right ventricular pressure was 100/0 and the pulmonary artery pressure 100/50). Thirty-year-old woman admitted in severe cardiac decompensation. (Angio-gram courtesy Dr. Wolfe Light, Queen Mary Veterans' Hospital, Montreal.)

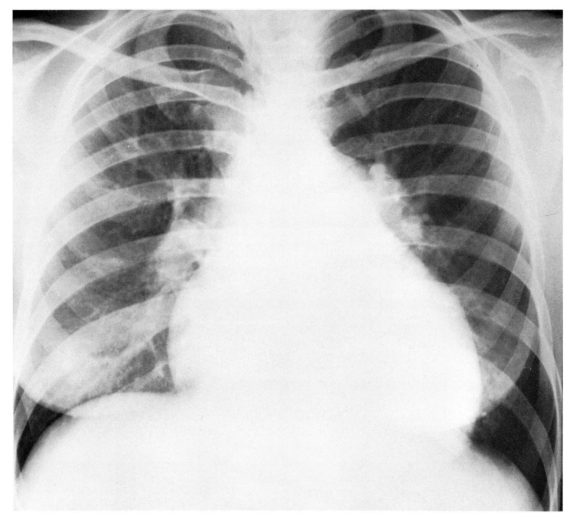

Figure 5–40.   **General Pulmonary Oligemia: Pulmonary Hypertension Secondary to Diffuse Systemic Sclerosis.**
This 37-year-old woman was admitted with right heart decompensation and severe dyspnea; a posteroanterior
roentgenogram reveals moderate cardiomegaly with a contour suggesting dilatation of the right heart chambers.
The hilar pulmonary arteries are large and taper rapidly as they proceed distally; the peripheral vascular markings
are narrow and attenuated, producing a picture of diffuse pulmonary oligemia. The lungs are not overinflated. At
necropsy, there was severe generalized pulmonary arteriosclerosis secondary to scleroderma; extensive involvement of the interstitial tissues by diffuse systemic sclerosis was not apparent on the premortem roentgenogram,
even in retrospect.

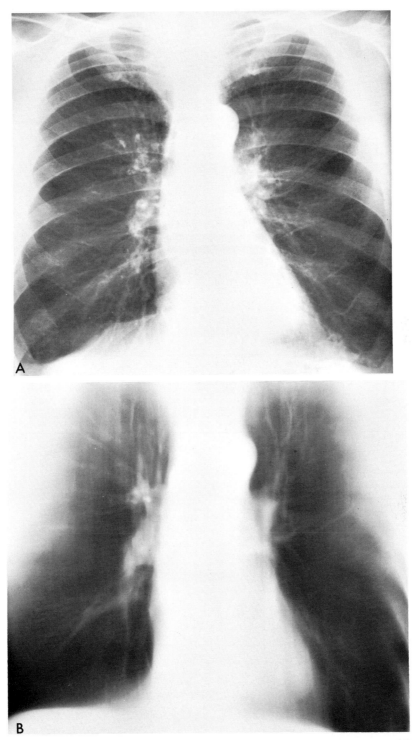

Figure 5–41. **General Pulmonary Oligemia: Emphysema.** A posteroanterior roentgenogram (A) reveals generalized reduction in the caliber of peripheral vessels throughout the lungs, seen to better advantage on a tomogram of both lungs in anteroposterior projection (B). There is severe generalized pulmonary overinflation (note the low flattened configuration of the diaphragm). There is no evidence of cardiomegaly and the hilar pulmonary arteries are not enlarged; thus, despite the generalized oligemia, there is no evidence of pulmonary arterial hypertension.

Table 5–12. Generalized Pulmonary Oligemia

	ETIOLOGY
DEVELOPMENTAL	Pulmonary artery stenosis or coarctation Congenital cardiac anomalies (a) Isolated pulmonic stenosis (b) Tetralogy of Fallot with pulmonary atresia (c) Persistent truncus arteriosus (type IV) (d) Ebstein's anomaly
INFECTIOUS	Schistosoma species
NEOPLASTIC	Metastases from trophoblastic neoplasms
THROMBOEMBOLIC	Widespread embolic disease to small arteries
CARDIOVASCULAR	**Chronic postcapillary hypertension (mitral stenosis)** Primary pulmonary hypertension Compression of the main pulmonary artery Vasoconstrictive (vasospastic) vascular disease

Table 5-12. *Generalized Pulmonary Oligemia (Continued)*

DIFFERENTIAL CHARACTERISTICS	COMMENTS
Absence of overinflation and expiratory air-trapping differentiates from emphysema. Pulmonary arteriography essential to differentiate from primary pulmonary hypertension or multiple peripheral embolization.	Diffuse pulmonary oligemia occurs when lesions are *multiple* and *peripheral*. Pulmonary arterial hypertension and cor pulmonale common. Associated cardiovascular anomalies frequent (60 per cent), particularly pulmonic stenosis. (*See* page 573.)
Cardiac enlargement present in some cases; no overinflation or air-trapping. Hila diminutive as a rule, permitting differentiation from primary pulmonary hypertension and multiple peripheral embolization (exception is poststenotic dilatation of main or left pulmonary artery in valvular pulmonic stenosis).	Pulmonary vascular pattern formed partly or wholly by hypertrophied bronchial circulation (may be studied by selective bronchial arteriography or flood aortography). (*See* page 577.)
Indistinguishable from pattern of primary pulmonary hypertension. Central pulmonary arteries can be huge. Absence of overinflation.	More common method of presentation is as diffuse reticulonodular pattern. (*See* page 719.)
Indistinguishable from primary pulmonary hypertension. No overinflation.	Acute cor pulmonale responds to treatment in some cases. (*See* page 797.)
Indistinguishable from primary pulmonary hypertension. There is no overinflation.	Multiple pulmonary emboli result in pulmonary artery hypertension; in contrast to emphysema, lung volume is either normal or decreased. (*See* page 840.)
Characteristic configuration of enlarged heart, particularly left atrium. Diffuse oligemia represents late stage of chronic venous and arterial hypertension.	**Commonly associated with episodes of interstitial or air-space edema. Roentgenographic evidence of hemosiderosis and ossific nodules in an occasional case.** (*See* **page 843.**)
Main and hilar pulmonary arteries are enlarged and show increased amplitude of pulsation fluoroscopically. Peripheral vessels diminutive. Absence of overinflation.	Preponderance in young women; familial tendency; dramatic response to intravenous injection of acetylcholine in some cases. (*See* page 840.)
Since the etiology is related to compression of the main pulmonary artery by a mass (*e.g.,* aortic aneurysm, or fibrosing mediastinitis), there will be roentgenographic evidence of a mediastinal abnormality in most cases.	A rare cause of pulmonary oligemia and cor pulmonale. (*See* page 841.)
Roentgenographic pattern indistinguishable from primary pulmonary hypertension.	Chronic vasoconstriction resulting from direct chemical-induced effects on the small arteries and arterioles—*e.g.,* chronic hypoxia, metabolic acidosis, and excessive amounts of catecholamines. (*See* page 841.)

Table continues

Table 5–12. *Generalized Pulmonary Oligemia (Continued)*

	ETIOLOGY
CARDIOVASCULAR *(Cont.)*	Syndrome of pulmonary hypertension and Raynaud's phenomenon
AIRWAYS DISEASE	Chronic obstructive emphysema Bullous disease of the lung

Table 5-12. *Generalized Pulmonary Oligemia (Continued)*

DIFFERENTIAL CHARACTERISTICS	COMMENTS
A syndrome occurring most commonly in middle-aged women, with a strong familial history, consisting of arthritis, Raynaud's phenomenon, and pulmonary hypertension.	Probably related to the collagen group of diseases, although the pulmonary vascular changes are considered by some to represent primary pulmonary hypertension. (*See* page 896.)
Large, central pulmonary arteries with rapid tapering peripherally. Generalized overinflation serves to differentiate this disease from others characterized by diffuse oligemia. Bullae may be present.	The oligemia may be predominant in the upper or lower lung zones or in one lung. Tomography may be of value in the assessment of diminution of pulmonary vasculature. (*See* page 993.)
Margins of bullae may be identified as curved, hair-line shadows. Hyperinflation is not as extreme as in chronic obstructive emphysema.	A pattern of diffuse oligemia is rare in bullous disease of the lungs without obstructive emphysema, but may be seen when bullae are numerous and have enlarged maximally. (*See* page 1023.)

Table 5–13

UNILATERAL, LOBAR, OR SEGMENTAL PULMONARY OLIGEMIA

The sheet anchor in the diagnosis of local pulmonary oligemia is reduction in caliber of the pulmonary arterial tree. The same three combinations of changes apply as in general pulmonary oligemia; the major difference between local and general oligemia is in its effect on pulmonary hemodynamics.

1. Small peripheral vessels; no overinflation; normal or small hilum. This is epitomized by lobar or unilateral hyperlucent lung (Swyer-James' or MacLeod's syndrome).

2. Small peripheral vessels; no overinflation; enlarged hilar pulmonary arteries (or an enlarged hilum). This combination is due almost invariably to unilateral pulmonary artery embolism without infarction.

3. Small peripheral vessels; overinflation; normal hilar pulmonary arteries. This combination is distinctive of obstructive emphysema.

In addition to the cases illustrated on the following pages, the following figures appearing elsewhere in the book may be referred to as representative of this pattern:

Figure	Page
2– 4	109
2– 11	124
4– 11	200
4–130	326
4–138	334
4–139	335
4–140	336
4–141	337
6– 1	570

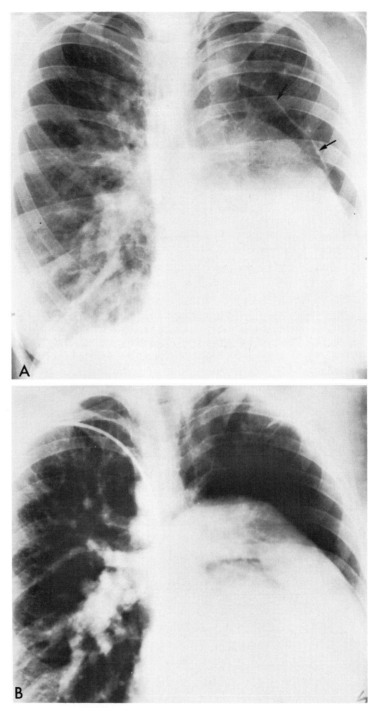

Figure 5-42.   **Local Pulmonary Oligemia: Agenesis of the Left Pulmonary Artery.** On the posteroanterior roentgenogram (A), there is evidence of marked shift of the mediastinum to the left. The visible portion of the left lung shows a severe diminution in the size of its vascular markings while those in the right lung are markedly increased in size; a left hilar complex cannot be identified. The overinflated right lung has extended across the anterior mediastinal septum into the left hemithorax, the vertical line shadow (*arrows*) representing four layers of pleura at the interface of the two lungs. A pulmonary angiogram (B) shows no evidence of a left pulmonary artery, the total right ventricular output passing into the right lung. As is so often the case in agenesis of the left pulmonary artery, this patient had a congenital intracardiac anomaly in the form of a ventricular septal defect.

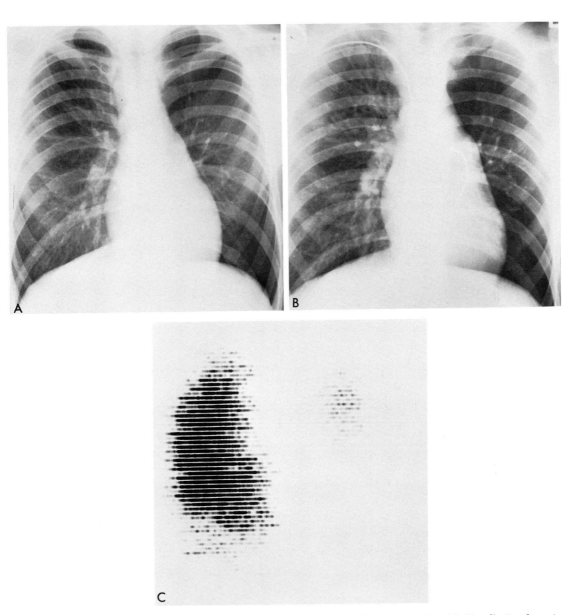

Figure 5–43. **Local Pulmonary Oligemia: Unilateral Emphysema (Swyer-James' or MacLeod's Syndrome).**
A posteroanterior roentgenogram of a 13-year-old asymptomatic boy (A) reveals considerable disparity in the
density of the two lungs, the left being generally more radiolucent. The vascular markings throughout the left
lung are diminutive, the disparity in blood flow to the two lungs being well illustrated in a pulmonary angiogram
(B) and in a lung scan (C). The left lung is of approximately normal volume compared to the right. (Courtesy Dr.
William Beamish, Royal Alexandra Hospital, Edmonton.)

Table 5–13. Unilateral, Lobar, or Segmental Pulmonary Oligemia

	ETIOLOGY
DEVELOPMENTAL	Hypogenetic lung syndrome
	Proximal interruption of the right or left pulmonary artery
	Anomalous origin of left pulmonary artery from the right
	Congenital bronchial atresia
INFECTIOUS	*Mycobacterium tuberculosis* (Primary)
	Staphylococcus aureus

Table 5–13. *Unilateral, Lobar, or Segmental Pulmonary Oligemia*
(Continued)

DIFFERENTIAL CHARACTERISTICS	COMMENTS
Anomalous vein forms "scimitar sign" which is diagnostic.	Partial hypoplasia of the *right* lung and right pulmonary artery; associated anomalies include dextrocardia, mirror-image bronchial tree, and anomalous venous drainage of right lung to inferior vena cava. Right lung supplied by systemic arteries, in part or in whole (*See* page 569.)
Absent or diminutive hilum. Differentiation from Swyer-James' (MacLeod's) syndrome by absence of air-trapping on forced expiration. Confirmation of diagnosis by pulmonary arteriography.	Involved lung hypoplastic and of reduced volume; supplied by hypertrophied bronchial circulation. Anomalous artery usually on side opposite aortic arch: when on *left*, high incidence of associated cardiovascular anomalies. (*See* page 571.)
If right main bronchus compressed, whole right lung may be radiolucent due to air-trapping—thus lung is *overinflated*. Confirmation by demonstration of posterior displacement of barium-filled esophagus due to interposition of anomalous artery between lower trachea and esophagus: arteriography diagnostic.	If anomalous artery compresses trachea rather than right main bronchus, both lungs will show overinflation and expiratory air-trapping. Severe compression may result in atelectasis of right lung. (*See* page 571.)
Almost invariably associated with a smooth, lobulated soft tissue mass, (due to inspissated mucus) distal to the point of atresia.	May involve a variety of segmental bronchi but most commonly the apicoposterior segment of the left upper lobe. Affected bronchopulmonary segments are air-containing due to collateral air-drift. (*See* page 583.)
Ipsilateral hilar lymph-node enlargement is present in most cases of primary tuberculosis. There is a predilection for anterior segment of upper lobe and medial segment of middle lobe.	Overinflation and oligemia result from partial bronchial obstruction. Although the majority of cases with this pattern are consequent upon extrabronchial compression from lymph nodes, some may develop as a result of bronchostenosis from tuberculous granuloma. Atelectasis may replace localized oligemia at a later stage. (*See* page 616.)
Large pneumatoceles develop as a complication of acute staphylococcal pneumonia and may fill an entire hemithorax. Air-fluid levels are present in some cases. Characteristically undergo rapid change in size.	Common in infants and children, rare in adults. (*See* page 595.)

Table continues

Table 5–13. *Unilateral, Lobar, or Segmental Pulmonary Oligemia*
(Continued)

ETIOLOGY	
NEOPLASTIC	Benign pulmonary neoplasms Bronchial adenoma Hamartoma Lieomyoma Fibroma Lipoma Myoblastoma Neurogenic neoplasms Chondroma Endometriosis Bronchogenic carcinoma Hodgkin's disease Lymphosarcoma group
THROMBOEMBOLIC	Pulmonary thromboembolism without infarction
INHALATIONAL	Foreign body aspiration
AIRWAYS DISEASE	Local obstructive emphysema

Table 5–13. *Unilateral, Lobar, or Segmental Pulmonary Oligemia*
(Continued)

DIFFERENTIAL CHARACTERISTICS	COMMENTS
Air-trapping and oligemia is frequently followed by obstructive pneumonitis or atelectasis. Rarely multiple areas involved with hamartoma.	Air-trapping and local oligemia result from partial endobronchial obstruction. Benign endobronchial neoplasms are rare causes of this pattern. (*See* pages 723-736.)
A segment, lobe, or whole lung may be affected. A mass is almost invariably identifiable. Air-trapping may be noted in expiratory film.	This is a rare manifestation of bronchogenic carcinoma. It may progress to a pattern of homogeneous segmental consolidation and atelectasis as a result of obstructive pneumonitis. Lymphatic spread of neoplasm to hilar lymph nodes occasionally results in compression of a bronchus, with resultant oligemia. (*See* page 736.)
Asymmetrical lymph-node enlargement in paratracheal, retrosternal, and hilar areas is almost invariable.	Local oligemia is a rare manifestation of endobronchial Hodgkin's. (*See* page 771.)
Usually in association with hilar and mediastinal lymph-node enlargement. Indistinguishable from Hodgkin's.	A rare manifestation of the secondary form of lymphosarcoma; results from partial endobronchial obstruction. (*See* page 784.)
Almost invariably associated with obstruction of a major pulmonary artery (*e.g.*, lobar). Affected artery is characteristically widened and of sharper-than-normal definition. The involved broncho-pulmonary segments may show moderate loss of volume — of value in differentiation from other causes of local oligemia.	**Local oligemia resulting from thrombo-embolism constitutes Westermark's sign. (*See* page 808.)**
Lower lobe predominance, invariably segmental in distribution. Foreign body identifiable as an opaque shadow in some cases.	**Air-trapping and local oligemia a more common manifestation of foreign body inhalation than atelectasis or obstructive pneumonitis. (*See* page 956.)**
In addition to showing air-trapping on expiration (as in Swyer-James' syndrome), affected zones are overinflated at TLC.	**Approximately 50 per cent of cases of emphysema have local rather than diffuse involvement of the lungs as assessed roentgenologically, although function tests usually indicate generalized disease. Affected areas may be upper zones or lower zones, more frequently the later. (*See* page 1006.)**

Table continues

Table 5–13. *Unilateral, Lobar, or Segmental Pulmonary Oligemia* *(Continued)*

	ETIOLOGY
AIRWAYS DISEASE *(Cont.)*	**Unilateral or lobar emphysema (Swyer-James' syndrome)**
	Bullae
IDIOPATHIC	Sarcoidosis
	Amyloidosis

Table 5–13. *Unilateral, Lobar, or Segmental Pulmonary Oligemia (Continued)*

DIFFERENTIAL CHARACTERISTICS	COMMENTS
Oligemia characteristically involves a whole lung, producing unilateral radiolucency; however, single lobes may be similarly affected. Both the hilar and peripheral vessels are diminutive, although structurally normal. The volume of affected lung at TLC is normal or reduced, seldom if ever increased. Air-trapping on expiration is a *sine qua non* to the diagnosis, and permits differentiation from agenesis of a pulmonary artery. Bronchiectasis is demonstrable in most cases.	There is convincing evidence that this abnormality results from acute pneumonia during infancy or childhood, frequency of viral etiology; infection of the peripheral airways leads to bronchiolitis obliterans and a morphologic picture virtually indistinguishable from emphysema. (*See* page 1033.)
Characterized by sharply defined, air-containing spaces bounded by curvilinear, hair-line shadows; range in size from 1 cm to the volume of a hemithorax. Vascular markings are absent; adjacent lung parenchyma is compressed. Overinflation and air-trapping are usual.	Predominantly unilateral in contrast to the bilateral disease described in Table 5–12. Unlike unilateral emphysema, the vasculature is absent rather than attenuated. (*See* page 1023.)
Oligemia results from partial bronchial obstruction and consequent air trapping and overinflation. Usually lobar or multilobar. Diagnosis may be suspected from symmetrical hilar and paratracheal lymph node enlargement.	A rare cause of local oligemia. Although bronchial compression from enlarged nodes may be the cause, obstruction more often results from endobronchial sarcoid deposits. (*See* page 1087.)
A manifestation of endobronchial amyloid deposits producing partial bronchial obstruction. Parenchymal lesions as well as endobronchial disease may be present in some cases.	A rare cause of local oligemia. Diagnosis is made on the basis of biopsy and the demonstration of multiple organ involvement. (*See* page 1121.)

Table 5–14

Pleural Effusion Unassociated With Other Roentgenographic Evidence of Disease in The Thorax

This title is self-explanatory. Effusion may be unilateral or bilateral. It must be emphasized that the lack of association with other abnormalities in the chest implies the absence of other *roentgenologically demonstrable* abnormality. Obviously, disease may be present but be roentgenographically invisible; for example, pulmonary involvement in rheumatoid disease may have no definite roentgenographic manifestations, although a considerable degree of pulmonary interstitial fibrosis may be apparent histo-

logically. Conversely, diseases in which pulmonary abnormality is obscured by an effusion (*e.g.*, lobar collapse due to an obstructing endobronchial cancer) are *not* included in this table, since the presence of underlying pulmonary disease would be clearly demonstrable roentgenographically after thoracentesis.

In addition to the cases illustrated on the following pages, the following figures appearing elsewhere in the book may be referred to as representative of this pattern:

Figure	Page
4–150	349
4–152	352

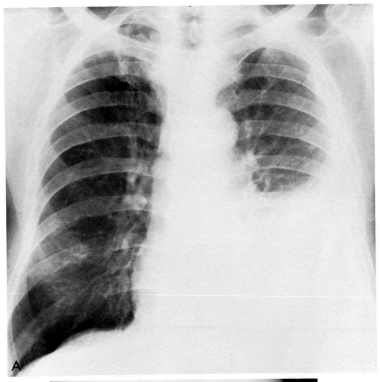

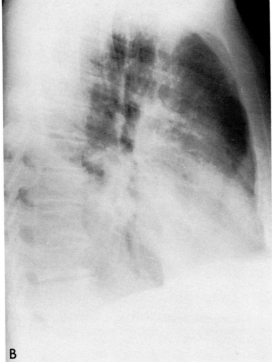

Figure 5–44. **Pleural Effusion in Rheumatoid Pleuropulmonary Disease.** Posteroanterior (A) and lateral (B) roentgenograms reveal the typical appearance of a moderate accumulation of fluid in the left pleural space. Following thoracentesis, the lungs were regarded as normal roentgenologically although subsequent examination of the lungs at necropsy established the presence of extensive changes compatible with rheumatoid disease.

Table 5–14. *Pleural Effusion Unassociated With Other Roentgenographic Evidence of Disease in the Thorax*

	ETIOLOGY	CHARACTER OF THE FLUID
INFECTIOUS	**Bacteria** *Mycobacterium tuberculosis*	Serous exudate. Predominantly lymphocytic reaction; erythrocytes may be present but seldom in great numbers. Blood glucose levels below 25 mg/100 ml highly suggestive (N.B.: differentiate from effusions of rheumatoid disease).
	Viruses All viruses and Mycoplasma	Serous exudate.
	Extrathoracic infection Pancreatitis	Usually serous exudate but may be serosanguinous. Pleural fluid amylase higher than serum.
	Subphrenic abscess	Serous exudate.
NEOPLASTIC	**Neoplasms Arising Within the Thorax** Lymphoma	Usually serosanguinous; specific gravity midway between exudate and transudate; may be chylous or chyliform.
	Neoplasms Arising Outside the Thorax Metastatic carcinoma	Serous exudate; varies in blood content from none to grossly hemorrhagic. Glucose content of greater than 79 mg/100 ml is common but not diagnostic.
	Ovarian neoplasms (Meigs' syndrome)	Usually serous exudate; occasionally serosanguinous.
	Carcinoma of the pancreas	Serous exudate.
	Retroperitoneal lymphoma	Serous exudate.

Table 5–14. *Pleural Effusion Unassociated With Other Roentgenographic Evidence of Disease in the Thorax (Continued)*

CRITERIA FOR PRESUMPTIVE DIAGNOSIS	CRITERIA FOR POSITIVE DIAGNOSIS	COMMENTS
Combination of positive tuberculin reaction and predominantly lymphocytic pleural fluid.	(a) Positive pleural biopsy. (b) Culture of tubercle bacilli from pleural fluid.	A negative tuberculin test virtually excludes the diagnosis. Strong tendency to subsequent development of active pulmonary tuberculosis if effusion not treated. Effusions rarely bilateral. A manifestation of primary tuberculosis more commonly in the adult (approximately 40 per cent) than in children (10 per cent). (*See* page 1146.)
None	Elevated agglutinin titer to offending organism.	May be bilateral. (*See* page 1149.)
Clinical picture of acute abdomen.	Elevated level of pleural fluid amylase.	May occur in acute, chronic, or relapsing pancreatitis. Majority of effusions *left*-sided. (*See* page 1157.)
Elevation and fixation of hemidiaphragm.	Gas and fluid in subphrenic space.	More commonly associated with basal pulmonary disease ("plate" atelectasis or pneumonitis). (*See* page 1157.)
Peripheral lymph-node enlargement, hepatosplenomegaly, and so forth.	Finding of typical cells in pleural fluid or biopsy of remote lymph node. White-cell count in leukemia.	This broad heading includes leukemia as well as Hodgkin's disease, lymphosarcoma, and reticulum-cell sarcoma. Approximately 30 per cent of cases have pleural effusion, but seldom without associated pulmonary or mediastinal-node involvement. (*See* page 1149.)
Identification of remote primary neoplasm.	Finding of characteristic tissue on needle biopsy or malignant cells in pleural fluid.	Most commonly from breast; also from pancreas, stomach, ovary, kidney. (*See* page 1150.)
Pleural fluid negative for malignant cells; pelvic mass.	Presence of ovarian neoplasm with ascites; disappearance of effusion following oophorectomy.	Ovarian neoplasm may be fibroma, thecoma, cystadenoma, adenocarcinoma, granulosa-cell tumor; occasionally fibromyoma of uterus. (*See* page 1157.)
Pleural fluid negative for malignant cells; clinical signs of intra-abdominal neoplasia.	Disappearance of fluid following removal of primary.	Effusion may occur without direct involvement of thorax by primary; probably related to transport of fluid into thorax via diaphragmatic lymphatics. (*See* page 1157.)
Pleural fluid negative for malignant cells; clinical signs of intra-abdominal neoplasia.	Disappearance of fluid following treatment of primary.	

Table continues

Table 5–14. *Pleural Effusion Unassociated With Other Roentgenographic Evidence of Disease in the Thorax (Continued)*

	ETIOLOGY	CHARACTER OF THE FLUID
IMMUNOLOGIC	Systemic lupus erythematosus	Serous exudate.
	Rheumatoid disease	Serous exudate; tends to be turbid and greenish-yellow. Predominance of lymphocytes. Glucose concentration characteristically low, with failure to rise on I.V. glucose infusion (failure of glucose-transport mechanism).
THROMBOEMBOLIC	Pulmonary embolism	Almost invariably serosanguinous.
TRAUMATIC	Closed-chest trauma	(A) Blood (hemothorax).
		(B) Chyle (chylothorax).
		(C) Contains ingested food (esophageal rupture).
INCIDENTAL CAUSES	Nephrotic syndrome and other causes of diminished plasma osmotic pressure	Transudate
	Acute glomerulonephritis	Transudate (?)
	Myxedema	Serous exudate.
	Cirrhosis with ascites	Transudate
	Hydronephrosis	Serous exudate.

Table 5–14. *Pleural Effusion Unassociated With Other Roentgenographic Evidence of Disease in the Thorax (Continued)*

CRITERIA FOR PRESUMPTIVE DIAGNOSIS	CRITERIA FOR POSITIVE DIAGNOSIS	COMMENTS
Clinical findings of typical rash, renal disease, heart murmur, and so forth.	Positive L.E.-cell test in association with characteristic clinical findings.	Occurs as isolated abnormality in slightly greater than 10 per cent of cases. Effusion usually small, but may be moderate or even massive; bilateral in about 50 per cent. Usually clears without residua. Often associated with pericardial effusion. (*See* page 1153.)
Clinical or roentgenologic changes of rheumatoid arthritis. High titer of rheumatoid factor in serum highly suggestive but not conclusive.	Biopsy of pleura showing typical rheumatoid granulation tissue.	Almost exclusively in men. Usually unilateral, on right slightly more often than on left. May antedate signs and symptoms of rheumatoid arthritis, but usually follows. Effusion often persists for several months. (*See* page 1153.)
History of sudden onset of pleural pain with or without peripheral thrombophlebitis. Rarely may observe relative diminution of peripheral vasculature roentgenologically.	Lung scan or pulmonary angiogram or both.	Frequency of effusion as sole manifestation of pulmonary embolism not precisely known, but probably very uncommon. (*See* page 1154.)
History	Thoracentesis and history.	May originate from chest wall, diaphragm, mediastinum, or lung. (*See* page 1155.)
History. Time lag between trauma and development of effusion.	Thoracentesis; lymphangiography.	Side of chylothorax depends on site of thoracic-duct rupture. (*See* page 1155.)
History	Thoracentesis; esophagogram.	Almost always left-sided. Generally due to surgical procedure. (*See* page 1156.)
General edema.	Thoracentesis; biochemical assay of serum and urine.	Effusion commonly infrapulmonary. (*See* page 1158.)
Usual findings of acute glomerulonephritis.	———	(*See* page 1158.)
Studies of thyroid activity.	———	Effusion occurs more often in pericardium. (*See* page 1158.)
Demonstration of cirrhosis and ascites (N.B.: exclude carcinoma of liver).	———	Ascitic fluid enters pleural space via diaphragmatic lymphatics (as in Meigs' syndrome). (*See* page 1158.)
Demonstration of hydronephrosis.	Disappearance of effusion following removal of urinary obstruction.	Mechanism not clear; possibly related to transport of fluid via diaphragmatic lymphatics. (*See* page 1158.)

Table continues

Table 5–14. *Pleural Effusion Unassociated With Other Roentgenographic Evidence of Disease in the Thorax (Continued)*

	ETIOLOGY	CHARACTER OF THE FLUID
INCIDENTAL CAUSES *(Cont.)*	Peritoneal dialysis	——
	Lymphedema	Exudate with high protein content.
	Familial recurring polyserositis	Serofibrinous exudate.

Table 5–14. *Pleural Effusion Unassociated With Other Roentgenographic Evidence of Disease in the Thorax (Continued)*

CRITERIA FOR PRESUMPTIVE DIAGNOSIS	CRITERIA FOR POSITIVE DIAGNOSIS	COMMENTS
Effusion developing during dialysis and clearing subsequently.	——	Mechanism as in Meigs' syndrome. (*See* page 1158.)
Clinical evidence of lymphedema elsewhere.	——	Occasional finding in Milroy's disease and in the syndrome of yellow nails, lymphedema, and pleural effusions. (*See* page 1158.)
Combination of symptoms and signs in specific racial groups.	——	Heredofamilial; limited to Armenians, Arabs, and Jews. Episodic acute attacks of abdominal and chest pain. Bilateral basal "plate" atelectasis may occur.

Table 5–15

**PLEURAL EFFUSION ASSOCIATED
WITH OTHER ROENTGENOGRAPHIC
EVIDENCE OF DISEASE IN THE THORAX**

This table includes all diseases in which unilateral or bilateral pleural effusion is associated with roentgenologic evidence of another abnormality in the thorax—local or general pulmonary disease, hilar or mediastinal lymph-node enlargement, cardiomegaly, diaphragmatic abnormality, disease of the bony thorax or chest wall, or any combination of these. This widely ranging list makes a long and rather cumbersome table; however, it seemed preferable to create a single, all-inclusive table than to subdivide diseases into separate categories according to the anatomic structures involved.

In addition to the cases illustrated on the following pages, the following figures appearing elsewhere in the book may be referred to as representative of this pattern:

Figure	Page
4–153	353
4–154	354
4–155	355
8– 20	773

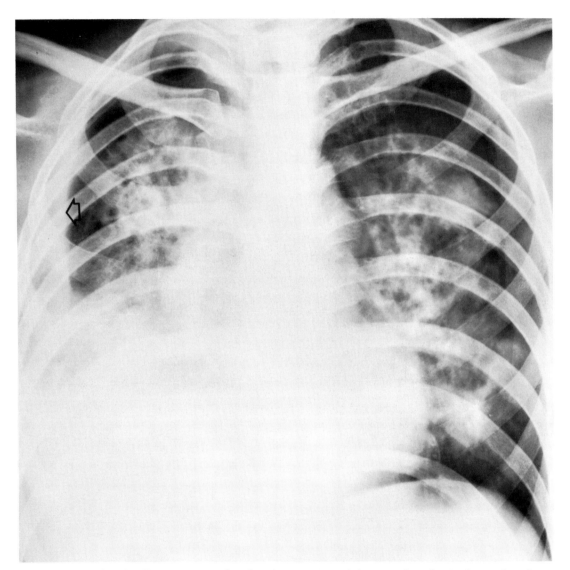

Figure 5–45. **Pleural Effusion Associated with Pulmonary Consolidation and Mediastinal Lymph-node Enlargement: Hodgkin's Disease.** A posteroanterior roentgenogram reveals a moderate accumulation of fluid in the right pleural space, possessing a somewhat atypical configuration (*arrow*) due to the presence of extensive underlying pulmonary disease. Bilateral hilar and right paratracheal lymph-node enlargement is also present. Proved Hodgkin's granuloma. (Courtesy Dr. David Berger, Royal Edward Chest Hospital, Montreal.)

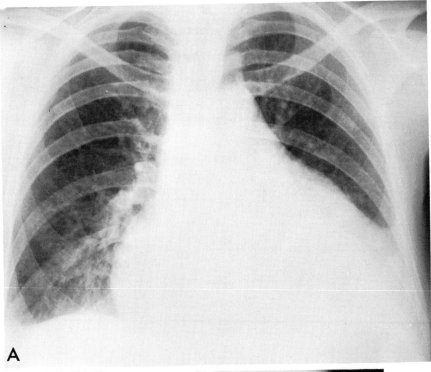

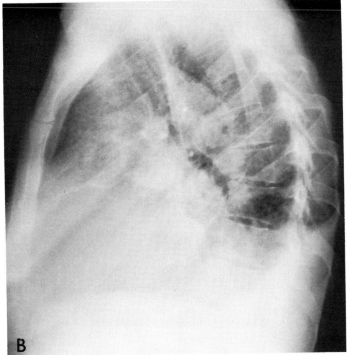

Figure 5–46. **Pleural Effusion Associated with Cardiomegaly: Systemic Lupus Erythematosus.** Posteroanterior (A) and lateral (B) roentgenograms reveal small bilateral pleural effusions obliterating the lateral and posterior costophrenic sulci. There is marked enlargement of the cardiac silhouette, due chiefly to a large pericardial effusion. The lungs are clear. Such a roentgenographic appearance could readily be produced by cardiac decompensation. Proved systemic lupus erythematosus.

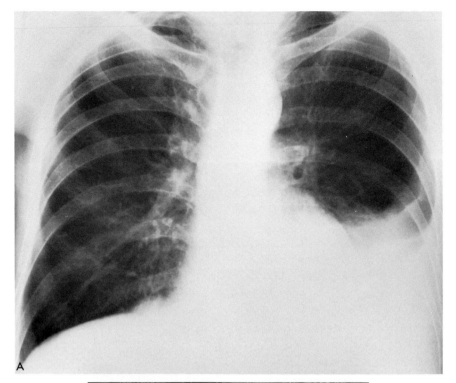

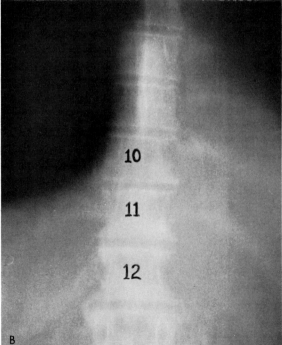

Figure 5–47. **Pleural Effusion Associated with Abnormality of the Bony Thorax: Hodgkin's Disease.** A posteroanterior roentgenogram (A) reveals pleural effusion of moderate size. Following thoracentesis, the underlying lung was thought to be normal roentgenologically. Because of the presence of back pain, the lower thoracic spine was roentgenographed and subsequently tomographed (B); there is erosion of both sides of the eleventh and twelfth thoracic vertebral bodies and of the left side of the tenth body due to invasion from Hodgkin's tissue in the paravertebral lymph-node chain.

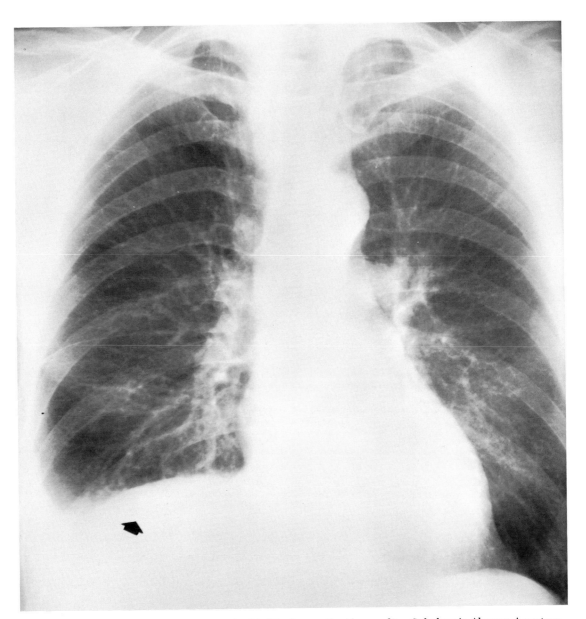

Figure 5–48. **Pleural Effusion Associated with Diaphragmatic Abnormality: Subphrenic Abscess.** A postero-anterior roentgenogram demonstrates a small right pleural effusion obliterating the right costophrenic sulcus. The right hemidiaphragm is moderately elevated and immediately beneath it there is a small accumulation of gas containing an air-fluid level (*arrow*). A more heavily penetrated roentgenogram revealed several foci of plate-like atelectasis in the region of the costophrenic angle. Subphrenic abscess two weeks following subtotal gastrectomy.

Table 5–15. *Pleural Effusion Associated With Other Roentgenographic Evidence of Disease in the Thorax*

	ETIOLOGY	CHARACTER OF THE FLUID
INFECTIOUS	**Bacteria**	
	Klebsiella pneumoniae (Friedlander's bacillus)	Purulent; predominant polymorphonuclear response.
	Pasteurella tularensis (tularemia)	Serous
	Staphylococcus aureus	Usually purulent but may be serous or serosanguinous.
	Diplococcus pneumonia	Serous
	Mycobacterium tuberculosis	Serous or purulent.
	Pasteurella pestis	Serous
	Streptococcus pyogenes	Varies from serous effusion to frank pus.

Table 5–15. *Pleural Effusion Associated With Other Roentgenographic Evidence of Disease in the Thorax (Continued)*

CRITERIA FOR PRESUMPTIVE DIAGNOSIS	CRITERIA FOR POSITIVE DIAGNOSIS	COMMENTS
Cavitating air-space pneumonia, often in upper lobes.	Culture of organism from sputum or pleural fluid.	Acute air-space pneumonia; cavitation frequent. Involved lobe may be expanded. (*See* page 1146.)
Combination of spherical or oval pulmonary densities with enlarged hilar nodes. History of animal exposure.	(a) Rising serum agglutinin titers against *P. tularensis.* (b) Isolation of the organism from sputum or pleural fluid.	Pleural effusion in 50 to 64 per cent of pneumonias. Hilar lymph-node enlargement frequent. Pulmonary and pleural involvement much more frequent in typhoidal form (50 to 77 per cent) than in nontyphoidal (8 to 26 per cent). (*See* page 1147.)
In infants and children, pneumonia and empyema almost pathognomonic, particularly with abscess and pneumatocele formation.	Identification of organism by smear or culture from sputum or pleural fluid.	Rapidly progressive pneumonia—typically confluent segmental bronchopneumonia; abscess and "pneumatocele" formation frequent in children. Empyema more common in adults; pleural reaction usually is less marked in adults although lung abscess common. (*See* page 1147.)
Typical roentgen characteristics of acute air-space pneumonia.	Isolation of organism.	Demonstrable effusion very uncommon in standard roentgenograms in erect position. (*See* page 1147.)
Granulomas on pleural biopsy; acid-fast organisms on smear of sputum or pleural fluid.	Culture of organism from sputum or pleural fluid.	Combined pleural effusion and roentgenographically demonstrable parenchymal disease an uncommon manifestation of either primary or reinfection tuberculosis. Effusion may occur as a manifestation of widely disseminated hematogenous disease or disease of the thoracic skeleton. (*See* page 1146.)
Combination of confluent pneumonia; enlarged peripheral lymph nodes, and history of animal exposure.	Isolation of organism from sputum, blood, or aspirate of lymph node.	Pulmonary disease may simulate acute pulmonary edema. (*See* page 609.)
	Smear or culture of organism from pleural fluid (may be very difficult to identify).	Inhomogeneous or homogeneous segmental bronchopneumonia; abscess formation variable. In children, commonly preceded by viral disease, especially exanthems. (*See* page 1147.)

Table continues

Table 5–15. *Pleural Effusion Associated With Other Roentgenographic Evidence of Disease in the Thorax (Continued)*

	ETIOLOGY	CHARACTER OF THE FLUID
INFECTIOUS *(Cont.)*	*Pseudomonas aeruginosa* *Escherichia coli* *Salmonella* species *Bacterium anitratum* *Hemophilus influenzae*	Purulent
	Malleomyces	Purulent
	Bacteroides species	Purulent
	Clostridium perfringens (B. welchii)	Purulent
	Fungi **Actinomyces israelii** (actinomycosis) **Nocardia** species	Purulent
	Blastomyces dermatitidis *Cryptococcus neoformans*	Serous exudate.
	Histoplasma capsulatum	Serous exudate.

Table 5–15. *Pleural Effusion Associated With Other Roentgenographic Evidence of Disease in the Thorax (Continued)*

CRITERIA FOR PRESUMPTIVE DIAGNOSIS	CRITERIA FOR POSITIVE DIAGNOSIS	COMMENTS
		Homogeneous segmental bronchopneumonia. (*See* page 600.)
		Patchy or confluent bronchopneumonia. (*See* page 606.)
Characteristically in patients with low resistance—*e.g.*, chronic diseases, alcoholism.	Isolation of organism.	Segmental bronchopneumonia; abscess formation variable. Involvement of GI tract may not be obvious. (*See* page 607.)
		Pneumonia, commonly with abscesses. Pyopneumothorax usual due to bronchopleural fistula. (*See* page 610.)
		Inhomogeneous segmental bronchopneumonia. In children, associated with acute upper-respiratory-tract symptoms. (*See* page 607.)
Exposure to animals in endemic areas (Far East).	Isolation of organism.	Bronchopneumonia with abscess formation; hilar-node enlargement. (*See* page 611.)
Characteristically in patients with low resistance—*e.g.*, chronic diseases, alcoholism.	Isolation of organism.	Segmental bronchopneumonia; incidence of infection higher than generally believed; organism requires anaerobic culture; may be intrapleural gas production. (*See* page 612.)
Combination of pleural effusion and gas in soft tissues (not postoperative or associated with pneumothorax).	Isolation of organism.	Segmental bronchopneumonia; gas in soft tissues. Gas-forming organisms may lead to pyopneumothorax. (*See* page 1147.)
Combination of cavitary pneumonia, pleural effusion (empyema), and chest-wall involvement should strongly suggest these etiologies.	**Isolation of organism from sputum, pleural fluid, or chest wall abscess.**	**Homogeneous nonsegmental air-space pneumonia almost invariable; abscess formation and chest wall involvement common, sometimes with rib destruction. Empyema necessitatis. (*See* page 1147.)**
None	Isolation of organism.	Effusion very uncommon in Blastomycosis and rare in Cryptococcosis. Associated with homogeneous nonsegmental air-space pneumonia; cavitation uncommon (15 per cent). Chest-wall involvement rare. (*See* page 1148.)
None to distinguish from primary tuberculosis; positive skin tests or serologic tests highly suggestive.	Isolation of organism.	Patchy parenchymal consolidation, commonly in lower lobes (primary infection); hilar-node enlargement common. Effusion very uncommon (2 per cent. (*See* page 1148.)

Table continues

Table 5–15. *Pleural Effusion Associated With Other Roentgenographic Evidence of Disease in the Thorax (Continued)*

	ETIOLOGY	CHARACTER OF THE FLUID
INFECTIOUS *(Cont.)*	*Aspergillus* species	Nonpurulent serous exudate.
	Viruses All viruses and Mycoplasma	Serous exudate.
	Parasites *Entamoeba histolytica* (amebiasis)	Usually serofibrinous but may become frankly purulent when secondarily infected. Occasionally fluid contains bile and cytolysed liver tissue and then possesses characteristic "chocolate-sauce" appearance.
	Paragonimus westermanii	Serous exudate.
	Echinococcus granulosus (hydatid disease)	Cloudy serous fluid.
	Extrathoracic Infection Subphrenic abscess	Serous exudate.
NEOPLASTIC	Bronchogenic carcinoma	Serous exudate; may be sanguinous.
	Lymphoma	Serosanguinous or chylous.

Table 5–15. *Pleural Effusion Associated With Other Roentgenographic Evidence of Disease in the Thorax (Continued)*

CRITERIA FOR PRESUMPTIVE DIAGNOSIS	CRITERIA FOR POSITIVE DIAGNOSIS	COMMENTS
None	Isolation of organism.	Usually an opportunistic invader in postoperative empyema cavity; does not form pus. (*See* page 1148.)
May be suggested by acute segmental pneumonia with combined interstitial and air-space elements. Clinical picture helpful.	Positive serologic tests.	Combined interstitial and air-space pneumonia (segmental). Effusion uncommon. (*See* page 1149.)
Combination of lower lobe consolidation, pleural effusion, and enlarged liver, especially in a patient with diarrhea.	Recovery of cysts or trophozoites from sputum, pleural fluid, or stool.	**Elevation and fixation of right hemidiaphragm; homogeneous consolidation of right lower lobe, with or without abscess formation. Organisms infiltrating from liver abscess through diaphragm into pleura and lung. May form bronchohepatic fistula. (*See* page 1148.)**
Thin-walled cystic spaces in lower lobes in a patient from an endemic area.	Recovery of ova from sputum or feces.	Isolated nodular shadows, usually in lower lobes, commonly with cavitation. "Metacercariae" migrate from free peritoneal space through diaphragm into the pleura and lung. (*See* page 1148.)
Effusion — commonly hydropneumothorax; floating scolices and daughter cysts producing "water-lily" sign.	Positive Casoni skin test or complement-fixation test. Recovery of hooklets from sputum or pleural fluid.	Skin effusion develops as a result of rupture of a pulmonary hydatid, a collapsed cystic space may be observed in the lungs; other solid hydatid cysts may be present. Rupture more commonly occurs into bronchus. (*See* page 1148.)
Elevated fixed hemidiaphragm with basal atelectasis and effusion (usually small).	Gas and fluid in subphrenic space.	Hemidiaphragm elevated and fixed; usually basal "plate" atelectasis, with or without pneumonia. (*See* page 1157.)
Obstructive pneumonitis with pleural effusion very strong presumptive evidence *per se*.	Recovery of cells from pleural fluid or sputum: positive pleural, bronchoscopic, or mediastinal-node biopsy.	Obstructive pneumonitis ("drowned lung"). May or may not be associated with hilar- or mediastinal-node enlargement. Although the effusion may not contain cells, its presence is ominous. (*See* page 1151.)
Combination of zones of consolidation (commonly separate from hilum) and pleural effusion, especially with enlargement of hilar and mediastinal nodes, constitutes strong presumptive evidence.	Biopsy of pleura or lymph node. Recovery of cells from pleural fluid.	Includes leukemia as well as Hodgkin's disease, reticulum-cell sarcoma, and lymphosarcoma. Single or multiple areas of consolidated lung of varying size — may be massive; usually homogeneous. Hilar and mediastinal nodes also may be enlarged. Parenchymal involvement seldom if ever the presenting feature. (*See* page 1149.)

Table continues

Table 5–15.   *Pleural Effusion Associated With Other Roentgenographic Evidence of Disease in the Thorax (Continued)*

	ETIOLOGY	CHARACTER OF THE FLUID
NEOPLASTIC *(Cont.)*	Metastatic carcinoma	Serous or serosanguinous.
	Mesothelioma	Almost invariably bloody; hyaluronic-acid levels may be elevated.
	Bronchiolar carcinoma	Serous or serosanguinous.
	Multiple myeloma	Commonly serosanguinous.
	Primary neoplasms of chest wall	Serosanguinous
	Neoplastic involvement of pleura by direct invasion	Serosanguinous
THROMBOEMBOLIC	Pulmonary embolism and infarction	Serosanguinous

Table 5–15. *Pleural Effusion Associated With Other Roentgenographic Evidence of Disease in the Thorax (Continued)*

CRITERIA FOR PRESUMPTIVE DIAGNOSIS	CRITERIA FOR POSITIVE DIAGNOSIS	COMMENTS
Combination of diffuse pulmonary densities and pleural effusion highly suggestive, particularly if heart size normal; differentiation from bronchiolar carcinoma may be difficult.	Identification of primary lesion; positive pleural biopsy; cells occasionally identified in pleural fluid or sputum.	(A) Hematogenous – generally nodular. (B) Lymphangitic – often predominantly linear but may have nodular component. Hilar and mediastinal nodes may be involved, but seldom a prominent roentgenographic feature. (*See* page 1150.)
In local variety, peripherally situated mass usually having obtuse angles with chest wall. In diffuse type, history of exposure to asbestos. Volume of ipsilateral hemithorax may be reduced despite massive opacification.	Recovery of cells from pleural fluid. Positive pleural biopsy.	Effusion uncommon in local variety but almost invariable in diffuse malignant type. Either local or diffuse variety may be obscured by pleural fluid. (*See* page 1152.)
High index of suspicion. Difficult to differentiate from metastatic neoplasm or widely disseminated lymphoma.	Malignant cells in pleural fluid or sputum. Biopsy.	Widely disseminated nodular densities of variable size, generally discrete but may be confluent in areas. Lymph nodes enlarged in 25 per cent of cases pathologically but may not be apparent roentgenologically. (*See* page 1152.)
Single or multiple soft-tissue masses arising from chest wall and protruding into thoracic space. Expansion of ribs almost pathognomonic.	Rib or chest-wall biopsy; characteristic changes in bone marrow; electrophoretic pattern of serum proteins. Plasma cells may be numerous in pleural fluid.	Pleural effusion uncommon. Destructive lesions of one or more ribs with or without expansion. Soft tissue masses commonly protrude into thorax. Also destructive lesions in shoulder girdles or thoracic spine. Lungs may be involved. (*See* page 1152.)
Combination of expanding lesion of chest wall and pleural effusion highly suggestive. May be indistinguishable from myeloma unless latter multiple.	Cells in pleural fluid or preferably direct biopsy.	Osteolytic, osteoblastic, or mixed neoplasms of ribs (or occasionally thoracic vertebrae) may extend into thoracic cavity. Primary mesenchymal neoplasms of intercostal spaces may act similarly. (*See* page 1152.)
In breast carcinoma, absence of breast shadow or history of mastectomy suggestive but not conclusive.	Typical cells in pleural fluid; pleural biopsy.	May occur occasionally from breast carcinoma, and rarely from liver or pancreas neoplasm. (*See* page 1152.)
Any basal shadow associated with diaphragmatic elevation and pleural effusion should suggest the possibility. Clinical picture usually distinctive.	Pulmonary angiogram supported by serum-enzyme changes – elevated LDH, normal SGOT, and elevated bilirubin.	Pulmonary changes vary from major segmental area of consolidation to line shadows of varying extent. Hemidiaphragm commonly elevated. Pleural effusion almost always small. (*See* page 1154.)

Table continues

Table 5–15. *Pleural Effusion Associated With Other Roentgenographic Evidence of Disease in the Thorax (Continued)*

	ETIOLOGY	CHARACTER OF THE FLUID
CARDIOVASCULAR	Congestive heart failure	Transudate
	Constrictive pericarditis	Transudate
	Obstruction of superior vena cava or azygos vein	Transudate
IMMUNOLOGIC	Systemic lupus erythematosus	Serous exudate.
	Rheumatoid disease	Exudate (*see* Table 5–14); low serum glucose values.
TRAUMATIC	Open- or closed-chest trauma	Blood (hemothorax). Chyle (chylothorax). Ingested food (esophageal rupture).

Table 5–15. *Pleural Effusion Associated With Other Roentgenographic Evidence of Disease in the Thorax (Continued)*

CRITERIA FOR PRESUMPTIVE DIAGNOSIS	CRITERIA FOR POSITIVE DIAGNOSIS	COMMENTS
Cardiac enlargement, usually general and "nonspecific." Clinical signs of cardiac decompensation.	Nature of the fluid on thoracentesis; its disappearance with treatment of cardiac decompensation.	Most commonly with failure of both sides of the heart. Frequently unilateral on the right, seldom on the left, but may be bilateral. (*See* page 1156.)
Signs of systemic venous hypertension.	Pericardial calcification with reduced amplitude of pulsation.	Effusion present in approximately 50 per cent of cases. (*See* page 1156.)
Clinical signs of superior venacava syndrome. Plain-film roentgenologic findings.	Angiography	——
Combination of bilateral pleural effusion, nonspecific cardiac enlargement and basal atelectasis or pneumonia should suggest the diagnosis.	Positive L.E.-cell preparation in association with characteristic clinical findings.	Pulmonary changes nonspecific—generally in form of basal "pneumonitis" or atelectasis; cardiac enlargement in 30 to 50 per cent of all cases, commonly due to pericardial effusion. Progressive loss of lung volume may be a characteristic. (*See* page 1153.)
Pleuropulmonary disease in patients with rheumatoid arthritis.	High titer of rheumatoid factor in blood suggestive but not conclusive.	Diffuse reticulonodular pattern, predominantly basal in distribution. Pleural effusion most commonly an isolated finding; incidence of coexistent pleural effusion and pulmonary disease not clear but probably independent. (*See* page 1153.)
Associated findings should allow precise diagnosis in majority of cases.	Thoracentesis always diagnostic with positive history.	Wide variety of changes, including fractured ribs, pulmonary hemorrhage or hematoma, mediastinal hematoma, aortic aneurysm, pneumothorax, pneumomediastinum. (*See* page 1155.)

Table 5–16

HILAR AND MEDIASTINAL LYMPH-NODE ENLARGEMENT

This table includes all conditions producing lymph-node enlargement within the thorax, either alone or in combination with other roentgenographic abnormalities. It is to be noted that a number of diseases are included in which node enlargement is a common manifestation in infants and children but uncommon in adults; since we have excluded much reference to pediatric diseases of the chest in the text, their inclusion here is a compromise to space limitation.

In addition to the cases illustrated on the following pages, the following figures appearing elsewhere in the book may be referred to as representative of this pattern:

Figure	Page
4–93	284
7–21	649
7–24	655
7–38	696
8– 7	745
8– 8	746
8–10	748
8–23	776
8–24	777
8–25	778
8–27	780

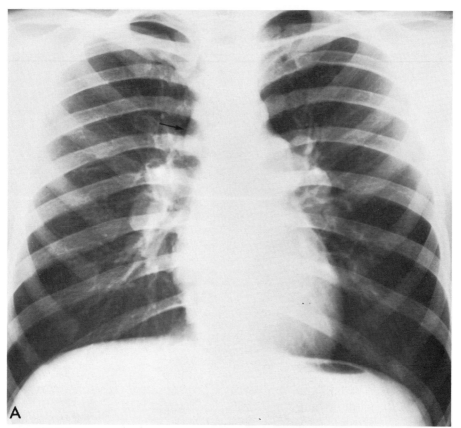

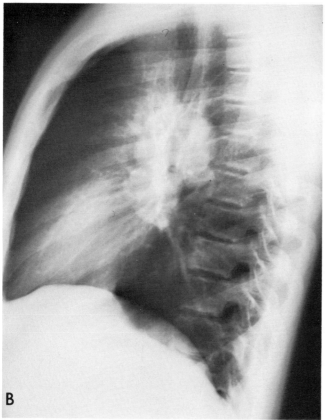

Figure 5–49. Hilar and Mediastinal Lymph-node Enlargement: Sarcoidosis. Posteroanterior (A) and lateral (B) roentgenograms reveal marked enlargement of both hilar shadows due to enlarged lymph nodes; the lobulated contour is particularly well demonstrated in lateral projection. Bilateral paratracheal and tracheobronchial lymph-node enlargement is also present, the azygos lymph node being clearly visible in posteroanterior projection (*arrow*). The lungs are clear. Proved sarcoidosis.

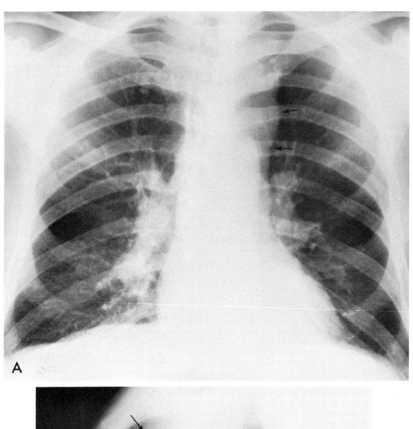

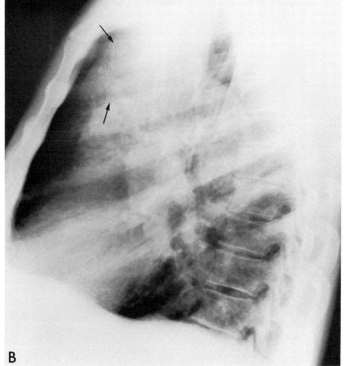

Figure 5–50.   **Hilar and Mediastinal Lymph-node Enlargement: Chronic Lymphatic Leukemia.** Posteroanterior (A) and lateral (B) roentgenograms demonstrate enlarged lymph nodes in both hila and in the anterior mediastinal (prevascular) compartment (*arrows* on both illustrations). Such enlargement of the anterior mediastinal chain is highly suggestive of lymphoma or leukemia.

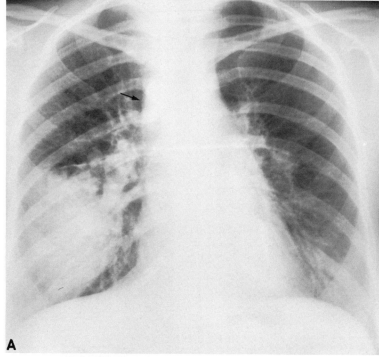

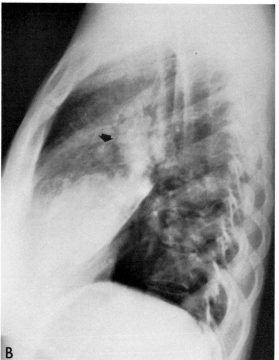

Figure 5–51.   **Combined Mediastinal Lymph-node Enlargement and Pulmonary Disease: Hodgkin's Disease.**
Posteroanterior (A) and lateral (B) roentgenograms reveal enlargement of paratracheal lymph nodes bilaterally;
note particularly the enlarged azygos node in the right tracheobronchial angle (*arrow*). In addition, there is almost
complete consolidation of the right middle lobe and a small well-defined nodule in the right upper lobe (*thick
arrow* in B). This combination of mediastinal-node enlargement and multilobar parenchymal disease strongly
suggests the diagnosis of lymphoma. Proved Hodgkin's disease (*see also* Figure 8–28, page 781).

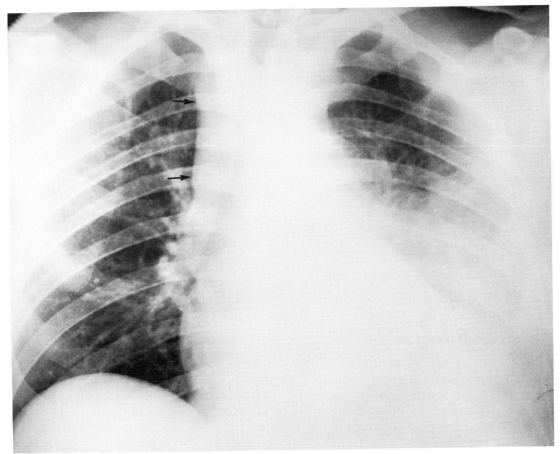

Figure 5–52. **Mediastinal Lymph-node Enlargement Associated with Pleural Effusion: Lymphosarcoma.** A posteroanterior roentgenogram reveals irregular nodular enlargement of the lymph nodes along the right paratracheal chain (*arrows*). A massive pleural effusion is present on the left. Following thoracentesis, enlargement of the left paratracheal lymph-node chain could be identified. The underlying lungs were normal roentgenographically.

Table 5–16. *Hilar and Mediastinal Lymph-Node Enlargement*

	ETIOLOGY	SYMMETRY	NODE GROUPS INVOLVED
INFECTIOUS	**Bacteria**		
	Mycobacterium tuberculosis (primary)	Unilateral in 80 per cent of cases.	Approximately 60 per cent hilar and 40 per cent combined hilar and paratracheal.
	Pasteurella tularensis	Unilateral	Hilar
	Hemophilus pertussis	Unilateral	Hilar
	Bacillus anthracis	Symmetrical	All
	Mycoplasma and Viruses		
	Mycoplasma pneumonia	Unilateral or bilateral.	Hilar
	Rubeola	Bilateral	Hilar
	ECHOvirus pneumonia	Bilateral	Hilar
	Varicella pneumonia	Bilateral	Hilar
	Psittacosis (ornithosis)	Unilateral or bilateral.	Hilar
	Infectious mononucleosis	Bilateral symmetrical.	Predominantly hilar.
	Fungi		
	Histoplasma capsulatum	May be unilateral or bilateral.	Hilar, mediastinal, or intrapulmonary.
	Coccidioides immitus	Unilateral or bilateral.	Hilar or paratracheal or both.
	Sporotrichum schenkii	Unilateral	Hilar
	Parasites		
	Tropical eosinophilia	Bilateral	Hilar

Table 5–16. *Hilar and Mediastinal Lymph-Node Enlargement (Continued)*

ADDITIONAL FINDINGS	COMMENTS
Almost always associated with ipsilateral parenchymal disease.	Rarely the presentation may be bilateral, symmetrical hilar-node enlargement as sole manifestation. (*See* page 616.)
Oval areas of parenchymal consolidation; pleural effusion common.	Ipsilateral hilar-node enlargement in 25 to 50 per cent of pneumonic tularemia. (*See* page 608.)
Ipsilateral segmental pneumonia.	Pneumonia is the result of secondary infection in some cases. (*See* page 608.)
Occasionally patchy nonsegmental opacities throughout lungs due to pulmonary hemorrhage; pleural effusion is common.	Node enlargement due to hemorrhage and edema; extension of inflammatory reaction into adjacent mediastinal tissues may obscure typical nodal configuration. (*See* page 599.)
Always with segmental inhomogeneous or homogeneous pneumonia.	Lymph node enlargement is rare in adults but common in children. (*See* page 678.)
Diffuse interstitial pattern throughout the lungs.	This pattern results from infection with rubeola virus itself and not from secondary infection. (*See* page 686.)
Accompanied by increase in bronchovascular markings.	Lymph-node enlargement rare in adults and pneumonia extremely rare in infants. (*See* page 688.)
Diffuse airspace pneumonia may mask hilar node enlargement.	(*See* page 689.)
Parenchymal involvement may be homogeneous consolidation or a diffuse reticular pattern.	Hilar-node enlargement has not been reported as sole manifestation of the disease. (*See* page 695.)
Splenomegaly.	Rarely associated with roentgenographic changes in the lungs. (*See* page 695.)
Enlarged nodes may obstruct airways through extrinsic pressure, resulting in pneumonitis.	Node enlargement is usually associated with parenchymal disease but may occur without, particularly in children. (*See* page 643.)
Node enlargement may occur with or without associated parenchymal disease.	Involvement of paratracheal lymph nodes should raise suspicion of imminent dissemination. (*See* page 652.)
Associated with parenchymal disease in some cases.	A rare form of mycotic infection. (*See* page 672.)
A widespread micronodular pattern throughout the lungs.	Diffuse parenchymal disease is usually not accompanied by node enlargement. (*See* page 709.)

Table continues

Table 5–16. *Hilar and Mediastinal Lymph-Node Enlargement (Continued)*

	ETIOLOGY	SYMMETRY	NODE GROUPS INVOLVED
NEOPLASTIC	Bronchogenic carcinoma	Unilateral almost invariably.	Hilar nodes almost invariably; paratracheal and posterior mediastinal nodes in some cases.
	Hodgkin's disease	Typically bilateral but asymmetrical; unilateral node enlargement is very unusual.	Paratracheal and bifurcation group involved as often or more often than bronchopulmonary group. Involvement of anterior mediastinal and retrosternal nodes frequent.
	The lymphosarcoma group	Bilateral but asymmetrical.	Similar to Hodgkin's disease.
	Leukemia	Usually symmetrical.	Mediastinal and bronchopulmonary.
	Metastatic lymphangitic carcinoma	Unilateral or bilateral.	Hilar or mediastinal or both.
	Bronchiolar carcinoma	Unilateral or bilateral.	Hilar or mediastinal or both.
INHALATIONAL	Silicosis	Symmetrical	Predominantly bronchopulmonary.
	Farmer's lung	Symmetrical	Bronchopulmonary
	Smallpox-handler's lung	Symmetrical	Bronchopulmonary
	Chronic berylliosis	Symmetrical	Bronchopulmonary

Table 5–16. Hilar and Mediastinal Lymph-Node Enlargement (Continued)

ADDITIONAL FINDINGS	COMMENTS
Involvement of the bifurcation or posterior mediastinal groups of nodes may displace the barium-filled esophagus.	Enlargement of mediastinal lymph nodes other than bronchopulmonary may be the sole abnormality roentgenographically and almost always indicates spread from an undifferentiated carcinoma. (*See* page 745.)
Pulmonary involvement occurs in less than 30 per cent of patients and is almost invariably associated with mediastinal-node enlargement. Pleural effusion in approximately 30 per cent of cases, usually in association with other intrathoracic manifestations. The sternum may be destroyed by direct extension from retrosternal nodes.	Intrathoracic involvement occurs in 90 per cent of patients at some stage of the disease, most commonly in the form of mediastinal lymph-node enlargement; the latter is seen on the initial chest roentgenogram of approximately 50 per cent of patients. (*See* page 771.)
Sometimes associated with pleuropulmonary involvement.	The most common intrathoracic manifestation of the disease; however, reticulum cell sarcoma tends to be manifested by parenchymal consolidation without associated node enlargement. (*See* page 784.)
Both pleural effusion and parenchymal involvement may be associated.	The most common roentgenographic manifestation of leukemia within the thorax (25 per cent of patients). A much more common manifestation of lymphocytic than of myelocytic leukemia. (*See* page 785.)
Usually associated with a diffuse reticular or reticulonodular pattern throughout the lungs, predominantly basal in distribution.	Septal (Kerley B) lines are frequently present. (*See* page 798.)
Node enlargement may occur in association with either local or diffuse pulmonary disease.	A rare finding in this neoplasm. (*See* page 770.)
Diffuse nodular or reticulonodular disease throughout both lungs. Pleural thickening in late stages. Eggshell calcification of lymph nodes occurs in approximately 5 per cent of cases and may also be observed in lymph nodes in the anterior and posterior mediastinum, the thoracic wall and occasionally the retroperitoneal and intraperitoneal nodes.	Enlargement of bronchopulmonary nodes may occur without roentgenographic evidence of pulmonary disease although this is a rare presenting picture. (*See* page 919.)
Diffuse micronodular disease invariably associated.	Enlargement of hilar lymph nodes is a rare finding in farmer's lung. (*See* page 909.)
Round opacities 5 to 15 mm in diameter scattered diffusely throughout lungs.	Moderate enlargement seen in the few cases reported in the literature. (*See* page 917.)
Diffuse micronodular pattern invariably associated.	Hilar node enlargement occurs in a minority of cases. (*See* page 946.)

Table continues

Table 5–16. *Hilar and Mediastinal Lymph-Node Enlargement (Continued)*

	ETIOLOGY	SYMMETRY	NODE GROUPS INVOLVED
IDIOPATHIC	Sarcoidosis	Almost invariably symmetrical, unilateral node enlargement occurring in 1 to 3 per cent of cases only. The outer borders of the enlarged hila are usually lobulated in contour.	Paratracheal, tracheobronchial, and bronchopulmonary groups. Paratracheal enlargement seldom if ever occurs without concomitant enlargement of hilar nodes.
	Diffuse interstitial pulmonary fibrosis (Hamman-Rich)	Symmetrical	Hilar
	Histiocytosis-X (Eosinophilic granuloma)	Symmetrical	Hilar and mediastinal.
	Idiopathic pulmonary hemosiderosis	Symmetrical	Hilar
AIRWAYS	Mucoviscidosis	Unilateral or bilateral.	Hilar

Table 5–16. *Hilar and Mediastinal Lymph-Node Enlargement (Continued)*

ADDITIONAL FINDINGS	COMMENTS
75 to 90 per cent of patients with sarcoid show mediastinal and hilar lymph-node enlargement and approximately 50 per cent of these will show diffuse parenchymal disease as well.	Seventy-five per cent of patients with hilar lymph-node enlargement show complete resolution of the enlarged nodes. Symmetrical appearance, lack of involvement of retrosternal nodes, and diminution of lymph node size with onset of diffuse lung disease aid in differentiating sarcoidosis from lymphoma and tuberculosis. (*See* Page 1087.)
Fine or coarse reticular pattern.	A rare finding. (*See* page 1104.)
Early diffuse micronodular pattern which may become coarse in later stages.	Intrathoracic lymph node enlargement is rarely a manifestation of this disease. (*See* page 1110.)
Composite alveolar and interstitial diffuse disease.	Predominantly in acute stage. (*See* page 1122.)
Diffuse increase in markings with hyperinflation and areas of atelectasis and bronchiectasis.	Hilar node enlargement is an uncommon finding in this disease. (*See* page 1062.)

Table 5–17

MEDIASTINAL WIDENING

The conditions listed in this table include all those responsible for increase in the width or mass of the mediastinum. Of necessity, there is considerable overlap of diseases in Tables 5–16 and 5–17; since enlargement of lymph nodes causes mediastinal widening, it is clear that all diseases listed in Table 5–16 must also be included in this category. In the present table, emphasis is placed on those diseases which cause widening of the mediastinal silhouette in which contour does *not* suggest node enlargement.

The headings in this table include *anatomic location* of the various disease processes within the mediastinal compartments: the designation +++ indicates that the process is almost invariably within that compartment, ++ that it predominates in that compartment, and + that it sometimes is located in that compartment. Thus, those diseases indicated by a single + in all compartments show no definite anatomic predilection. Where possible, the order in which the diseases have been listed has been arranged to comply with predominant anatomic location; thus, under *Neoplasms*,

tumors which tend to occupy the anterior compartment are listed first, the middle compartment second, and the posterior compartment last.

No attempt has been made to include diseases of the heart since such clearly is outside the scope of this book. Similarly, abnormalities of mediastinal contour which relate directly or indirectly to cardiac anomalies have been excluded (*e.g.,* the "snowman" configuration of anomalous pulmonary venous return).

Emphasis is placed on benign conditions in the illustrative cases that follow; mediastinal tumors are illustrated in Chapter 17. In addition to the cases illustrated on the following pages, the following figures appearing elsewhere in the book may be referred to as representative of this pattern:

Figure	Page
2–13	126
4–97	288
6– 8	585
6– 9	586
7–22	650
8–11	749

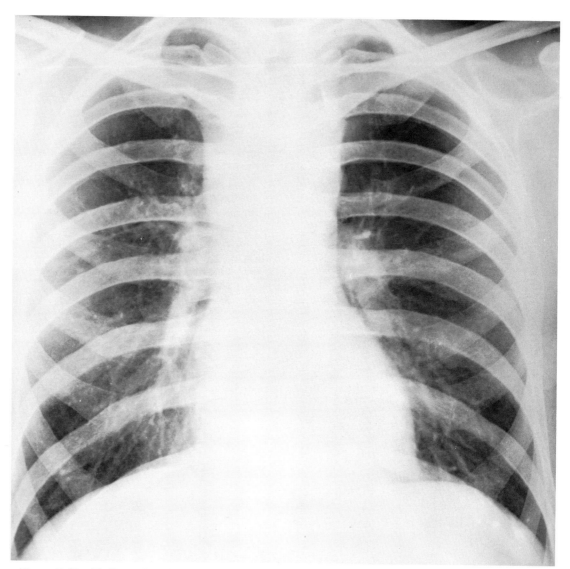

Figure 5–53. **Mediastinal Widening: Mediastinitis Secondary to Histoplasmosis.** This 30-year-old man presented clinically with a superior vena caval syndrome. A posteroanterior roentgenogram reveals moderate widening of the superior mediastinum, contour being smooth rather than nodular as might be expected from lymph-node enlargement. Multiple tiny punctate calcifications were present throughout the spleen (not visualized on this illustration), lending support to other evidence for a diagnosis of histoplasmosis.

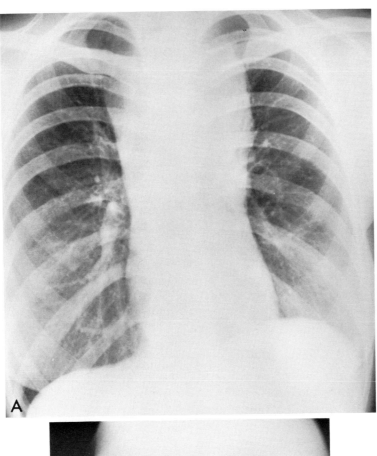

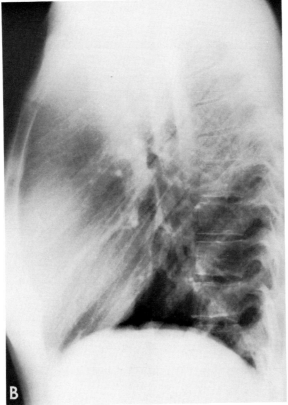

Figure 5–54. **Mediastinal Widening: Malignant Thymoma.** Posteroanterior (*A*) and lateral (*B*) roentgenograms reveal a marked widening of the upper mediastinum by a smooth, sharply circumscribed soft tissue mass of homogeneous density situated predominantly in the anterior mediastinal compartment (note the poorly defined increase in density in the anterior portion of the thorax in lateral projection). The elevation of the left hemidiaphragm was unexplained. Proved malignant thymoma.

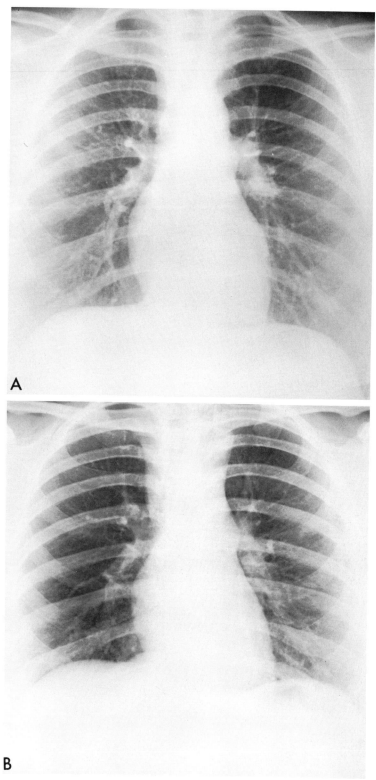

A

B

Figure 5–55. **Mediastinal Widening: Lipomatosis.** In *A* is reproduced a posteroanterior roentgenogram of a 28-year-old woman with thrombocytopenic purpura; no abnormalities are identified (note particularly the normal appearance of the mediastinal silhouette). At this time, the patient was placed on corticosteroid therapy and during the following three months she developed obvious clinical evidence of iatrogenic Cushing's disease. Three months after the institution of therapy, a posteroanterior roentgenogram (*B*) revealed bilateral widening of the superior mediastinum caused by deposition of fat. The mediastinal widening disappeared with reduction in corticosteroid dosage.

558

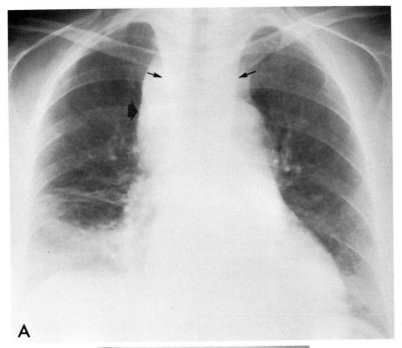

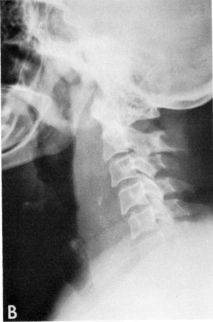

Figure 5–56. **Mediastinal Widening: Hemorrhage.** Approximately one year prior to this roentgenogram, this 49-year-old woman suffered a mild myocardial infarction for which she was placed on anticoagulant therapy. On the day of this roentgenogram, she developed acute shock, with ecchymosis covering most of the skin of the body and with hematuria and melena. A posteroanterior roentgenogram (A) reveals moderate widening of the upper half of the mediastinum—apparently in two separate anatomic regions: a rather lobulated swelling in the right paratracheal region (*thick arrow*), and a smooth sharply demarcated shadow extending from the thoracic inlet along the paravertebral areas bilaterally (*thin arrows*). A lateral view of the soft tissues of the neck (B) reveals marked swelling of the retropharyngeal and retrotracheal soft tissues. Both the retropharyngeal fullness and the mediastinal widening resulted from hemorrhage secondary to long-standing anticoagulant therapy. The right lower lobe parenchymal disease observed in A was thought to be due to aspiration.

Table 5-17.   *Mediastinal Widening*

	ETIOLOGY	ANTERIOR	LOCATION MIDDLE	POSTERIOR
DEVELOPMENTAL	Bronchogenic cyst	+	++	+
	Diverticula of the pharynx or esophagus			+++
	Mesothelial cyst (pericardial and pleuropericardial cysts and diverticula)	+	++	
	Gastroenteric cyst			+++
	Neurogenic cyst			+++
	Meningocele			+++
INFECTIOUS	Chronic granu- lomatous and fibrous mediastinitis	+	+	+
	Granulomatous mediastinal lymphadenitis	+	++	+
	Acute mediastinitis	+	+	+
	Suppurative spondylitis			+++
NEOPLASTIC	Thyroid tumors	+++		+
	Thymoma	+++		

Table 5–17. *Mediastinal Widening (Continued)*

Contour	Additional Findings	Comments
Round or oval, well-defined. Contour may be affected by contact with more solid structures.	May compress tracheobronchial tree or esophagus.	Cyst may be multilocular. Seldom communicates with tracheobronchial tree. (*See* page 582.)
Cyst-like structure in superior (pharyngeal) or inferior (esophageal) regions.	Invariably communicate with pharynx or esophagus. May displace contiguous esophagus.	Aspiration pneumonia may develop from pharyngeal (Zenker's) diverticulum. (*See* page 1211.)
Usually round, oval, or "teardrop" in appearance with smooth margin.	Variation in shape of cyst may occur on changing position of patient.	Almost always asymptomatic. (*See* page 1193.)
Oval, round, or molded by adjacent structures.	Rarely contain air.	Very rare and seen mostly in infants. (*See* page 1210.)
Oval or lobulated, sharply defined, homogeneous.	Spinal anomalies in many cases. Rarely air is found in cyst.	Often discovered in infancy. May reach large size, and may be unilateral or bilateral. (*See* page 1210.)
Sharply circumscribed, solitary or multiple, unilateral or bilateral.	Frequently spine and rib deformities. No calcification.	Usually communicates with spinal subarachnoid space. (*See* page 1210.)
Lobulated, usually in right paramediastinal area.	**May show calcification. Compression of S.V.C. or other vessel in some cases.**	**The cause of approximately 10 per cent of mediastinal widening.** (*See* page 1171.)
One or more masses, unilateral or bilateral.	**Calcification common in infectious granulomas.**	Hilar or paratracheal lymphnode enlargement in most cases. especially sarcoidosis. (*See* page 1167.)
Symmetrical widening due to diffuse involvement or localized due to abscess formation.	May be air in mediastinum.	Most cases due to esophageal rupture. (*See* page 1166.)
Widening of lower mediastinum with fusiform mass.	Erosion or destruction of vertebrae at level of paravertebral mass.	Tomography may be helpful. (*See* page 1214.)
Smooth or lobulated, well-defined.	**Compression of trachea and/or esophagus. Calcification not infrequent.**	Almost invariably occur superiorly. (*See* page 1184.)
Smooth or lobulated, oval or round. May protrude to either side or bilaterally.	**Contains calcium in some cases.**	Usually occurs superiorly. Tomography, angiography, and mediastinography helpful. (*See* page 1180.)

Table continues

Table 5-17. *Mediastinal Widening (Continued)*

ETIOLOGY	ANTERIOR	LOCATION MIDDLE	POSTERIOR
Germinal cell neoplasms (1) **Teratoma and dermoid cyst** (2) **Seminoma** (3) **Choriocarcinoma** (4) **Embryonal carcinoma**	+++		+
Parathyroid tumors	+++		
Lipoma (or sarcoma)	++	+	+
Fibroma (or sarcoma)	+++		+
Hemangioma (or sarcoma)	++		+
Lymphangioma (hygroma)	+++		
Lymphoma and leukemia	++	+++	
Metastatic lymph-node enlargement	+	+++	+
Mediastinal lymph-node hyperplasia	+	+++	+
Neurogenic neoplasms	+	+	+++
Esophageal neoplasms			+++

NEOPLASTIC *(Cont.)*

Table 5–17. Mediastinal Widening (Continued)

CONTOUR	ADDITIONAL FINDINGS	COMMENTS
Smooth or lobulated, oval or round. May protrude to either side or bilaterally.	Calcification, bone, teeth, or fat may be identified in teratomas and dermoid cysts.	Tomography, angiography, and mediastinography helpful. (*See* page 1182.)
Smooth or lobulated.	Evidence of hyperparathyroidism in the thoracic skeleton. Mass may displace esophagus.	Pneumomediastinography or arteriography may reveal smaller lesions. Hypercalcemia and hypophosphatemia. (*See* page 1186.)
"Hour-glass" appearance rarely. May bulge to either side and frequently extends into lower anterior mediastinum.	Difference in radiolucency from other portions of mediastinum may be apparent.	Symmetrical widening of the upper mediastinum and increase in size of epicardial fat pads may occur with corticosteroid therapy. (*See* page 1186.)
Well-circumscribed.	Distortion of esophagus by esophageal fibrosarcomas.	Very rare and usually do not produce symptoms. (*See* page 1188.)
May be well-circumscribed and multiple. Occasionally diffusely invasive.	Phleboliths are diagnostic if present. Angiography may reveal anomalous vessels, rib hypertrophy or erosion.	Vary from benign hemangiomas to malignant endotheliomas. (*See* page 1188.)
Widened mediastinum in cervicomediastinal area.	Soft tissue mass frequently present in neck.	Benign to invasive. Chylothorax rarely. (*See* page 1188.)
Symmetrically widened mediastinum or solitary or multiple lobulated masses.	Pulmonary consolidation and pleural effusion in some cases.	Most common mediastinal "mass." Tomography may delineate individual nodes. (*See* pages 771, 790 and 1188.)
Commonly unilateral with bronchogenic carcinoma. Predominant involvement may occur in paratracheal or bronchopulmonary groups.	Phrenic nerve involvement may result in diaphragmatic paralysis.	Primary usually bronchogenic carcinoma. May originate from upper G.I. tract, prostate, kidney, and so forth. (*See* page 1189.)
Usually solitary and sharply circumscribed.	No calcification.	In anterior mediastinum a multilobulated appearance may suggest thymic or teratoid tumors. (*See* page 1192.)
Round or oval, well-circumscribed. Rarely dumbbell shaped.	Majority are paravertebral in location, usually unilateral. Rib or vertebral erosion. Occasionally pleural effusion. Rarely calcification with tumor.	Myelography and aortography may be required. Chemodectomas may occur anywhere in mediastinum. (*See* page 1205.)
Smooth, rounded margin; usually unilateral.	Smooth compression of esophageal lumen on barium swallow.	Usually leiomyomas. (*See* page 1211.)

Table continues

Table 5–17. *Mediastinal Widening (Continued)*

ETIOLOGY	ANTERIOR	LOCATION MIDDLE	POSTERIOR
NEOPLASTIC *(Cont.)*			
Bone and cartilage neoplasms	+		+++
Extramedullary hematopoiesis			+++
CARDIOVASCULAR			
Aortic aneurysm	+	+	+
Elongation or aneurysm of the innominate artery		+++	
Superior vena caval dilatation		+++	
Azygos and hemi-azygos dilatation			+++
Dilatation of pulmonary artery		+++	
Mediastinal effusion	+		+
Aortic vascular ring		+	+
TRAUMATIC			
Pneumomediastinum	+	+	+
Mediastinal hematoma	+	+	+
Fracture of vertebra with hematoma			+++
INCIDENTAL			
Esophageal hiatus hernia			+++

Table 5–17. *Mediastinal Widening (Continued)*

CONTOUR	ADDITIONAL FINDINGS	COMMENTS
Rounded, paravertebral mass.	Destruction of affected bone, often associated with soft tissue mass protruding into and compressing lung.	(*See* page 1214.)
Lobulated or smooth, single or multiple, often bilateral.	Spleen may be enlarged.	Anemia and hepatosplenomegaly. (*See* page 1214.)
Fusiform or saccular.	Erosion of bony thoracic cage where pulsatile aneurysm contiguous. Calcification may be present in wall.	Aortography may be needed for definitive diagnosis. (*See* page 1201.)
Smooth, lateral bulging, convex laterally from level of aortic arch upwards.	Tortuous thoracic aorta due to atherosclerosis may also be noted.	Angiography may be required for definitive diagnosis. (*See* page 1205.)
Smooth, extending from hilum along right paramediastinal border.	Signs of etiology—e.g., cardiac dilatation, mediastinal mass, and so forth.	Secondary to central pressure rise or to compression and obstruction. (*See* page 1197.)
Smooth, round or oval mass at tracheobronchial angle.	Change in size with Valsalva and Mueller procedures and with change in body position.	Azygography may be required for definitive diagnosis. (*See* page 1197.)
Smooth	Stenotic pulmonary valve or peripheral vascular attenuation in secondary types.	Angiography may be required to differentiate from mediastinal tumors. (*See* page 1197.)
Smooth; may possess a wide variety of shapes.	Cardiac enlargement in some instances.	Rapid changes with treatment of cause. May look like pericardial effusion if anterior.
A vessel detected between trachea and esophagus.	Compression of esophagus or trachea.	Usually detected in first year of life (*See* page 1205.)
Smooth; unilateral or bilateral.	Unilateral or bilateral pneumothorax. Subcutaneous and interstitial emphysema.	Readily diagnosed by presence of mediastinal air. (*See* page 1174.)
May be local or diffuse, commonly in upper mediastinum.	Rarely S.V.C. compression.	History of trauma or dissecting aneurysm. (*See* page 1179.)
Smooth paravertebral swelling, usually bilateral.	Vertebral and rib fractures.	(*See* page 1214.)
Retrocardiac mass of variable size containing air and fluid; usually smooth.	May contain several fluid levels; rarely completely opaque. Barium usually outlines contents.	Contains stomach, rarely bowel omentum, liver, or spleen. (*See* page 1211.)

Table continues

Table 5-17. *Mediastinal Widening (Continued)*

	ETIOLOGY	ANTERIOR	LOCATION MIDDLE	POSTERIOR
INCIDENTAL *(Cont.)*	Herniation through foramen of Morgagni	+++		
	Herniation through foramen of Bochdalek			+++
	Megaesophagus			+++

Table 5–17. Mediastinal Widening (Continued)

CONTOUR	ADDITIONAL FINDINGS	COMMENTS
Round or oval; usually to right of pericardium.	If completely radio-opaque a pneumoperitoneum may differentiate from epicardial fat pad or pericardial cyst.	Often in asymptomatic individuals (*See* page 1193.)
Round or oval retrocardiac density. Unilateral and rarely bilateral.	———	Occasionally contains bowel loops, more often omentum or solid abdominal viscera. (*See* page 1214.)
Broad vertical shadow on the right side of the mediastinum.	Air in lumen with fluid level at varying distance from diaphragm.	Usually the result of scleroderma or achalasia. (*See* page 1211.)

6

PULMONARY ABNORMALITIES OF DEVELOPMENTAL ORIGIN

AGENESIS, APLASIA, AND HYPOPLASIA OF
   THE LUNGS
ANOMALIES OF THE PULMONARY
   VASCULATURE
   HYPOGENETIC LUNG SYNDROME
   ANOMALOUS PULMONARY VENOUS DRAINAGE
   ABSENCE (PROXIMAL INTERRUPTION) OF THE
      RIGHT OR LEFT PULMONARY ARTERY
   ANOMALOUS ORIGIN OF THE LEFT PULMONARY
      ARTERY FROM THE RIGHT
   PULMONARY ARTERY STENOSIS OR COARCTATION
   CONGENITAL ANEURYSMS OF THE PULMONARY
      ARTERIES
   PULMONARY ARTERIOVENOUS FISTULA
   VARICOSITIES OF THE PULMONARY VEINS
   ANOMALIES OF THE HEART AND GREAT

   VESSELS, RESULTING IN INCREASED
      PULMONARY BLOOD FLOW
   ANOMALIES OF THE HEART AND GREAT
      VESSELS, RESULTING IN DECREASED
      PULMONARY BLOOD FLOW
   SYSTEMIC ARTERIAL SUPPLY TO THE LUNG
BRONCHOPULMONARY SEQUESTRATION
   INTRALOBAR SEQUESTRATION
   EXTRALOBAR SEQUESTRATION
CONGENITAL BRONCHIAL CYSTS
   PULMONARY BRONCHIAL CYSTS
   MEDIASTINAL BRONCHIAL CYSTS
CONGENITAL BRONCHIAL ATRESIA
CONGENITAL CYSTIC ADENOMATOID
   MALFORMATION OF THE LUNG

Before reading this chapter, the reader is urged to refer to the section on Development of the Lung in Chapter 1 (*see* page 58), or, if desired, to more comprehensive works on the subject.[827, 828]

AGENESIS, APLASIA, AND HYPOPLASIA OF THE LUNGS

Factors which interfere with the formation of the lungs must become effective not later than 26 days after conception.[827] Three different degrees of arrested development may occur:[828]

1. *Agenesis*, in which there is complete absence of one or both lungs; there is no trace of bronchial or vascular supply or of parenchymal tissue.

2. *Aplasia*, in which there is suppression of all but a rudimentary bronchus which ends in a blind pouch; there are no vessels or parenchyma.

3. *Hypoplasia*, in which the bronchus is fully formed but is reduced in size and ends in a fleshy structure which usually lies within the mediastinum.[828–830] Rudimentary pulmonary parenchyma may be present around the bronchial stump and often is the site of cystic malformation.[831] Small rudi-

mentary vessels are present in most cases. Hypoplasia usually involves a whole lung but may affect only one lobe,[828] in which case the clinical and roentgenographic manifestations are different.

The incidence of these anomalies is low; for example, chest roentgenography has been reported to show aplasia in one in 10,000 cases;[832] and in a review in 1955, Valle[830] found only 120 cases of agenesis reported in detail. There is no clear-cut sex or lateral predominance.[830] Wilson and Warkany,[833] who found lung agenesis in rat fetuses of mothers deprived of vitamin A, suggested that such deprivation may be a contributory etiologic factor, although an earlier report by Warkany[834] pointed out that a sufficiently severe degree of malnutrition of this type is unlikely to occur in man.

ROENTGENOGRAPHIC MANIFESTATIONS. The findings in cases of agenesis, aplasia, or whole-lung hypoplasia are as might be expected with total or almost total absence of aerated lung in one hemithorax. The marked loss of volume is indicated by the approximation of ribs, elevation of the ipsilateral hemidiaphragm, and shift of the mediastinum. In most cases the contralateral lung is greatly overinflated, with herniation across the anterior mediastinal septum into the involved hemithorax;[832, 835, 836] this herniation of air-containing lung to the side of the agenesis may lead to some confusion in diagnosis. Tomography, bronchography, and angiography may all be required to establish the degree of underdevelopment[832, 835, 837–840] or to differentiate agenesis from other conditions which may closely mimic it roentgenographically—total atelectasis from any cause, severe bronchiectasis with associated collapse, and possibly advanced fibrothorax; in fact, in some cases it may be very difficult, even on examination of the pathologic specimen, to establish with certainty that the lesion is congenital rather than the result of early acquired infection.[841]

About 60 per cent of patients with agenesis of the lung are said to have other congenital anomalies; in fact, manifestations of the other lesions may exceed those of the agenesis itself.[836, 837, 842, 843] Perhaps the most frequent of the wide variety of associated anomalies are patent ductus arteriosus,[844] tetralogy of Fallot,[845] anomalies of the great vessels,[845–849] bronchogenic cysts,[850, 851] congenital diaphragmatic hernia,[835, 852, 853] and anomalies of the bones.[835]

Berdon and associates[4118] studied the prognosis of newborn infants with combined pulmonary hypoplasia and diaphragmatic hernia; since the bronchial tree, the diaphragm, and the gut develop rapidly between the eighth and twelfth weeks, interference with one may affect the others; thus, if the diaphragm fails to close, herniation of abdominal contents (particularly midgut) into the thorax may retard bronchial and bronchiolar subdivision. Obviously, the degree of resultant hypoplasia depends on timing—if interference occurs at 12 weeks, pulmonary underdevelopment is mild. Prognosis appears to depend largely on the severity of the hypoplasia.

CLINICAL MANIFESTATIONS. Patients with agenesis of the lung usually have no acutely distressing symptoms, and many are totally asymptomatic and live normal lives. However, the anomaly appears to predispose patients to respiratory infection, and many of these people die before the second decade, whether from the anomaly itself or from other associated congenital malformations. The diagnosis cannot be made by physical examination, but the presence of the defect may be suspected from asymmetry of the two sides of the thorax and from reduction in respiratory movement and absence of air entry in the involved side. Often, however, the chest is symmetrical and normally developed, and relatively normal breath sounds may be heard over the herniated contralateral lung.

ANOMALIES OF THE PULMONARY VASCULATURE

Hypogenetic Lung Syndrome

This rare congenital anomaly consists of partial hypoplasia of the right lung and of the right pulmonary artery, dextrocardia, and anomalies of the right bronchial tree (commonly mirror-image), with anomalous pulmonary venous return from the right lung to the inferior vena cava, either below the diaphragm or at the junction of this vessel with the right atrium (Figure 6–1). The hypogenetic right lung is supplied by systemic arteries, thus producing a left-to-right (arteriovenous) shunt.

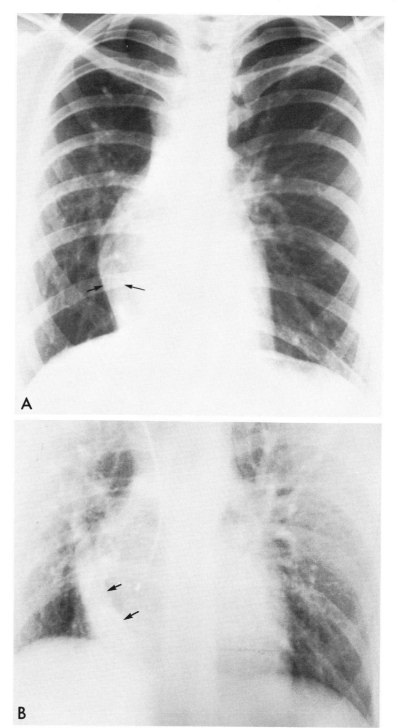

Figure 6–1. **Hypogenetic Lung Syndrome.** A posteroanterior roentgenogram (*A*) of a 15-year-old asymptomatic girl reveals slight loss of volume of the right lung as evidenced by shift of the mediastinum. The right hilum is diminutive and of abnormal configuration. Similarly, the bronchovascular pattern throughout the right lung is distinctly abnormal, the main markings being a network of irregular channels in the mid-lung zone. A broad band-shadow can be identified in the plane of the right heart border descending toward the right cardiophrenic angle (*arrows*); this shadow represents the "scimitar" shadow of anomalous pulmonary venous drainage. Pulmonary angiography revealed a right pulmonary artery to be present but to be much smaller than normal; all blood entering the right lung drained via the anomalous vein (indicated by *arrows* in *B*). The levogram phase of the contrast study permitted visualization of several small bronchial arteries entering the right lung. (Courtesy Dr. Bruce Bird, St. Michael's Hospital, Toronto.)

In some cases the anomalous vein is visible roentgenologically as a broad, gently curved shadow descending to the diaphragm just to the right of the heart; this shadow is shaped like a scimitar—thus the designation *scimitar syndrome* (Figure 6–1).[846, 847, 854–857] Most commonly—in 41 of 46 cases in one series[858]—the entire right lung is drained by the anomalous vein. According to Kiely and colleagues,[851] 67 cases of scimitar syndrome had been reported by 1967; these authors emphasized that usually the diagnosis can be made on a plain posteroanterior roentgenogram, as in 57 of the 67 published cases.

Anomalous Pulmonary Venous Drainage

Both partial and total anomalous pulmonary venous drainage consist of an extra-cardiac left-to-right shunt; in addition, total anomalous connection provides a right-to-left shunt through an obligatory septal defect. The increased pulmonary blood flow which results may be recognized by increase in the size of the central and peripheral pulmonary arteries; sometimes the anomalous vein can be identified on plain roentgenograms, although pulmonary angiography is necessary for confirmation and for elucidation of the specific anatomic variation (Figure 6–2).

Partial obstruction of the venous return results in pulmonary venous hypertension and a characteristic roentgenographic combination of interstitial pulmonary edema and a normal-sized heart. Obstruction may occur from various causes and is not related solely to an infradiaphragmatic site of communication.[860]

Rarely, a large vein may drain blood from one pulmonary lobe to an ipsilateral lobe, simulating the scimitar syndrome.[861]

Absence (Proximal Interruption) of the Right or Left Pulmonary Artery

This rare anomaly preferably is designated "proximal interruption" of the right or left pulmonary artery, since the vessels within the lung usually are intact and patent.[862] The ipsilateral lung is hypoplastic and of reduced volume; its arterial supply is derived from a hypertrophied bronchial circulation. Despite its reduced

volume, the lung usually is hyperlucent—a finding which, when taken in conjunction with the diminutive hilar shadow, may lead to the erroneous diagnosis of the acquired disease known as Swyer-James or MacLeod's syndrome. However, differentiation may be readily accomplished by roentgenography in full expiration—patients with the Swyer-James syndrome show ipsilateral air trapping due to bronchiolar obstruction, a sign which is absent in cases of proximal interruption of a pulmonary artery (*see* Figure 4–138, page 334). If further confirmation is required, pulmonary arteriography should permit visualization of a diminutive but patent pulmonary arterial circulation in patients with acquired unilateral emphysema.

The anomalous pulmonary artery usually occurs on the side opposite the aortic arch.[863] When the proximal interruption is on the left, there is a high incidence of associated congenital cardiovascular anomalies, particularly tetralogy of Fallot and septal defects. Associated congenital anomalies are much less frequent when the pulmonary artery anomaly is on the right.

Anomalous Origin of the Left Pulmonary Artery from the Right

Of the many recognized anomalous origins of the pulmonary arteries,[863] that in which the left pulmonary artery arises from the right pulmonary artery is of particular interest because of the effects it produces on the lungs. From its point of origin from the right pulmonary artery, the aberrant left artery passes posteriorly to the right of the right main bronchus or lower trachea and then turns sharply to the left and passes between the esophagus and trachea in its course to the left hilum. Its intimate relationship to the right main bronchus and to the trachea results in compression of these structures and various degrees of obstructive overinflation or atelectasis of the right or both lungs.[863] Airway obstruction usually becomes manifest shortly after birth and may be severe. The demonstration of local posterior displacement of the barium-filled esophagus in the region of the lower trachea makes the diagnosis virtually certain; this may be confirmed by pulmonary angiography. Since the lesion is surgically correctable, its early recognition is vital.

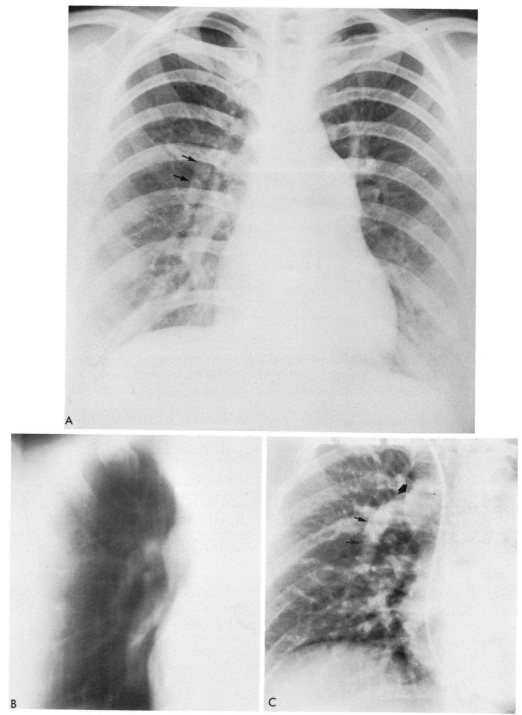

Figure 6–2. **Partial Anomalous Pulmonary Venous Drainage.** A posteroanterior roentgenogram (*A*) of an asymptomatic 18-year-old female reveals slight prominence of the main pulmonary artery segment on the left border of the heart; the pulmonary vascular markings are either normal or slightly increased in caliber. Situated immediately lateral to the descending branch of the right pulmonary artery is a vascular channel whose width appears to increase from below upward (*arrows*). An anteroposterior tomogram with the patient in the supine position (*B*) shows the abnormal vascular shadow to better advantage; in addition, there is moderate enlargement of the azygos vein, suggesting that the abnormal vessel is an anomalous pulmonary vein draining into the azygos. The venous phase of a pulmonary angiogram (*C*) shows opacification of the anomalous pulmonary vein (*thin arrows*) and of the enlarged azygos vein (*thick arrow*), confirming the diagnosis of partial anomalous pulmonary venous drainage. Since normal pulmonary veins can be identified from the lower lobe, it is assumed that the anomalous drainage occurred from both the upper and middle lobes.

Pulmonary Artery Stenosis or Coarctation

This rare anomaly is characterized by single or multiple coarctations of the pulmonary arteries, commonly associated with poststenotic dilatations.[741-746] The stenoses may be short or long, peripheral or central, unilateral or bilateral. When the lesions are multiple and situated peripherally, plain roentgenograms may reveal no more than diffuse pulmonary oligemia and signs of pulmonary arterial hypertension and cor pulmonale. Multifarious associated anomalies may be present, including infundibular, vascular, or supravalvular pulmonic stenosis (in 60 per cent of cases[745]) and atrial septal defect.[747] The precise morphologic nature of the abnormality may be obscure without selective pulmonary angiography, and this procedure is essential to positive diagnosis. Winfield and colleagues[746] stressed the necessity for pulmonary angiography in all cases of presumed pulmonary valvular stenosis, to rule out associated peripheral pulmonary coarctation: surgical relief of the pulmonic stenosis in the presence of peripheral coarctations may precipitate severe pulmonary hypertension.

Congenital Aneurysms of the Pulmonary Arteries

These are rare and are said to be associated almost invariably with other pulmonary abnormalities, such as arteriovenous fistulas or bronchopulmonary sequestration.[863] Aneurysms of the central pulmonary arteries, which occur most often in association with congenital cardiovascular anomalies and may be present at birth, usually are the result of such disturbed hemodynamics as the jet of blood and turbulence created by a pulmonary valvular stenosis. This type of poststenotic dilatation affects the left pulmonary artery much more commonly than the right; in fact, enlargement of the main pulmonary artery and its left branch in conjunction with a normal right hilum should strongly suggest the diagnosis of pulmonary valvular stenosis.

Although sometimes "aneurysmal" in degree, enlargement of the main pulmonary artery and of its major branches in response to increased flow—as in left-to-right intracardiac shunts—or to increased pulmonary artery pressure from any cause is seldom "congenital." Ellis and associates[863] stated that the diagnosis of congenital pulmonary valvular insufficiency should be considered a likely possibility if huge central pulmonary arteries can be identified roentgenographically within the first few days of life.

Pulmonary Arteriovenous Fistula

Communication between blood vessels is abnormal in a wide variety of both congenital and acquired disease of the lungs. Acquired fistulas are more properly designated "vascular shunts," since they occur not only *from artery to vein* (for example, in cases of metastatic carcinoma from the thyroid,[864] in schistosomiasis, and in cirrhosis of the liver[865, 866]), but also *from artery to artery* (epitomized by the bronchial-artery to pulmonary-artery shunts that develop in many pulmonary diseases associated with chronic ischemia or chronic infection, such as bronchiectasis), and *from vein to vein* (such as the bronchial-vein to pulmonary-vein shunt in advanced pulmonary emphysema). These acquired "shunts" are dealt with in relation to the specific disease entities; in the present section, discussion is restricted to abnormal communications of congenital origin.

The term "congenital arteriovenous fistula" usually connotes an abnormal vascular communication within the pulmonary circulation—from pulmonary artery to pulmonary vein—although it should be remembered that pulmonary sequestration constitutes a congenital arteriovenous communication in which a systemic vessel under high pressure connects with relatively thin-walled pulmonary vessels under low pressure. Congenital pulmonary arteriovenous fistula or aneurysm is considered to be due to a defect in the terminal capillary loops which allows dilatation and the formation of thin-walled vascular sacs supplied by a single distended afferent artery and drained by a single distended efferent vein.[876, 877] In addition to this relatively simple arteriovenous communication between a single artery and vein, a more complex aneurysm has been described with multiple feeding arteries and draining veins;[869] many of these lesions involve the entire blood supply of a lobe or segment and may have arterial communication with the neighboring chest wall or adjacent lung segments.[867, 868] This complex type of communication is associated most commonly with the classical clinical picture of cyanosis, polycythemia, and clubbing of the fingers.

Approximately one third of cases of pulmonary arteriovenous fistula have multiple lesions in the lungs; some resected specimens contain small fistulas which were not apparent on plain roentgenography[869, 870]—a point of obvious importance in investigation when resectional surgery of a known fistula is contemplated.

From 40 to 65 per cent of patients with arteriovenous fistulas in the lungs have arteriovenous communications elsewhere, including the skin, mucous membranes, and other organs.[865, 869, 871, 872] This condition, known as *hereditary hemorrhagic telangiectasia* or Rendu-Osler-Weber's disease,[873] is of simple dominant non-sex-linked transmission. Although it is assumed that the congenital vascular defect is present at birth, it seldom becomes manifest clinically until adult life when the vessels have been subjected to pressure over several decades.[876] In one family of 91 individuals known to have this condition,[876] 14 (15 per cent) were found to have arteriovenous fistulas in the lungs, a finding which exemplifies the need for thorough investigation for pulmonary lesions in all cases of cutaneous or mucous-membrane telangiectasis. Many of these congenital fistulas are situated just beneath the pleura,[868] between lobules, along bronchovascular bundles, and just deep to the interlobar and mediastinal pleura.[877]

ROENTGENOGRAPHIC MANIFESTATIONS. Pulmonary arteriovenous fistulas are seen more commonly in the lower lobes than in the middle or upper lobes[865, 877] and are single in about two thirds of cases.[639, 869] The classical appearance is of a round or oval homogeneous mass of unit density, somewhat lobulated in contour but sharply-defined, most often in the medial third of the lung, ranging from less than 1 cm to several centimeters in diameter (Figure 6–3). Identification of the feeding and draining vessels, which is essential to the diagnosis, may be difficult with plain roentgenograms and often requires tomog-

raphy. The artery and vein usually can be distinguished relatively easily, the artery relating to the hilum and the vein deviating from the course of the artery toward the left atrium. The increased blood flow on the involved side may be manifested fluoroscopically by increased amplitude of pulsation of the hilar vessels.[865, 875, 877] In a minority of cases a fairly extensive racemose opacity, somewhat ill-defined but homogeneous in density, occupies much of one bronchopulmonary segment;[639] this represents a more complex angiomatous mass possessing several feeding and draining vessels.[869]

The vascular nature of these lesions may be suggested roentgenographically by the demonstration of decrease and increase in their size during the Valsalva and Mueller maneuvers respectively;[639, 640, 877] a change in size may be evident also on roentgenograms exposed in the erect and recumbent positions. Precise identification of the feeding and draining vessels requires tomography in both frontal and lateral projections when the orientation of the vessels is such that it permits visualization in one and not the other. Angiography may be required to confirm the diagnosis but, in any event, is mandatory in any patient on whom resectional surgery is contemplated. *Care must be exercised in obtaining angiographic visualization of all portions of both lungs;* it is not enough to perform selective angiography of the lung in question, since lesions may be present in the contralateral lung and may not be visible on the plain roentgenogram (Figure 6–3).[639, 640, 870] In fact, multiple tiny fistulas have been demonstrated in patients with normal plain roentgenograms,[876] notably in asymptomatic siblings of patients with proven fistulas and in patients in whom the diagnosis was suspected clinically because of polycythemia and cyanosis.[878] In such circumstances, detection of their presence must depend on angiographic demonstration. In some cases plain roentgenography does not reveal lesions because they are obscured by hemorrhage into contiguous parenchyma or occasionally by atelectasis resulting from bronchial compression.[865] Calcification, which has been reported in some cases,[876] probably is due to phleboliths.

Even without angiography, positive identification of the feeding artery and

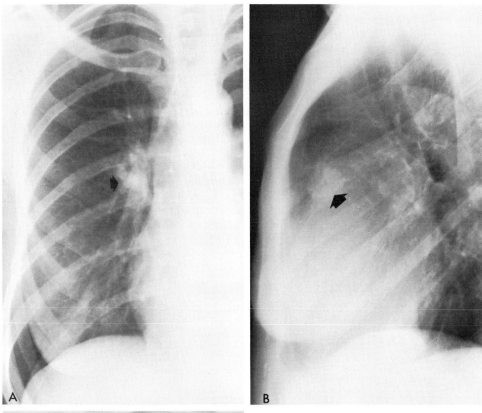

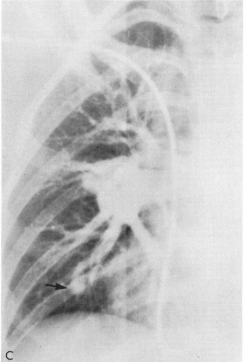

Figure 6–3. **Pulmonary Arteriovenous Fistula.** Views of the right hemithorax from posteroanterior (*A*) and lateral (*B*) roentgenograms reveal a somewhat lobulated soft tissue mass measuring about 2 cm in diameter situated in the anterior segment of the right upper lobe (*arrow* in both projections); the mass is partly superimposed on the right hilum in posteroanterior projection; in lateral projection, the shadows of a feeding artery and draining vein could be vaguely discerned. A view of the right lung following injection of contrast medium into the pulmonary artery (*C*) reveals a somewhat racemose accumulation of opacified vessels which are poorly visualized because of superimposition of the hilar pulmonary arteries. To be noted, however, is a second, much smaller arteriovenous fistula in the right lower lobe (*arrow*) which could be identified on the posteroanterior roentgenogram only in retrospect.

draining vein establishes the diagnosis beyond any reasonable doubt. When such vessels are not convincingly demonstrable, the differential diagnosis is from any solitary pulmonary nodule. The relative rarity of this lesion compared with other solitary nodules is apparent in Bateson's series[608] in which only one of 155 such lesions was a pulmonary arteriovenous aneurysm.

A study of cirrhosis by Berthelot and colleagues[880] yielded evidence that the hypoxemia common in this condition may be due to a myriad of shunting spider angiomata in the lungs; sometimes these are manifested roentgenographically by a diffuse, rather ill-defined nodular pattern.

CLINICAL MANIFESTATIONS. Some pulmonary arteriovenous fistulas give rise to symptoms.[639, 865, 868] Of the family of 91 individuals with hereditary telangiectasia referred to previously, eight of the 14 patients with pulmonary arteriovenous fistulas were asymptomatic.[876] By contrast, Moyer and colleagues,[865] in a study of 21 cases and a review of the literature, found the majority of patients to be symptomatic; however, the majority of these had multiple telangiectasia and symptoms may have related to involvement of organs other than the lungs, including the upper respiratory tract (epistaxis), the gastrointestinal tract (hematemesis), and the brain (cerebrovascular hemorrhage).

In addition to hemoptysis, which is the most common presenting complaint, the only other common symptom referable to the lungs is dyspnea, which is present in 60 per cent of cases.[865] *Signs* suggestive of a pulmonary arteriovenous fistula include cyanosis, finger-clubbing, and a continuous murmur or bruit audible over the lesion or lesions.[865, 866] The presence of telangiectasis in the skin or mucous membranes is an obviously important clue. Rarely, hemothorax gives rise to pleuritic pain, with the attendant signs of friction rub, decreased breath sounds, and dullness on percussion.[869, 876] The high incidence of cerebral symptoms associated with pulmonary arteriovenous aneurysms has been attributed to metastatic abscesses, hypoxemia, cerebral embolus, cerebral thrombosis on the basis of secondary polycythemia, and cerebral hemorrhage from intracerebral arteriovenous aneurysm.[639, 865, 867, 868, 871, 877, 881] It is of interest that cerebral symptoms are transitory in many cases and are not uncommon in patients with heriditary hemorrhagic telangiectasis even in the absence of pulmonary arteriovenous fistulas; these episodes have never been satisfactorily explained.[876] Although the majority of patients with arteriovenous aneurysms have polycythemia,[865] repeated hemorrhages from the nose or from the lungs may lead to anemia.[871, 875, 882]

Arterial blood-gas analysis and cardiac catheterization may provide useful data in confirming the diagnosis: PO_2 and arterial oxygen saturation are decreased, cardiac output is increased, and the pulmonary artery pressure is normal.[865, 883] The electrocardiogram usually is normal, constituting a useful sign in differentiation from congenital heart disease.[865] Blood volume studies reveal increase in the red blood cell mass in many cases, with normal or near normal plasma volume.[865]

Varicosities of the Pulmonary Veins

This rare abnormality, which may be either congenital or acquired, consists of abnormal tortuosity and dilatation of a pulmonary vein just before its entrance into the left atrium. It usually occurs without symptoms, but hemoptysis and some fatal cases have been reported.[641, 884] In most cases the lesion is apparent as a round or oval homogeneous mass of unit density, somewhat lobulated but well-defined in contour, in the medial third of either lung. On the left, the lingular vein is usually affected, and, on the right, a branch of the inferior pulmonary vein in the region of the medial basal segment of the right lower lobe.[884–887] In 1966 a search of the world literature revealed only 20 cases,[888] at least four of them associated with pulmonary venous hypertension.[886]

The roentgenologic differential diagnosis includes all mass lesions occurring in the lungs. The Valsalva and Mueller maneuvers may result in a change in size in the lesion and thereby indicate its vascular nature, in which case angiography usually is necessary to differentiate from arteriovenous aneurysm:[641, 890] in cases of venous varicosity opacification is apparent in the venous phase only, whereas in arteriovenous fistula it occurs in the arterial phase also.[886] Opacification may develop more slowly in the varicosity than in normal pulmonary veins, and because of sluggish flow may drain more slowly.[641] Compression atelectasis of the surrounding lung has been reported,[885] and, in one case[889] chronic collapse of the right middle lobe was attributed to bronchial obstruction by the dilated vein.

Anomalies of the Heart and Great Vessels, Resulting in Increased Pulmonary Blood Flow

These anomalies include atrial and ventricular septal defect, patent ductus arteriosus, aorticopulmonary window, and anomalous pulmonary venous drainage. The left-to-right shunt results in some degree of increased pulmonary blood flow (see Figure 1–64A, page 88) which may be recognizable roentgenologically as an increase in size and amplitude of pulsation in the central and peripheral pulmonary arteries. This subject is considered in greater detail in Chapter 10 (see page 835).

Anomalies of the Heart and Great Vessels, Resulting in Decreased Pulmonary Blood Flow

By far the most common cause of general pulmonary oligemia due to diminished flow is a congenital cardiac anomaly of the right ventricular outflow tract (isolated pulmonic stenosis, tetralogy of Fallot with pulmonary atresia, type-IV persistent truncus arteriosus, and Ebstein's anomaly) (see Figure 5–38, page 500). The caliber of the pulmonary vessels usually reflects the severity of the decrease in flow, the hila usually being diminutive and the peripheral vessels correspondingly small (an exception occurs in valvular pulmonic stenosis, in which poststenotic dilatation may cause enlargement of the main or left pulmonary artery). The reduction in flow throughout the lungs is more or less uniform, although both physiologic[163] and roentgenologic[737] studies have shown discrepant flow through the two upper zones in patients with isolated pulmonic stenosis or the tetralogy of Fallot. However, it is not clear from these reports on which side the greater flow usually occurs: flow was greater in the left lung during physiologic studies using carbon dioxide labeled with ^{15}O,[163] and was greater in the right

lung during angiographic investigation.[737] The mechanics producing asymmetric flow are not thoroughly understood.

Since decrease in the pulmonary circulation always engenders increased bronchial collateral flow,[68, 69, 292, 293] the pulmonary vascular pattern throughout the lungs may be formed partly or wholly by a greatly hypertrophied bronchial arterial system. This extensive systemic arterial supply is particularly evident in tetralogy of Fallot and in type-IV persistent truncus arteriosus. Although pulmonary arterial flow is negligible in these cases, the diminutive vascular markings throughout the lungs may represent the pulmonary arterial tree, being filled through systemic-pulmonary-artery anastomoses. The extent of collateral circulation may be best appreciated by selective bronchial arteriography, although the anomalous supply usually is of sufficient magnitude to permit roentgenologic visualization during aortic flooding or even during the levogram phase of angiocardiography. It has been suggested[739] that the absence of a pulmonary artery and the presence of atypical vessels arising from the aorta may be detected by tomography in frontal and lateral projections.

Systemic Arterial Supply to the Lung

A portion of lung—which may be normal or dysplastic[891]—may be supplied by a systemic artery arising from the aorta or one of its branches.[1692] Since drainage is via the pulmonary veins, the shunt is left-to-left.[857] The most common form of this anomaly is pulmonary sequestration.

BRONCHOPULMONARY SEQUESTRATION

This is a congenital pulmonary malformation in which a portion of pulmonary tissue is detached from the remainder of the normal lung and receives its blood supply from a systemic artery. The anomaly exists in two forms, *intralobar* and *extralobar*. The embryologic pathogenesis of these malformations is disputed,[828, 892–894] but it is highly probable that the two forms are not related embryologically.[895, 896] Intralobar and extralobar sequestrations rarely exist concomitantly.[906] Preoperative diagnosis is important in view of the hazards involved in severing the anomalous systemic vessel during surgical resection.

Intralobar Sequestration

In 1964, 250 cases of intralobar sequestration were traced in the literature,[651] although there is no question that the true incidence is much higher than this figure would suggest. This congenital pulmonary malformation consists in a nonfunctioning portion of lung within the visceral pleura of a pulmonary lobe. It derives its systemic arterial supply from the aorta or one of its branches, most commonly the descending thoracic aorta but occasionally the abdominal aorta, intercostal vessels, or aortic arch. Turk and Lindskog[288] reported the following arterial origins in the 114 cases they reviewed: descending thoracic aorta, 74; abdominal aorta, 25; intercostal artery, 5; and aortic arch, 1; 17 patients had multiple aberrant vessels. Venous drainage is invariably via the pulmonary venous system, producing a left-to-left shunt. Although the precise embryologic pathogenesis is not known, the primary defect appears to be a failure of the normal pulmonary artery to supply a peripheral portion of the lung, whose arterial supply then is derived from a persisting ventral branch of the primitive dorsal aorta. In approximately two thirds of cases the sequestered portion of lung is situated in the left paravertebral gutter in the region of the posterior bronchopulmonary segment of the lower lobe; in the remainder it occupies the same anatomic region in the right lower lobe.[288, 651] The upper lobes are rarely involved;[288, 653] in these cases the anomalous vessel commonly arises from the ascending thoracic aorta or one of its major branches, and associated cardiac malformations are very common.[893] For reasons unknown, intralobar sequestration is never seen in neonates at necropsy and, except for the rare lesion in an upper lobe, is not associated with other anomalies. Characteristically the sequestered segment is a closed system unconnected with the normal bronchial tree, but communication may develop as a result of infection in the sequestered lung. Three cases were reported[897] of communication between accessory lung tissue and the gastrointestinal tract—congenital bronchopulmonary-foregut malformation.

PATHOLOGIC CHARACTERISTICS. The affected segment typically is cystic, the spaces being filled with mucus, or, when infection is present, pus. The epithelium ranges from ciliated columnar epithelium indistinguishable from that of a normal bronchus (which is most common) to flat epithelium. Respiratory structures and the pulmonary tissue between the dilated bronchi and cysts are poorly developed and lack pigmentation, and the latter tissue consists predominantly of connective tissue, with inflammatory reaction in some cases. The anomalous vessel usually enters the lung by way of the lower part of the pulmonary ligament and typically is much larger than might be expected from the volume of tissue supplied. Histologically, this vessel is an elastic artery, with intimal thickening and arteriosclerotic changes in many cases.

ROENTGENOGRAPHIC MANIFESTATIONS. The roentgenographic appearance depends in large measure on whether the sequestered segment has been the site of infection and as a result has developed communication with the airways of contiguous lung tissue. When no communication exists, the anomalous tissue appears as a homogeneous mass of water density in the posterior portion of a lower lobe (usually the left) and almost invariably contiguous to the diaphragm. It is round, oval, or triangular and typically is sharply circumscribed. When infection has resulted in communication with the bronchial tree, the roentgenologic presentation is of an air-containing cystic mass with or without air-fluid levels (Figure 6–4).[289, 651, 652, 898] The cysts may be single and very large, but more commonly are multiple.[893, 899] Cases have been reported[901] in which serial roentgenography of homogeneous sequestered segments showed the development of cysts as a result of infection. The infectious process which first involves the sequestered segment often affects the surrounding parenchyma also, thereby obscuring the underlying anomaly with pneumonic consolidation; the cystic nature of the underlying mass may not become manifest until the pneumonia resolves (Figure 6–5). The size of the lesion may vary considerably with time, depending on the amount of gas and fluid within it. Bronchographic contrast medium

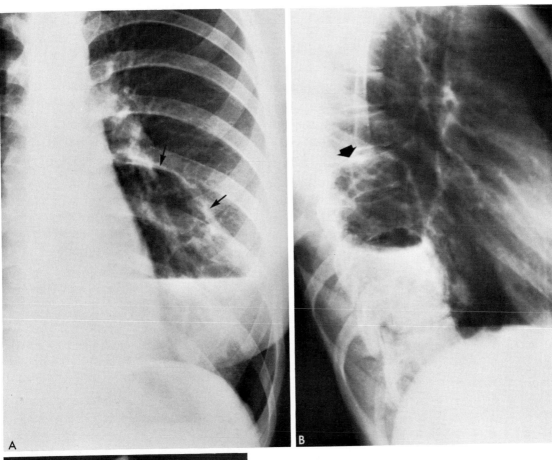

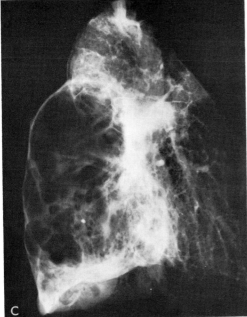

Figure 6–4. **Intralobar Pulmonary Sequestration.**
Views of the left hemithorax in posteroanterior (A) and
lateral (B) projections demonstrate a large, sharply circumscribed mass in the posteroinferior portion of the left
hemithorax, containing a well-defined air-fluid level. The
wall of the cavity is thin but sharply circumscribed (*arrows*
in both projections). At thoracotomy, the anomalous systemic artery supplying the sequestered portion of lung
was found to arise directly from the descending thoracic
aorta. In C is illustrated a roentgenogram in lateral projection of the resected left lower lobe; the cyst appears
to be multiloculated.

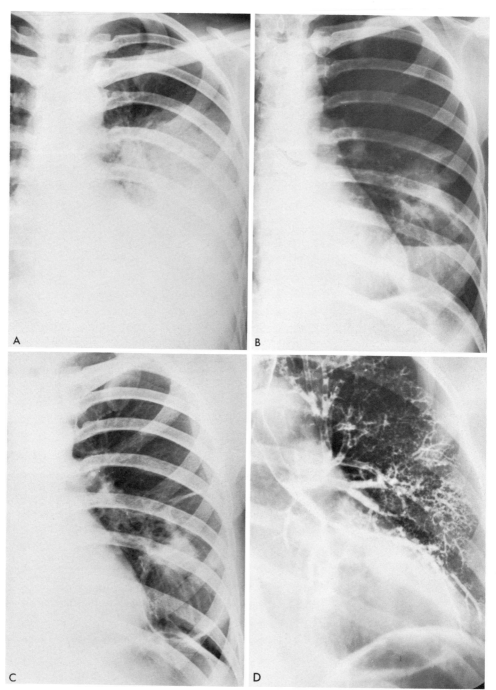

Figure 6–5.   **Intralobar Pulmonary Sequestration.** A view of the left hemithorax from a posteroanterior roent-genogram (A) reveals massive air-space consolidation of the lower two thirds of the left lung; note the air bronchogram in the upper portion of the consolidation. Three weeks later (B), there is almost complete resolution of the pneumonia, but there remains a rather well-defined mass lying contiguous to the left hemidiaphragm and possessing a prominent air-fluid level. Two months later (C), the fluid has disappeared, leaving a thin-walled cyst measuring several centimeters in diameter and showing an irregular nubbin of tissue in its superior portion. At this time, a bronchogram (D) demonstrates the basal bronchi to be festooned around the cystic space, a finding which is characteristic of intralobar pulmonary sequestration. At thoracotomy the anomalous systemic vessel was seen to enter the sequestered mass from the diaphragm.

rarely if ever enters the lesion; the opacified bronchial tree appears festooned around the mass, a distinctive and in fact almost diagnostic finding (Figure 6–5).

Although the diagnosis of bronchopulmonary sequestration may be strongly suspected from the preceding findings, definitive diagnosis depends upon opacification of the anomalous vessel by angiography.[289, 651, 652, 898] This is best accomplished by percutaneous aortography, either by flood technique or by selective catherization of the anomalous vessel. In some cases the anomalous vessel is apparent on plain roentgenograms or on tomograms as a finger-like appendage extending posteriorly and medially from the mass toward the aorta;[652, 896, 902] in one report, pneumoperitoneum permitted visualization of the vessel extending across the gas-filled subphrenic space from the aorta to the diaphragm.[320]

CLINICAL MANIFESTATIONS. The clinical picture is nonspecific. Most patients are asymptomatic until an acute respiratory infection develops, and in many cases this does not happen until they are adult.[651, 896, 898, 902–904] Signs and symptoms then are those of acute lower-lobe pneumonia, the basic defect becoming apparent only as a result of roentgenologic observation of the sequence of changes during resolution of the infection. Complications are infrequent; in one reported case an aspergilloma developed in a cyst,[903] and spontaneous pneumothorax as a result of cyst rupture is said to occur rarely.[652]

Extralobar Sequestration

The extralobar type of sequestration differs from the intralobar variety in many respects. Embryologically, it develops as complete ectopia of a segment of pulmonary tissue in the form of an accessory lobe or segment which is enclosed in its own visceral pleura (in contrast to an intralobar sequestered segment, which is enclosed within the visceral pleura of the affected lobe). In essence it is a primitive accessory lung bud. Anatomically, extralobar sequestration is related to the left hemidiaphragm in 90 per cent of cases;[829] it may be situated between the inferior surface of the lower lobe and the diaphragm, below the diaphragm, or within the substance of the diaphragm. In contrast to the intralobar variety, it drains via the systemic venous system—either the inferior vena cava or the azygos or hemiazygos system—and creates a hemodynamic communication in the form of a left-to-right shunt. The systemic arterial supply is commonly from the abdominal aorta or one of its branches, and the vessels may be multiple and small.[651] In contrast to intralobar sequestration, the extralobar anomaly is often seen at necropsy of neonates and frequently is associated with other congenital anomalies.[289, 651, 652, 829, 892, 905] Eventration or paralysis of the ipsilateral hemidiaphragm may be present.

Since an extralobar sequestered segment is enveloped in its own pleural sac, the chances of its becoming infected are greatly reduced; consequently, its chief mode of presentation, whether intrathoracic or intra-abdominal, is as a homogeneous soft-tissue mass. Distinguishing the intralobar or extralobar character of an intrathoracic non-air-containing sequestered segment *in vivo* can be accomplished by angiography: the course of the contrast medium through the venous phase reveals drainage via the pulmonary venous system (intralobar sequestration) or the systemic venous system (extralobar sequestration).[651]

CONGENITAL BRONCHIAL CYSTS

With one ethnologic exception (*see later*), a bronchial or bronchogenic cyst is a rare congenital anomaly resulting from an abnormality of budding or branching of the tracheobronchial tree during its embryologic development. Both the respiratory tract and the esophagus derive from the primitive foregut, which divides into a dorsal segment to form the esophagus and a ventral segment which differentiates into the tracheobronchial tree. Congenital anomalies arising from the dorsal segment, known as enteric or neurenteric cysts, are considered in the chapter on the mediastinum (*see* Chapter 17).

Bronchial cysts develop in the pulmonary parenchyma or mediastinum, or rarely within or beneath the diaphragm.[915] Rogers and Osmer[654] reported 46 pathologically proved cases seen over a period of 15 years: 32 were within the pulmonary parenchyma and 14 in the mediastinum; the average age at thoracotomy was 24 years, in a range of 14 months to 48 years. The anomaly appears to have a predilection for males.[850, 916] An ethnologic relationship was uncovered recently in Israel, where an extraordinarily high incidence of the anomaly was found in Yemenite Jews not only in comparison with Jews from other countries but also with other populations throughout the world.[918, 919]

The cysts are thin-walled and are lined by respiratory epithelium and usually are filled with mucoid material. Their walls may contain mucous glands, cartilage, elastic tissue, and smooth muscle. Calcium is rarely deposited in the wall of the cyst[920] but has been found in cyst contents.[921] They do not communicate with the tracheobronchial tree unless they become infected, in which case the mucus may be replaced by pus or by pus and air.

Pulmonary Bronchial Cysts

The pulmonary parenchyma is the most common location.[654] There is a predilection for the lower lobes—in one report of 32 cases, almost two-thirds were located there—with equal distribution in the two lungs.[654] In some cases the cysts are supplied by a systemic vessel and then may just as correctly be regarded as pulmonary sequestration. Sometimes their histologic appearance may simulate bronchiectasis with little or no evidence of a congenital origin. Culiner[922] considers intralobar bronchial cystic disease to be part of a "sequestration complex" and congenital cystic bronchiectasis to be a variant of a single complex of bronchovascular anomalies.

ROENTGENOGRAPHIC MANIFESTATIONS. The typical appearance is of a sharply circumscribed, solitary, round or oval shadow of unit density, usually in the medial third of the lungs (Figure 6–6); serial roentgenography usually but not always shows little change in the size and shape of the mass with time (Figure 6–7). Characteristically, the lesions do not communicate with the tracheobronchial tree until they become infected, an event which occurs eventually in approximately 75 per cent of cases. Once communication has been established, the cyst will contain air, with or without fluid.[654] If the patient presents originally with an infected bronchogenic cyst, the usual sharp definition of the shadow may be obscured by consolidation of surrounding parenchyma; in such circumstances the true nature of the cyst becomes apparent only when the surrounding pneumonitis has resolved.

It may be difficult to differentiate congenital bronchogenic cysts from acquired cystic lesions; even pathologists may find it impossible to establish the origin with certainty once a congenital lesion has been infected, since the respiratory epithelium which lines the congenital cyst may be destroyed by the infection. Most acquired pulmonary cysts are residua of remote lung abscesses, and a history of an acute respiratory episode may be of help in diagnosis. A bulla may be identical in appearance to a communicating bronchogenic cyst, and unless pulmonary emphysema is present to indicate the true nature of the process, histologic examination may be requisite to differentiation.

CLINICAL MANIFESTATIONS. The majority of uninfected bronchogenic cysts occasion no symptoms and are discovered by accident on a screening chest roentgenogram. Symptoms, of which hemoptysis is the most common, almost invariably relate to infection in and around the cyst.[916, 923–925] In contrast to emphysematous bullae, pneumothorax is a rare complication; but air embolism was reported in several patients who underwent decompression after construction work in a tunnel.[726]

In neonates, a communication between a cyst and the tracheobronchial tree may incorporate a check-valve mechanism which may result in rapid expansion of the cyst; such an air space may become so large as to compress the mediastinum, with resultant cardiac embarrassment and even death.

Mediastinal Bronchial Cysts

Maier classified mediastinal bronchogenic cysts into five types: (1) paratracheal, (2) carinal, (3) hilar, (4) paraesophageal, and (5) miscellaneous.[926] The majority are situated in the vicinity of the carina, often attached by a stalk to one of the major airways; in this location even a small cyst can cause symptoms by pressure on surrounding structures.[654, 928] Mediastinal cysts may arise within the pericardium, usually between the root of the aorta and the superior vena cava; in this

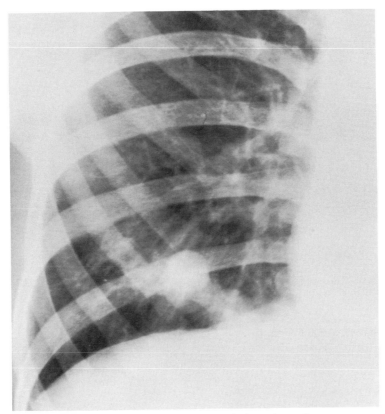

Figure 6–6. **Pulmonary Bronchogenic Cyst.** A view of the right hemithorax from a posteroanterior roentgeno-gram reveals a sharply circumscribed, somewhat lobulated mass in the lower portion of the right lung. The mass is homogeneous and shows no evidence of calcification. Proved bronchogenic cyst. Seventeen-year-old asymptomatic male.

location they may displace the mediastinal vessels and the heart.[284, 920] Of 14 pathologically proved mediastinal bron-chogenic cysts,[654] two (14 per cent) were found in the superior mediastinum, five (35 per cent) in the mid-mediastinum, and seven (50 per cent) in the posterior medi-astinum.

ROENTGENOGRAPHIC MANIFESTATIONS. Mediastinal bronchogenic cysts usually present as clearly defined masses of homo-geneous density just inferior to the carina and often protruding slightly to the right, thus overlapping the right hilar shadow (Figure 6–8). The majority are oval or round, and the shape may vary with in-spiration and expiration. They may dis-place the esophagus and, although situated on a somewhat higher plane, may be misinterpreted as left atrial enlarge-ment.[920, 928, 929] Unlike pulmonary bron-chogenic cysts, the mediastinal variety rarely communicates with the tracheo-bronchial tree (Figure 6–9). They are al-ways solitary but many are multiloculated.

CLINICAL MANIFESTATIONS. Medi-astinal bronchogenic cysts may become very large without causing symptoms; however, those located in the subcarinal area may cause pressure symptoms even when quite small and without being roent-genologically visible.[930] The possibility of such a lesion should be taken into con-sideration in any patient with signs and symptoms of major airway obstruction. Symptoms include dyspnea on effort, stri-dor, and persistent cough.[928, 930, 931] When a mediastinal cyst becomes infected—which seldom happens—the patient may have fever and, in some cases, retrosternal pain.

CONGENITAL BRONCHIAL ATRESIA

This rare anomaly consists of local oblit-eration of the lumen of a bronchus, most commonly the apicoposterior segmental bronchus of the left upper lobe at its point of origin (*see* Figure 4–130, page

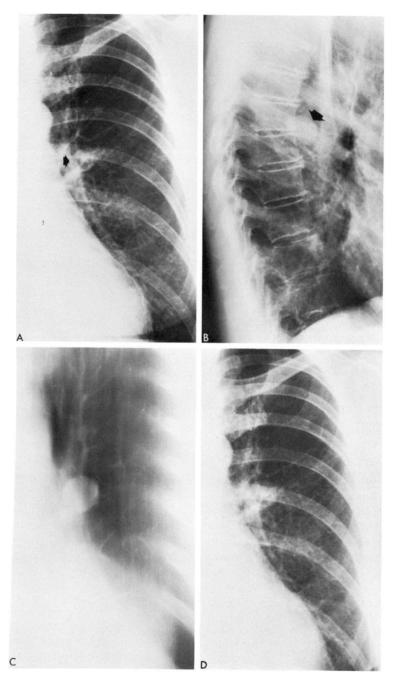

Figure 6-7. **Pulmonary Bronchogenic Cyst.** Views of the left hemithorax from posteroanterior (*A*) and lateral (*B*) roentgenograms demonstrate a smooth, sharply circumscribed soft tissue mass measuring slightly more than 2 cm in diameter situated immediately behind the left hilum (*arrow* in both projections). The sharp definition and homogeneous density are more easily appreciated on an anteroposterior tomogram (*C*). Roentgenograms during the Valsalva and Mueller maneuvers (not reproduced) revealed no change in the size or configuration of the mass. The mass proved on resection to be a bronchogenic cyst. Although it is unusual for such lesions to grow, serial roentgenograms of the chest of this 51-year-old asymptomatic woman had shown gradual increase in the size of the lesion since three years previously (*D*). (Standard roentgenograms courtesy Dr. John Silny, Sherbrooke Hospital, Sherbrooke, Quebec; tomogram courtesy Dr. David Berger, Royal Edward Chest Hospital, Montreal.)

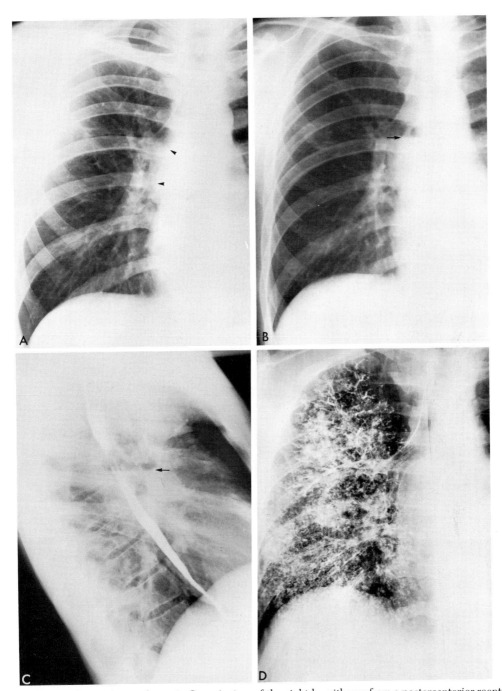

Figure 6–8. **Mediastinal Bronchogenic Cyst.** A view of the right hemithorax from a posteroanterior roentgeno-gram (A) reveals a smooth upward displacement of the right main- and intermediate-stem bronchi (*arrows*) by a homogeneous mass situated within the mediastinum. This 25-year-old man had been in a severe car accident two weeks previously and the mass was regarded as a traumatic mediastinal hematoma. The patient was readmitted three weeks later with an acute respiratory infection; at this time, posteroanterior (B) and lateral (C) roentgeno-grams demonstrated a prominent air-fluid level within the soft tissue mass (*arrows*); the esophagus is displaced slightly to the left. A bronchogram performed at this time (D) shows the upward displacement of the right main-and intermediate-stem bronchi; no contrast medium entered the cyst. At thoracotomy, the mass was found to be a bronchogenic cyst attached to the *left* main-stem bronchus. Histologically, the cyst wall showed an intense non-specific inflammation. (Courtesy Dr. Gerald Maguire, Montreal General Hospital.)

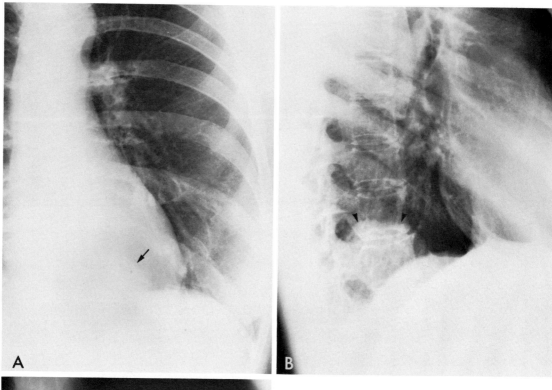

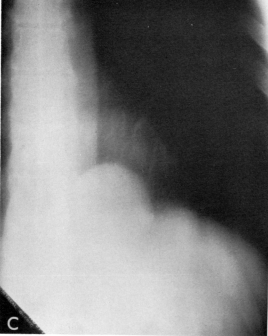

Figure 6–9. **Mediastinal Bronchogenic Cyst.** Views of the left hemithorax in posteroanterior (*A*) and lateral (*B*) roentgenograms reveal a smooth, sharply circumscribed soft tissue mass situated in the posterior costophrenic sulcus (*arrows* in both projections). An anteroposterior tomogram (*C*) shows the mass to be homogeneous and uncalcified; the relationship of the mass to the posterior mediastinal line suggested that it originated from the lungs or pleura rather than from the mediastinum although at thoracotomy, it was found to lie within the mediastinum.

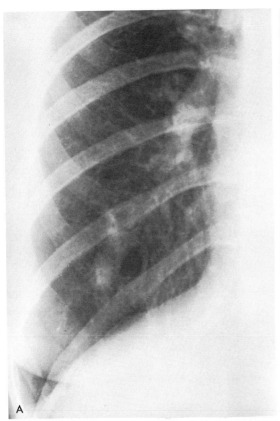

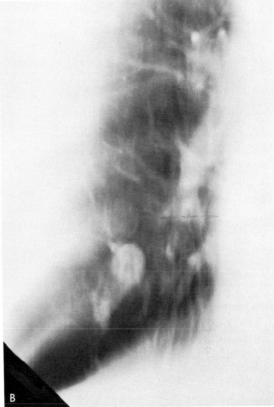

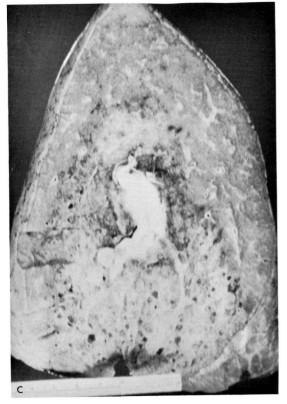

Figure 6-10. **Congenital Atresia of the Lateral Basal Bronchus, Right Lower Lobe.** A view of the right hemithorax from a posteroanterior roentgenogram (A) reveals a sharply circumscribed, finger-like mass measuring approximately 1 cm in width and 4 cm in length; the right lung is otherwise normal. An anteroposterior tomogram (B) shows the mass to be homogeneous in density and to diminish slightly in caliber as it proceeds distally. A bronchogram was not performed. The right lower lobe was resected (C). Pathologically there was seen to be a normal complement of segmental bronchi; just beyond its origin, the first division of the lateral segmental bronchus was found to be totally atretic; distal to the point of atresia, the bronchus was dilated to approximately 2.5 cm and contained thick inspissated mucus; distal to this, the smaller branches of the bronchial tree were found to be irregularly dilated. There was no evidence of an inflammatory cause for the bronchial atresia and it was considered to be of congenital origin. This anomaly more commonly affects the apicoposterior segment of the left upper lobe. (Roentgenograms courtesy Dr. P. J. Fitzgerald, Lakeshore General Hospital, Pointe Claire, Quebec.)

326).[699, 700, 832] Occasionally other segmental bronchi are affected—we have seen an example in a basal bronchus of the right lower lobe (Figure 6–10). The bronchial tree peripheral to the point of obliteration is patent. Mucus is secreted in the bronchial tree distal to the obstruction, leading to dilatation of the bronchus over a distance of 4 to 5 cm. The result is a well-circumscribed, somewhat elliptical, soft-tissue mass situated (in left upper lobe atresia) just above the left hilum in the anatomic position of the apicoposterior bronchus. An invariable accompaniment is collateral air drift between the obstructed bronchopulmonary segments and the anterior segment, giving rise to overinflation of the involved segments. The reduction in ventilation results in decreased perfusion, leading to diminution in vascular markings. The combination of overinflation and a well-circumscribed, elliptical, suprahilar mass produces a distinctive roentgenographic picture. These patients are asymptomatic, and usually the anomaly is discovered on a screening chest roentgenogram.

CONGENITAL CYSTIC ADENOMATOID MALFORMATION OF THE LUNG

This anomaly, which seems to be apparent only in infants, consists in a mass of disorganized pulmonary tissue within a lobe. Irregular cystic spaces occupy much of the mass, with no attempt at division into discrete lobules. The lesion lacks a well-defined bronchial system but communicates with the bronchial tree, a fact which differentiates this anomaly from intralobar sequestration; further, it is supplied by the pulmonary circulation.

Histologically, the mass is composed of an overgrowth of bronchioles with polypoid changes in the mucosa.[933] Roentgenologically, the lesion is space-occupying and produces expansion of the ipsilateral hemithorax with shift of the mediastinum to the contralateral side. The mass comprises numerous air-containing cysts scattered irregularly through tissue of unit density. Clinically, the patient may be cyanotic and may evidence respiratory embarrassment.[935]

7

INFECTIOUS DISEASES OF THE LUNGS

PNEUMONIA DUE TO GRAM-POSITIVE
AEROBIC BACTERIA
    DIPLOCOCCUS PNEUMONIAE
        The Causative Organism
        Epidemiology
        Pathologic Characteristics
        Roentgenographic Manifestations
        Clinical Manifestations
    STAPHYLOCOCCUS AUREUS
        The Causative Organism
        Epidemiology
        Pathologic Characteristics
        Roentgenographic Manifestations
        Clinical Manifestations
    STREPTOCOCCUS PYOGENES
        The Causative Organism
        Epidemiology
        Pathologic Characteristics
        Roentgenographic Manifestations
        Clinical Manifestations
    BACILLUS ANTHRACIS
        Pathologic Characteristics
        Roentgenographic Manifestations
        Clinical Manifestations
    LISTERIA MONOCYTOGENES
PNEUMONIA DUE TO GRAM-NEGATIVE
AEROBIC BACTERIA
    PSEUDOMONAS AERUGINOSA
        Epidemiology
        Pathologic Characteristics
        Roentgenographic Manifestations
        Clinical Manifestations
    PSEUDOMONAS PSEUDOMALLEI
        The Causative Organism
        Epidemiology
        Roentgenographic Manifestations
        Clinical Manifestations
    KLEBSIELLA AND AEROBACTER SPECIES
        Pathologic Characteristics
        Roentgenographic Manifestations
        Clinical Manifestations
    ESCHERICHIA COLI
    BACILLUS PROTEUS
    SALMONELLA SPECIES
    SERRATIA MARCESCENS
    HEMOPHILUS INFLUENZAE
    HEMOPHILUS (BORDETELLA) PERTUSSIS
    PASTEURELLA TULARENSIS
    PASTEURELLA PESTIS

PASTEURELLA SEPTICA
BACTERIUM ANITRATUM
BRUCELLA SPECIES
MALLEOMYCES MALLEI
PNEUMONIA DUE TO ANAEROBIC ORGANISMS
    BACTEROIDES SPECIES
    MICROAEROPHILIC STREPTOCOCCUS
    FUSIFORM BACILLI AND SPIROCHETES
        Acute Lung Abscess Secondary to Aspiration
    CLOSTRIDIUM PERFRINGENS
MYCOBACTERIAL INFECTIONS OF THE
LUNGS
MYCOBACTERIUM TUBERCULOSIS
        Epidemiology
        The Causative Organism
        Allergy and Immunity
    PRIMARY PULMONARY TUBERCULOSIS
        Pathologic Characteristics
        Roentgenographic Manifestations
        Clinical Manifestations
    REINFECTION TUBERCULOSIS
        Pathologic Characteristics
        Roentgenographic Manifestations
        Clinical Manifestations
        Extrapulmonary Tuberculosis
        Laboratory Procedures in Diagnosis
    ANONYMOUS MYCOBACTERIA
        The Causative Organisms
        Epidemiology
        Pathologic Characteristics
        Roentgenographic Manifestations
        Clinical Manifestations
MYCOTIC INFECTIONS OF THE LUNG
    HISTOPLASMOSIS
        The Causative Organism
        Epidemiology
        Primary Histoplasmosis
        Chronic or Reinfection Histoplasmosis
        Disseminated Histoplasmosis
        Laboratory Studies
    COCCIDIOIDOMYCOSIS
        The Causative Organism
        Epidemiology
        Benign Coccidioidomycosis
        Disseminated Coccidioidomycosis
        Laboratory Studies
    NORTH AMERICAN BLASTOMYCOSIS
        The Causative Organism
        Epidemiology

Roentgenographic Manifestations
Clinical Manifestations
Laboratory Studies
CRYPTOCOCCOSIS
The Causative Organism
Epidemiology
Roentgenographic Manifestations
Clinical Manifestations
Serologic Studies
ACTINOMYCOSIS
The Causative Organism
Roentgenographic Manifestations
Clinical Manifestations
NOCARDIOSIS
The Causative Organism
Roentgenographic Manifestations
Clinical Manifestations
ASPERGILLOSIS
The Causative Organism
Primary Aspergillosis
Secondary Aspergillosis
Serologic Studies
CANDIDIASIS (MONILIASIS)
The Causative Organism
Roentgenographic Manifestations
Clinical Manifestations
PHYCOMYCOSIS (MUCORMYCOSIS)
The Causative Organism
Roentgenographic Manifestations
Clinical Manifestations
GEOTRICHOSIS
SPOROTRICHOSIS
SOUTH AMERICAN BLASTOMYCOSIS
ALLESCHERIASIS
TORULOPSIS GLABRATA
INFECTIONS OF THE LUNG DUE TO THE
VIRUSES, MYCOPLASMA PNEUMONIAE, AND
THE RICKETTSIAE
RESPIRATORY SYNDROMES
CORYZA
ACUTE PHARYNGITIS/TONSILLITIS INFECTIONS
ACUTE RESPIRATORY DISEASE (ARD)
ACUTE LOWER RESPIRATORY TRACT DISEASE
Primary Atypical Pneumonia (PAP)
Pneumonia due to Mycoplasma pneumoniae
RESPIRATORY INFECTIONS DUE TO VIRUSES
MYXOVIRUS RESPIRATORY INFECTIONS
Influenza Virus Infection
Parainfluenza Virus Infection
Respiratory Syncytial Virus Infection
Measles (Rubeola) Respiratory Infection

PICORNAVIRUS RESPIRATORY INFECTIONS
Coxsackie Virus Respiratory Infection
ECHO Virus Respiratory Infection
Poliovirus Respiratory Infection
Rhinovirus Respiratory Infection
REOVIRUS RESPIRATORY INFECTION
ADENOVIRUS RESPIRATORY INFECTION
HERPES VIRUS RESPIRATORY INFECTIONS
Varicella-Zoster Respiratory Infection
Cytomegalovirus Respiratory Infection
MISCELLANEOUS VIRUS AND PRESUMED VIRUS
INFECTIONS
BEDSONIA RESPIRATORY INFECTIONS
Ornithosis (Psittacosis)
INFECTIONS DUE TO OTHER BEDSONIA
ORGANISMS
RESPIRATORY INFECTIONS DUE TO
RICKETTSIA
Q-fever Pneumonia
"Scrub-typhus" Pneumonia
RENAL TRANSPLANTATION PNEUMONIA
PARASITIC INFESTATION OF THE LUNG
PROTOZOAN INFESTATION
AMEBIASIS
Pathologic Characteristics
Roentgenographic Manifestations
Clinical Manifestations
TOXOPLASMOSIS
Pathologic Characteristics
Roentgenographic Manifestations
Clinical Manifestations
PNEUMOCYSTIS CARINII INFESTATION
Pathologic Characteristics
Roentgenographic Manifestations
Clinical Manifestations
METAZOAN INFESTATION
NEMATHELMINTH (ROUND-WORM)
INFESTATION
Ascariasis
Strongyloidiasis
Ancylostomiasis (Hookworm Disease)
Trichinosis
Filariasis
Pulmonary Larva Migrans
PLATYHELMINTH (FLAT-WORM) INFESTATION
Echinococcosis (Hydatid Disease)
Cysticercosis
Paragonimiasis
Opisthorciasis
Schistosomiasis
ARTHROPOD INFESTATION
Pentastomiasis

Infection of the parenchyma of the lung is called pneumonia or pneumonitis. Three major groups of pneumonias may be recognized on the basis of pathogenesis, each possessing different morphologic and roentgenologic characteristics which usually permit their differentiation. (1) Some organisms—notably *Diplococcus* *pneumoniae*—reach the peripheral air spaces of the lung, where they incite inflammatory edema which spreads centripetally from unit to unit through communicating channels (the pores of Kohn and canals of Lambert); this is designated "air-space pneumonia" or "alveolar pneumonia" (the term "lobar pneumonia," although in common use, is not recommended: only seldom are these pneumonias lobar in extent, and the term gives little indication of the pathogenesis of the parenchymal consolidation). (2) Other organisms—for example, *Staphylococcus aureus*—initiate an inflammatory response in the conducting airways of the lung and their surrounding parenchyma; this type of pneumonia is designated "bronchopneumonia" or "lobular pneumonia." (3) The viral organisms and *Mycoplasma* tend to affect the interstitial tissues predominantly and thus produce a pattern which is designated "interstitial pneumonia or pneumonitis." Although it is not always possible to fit an individual case into one of these categories, recognition of these patterns is of obvious importance for the prompt institution of specific therapy.

The clinical diagnosis of pneumonia often is suggested by the symptoms of cough, expectoration, chills and fever, and particularly pleural pain. In many cases physical signs indicate the location of the disease, although the classical signs of parenchymal consolidation—inspiratory lag, impaired percussion, bronchial breathing, fine rales, and whispering pectoriloquy—are heard much less often than formerly, presumably because the prompt institution of antibiotic therapy prevents the majority of acute pneumonias progressing to the full-blown stage of so-called "hepatization." Physical examination of the chest usually reveals only fine rales and a decrease in breath sounds. Although occasionally it is possible to detect on physical examination minor degrees of pneumonia for which there is no roentgenographic evidence, more often there is a complete absence of physical signs in cases showing major areas of parenchymal consolidation roentgenographically. Thus in a study of 200 patients with pneumonia, Osmer and Cole[949] could correlate roentgenographic evidence of parenchymal consolidation with physical signs in only 83 patients (41.5 per cent). Also, in some cases roentgenographic evidence of pneumonia is present without accompanying physical signs in one area, and *vice versa* in other areas. These inconsistencies suggest that the manifestations of pneumonia vary considerably, depending upon the degree of inflammation and the stage of the disease process.

In a significant percentage of patients the organism or organisms responsible for the pneumonia are not detectable. Sometimes when a pathogen (or potential pathogen—for example, an "opportunistic" organism) is grown on sputum culture the clinical history is inconsistent with the picture usually attributed to that etiology. Sometimes the reason for this inconsistency is obvious; for example, before admission to hospital the patient may have received antibiotics without prior bacteriologic study, and such therapy probably eliminated the responsible pathogen (in many cases *Diplococcus pneumoniae*). Similarly, antibiotic therapy may have altered the upper respiratory tract flora and enabled resistant organisms to multiply, thereby leading the physician to the erroneous conclusion that the resistant organism is responsible for the disease process. Since healthy subjects may harbor pathogenic bacteria in their upper respiratory tract, isolation of specific pathogens does not *necessarily* indicate the etiology of parenchymal disease, and such bacteriologic findings must be interpreted in the light of clinical features and roentgenographic patterns. Repeated heavy growth of the same organism on culture of purulent expectorated material obviously strengthens the likelihood of that organism being etiologically responsible for the disease; and culture of the same organism from both blood and sputum provides convincing evidence of this.

It is very likely that most bacterial pneumonias follow a viral infection,[950] indicating a possible synergistic action between bacteria and viruses. This theory is supported by the frequent finding of streptococcal and staphylococcal pneumonias in patients who die during influenzal epidemics; similarly, greater concentrations of *Hemophilus influenzae* and *Diplococcus pneumoniae* have been cultured from the throats of children with upper respiratory tract disease.[950] Failure to isolate a bacterial pathogen from the sputum of patients with pneumonia usually leads to a diagnosis of virus pneumonia, a label which may be supported by clinical, roentgenologic, and laboratory evidence and which in a percentage of cases may be confirmed by subsequent isolation of the organism or by a rise in titer of the antibody to a specific virus during the convalescent period. Recent studies in patients with bacterial infections have shown a significantly higher percentage of neutrophils which reduce nitroblue-tetrazolium than in normal subjects or in patients with non-bacterial infectious diseases; this observation may prove useful as a diagnostic method in the future.[951]

In the preantibiotic era the term pneumonia was considered to be almost synonymous with infection of the lung by *Diplococcus pneumoniae*. As a result of the high susceptibility of *D. pneumoniae* to the sulfonamides and penicillin and its failure to develop resistance to these drugs, full-blown cases of diplococcal pneumonia are seen much less commonly in hospitals nowadays; undoubtedly many of these patients are treated at home without bacteriologic confirmation. In hospital populations today, pneumonia is more often a problem of pulmonary infection in patients with lowered resistance resulting from other chronic disease; many are caused by pathogens or opportunistic organisms resistant to some or all known antibiotics.

Over the last three decades a considerable change has occurred in the organisms responsible for terminal pneumonia; Kneeland and Price[952] showed that organisms which were etiologically responsible in 1947[953] — *D. pneumoniae, H. influenzae*, and *beta*-hemolytic *Streptococcus* — were rarely so in 1960; streptococci and influenza bacilli had completely disappeared as causes of terminal pneumonia, and *D. pneumoniae* was isolated only in those patients not given antibiotics terminally. Today the most common etiologic agents in terminal pneumonia are *Staph. aureus* (usually resistant to the various penicillins) and *Ps. aeruginosa* (an organism which often flourishes terminally, despite broad-spectrum antibiotic therapy, and which often is completely resistant to antibiotics *in vitro*), and less commonly other Gram-negative organisms including the *Klebsiella-Aerobacter* group, *Proteus*, and *E. coli;* unlike pseudomonas, the last three do not appear to flourish in patients who are receiving antibiotics.[952] Patients with disease of the reticuloendothelial system appear to be particularly prone to the development of overwhelming infections from opportunistic organisms, not only bacterial but also viral and mycotic. Kneeland and Price also found that patients with severe liver disease manifested increased susceptibility to pneumonia, at the same time showing diminished capacity for inflammatory response. Although the precise mechanism by which viral infections predispose patients to super-infection with bacteria is unknown, it is thought that depression of bacillary movement due to destruction of cilia may be at least partly responsible.

The majority of pneumonias develop through inhalation or aspiration of the causative organism, and some result from direct infection of the blood stream from a primary site elsewhere or from bacterial contamination of an "intracatheter" inserted for purposes of intravenous therapy,[954] almost invariably in hospital patients. Gram-positive and more often Gram-negative bacterial septicemias may cause severe congestion, edema, hemorrhage, and thromboses of the pulmonary capillaries,[955, 956] with a clinical and roentgenologic picture simulating diffuse pulmonary edema. Since systemic hypotension commonly accompanies this form of infection the pulmonary involvement has been entitled "shock lung."[335c, 956]

Empyema as a complication of pneumonia occurs much less frequently since the advent of antibiotics. Fluid aspirated on thoracentesis frequently is sterile on culture. In approximately 20 per cent of cases, the empyema fluid grows multiple organisms,[957, 958] the most common of which are coagulase-positive *Staphylococcus aureus* and various Gram-negative organisms. Empyema rarely occurs in association with pneumonia due to *D. pneumoniae*, probably because antibiotic therapy prevents progression of the disease to an advanced stage; occasionally, however, pneumococcal pneumonia may be associated with sterile empyema. Improved therapy has resulted in the infrequent development of tuberculous empyema, which formerly was common.

PNEUMONIA DUE TO GRAM-POSITIVE AEROBIC BACTERIA

DIPLOCOCCUS PNEUMONIAE

The Causative Organism

Although over 75 varieties of pneumococci have been identified, the great majority of pneumonias in man are caused by types I, III, IV, and VII. The organism is Gram-positive and usually is seen on smear in pairs or in short chains; it has a capsule which swells when placed in homologous antiserum. *D. pneumoniae* grows readily on blood agar; the injection of bacteria-laden sputum into the peritoneum of mice frequently produces death within hours.

Epidemiology

Although there is little doubt that many patients with pneumococcal pneumonia treated with antibiotics are either cured in their homes or are rendered culturally sterile by the time of admission to hospital, Austrian[959] showed that the incidence of bacteremic pneumococcal infections is unchanged. Fulminating cases are particularly common in vagrants or alcoholics. The disease is seen most often in males between the ages of 30 and 50, the responsible organisms usually being types I, III, IV, and VII. Type-III *Diplococcus pneumoniae* appears to show a predilection for older patients and in the preantibiotic era often was fatal. Type-II pneumococcus, formerly a common cause of pneumonia, has virtually disappeared.[959] *D. pneumoniae* infections occur most commonly during the winter and early spring and show a distinct increase in incidence during influenzal epidemics.

Pathologic Characteristics

D. pneumoniae is aspirated into the lungs from the upper respiratory tract and flows under the influence of gravity to the most dependent portion of the lungs.[554, 562, 563, 568] Thus, like any aspiration pneumonia, it shows an anatomic bias for the lower lobes and posterior segments of the upper lobes. Organisms penetrate to the most peripheral air spaces of the lung, where initially they incite an outpouring of inflammatory edema which permits rapid multiplication of the organism. Centripetal propagation of the bacteria-laden exudate proceeds rapidly, with spread from alveolus to alveolus and from acinus to acinus via the communicating pores of Kohn. This centripetal spread accounts for the homogeneity of consolidation, seen both morphologically and roentgen-ologically, and for its nonsegmental distribution: the mechanism of spread does not respect segmental boundaries. With progression of the inflammatory response there is engorgement of the capillaries in the alveolar septa and the appearance of polymorphonuclear leukocytes and erythrocytes in the alveolar exudate. Still later, there occurs the stage of "gray hepatization" in which the alveoli remain airless but become filled with fibrin and large numbers of polymorphonuclear cells; at this stage, congestion disappears and the alveolar capillaries become inconspicuous. Resolution follows, during which macrophages invade the alveoli and engulf the bacteria-containing polymorphonuclear leukocytes; once again, the capillaries open and blood flows through them. Incomplete resolution may occur, fibrosis developing chiefly in the peribronchial and subpleural regions of the lungs.[961]

Roentgenographic Manifestations

The roentgenographic pattern of acute pneumococcal pneumonia should be readily apparent from the pathologic description. Characteristically, there is homogeneous consolidation of lung parenchyma (*see* Figures 4–5 to 4–7, page 194). Since the consolidation begins in the peripheral air spaces of the lung, it almost invariably abuts against a visceral pleural surface, either interlobar or over the convexity. Where consolidation is not related to a visceral pleural surface its margin usually is fairly well defined (*see* Figure 4–68, page 261). Because of the mechanism of spread there is no respect for segmental boundaries, a point of major importance in differentiating acute air-space pneumonia from bronchopneumonia. Contrary to the implication of the commonly-employed term "lobar" pneumonia, only seldom is a complete lobe consolidated (Figure 7–1).[568] An air bronchogram is almost invariable, and its absence should cast doubt upon the diagnosis. Since the pathologic process is one of replacement of air by inflammatory exudate, loss of volume is either slight or absent during the acute stage of the disease; during resolution, however, some degree of atelectasis is common, due presumably to the presence of exudate within airways and resultant obstruction. Most frequently the disease is confined to one lobe, but

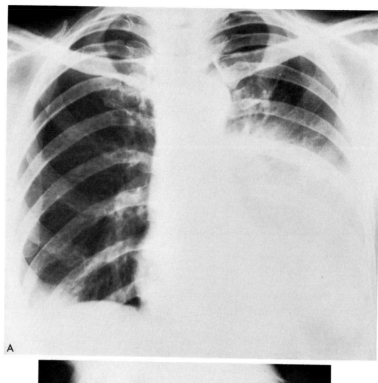

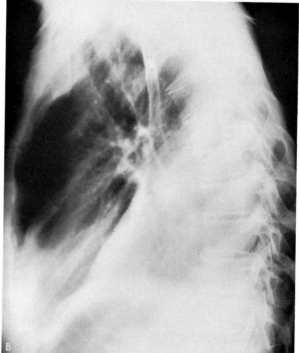

Figure 7–1. **Acute Pneumococcal Pneumonia.** Posteroanterior (*A*) and lateral (*B*) roentgenograms reveal homogeneous consolidation of the whole of the left lower lobe; there is no loss of volume; an air bronchogram is present. In addition, a small area of consolidation is present in the right costophrenic angle representing early infection of the right lower lobe. Involvement of more than one lobe in acute pneumococcal pneumonia is uncommon. Heavy growth of *Diplococcus pneumoniae* in the sputum.

sometimes the infection develops simultaneously in two or more lobes (Figure 7–1), in which case the prognosis tends to be less favorable. With appropriate therapy roentgenologic resolution is fairly rapid, complete clearing occurring within ten to 14 days; in untreated patients, resolution may take as long as seven weeks.[962] Cavitation is rare, although Danner and his associates[963] recently described two cases of acute pneumococcal pneumonia in which massive pulmonary gangrene occurred, with sloughing of irregular masses of necrotic lung into a large central cavity; the necrosis was considered to be due to vascular thrombosis. This rare complication of acute air-space pneumonia—only ten cases had been reported by 1968[963]—is said to occur in both pneumococcal and Friedländer's infections.

In contrast to its frequency in the pre-antibiotic era, roentgenographically demonstrable associated pleural effusion is very uncommon today.

Clinical Manifestations

The usual clinical presentation of acute pneumococcal pneumonia is abrupt, with fever, shaking chills, cough, slight expectoration, and intense pleural pain. On close questioning the majority of patients admit to an upper respiratory infection before the onset of the more dramatic symptoms. Fever may be as high as 106° F. The cough may be nonproductive at first but soon results in the expectoration of bloody, "rusty," or greenish material. In debilitated and alcoholic patients, extreme cyanosis may be present and shock may ensue rapidly. Typical findings on physical examination include decreased breath sounds, crepitations, and impaired percussion over the site of the pneumonia, with bronchial breathing, bronchophony, and whispering pectoriloquy audible on auscultation in a small percentage of patients. During resolution, the crepitations increase at first and then slowly disappear as normal breath sounds return. A friction rub is audible over the consolidated lung in many cases.

Although fairly common in the preantibiotic days, complications of acute pneumococcal pneumonia—empyema, meningitis, endocarditis, and pericarditis—now are seen rarely. Perhaps the most common

complication is superinfection, usually by Gram-negative organisms and commonly in patients who have received huge doses of penicillin or a combination of antibiotics.

Although the diagnosis of acute pneumococcal pneumonia may be strongly suspected from the clinical picture and the roentgenographic pattern, a definitive diagnosis requires isolation of the organism. The demonstration of cocci on a smear is helpful but not confirmatory. Culture on blood agar is a lengthy process, whereas inoculation of sputum into the peritoneum of guinea pigs provokes a reaction the same day; swelling of the capsule of the organism in the presence of specific antiserum is visible microscopically, permitting identification not only of the *D. pneumoniae* but also of its type. Bacteremia is common in pneumococcal pneumonia, and a positive blood culture is diagnostic.

The white-cell count usually is over 20,000 per c mm, in a range of 10,000 to 40,000 per c mm; polymorphonuclear leukocytosis, with many band forms, is common. However, leukopenia develops in many extremely ill patients. Analysis of arterial blood gas may show mild or even severe hypoxemia during the stage of "red hepatization." In most cases the PCO_2 is reduced, and the minute ventilation indicates hyperventilation with small tidal volume.

STAPHYLOCOCCUS AUREUS

The Causative Organism

Staphylococcus aureus is a Gram-positive organism which, on smear, usually appears in clumps; it grows readily on blood agar, usually in a golden-yellow colony surrounded by hemolysis. Among other substances produced by the organism are coagulase, hemolysins, and enterotoxin. Its pathogenicity for man is related in particular to its ability to produce coagulase (coagulase-negative strains rarely cause human disease).

Epidemiology

Staphylococcus aureus has replaced *Streptococcus pyogenes* as the most common cause of bronchopneumonia, frequently complicating virus infections or developing in hospital patients whose resistance has been lowered by disease or recent operation. The emergence of the staphylococcus as an important and often virulent pathogen is related to its ability to develop antibiotic resistance and to the contamination of the hospital environment, where the majority of cases occur.

Infants during the first year of life are particularly prone to the development of staphylococcal pneumonia;[635, 964-966] in fact, it is the most common bacterial cause of death due to respiratory tract infection in this age group.[967] Newborn babies usually acquire the infection while in hospital; the periumbilical region commonly is affected first, and subsequently the upper respiratory passages.

Staphylococcal pneumonia rarely develops in healthy adults. Sometimes the infection follows an attack of influenza, a complication which may well be the most common cause of death during influenzal epidemics. More commonly, however, the pneumonia develops in hospital patients who are debilitated or have recently undergone operation;[968-970] those who are receiving antibiotic therapy, particularly with multiple drugs, are most susceptible. Patients acquire their infections directly or indirectly from active staphylococcal lesions rather than from asymptomatic carriers. Prolonged stay in hospital increases the risk of infection; in fact, studies have shown a direct correlation between length of hospital stay and the development of positive cultures for coagulase-positive staphylococci from bronchial swabs.[971]

Pathologic Characteristics

The pathologic findings in staphylococcal pneumonia depend upon the rapidity with which the disease progresses. In acute fulminating cases the picture may be one of severe hemorrhagic pulmonary edema; the disease begins in the conducting airways and histologically the bronchi show destruction of epithelium and infiltration with polymorphonuclear leukocytes; the alveoli are filled with proteinaceous material, blood, and a few polymorphonuclear cells; organisms abound in both bronchial and alveolar exudate. In cases of insidious progression of the disease the pathologic picture is one of consolidation of acinar units surrounding the airways. Peribronchial abscesses form which subsequently communicate with the lumen of the airways; these communications permit entry of air into the abscess pockets and the development of the characteristic pneumatoceles. These pneumatoceles may rapidly become enormous, particularly in children, presumably as a result of check-valve obstruction at the site of perforation.[729, 966] In some cases of fulminating staphylococcal pneumonia the development of staphylococcal septicemia results in generalized infiltration of the interstitium of the lungs with polymorphonuclear leukocytes and mononuclear phagocytic cells.[961]

Pleural effusion is fairly common and may be serous or serosanguinous; more commonly, however, and particularly in infants and children, the pleural reaction is purulent.

Roentgenographic Manifestations

Since the pathogenesis of acute staphylococcal pneumonia is related to the bronchial tree, resultant parenchymal consolidation typically is segmental in distribution. Depending on the severity of involvement, the process may be patchy or homogeneous, the latter representing confluent bronchopneumonia and being the more common method of presentation in our experience (see Figure 5–5, page 394). Acute inflammatory exudate fills the airways, so that some degree of segmental collapse may accompany the consolidation; for the same reason an air bronchogram is seldom observed, and its presence should cast some doubt upon the diagnosis.

The roentgenographic pattern differs somewhat in children and adults. *In children*, consolidation develops very rapidly, usually involves a whole lobe, and may be multilobar. A distinctive characteristic is the development of pneumatoceles, which are reported to occur in 40 to 60 per cent of child patients (see Figure 4–94, page 285).[13, 635, 965, 966, 972] These cystic spaces are commonly thin-walled and are thought to result from check-valve obstruction of a communication between a peribronchial abscess and the lumen of a bronchus. They may be enormous—the size of a hemithorax or larger, in which case they may simulate tension pneumothorax. Many pneumatoceles contain fluid levels. They appear usually during the first week of the pneumonia and always disappear spontaneously, within six weeks[966] or after persisting for as long as several months.[729, 965] Huxtable and her associates[972] followed up 22 children with acute staphylococcal pneumonia for an average of 43 months: pneumatocele developed in 20, pneumothorax in 15, and pleural effusion in all 22. Complete roentgenographic resolution occurred in 19 patients, minor residua consisting of minimal pleural thickening in three. Pleural effusion (or empyema) occurs in over 90 per cent of child cases,[13, 635, 965, 966, 972] and during the acute stage of the disease may mask the parenchymal consolidation.[965, 969]

In adults, the disease is bilateral in over 60 per cent of cases.[969, 973] Abscess formation with subsequent communication with the bronchial tree and the appearance of fluid-containing cavities is fairly common, ranging in incidence from 25 per cent[969] to 75 per cent.[973] Abscesses characteristically show a very irregular shaggy inner wall (*see* Figure 4–79, page 271) and may be multiple. As in children, enlargement of the cavity may occur through check-valve obstruction of the bronchial communication but is manifested simply by enlargement of the abscess cavity rather than by development of the thin-walled pneumatoceles so characteristic of the disease in infants and children. Resolution commonly takes several weeks; when abscess formation has occurred a residual thin-walled bulla may remain. In one of our patients bronchography revealed free communication between this bulla and the bronchial tree (*see* Figure 4–146, page 343). Pleural effusion or empyema occurs in approximately 50 per cent of adult patients, and its presence is a useful sign in differentiating staphylococcal pneumonia from that caused by other cocci.[969]

The common method of development of acute staphylococcal pneumonia is by inhalation or aspiration of the organism but occasionally organisms reach the lung in septic emboli, via the blood stream, frequently from pelvic veins. Then the roentgenographic appearance is one of multiple nodular masses throughout the lungs, sometimes with poorly defined borders (*see* Figure 5–24, page 457); they may be confluent and resemble homogeneous consolidation. Pyemic abscesses may erode into the bronchial tree and produce air-containing cavities, frequently with fluid levels; in such circumstances the roentgenographic appearance simulates Wegener's granuloma or multiple excavating metastatic lesions.

Clinical Manifestations

The clinical picture varies, depending on the patient's age, the degree of his debilitation, and whether the pneumonia is superimposed on influenzal infection. In infants, the onset often is abrupt, with high fever, tachypnea, and cyanosis; prompt treatment is necessary to save the patient's life. In children and adults who acquire the infection following influenza—up to 14 days after the onset of influenza[968]—or in the very occasional case in which the disease develops outside hospital in an otherwise healthy subject, the onset is also abrupt, with pleural pain, cough, and the expectoration of purulent yellow or brown material, sometimes blood streaked. When the infection develops in hospital, either after an operation[970] or as a complication of a chronic disease which is being treated with corticosteroids or multiple antibiotics,[969, 973] the onset often is insidious and is characterized by cough, fever, and the expectoration of purulent, blood-streaked material, but rarely by chest pain and chills. In this group it is of the utmost importance that a diagnosis be made and appropriate therapy instituted promptly, since the mortality rate is high. Physical signs vary and include signs of consolidation with bronchial breathing, patchy areas of rales, rhonchi, and decreased breath sounds, usually with signs of pleural effusion. Large pneumatoceles may be present, giving rise to a hyperresonant percussion note.

The diagnosis of staphylococcal pneumonia should be suspected whenever pneumonia develops soon after influenza or in a hospital patient. In infants, the roentgenographic demonstration of pneumonia associated with pneumatocele formation is almost pathognomonic. In all patients the diagnosis should be confirmed by sputum culture; in the majority, a heavy growth—sometimes pure—of *Staph. aureus* is obtained. The white-cell count usually is elevated to between 16,000 and 25,000 per c mm, with polymorphonuclear leukocytosis, but leukopenia may be present in severely ill patients. Positive blood cultures have been found in as many as 50 per cent of patients[973] but probably are not as common as in acute pneumococcal pneumonia.

Complications of acute staphylococcal pneumonia include meningitis, metastatic abscesses (particularly to the brain and kidneys), and acute endocarditis which may develop in patients without valvular disease. Pneumothorax, pyopneumothorax, and empyema occur so frequently that they should be considered as manifestations of the disease rather than as complications.[964, 1029–1031]

STREPTOCOCCUS PYOGENES

The Causative Organism

This Gram-positive organism (Lancefield group-A *beta*-hemolytic *Streptococcus*) appears on smear in the form of chains. Culture on blood agar is very rapid, colonies being identifiable microscopically and serologically within 24 hours; the colonies show typical *beta*-hemolysis surrounding them. The organism may be cultured from the sputum or from the pleural effusion which commonly accompanies the pneumonia. It is very sensitive to penicillin and, unlike *Staph. pyogenes*, has not developed resistant strains.

Epidemiology

Until the advent of antibiotics, *Strep. pyogenes* was the most common cause of bronchopneumonia, a disease which affected predominantly the young and the elderly. Commonly it followed attacks of measles and pertussis, and in the influenza pandemic following World War I was a common and serious complication. Acute streptococcal pneumonia is rarely seen nowadays, although occasional reports still appear of cases of upper respiratory infections[974] in epidemic form[1026] and as complications of measles and other childhood exanthemata;[1027] it rarely follows streptococcal pharyngitis or tonsillitis. The infection occurs most commonly during the coldest months. The organism enters the lungs by inhalation and aspiration and under the influence of gravity passes to the most dependent portions; thus the disease is almost invariably localized to the lower lobes.

Pathologic Characteristics

The morphologic characteristics of acute streptococcal pneumonia are almost identical to those of the staphylococcal variety; as with the latter, the severity of the disease clinically correlates with the morphologic findings. In the preantibiotic era, many patients with the acute fulminating disease died within 36 hours, necropsy revealing severe serosanguineous pleural effusion and hemorrhagic edema of the lung parenchyma, particularly of the lower lobes; acute bronchial and bronchiolar inflammation was present, with infiltration of polymorphonuclear leukocytes and shedding of epithelium. The alveoli and airways invariably were filled with edema fluid, red blood cells, and micro-organisms. Alveolar-wall necrosis and cavities developed in those who survived for four to five days.

In patients with less acute disease—commonly associated with whooping cough or measles—the pathologic picture differs and is similar to that of acute staphylococcal pneumonia: peribronchial consolidation is associated with fairly severe bronchial and bronchiolar epithelial damage and with infiltration with polymorphonuclear leukocytes and lymphocytes. The peripheral parenchyma shows a combination of inflammatory edema and collapse.

Empyema is almost invariable in fatal cases of acute streptococcal pneumonia.

Roentgenographic Manifestations

In most respects the roentgenographic characteristics are indistinguishable from acute staphylococcal pneumonia—homogeneous or patchy consolidation in segmental distribution, associated with some degree of loss of volume, typically affecting the lower lobes and sometimes bilateral. There is not the same tendency for the development of pneumatoceles or pyopneumothorax as in acute staphylococcal pneumonia, although lung abscesses and cavities may develop and empyema is common (the latter was an inevitable accompaniment in the preantibiotic era).

Clinical Manifestations

The onset of acute streptococcal pneumonia is usually abrupt, with pleural pain, shaking chills, fever, and cough productive of purulent and often blood-tinged material. Patchy areas of decreased breath sounds may be heard at the lung bases, together with rales and rhonchi; signs of pleural effusion are usually detected.

Positive diagnosis depends on culture of the organism from sputum, pleural fluid, or occasionally blood. Antisera may be used to identify the type of organism. In the later stages of the disease, antibodies may be found in the serum, and the titer of anti-streptolysin O may indicate the diagnosis. There is commonly a polymorphonuclear leukocytosis, with a mixture of mature and immature cells.

Complications include significant residual pleural thickening (in 15 of 20 patients in one series[1026]), bronchiectasis (especially in children in whom the disease develops in conjunction with an exanthem), and rarely glomerulonephritis.[974]

BACILLUS ANTHRACIS

Anthrax is chiefly a disease of cattle, sheep, and goats; although infections in man were not uncommon in previous centuries, prophylactic measures employed in the twentieth century have been successful in largely eradicating the disease. *Bacillus anthracis* is a large Gram-positive, spore-forming, rod-shaped organism that may contaminate the fur of animals and be imported in wool or hides; thus the disease is most common in sorters and combers in the wool industry. The organism is exceptionally virulent, and laboratory workers who come in contact with it are at considerable risk. Cases have been reported in persons living in the neighborhood of a tannery.[1032] No seasonal predilection is apparent. The infection is predominantly cutaneous in some cases.

Pathologic Characteristics

After their inhalation, the spores of the organism reach the alveoli where they are engulfed by macrophages which pass via the lymphatics to the hilar lymph nodes; here the spores germinate into the vegetative form of the organism. Multiplication of the vegetative form is accompanied by hemorrhage and edema in the lymph nodes and the surrounding mediastinal connective tissues. Dissemination then occurs via the blood stream to the lungs—causing hemorrhagic pneumonitis—and to the meninges, spleen, and intestines. Hemorrhagic pleural effusion is common. Entry of the organism into the body through the skin may give rise to bacteremia and result in pulmonary disease.

The most dramatic pathologic finding in the thorax is the hemorrhagic edema of hilar lymph nodes and surrounding mediastinal tissues. In the lungs, hemorrhagic foci may be found in the peripheral air spaces, and the larger bronchi may be filled with blood and mucus. Polymorphonuclear leukocytes are not present in the inflammatory exudate unless there is secondary pyogenic infection. The spleen may be enlarged.

Roentgenographic Manifestations

The characteristic roentgenologic finding is mediastinal widening resulting from lymph-node enlargement; this is of particular diagnostic significance if it develops acutely in a patient with a history of occupational exposure. Patchy nonsegmental opacities may develop throughout the lungs, presumably due to hemorrhagic edema. Pleural effusion is common.

Clinical Manifestations

The initial symptoms following the inhalation of spores of *Bacillus anthracis* are nonspecific, consisting of mild fever, myalgia, nonproductive cough, and frequently a sensation of precordial oppression. The second stage of the disease begins abruptly within a few days and is characterized by acute dyspnea, cyanosis, tachycardia, fever, and sometimes shock. Diffuse diaphoresis and subcutaneous edema of the chest and neck may develop, and stridor may result from compression of the airways by enlarged lymph nodes. Expectorated material usually is bloody and frothy. Physical examination may reveal widespread crepitations and signs of pleural effusion, with evidence of meningitis in some cases. Most patients die within 24 hours after the onset of the second stage.

The organism may be cultured on peptone agar, from the blood, cerebrospinal fluid, and sputum. However, if life-saving therapy is to be instituted promptly, the diagnosis cannot await positive culture and must be made on the basis of a history of acute febrile illness in a person occupationally exposed to anthrax spores and showing roentgenographic evidence of mediastinal widening.

LISTERIA MONOCYTOGENES

Listeriosis is a rare infectious disease in which pulmonary and pleural involvement is very uncommon. Infection with *Listeria monocytogenes* usually affects the meninges and the endometrium, and in the latter location is suspected of being a cause of repeated abortion. Of 18 cases reported in 1967, all had neoplasms, 16 of the reticuloendothelial system.[4319]

Listeria monocytogenes is a Gram-positive rod, approximately 0.5μ wide and 1 to 3μ long, which grows well on most standard culture media. The organism closely resembles the diphtheroids and is recognized by its hemolytic activity on blood agar and its motility when incubated at room temperature.[1034]

Listeriosis may develop following the inhalation of, ingestion of, or direct contact with contaminated food or animal products. Pulmonary or pleural involvement, which is rare, presumably occurs via the blood stream. Of the 18 patients reported by Louria and his associates,[4319] one had diffuse right lower-lobe parenchymal consolidation and pleural effusion, and another had pleural effusion only. Buchner and Schneierson[1034] recently described ten cases of listeriosis, several of which had lung lesions, with cavitation in one case.

There is some evidence to suggest that this organism may cause a clinical picture not unlike infectious mononucleosis. Infection can be transmitted venereally.[4319]

PNEUMONIA DUE TO GRAM-NEGATIVE AEROBIC BACTERIA

PSEUDOMONAS AERUGINOSA

Epidemiology

Because of their resistance to almost all antibiotics, pulmonary infections due to *Ps. aeruginosa* have become the most dreaded of pneumonias acquired in hospitals. The organism is a Gram-negative bacillus which occasionally can be cultured from the sputum of subjects who are in good health, particularly those who have received antibiotic therapy recently. As with staphylococcal pneumonia, most cases occur in the young or in elderly patients with debilitating disease; infection frequently is acquired in hospital.

Ps. aeruginosa shows a great propensity to grow and multiply in liquid media, even in a number of the "antiseptic" solutions generally used for "sterilization" of aspiration equipment. The antiseptic solutions used to eradicate staphylococcal organisms from the umbilical region of newborn infants frequently are ineffective against *Ps. aeruginosa*. Epidemics in nurseries have been traced to contamination of faucet aerators and delivery-room resuscitators.[1035] Although the organism is often recovered from throat swabs of hospital staff and patients, it is normally a commensal at this site; this observation is simply an indication of the wide dissemination of the organism.[1036, 1037] Recovery of the organism by throat swabbing of patients in a hospital ward does not necessarily indicate that in those cases the bacillus is acting as a pathogen.[1038] Most patients who acquire the disease either have been in contact with a heavily infected source, such as patients with wounds, burns, urinary-tract infections, and, particularly, respiratory-tract involvement, or have aspirated large numbers of bacilli through contamination of saline, soap, antiseptic solutions, creams, jellies, or other substances used in the care of tracheostomy sites or as repositories for suction catheters.[1037–1040] In our experience the most common source of infection in hospital patients is the heavily contaminated nebulizer attached to artificial ventilators.

Inhalation of the organism may result in pneumonia, particularly in infants and children with congenital heart disease.[1041] In the adult, most infections develop in patients suffering from chronic lung disease, congestive heart failure, diabetes mellitus, alcoholism, or kidney disease;[1042] patients with tracheostomies are particularly susceptible, especially in the early postoperative period.[1036, 1038]

In summary, pseudomonas pneumonia is

most likely to develop in hospital patients with debilitating disease, usually on multiple antibiotic and often corticosteroid therapy, with a tracheostomy—especially when frequent suction is required or as an artificial aid in ventilation. It is equally true, however, that the disease develops in only a proportion of patients fulfilling these criteria, indicating that some natural defensive mechanism must be present in the respiratory tract of even the critically ill.[1038] Entry of the organism into the body may be directly via the blood stream, usually secondary to contamination at the site of an indwelling intravenous catheter.[954]

Pathologic Characteristics

At necropsy, patients who have acquired their disease through aspiration usually show affection of the posterior segments of the lower lobes. Microabscesses may be identified in the peribronchial tissues with necrosis of the alveolar walls within the lung parenchyma. These abscesses may be walled off and contain many polymorphonuclear cells. Focal areas of atelectasis and emphysema may be present; almost invariably at necropsy, there is a hemorrhagic or purulent pleural effusion.[1042, 1043]

A somewhat different pathologic picture is found in those patients in whom pneumonia resulted from pseudomonas bacteremia.[1042] Nodular infarcts develop, with massive Gram-negative bacillary infiltration of arterial and venous walls. A distinctive skin lesion known as *ecthyma gangrenosa* may develop which begins as a vesicle and later becomes necrotic; these lesions range from a few millimeters to several centimeters in diameter and their center is black.

Roentgenographic Manifestations

The roentgenographic pattern of acute *Ps. aeruginosa* pneumonia is said to be quite unlike that of other Gram-negative pneumonias and to resemble more closely the pattern seen in acute staphylococcal pneumonia.[1042] The posterior segments of the lower lobes are most commonly involved but several lobes may be affected. Multiple small nodules 0.3 to 0.5 cm in diameter may be present, often associated with small areas of radiolucency, presumably the roentgenographic counterpart of

the microabscesses seen at necropsy. These nodules tend to coalesce into homogeneous areas of consolidation 2 cm or more in diameter (Figure 7-2).[1042] We have seen one patient in whom massive homogeneous consolidation of much of both lungs occurred, simulating acute airspace pneumonia; an air bronchogram was apparent everywhere (Figure 7-3). Pleural effusions are common.

In patients who acquire the disease as a result of bacteremia, the roentgenographic pattern is more diffuse and patchy.

Clinical Manifestations

Most but not all patients with pseudomonas pneumonia are in hospital at the time they acquire the infection, and almost invariably they have underlying disease which has resulted in loss of resistance. An upper respiratory infection may precede the pneumonia whose onset is typically abrupt, with chills, fever, severe dyspnea, and cough productive of copious yellow or green, occasionally blood-streaked, sputum. Although empyema is common, pleural pain is said to be infrequent. Bradycardia is the rule. The temperature curve is unusual in that it peaks in the mornings rather than in the evenings.[1042] The white-cell count usually is normal in the early stages but commonly rises to an average of about 20,000 per c mm. Eosinophilia has been reported.[1042]

In the bacteremic form of the disease, it may be extremely difficult to make the diagnosis during the early stages, and only the appearance of circulatory collapse or the typical skin lesions suggests the etiology. When the disease is secondary to inhalation, the diagnosis usually is made by repeated culture of heavy—sometimes pure—growths of *Ps. aeruginosa*. Blood cultures should be made whenever the diagnosis is suspected: in those in whom the organism has gained entry via the blood stream, positive blood culture may antedate by several days the discovery of the organism in the sputum.

PSEUDOMONAS PSEUDOMALLEI

The Causative Organism

Pseudomonas pseudomallei (Malleomyces pseudomallei, Loefflerella whitmore),

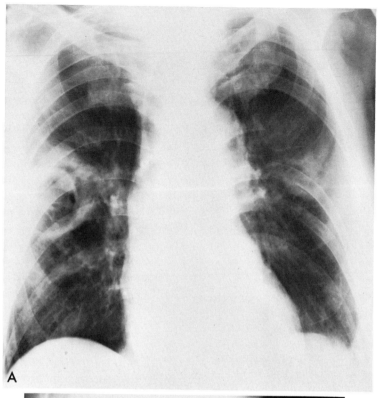

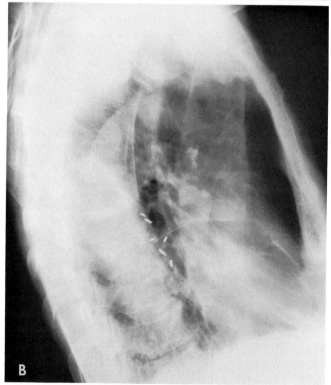

Figure 7–2. **Lung Abscess Due to *Pseudomonas aeruginosa*.** This 78-year-old man had had an esophageal resection with esophagogastric anastomosis for esophageal ulcer and stricture ten days prior to these anteroposterior (A) and lateral (B) roentgenograms. Abscesses are present in both lungs, situated in the superior segment of the lower lobes. The abscesses were preceded by relatively homogeneous parenchymal consolidation; the nodular phase described in the text was not observed in this patient. Repeated heavy growth of *Pseudomonas aeruginosa* in the sputum was regarded as strong presumptive evidence that this was the etiologic agent.

Figure 7–3. Acute Air-space Pneumonia Due to *Pseudomonas aeruginosa.* This 38-year-old woman was admitted to hospital in a deep coma as a result of an overdose of barbiturates; she had been placed on high doses of corticosteroids and antibiotics and required continuous artificial ventilation. Several days after admission, an anteroposterior roentgenogram (*A*) demonstrated massive air-space consolidation of all lobes of both lungs, the superior portion of the left upper lobe being least involved. An air bronchogram was present in all areas. The patient expired three days after the roentgenogram illustrated in *A*; a postero-anterior roentgenogram (*B*) exposed in the erect position in the autopsy theater demonstrates almost total opacification of both lungs, homogeneity being disturbed only by a well-defined air bronchogram. The left pneumothorax was thought to result from vigorous forced ventilation in which high positive pressures were employed in an attempt to improve the severely compromised alveolar ventilation. The pneumoperitoneum was unexplained. *Pseudomonas aeruginosa* was recovered in pure culture from the sputum and directly from the lung.

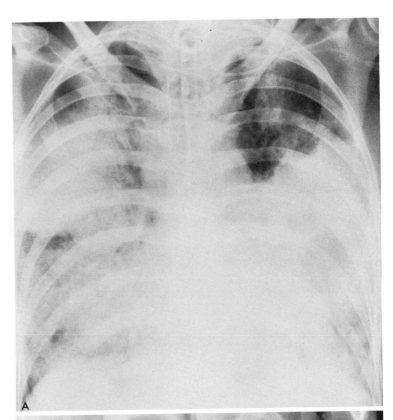

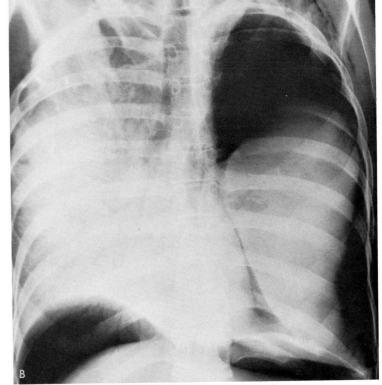

like *Ps. aeruginosa*, is a motile pleomorphic Gram-negative rod with one or two flagellae at one pole; it does not possess a capsule. It can be isolated on all culture media under both aerobic and anaerobic conditions. It shows specific enzyme reactions and sugar fermentation which permit it to be differentiated from *Malleomyces mallei*, the organism responsible for glanders.

Epidemiology

Melioidosis, the disease caused by *Ps. pseudomallei*, occurs principally in rodents, cats, and dogs and is endemic in Ceylon, India, Burma, and the East Indies, where the organism has been found in the soil. Only rare sporadic cases have been encountered in North America.[1044] The disease does not appear to have any seasonal, age, or sex predominance. In endemic areas, serologic tests have shown the disease to be of widespread distribution, most patients being asymptomatic. Man is believed to acquire the infection through cutaneous or respiratory portals of entry or following ingestion of food contaminated by animal excreta;[1044] man-to-man transmission does not occur.[1045]

Pathologically, multiple small abscesses are found throughout the lungs, spleen, lymph nodes, liver, and kidneys.

Roentgenographic Manifestations

Both roentgenographically and clinically, two distinct patterns have been described—the acute and the chronic.[1046] The more common—the acute—is characterized by a roentgenographic pattern consisting in irregular nodular densities measuring 4 to 10 mm in diameter widely disseminated throughout both lungs. These have indistinct borders and tend to enlarge, coalesce, and cavitate as the disease progresses. In this later stage, the chest roentgenogram may reveal local groups of confluent shadows resembling homogeneous consolidation involving a single or multiple lobes. Patients with the acute form of the disease may die suddenly, in which circumstances the chest roentgenogram suggests pulmonary edema.

The chronic form of the disease,[1045] which has been described as "unresolved pneumonia," often is associated with cavitation but without hilar lymph-node en-largement; the roentgenographic appearance is said to simulate tuberculosis.[1044] Roentgenographically demonstrable pleural effusion does not occur.[1046]

Clinical Manifestations

The onset of acute melioidosis usually is abrupt but may be preceded by a brief period of malaise, anorexia, and diarrhea. The symptoms of high fever, chills, cough, expectoration of purulent blood-streaked material, dyspnea, and pleuritic pain may be followed rapidly by evidence of bacteremic dissemination, including miliary visceral and osseous abscesses, leading to prostration and resulting in death within a few days.[1044, 1045, 1047, 1048] In their 1957 review of over 300 cases, Prevatt and Hunt[1048] found that the great majority of patients presented with this picture of acute fulminating, usually fatal disease. A more recent report suggests that most cases are chronic, with a clinical and roentgenographic picture which mimics pulmonary tuberculosis so closely that only a negative tuberculin skin test and a history of residence in an endemic area will suggest the diagnosis.[1045] In chronic cases the lungs appear to be the organs predominantly involved; many patients show signs of abscesses in viscera, bones, joints, and skin.[1044, 1045, 1048] Underlying disease increases susceptibility to the infection.[1047]

The white-cell count may be normal or may show moderate leukocytosis with neutrophilia. Cultures should be made of sputum, urine, blood, and, if symptoms indicate meningeal spread, cerebrospinal fluid. There is no specific skin test; an agglutination test may aid in diagnosis when cultures are negative.

One case has been reported in a formerly healthy cleaner of air conditioners who acquired acute necrotizing pneumonia due to *Pseudomonas* "eugonic oxidizer Group I" (*Pseudomonas* E.O.-I).[1703] Lung biopsy showed a pathologic picture very similar to acute *Ps. pseudomallei* pneumonia.

KLEBSIELLA AND AEROBACTER SPECIES

The *Klebsiella* and *Aerobacter* organisms have been grouped together because of their antigenic similarities. Pneumonias caused by these organisms are of two types: (1) acute fulminating air-space pneumonia caused by the Friedländer's bacillus (*Klebsiella pneumoniae, K. edwardsii edwardsii*, and *K. edwardsii atlantae*), which comprises 1 to 5 per cent of all acute alveolar pneumonias; and (2) a more chronic insidious pneumonia which occurs in patients with underlying chronic pulmonary disease caused by the various strains of *Aerobacter*. Acute fulminating pneumonia usually occurs in males in the sixth and seventh decades of life, almost invariably in association with an underlying disease, such as diabetes or alcoholism. The mortality rate is approximately 50 per cent, death occurring within 48 hours of the onset of the disease. In the more chronic form of *Klebsiella-Aerobacter* infection, patients almost invariably have some form of chronic lung disease, such as asthma, chronic bronchitis, emphysema, bronchiectasis, or diffuse interstitial fibrosis or granulomatosis. The chest roentgenogram of such patients may show local pneumonic consolidation and the etiologic significance of *Klebsiella-Aerobacter* organisms in the sputum of these patients is not yet clear.

Hospital outbreaks of acute *Klebsiella* pneumonia have been traced to aerosol solutions used in nebulizers[1049] and to a hand cream employed by nurses in an intensive-care unit.[1050] Poor oral hygiene is practiced in many cases and may well be the source of the organism.

Klebsiella organisms are Gram-negative encapsulated bacilli which culture on agar as large mucoid gelatinous colonies. Antigenic types I to VI (Friedländer's bacillus) may be identified on typing with antisera; in contrast to many other types of *Klebsiella-Aerobacter* organisms, these six types are extremely virulent for mice.

Pathologic Characteristics

As with other organisms such as *Diplococcus pneumoniae* which cause acute air-space pneumonia, *Klebsiella* gains entry by inhalation and flows by gravity to the most dependent portions of the lung; thus the areas most commonly involved are the posterior portion of an upper lobe or the superior portion of a lower lobe. Acute pneumonia usually is unilateral and most frequently involves the right lung.

Grossly, the consolidated lung is reddish-gray, with cavitation in many cases. Histologically the peripheral air spaces are filled with edema fluid containing many Gram-negative bacilli; mononuclear cells which are present initially are replaced later by polymorphonuclear leukocytes.[961] Extension to the pleura with resultant empyema is common. Massive lung necrosis may lead to the formation of huge cavities.[569, 961]

Roentgenographic Manifestations

As an acute air-space pneumonia, acute Friedländer's pneumonia may be expected to show the same general roentgenographic features as acute pneumococcal pneumonia—homogeneous parenchymal consolidation containing an air bronchogram but showing no precise segmental distribution (unless a whole lobe is involved—a frequent occurrence). Three features of acute Friedländer's pneumonia help to differentiate it from acute pneumococcal pneumonia: (1) a tendency for the formation of voluminous inflammatory exudate such that the volume of affected lung is increased above normal, with resultant bulging of interlobar fissures (*see* Figure 4–101, page 294);[569, 1051, 1052] (2) a tendency to abscess and cavity formation which is common in acute *Klebsiella* pneumonia and rare in acute pneumococcal pneumonia; and (3) pleural effusion (or empyema) which occurs much more frequently in pneumonia of *Klebsiella* etiology. Expansion of a lobe is not an invariable finding however, and the association of acute air-space pneumonia in a lobe which is of normal volume or of reduced volume should not cause one to exclude a Friedländer's etiology.[569, 1053] Abscesses and unilocular or multilocular cavities usually develop rapidly if the patient survives the initial 48 hours. The separation of large masses of necrotic lung into an abscess cavity is reported to occur rarely, with about the same frequency as in acute pneumococcal pneumonia.[963]

Sometimes the acute disease undergoes only partial resolution and passes into a chronic phase with cavitation and persistent positive cultures for *Klebsiella pneumoniae*. In these circumstances the roentgenographic picture closely simulates fibroproductive tuberculosis.

Clinical Manifestations

Acute pneumonia tends to develop in elderly, debilitated persons, especially alcoholics. The onset usually is abrupt, with prostration, pain on breathing, cyanosis, moderate fever, and severe dyspnea; expectoration usually is greenish, purulent, and blood-streaked, and occasionally brick-red and gelatinous. Malaise, chills, and shortness of breath may be present for some time,[569] but on admission to hospital many patients are in shock.

Physical signs usually are those of parenchymal consolidation—bronchial breathing, impaired percussion, whispering pectoriloquy, and rales; breath sounds are decreased when pus in the airways results in bronchial obstruction.

The white-cell count usually is moderately elevated; when it is normal or reduced the prognosis is most unfavorable.[569] Bacteremia is fairly common.[569, 1050]

The diagnosis should be suspected from the clinical picture and the roentgenographic findings; should a smear of sputum show a preponderance of Gram-negative bacilli, antibiotic therapy should be instituted immediately; to await the results of culture is to court disaster. Complications include empyema and occasionally pericarditis and meningitis.

ESCHERICHIA COLI

E. coli is a rare cause of bronchopneumonia and tends to affect debilitated patients and occasionally neonates, the latter due presumably to aspiration of amniotic fluid.[1054] *E. coli* is a Gram-negative bacillus frequently found in the nose and throat of patients receiving antibiotic therapy. In patients with chronic lung disease or chronic extrapulmonary diseases such as diabetes mellitus or renal or cardiovascular disease, the organism may penetrate to the lower respiratory tract and incite acute or subacute pneumonia. Of approximately 1900 hospital cases of pneumonia over a 30-month period, Tillotson and Lerner[1055] found 82 (4.3 per cent) to be due to Gram-negative organisms; 20 of these were considered to be due to *E. coli* on the basis of two relatively pure cultures from the blood or pleural fluid. Patients ranged in age from 17 to 84 years, with a mean of 53

years; there was no sex or race predominance. Many had gastrointestinal or genitourinary disease, suggesting that lung involvement was usually, although not invariably, secondary to bacteremia. The infections occurred most commonly in the winter and spring.

Morphologically, necropsy of patients who die within 48 hours after onset reveals hemorrhagic pneumonia, usually of the lower lobes, with interstitial mononuclear infiltration, capillary engorgement, and exudation of protein into the alveoli.[956] *Roentgenographic appearances* are those of patchy or confluent bronchopneumonia; associated pleural effusion is said to be fairly common.[1043, 1055]

Clinically, the usual history is of pre-existing chronic disease, with abrupt onset of fever, chills, dyspnea, pleuritic pain, cough, and expectoration of yellow—rarely blood-tinged—sputum. Gastrointestinal symptoms including nausea, abdominal pain, dysphagia, diarrhea, and vomiting may be present. The onset may be fulminating, with shock leading rapidly to death. The classical signs of consolidation are lacking, the sole finding on physical examination being basal rales; empyema may lead to decreased breath sounds and dullness or flatness on percussion. The white-cell count may be decreased or may be increased to over 20,000 per c mm.

Diagnosis requires a predominant or pure growth of *E. coli* on culture; occasional colonies are of no significance, particularly in patients receiving antibiotic therapy. Positive culture from the blood or pleural fluid is strong evidence that the organism is pathogenic.

BACILLUS PROTEUS

Up-to-date information on acute *Bacillus proteus* pneumonia was provided in 1968 by Tillotson and Lerner,[1056] who reviewed the literature and reported six more cases of pneumonia presumed to be caused by various species of this organism. Many affected patients have chronic pulmonary disease and some have chronic extrathoracic disease such as diabetes mellitus or alcoholism. Like *E. coli*, *Proteus* is more commonly a cause of kidney infection.

The organism is thought to gain entry to

the lungs by inhalation. Both morphologically and roentgenographically, the picture is one of acute air-space pneumonia similar in most respects to that of *Diplococcus pneumoniae* and more particularly the *klebsiella* organisms. Nonsegmental homogeneous consolidation occurs predominantly in the posterior portion of the upper lobes or the superior portion of the lower lobes; abscess formation is frequent, being observed in five of the six cases described by Tillotson and Lerner.[1056] In four of their cases, loss of volume of the affected lobe was evidenced by deviation of the trachea toward the side of the lesion. Pleural effusion is uncommon.

Clinically, the onset and course of acute *Proteus* pneumonia is more insidious than is usual in the other Gram-negative pneumonias. For several weeks before admission to hospital, patients may complain of a general lack of well-being and worsening of the symptoms of their chronic pulmonary disease; as these symptoms become more severe, pleural pain develops, with cough productive of purulent yellow sputum which sometimes is blood-streaked. There is moderate fever but no evidence of shock. Physical signs of pulmonary consolidation were present in every case reviewed by Tillotson and Lerner; a moderate leukocytosis with a shift to the left was common; blood cultures were negative.

SALMONELLA SPECIES

Salmonella species are Gram-negative bacteria which rarely affect the lungs; they include *S. typhi*, *S. choleraesuis*, *S. typhimurium*, and occasionally others such as Group-C organisms. Although they are more commonly pathogens in the gastrointestinal tract, any of these organisms may cause bronchopneumonia secondary to aspiration, or diffuse pneumonitis secondary to bacteremia. Infections usually develop during the warm months although sporadic cases may occur the year around. The disease was much more common in former years because of inadequate hygienic control.[1057] Patients with disseminated malignant disease apparently are predisposed to the infection.[1058]

Morphologic characteristics depend largely on the mode of infection, aspiration of organisms causing focal bronchopneumonia, and bacteremia resulting in diffuse bilateral suppurative disease. Suppuration and necrosis lead to cavity formation and empyema.[1059-1062]

Roentgenographically, the pattern is one of segmental bronchopneumonia if the organism gains entry by aspiration;[1057] cavitation and pleural effusion (empyema) are common.[1060, 1061] An acute miliary pattern has been described in cases of proved salmonella bacteremia.[1059]

Clinically, the course of the disease usually is prolonged, with chills, fever, and pleural pain; cough often is nonproductive but eventually may produce purulent expectoration. The white-cell count varies from leukopenic to moderately leukocytic. The species type can be identified by biochemical and agglutination tests.

SERRATIA MARCESCENS

This organism is a Gram-negative bacillus commonly saprophytic in soil and occasionally pathogenic for man. Sometimes it produces a red pigment whose appearance simulates blood on expectorated material (pseudohemoptysis). Barrett and his co-workers[1063] stated that infections from this organism are increasing in incidence, the majority involving the urinary tract. The organism tends to be opportunistic, affecting patients with underlying disease.

Pathologic, roentgenologic, and clinical manifestations which could be ascribed to infection with this organism have not been described. In the hospital epidemic described by Ringrose and colleagues,[1064] the organism was cultured from pleural fluid in one patient and directly from a lung biopsy in another—strong indications that *Serratia marcescens* sometimes is pathogenic.

HEMOPHILUS INFLUENZAE

Hemophilus influenzae is the most common organism cultured from purulent expectoration of patients with chronic pulmonary disease, although some doubt still exists as to its pathogenicity. Of its many strains, six have capsules and may be differentiated into types a to f according to the nature of their capsular polysac-charides. Type-b strains are those usually believed to cause disease in man.[1065, 1066] Evidence that this organism produces at least a surface bacterial infection in patients with chronic bronchitis and bronchiectasis is provided by the observations that purulent expectoration may be cleared by antibiotic therapy[1067, 1068] and that antibodies may be demonstrated in the sera of affected patients.[1704]

H. influenzae has been shown to be responsible for epiglottitis, bronchitis, bronchiolitis, and segmental bronchopneumonia in very young children.[1065, 1066, 1070] As a primary pathogen, it usually causes acute inflammation of the mucous membranes of the airways, although when it follows respiratory virus disease, particularly acute infection with the influenza virus, it may penetrate the bronchial wall and cause an inflammatory reaction in the peribronchiolar tissues—typical bronchopneumonia.[961]

Roentgenographically, acute bronchopneumonia occurs usually in the lower lobes and may be bilateral (*see* Figure 5–11, page 414).[1069] In adults the organism occasionally induces acute air-space pneumonia simulating that caused by *D. pneumoniae*.[1069, 1071]

The acute disease in infants may be very severe, with extremely severe dyspnea, high fever, and cyanosis resulting chiefly from acute bronchiolitis. Empyema is frequent.[1070] The white-cell count may be normal or may reveal moderate leukocytosis. The organism may be cultured from the sputum, blood, or pleural fluid.[1070]

HEMOPHILUS (BORDETELLA) PERTUSSIS

This Gram-negative organism causes whooping cough (pertussis). Although it has been assumed that this disease was largely eradicated by immunization, recent studies suggest that immunity may not be as long-lasting as was thought and that the disease may be occurring more often in adults.[1072] Pathologically, acute pertussis is characterized by endobronchitis and endobronchiolitis, which may progress to peribronchitis, interstitial pneumonitis, ulceration of the bronchial epithelium, and bronchial obstruction.[961]

In a review of the chest roentgenograms of 556 children with pertussis, Fawcitt and Parry[1073] found various combinations of atelectasis (48 per cent), segmental pneumonia (26 per cent) usually in the lower lobes or middle lobe, and hilar lymphnode enlargement (30 per cent). No necropsies were performed, so there is no proof that the pneumonia was caused by *H. pertussis*—it could have resulted from secondary infection. A fairly common although not distinctive feature of the pulmonary disease is its tendency to conglomerate contiguous to the heart, thus obscuring the cardiac borders; this has been designated the "shaggy-heart sign,"[325] and it has been suggested that its presence connotes a more severe and prolonged illness.

Acute pertussis usually affects children below the age of two years and is associated with the characteristic clinical picture of paroxysmal cough ending in a whoop. Adults rarely show the fullblown picture of "whoop" associated with vomiting, usually manifesting no more than a short-lived mild paroxysmal cough; thus it may be more difficult to diagnose the condition in adults. Acute pertussis engenders a moderate to severe degree of lymphocytosis. Diagnosis depends on positive culture from nasopharyngeal swabbing on Bordet-Gengou medium; a fluorescent antibody technique has proved of some use in diagnosis.

PASTEURELLA TULARENSIS

Pasteurella tularensis is responsible for tularemia, a disease largely affecting rodents and small mammals; insects act as both reservoirs and vectors. The organism is a Gram-negative, nonmotile bacillus which grows best on blood-glucose-cysteine agar or after inoculation of purulent material into mice. Acute pulmonary tularemia is relatively rare compared with other bacterial pneumonias but has been reported from all areas of the U.S.A., Canada, and Scandinavia. Man may be infected via various routes: the organism may gain entry through an open sore on the hands while he is skinning infected rabbits; certain insects (ticks, deer flies, and mosquitoes) may transmit the disease from animal to man through a bite (in addition, the tick may pass the organism on to its offspring); or the disease may be acquired by the ingestion of contaminated meat from infected animals or the inhalation of culture material in the laboratory.

Four forms of the disease have been described, depending on pathogenesis: (1) *the ulceroglandular form*, consisting in an ulcerated cutaneous lesion and regional lymph-node enlargement; (2) *the oculoglandular form*, in which the organism enters the eye and results in acute inflammation; (3) *the typhoidal form*, which is associated with bacteremia and is seen chiefly following the ingestion of contaminated meat but may follow any mode of entry; and (4) *the pulmonary form*, which results from the inhalation of organisms, chiefly by laboratory workers.

Pathologically, the pulmonary form is manifested in the peripheral parenchyma between interlobular septa. The regional lymph nodes usually are enlarged and contain abscesses. Histologically, there is widespread necrosis surrounded by an inflammatory zone containing mononuclear cells and polymorphonuclear leukocytes. The alveolar cells become swollen and there is mononuclear-cell infiltration of the alveolar walls; the inflammatory exudate is chiefly intra-alveolar. Only occasionally does an abscess perforate the bronchial wall and form a cavity, giving rise to the subsequent expectoration of necrotic material. Arteritis and thrombosis are apparent in the pulmonary arteries.

Roentgenographically, the pattern is said to be distinctive; homogeneous consolidation occurs within the substance of any lobe, tends to be oval, and has been likened to an acute lung abscess before cavitation develops.[1075] The margin of the consolidation has been described both as well-circumscribed[1075] and indistinct.[474, 1074] Oval areas of parenchymal consolidation averaging approximately 2×8 cm were identified in 15 of 17 cases described by Overholt and his colleagues;[474, 1074] in 12 cases the lesions were solitary, without lobar predilection, and in three they were multiple; a similar pattern was described previously.[1076] Other reported roentgenographic changes include "stringy" peribronchial shadows and "diffusely scattered lesions."[1076] Hilar lymph-node enlargement occurs in 25 to 50 per cent of cases,[1074, 1076, 1077] and pleural effusion occurs with about the same frequency. The hilar-node enlarge-

ment is characteristically ipsilateral. Cavitation is rare.

The diagnosis of tularemia may be suspected first because of occupational exposure: a butcher, a hunter, or a laboratory worker gives a history of recently skinning or eating wild rabbits or a patient reports being bitten recently by a tick; exposure is followed by the development of a peripheral cutaneous ulcer, enlarged draining lymph nodes, acute pulmonary infection, and typhoidal-like symptoms. Pneumonia develops in approximately one third of patients with the ulceroglandular form of the disease and in three quarters of those with the typhoidal form.

The primary form of pulmonary parenchymal involvement occurs chiefly in laboratory workers,[1074] symptoms appearing within two to six days of exposure; symptoms include a feeling of substernal tightness, dry cough, and pleuritic chest pain; somewhat later the cough may become productive, occasionally of bloody material. Physical findings in the chest usually are minimal.

Cultures may be made directly from skin lesions, lymph nodes, or sputum. Blood cultures are rarely positive. Inoculation into mice or guinea pigs produces necrotic foci in the liver, spleen, and lymph nodes, and cultures should be made from these organs on blood-glucose-cysteine agar. The white-cell count usually is normal or low; leukocytosis is rare. Serial agglutination tests, with or without positive cultures, will permit positive diagnosis, a rise in antibody titer occurring on the eighth to tenth day after onset of infection. A highly specific tuberculin-like delayed-reaction skin test has been reported, which becomes postive during the first week of the disease coincidentally with the development of agglutinins.[1078]

PASTEURELLA PESTIS

This organism is the cause of plague, a disease which used to occur in world-wide pandemics but which now has been largely controlled by public-health measures. *Pasteurella pestis* is a short ovoid bipolar Gram-negative bacillus containing a potent endotoxin; it grows rather slowly on blood agar and is highly virulent for mice and guinea pigs.

Although in the western world at least,

the plague generally is considered a disease more of historic interest than of professional concern, reports have appeared in recent years of a case in a laboratory worker in Maryland, U.S.A.,[1079] and of an epidemic in Vietnam;[1080] endemic areas still remain in Asia, Africa, and South America. Epidemics in man usually are preceded by an outbreak of plague in the local rodent population, usually in rats but also in squirrels and tarabagans. Fleas (usually the rat flea, *Xenopsylla cheopis*) from infected rodents disseminate the disease in man: after a blood meal and while still adherent to the host they regurgitate large numbers of bacilli, which give rise within one to five days to a local lesion usually on the leg. Regional lymph nodes become enlarged and extremely tender, and the overlying skin becomes firm and purplish: this is known as bubonic plague. Bacteremia and septicemia resulting from these infected buboes may lead to secondary pneumonia; once the organism has gained entry to the lungs the infection may be passed from man to man by airborne transmission. The mortality rate without antibiotic therapy is 100 per cent.

Pathologically, plague pneumonia is characterized by severe bronchitis and alveolitis; patchy areas of parenchymal disease tend to become confluent, with the formation of large areas of nonsegmental homogeneous consolidation. The consolidated area is grayish-red and is surrounded by a hemorrhagic zone. Microscopically, severe hemorrhagic pulmonary edema is seen, the alveolar exudate containing polymorphonuclear leukocytes, macrophages, and many organisms; hyaline membranes may be present.

Roentgenographically, the pattern is one of nonsegmental homogeneous parenchymal consolidation, which may be extensive and occasionally simulates diffuse bilateral pulmonary edema but does not cavitate. Pleural effusion may be present. Until the advent of antibiotics, plague pneumonia was invariably fatal within two to four days; appropriate antibiotic therapy now results in complete resolution in the majority of cases.[1080]

The diagnosis of bubonic plague should be suspected from the combination of confluent pneumonia, tender enlarged peripheral lymph nodes, and a history of contact with rats in an endemic area. Primary pneumonic plague is fulminating, with high fever, dyspnea, cyanosis, and a rapidly downhill course. Cough and the expectoration of bloody frothy material may occur. Pleural pain is common.

An unusual syndrome has been described by Conrad and his associates[1080] occurring exclusively in women in endemic areas; these women examine each other's hair for lice and fleas, which they kill by biting them; the result is as might be anticipated—acute peritonsillar abscesses and pneumonia.

The diagnosis may be established by culture of the sputum, blood, or material aspirated from an enlarged lymph node; similarly, mouse or guinea-pig inoculation provokes a diagnostic reaction. Most patients have mild to moderate leukocytosis. Antibodies are present during the second week of the illness and may be demonstrated by agglutination or complement-fixation tests.

PASTEURELLA SEPTICA

This organism usually affects domestic, farm, and wild animals which rarely infect man through a bite or scratch. Like *Pasteurella pestis*, *P. septica* (*P. multocida*) is a small Gram-negative bipolar-staining nonmotile rod which grows slowly on ordinary media.

When the organism is isolated in man, usually it is found in the sputum of patients with bronchiectasis; thus the roentgenographic features are nonspecific. The diagnosis may be made by culture of a heavy growth of the organism from patients with chronic lung disease who have a history of close contact with dogs, cats, cattle, or sheep.[1081] The finding in 1967 of a significant titer of serum agglutinins in one patient and the discovery of clumps of the organism in material aspirated from liver abscesses in another[1081] suggest that *P. septica* may operate as a pathogen more frequently than had been suspected.

BACTERIUM ANITRATUM

B. anitratum is an extremely rare cause of pneumonia;[1082, 1084] it is a large (0.8μ) Gram-negative diplococcus which is encapsulated and may be either motile or nonmotile. It is distinguished from *Neisseria* by the large white or mucoid colonies it forms on agar and by its inability to reduce nitrates.[1082]

In the lungs, *B. anitratum* can produce severe acute air-space pneumonia, even in patients without underlying disease.[1085] Empyema is frequent,[1082, 1084] and the organism has been cultured and was presumed to be the cause of empyema in patients with bronchopleural fistulae.[1084]

Clinically, patients complain of pleuritic pain, fever, nausea and vomiting, and purulent expectoration. Leukocytosis is usual.

BRUCELLA SPECIES

Brucella organisms (*B. melitensis, B. abortus, B. suis*) cause pneumonia very rarely. In a review of 228 cases of bacteriologically proved brucellosis, Pfischner and associates[1083] found complaints of respiratory symptoms (cough, sputum, or chest pain) in only a very small percentage; minor abnormalities were detected on physical examination of the chest in 34 patients (15 per cent) but none showed roentgenographic evidence of pulmonary disease. Small fleeting pneumonias and granulomatous lesions have been described.[961, 1086]

Brucella organisms are Gram-positive rods which require exposure to 10 per cent carbon dioxide for culture. The various species are differentiated on the basis of biochemical and serologic tests.

Symptoms of brucellosis include musculoskeletal pain, sweats, chills, and malaise. Splenomegaly and peripheral lymph-node enlargement are found in 50 per cent of patients. The white-cell count is normal or low. Agglutination and skin tests are dependable and specific.

MALLEOMYCES MALLEI

This organism is the cause of glanders, a disease primarily of horses and rarely of man. It has been reported from many areas throughout the world but appears to be controlled in the western hemisphere. The disease is communicated from horses to horses or man, and from man to man.

M. mallei is a Gram-negative bacillus; it grows on ordinary culture media and is antigenically separable from *Ps. pseudomallei*, the organism responsible for melioidosis.

The usual manifestation of glanders is as cellulitis of the face, commonly with extension to regional lymph nodes. Involvement of the lungs is characterized by acute pneumonia, usually with abscess formation, empyema, and hilar lymph-node enlargement.

Like melioidosis, the clinical picture varies from an acute fulminating disease to chronic granulomatous disease simulating tuberculosis; it is possible that the majority of patients are asymptomatic. The disease should be suspected in persons residing in Asia or South America who are exposed to horses and in whom oral and nasal ulcers develop, with nodules along the lymphatics, and acute or chronic pneumonia. The organism grows readily on ordinary culture media and is fatal to guinea pigs on inoculation. The white-cell count may be normal or low. Agglutination and complement-fixation tests are available, and a skin test using a sterile culture filtrate known as mallein is highly specific.

PNEUMONIA DUE TO ANAEROBIC ORGANISMS

Pneumonia and empyema resulting from organisms which require anaerobic conditions for culture frequently are associated with oropharyngeal sepsis in persons with poor oral hygiene; in such circumstances, responsible organisms include fusiform bacilli, spirochetes, and microaerophilic streptococci. When pulmonary involvement is associated with infections of the gastrointestinal and genitourinary systems, the causative organisms usually are *Bacteroides* species and *Clostridium perfringens*. Most laboratories do not routinely culture under anaerobic conditions, and it is probable that many cases of pneumonia due to anaerobic organisms are falsely attributed to various potential pathogens that grow readily on standard culture media and are commonly found in the upper respiratory tract of healthy people. Although it is likely that lung abscesses due to anaerobic organisms are more frequent than is indicated by the results of routine (aerobic) cultures, general improvement in oral hygiene undoubtedly has resulted in a marked reduction in the frequency of such infections. The pneumonia and abscesses that result from aspiration in association with poor oral hygiene usually develop in the posterior portions of the lungs indicating that aspiration tends to occur when patients are supine, while they are sleeping or are comatose as a result of alcoholic overindulgence or drug-taking.

BACTEROIDES SPECIES

Bacteroides species include two organisms which are known to cause human infection, *B. fragilis* and *B. fungiformis.* These organisms, which are found normally in the gastrointestinal and genital tracts, are Gram-negative, nonmotile, anaerobic, pleomorphic rods which vary from minute coccoid to long filamentous forms. Infections usually involve the pharynx (particularly the tonsils and peritonsillar area), the female genital tract, the bowel, and the peritoneum.[1087] Pneumonia tends to develop predominantly in two groups of patients, women in their thirties who have pelvic inflammatory disease and elderly men.[1088] Of 82 patients with pneumonia and empyema caused by Gram-negative organisms, Tillotson and Lerner[1088] found 11 (13 per cent) to be due to *Bacteroides* species. These authors felt that other disease was present in most cases and probably contributed to increased susceptibility; it is clear, however, that concomitant disease need not necessarily be present, since cases have been described in persons who were in the best of health at the time of onset of pneumonia and empyema.[1089, 1090]

The lungs may be affected in either of two ways. (1) Aspiration of infected material from the upper respiratory tract may result in pneumonia which tends to involve the posterior portions of the lungs; and (2) septic infarctions may result from emboli arising in veins in the peritonsillar area or pelvis, thrombosis developing as a result of local infection in the pharynx, genitourinary system, or gastrointestinal tract. Infarcts usually occur in the lower lobes and commonly are associated with abscess formation. It is probable that this form of the disease is more common than

is generally suspected, since anaerobic cultures are carried out so seldom.

These organisms, either alone or more commonly in combination with microaerophilic streptococci, penetrate deep into the respiratory bronchioles and alveoli, where they cause acute air-space pneumonia. Necropsies have revealed moderate interstitial and alveolar mononuclear-cell infiltration, with small abscesses associated with polymorphonuclear infiltrates in some cases.[1088]

Roentgenographically, the disease is usually localized to the lower lobes and is in the form of patchy or confluent nonsegmental homogeneous consolidation.[1088] Cavitation is particularly common in those cases believed to be due to septic infarcts. Empyema is almost invariable and may be associated with sufficient gas production to be visible roentgenographically. The empyema may obscure the underlying parenchymal disease.

Clinically, patients characteristically have little or no fever and do not appear acutely ill; although the onset usually is insidious, it may resemble acute pneumonia of other etiology. Expectorated material may be foul-smelling and sometimes contains blood.[1088] Some of these patients complain of pleural pain, and bacteremia may give rise to shaking chills. Physical findings vary considerably but may be characteristic of parenchymal consolidation. The white-cell count is above 15,000 in most cases and as high as 25,000 per c mm in some, with many polymorphonuclear leukocytes. Anemia is common, as illustrated by the group of patients described by Tillotson and Lerner[1088] whose average hemoglobin was 8.8 g. Pleural fluid tends to be thick and foul-smelling and may contain blood and many polymorphonuclear leukocytes.

When pneumonia develops in patients with poor oral hygiene, pharyngeal infection or disease of the gastrointestinal or genitourinary tracts (particularly if there is evidence of thrombophlebitis in the areas of infection), *Bacteroides* species should be strongly suspected as a possible etiology. Aspiration from the pleural cavity of foul greenish material which shows many Gram-positive pleomorphic organisms on smear is strong supporting evidence for the diagnosis; confirmation may be obtained by anaerobic culture on solid enriched media or in thioglycollate broth.

Microaerophilic Streptococcus

Microaerophilic streptococci often are found in association with *Bacteroides* species in patients with aspiration pneumonia and abscesses. They are Gram-positive anaerobic organisms, usually smaller than the common aerobic streptococci, and grow in short or long chains. Culture should be carried out in an anaerobic atmosphere containing 10 per cent carbon dioxide.[1091]

The roentgenographic picture is one of segmental bronchopneumonia, often associated with abscess formation and cavitation. Empyema develops in most cases; aspiration may permit isolation of the organism in pure culture.[1091] The disease usually is insidious in onset, and the diagnosis seldom is suspected until purulent, foul-smelling sputum or empyema fluid become evident.

Fusiform Bacilli and Spirochetes

The fusiform bacilli (*Fusobacterium melaninogenicum, F. fusiformis, F. ramosus,* and *F. fragilis*) and oral treponemata (*Borrelia vincenti*) act in concert to produce gingivitis, pharyngitis (Vincent's angina), and aspiration pneumonia. Fusiform bacilli are small Gram-negative anaerobic nonmotile organisms with tapered ends which may be distinguished from Bacteroides by biologic and biochemical reactions. The advent of antibiotics and the adoption of the sitting rather than supine position for tonsillectomy have reduced to a remarkable degree the incidence of pulmonary infection due to these organisms, although occasional cases are still seen particularly in alcoholics with poor oral hygiene who tend to aspirate during alcoholic coma.

The pathologic and roentgenographic findings associated with aspiration of infected material depend in large measure on the consistency of the material: if it is watery, it will penetrate to the peripheral air spaces, with resultant air-space edema, pneumonia, and sometimes abscess formation; if the material is bulky or contains solid particles, it may impact in larger airways, with consequent suppurative bronchitis, segmental bronchopneumonia, and eventually bronchiectasis.

Pneumonia caused by fusiform bacilli and spirochetes should be suspected in any patient with gingivitis or Vincent's angina whose breath or expectorated purulent material develops a foul odor. Smears of sputum showing a predominance of *Fusiform bacilli* and *Spirochetes* will confirm the suspicion.

Acute Lung Abscess Secondary to Aspiration

One of the complications of aspiration pneumonia is acute lung abscess. Purulent gingivitis may lead to the contamination of aspirate by organisms which are commonly found in the mouth but which may increase greatly in numbers when aspirated with purulent material into the bronchial tree. Acute inflammation and necrosis develop distal to a partly or completely obstructed bronchus. Multiple organisms are usually present, including anaerobic streptococci, fusiform bacilli, and *Spirochaetaceae;* in one series of 31 patients with lung abscess, the organism changed from Gram-positive to Gram-negative in 90 per cent of cases.[1699]

Roentgenographically, aspiration pneumonia usually presents as segmental homogeneous consolidation or as a peripheral mass. Despite the development of extensive necrosis, liquefied material may not gain access to the bronchial tree, with the result that the mass may persist unchanged for many weeks while the patient receives intermittent and inadequate antibiotic therapy. Only when perforation occurs into the bronchial tree will the true nature of the lesion become apparent. Acute lung abscess typically presents as a thick-walled irregular cavity in the posterior portion of the lung. An air-fluid level is commonly observed and there may be some degree of consolidation in the surrounding parenchyma. Early diagnosis is important, since the organisms leading to this complication are almost invariably sensitive to penicillin;[1092] in fact, the use of antibiotics has resulted in a marked decrease in the incidence of lung abscess secondary to aspiration.[1700-1702]

It is to be emphasized that not all lung abscesses resulting from aspiration are acute; both onset and course may be chronic and insidious and may be associated with a rather unimpressive history. Clubbing is not uncommon in these more chronic forms.[1702]

CLOSTRIDIUM PERFRINGENS

C. perfringens (*C. welchii*) is an anaerobic Gram-positive bacillus which frequently is a saprophytic contaminant in patients with burns or injuries to the skin and muscle. Pneumonia develops in some cases, either as primary disease or in association with bacteremia following attempted criminal abortion.[1093, 1094] Primary pneumonia usually occurs in patients with underlying pulmonary or cardiac disease;[1094] empyema is common and may be present as a pyopneumothorax as a result of gas formation by the bacilli. The diagnosis may be suspected from the presence of foul-smelling pus aspirated from the pleural space.

Two other organisms of the genus *Clostridium*—*C. tetani* and *C. botulinum*—may be associated with respiratory disease of the neuromuscular type (*see* page 1260).

MYCOBACTERIAL INFECTIONS OF THE LUNGS

Various species of the genus *Mycobacterium* may cause disease of the lungs and pleura and by far the most important of these is *M. tuberculosis*, which is responsible for 95 to 99 per cent of pulmonary mycobacterial infections. *Mycobacterium bovis*, formerly a common cause of disease, usually in children and often involving lymph nodes, gastrointestinal tract, and bones, has all but disappeared from the North American continent, due to control of the disease in cattle and the pasteurization of milk. Disease due to *M. bovis* is still prevalent in areas where hygiene is inadequate to eradicate the organism; pulmonary involvement occurs chiefly by dissemination from extrapulmonary foci. Since the pathologic and roentgenographic manifestations of disease caused by *M. bovis* and *M. tuberculosis* are identical, no further discussion of the former appears warranted except to emphasize the importance of identifying the organism on culture in suspicious cases, because of its insensitivity to drugs ordinarily employed in the treatment of tuberculosis. *Mycobacterium avium* also is responsible for a small number of cases of pulmonary disease in humans; this organism has different cultural characteristics from *M. tuberculosis* and *M. bovis*, and is highly pathogenic to birds and swine; culturally it strongly resembles Runyon's group-III atypical mycobacteria.

With the control of *M. tuberculosis* and the improvement in methods of culture in recent years, several other mycobacteria—the atypical, anonymous, or unclassified mycobacteria (*see* page 640)—have been recognized as infrequent causes of pulmonary disease. The pathologic and roentgenographic changes produced by this group of organisms are virtually identical to those of *M. tuberculosis*.

MYCOBACTERIUM TUBERCULOSIS

Epidemiology

Although according to the National Tuberculosis Association[1095] any mycobacterial disease of the lungs other than that caused by *M. leprae* can be designated as tuberculosis, the term usually implies and sometimes is restricted to infections caused by *M. tuberculosis*. Tuberculosis is world-wide in distribution but is found in greatest incidence where there is crowding and poverty. At the turn of the century it was the most common cause of death in the U.S.A., but in subsequent decades the tremendous progress made in both diagnosis and therapy have greatly reduced both the rate of infection and the mortality rate, particularly the latter. In 1965, in the U.S.A. an estimated 35 million persons were tuberculin-sensitive, 320,000 were registered as having tuberculosis and 105,000 of these had active disease.[1096] Although these figures show that a problem still exists in the U.S.A., the true magnitude of the impact of tuberculosis on society may be recognized more clearly by a consideration of the situation in India, where public-health measures in the main are primitive and a large proportion of the population is illiterate. Whereas less than 20 per cent of the total population of the U.S.A. had positive tuberculin skin tests in 1965, in India 27 per cent of children under the age of five years are positive reactors and 90 per cent of the 40-year-olds are strong reactors to tuberculin. Of even greater significance is the observation that 1.5 per cent of the population of India is estimated to have tuberculosis on the basis of roentgenographic abnormalities in the chest.[1097]

Although active pulmonary tuberculosis may develop at any age, infants, adolescents at the age of puberty, and the aged are particularly susceptible. Negroes appear to be much more susceptible to infection than Caucasians. In women there is a tendency for the incidence to level off or even fall slightly after the child-bearing period, whereas in men the incidence increases gradually into the late fifties. In recent years the older male has been shown to be a frequent source of newly acquired infection.[1098-1100] The high incidence of active pulmonary tuberculosis in this age group may be explained partly by the fact that many of these people are indigent and poorly nourished and live in an environment lacking modern sanitary conveniences; undoubtedly a much more significant factor is that this older age group represents the survivors of a child population which was heavily infected early in the twentieth century and which is now showing endogenous reactivation of the disease.

The Causative Organism

Mycobacteria are aerobic nonmotile rods. They possess an affinity for certain aniline dyes (particularly carbol fuchsin) which are not removed on exposure to acid—thus, they are acid-fast. Enrichment of the ordinary laboratory media by the addition of egg, potato, blood, or albumin is required to produce growth on culture. Growth is slow, requiring two to eight weeks; the colonies are opaque, white to cream, and have a wrinkled surface. M. tuberculosis is highly pathogenic for guinea pigs but not for rabbits or chickens. Strains which have become isoniazid-resistant lose their pathogenicity for guinea pigs and the endogenous catalase which is normally present in M. tuberculosis. Man acquires pulmonary tuberculosis by inhalation of droplets carrying this organism. In most cases, this means repeated or constant contact with an individual who has cavitary disease and whose sputum is highly positive for the bacilli. Disease in a child can be traced to parents or grandparents as a source of infection in many cases.

Allergy and Immunity

Reaction of the body to the tubercle bacillus depends upon the natural immunity of the host and upon the presence or absence of tissue hypersensitivity and acquired immunity. The tissues of an individual who has never previously been infected show an entirely different response to exogenous *tuberculosis* than will those of a person previously infected who is reinfected either from an exogenous source or from reactivation of dormant bacilli within his body. The reasons for these differences lie within the still vague and controversial properties of allergy and immunity with respect to *tuberculosis*.

If man or an appropriate animal is infected with tubercle bacilli or is vaccinated with attenuated organisms such as BCG (bacillus of Calmette and Guerin), the tissues become sensitive to the protein (tuberculin) of the organism: this represents *hypersensitivity* or *allergy*. When such a person or animal subsequently is injected with extracts of *tuberculosis*,* an area of edema develops (with or without erythema) at the site of intradermal injection; this area measures 10 mm or more in diameter and indicates reaction to the organism. Most authorities believe that "acquired allergy" brings with it some degree of "acquired immunity," a conclusion based on animal experimentation as well as on the difference in morphologic changes in the person who is primarily infection compared with those in the person who is "reinfected." This "acquired immunity" is cellular in type; humoral antibodies have been demonstrated by hemagglutination and agar-diffusion precipitation techniques but their immunologic significance is not yet known.

The basic tissue response in patients sensitized by previous infection or vaccination is "caseous necrosis." Although this reaction usually is accepted as being allergic in type, there is no doubt that it also

---

*PPD (purified protein derivative) prepared from a single strain of M. *tuberculosis* and precipitated with ammonium sulphate; or OT (old tuberculin) prepared by heat sterilization of cultures of tubercle bacilli in liquid medium and subsequent evaporation of the filtrate to one-tenth its volume.

serves to destroy numerous mycobacteria, thus providing a useful defensive role. This property of sensitivity and immunity acquired from previous infection also appears to act by localizing the disease process.

Although controversy still remains as to the mechanism of acquired immunity in tuberculosis and its relationship to allergy, there is even less known about the property of *natural resistance* to tuberculous infections. It seems that the white man has a natural resistance to tuberculosis which is considerably greater than that of his black brother. Natural resistance appears to vary with age, since infants and pubertal adolescents are more prone to the infection. Undoubtedly persons under physical strain and with poor nutrition are more susceptible to infection, particularly those with underlying diseases such as diabetes, silicosis, measles, or alcoholism.

Since patients who have been exposed for the first time show different pathologic, roentgenologic, and clinical features than those who are superinfected or have reactivation of previous disease, it is logical to consider the disease processes under the separate headings of "primary tuberculosis" and "secondary or reinfection tuberculosis." However, it should be remembered that the pathologically and roentgenologically apparent changes produced by so-called "reinfection" tuberculosis are conditioned by allergy and acquired immunity; since these qualities of tissue reaction develop within four to six weeks after primary infection, it is obvious that the "reinfection" type of response may occur from the primary infection itself if it is not promptly checked by the natural defense mechanisms of the body. Progression of the primary complex to chronic destructive or "reinfection" tuberculosis without a latent interval has been called progressive primary tuberculosis.[1101]

PRIMARY PULMONARY TUBERCULOSIS

Primary pulmonary tuberculosis occurs predominantly in children and is particularly prevalent in geographic areas where control measures are inadequate. However, primary tuberculosis in the adult is increasing in incidence as a result of new infection being acquired by people residing in areas where prophylactic and therapeutic measures resulted in a low incidence of infection during childhood.

Pathologic Characteristics

The reaction to the tubercle bacillus in a previously uninfected host depends upon both the number of organisms aspirated and the inherent resistance of the host. The initial reaction is exudative and consists of dilation of capillaries, swelling of endothelial and alveolar lining cells, and an outpouring of fibrin, macrophages, and polymorphonuclear leukocytes into the alveolar spaces. During this stage, alveolar structure remains intact. With the onset of hypersensitivity—usually by six weeks after initial infection—caseous necrosis develops in the center of the lesion. Coincident with caseation (which tends to remain solid), the large number of microorganisms present in the exudative phase tend to disappear. Once caseation has occurred, the process of healing begins, with invasion by fibroblasts, progressive hyalinization, and, if the lesion is sufficiently large, calcification and occasionally ossification.

Extension of the parenchymal infection to regional lymph nodes via lymphatic channels is common, so that enlargement of regional lymph nodes is a frequent manifestation; organisms from the involved nodes may gain access to the blood stream. Hematogenous dissemination probably is common but seldom produces the full-blown clinical picture of miliary or extrapulmonary tuberculosis, because of the limited number of organisms that cause the bacteremia and the native immunity of the host.

Spread of the infection may occur into the pleural or pericardial cavities from caseous foci in lung parenchyma adjacent to these serous membranes. Lymphatic spread may occur from the pleura, usually to the upper lumbar vertebrae.

In a minority of patients, primary disease may progress directly to a chronic destructive form of "reinfection" tuberculosis; this transition occurs particularly in infants under the age of one, is uncommon between the ages of two and 12 years, and has been estimated to occur in about 10 per cent of cases in adolescents and young adults.[1101]

Roentgenographic Manifestations

Primary infection with the tubercle bacillus within the thorax usually affects one or a combination of four structures—the pulmonary parenchyma, the mediastinal and hilar lymph nodes, the tracheobronchial tree, and the pleura. One of the most complete analyses of the roentgenologic changes of primary tuberculosis was reported recently by Weber and his associates;[1102] of 235 children with primary tuberculosis admitted to a large sanitorium in Massachusetts over a six-year period, 85 were selected for study by these authors on the basis of positive culture of *M. tuberculosis*. Chest roentgenograms were available on 83 of the 85 patients.

PARENCHYMAL INVOLVEMENT. The upper lobes were slightly more frequently involved than the lower, although there were no significant differences between left and right lungs or between anterior and posterior segments. This tendency to predominant involvement of the upper lobes has been noted by others,[1103, 1104] although Jacobson and Shapiro reported that parenchymal disease frequently but not invariably locates in the apex of a lower lobe.[1105] Occasionally more than one area of parenchymal consolidation is present. Sometimes an entire lobe may be consolidated, often the right middle lobe; lobar involvement probably is due to a combination of parenchymal consolidation (due to direct invasion by the organism) and atelectasis (resulting from bronchial obstruction due to enlarged lymph nodes or endobronchial disease).

The parenchymal reaction typically is that of air-space consolidation, ranging in diameter from 1 to 7 cm (Figure 7–4). The consolidation tends to be homogeneous in density and to have ill-defined margins except where it abuts against a fissure. Parenchymal involvement in primary disease in adults appears to differ little from that seen in children.

LYMPH-NODE INVOLVEMENT. Hilar or paratracheal lymph-node enlargement is the roentgenographic finding that clearly differentiates primary from "reinfection" tuberculosis (Figure 7–4). Of the 83 cases studied by Weber and his colleagues,[1102] 80 showed clear-cut roentgenographic evidence of hilar or paratracheal lymph-node enlargement (or both); because of

obliteration of the hilar and mediastinal shadow by contiguous pulmonary disease it was impossible to assess accurately the presence or absence of node enlargement in the remaining three. In 13 of the 80 cases, node enlargement was bilateral and hilar, in 34 it was predominantly unilateral and hilar, and in 33 it was unilateral and both hilar and paratracheal, predominantly on the right side. Lymph-node enlargement appears to be less frequent in adults than in children (Figure 7–5); Stead and his associates[1101] observed node enlargement in only 16 (43 per cent) of 37 adult patients whom they considered to have primary disease largely on the basis of conversion of the tuberculin reaction.

From these studies it appears that the diagnosis of primary pulmonary tuberculosis should be held in some doubt in the absence of lymph-node enlargement, particularly in children. It has been pointed out that in some cases lymph-node enlargement is the only detectable roentgenographic evidence of primary tuberculosis,[1105] even in adults.[1106]

AIRWAY INVOLVEMENT. Tracheobronchial disease is common and usually is the result of the compression of bronchi by enlarged lymph nodes;[1102, 1107] less commonly, tuberculous granulation tissue may accumulate in the mucosa of the bronchi and may be identified bronchoscopically.[1102, 1108] Weber and his co-workers[1102] identified tracheobronchial changes in 23 (28 per cent) of their 85 patients, including secondary mucosal edema due to pressure from contiguous inflamed lymph nodes. In five cases there was a small opening in the bronchial wall where caseation necrosis in a contiguous lymph node had perforated it; such a change may produce partial or complete occlusion of a bronchus, with resultant peripheral atelectasis, or may actually cause disappearance of segmental or lobar collapse. Atelectasis was identified in 25 (30 per cent) of Weber and his associates' series, and in four it was preceded by obstructive "emphysema." This sequence of obstructive overinflation followed by either atelectasis or combined collapse and consolidation has been noted by others also.[1107, 1108] Of the 25 patients with atelectasis reported by Weber and his colleagues,[1102] the anatomic distribution of collapse was as follows: right upper lobe, six; right middle lobe, one; right middle fers considerably from primary disease in that the tissue reaction appears directed toward localizing the infection and destroying the tubercle bacilli causing it. The disease tends to be largely limited to the apical and posterior segments of the upper lobes and to the superior segment of the lower lobes. The exudative phase is associated with a greater polymorphonuclear leukocytic infiltration than occurs in primary disease, although sometimes there is an outpouring of fibrin into the alveoli, with a paucity of cellular response. Histologically this phase consists in foci of caseous necrosis with surrounding edema, hemorrhage, and mononuclear-cell infiltration. These caseous foci may liquefy and empty into a bronchus, with dissemination of tubercle bacilli through the airways into other areas of the lungs; thus, this may result in a multitude of small foci of air-space disease roentgenologically visible as acinar shadows (see Figure 1–3, page 5). In addition to caseous necrosis, the other hallmark of reinfection tuberculosis is the *tubercle*. Tubercles usually develop at the periphery of a necrotic lesion and are the result of an accumulation of mononuclear macrophages which swell and become pale and which then are known as epithelioid cells. Also, giant cells of Langhan's type which develop in the margins of the tubercles are believed to originate from mononuclear macrophages. The tubercle is surrounded by lymphocytes, fibroblasts, and collagenous tissue. Although necrosis is not necessarily seen in relation to all granulomas, central caseation inevitably develops with time. In more fulminating disease, the exudative lesion predominates and the picture may be one of acute tuberculous pneumonia with consolidation of an entire lobe. More commonly the pattern is one of gradually progressive disease, presumably as a result of dissemination of liquefied caseous material within the airways.

Healing occurs by fibrosis and contracture. The terms "fibrocaseous" and "productive" tuberculosis denote a pattern of cavitation with surrounding thickened fibrotic walls, slow formation of tubercles, and fibrotic replacement. Pathologically, the examination of resected lungs at necropsy reveals some degree of healing in almost all cases of secondary tuberculosis even when the disease is progressing in other areas. Zones of exudation and perifocal edema may disappear completely. Necrotic areas become hyalinized or replaced by collagen or fibrous tissue and may shrink to a point of invisibility. More commonly a slowly progressive invasion of fibroblasts occurs in and around areas of caseous necrosis, reducing the extent of involvement and walling off the caseous foci, thus preventing dissemination via the airways. Calcium may be deposited in caseous foci, although this phenomenon is less common in reinfection than in primary tuberculosis. Since viable tubercle bacilli may be recovered from calcified lesions, the presence of calcification is no proof of cure. Chemotherapy tends to accelerate the process of healing and, in fact, the roentgenographic disappearance of acute exudative disease may be so rapid as to simulate resolution of nontuberculous pneumonia.[1114, 1115] Chemotherapy also has the effect of accelerating the fibrotic reaction; in a serial biopsy study of patients receiving chemotherapy for tuberculous pleurisy, Sohn and associates[1116] found that fibrosis had largely replaced the typical granulomatous appearance by the third month after initiation of treatment; at this stage the changes could be interpreted as no more than nonspecific pleuritis. Even caseous lesions appear to undergo rapid fibrosis in patients receiving chemotherapy; cavities containing caseous material may show inspissation of contents and obliteration of the draining bronchus either by fibrosis or by organization of the exudate within the bronchus. Open cavities often contain no viable organisms and follow-up studies have shown that the relapse rate of "open negative" cavities is virtually nil with modern chemotherapy; occasionally, however, viable organisms may remain in open cavities that are small and thick-walled.[1117]

Roentgenographic Manifestations

ANATOMIC DISTRIBUTION. A characteristic although not unique manifestation of reinfection tuberculosis is a tendency to be localized to the apical and posterior segments of the upper lobes.[648] It has been postulated that this location is related to the high Po_2 in these zones, the result of high ventilation-perfusion ratios.

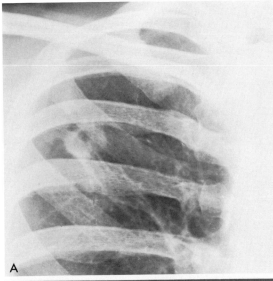

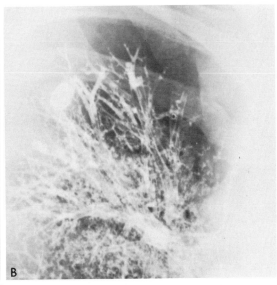

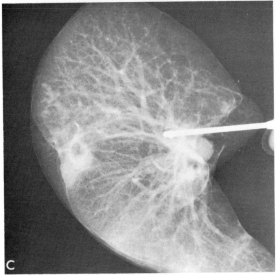

Figure 7-10. **Tuberculous Cavitation: Communication with the Bronchial Tree.** A view of the upper half of the right lung from a posteroanterior roentgenogram (A) reveals a sharply demarcated shadow measuring approximately 2 cm in diameter containing a central radiolucency characteristic of a cavity. Positive sputum. At bronchography (B), opacification of the cavity is well illustrated (such communication occurs in about 50 per cent of tuberculous cavities). A roentgenogram of the resected lobe (C) shows the subpleural location of the lesion and reveals a local indrawing of pleura due probably to cicatrization. Since the contrast material used in bronchography was not barium sulfate, the "wall sign" could not be assessed.

dation; the latter feature has not been observed by us in acute air-space pneumonia of other etiology.

MILIARY TUBERCULOSIS. Although hematogenous dissemination of tubercle bacilli throughout the body is a common occurrence in primary tuberculosis, there is seldom clinical or roentgenographic evidence of miliary spread or multiple organ involvement, presumably because of the small number of bacilli causing the bacteremia and the resistance of the host. If large numbers of tubercle bacilli enter the blood stream, however, there is widespread invasion of tissues and organs. In the lung this is manifested by the appearance of tiny discrete foci widely and uniformly distributed throughout both lungs. (Figure 7-13; *see also* Figure 4-59, page 250). The time interval between dissemination and the development of roentgenographic evidence of disease probably is six weeks or more, during which time the foci are too small for roentgenographic visualization. When they do become visible their appearance is distinctive—tiny, absolutely discrete, pinpoint shadows evenly distributed throughout both lungs. When first visible they measure little more than 1 mm in diameter; in the absence of adequate therapy they may reach 2 to 3 mm in diameter before the patient dies. By this time they may have become almost confluent, presenting what has been termed a "snow-storm" appearance. Rarely, patients die from miliary tuber-

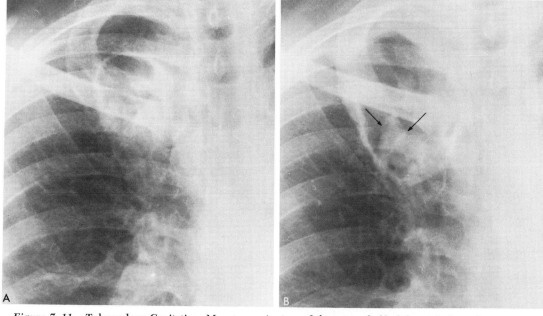

Figure 7–11. **Tuberculous Cavitation: Mycetoma.** A view of the upper half of the right lung from a postero-anterior roentgenogram (*A*) shows a well-defined cavitary lesion measuring approximately 4 cm in diameter. The wall of the cavity is thin but sharply circumscribed. An air-fluid level is not present. Positive sputum. Six weeks later (*B*), the cavity is much larger and now relates to the apical and mediastinal pleura; its wall is somewhat thicker, particularly inferiorly and laterally; a well-defined intracavitary structure can now be identified (*arrows*) which on further study was seen to move freely within the cavity. Proved mycetoma or intracavitary fungus ball in a tuberculous cavity. Increase in the thickness of a cavity wall has been reported to occur frequently in association with a developing mycetoma.

culosis (proved pathologically) without demonstrable abnormality on the chest roentgenogram.[1126]

With appropriate treatment, improvement may be extremely rapid, clearing usually occurring much faster than in nonhematogenous pulmonary tuberculosis.[1127] Roentgenographically, resolution usually is complete and without residua.[1126, 1128] In a review of 68 adult patients with miliary tuberculosis, of whom 23 were followed roentgenographically while under treatment, Biehl[1126] found considerable improvement in nine patients within three weeks of the institution of therapy; in five the chest film was completely normal within five weeks, and in four complete clearing required seven to 22 months. The chest roentgenograms had returned to normal at 16 weeks in the majority of cases and failed to clear completely in only one. The period required to show complete roentgenographic resolution correlated roughly with the extent of initial involvement and with the promptness with which improvement oc-

curred initially. Clearing was shown to occur much more slowly in older than in younger patients.

Although the source of dissemination of tubercle bacilli usually is apparent either clinically or roentgenographically (Figure 7-14), the primary focus is not obvious, even at necropsy, in many cases of miliary tuberculosis.[1126]

TUBERCULOUS BRONCHIECTASIS. Two mechanisms may be involved in the pathogenesis of tuberculous bronchiectasis: (1) the bronchial wall is infected during the active phase of the disease, and the fibrosis and cicatrization which occurs during healing leads to irreversible bronchial dilatation (Figure 7-15); (2) a segmental bronchus is obstructed by compression of enlarged lymph nodes in primary tuberculosis or by bronchostenosis secondary to endobronchial disease, and the result is obstructive pneumonitis and subsequent bronchiectasis. Since the vast majority of cases of reinfection tuberculosis affect the apical and posterior segments of an upper lobe, thereby facili-

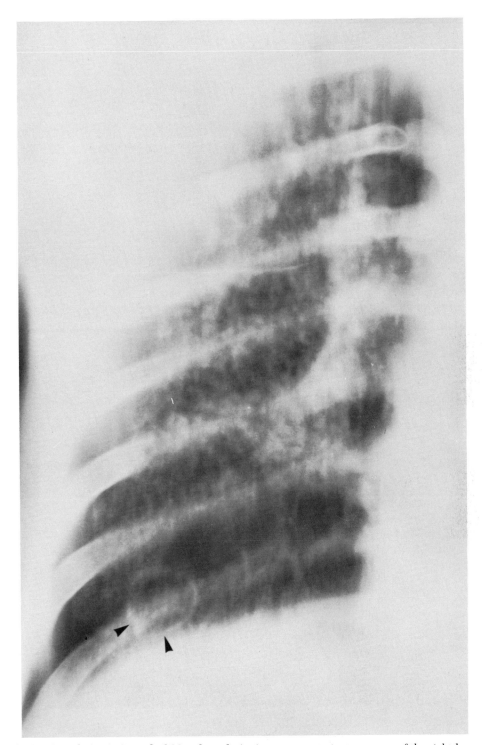

Figure 7–12. **Bronchogenic Spread of *M. tuberculosis.*** An anteroposterior tomogram of the right lung reveals a sharply-defined, thin-walled cavity in the lung base (*arrows*). Throughout the upper two thirds of the lung are numerous, fairly discrete, homogeneous shadows ranging from 4 to 6 mm in diameter—typical acinar shadows. This combination of findings is characteristic and almost pathognomonic of bronchogenic spread of *M. tuberculosis.* The basal cavity was the source of the organisms. *See also* Figures 1–3, page 5, and 4–78, page 270. (Courtesy Dr. David Berger, Royal Edward Chest Hospital, Montreal.)

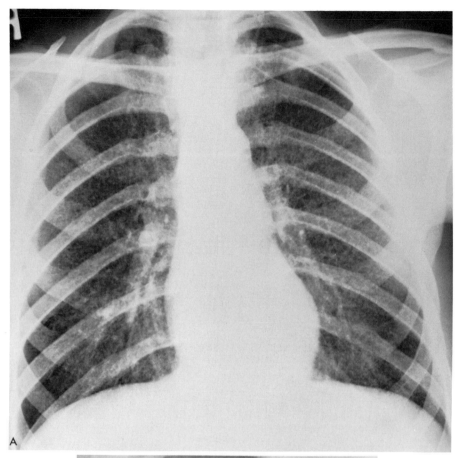

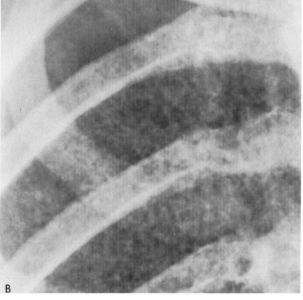

Figure 7–13. **Miliary Tuberculosis.** A posteroanterior roentgenogram (A) shows a myriad of tiny, discrete nodules scattered uniformly throughout both lungs, seen to better advantage in a magnified view of the upper portion of the right lung (B). The shadows are perfectly discrete. Nineteen-year-old man who subsequently developed tuberculous meningitis and expired. As is often the case, there is no roentgenologic evidence in the chest of a source for the widespread hematogenous dissemination.

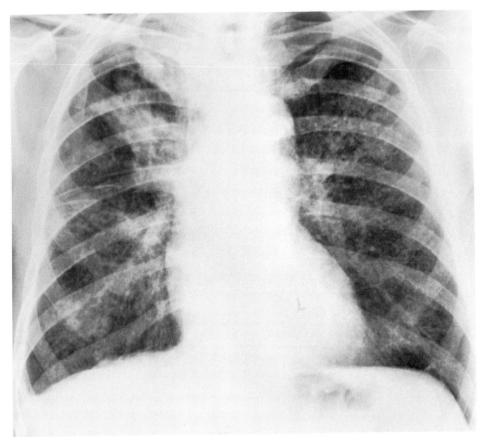

Figure 7–14. **Miliary Tuberculosis.** A posteroanterior roentgenogram reveals a pattern of widely disseminated, nodular shadows throughout both lungs; the shadows are perfectly discrete and uniformly distributed although somewhat larger than the lesions seen in Figure 7–13. In contrast to the situation in Figure 7–13, however, a rather large area of parenchymal consolidation is present in the right upper lobe, representing the source for the hematogenous dissemination; such evidence is the exception rather than the rule in miliary tuberculosis.

tating bronchial drainage, bronchiectasis usually is asymptomatic. Hemoptysis occurs in some cases.

TUBERCULOUS BRONCHOSTENOSIS. In children with primary tuberculosis the tracheobronchial tree is involved chiefly as a result of pressure from enlarged lymph nodes. In reinfection tuberculosis, endobronchial involvement is fairly frequent and occurs particularly in airways that drain a pulmonary cavity. Ulceration of the bronchial mucosa leads eventually to fibrosis and cicatricial bronchostenosis. Of considerable importance is the fact that tuberculous bronchitis may occur in the absence of demonstrable roentgenographic abnormality; ulceration of the bronchial mucosa, which may be identified bronchoscopically although inapparent roentgenographically, often is the source of positive sputum. If the diagnosis is not made promptly and appropriate antituberculosis therapy instituted at once, cicatricial bronchostenosis is almost inevitable with its resultant obstructive atelectasis, pneumonitis, and bronchiectasis (*see* Figure 4–49, page 238). Clinical evidence of a persistent respiratory wheeze may suggest the diagnosis.

TUBERCULOMA. A tuberculoma, which may be a manifestation of either primary or reinfection tuberculosis, is a round or oval lesion situated most commonly in an upper lobe, the right more often than the left.[1129] Tuberculomas range in size from 0.5 to 4 cm or more in diameter and typically are smooth and sharply circumscribed;[612, 1129] up to 25 per cent may be smooth and lobulated.[1129] Small discrete shadows in the immediate vicinity of the main lesion—"satellite" lesions—may be identified in as many as 80 per cent of

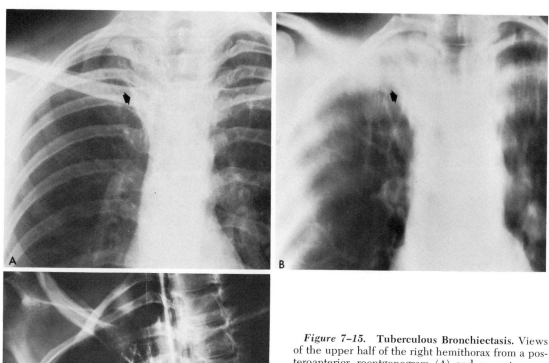

Figure 7–15. **Tuberculous Bronchiectasis.** Views of the upper half of the right hemithorax from a posteroanterior roentgenogram (*A*) and an anteroposterior tomogram (*B*) demonstrate marked loss of volume of the apical segment of the right upper lobe (lateral margin of collapsed segment at *arrows*). The loss of volume is evidenced by local displacement of the trachea to the right and by elevation of the right hilum. A right bronchogram (*C*) shows considerable crowding and uniform dilatation of all branches of the apical segmental bronchus. Proved chronic fibroproductive tuberculosis.

cases.[1129] There may be irregular thickening of the wall of the draining bronchus and, in a small percentage of patients, actual bronchostenosis.

The majority of these lesions remain stable for a long time[1130] and many calcify. The larger the lesion the more likely it is to be active (Figure 7–16), and it has been suggested that tuberculomas measuring more than 3 cm in diameter should be resected.[1130, 1131]

The differential diagnosis of tuberculomas is considered in detail in the section on solitary pulmonary nodules (*see* page 765)

Clinical Manifestations

Most cases of tuberculosis come to the attention of a physician following the discovery of disease on a screening chest roentgenogram. When the diagnosis has been suggested as the result of such a procedure, and the tuberculin reaction is positive, further investigation and follow-up will reveal inactive disease in the majority of cases. Most of these patients will fail to give a history indicative of an active phase of the disease, although some will recollect a particularly severe bout of "pneumonia" with a rather protracted course and persistent pleuritic pain and fever but not documented by chest roentgenography. Many have a family history of one or both parents having suffered from the disease or having died from it.

Only a small percentage of patients with evidence of disease suggesting tuber-

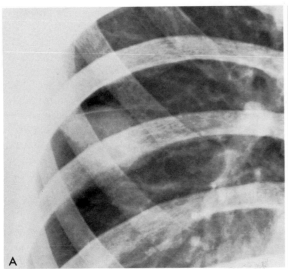
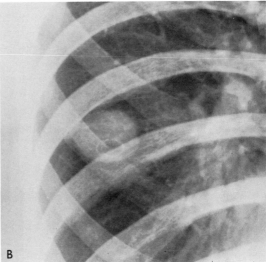
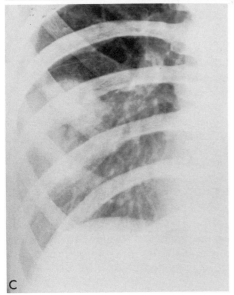

Figure 7–16. **Tuberculoma with Breakdown.** A view of the right mid-lung from a posteroanterior roentgenogram (A) reveals a sharply-circumscribed, oval shadow measuring approximately 3 cm in diameter; a small, calcific ring shadow can be identified in the center of the lesion. The surrounding lung parenchyma is normal. Two years later (B), the shadow is slightly smaller in size and the central ring calcification more evident. Two years later, the patient developed an abrupt onset of an acute respiratory illness; a roentgenogram at that time (C) revealed breakdown of the tuberculoma and the development of acute air-space disease in the surrounding parenchyma. The lobe was resected; proved exudative tuberculosis.

culosis on mass roentgenography will be found to have active disease; mass roentgenography for tuberculosis case-finding has been reported to be responsible for the detection of 10 to 30 per cent of active cases of the disease.[1132, 1133] The yield of positive cases is particularly high if patients are referred for roentgenographic examination by their own physicians.[1133] The routine hospital admission chest roentgenogram also is of major value as a means of detecting early cases:[1134] Allen found that 58 per cent of all cases of tuberculosis in patients admitted to one hospital were discovered by this technique.[1134] Such routine roentgenography is particularly important for antenatal patients.[1135] Whether

or not disease detected during such surveys is active, the majority of patients are well, deny symptoms, and often are somewhat incredulous of the diagnosis.

It is to be emphasized that the diagnosis of tuberculosis discovered on screening chest roentgenography should not be entertained without a positive tuberculin skin test; a negative skin test virtually excludes the diagnosis. This is a most important consideration, since many patients— 59 per cent in one series[1136]—have roentgenograms compatible with tuberculosis, yet have negative tuberculin reactions and subsequently are proved to have disease of nontuberculous etiology.

Many patients with even advanced active pulmonary tuberculosis refuse to admit that they are ill; such patients often are indigent or alcoholic, and it is only with the well-being that comes with treatment that a previous poor state of health is recognized in retrospect. Symptoms when present frequently are nonspecific and do not direct the attention of the patient or the physician to the lungs—tiredness, weakness, anorexia, loss of weight, and a low-grade fever in the afternoon or evening. Direct questioning may elicit a history of recent onset of unproductive or mildly productive cough. Less commonly, patients present with respiratory symptoms, usually a cough which persists after an upper respiratory infection and which may be mildly productive and occasionally associated with hemoptysis. Sometimes the initial complaint is pleuritic chest pain, frequently with fever, and although this symptom is more common in adults a majority of these patients are believed to have primary tuberculosis. Very rarely pleuritic chest pain is associated with spontaneous pneumothorax. Hoarseness usually is a manifestation of laryngeal involvement and is indicative of active disease; in most cases it is associated with a positive sputum. Shortness of breath is uncommon and usually indicates long-standing productive disease. A relatively rare form of onset is that which suggests acute pneumonia, with high fever, sweating, productive cough, pleuritic pain, and tachycardia; such an onset may not be recognized as relating to tuberculous disease.

The past history or family history may provide a clue to the diagnosis; for example, a patient may be known to have had pleurisy with effusion or proved active tuberculosis which was inadequately treated. A history of contact, usually in the family, is common. Patients with chronic disabling diseases such as diabetes or alcoholism, and those receiving corticosteroid therapy, are more susceptible to tuberculosis. Diabetics are particularly prone to develop the disease, often of far-advanced type; of 106 patients with both diabetes and tuberculosis studied by Holden and Hiltz,[1137] 48 were diagnosed as having tuberculosis before the onset of diabetes, 40 were known to have diabetes at the time of onset of the tuberculosis, and in the remaining 18 cases the diag-

noses were made simultaneously. Another study suggested correlation between tuberculosis and the consumption of alcohol, without the generally accepted features of alcoholism.[1138] The development of tuberculosis in patients on long-term corticosteroid therapy[1139] occurs with sufficient frequency that it is considered wise to place tuberculin reactors requiring this form of therapy on prophylactic isoniazid medication. Acute tuberculous infection may develop in association with granulocytopenia; miliary dissemination has been reported to occur in 3 to 4 per cent of patients with myeloid leukemia.[1140] Patients with silicosis also are particularly susceptible to tuberculosis (see page 931).

Every patient with suspected pulmonary tuberculosis should undergo complete physical examination, particularly with reference to the possibility of extrapulmonary lesions. Examination of the chest itself is unrewarding in many cases and rarely provides information of assistance in diagnosis. If an apical lesion is identified on the chest roentgenogram, the presence of posttussic rales on auscultation strongly suggests activity. Physical signs in acute tuberculous pneumonia are the same as in air-space pneumonia of other etiology. In patients with recent bronchial dissemination of disease, rales and rhonchi may be heard extensively over both lungs; diffuse rhonchi may be an indication of tuberculous bronchitis. Cavernous breathing is rarely audible over a peripheral cavity. In chronic pulmonary tuberculosis, rhonchi, prolonged expiration, and decreased breath sounds may indicate a considerable degree of lung destruction associated with secondary "emphysema." When onset of disease is characterized by pain on respiration, a friction rub or signs of pleural effusion or pneumothorax may be heard. Rarely, clinical findings may suggest compression of mediastinal structures by enlarged tuberculous lymph nodes; pericarditis, bronchoesophageal fistula,[1141] erosion of the aorta,[1142] spontaneous paralysis of the phrenic nerve,[1143] and superior vena caval syndrome[2123] have all been reported as complications of tuberculosis involving the mediastinum in adults.

Miliary tuberculosis presents a clinical picture somewhat different from that of other forms of pulmonary involvement.

Negroes appear to be particularly susceptible to this form of the disease; of 68 adult patients with miliary tuberculosis described by Biehl,[1126] 58 were Negro and ten Caucasian; males predominated and 28 patients (41 per cent) were over the age of 60 years. In this series, five of the 14 females under the age of 40 years were pregnant at the time of admission to hospital or had delivered within the ten months before admission. The clinical onset of the disease tends to be insidious, the stated length of illness ranging from three to 15 weeks. Cough, weight loss, weakness, anorexia, and night sweats are common symptoms; signs ascribed to meningeal involvement occur late. In only three of Biehl's cases was there a previous history of known tuberculosis. Funduscopic examination reveals choroidal tubercles in some cases,[4321] and although these lesions are not pathognomonic of tuberculosis they serve to confirm a diagnosis suspected because of a roentgenographic pattern of miliary disease. In contrast to the frequency of hepatosplenomegaly in miliary tuberculosis in children, splenic enlargement was found in only one patient in Biehl's series.

The diagnosis of miliary tuberculosis should be considered in any patient showing a combination of fever and a miliary roentgenographic pattern: other subacute or chronic pulmonary diseases may show a similar roentgenographic picture but seldom are associated with pyrexia.

CLINICAL COURSE. Clinically apparent disease rarely develops in positive tuberculin reactors whose roentgenograms show no abnormality, a fact borne out by the subsequent development of disease in only 35 (2.8 per cent) of the 1323 student nurses with positive tuberculin reactions who were followed up by Myers and his associates.[1144] Chace and his colleagues[1145] reported significant findings in their three-year follow-up study of two groups of Naval and Marine Corps personnel. Active tuberculosis developed in 16 (6 per cent) of the 268 men who were considered to have inactive disease roentgenologically but who were positive reactors, but developed in none of the 493 without roentgenographic evidence of significant abnormality. Reimann[1096] stated that 15 to 30 per cent of patients treated with strepto-

mycin and isoniazid have reactivation of their disease within four years, although a follow-up study of 210 patients treated in a sanatorium[1146] showed relapse in only 6 per cent over a period of six years in contrast to a 37 per cent incidence of relapse observed in a similar series ten years earlier.

Sensitivity studies in patients with reactivated tuberculosis sometimes reveal organisms which are insensitive to the commonly used antituberculous drugs; even some cases of primary tuberculosis may be caused by organisms which are resistant to streptomycin and paraaminosalicylic acid.[1147]

Parenchymal disease rarely develops after adequately treated tuberculous pleural effusion;[1148] it is to be emphasized that, in this context, "adequate therapy" means chemotherapy, since bed rest alone has been shown to be associated with the development of parenchymal lesions in 28 per cent of cases.[1148]

RELATIONSHIP BETWEEN PULMONARY TUBERCULOSIS AND BRONCHOGENIC CARCINOMA. The coexistence of pulmonary tuberculosis and bronchogenic carcinoma has been reported by several authors, and a pathogenetic relationship has been inferred.[1149–1151] Carcinoma of the bronchus involved an area of lung containing pre-existing tuberculosis in 50 per cent and 75 per cent of cases respectively in two series.[1150, 1151] However, certain aspects of these two diseases suggest that their coexistence may be no more than coincidental: for example, both bronchogenic carcinoma and tuberculosis tend to involve predominantly the upper lobes; similarly, the incidence of tuberculosis is increasing in patients in the older age group, when bronchogenic carcinoma is more prone to develop.[1152] In one well-controlled study,[1153] 54 patients with coexisting bronchogenic carcinoma and tuberculosis were compared with 41 nontuberculous patients with bronchogenic carcinoma; the carcinoma was located in the same general area in both series, and it was concluded that in these cases at least there was no significant relationship between the two diseases. In two other series, of 140[1154] and 100[1155] cases of coexistent disease, it was concluded that the high incidence in males, the location, the variety, and the frequency of the various primary lung neoplasms were the same as would be expected in bronchogenic carcinoma without coexisting tuberculosis.

Until convincing evidence is provided to the contrary, we are of the opinion that the coexistence of pulmonary tuberculosis and bronchogenic carcinoma is no more than coincidental.

RELATIONSHIP BETWEEN PULMONARY TUBERCULOSIS AND SARCOIDOSIS. Most specialists in pulmonary disease have encountered one or more patients who, despite a typical clinical and pathologic picture of sarcoidosis, subsequently have acid-fast organisms in their sputum. Since strong evidence is now emerging to the effect that sarcoidosis is caused by atypical mycobacteria, it is possible that the acid-fast organisms in such cases were not *M. tuberculosis*. There is no doubt, however, that *M. tuberculosis* is isolated from the sputum of more patients thought to have sarcoidosis than could be accepted as purely coincidental. It must be admitted that in such situations the tuberculosis may be a complication of sarcoidosis; in fact, the two diseases were coexistent in 29 (13 per cent) of 230 cases of sarcoidosis studied by Scadding.[1156] This same investigator found calcified tracheobronchial nodes in 16 (12 per cent) of 136 patients with sarcoidosis, a percentage almost identical to the incidence of calcified nodes in 256 patients with sarcoidosis studied by Israel and associates.[1157]

It is clear that this long-debated question of the relationship of these two diseases is not settled. It is recommended that patients with persisting pulmonary sarcoidosis, particularly Negroes (since coexistence of the two diseases is more common in this race[1158]) should be watched closely for the development of tuberculosis, with periodic sputum examination and skin testing. Corticosteroid therapy should never be administered without concomitant antituberculosis therapy in patients with sarcoidosis.

Extrapulmonary Tuberculosis

With the exception of tuberculous pleuritis, extrapulmonary involvement in tuberculosis is seldom seen today, perhaps because of improved methods of treatment. However, *M. tuberculosis* is responsible for chronic febrile disease occasionally, particularly in Negroes.

Hematogenous dissemination is a frequent complication of primary tuberculosis and many years may elapse before the involvement of many tissues and organs becomes clinically manifest. Perhaps the most common form of extrapulmonary tuberculosis in the adult is genitourinary, and the discovery of pyuria, hematuria, and albuminuria in a patient who has had pulmonary tuberculosis or who shows roentgenographic evidence of a healed pulmonary lesion should suggest tuberculosis as a possible etiology. The diagnosis of tuberculosis of the kidney and bladder may be established by intravenous pyelography and by urine culture. Tuberculosis of the female genital system usually occurs in the form of salpingitis and oophoritis, manifested clinically by pelvic pain and menstrual disturbances; it is to be noted, however, that menstrual disorders are frequent in pulmonary tuberculosis without genital involvement and their presence need not necessarily mean extension of the disease. In the male, epididymitis, seminal vesiculitis, and prostatitis may occur in some cases. Although formerly common in children, bone and joint involvement, either from hematogenous dissemination or from direct extension via the lymphatic system from the pleura to the thoracic and lumbosacral spine, is rarely seen today. Involvement of the hilar and mediastinal lymph nodes is almost invariable in primary tuberculosis. Control of *Mycobacterium bovis* has resulted in a marked reduction in the frequency of cervical lymph-node involvement (scrofula) and its occurrence now probably is due to atypical mycobacteria (*see* page 642). Rarely, general superficial lymph-node enlargement may be the presenting picture in disseminated tuberculosis.

Reference has been made to the extension of tuberculosis to mediastinal organs. The most common complicating infection in this area is tuberculous pericarditis which, in healing, may result in a markedly thickened membrane and constrictive pericarditis.

Involvement of the central nervous system usually is a late manifestation of miliary tuberculosis, and this complication can be avoided by the prompt institution of adequate treatment.[1159] Tuberculous meningitis causes headache, somnolence, irritability, vomiting, and sometimes neck stiffness; the diagnosis is made by culture of the tubercle bacillus from the cerebrospinal fluid. Although a low sugar and chloride content in the CSF may suggest the diagnosis, it should be borne in mind that these biochemical abnormalities are present in cryptococcal and coccidioidal meningitis also.[1160]

Chemotherapy has largely averted the involvement of the upper respiratory and gastrointestinal tracts that formerly was fairly common in cases of advanced pulmonary disease caused by *M. tuberculosis* or *M. bovis*. The gastrointestinal tract usually is affected in the ileocecal area or around the rectum, the latter leading to perianal or ischiorectal abscesses.

Laboratory Procedures in Diagnosis

TUBERCULIN SKIN TEST. An intradermal skin test using old tuberculin (OT) or purified protein derivative (PPD) from strains of *Mycobacterium tuberculosis* is an invaluable diagnostic tool in the detection of active tuberculosis (*see* Chapter 3, page 174). Great care must be exercised in the performance of the skin test, since false negative reactions may result from faulty technique. The material must be fresh and should be injected through disposable 26- or 27-gauge short-bevelled needles; 0.1 ml of solution should be injected intradermally on the volar aspect of the forearm, with the needle bevel pointing upward.[1161] The skin tests should be "read" within 48 to 72 hours, when the longest axis of the raised edematous wheal should be measured; the degree of erythema is of no significance and need not be estimated. When material of intermediate strength (PPD–S 5 T.U. or OT 1:1000) was injected, a raised edematous area measuring 5 mm or more should be considered significant; the larger the wheal the greater the significance. If the clinical and roentgenographic evidence strongly suggests a diagnosis of tuberculosis, it is wise to use PPD first strength or OT 1:10,000 initially. If the patient fails to react to intermediate-strength PPD or OT 1:1000, second-strength PPD (PPD–S 250 T.U.) or OT 1:100 may be used, although a positive reaction at these strengths is considerably less significant. Multiple puncture techniques such as the Heaf and the Disk Tine tests, are useful for epidemiologic surveys, particularly in children.

The patch test is no longer considered reliable.

A negative tuberculin skin reaction using both intermediate and second-strength PPD, and OT 1:1000 and 1:100, almost excludes the possibility of tuberculosis,[1136] although certain exceptions to this general rule must constantly be borne in mind: patients who are seriously ill with tuberculosis may show negative reactions, particularly if the tuberculosis is miliary; in one series of 26 patients with miliary tuberculosis, only 16 (61 per cent) showed positive tuberculin tests; eight of the ten nonreactors in this group died.[1126] False negative reactions also may occur in patients with sarcoidosis, those receiving corticosteroid therapy, and in pregnant women. There seems little doubt that atypical mycobacterial infections may cause cross-reactions leading to edematous areas 5 to 10 mm in diameter.

BACTERIOLOGIC INVESTIGATION. A definitive diagnosis of pulmonary tuberculosis requires culture of *M. tuberculosis*, although a smear showing acid-fast organisms is virtually diagnostic in a patient showing clinical and roentgenographic findings suggestive of the disease. Material for diagnosis comes from sputum, gastric and bronchial lavage, or a laryngeal swab. Sometimes, organisms may be identified on smear or may be cultured from tissue material obtained from the pleura, lymph nodes, or directly from the lung. Sputum is the most valuable source of organisms and, in patients who do not expectorate spontaneously, inhalation of a warmed solution of propylene glycol may induce sputum production (*see* Chapter 3, page 164). Specimens of sputum obtained immediately after bronchoscopy are particularly valuable. Material smeared on a glass slide should be stained by the Ziehl-Neelson method. This stain reveals the organisms to be Gram-negative and acid-fast; since certain diptheroids and *Nocardia* species also may show an acid-fast stain, culture is required for final identification.

Material for culture should be concentrated and generally should be collected over a period of three days, since the larger quantity renders identification more likely. Smears are made on egg yolk and potato media and are incubated at 37° C for up to eight weeks. The characteristics of the colony serve to differentiate *Myco-*

bacterium tuberculosis from other mycobacteria. By culturing three specimens on two different media, one group of investigators[1136] was able to recover tubercle bacilli from 22.5 per cent of patients considered to have primary disease and 95 per cent of patients with reinfection. Every biopsy specimen should be submitted for both pathologic and bacteriologic study; although the finding of caseous necrosis in a granuloma may be strong evidence for the diagnosis of tuberculosis, mycotic infections may show a similar histologic picture. Since organisms seldom are seen and only rarely cultured from granulomas in pleural biopsy specimens, however,[428] the mere presence of a granuloma in the pleural membrane usually is regarded as acceptable evidence of tuberculous pleuritis. The same cannot be said of liver biopsies, since many other diseases cause granuloma formation in this organ. Although positive cultures are obtained in about two thirds of cases of miliary tuberculosis — usually from the sputum or gastric contents and less commonly from the urine or cerebrospinal fluid[1126] — the seriousness of this form of tuberculosis constitutes an indication for direct lung biopsy while awaiting results of culture. Our policy is to assume that a patient with pyrexia and a miliary pattern on a chest roentgenogram has miliary tuberculosis which warrants immediate institution of treatment; lung biopsy is performed two to three weeks later to confirm the diagnosis, especially if it is felt that inadequate specimens of sputum or gastric washings have been obtained for culture. Positive diagnosis is of utmost importance in such cases, since at least 18 to 24 months of therapy is required.

Antibodies may be produced by patients with tuberculosis and may be demonstrated by a gel double-diffusion method or by a hemagglutination technique; unfortunately, so many false-negative reactions occur with these tests that they are of little or no diagnostic value.

The white-cell count in tuberculosis usually is within normal limits but may be elevated to between 10,000 and 15,000 per c mm. The differential count sometimes shows a decrease in lymphocytes and an increase in monocytes.

Bronchoscopy should be performed in any patient with tuberculosis who manifests evidence of tracheobronchial involvement — the presence of rhonchi, a positive sputum without roentgenographic abnormality,[1163] or local atelectasis, obstructive pneumonitis, or emphysema.

PULMONARY FUNCTION TESTS. In the absence of chronic bronchitis and emphysema, patients with pulmonary tuberculosis — even when advanced — show little impairment of respiratory function. This probably is due to the fact that the lower lobes and anterior segments of the upper lobes usually are spared; in addition, since the disease interferes with both ventilation and perfusion to an equal degree, ventilation/perfusion abnormalities do not develop.[1164] Pulmonary function tests are useful in assessing patients before surgery and to determine objectively the degree of disability in patients with diffuse chronic destructive tuberculosis. If a lobe or lung is to be removed as the presumed source of continuing positive sputum, it is of considerable importance to determine the patient's breathing reserve before operation, to avoid rendering him a respiratory cripple. Bronchospirometry plays a major role in the assessment of such patients, by permitting selective measurement of ventilation and oxygen uptake.

ANONYMOUS MYCOBACTERIA

A small but perhaps increasing proportion of mycobacterial infections of the lung are caused by organisms other than *M. tuberculosis*, *M. bovis*, or *M. avium*; these are referred to variously as "anonymous," "atypical," "chromogenic," or "unclassified" mycobacteria.

The Causative Organisms

Characteristics common to all of the anonymous mycobacteria include ready growth on culture at 25 or 37° C (in contrast to *M. tuberculosis*, which grows only at 37° C) and their nonpathogenicity in guinea pigs. Based on cultural characteristics — morphology, presence, or absence of pigment, and rate of growth — Runyon[1165] classified these organisms into four groups.

GROUP I — THE PHOTOCHROMOGENS. The organisms in this group probably are quite homogeneous and have been given the species designation *M. kansasii*. They sometimes cause pulmonary disease, and occasionally cervical adenitis and disseminated disease. This group is recognized on culture by the fact that the colonies turn yellow when exposed to light. The exact source of the organism in nature is not known but is thought to be milk or soil.

GROUP II—THE SCOTOCHROMOGENS. These organisms occasionally involve the lungs but more characteristically cause a scrofula-like picture. Colonies on culture show a yellow pigment which turns orange on exposure to light. The organism has been cultured from soil, water, and the sputum of healthy subjects.

GROUP III—INCLUDING THE BATTEY BACILLUS. This group contains several different species; as a cause of human pulmonary disease, the important strain is the Battey bacillus. Colonies on culture are white to beige and seldom show pigment; they take two to four weeks to reach full growth. The Battey bacillus has been cultured from soil and milk and exists predominantly in the south-eastern U.S.A. It rarely causes widely disseminated disease.

GROUP IV—THE NONCHROMOGENS. This group is known also as the "rapid growers"[1181] since these organisms take only three to five days to reach full growth on culture. Their color characteristics are identical to those of group III and the only method of differentiating the two is by rate of growth. Interest in this group is limited to *M. fortuitum*, an organism prevalent in soil and only rarely pathogenic for man. In almost all cases it has been isolated from the sputum along with *M. tuberculosis*, and only rarely is the sole mycobacterial organism found on culture.

Epidemiology

Studies carried out in the U.S.A. indicate that these organisms are the cause of mycobacterial pulmonary disease in about 1 per cent of patients admitted to sanatoria.[1166-1168] The incidence varies geographically, *M. kansasii* being more prevalent in the southern and mid-western States and the Battey bacillus in the south-eastern States. In certain endemic areas, such as Cook County, Illinois, the incidence of pulmonary disease due to *M. kansasii* is as high as 7 per cent of patients admitted to tuberculosis sanatoria.[1169] A

Veterans' Administration–Armed Forces study indicated a 21 per cent incidence of anonymous mycobacteriosis in the south;[4110] in a preliminary clinical and epidemiologic study, Hsu[1170] found a higher incidence of anonymous mycobacterial infection in children in Houston, Texas, than of infection due to *M. tuberculosis*. Other authors[1171, 1172] have reported an incidence of 3 to 4 per cent.

Anonymous mycobacteria, particularly the scotochromogens, may be isolated from sputum or tissues of patients without clinical evidence of the disease. In a study of 1610 patients admitted to a Connecticut hospital, Warring[1168] found only 15 (0.9 per cent) to have pulmonary disease presumed to be caused by mycobacteria other than tuberculosis, whereas 5 per cent of hospital patients and 6 per cent of clinic patients showed anonymous mycobacteria on culture which were considered to be saprophytes, commensals, or contaminants. Other authors[1172, 1173] also have described isolation of anonymous mycobacteria in association with *M. tuberculosis* where the latter organism was considered to be the true pathogen. In a study carried out in upstate New York, Heitzman and his associates[1174] isolated anonymous mycobacteria from 36 patients; in nine of these the organisms were *M. kansasii* and in four the scotochromogens; not a single case of Runyon group-III nonchromogenic organisms (Battey bacillus) was found in this geographic area.

Since antigens were developed for group-I photochromogens (PPD-Y), group-II scotochromogens (PPD-G), and group-III nonphotochromogens (PPD-B), skin testing has shown widespread infection with these organisms, both in the U.S.A. and elsewhere. Undoubtedly many children who show weak positive reactions to *M. tuberculosis* represent examples of cross-sensitization with either the Battey bacillus or *M. kansasii*.[1175, 1176] Persons who show stronger positive response (10 mm or more of induration) with PPD antigens of anonymous mycobacteria than with standard PPD probably represent examples of nontuberculous mycobacterial infections. Studies on Caucasian navy recruits[1173] showed that 40 to 74 per cent of those who had been life-time residents in the southern and south-eastern United States reacted positively to

PPD-B, and there was good correlation between the percentage of positive reactors to this antigen and the number of reported cases of human disease due to Battey-type organisms. In this group the majority of positive reactors to group-I antigen (PPD-Y) came from Illinois, Kansas, and Texas; 48.7 per cent showed a positive reaction to PPD-G, which seems out of proportion to the percentage of cases of active pulmonary disease considered to be due to these scotochromogens.

Anonymous mycobacteria frequently have been isolated from soil and water and more recently from milk,[1177] and infection by these organisms seems to be predominantly in farmers, at least in some series.[1166] Some cases have been documented in children known to have eaten soil.[1170] The majority of studies indicate that disease due to anonymous mycobacteria is rarely communicable from man to man.[1167, 1169, 1173, 1178]

Pathologic Characteristics

The pathology of pulmonary disease due to anonymous mycobacteria is in all respects identical to that caused by *M. tuberculosis*.[1167, 1169, 1173, 1174]

Roentgenographic Manifestations

The roentgenographic pattern of pulmonary disease due to anonymous mycobacteria cannot be accurately differentiated from that due to *M. tuberculosis*, although the changes usually are those of advanced disease.[1169, 1173, 1179, 1180] Certain features, however, seem to be more suggestive of anonymous mycobacteriosis:[1169, 1174, 1178, 1181] (a) there is a greater tendency to cavitation, particularly with the formation of multiple thin-walled cavities; (b) exudative lesions are very uncommon; (c) hematogenous dissemination is rare (although Tsai and colleagues[1181] stated that there is a greater incidence of bronchogenic spread); and (d) pleural effusion is rare. Despite these features, the roentgen patterns of the two groups of diseases are equally protean and are virtually indistinguishable in individual cases.

Clinical Manifestations

The clinical picture of anonymous mycobacteriosis is indistinguishable from tuberculosis,[1167, 1173, 1177] although middle-aged and elderly persons appear to be more commonly affected, particularly those with associated disease such as chronic bronchitis and emphysema.[1169, 1179] Many of these patients die of cor pulmonale. Except for involvement of the cervical lymph nodes by group-II organisms,[1169] extrapulmonary disease is rare. Disseminated anonymous mycobacteriosis associated with pancytopenia is said to occur usually in patients with underlying disease of the reticuloendothelial system or in those receiving immunosuppressive therapy.[1182-1184] It is assumed that the reticuloendothelial disease and pancytopenia create a fertile ground for opportunistic invasion by anonymous mycobacteria, a relationship which also has been described in miliary tuberculosis.[1140]

MYCOTIC INFECTIONS OF THE LUNG

Recent years have seen an increasing recognition of the frequency with which fungi are concerned in lung infections. Our increased awareness probably derives from two factors, an apparent increase in the incidence of these diseases, notably histoplasmosis, and the relatively recent discovery of chemotherapeutic agents, particularly amphotericin-B, which are highly effective in combating these diseases. Some of these organisms—such as *Histoplasma capsulatum, Coccidioides immitis,* and *Blastomyces dermatitidis*—can cause infection in otherwise healthy subjects, whereas others—such as *Aspergillus fumigatus* and *Candida albicans*—are almost entirely saprophytic or "opportunistic" in that they affect susceptible individuals who are already ill, especially those receiving antibiotic or corticosteroid therapy. The majority of fungus infections produce benign illness, often without symptoms, and may be recognized only in retrospect because of a positive skin reaction to a specific mycotic antigen. In some instances, however, fungi may become rapidly disseminated throughout the body and produce acute, subacute, or chronic disease that may be fatal.

Most fungi live in two forms—mycelial and yeast—changing from one to another with changes in environment. The source of contamination is almost invariably the soil, which in turn may have been contaminated by animals infected with the organism. Although occasional cases have been reported which suggest that fungus infection may be transmitted from human to human, this must be very rare—if, indeed, it occurs at all. Certain fungi, such as *Histoplasma capsulatum* and *Coccidioides immitis*, are highly endemic in distribution, probably because of soil characteristics in specific areas. The Actinomycetaceae, which include *Actinomyces israelii* and *Nocardia* species, are sometimes classified as bacteria.

Pathologically, fungi in the lungs, as elsewhere, produce granulomas which are nonspecific in type and in no way different from those of tuberculosis or sarcoidosis. Pathologic diagnosis rests upon the finding of the organisms in tissue.

HISTOPLASMOSIS

The Causative Organism

The organism *Histoplasma capsulatum* lives in the mycelial form as a saprophyte in moist soil of appropriate chemical composition; it gains entry into humans by inhalation and then assumes its yeast form and resides in the cytoplasm of cells; it is oval and measures 3 to 5μ in diameter. The diagnosis of histoplasmosis seldom is made through identification of the organism in smears of expectorated material, pleural fluid, or bone marrow. Culture is a more reliable technique and in suspected cases the body fluids, bone marrow or tissue should be cultured both on glucose agar at 30° C and on cysteine blood agar at 37° C; growth usually takes two to three weeks. Final identification depends on the demonstration of tuberculate spores in mycelial growth. Positive cultures rarely are obtained in cases of primary disease and may require inoculation into mice and subsequent culture of the animals' spleen and liver in cases of chronic disease without cavitation.[478] Cultures of sputum or gastric aspirate are more often positive in the cavitary form of the disease,[1185, 1186] and blood, bone marrow, and tissue from biopsies are the major source of the fungus in cases of disseminated disease.[1187]

Immunofluorescent techniques are useful in identifying *H. capsulatum* in culture material and biopsy specimens.[1188] This procedure requires the preparation of an anti-histoplasma fluorescein-tagged globulin which is used in staining the material suspected of harboring the organisms; microscopy with ultraviolet light reveals fluorescence in the yeast cells.

Pathologically, *Histoplasma capsulatum* produces granulomas, sometimes with central caseation. Biopsy or necropsy material should be stained by the periodic-acid–Schiff (PAS) method or with one of the tissue silver stains, the best of which appears to be Gomori methamine-silver-nitrate.[1189]

Epidemiology

Most reports of the disease have come from North America, particularly the central and eastern portions and notably in the Ohio, Mississippi, and St. Lawrence River valleys, which are regarded as endemic areas. It has also been reported from South and Central America, India, Malaya, and Cyprus;[1190, 1191] it is rare in Europe and Australia and almost nonexistent in England and Japan. Since the disease may be acquired during only a brief stay in an endemic area, it is not unusual in these days of rapid and frequent travel to discover cases in countries usually considered to be free of the disease.[1191, 1194–1196]

In Africa, a somewhat different clinical picture is produced by an organism which some feel is quite distinct from *H. capsulatum* and which has been called *Histoplasma duboisii*.[1192] This variety appears to involve mainly the skin and bones and seldom the lungs, suggesting a different mode of entry.[1192, 1193]

In endemic areas, positive histoplasmin skin tests may be found in as many as 80 per cent of the population,[1197] and serial postmortem examinations reveal splenic calcification in 50 per cent,[1198] a finding which is thought to indicate a benign insidious dissemination. Even in areas of high endemicity, the infection is unevenly distributed, a fact which probably reflects "point sources" of heavily contaminated soil in areas of bird or bat roosting or of soil contaminated by chicken or pigeon excreta.[1199, 1201-1209] The excreta of birds and bats is considered to foster growth of the saprophytic organism in the soil and, in fact, *H. capsulatum* has been isolated from the organs of bats[370] and dogs.[1210]

Persons of all ages may be affected, and the disease is particularly virulent in infants,[1211] the elderly, and patients with lymphoma or on corticosteroid therapy.[1212] Histoplasmosis is particularly common as a symptom-producing disease in Caucasian males and extremely uncommon in Negroes[478, 1213] but skin-test surveys indicate that probably the infection is equally common in Negroes and females also.[1212]

Symptoms and roentgenographic manifestations very likely relate to the degree of exposure.[1201] The incubation period varies from five to 18 days as roughly determined from the many dramatic instances of exposure in "epidemic histoplasmosis."[1201–1203, 1209] Because of the frequency of local pulmonary calcifications associated with negative tuberculin tests, chronic pulmonary reinfection is thought to be endogenous in origin.

Histoplasmosis is manifested in various fairly well-defined clinical presentations and roentgenographic patterns. These varieties may be grouped into three categories: (1) primary disease, which usually is benign; (2) chronic disease or reinfection; and (3) disseminated histoplasmosis.

Primary Histoplasmosis

BENIGN TYPE. This common form of histoplasmosis is frequently discovered on a screening chest roentgenogram or, in retrospect, when calcified nodules in the lung periphery and in draining hilar lymph nodes are found associated with a positive histoplasmin skin test.[1199] Onset of the disease may be ushered in by mild respiratory symptoms such as fever[1213, 1215] or erythema nodosum.[447, 1216, 4322] The chest roentgenogram shows one or more ill-defined nonsegmental opacities, more frequently in the lower than the upper zones (Figure 7–17). Hilar lymph-node enlargement may be present; unlike tuberculosis, histoplasmosis rarely gives rise to pleural effusion.[477] Despite the mild or asymptomatic response to the invasion of this micro-organism, widespread dissemination may occur, as revealed by the remarkable finding of close to 50 per cent

of cases with typical punctate splenic calcifications in some endemic areas.[1218, 1219]

PNEUMONIC TYPE. This form of the disease is more acute and is characterized roentgenographically by homogeneous parenchymal consolidation of nonsegmental anatomic distribution; thus, it may simulate acute air-space pneumonia of bacterial origin. Unlike the latter, however, the disease tends to clear in one area and appear in another. Hilar lymph-node enlargement occurs in many cases.[1201, 1211, 1213] The symptoms include cough with mucopurulent sputum and sometimes hemoptysis, and headaches, pleuritic pain, or pain in the limbs and

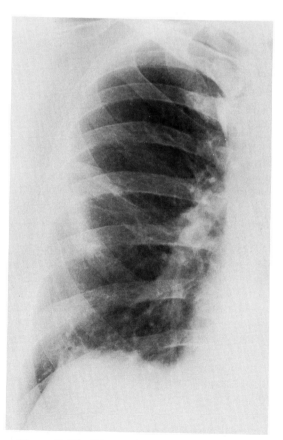

Figure 7–17. **Benign Pulmonary Histoplasmosis.** A view of the right lung from a posteroanterior roentgenogram reveals an indistinctly defined, hazy consolidation of the axillary portion of the right lung, situated within the middle lobe. There is slight enlargement of hilar lymph nodes. This 41-year-old man had mild symptoms consisting of unproductive cough and anorexia; a histoplasmin skin test was strongly positive; the illness occurred during a mild epidemic of acute histoplasmosis. *See* Figure 7–20.

back. Fever may be present. Physical signs include rales, a friction rub, and occasionally signs of consolidation. The differential diagnosis should include acute viral or bacterial pneumonia;[1201, 1211, 1213, 1215] however, since hilar lymph-node enlargement is very uncommon in either of these conditions, this finding should lend emphasis to the diagnosis of acute histoplasmosis, particularly in endemic areas.

THE HISTOPLASMOMA. This relatively common form of pulmonary histoplasmosis is the usually solitary, nodular shadow or "coin" lesion, typically sharply circumscribed and seldom more than 3 cm in diameter.[1189, 1213, 1220] These lesions occur more frequently in the lower than in the upper lobes, often with satellite lesions nearby;[488] many of them calcify, producing the "target" lesion that is virtually pathognomonic of this disease (Figure 7-18; see also Figure 5-17, page 436). Associated hilar lymph-node calcification is common, although concomitant node enlargement (as observed in one of our cases) must be very unusual (Figure 7-19). Multiple histoplasmomas seldom exceed four or five in number and often differ considerably in size; serial roentgenograms over months or years may reveal moderate growth of these lesions, to a point in fact where concern may arise as to the possibility of a metastatic etiology (Figure 7-20). A histoplasmoma usually is discovered as a chance finding and very probably represents a residual lesion from an active primary focus. Staining may reveal organisms within these lesions but culture usually is sterile. In the absence of central calcification, the differential diagnosis must include all other etiologies of "coin" lesions (see Table 5-6, page 440).

LYMPH-NODE INVOLVEMENT. Histoplasmosis is sometimes manifested by unilateral or bilateral enlargement of hilar, mediastinal, or intrapulmonary lymph nodes without roentgenographic evidence of parenchymal disease. This form is particularly common in children[1211] but occurs in adults also. Most patients are asymptomatic during the active phase of the disease;[1202, 1213, 1215] however, with healing and subsequent calcification, extrinsic pressure of enlarged nodes on the airways, particularly the right middle-lobe bronchus, may cause obstruction and resulting distal infection or atelectasis (see Figure 4-50, page 239).[1211, 1213, 1215, 1221-1223] Calcification of lymph nodes, usually of the bronchopulmonary group, may be associated with erosion into the bronchial lumen—broncholithiasis (Figure 7-21). Cough and hemoptysis usually result. In many cases, tomography and bronchography reveal parabronchial calcification and thereby indicate the nature of the underlying abnormality, and appropriate staining of expectorated material may reveal H. capsulatum.[1222, 1224]

MEDIASTINAL INVOLVEMENT. Various clinical and roentgenologic presentations may result from mediastinal lymph-node involvement or from actual extension of the pulmonary infection into the mediastinal space with production of granulomatous and fibrotic mediastinitis. Special roentgenologic techniques are necessary to delineate the extent of the disease in most of these cases. Four main types of involvement may be recognized.

1. *Pericarditis.*[477, 1221, 1225] Pericardial effusion may be apparent roentgenographically as enlargement of the cardiovascular silhouette. Mediastinal lymph-node enlargement frequently coexists. Calcification of the pericardium or constrictive pericarditis may develop subsequently.[1226, 1227]

2. *Esophageal encroachment.* During either the active or healed stage of the disease, enlarged posterior mediastinal lymph nodes may encroach upon the esophagus and displace or partially obstruct it. Healing of the affected lymph nodes may create cicatrices on the esophagus, leading to traction diverticulum.[1211, 1228]

3. *Superior-vena-caval obstruction.* Encroachment on the superior vena cava by enlarged mediastinal nodes may result in the classical picture of the superior-vena-caval syndrome.[1225, 1228-1231] Angiography is usually required for proper assessment (Figure 7-22).[1228-1231]

4. *Pulmonary arterial and venous obstruction.* Occasionally, severe mediastinitis with granuloma formation and fibrosis results in obstruction of pulmonary arteries and veins as they leave and enter the mediastinum. The effects on the lungs are predictable and are more commonly local than general—oligemia, or the manifestations of pulmonary venous hypertension, respectively. Because of the severity of mediastinal involvement, this variety commonly is associated with one

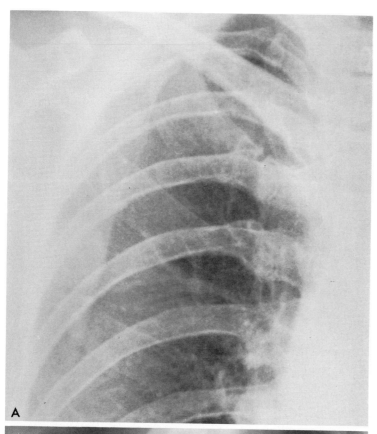

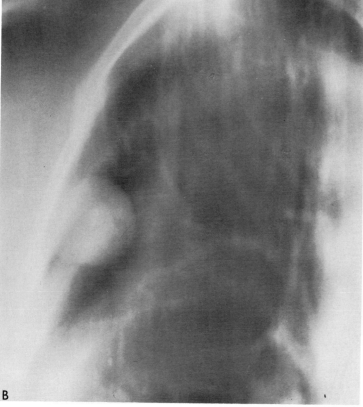

Figure 7–18. **Histoplasmoma.** Views of the upper half of the right lung from a posteroanterior roentgenogram (A) and an anteroposterior tomogram (B) show a sharply-demarcated, circular shadow measuring 2.8 cm in diameter situated just deep to the visceral pleura. The density is homogeneous except for a central, punctate deposit of calcium. Such central calcification represents the characteristic appearance of chronic granulomatous infection due to histoplasmosis (the "target" lesion). Fifty-one-year-old asymptomatic woman whose chest roentgenogram was normal one year previously. (Courtesy Dr. Max J. Palayew, Jewish General Hospital, Montreal.)

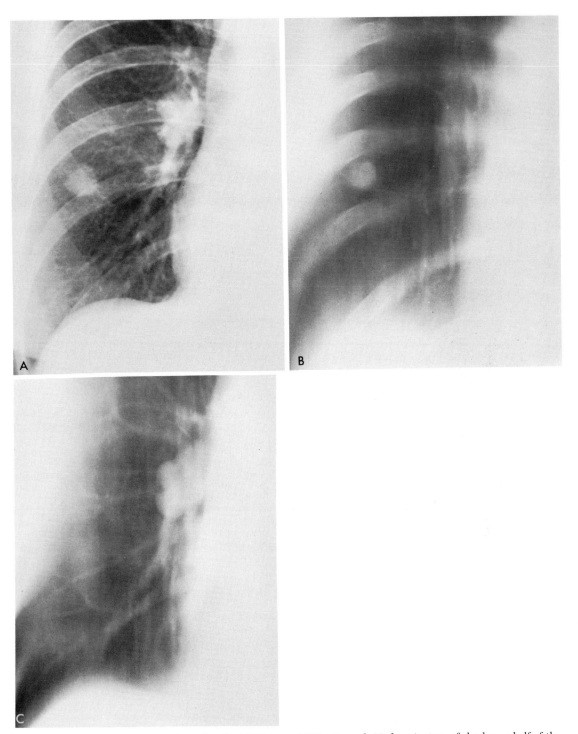

Figure 7–19.   **Histoplasmoma Associated with Enlarged Hilar Lymph Nodes.** A view of the lower half of the right hemithorax from a posteroanterior roentgenogram (A) reveals a solitary, sharply-circumscribed nodule measuring 15 mm in diameter situated in the lower portion of the right lung. A nodular outline of the right hilum suggests lymph-node enlargement. Tomographic sections of the right lung at different levels (B and C) show the lesion to be homogeneous in density and to contain no calcium; on the hilar cut (C), the configuration is typical of enlarged lymph nodes. This combination of changes is uncommon in histoplasmoma. The lesion was resected and its etiology established. (Courtesy Dr. David Berger, Royal Edward Chest Hospital, Montreal.)

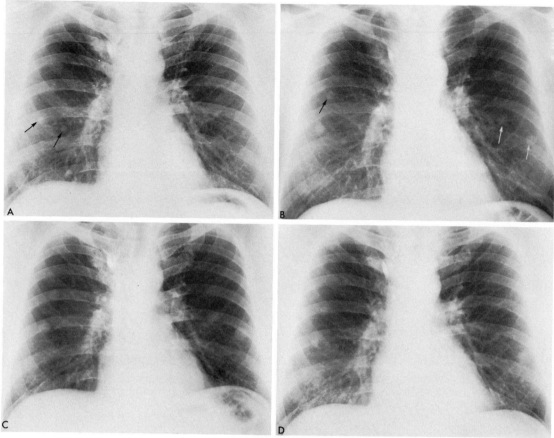

Figure 7-20. **Multiple Histoplasmomas Showing Growth.** These four roentgenograms are of the same patient illustrated in Figure 7–17 and were made during the four years following that acute benign episode. In *A*, two small nodules measuring 6 cm in diameter can be identified in the mid right lung (*arrows*). One year later (*B*), the lateral of these two lesions has increased considerably in size and now measures 12 mm. In addition, there has developed a third nodule in the right lung (*arrow*) and two lesions in the left lung, each measuring 14 mm in diameter (*arrows*). Six months later (*C*), three of the nodules have undergone still further growth and now measure approximately 16 mm in diameter. Eighteen months later (*D*), all lesions have diminished considerably in size. During this four-year period, the patient remained asymptomatic. The diagnosis of multiple histoplasmomas is presumptive and is based largely on the previous episode of acute benign disease.

or more of the three manifestations described previously. In such situations, a suspicion of mediastinitis as the underlying mechanism should be heightened by the roentgenologic observation of widening of the mediastinal shadow.

ACUTE DIFFUSE NODULAR DISEASE. This is the "epidemic" form of the disease which typically develops in groups of people heavily exposed to organisms in caves inhabited by bats or in a locale where soil is heavily contaminated by bird excreta.[1201, 1214, 1232-1236] Symptoms may be very mild and, in fact, exposure may not be recognized until many years later when multiple calcific nodules are seen roentgenologically in the lungs. On the other hand, overwhelming exposure may result in severe illness and death.[1203, 1204] Following heavy exposure and despite symptoms, the roentgenogram may show no abnormalities for a week or more; eventually, widely disseminated, fairly discrete nodular shadows appear throughout the lungs, individual lesions measuring up to 3 or 4 mm in diameter,[1232] with hilar lymph-node enlargement in the majority of cases.[1201-1204, 1232, 1233, 1236, 1237] These shadows may clear completely in two to eight months or may fibrose and persist. Frequently, the chest roentgenogram one to several years later reveals widely disseminated punctate calcifications representing the end result of the acute disseminated disease (*see* Figure 5-25, page 458).[1203, 1214, 1232, 1236]

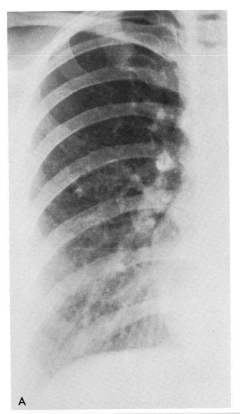

Figure 7–21. **Broncholithiasis.** A view of the right hemi-thorax from a posteroanterior roentgenogram (A) reveals a calcified lymph node measuring approximately 12 mm in diameter contiguous to the lateral aspect of the intermediate-stem bronchus. A partly calcified parenchymal shadow can be identified in the mid-lung. Anteroposterior (B) and lateral (C) tomographic sections show the intimate relationship of the irregularly calcified node to the intermediate-stem bronchus (*arrow*); in addition, a second calcified node can be identified in relation to the anterior wall of the trachea (*arrow* in C). This 42-year-old woman had had repeated episodes of mild hemoptysis; on several occasions, she had coughed up small hard particles representing detached fragments of calcified lymph node. (Courtesy Dr. G. Wightman, Queen Elizabeth Hospital, Montreal.)

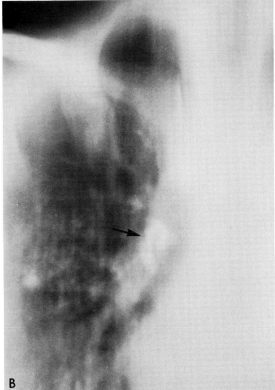

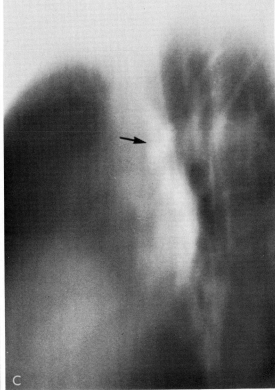

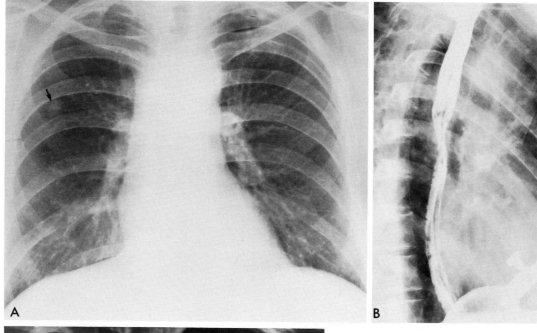

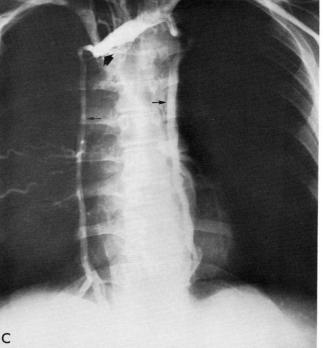

Figure 7–22. **Mediastinal Histoplasmosis: Superior Vena Cava Obstruction.** A posteroanterior roentgenogram (*A*) shows a somewhat widened upper mediastinum possessing a smooth contour. A partly calcified nodule can be identified in the upper portion of the right lung (*arrow*). This 51-year-old man presented with a typical picture of obstruction of the superior vena cava; in addition to the typical symptoms and signs referable to the head and neck and upper extremites, the patient complained of "hemoptysis" which on further questioning and examination was found to be arising from the esophagus rather than the lungs and to be due to "downhill" esophageal varices (*B*). A roentgenogram of the thorax following the rapid injection of contrast medium into an antecubital vein (*C*) reveals complete obstruction of the superior vena cava just proximal to the junction of the right and left innominate veins (*thick arrow*). Filling of the internal mammary veins can be identified on both sides (*thin arrows*), representing part of the extensive collateral circulation. Note the multiple small calcifications throughout the spleen; this finding in addition to a strongly positive histoplasmin skin test comprised highly suggestive evidence for the diagnosis of mediastinal histoplasmosis.

Chronic or Reinfection Histoplasmosis

In contrast to the types already mentioned, the chronic form of the disease is considered to be on the basis of reinfection, probably endogenous in origin. Two more-or-less well-defined groups may be recognized—early chronic pulmonary histoplasmosis and a more advanced cavitary type.

EARLY CHRONIC DISEASE. Roentgenographically, this form of the disease is characterized by fairly sharply circumscribed zones of parenchymal consolidation, usually in the upper lobes (see Figure 4–116, page 312) and tending to involve one area after another; considerable loss of lung volume may result.[478] Symptoms include mild fever, weight loss, malaise, anorexia, cough, and chest pain.

CHRONIC CAVITARY DISEASE. Cavitation occurs most commonly in men over the age of 40. The roentgenographic appearance closely simulates reinfection tuberculosis,[1238, 1239] and in some cases the two diseases coexist.[478, 1240] One or more cavities may be identified, usually in the upper lobes, with surrounding parenchymal consolidation of varied extent.[1187] A calcified primary lesion is apparent in a remote location, usually a lower lobe, in many cases. This form of the disease gradually progresses,[1187] and the prognosis is poor if adequate treatment is not instituted.[1187, 1241, 1242]

Disseminated Histoplasmosis

As already discussed, the widespread dissemination of H. capsulatum via the blood stream may be unrecognized until multiple punctate calcifications are identified throughout the spleen a long while after primary infection. However, disseminated disease may occur in a much more virulent form, and in these cases the prognosis is poor if the patient is not adequately treated.[1187, 1211] It develops most often in infants under the age of one year and in adults over 40,[1187, 1211] in either the primary and/or the reinfection type of the disease. The clinical findings are predominantly extrapulmonary—hepatosplenomegaly, general lymph-node enlargement, ulcers of the mouth or larynx, and, in some cases the signs and symptoms of adrenal insufficiency. Roentgenographically, the chest may be normal or show only hilar lymph-node enlargement.[1187, 1211] Approximately half of these patients have acute pneumonia, with or without cavitation, or a widely disseminated miliary pattern of infection (Figure 7–23).

Laboratory Studies

HEMATOLOGY. The number of white cells usually is normal but may increase to 13,000 per c mm in the acute epidemic form[1203] and to 20,000 per c mm in cases of cavitary disease;[1187] both leukopenia and anemia develop in approximately 50 per cent of cases of disseminated disease.

SEROLOGY. In many cases of histoplasmosis the diagnosis must be based on serologic tests, including agglutination, precipitation, and complement-fixation procedures. The yield of positive results is greater if both mycelial and yeast antigens are used and if both agglutination and complement-fixation tests are done.[487] A modification of the standard agglutination test that is more easily and quickly performed and that yields less false positive results is the latex-agglutination test.[1217] The histoplasmin latex-agglutination test (HLA) is satisfactory for detecting primary pulmonary disease but is positive in only 50 per cent of cases of chronic disease with significant complement-fixing antibody titers.[1244] Serologic tests become positive approximately one month after primary infection. A difference in titer in serial determinations is more significant than the result of a single test, but values of 1:4 for mycelial and 1:16 for yeast antigens are strong evidence of activity. A rise in titer is detectable in 95 per cent or more of cases of primary disease;[478] 76 per cent of cases of chronic pulmonary histoplasmosis have titers in the significant range[1245] but only 10 to 12 per cent of cases with residual "coin" lesions have yeast-phase antigen titers of 1:32 or more;[488, 1245] and 61 per cent of patients with disseminated disease have titers above 1:8.[1187] Unlike the series of events in coccidioidomycosis, the degree of dissemination of histoplasmosis is not necessarily related to the height of antibody formation—benign primary cases may have levels as high as 1:2048. The more severe and persistent infections in histoplasmosis frequently are associated with a relatively

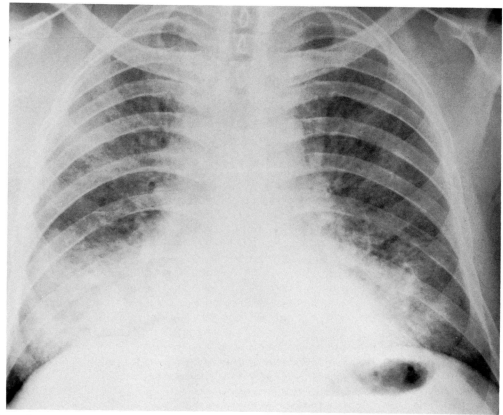

Figure 7–23. **Acute Disseminated Histoplasmosis.** A posteroanterior roentgenogram shows extensive involvement of both lungs by a process characteristic of air-space consolidation. In most areas, the shadows are confluent; an air bronchogram can be identified. This 40-year-old man had had proved Hodgkin's disease for many years, manifested roentgenologically by hilar and mediastinal lymph-node enlargement. He was receiving high doses of corticosteroids and antineoplastic drugs at the time of onset of acute disseminated histoplasmosis; it is clear that the dissemination occurred from an endogenous source although the site was not discovered.

low titer of activity which fails to fall to normal over a period of months.[1244]

As in tuberculosis, the histoplasmin skin test indicates only that the patient has been exposed to *H. capsulatum* either remotely or recently and that an allergic reaction has developed. The skin test is particularly useful if a positive result is obtained on a patient known to have had a negative result previously, and it strongly favors the diagnosis if the clinical history suggests exposure two or more weeks before the development of the positive cutaneous reaction. Since skin testing itself may produce antibodies, it is most important that blood should be drawn at the time of skin testing—or at least within the next four or five days—to provide a "control" sample and thereby avoid false positive serologic results. Positive reaction to a histoplasmin skin test, which consists in the intradermal injection of 0.1 ml of 1/100

solution, develops within two to three days.[487, 1212] The test provokes a positive reaction in 90 to 100 per cent of cases of acute pulmonary disease,[1212] in 97 per cent of cases of pathologically proved active residual lesions,[488] and in 83 per cent of cases of untreated chronic pulmonary disease,[1212] whereas a positive reaction develops in no more than 55 per cent of cases of disseminated disease.[1187, 1212] Because of the likelihood of cross-reactions, skin testing should be made simultaneously with histoplasmin, tuberculin, blastomycin, and coccidioidin, the greatest reaction indicating the likely etiology of the mycosis.

COCCIDIOIDOMYCOSIS

Coccidioidomycosis is a highly infectious mycotic disease usually but not always localized to the lungs; it appears to be limited to the western hemisphere and particularly to the south-western U.S.A.

The Causative Organism

The etiologic agent of coccidioidomycosis is the pathogenic soil fungus *Coccidioides immitis*. In tissue, the fungus has the form of a spherule—a round, thin-walled cell 20 to 80μ in diameter and containing a multitude of 2 to 4μ endospores. The spherules are rarely found in the sputum but may be identified in abscess and tissue specimens cultured on Sabouraud's glucose medium at 30° C. Mycelial growth appears as hyphae-containing rectangular arthrospores in two- to eight-day cultures and may occur in cavities *in vivo*. If mycelia grown from culture are inoculated into mice or guinea pigs, spherules develop in the animal and may be found in exudate; the spherule is often seen in the center of a giant cell in tissue stained by periodic-acid–Schiff, Gridley, Gomori, or Bauer stain. Pathologically, the tissues react to this organism by granuloma formation identical to that seen in other mycoses, tuberculosis, and sarcoidosis.

Epidemiology

The endemic area of coccidioidomycosis includes parts of California (particularly the San Joaquin Valley), Nevada, Arizona, Texas, Utah, New Mexico, and northern Mexico;[1246] a few cases have been reported from Central and South America.[1247] The disease is acquired from inhalation of the organism from contaminated soil. Requirements for proliferation of the mycelial form of the fungus include an alkaline soil free from severe frost and a dry season following a wet one. The mycelial form of the fungus produces arthrospores which are carried in the air and inhaled.[1248] Epidemics may occur following the disturbance of soil in preparation for construction,[1249] and therefore may be kept to a minimum by adequate dust-control programs.[1250] It is not spread directly from man to man, although one report describes six cases developing from exposure to a patient who had a draining sinus and whose plaster cast and surgical dressings served as culture medium for proliferation of arthrospores;[1251] simple hygienic precautions should prevent this form of spread.[1252]

The incidence of infection is very high in endemic areas: 25 per cent of persons newly arrived in such an area may be expected to have positive skin tests at the end of one year, and 50 per cent at the end of four years. Most of these conversions from negative to positive skin tests take place without recognizable symptoms. A few cases have been reported outside the endemic area in which the source of infection was contaminated soil, food, cotton, or wool shipped from an endemic area.[1247]

Statistics accumulated from several reported series indicate that of approximately 6000 cases of infection, 2000 will give rise to symptoms and 4000 will not. Of the former, 1 per cent (20 patients) will have prolonged illness lasting weeks or months, and the disease will become disseminated in one of these cases. Although disseminated disease is thus very uncommon—one in 6000 cases—it occurs 20 times more frequently in the Filipino and Negro than in the Caucasian.[188] The incubation period is from one to four weeks.

Coccidioidomycosis may be manifested by various clinical pictures and roentgenographic patterns which are best considered under the headings *benign* and *disseminated* disease.

Benign Coccidioidomycosis

ASYMPTOMATIC AND "FLU-LIKE" DISEASE. It has been estimated that 60 to 80 per cent of cases are completely asymptomatic. The frequency with which it is recognized is probably dependent on how closely it is looked for and also to some extent on the degree of exposure. Some patients have influenza-like episodes, with fever, cough, and myalgia, sometimes with arthralgia and conjunctivitis. This syndrome is seen in minor epidemics,[1200, 1249] and in one series of 210 laboratory workers was recognized in two-thirds.[476]

Roentgenographically the changes are said to consist of "fleeting" areas of parenchymal consolidation, usually in the upper lobes, and which tend to leave residual thin-walled cavities.[617]

PNEUMONIC TYPE. Parenchymal consolidation is predominantly lower lobe in site and may be homogeneous or mottled, segmental or nonsegmental.[188] Pleural effusion may occur, without associated parenchymal disease in some cases.[1254] Symptoms include fever, dry cough, occasional bloody expectoration, chills, muscle and joint pains, and, in less than 5 per cent of patients, pleuritic pain.[1255] Rales and rhonchi may be heard on auscultation, and rarely there are signs of consolidation over the lower lobes. Toxic cutaneous erythemas may develop; erythema nodosum or multiforme occurs in 5 to 20 per cent of patients and was present in 50 per cent in one epidemic.[1249]

NODULAR LESIONS (WITH OR WITHOUT CAVITATION). Well-defined nodules from 0.5 to 3 cm in diameter may occur singly or in multitudes; roentgenographically they offer no distinguishing features from other granulomas. These nodules are the residua of active parenchymal infection and probably are the equivalent of the reinfection type of histoplasmosis. As in histoplasmosis, chronic disease probably indicates exacerbation from an endogenous source rather than exogenous reinfection. The nodules may calcify. Dissemination seldom occurs, even when the lesion is active locally.[1254]

Nodules may excavate to form thin-walled or thick-walled cavities.[1255, 1256] Cavitation occurs predominantly in the upper lobes[1256] and, unlike tuberculosis, may develop in the anterior segment of an upper lobe.[617] Cavitary disease is associated with pneumothorax and empyema in approximately 2 per cent of cases.[1254, 1257]

Many patients, even those with cavitary disease, are asymptomatic, and the nodules may not be discovered for months or years after they have left an endemic area.[1256, 1258-1260] The cavities may be associated with hemoptysis or with secondary infection and abscess formation; such lesions may heal, resulting in residual fibrotic scars.

LYMPH-NODE INVOLVEMENT. Unilateral or bilateral enlargement of lymph nodes in the hilar or paratracheal regions may occur, even in the absence of parenchymal disease, and in many cases without symptoms (Figure 7–24). Involvement of the paratracheal nodes may indicate the imminence of dissemination of the disease,[1261] although even the scalene nodes may be affected without clinical or serologic evidence of such progression.[1262] A recent case report described a child in whom secondary stenosis of the trachea developed following involvement of a paratracheal node.[1693]

Disseminated Coccidioidomycosis

The acute "miliary-like" roentgenographic pattern seen in histoplasmosis due to the inhalation of a large number of organisms does not occur in coccidioidomycosis.[1201, 1214, 1232-1236] A diffuse micronodular pattern indicates widespread dissemination via the blood stream, as in tuberculosis; it usually is seen early in the course of the infection and rarely more than two months after onset.[1261] As indicated previously, it is a rare manifestation of the disease, being recorded in only one of 6000 cases.[188] It is to be emphasized that miliary involvement of the lungs is by no means an invariable development in disseminated disease, which usually can be suspected four weeks after its onset on the basis of weight loss, persistent fever, slow clearing of local lesions on the chest roentgenogram, and clinical signs of extrapulmonary spread. Lymph nodes, skin, and subcutaneous tissues may all be involved, sometimes with sinus formation, and spread may occur to the meninges, liver, spleen, kidneys, adrenals, bone (with formation of osteolytic lesions), and occasionally the endocardium and pericardium. Unlike extrapulmonary spread in many other fungus infections, that in coccidioidomycosis is seldom associated with corticosteroid therapy.[1263]

Laboratory Studies

HEMATOLOGY. The hemoglobin value is decreased in many cases of disseminated disease. The white-cell count is normal or moderately elevated in most patients, often with a significant degree of eosinophilia, particularly in the presence of erythema nodosum.

SEROLOGY. Serologic tests include agglutination, complement-fixation, immunodiffusion (ID), and latex-particle agglutination (LPA) tests; the last two are recent invaluable additions for screening sera.[1244] The agglutination reaction becomes positive two to three weeks after exposure, and complement fixation usually a little later; however, the complement-fixation

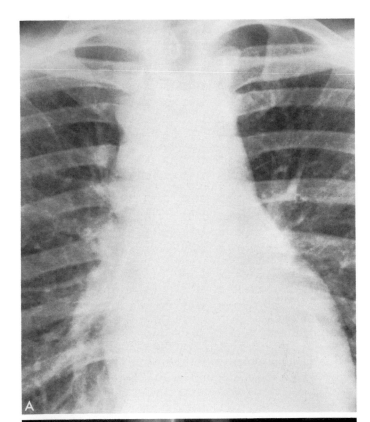

Figure 7-24. **Lymph-node Coccidioidomycosis.** Views of the mediastinum from a posteroanterior roentgenogram (*A*) and an anteroposterior tomogram (*B*) reveal marked enlargement of lymph nodes in the paratracheal chain bilaterally and to a lesser extent in the right hilum. The lungs are clear. This 29-year-old man had recently visited the San Joaquin Valley in California; symptoms were very mild and of a constitutional nature. (Courtesy Dr. H. J. Prichard, Long Beach, California.)

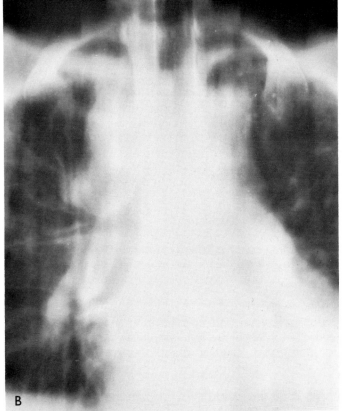

reaction never becomes positive in a large percentage of cases of primary infection with positive precipitin reactions.[1244] If these tests remain positive after six months, or if the complement-fixation titer rises above 1:16, dissemination has very likely occurred. Serologic tests are positive in 92 per cent of symptomatic patients with benign disease and in 60 per cent of patients with residual lesions.[1264] The complement-fixation reaction in the cerebrospinal fluid is positive in 75 per cent of patients with meningitic spread of the disease and is diagnostic of such progression. Skin testing is done with a mycelial filtrate (coccidioidin), using 0.1 ml of 1/100 solution; it is read at 24 and 48 hours. In the benign nondisseminated form of the disease the skin test is positive in almost 100 per cent of patients within three weeks of the onset of the infection; it may revert to negative within two years but can remain positive for as long as ten years. In disseminated disease the skin test is usually negative (70 per cent of patients), and a combination of this finding with a complement-fixation titer of more than 1:16 is practically pathognomonic of dissemination.

North American Blastomycosis

North American blastomycosis is a granulomatous mycotic infection caused by the fungus *Blastomyces dermatitidis*. The name is actually a misnomer, since the disease is not confined to North America and has been reported from Central and South America and from Africa.[1265] The major target organs are the skin and the lungs, but bone and other organs are involved in some cases.

The Causative Organism

Blastomyces dermatitidis is a dimorphic organism which occurs in mycelial phase in the soil and in yeast phase in humans and animals. In man, the organism is found in pus, sputum, urine, cerebrospinal fluid, and blood and may be identified on wet smear when sputum or pus is mixed with an equal quantity of sodium or potassium hydroxide.[1266] On Sabouraud's glucose agar it grows slowly as mycelia, its oval or round conidia being attached to hyphae or carried on short lateral conidiophores. On blood agar at 37° C it grows as yeast with five to 20 single-budding, double-refractile, walled organisms. Organisms may be identified in tissue stained with PAS, Gridley, Gomori, or Bauer stains. *B. dermatitidis* is pathogenic in mice and guinea pigs and in these animals, as in man, produces nonspecific granulomata which cannot be differentiated from other infectious granulomas.

Epidemiology

Although the precise incidence of North American blastomycosis is unknown, this infection is considerably less common than histoplasmosis, which occurs in roughly the same geographic areas. Middle-aged males are most commonly involved, male predominance being 6:1 to 15:1;[1266-1268] in one epidemic, however, seven of 11 cases occurred in children under the age of 16.[1269] There appears to be no racial predominance.[1267] The disease is confined largely to the western hemisphere, most cases being seen in the central[1267] and south-eastern U.S.A.[1266, 1270] and in Canada.

The fungus is believed to reside in the soil and, certainly, most cases occur in persons with a heavy soil exposure.[1266, 1268, 1270] Rarely—in laboratory workers—the disease is acquired through direct inoculation through the skin,[1271, 1272] in which circumstances the disease usually remains local but may extend to remote sites.[1272] Point sources of infection have not been proven, even in rare reports of epidemics.[1269] The disease is just as common in dogs as in man,[1267] but there is no proof of transmission from man to man or from animal to man,[1273] and the rare occurrence of the disease in two persons living in close contact probably evidences a common source of infection rather than transmission from one to the other.[1274]

Although *B. dermatitidis* is considered to be a primary pathogen and not an opportunistic fungus, many affected persons have underlying disease; for example, in one report,[1266] 34 of 40 patients had what might be considered predisposing conditions, including pulmonary emphysema, tuberculosis, and slight elevation of blood sugar after glucose loading; in another report, four of five patients had underlying disease.[1275]

Roentgenographic Manifestations

The roentgenologic findings in pulmonary blastomycosis are entirely nonspecific, none of the changes being characteristic or diagnostic of the disease.[1266, 1276] The usual pattern is one of acute air-space pneumonia, more often nonsegmental (Figure 7–25); consolidation usually is homogeneous but may be patchy;[1266, 1268, 1270, 1277, 1278] and the upper lobes are more frequently affected than the lower, in a ratio of about 3:2.[1266] Cavitation is uncommon, occurring in no more than 15 per cent of cases.[1266, 1270]

Single or multiple nodular "coin" lesions occur much less frequently than in histoplasmosis or coccidioidomycosis, and none was detected in one series of 18 cases.[1276] A widely disseminated nodular or miliary pattern is infrequent;[1266, 1278] hilar and mediastinal lymph-node enlargement and pleural effusion are very uncommon,[1270] and the latter invariably is associated with parenchymal disease. Calcification of parenchymal lesions is extremely rare. Osteolytic lesions in the thoracic skeleton usually are associated with superficial abscesses (Figure 7–25).[1266]

Clinical Manifestations

Unlike histoplasmosis and coccidioidomycosis, blastomycosis causes symptoms in the majority of patients. Although the fungus is believed to enter the body via the lungs in almost all cases, the pulmonary lesion may not be symptom-producing and often is discovered roentgenographically during the investigation of symptomatic extrapulmonary disease.[1267] Symptoms of pulmonary disease occur in only one third to one half of cases and consist of cough, expectoration of foul-smelling, purulent, and sometimes bloody sputum, and occasionally chest pain.[1267, 1268] Low-grade fever rarely occurs.[1266] Rales and rhonchi may be heard in some cases, but signs of parenchymal consolidation are seldom apparent.[1268] Pleural effusion is said to occur in 2 per cent of patients.[1270] Bone lesions, which occur in about 25 per cent of cases,[1263, 1266] sometimes develop by direct extension from the pleura to the ribs.[1268, 1279]

Skin lesions are seen just as commonly as lung lesions and tend to resemble neoplasms.[1266, 1270] A remarkable hyperplasia of the epidermis results in verrucous granulomas and subcutaneous nodules that may develop into chronic draining sinuses[1269] and ulcerative lesions.[1266] The genitourinary system is involved in 10 per cent of male patients.[1270] The central nervous system is affected in some cases,[1280, 1281] and rare reports of adrenal insufficiency have appeared.[1282] Laryngeal involvement is infrequent.[1283] Pneumothorax[1268] and intestinal lesions[1270] have been reported to develop in patients with blastomycosis who are receiving corticosteroid therapy. Fulminating pneumonia, simulating acute bacterial pneumonia, develops in some cases.[1265]

If untreated or inadequately treated, the course of North American blastomycosis is one of frequent remissions and exacerbations,[1268] with death occurring in approximately 30 per cent of patients; prognosis is much improved with adequate therapy with amphotericin-B.[1284]

Laboratory Studies

HEMATOLOGY. The leukocyte count is normal or only moderately raised in most patients,[1266] although it is said to be over 30,000 per c mm in some cases of extensive disease.[1275] Anemia may be present in cases of the chronic form of the disease.[1266]

SEROLOGY. The yeast-phase complement-fixation test and serologic and skin tests, using both mycelial and yeast antigens, are of no practical value in most cases.[1244, 1266, 1276] Cross-reactions with histoplasmin and coccidioidin occur frequently, and a positive blastomycin test should be considered as significant only when its reaction is stronger than that to histoplasmin and coccidioidin.[487, 498, 1270]

CRYPTOCOCCOSIS

Cryptococcosis is a granulomatous disease caused by the organism *Cryptococcus neoformans*, a fungus which is not dimorphic and which exists in yeast form in soil and in animals and man.

The Causative Organism

The yeast cell of *Cryptococcus neoformans* is a spherical single-budding,

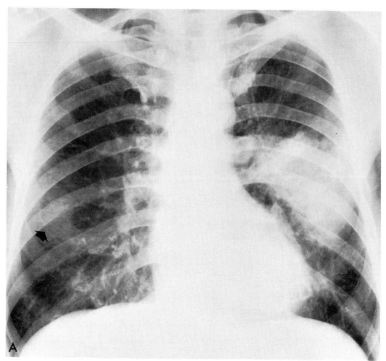

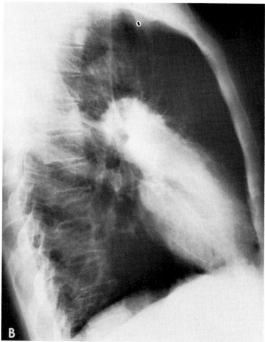

Figure 7–25. **North American Blastomycosis.** This 55-year-old male immigrant was well until two months prior to admission, at which time he developed an abrupt onset of pleuritic pain in the left side of his chest. He had had a 20 lb weight loss during the previous year. One month prior to admission a right lower molar tooth had been extracted, followed by the development of swelling below the right eye. Two weeks before admission, he developed a painful swelling of the right side of his chest in the anterior axillary line. On admission, roentgenograms of the chest in posteroanterior (*A*) and lateral (*B*) projections demonstrated a large, poorly-defined shadow of homogeneous density in the lingula; the consolidation is nonsegmental and shows no evidence of an air bronchogram. In addition, the posteroanterior roentgenogram reveals destruction of the anterior portion of the right fifth rib (*arrow*). *Blastomyces dermatitidis* was cultured from a 24-hour sputum collection, from pus aspirated from the swelling under the right eye and from fluid aspirated from the swelling over the right fifth rib.

double-refractile organism 4 to 15μ in diameter. Except for the presence of a thick capsule, the organisms might easily be confused with mononuclear leukocytes or erythrocytes. Identification may be made by mixing material from sputum, cerebrospinal fluid, or urine with a drop of India ink and examining it wet under a cover slip. Hematoxylin and eosin stain of tissue material often is unsatisfactory, but the organism stains jet black with the silver-chromate technique;[1285] the PAS method also may be used for tissue, and Vogel and his associates reported using the fluorescent antibody technique to detect the organism.[1286, 1287]

Cultures of sputum yield very few positive results,[1288] although spinal-fluid culture is more rewarding.[1289] Glucose or blood agar is used as culture medium, the latter being useful in differentiating pathogenic from nonpathogenic strains,[1290] and produces growth in 48 hours to several weeks. Cultures of lesions removed at operation may fail to produce growth despite a characteristic appearance on tissue staining, a combination which presumably indicates nonviable organisms.[1291] Mice are highly susceptible, and their organs should be cultured two to four weeks after intraperitoneal inoculation.

The granulomatous lesion consists of a "caseous" necrotic center surrounded by moderately well-developed connective tissue containing groups of lymphocytes and occasional giant cells and plasma cells. There is nothing specific about the granuloma, and pathologic diagnosis depends on precise identification of the organism.

Epidemiology

C. neoformans is considered to be of world-wide distribution;[1290, 1292] it lives in soil and shows particular affinity for soil contaminated by pigeon excreta.[1290, 1293, 1294] There is no proof of transmission from animal to man or from man to man. The disease may affect persons of any age but is most common in middle-aged males;[1288, 1295] in a recent review of 101 pulmonary cases, 82 per cent were males and 87 per cent Caucasian.[1288] The respiratory tract is the portal of entry into the body in most if not all cases, although some patients present with a normal chest roentgenogram and symptoms and signs of extrapulmonary involvement, usually of the central nervous system. The organism has a particular affinity for the central nervous system, due, according to Littman,[1290] to nutrients (thiamine, glutamic acid, and certain carbohydrates) in the cerebrospinal fluid.

As with blastomycosis, a benign asymptomatic form of disease has not been described, due possibly to a failure of recognition because of the lack of satisfactory skin tests to identify positive reactors with mild symptoms. Although the organism is a relatively rare primary pathogen, it may occur also as an opportunistic invader, one third of the cases in one series occurring in patients with Hodgkin's disease or allied reticuloendothelial abnormalities.[1290]

Roentgenographic Manifestations

The most common form of pulmonary involvement roentgenographically is a fairly well circumscribed mass ranging in diameter from 2 to 8 cm and occasionally up to 10 cm (Figure 7–26).[1285, 1290-1292, 1295-1297] The lesions are usually single; in the majority of cases the disease is confined to one lobe,[1288, 1292] most frequently a lower lobe.[1288, 1292, 1298, 1299] The masses are located peripherally in most cases but present as segmental consolidation in some.[1295, 1296, 1300, 1301] Cavitation is relatively uncommon compared with the incidence in other mycoses[1288, 1295, 1298, 1302] and in one review of the literature was cited as occurring in 16 of 101 cases.[1288] Widely disseminated disease may be associated with a miliary pattern or with multiple diffuse ill-defined shadows.[1290, 1298, 1303] Hilar and mediastinal lymph-node enlargement is unusual, although in one proved case there was massive bilateral node enlargement (Figure 7–27).[1295] Calcification is extremely rare,[1290, 1292, 1295] and pleural effusion seldom occurs.

Clinical Manifestations

Pulmonary involvement frequently is asymptomatic, and, since sputum cultures usually are unrewarding,[1288] the diagnosis of pulmonary cryptococcosis is often made by the pathologist from tissue removed at thoracotomy.[1288, 1295] When symptoms do occur in disease confined to the lungs they

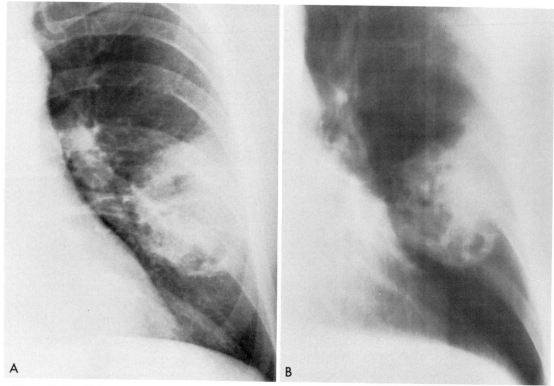

Figure 7–26. **Pulmonary Cryptococcosis.** Views of the left hemithorax from a posteroanterior roentgenogram (A) and an anteroposterior tomogram (B) reveal a well-circumscribed mass situated in the axillary portion of the left lower lobe; its lateral aspect abuts against the visceral pleura. Several irregular areas of radiolucency are present throughout the mass, representing multiple foci of cavitation. The appearance of the mass is quite characteristic of cryptococcosis although the cavitation is somewhat unusual. *Cryptococcus neoformans* was cultured from the sputum.

are usually mild and include cough, scanty mucoid and rarely bloody sputum, and chest pain and low-grade fever in some cases.[1285, 1288, 1290, 1295, 1298] A history of exposure to pigeon excreta may suggest the diagnosis.[1290, 1293, 1304, 1305] Physical examination of the chest occasionally reveals rales and rhonchi and rarely signs of consolidation. Extrapulmonary spread occurs much more commonly if there is underlying chronic disease, particularly of the reticuloendothelial system,[1288] and there is some evidence that corticosteroid therapy facilitates dissemination.[1288, 1300, 1306]

A common method of presentation clinically is in the form of a low-grade meningitis, and in some of these patients the chest roentgenogram is normal; the cerebrospinal fluid contains leukocytes and cryptococci, the latter easily mistaken for lymphocytes or red blood cells, and has a low sugar and high protein content. More rarely the neurologic picture is that of an expanding intracranial lesion[1303] or of a psychiatric problem.[1290, 1307] Acneform skin lesions, osteolytic bone lesions, and genitourinary involvement occur in some cases,[1289, 1290] and dissemination to lymph nodes, liver, and spleen may result in a clinical picture suggesting sarcoidosis.[1301]

Serologic Studies

Skin tests are not very helpful because of an extreme degree of cross-reactivity with other fungi,[1308] but serologic tests for both antigens and antibodies, which have been employed in only a limited number of patients, show considerable promise.[1307, 1309–1311] Circulating antigens appear to indicate continuing disease and are highly specific for cryptococcosis, whereas antibodies are found only after therapy, when patients' sera or cerebrospinal fluid has become culturally negative and antigen titers have decreased.[1309] Fluorescent

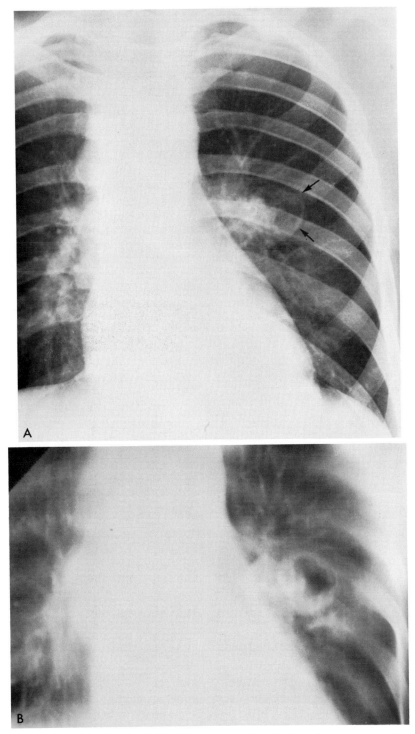

Figure 7-27. **Pulmonary and Lymph-node Cryptococcosis.** Selected views from a posteroanterior roentgenogram (A) and an anteroposterior tomogram (B) demonstrate a sharply-circumscribed cavity in the parahilar area of the left lung (*arrows* in A); the wall of the cavity is fairly thick and its inner surface somewhat irregular and shaggy. An irregular nodular contour of the upper half of the mediastinum, particularly on the right, indicates enlarged mediastinal nodes. Both the cavitation and the node enlargement are reported to be unusual manifestations of cryptococcosis. *Cryptococcus neoformans* was cultured from the sputum.

or C.F.-positive tests for antibody have been recorded in patients with positive cold-agglutination tests and in those with histoplasmosis or blastomycosis.[1310] The complement-fixation test appears to be more sensitive than either a modified latex-fixation or slide-agglutination test.[1309]

ACTINOMYCOSIS

In man, actinomycosis is caused by the organism *Actinomyces israelii*, a pleomorphic organism which exists in rod-shaped bacterial form in the mouth and tonsillar crypts and in mycelial form in tissues. The morphologic and cultural characteristics of *A. israelii* are similar if not identical to those of *A. bovis*, the organism which causes "lumpy jaw" in cattle.

The organism is found commonly in dental caries and at gingival margins in individuals with poor oral hygiene, and pulmonary infection is believed to occur through aspiration of the organism in such individuals. Before the advent of antibiotics, actinomycosis was the most commonly diagnosed fungus disease, presenting the fairly typical clinical picture of empyema and sinus tracts in the chest wall; this advanced stage of the disease is rarely seen now.

The organism has not been found in soil. Males are affected slightly more often than females. There is no occupational predilection or seasonal variation.[1312]

The Causative Organism

The finding of white or yellow "sulfur granules" in the sputum or in exudate from sinus tracts is highly suggestive of the diagnosis. These granules are 1 to 2 mm in diameter and consist of mycelial clumps with very thin hyphae possessing peripheral radiations, with or without clubbing at the ends. The sulfur granules should be mixed with a drop of potassium hydroxide and examined under a cover slip, with Gram staining to detect the Gram-positive filamentous mycelia and an acid-fast stain to permit differentiation from *Nocardia*, since some species of the latter organism are acid-fast.

Despite the highly suggestive nature of sulfur granules, culture is required for confirmation of the diagnosis.[1312]

Anaerobic conditions are required for culture; the medium used is an enriched agar plate maintained at 37° C or Brewer's thioglycollate medium. Growth appears in three or four days and when stained and studied under the microscope is found to contain masses of Gram-positive delicate branching hyphae, sometimes with small fragments simulating diphtheroids.

Roentgenographic Manifestations

The typical pattern is one of acute airspace pneumonia, commonly in the periphery of the lung and with a predilection for the lower lobes, but without recognizable segmental distribution; it is thus indistinguishable from acute diplococcal pneumonia. Once the pneumonia has developed, the subsequent course of events depends largely upon whether antibiotic therapy is instituted. With appropriate therapy, resolution may be expected to occur without complications; if therapy is not instituted, lung abscess is common (Figure 7–28), with extension of the infection into the pleura and the development of empyema, and subsequent spread into the chest wall, with osteomyelitis of the ribs and abscess formation in these areas. Rarely the disease becomes disseminated, with the development of a miliary pattern roentgenographically. Even more rarely, a soft-tissue mass may be identified in the chest wall, without associated pulmonary disease.[1277, 1312, 1313]

Clinical Manifestations

The most common clinical presentation of actinomycosis is an osteomyelitis of the mandible and an abscess in contiguous soft tissues, often following dental extraction (cervicofacial actinomycosis), and the next most common is gastrointestinal infection; primary pulmonary actinomycosis is relatively uncommon.

The initial clinical manifestations of pulmonary involvement consist of nonproductive cough and low-grade fever; subsequently the cough becomes productive of purulent and, in many cases, blood-streaked sputum. The temperature rises, and pain on breathing develops as the infection spreads to the pleura and chest wall. Rarely, a sinus tract may result in a bronchocutaneous fistula, or the infection

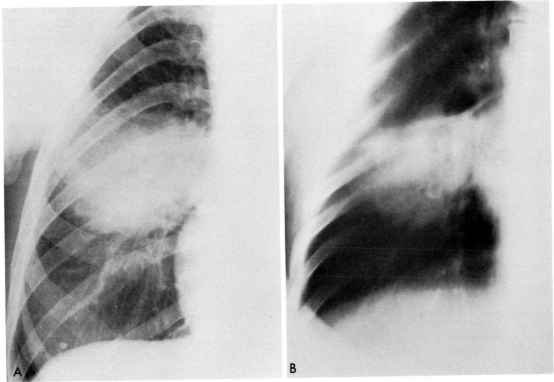

Figure 7–28. **Pulmonary Actinomycosis.** Views of the right hemithorax from a posteroanterior roentgenogram (A) and an anteroposterior tomogram (B) reveal a poorly-defined area of consolidation localized to the superior segment of the right lower lobe. Although the mass appears to be homogeneous on the standard roentgenogram, the tomogram reveals a well-defined central cavity measuring approximately 2 cm in diameter; extending into the cavity from its inferior wall is a nubbin of tissue on a stalk (? the beginning of a mycetoma). The diagnosis of actinomycosis was made histologically following resection.

may penetrate through the diaphragm or into the mediastinum. Although the majority of cases of pulmonary disease are the result of aspiration of infected material from the oropharynx, the lungs may become involved secondarily from extension of the disease through the esophagus or diaphragm from primary sites in the gastrointestinal tract.

Physical examination of the chest may reveal signs of consolidation; rarely, a soft-tissue mass is evident in the chest wall. As the disease progresses, weight loss, anemia, and finger-clubbing may occur,[1312, 1314] and secondary amyloidosis has been described.[1315] The development of pleural effusion almost certainly indicates an empyema. Dissemination of actinomycosis to many extrapulmonary locations is rare.[1312]

The white-cell count is normal or moderately increased, and anemia may develop in subacute or chronic cases.[1312]

NOCARDIOSIS

Nocardia species inhabit the soil and are of world-wide distribution.[1316] In tropical and subtropical climates, species of the organism are the main cause of mycetoma of the foot (Madura foot or Maduromycosis). In North America, the organism chiefly responsible for pulmonary disease is *Nocardia asteroides*. Both the clinical and the morphologic appearance of the mycelium in tissue closely resembles those of actinomycosis. *N. asteroides* is rarely if ever a saprophyte in the human respiratory tract and is an uncommon laboratory contaminant.[1317] Whereas formerly nocardiosis was seen almost exclusively as a primary pulmonary pathogen, nowadays it is more frequently recognized as an opportunistic invader superimposed on pre-existing chronic disease, often in patients receiving glucocorticosteroids.[1317–1319]

There is a male sex predominance of 2:1

but there does not appear to be any predilection for race or age group. Man presumably contracts the disease from exposure to contaminated soil; spread does not occur from animal to man or from man to man.

The Causative Organism

N. asteroides is a Gram-positive organism consisting of delicate branching filamentous hyphae; it is sometimes acid-fast but may lose this characteristic to some degree during tissue fixation.[1316] The organism may be identified on smears or cultures of exudate from the lung, subcutaneous abscesses, and occasionally the joints, or of blood or cerebrospinal fluid. Aerobic culture is made on glucose agar at 30° C or on blood agar at 37° C; some colonies may take as long as four weeks to appear.[1316, 1320] Care must be taken to differentiate this organism on culture from *Mycobacterium fortuitum*.[1321] Granules resembling those of actinomycosis are seen occasionally. Tissues should be stained by Gram and Giemsa stains; hematoxylin and eosin and PAS stains usually are unsatisfactory.

The pathologic lesion is a combination of granuloma formation and suppuration; the morphologic appearance of the organism in tissue is indistinguishable from that of actinomycosis.

Roentgenographic Manifestations

Although the roentgenographically apparent changes vary considerably, they are in most respects similar to those of actinomycosis.[1277] The most frequent manifestation is air-space pneumonia, usually homogeneous and nonsegmental[1316, 1322] but sometimes patchy and inhomogeneous.[1317] Cavitation is not infrequent[1317, 1320, 1323] and, as with actinomycosis, the infection may extend into the pleural space, with resultant empyema. Involvement of the chest wall is rare nowadays, as is widespread dissemination.[1321] Typical "coin" lesions may develop,[1316] and broncholith formation subsequent to involvement of hilar lymph nodes has been reported.[1224]

Clinical Manifestations

Cough, purulent sputum (sometimes blood-streaked), pleural pain, and night sweats are the most common symptoms. Physical examination may reveal rales over the area of involvement and occasionally signs of consolidation or pleural effusion.[1316, 1320, 1322] The course is usually chronic but in patients with lowered resistance an acute fulminating nocardial pneumonia may develop.[1321, 1366] The infection may spread to other areas of the body, most commonly manifested in cerebral[1318, 1320, 1322, 1324] or subcutaneous abscesses.[1320] Empyema, rib osteomyelitis, and subcutaneous abscesses develop in a small percentage of cases.[1320]

Since this infection is superimposed on some other disease in the majority of instances, the signs and symptoms of the primary disease may confuse the clinical picture. Although nocardiosis may co-exist with any chronic condition,[1317, 1320] patients with disease of the reticuloendothelial system—and, for reasons not known, alveolar proteinosis—appear to be the most susceptible.[1317-1319]

The white-cell count usually is moderately elevated, with neutrophilia; lymphocytosis or leukopenia develop in a few cases.[1316] Animal inoculation and serologic tests are of no diagnostic value. The use of skin tests has not been reported in man, but a recently described antigen has shown significant specificity for infections with *N. asteroides* in guinea pigs.[1325]

ASPERGILLOSIS

Aspergillosis is a mycotic disease caused by a variety of species of the dimorphic fungus *Aspergillus*. Although many species of Aspergillus can cause disease in man, the responsible organism is almost invariably *Aspergillus fumigatus*, and much less commonly *Aspergillus niger*. Aspergillus species is ubiquitous in nature and occurs as a saprophyte in the upper respiratory tract and as a contaminant in the laboratory. It is found more commonly in the sputum of patients with bronchial asthma than in the general population, an incidence which appears to be especially notable in the British Isles;[1326] in one series, isolation of the organism was considered more than a coincidental finding in 50 per cent of cases.[1327] Although the usual portal of entry is the respiratory tract, the skin and mucous membranes may be directly affected, and entry by way of the gastrointestinal tract or the genito-urinary tract occurs occasionally.[1328]

The disease is of world-wide distribution although it is more commonly reported from France and England than from North America. It shows a male sex predominance of about 3:1.[1329, 1330] There is no evidence of transmission from animal to man or from man to man.

The original description of a primary form of the disease associated with exposure to grain and birds may have been overemphasized, although an occasional case of this type of occupational exposure is still reported.[1328] The most common existence of the organism in the lung is as a saprophyte in residual cavities or in mucous plugs in patients with pre-existing hypersensitivity. When this normally saprophytic fungus invades tissues, almost invariably there is some underlying disease or lack of resistance—for example, during immunosuppresive therapy following renal transplantation, or corticosteroid, antibiotic, antineoplastic, or cytotoxic therapy, or irradiation, for a debilitating disease.[1328, 1331, 1332]

The Causative Organism

Microscopically, all species of *Aspergillus* are characterized by conidiophores which expand into large vesicles. The mycetoma is composed of intertwined hyphae matted together with fibrin, mucus, and cellular debris (*see* Figure 4–82C, page 273). A similar ball of fungus is seen occasionally in infections with *Candida albicans*, streptomyces, *Allescheria boydii*, and *Nocardia asteroides*.[1329, 1333, 1334] Organisms may be absent or sparse in the sputum of patients with intracavitary disease[1336, 1355] or bronchial asthma productive of mucous plugs.[1327]

The conclusive diagnosis of aspergillosis in those forms of the disease other than pulmonary mycetoma may be difficult. Infection may be strongly suspected if this organism and no other pathogens can be cultured repeatedly from the sputum, but conclusive evidence for *Aspergillus* species playing the role of a pathogen necessitates the microscopic demonstration of tissue invasion. Aspergillus as a cause of empyema postoperatively has been identified by culture of pleural exudate.[1337]

Tissue reaction to *Aspergillus* consists in a granuloma similar in many respects to that caused by other fungi. When the fungus exists as a saprophyte in a pre-existing cavity, the "fungus ball" consists of a mass of mycelia in altered blood. The cavity itself may be lined with bronchial epithelium, granulation tissue, or, occasionally, cells of a bronchogenic neoplasm. In those cases in which the organism is more invasive, acting either as a primary pathogen or as an opportunistic micro-organism, necrosis will be found in addition to the granulomatous process.

Infections caused by *Aspergillus* may be divided into "primary" and "secondary" types, the former representing the invasion of tissues in a previously healthy person and the latter designating infection superimposed upon a predisposing condition which has resulted in lack of resistance. It is to be emphasized that these terms, both in this book and in the literature, do not connote "original infection" and "reinfection" as understood in relation to pulmonary tuberculosis.

Primary Aspergillosis

Primary infection with *Aspergillus* is exceedingly rare. In the early French medical literature there is reference to an occupational hazard in squab-feeders who held grain in their mouths before feeding it to the birds, and in chimney sweeps and fur cleaners who used rye flour as a grease remover. More recent work has not substantiated the suggestion that grain contaminated with aspergillus spores constitutes a significant hazard,[1338] and in most of the few instances in which aspergillosis is said to have developed in otherwise healthy persons there was no history of significant occupational exposure.[1339-1342]

The roentgenographic pattern of primary aspergillosis is one of nonsegmental, homogeneous consolidation which may progress to abscess formation;[1343] in the absence of cavitation, the appearances are indistinguishable from those of acute diplococcal pneumonia. Clinically, the picture is one of chronic granulomatous infection, with low-grade fever, cough, sometimes purulent expectoration, hemoptysis, and chest pain. Thoracic tissues, including the mediastinum, may be extensively involved; the disease may be fatal.[1344]

Secondary Aspergillosis

PULMONARY MYCETOMA. A mycetoma may be defined as a conglomeration of intertwined hyphae of aspergillus matted together with fibrin, mucus, and cellular debris, situated within a pulmonary cavity (see Figure 4–82, page 273). The evidence is overwhelming that in the great majority of cases the fungus is present as a pure saprophyte: (1) the underlying cavity almost invariably can be ascribed to other causes such as bronchiectasis, tuberculosis, histoplasmosis, bronchial cysts, chronic bacterial abscess, or carcinoma;[1327, 1329, 1330, 1345-1349] (2) invariably the organism is in a mycelial form; and (3) the walls of the cavity show no evidence of invasion by the organism.[1345] The diagnosis is readily apparent in the typical roentgenographic features but can be confirmed only with the surgically removed specimen, since fungi are infrequently expectorated in this form of aspergillosis.[1335, 1336, 1340, 1347, 1350] If the characteristic roentgenographic pattern is lacking, the diagnosis may be suspected by the finding of a positive precipitin test.[490, 1334]

The invariable roentgenographic appearance of pulmonary mycetoma is of a solid rounded mass of unit density within a spherical or ovoid cavity, separated from the wall of the cavity by a crescent-shaped air space. Fluid levels are not seen within the cavities.[1345] The intracavitary fungus ball occurs much more commonly in the upper than in the lower lobes, probably because it so frequently occupies a tuberculous cavity.[1277, 1329, 1330, 1334, 1340, 1345] Most of the cavities are thin-walled,[1330, 1345] and in one series averaged 5.5 by 3.5 cm in diameter;[1330] they are often contiguous to a pleural surface, which may be thickened. The fungus ball should move when the patient changes position, an observation that is facilitated by tomography.[1333, 1345, 1352, 1353] Calcification of the mycelial mass may occur in the form of scattered small nodules, as a fine rim around the periphery of the mass or as an extensive process involving the greater part of the mycelial ball.[1330, 1345, 1354] The ball may vary in size[1355] or may show a remarkable constancy over many years.[1345] The differential diagnosis should include a fragment of tissue in a carcinoma which has undergone necrosis, a mass of necrotic lung in an abscess, a disintegrating hydatid cyst, and an intracavitary blood clot. A precipitin test usually permits differentiation.

Thickening of the walls of tuberculous cavities has been described as an early roentgenographic sign of secondary aspergillosis, antedating the formation of a fungus ball.[1356] It is said that bronchographic contrast material usually does not enter a cavity with a pulmonary mycetoma.[1353, 1357]

Clinically, most patients with intracavitary aspergilloma are healthy,[1345] but some may show evidence of chronic wasting, presumably as a result of the primary disease responsible for the cavity.[1329] Cough and expectoration are frequent,[1327, 1337, 1345, 1346] and hemoptysis is particularly apt to occur, having been reported in 45 per cent of cases in one series[1329] and in 67 per cent in another.[1345]

HYPERSENSITIVITY ASPERGILLOSIS. This form of the disease is characterized by the presence in segmental bronchi of mucous plugs containing aspergilli and eosinophils. Most patients give a history of long-standing bronchial asthma but in some the initial episode of bronchospasm coincides with the discovery of aspergilli in the sputum.[1330]

The roentgenographic pattern of this form of aspergillosis is identical to that described for mucoid impaction[1358-1360] (see page 1055). Homogeneous finger-like shadows of unit density are present in a precise bronchial distribution, usually involving the upper lobes and typically occupying the more central segmental bronchi rather than the peripheral branches of the bronchial tree (Figure 7–29).[1360] The impacted bronchi may relate to atelectatic areas in the involved segment; in our experience, atelectasis often is notable by its absence, a fact which is explained by the presence of collateral airdrift. Cases of involvement of an entire lung have been described.[1361] The shadows tend to be transient, although they may persist unchanged for weeks or even months, or may increase in size. Segmental collapse and consolidation may develop coincident with clinical exacerbation.[1330] When the lesion resolves, it leaves cylindrical or saccular dilatation of the bronchi at the site of the previous mucoid impaction.[1326, 1327] There is a tendency for these lesions to recur in the same segmental

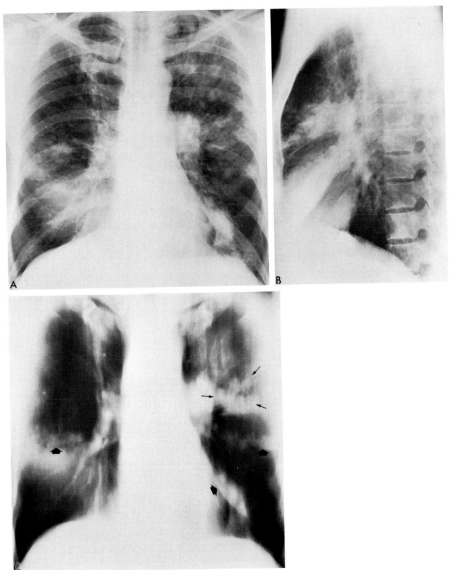

Figure 7–29. **Hypersensitivity Aspergillosis.** Posteroanterior (*A*) and lateral (*B*) roentgenograms reveal extensive bilateral pulmonary disease, all lobes of the lung being affected by a process possessing an unusual mixed pattern. In the left upper lobe, the pattern appears to be one of air-space consolidation, confluent shadows of homogeneous density being associated with an air bronchogram; the medial segment of the right middle lobe shows a combination of atelectasis and consolidation; broad areas of consolidation extend into the anterior basal segment of the left lower lobe and the anterior segment of the left upper lobe. A full lung tomogram in antero-posterior projection (*C*) shows numerous broad-band shadows bilaterally, each measuring approximately 1 cm in diameter and extending in a distribution compatible with the bronchovascular bundles (*thick arrows*). In the midportion of the left lung, one of these shadows possesses a Y-configuration (*thin arrows*). These band shadows are caused by inspissated mucus within markedly dilated bronchi; the Y-shaped shadow in the left mid-lung represents a bifurcating bronchus impacted with mucus. Note that with the exception of the right middle lobe, all impacted bronchi are unassociated with consolidation or atelectasis of the lung distal to them presumably as a result of effective collateral air-drift. This 42-year-old man had an industrial exposure to powdered casein, samples of which grew *Aspergillus fumigatus*; he presented with fever, productive cough and dyspnea; there was a moderate peripheral eosinophilia; *Aspergillus fumigatus* was recovered from the sputum.

bronchus, suggesting that previous bronchial damage predisposes locally to further episodes.[1360] Coexistent aspergilloma and hypersensitivity aspergillosis have been reported.[1362]

Clinically, these patients have fever, cough, purulent expectoration sometimes with hemoptysis, and expectoration of mucous plugs. Dyspnea may be very severe and leukocytosis with eosinophilia develops in most cases. There is reason to believe that in this syndrome the fungus is more than a saprophyte, since many of these patients with a positive skin reaction to the aspergillus extract have a positive reaction to the precipitation test for antibodies also;[1326, 1327, 1350, 1361] in addition, the first attack of bronchospasm commonly is associated with recovery of the organism from the sputum. Inhalation of aspergillus extract can result in a decrease in forced expiratory volume, indicating positive bronchial sensitivity to this organism.[1326]

ASPERGILLOSIS WITH CHRONIC DEBILITATING DISEASE. This form of aspergillosis can occur as an added infection in patients with various chronic pulmonary diseases and in those with extrapulmonary disease, particularly when they are being treated with corticosteroids, antibiotics, or antineoplastic or immunosuppressive drugs.[1328, 1331, 1332, 1352] The aspergillosis may be the major cause of death in some cases,[1331] mainly because the lack of resistance permits widespread dissemination of the organism throughout the body, including the brain[1331] and the endocardium.[1328]

The roentgenographically apparent changes vary with the nature of the underlying pulmonary disease and with the presence or absence of dissemination. Sometimes the fungus may be superimposed on bacterial pneumonia, in which circumstances it may present as a pulmonary mycetoma. More often, however, pulmonary involvement is in the form of single or multiple areas of pneumonic consolidation, which may cavitate (Figures 7–30 and 7–31).[1328] Miliary spread throughout the lungs is very rare.

Serologic Studies

Several reports have indicated that skin and serologic tests play a very important role in implicating aspergillus as a pathogen rather than as a saprophyte.[489, 491, 1326, 1327, 1350, 1352, 1360, 1364] The complement-fixation test is highly specific and is positive in active cases. In a study of 307 patients with asthma, Longbottom and Pepys[491] found that 9 per cent had precipitins to aspergillus; in addition, they found that 63 per cent of those who had transient pulmonary opacities and eosinophilia had positive reactions to the test, and that in 98 per cent of the 57 patients with mycetoma the serum contained precipitating antibodies which tended to disappear following surgery. In another series, 49 of 58 patients with mycetoma proved at operation were serologically positive.[1364] Skin reactions, of the immediate and late Arthus types, develop in a large percentage of patients who show the clinical picture of hypersensitivity aspergillosis; in cases of pulmonary mycetoma, the skin reaction usually is negative, whereas the test for humoral precipitating antibodies almost invariably provokes positive reactions.[491, 1326]

CANDIDIASIS (MONILIASIS)

Pulmonary infection with various species of *Candida* is rare and almost invariably occurs in infants, the elderly, or persons debilitated by chronic disease.[1366] It is a common saprophyte of the upper respiratory tract and is present in a higher percentage of hospital patients and hospital employees than of medical students[560] or the nonhospital population.[1368] In one series of 166 patients admitted consecutively to a general medical ward,[1369] monilia were isolated from the throat swabs of 28 per cent and from the rectal swabs of 8.4 per cent; furthermore, the percentage of positive cultures after five days increased considerably, but only in those patients who meanwhile had been treated with antibiotics.[1369] A high yield of positive cultures in patients receiving antibiotic therapy is well recognized,[472, 1371] and it has been shown that the infection persists for as long as two weeks after discontinuation of the therapy.[1370] Similarly, experimental studies on animals revealed an increased likelihood of infection when glucocorticoids were administered before initiating infection.[1372]

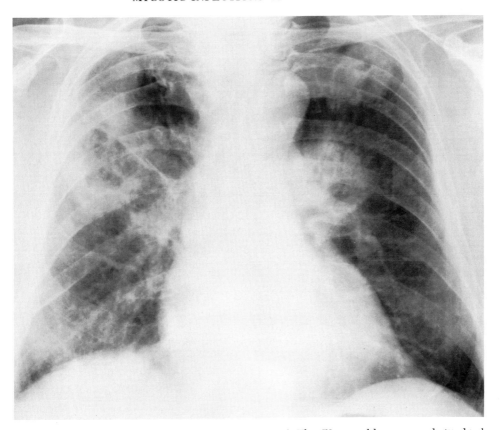

Figure 7–30. **Primary Pulmonary Aspergillosis (Opportunistic).** This 70-year-old man was admitted to hospital with the diagnosis of pemphigus vulgaris which required high doses of corticosteroid therapy for control. He was also diabetic. Within three weeks of the beginning of corticosteroid therapy, he developed a cough productive of moderate amounts of mucopurulent sputum which, over a brief period of time, became copious in amount and blood-tinged. Constitutional symptoms were mild. This posteroanterior roentgenogram reveals large thick-walled cavities in both lungs, possessing irregular shaggy inner linings. *Aspergillus fumigatus* was cultured both from the sputum and from creamy pus aspirated directly from one of the cavities.

The lung is a relatively rare site of monilial infection, the oropharynx, vagina, and skin being much more commonly affected. Susceptible individuals develop fungemia, with dissemination of the organism throughout the body and subsequent granuloma formation in the tissues. Rifkind and associates, who described the necropsy findings in 51 patients who had undergone renal transplantation, found systemic fungus infection in 23; *Candida* was the most common organism involving the lungs, being found in eight cases.[1332] Endocarditis may result, a development to which drug addicts, for no known reason, appear to be particularly susceptible; in four of five cases of monilial endocarditis reported, the etiologic agent was *Candida parakrusei.*[1373]

Although occupational hazard has not been reported to result in pulmonary mon-

iliasis, the cutaneous variety of the disease occurs in fruit packers. Similarly, Castellani reported a higher incidence of bronchitis in tea-tasters in Ceylon.[1374]

The Causative Organism

In man, almost all of these infections are due to *Candida albicans*. Wet preparations with potassium hydroxide under a cover slip show the budding yeast-like fungus to be 2 to 4μ in diameter and to have a thin wall. Candida is a dimorphic fungus and is thought by some[1375] to be more likely a pathogen if both yeast and mycelial forms are isolated from body fluids or tissues. The organism may be identified in tissue stained with hematoxylin and eosin or with PAS. *Candida albicans* is readily identifiable by its cultural characteristics

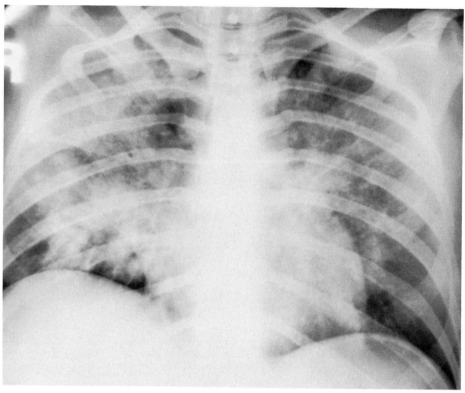

Figure 7–31. **Disseminated Aspergillosis (Opportunistic).** This 27-year-old woman was admitted to hospital with complaints referable to multiple systems which eventually proved to be due to systemic lupus erythematosus. For this she received corticosteroid therapy to which was added high doses of antibiotics when she developed clinical and roentgenologic evidence of pneumonia. This anteroposterior roentgenogram reveals extensive bilateral pulmonary disease characterized by confluent air-space consolidation; a well-defined air bronchogram can be identified in most areas. The patient's clinical condition rapidly deteriorated and she died in severe respiratory distress four days after this roentgenogram. At necropsy, in addition to the characteristic findings of systemic lupus erythematosus, there was evidence of multi-system involvement by *Aspergillus fumigatus,* most pronounced in the lungs, heart, and kidneys.

on corn-meal agar, on which it produces thick-walled chlamydospores.

Rarely, other species of *Candida* have been reported to cause disease in susceptible persons.[1033] Laboratory animals may be affected by some species, particularly if they are receiving glucocorticoids or have been rendered diabetic with alloxan.

Roentgenographic Manifestations

Roentgenologic patterns in candidiasis are in no way specific. The most common presentation is patchy segmental homogeneous consolidation;[1277, 1313] nonsegmental air-space consolidation also may occur. Miliary dissemination has been described (Figure 7–32),[1277, 1376] as have cases of cavitation in consolidated lung, with or without the formation of fungus ball.[1329, 1333, 1377]

Clinical Manifestations

There is nothing distinctive about the clinical picture of pulmonary candidiasis. The diagnosis should be considered in patients with roentgenographic evidence of acute or chronic pulmonary disease who have repeated and heavy growth of *C. albicans* in sputum which otherwise is free of pathogenic organisms. Since cases are extremely rare in the absence of underlying chronic disease, especially in patients on antibiotic or corticosteroid therapy,[1376] and since the organism is very commonly a saprophyte in the respiratory tract, conclusive diagnosis requires demonstration of the organism in tissues.[560, 1375, 1376]

When associated with the finding of the organism in a catheter specimen of urine, the development of fungemia in a patient

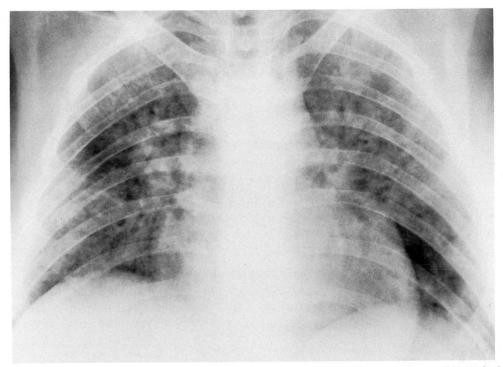

Figure 7-32. **Disseminated Candidiasis (Opportunistic).** This 19-year-old man had acute blastic leukemia for which he was receiving high doses of antineoplastic drugs and corticosteroids. During this course of therapy, he developed clinical evidence of diffuse pneumonia. This anteroposterior roentgenogram reveals widespread involvement of both lungs by patchy and confluent areas of air-space consolidation; an air bronchogram is clearly visible in most areas. At necropsy, there was found widespread organ involvement by *Candida albicans.*

with an appropriate clinical picture is strong evidence for dissemination.[1378] However, candidemia may be only a transient contamination of the blood stream and does not always result in tissue invasion;[1378] consequently, a positive blood culture does not necessarily indicate dissemination of the disease. Skin and agglutination tests are available[487] but cannot be relied upon to indicate pathogenicity of the organism.

The symptoms of pulmonary involvement include cough, expectoration of purulent material, and hemoptysis. One should bear in mind that symptoms and signs may be masked by the underlying disease responsible for the lack of resistance. Patients with disseminated moniliasis should be treated with amphotericin-B.

PHYCOMYCOSIS (MUCORMYCOSIS)

Although this disease commonly is referred to as mucormycosis, it is preferable to employ the designation phycomycosis and thereby include infections caused by other members of the class *Phycomycetes—Absidia, Rhizopus,* and *Mucor* species. These fungi appear to be world-wide in distribution and are found on bread and fruit and in soil. Infection is probably exogenous, the spores entering the paranasal sinuses and lung by inhalation. The disease occurs almost invariably in patients with underlying disease,[1379] especially during treatment with corticosteroids or antibiotics. The most common underlying diseases are diabetes (present in 21 of 55 cases in one series),[1379] lymphoma, and leukemia;[1379, 1380] one case has been reported in a patient who had a normal blood-sugar level at the time phycomycosis was diagnosed but in whom diabetes which required insulin therapy developed subsequently.[1381]

The Causative Organism

The organism has a distinctive appearance in tissue, consisting in wide, nonseptate hyphae; despite this distinctive appearance, however, culture is required for confirmation of diagnosis. Growth occurs readily on Sabouraud's glucose agar, and microscopic examination reveals hyphae bearing large globular sacs 100μ in diameter; these sacs, known as sporangia, contain round or elliptical spores measuring 6 to 8.5μ. The organism is a common laboratory contaminant. In man the infection is characterized by acute inflammation and by vascular thrombosis caused by invasion of the walls and lumina of blood vessels by the fungus; such thrombosis frequently results in infarction.

Roentgenographic Manifestations

Lung involvement usually is segmental and homogeneous, manifested in primary pneumonia caused by the organism or, less commonly, pulmonary infarction secondary to invasion of a pulmonary artery by the fungus.[1379, 1382, 1383] Cavitation may occur.[1381]

Clinical Manifestations

The only distinctive part of the clinical picture in phycomycosis is the tendency to involvement of the paranasal sinuses, particularly in patients with diabetes mellitus. Extension may occur to the orbits and cranium, with the development of orbital cellulitis and meningoencephalitis.[1383] It is not usual for patients with diabetes to present with this clinical picture without evidence of associated pulmonary disease. The tendency for the organism to invade blood vessels is illustrated by the several cases of occlusion of coronary arteries with resultant myocardial infarction which have been reported in the literature.[1384]

GEOTRICHOSIS

This rare fungus infection may exist in either a bronchial or a pulmonary form. It is not uncommon to find the causative organism (*Geotrichum* species) as a saprophyte in the sputum of patients with chronic pulmonary disease and even in the mouths and gastrointestinal tracts of normal subjects. There are no known endemic areas, occupational hazards, or age, sex, or racial predispositions. The disease is presumed to be of endogenous origin.

The sputum may contain large, rectangular arthrospores with rounded ends; culture on Sabouraud's glucose agar may sustain a growth of hyphae attached to the elongated arthrospores, which may become oval or spherical when separated from the hyphae.

The chest roentgenogram is not in any way distinctive. The bronchial form of the disease may show no roentgenographic abnormalities[1385] or merely an accentuation of basal pulmonary markings.[1386] The pulmonary form usually involves the upper lobes in the form of parenchymal consolidation, frequently associated with thin-walled cavities.[1313]

Clinically, the bronchial type is associated with a picture of bronchitis or asthma, with eosinophilia in some cases.[1385, 1386] Purulent expectoration may be copious in both the bronchial and pulmonary types of the disease, and the sputum may be very gelatinous. Fever and hemoptysis are present in most cases of the pneumonic form of the disease. Rales, rhonchi, and occasionally signs of consolidation may be detected.

A skin test and an agglutination test are available and are very useful in diagnosis.[1386]

SPOROTRICHOSIS

Sporotrichosis in man is caused by the organism *Sporotrichum schenckii*, a dimorphic fungus of world-wide distribution. It is a saprophyte in soil, peat moss, decaying vegetable matter, and on thorns, but not in the human respiratory tract. There is a distinct occupational hazard to farmers, laborers, and florists, with the result that there is a significant male sex predominance. Animals also may be infected, and it has been suggested that the disease may be transmitted from animals to man.[1387]

The organism is readily isolated from the sputum,[1387] where it may be seen on smear. Culture at 30° C on Sabouraud's agar reveals delicate hyphae supporting conidiophores terminating in clusters of pyriform conidia. Enriched media at 37° C or mouse tissues may support a growth of the cigar-shaped, Gram-positive, yeast-like forms. *Spor. schenckii* cannot be positively identified in tissues[1388] but stains well with methionine silver.[1387]

Primary pulmonary disease is extremely rare, only 22 authenticated cases having been published in the literature.[1387]

Roentgenographically, the disease may be manifest in any portion of the lung, and the number of variations in its presentation are almost as great as the number of cases reported. Changes include isolated nodular masses which may cavitate, leaving thin-walled cavities;[1387, 1389-1391] segmental parenchymal consolidation, hilar lymph-node enlargement, which occurs in a high percentage of cases and may cause bronchial obstruction;[1387, 1389] and, in some cases, pulmonary disease which spreads through the pleura into the chest wall, creating a sinus tract.[1387]

The reaction to the organism in the tissues is usually suppurative but may be granulomatous.

Clinical manifestations vary from mild acute bronchitis to pneumonia which may be associated with severe malaise, cough, and fever. In man, most infections are cutaneous, with spread to regional lymph nodes; such may occur in epidemic form. Commonly, a pustule forms on the hand and the infection spreads along the lymphatic channels, forming nodules which may ulcerate; bones and joints may be directly involved from the cutaneous and lymph-node spread, and blood-stream invasion has been reported.[1392] Anemia and polymorphonuclear leukocytosis may develop.

Agglutination and complement-fixation tests sometimes are helpful to diagnosis,[1387] and a skin test also is available.

SOUTH AMERICAN BLASTOMYCOSIS

The dimorphic organism causing South American blastomycosis is limited to South and Central America and is most commonly reported from Brazil; it is considered to be exogenous in origin, but the site of its residence in nature is unknown. The disease shows a striking male predominance of 10:1[1393] and occurs especially in manual laborers and farmers, suggesting an occupational link.

In tissues or exudates cultured on media at 37° C, the organism is a multiple budding yeast form 2 to 16μ in diameter. Cultures on Sabouraud's glucose-agar medium at less than 30° C grow mycelia with branching hyphae and conidia. The organism is pathogenic for mice and guinea pigs.

The clinical picture usually consists in mucocutaneous lesions of the face and mouth, with or without lymph-node involvement in the neck and axillae. Clinically significant pulmonary involvement arises only through blood-stream dissemination, from infection in the gastrointestinal tract (chiefly from ulcerated lesions in the ileocecal area), or following tooth extraction;[1393] the fungemia may lead to involvement of the liver, spleen, and lungs. Since pulmonary involvement occurs via the blood stream, a miliary pattern is apparent roentgenographically in these cases.[1393] Skin and serologic tests are useful in diagnosis. The number of persons with positive skin tests in endemic areas suggests the existence of a benign, asymptomatic form of the disease.

ALLESCHERIASIS

The fungus, *Allescheria boydii*, is one of several that cause Maduromycosis, and sometimes gives rise to opportunistic infection in the lungs.[1394-1396] The *roentgenologic pattern* is of cavitation, sometimes enclosing a fungus ball.[1394, 1395] The patient may be asymptomatic or may have symptoms or signs of an underlying disease. The fungus may be cultured from sputum or blood and is identified by its ability to form ascospores.

TORULOPSIS GLABRATA

Like candida and cryptococcus, this organism is a member of the family *Cryptococcaceae*. It is a non-spore-forming yeast which reproduces by budding but which fails to produce septate hyphae. Infections in man are opportunistic and usually involve the urinary tract. Pulmonary involvement is rare.[1397-1399] A mycetoma due to this organism was a chance finding at postmortem examination in one reported case of a tuberculous cavity.[1399]

In tissue, *Torulopsis glabrata* is an ovoid, slightly elongated structure measuring $2 \times 4\mu$. The fungus can be demonstrated in tissues with PAS, silver methanamine, or hematoxylin and eosin stains.

INFECTIONS OF THE LUNGS DUE TO THE VIRUSES, *MYCOPLASMA PNEUMONIAE,* AND THE RICKETTSIAE

Many respiratory tract infections due to viruses and to *Mycoplasma pneumoniae* begin in the upper respiratory passages. Some viruses, including certain enteroviruses and the chicken-pox and measles viruses, frequently propagate in the upper respiratory tract, whence they disseminate throughout the body without producing respiratory symptoms. Others typically remain confined to the respiratory mucous membrane, where they cause a spectrum of disease ranging from mild, virtually asymptomatic rhinitis to widely disseminated, sometimes fatal, air-space pneumonia. Specific respiratory viruses tend to produce fairly well-defined clinical syndromes, although each is capable of producing any of the respiratory syndromes, depending upon the characteristics of the inoculum and the resistance of the host. The virulence and dose of the organism undoubtedly play a large role in determining whether the infection is confined to the nose and throat or whether it extends to the upper and lower respiratory tract. Experimental work has indicated that the size of the aerosol particle that carried the virus may be a major factor in determining the site of infection:[1400] large aerosol particles tend to deposit in the nasopharynx, resulting in an influenza-like infection with little or no involvement of the lower respiratory tract; small aerosol particles measuring 3μ or less are carried deep into the lungs, where they produce clinical and roentgenographic evidence of acute bronchitis, bronchiolitis, or pneumonia. When the rhinovirus is carried in small aerosol particles, it can produce tracheobronchitis experimentally, whereas under clinical conditions it usually produces no more than acute coryza. The resistance of the host is important in that it affects not only his ability to cope with the infection but also the extent to which the affecting agent may penetrate the defenses of the respiratory tract.

The age of the host also plays a role in determining the extent of infection, resistance in the very young and old being limited by immunologic and constitutional factors.[1401] For example, the rhinovirus—the common cause of acute coryza in adults—may produce a clinical picture of croup, bronchitis, bronchiolitis, and even bronchopneumonia in children.[1400] Also, underlying debilitating diseases, such as the reticuloendothelioses and specific immunoglobulin and cellular deficiency states, may increase individual susceptibility to respiratory virus infection. The influence of exposure and cold in reducing host resistance has been debated for many years but there is good evidence that temperature and humidity have little if any effect on susceptibility to disease.[1402] Women appear to be more susceptible just before and just after the menstrual period, but show an unusual resistance to respiratory viral infections during it.[1400]

It is probable that local factors play an even greater role than constitutional factors in modifying the extent to which viruses penetrate the respiratory tract. Normally, the lower respiratory tract is sterile, and experimental studies demonstrated a remarkable ability of the healthy lung to rid itself of microorganisms.[471, 1403] Rapid clearing of microorganisms depends largely on the presence of a healthy mucous membrane with active cilia and an appropriate consistency of the mucous that lines the respiratory tract; it also appears to relate to the presence of immunoglobulin A in mucous secretion.[1404] These local defense mechanisms can be diminished by the inhalation of fumes—particularly cigarette smoke[1405, 1406]—or aerosols that damage respiratory tract epithelium and inhibit ciliary activity; obstruction of air passages, either local or diffuse, may prevent adequate clearance of organisms from the distal airways, with resultant general bronchitis or local bronchopneumonia; patients with asthma, bronchogenic carcinoma, or chronic bronchitis and emphysema are subject to repeated infections, many of which are viral in origin. In a controlled study of patients with chronic bronchitis, Stenhouse[1407] found eight (14 per cent) of 56 acute exacerbations of bronchitis to be due to rhinovirus, as documented by culture and by a rise in neutralizing antibody titers; a control group showed only febrile or afebrile rhinorrhea. Although infections with the respiratory viruses usually are restricted to the upper respiratory tract, the clinical presentation may be that of pneumonia when the organism appears in epidemic form, as when civilian and military personnel are grouped closely together; examples of such an occurrence include the epidemics of adenovirus pneumonia reported by Miller and his associates in naval recruits[1408] and the severe air-space pneumonia reported in epidemics of influenza (*vide infra*).

RESPIRATORY SYNDROMES

CORYZA

Acute coryza (the common cold) is a syndrome which includes rhinorrhea, nasal obstruction, and occasionally cough and sore throat, without accompanying severe systemic or lower respiratory tract involvement. Although it has been known for many years that coryza may be caused by a number of the respiratory viruses, it was not until 1965, when Hoorn and Tyrrell[1409] identified the rhinoviruses, that these were recognized as the cause of up to 40 per cent of cases of coryza in adults and only a slightly smaller percentage in children.[1400, 1407, 1410] Like the enteroviruses, the rhinoviruses form a group within the large family of *Picornaviruses*. These organisms grow on tissue culture and are among the smallest of the viruses.[1411] A small percentage of cases of coryza are caused by other viruses including influenza, parainfluenza (especially types I and III), the adenoviruses, respiratory syncytial virus, coxsackie virus A-21, some ECHO viruses, and *Mycoplasma pneumoniae*.[1400, 1411] Despite these multiple etiologies, in a substantial number of cases of common cold the responsible organism defies identification. Tyrrell and Bynoe[1412] produced coryza in volunteers from an inoculum which could not be propagated even on organ culture; this "new" respiratory virus is morphologically identical and indistinguishable from those that cause avian infectious bronchitis and mouse hepatitis. Neutralizing antibodies to this "new" virus have been demonstrated, and 29 per cent of 215 sera collected between 1957 and 1967 from children and adults in Great Britain contained this neutralizing antibody.[1413, 1414] No instances of lower respiratory infection were noted in the small study of inoculated volunteers conducted by Bradburne and associates.[1413]

ACUTE PHARYNGITIS/TONSILLITIS INFECTIONS

Only a small percentage of cases of acute pharyngitis and tonsillitis are caused by viruses (including adenoviruses and the coxsackie, herpes simplex, influenza, and parainfluenza viruses). The most common etiologic agent in this group is not a virus but a bacterium, beta-hemolytic streptococcus, which is said to be responsible for 25 to 35 per cent of cases.[1410] This streptococcus usually is of the Lancefield group-A type, but infections due to organisms from groups B, C, and G also have been described.[1415] The etiologic agent is unknown in approximately 30 per cent of cases of this clinical syndrome.[1410]

ACUTE RESPIRATORY DISEASE (ARD)

This is an ill-defined group of upper respiratory tract infections which cannot be classified as one of the other respiratory syndromes because the nose does not run enough, the throat is not sore or red enough, and the cough is not severe or paroxysmal enough.[1410] Fever is a constant feature, and malaise and generalized aching are almost always present. Physical signs are sparse, but redness of the throat and occasional rales are common. The etiology of the syndrome varies in population groups studied over a period of years;[1415] 15 to 35 per cent are believed to be caused by influenza virus, 2 to 9 per cent by parainfluenza virus, approximately 4 per cent by the respiratory syncytial virus and 3 per cent by adenovirus. The last named appears to be responsible for a large percentage of cases of ARD in military recruits.[1400, 1410] Although the etiology of a minority of cases of ARD remains undetermined, the responsible agent is being identified far more frequently now than it was ten years ago, when only 16 to 17 per cent of cases could be ascribed to a specific organism.[1410, 1416]

ACUTE LOWER RESPIRATORY TRACT DISEASE

This term includes acute bronchitis, bronchiolitis, bronchopneumonia, and primary atypical pneumonia. In adults, the most common etiologic agent is *Mycoplasma pneumoniae*, said to be responsible for 25 to 60 per cent of all nonbacterial pneumonias;[1410] other agents include the adenoviruses and influenza virus; and in approximately 40 per cent of cases the etiologic agent is not identified. In infants and small children, the chief etiologic agent in acute bronchiolitis and bronchopneumonia of nonbacterial origin is the respiratory syncytial virus; these infections frequently occur in epidemic form.[1417, 1418]

Primary Atypical Pneumonia (PAP)

GENERAL COMMENTS AND EPIDEMIOLOGY. Approximately 25 years ago it was recognized that a certain percentage of cases of pneumonia did not respond to sulfonamides and penicillin and that this group possessed clinical and roentgenographic manifestations which set them apart from the usual bacterial pneumonia. The onset of pneumonia tended to be insidious and was associated with a moderate degree of fever, cough (productive of only small amounts of mucoid material), sparse physical signs, and often a normal white-cell count. The roentgenographic pattern also was somewhat different from the usual bacterial pneumonia in that it consisted of multiple patchy areas of homogeneous density, usually in the lower lobes. The demonstration of cold agglutinins (serum macrogammaglobulins which agglutinate human-type O cells at 0° C but not at 37° C) in patients with these clinical and roentgenographic manifestations led to the inclusion of this phenomenon as one of the criteria for diagnosis of this type of pneumonia, called primary atypical pneumonia (PAP).[1419] In 1944, Eaton and his colleagues[1420] isolated a specific agent on culture embryos which appeared to be responsible for at least some of the cases of PAP. In 1957, Liu[493] identified the responsible organism in the sputum of patients by an antigen-antibody reaction, using fluorescein-labeled antibody on frozen section of infected chick embryo lungs. Subsequent studies revealed that the Eaton agent was a pleuro-pneumonia-like organism (PPLO) which has since been designated *Mycoplasma pneumoniae*. The cold-agglutination test has been shown to be rather nonspecific, in that it is positive in cases other than those that could be identified culturally or serologically as due to *M. pneumoniae*; conversely, some infections due to *M. pneumoniae* do not produce cold-agglutinating antibodies. Griffin and Crawford[482] identified cold-agglutinin reactive sera in 172 patients with primary atypical pneumonia, and only 41 of these proved to be due to *M. pneumoniae* on culture and serologically. Cold agglutinins usually develop in the second week of illness and reach a maximum titer in the third or fourth week, after which they usually disappear. A titer of 1:32 or greater usually is considered positive, and a four-fold or greater rise in titer in convalescent serum is required for demonstration of activity.[484] Of a series of cases of primary atypical pneumonia studied by George and associates,[481] 43 per cent were considered due to *M. pneumoniae*, 7 per cent to adenovirus, and the remainder were of undetermined etiology; a cold-agglutinin titer of 1:32 or higher was found in 57 per cent of patients with *M. pneumoniae* infection, 17.6 per cent of those due to adenovirus, and in 43 per cent of those of undetermined etiology. A four-fold rise in titer was seen in 59 per cent of patients with mycoplasma infections and in only 29 per cent of those in whom the etiology was undetermined; in none of the cases in which adenovirus was the responsible organism was a four-fold rise in titer demonstrated.

In different series, analysis of cases judged on clinical and roentgenographic grounds to satisfy the criteria of PAP has shown that *Mycoplasma pneumoniae* is responsible for approximately 50 per cent of cases.[479, 481, 483] In epidemics, however, other organisms, particularly type-IV adenovirus, may predominate; for example, type-IV adenovirus was the responsible organism in 80 per cent in one series of 88 cases of PAP.[1408] In addition to the two main organisms responsible for PAP—*M. pneumoniae* and the adenoviruses[483]—other organisms that may produce the generally accepted clinical and roentgenographic features are influenza, parainfluenza, and respiratory syncytial viruses, as well as the etiologic agents responsible for psittacosis, Q-fever, and histoplasmosis.[479, 484]

Although primary atypical pneumonia may occur at any time throughout the year, cases due to *M. pneumoniae* show a peak incidence in the late summer and autumn and those due to adenovirus occur predominantly during the winter months.[481, 483]

PATHOLOGIC CHARACTERISTICS. The pathology of the various pneumonias caused by virus and virus-like organisms is somewhat different from that due to bacteria, presumably because of the intracellular invasion by viruses. Since acute virus pneumonia is seldom fatal there is a paucity of pathologic reports; many of the patients who do die have superimposed bacterial infection which masks the original viral reaction.

There is little doubt that the virulence of the infecting agent plays a major role in determining the resultant pathologic change. An overwhelming infection with virulent organisms tends to produce a severe, diffuse, hemorrhagic edema of the parenchymal air spaces, with subsequent polymorphonuclear infiltration; a smaller dose of less-virulent organisms produces proliferation of the respiratory epithelium of the bronchi, bronchioles, and alveoli, with infiltration of mononuclear cells in the bronchial walls, the peribronchiolar tissues, and sometimes the alveolar walls.[961] The process is predominantly interstitial, the acute inflammatory reaction in the peribronchial and peribronchiolar tissue extending along blood vessels and lymphatics into interlobular septa.[484]

ROENTGENOGRAPHIC MANIFESTATIONS. Primary atypical pneumonia tends to involve the lower lobes, more often the left, and is limited to a single lobe in about 50 per cent of cases. Occasional involvement of an upper lobe may result in a pattern simulating tuberculosis. George and associates[481] described the roentgenographic pattern of pneumonia due to *Mycoplasma pneumoniae* and the adenoviruses as segmental consolidation (Figure 7–33). Our own experience with 36 patients with proved mycoplasma and viral pneumonia[1424] has revealed a sequence of changes that we regard as highly suggestive of the diagnosis (*see* Figure 4–57, page 247). The early change is a fine reticular pattern of segmental distribution seldom involving more than one lobe; this pattern corresponds to a phase of acute interstitial inflammation. In the second phase, the acute inflammation extends to the air spaces of the lung, with production of patchy areas of air-space consolidation in which individual acinar shadows may be identified. The third phase indicates the early stage of resolution and consists in the disappearance of signs of air-space consolidation but persistence of the reticular pattern that represents interstitial inflammation. The development of new areas of consolidation during treatment is not uncommon, and there may be some loss of volume. Roentgenographically demonstrable pleural effusion is rare.[481, 484, 1424]

CLINICAL MANIFESTATIONS. Symptoms usually are rather unimpressive, often to a degree where marked discrepancy exists between the mildness of symptoms and the severity of the roentgenographic changes.[484] Fever usually is low-grade but may rise to 103° F. Cough is usual and may be either dry or productive of mucoid or purulent material, and the patient may complain of symptoms relating to the upper respiratory tract. Hemoptysis and pleural pain are most uncommon, although intercostal or retrosternal pain may be complained of on coughing. Findings usually consists of a local decrease in breath sounds, a few rales, and occasionally frank signs of consolidation with bronchial breathing. The clinical picture is in sharp contrast to that of acute bacterial pneumonia, which has an acute onset, chills, bloody sputum, pleural pain, frank signs of consolidation, and severe respiratory distress.[479]

PAP rarely gives rise to leukocytosis; in 75 to 80 per cent of cases reported by George and his associates,[481] the white-cell count was below 10,000 per c mm. (In any case of pneumonia, a white-cell count above 15,000 per c mm should suggest a bacterial etiology.[479]) Eosinophilia develops in few cases.[484] In a study of leukocyte response during acute viral respiratory disease in 113 volunteers who were exposed to a number of different virus agents, Douglas and his associates[1022] found a mild leukocytosis of 10,000 to 13,000 per c mm at the onset of illness, often followed by leukopenia at a stage when nonviral pneumonia would have shown further leukocytosis; lymphopenia

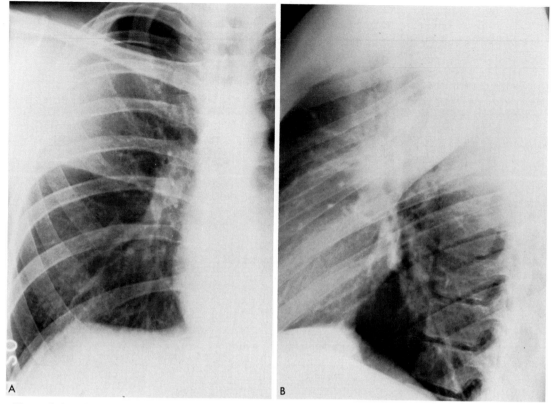

Figure 7–33.   **Primary Atypical Pneumonia (Mycoplasma).** Views of the right hemithorax from posteroanterior (A) and lateral (B) roentgenograms demonstrate homogeneous consolidation of the posterior bronchopulmonary segment of the right upper lobe; the density is somewhat granular in texture. The consolidation abuts against the posterior portion of the minor fissure, in keeping with the anatomic distribution of this segment. Twenty-eight-year-old man; moderate leukopenia; positive complement fixation to *Mycoplasma pneumoniae.* Although this pattern of homogeneous consolidation occurs in some cases of acute viral or Mycoplasma pneumonia, in our experience it is not as common (nor as characteristic) as a mixed interstitial and air-space pattern as illustrated in Figure 4–57, page 247.

preceded by increase in lymphocytes occurred in those volunteers who were more severely ill. These authors showed the leukocyte count to be of no value in differentiating the different viral etiologies.

Results of pulmonary function tests in patients with PAP were described by Berven.[1426] A degree of hypoxemia was noted on exercise in some cases. Impairment of pulmonary function persisted in the postinfectious phase, despite return of the chest roentgenogram to normal, and he stated that the diffusing capacity may be decreased for up to six months after clinical cure.

Pneumonia due to *Mycoplasma pneumoniae*

GENERAL COMMENTS AND EPIDEMI-OLOGY. Although the pleuro-pneumonia-like organism (PPLO), *Mycoplasma*

pneumoniae, is not a true virus and is more correctly included among the bacteria, it is generally accepted as the most common cause of nonbacterial pneumonia (comprising 10 to 33 per cent of all pneumonias in the civilian population and approximately one-third in marine recruits[1427]). Several serologically distinct species of mycoplasma have been recognized—*M. hominis, M. salavarium, M. orale, M. fermentans,* and *M. pneumoniae;* the last named is the only species clearly pathogenic for man, although the others may act as saprophytes.

Mycoplasma pneumoniae grows readily on enriched agar or beef broth and has been cultured in tissue and in chorioallantoic membrane of chick embryos.[484, 1428]

Unlike adenovirus pneumonia, which tends to occur almost exclusively during the winter months, infections with *Mycoplasma pneumoniae* occur throughout the year, with a peak during the autumn and early winter.[481, 483, 1427, 1429, 1430] Mycoplasma pneumonia occurs most often in the age group 5 to 19 years, infection in younger children usually producing no symptoms, and in somewhat higher incidence in males than in females.[1427, 1429, 1431, 1432]

Although nearly all infections with this organism are mild,[1430] careful inquiry into family groups usually reveals symptoms in the majority of affected persons.[1431–1433] In a study by Balassanian and Robbins,[1433] two thirds of the patients were symptomatic, most of them presenting a clinical and roentgenographic picture of primary atypical pneumonia; asymptomatic infection tended to occur in children under the age of five years. In a follow-up study for several months after the acute episode these same authors found a four-fold increase in antibody titers in all members of a family.[1433] Despite the presence of circulating antibody and the administration of tetracycline, shedding of mycoplasma organisms may continue after the patient has recovered from infection.[1433, 1434] These "carriers" have been found in military populations,[483] in student groups,[1410] and even in civilian communities.[1431] Infection is acquired by droplet inhalation and has been produced by this means in volunteers.[1434, 1435] The incubation period is about three weeks in naturally acquired disease and approximately ten days in volunteers, the shorter incubation period in the latter being due to the placement of the large inoculum directly in the respiratory tract.[1427, 1432]

PATHOLOGIC CHARACTERISTICS. To our knowledge, there are no specific morphologic features of mycoplasma pneumonia that distinguish it from acute viral pneumonia. The inflammatory reaction is predominantly interstitial, with extension of the process into alveoli in the more severe infections (see page 677).

ROENTGENOGRAPHIC MANIFESTATIONS. According to Rosmus and his colleagues,[1424] the roentgenographic pattern of acute mycoplasma pneumonia is indistinguishable from that of many of the viruses (see page 677). In the early stages it is characterized by a rather fine reticular pattern representing the acute interstitial inflammatory stage of the disease. This is followed by signs of air-space consolida-

tion of patchy distribution, often with acinar shadows (see Figure 4–57, page 247). With resolution, the process is reversed, the air-space consolidation disappearing first and then the interstitial disease. In a study of 116 cases followed serially, George and associates[481] found that roentgenographic resolution averaged 11 days, clearing being complete in all cases within 25 days. In contrast to the nonsegmental distribution of acute bacterial air-space pneumonia (caused by *Diplococcus pneumoniae*, for example) mycoplasma pneumonia tends to be segmental; of a series of 79 cases reported by Alexander and associates,[1429] only two had a roentgenographic picture that could be confused with bacterial pneumonia, and both of these were readily identified as being of mycoplasma or viral origin, on the basis of clinical findings and white-cell count. Involvement is predominantly of the lower lobes, only five of 39 cases studied by Grayston and associates[1436] having upper-lobe involvement. Hilar lymph-node enlargement is rare in adults,[1424] although it was present in eight of 30 children in one study.[1437] Pleural effusion usually is found only occasionally, although in one series small effusions were noted in four of 20 cases.[1438] Unusual findings in a few of the 116 cases reported by George and associates[481] included Kerley B lines and pneumatoceles.

CLINICAL MANIFESTATIONS. Pneumonia due to *Mycoplasma pneumoniae* usually is more prolonged and severe than that due to the viruses, lasting for an average of two to three weeks.[1439] Symptoms include cough, which usually is nonproductive but sometimes associated with mucoid expectoration, headache, malaise, fever, and sometimes chills.[1435, 1440] Upper respiratory tract involvement, characterized by sore throat and nasal symptoms, is noted in approximately half the cases[481, 1427] and is indistinguishable from disease caused by various respiratory viruses.[1427] The incidence of upper respiratory symptoms in mycoplasma pneumonia varies: George and associates[481] found them to occur less often, and Evans[1410] equally as often as in virus pneumonia. Headache and fever are said to be more common, and rhinitis and gastrointestinal symptoms less common than in other pneumonias.[1429] Among the upper respiratory symptoms and signs of particular interest is bullous myringitis, a manifestation which was originally described in volunteers infected with Eaton agent[1435] but which subsequently has been described in a few cases with naturally acquired infections.[1411, 1431, 1432] A maculopapular rash develops over the trunk and back of some patients.[1431] Physical examination of the lungs usually reveals rales and decrease in breath sounds at the lung bases, and signs of frank consolidation have been described in some instances.[481]

Complications of *Mycoplasma pneumoniae* infections are not common but may be very serious. In addition to the myringitis, which could be considered a manifestation of the disease rather than a complication, meningoencephalitis or meningitis may develop,[1427] resulting in a high protein content and many mononuclear cells in the cerebrospinal fluid in some cases; these complications infrequently are fatal. Toxic psychosis developed in two members of the family group studied by Balassanian and Robbins.[1433] Other complications include the development of hemagglutination or hemolysis (presumably due to the cold agglutinins), and peripheral thrombophlebitis with subsequent pulmonary thromboembolic disease. These complications appear to occur only in patients who have very high titers of cold agglutinins; in one case report of a woman who experienced a hemolytic crisis with approximately 50 per cent decrease in hematocrit, the cold agglutinin titer was 1:8192.[1433] Three cases of pneumonia associated with polyarthritis have been described in which the diagnosis of mycoplasma pneumonia was made by complement fixation, all three having negative anti-streptolysin-O titers;[2071] the relationship of this acute arthritis to the more chronic joint disease associated with the syndrome of PPLO is not clear.

Other rare complications include thrombocytopenic purpura and various skin eruptions, of which the most important is erythema multiforme or the Stevens-Johnson syndrome.

Stevens-Johnson Syndrome. Erythema multiforme originally was described by Hebra in 1866[1441] as a descriptive term for red or violet macules, papules, vesicles, or bullae usually distributed widely and symmetrically over most of the skin of the body and sometimes the mucous membranes. The syndrome described by Stevens and Johnson[1442] in 1922 usually is reserved for the more severe cases of erythema multiforme associated with a systemic reaction including high fever, stomatitis, ophthalmia, and occasionally involvement of the lungs. Association of this syndrome with primary atypical pneumonia was noted by many observers over the last quarter century, and in 1967 Fleming and associates[1443] reviewed the literature pertaining to this relationship. Ludlam and associates[1444] were the first to report a positive complement-fixation test for *Mycoplasma pneumoniae* in patients with this syndrome, and their findings have been confirmed by many others.[481, 1443, 1445, 1446] *M. pneumoniae* has been isolated both from the nasopharynx[1443] and from blister fluid in patients with erythema multiforme.[1445] Not all patients have roentgenographic evidence of pneumonia; this was detected in only 9 of 56 patients studied at the Johns Hopkins Hospital, although many of the patients did not have chest roentgenograms because there was no clinical indication of pulmonary involvement.[1447] When pneumonia is present, the roentgenographic pattern is said to be identical to that of mycoplasma pneumonia.[1446]

In some patients at least, drug therapy may be implicated in the etiology of Stevens-Johnson syndrome. Bianchine and associates,[1447] who made a very thorough retrospective study of 130 patients with erythema multiforme, divided their patients into three groups: (1) those in whom an upper respiratory infection was present for one day to two or more weeks before the clinical syndrome became manifest and who were given no drug therapy (20 per cent of the cases); (2) the largest group, comprising 50 per cent of the series, also had an onset suggesting an upper respiratory infection but the syndrome appeared at varying intervals following inception of drug therapy; (3) the remainder of the cases (30 per cent) showed no evidence of upper respiratory prodromata but were receiving drug therapy before the appearance of the syndrome. Subsidence of the cutaneous reaction after drugs are stopped, and exacerbations with challenge, support the conclusion that drug therapy is intimately involved in the etiology in some cases.[1447, 1448] Thus it appears that the Stevens-Johnson syndrome is related to infection with *Mycoplasma pneumoniae* in some cases and to drug therapy in others. In this regard it is of interest that the age incidence of patients with Stevens-Johnson syndrome is virtually identical to that of *Mycoplasma pneumoniae* infection.[1445, 1447]

LABORATORY PROCEDURES IN DIAGNOSIS. The white-cell count in mycoplasma pneumonia usually is normal but in a small percentage of cases may reach 20,000 per c mm. Andrewes[1411] found an average count of 9,500 per c mm in 67 patients, in a range of 3,800 to 20,700, and in George and colleagues' series of patients with mycoplasma or adenovirus infections the average count was less than 10,000 per c mm.[481] By contrast, Evans[1410] found the white-cell count to be a differentiating feature between mycoplasma pneumonia and virus pneumonias in general, in that the leukocyte count was raised in twice as many cases of nonmycoplasma pneumonia as in infections due to this organism. Eosinophilia was observed in eight of 67 patients in one series.[1411]

Since culture of *Mycoplasma pneumoniae* on agar or in broth takes one to three months, and since recovery always occurs within this period, this procedure is useful only as a means of retrospective diagnosis. Similarly, the demonstration of four-fold rise in specific antibody titer may take several weeks and therefore is of little use in establishing the diagnosis during the acute phase of the disease. These facts emphasize the importance of suggesting the diagnosis from the fairly characteristic roentgenographic pattern. For many years a four-fold rise in cold-agglutinin titer during the period of acute illness has been considered a useful indication of primary atypical pneumonia. There is little doubt that *Mycoplasma pneumoniae* infection is the most common respiratory cause for the production of cold agglutinins; however, they are found in not more than 50 per cent of cases,[481, 1427, 1435, 1439, 2664] and they develop in virus pneumonia also; in fact, approximately one quarter of cold-agglutinin-positive pneumonias are not due to *M. pneumoniae*.[1427]

Another nonspecific serologic test sometimes used to identify primary atypical pneumonia is the development of agglutinins for streptococcus MG, a ubiquitous oral bacterium. Agglutinins for this organism develop in only a small proportion of patients with mycoplasma pneumonia,[1427] and a significant titer was present in only one of the 25 volunteers inoculated with the organism by Rifkind and his colleagues.[1435] Increase in the titer of cold hemagglutinins and streptococcus-MG agglutinins appears to be related to the severity of *M. pneumoniae* infection,[495, 1433] but there may be no significant increase in cases of Stevens-Johnson syndrome due to *Mycoplasma pneumoniae*.[1444, 1445]

Of much greater diagnostic value are the techniques that show specific antibodies to *Mycoplasma pneumoniae*, including immunofluorescence microscopy and complement-fixation tests:[1450] the former reveals antibodies and the latter a fourfold rise in titer of the antibodies in virtually every culturally proved case of mycoplasma pneumonia.[1433, 1435, 1450] Immunofluorescence microscopy of sputum or pleural fluid containing *Mycoplasma pneumoniae* organisms directly stained with fluorescent antibody is particularly valuable in that it allows for early diagnosis.[1427]

RESPIRATORY INFECTIONS DUE TO VIRUSES

The respiratory viruses may be divided into two large groups on the basis of the type of nucleic acid they contain. The viruses and rickettsia are composed of an outer coat of protein and an inner core of either ribose nucleic acid (RNA) or desoxyribose nucleic acid (DNA) or a combination of the two. The RNA group includes the myxoviruses, picornaviruses, and reoviruses; the DNA group includes adenoviruses and herpes viruses. The rickettsia and the etiologic agent of ornithosis contain both types of nucleic acid.

MYXOVIRUS RESPIRATORY INFECTIONS

The myxoviruses capable of producing respiratory infections include influenza, parainfluenza, respiratory syncytial virus, and measles (rubeola) virus. *Influenza virus* infection usually involves only the upper respiratory passages, including the trachea and major bronchi, and is particularly prone to affect school children and young adults; however, in a small percentage of patients—particularly the aged or chronically ill—it may be responsible for fulminating pneumonia. *Parainfluenza viruses* characteristically affect children and are the cause of croup; in infants and young children they may cause severe bronchiolitis and bronchopneumonia; adults show a strong resistance to infection. The *respiratory syncytial virus* also tends to affect infants and small children and sometimes results in severe bronchiolitis and bronchopneumonia. *Measles virus* may cause pneumonia also, although it is probable that the majority of pneumonias in measles are the result of secondary bacterial infection. A distinctive pathologic entity known as giant-cell pneumonia is found in patients infected with the measles virus who appear to be incapable of producing antibodies.

Influenza Virus Infection

GENERAL COMMENTS AND EPIDEMIOLOGY. Influenza is an acute infectious disease caused by the inhalation of influenza virus into the upper respiratory tract; clinically it is characterized by fever, myalgia, nonproductive cough, protracted weakness and lethargy, and often upper respiratory symptoms. The influenza virus can be divided into groups A, B, C, and D, each with a specific antigen demonstrable by complement-fixation testing. Groups A and B can be further divided into subgroups on a basis of neutralization and hemagglutination-inhibition tests. The influenza A virus commonly appears in epidemic form and is the responsible organism in the majority of cases of pneumonia. In contrast to the other respiratory myxoviruses, which produce infection only in infants and small children, influenza virus infects persons from five years of age to early adulthood.[1451, 1452]

Influenza is a very contagious disease, and during epidemics and pandemics the majority of the population contract it in some degree from asymptomatic infection to fulminating pneumonia and death. Acute chest complications developed in 28 (3 per cent) of the 930 patients diagnosed

and treated by Fry[1466] during the 1957 epidemic of Asian influenza; 18 had pneumonia and 10 had acute bronchitis.

The influenza A virus is an obligate human parasite which is transmitted from human to human by droplet infection. It shows a remarkable ability to mutate, so that an ever-increasing number of distinctive antigenic subgroups are being discovered, the most recent being the Hong Kong/68 A_2 variant.[1453] The incubation period of influenza virus infection is 24 to 48 hours, allowing for rapid spread of disease. Antibody formation to specific strains occurs with infection or vaccination and confers immunity for one to two years. Cross reactions occur, however, and the demonstration of antibodies to a specific strain does not necessarily signify immunity, since such antibodies may have been produced by an entirely different strain.[1454]

Pneumonia is an uncommon but dreaded complication of influenza infection; although many cases are localized and of mild-to-moderate severity, pneumonia is sometimes overwhelming and fatal. Most cases of pneumonia are recognized during epidemics or pandemics such as that of 1957/1958; when it develops as an endemic infection, it is often misdiagnosed or undiagnosed.[1455] In perhaps one third of cases of severe pneumonia—which may be fatal—the illness develops abruptly in persons who are apparently in good health;[1456-1458] it is now well recognized, however, that the majority have ˙some predisposing condition, such as heart disease, particularly rheumatic mitral stenosis,[1455, 1458-1461] pregnancy,[1458, 1459] chronic bronchitis, or diabetes.[1460, 1462] The strange predilection for patients with mitral stenosis to contract overwhelming alveolar spread of influenzal infection may be related to the presence of air-space edema (secondary to left atrial hypertension), which permits rapid dissemination of organisms from unit to unit through the pores of Kohn. Experimental studies have shown that sublethal inoculations of virus into the upper respiratory tract of mice may cause fulminating pneumonia if fluid is dropped into the nose or trachea also.[1461]

In the 1918/1919 influenza pandemic, hemolytic streptococcus was a common cause of superinfection and probably was responsible for many deaths. In the pandemic of 1957/1958, *Staphylococcus aureus* replaced the streptococcus and undoubtedly was the pathogen that contributed to the fatal outcome in a large proportion of cases. Superinfection is not necessary for a fatal outcome, however, for there seems no doubt that the influenza virus alone is capable of producing an overwhelming pneumonitis which may lead to death within 24 hours.[1461] The influenza virus was the only pathogen recovered from the lung in some patients post mortem,[1457, 1463] and in at least some of these, recovery of the virus from extrapulmonary organs indicated the presence of viremia.[1457]

PATHOLOGIC CHARACTERISTICS. The influenza virus causes proliferation and necrosis of epithelial cells lining the respiratory tract. Initially, changes consist in destruction of bronchial epithelium, including ciliated cells, goblet cells, and many of the bronchial mucous-gland secretory cells. The superficial cells undergo necrosis, exposing the basal layer. The bronchial walls are edematous and infiltrated with lymphocytes, and edema and inflammation extend into the peribronchial tissues and alveoli, which also are infiltrated with mononuclear cells. These changes extend all the way to the respiratory bronchioles and alveolar ducts and may be associated with capillary thrombosis, necrosis, aneurysm formation, and hemorrhage. Regeneration of the epithelium of the respiratory bronchioles and alveolar ducts starts five to seven days after the inception of inflammation.[1464] In the small percentage of cases in which fulminating air-space pneumonia is fatal within 48 hours, in addition to the changes in the airways, the alveoli are filled with edema fluid, red blood cells, fibrin, mononuclear cells, and not uncommonly hyaline membranes;[1457, 1458] Hers and associates[1464] identified staphylococci as a secondary invader in 60 per cent of their 148 confirmed cases of this type. In patients who survive the first few days, pathologic changes due to the virus infection may be obscured by the destructive influence of the staphylococcus (*see* page 596).

ROENTGENOGRAPHIC MANIFESTATIONS. The roentgenographic pattern varies considerably, depending upon the virulence of the organism, the resistance of the host, and the presence or absence of superinfection. Involvement may be local or general. The former usually is in the form of segmental consolidation, which may be homogeneous or patchy,[1465, 1466] most commonly in the lower lobes, and either unilateral or bilateral; serial chest roentgenograms may show poorly defined patchy areas of consolidation, 1 to 2 cm in diameter, which rapidly become confluent. In the cases described by Galloway and Miller,[1465] the disease was unilateral or bilateral in approximately equal incidence and roughly a quarter of the latter had widespread dissemination throughout both lungs; the roentgenographic pattern in these cases was one of diffuse patchy air-space disease resembling pulmonary edema, a pattern also observed by Soto and his coworkers (Figure 7–34).[1458] In the series studied by Kaye and his associates,[1455] these appearances of edema showed no response to treatment for cardiac failure. Pleural effusions occur but are comparatively rare.[1465] The average period of resolution is approximately three weeks.[1465]

CLINICAL MANIFESTATIONS. The symptoms of influenza consist of a dry cough, pain in the back and the leg muscles, chilly sensations, headache, conjunctivitis, sometimes substernal burning pain, and a fever of 101° or more for three to five days. Rhinorrhea and pharyngitis are not major manifestations of the clinical picture. When pneumonia develops, symptoms and signs depend on the nature and extent of the affection.

Louria and associates[1459] described three distinct lower respiratory tract syndromes in influenza. The mildest of these is believed to represent bronchiolitis and is unassociated with roentgenographic abnormality in the chest; patients may have hemoptysis, and local or diffuse rales and rhonchi may be audible. The second form is more common and occurs when superinfection with staphylococci, pneumococci, *H. influenzae*, or streptococci develops within two weeks after the initial virus infection. These patients expectorate purulent sputum which may be rusty or bloody and may complain of pleural pain. The third form is a much more fulminating type of pneumonia which develops within 12 to 36 hours after the initial symptoms and may be due to either the virus alone or to a combination of the virus and

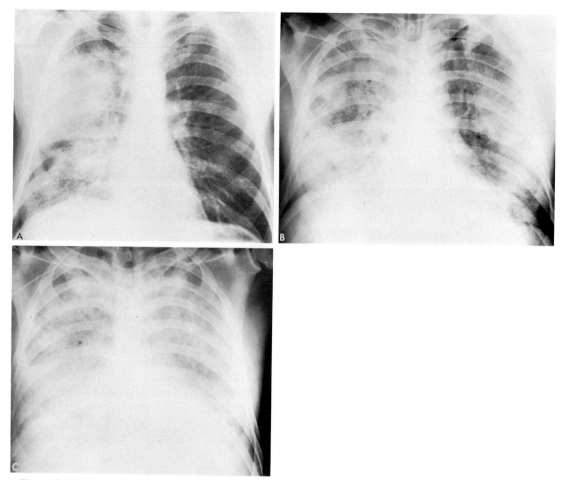

Figure 7–34. **Acute Influenza Virus Pneumonia.** This 32-year-old man was admitted to hospital with a three day history of progressive dyspnea, cough productive of whitish-yellow sputum, right-sided pleuritic chest pain, chills, and fever. His white cell count was 3500, consisting of 54 per cent lymphocytes and 46 per cent neutrophils. A posteroanterior roentgenogram on the day of admission (*A*) reveals extensive homogeneous air-space consolidation of the right upper lobe, with patchy shadows of air-space consolidation of the right lower lobe; the left lung is clear. Two days later (*B*), consolidation of the right lower lobe has become almost uniform and there has occurred extension of the air-space disease throughout the whole of the left lung; at this time, the roentgenographic appearance would be compatible with diffuse pulmonary edema. Twenty-four hours later (*C*), both lungs are almost completely consolidated, the only visible air being present within the bronchial tree (a diffuse air bronchogram). Shortly after admission, the patient became comatose and never regained consciousness; even with assisted ventilation on 100 per cent oxygen, the P_{O_2} was below 40 and P_{CO_2} between 80 and 90. Virology studies revealed a titer of 1/128 CFT for influenza A_2 and of 1/32 CFT for influenza B; a hemagglutination-inhibition test was positive to a titer 1/160 for influenza A_2, Hong Kong variant. In addition, respiratory syncytial virus and influenza virus were cultured from the blood, the sputum and directly from the lung at necropsy. (Courtesy Dr. Adolf Glay, St. Mary's Hospital, Montreal.)

staphylococcal superinfection. These patients are extremely ill, showing rapid development of dyspnea, cyanosis, and frothy blood-stained sputum which on culture may show a pure growth of coagulase-positive *Staphylococcus aureus*.[1467] Patients in this group tend to be those with underlying mitral stenosis or chronic bronchitis and who are pregnant. Oswald and his colleagues[1460] compared the clinical picture presented by patients with and

without bacteriologic evidence of staphylococcal superinfection and showed the former to be more severe and to be associated with a higher fatality rate. A study carried out by the British Public Health Laboratory Service[1468] in 1957 revealed the incidence of staphylococcal superinfection to rise in direct relationship to the length of hospitalization, 13 per cent of patients who died within the first two days of admission showing this organism on culture, whereas 80 per cent of those who were hospitalized and who survived for eight days or more harbored *Staphylococcus aureus*. In the series reported by Oswald and his co-workers,[1460] 15 per cent manifested mental changes including confusion, delirium, and coma; these were ascribed to respiratory failure, since many of these patients had chronic bronchitis. In the 1957/1958 epidemic in India, a small proportion of patients had liver disorders, as revealed by a rise in serum bilirubin values, and neurologic changes.[1469]

The white-cell count is usually normal in uncomplicated influenza but leukopenia develops in some cases, and, when severe, it is a poor prognostic sign. Overwhelming infection commonly results in a neutrophilia of 20,000 or more per c mm. Superinfection with staphylococci is evidenced by the production of purulent sputum containing polymorphonuclear cells. The influenza group responsible for the infection may be identified by complement-fixation testing, and the sub-group by the demonstration of specific hemagglutination-inhibition or neutralization antibodies. One method of rapidly diagnosing influenza consists in staining nasal smears directly with fluorescent antibody to influenza viruses prepared in guinea pigs.[1470] The virus may be isolated by culture of the sputum in monkey kidney or chick embryo, growth occurring in 3 to 21 days.

Parainfluenza Virus Infection

In 1958 a new group of myxoviruses was identified by a technique of hemadsorption with guinea-pig erythrocytes,[1471] and now have been classified as types I, II, and III hemadsorption or parainfluenza viruses. They are responsible for a small percentage of cases of coryza in adults, but in infants and young children may cause severe croup and lower respiratory tract disease.[1418, 1471–1473] Parainfluenza virus infections occur predominantly in the winter months and may assume epidemic proportions; in such circumstances they may account for a high proportion of the cases of pneumonia, croup, and acute bronchiolitis in nursery outbreaks.[1418, 1474] In a study of 200 University of Wisconsin students with acute respiratory illness, Evans[1475] found 8.5 per cent to be due to hemadsorption type-I and 1.5 per cent to hemadsorption type-II viruses. Although the majority of the infections were restricted to the upper respiratory tract, two were associated with pneumonia. The disease presumably is transmitted by droplet infection. Pathologic characteristics have not been described, since almost invariably the infections are mild and self-limiting.

The roentgenographic changes in the chest which are relatively nonspecific, are said to consist in diffuse or local accentuation of lung markings due to peribronchial and peribronchiolar "infiltrations."[469]

In children the symptoms are those of croup, sometimes associated with intermittent rales indicating an associated bronchiolitis;[1418] the usual manifestation in adults is in the form of acute pharyngitis and tonsillitis.[1475] The white-cell count usually is normal although it increases to 15,000 per c mm in some cases of croup or pneumonia. The organism may be isolated by the culture of sputum on monkey tissue; growth requires 3 to 21 days. Neutralization and complement-fixation tests may be employed for diagnosis, as may hemadsorption with guinea-pig erythrocytes.

Respiratory Syncytial Virus Infection

The respiratory syncytial virus (RSV) is responsible for a small percentage of cases of coryza in children and adults and is a major cause of severe bronchiolitis and bronchopneumonia in infants and small children.[967, 1417, 1452, 1476, 1477] Epidemic outbreaks of acute bronchiolitis have been described.[1417, 1478, 1479]

This myxovirus was originally isolated in 1956 and 1957 from chimpanzees with coryza and from infants with croup and pneumonia, and was originally known as the chimpanzee coryza agent (CCA).[1480, 1481] Infections occur predominantly during the winter months and early spring; the incubation period ranges from three to five days.[1478, 1480]

Infants and young children under the age of four are particularly susceptible to infection with this virus,[1482] with lower respiratory tract involvement in a third to a half,[1478, 1482] and it has been estimated that the disease is fatal in 2 to 5 per cent of affected children.[1483] In an extensive study of acute respiratory illness by Reilly and co-workers[1476] the respiratory syncytial virus was found to be responsible for 14 per cent of all cases of mild upper respiratory illness and for 34 per cent of lower respiratory tract disease.

Disparity has been noted between the severity of respiratory symptoms and the relative paucity of roentgenographic changes.[1479] In infants, the chest roentgenogram is reported to show patchy areas of consolidation interspersed with zones of emphysema.[1478]

Symptoms include severe rhinitis, cough, and fever, associated with mild pharyngitis or conjunctivitis.[1480, 1482] In the presence of bronchiolitis or pneumonia, wheezing, dyspnea, cyanosis, and retraction of the rib cage are noted, in addition to physical signs of parenchymal consolidation.

Infection with this organism appears to result in most effective immunity, since adults who are challenged with the virus manifest no symptoms or signs or, at most, have symptoms of a mild common cold.[1452, 1480, 1483] The infection can be detected by complement-fixation and neutralization tests, and Gardner and McQuillin showed the great value of the immunofluorescent antibody technique in the early diagnosis of this infection.[1484]

Measles (Rubeola) Respiratory Infection

Segmental pneumonia and atelectasis occur commonly in patients with measles and in the majority are the result of superinfection with various bacteria; however, by inducing pathologic changes in the epithelial cells lining the airways and the alveoli, the measles virus itself may affect the lung directly. This virus is the most common if not the only organism responsible for the entity known as giant-cell pneumonia.

Measles is a disease of small children that occurs predominantly in the late winter and early spring. The incubation period averages 11 days, and prodromal symptoms, including fever, malaise, myalgia, headaches, conjunctivitis, sneezing, coughing, and nasal discharge may be noted for two to four days before the appearance of the typical blotchy erythematous rash. The measles virus may be recovered from nasopharyngeal secretions and presumably is transmitted by droplet infection.

PATHOLOGIC CHARACTERISTICS. Predominant changes consist in degeneration and hyperplasia of the epithelial cells of the bronchi and bronchioles; the epithelium may separate from its basement membrane and be detached into the lumen of the airways. Hyperplastic changes in the epithelial cells in the distal bronchi and bronchioles may be associated with active mitosis. Inflammatory exudate appears in the alveolar septa adjacent to the bronchi and bronchioles, the cellular infiltration consisting largely of lymphocytes and plasma cells and only occasional polymorphonuclear leukocytes.[961] Multinucleated epithelial giant cells containing intracytoplasmic inclusion bodies may be found in the respiratory epithelium at all levels of the airways. Although giant cells identical to these may develop in tissue culture of many viruses (including varicella, herpes zoster, herpes simplex, and various adenoviruses), the ability to produce this giant-cell reaction *in vivo* appears to be specific to measles; the measles virus is the only organism isolated to date in cases of true giant-cell pneumonia in man.[1485, 1486] In addition to the giant cell that forms part of the pathologic picture of giant-cell pneumonia, an entirely different type—the Warthin-Finkelbey giant cell—develops commonly in patients with measles; these cells appear in lymphoid tissue throughout the body during the prodromal stage of the disease and disappear soon after the rash becomes manifest.

ROENTGENOGRAPHIC MANIFESTATIONS. Primary pneumonia due to the measles virus produces a widespread reticular pattern throughout the lungs, indicating the location of the disease. Hilar lymph-node enlargement is the rule.[1485] The pneumonia that results from bacterial superinfection typically is segmental in distribution and usually affects the lower lobes, sometimes bilaterally; some degree of atelectasis is very common.

In children with measles, in addition to the interstitial pneumonitis with giant-cell formation caused by the virus itself, segmental pneumonia and atelectasis develop in many cases, usually the result of superinfection with *Diplococcus pneumoniae, Staph. aureus, H. influenzae,* or *Strep. hemolyticus.* In a survey of 897 patients with measles, Fawcitt and Parry[1073] found atelectasis in 28 per cent and pneumonia in 26 per cent; 64 per cent of the children showed roentgenographic evidence of hilar lymph-node enlargement. Follow-up studies of these patients revealed slow resolution (up to a year) of the atelectatic foci in some, although permanent pulmonary residua were rare.

CLINICAL MANIFESTATIONS. Giant-cell pneumonia characteristically develops before or coincident with the peak of the measles exanthem, often during the course of reticuloendothelial disease. Some patients appear to lack specific antibodies, and in these the pneumonia has been reported to occur after the exanthem has subsided;[1487] in such patients, the measles virus (which usually disappears rapidly once the rash is manifest) may persist and may be found in the upper respiratory tract for unusually long periods. Enders and associates[1488] isolated measles virus at necropsy from three typical cases of giant-cell pneumonia without signs or symptoms of clinical rubeola. Giant-cell pneumonia rarely occurs in adults.[1489, 1490]

The secondary bacterial pneumonia usually develops several days after the rash and when the patient's condition has begun to improve; its presence may be suspected when cough, purulent expectoration, tachycardia, rise in fever, and sometimes pleural pain, develop during early convalescence.

The white-cell count in giant-cell pneumonia usually is normal but may be low; in the presence of secondary bacterial pneumonia, polymorphonuclear leukocytosis commonly develops. The measles virus can be isolated on tissue cultures of throat washings or blood, and giant cells may be identified on throat smears and in urinary sediment.[1491]

PICORNAVIRUS RESPIRATORY INFECTIONS

The picornaviruses comprise a group of small organisms which contain RNA; the enteroviruses, which are a subgroup, comprise the various strains of Coxsackie and ECHO viruses. These organisms cause a great variety of clinical diseases of which affection of the respiratory tract is only one. Respiratory infection is usually limited to the upper tract and tends to be mild in degree; pneumonia is rare.[1492]

Coxsackie Virus Respiratory Infection

Coxsackie viruses may be differentiated from the other enteroviruses (ECHO and polio) by their pathogenicity for mice and hamsters and their lack of pathogenicity for monkeys. The Coxsackie viruses may be divided into two major groups: *group A*, which contains 24 serologic subtypes and is differentiated on the basis of production of flaccid paralysis in mice; and *group B*, which contains six serologic subtypes and causes spastic paralysis in mice. Coxsackie-A viruses typically produce vesicular and ulcerative lesions on the soft palate and occasionally aseptic meningitis; some strains (A-21 and A-24) are responsible for a small proportion of upper respiratory infections resembling the common cold. Coxsackie-B virus causes a great variety of clinical patterns, including aseptic meningitis, Bornholm disease, myocarditis, pericarditis, acute meningoencephalitis, and orchitis.[1493–1497]

Coxsackie virus infections usually occur in local or widespread epidemics during the summer months and early autumn. Pneumonia has been reported to occur rarely in Coxsackie-A infection[1498] and in association with pleurodynia due to Coxsackie-B (Bornholm disease).[1492, 1499] The B-5 strain has also been reported to cause linear atelectasis and pleural effusion.[1500]

The pathology of Coxsackie virus infection has not been described, since the disease is never fatal.

In the few cases of Coxsackie virus pneumonia that have been described, the roentgenographic pattern is said to consist of a fine perihilar "infiltration";[1498] parenchymal consolidation in the lung bases may occur in association with pleurodynia.[1694]

Symptoms may be limited to involvement of the upper respiratory tract, with rhinitis, pharyngitis and a dry cough, or may be related to epidemic pleurodynia and consist of intermittent severe recurring aching and gripping pain involving the lower thoracic and upper abdominal regions. Pleurodynia is usually accompanied by difficulty in breathing and by fever ranging from 100° to 103° F. The disease is characterized by remissions and by exacerbations that may last several weeks. There may be signs of meningitis and headache as a result of it, and signs of myocarditis, pericarditis, and orchitis. The white-cell count ranges from slight leukopenia to mild leukocytosis.[1498] The organism may be isolated by culture on monkey kidney of material from throat or rectal swabs or of serum, cerebrospinal fluid, urine, or stool. Strain-specific neutralization antibody tests are available.

ECHO Virus Respiratory Infection

The Enteric Cytopathic Human Orphan viruses include some 26 strains which cause a great variety of clinical manifestations, including fever, diarrhea, maculopapular and petechial rashes, aseptic meningitis[1695] and occasionally pneumonia.[1696, 1697] Respiratory disease occurs predominantly in infants, and in the few adults affected it simulates the common cold.

Involvement of the lung by this organism is said to produce a roentgenographic pattern of increase in the bronchovascular markings associated with bilateral hilar lymph-node enlargement.[1696] Butterfield and associates[1697] described the changes in eight premature infants affected during an epidemic involving a hospital nursery: the infants who survived the infection showed roentgenographic evidence of cystic emphysematous changes in their lungs; necropsy of the one who died revealed bilateral parenchymal consolidation and pneumatocele formation, and tissue culture grew type-19 ECHO virus.

The white-cell count usually is within normal limits, with relative lymphocytosis; leukocytosis develops in some cases. Diagnosis depends upon demonstration of the organism on human and simian cell-tissue culture, or by a four-fold increase in titer of neutralization and complement-fixation antibodies.

Poliovirus Respiratory Infection

The effects of the polioviruses on the thorax are indirect only; paralysis of the muscles of respiration results in alveolar hypoventilation and respiratory failure. Since static chest roentgenograms are normal, this subject is dealt with in more detail in the section on respiratory disease associated with a normal chest roentgenogram (*see* Chapter 19).

Rhinovirus Respiratory Infection

This most recently discovered member of the picornavirus group is responsible for a high percentage of upper respiratory coryza-like infections. Occasionally it produces lower respiratory tract disease in infants (*see* page 674).

REOVIRUS RESPIRATORY INFECTION

Sporadic reports of pneumonia caused by reoviruses have appeared in the literature.[1501–1504] The case described by Tillotson and Lerner[1501] was a five-year-old child who presented with a maculopapular rash and diffuse bilateral bronchopneumonia; at necropsy, the trachea and major bronchi were obstructed by a large mucous plug which on culture grew reovirus type III. Histologically, the lungs showed interstitial pneumonitis with a characteristic mononuclear infiltration similar to other virus pneumonias. The white-cell count was 19,000 per c mm, with polymorphonuclear leukocytosis.

ADENOVIRUS RESPIRATORY INFECTION

The adenoviruses are one of the two major groups of viruses that contain DNA and are responsible for respiratory infections (the other group are the herpes viruses). Respiratory infections caused by the adenoviruses range from the common cold to severe pneumonia. Twenty-eight immunologically distinct members of this group have been described, but most respiratory infections are caused by types III, IV, or VII, frequently in epidemic proportions. Epidemics are particularly prone to occur among military populations recently removed from civilian life; if the eight-week period of basic combat training is during the colder months, adenovirus infection rates approach 100 per cent of susceptible recruits, and approximately 50 per cent of those drafted will be sick enough to require hospitalization.[1508] Summer epidemics have been reported in children in association with swimming pools and summer camps.[1505]

All types of adenoviruses have a common complement-fixing antigen, and they can be differentiated by serum neutralization tests.

Lower respiratory infection with adenovirus is fairly common and may occur in epidemic form.[1408, 1506, 1507] In the epidemic of adenovirus type-VII disease reported by Dascomb and Hilleman,[1506] 16 per cent of the patients had pneumonia and 67 per cent had acute bronchiolitis. Lang and associates[1507] described an epidemic of adenovirus type-21 bronchopneumonia in Polynesian children: 2 of the 25 patients died and 15 (60 per cent) had residual lung damage, consisting of fairly severe bronchiectasis in five (20 per cent). MacPherson and Gold[3386] recently drew attention to the etiologic relationship between acute adenoviral pneumonia in children and the subsequent development of unilateral translucent lung (Swyer–James syndrome). The disease is acquired by droplet infection and the incubation period is four to five days. The pathologic changes have not been described.

The roentgenographic pattern is very similar to that seen in mycoplasma pneumonia (see page 677). The lower lobes are predominantly affected, usually unilaterally.[481] Pleural effusion is rare.

The adenoviruses are perhaps the most common cause of ARD (acute respiratory disease), a somewhat ill-defined syndrome of fever, pharyngitis, cough, hoarseness, chest pain, and conjunctivitis; fever tends to persist for four to five days.[1505] Pneumonia usually is mild and always is associated with typical upper respiratory symptoms as well as those due to the pneumonia.[481, 1505] The pneumonia may be severe, with productive cough in the later stages; pleural pain rarely occurs. Physical findings include pharyngitis, which frequently is exudative and closely resembles that due to streptococcal infection, and diffuse rales and rhonchi indicative of bronchiolitis but in some cases with definite signs of consolidation.[481, 1506]

Adenoviruses grow readily in tissue culture of human and simian cells, producing a distinctive destruction of tissue referred to as cytopathogenesis. The white-cell count usually is normal but may be slightly increased, and in very ill patients may reach values over 30,000 per c mm.[1506] Although the cold-agglutination test usually is reported to give negative results,[1505, 1506] George and associates[481] found cold-agglutinin titers of 1:32 or

higher in 17.6 per cent of patients with adenovirus infection; however, a four-fold rise in titer occurred in none of their cases.

HERPES VIRUS RESPIRATORY INFECTIONS

The herpes viruses are the second group of organisms containing DNA, and include varicella-zoster (chicken-pox) virus, cytomegalovirus (the etiologic agent of cytomegalic inclusion disease), and herpes simplex virus. The last-named may cause fatal disease in infants who acquire the infection from mothers who have recurrent herpetic vulvovaginitis.

Varicella-Zoster Respiratory Infection

GENERAL COMMENTS AND EPIDEMIOLOGY. The virus of varicella-zoster may invade the lungs and cause diffuse pneumonia. Although the pneumonia may be severe and rapidly fatal, sometimes it is relatively mild and is recognized only in retrospect on the basis of roentgenographic evidence of widespread microcalcifications throughout the lungs in a patient who gives a history of having had chicken pox during adult life.[1509]

The overall incidence of pneumonia in chicken pox appears to be about 14 per cent,[1510, 1511] although the incidence in adults admitted to hospital may be as high as 50 per cent.[1512, 1513] Only 14 cases of acute chicken-pox pneumonia could be found in the literature up to 1956,[1516] whereas 246 cases had been reported by 1967;[1510] this apparent increase in incidence during the past decade may be due partly to increased awareness of this manifestation of varicella. Ninety per cent of affected patients are aged 19 years or over, and more than 75 per cent of cases occur in the third to fifth decades. This high incidence of pneumonia in the adult population is in contrast to the incidence of varicella itself—50 per cent occurs in children less than six years of age and only 19 per cent in adults.[1510, 1514, 1515]

In both adults and children, pre-existing reticuloendothelial disease and corticosteroid and broad-spectrum antibiotic therapy may predispose patients to primary varicella pneumonia.[1517] Similarly, both the incidence and the mortality rate from pneumonia are much higher in pregnant women;[1510, 1512, 1514, 1518] in the large series reviewed by Triebwasser and associates,[1510] the mortality rate was 11.4 per cent in male and nonpregnant female patients, whereas 41 per cent of the 17 pregnant women died from the disease.

There is no particular race or sex predilection.[1510, 1514] Varicella tends to occur during the colder months and is thought to be transmitted by droplet infection. Viremia develops promptly following deposition of the virus in the upper respiratory tract. The incubation period averages 14 days and ranges from three to 21 days.

PATHOLOGIC CHARACTERISTICS. The varicella virus shows an affinity for epithelial cells and may invade any organ of the body. In the lungs, there is a combination of swelling, proliferation, and desquamation of alveolar septal cells and a predominantly mononuclear-cell infiltration. Fibrinous exudate fills the alveoli and sometimes forms "hyaline membranes." Focal areas of hemorrhage are common. Intranuclear inclusion bodies are found in septal cells, giant cells, fibroblasts, capillary endothelium, and epithelium of the airways. The bronchi and bronchioles may be filled with exudate and blood. The skin shows papules, vesicles, and pustules which, in cases of pneumonia, almost invariably extend into the oropharynx, the trachea, and larger bronchi. Vesicles may be found on the pleural and peritoneal membranes also.[1510, 1513, 1515, 1516, 1519, 1520]

ROENTGENOGRAPHIC MANIFESTATIONS. The characteristic roentgenographic pattern is one of patchy, diffuse air-space consolidation, and reports of nodular or "miliary-like" densities[1515, 1516] undoubtedly represent semantic variation on the same theme (Figure 7–35). The acinar shadows usually are fairly discrete in the periphery of the lung but show a tendency to coalesce near the hila and in the lung bases.[1510, 1512, 1514, 1519] In a minority of cases the changes have been described as transitory, some areas of air-space consolidation clearing while new areas appear.[1515, 1520] Hilar lymph-node enlargement may be present but may be difficult to appreciate because of contiguity of the parenchymal consolidation in the perihilar parenchyma.[1510, 1514, 1515, 1520] One case was reported to show central rarefaction in a zone of confluent consolidation.[1522] Roentgenographically demonstrable pleural effu-

sion is very uncommon and when present is small.

Roentgenographic clearing may take from nine days to several months;[1515, 1521–1523] in fact, six (30 per cent) of the 20 patients studied by Sargent and his co-workers[1520] showed roentgenographic evidence of widespread nodulation six years after the infection; they considered the nodules to represent residual scarring.

An interesting and apparently unique manifestation of acute chicken-pox pneumonia which was first described by MacKay and Cairney[1524] in 1960 and subsequently by other investigators in 1964[625] and in 1965,[1509] consists in tiny widespread calcifications throughout both lungs in persons who have a remote history of chicken pox during adult life (Figure 7–36). The calcifications occur in various sizes and numbers but seldom are more than 2 to 3 mm in diameter; they predominate in the lower half of the lungs. Calcification of hilar lymph nodes does not occur.

CLINICAL MANIFESTATIONS. Acute chicken-pox pneumonia occurs predominantly in adults who have severe cutaneous manifestations of the disease. Symptoms, signs, and roentgenographic changes develop two to three days after the appearance of the vesicular eruption, and history frequently reveals contact with an affected child three to 21 days before the onset of the acute illness. The onset often is marked by high fever which may precede the rash by two to three days. The rash may be scarlatiniform in its early stages but rapidly becomes maculopapular, vesicular, and pustular. In the rare cases of pneumonia in association with herpes zoster, the vesicles and papules are limited to one side of the body and show a peripheral nerve distribution.[1525, 1526]

The symptoms of pneumonia develop within a few days of the onset of the rash and consist of cough, shortness of breath, hemoptysis, tachypnea, pleuritic chest pain, and cyanosis, with fever as high as 105° F. Purulent expectoration is not a feature.[1510, 1514, 1515, 1520] When pneumonia develops, rash tends to be unusually severe and often extends on to the mucosa of the mouth and pharynx.[1520] Abdominal pain may be suggestive of "acute abdomen," and back pain may simulate that due to a herniated intervertebral disc.[1510]

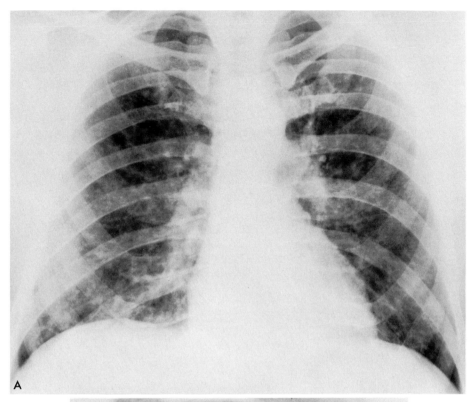

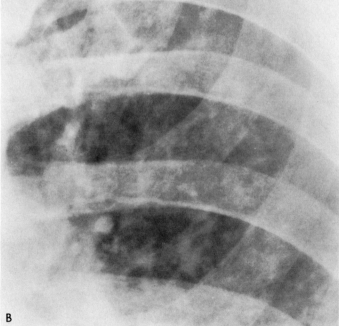

Figure 7–35. **Acute Varicella-zoster (Chicken-pox) Pneumonia.** A posteroanterior roentgenogram (*A*) reveals widespread involvement of both lungs by a process characterized by patchy air-space consolidation. Typical acinar shadows can be identified in most areas, as seen in a magnified view of the left upper lung (*B*). There is no evidence of hilar lymph-node enlargement. Thirty-year-old man with florid chicken pox; the appearance of clinical and roentgenologic signs of pneumonia coincided with the development of the rash. Uneventful recovery. (Courtesy Dr. Joseph Bloom, Montreal.)

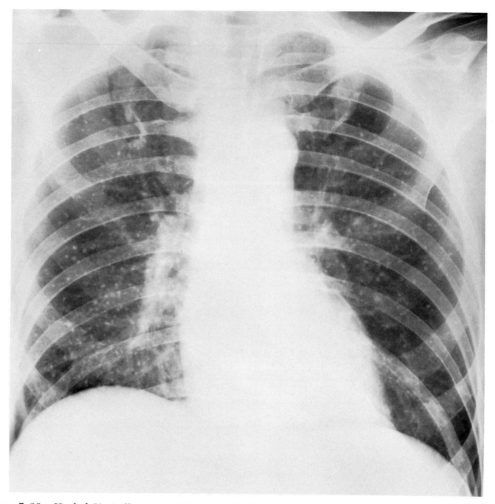

Figure 7–36. **Healed Varicella-zoster (Chicken-pox) Pneumonia.** A posteroanterior roentgenogram demonstrates a multitude of tiny calcific shadows measuring 1 to 2 mm in diameter scattered widely and uniformly throughout both lungs. This 42-year-old asymptomatic man had had florid chicken pox fifteen years previously; the presence of acute pneumonia was recognized at the time. (Courtesy Dr. Romeo Ethier, Montreal Neurological Hospital.)

Despite the extensive roentgenographic changes, in many cases the physical findings are unremarkable or absent.[1515, 1520] In one series, rales were heard in one or both lungs in 11 of the 20 patients (55 per cent).[1520] The temperature usually returns to normal within four days but may remain elevated for several days. Clinical improvement usually antedates roentgenographic clearing by several weeks. Complications include subcutaneous emphysema, hepatitis, nephritis, myocarditis, thrombocytopenia, and adrenal hemorrhage.[1510, 1513] Although it is probable that many cases of varicella pneumonia are mild and may be overlooked, a mortality rate as high as 11 per cent has been reported[1510] and patients with acute

pneumonia may die suddenly without warning indications.[1514]

The white-cell count is less than 10,000 per c mm in the majority of cases but exceeds this figure and is associated with polymorphonuclear leukocytosis in approximately one-third.[1510, 1520] Complement-fixing, neutralizing, and fluorescent antibodies are found in both varicella and herpes zoster infections, appearing about the fifth day of illness; paired titers determined in the acute and convalescent stages may be used to confirm the diagnosis,[1510] and the characteristic "type A intranuclear inclusion bodies" have been found in the sputum of one patient with acute varicella pneumonia.[1528]

Bocles and associates[1529] studied the

pulmonary function of adult patients with acute varicella, with and without pneumonia. In the absence of pneumonia, pulmonary function was completely normal. Patients with pneumonia showed a significant decrease in diffusing capacity (which persisted up to eight years after the acute illness) but normal ventilatory function. Arterial oxygen saturation was reduced in two of seven cases studied by Triebwasser and his colleagues.[1510] Some patients may have both hypoxemia and hypercarbia and may require artificial ventilation.[1530]

Cytomegalovirus Respiratory Infection

GENERAL COMMENTS AND EPIDEMIOLOGY. The cytomegalovirus (CMV) is the cause of cytomegalic inclusion disease (CID), a condition predominantly affecting neonates and small infants, and adults with underlying reticuloendothelial disease, immunologic deficiencies, or receiving immunosuppressive therapy. The disease is rare but is being recognized more frequently, particularly in recipients of transplanted kidneys and in those requiring extracorporeal circulation during surgery.[1531, 1532, 1563] Pulmonary disease may occur in infants but is much more common in the adult;[1533] it has been reported coexistent with *Pneumocystis carinii* pneumonia.[1564]

The cytomegalovirus is a common parasite of rodents. It has been recovered from the saliva of some infants without evidence of infection, presumably residing in the salivary glands; similarly, the virus has been recovered from the organs of persons who have shown no clinical evidence of disease and no specific histologic lesions at necropsy. Thus it is clear that the virus can exist as a commensal or saprophyte in man, even though it can also cause pathologic changes that may be fatal.

Congenital cytomegalic inclusion disease is acquired *in utero* from a mother who harbors the infection but shows no clinical evidence of it; the infants are jaundiced, hepatosplenomegaly and thrombocytopenic purpura develop, and those who survive usually have cerebral damage.[1533, 1534] As with the asymptomatic "carrier" mothers, adults and small children also may have a latent virus whose activity is triggered by immunosuppressive therapy or by immunologic deficiency secondary to reticuloendothelial disease or hypogammaglobulinemia.[1533, 1535–1537] In infants other than neonates, cytomegalovirus infection may be acquired from maternal milk.[1538] Serologic studies suggest that most patients in whom the infection develops after renal transplantation had prior exposure to CMV;[1532] where a latent form of infection cannot be incriminated, it is possible that patient-to-patient transmission occurs through oropharyngeal secretions, or perhaps the recipient of a renal graft may acquire infection from that kidney or from transfused fresh blood.[1532]

PATHOLOGIC CHARACTERISTICS. The characteristic histologic change due to cytomegalovirus infection is the presence of intranuclear and intracytoplasmic inclusion bodies in the parenchymal cells of the salivary glands, liver, kidneys, adrenals, and lungs. In the last named, both the bronchiolar and alveolar epithelial cells become greatly enlarged and eventually are detached so as to lie in the bronchial and alveolar lumen. The alveoli are filled with a serosanguinous exudate and the interstitium of the lung shows edema and mononuclear-cell infiltration.[961, 1534, 1536] Abundant hyaline membranes have been described,[1534] and inclusion bodies have been reported to occur in large numbers in the mediastinal lymph nodes.[1534]

ROENTGENOGRAPHIC MANIFESTATIONS. The usual pattern of cytomegalovirus disease of the lungs consists in diffuse nodular shadows up to 2 mm in diameter, particularly numerous in the outer third of the lungs (Figure 7–37).[1563] Air-space consolidation may be evident in the form of acinar shadows, but not as prominently as in *Pneumocystis carinii* pneumonia—which is one of the main conditions to be differentiated.[1534, 1535] Neither pleural effusion nor cavitation has been reported.

CLINICAL MANIFESTATIONS. In neonates and young infants, the clinical features include jaundice, hepatosplenomegaly, thrombocytopenic purpura, and sometimes diffuse interstitial pneumonia. Most of those who survive the acute illness are severely mentally retarded, with microcephaly, seizures, deafness, spasticity, and other signs of cerebral invasion.

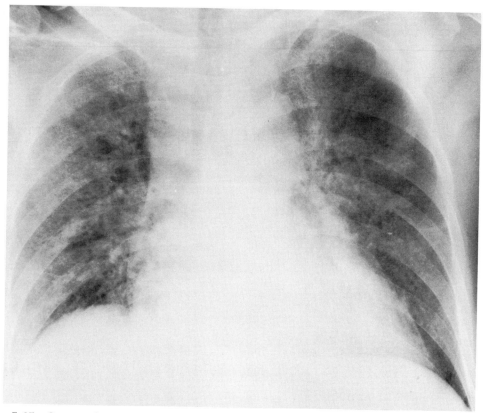

Figure 7–37. **Cytomegalovirus Pneumonia.** This anteroposterior roentgenogram shows widespread involvement of both lungs by a process whose basic pattern is finely reticulonodular. In some areas, particularly the peripheral portion of the right lung, the shadows are so numerous as to be confluent, suggesting air-space consolidation. The upper half of the mediastinum is widened and lobulated in contour suggesting lymph-node enlargement. This 35-year-old woman had been the recipient of a kidney transplant and was receiving immunosuppressive and corticosteroid therapy.

In small children and adults, symptoms caused by pulmonary invasion include progressive dyspnea and cyanosis; paroxysms of coughing and hemoptysis have been reported to occur.[1534]

Sullivan and colleagues[1537] documented seroconversion in nine of 12 children with leukemia: the cytomegalovirus antibodies appeared without significant clinical signs of infection in five and following a mild febrile episide in four. A postperfusion syndrome consisting of fever, malaise, hepatosplenomegaly, lymphadenopathy, jaundice, atypical lymphocytosis, and occasionally eosinophilia and anemia was reported in children following extracorporeal circulation.[1531] The clinical picture appears two to four weeks after surgery and is associated with a rise in titer of cytomegalovirus antibody, with or without positive culture of the organism, and a negative Paul-Bunnell test.

Cytomegalovirus may be isolated from the urine or sputum[1532, 1535] and has been recovered from the cervix after abortion and from milk expressed from the breast after delivery.[1538] In the absence of leukemia, the white-cell count is either low normal or leukopenic.[1535, 1536] Complement-fixation and agglutination tests are useful in diagnosis,[1534] but it must be remembered that gamma-G antibody can cross the placenta and thus be passively transferred from the mother to the infant; only gamma-M antibody is not transferred across the placenta, so that detection of this antibody by fluorescence microscopy is a rapid means of confirming the diagnosis. Culture of the virus requires up to one month. Intranuclear inclusion bodies may be identified in epithelial cells in the urine.[1533]

MISCELLANEOUS VIRUS AND PRESUMED VIRUS INFECTIONS

The virus of *lymphocytic choriomeningitis* has been recognized as the cause of fatal bronchopneumonia in two well-documented cases.[1540] Necropsy in both cases showed alveolar exudate containing polymorphonuclear cell infiltration, with hemorrhagic pneumonia in one. Both patients had initial leukopenia and subsequent leukocytosis with immature polymorphonuclear cells.

Infectious mononucleosis, a presumed but not proved virus infection, may be associated with hilar lymph-node enlargement (Figure 7–38). Hoagland[1541] found slight enlargement of hilar lymph nodes without associated parenchymal disease in three of 200 cases, and one of our patients who had grossly enlarged hilar nodes had normal roentgenographic findings in the lungs; the lymph nodes became normal in size in one month. Wechsler and associates[1542] described an epidemic of 556 cases of infectious mononucleosis, 30 of whom had abnormal physical findings in the chest and 14 of these having roentgenographic evidence of pneumonitis of a pattern indistinguishable from that of primary atypical pneumonia. Although lymph nodes were palpable in the neck, no enlargement of hilar lymph nodes was identified roentgenographically. Roentgenographic clearing occurred rapidly in all cases. All of these patients complained of the typical angina and had the abnormal peripheral-blood picture associated with this disease.[1542] Spasmodic cough was a common symptom, with production of small amounts of tenacious sputum.

Cat-scratch disease, presumed to be due to a virus (although this has not been isolated), has been reported to cause pneumonia; consolidation involved the right middle and lower lobes.[1543] The diagnosis should be suspected from a history of a cat scratch, the appearance of an indolent ulcer or vesicle on the skin, and the presence of enlarged draining lymph nodes containing sterile pus. Specific skin testing is positive in almost 100 per cent of cases.[1544]

BEDSONIA RESPIRATORY INFECTIONS

Members of this group of organisms are perhaps more correctly regarded as small bacteria than viruses. In contrast to the myxoviruses and picornaviruses (which are RNA organisms) and the adenoviruses and herpes viruses (which are DNA organisms), the Bedsonia viruses contain both RNA and DNA. These organisms are responsible for the diseases known as ornithosis (psittacosis), lymphogranuloma venereum, and trachoma.

Ornithosis (Psittacosis)

GENERAL COMMENTS AND EPIDEMIOLOGY. Ornithosis results from the inhalation of dry excreta from infected birds of any type—poultry and domestic and wild birds. Since psittacosis refers strictly to disease in parrots, the designation ornithosis is preferable. In man, the disease ranges from an asymptomatic state through a mild febrile illness to a severe typhoid-like clinical picture with evidence of widespread dissemination of the organism throughout the body. The disease is diagnosed infrequently, and it is probable that many cases are labeled as primary atypical pneumonia despite the fact that careful history-taking and serologic testing should permit ready differentiation. The incidence is low; in a study of 539 patients with serologically proved pneumonia, Stenström and associates[1545] found 29 (5 per cent) fulfilling the criteria of ornithosis. The disease occurs both sporadically and in epidemic form, the latter usually among poultry workers exposed to chickens, ducks, and turkeys.[1546] The disease may be acquired at any season of the year but the incidence rises somewhat during the cold months and early spring.[1547] The mortality rate has been estimated at between 10 and 40 per cent.[1546]

Patients who acquire the disease may give a history of exposure to parakeets,[1548] pigeons or budgerigars,[1547, 1549] or poultry.[1546] The responsible bird or birds may have been known to be ill or may have died from disease, but not necessarily. The disease may be acquired from an infected bird recently purchased from a dealer who shows no evidence of the disease, the dealer having acquired immunity. There is evidence that transmis-

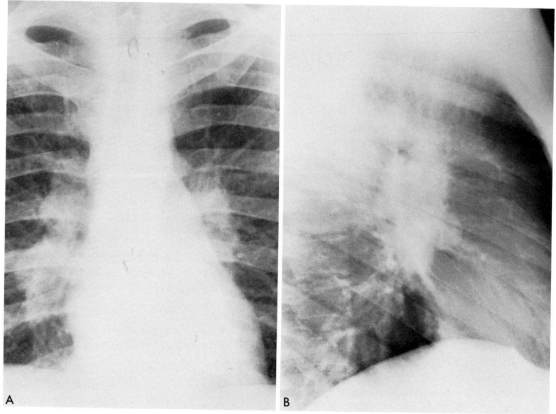

Figure 7–38. **Infectious Mononucleosis.** This 17-year-old man presented with a history and physical findings compatible with infectious mononucleosis; he had a leukocytosis of 18,000, 50 per cent of which were atypical lymphocytes; serial studies revealed a rising heterophil antibody titer. Views of the mediastinum from postero-anterior (A) and lateral (B) roentgenograms demonstrate marked enlargement of both hila, the lobulated contour being typical of lymph-node enlargement. The mediastinal lymph-node chains are not affected. There is no evidence of pulmonary or pleural disease. One month later, a chest roentgenogram was normal.

sion occurs occasionally from human to human.[1549] The rather abrupt increase in the incidence of the disease noted by Barrett and Greenberg[1549]—61 cases occurred in 1964, as compared with an average of two to three in previous years—suggested to these authors that epidemics may originate from an infected wild bird population if climatic conditions allow desiccation of excreta and subsequent dissemination of infected dust. The organism is resistant to drying and remains viable for at least one month at normal temperatures.

PATHOLOGIC CHARACTERISTICS. The pathologic changes in ornithosis are similar to those of other viral pneumonias, although considerable hemorrhagic consolidation may occur in the more severe cases. Regional lymph nodes may be enlarged. Proliferation, necrosis, and desqua-

mation of epithelial cells lining bronchi, bronchioles, and alveoli occur, and the alveolar septa become congested and edematous. The alveoli and interstitial tissues may contain lymphocytes and large phagocytes, and the epithelial cells contain intracytoplasmic inclusion bodies. Hyaline capillary thromboses occur in the alveolar walls.[961]

ROENTGENOGRAPHIC MANIFESTATIONS. The roentgenographic pattern varies; it has been described as showing a homogeneous "ground-glass" opacity, often containing small areas of radiolucency;[1549] and a patchy reticular pattern radiating out from the hilar areas or involving the lung bases has been noted.[1545, 1548, 1550] Segmental or lobar consolidation with or without atelectasis also occurs occasionally.[1548, 1549, 1551] Enlargement of hilar lymph nodes was a common feature in the 29 patients described by Stenström and co-workers.[1545] A miliary-like pattern has been described in one patient.[1552]

Roentgenographic resolution often is delayed for many weeks after clinical cure has occurred. Barrett and Greenberg[1549] and Brezina[2108] found the interval between the first abnormal roentgenogram and complete roentgenographic resolution to average six weeks, with a range of one to 20 weeks, and Stenström and associates[1545] found 48 per cent of 29 cases to show persisting roentgenographic abnormality at six weeks and 17 per cent for more than nine weeks.

CLINICAL MANIFESTATIONS. The clinical picture of ornithosis ranges from a mild febrile episode to severe pneumonia indistinguishable from acute bacterial pneumonia.[1548] In the more severe cases the clinical presentation tends to simulate typhoid and may include bradycardia and even "rose spots."[1549, 1550, 1553] The patient may present with fever but without either clinical or roentgenographic local signs in the chest. Cough usually is dry but may be productive of nonpurulent mucoid material;[1546, 1548, 1549] hemoptysis occurs in few cases and pleuritic pain is uncommon. Some patients complain of sore throat.[1548] Dyspnea may be very severe in cases of overwhelming infection. Systemic symptoms and signs include malaise, anorexia, shaking chills, nausea and vomiting, polyarthritis, myalgia, headache, abdominal pain, delirium, and unconsciousness.[1548, 1549, 1550] Physical signs often are scanty or absent and may consist only of basal crepitations;[1549] signs of frank parenchymal consolidation have been described, and a friction rub may be heard.[1548] Hepatosplenomegaly is not uncommon and superficial lymph-node enlargement has been noted.[1550] Sarner and Wilson[1555] described five cases in women who showed a clinical picture of erythema nodosum and had elevated titers of complement-fixation antibodies to ornithosis.

The white-cell count ranges from normal to moderately increased[1548, 1549] and a significant degree of eosinophilia may develop;[1548] proteinuria and abnormal results of liver function tests are found in some cases.[1548]

The organism may be recovered from the sputum during the first two weeks of illness or from the blood during the first four days. Viremia is usual and may be demonstrated by inoculation of blood into mice. The virus can be isolated by culture of spleen or liver tissue in the intraperitoneal cavity of mice, in chicken embryos, and on tissue; growth occurs in five to 30 days. Complement-fixation antibodies appear in the second to fourth week of the disease. In one series,[1545] 5 of 27 patients had positive Wassermann or Kahn reactions. Electrocardiographic abnormalities are said to be frequent.[1553]

INFECTIONS DUE TO OTHER BEDSONIA ORGANISMS

Lymphogranuloma venereum has been reported in association with atypical pneumonia in one patient;[1556] axillary and inguinal lymph nodes became enlarged one month after the onset of pneumonia of the right lower lobe, and both the Frei test and complement-fixation test were positive.

An acute form of Hamman-Rich syndrome has been reported to occur in a man who worked on a cattle ranch and who was exposed to epizootic bovine abortion agent; organisms of the Bedsonia group were isolated from the blood at necropsy. The cattle with whom the patient came in contact had a high incidence of abortions and the organism was isolated from aborted fetuses.[1557]

RESPIRATORY INFECTIONS DUE TO RICKETTSIAE

The major respiratory disease caused by the rickettsiae is Q-fever pneumonia. Pneumonia occurs occasionally in endemic or scrub typhus but is an inconstant finding in other forms of rickettsial disease such as epidemic typhus and Rocky Mountain spotted fever. Rickettsia are both intracellular and extracellular organisms.

Q-Fever Pneumonia

GENERAL COMMENTS AND EPIDEMIOLOGY. Infection with the rickettsial organism *Coxiella burnetii* produces a febrile illness that often simulates influenza or typhoid; the disease is associated with an abnormal chest roentgenogram in one third to one half of clinically recognized cases.[475] Q-fever appears to be rare, but it is probable that many sporadic cases are missed, the diagnosis being made most commonly when an epidemic occurs among abattoir workers[1559] or laboratory workers handling infected specimens.[475] The disease is world-wide in distribution, having been described originally in Australia (thus Queensland fever) and subsequently in the U.S.A. and Europe.

The organism has been isolated from insects, arachnids, birds, rabbits, and domestic animals, apparently being transmitted by the bite of a diseased tick or mite. Although a few cases may develop in humans as a result of a tick or mite bite, undoubtedly the most common mode of transmission is by inhalation of contaminated dust particles. Some cases may follow ingestion of raw milk; pasteurization destroys the organism. The infection apparently is prevalent among livestock in the U.S.A.,[1560] and, as a consequence, farmers and persons working in stockyards are particularly susceptible.[1559] The disease appeared not to be transmitted from man to man in the large outbreak described by Pavilanis and colleagues,[1559] in that the infection developed only in persons directly exposed to animals, the hospital staff and families of the patients who were treated at home showing no evidence of the disease. It is a self-limiting disease and the mortality rate is low, probably less than 1 per cent.[1561]

PATHOLOGIC CHARACTERISTICS. The pathologic changes are similar to those of virus pneumonia and are not in any way diagnostic. Both the interstitium and alveoli show edema, mononuclear-cell infiltration and extravasation of red blood cells. Peribronchial, peribronchiolar, and perivascular cellular infiltration may be present, and considerable amounts of fibrin may be deposited in the alveoli and in the lumen of the small bronchioles. Rickettsia can be identified in the alveolar spaces and within desquamated cells in some cases.[961]

ROENTGENOGRAPHIC MANIFESTATIONS. Homogeneous parenchymal consolidation occurs which is segmental in distribution and affects predominantly the lower lobes (Figure 7–39).[475, 1561] Pleural effusion occurs in some cases but hilar lymph-node enlargement has not been reported.

CLINICAL MANIFESTATIONS. The onset of the disease may be associated with no more than malaise that may last for several days before the development of fever, headaches, chills, severe myalgia, arthralgia, and, in a minority of cases, nausea, vomiting, and diarrhea. The incubation period is from one to five weeks, averaging about 14 days.[475, 1561]

Involvement of the upper respiratory tract is common and is associated with a dry cough which often is troublesome. Physical examination of the lungs commonly reveals a paucity of findings despite fairly extensive parenchymal disease apparent roentgenographically.[1561] Fever is frequently remittent; it may last for several weeks but averages eight to 12 days.[1561] The clinical picture varies considerably from case to case; patients without roentgenographic abnormality in the chest usually have predominantly extrapulmonary symptoms and signs. Phlebitis may occur, and the complications from this may be more drawn-out and disabling than the original infection.[1561] Headache may be severe, but lymphocytic meningitis is rare. The illness may relapse and recur.[475] Jaundice resulting from hepatic involvement may be the presenting clinical manifestation; splenomegaly occurs in a minority of patients.

Of 50 cases in one series[475] one-third had a white-cell count above 13,000 per c mm, and only one had a count above 15,000. The organism may be isolated from the urine, blood, sputum, or pleural fluid. Inoculation of material into the peritoneal cavity of guinea pigs is a useful method of isolating the organism, and culture may be established in eggs; growth of the organism occurs in four to 14 days. Complement-fixing and agglutinating antibodies appear within two to three weeks, and the titer is maximal approximately 30 days after the onset of clinical symptoms.[475]

"Scrub-Typhus" Pneumonia

"Scrub-typhus" is caused by *Rickettsia tsutsugamushi*. The disease occurs in the south-west Pacific, in south-east Asia and Australia, and in Japan and shows its highest incidence during the hottest months. Man is infected by the bite of a mite resulting in a local lesion associated

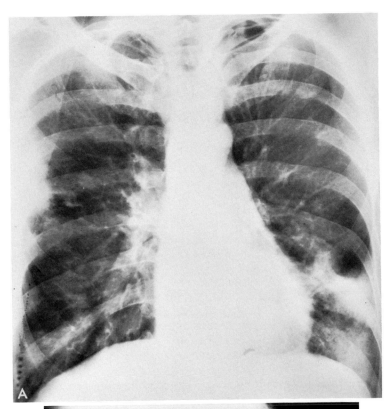

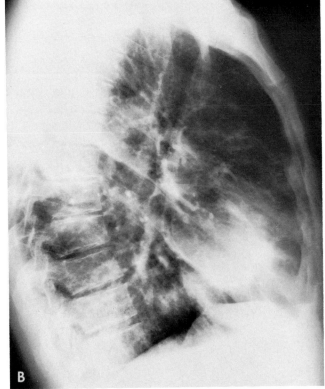

Figure 7–39. **Q-fever Pneumonia.** This 37-year-old man had had mild symptoms described as a "chest cold" for three weeks prior to admission; on the morning of admission, he was awakened with a severe pain in the left side of the chest, made worse by deep breathing. Posteroanterior (A) and lateral (B) roentgenograms reveal local areas of homogeneous consolidation in the right upper and lower lobes, the lingula, and the left lower lobe. In no area is the consolidation truly segmental although the pattern is typically one of air-space consolidation. This lack of segmental distribution is said to be atypical in Q-fever pneumonia. Four serum samples showed a rising titer of complement-fixing antibodies to *Coxiella burnetii* during the four weeks following these roentgenograms, maximum being 1:256. Roentgenologic resolution was slow and was not complete at the time of the last available roentgenogram five weeks later. (Courtesy Dr. John Silny, Sherbrooke Hospital, Sherbrooke, Quebec.)

with enlargement of draining lymph nodes. The pneumonia may be interstitial in type but sometimes is in the form of homogeneous consolidation. Clinically, the picture is one of a maculopapular rash, fever, splenomegaly, cough (often with hemoptysis), myocarditis, and encephalitis. The white-cell count may be normal or leukopenic. Organisms may be recovered from the peritoneal cavity of mice injected with blood from patients with the disease. Agglutinins to proteus OX-K antigen appear during the second or third week, and specific complement-fixing antibodies also may be demonstrable.

RENAL-TRANSPLANTATION PNEUMONIA

Patients with transplanted organs are particularly susceptible to infection because of the continuous corticosteroid and immunosuppressive therapy they receive. As in other situations in which the immune mechanism is defective, infections may occur from various organisms, many of which are usually considered to be nonpathogenic. In a study of 111 patients, Goodman and associates[1563] attempted to correlate roentgenographic findings with pathologic data and found that in about one third of cases they could identify the etiologic agent on the basis of roentgenographic findings: a pattern of fine nodular densities, approximately 2 mm in diameter, in the outer two thirds of the lung fields, suggested cytomegalovirus disease; homogeneous air-space consolidation indicated bacterial infection with *Pseudomonas* species, *Diplococcus pneumoniae, Staph. aureus,* or *Klebsiella* species; cavitary disease almost invariably indicated a fungus infection; and widely disseminated acinar shadows could be produced by any of these organisms as well as by *Pneumocystis carinii.*

Rifkind and associates[1564] described six patients who, while receiving decreasing doses of prednisone, contracted bilateral air-space disease associated with fever, mild productive cough, dyspnea, and cyanosis. Five of the six showed positive cold-agglutinin reactions, but complement-fixation tests for *Mycoplasma pneumoniae* gave negative results in the three cases so tested. Necropsy of the one patient who

died revealed combined *Pneumocystis carinii* and cytomegalovirus infection, either or both of which may have been responsible for the diffuse pneumonia (Figure 7–40). These authors, however, suggested the alternative possibility that the patients may have had an "immunologic response." Similarly, Hamburger and associates[1565] described three patients who had undergone renal homotransplantation and in whom pulmonary disease developed associated with fever and dyspnea, without demonstrable microbial infection. One of these patients died, and *Pneumyocystis carinii* was found at necropsy; in one the illness responded to prednisone therapy, suggesting that the pulmonary reaction may have been allergic in origin. Slapak and his colleagues[1566] recently ascribed post-transplantation pulmonary disease to an immunologic reaction in the lungs, on the basis that it develops coincidentally with reduction in steroid therapy and responds to an increase in dosage of corticosteroids.

Pulmonary function studies in such patients have shown decrease in diffusing capacity and in arterial P_{O_2}.[1564, 1566]

PARASITIC INFESTATION OF THE LUNG

Parasitic diseases of the thorax may be manifested either as a hypersensitivity reaction—for example Loeffler's syndrome (*see* page 870)—or as changes resulting from direct invasion of the pleura or lungs. Although pulmonary parasitic disease is rarely encountered and much more rarely acquired in North America, an ever-increasing amount of travel to countries where parasitic infestations are endemic, and the migration of people from such countries to North America, requires knowledge of these diseases and their diagnostic features. In the Near and Far East, Africa, and South America, parasitic diseases vary in type from country to country, and are more common in rural than in urban areas because of lack of public-health measures. A report from a pulmonary service in a Cairo hospital[1567] described 90 patients with parasitic infestation among 5014 admissions, an incidence of 1.7 per cent. On the pulmonary service of the Royal Victoria Hospital, the

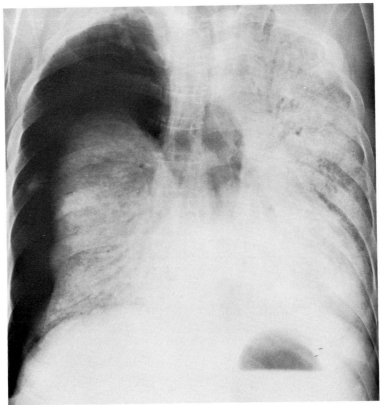

Figure 7-40. **Renal Transplantation Pneumonia.** This roentgenogram (exposed postmortem in the autopsy theater in posteroanterior projection, erect position) is of a 32-year-old woman who had been the recipient of a renal transplant and who was receiving high doses of immunosuppressive drugs and corticosteroids. It shows widespread involvement of both lungs by a process whose pattern is granular rather than homogeneous; evidence of air-space consolidation is provided by a well-defined air bronchogram. At necropsy, the lungs showed evidence of combined cytomegalovirus and *Pneumocystis carinii* pneumonia. This roentgenographic pattern is regarded as characteristic of mixed interstitial and air-space disease. The right tension pneumothorax was thought to result from vigorous attempts at resuscitation.

incidence of pulmonary parasitic disease is much lower than this—but it is significant that, over the past ten years, we have seen examples of almost all the infestations described in this section.

In the majority of patients, the presence of parasitic disease is suspected because of the finding of peripheral blood eosinophilia in a patient who has resided in an endemic zone. Confirmation of pleuropulmonary involvement requires the demonstration of ova or larvae in the sputum or pleural fluid; strong circumstantial evidence may be obtained in some cases from the finding of ova or larvae in the stools, or from positive serologic tests. Often, the chest roentgenogram shows a pattern which is either strongly suggestive or even diagnostic of a specific parasitic disease.

PROTOZOAN INFESTATION

AMEBIASIS

Amebiasis is predominantly a disease of the colon—amebic dysentery—which follows ingestion of the cysts of *Entamoeba histolytica*. Ulceration of the colon results from the liberation of cytolytic enzymes by the vegatative form of the parasite (the trophozoite), this enzyme digesting surrounding tissue and permitting the organism to penetrate into the submucosa and into the circulation of the bowel wall. The organism may embolize either to the liver via the portal vein or, rarely, directly to the lungs via hemorrhoidal veins or the lymphatics. Within the liver, liberation of cytolytic enzyme results in the formation of abscesses which occasionally penetrate the diaphragm into the pleural cavity or lung. Liver abscesses (which are more common in the right lobe) may extend into the subphrenic space and form a subdiaphragmatic abscess; in such cases, intrathoracic complications such as pleural effusion and basal pulmonary disease are secondary to the subphrenic inflammation rather than to direct invasion by the parasite. Also amebae may penetrate the diaphragm and infect the pleura or lung, without an associated subphrenic abscess. Rarely, a hepatobronchial fistula develops and is associated with minimal abnormality on the chest roentgenogram.[1568]

Amebic dysentery is a disease of worldwide distribution, with areas of high endemicity, especially where hygiene and therapeutic measures are inadequate. Amebic colitis shows no age or sex predominance, although for some unknown reason pleuropulmonary involvement occurs most frequently between the ages of 20 and 40 years and is far more common in men than in women, in a ratio of 10 to 15:1.[961] In 1936, Ochsner and DeBakey[1569] estimated that the liver is involved in 5 to 20 per cent of patients with intestinal amebiasis; and it was stated later that pleuropulmonary disease develops in about 15 to 20 per cent of patients with liver involvement.[1570, 1571]

Pathologic Characteristics

Over 95 per cent of amebic lung abscesses are contiguous to the diaphragm — the lower lobes, right middle lobe, and lingula, and in 75 per cent an extension is pathologically demonstrable from the liver through the diaphragm into the lungs.[961] On section, a lung abscess is seen to be filled with a dark reddish-brown liquid resembling anchovy or chocolate sauce; the lung peripheral to the abscess may be collapsed, hemorrhagic, or edematous. Histologically, in the acute stage an inflammatory exudate containing polymorphonuclear leukocytes may surround the area of necrosis, but in well-established or chronic abscesses the cells become lymphocytic and histiocytic in type; there may be minimal fibrosis. *Entamoeba histolytica* may be identified in the margin of the abscess contiguous to normal lung.

Roentgenographic Manifestations

The combination of right-sided pleural effusion and basal pulmonary disease comprise the usual picture of pleuropulmonary amebiasis. The pleural effusion is most commonly a sterile exudate secondary to subdiaphragmatic amebic abscess, but in a small percentage of cases it results from direct invasion of the pleura subsequent to breaching of the diaphragm by the organism. The parenchymal abnormality may be no more than horizontal line shadows due to plate atelectasis just above an elevated hemidiaphragm;[1568, 1572, 1573] more commonly, however, pulmonary parenchymal involvement consists of an ill-defined homogeneous consolidation involving the right lower or middle lobes and presenting no clear-cut segmental distribution, associated with pleural effusion. Some of these progress to abscess formation and subsequently to cavitation.[1572] Parenchymal consolidation, with or without cavitation, develops in a site remote from the diaphragm, such as the upper lobes, in a small percentage of cases, presumably as a result of direct extension to the lungs from the colon and without intermediate liver abscess. A band-like shadow may be seen extending from the pulmonary hilum to the diaphragm in patients in whom hepatobronchial fistula develops without associated parenchymal consolidation or abscess formation.[1568, 1572]

Clinical Manifestations

The possibility of pleuropulmonary amebiasis should be suspected in any patient who has resided in an endemic area, who has symptoms and signs of amebic dysentery, and who complains of right upper-quadrant abdominal pain and a dry cough. The dry cough which characterizes the early stages of pleuropulmonary involvement later may become productive of "chocolate-sauce" material, indicating hepatobronchial communication, and then may be accompanied by a marked degree of cachexia suggesting the possibility of tuberculosis or cancer.[1571] An amebic etiology should be suspected if adequate antibiotic therapy of basal pleuropulmonary disease has produced no obvious response.[1574]

Leukocytosis is usually moderate in degree and eosinophilia may occur. The diagnosis is made by the demonstration of trophozoites in the sputum or pleural exudate. The combination of pleuropulmonary disease and the presence of trophozoites or cysts in the stool is strongly suggestive of the diagnosis.

TOXOPLASMOSIS

Toxoplasmosis is a protozoan disease resulting from infestation with *Toxoplasma gondii*, an obligate intracellular organism measuring 4 to 7 by 2 to 4μ in size. Its nucleus stains red and its cytoplasm blue with Rowanowsky-type stain. Toxoplasmosis is world-wide in distribution but in the majority of patients gives rise to no symptoms, the diagnosis being established by the demonstration of antibodies in the blood. Natural infestation occurs in many species of birds and mammals.

In man, the most common form of the disease is congenital, due to intrauterine transmission from a mother with latent infection, usually in the late stages of pregnancy. Congenital toxoplasmosis commonly severely damages the central nervous system and gives rise to affections such as hydrocephalus, microcephalus, and choroido-retinitis; rarely, pulmonary involvement may occur as a consequence of widespread dissemination of the organism.

The majority of cases of the acquired form of the disease probably result from the ingestion of contaminated meat; in one study a significantly greater incidence of positive skin tests was found in children who ate poorly cooked meat.[1575] Several examples have been reported of transmission of the disease in the laboratory,[1576] and one in which the organism was transmitted in a transplanted kidney.[1577]

Pathologic Characteristics

In the lung, the alveolar lining cells proliferate and some are desquamated. These cells contain characteristic "toxoplasma cysts," spherical or oval masses with ill-defined walls containing large numbers of round or oval pointed parasites; the cyst wall is produced by the toxoplasma organisms and is not a host reaction.[1576] Some of the alveoli contain a gelatinous exudate in which parasites may be identified. The interstitial tissues are infiltrated with plasma cells, lymphocytes, and a few eosinophils, and in some cases have areas of necrosis. The encysted aggregates of toxoplasma organisms are protected from the action of antibodies by their surrounding membranes. In the six cases of toxoplasmosis in adults described by Sexton and associates,[1578] myocarditis was a constant finding, hepatitis and splenitis were present in four, and brain and lymph-node involvement was identified in some.

Roentgenographic Manifestations

Pulmonary toxoplasmosis is part of a general infestation. Usually it is manifested by a focal reticular pattern resembling acute virus pneumonia, sometimes associated with air-space consolidation. Hilar lymph-node enlargement is common.[1579, 1580] The roentgenographic changes in the lungs[1581] in two adults whose clinical presentations had been previously reported[1582] consisted in combined interstitial and air-space disease which was likened to "atypical pneumonia"; in the early stages of the disease the pattern was said to simulate pulmonary congestion and diffuse interstitial pulmonary edema, but without associated cardiac enlargement.

Clinical Manifestations

Toxoplasmosis may give rise to a clinical picture not unlike that of infectious mononucleosis, with low-grade fever and peripheral lymph-node enlargement. These symptoms may persist for several weeks or months and usually are associated with anemia and lymphocytosis; the heterophil-antibody test is negative.[1579] The rare disseminated form of the disease gives rise to pneumonitis associated with nonproductive cough, tachypnea, dyspnea, and cyanosis; physical examination is said to reveal rales and impairment of the percussion note.[1579] In some cases acquired disease becomes widely disseminated, involving the lungs, liver, heart, skin, muscle, brain, and meninges, and evident in a maculopapular rash, high fever, and extreme prostration. Another form of clinical presentation in adults, which was described by Pinkerton and Henderson,[1582] consists in a spotted-fever-like syndrome with acute pneumonia.

It is to be appreciated that these clinical presentations are uncommon and that toxoplasmosis in the adult is usually a latent infection; in a review of the subject, Feldman[1576] stated that inhalant toxoplasmosis usually is unassociated with recognizable clinical manifestations.

The congenital form of the disease commonly leads to severe damage to the central nervous system, sometimes resulting in permanent blindness and mental retardation; death may result from widespread dissemination. In a four-year study of 189 members of 37 families in Syracuse, N.Y., Lamb and Feldman[1583] showed that the titer of antibodies was greater than 1:8 in only 5 per cent of their subjects under the age of 20, but it was positive in 30 per cent of those 20 years of age or over. Over the four-year period of surveillance, these authors recorded the appearance of antibodies in three children, none of whom showed clinical evidence of the disease.

Three commonly available serologic tests are used in the diagnosis of toxoplasmosis: the Sabin-Feldman dye test,[1584] a complement-fixation test, and a hemagglutination test. The dye test consists in incubation of toxoplasma organisms in suspected serum, with methylene blue to stain the toxoplasma organisms for antigen-antibody reaction; a positive dye test (1:8) indicates that the patient has or has had the disease, and a four-fold rise in titer is requisite to the diagnosis of active disease. The value of the hemagglutination test lies in the fact that viable organisms are not required. A fluorescent antibody test also has been developed and is of some aid in diagnosis.[1576] A tuberculin-type skin test, employing material obtained from mouse peritoneal exudate or from infected embryonated eggs may show no reaction for several months and often yields false negative results.[1576]

PNEUMOCYSTIS CARINII INFESTATION

Pneumonia due to this organism was originally described in Europe as a disease of infants—interstitial plasma-cell pneumonia—and only subsequently was shown to be due to Pneumocystis carinii and to occur in older children and adults also. Pneumocystis carinii usually is classified as a protozoan although all attempts to culture it have failed; the manner in which it divides, by giving rise to new daughter parasites, is more suggestive of fungus-type nuclear division than of that usual in protozoa.[961] In fact, there is a considerable body of opinion that so-called Pneumocystis carinii pneumonia is not a parasitic infestation but is an unusual fungus infection whose reaction in the lung has been altered by superinfection, possibly from a virus.[1585]

Pneumocystis carinii is a saprophyte found in the lungs of many animals, including the rat, mouse, rabbit, and dog;[1586] it may be that it exists as a saprophyte in man except in those cases in which some other disease process favors its growth as an opportunistic invader. Characteristically it occurs in persons with impaired defense mechanisms, due either to gammaglobulin deficiency[1587–1590] or to primary malignancy of the reticuloendothelial system; in the latter it occurs most often in cases treated with corticosteroids or antimicrobial or cytotoxic agents.[1591–1594] Affected infants most commonly are born prematurely and the infection becomes apparent between the ages of 2 and 5 months; in these infants, the disease commonly is institutional, occurring sporadically and in small epidemics in children's hospitals and nurseries. In Rifkind and associates' series of ten patients with transplanted kidneys in whom this infection developed, all were in one of two hospitals, an indication of colonization of this commensal.[1595] Pneumocystis carinii pneumonia has been reported to develop following renal transplantation in both children and adults, but in these cases, as in other situations where it is isolated, the organism's etiologic role in the pneumonia remains in doubt.[1564–1566, 1595] The route of infection in man probably is by inhalation, since there is no evidence for parasitemia.

Pathologic Characteristics

Grossly, the lungs are pinkish-white and bulky. There is considerable variation in the severity of changes seen histologically. Mild cases may show only minimal alveolar septal infiltration with lymphocytes and occasional plasma cells, associated with proliferation of alveolar lining cells and small numbers of *Pneumocystis carinii* organisms within edema fluid in the alveolar spaces. In more severely affected cases, the changes consist of widespread interstitial and alveolar edema, with lymphocytic and plasma-cell infiltration, necrosis of alveolar walls, and many masses of intra-alveolar pneumocystis organisms.[961, 1599] Little or no fibrosis occurs. The organisms lie in groups, as many as eight vegetative forms each measuring 1μ in diameter, lying together within the foamy alveolar edema; they stain with periodic acid–Schiff (PAS) or Gomori's methenamine silver stain and not with hematoxylin and eosin.[1599, 1600] The association of cytomegalic inclusion disease (*see* page 693) with *Pneumocystis carinii* pneumonia is frequent; in ten cases of *Pneumocystis carinii* pneumonia studied by Rifkind and associates,[1595] culture of the exudate grew cytomegalovirus in seven.

Roentgenographic Manifestations

In the early stages of the disease a granular or reticulogranular pattern is apparent, particularly in the perihilar areas.[1601-1605] With progression of the disease the pattern becomes one of air-space consolidation, patchy areas of homogeneous consolidation being interspersed with focal areas of atelectasis and emphysema, particularly in the peripheral zones (Figure 7–41). The changes are diffuse and may resemble those of pulmonary edema; the pattern is said to be distinctive and almost diagnostic of the disease in patients who have had renal transplantation.[1563] There is no roentgenographic evidence of pleural effusion or hilar lymph-node enlargement.[1586, 1599, 1601]

Clinical Manifestations

In premature infants, the clinical course may be very stormy and may end in sudden death within a few hours or days; severe dyspnea, tachypnea, and cyanosis may develop.[1603] More commonly, both in children and in adults, the course is more insidious, with a dry hacking cough, cyanosis, dyspnea, and little or no fever; pleural pain and hemoptysis do not occur. Physical signs are minimal and include a few scattered rales or rhonchi.[1599, 1600, 1606]

It is said that the clinical course of the disease lasts for six to eight weeks but that roentgenographic changes may persist much longer.[1603] The white-cell count is slightly to moderately increased, with polymorphonuclear leukocytes predominating.

Although the disease may be strongly suspected from the roentgenographic picture, the severe cyanosis and dyspnea, and the lack of other symptoms or clinical signs, demonstration of the organism is required for definitive diagnosis. The organism is identified in material aspirated from the tracheobronchial tree in some cases and but rarely in the sputum; in the majority, aspiration biopsy of lung parenchyma is required.

METAZOAN INFESTATION

NEMATHELMINTH (ROUND-WORM) INFESTATION

Ascariasis

The adult Ascaris worm lives in the small intestine, where it produces eggs which are passed in the feces. The first two larval stages develop within the egg after it has reached soil; since larval development is inhibited by direct sunlight and excessive heat, a peak incidence of the disease usually is reported during those seasons when the soil is moist and cool.[1607, 1608] Man contracts the disease by ingesting eggs in water or food, or more commonly from contaminated soil under the finger nails. Larvae which are still within the shell of the ovum hatch within the small intestine and then enter the blood stream and pass to the lung capillaries; they migrate into the alveolar spaces, move up the airways to the larynx and are swallowed; on reaching the small bowel, they complete their Odyssey by developing into mature worms.

Thus the pulmonary disease is caused by the third-stage larvae in their passage through the lungs; the response is allergic in type and invariably associated with blood eosinophilia. Since the disease is benign, pathologic data are not available.

Roentgenographically, patchy areas of homogeneous consolidation are visible; in many cases they are transient and without

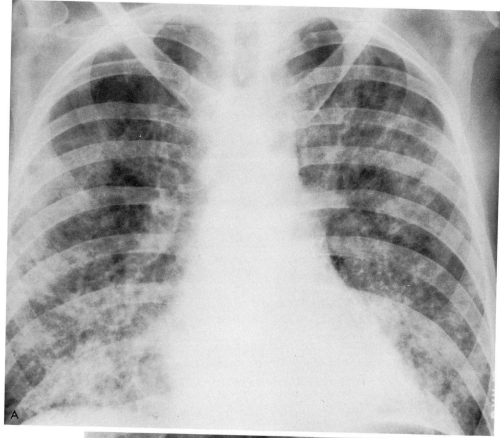

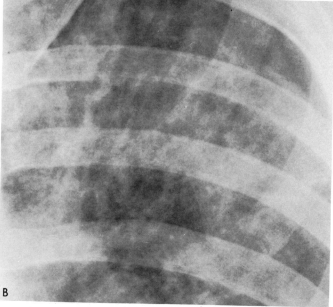

Figure 7–41. Pneumocystis carinii Pneumonia. This 32-year-old man had been the recipient of a renal transplant and was receiving immunosuppressive and corticosteroid therapy. An anteroposterior roentgenogram (*A*) shows widespread involvement of both lungs by patchy areas of air-space consolidation, in some areas discrete and in others confluent. A mixed acinar and reticular pattern appears to be present in most areas as illustrated in a magnified view of the upper half of the left lung (*B*). A photomicrograph (*C*) shows the typical appearance of *Pneumocystis carinii* organisms obtained by direct needle aspiration of the lung and stained with Grocott methenamine silver.

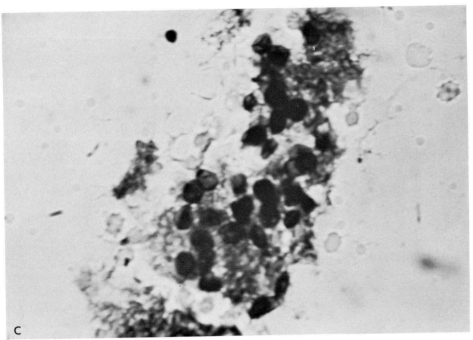

Figure 7-41. Continued.

clear-cut segmental distribution in the characteristic pattern originally described by Loeffler (*see* page 870). The shadows may be several centimeters in diameter, and in cases of moderate severity tend to be rather discrete and concentrated in the perihilar regions. With more severe involvement, the shadows tend to become confluent and assume a lobular pattern.[1607]

Symptoms consist of nonproductive cough, substernal chest pain, and, in more severe cases, hemoptysis and dyspnea. Of the 108 cases reported by Gelpi and Mustafa,[1607] 16 (15 per cent) of the patients complained of a transient, intensely pruritic skin eruption which appeared within four to five days after the onset of respiratory symptoms. Low-grade fever may be present, and scattered rhonchi and rales may be heard over the lungs. Leukocytosis of 20,000 to 25,000 per c mm is common, with an eosinophilia ranging from 30 to 70 per cent.

The diagnosis of pulmonary ascariasis is made by the discovery of larvae in the sputum or gastric aspirate;[1609] the identification in the stools of adult worms or of typical mammillated outer-shelled ova is strong evidence for the diagnosis, particularly in a patient with leukocytosis and eosinophilia.

Strongyloidiasis

Strongyloides stercoralis is a nematode whose life cycle has a larval stage which causes pulmonary disease during migration through the lungs. The disease is world-wide in distribution, being endemic in rural areas where the climate is warm and the soil moist. Its highest geographic incidence is throughout much of southeast Asia, India, the U.S.S.R., Africa, Central America, northern South America, and the southern U.S.A.

As with the hookworms, *Ancylostoma duodenale* and *Necator americanus*, the filariform larvae infect man through penetration of the skin; consequently, the disease is seen in those geographic areas where barefoot man walks on soil contaminated by feces. Following penetration of the skin, the larvae reach the lung by way of the blood stream, migrating from the capillaries into the alveoli and then climbing the bronchi and trachea to descend into the bowel via the esophagus. The subsequent course within the bowel is different from that of *Ascaris*, whose eggs leave the human in the feces; within the bowel, *Strongyloides* develops rhabditiform larvae that may be passed as such in the stool or may progress to the next stage—filariform larvae; thus, autoinfection may occur through penetration of the intestinal mucosa or perianal skin and the establishment of a cycle within the host without leaving the body. The pulmonary disease in man is associated with migration of the worm from the pulmonary capillaries into the alveolar spaces. Occasionally, during this migration the larvae may become retarded in their voyage by bronchial secretions and may mature into the adult form within the lung parenchyma.

Strongyloides may exist independently of the human host as a free-living form in the soil; here they develop into male and female worms, the latter laying eggs which hatch into rhabditiform larvae which in turn are capable of maturing into adults; thus, if conditions are favorable, sexual reproduction and indefinite survival is possible in soil alone.

The benign nature of the disease precludes detailed pathologic studies, although alveolar hemorrhage and edema have been reported to occur as a result of the presence of the larvae.[961]

Roentgenographically, the findings are no different from ascariasis or hookworm disease and consist of nonsegmental patchy areas of homogeneous consolidation.

Clinically, penetration of the skin by larvae may produce erythematous papular eruptions. Abdominal pain is the most common symptom and often is associated with diarrhea alternating with constipation; anemia may be present. Severe infections are characterized by repeated attacks of bronchospasm associated with dyspnea and sometimes with hemoptysis. A fatal form of strongyloidiasis has been described in patients receiving corticosteroids,[1610] the clinical picture including diarrhea, vomiting, abdominal pain and distension, hypokalemia, hypoproteinemia, and shock; pulmonary congestion, bronchopneumonia, pleural effusion, and pulmonary infarctions were found at autopsy.

A mild to moderate leukocytosis with eosinophilia is found in the peripheral blood. The diagnosis is made by the finding of larvae in the sputum or in the stool.

Ancylostomiasis (Hookworm Disease)

The nematodes *Ancylostoma duodenale* and *Necator americanus* exist in filariform

larval stage in soil. They infect man by penetrating the skin so that, as with *Strongyloides*, a combination of warm climate, moist contaminated soil, poor hygiene, and bare feet are required for completion of the life cycle. The larvae reach the pulmonary capillaries by way of the systemic veins, migrating from the capillaries into the alveoli and then by way of the bronchi and trachea into the esophagus and small intestine. In the small bowel they mature into adult hookworms which produce eggs which are passed in the feces.

The major manifestation of hookworm disease is anemia which results from the tendency of these worms to feed mainly on blood. Pulmonary disease appears to be less common than in Strongyloides infestation, but in cases of severe infection, transient cough and hemoptysis may occur and nonsegmental homogeneous consolidation may be apparent roentgenographically. Anemia and eosinophilia characterize the blood picture. Patients typically are pale, weak, and emaciated. The diagnosis is made by the finding of ova or mature worms in the stools.

Trichinosis

Trichinosis follows the ingestion of larvae of the round worm *Trichinella spiralis*. Its major manifestations in man are muscular rather than pulmonary, although involvement of the respiratory muscles may lead to dyspnea and tachypnea.[1611] The disease is world-wide in distribution and is found wherever uncooked contaminated meat, particularly pork, is eaten. Live encysted larvae in uncooked meat reach the small intestine, where they mature; the male and female adults mate within the intestine, and, when the eggs hatch, the larvae penetrate the duodenal wall and are carried to the lungs, through the pulmonary circulation into the systemic circulation, and thence to striated muscles throughout the body, including the diaphragm and the pectoral and intercostal muscles. Within muscle, the coiled Trichina worm incites an inflammatory response which gives rise to cyst formation; the cyst wall becomes calcified six to 18 months after infestation.

Roentgenographically there are no abnormalities related to the lungs, the larvae producing no reaction in their passage through the pulmonary circulation. Pleural effusion occurs rarely. Calcification in the walls of the larval cysts within the respiratory muscles may be detected on chest roentgenograms as oval opacities measuring 0.8 to 1.0 mm in their longest diameter.

Clinically, no symptoms result from the passage of the parasite through the lungs. Diarrhea develops two to four days after the ingestion of contaminated meat; by the seventh day, fever, muscular pains, facial edema, and, in some cases, central nervous system symptoms, may occur. Deposition of the larvae in skeletal muscles occurs by the tenth day and may cause muscle pain. If the respiratory muscles are affected the patient may complain of shortness of breath.

Leukocytosis with a variable degree of eosinophilia is common; the skin test and serologic tests become positive three weeks after infestation. The diagnosis may be suspected from the clinical picture, particularly if supported by a history of the ingestion of uncooked pork.

Filariasis

Filariasis results from infection of the blood, skin, and lymph nodes by various types of thread-like nematodes. The most common of these is *Wuchereria bancrofti*, which causes Bancroftian filariasis, a disease characterized by subcutaneous, raised, tender red areas, lymphangitis, epididymitis, orchitis, and lymphatic obstruction leading to elephantiasis of the legs, scrotum or vulva, arms, and breasts. Patients with pulmonary disease due to microfilariae do not usually manifest these cutaneous and lymphatic changes but present with two rather characteristic syndromes—tropical pulmonary eosinophilia, and "coin" lesions due to the larvae of *Dirofilaria immitis*.

Tropical pulmonary eosinophilia is a disease confined to the tropics, in a geographic distribution identical to that of Bancroftian filariasis—India and Pakistan, Malaysia, southern Asia, North Africa and in certain areas of South America. The clinical presentation is one of bronchial asthma associated with moderately severe leukocytosis and eosinophilia and with a chest roentgenogram showing a diffuse reticulonodular pattern. Most cases occur between the ages of 20 and 40 years, and only occasionally in children or the elderly. It appears to show a male sex predominance.[1612] Indians and Pakistanis appear to be particularly susceptible, even in geographic areas where they make up a minority of the population;[1613] Caucasians are rarely affected.

The pathogenesis of the disease is still incompletely understood. There is a good deal of evidence that most if not all cases are caused by microfilaria which, for some unknown reason, do not pass through the full cycle to the mature worm as is generally the case in Bancroftian filariasis. Circumstantial evidence that microfilariae are the etiologic agent lies in the fact that 95 per cent of patients show a positive reaction to an antigen prepared from *Dirofilaria immitis*[1614] and in the clinical and roentgenographic response to drugs such as arsenic and diethylcarbamazine.[1615–1617] However, in one series of 26 patients with the typical clinical picture of tropical eosinophilia and whose lungs were biopsied, only three showed histologic evidence of microfilaria.[1618]

Man is infected from the bite of a mosquito which introduces filariform larvae into the skin; mature worms subsequently develop from which microfilariae are discharged.

Pathologically, microfilaria of the *W. bancrofti* type were identified by Webb and associates[1619] in the centers of pulmonary lesions removed surgically. Udwadia[1612] provided detailed descriptions of the pathologic changes in 30 biopsied cases: in the early stages, there is an outpouring of histiocytes into the alveolar spaces and interstitial tissues; later, the lung tissue develops a hypersensitivity reaction, with eosinophilic infiltration; six months to five years after the onset of symptoms, eosinophils have disappeared, and there is histiocytic infiltration with fibrosis. Debris may be present, surrounded by foreign-body giant cells.[961]

Roentgenographically, the lungs are involved diffusely and symmetrically. The pattern is one of general increase in linear markings, frequently associated with nodules ranging from 2 to 5 mm in diameter, predominantly involving the mid and lower lung zones (Figure 7–42). Hilar lymph-node enlargement occurs in some

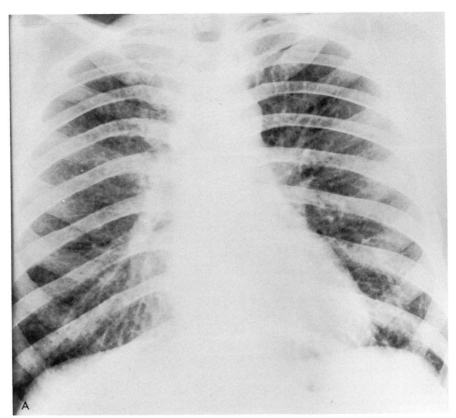

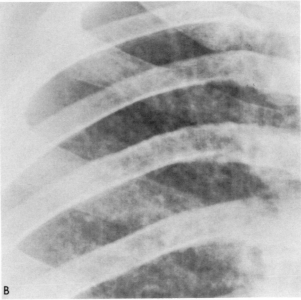

Figure 7–42. **Tropical Eosinophilia.** This posteroanterior roentgenogram was of a 25-year-old male who was a native of India. He had formerly been a long-distance runner of some international repute and recently had noted the onset of dyspnea on severe exertion. The roentgenogram reveals a widespread reticulonodular pattern evenly distributed throughout both lungs; in some areas, such as the upper portion of the right lung (*B*), the pattern appears to be predominantly nodular, individual shadows measuring up to 2 mm in diameter. There was a high blood eosinophilia. The chest roentgenogram returned to normal within three weeks of the institution of appropriate therapy.

cases.[1612, 1613, 1620] The chest roentgenogram may show complete clearing with appropriate therapy, but the changes may be permanent,[1621] indicating the fibrotic interstitial reaction observed by Udwadia.[1612]

The main symptom is cough, usually productive of small amounts of mucoid or mucopurulent material; coughing tends to be particularly bothersome at night, when it appears in paroxysms sometimes with the production of blood-streaked sputum. Attacks of coughing and dyspnea may be so severe as to suggest status asthmaticus. Weight loss, fatigue, and low-grade fever may be observed. Slight enlargement of the liver and spleen is frequent.[1613, 1620, 1622] Superficial lymph-node enlargement is rare. Physical signs of bronchospasm may be present on examination. Leukocytosis is usually marked — a count of 60,000 white cells per c mm is not unusual — associated with extreme degrees of eosinophilia, sometimes as high as 60 per cent.

The diagnosis may be suspected from the combination of the clinical picture and a diffuse reticulonodular pattern roentgenographically in a patient who has resided in an endemic zone. Confirmation may be provided by a complement-fixation test and a skin test using *D. immitis* antigen; microfilaria may be identified in a lung biopsy or rarely in nocturnal specimens of blood. One case has been reported in which an adult filarial worm was found embedded in the left axilla associated with classical pulmonary symptoms and roentgenographic findings of tropical eosinophilia.[1623]

Pulmonary function tests show either a restrictive pattern or a combined restrictive and obstructive pattern.[1617] In the combined pattern, flow rates, residual volume and vital capacity are diminished, the decrease in flow rate being disproportionately greater than the decrease in vital capacity. Pulmonary function aberrations may become irreversible, indicative of fibrotic changes observed roentgenographically and pathologically. These patients may have chronic hypoxemia, although PCO_2 is always normal and pulmonary arterial pressures are within normal limits.

DIROFILARIA IMMITIS "COIN" LESION. Since 1964 at least 13 cases have been reported of solitary pulmonary nodules or "coin" lesions which on removal were found to contain *Dirofilaria immitis*, the "heart worm" of the dog.[1624-1627] A mosquito transmits the microfilaria from a fur-bearing animal, usually a dog or a cat, to the human host, where maturation of the microfilaria occurs in the right side of the heart or in the pulmonary artery; the mature worm detaches and becomes impacted in a pulmonary arteriole, where it incites a fibroblastic reaction in the surrounding tissues. The center of the resultant well-circumscribed mass may become necrotic and undergo cavitation, rendering identification of the worm difficult.[1625, 1626] Impaction of the worm in a larger branch of the pulmonary artery may result in a roentgenographic shadow simulating pulmonary infarction. Cases published to date have been asymptomatic, pulmonary resection having been performed because of a suspicion of bronchogenic carcinoma.

Pulmonary Larva Migrans

This parasitic disease results from infestation of the larvae of the dog or cat round worm, *Toxocara canis* and *T. cati*. It is probably world-wide in distribution but the majority of reports have come from North America, England, Australia, and Mexico. The disease occurs predominantly in children who swallow soil contaminated by eggs passed in the feces of dogs and cats. The eggs develop into larvae in the intestine, whence they pass into the blood stream and are carried to the liver, brain, eyes, lungs, cardiac muscle, lymph nodes, and other tissues (visceral larva migrans). Multiple lesions are found in many organs throughout the body, consisting of granulomatous foci containing eosinophils, lymphocytes, epithelial cells, and giant cells surrounding the larvae.

Roentgenographically the chest shows evidence of local or diffuse patchy areas of ill-defined pneumonitis.

Children with this disease may be asymptomatic or may complain of cough, wheezing, dyspnea, cyanosis, abdominal pain, and neurologic symptoms. Hepatosplenomegaly is usually present. Leukocytosis of 40,000 or more is common, usually associated with extreme eosinophilia of at least 30 per cent. Hyperglobulinemia, anemia, and increased erythrocyte sedimentation rate may be noted. The diagnosis may be made by the identification of eosinophilic granulomas containing larvae in liver biopsy.

PLATYHELMINTH (FLAT-WORM) INFESTATION

Echinococcosis (Hydatid Disease)

GENERAL COMMENTS AND EPIDEMIOLOGY. Hydatid disease is caused by the parasite *Echinococcus granulosus*, a member of the class *Cestoda* (the tape worms). *Echinococcus granulosus* is a small tape worm whose definitive host is the dog or wolf and whose intermediate host is a variety of mammals, including sheep and man. There are two types of hydatid disease, the *pastoral variety* which is the more common of the two and in which the usual intermediate host is the sheep, and the *sylvatic form* which very likely is caused by a different strain of tape worm and in which the dog and moose are the usual intermediate hosts. There are some differences in the roentgenographic and clinical features of the pastoral and sylvatic forms of the disease although their epidemiology and pathology are identical. Pastoral echinococcosis is particularly common in the sheep-raising Mediterranean regions and in Australia, New Zealand, and Africa. The sylvatic form is seen primarily in Alaska and northern Canada. Nearly all cases of hydatid disease in southern Canada and in the United States occur in immigrants.[1628, 1629] Males appear to be slightly more commonly affected than females;[616, 1630] the age incidence ranges from six to 50 years,[1631] about one third of patients being children under the age of 15.[1630]

The minute tape worm *Echinococcus granulosus* lives within the small intestine of the dog which is the definitive host; millions of ova are passed on to pastures where sheep and cattle may be grazing. These animals, and occasionally man, ingest the ova, which subsequently develop into larvae in the duodenum. The larvae enter the blood stream and pass to the liver and lungs; if they penetrate these two capillary sieves, they may reach the spleen, kidneys, brain, or skeleton. Only a few of these larvae survive the natural defenses of the host, and it may be as long as 20 years before those that do survive give rise to symptoms as a result of the formation of an hydatid cyst.[1632] The life cycle of the parasite is completed when the definitive host, the dog, feeds on the remains of an intermediate host—sheep or cattle—harboring the larval or cystic stage of the disease, and thereby permits the development of adult worms.

The anatomic bias for the liver and lungs shown by hydatid cysts varies considerably in reported series; for example, in pastoral echinococcosis, lung cysts have been reported to be more common than liver cysts,[616] less common than liver cysts,[1633, 1634] and of equal incidence.[1630, 1631, 1635, 1636] In sylvatic hydatid disease, lung cysts show a distinct preponderance over liver cysts.[1634, 1637] The recent literature suggests that a higher proportion of lung cysts are seen nowadays, probably due to the extension of screening chest roentgenography in endemic areas.

PATHOLOGIC CHARACTERISTICS. Thoracic hydatid cysts occur predominantly within the lung parenchyma, only 2 to 5 per cent developing in the mediastinum, pleural cavity or diaphragm.[1638–1640] In its early stages, the cyst is a spherical or oval mass surrounded by a layer of fibrous tissue formed by the host and sometimes known as the pericyst. The hydatid cyst itself is composed of two layers, a laminated layer which forms the chitinous outer membrane of the cyst (the exocyst) and a thin inner lining formed by a syncytium of cells (the germinal layer or endocyst), from which daughter cysts grow and protrude into the fluid-filled cyst cavity. Rarely elsewhere—and almost never in the lung—daughter cysts may grow outward, invading the host tissue and behaving in many respects like an infiltrating neoplasm; this form of growth is known as multilocular or alveolar-type hydatid disease in contrast to the commoner unilocular cyst.

Pulmonary hydatid cysts may rupture into the surrounding bronchi, resulting in expulsion of the cyst contents and their replacement with air. Sometimes only the pericyst may be eroded, permitting communication between the bronchial tree and the potential space between the exocyst and pericyst; when this occurs, air accumulates around the exocyst so that the germinal layer tends to collapse. Rupture of a cyst into a bronchus is commonly followed by secondary infection which tends to kill the parent cyst but permits the daughter cysts to survive. Rarely a cyst may rupture into the pleural cavity, producing pyopneumothorax.

Rupture of the cyst is said to occur far more frequently in the pastoral type than in the sylvatic type.[1634] Daughter cysts develop both from the germinal layer itself and from small vesicular modifications of the germinal layer known as brood capsules which in turn bud the scolices with their many hooklets.

ROENTGENOGRAPHIC MANIFESTATIONS. Characteristically, pulmonary echinococcal cyst presents as a solitary, sharply circumscribed, spherical or oval mass of unit density surrounded by normal lung (Figure 7–43).[616, 1630, 1634, 1641] Cysts are multiple in 20 to 30 per cent of patients.[616, 1630] Their size ranges from 1 cm to over 10 cm in diameter; the larger cysts usually are of the pastoral type, the sylvatic variety rarely exceeding 10 cm.[1634] In a study of the growth-rate characteristic of hydatid cysts in ten patients, Bloomfield[616] found the doubling time to range from 16 to 20 weeks.

The majority of pulmonary hydatid cysts are situated in the lower portions of the lungs, usually the lower lobes and then more often posterior than anterior in position, and somewhat more commonly in the right than in the left.[1630, 1631, 1638, 1641] The greater incidence of cysts in the right lower lobe than in the left probably is due to the occasional case which develops as a result of extrusion through the diaphragm from the right lobe of the liver.

Although commonly sharply circumscribed, hydatid cysts sometimes possess a bizarre, irregular shape, an unusual characteristic that has been attributed to the fact that, as the cyst grows, it impinges on relatively rigid structures such as bronchovascular bundles and thus becomes indented and lobulated (*see* Figure 5–22, page 450).[616, 1631] When a cyst relates to the diaphragm, chest wall, or mediastinum, it tends to flatten against these structures, although compression of mediastinal structures may occur. The fluid content of a cyst may be evidenced by a change in shape on roentgenograms exposed in maximal inspiration and expiration or in erect and recumbent positions.[1630, 1642]

Although the diagnosis of hydatid cyst may be suggested by their rather bizarre lobulated shape, they commonly present as a homogeneous mass indistinguishable from other causes of solitary "coin" lesions or of masses such as bronchogenic carcinoma. The diagnosis becomes obvious only when communication develops between some portion of the cyst and the bronchial tree. Communication may occur in two ways, each of which has distinctive roentgenographic characteristics. Rupture may occur between the pericyst and the exocyst, permitting air to enter between these layers and presenting an appearance of a thin crescent of air around the periphery of the cyst—the "meniscus sign," the "double-arch sign," the "moon sign," or the "crescent sign."[616, 1630, 1632, 1637, 1641, 1643] Despite the emphasis that has been placed on this sign in the literature, McPhail and Arora[1630] observed it in only 5.4 per cent of their 49 patients; it is a rare manifestation of the sylvatic type of infestation, being observed in none of the 101 patients studied by Wilson and colleagues.[1634] The second form of bronchial communication occurs directly with the endocyst, permitting expulsion of cyst contents and the production of an air-fluid level roentgenographically; the presence of cyst fluid in the surrounding parenchyma may simulate pneumonic consolidation.[1630] Occasionally, both forms of communication may be manifest, showing an air-fluid level within the cyst and a "crescent sign" around its periphery.[1632, 1643] After rupture of the cyst into the bronchial tree, the cyst membrane sometimes floats on the surface of the fluid within the cyst, giving rise to the classic "water-lily" sign or the "sign of the camalote."[616, 1632, 1682] This sign also may be seen in pleural fluid following rupture of the cyst into the pleural space, with resultant hydropneumothorax or pyopneumothorax.[1639] The "water-lily sign" is rare in the sylvatic form of the disease, having been observed in only one of the 101 patients studied by Wilson and his associates;[1634] despite this rarity, however, the sylvatic form of hydatid cyst shows a strong predisposition to rupture spontaneously into the bronchial tree, with subsequent complete cure in most instances.[1637] By contrast, the pastoral form of hydatid

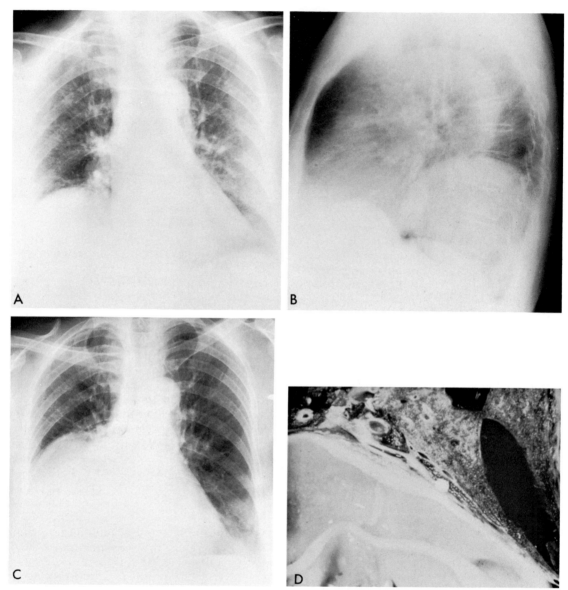

Figure 7–43. **Echinococcus (Hydatid) Cyst.** Posteroanterior (*A*) and lateral (*B*) roentgenograms reveal a large sharply-circumscribed, homogeneous mass in the lower portion of the right hemithorax, situated within the substance of the right lower lobe. One week later (*C*), the mass had increased markedly in size although still showing sharp definition where it related to air-containing lung. This 60-year-old woman had emigrated to Canada from Greece three months previously; her chief complaint was right costovertebral angle pain which had become very severe just prior to admission. The Casoni skin test was strongly positive. The right lower lobe was resected. Pathologically, the cyst was found to measure 9 × 7 cm (*D*); the cyst cavity was lined by a glistening white membrane to which were attached numerous minute white scolices. The entire surface of the germinative membrane was studded by small scolices; the surrounding lung tissue was compressed to form a pseudocapsule. In the photograph of a portion of the gross specimen, three layers can be identified—the adventitial layer (pericyst) formed by compressed lung, the middle or laminated membrane (the exocyst), and the germinal layer (endocyst) to which are attached daughter cysts.

cyst rarely disappears completely following rupture, a residual cavity commonly remaining that often becomes infected; McPhail and Arora[1630] recorded spontaneous disappearance of a pastoral cyst following rupture in only 10 per cent of their cases.

Calcification of pulmonary hydatid cysts is extremely rare,[616] presumably because growth is so rapid and rupture so frequent that calcification has no chance to develop; in many series, calcification has not been observed,[1638, 1642] although it developed in three of the 49 patients studied by McPhail and Arora.[1630]

Rib erosion occurred in two of 13 cases of pulmonary hydatid disease reported by Jonathan.[1645]

Mediastinal echinococcosis is relatively rare compared with the pulmonary form. In a review of 74 cases—some with more than one cyst—from the literature, and six new cases, Rakower and Milwidsky[1646] found cysts in the posterior mediastinum in 65 per cent, in the anterior mediastinum in 36 per cent and in the middle mediastinum in 9 per cent. In the posterior mediastinum—the most common location—the cysts tend to erode ribs and vertebrae and to compress the spinal cord; of the posterior mediastinal cysts described by Rakower and Milwidsky,[1646] 67 per cent were associated with bone erosion. Cysts located in the anterior mediastinum may compress the trachea, and those in the mid-mediastinum may compress and erode great vessels.

CLINICAL MANIFESTATIONS. The majority of intact pulmonary hydatid cysts occasion no symptoms.[1638] The sylvatic form, particularly, produces symptoms only rarely and is said to be unassociated with serious complications.[1638] Occasionally an unruptured cyst may be responsible for a nonproductive cough and minimal hemoptysis.[1631] When the cyst ruptures, either spontaneously or as a result of secondary infection, there is an abrupt onset of cough, expectoration, and fever; an acute hypersensitivity reaction may develop, with urticaria, pruritus and sometimes hypotension. The patient may complain of chest pain. The sputum may become purulent and may contain fragments of hydatid membrane; rarely, microscopic examination of the sputum reveals hooklets from the scolices.[1632] A few cases have been described in which a cyst developed at the thoracic inlet and resulted in symptoms and signs of a superior pulmonary sulcus tumor,[1647, 1648] a clinical syndrome much more frequently associated with bronchogenic carcinoma (*see* page 753). Hydatid cysts arising in the posterior mediastinum may be associated with pain as a result of bone erosion; those in the anterior mediastinum may cause severe dyspnea as a result of tracheal compression; and the rare involvement of the middle mediastinum may lead to catastrophic hemorrhage due to erosion of great vessels.

Unlike many other parasitic diseases, eosinophilia is uncommon in echinococcosis, occurring in no more than 20 to 25 per cent of cases; McPhail and Arora[1630] found an eosinophil count of less than 6 per cent in the majority of their cases, although it was as high as 52 per cent in some. Severe eosinophilia usually is associated with anaphylaxis following cyst rupture.

Laboratory aids to diagnosis include the occasional identification of hooklets from scolices in the sputum and a skin test (the Casoni test) using an antigen made from hydatid fluid; the latter is positive in 60 to 65 per cent of patients.[1629, 1631, 1636, 1645] A new antigen made from scolices which was first described in 1968[1649] gave a positive reaction in 78 per cent of cases, compared with only 17 per cent positive results with hydatid-fluid antigen.

Cysticercosis

Cysticercosis is a parasitic infestation caused by various tape worms, particularly *Taenia solium*, members of class *Cestoda*. The disease is common in Africa, India, and China.[1650] Man occasionally serves as the intermediate host, infestation occurring in one of three ways: (1) eggs may be ingested in contaminated soil or water; (2) autoinfection may occur by anus-to-mouth contamination in patients infected with adult worms; and (3) rarely, autoinfection may occur through regurgitation of eggs from the lower to the upper intestine. The eggs loose their shells in the upper small bowel, the emerging oncospheres penetrating the mesenteric veins and being carried to various organs and tissues of the body, particularly muscle, brain, and eyes; over a period of 60 to 70 days, the oncospheres undergo metamorphosis into cysticerci (*Cysticercus cellulosae*). Thoracic involvement occurs through deposition of the cysticerci in the respiratory muscles where their presence may occasion pain. Roentgenographically, they may be identified as oval calcified shadows measuring 3 by 10 mm; they are usually multiple but occasionally solitary.[1651]

Paragonimiasis

GENERAL COMMENTS AND EPIDEMIOLOGY. Paragonimiasis is caused by the fluke *Paragonimus westermanii (Distoma pulmonale)*, a member of the class *Trematoda*. This parasite was first identified in a variety of wild and domestic animals and was subsequently shown to be the cause of human lung disease in Korea, Formosa, Japan, parts of China, the Philippine Islands, Indonesia, New Guinea, south-east Asia, and certain countries in Africa and South America. Wild and domestic animals in North America have been found to harbor the parasites, and it seems that human beings can acquire the disease on this continent without having visited areas which are usually regarded as endemic.[1652] The ova are destroyed by heating to 55° C for five minutes. The disease occurs in patients of all ages but tends to be particularly severe in young children.[1653]

The life cycle of *Paragonimus westermanii* is one of the most fascinating of all parasites. Within the lungs of man or animals the larval form (metacercariae) develop into adult flukes which deposit eggs in burrows in lung parenchyma. The eggs are coughed up or are swallowed and excreted in the feces. Under suitable moist conditions, the eggs develop into ciliated miracidia which infest fresh-water snails. Within the snail, further larval forms develop which are liberated as cercariae after approximately two months; these are actively motile parasites which penetrate the soft periarticular tissues of certain species of crayfish and crabs. Man is infected either by eating raw or improperly cooked crabs or crayfish or by drinking water contaminated by them. Metacercariae are liberated in the jejunum, whence they penetrate the wall of the

small bowel into the peritoneal cavity; from there they penetrate the diaphragm and enter the pleural space and, eventually, the lung. Within the lung — usually the lower lobe — the metacercariae mature into adult flukes, which produce ova to begin the cycle all over again. The mature parasite lives for many years in the lung and produces ova continuously.

PATHOLOGIC CHARACTERISTICS. Since the disease usually is mild and seldom is fatal, there is a paucity of data regarding its pathology. Spencer[961] described three different forms of reaction within the lung: a nonsuppurative, chronic granulomatous reaction containing numerous ova; a suppurative lesion with caseation; and a chronic ulcerative condition. Necrosis is believed to be the result of the toxic action of dead parasites, which may be identifiable in the center of such lesions; surrounding the necrosis there is a zone of vascular granulation tissue containing lymphocytes, plasma cells, and a few eosinophils. Necrotic and granulomatous lesions have been said to form around the chitinous cuticle of the foreign-body parasitic eggs.[1654] Ova may be identified throughout the lung tissue. Both flukes and ova may be carried to the brain, resulting in fatal encephalitis.

ROENTGENOGRAPHIC MANIFESTATIONS. Perhaps the most comprehensive report of the roentgenographic changes in pulmonary paragonimiasis has been provided by Suwanik and Harinsuta[1655] from a study of 38 patients in an endemic area in Thailand. The most characteristic pattern is one of ring shadows of thin-walled cysts ranging from 6 mm to 4 to 5 cm in diameter and typically presenting a crescent-shaped opacity along one aspect of their inner lining. They are usually multiple but may be solitary (Figure 7–44). A characteristic feature is the presence of irregular tracks or burrows extending from one cyst to another, with a lumen up to 5 mm in diameter (compared with the expected bronchial diameter of 2 to 3 mm). Tomography may be of considerable value in visualizing these burrows; in at least one patient, bronchography demonstrated communication between slightly dilated bronchioles and cystic cavities;[1655] such a picture may simulate severe cystic bronchiectasis (Figure 7–45). Another roentgenographic manifestation is hetero-

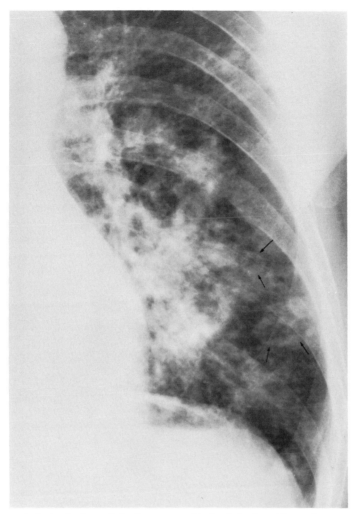

Figure 7–44. **Paragonimiasis.** A view of the lower two thirds of the hemithorax from a posteroanterior roent-genogram reveals extensive parenchymal disease of which the most characteristic change consists of irregular cystic spaces possessing walls of moderate thickness (*arrows*). In the medial portion of the lobe, consolidation of lung parenchyma is more confluent. Fluid obtained from the left lower lobe by aspiration needle biopsy contained the fluke *Paragonimus westermani.* (Courtesy Dr. David Berger, Royal Edward Chest Hospital, Montreal.)

geneous, nonsegmental consolidation which may mimic reinfection tuberculosis when it affects an upper lobe (Figure 7–46).

Less frequent roentgenographic abnormalities include nodular shadows 3 to 4 cm in diameter usually situated in the peripheral portion of the lower lobes. Rarely, irregular line shadows and pleural thickening may be identified. Pleural effusion or pneumothorax have been described, presumably resulting from transgression of the pleura by the metacercariae. In the late stages of the disease, the lesions have been known to undergo calcification.[1656]

CLINICAL MANIFESTATIONS. Hemoptysis is almost invariably present[1652, 1653, 1657] and may occur sporadically for months or years in the absence of other signs of illness. Shortness of breath, mild fever, anorexia, and weight loss may be observed, and the development of pleural effusion or pneumothorax may result in pleural pain; diarrhea, epileptic seizures and hemiplegia develop in a small percentage of cases. Symptoms may not develop for at least one year after the presumed time of the infestation.

Neither leukocytosis nor eosinophilia usually is present, although both may

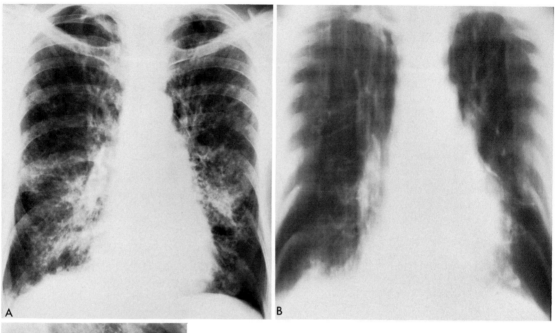

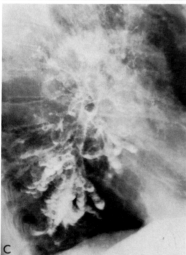

Figure 7–45. **Paragonimiasis.** A posteroanterior roentgenogram (*A*) reveals extensive bilateral parenchymal disease characterized by very coarse reticulonodular pattern. In the left base are several well-defined cystic spaces possessing walls of moderate thickness; a similar cyst can be identified in the upper portion of the left lung. A full lung tomogram in anteroposterior projection (*B*) shows the cystic spaces in the left base to excellent advantage. Severe cystic bronchiectasis of all basal bronchi of the left lower lobe is apparent bronchographically (*C*). A left lower lobectomy was performed and the fluke *Paragonimus westermani* was identified in the resected specimen. This 38-year-old man is a native Montrealer who has never left Canada. Examination of peripheral blood showed a striking eosinophilia. (Courtesy Dr. David Berger, Royal Edward Chest Hospital, Montreal.)

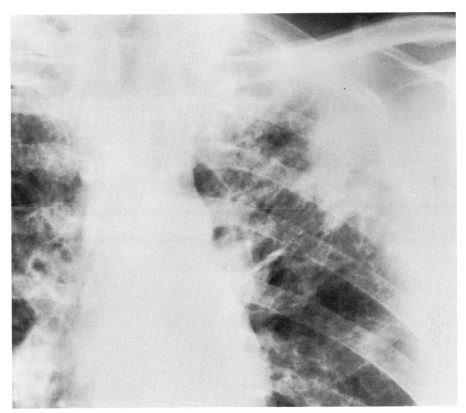

Figure 7–46. **Paragonimiasis.** A view of the upper half of the left hemithorax from a posteroanterior roentgenogram reveals inhomogeneous consolidation of the left upper lobe, situated predominantly in the posterior and apical bronchopulmonary segments; a small pleural effusion is present. The roentgenologic appearance strongly suggested reinfection pulmonary tuberculosis. The fluke *Paragonimus westermani* was identified in the sputum; there was no evidence of *M. tuberculosis*. Complete roentgenologic resolution occurred in two months on appropriate therapy. Thirty-six-year old immigrant Filipino. Prior to identification of the parasite, the diagnosis was suggested by the patient's recent immigrant status from Malaysia. (Courtesy Dr. David Berger, Royal Edward Chest Hospital, Montreal.)

develop temporarily when the metacercariae enter the pleural cavity.[1652] Some of the patients are anemic.

The diagnosis is made by the finding of typical operculated eggs in the sputum or stool. Béland and his associates[1652] stated that the eggs may be readily identified by staining with the Papanicolaou method. A complement-fixation test and skin test are available but appear to be of limited value, since the diagnosis is readily made by the demonstration of eggs in the sputum or stool.

Opisthorciasis

Pulmonary involvement by *Opisthorchis felineus*, the liver fluke (class *Trematoda*) is extremely rare in man, only one case

having been reported.[1658] In this case, an abscess ruptured through the right hemidiaphragm, resulting in a large abscess in the right lower lobe. The patient coughed up greenish sputum which was found to contain bile; at post mortem, the connection between the liver and lung was readily demonstrated. This complication of rupture of an abscess through the diaphragm into the lung is much more commonly seen in amebiasis and echinococcosis, particularly the former.

Schistosomiasis

GENERAL COMMENTS AND EPIDEMIOLOGY. Three blood flukes (class *Trematoda*) cause disease in man—*Schistosoma mansoni*, *S. japonicum*, and *S. haemato-*

bium. Two forms of pulmonary disease may be recognized, a transitory process simulating Loeffler's syndrome which occurs coincidentally with the passage of cercariae through the pulmonary capillaries, and a more serious form of pulmonary arterial hypertension, occasionally acute and fulminating but more commonly insidious and chronic, the result of dissemination of schistosoma eggs throughout the pulmonary vascular tree. Schistosoma infestations must be seriously considered as the etiology of cor pulmonale in any person residing in an endemic area.

Both S. mansoni and S. haematobium are endemic in Egypt and Africa, and the former in the West Indies and South America also; S. japonicum is found in China, Japan, and the Philippines. The great majority of patients with schistosomiasis seen in the United States and Canada are Puerto Ricans infested with S. mansoni, and it has been estimated that 11 per cent of all Puerto Ricans have schistosomiasis.[1659] In one study of 103 Puerto Rican males residing in the United States, 29 were found to harbor eggs of S. mansoni and 45 to have positive skin tests for schistosomiasis.[1660]

The eggs of S. mansoni and S. japonicum are deposited primarily in the liver, so that symptoms and signs are predominantly those of cirrhosis and hepatosplenomegaly. By contrast, S. haematobium affects the urinary bladder chiefly, and hematuria is the major symptom. Pulmonary involvement occurs in approximately a third of patients with S. haematobium and S. mansoni infestation;[704, 1661] however, despite the presence of eggs in the lungs, the clinical picture of cor pulmonale develops in only 2 to 6 per cent of these patients.[704] Although cor pulmonale secondary to S. japonicum infestation usually is considered to be an uncommon complication,[1662, 1663] a recent report suggested that pulmonary involvement is far more common than is generally recognized.[1664]

Significant pulmonary disease due to S. mansoni usually appears between the ages of 12 and 35 years and seldom if ever before the age of ten years.[1665, 1666]

The life cycle of the blood fluke is complex and fascinating. Man acquires the infestation by drinking, swimming, working, or washing in fresh water containing the infective cercariae. The larvae penetrate the skin or less commonly the mucosa of the mouth or pharynx, and pass via the venous circulation to the pulmonary capillaries; they flow through the pulmonary capillary sieve to the systemic circulation, and in order to survive, must enter the mesenteric vessels and subsequently the intrahepatic portion of the portal system. There they develop into adolescent worms which subsequently migrate against the portal blood flow to the mesenteric, bladder, and pelvic venules. The adult male and female worms copulate in these venules and then the females migrate to smaller venous channels in the submucosa and the mucosa of the bowel and bladder and lay their eggs.[1666] Many of these eggs subsequently are extruded into the lumen of the bowel and urinary bladder and are passed in the feces or urine; those which reach fresh water develop into larvae which enter snails. Several transformations take place within the snail, infective cercariae eventually emerging; penetration of the skin of a person in contact with the contaminated water then completes the Odyssey. Some of the eggs deposited by the female worm in the mucosa and submucosa of the bowel and bladder enter the venous system: the eggs of S. mansoni and S. japonicum are deposited in the liver and those of S. haematobium in the lungs. Affection of the lungs by eggs of S. mansoni and S. japonicum is thought to occur only when the liver has become cirrhotic as a result of previous schistosomal reaction and has established anastomotic channels that permit migration of the ova between the portal and systemic venous systems.[1664, 1666, 1667]

PATHOLOGIC CHARACTERISTICS. In their passage through the lung capillaries the metacercariae may incite a local tissue reaction evidenced by transient petechial hemorrhages and foci of eosinophilic and leukocytic infiltration, a picture which fits the usually accepted pathologic criteria of Loeffler's syndrome.[1664] Much later in the cycle, eggs deposited in the venules of the mucosa and submucosa of the bowel and urinary bladder traverse the systemic veins and reach the right side of the heart and become impacted in arterioles ranging from 50 to 100μ in diameter. The ova measure 40 to 70 by 100 to 170μ.[704] A small percentage of ova may lodge in larger arteries, perhaps due to the sticky nature of their shell.[961] After the ovum becomes lodged in a pulmonary vessel, it digests its way through the vessel wall, producing a focal obliterative arteriolitis. The ovum finally reaches the perivascular tissues, where it initiates a tissue reaction which ultimately results in the formation of a granuloma. Infiltration with histiocytes, eosinophilic leukocytes, lymphocytes, and multinucleated giant cells occurs in the tissues surrounding the extruded egg, and this inflammatory reaction eventually becomes fibrotic.[704, 1661, 1666] When vascular lesions are widespread, a diffuse obliterating endarteritis occurs which restricts the capacity of the pulmonary vascular bed and results in increase in pulmonary artery pressure. In larger arteries, a similar process may take place with partial or complete extrusion of the eggs and subsequent development of a granulomatous lesion which may eventually completely obstruct blood flow through the vessel. Recanalization of obstructed arterioles may lead to the appearance of angiomatoid lesions characteristic of any form of pulmonary hypertension.[704, 961] Similarly, nonspecific medial hypertrophy of the small arteries may result (see page 833).[1661] In addition to these vascular and perivascular lesions, a considerable degree of interstitial pulmonary fibrosis may develop.[1666, 1668]

Some adult worms may reach the pulmonary vessels, where they tend to incite no reaction until they die and then they produce panarteritis, thrombosis, and occlusion of the arterial lumen. It is probable that fertilization may occur within the pulmonary vessels, with subsequent production of ova there.

ROENTGENOGRAPHIC MANIFESTATIONS. Pulmonary arterial hypertension due to pulmonary schistosomiasis is indistinguishable from that due to any other cause, there being a marked degree of dilatation of the main pulmonary artery and its branches with rapid tapering toward the periphery (see Figure 5–39, page 501).[704] Some cases, perhaps the majority, show a diffuse miliary or reticulonodular pattern presumably due to the migration of ova through vessel walls and subsequent reaction to this foreign body.[704, 1660, 1662, 1664, 1669, 1670] The appearance of the chest roentgenogram varies considerably, depending upon the number of eggs that reach the lung and the time of roentgenography in relation to the formation of perivascular granulomas following extrusion of the eggs. Areas of pneumonic

consolidation are said to develop around dead adult worms that occlude arteries.[704] Pleural effusion does not occur, although focal pleural thickening may develop. Occasional case reports have appeared in which pulmonary nodules or "coin" lesions observed roentgenographically were due to granuloma formation or infarction caused by adult schistosomal worms.[1671, 1672]

CLINICAL MANIFESTATIONS. Extrathoracic symptoms caused by involvement of the urinary and intestinal tracts include dysuria and terminal hematuria, and diarrhea mixed with blood, pus, and mucus. Showers of eggs reaching the pulmonary arterioles produce dry cough, dyspnea, and palpitations. With the development of pulmonary hypertension, an ejection systolic murmur, with or without an early diastolic murmur, a loud second pulmonic sound and a left parasternal heave may appear; signs of cardiac decompensation may develop. Diffuse scattered rales or rhonchi may be the only audible sounds on auscultation over the lungs. Hepatosplenomegaly develops in patients with S. mansoni and S. japonicum infestation.

In addition to the late manifestations due to cor pulmonale, a Loeffler-like syndrome has been described, with transient pulmonary consolidation and eosinophilia, presumably due to the passage of metacercariae through the pulmonary capillaries.[1664, 1666] Also, some cases have been reported of the acute onset of cyanosis, hypoxemia, and bilateral pulmonary edema, thought to constitute an allergic reaction due to the sudden mobilization of many eggs to the lungs.[1659, 1673] It is of some interest that a Loeffler-like picture similar to that which occurs with passage of the larvae through the lungs may be observed when the patient with schistosomiasis is given chemotherapy.

Unlike paragonimiasis, in which the mature worm may penetrate and lay eggs in the conducting airways, pulmonary schistosomiasis is largely a disease of the vasculature and perivascular interstitial tissues; consequently, hemoptysis occurs only rarely and when present is apparently provoked by erosion of a pulmonary artery by larval transgression.[1674] Since there is no tendency to involvement of the airways, ova are seldom found in the sputum.[704, 1664]

In patients with suspected schistosomiasis, concentrated specimens of stool and urine should be examined repeatedly for ova. Infestation is demonstrable in many cases by the finding of eggs in biopsy specimens of the rectal and bladder mucosa, but examination of the sputum seldom reveals ova, and lung biopsy usually is required to establish the presence of pulmonary involvement.[1660, 1675, 1676]

The ova of the three varieties of schistosoma have specific characteristics that permit ready differentiation; specific skin tests and precipitin tests are available.[1660, 1664] Moderate leukocytosis and eosinophilia usually are present, the latter to as high as 33 per cent.[704] In patients with cor pulmonale, the electrocardiogram reveals right axis deviation, right ventricular hypertrophy, and incomplete right bundle branch block.[704, 1669]

Pulmonary function tests in pulmonary schistosomiasis with cor pulmonale may be completely normal, even when catheterization reveals high pulmonary artery pressure. A slight reduction in vital capacity and flow rates has been recorded.[704, 1665] Patients tend to hyperventilate and have raised ventilatory equivalents with an increase in dead space. Compliance is reduced, presumably as a result of interstitial fibrosis and destruction of lung elasticity.[1668] Zaky and associates[1668] detected hypoxia of 89 to 94 per cent in less than 10 per cent of their patients and only those with pulmonary hypertension at rest or on exercise. It is probable that the hypoxemia is due to shunting between portal and pulmonary veins.[1677]

ARTHROPOD INFESTATION

Pentastomiasis

The tongue worms, *Linguatula serrata* and *Armillifer armillatus*, are arachnids whose larval stage may infest man. *L. serrata* is said to be present on every continent,[1678] although most reports of human infestation have originated in southern Germany, Switzerland, Brazil, and Chile.[1650, 1679] The adults of this arachnid live in the upper respiratory passages of pigs, foxes, and wolves, and the females lay eggs which are discharged in sputum and mucus from the respiratory tract of these animals. The larval hosts include rabbits and hares, domestic animals, and, occasionally, man. The eggs hatch when swallowed by the larval host; four- to six-legged larvae emerge in the intestine and migrate to the liver, spleen, lymph nodes, and lungs, where they are transformed into nymphs, which become encapsulated and eventually calcified. *Armillifer armillatus* has a similar life cycle, occurring predominantly in Negroes in central Africa but having been reported also from Java, Manila, Sumatra, and China. The adult arachnid lives in the respiratory passages and body cavities of reptiles, birds, and mammals.

Chest roentgenograms in these patients reveal numerous discrete calcifications 4 to 6 mm in diameter, usually in the form of an incomplete ring shadow.[1678, 1680] Necropsies have revealed lesions in 4 to 5 per cent of the population in some areas of Africa and Chile.[961, 1650] The infestation is apparently nonsymptom-producing in man.

INDEX

INDEX

of first authors of cited literature

Reference numbers are in **bold face** and are followed by the numbers of the pages on which they are cited.

Aaby, G. V., **3499**: 1067
Aach, R., **2185**: 784
Abbott, O. A., **869**: 573, 574, 576; **3272**: 1105
Abdel-Hakim, M., **1567**: 700
Abelmann, W. H., **4288**: 1263
Abernathy, R. S., **1268**: 656, 657
Abouav, J., **2067**: 761
Abrahams, E. W., **625**: 283, 690
Abrams, H. L., **249**: 121
Abrams, L. D., **430**: 161
Abrantes, P., **1649**: 715
Adams, C. W., **2273**: 805
Adams, E. B., **3776**: 1125, 1255
Adams, J. M., **1505**: 688, 689
Adamson, R. H., **4273**: 1260
Addington, W. W., **3318**: 1018
Adhikari, P. K., **2611**: 889, 894, 1252
Adler, D., **1707**: 723
Adler, H., **1119**: 623
Aggarwal, M. L., **1643**: 713
Agnos, J. W., **1772**: 732
Agostoni, E., **130**: 65, 341; **131**: 66
Ahlmark, A., **2796**: 919; **2855**: 937, 939
Aho, A., **2492**: 867, 879; **3583**: 1093, 1160
Aikens, R. L., **444**: 163
Akkaynak, S., **1574**: 702
Alarcón-Segovia, D., **2490**: 867, 868
Albers, W. H., **2449**: 857
Albert, B. L., **1247**: 653
Aldrich, R. A., **2673**: 902
Aledort, L. M., **3783**: 1125
Alexander, C., **4098**: 1219, 1220
Alexander, E. R., **1429**: 679
Alexander, H. L., **3110**: 981, 982
Alexander, J. K., **372**: 148, 1259, 1262, 1263; **2335**: 822; **4302**: 1267
Alivisatos, G. P., **2859**: 937
Allan, W., **459**: 164, 177, 178, 764
Allen, A. R., **1136**: 635, 639, 640; **2537**: 874
Allen, W. E., Jr., **1134**: 635
Allison, P. R., **282**: 125; **4134**: 1230
Al-Mallah, Z., **3497**: 1066, 1067
Altemus, L. R., **2239**: 794, 798
Altman, R., **1492**: 687
Altmann, K., **84**: 46

Amatruda, T. T., Jr., **2089**: 762
American College of Chest Physicians, **2911**: 946, 947
American Thoracic Society, **3116**: 982, 995
Amos, J. A. S., **2350**: 824, 827
Amundsen, P., **168**: 99, 286; **271**: 125
Andér, L., **3684**: 1109
Andersen, H. A., **460**: 158, 159
Anderson, A. E., Jr., **3231**: 997; **3700**: 1116
Anderson, C. M., **3470**: 1064
Anderson, D. O., **3139**: 984
Anderson, N. W., **1199**: 643, 644
Anderson, R., **3633**: 1103, 1104
Anderson, R. C., **862**: 571
Anderson, R. P., **3504**: 1067
Andrewes, C. H., **1411**: 675, 680, 681
Andrews, B. F., **2670**: 900
Andrews, G. S., **2111**: 763, 764, 765
Andrews, J. T., **2226**: 793
Andrews, N. C., **409**: 159, 160; **815**: 119, 123, 624
Andriole, V. T., **3823**: 1131
Angeloni, J. M., **968**: 596, 597
Angervall, L., **2893**: 943
Anjilvel, L., **2821**: 933
Annamalai, A., **866**: 573, 576
Annotations, Lancet, **4311**: 1268
Anthonisen, N. R., **910**: 185; **912**; 185, 1021; **913**: 185; **2454**: 857
Anton, H. C., **2830**: 934, 936; **3806**: 1128, 1129, 1160
Antweiler, H., **2725**: 908
Appenzeller, O., **738**: 153
Apthorp, G. H., **878**: 574
Arany, L. S., **1183**: 642; **2164**: 770
Arden, M. J., **2184**: 782
Arean, V. M., **1792**: 733
Areechon, W., **852**: 569
Armen, R. N., **302**: 127; **3977**: 1167, 1174
Arnett, N. L., **3705**: 1116
Arnois, D. C., **702**: 328
Arnold, W. H., Jr., **3313**: 1018
Arnoldsson, H., **2722**: 908
Aronoff, A., **2551**: 879
Aronovitch, M., **415**: 160
Aronson, P. R., **4309**: 1268
Arora, Y. C., **2325**: 816
Arrigoni, A., **2905**: 945

Arrington, C. W., **435**: 162
Arruda, R. M. de, **1715**: 724, 725
Artenstein, M. S., **1496**: 687
Arvidsson, H., **741**: 573, 841
Asch, T., **319**: 129; **4144**: 1232
Aschoff, L., **5**: 5, 191, 192
Ashbaugh, D. G., **3868**: 1135, 1136; **3869**: 1135
Ashcroft, T., **2822**: 933; **3206**: 989
Asher, R., **357**: 145
Ashley, D. J. B., **1769**: 732; **1802**: 734; **1889**: 738
Askergren, A., **1734**: 730
Atkinson, A. J., **1308**: 660
Aubert, L., **2656**: 897, 1122
Auerbach, O., **1862**: 737, 739, 984; **1863**: 737, 739; **1864**: 737, 739
August, J. T., **1782**: 733
Austen, F. K., **371**: 148, 1017
Austrian, R., **959**: 593
Ausubel, H., **4166**: 1239
Avery, M. E., **53**: 34; **3395**: 1043, 1044
Avila, R., **2776**: 916
Avnet, N. L., **4104**: 1220
Ayres, S. M., **3343**: 1021
Azen, E. A., **3792**: 1128
Azzopardi, A., **11**: 3
Azzopardi, J. G., **2052**: 761

Baar, H. S., **2952**: 950
Babbitt, D. P., **1202**: 643, 644, 645
Bacharach, T., **3626**: 1103; **3638**: 1104
Bachman, A. L., **296**: 127; **3519**: 1077
Backer, O. G., **4179**: 1240
Bacon, A. P. C., **2256**: 801
Bader, M. E., **2839**: 936
Badger, T. L., **1161**: 639; **3851**: 1132
Baehner, R. L., **2681**: 904
Baer, R. B., **3539**: 1087
Baetjer, A. M., **1881**: 738
Baggenstoss, A. H., **2513**: 871
Baghdassarian, O. M., **2966**: 952; **3873**: 1136, 1137
Bagshawe, K. D., **2222**: 792, 797, 803; **2230**: 793, 797
Bahk, Y. W., **2505**: 871
Baird, J. A., **118**: 72, 162, 758
Baird, R. B., **3483**: 1066
Baker, D. H., **318**: 129, 1224
Baker, G. L., **643**: 289, 958, 959
Baker, R. D., **1198**: 643
Baker, R. R., **2292**: 806, 824, 826
Balassanian, N., **1433**: 679, 680, 681
Baldry, P. E., **2249**: 801; **3210**: 989
Baldus, W. P., **2754**: 910
Baldwin, E. deF., **3305**: 1017
Baldwin, J. N., **1717**: 724, 725, 730; **2030**: 760
Balentine, J. D., **3879**: 1137, 1139
Balkin, S. S., **1057**: 607
Ball, J. D., **2856f**: 937, 942, 945
Ball, K. P., **706**: 329, 806, 809
Ball, R. E., Jr., **3457**: 1063
Ball, W. C., Jr., **102**: 50, 51, 185
Banfi, A., **2177**: 775
Bang, A. N., **2353**: 825, 826
Bannister, W. K., **4327**: 959
Barabas, A. P., **3887**: 1142
Barach, A. L., **458**: 164, 764
Baraff, A. S., **3057**: 973

Barber, L. M., **507**: 175
Barden, R. P., **322**: 129; **323**: 129, 1006; **2099**: 762; **3274**: 1005
Bariéty, M., **311**: 128, 1166; **1901**: 739; **2007**: 758
Barker, G. S., **3143**: 984
Barkov, D. A., **1640**: 712
Barnes, M. G., **1557**: 697
Barnhard, H. J., **325**: 608; **1023**: 129, 180, 1005
Baron, M. G., **2188**: 784, 785
Barrett, F. F., **1063**: 607
Barrett, N. R., **3988**: 1171
Barrett, P. K. M., **1549**: 695, 696, 697
Barrie, H. J., **2943**: 948
Barrowcliff, D. F., **3717**: 910
Barry, C. T., **3328**: 1020
Barry, W. F., Jr., **797**: 357
Bartlett, J. P., **1807**: 734, 735
Bartter, F. C., **2085**: 761
Bashour, F. A., **3589**: 1093
Bass, H., **911**: 185
Bässler, R., **3793**: 1128
Bates, D. V., **1**: 2, 48, 142, 160, 185, 253, 338, 920, 931, 979, 980, 995, 1000, 1039, 1089, 1099, 1118, 1119, 1128, 1159, 1163, 1243, 1267; **78**: 43, 86, 183; **557**: 184, 185; **688**: 314, 990, 991; **3076**: 979
Bates, J. H., **4317**: 1269
Bateson, E. M., **608**: 260, 576, 731, 765, 769, 794, 801; **609**: 260; **1744**: 731; **1752**: 731; **1812**: 735; **4032**: 1184
Batson, J. M., **3613**: 1102
Batten, J., **3473**: 1064
Baum, G. L., **560**: 168, 668, 670; **919**: 582; **1222**: 645; **1241**: 651; **1273**: 656; **2414**: 842, 1017
Baume, P., **3955**: 1162
Baxter, J. D., **3501**: 1067
Bech, A. O., **2946**: 948
Beck, R. E., **245**: 120
Becker, A. H., **4003**: 1175
Becklake, M. R., **2816**: 931, 936, 942, 947, 948; **2954**: 950, 951; **3165**: 985
Bedell, G. N., **4239**: 1259
Beem, M., **1481**: 685; **3416**: 1051; **3417**: 1051
Beerel, F., **3339**: 1021
Beerman, H., **379**: 153
Beers, R. F., Jr., **3073**: 979
Befeler, B., **4067**: 1197
Behrendt, D. M., **4062**: 1193
Beier, F. R., **3482**: 1066
Beilin, D. S., **183**: 101, 808, 812, 816
Béland, J. E., **1391**: 673; **1652**: 716, 717, 719
Belcher, J. R., **1349**: 666; **1932**: 740
Belgrad, R., **2158**: 770, 771
Belin, L., **2717**: 908
Belin, R. P., **2392**: 831
Bell, A. L., Jr., **774**: 847; **775**: 847
Bell, D., **1385**: 672
Bell, J. W., **2166**: 771
Bell, T. K., **2347**: 823
Belli, N., **3760**: 1122
Bellini, F., **628**: 283, 921
Belsey, R., **3007**: 959
Benda, R., **2658**: 897, 1122
Bendel, W. L., Jr., **1912**: 740
Bendkowski, B., **3101**: 981
Bennett, D. E., **1217**: 651
Benoit, F. L., **3764**: 1123
Bensch, K. G., **1918**: 740

Bentivoglio, L. G., **105**: 50, 1006, 1021; **3284**: 980
Bentley, D. W., **954**: 592, 601
Benton, C., **4091**: 1210, 1214
Berdon, W. E., **859**: 1197; **900, 4118**: 569, 1225
Berendes, H., **2679**: 904
Berenson, M., **4284**: 1261
Berger, H. W., **2578**: 882, 883
Berger, R. L., **448**: 163
Bergh, N. P., **451**: 163, 1166
Bergman, F., **1294**: 659; **3745**: 1121
Bergmann, M., **2990**: 955, 956; **2991**: 955, 956
Bergofsky, E. H., **4192**: 1243, 1245
Berkheiser, S. W., **1945**: 741
Berkson, J., **178**: 100, 104
Berlyne, G. M., **1974**: 1085
Berman, B., **2022**: 760
Berman, D. A., **2540**: 874
Bernard, E., **3477**: 1064
Bernatz, P. E., **4138**: 1230
Berne, A. S., **314**: 128, 369, 1163; **316**: 128, 756; **3969**: 1166
Bernhardt, H., **467**: 165, 177
Bernheimer, H., **1740**: 730
Bernou, A., **224**: 116
Bernstein, C., **4158**: 1236, 1239
Bernstein, I. L., **3047**: 972
Berrigan, T. J., Jr., **2374**: 828, 829
Berris, B., **3003**: 959
Berry, E. H. J., **1635**: 712
Bersack, S. R., **3369**: 1027
Berte, S. J., **3582**: 1093
Berthelot, P., **880**: 576, 1264
Berven, H., **1426**: 678
Bessler, W. T., **254**: 122
Bessolo, R. J., **858**: 571
Béthoux, L., **527**: 177
Beton, D. C., **2974**: 954
Betts, R. A., **4111**: 1224, 1229, 1230
Beumer, H. M., **1449**: 1075
Bevan, P. G., **674**: 301, 304, 1085
Beyer, A., **3675**: 1106, 1160
Bianchi, F. A., **2610**: 889, 890, 893, 894, 897
Bianchine, J. R., **1447**: 680, 681
Bickerman, H. A., **457**: 164
Bickers, J. N., **3698**: 1111, 1116
Bidstrup, P., **4173**: 1240
Bidstrup, P. Lesley, **1870**: 737, 738
Biehl, J. P., **1126**: 630, 637, 639, 640
Bierman, C. W., **3102**: 981, 1160
Bindelglass, I. L., **757**: 843
Bindschadler, D. D., **1310**: 660, 662
Bingham, J. A. W., **4122**: 1229
Birkhäuser, H., **1894**: 739
Bischoff, M. E., **2532**: 873, 874
Bishop, J. M., **2758**: 911
Bittar, E. E., **515**: 176, 1157
Björk, L., **235**: 119; **2334**: 822
Björk, V. O., **872**: 574
Black, R. A., **1397**: 673
Blackburn, C. R. B., **2737**: 909, 918
Blackman, J., **1770**: 732
Blackwell, J. B., **1341**: 665
Blaese, R. M., **2675**: 902
Blakemore, W. S., **3303**: 1017
Blankenberg, H. W., **1381**: 671
Blendis, L. M., **3222**: 1197
Bleyer, J. M., **612**: 260, 633

Block, A. J., **3317**: 1018
Blomquist, G., **2619**: 890, 1211
Bloomer, W. E., **35**:10, 12
Bloomfield, J. A., **616**: 273, 712, 713, 715
Blount, H. C., Jr., **3954**: 1162
Blumenthal, M. N., **3066**: 974
Blundell, J. E., **2329**: 821, 1160
Bluth, I., **1706**: 723, 724, 725, 730
Bobrowitz, I. D., **1896**: 739
Boch, H. B., **4115**: 1225
Bock, K., **4064**: 1197
Bocles, J. S., **1529**: 692
Bodey, G. P., **3996**: 1174
Bodman, S. F., **4044**: 1188
Bogdonoff, M. L., **2301**: 806
Bogsch, A., **4059**: 1192
Bohlig, H., **2935**: 948
Boijsen, E., **287**: 127
Boland, E. W., **4196**: 1245
Bolande, R. P., **3262**: 1001
Bonanni, P. P., **3643**: 1105
Bonard, E. C., **2606**: 889, 890, 893
Bonbrest, H. C., **2471**: 864
Bonmati, J., **1292**: 659
Bonnell, J. A., **2975**: 954; **2976**: 954
Bonstein, H., **1128**: 630
Bonte, F. J., **2961**: 952; **3951**: 1166
Boone, M. L., **4157**: 1236
Booth, J. B., **843**: 569
Borek, Z., **3957**: 1164
Boren, H. G., **3229**: 995
Borgström, K., **2215**: 1076; **2461**: 860, 861
Borman, J. B., **4283**: 1261
Bornstein, P., **2037**: 760
Borrie, J., **1683**: 712, 713, 715
Boruchow, I. B., **2017**: 759
Botham, S. K., **3720**: 934
Botti, R. E., **3587**: 1093
Boucot, K. R., **1848**: 736, 737, 757; **1849**: 736; **1928**: 740; **1933**: 740; **1950**: 742; **1982**: 757; **3136**: 984
Bouhuys, A., **2715**: 908; **2719**: 908; **2721**: 908; **2724**: 908; **2731**: 908; **2733**: 908; **3033**: 971; **3724**: 908
Bourassa, M. G., **845**: 569
Boushy, S. F., **3322**: 1019; **3361**: 1024, 1027; **3604**: 1099
Bousvaros, G., **747**: 573
Bowden, D. H., **3465**: 1064
Bowen, A., **789**: 345
Bowen, D. A. L., **3486**: 1066
Bower, B. F., **2063**: 761; **2090**: 762
Bower, G., **1712**: 724, 725, 730; **3146**: 984
Bowers, D., **3415**: 1051
Boyd, D. H. A., **3754**: 1122, 1125, 1128
Boyd, D. P., **4128**: 1230
Boyden, E. A., **27**: 10, 13; **28**: 10, 12; **33**: 10; **34**: 10, 11, 13; **125**: 63; **821**: 61; **828**: 568, 569, 577
Brachman, P. S., **1032**: 599
Bradburne, A. F., **1413**: 675
Bradford, J. K., **2766**: 915
Brady, L. W., **3522**: 1085
Brady, R. O., **3882**: 1139; **3884**: 1142
Brailey, A. G., Jr., **1517**: 689
Brailsford, J. F., **132**: 75
Braimbridge, M. V., **3004**: 959, 1067
Brain, Lord, **1999**: 758, 759
Brannan, H. M., **2567**: 882; **3781**: 1125, 1128
Braun, D. C., **2850**: 937

Breckenridge, R. T., **2287**: 806
Bretland, P. M., **1680**: 722
Brett, G. Z., **1978**: 756; **1981**: 756
Brewin, T. B., **355**: 145, 782
Brezina, K., **2108**: 697
Bridgman, A. H., **984**: 157, 159, 163
Briggs, G. W., **3737**: 1121
Bringhurst, L. S., **2759**: 911
Brink, G. C., **2817**: 931, 933
Brinkman, G. L., **1962**: 753, 1151; **2696**: 1016; **3142**: 984; **3167**: 985
Bristol, L. J., **2734**: 908, 937, 939
British Public Health Laboratory Service, **1468**: 684
Brock, R. C., **37**: 11
Brodsky, I., **3826**: 1131
Brody, J. S., **682**: 309
Bron, K. M., **598**: 249, 253, 830
Brönnestam, R., **489**: 169, 668
Bronson, S. M., **3755**: 1122, 1128
Brouet, G., **3914**: 1157
Brown, B. St. J., **578**: 198, 289, 324, 956, 958
Brown, C. T., **2789**: 919
Brown, G., **2654**: 897
Brown, H. M., **3054**: 972
Brown, H. W., **4303**: 1267
Brown, J., **3750**: 1122
Brown, J. H., **2786**: 919
Brown, K. E., **1138**: 636
Brown, N. M.: **3478**: 1064
Brown, W. G., **263**: 122
Browne, J. S. L., **3304**: 1017
Brownstein, M. H., **4292**: 1264
Bruderman, I., **4189**: 1243, 1245
Brugsch, H. G., **2823**: 933
Bruneau, R., **2199**: 785, 1150, 1158, 1159
Brünner, A., **4137**: 1230
Brünner, S., **836**: 569; **925**: 582; **1957**: 753; **2963**: 952
Bruns, P. D., **3875**: 1137, 1139
Bruwer, A. J., **3727**: 1119; **3778**: 1125
Bryan, A. C., **914**: 185
Bryan, G. T., **3453**: 1063
Bryant, L. R., **2348**: 823
Bryk, D., **886**: 576
Bucci, G., **155**: 87
Buchberger, R., **1930**: 740, 741
Bücheler, E., **850**: 569, 582
Bucher, U. G., **2650**: 897
Buchner, L. H., **1034**: 600
Buck, A. A., **3537a**: 1087; **3537b**: 1087; **3537c**: 1087; **3537d**: 1087
Buckingham, W. B., **4063**: 1197
Buckley, C. E., III, **3426**: 1052; **3551**: 1088, 1089
Buddington, W. T., **915**: 581
Buechner, H. A., **2761**: 915; **2767**: 915
Buerger, L., **3780**: 1125
Buescher, E. L., **1508**: 688
Bugyi, B., **2788**: 919
Bühlmann, A., **4188**: 1243
Bukantz, S. C., **2129**: 765
Bulger, R. J., **3295**: 1017
Bulgrin, J. G., **2491**: 867, 869, 1153
Bumgarner, J. R., **1823**: 735, 1162
Bünger, P., **3852**: 1132
Burbank, B., **1319**: 663, 664
Bürgel, E., **589**: 225
Burgen, A. S., **812**: 66
Burgi, H., **1015**: 175

Burke, H. E., **456**: 164
Burke, R. M., **1120**: 623
Burman, S. O., **401**: 157
Burmeister, R. W., **974**: 598, 599; **1079**: 610
Burn, J. I., **2221**: 792
Burns, M. W., **1704**: 608, 986
Burr, J. M., **3610**: 1102
Burrell, L. S. T., **3729**: 1119, 1159
Burrows, B., **3129**: 983, 984; **3204**: 988, 1008, 1023; **3244**: 1000, 1016, 1018; **3286**: 1016, 1020, 1021
Burrows, D., **3075**: 979
Burrows, F. G. O., **2561**: 882, 883, 888
Burton, G. G., **1514**: 689, 690, 692
Burton, R. M., **2234**: 793, 797
Burwell, C. S., **4235**: 1259
Butler, J., **108**: 51
Butterfield, J., **1697**: 688
Buxton, J. T., Jr., **2395**: 831
Byrd, R. B., **1920**: 740, 746, 757; **1921**: 740, 757; **1922**: 740, 757; **2101**: 762, 763

Cadham, F. T., **2739**: 909
Caffey, J., **4123**: 1229
Caffrey, P. R.: **3839**: 1131
Caldicott, W. J. H., **2684**: 904
Caldwell, D. M., **2795**: 919, 921
Calenoff, L., **841**: 569
Callerame, M. L., **1594**: 704
Cameron, D. G., **3986**: 1171
Cameron, G. R., **2468**: 864
Camiel, M. R., **2095**: 762
Camp, J. D., **2028**: 760
Campbell, A. H., **1858**: 737; **3498**: 1066, 1067; **4198**: 1245
Campbell, C. C., **1244**: 651, 652, 654, 656, 657
Campbell, D. C., Jr., **1692**: 577; **1804**: 734
Campbell, E. J. M., **351**: 142; **556**: 180; **3320**: 1019
Campbell, G. D., **525**: 177; **1288**: 659, 660; **2577**: 882, 883
Campbell, H. E., **4070**: 1197, 1201
Campbell, I. K., **2933**: 948
Campbell, J. A., **905**: 581, 1214, 1220, 1229, 1230, 1232; **2593**: 888
Campbell, J. M., **2740**: 909
Campbell, M. J., **1327**: 664, 665, 666, 668, 1055
Cander, L., **82**: 43, 86
Canfield, C. J., **3772**: 1123
Cannon, P. J., **4280**: 1261
Cantarow, A., **3931**: 1158, 1159
Capers, T. H., **2130**: 765; **3870**: 1136
Capitanio, M. A., **1586**: 704, 705; **1605**: 705
Caplan, A., **2557**: 882, 888; **2592**: 888, **2877**: 942
Carabasi, R. J., **3685**: 1109; **4169**: 1239
Carbone, P. P., **1331**: 665, 668
Cardell, B. S., **687**: 314, 977
Carey, J. M., **1154**: 637
Carey, V. C. I., **2060**: 761; **2074**: 761
Carithers, H. A., **1544**: 695
Carlens, E., **402**: 157, 163, 764, 1166; **3966**: 1166
Carlile, W. K., **1323**: 664
Carlotta, D., **383**: 154
Caro, C. G., **83**: 45
Carpathios, J., **2809**: 921
Carr, D. T., **431**: 161; **466**: 165; **502**: 175, 869; **508**: 175; **509**: 175, 882, 883, 1153, 1154; **3485**: 1066
Carrington, C. B., **1827**: 736; **2527**: 873, 874

Carroll, D., **4238:** 1259
Carski, T. R., **497:** 174
Carson, M. J., **2683:** 904
Carter, S. J., **217:** 116, 117
Casey, J. F., **3017:** 965
Castellani, A., **1374:** 669
Castellino, R. A., **4069:** 1197
Castellot, J. J., **1263:** 654, 657
Castleman, B., **335e:** 816; **1830:** 736, 1192; **2068:** 761; **4051:** 1192
Cathcart, R. T., **2879:** 942
Catterall, M., **2616:** 890, 894
Caughey, J. E., **3405:** 1048
Cauna, D., **2820:** 933
Cavina, C., **3925:** 1158
Cece, J. D., **3458:** 1063
Celoria, G. C., **2643:** 896
Centerwall, W. R., **2669:** 900, 902
Chace, J. F., **1145:** 637
Chait, A., **2291:** 806, 826
Chakravarty, S. C., **472:** 168, 668, **1370:** 668
Chamberlain, D. A., **3311:** 1018
Chamberlin, G. W., **600:** 249
Chandor, S. B., **450:** 163, 764
Chang, C. H., **76:** 41, 98; **2322:** 809; **2473:** 864
Chanock, R. M., **1430:** 679; **1471:** 685; **1474:** 685
Chapman, I., **3892:** 1143
Chapman, J. S., **1177:** 642; **3547:** 1088; **3548:** 1088; **3549a:** 1088; **3549b:** 1088; **3549c:** 1088; **3550:** 1088
Chasler, C. N., **3994:** 1174
Chatgidakis, C. B., **2591:** 888; **3172:** 985; **3731:** 1119
Cheris, D. N., **2413:** 841
Cherniack, N., **3406:** 1051
Cherniack, R. M., **4262:** 1260
Chest Conference, University of California, School of Medicine, **1257:** 654
Chester, E. H., **1425:** 1075
Chesterman, J. T., **1554:** 1075; **3402:** 1044
Chick, E. W., **498:** 175, 657
Chin, E. F., **4102:** 1220, 1224
Chinachoti, N., **3848:** 1131, 1134
Chrétien, J., **551:** 178; **2110:** 763, 765
Chrispin, A. R., **2320:** 808
Christianson, L. C., **1167:** 641, 642
Christie, R. V., **694:** 324, 1000, 1019
Christoforidis, A. J., **234:** 119; **265:** 119, 123; **3670:** 1106, 1109; **3975:** 1167, 1175
Chrysospathis, P., **1641:** 713
Churg, J., **2541:** 874
Chwalibogowski, A., **1029:** 598
Ciba Guest Symposium Report, **3119:** 983, 993, 1023
Cicero, R., **266:** 124
Cifarelli, F. P., **1633:** 712
Cimmino, C. V., **134:** 75; **135:** 75; **136:** 75; **137:** 75, 76; **4195:** 1245
Cimons, I. M., **1530:** 693
Citron, K. M., **3579:** 1090; **3948:** 1160
Clagett, O. T., **2240:** 794; **4031:** 1184
Clain, A., **2000:** 758
Clara, M., **25:** 10
Clark, J. B., **4178:** 1240, 1241
Clark, N. S., **3391:** 1043, 1044, 1048
Claxton, C. P., Jr., **2077:** 761
Clayton, Y. M., **1368:** 668
Clements, J. A., **48:** 34; **49:** 34; **57:** 34, 304, 816; **874:** 207
Cliffton, E. E., **1938:** 740, 763

Clinical Staff Conference, National Cancer Institute, **1298:** 659, 660; **2072:** 761, 762
Clouse, M. E., **2384:** 830
Clyde, W. A., Jr., **495:** 174, 681
Coates, E. O., Jr., **3455:** 1063; **3476:** 1064
Coates, H. V., **1483:** 685, 686
Coates, J. R., **3784:** 1125
Coburn, J. W., **1262:** 654
Cochrane, A. L., **2813:** 931; **2856e:** 937, 939, 940; **2944:** 948
Cockshott, W. P., **1192:** 643; **2223:** 793
Cohen, A. A., **1297:** 659
Cohen, G., **4010:** 1179
Cohen, H., **2288:** 826
Cohen, H. I., **2736:** 909, 917
Cohen, S., **1845:** 736, 737, 739, 740, 742, 745, 746, 753, 757, 758, 764
Cohen, W. N., **1604:** 705
Cohn, J. E., **4229:** 1258
Cole, C. W. D., **2903:** 945
Cole, W. R., **3858:** 1134
Colebatch, H. J. H., **63:** 35
Coleman, A. J., **4312:** 1268
Coleman, M. T., **1453:** 682
College of General Practitioners, **3124:** 983
Collier, C. R., **555:** 180
Collins, J. J., Jr., **728:** 341
Collins, N. P., **1906:** 739, 740
Collins, V. P., **661:** 301, 769
Collins-Williams, C., **1404:** 674
Colp, C. R., **2371:** 827
Colwell, J. A., **1261:** 654
Comings, D. E., **3971:** 1166, 1171
Comroe, J. H., Jr., **2:** 2, 806, 807, 812; **3:** 2; **393:** 156
Conant, N. F., **1313:** 662, 670, 672
Condon, R. E., **3744:** 1121
Condon, V. R., **1713:** 724, 730
Conference at Royal Northern Hospital on Sarcoidosis, **3595:** 1099, 1102
Coni, N. K., **856:** 571
Conklin, E. F., **455:** 164
Conn, H. O., **380:** 153, 1017
Connor, E., **2949:** 950
Connor, T. B., **2070:** 761
Conquest, H. F., **1913:** 740
Conrad, F. G., **1080:** 610; **1240:** 651
Conte, B. A., **396:** 156
Coodley, E. L., **1301:** 659, 660
Cooley, J. C., **3941:** 1160, 1175
Cooley, R. N., **277:** 125; **2289:** 806, 822, 823
Coombs, R. R. A., **3026:** 970
Coons, A. H., **1009:** 174
Coope, R., **373:** 151
Cooper, A. S., **3757:** 1122
Cooper, A. W., **3181:** 986
Cooper, G., Jr., **2004:** 1076, 1085
Cooper, M. D., **2674:** 902; **2678:** 902
Cope, C., **347:** 138, 161; **426:** 161; **998:** 161
Copps, S. C., **1431:** 679, 680
Corazzo, L. J., **3306:** 1018
Cornelius, E. A., **602:** 249, 951
Cornell, S. H., **921:** 582; **3908:** 1156
Cornog, J. L., Jr., **1552:** 697
Cornwall, C. J., **3194:** 987
Corpe, R. F., **1117:** 622, 624
Corriere, J. N., Jr., **1688:** 1158
Corry, P., **813:** 106

Cortes, F. M., **1675**: 722
Costa, N., **1911**: 739, 740
Coté, J., **4006**: 1179
Cottom, D. G., **3379**: 1032
Cotton, R. E., **3742**: 1121, 1122
Coulter, W. W., Jr., **575**: 197
Coursin, D. B., **2659**: 897
Court, P., **2023**: 760
Court, S. D. M., **1401**: 674
Courtice, F. C., **811**: 66
Coury, C., **382**: 154
Cowdrey, C. R., **343**: 137
Cox, J. S. G., **3028**: 970
Coy, P., **1835**: 736
Craig, D. B., **4329**: 911, 915
Craig, J. M., **935**: 588
Craighead, C. C., **3952**: 1161, 1239
Craighead, J. E., **1532**: 693, 694
Cramblett, H. G., **1696**: 688
Cranz, H. J., **583**: 217
Crile, G., Jr., **4036**: 1184
Crittenden, I. H., **4127**: 1229
Croft, P. B., **2015**: 758
Crofts, N. F., **1808**: 734, 735; **2277**: 805
Cromie, J. B., **3240**: 999
Crompton, G. K., **3063**: 974
Crone, P. B., **1417**: 676, 685
Cross, H. E., **2381**: 830
Crow, H. E., **1166**: 641, 642
Crow, N. E., **2254**: 801
Croxatto, O. C., **3394**: 1043
Cruickshank, B., **2566**: 882
Crutcher, R. R., **1820**: 735
Cruthirds, T. P., **1390**: 673; **3711**: 118
Cruz, T., **1610**: 708
Cruze, K., **2116**: 764
Cudkowicz, L., **95**: 47; **2569**: 882; **3242**: 1000
Cueto, J. C., **4088**: 1207, 1210
Culiner, M. M., **579**: 198, 199, 302; **701**: 325, 1035; **922**: 582; **1949**: 1085; **3444**: 1062
Cullen, J. H., **4241**: 1259
Cullen, K. J., **3133**: 984
Cummings, M. M., **3533**: 1087; **3536**: 1087; **3543**: 1088; **3545**: 1088
Cunningham, G. J., **4216**: 1252
Cunningham, R., **3774**: 1123, 1124
Curran, J. D., **619**: 274, 801
Curran, W. S., **528**: 177; **3045**: 972
Currarino, G., **4183**: 1241
Curry, F. J., **1173**: 641, 642; **1213**: 644, 645, 1148
Curtis, G. H., **2930**: 947
Cutforth, R. H., **2373**: 827

Dabbs, C. H., **920**: 582, 583
Dahlgren, S., **986**: 159
Dailey, R., **1703**: 604
Dalen, J. E., **2400**: 834
D'Alessio, D. J., **369**: 148
Daley, R. H., **160**: 97
Dalgaard, J. B., **3484**: 1066
Dalldorf, F. G., **955**: 592
Dalton, C. J., **133**: 75
Daly, J. F., **1108**: 617, 620
Daly, J. J., **3095**: 980
Danaraj, T. J., **1614**: 709; **1621**: 711

Danes, B. S., **3454**: 1063
D'Angio, G. J., **2236**: 793, 794, 801, 1160
Daniel, R. A., Jr., **4012**: 1179, 1184, 1193, 1205, 1210, 1211
Daniels, A. C., **437**: 162; **1571**: 702, 1148
Danilenko, S. I., **1841**: 736, 740, 741
Danner, P. K., **963**: 273, 595, 605
Darch, G. H., **3999**: 1175
Darke, C. S., **940**: 127; **1760**: 731
Dascomb, H. E., **1506**: 689
d'Assumpcao, C., **3104**: 981
Daughtry, D. C., **1843**: 1076; **2009**: 758, 759, 761, 762
Davenport, A., **2726**: 908
Davidson, J. K., **725**: 341
Davidson, L. A., **3294**: 1017
Davidson, M., **1811**: 735
Davidson, M. B., **3758**: 1122
Davies, C. N., **2787**: 919
Davies, D., **3666**: 1106
Davies, D. T., **962**: 595
Davies, G. M., **3425**: 1052
Davies, H., **4184**: 1241, 1243
Davies, R., **1819**: 735
Davies, T. A., **2980**: 954
Davis, C. M., **2995**: 956, 958
Davis, E. W., **2105**: 763, 765; **2135**: 765
Davis, J. G., **928**: 582, 583; **4075**: 1201
Davis, L. A., **126**: 64; **1112**: 620
Davis, S., **1686**: 348
Davison, P., **2286**: 806, 826
Dawson, J., **3726**: 1119
Dawson, P. J., **2183**: 782
Dayman, H., **58**: 34, 1020
Deal, C. W., **1939**: 740
Dean, G., **1837**: 736
DeAngelis, C. E., **1809**: 735
Deck, F. W., **2251**: 801
Deeley, T. J., **3516**: 1077, 1085
Dees, S. C., **3437**: 1058
DeFrancis, N., **419**: 161
de Haller, R., **26**: 10
Dekker, E., **3078**: 979; **3250**: 1001; **3337**: 1020
Delahaye, R. P., **1573**: 702, 1148
Delaney, L. T., Jr., **2953**: 950
Delarue, N. C., **417**: 160; **1871**: 737, 738
De Lavergne, E., **1084**: 610, 611
del Castillo, J. J., **740**: 841
DeLeeuw, N. K. M., **3791**: 1128
deLeon, E. P., **1664**: 720, 721, 722
Dellipiani, A. W., **2640**: 896
Del Valle, J., **1203**: 643, 644, 648, 651
Demasi, C. J., **2522**: 873
DeMuth, G. R., **3481**: 1064; **3560**: 1064
Demy, N. G., **1874**: 737, 936, 1164
DeNardi, J. M., **2914**: 946
Dennis, J. M., **1076**: 609, 1147
Denny, J. J., **2932**: 947
Denny-brown, D., **2013**: 758
Denson, H. B., **3777**: 1125, 1128
Dent, C. E., **3611**: 1102
Denton, J. F., **1272**: 656
Denton, R., **3209**: 989
De Paula, A., **1233**: 648, 654
Depierre, R., **2218**: 792, 801
DeRemee, R. A., **3677**: 1109
Derham, R. J., **1111**: 620, 621

Dermksian, G., **3363**: 1024, 1160
Derra, E., **4011**: 1179, 1180
Desforges, G., **4132**: 1230, 1232
Desmonts, G., **1575**: 703
De Souza, R. C., **2081**: 761
De Torregrosa, M. V., **518**: 176
D'Ettorre, A., **3949**: 1160
De Villiers, A. J., **1875**: 738
De Villiers, J. C., **4154**: 1236
DeVita, V. T., **2216**: 792, 1150
Devlin, H. B., **2973**: 954
Dexter, L., **93**: 47; **281**: 125, 806; **335g**: 806, 827
Diaconita, G. H., **1654**: 716
Diament, M. L., **4295**: 1264: **4296**: 1264
Dickie, H. A., **2747**: 910
Dighiero, J., **742**: 573, 841
Diller, W. F., **1422**: 1069
Dilley, J. J., **3413**: 1051
Dimich, I., **848**: 569
Dines, D. E., **966**: 596, 597; **2207**: 790
Dinsmore, R. E., **2620**: 890
Diosi, P., **1538**: 693, 694
DiRienzo, S., **59**: 34, 35, 122; **257**: 122; **258**: 122, 1020
di Sant'Agnese, P. A., **3023**: 1063, 1064; **3131**: 1063, 1064; **3445**: 1063, 1064; **3462**: 1063
Disney, M. E., **1499**: 687; **1694**: 687
Ditto, W. R., **3787**: 1125
Divertie, M. B., **2497**: 869, 875, 879, 889, 890, 893, 894; **3807**: 1129; **4048**: 1188
Dockerty, M. B., **3920**: 1157
Doctor, L., **2564**: 882
Dodd, G. D., **2252**: 801
Dodge, H. J., **1205**: 643
Dodson, W. H., **506**: 175, 882, 883, 1146, 1153, 1154
Doehnett, H. R., **3844**: 1131, 1134
Dohan, F. C., **3159**: 985
Doig, A. T., **2896**: 943
Dolan, D. L., **4172**: 1240
Dolan, T. F., Jr., **1324**: 664
Doll, R., **1869**: 737, 738; **1878**: 738; **2846**: 936
Doll, S. G., **4263**: 1260
Dollery, C. T., **163**: 97, 577, 838; **4193**: 1245
Domm, B. M., **3739**: 1121
Domz, C. A., **2667**: 900
Don, C., **2255**: 801
Doniach, I., **2427**: 851, 1121
Donner, M. W., **1382**: 672
Donohoe, R. F., **422**: 161; **432**: 161
Donohoo, C. M., **1352**: 666, 668
Donohue, W. L., **3652**: 1105
Dontas, N. S., **4038**: 1186
Döpper, T., **1644**: 1075
Doppman, J., **1759**: 731
Doppman, J. L., **768**: 845
Dore, E. K., **2699**: 1021
Dorn, H. F., **1847**: 736, 737
Dornhorst, A. C., **567**: 192, 205, 289, 371; **3389**: 1039
Dossetor, J. B., **2093**: 762; **4315**: 1268, 1269
Dotter, C. T., **270**: 125
Doubleday, L. C., **4205**: 1246
Douglas, A. C., **3367**: 1027
Douglas, J. W. B., **3161**: 985
Douglas, R. G., Jr., **1022**: 178, 677
Dovenbarger, W. V., **1746**: 731
Doyle, A. E., **734**: 835
Doyle, A. P., **3824**: 1131
Doyle, F. H., **142**: 78, 127, 1197

Dozois, R. R., **3970**: 1166, 1171
Dreessen, W. C., **2863**: 939
Drennan, J. M., **1771**: 732
Drevvatne, T., **611**: 260
Drinković, I., **3845**: 1131, 1134
Drips, W., Jr., **1250**: 653
Drouhet, M. E., **1364**: 668
Dubois, A. B., **88**: 46
Ducloux, J. M., **1572**: 702
Dudley, H. R., **2921**: 947
Duguid, H. L. D., **2118**: 764
Duguid, J. B., **2873**: 940
Duke, W. M., **4087**: 1207
Dulfano, M. J., **230**: 117, 993, 1006; **3291**
Dumas, L. W., **2587**: 883
Dunbar, J. S., **240**: 119, 123; **795**: 357, 359, 1158; **4161**: 1239
Duncan, D. A., **3763**: 1123
Dunkin, R. S., **3353**: 1022
Dunmore, L. A., Jr., **3694**: 1111, 1116
Dünner, L., **2794**: 919
Dunnill, M. S., **148**: 58; **344**; **345**: 137; **3068**: 975, 1058
DuPont, H. L., **3983**: 1171
Durant, T. M., **285**: 125
Dutra, F. R., **1873**: 737; **2797**: 919
Dutton, R., Jr., **3296**: 1017
Düx, A., **945**: 127
Dworkin, H. J., **334**: 133
Dwyer, E. M., Jr., **3946**: 1160
Dysinger, P. W., **3134**: 984

Eadie, M. B., **3187**: 986
Earle, J. H. O., **1191**: 643
Eastridge, C. E., **2047**: 760; **2083**: 761
Eaton, M. D., **1420**: 676
Ebert, P. A., **4129**: 1230, 1232
Ebisawa, I. T., **1470**: 685
Eckmann, B. H., **1251**: 653
Edenfield, R. W., **2861**: 939
Edge, J. R., **1195**: 643; **4029**: 1184
Editorial, **1709**: 724; **2482**: 864; **2562**: 882; **2633**: 895; **2648**: 896; **2704**: 907, 909, 910; **2843**: 936, 937; **3590**: 1093, 1103; **3890**: 1143; **4269**: 1260; **4300**: 1266
Edling, N. P. G., **203**: 115, 132, 931; **2938**: 948
Edwards, G., **3177**: 986
Edwards, L. B., **3546**: 1088
Edwards, S. R., **3924**: 1158
Edwards, W. M., **2136**: 765, 769
Efron, G., **4133**: 1230, 1232
Ehrenhaft, J. L., **2700**: 794
Eichenholz, A., **4313**: 1268
Eikas, J., **1653**: 716, 717
Eimind, K., **3488**: 1066
Eisenstadt, H. B., **2835**: 936
Elder, J. C., **714**: 331
Elder, J. L., **3788**: 1128
Eldridge, F., **2524**: 873; **3351**: 1022
Elliott, F. M., **66**: 36
Elliott, G. B., **1767**: 732
Elliott, R. C., **463**: 165
Ellis, C. A., **1378**: 671
Ellis, K., **572**: 193, 1135; **601**: 249, 1090, 1093, 1104; **863**: 571, 573

Ellis, R. H., **1081**: 610; **1361**: 666, 668, 1055
Ellison, L. T., **3302**: 1017
Ellison, R. C., **2276**: 805
Ellman, P., **870**: 574; **2179**: 775, 779; **2563**: 882
El Mallah, S. H., **1672**: 721
Elmes, P. C., **2844**: 936
Elmqvist, D., **2018**: 759
El-Rai, F. M., **1504**: 688
Elwood, P. C., **2732**: 908; **2845**: 936, 937
Emanuel, D. A., **2750**: 910; **2778**: 916; **2779**: 916
Embil, J. A., **1531**: 693, 694
Emerson, G. L., **1905**: 739, 742, 745, 746, 753, 757
Emerson, P. A., **3930**: 1158
Emery, J. L., **3993**: 1174
Emirgil, C., **2245**: 798, 801, 803
Emmanuel, G., **3341**: 1021
Emmons, C. W., **1207**: 643; **1208**: 643; **1293**: 659, 660
Emson, H. E., **971**: 596
Enders, J. F., **1488**: 687
Endress, Z. F., **1519**: 690
Engel, F. L., **2038**: 760
Engel, S., **3422**: 1052
English, J. M., **2960**: 952
Enriquez, P., **3693**: 1111, 1116, 1118
Enticknap, J. B., **2842**: 936, 937
Entwistle, C. C., **2104**: 763
Enzer, N., **2897**: 943
Epstein, B. S., **4099**: 1219, 1224
Epstein, S. W., **3327**: 1020
Erasmus, L. D., **2629**: 894
Erdélyi, J., **2793**: 919
Eriksen, K. R., **3978**: 1167
Eriksson, S., **3261**: 1001
Erlich, H., **395**: 156
Errion, A. R., **1162**: 1069, 1075
Escovitz, W. E., **1739**: 730
Ettman, I. K., **3494**: 1066, 1067
Evans, A. S., **479**: 169, 676, 677; **1410**: 675, 676, 679, 681; **1475**: 685
Evans, D. M., **1762**: 731
Evans, E. H., **2984**: 955
Evans, K. T., **2231**: 793, 797
Evans, W., **750**: 840; **751**: 840
Evans, W. H. M., **2783**: 917
Evarts, C. M., **2380**: 830
Everhart, F. J., **861**: 571
Eyal, Z., **3014**: 965
Eyckmans, L., **2774**: 916
Eygelaar, A., **4212**: 1249
Eyler, W. R., **1689**

Fabel, H., **2393**: 831
Fadell, E. J., **4246**: 1259
Fagan, C. J., **637**: 286, 341, 1069, 1075
Fagge, C. H., **375**: 153
Faiman, C., **2096**: 762
Fainsinger, M. H., **1682**: 273, 713
Falkenbach, K. H., **1603**: 705
Falsetti, H. L., **4243**: 1259
Farid, Z., **704**: 329, 720, 721, 722, 841
Farmer, R. G., **2607**: 889, 890, 893
Fattal, A. R., **1210**: 644
Faulds, J. S., **2901**: 945

Faust, E. C., **1650**: 715, 722
Favis, E. A., **228**: 116, 627; **2211**: 792, 1152
Fawcitt, J., **1073**: 608, 686
Feinberg, S. B., **1601**: 705; **3864**: 1135
Felder, S. L., **4114**: 1225
Feldman, D. J., **802**: 362
Feldman, F., **1796**: 734
Feldman, H. A., **1576**: 703, 704
Feldman, P. A., **1778**: 732
Feldman, R., **3441**: 1058, 1062
Feldstein, A. M., **521**: 176
Felson, B., **21**: 6, 192; **69**: 37, 59, 60, 61, 80, 81, 83, 113, 193, 213, 220, 324, 362, 577, 1197, 1218, 1220; **119**: 59, 61, 62; **657**: 291, 297; **822**: 78; **1052**: 605; **1228**: 645; **1684**: 297; **3424**: 1052; **3571**: 1090; **3572**: 1090; **3674**: 1106; **4001**: 1175
Fennessy, J. J., **255**: 122, 177; **543**: 177, 764; **994**: 159, 161
Feraru, F., **724**: 341, 1159
Ferencz, C., **2403**: 840
Ferguson, G. C., **2585**: 883, 1153
Ferguson, T. B., **3980**: 1167
Ferris, E. J., **283**: 125, 822
Fielding, J., **3310**: 1018
Fierer, J., **1035**: 600
Fifer, W. R., **1701**: 613, 961; **3710**: 1116, 1118
Figiel, S. J., **4078**: 1201
Figley, K. D., **2712**: 907, 972
Figley, M. M., **2314**: 807, 808, 809, 816, 821
Fine, G., **4035**: 1184
Finegold, S. M., **1091**: 613; **1328**: 665, 668
Finestone, A. W., **3561**: 1090
Fink, A., **4177**: 1240, 1241
Fink, J. N., **2772**: 915, 916; **2773**: 916
Finlayson, D. M., **1629**: 712, 715
Finley, T. N., **98**: 48
Fischel, R. E., **4124**: 1229
Fischer, D. A., **1171**: 641
Fischer, D. S., **4281**: 1261
Fischer, E., **627**: 283
Fischer, F. K., **3219**: 993
Fish, R. G., **1282**: 657
Fisher, A. M., **973**: 597, 598; **2173**: 774, 775, 779, 782, 1149
Fisher, J. H., **3668**: 1106
Fishman, A. P., **91**: 46; **3356**: 1023
Fisk, G. C., **4271**: 1260
Fissel, G. E., **1237**: 648
Fitzpatrick, H. F., **2168**: 771
Fitzpatrick, M. J., **1840**: 736, 740
Flaherty, R. A., **729**: 341, 596, 597
Flanagan, P., **1908**: 739, 740, 763
Flatley, F. J., **154**: 87; **2588**: 883
Fleck, A. C., **1132**: 635
Flecker, A., **2262**
Fleischner, F. G., **141**: 78; **196**: 113, 745; **259**: 122, 193; **3350**: 816; **570**: 193; **581**: 199, 301, 302; **644**: 289, 806, 807, 808, 812, 816, 821, 826; **670**: 301; **671**: 301, 302, 305, 816; **675**: 302; **678**: 308; **718**: 334, 808; **792**: 345, 348, 351, 352, 353, 357, 359; **1953**: 745; **2302**: 806, 808, 821, 825, 826; **2317**: 808; **2318**: 808, 809, 821, 825; **2338**: 822, 823, 2463: 860; **3217**: 991; **3249**: 1000, 1011
Fleming, H. A., **2278**: 805; **2425**: 851
Fleming, J. A. C., **2069**: 1076
Fleming, J. S., **4068**: 1197
Fleming, P. C., **1443**: 680

Fleming, P. R., **780**: 852, 857
Fletcher, C. M., **2878**: 942; **3118**: 983; **3121**: 983; **3130**: 983, 984
Flint, F. J., **3298**: 1017
Floyd, F. W., **3376**: 1032
Foe, R. B., **3176**: 964
Foldes, F. F., **4268**: 1260
Foley, F. D., **3236**: 999
Fontana, R. S., **408**: 158, 164; **538**: 177, 764
Forbes, G., **3013**: 965
Forbes, J. A., **1479**: 685, 686
Ford, D. K., **2686**: 904
Ford, F. D. C., **3625**: 1103
Ford, R. M., **2509**: 871, 872
Foreman, S., **3372**: 1027
Forester, C. F., **4230**: 1258
Fors, B., **3747**: 1121
Forsee, J. H., **1220**: 645
Forster, R. E., **100**: 48
Forsyth, B. R., **483**: 169, 676, 677, 679
Foshay, L., **1078**: 609
Fouché, R. F., **717**: 334, 806; **3383**: 1035, 1039
Fowler, N. O., **2396**: 826, 833
Foy, H. M., **1432**: 679, 680
Fraimow, W., **599**: 249, 253, 830, 831; **3665**: 1106, 1119; **3833**: 1131; **3835**: 1131
Franchel, F., **1720**: 725
Francis, K. C., **2224**: 793
Francis, T., Jr., **1451**: 682
Frank, H. D., **1733**: 730
Frank, R. C., **2748**: 910, 911
Franken, E. A., Jr., **697**: 324, 1033; **4023**: 1182
Frankland, A. W., **2989**: 918, 972
Franklin, W., **3149**: 984
Franseen, C. C., **411**: 159
Fraser, R. G., **38**: 12, 35, 122, 977, 993, 1001, 1011, 1014; **72**: 41, 117, 328, 330, 336, 975, 993, 1006; **261**: 122, 993, 1014; **568**: 192, 193, 289, 568, 593
Fraser, R. S., **4221**: 1255
Frayser, R., **1665**: 720, 722
Fred, H. L., **2293**: 806; **2331**: 821, 823; **2478**: 864
Freed, T. A., **946**: 1201
Freedman, S., **3326**: 1020
Freeman, G., **3158**: 985
Freeman, R. M., **3800**: 1128
Freiman, D. G., **335d**: 806, 822; **2268**: 804, 805, 806, 824; **3541**: 1087, 1099
Freundlich, I. M., **2827**: 933, 934, 936, 1163, 1169
Friede, E., **2894**: 943
Friedel, H., **541**: 177
Friedenberg, R. M., **1114**: 622
Friedman, E., **128**: 64
Friedman, J. L., **1221**: 645
Friedman, O. H., **406**: 158, 1103
Friedman, R. L., **800**: 357
Friedreich, N., **3856**: 1132; **3857**: 1132
Fritts, H. W., Jr., **2399**: 834
Fritze, E., **4326**: 888
Froman, C., **4301**: 1266
Frostad, S., **650**: 291, 620; **1109**: 620
Fry, D. L., **3248**: 1001, 1020
Fry, J., **1466**: 682, 683
Fry, L., **2076**: 761
Fry, W. A., **2415**: 842
Fukushima, K., **1339**: 665
Fuller, C. J., **2751**: 910
Fuller, D. N., **899**: 578

Furcolow, M. L., **1197**: 643; **1212**: 644, 652; **1232**: 648, 654; **1267**: 656, 657; **1284**: 657
Furgerson, W. B., Jr., **2657**: 897, 1122
Fusco, F. D., **2097**: 762
Fyles, T. W., **3086**: 980

Gabriele, O. F., **1383**: 672
Gaensler, E. A., **407**: 158; **558**: 159, 160; **2928**: 947; **3245**: 1000, 1016; **3688**: 1109, 1110
Gahagan, T., **2308**: 807
Gailitis, J., **2956**: 950
Galatius-Jensen, F., **1824**: 735, 1162
Gallacher, P. G., **896**: 577, 581
Gallo, R. C., **3309**: 1018
Galloway, R. W., **623**: 283, 851; **1465**: 683
Galofré, M., **1917**: 740
Gandevia, B., **223**: 116; **346**: 116; **2981**: 954
Gannon, W. E., **1822**: 735
Ganter, G., **787**: 345
García-Palmieri, M. R., **1667**: 720
Gardner, D. L., **1085**: 611; **2603**: 889
Gardner, P. S., **967**: 596, 685; **1477**: 685; **1484**: 686
Gardner, W. D., **566**: 192
Garland, L. H., **169**: 99, 100, 102, 104; **170**: 99, 104; **171**: 99, 104; **645**: 290, 736, 739, 740, 741; **666**: 301, 769; **667**: 301, 741, 769; **1940**: 741; **1979**: 756; **2493**: 867, 868, 875, 890
Garland, T., **4222**: 1255
Garrell, M., **2508**: 871, 872
Gary, J. E., **2924**: 947
Gatzek, H. F., **221**: 116
Gault, M. H., **2046**: 760
Gay, B. B., Jr., **745**: 573, 841
Géher, F., **1656**: 717
Gelfand, M., **1235**: 648, 654
Gelfand, M. L., **3442**: 1062
Gelfman, N. A., **2042**: 760
Gellman, D. D., **2253**: 801
Gelpi, A. P., **1607**: 705, 707
Georg, J., **820**: 47, 1023
George, R. B., **481**: 169, 676, 677, 680, 681, 689
Geraci, J. E., **1295**: 659, 660
Gerald, B., **2416**: 842
Gerard, F. P., **898**: 578, 581
Gerlach, U., **519**: 176
Gerle, R. D., **897**: 578; **2257**: 801
Gernez-Rieux, C., **473**: 168
Gerrits, J. C., **2144**: 766
Gerritsen, W. B., **2959**: 952
Ghon, A., **1110**: 620
Giammalvo, J. T., **752**: 841
Gibson, D. G., **2462**: 860, 861
Gierson, H. W., **1160**: 639
Gilbertsen, V. A., **1976**: 756
Gildenhorn, H. L., **324**: 129
Gillman, P. M., **4279**: 1261
Gilmartin, D., **4159**: 1236
Gilroy, J. A., **2205**: 790, 791
Gilson, J. C., **2150**: 907, 933; **2729**: 908; **2880**: 942; **2881**: 942
Gimes, B., **884**: 576
Ginsburg, J., **388**: 154
Giovacchini, R. P., **2993**: 956
Gish, J. R., **2149**: 1076
Glauser, E. M., **3390**: 1043

Glay, A., **3768:** 1123; **3802:** 1128, 1131
Glazier, J. B., **104:** 50, 51, 97
Gleason, D. C., **2446:** 855
Glenert, J., **504:** 175
Glick, L. M., **1082:** 610, 611
Glick, S. M., **1497:** 687
Glynn, A. A., **3067:** 975
Gocke, T. M., **3123:** 983
Godfrey, R. C., **2998:** 956, 958
Gold, J. A., **2127:** 765
Gold, W. M., **2391:** 831; **2502:** 869
Goldberg, B., **1330:** 665, 666, 1055
Goldberg, M. F., **2064:** 761
Goldberg, N. M., **1094:** 614
Goldenberg, D. B., **824:** 83, 84, 85, 1235
Goldenberg, G. J., **3577:** 1090
Goldenthal, S., **198:** 115, 132, 1005
Golding, F. C., **726:** 341, 582
Goldman, H. I., **152:** 86, 87, 91, 179
Goldman, K. P., **1886:** 738; **1934:** 740
Goldman, M., **514:** 176, 1157
Goldmeier, E., **180:** 101, 769
Goldring, D., **2655:** 897
Goldring, R. M., **3466:** 1064
Goldsmith, H. S., **2247:** 798, 1151
Goldstein, E., **1069:** 608; **1306:** 660
Goldstein, J., **2103:** 763; **2194:** 785
Goldstein, M. J., **1959:** 753
Goltz, R. W., **3263:** 1001
Gómez, G. E., **3841:** 1131, 1132, 1134
Gondos, B., **140:** 78; **2604:** 889, 890
Gonick, P., **2225:** 793
Gonzalez, E., **3358:** 1023
Gonzalez-Angulo, A., **607:** 253, 1106, 1109
González de Vega, N., **1678:** 722
González-Licea, A., **3663:** 1106
Good, A. E., **4199:** 1245
Good, C. A., **621:** 277, 765, 769; **890:** 576; **1718:** 724, 725; **1956:** 746, 753; **2266:** 769
Goodburn, G. M., **494:** 174
Goodman, M. L., **1624:** 711
Goodman, N., **1539:** 771; **1563:** 693, 700, 705
Goodpasture, E. W., **3752:** 1152
Goodwin, J. F., **335r:** 825, 826, 827
Goodwin, R. A., Jr., **478:** 169, 643, 644, 651
Gordon, M. A., **1307:** 660
Gordon, R. B., **1494:** 687
Gordon, W., **3740:** 1121
Gore, I., **2351:** 825
Gorham, G. W., **3411:** 1051
Gorham, L. W., **2295:** 806, 826; **2359:** 826
Gorlin, R., **94:** 47; **1367:** 47; **2432:** 851
Göthe, C.-J., **3544:** 1088
Goudemand, M., **2204:** 789, 1253
Gough, J., **340:** 340; **2599:** 888; **2856c:** 937, 943, 945; **2872:** 244, 940, 942; **3198:** 997, 999
Gough, J. H., **2385:** 830
Gould, D. M., **592:** 240; **2489:** 867, 868, 869, 1153
Gourlay, R. H., **964:** 596, 598
Gowenlock, A. H., **2054:** 761
Gracey, D. R., **3660:** 1105
Graham, J. R., **3987:** 1171
Gramiak, R., **642:** 287, 733, 1162
Grant, I. W. B., **2208:** 790
Grant, J. L., **4257:** 1260
Grant, L. J., **3703:** 1116
Grantham, J. J., **2091:** 762

Gray, B., **2124:** 764
Gray, F. D., Jr., **3667:** 1106
Gray, J. M., **3998:** 1175
Gray, K. G., **1011:** 174
Grayston, J. T., **1436:** 679
Green, R. A., **1761:** 731; **2202:** 789, 1253; **4080:** 1205
Greenberg, G., **3614:** 1102
Greenberg, H. B., **113:** 66; **2275:** 805, 825
Greenberg, M. J., **3849:** 1132
Greenberg, S. D., **1900:** 739
Greenburg, L., **3193:** 987
Greene, J. G., **2011:** 758, 759
Greenfield, G. B., **2024:** 760
Greenfield, H., **1768:** 732, 1253
Greening, R. R., **182:** 101, 118; **1423:** 1069, 1075; **2807:** 921
Greenspan, R. H., **269:** 124, 125, 127; **976:** 124; **1059:** 607; **1681:** 249; **3569:** 1090, 1129; **3854:** 1132
Greenwell, F. P., **218:** 116, 117
Greer, Allen E., **1359:** 666, 1055, 1058
Greer, Alvis E., **1277:** 657, 662, 664, 666, 670
Gregg, I., **3940:** 993
Gregory, P. H., **2746:** 909, 910
Griffin, J. P., **482:** 169, 676
Grimes, O. F., **723:** 341, 1027, 1159
Griner, P. F., **2364:** 827
Grist, N. R., **1452:** 682, 685, 686; **1547:** 695; **3189:** 986
Groen, A. S., **1968:** 756
Gross, N. J., **3288:** 1017
Gross, P., **2703:** 907, 909; **2968:** 954; **3641:** 1105
Grossman, L. A., **2575:** 882, 883
Gudbjerg, C. E., **242:** 119, 1044, 1253; **1747:** 731; **3404:** 1048
Guenter, C. A., **3260:** 1001
Guha, P. K., **1275:** 656, 657
Guidry, L. D., **3015:** 965
Gupta, A. K., **1944:** 741, 757
Gupta, R. L., **4131:** 1230
Gupta, S. K., **1143:** 636
Gurewich, V., **335l:** 807, 826; **3795:** 1128
Gusinde, R. E., **2119:** 764
Gyllenswärd, Å., **743:** 573, 841

Haber, S., **4086:** 1207
Häberlin, F., **3843:** 1131
Hacking, P. M., **860:** 571, 861
Hackl, H., **1895:** 739
Hackney, J. D., **4245:** 1259
Haddad, J. K., **2970:** 954
Haddad, R., **3671:** 1106
Haegelin, H. F., **2339:** 822
Hagen, H., **885:** 576, 577
Hahne, O. H., **1061:** 607
Hainer, J. W., **4171:** 1240
Hale, F. C., **3334:** 1020
Hale, L. W., **2792:** 919; **2838:** 939; **2856b**
Hall, E. R., Jr., **2192:** 785
Hall, J. W., III, **2515:** 872
Hall, T. C., **2927:** 947
Hallett, W. Y., **3471:** 1064
Hallgrimsson, J., **2387:** 830
Hallman, G. L., **4083:** 1205
Halmagyi, D. F., **3100:** 981
Ham, J. C., **3420:** 1051
Hambrick, G. W., Jr., **2027:** 760

Hamburger, J., **1565:** 700, 704
Hamburger, M., **562:** 192, 593
Hamel, N. C., **1149:** 637
Hamer, J., **3681:** 1109
Hamer, N. A. J., **3601:** 1099
Hamilton, J. D., **3316:** 1017, 1018
Hamilton, W., **1872:** 1085
Hamlin, W. B., **1600:** 705
Hamman, L., **376:** 153; **3639:** 1105; **3640:** 1105
Hammarsten, J. F., **513:** 176, 1157
Hammond, D., **3771:** 1123
Hammond, E. C., **1836:** 736, 737; **1854:** 737
Hammond, J. D. S., **3350:** 1022
Hampton, A. O., **2324:** 816
Hampton, C. S., **110:** 150
Hamre, D., **1416:** 675
Han, T., **1058:** 607
Hanashiro, P. K., **3032:** 971
Hanbury, W. J., **1929:** 740; **1931:** 740, 741
Hanford, R. B., **4096:** 1214, 1216
Hanshaw, J. B., **1533:** 693, 695
Hanson, D. J., Jr., **4041:** 1186
Harbitz, F., **3836:** 1131
Hardaway, R. M., **335c:** 592
Harden, K. A., **3573:** 1090
Harding, H. E., **2892:** 943
Hardy, H. L., **2849:** 936; **2910:** 946, 947; **2912:** 946; **2917:** 946
Hardy, J. D., **1698:** 1075, 1161; **4040:** 1186
Hardy, M. A., **1163:** 640
Hare, W. S. C., **1965:** 756; **3968:** 1166
Harford, C. G., **1461:** 682, 683
Hargreave, F. E., **2765:** 915; **2771:** 915, 916
Harington, J. S., **512:** 176, 1152, 1164
Harley, H. R. S., **781:** 852, 857
Härmä, R. A., **3972:** 1167, 1174
Harold, J. T., **2246:** 798, 801
Haroutunian, L. M., **1158:** 638
Harrell, E. R., **1271:** 656
Harrington, S. W., **4112:** 1224, 1229
Harris, D. K., **2986:** 955
Harris, G. B. C., **760:** 843, 861
Harris, P., **771:** 833
Harrison, C. V., **770:** 844, 847
Harrison, G. M., **3480:** 1064
Harrison, J. F., **4139:** 1230
Harrold, B. P., **3734:** 1119, 1121
Hartung, W., **338:** 136
Hartweg, H., **2203:** 789, 1149; **3568:** 1090
Harvey, J. C., **1312:** 662, 663
Hashida, Y., **4146:** 1232, 1235
Hatch, H. B., Jr., **1972:** 756; **2043:** 760
Hatch, T. F., **2799:** 919
Hathaway, B. M., **1316:** 663, 664
Hattori, S., **397:** 157, 177, 764; **2121:** 764
Hauser, T. E., **2244:** 798, 801
Havard, C. W. H., **2191:** 785
Haverling, M., **1730:** 1075
Hawker, J. M., **3876:** 1137, 1139
Hawkins, J. A., **1302:** 659; **2160:** 770, 771
Hawley, C., **1279:** 657
Hayada, Y., **1970:** 756
Hayashi, S., **1774:** 732
Hayes, D. S., **2594:** 888
Hayman, L. D., **2621:** 893
Haynes, W. F., Jr., **1406:** 674, 984
Hayslett, J., **486:** 169
Hazard, J. B., **2913:** 946

Heard, B. E., **2440:** 854; **3226:** 995; **3238:** 999, 1000; **3733:** 1119; **3735:** 1119, 1121
Heard, K. M., **2651:** 897
Heath, D., **749:** 840; **2422:** 844
Hebra, F., **1441:** 680
Hecht, H. H., **2420:** 842
Hedvall, E., **2115:** 764; **3620:** 1103
Hegetschweiler, W., **3300:** 1017
Heim, G., **3221:** 993
Heimburg, P., **293:** 127, 577
Heimburger, I. L., **1724:** 725
Heimlich, H. J., **1985:** 757, 1160
Heine, F., **404:** 158; **1785:** 733
Heinemann, H. O., **4287:** 1263
Heiner, D. C., **499:** 175
Heitzman, E. R., **683:** 309; **1174:** 641, 642
Helin, M., **1500:** 687
Helm, W. H., **3401:** 1044
Hemley, S. D., **2044:** 760
Henderson, A. H., **1360:** 666, 668
Hendren, W. H., III, **635:** 286, 596, 597
Henggeler, C., **1608:** 705
Hennell, H., **2514:** 871, 875
Hennessy, A. V., **3182:** 986
Henry, W. J., **577:** 197
Hensler, N. M., **462:** 165
Hentel, W., **3205:** 988; **3396:** 1043
Hepper, N. G. G., **1991:** 758; **2635:** 896; **4190:** 1243
Heppleston, A. G., **3239:** 999
Herbert, F. A., **3661:** 1105, 1109
Herlinger, H., **1620:** 711
Herlitzka, A. J., **4016:** 1180
Herrera-Llerandi, R., **1568:** 702, 1148
Herrmann, R. A., **4282:** 1261
Herrnheiser, G., **2457:** 858, 859
Hers, J. F., **1464:** 683
Herxheimer, H., **2713:** 907; **3034:** 971; **3036:** 971
Hessén, I., **786:** 112, 343, 345, 351, 352, 357, 786, 1253; **3392:** 1043
Heuck, F., **2908:** 945
Hewer, R. L., **4264:** 1260
Heycock, J. B., **3419:** 1051, 1052
Hicken, P., **772:** 842
Hickie, J. B., **1289:** 659, 660
Hickok, D. F., **3938:** 1159
Higgins, I. T. T., **3168:** 985; **3169:** 985; **3170:** 985
Higgins, J. A., **804:** 362, 1156
Hildeen, T., **2429:** 851
Hill, D. M., **3723:** 954
Hill, H. E., **434:** 161
Hill, M. C., **320:** 120, 581
Hill, R. B., Jr., **2666:** 900
Hilleman, M. R., **485:** 169
Hinaut, G., **1348:** 666
Hinshaw, H. C., **188:** 104, 653, 654, 770, 879, 893, 1064
Hinson, K. F. W., **531:** 177, 764
Hinton, J. M., **2126:** 765
Hirai, J., **1670:** 721
Hirsch, J. G., **3634:** 1103, 1104
Hirschfeld, J. H., **3366:** 1027; **4218:** 1253
Hoagland, R. J., **1541:** 695
Hochberg, L. A., **2197:** 785
Hochholzer, L., **4033:** 1184, 1189, 1192, 1214, 1216
Hodge, J., **4013:** 1179, 1180, 1188
Hodson, C. H., **876:** 573, 574, 576
Hodson, C. J., **660:** 291; **686:** 313, 975, 991; **2455:** 858; **3460:** 1063; **3525:** 1085; **3753:** 1122, 1123, 1125

Hoferichter, J., **923**: 582
Hoffbrand, B. I., **2494**: 867, 868, 869, 1153, 1252; **3512**: 1076, 1085
Höffken, W., **1357**: 666; **1880**: 738
Hoffman, E., **4217**: 1252
Hoffman, G. H., **4072**: 1197
Hoffman, L., **1130**: 634
Hoffman, Lee, **3701**: 1116, 1118
Hogg, J. C., **3020**: 968, 988, 1052
Holdaway, M. D., **1065**: 608
Holden, H. M., **1137**: 636; **1902**: 739
Holden, W. S., **237**: 119; **250**: 121, 122
Holder, T. M., **933**: 588
Holesh, S., **2174**: 774, 779
Holin, S. M., **1963**: 756, 765, 766
Hollaey, H. S., **111**: 56, 179, 1259
Holland, J., **909**: 185
Holland, R. A. B., **3678**: 1109; **3679**: 1109
Holland, R. H., **1884**: 738
Holland, Robert H., **2584**: 1136
Holland, W. W., **3160**: 985
Hollander, J. L., **2582**: 883
Holling, H. E., **385**: 154
Holman, C. W., **1000**: 162; **2106**: 763, 764, 1253
Holmes, L. B., **3412**: 1051
Holmes, R. B., **569**: 193, 262, 605, 606
Holt, G. W., **2016**: 759
Holt, L. E., Jr., **3942**: 1160
Holzel, A., **3927**: 1158
Honda, M., **1125**: 627
Honey, M., **3576**: 1090
Hood, R. H., Jr., **1927**: 740, 741, 763, 764
Hood, R. M., **1598**: 1075; **2544**: 875; **4293**: 1264
Hoorn, B., **1409**: 675
Hoover, C. F., **3321**: 1019
Horler, A. R., **2555**: 879
Horn, C., **1729**: 1005, 1006
Hornbaker, J. H., Jr., **2196**: 785
Horns, J. W., **3502**: 1067
Hornykiewytsch, T., **71**: 41, 117
Horrocks, J. E., **520**: 176
Horsfield, K., **3228**: 995, 997
Horstmann, D. M., **469**: 165, 685; **1418**: 676, 685
Hoschek, R., **2909**: 945
Hosty, T. S., **1204**: 643, 648
Houk, V. N., **3384**: 1035, 1039
Hourihane, D. O'B., **2819**: 933, 934, 936, 1163, 1164; **2841**: 936, 937, 1164; **2847**: 936, 937, 1164
Houston, C. S., **2475**: 864
Howat, H. T., **2782**: 917
Howells, J. B., **2153**: 770, 771
Howes, J. M., **1260**: 654
Howland, W. J., Jr., **3491**: 1066
Hsieh, Y-C., **3196**: 987, 1232
Hsu, K. H. K., **1170**: 641, 642
Huang, C. T., **2488**: 867, 869, 882, 889, 1252; **2495**: 869, 1252; **2501**: 869
Huang, N. N., **3451**: 1063
Huckabee, W. E., **4314**: 1268, 1269
Huckstep, R. L., **387**: 154, 760
Huff, R. W., **2472**: 864
Hughes, D. L., **310**: 128, 1166
Hughes, D. T. D., **2623**: 894
Hughes, E. W., **3649**: 1105
Hughes, J. M. B., **2444**: 845
Hughes, J. P., **2438**: 852
Hughes, R., **367**: 147

Hughes, R. T., **2442**: 854, 858
Hülsoff, T., **832**: 569, 588
Hultgren, H. N., **2476**: 864; **2477**: 864; **2479**: 864
Hunnicutt, T. N., Jr., **2890**: 943
Hunt, W., III, **1344**: 665
Hunter, C. C., Jr., **3257**: 1001
Hunter, D., **2768**: 915, 917; **2784**: 917, 955
Hunter, D. D., **881**: 576
Huppertz, A., **2870**: 945
Hurley, H. J., **3542**: 1088
Hurst, A., **363**: 147
Hurtado, A., **2474**: 864
Hurwitz, J. K., **1227**: 645
Hurwitz, M., **597**: 249, 253, 291, 294, 1163
Hurwitz, P. A., **3929**: 1158
Hutcheson, J. B., **2145**: 766; **3432**: 1055
Hutchinson, W. B., **808**: 369, 1152, 1163, 1164; **1825**: 735, 736
Huxtable, K. A., **972**: 596, 597
Hyatt, R. E., **2869**: 939
Hyde, L., **1255**: 654; **3936**: 1159
Hyman, G. A., **1727**: 725, 730
Hymes, A. C., **2035**: 760

Iacocca, V. F., **3450**: 1063; **3452**: 1063
Ikins, P. M., **315**: 128, 756
Inada, K., **4052**: 1192
Incaprera, F. P., **2516**: 872
Inkley, S. R., **3990**: 1171
Inman, W. H. W., **2280**: 805
Ioannou, J., **1941**: 741, 763
Irwin, A., **1353**: 666
Isard, H. J., **313**: 128
Ising, U., **1781**: 732
Israel, H. L., **1157**: 638; **2267**: 804, 825, 826; **2503**: 871, 873, 1153; **2920**: 946; **3529**: 1087; **3558**: 1089; **3629**: 1103; **3632**: 1103
Israël-Asselain, R., **3653**: 1105; **3956**: 1164; **4121**: 1225, 1229
Ivie, J. M., **1075**: 609; **1077**: 609
Iwai, K., **3586**: 1093
Iwanaga, K., **1954**: 746

Jack, I., **3183**: 986
Jackson, C. S., **36**: 11
Jackson, C. T., **2375**: 828
Jackson, D. C., **3885**: 1142
Jackson, F. I., **191**: 105
Jacobs, L. G., **1291**: 659; **2811**: 921, 931
Jacobson, G., **267**: 124; **778**: 847, 852, 857, 1006; **942**: 107; **2810**: 921; **2942**: 932; **3243**: 1000
Jacobson, H. G., **1105**: 617, 623
Jacox, R. F., **1535**: 693, 694
Jacques, J. E., **719**: 335
Jaffé, E. R., **4297**: 1264, 1266
Jaffe, R. B., **2305**: 806
Jahn, O., **358**: 146, 147
James, A. E., **1046**: 604
James, A. E., Jr., **2535**: 874
James, D. G., **3531**: 1087, 1103; **3562**: 1090; **3591**: 1093; **3631**: 1103, 1104
James, W. R. L., **2874**: 940
Jameson, A. G., **186**: 48, 53
Jamplis, R. W., **2114**: 764; **4021**: 1181; **4056**: 1192
Janetos, G. P., **3950**: 1160
Janigan, D. T., **1486**: 686

Janower, M. J., **2005**: 758
Jarnum, S., **1590**: 704
Järvinen, K. A. J., **526**: 177; **3270**: 1005
Jawahiry, K. I., **1661**: 720, 721
Jefferson, K. E., **70**: 37, 97
Jelihovsky, T., **2698**: 735
Jennings, F. L., **2033**: 1076, 1077
Jensen, K. G., **668**: 301, 731
Jensen, K. M., **3364**: 1024
Jensen, V., **893**: 577, 578
Jepson, E. M., **1315**: 663
Jerry, L. M., **3669**: 1106
Jessamine, A. G., **4197**: 1245
Jesseph, J. E., **40**: 12
Jewett, T. C., Jr., **1031**: 598; **2996**: 956
Jimenez, J. P., **2965**: 952
Joffe, B., **1249**: 653, 654
Joffe, N., **1104**: 617, 621; **4209**: 1246
Johansson, S. G. O., **3027**: 970; **3192**: 970
Johnson, H. R. M., **2972**: 954
Johnson, J. E., III, **475**: 168, 698; **476**: 168, 653; **1558**: 909
Johnson, R. L., Jr., **80**: 43
Johnson, R. M., **2213**: 792, 794
Johnson, R. S., **3430**: 1055, 1058
Johnson, T. H., Jr., **1691**: 1232
Johnston, P. W., **2143**: 766
Johnston, R. F., **3493**: 1066, 1067; **3911**: 1157, 1158
Johnston, R. N., **360**: 146, 147
Joint Tuberculosis Council Report, **1098**: 615
Jonathan, O. M., **1645**: 715
Jones, C. C., **3818**: 1131
Jones, E. R., **4206**: 1246
Jones, F. L., Jr., **1252**: 653
Jones, H. E., **842**: 569
Jones, N. L., **3122**: 983, 1016, 1020
Jones, R. H. T., **3077**: 979
Jones, R. S., **3064**: 974
Jonsson, B., **156**: 87
Jonsson, S. M., **2032**: 760
Jordan, J. D., **2602**: 889
Jordan, J. W., **2597**: 888; **2918**: 946
Jorgens, J., **195**: 113
Joseph, M., **368**: 147; **2006**: 758
Joseph, R. R., **3594**: 1099
Joseph, W. L., **4014**: 1179, 1181, 1189
Joske, R. A., **1502**: 688
Joyner, C. R., **1005**: 165
Joynt, G. H. C., **1365**: 1069, 1075
Judd, D. R., **3505**: 1067
Jue, K. L., **846**: 569, 571
Jungblut, R., **3808**: 1182
Just-Viera, J. O., **2366**: 827

Kafka, V., **906**: 577
Kagan, I. G., **1660**: 720, 721, 722
Kageyama, K., **1984**: 757
Kahn, P. C., **294**: 127, 756
Kaida, K., **1799**: 734
Kain, H. K., **1525**: 690
Kalbian, V. V., **3574**: 1090, 1103
Kallqvist, I., **1810**: 735
Kamat, S. R., **3347**: 1022
Kamberg, S., **3741**: 1121, 1122
Kamen, S. E., **229**: 116, 627

Kanagami, H., **3521**: 1085
Kane, I. J., **216**: 116; **659**: 291
Kantor, M., **2600**: 888
Kapila, C. C., **1469**: 685
Kaplan, H., **3592**: 1099
Kaplan, N. M., **1071**: 608
Kapur, K. K., **1001**: 162
Kariks, J., **1622**: 711
Karlish, A. J., **3475**: 1064
Karlson, K. E., **3981**: 1167
Karon, E. H., **3128**: 983; **4167**: 1239
Karp, H. R., **4304**: 1267
Kartagener, M., **3407**: 1051
Karwowski, J., **210**: 115, 132
Kass, E. H., **362**: 147, 986
Katz, A. M., **1628**: 712
Katz, D., **1398**: 673
Katz, I., **3496**: 1066; **4053**: 1192
Katz, R. L., **1304**: 660
Katz, S., **624**: 283
Katznelsen, D., **3459**: 1063
Kaufman, B. J., **4240**: 1259
Kaufman, G., **1766**: 732
Kaunitz, L., **790**: 345
Kawamori, Y., **464**: 165
Kaye, D., **1455**: 682, 683
Kaye, J., **2328**: 821; **3267**
Kazantzis, G., **2978**: 954
Keating, D. R., **705**: 329, 806, 808, 809
Keatinge, G. F., **3173**: 985
Keats, T. E., **763**: 843; **823**: 78; **2029**: 760; **2386**: 830; **4160**: 1239
Keay, A. J., **1012**: 174
Keers, R. Y., **1756**: 731
Kegel, R. F. C., **1632**: 712, 713, 715
Keith, T. A., III, **3180**: 986
Kelalis, P. P., **3069**: 975
Keller, R. H., **1180**: 642
Kelman, G. R., **791**: 154
Kendig, E. L., Jr., **1176**: 641; **3538**: 1087
Kennedy, A. C., **4164**: 1239
Kennedy, J. H., **1377**: 670; **2040**: 760
Kennedy, W. P. U., **3773**: 1123, 1125
Kent, D. C., **924**: 582; **3563**: 1090; **3600**: 1099
Kent, E. M., **4084**: 1205
Kent, G., **3855**: 1132
Kent, T. H., **1300**: 659, 660
Kerley, P., **120**: 60, 362; **676**: 306; **735**: 838, 851; **948b**: 306, 309; **948c**: 306, 309; **2456**: 858
Kern, R. A., **3050**: 972
Kerr, A., Jr., **349**: 141, 142
Kerr, W. J., **4234**: 1259
Keshishian, J. A., **4135**: 1230
Kessel, L., **2228**: 793
Keszler, P., **2142**: 766
Kettel, L. J., **997**: 161
Kevy, S. V., **1027**: 598, 1147
Khomyakov, Y. S., **793**: 348
Khoo, F. Y., **1613**: 709, 711
Khoury, G. H., **2418**: 842, 843; **4047**: 1188
Kieffer, S. A., **716**: 331
Kiely, B., **851**: 569, 571
Kihara, F., **840**: 569
Kilbourne, E. D., **1463**: 687
Kilburn, K. H., **2209**: 790; **3293**: 1017, 1081; **4276**: 1261; **4277**: 1261; **4306**: 1268
Kilman, J. W., **652**: 291, 578, 581

Kim, B. M., **534**: 177, 564
Kimball, H. R., **1311**: 660
Kinare, S. G., **2210**: 790, 791
Kingsbury, E. W., **1325**: 664
Kinloch, J. D., **2055**: 761
Kinney, V. R., **2539**: 874
Kirchheiner, B., **3585**: 1093
Kirkpatrick, C. H., **2660**: 899
Kirkpatrick, J. A., Jr., **3926**: 1158
Kirkpatrick, R. H., **2691**: 905
Kitchin, A. H., **3354**: 1022
Kittredge, R. D., **1106**: 617; **2159**: 770, 771; **3708**: 1116, 1118; **3947**: 1160
Kiviluoto, R., **807**: 366, 367, 933, 936, 1163
Klassen, K. P., **3213**: 990
Klatte, E. C., **2200**: 789
Klaus, M., **52**: 34
Klein, E. W., **617**: 273, 653, 654
Kleinerman, J., **2871**: 940; **3340**: 1021
Kleinfeld, M., **2834**: 936; **2837**: 936; **2857**: 937; **2860**: 937; **2947**: 950; **2948**: 950
Klingenberg, I., **117**: 72, 162
Klite, P., **370**: 148, 644
Klocke, R. A., **3690**: 1110
Kneeland, Y., Jr., **952**: 592
Knight, V., **1480**: 685, 686
Knott, J. M. S., **3268**: 1005
Knowles, J. H., **2008**: 758, 760, 762, 763
Knudson, R. J., **1855**: 737, 739; **2162**: 770, 771; **3094**: 980; **3699**: 1111, 1116
Knyvett, A. F., **626**: 283; **1509**: 689, 690
Koblet, H., **3247**: 1001
Koch, B., **3647**: 1105, 1106, 1109
Koch, D. A., **3421**: 1052
Koenig, M. G., **4275**: 1261
Koerner, H. J., **4043**: 1188
Koffler, D., **1489**: 687
Köhler, A., **145**: 84
Kontos, H. A., **352**: 142
Kopp, W. L., **2439**: 853
Korn, D., **2300**: 806, 822
Korn, D. S., **2738**: 909, 918
Kornblum, D., **2538**: 874
Körösi, A., **3974**: 1167
Korpela, A., **1838**: 736
Kossel, A., **1593**: 704
Kotin, P., **1893**: 739
Kourilsky, R., **205**: 115, 132; **209**: 115, 132; **212**: 115, 132
Kovach, R. D., **2049**: 760
Kovarik, J. L., **1777**: 732, 733; **1817**: 735, 1160
Kozinn, P. J., **1375**: 669, 670
Kozuka, T., **889**: 577
Krahl, V. E., **335a**
Krause, G. R., **587**: 220
Kreel, L., **312**: 128; **978**: 127; **2198**: 785
Kress, M. B., **2151**: 770, 771
Kretschy, A., **4213**: 1263; **4251**: 1259, 1263
Krige, L., **2831**: 934, 936, 1163
Kriss, N., **1521**: 690
Kritzler, R. A., **2687**: 905
Kroeker, E. J., **3816**: 1129, 1131
Kroening, P. M., **1550**: 696, 697
Krohn, J., **1907**: 739
Krokowski, E., **3838**: 1131
Kronenberger, F. L., **2955**
Krugman, S., **1513**: 689, 690, 692

Krumholz, R. A., **416**: 160; **992**: 159, 160; **3151**: 984
Kubásek, M., **2741**: 909
Kuida, H., **2484**: 864, 865
Kuisk, H., **604**: 253, 1106, 1109
Kulczycki, L. L., **3469**: 1064
Kümmerle, F., **4140**: 1232
Kuncaitis, J., **1062**: 607
Kundel, H. L., **4073**: 1001
Kuper, S. W. A., **1019**: 177; **1020**: 177, 623
Kurlander, G. J., **798**: 357
Kuschner, M., **1860**: 737
Kusui, K., **2001**: 758
Kuykendall, S. J., **1285**: 659, 660
Kwaan, H. M., **3965**: 1166
Kyllönen, K. E. J., **904**: 581
Kyttä, J., **1946**: 741

Laënnac, R. T. H., **374**: 151
LaFleche, L. R., **3722**: 950
Laforet, E. G., **4005**: 1179
Lagos, J. C., **3732**: 1119
Lahey, F. H., **4037**: 1184
Lai, K. S., **2410**: 840
Laios, N. C., **3709**: 1116, 1118
Laipply, T. C., **3728**: 1119, 1159
Lal, S., **441**: 162
Lalli, A. F., **989**: 159
Lamb, G. A., **1583**: 704
Lambert, H. P., **1438**: 679; **2071**: 680, 761
Lambert, M. W., **14**: 4
Lammers, B., **2716**: 908
Lamy, P., **2002**: 758
Lanceley, J. L., **1193**: 643
Landing, B. H., **2680**: 904
Landis, F. B., **3815**: 1129, 1131
Landmann, H., **1657**: 717
Landrigan, P. L., **1362**: 668
Lane, R. E., **3164**: 985; **3234**: 999
Lane, W. Z., **960**: 1069
Lang, W. R., **1507**: 689
Langbein, I. E., **3636**: 1201
Langston, H. T., **1996**: 758
Lansing, A. M., **576**: 197
Lanzoni, V., **4227**: 1258
Larizadeh, R., **1597**: 1075, 1161
Larose, J. H., **3524**: 1085
Larson, R. E., **1276**: 657
Larson, R. K., **3148**: 984; **4108**: 1224
Laski, B., **3651**: 1105
Lasser, E. C., **201**: 115, 132, 1219
Lattes, R., **1813**: 735
Lauby, V. W., **410**: 159, 160, 763
Laur, A., **2323**: 809
Laurenzi, G. A., **471**: 168, 674, 986; **720**: 338, 1027; **1403**: 674; **3214**: 990
Laurie, W., **546**: 177, 764
Laustela, E., **4045**: 1188; **4105**: 1220; **4130**: 1230
Laval, P., **1948**: 741
Lavender, J. P., **159**: 97; **767**: 845; **4107**: 1224
Law, W. R., **2969**: 954
Lawrence, J. R., **4223**: 1255
Lawrence, L. T., **4253**: 1260
Laws, J. W., **213**: 115, 132; **708**: 329, 1002, 1005, 1008, 1014, 1015, 1024
Lawson, J. P., **805**: 366, 936

Leading Article, Brit. Med. J., **1010**: 174; **1013**: 174; **1037**: 600; **1041**: 600; **1184**: 642; **1414**: 675; **1462**: 682; **1493**: 687; **1695**: 688; **1833**: 736, 740; **1859**: 737; **2010**: 758, 760; **2171**: 773, 774; **2283**: 805; **2284**: 805; **2580**: 883; **2676**: 902; **2697**: 916; **2818**: 933; **2977**: 954; **3071**: 978; **3605**: 1099; **4034**: 1184

Leading Article, Lancet, **1334**: 665, 666; **2058**: 761; **3025**: 970; **3053**: 972, 973; **4226**: 1258

Leahy, D. J., **3385**: 1035, 1039

Leake, E., **3657**: 1105, 1119, 1121

Leape, L. L., **3374**: 1032, 1033

Leathart, G. L., **2840**: 936

Lebacq, E., **3622**: 1103

Leckie, W. J. H., **442**: 162, 764

Ledbetter, M. K., **3081**: 980

Lee, F. I., **2560**: 879, 882

Lee, P. R., **2583**: 883, 1153

Lee, S. H., **1915**: 740, 741

Lees, A. W., **2112**: 764; **3464**: 1064

Leff, I. L., **2548**: 879

Leggat, P. O., **420**: 161, 763; **3290**: 1017

Lehar, T. J., **1919**: 740, 757

Le Hegarat, R., **1356**: 666

Leib, G. M. P., **2957**: 951

Leibovici, D., **4046**: 1188

Leigh, T. F., **4009**: 1179, 1180, 1186, 1188, 1193, 1210; **4019**: 1181, 1186, 1188, 1197, 1216; **4090**: 1180

Leilop, L., **535**: 177, 764

Leland, O. S., Jr., **335h**: 827

LeMay, M., **2250**: 801

Le Melletier, J., **3006**: 959

Lemle, A., **3680**: 1109

Lemon, F. R., **1852**: 737

Lemon, W. S., **3910**: 1157

Lenk, R., **3370**: 1027

Lennon, E., **1651**: 716

Lennon, E. A., **143**: 80, 1218

Lentino, W., **647**: 291

Lenz, H., **4101**: 1220

Leoncini, B., **995**: 160

Lerner, A. M., **1498**: 687, 688; **1503**: 688

Lerner, M. A., **539**: 177, 756, 757, 764, 1253

Le Roux, B. T., **1750**: 731; **1888**: 738; **4120**: 1225, 1229

Lertzman, M., **3308**: 1018

Lester, C. F., **1283**: 657

Lester, C. W., **4182**: 1241, 1243

Leuallen, E. C., **1016**: 175

Levant, M. N., **3277**: 1006

Levene, N., **1336**: 665, 666

Levin, B., **681**: 240, 309, 798; **762**: 862

Levin, E. J., **1345**: 666

Levin, H. G., **1522**: 690

Levin, J., **2102**: 763

Levine, H., **424**: 161, 763; **2581**: 883

Levine, M. A., **764**: 843

Lévi-Valensi, P., **2906**: 945

Levy, A. M., **2417**: 842

Lewis, A. G., Jr., **1179**: 642

Lewis, F. A., **1472**: 685

Lewis, J. G., **3695**: 1111, 1116, 1118

Lewis, J. M., **2050**: 760

Lewis, P. J., **3031**: 971

Lewis, R., **2706**: 907; **3058**: 973

Lichtenstein, H., **3509**: 1076, 1077

Lichtenstein, L., **3692**: 1110

Liddle, G. W., **2036**: 760

Lieben, J., **2931**: 947

Lieber, A., **2433**: 852

Lieberman, J., **932**: 207; **3863**: 1135

Liebow, A. A., **67**: 37; **96**: 47, 127; **292**: 127, 577; **727**: 1791: 733; **1983**: 757, 758; **2309**: 807, 1251; **3198c**: 1110; **3687**: 1109, 1110

Light, J. P., **241**: 119

Lilker, E. S., **4220**: 1255

Lillard, R. L., **3992**: 1174, 1175

Lillehei, J. P., **465**: 165

Lillington, G. A., **446**: 163, 1093, 1103; **4250**: 1259

Lincoln, E., **1159**: 638

Lindars, D. C., **4328**: 888

Lindesmith, L. A., **4267**: 1260

Lindig, W., **1977**: 756

Lindskog, G. E., **3937**: 1159

Linton, A. L., **2084**: 761

Lisa, J. R., **1942**: 741

Lister, W. B., **2885**: 942, 943

Little, C. C., **1867**: 737

Little, J. B., **1856**: 737, 738

Littman, M. L., **1185**: 643; **1186**: 643; **1290**: 659, 660; 1299: 659

Littmann, D., **335n**: 827

Liu, C., **493**: 174, 676

Liu, J., **1662**: 720, 721

Livingston, H. J., **3712**: 1118

Livingston, S., **3659**: 1105

Livingstone, C. S., **1588**: 704

Llamas, R., **2303**: 806, 807, 808, 809, 812, 822, 826, 827

Lloyd, M. S., **405**: 158

Lloyd, T. C., Jr., **109**: 51; **3019**: 968, 1020

Locke, G. B., **603**: 253, 879, 882, 883, 889, 1154

Lockey, S. D., **1089**: 612

Locks, M. O., **2061**: 761

Lodge, T., **2556**: 879, 1154; **2568**: 882, 931

Lodin, H., **139**: 76, 116, 217; **222**: 116, 1240; **1333**: 665, 666, 670

Lodwick, G. S., **1952**: 745

Loehry, C. A., **2271**: 805

Loeschcke, H., **7**: 3

Loew, M., **2178**: 775

Loewen, D. F., **1238**: 651

Löfgren, S., **3593**: 1099, 1103; **3612**: 1102

Logan, W. D., Jr., **1755**: 731; **3409**: 1051

Logue, R. B., **2443**: 854, 1156

Loken, M. K., **331**: 133

Longbottom, J. L., **491**: 169, 668; **1350**: 666, 668

Longcope, W. T., **3526**: 1087, 1089, 1093, 1099, 1102, 1104

Loop, J. W., **4186**: 1243

Loosli, C. G., **561**: 192; **564**: 192

Lopez-Majano, V., **979**: 133, 823

Lordon, R. E., **3557**: 1088

Lorian, V., **1008**: 168

Loudon, R. G., **1281**: 657

Lougheed, M. N., **2117**: 1076, 1077

Louhimo, I., **1751**: 731

Louis Bar, D., **2668**: 900

Louria, D. B., **1033**: 670; **1343**: 665; **1372**: 668; **1395**: 673; **1459**: 682, 683; **4319**: 600

Lovejoy, F. W., Jr., **3156**: 985

Lovette, J. B., **3819**: 1131

Low, L. R., **297**: 127, 756

Lowe, W. C., **2100**: 762, 763

Lowman, R. M., **4095**: 1214

Lowry, T., **2950**: 950, 951

Loyd, H. M., **149**: 86, 131, 180, 969, 1005

Lubert, M., **582**: 211, 220, 221, 231; **584**: 218, 219, 221; **586**: 220, 221, 291

Lucas, R. V., Jr., **761**: 843, 861; **4066**: 1197
Ludlam, G. B., **1444**: 680, 681, 897
Luhr, J., **3436**: 1058
Lull, G. F., Jr., **1231**: 645; **3817**: 1131
Lundin, P., **3743**: 1121, 1162
Lundsgaard, C., **389**: 154
Lunn, J. A., **2714**: 907, 909, 918
Lunn, J. E., **3162**: 985
Luoto, L., **1560**: 698
Luridiana, N., **236**: 119, 122
Lyell, A., **1445**: 680, 681
Lynch, E. C., **615**: 270
Lynch, H. J., **496**: 174
Lynch, P. A., **190**: 105
Lyons, H. A., **276**: 125, 756; **4028**: 1179, 1180, 1182, 1189, 1193, 1210
Lyons, J. P., **2824**: 940; **2883**: 942

Maassen, W., **452**: 163; **3967**: 1166
Macartney, J. N., **1335**: 666
Macfarlane, J. C. W., **1943**: 741, 765
Macieira-Coelho, E., **1666**: 720, 721
MacKay, I. R., **3645**: 1105
MacKay, J. B., **1524**: 690
MacKeen, A. D., **2369**: 827
MacKinnon, J., **1139**: 639
Macklem, P. T., **61**: 35, 122, 993, 1001, 1011, 1014, 1020; **62**: 35; **185**: 35, 968; **3191**: 967, 1052; **3323**: 1019; **3342**: 1021
Macklin, C. C., **3105**: 981, 1159, 1174
Macklin, M. T., **975**: 981, 1159, 1174
MacLean, K. S., **540**: 177
MacLean, L. D., **981**: 133, 823; **2486**: 865
MacLeod, M., **2653**: 897
MacLeod, W. M., **711**: 330, 331, 1033, 1044, 1052
MacPherson, P., **3623**: 1103
MacPherson, R. I., **3386**: 689, 1035
Madani, M. A., **1754**: 731
Madden, T. J., **4085**: 1207
Maddison, F. E., **2310**: 807
Maddock, R. K., Jr., **3798**: 1128
Maddy, K. T., **1248**: 653
Madrid, G. S., **1246**: 653
Magbitang, M. H., **4071**: 1001, 1197
Mahon, W. E., **2780**: 917
Mahrer, P. R., **2618**: 890
Maier, H. C., **926**: 582; **3898**: 1151
Mair, A., **2723**: 908
Maisel, J. C., **3336**: 1020
Majcher, S. J., **2056**: 761
Malamos, B., **4093**: 1214
Malmberg, R., **3964**: 1109
Maloney, J. V., Jr., **438**: 162
Mancall, E. L., **2020**: 759
Mandelbaum, I., **3380**: 1033
Mandl, M. A. J., **2677**: 902
Maneke, M., **4176**: 1240
Manfredi, F., **991**: 159, 160; **1053**: 605; **3963**: 1164
Mankiewicz, E., **1259**: 654; **3552**: 1088; **3553**: 1088; **3554**: 1088; **3555**: 1088
Mann, B., **2815**: 931
Manson-Bahr, Sir P. H., **470**: 165; **1679**: 722
Marchal, M., **204**: 115, 132; **206**: 115, 132; **208**: 115, 132
Marchand, E., **1669**: 721, 722
Marchand, M., **2891**: 943
Marchand, P., **4136**: 1230
Margolin, H. N., **712**: 331, 1035, 1039

Margulis, A. R., **2661**: 899, 900
Mark, L. K., **2232**: 793
Markel, S. F., **1708**: 723, 724, 725
Markewitz, M., **2235**: 793
Marks, L. J., **2034**: 760
Marland, P., **3575**: 1090
Marmorshtein, S. I., **684**: 311
Marschke, G., **3042**: 972
Marshall, R., **2304**: 806; **4214**: 1252
Marshall, R. J., **1229**: 645
Marston, E. L., **3973**: 1167, 1174
Martel, W., **3900**: 1154
Martin, H. B., **16**: 4, 198; **3241**: 1000
Martin, J. E., Jr., **2866**: 939
Martin, J. J., **2175**: 774, 775, 777, 779, 782, 1149
Maruyama, Y., **274**: 125; **2376**: 828, 829; **3506**: 1067
Masi, A. T., **2605**: 889, 894
Mason, M. K., **1773**: 732
Mason, W. E., **1829**: 736; **1967**: 756
Massaro, D. J., **1127**: 630; **2075**: 761; **3315**: 1018; **3616**: 1102; **3654**: 1105, 1106, 1252; **3655**: 1105; **4321**: 637
Massenti, S., **1747**: 715
Masson, P., **2652**: 897
Masson, P. L., **3211**: 990; **3212**: 990
Massoud, A., **492**: 169, 908
Massumi, R. A., **4233**: 1258
Mather, C. L., **3825**: 1131
Mathews, W. H., **3738**: 1121
Maunsell, K., **3052**: 972
Maurer, E. A., **321**: 129; **1818**: 735, 1160
Maxon, F. C., Jr., **2982**: 954
May, C. J., **1788**: 733
May, J. R., **1067**: 608; **1068**: 608; **3178**: 986; **3179**: 986
May, R. L., **3375**: 1032, 1033
Mayer, E., **3253**: 1001
Mayock, R. L., **618**: 274, 627; **2967**: 954; **3527**: 1087, 1093, 1099, 1102, 1104
Mays, E. E., **2579**: 883
Mays, E. T., **295**: 127
McAdams, A. J., Jr., **2951**: 950
McAdams, G. B., **3664**: 1106
McAlister, W. H., **573**: 193
McBride, R. A., **1379**: 671, 672
McCall, C. B., **3797**: 1128
McCallum, R. I., **2919**: 946
McCarthy, D. S., **4141**: 1055
McClure, C., **2140**: 766
McConnell, E. M., **1490**: 687
McCormack, W. M., **4278**: 1261
McCormick, P. W., **3002**: 959
McCort, J. J., **115**: 72; **3581**: 1091, 1093
McCreary, C. B., **1097**: 615
McCredie, M., **2445**: 855
McDaniel, H. G., **2039**: 760
McDearman, S. C., **500**: 175
McDonald, J. R., **1753**: 731
McDowell, C., **3803**: 1128, 1131
McDowell, L. A., **1133**: 635
McFadden, E. R., Jr., **3087**: 980
McGaff, C. J., **151**: 86
McGee, A. R., **2242**: 797
McGregor, M. B. B., **2528**: 873, 874
McIlroy, M. B., **336**: 134
McKerrow, C. B., **2718**: 908; **2728**: 908
McKusick, V. A., **2671**: 900, 902; **3264**: 1001; **3648**: 1105, 1106, 1109
McLaughlin, A. I. G., **2856a**; **2889**: 943; **2899**: 943, 945; **2900**: 943, 945; **2902**: 945; **2939**: 948

McLaughlin, J. S., **3831**: 1131
McLaughlin, R. F., Jr., **3237**: 999
McLean, D. M., **1473**: 685
McLean, K. H., **3232**: 198, 997; **3251**: 198, 1001
McLelland, L., **1482**: 685, 686
McLetchie, N. G. B., **3702**: 1116
McNeill, R. S., **3062**: 974
McNicol, M. W., **3314**: 1018; **3349**: 1022
McPhail, J. L., **1630**: 712, 713, 715
McQuarrie, D. G., **1903**: 739
McVay, L. V., Jr., **1090**: 612
Mead, J., **51**: 34; **56**: 34, 304, 816; **3333**: 1020
Mearns, M., **2517**; **3447**: 1063
Medearis, D. N., Jr., **1534**: 693, 694
Medeiros, A. A., **4322**: 644
Medical Research Council Report, **3117**: 982; **3163**: 985
Medlar, E. M., **1100**: 615, 621
Meeting of Experts on the International Classification of Radiographs of the Pneumoconioses, **2805**: 921, 931
Megahed, G. E., **3153**: 984
Meigs, J. V., **3912**: 1157; **3917**: 1157
Meisner, P., **3079**: 979, 980
Melamed, M. R., **1964**: 756, 764, 1253
Melhem, R. E., **782**: 852, 857; **3714**: 1118
Mellman, W. J., **1175**: 641
Melmon, K. L., **1726**: 726, 730; **2405**: 840; **3609**: 1093
Mélon, J., **3037**: 971
Meltzer, H., **1637**: 712, 713
Melzer, H., **1553**: 697
Mendeloff, A. I., **2248**: 798, 801
Mendelson, C. L., **3001**: 958
Mendenhall, E., Jr., **3814**: 1129
Mendl, K., **4211**: 1249
Menon, N. D., **2481**: 864
Merckx, J. J., **1172**: 641
Merendino, K. A., **39**: 12
Mermelstein, R. H., **1512**: 689, 690
Merriam, J. C., Jr., **2997**: 956, 958
Mertz, J. J., **1049**: 605
Merwarth, C. R., **3352**: 1022
Messite, J., **2853**: 937
Mestitz, P., **429**: 161; **524**: 176, 826, 1146
Métras, H., **252**: 122
Metyš, R., **1748**: 731
Meyer, A., **3618**: 1103, 1104
Meyer, E. C., **1155**: 637; **3672**: 1106
Meyer, P. C., **1961**: 753, 757, 792, 793, 1149, 1150, 1151
Meyers, H. I., **965**: 596, 597
Miall, W. E., **2598**: 888
Michael, M., Jr., **3535**: 1087
Michel, R. D., **2802**: 920
Michelassi, P. L., **2237**: 794, 1160
Michelson, E., **73**: 41, 117, 328
Middlemass, I. B. D., **197**: 113
Milic-Emili, J., **101**: 50, 65; **4291**: 1264
Milledge, R. D., **308**: 128, 1197; **638**: 286, 1119
Miller, A. A., **2884**: 942
Miller, A. J., **356**: 145
Miller, D. B., **1230**: 645
Miller, D. L., **3207**: 989
Miller, F. L., **414**: 160, 763
Miller, G. A., **2999**: 958
Miller, H. C., **2229**: 793

Miller, J. M., **4201**: 1245
Miller, L. F., **1408**: 675, 676, 689
Miller, M. A. L., **1780**: 732, 733
Miller, R. D., **2613**: 889, 894
Miller, W. S., **4**: 3, 8
Miller, W. T., **3916**: 1157, 1232
Millett, J., **3918**: 1157
Milliken, J. A., **2985**: 955
Milne, E. N. C., **784**: 852, 857; **1421**: 1069; **2345**: 1005; **3282**: 1008, 1011, 1015; **4323**: 794
Minarik, L., **1123**: 624
Minnis, J. F., Jr., **722**: 341
Mintz, G., **2634**: 895
Mishkin, F. S., **3082**: 980; **3083**: 980
Miskovits, G., **1973**: 756
Mitchell, C. E., **3915**: 1157
Mitchell, J., **2936**: 948; **2937**: 948
Mitchell, R., **2141**: 766
Mitchell, R. S., **3154**: 984, 988, 1016; **3254**: 1001; **3287**: 1016
Mithoefer, J. C., **4285**: 1261, 1266
Mitus, A., **1487**: 687; **1491**: 687
Miyaji, T., **1916**: 740, 741
Mobbs, G. A., **1815**: 735
Mody, K. M., **1151**: 637
Moersch, H. J., **1716**: 724, 725; **4042**: 1192
Moersch, R. N., **2701**: 794
Moës, C. A. F., **304**: 127
Mogabgab, W. J., **1415**: 675
Mohri, N., **3770**: 1123
Mokrohisky, J. F., **3919**: 1157
Molander, D. W., **3897**: 1149
Molnar, W., **244**: 119, 756
Moloshok, R. E., **2692**: 905
Momose, T., **2915**: 946
Monod, O., **1337**: 665, 666, 1148
Montes, M., **278**: 125; **1828**: 736
Montgomery, R. D., **2156**: 770, 894
Moody, D. L., **2241**: 794
Moolten, S. E., **2180**: 777
Moore, F. H., **3644**: 1105
Moore, M. E., **1135**: 635
Moore, M. T., **3658**: 1105
Moore, W., **1448**: 681
Moran, T. J., **3000**: 958; **3011**: 965
Morgan, A. D., **1787**: 733; **3982**: 1171
Morgan, E. H., **970**: 596, 597
Morgan, W. K. C., **2558**: 879, 883, 888; **2596**: 888; **2898**: 943
Morgan-Hughes, J. A., **350**: 142
Mori, P. A., **3269**: 1005
Mori, S., **1790**: 733
Mork, J. N., **3811**: 1129
Morrell, M. T., **2270**: 805
Morris, J. A., **1454**: 682
Morris, J. J., **4119**: 1225
Morrison, G., **3991**: 1171
Morrison, M. C. I., **2354**: 825
Morrissey, J. F., **2510**: 871, 872
Morrow, J. D., **2428**: 851
Morse, L. J., **1050**: 605, 606
Morse, S. J., **1072**: 608
Morton, D. L., **2014**: 758, 759
Moser, K. M., **2343**: 823
Mosetitsch, W., **3746**: 1121, 1122; **4180**: 1241
Moss, P. D., **4305**: 1267

Moss, W. T., **3517:** 1077; **3518:** 1077
Mostecký, H., **1801:** 734
Motley, H. L., **753:** 841
Motoyama, E. K., **4310:** 1268
Mounier-Kuhn, P., **3495:** 1066
Mounts, R., **2294:** 806
Moyer, J. H., **865:** 573, 574, 576
Mufson, M. A., **1439:** 679, 681
Muir, D. C. F., **2518:** 873; **3474:** 1064
Mullaney, P. J., **1909:** 739
Müller, R., **785:** 112, 343, 345, 348, 1253
Mulvey, R. B., **794:** 351
Munk, J., **695:** 324
Munnell, E. R., **2161:** 770
Munro, J. F., **3799:** 1128
Munt, D. F., **2727:** 908
Murai, M., **847:** 569, 571
Murasawa, K., **1899:** 739
Murphy, G. B., Jr., **2945:** 948
Murphy, K. J., **3769:** 1123, 1125
Murray, J. F., **477:** 168, 644, 645; **1201:** 643, 644, 645, 648, 658; **1320:** 664, 1148; **4194:** 1245
Murray, M. J., **2520:** 873
Murray, R., **2711:** 907
Muschenheim, C., **3686:** 1109
Myers, C. E., **1885:** 738
Myers, J. A., **1113:** 621; **1144:** 637
Myers, N. A., **3381:** 1033
Myers, W. P. L., **2059:** 761; **2082:** 761, 762
Myhre, J. R., **2496:** 869, 1252

Nadeau, P. J., **3697:** 1111, 1116
Nadel, J. A., **335k:** 807; **817:** 123; **2306:** 807; **2372:** 827; **2412:** 841; **3140:** 984
Naeye, R. L., **2615:** 889; **4187:** 1243
Nagakura, Y., **1103:** 617
Nagelschmidt, G., **2801:** 920, 934
Nahmias, B. B., **3683:** 1109
Nairn, J. R., **3388:** 1039
Naito, H., **2506:** 871
Nash, F. A., **1925:** 740, 756
Nash, G., **3877:** 1137, 1139
Nath, K., **1615:** 709
Nathan, M. H., **662:** 301, 769
National Tuberculosis Association, **1095:** 614
Naylor, B., **550:** 178
Neder, G. A., Jr., **3440:** 1058, 1062
Neill, C. A., **854:** 571
Neilson, D. B., **1456:** 682
Nelson, S. W., **41:** 12; **264:** 123; **530:** 206, 1160; **3400:** 1048
Nelson, W. P., **888:** 576; **3989:** 1171
Nessa, C. G., **2448:** 856, 857
Neu, H. C., **1321:** 664
Neuhauser, E. D., **754:** 841; **1585:** 704
Newell, R. R., **177:** 100, 101, 118, 769; **4320:** 623
Newhouse, M. L., **3959:** 1164
Newhouse, M. T., **153:** 35, 53, 806
Newman, F., **79:** 43, 86
Newman, W., **4236:** 1259
Nice, C. M., Jr., **2487:** 867; **3456:** 1063
Nichol, K. P., **950:** 591
Nicholas, J. J., **3821:** 1131
Nickell, W. K., **4207:** 1246
Nicklaus, T. M., **1024:** 180; **2694:** 873; **3266:** 1002, 1005, 1006, 1014, 1015

Nickol, K. H., **3782:** 1125, 1160
Nicks, R., **1636:** 712, 715
Nicod, J.-L., **2812:** 931
Niden, A. H., **184:** 34; **425:** 161
Nielsen, P. B., **892:** 577, 581
Nigogosyan, G., **4145:** 1232
Nisbet, H. I. A., **3775:** 1255
Nohl, H. C., **116:** 72; **439:** 162
Nolan, J. P., **3584:** 1093
Nome, O., **2964:** 952
Nordenström, B. E., **247:** 120, 121, 959; **253:** 122; **256:** 122, 158; **291:** 127; **673:** 301; **730:** 838; **819:** 47; **988:** 159, 160, 763; **1002:** 163; **1003:** 163
Norman, J. C., **4004:** 1179
Norris, G. F., **2929:** 947
Northway, W. H., Jr., **3867:** 1135, 1137, 1139
Nozaki, S., **2814:** 931
Nugent, C. A., **4219:** 1255
Nyboer, J., **326:** 132

Oakley, C., **2282:** 805
Ochsner, A., **1569:** 702; **4147a:** 1246; **4147b:** 1235
Ochsner, A., Jr., **4203:** 1246, 1249
Ochsner, J. L., **4030:** 1184, 1188, 1193, 1210
Ochsner, S., **1784:** 733; **1797:** 734
Oderr, C., **43:** 33; **211:** 115, 132, 1005; **215:** 115, 132
O'Donovan, T. P., **4079:** 1205
Oechsli, W. R., **656:** 261, 919, 921
Ogilvie, A. G., **3109:** 981
Ogilvie, C., **2882:** 942
Ognibene, A. J., **2559:** 879, 882, 889; **2565:** 882; **3756:** 1122
Ohara, I., **4082:** 1205
Oka, S., **2139:** 766; **3804:** 1128; **3822:** 1131; **3842:** 1131; **3860:** 1134
O'Keefe, M. E., Jr., **2264**
Okel, B. B., **4307:** 1268
Okuda, K., **3439:** 1058
Olazábal, F., Jr., **2358:** 826
Oldfield, F. S. J., **1399:** 673
Oliner, H., **3656:** 1105, 1119
Olkon, D. M., **86:** 46
Olsen, C. R., **533:** 177, 764; **3329:** 1020
O'Neill, R. P., **3850:** 1132, 1134
Onuigbo, W. I., **440:** 162, 758; **1992:** 758; **1993:** 758; **1994:** 758; **1995:** 758
Oosthuizen, S. F., **596:** 244, 366, 921; **2833:** 936
Opie, L. H., **2617:** 890
Oppenheimer, E. A., **1021:** 177; **3338:** 1021
Oram, S., **2614:** 889
Ordman, D., **3049:** 972
Orell, S. R., **744:** 573, 841
Oreskes, I., **3615:** 1102
Ormond, R. S., **138:** 75, 76; **733:** 835; **777:** 847; **2332:** 822
Orzalesi, M. M., **3074:** 979; **3472:** 1064; **4181:** 1241
Oseasohn, R., **1457:** 682, 683
Oshima, Y., **3060:** 973, 985
Oshiro, M., **3943:** 1160
Osmer, J. C., **949:** 591
Oswald, N. C., **1140:** 636, 642; **1460:** 682, 684, 685; **1562; 3126:** 984, 1016; **3132:** 983
Overholt, E. L., **474:** 168, 609; **1074:** 609; **3408:** 1051; **3766:** 1123; **4228:** 1258
Overholt, R. H., **3039:** 972; **3040:** 972
Owen, G. E., **1225:** 645

Owen, W. G., **3961**: 1164
Ozgelen, F., **2120**: 764
Ozonoff, M. B., **3103**: 981

Pace, W. R., Jr., **2636**: 896, 1253
Pader, E., **4061**: 1193
Padgett, G. A., **3891**: 1143
Page, M. I., **2749**: 910
Pagel, W., **2125**: 765
Paglicci, A., **2214**: 792, 793, 794, 798
Pain, M. C. F., **3357**: 1023
Pajewski, M., **232**: 117
Palayew, M. J., **1215**: 644, 645
Palmer, K. N. V., **3092**: 980; **3093**: 980, 1022; **3096**: 980, 982; **3099**: 980; **3312**: 1018; **4294**: 1264
Palmer, P. E., **1265**: 656, 657
Palmer, P. E. S., **839**: 569
Palmer, W., **748**
Pancoast, H. K., **1988**: 753, 758; **1989**: 753, 758
Papadopoulos, C. N., **4316**: 1268
Papavasiliou, C. G., **2026**: 760; **4094**: 1214, 1216
Paré, J. A. P., **4252**: 1260
Parish, D. J., **2057**: 761
Parish, W. E., **2742**: 909
Park, B. H., **951**: 592
Parker, B. M., **2272**: 805, 807, 825, 826
Parkhurst, G. F., **1384**: 672
Parkin, T. W., **2547**: 879
Parkinson, J. E., **3883**: 1142
Parks, R. E., **1758**: 1076
Parmley, L. F., **4077**: 1201
Parmley, L. F., Jr., **2298**: 806
Parnell, J. L., **1405**: 674, 984
Parsons, F. G., **825**: 84
Parsons, W. D., **1876**: 738
Passey, R. D., **1857**: 737
Pate, J. W., **2003**: 758
Paterson, J. F., **2803**: 920
Patterson, C. D., **2570**: 882
Pattle, R. E., **45**: 34; **46**: 34; **55**: 34, 304, 816
Paul, R., **1671**: 721; **3171**: 985
Paulson, D. L., **2131**: 765
Pavilanis, V., **1559**: 698
Payne, C. B., Jr., **3324**: 1020
Payne, M., **3135**: 984
Peabody, J. W., Jr., **731**: 341, 753; **1314**: 663; **1958**: 753
Peace, R. J., **1536**: 693, 694
Pearson, C. M., **4170**: 1240
Pearson, F. G., **2107**: 763, 764
Pearson, J. E. G., **4163**: 1239
Pecora, D. V., **468**: 165, 168; **3175**: 986
Pedersen, J., **4247**: 1259
Pek, S., **1526**: 690
Peleg, H., **1723**: 725, 731, 732, 733, 735
Pelzer, A.-M., **3150**: 984
Pendergrass, E. P., **2785**: 919, 942; **2808**: 921, 934; **2887**: 943; **2888**: 943; **2907**: 945
Pepys, J., **1326**: 664, 666, 668, 1055; **2705**: 907, 910, 911; **2743**: 909; **2752**: 910, 911; **2781**: 917; **3029**: 970; **3055**: 972
Perkins, R. L., **1206**: 643
Permutt, S., **85**: 46
Pernod, J., **2157**: 770
Peter, R. H., **1617**: 709, 711
Peters, G. A., **3138**: 984
Petersen, A. G., **2430**: 851

Petersen, J. A., **796**: 357, 359
Petersen, R. W., **307**: 128, 1197
Peterson, H. G., Jr., **571**: 193, 1135
Peterson, K. L., **2336**: 822
Peterson, O. L., **1419**: 676
Petty, T. L., **2574**: 882
Pfischner, W. C. E., Jr., **1083**: 611
Pfister, A. K., **1278**: 657
Pfitzer, E. A., **3721**: 950
Pfuetze, K. H., **1169**: 641, 642; **1178**: 642, 1146
Phelps, H. W., **3059**: 973
Philipps, E., **2467**: 861
Phillips, A. W., **2994**: 956
Phillips, F. J., **243**: 119
Phillips, I., **1040**: 600
Phillips, S., **1146**: 637
Phillips, T., **2137**: 765, 766
Phillips, T. L., **3514**: 1077
Pichel, R. R., **1731**: 730
Pierce, A. K., **1039**: 600
Pierce, J. A., **42**: 33; **864**: 573, 797; **3252**: 1001; **3373**: 1027
Pieri, J., **3489**: 1066
Piiper, J., **187**: 86, 91
Pilheu, J. A., **2109**: 763
Pillay, V. K. G., **1366**: 664, 668
Pimentel, J. C., **1354**: 666
Pines, A., **1148**: 637, 1146
Pinkerton, H., **1582**: 703, 704
Piper, W. N., **2609**: 889
Pirnar, T., **4155**: 1236
Pischnotte, W. O., **2265**
Pitman, R. G., **732**
Pitt, B., **3289**: 1017
Plachta, A., **1783**: 733
Plair, C. M., **1850**: 737
Plenk, H. P., **3809**: 1129, 1131
Plum, G. E., **3907**: 1156
Plummer, N. S., **3540**: 1087
Pock-Steen, O. C., **1705**: 723, 724, 725, 730
Poe, N. D., **980**: 133
Pohl, R., **1898**: 739, 758; **4165**: 1239
Polachek, A. A., **2362**: 826
Polgar, G., **3448**: 1063, 1064, 1066
Pollard, A., **1732**: 730
Poller, S., **641**: 286, 576, 577
Pongor, F., **3713**: 1118
Ponnampalam, J. T., **1234**: 648, 654
Pontius, J. R., **3399**: 1048
Pontoppidan, H., **3346**: 1022; **3881**: 1137, 1139
Poole, G., **359**: 146, 147
Poppius, H., **648**: 291, 662
Porro, F. W., **2851**: 937; **2858**: 937
Porter, G. H., **3588**: 1093
Portner, M. M., **2589**: 883, 888
Portnoy, L. M., **3853**: 1132
Posen, S., **317**: 128, 1186
Posner, E., **1980**: 756; **2790**: 919
Potchen, E. J., **2344**: 823
Powell, A. H., **3790**: 1128
Pratt, P. C., **3874**: 1137, 1139
Prevatt, A. L., **1048**: 604
Prichard, M. M. L., **2459**: 859
Pridgen, J. E., **4270**: 1260
Prignot, J., **2875**: 940, 942
Prijyanonda, B., **1658**: 719
Princi, F., **2979**: 954

Priviteri, C. A., **251**: 121, 959
Procknow, J. J., **1214**: 648, 654; **1274**: 656; **1347**: 666
Proffitt, R. D., **1609**: 707
Prowse, C. B., **3748**: 1122
Prowse, C. M., **3387**: 1039
Pruzanski, W., **3008**: 959; **3716**: 1118
Pryce, D. M., **894**: 577
Pugsley, H. E., **1239**: 651
Puhr, L., **3837**: 1131
Pump, K. K., **8**: 2; **23**: 7
Purcell, R. H., **1427**: 678, 679, 680, 681; **1440**: 679
Purriel, P., **1648**: 715
Pursel, S. E., **361**: 147
Pyke, D. A., **394**: 156

Quie, P. G., **2682**: 904
Quinlan, J. J., **916**: 582
Quinlan, M. F., **3215**: 990
Quinn, J. L., III, **330**: 133, 823; **1485**: 686

Rabin, C. B., **1721**: 725; **3893**: 1145, 1149, 1150, 1154
Rabinov, K., **990**: 159; **1690**: 376, 793
Racz, I., **918**: 582
Radford, E. P., Jr., **47**: 34
Rahn, H., **917**: 197
Raich, R. A., **1317**: 663, 664; **1623**: 711
Rainer, W. G., **260**: 122, 1011
Rainey, R. L., **1280**: 657
Rajasuriya, K., **3619**: 1103, 1104
Rakower, J., **1639**: 712, 713, 1149; **1646**: 715; **3382**: 1033, 1039; **3580**: 1091
Ramah, S. J., **1086**: 611
Ramirez, G., **1376**: 670
Ramirez-Rivera, J., **2601**: 888; **3810**: 1129; **3812**: 1129, 1131; **3820**: 1131; **3828**: 1131; **3829**: 1131; **3830**: 1131
Ramos, H. S., **1561**: 698
Ramos, J. G., **87**: 46
Ranke, E. J., **1947**: 741
Rankin, J., **2744**: 909, 910, 911, 916; **2756**: 911
Ranney, E. K., **1518**: 690
Ranniger, K., **651**: 291, 578, 581, 1235; **944**: 127
Ransome-Kuti, O., **4002**: 1175
Rao, N. V., **423**: 161
Raphael, H. A., **3984**: 1171
Raphael, M. J., **4008**: 1179
Rapoport, A., **2219**: 792
Raskin, P., **3048**: 972
Rasmussen, P., **4152**: 1236; **4153**: 1236
Rawson, A. J., **2645**: 896
Ray, R. L., **3805**: 1128, 1131
Rayl, D. F., **816**: 122
Rayl, J. E., **262**: 122
Rea, D., **3905**: 1156
Read, J., **99**: 48, 1109; **3114**: 982; **3646**: 1105
Ream, C. R., **4274**: 1260
Rebuck, A. S., **3061**: 974
Recant, L., **3715**: 118
Reed, C. E., **2770**: 915, 916
Reed, E. S., **2867**: 939
Reed, J. O., **4113**: 1224, 1225, 1229
Reed, W. B., **2672**: 900, 902
Rees, H. A., **3091**: 980; **3097**: 980; **3098**: 980, 981; **3107**: 981

Rees, R. S. O., **2401**: 838
Rees, S., **2402**: 838
Reese, O., Jr., **428**: 161, 640
Reeves, J. T., **2460**: 860
Refsum, H. E., **3292**: 1017, 1018
Regan, G. M., **982**: 156
Reich, S. B., **580**: 198, 1001
Reichel, G., **3166**: 985
Reid, D. D., **3120**: 983
Reid, J. A., **707**: 329, 1000
Reid, J. D., **1196**: 643
Reid, J. M., **696**: 324, 1032, 1033; **1935**: 740
Reid, L. M., **158**: 3, 97, 120; **542**: 315; **672**: 309; **713**: 331, 1033, 1035, 1039; **2326**: 816; **3035**: 1033; **3157**: 985; **3197**: 987, 988; **3198**: 987, 988, 989, 990, 1001, 1016; **3203**: 988; **3223**: 993, 1011; **3224**: 993; **3265**: 1014, 1015, 1035; **3278**: 1015; **3279**: 1015; **3280**: 1011, 1015, 1024, 1027, 1052; **3283**: 993, 1011; **3403**: 1044
Reilly, C. M., **1476**: 685
Reimann, H. A., **1096**: 614, 637
Rele, J. R., **1853**: 737, 738
Renzetti, A. D., Jr., **4202**: 1245
Resink, J. E., **181**: 101, 245, 921
Resnick, M. E., **2201**: 789, 790, 1253
Restrepo, A., **1393**: 673
Restrepo, G. L., **3202**: 988
Reuter, S. R., **1969**: 756
Revill, D., **873**: 574
Reynolds, E. S., **1577**: 703
Reynolds, J., **987**: 1069, 1075, 1076, 1155, 1156; **2962**: 952
Rezek, P. R., **3449**: 1063
Rice, R. L., **353**: 142, 1268
Richards, B. T., **2533**: 873, 874
Richards, D. W., **3371**: 1027; **4324**: 834
Richards, R. L., **2626**: 894
Richardson, P., **2389**: 830
Richert, J. H., **436**: 162, **488**: 169, 651, 652; **1676**: 722
Richman, S. M., **2447**: 856
Richter, K., **739**: 577
Richter, T., **4258**: 1260
Rickards, A. G., **2595**: 888
Riddle, H. F. V., **2735**: 909, 917
Ridgeway, N. A., **1389**: 673
Riebel, F. A., **176**: 99, 102
Rienhoff, W. F., III, **1936**: 740, 758
Rietz, K.-A., **4039**: 1186
Rifkind, D., **1332**: 665, 668, 669; **1435**: 679, 680, 681; **1564**: 693, 700, 704; **1595**: 704, 705
Rigatto, M., **4109**: 1224
Rigby, R. A., **956**: 592, 606
Riggs, B. L., Jr., **2045**: 760
Riggs, W. Jr., **1211**: 644, 645, 651
Rigler, L. G., **165**: 98, 99; **194**: 112, 345; **610**: 260, 742; **664**: 301, 742, 757; **685**: 312; **799**: 357; **1951**: 745; **2260**: 1251, 1252, 1253; **2263**: 2458: 859
Riley, C. M., **2689**: 905; **2693**: 905
Riley, E. A., **1346**: 666; **4100**: 1219
Riley, R. L., **164**: 97
Rimington, R. A., **1047**: 604
Ring, A., **2319**: 808, 809
Ringrose, R. E., **1064**: 607
Rinker, C. T., **301**: 127, 756; **1966**: 756
Riordan, J. F., **2485**: 865
Ritchie, B., **2624**: 894, 1252
Ritter, H., **121**: 61

Ritvo, M., **1051**: 605
Roach, S. A., **2720**: 908
Robbins, J. B., **1589**: 704
Robbins, L. L., **585**: 220, 291; **629**: 220, 291; **630**: 220, 291; **631**: 220, 291; **632**: 220, 291; **633**: 220, 291; **634**: 220, 291; **2189**: 784, 785, 789; **3010**: 964
Robbins, S. L., **4018**: 1180
Roberton, N. R. C., **3880**: 1137, 1139
Roberts, G. B. S., **1467**: 684
Roberts, H. J., **2080**: 761
Roberts, J. C., **2170**: 771
Robertson, A. J., **679**: 151; **2856d**: 937, 939; **2904**: 945
Robertson, C. K., **565**
Robertson, J. L., **2572**: 882, 883
Robertson, O. H., **549**: 192; **554**: 192, 593; **563**: 192, 289, 593
Robillard, G., **1602**: 705
Robin, E. D., **1611**: 708; **2367**: 827; **2368**: 827; **2450**: 857
Robinson, A., **977**: 132
Robinson, A. E., **4210**: 1249
Robinson, B. R., **2519**: 873, 1153
Robitaille, G. A., **3888**: 1142
Robson, A. O., **1883**: 738; **3065**: 974
Roche, A. D., **2791**: 919
Roche, G., **1821**: 735, 1162
Rockey, E. E., **1865**: 737
Rodman, M. H., **1816**: 735
Rodman, T., **2507**: 871; **3520**: 1085; **4254**: 1260; **4255**: 1260, 1263; **4286**: 1263; **4289**: 1264
Rodnan, G. P., **2608**: 889; **2628**: 894
Rodríguez, H. F., **1674**: 721
Roehm, J. O. F., Jr., **855**: 571
Roelsen, E., **2154**: 770, 771
Rogers, L. F., **654**: 291, 581, 582, 583
Rohrs, L. C., **2987**: 955
Rokseth, R., **2431**: 851
Roland, A. S., **3707**: 1116
Roque, F. T., **1115**: 622
Rose, A. L., **2631**: 894, 895, 896, 1262
Rose, G. A., **2534**: 874, 875, 879; **2545**: 875
Rose, H. A., **2186**: 784, 785
Roseman, D. M., **3913**: 1157
Rosen, F. S., **2662**: 899, 900, 902; **2690**: 902
Rosen, S. H., **3801**: 1128, 1129, 1131
Rosen, S. W., **2098**: 762
Rosenbaum, H. D., **1763**: 731, 732
Rosenberg, B. F., **545**: 177, 801
Rosenberg, D. M. L., **2356**: 826
Rosenberg, L. E., **3889**: 1142
Rosenberg, M., **4142**: 1232
Rosenberg, S. A., **2187**: 784, 785
Rosenblatt, G., **392**: 155
Rosenblatt, M. B., **2165**: 770; **3899**: 1151
Rosenthal, L., **333**: 133
Rosenthall, L., **328**: 133
Rosenzweig, D. Y., **3335**: 1020
Rosmus, H. H., **1424**: 677, 679
Ross, C. A., **3186**: 986
Ross, E. J., **2087**: 762
Ross, J. D., **1386**: 672
Rotem, Y., **3840**: 1131, 1132
Rothstein, E., **3922**: 1158
Rotta, A., **2421**: 843
Roughton, F. J., **77**: 43, 86, 183
Roujeau, J., **606**: 253, 1119; **3730**: 1119, 1159

Roussel, J., **1882**: 738
Rouvière, H., **114**: 72, 162, 758
Rowlandson, R., **2702**: 794
Rowley, P. T., **3889**: 1142
Rowley, W. E., **1587**: 704
Roy, P. H., **1017**: 175
Royal College of General Practitioners, **2279**: 805
Rubin, E. H., **1793**: 733; **2552**: 879, 882; **3368**: 1027; **4215**: 1252
Rubin, H. M., **1187**: 643, 651, 652
Rubin, P., **614**: 269
Ruckley, C. V., **3939**: 1159, 1160
Rudberg-Roos, I., **3530**: 1087, 1093, 1103, 1104
Rudhe, U., **3997**: 1174, 1175
Rumbaugh, I. F., **1699**: 613, 960
Rundle, F. F., **193**: 108
Runyon, E. H., **1165**: 640
Russakoff, A. H., **505**: 175
Rutishauser, M., **646**: 290, 746
Rutishauser, W. J., **129**: 65
Ryan, D., **225**: 116
Ryder, J. B., **1122**: 624
Rytel, M. W., **484**: 169, 676, 677, 678

Sabga, G., **853**: 569
Sabin, A. B., **1584**: 704
Sackner, M. A., **150**: 86; **2622**: 894
Sacks, R. P., **3507**: 1067
Sadrieh, M., **1631**: 712, 713, 715
Sagel, S. S., **1757**: 731
Sakula, A., **1194**: 643; **2227**: 793; **2760**: 911; **3487**: 1066
Saliba, A., **1340**: 665, 666
Salmon, H. W., **3985**: 1171
Saltzman, H. A., **354**: 143
Saltzstein, S. L., **1826**: 735, 785
Salvaggio, J. E., **2763**: 915; **2764**: 915
Salvato, G., **3208**: 989
Salvin, S. B., **487**: 169, 651, 652, 657, 671
Salzman, E., **1683**: 283
Sammons, B. P., **868**: 574, 576; **3220**: 993
Samter, M., **3070**: 978
Samuels, M. L., **2182**: 777; **3794**: 1128
Sander, O. A., **2895**: 943; **2941**: 948
Sanders, C. F., **908**: 83
Sanders, D. E., **275**: 125, 756
Sanders, J. S., **883**: 576; **1776**: 732, 1253
Sanderud, K., **3152**: 984
Sandiford, B. R., **3418**: 1051
Sandler, M., **1725**: 725, 730
Sandor, F., **4266**: 1260
Sanghvi, L. M., **3909**: 1156
Sansone, S., **985**: 158
Sante, L. R., **1581**: 703
Santy, P., **4148**: 1235
Sargent, E. N., **939**: 120; **1520**: 690, 692; **1527**
Sarner, M., **1555**: 697
Sarnoff, S. J., **2469**: 864; **2470**: 864
Sasahara, A. A., **335s**: 826, 827; **2365**: 827
Sasamoto, H., **2397**: 833
Saslaw, S., **1216**: 644
Sato, S., **2243**: 797
Sautter, R. D., **2290**: 806
Sawazaki, H., **3423**: 1052
Saxton, G. A., Jr., **4259**: 1260

Saxton, J., **3378:** 1032

Scadding, J. G., **377:** 153; **1156:** 638; **3532:** 1087, 1090, 1091, 1104; **3662:** 1105; **3673:** 1106, 1109

Scakner, M. A., **2622:** 894

Scalettar, R., **4249:** 1259

Scannell, J. G., **29:** 10, 13; **30:** 10, 13; **31:** 10

Scarrow, G. D., **709:** 329, 1006, 1008; **3275:** 1006

Scatliff, J. H., **814:** 116

Schaffner, **123:** 62

Schaffner, W., **1548:** 695, 696, 697

Schattner, A. S., **1659:** 720, 721

Scheer, R. L., **3761:** 1123, 1128

Scheff, S., **146:** 83

Schermuly, W., **3578:** 1090

Schieppati, E., **453:** 163, 764

Schimke, R. N., **2639:** 896

Schlesinger, M. J., **341:** 137

Schleusener, A., **3258:** 1001

Schmidt, A., **3934:** 1159

Schmidt, H. W., **2549:** 879

Schmidt, P. G., **1131:** 634

Schmidt, S., **199:** 115, 132, 1219; **200:** 115, 132, 1219, 1224; **202:** 115, 132, 1219

Schneckloth, R. E., **1738:** 730

Schneider, H. J., **4081:** 1205

Schneider, I. C., **391:** 155

Schneider, L., **399:** 157, 757, 1253; **806:** 366, 936

Schneider, R. M., **1243:** 1069

Schneider, R. M., **3689:** 1109, 1110

Schneierson, S. J., **3928:** 1158

Schoemperlen, C. B., **3410:** 1051

Schoen, I., **3886:** 1142

Schoenmackers, J., **3273:** 1005

Schoettlin, C. E., **2709:** 907, 973

Scholz, D. A., **4022:** 1182

Schonell, M. E., **2363:** 827

Schools, G. S., **510:** 175, 883, 1153

Schowengerdt, C. G., **3979:** 1167, 1171

Schrenk, H. H., **2695:** 907

Schröder, W., **692:** 324

Schub, H. M., **3895:** 1146, 1148

Schüler, P., **2836:** 936

Schultz, E. H., Jr., **3005:** 959

Schultz, J. C., **1599:** 705

Schultze, G., **13:** 596, 597, 1147

Schulz, H., **97:** 3, 48

Schulze, W., **2394:** 831

Schuster, B., **776:** 847

Schuster, G., **903:** 581

Schuster, S. R., **3467:** 1064

Schwartz, A., **1363:** 1069

Schwartz, I., **461:** 164

Schwartz, S., **298:** 127

Schwartz, W. B., **2079:** 761; **2086:** 762

Schwarz, E., **934:** 1067

Schwarz, J., **1218:** 644; **1329:** 665, 666, 670

Schwedel, J. B., **779:** 852, 857

Schweich, A., **3945:** 1160

Schweisguth, O., **4089:** 1207

Schweppe, H. I., **1702:** 613, 961, 964

Schwippert, H., **2113**

Scotland, Department of Health, Scientific Advisory Committee on Medical Administration and Investigation, **1054:** 606

Scott, S. M., **1388:** 673

Seal, R. M. E., **3718:** 910

Secker-Walker, R. H., **2346:** 823, 824

Secrest, P. G., **3490:** 1066

Seebohm, P. M., **3246:** 1000

Seeler, A. O., **2854:** 937

Seelig, M. S., **1371:** 668

Segal, E. L., **1189:** 643, 645

Segal, M. S., **3043:** 972

Segarra, F. O., **398:** 157; **649:** 291, 623

Seidelin, R., **2958:** 952

Seidler, R. C., **4097:** 1214

Seiler, E., **3534:** 1087

Selby, H. M., **1844:** 736, 740, 742, 745, 757

Seldinger, S. I., **286:** 125

Selenkow, H. A., **3596:** 1099

Selikoff, I. J., **1861:** 737, 936, 937; **2665:** 737, 936, 1164; **3018:** 937; **3962:** 1164

Sell, S. H. W., **1188:** 643

Sellers, R. D., **3603:** 1099

Seltzer, C. S., **1868:** 737

Seltzer, R. A., **4204:** 1246

Semple, T., **378:** 153; **2021:** 759, 760

Sepúlveda, G., **2436:** 852

Serviansky, B., **620:** 277, 621; **1219:** 644

Setnikar, I., **1687:** 351, 353

Severinghaus, J. W., **65:** 35, 53; **2370:** 827

Sevitt, S., **335t:** 805; **2274:** 805, 825

Sexton, R. C., Jr., **1578:** 703

Seybold, W. D., **4020:** 1181

Shackelford, R. T., **3904:** 1156

Shah-Mirany, J., **1153:** 637

Shaldon, S., **4290:** 1264

Shames, J. M., **1742:** 730

Shane, S. J., **2404:** 840

Shanker, A., **1616:** 709

Shanklin, D. R., **3878:** 1137, 1139

Shapiro, J. B., **3438:** 1058

Shapiro, M., **2025:** 760

Sharma, O. P., **3607:** 1099

Sharnoff, J. G., **2526:** 873

Sharp, J. T., **2452:** 857; **2453:** 857; **3145:** 984; **4244:** 1259

Shauffer, I. A., **826:** 84; **4150:** 1235

Shaver, C. G., **2934:** 948

Shaw, D. B., **4191:** 1243, 1245

Shaw, R. K., **433:** 161

Shaw, R. R., **3429:** 1055

Sheehan, V. A., **3431:** 1055

Sheehy, T. W., **1045:** 604

Sheers, G., **2862:** 939

Sheffner, A. L., **1007:** 168

Sheft, D. J., **605:** 253, 1106, 1109

Sheinmel, A., **2172:** 774, 775, 777, 779

Sheldon, G. C., **1543:** 695

Shepard, F. M., **3866:** 1135

Shepherd, J. T., **2398:** 834, 840

Sherman, W. T., **2437:** 852

Sherrick, D. W., **17:** 320, 331

Shields, T. W., **447:** 163, 644, 764; **2663:** 758

Shih, M. H., **1842:** 736

Shima, M., **2916:** 946

Shkrob, O. S., **1975:** 756

Shope, R. E., **1141:** 636

Shopfner, C. E., **907:** 83

Short, D. S., **773:** 847

Shuford, W. H., **303:** 127

Shwachman, H., **3468:** 1064

Sibley, J. C., **3894:** 1146

Sicard, J. A., **233:** 118

Siddons, A. H., **1904:** 739; **3012:** 965
Sidransky, H., **1380:** 671
Siegal, W., **2852:** 937
Siegel, R. S., **4151:** 1236
Siegenthaler, W., **1551:** 696
Sieker, H. O., **4237:** 1259; **4248:** 1259
Siemsen, J. K., **2019:** 759
Sieniewicz, D. J., **2586:** 883, 888; **2590:** 888
Sieracki, J. C., **3813:** 1129
Sievers, K., **2571:** 882
Sigrest, M. L., **501:** 175
Silber, R., **2483:** 864
Silbiger, M. L., **1596:** 1075; **2649:** 896, 897
Siltzbach, L. E., **3635:** 1103
Silverman, I., **412:** 159
Šimeček, C., **454:** 163, 764; **983:** 157
Similä, S., **3621:** 1103
Simmel, E. R., **4299:** 1264
Simmons, D. H., **90:** 46, 841
Simon, G., **75:** 41, 116; **122:** 61, 76, 77, 80, 107, 217,
    220, 287, 301, 311, 312, 313, 322, 1005; **124:** 62;
    161: 81, 1219; **162:** 97; **588:** 223; **689:** 314, 990, 991,
    993; **690:** 315; **693:** 324, 1002, 1005, 1008; **699:**
    324, 588; **1685:** 305, 315; **2193:** 779; **2327:** 818;
    3216: 990, 991, 992, 1011; **3271:** 1005; **3285:** 993
Simon, H., **1960:** 753, 758
Simon, M., **335p:** 822; **755:** 841, 851, 852, 857; **765:**
    845; **769:** 845
Simonetti, C., **226:** 116
Simopoulos, A. P., **901:** 578
Simpson, D. G., **1164:** 640
Simpson, H., **3089:** 980
Sinclair, D. J., **1998:** 758
Singer, D., **2311:** 807
Singer, D. B., **1764:** 732, 1253
Singh, D., **1107:** 617
Singh, I., **2419:** 842, 843; **2480:** 864
Singshinsuk, S., **759:** 843
Sison, B. S., **421:** 161
Sjoerdsma, A., **1735:** 730
Sjögren, H., **2646:** 896
Skinner, D. B., **300:** 127, 756; **449:** 163
Skorneck, A. B., **384:** 154; **4168:** 1239
Slager, U. T., **3762:** 1123
Slapak, M., **1566:** 700, 704
Sleeper, J. C., **2408:** 840
Sleggs, C. A., **3958:** 1164
Slutzker, B., **3827:** 1131
Smadel, J. E., **1540:** 695
Small, M. J., **1258:** 654
Smart, J., **418:** 159; **3332:** 1020
Smart, R. H., **2798:** 919
Smellie, H., **3559:** 1090, 1091, 1252; **3564:** 1090
Smillie, W. G., **953:** 592
Smith, A. R., **2832:** 936, 937, 939, 1163
Smith, B. S., **3255:** 1001; **3786:** 1125
Smith, C. B., **1434:** 679
Smith, C. E., **1264:** 656
Smith, D. T., **1014:** 174
Smith, F. R., **32:** 10
Smith, G., **4065:** 1197
Smith, G. T., **335i:** 785, 804, 805, 807, 808; **2269:** 804,
    806
Smith, J. C., **3235:** 999; **3510:** 1076, 1077; **3513:** 1077
Smith, J. G., Jr., **1269:** 656, 657
Smith, J. M., **3024:** 969
Smith, K. W., **655:** 291, 934, 936

Smith, L., **4126:** 1229, 1230
Smith, R. A., **837:** 569; **895:** 577; **1887:** 738, 757
Smith, R. B. W., **2710:** 907, 973
Smith, W. E., **3767:** 1123
Smith, W. G., **413:** 159; **3434:** 1058; **3935:** 1159
Smith, W. M., **2642:** 896
Smith, W. G., **996:** 160
Smithers, D. W., **1800:** 739; **2146:** 769
Smits, B. J., **1369:** 668
Smyllie, H. C., **390:** 155; **3106:** 981
Smythe, P. M., **4225:** 1255
Snelling, M. R. J., **1839:** 736
Snider, G. L., **958:** 592; **3233:** 997; **3602:** 1099, 1252
Snider, T. H., **3834:** 1131
Sniffen, R. C., **1711:** 724
Snodgrass, P. J., **335f:** 827
Sobel, M., **1987:** 758
Sochocky, S., **1129:** 633, 634; **1765:** 732; **2152:** 770
Sodeman, W. A., **2762:** 915
Soergel, K. H., **3751:** 1122, 1123, 1125, 1128; **3765:**
    1123
Sohn, E., **1116:** 622
Sokoloff, L., **3630:** 1103
Sokolov, R. A., **2543:** 874
Sollaccio, P. A., **2523:** 873
Solovay, J., **3953:** 1162
Sommer, F., **231:** 117
Sommerville, R. G., **3184:** 986
Somner, A. R., **400:** 157, 757, 763, 1253
Sones, M., **3637:** 1104
Sorsdahl, O. A., **1118:** 1069, 1075
Sosman, M. C., **574:** 193, 249, 1131, 1132, 1134
Soto, P. J., **1458:** 682, 683
Southard, M. E., **1516:** 689, 690
Southworth, R., **2163:** 770
Souza, R. C., **1914:** 740
Sowerbutts, J. G., **929:** 583
Spear, G. S., **2536:** 874
Spear, H. C., **1627:** 711
Speizer, F. E., **3111:** 982; **3112:** 982; **3113:** 982; **3174:**
    985
Spencer, H., **961:** 593, 596, 605, 608, 611, 677, 686,
    693, 696, 698, 702, 704, 705, 708, 709, 716, 720, 721,
    722, 732, 794, 848, 897, 1106, 1116, 1129; **2546:** 875
Sperling, D. R., **2409:** 840
Spickard, A., **1400:** 674, 675
Spinka, J., **1789:** 733, 1253
Spittell, J. A., Jr., **2355:** 826, 827
Spittle, M. F., **2238:** 794
Spock, A., **3446:** 1063
Spodick, D. H., **553:** 178
Spratt, J. S., Jr., **179:** 101, 769; **665:** 301, 769
Sprecace, G. A., **3785:** 1125
Springett, V. H., **1834:** 736, 737, 757
Sproule, B. J., **2379:** 830, 1135
Stack, B. H. R., **3642:** 1105, 1109
Staines, F. H., **2755:** 910
Stallybrass, F. C., **1338:** 665
Stamm, **1025:** 186
Standerfer, J. E., **882:** 576
Standertskjöld-Nordenstam, C., **214:** 115, 132
Stanford, W., **4055:** 1192
Staple, T. W., **698:** 324, 1032, 1033
Stark, J. E., **3185:** 986
Staub, N. C., **22:** 7, 35, 43, 46, 48, 51, 52, 86; **89:** 46;
    92: 47, 53
Stead, W. W., **1099:** 615; **1101:** 616, 617, 620, 621

Steckel, R. J., **246**: 120
Steel, S. J., **993**: 159
Steele, J. D., **613**: 260; **1745**: 731, 765, 766, 769, 794, 801; **2133**: 765, 766
Stein, G. N., **2316**: 812, 816, 821, 1155
Stein, H. F., **1806**: 734
Stein, M., **335**: 807
Stein, P. D., **2337**: 822
Steinberg, B., **3691**: 1110
Steinberg, I., **273**: 125; **284**: 125, 127, 583; **639**: 286, 574, 576; **838**: 569; **867**: 574, 576; **871**: 574, 576; **887**: 576; **2123**: 636; **3016**: 965; **3398**: 1044; **4074**: 1201; **4076**: 1201
Steinborn, K. E., **4260**: 1260
Steiner, H. A., **835**: 569
Steiner, M., **1147**: 637
Steiner, R. E., **207**: 115, 132; **756**: 841; **2423**: 848
Steinmetz, W. H., **4025**: 1182, 1184
Stender, H. St., **593**: 240, 854
Stengel, B. F., **2576**: 882, 883, 888
Stenhouse, A. C., **1407**: 674, 675; **3188**: 986
Stenseth, J. H., **788**: 154
Stenström, R., **1545**: 695, 696, 697
Stephanopoulos, C., **3921**: 1157
Sterling, G. M., **3046**: 972; **3141**: 984
Stern, H., **3190**: 986
Stern, H. S., **332**: 133
Stern, W. Z., **305**: 128, 1197
Sternberg, W. H., **2190**: 785
Sterner, G., **1478**: 685, 698; **2664**: 681
Stevens, A. E., **1986**: 757; **2352**: 825
Stevens, A. M., **1442**: 680
Stevens, E., **1028**: 1069
Stevens, P. M., **2435**: 852
Stewart, P. B., **809**: 66, 1149; **810**: 66
Stoker, D. J., **1190**: 643
Stolberg, H. O., **595**: 240, 246, 309, 777, 779, 1149
Stoloff, I. L., **2169**: 771
Stone, D. J., **3365**: 1024, 1027; **3567**: 1090, 1093; **4265**: 1260
Stoney, W. S., **279**: 125
Storer, J., **930**: 583, 1253; **4049**: 1192
Storey, C. F., **2167**: 771, 1152
Stork, W. J., **877**: 573, 574, 576
Stott, H., **2730**: 908, 917
Stout, A. P., **1795**: 734
Stovin, P. G. I., **758**: 843, 861; **3377**: 1032
Strand, R. D., **3719**: 918
Strang, C., **1955**: 746
Strang, L. B., **3072**: 979; **3861**: 1135
Strauss, W. G., **2521**: 873
Strax, T. E., **4007**: 1179
Streete, B. G., **1749**: 1076; **4015**: 1179
Streeter, G. L., **827**: 568
Stretton, T. B., **2553**: 879, 882
Strickland, B., **2176**: 775, 779, 782
Strickland, N. J., **2062**: 761
Strott, C. A., **1741**: 730
Strug, L. H., **1924**: 740
Stuart-Harris, C. H., **3127**: 983
Stur, O., **3461**: 1063
Sturm, A., Jr., **4156**: 1236
Sturtevant, H. N., **3427**: 1052
Sturzenegger, H., **1814**: 735
Sugg, W. L., **4092**: 1214
Sugita, K., **3944**: 1160
Suhs, R. H., **3397**: 1043

Sullivan, M. P., **1537**: 693, 694
Sumerling, M. D., **309**: 128
Sundberg, R. H., **3009**: 964, 965
Sunderman, F. W., **2511**: 871
Surprenant, E. L., **938**: 119; **3325**: 1020; **3492**: 1066
Sutherland, G. R., **936**: 115
Sutherland, I., **3556**: 1088
Sutinen, S., **691**: 324, 1014, 1015
Sutnick, A. I., **879**: 207; **927**: 207; **2307**: 807, 812
Sutter, V. L., **1038**: 600, 601
Sutton, D., **289**: 127, 578, 581
Suwanik, R., **1655**: 716
Swann, N. H., **1495**: 687
Swanson, A. G., **3319**: 1018
Swedlund, H. A., **3044**: 972
Sweet, H. C., **3230**: 997; **3331**: 1020
Sweet, R. S., **1044**: 604
Sweeting, J., **1093**: 614
Sweetman, W. R., **2212**: 792
Swenson, E. W., **64**: 35, 53; **335m**: 807
Swensson, Å., **2983**: 954
Swensson, N. L., **3923**: 1158, 1159
Swierenga, J., **3789**: 1128
Swyer, P. R., **710**: 330, 1033, 1039, 1044, 1052; **3872**: 1136
Sybers, R. G., **3779**: 1125, 1128

Tacquet, A., **511**: 176, 1152, 1164
Taft, P. D., **552**: 178
Tai, E., **3088**: 980
Taiana, J. A., **1642**: 713, 715
Takahashi, M., **2388**: 830; **3704**: 1116
Takaro, T., **268**: 124
Takeuchi, A., **875**: 574, 576
Takino, M., **3041**: 972
Tala, P., **1714**: 724, 725
Talal, N., **2195**: 785; **2647**: 896
Talamo, R. C., **366**: 147, 1001; **3256**: 1001
Talbot, P. S., **3598**: 1099
Talbott, J. A., **2550**: 879
Taleghani-Far, M., **1318**: 663, 664
Tamas, A., **4103**: 1220
Tamir, M., **2971**: 954
Tammeling, G. J., **849**: 569
Tan, D. Y. M., **1515**: 689, 690, 692
Tanaka, S., **2992**: 955
Tannehill, A. W., Jr., **1626**: 711
Tannenberg, J., **3393**: 1043
Taplin, G. V., **327**: 133
Tarkoff, M. P., **3259**: 1001
Tarnowski, C. E., **445**: 163
Tashjian, A. H., Jr., **2065**: 761; **2066**: 761
Tauxe, W. N., **2342**: 823
Tauzon, R. A., **1625**: 711
Tavel, M. E., **4308**: 1268
Taylor, A. B., **1910**: 739, 740
Taylor, A. J., **503**: 175
Taylor, D. A., **4174**: 1240
Taylor, D. M., **2073**: 761
Taylor, F. B., Jr., **3862**: 1135
Taylor, R. L., **3608**: 1102
Taylor, R. R., **2259**
Taylor, T. L., **2498**: 869, 1153
Taylor-Robinson, D., **1428**: 678; **1450**: 681
Teates, C. D., **3515**: 1077; **3523**: 1085

Teates, D., **3511**: 1076
Tebrock, H. E., **2925**: 947
Teculescu, D. B., **3090**: 980
Tellesson, W. G., **1355**: 665, 666
Temple, H. L., **658**: 291
Templeton, A. W., **1926**: 1085; **2138**: 765; **4027**: 1182
Ten Eyck, E. A., **1786**: 733, 1162
Teplick, J. G., **2321**: 808
Terrell, E. E., **364**: 192
Terris, M., **3528**: 1087, 1088
Thalhammer, O., **1580**: 703
Theodos, P. A., **2876**: 940, 942
Theologides, A., **1579**: 703
Theron, C. P., **2806**: 921
Theros, E. G., **3749**: 1125
Thibault, P., **2233**: 793
Thomas, B. M., **1722**: 725, 730
Thomas, D. P., **335b**: 807; **2299**: 806
Thomas, E. W. P., **2637**: 896
Thomas, H. S., **999**: 162, 163
Thombs, D. D., **1437**: 679, 1149
Thompsett, D. H., **342**: 137
Thompson, C. A., **1523**: 690
Thompson, E. N., **2361**: 826
Thompson, G. S., **2051**: 760
Thompson, J., **3706**: 1116
Thomson, A. E., **4261**: 1260
Thomson, W. N., **2500**: 869, 875
Thorn, N. A., **2088**: 762
Thorne, P. S., **3906**: 1156
Thorsøe, H., **4000**: 1175
Thurlbeck, W. M., **12**: 3, 134; **337**: 135, 137; **947**: 987, 988, 997, 999, 1016; **2923**: 947; **3199**: 988; **3200**: 988; **3201**: 988; **3218**: 991, 999, 1002, 1008, 1014, 1015, 1017, 1018, 1020, 1021, 1022, 1023, 1253; **3227**: 995, 1000; **3281**: 1014, 1015
Tierney, D. F., **50**: 34, 304, 816
Tillotson, J. R., **1042**: 600, 601; **1043**: 601, 606; **1055**: 606; **1056**: 606, 607; **1088**: 612; **1501**: 688
Timbrell, V., **2828**: 933; **3276**: 907
Timmerman, J. C., **4272**: 1260
Ting, E. Y., **721**: 1224; **4318**: 338
Ting, Y. M., **1351**: 1069
Tinne, J. E., **1036**: 600
Titus, J. L., **1831**: 736
Toigo, A., **1342**: 665
Tomlin, P. J., **3443**: 1062
Tong, J. L., **1396**: 673
Tooley, W. H., **54**: 34
Torrance, D. J., Jr., **2313**: 807, 808, 809, 812, 816, 821
Torres, G., **3348**: 1022
Totten, R. S., **2753**: 910
Tow, D. E., **2315**: 807, 823, 824
Towey, J. W., **2777**: 916
Town, J. D., **2886**: 943
Townley, R. G., **2530**: 873, 874
Trackler, R. T., **801**: 359
Tralka, G. A., **1794**: 734
Trapnell, D. H., **112**: 66; **594**: 240, 309; **677**: 66, 306, 308, 309; **680**: 309
Travis, D. M., **4200**: 1245
Travis, R. E., **1394**: 673
Trench, N. F., **1030**: 598
Trevathan, R. D., **1387**: 672, 673
Triebwasser, J. H., **1510**: 689, 690, 692, 693
Trinidad, S., **2258**: 801
Trivedi, S. A., **4208**: 1246

Trombold, J. S., **3902**: 1155
Trossman, C. M., **931**: 583
Troupin, R. H., **1728**: 724, 725
Truitt, G. W., **3051**: 972
Tsagaris, T. J., **2407**: 840
Tsai, S. H., **1181**: 641, 642; **3435**: 1058; **3976**: 1167, 1174
Tscherne, H., **2378**: 830
Tschumy, W., Jr., **2512**: 871
Tsitouris, G., **4256**: 1260
Tsuboi, E., **2122**: 764
Tucker, R. M., **3759**: 1122
Tuddenham, W. J., **172**: 99, 100, 102, 104, 105, 106, 297; **173**: 99; **174**: 99; **175**: 99; **189**: 105
Tuffanelli, D. L., **2625**: 894
Tuft, L., **3108**: 981
Tuhy, J. E., **2529**: 873, 874
Tunevall, G., **480**: 169
Tung, K. S. K., **4057**: 1192
Turiaf, J., **831**: 568; **3570**: 1090
Turk, L. N., III, **288**: 127, 578
Turner, J. A., **1446**: 680
Turner, P., **2092**: 762
Turner-Warwick, M., **68**: 37, 47, 127, 154, 577; **3676**: 1109
Twining, E. W., **18**: 5; **948a**: 306, 309
Tyler, W. S., **10**: 3
Tyrrell, D. A. J., **1402**: 674; **1412**: 675
Tyson, M. D., **1743**: 1076

UCLA Interdepartmental Conference, **2341**: 823, 826
Udwadia, F. E., **1612**: 709, 711; **1618**: 709
Uhley, H. N., **2451**: 857
Ulm, A. H., **2383**: 830
Umiker, W. O., **529**: 177, 764; **532**: 177, 736, 764; **536**: 177, 764; **537**: 177, 764; **547**: 178, 764; **548**: 178; **1832**: 736
Unfug, H. V., **4050**: 1192
Unger, J. D., **2775**: 916
Urschel, H. C., **1358**: 666, 1055, 1058; **3960**: 1164

Vadas, G., **3725**: 1118, 1119, 1159
Valle, A. R., **830**: 568, 569
Vallebona, A., **219**: 116
Vance, J. W., **2132**: 765
Van Der Schaar, P. J., **403**: 157, 764
Van de Weyer, K. H., **640**: 286, 574
Van Epps, E. F., **2406**: 840
Van Heerden, J. A., **1006**: 167
Vanier, T., **3307**: 1018
Varma, B. N., **3859**: 1134
Varriale, P., **2542**: 874
Vassar, P. S., **1736**: 730
Vaughan, B. F., **715**: 331; **2181**: 777; **4125**: 1229
Velican, C., **2804**: 920, 1252
Veneziale, C. M., **4054**: 1192
Vessey, M. P., **2281**: 805
Veterans Administration–Armed Forces Cooperative Study on Histoplasmosis, **1242**: 651
Veterans Administration–Armed Forces Study on the Chemotherapy of Tuberculosis, **4110**
Veterans Administration Cooperative Study of Blastomycosis, **1270**: 656, 657

Veterans Administration Cooperative Study on Histoplasmosis, **1245**: 651

Viamonte, M., Jr., **290**: 127; **783**: 852, 857; **857**: 571, 577

Vieta, J. D., **3896**: 1149

Vigliani, E. C., **2800**: 920

Vineberg, A. M., **2333**: 1017

Vinik, M., **1070**: 608

Viola, A. R., **3362**: 1024, 1027, 1032

Viswanathan, R., **3846**: 1131

Vogel, C. L., **1606**: 705

Vogel, M. D., **2048**: 760

Vogel, R. A., **1286**: 659; **1287**: 659

Vogl, A., **386**: 154; **4106**: 1220

Voisin, C., **490**: 169, 666

Volini, F. I., **1142**: 636

Volk, T. E., **1087**: 612

von Gsell, O., **1866**: 737

von Hayek, H., **15**: 4, 10, 12, 35, 61, 62, 80, 240; **24**: 10, 48

von Neergaard, K., **44**: 33

Vorwald, A. J., **2864**: 939

Wachtel, F. W., **4175**: 1240

Wacker, W. E. C., **522**: 176, 1155; **523**: 176, 826, 1155

Wada, N., **1890**: 738

Wada, S., **1891**: 739

Wada, Y., **2504**: 871

Waddell, J. A., **700**: 324, 588

Wade, G., **2644**: 896

Wagenvoort, C. A., **891**: 577, 734

Wagner, H. N., Jr., **329**: 133, 823; **335q**: 133; **941**: 133; **1971**: 756; **2340**: 822

Wagner, J. C., **2826**: 933, 936, 937, 1164

Wagoner, J. K., **1877**: 738; **1892**: 739

Walker, J. M., **3796**: 1128

Walker, S. H., **1066**: 608

Walker, W. A., **306**: 128

Walker, W. C., **2573**: 882

Wall, C. A., **902**: 581

Wallace, S. L., **3628**: 1103

Walske, B. R., **2134**: 765, 766

Walter, J. E., **1309**: 660, 662

Walton, E. W., **2531**: 873, 874

Walton, J. N., **2630**: 894

Wan Teh-Hsing, **4017**: 1180

Wang, C. C., **3736**: 1121, 1122

Ward, H. P., **4242**: 1259

Ward, P., **2217**: 792, 793, 1150

Ward, R., **2554**: 879, 882, 883

Ware, G. W., **3503**: 1067

Warfvinge, L. E., **2128**: 765

Waring, W. W., **3433**: 1055, 1063

Warkany, J., **834**: 569

Warner, R. R. P., **1737**: 730

Warraki, S. E., **2988**: 955; **4143**: 1232

Warren, S., **1997**: 758

Warring, F. C., Jr., **1168**: 641

Wasserman, K., **3832**: 1131

Watabe, T., **3297**: 1017

Watanabe, S., **3330**: 1020

Waterhouse, B. E., **4060**: 1192

Waters, M. H., **3847**: 1131, 1134

Watson, A. J., **2865**: 939

Watson, W. L., **1923**: 740, 770, 771

Wayl, P., **1152**: 637

Weary, P. E., **2688**: 905

Weaver, A. L., **2627**: 894

Webb, J. K. G., **1619**: 709

Webb, W. R., **818**: 34; **1779**: 732

Webber, M. M., **127**: 64

Weber, A. L., **1102**: 617, 620, 621; **2926**: 947

Weber, D. M., **1511**: 689

Weber, H. H., **248**: 120

Webster, B. H., **1570**: 702

Webster, I., **2825**: 933, 936, 937

Webster, J. R., Jr., **2357**: 826; **3125**: 983, 984

Wechsler, H. F., **1542**: 695

Weed, L. A., **1224**: 645, 664; **1322**: 664

Weg, J. G., **2390**: 830; **4231**: 1258

Wegener, F., **2525**: 873

Weibel, E. R., **9**: 3, 137; **81**: 43, 86, 91; **339**: 136

Weidner, W., **2330**: 821, 822, 823

Weilgoni, M., **4149**: 1235

Weill, H., **6**: 192; **2707**: 907, 973; **2708**: 907, 973; **2769**: 915

Weinstein, A. S., **147**: 85

Weisel, William, **669**: 301, 731, 769

Weisel, Wilson, **1719**: 725, 730, 1253

Weiss, L., **1710**: 724

Weiss, W., **427**: 161; **663**: 301, 769; **803**: 362; **1060**: 607; **1092**: 613, 961; **1937**: 740, 769; **2148**: 769; **3147**: 984

Weisser, A., **2465**: 861

Weitzner, S., **1805**: 734

Welch, C. C., **1026**: 598, 599, 1147

Welch, H., **3030**: 970

Welch, M. H., **4330**: 1006

Wellington, J. L., **1798**: 734; **3903**: 1155

Wells, R. E., Jr., **3195**: 987

Wendt, V. E., **2411**: 841

Wenger, M. E., **4026**: 1182, 1184

Wenzel, F. J., **2745**: 909, 910

Werk, E. E., Jr., **2041**: 760

Werner, W. A., **1303**: 659, 660

Wessell, H. U., **1673**: 721

Wessler, S., **4224**: 1255

West, J. B., **103**: 50, 51; **106**: 50; **107**: 51, 52, 185; **766**: 845; **2441**: 854

West, J. R., **3682**: 1109

West, W. O., **3299**: 1017; **3617**: 1102

Westermark, N., **157**: 87, 808, 1155; **167**: 98

Westra, D., **227**: 116

Wetherhold, J. M., **4298**: 1264

Wheeler, P. C., **844**: 569

Whitaker, W., **622**: 283

White, F. C., **1150**: 637

White, H., **3463**: 1063

White, W. F., **1591**: 704

Whitehouse, G., **2426**: 851, 1066

Whitfield, A. G. W., **3932**: 1153

Whitley, J. E., **166**: 98; **736**: 4325: 838

Whittaker, L. D., Jr., **4117**: 1125

Whittenberger, J. L., **3155**: 984

Wholey, M. H., **591**: 240, 246, 253

W. H. O. Technical Report, **2434**: 852; **3225**: 852, 995

Widdicombe, J. G., **238**: 119, 140; **348**: 140

Wiener, L., **2382**: 830

Wiener, S. N., **2296**: 806, 808, 809, 821, 822, 826

Wier, J. A., **829**: 568, 581, 1235

Wiernik, G., **3345**: 1026, 1077

Wiita, R. M., **969**: 596, 597

Wikler, A., **1373**: 669
Wilcox, K. R., **1209**: 643, 644
Wilder, C. E., **943**: 127
Wilens, S. L., **2285**: 806
Wilhelmsen, L., **2360**: 826, 827
Wilk, S. P., **220**: 116
Wilkinson, P. C., **2012**: 758
Williams, A. W., **3696**: 1111, 1116
Williams, B., **1528**: 692
Williams, E. D., **2053**: 761
Williams, H., **3500**: 1067
Williams, J. F., Jr., **3355**: 1022, 1023
Williams, J. R., **280**: 125, 807, 809, 816, 821, 822; **636**: 286, 1069; **1124**: 1069; **1253**: 1069, 1075; **2312**: 807; **2377**: 829, 1069, 1075; **3901**: 1155, 1156, 1161
Williams, J. V., **2757**: 911
Williams, K. R., **3933**: 1159
Williams, M. H., Jr., **3084**: 980; **3115**: 982, 1058, 1062; **3344**: 1021, 1023; **3359**: 1023; **3360**: 1023
Williams, R., **2829**: 934
Williams, R. T., **2094**: 762
Williams, W. J., **1879**: 738; **2848**: 936; **2922**: 947
Willis, R. A., **2220**: 792, 797
Willson, J. K. V., **239**: 119, 120
Wilson, D. E., **1392**: 673
Wilson, J. F., **1634**: 712, 713
Wilson, J. G., **833**: 569; **2466**: 861
Wilson, J. T., **443**: 162
Wilson, L. L., **1305**: 660
Wilson, M. G., **3871**: 1136
Wilson, M. M., **559**: 168
Wilson, R. E., **3995**: 1174
Wilson, R. H., **3144**: 984
Wilson, R. J., **2612**: 889, 894, 1252
Wilson, T. M., **1121**: 624
Wilson, W. J., **737**: 577
Wilson, W. R., **2424**: 851; **4232**: 1258
Wimpfheimer, F., **365**: 147, 1001
Winfield, M. E., **746**: 573, 841
Winkelmann, R. K., **2632**: 894, 895
Winkler, A. W., **2078**: 761
Winn, W. A., **1200**: 653; **1254**: 654; **1256**: 654
Winnacker, J. L., **3597**: 1099, 1102
Winslow, W. A., **2499**: 869, 1153
Winter, B., **1693**: 654
Winterbauer, R. H., **2638**: 896
Winters, W. L., Jr., **2641**: 896
Wisoff, C. P., **3428**: 1052
Witorsch, P., **1266**: 656, 657
Witten, D. M., **653**: 291, 578
Wittenborg, M. H., **144**: 80, 81, 1218
Wohlfeld, G. M., **3865**: 1135
Wójtowicz, J., **74**: 41, 117, 328
Wolcott, M. W., **1700**: 613, 961
Wolfe, J. N., **1296**: 659
Wolfel, D. A., **299**: 127; **2206**: 790, 791, 1249; **4058**: 1192

Wolff, G., **2147**: 769
Wolfson, J. J., **2685**: 904
Wolopitz, A., **1236**: 648, 654
Wood, J. A., **3479**: 1064
Wood, P., **2297**: 806
Wood, W. H., Jr., **1556**: 697
Woodruff, C. E., **1897**: 739, 758; **1990**: 758
Woodruff, J. H., **2155**: 770, 771
Woods, L. P., **1223**: 645
Woodward, S. C., **1592**: 704
Woolcock, A. J., **3021**: 968, 979, 1019, 1052; **3022**: 968, 980; **3080**: 979, 980; **3085**: 980
Wooley, C. F., **1226**: 645
Woolner, L. B., **544**: 177, 757, 764, 1253
Wright, G. L. T., **3056**: 973
Wright, R. R., **60**: 34, 1001
Wrinch, J., **2464**: 860
Wróblewski, F., **516**: 176; **517**: 176, 765
Wurm, K., **3565**: 1090; **3566**: 1090
Wyatt, J. P., **2868**: 939; **2940**: 948
Wychulis, A. R., **3508**: 1067
Wyman, S. M., **272**: 125
Wynder, E. L., **1846**: 736; **1851**: 737; **3137**: 984
Wynn-Williams, N., **3624**: 1103; **4162**: 1239

Yacoub, M. H., **381**: 153, 759
Yacoubian, H., **1775**: 732
Yam, L. T., **1018**: 177
Yeh, T. J., **957**: 592
Yen, H. C., **1663**: 720
Young, D. G., **4116**: 1225, 1229
Young, R. C., Jr., **3606**: 1099
Young, R. L., **3599**: 1099, 1252; **3627**: 1103
Young, W. A., **3650**: 1105, 1106, 1160
Yow, E. M., **1546**: 695, 697
Yu, P. N., **703**: 329, 840
Yue, W. Y., **1004**: 164, 165
Yurick, B. S., **4024**: 1182, 1184

Záček, V., **2261**
Zaid, G., **3038**: 971
Zak, F. G., **1803**: 734, 1252
Zaky, H. A., **1668**: 721, 722; **1677**: 722
Zamorano, J., Jr., **1182**: 642
Zasly, L., **3301**: 1017
Zatuchni, J., **2031**: 760; **2349**: 823
Zdansky, E., **590**: 228
Zelefsky, M. M., **937**: 115, 132
Zerfas, A. J., **3414**: 1051
Zinn, B., **192**: 108
Ziskind, M. M., **19**: 6, 192, 798; **20**: 6, 192
Zorab, P. A., **4185**: 1241, 1243

SUBJECT INDEX

Note: Page numbers in *italics* indicate illustrations; (t) indicates table.

Abrams needle, 161
Abscess, 266
  carcinoid bronchial adenoma producing, 728
  lung. See *Lung abscess.*
  mediastinal and acute retropharyngeal, *1168-1169*
  pyemic, *457*
    differential diagnosis of, 460-461(t)
  subphrenic, *531*, 1232, *1233, 1234*
    differential diagnosis of, 520-521(t), 536-537(t)
    pleural effusion in, 1157
Acanthosis nigricans, 760
Acid-base balance of blood, disturbances in, 56, 57(t)
Acidosis, 47
Acinar, use of term, 6
Acinar interstitial space. See *Parenchymal interstitial space.*
Acinar shadow(s), 5, 6, *190, 191*
  causes of, 192
  in metastatic disease, 799
  with air-space edema, 855
Acinar units, diffusion of gas in, 47
    measurement of, 183
  perfusion of, 43
    measurement of, 183
Acinar ventilation, 30
  mechanics of, 31
    measurement of, 181
"Acino-nodose" lesion, 5, 191
Acinus(i). See also entries under *Lung parenchyma* and *Parenchymal.*
  anatomy of, 2-5
  as roentgenologic unit, 5-7
  diagram of, in centrilobular emphysema, *998*
  function of, 7-8
  parts of, 2
ACTH (adrenocorticotrophic hormone), in bronchial adenoma, 730
Actinomyces israelii, 662-663. See also *Actinomycosis.*
  differentiation from *Nocardia*, 662
  in differential diagnosis, 386-387(t), 400-401(t), 416-417(t), 428-429(t), 534-535(t)
  pleural effusion due to, 1147
Actinomycosis, 662-663. See also *Actinomyces israelii.*
  cervicofacial, 662
  differential diagnosis of, 386-387(t), 400-401(t), 416-417(t), 534-535(t)
  pulmonary, *663*
ADE (alveolar-duct emphysema), 999
Adenocarcinoma, 740, 755, *930*
  clear-cell, *451*
  peripheral, *263, 264*

Adenoma, bronchial, *200, 223*, 724-730
  ACTH (adrenocorticotrophic hormone) in, 730
  carcinoid, 724, *726, 727*
    producing obstructive pneumonitis and abscess formation, 728
    solitary nodule of, 729
  clinical manifestations of, 725
  differential diagnosis of, 400-401(t), 442-443(t)
  pathologic characteristics of, 724
  roentgenographic manifestations of, 725
  salivary gland types of, 724
  mucoepidermoid, 725
  pleomorphic, 724
Adenomatoid malformation of lung, cystic, congenital, 588
  differential diagnosis of, 410-411(t)
Adenoviral pneumonia, 689
Adenovirus(es), differential diagnosis of, 400-401(t), 410-411(t), 416-417(t)
Adenovirus respiratory infection, 688-689
ADH (antidiuretic hormone), inappropriate secretion of, in bronchial carcinoma, 761
Adventitious sounds, 152, 152(t)
Aerobacter species, 604-606. See also entries under *Klebsiella.*
Agammaglobulinemias, 899
  acquired, primary, 900, *901*
    secondary, 900
  congenital, 899
  Swiss-type, 902
Agenesis, of left pulmonary artery, *510*
  of lung, 568-569
Air, inspired, distribution of, measurement of, 184
Air bronchogram, 193
  absence of, in atelectasis, 220
Air cyst, pulmonary, 336, 341
Air drift, collateral, 4, 198
  interference of, 203
  interlobar, *200*
  with air-trapping, *201*
Air pollution, influence on chronic bronchitis, 984
Air sign, extrapleural, 1175
Air-gap roentgenographic technique, 105
Air-space atelectasis, air-space consolidation and interstitial pulmonary disease, 256, *258*
Air-space consolidation, 7, *190*
  absence of collapse in, 193
  air-space atelectasis and interstitial pulmonary disease, 256, *258*
  and interstitial pulmonary disease, 256, *257*
  in acute pulmonary edema, 7

Air-space consolidation (*Continued*)
  nonsegmental distribution of, 192
  peripheral, *189*
  roentgenologic signs of, 194
Air-space disease, 842. See also *Lung disease.*
  and interstitial pulmonary disease, *246, 247,* 256-
    258
  roentgenologic signs of, 189-239
Air-space pneumonia. See *Pneumonia, air-space.*
Air-trapping, bullae showing, *1026*
  collateral air drift with, *201*
  in spasmodic asthma, *323*
  inspiratory-expiratory roentgenography for investi-
    gation of, 108, *109*
  overinflation with, *324*
Airways, and pulmonary ventilation, 8-36
  diseases of, 966-1067
    with normal roentgenogram, 1253-1255
  resistance of, 34
  roentgenology of, 10-13
  small, disease of, 1052-1055, *1056-1057*
    differential diagnosis of, 488-489(t)
Airway anastomoses, direct, 4, 198
Airway obstruction, 326
  assessment of, in chronic obstructive pulmonary dis-
    ease, 1019
  due to bronchogenic carcinoma, 742
  peripheral, effects of, *203*
    resorption atelectasis due to, *204*
Airway resistance, measurement of, 182
    direct, in chronic obstructive pulmonary disease,
    968
  use of mouth pressure for determining, 183
Albumin, macroaggregates of, 132
Aleutian-mink disease, 1143
Allescheria boydii, 673
Allescheriasis, 673
Aluminosis, 947-948
  differential diagnosis of, 486-487(t)
Alveolar dead space, 51
Alveolar ducts, 2, *2*
Alveolar gas, composition of, 30
    measurement of, 180
Alveolar hypersensitivity, 908-918
  diseases of, differential diagnosis of, 484-485(t), 496-
    497(t)
Alveolar hypoventilation syndromes, 842
Alveolar perfusion, 50
Alveolar pneumonia, 590
  acute, consolidation in, 192
Alveolar pores, 4. See also *Pores of Kohn.*
Alveolar sacs, 2, *2*
Alveolar ventilation, 50
Alveolar-capillary gas exchange, 30
"Alveolar-filling" diseases, 6
"Alveolarization," 120
Alveolitis, allergic, extrinsic, 907. See also *Hyper-
    sensitivity, alveolar.*
  fibrosing, 253. See also *Hamman-Rich disease.*
  necrotizing, 879
    differential diagnosis of, 470-471(t)
Alveolocapillary membrane, diffusion across, 47
Alveolus(i), 2, *2*
Amebiasis, 701-703
  differential diagnosis of, 386-387(t), 428-429(t), 536-
    537(t)
  pleuropulmonary, 702
Amebic dysentery, 701

Aminoaciduria, renal, cor pulmonale and familial re-
    tardation of growth, 1142-1143
Amosite, 933
"Amphoric" breathing, 151
Amyloidosis, bronchopulmonary, 1121-1122
  differential diagnosis of, 404-405(t), 446-447(t), 462-
    463(t), 490-491(t), 516-517(t)
Anastomoses, airway, direct, 4, 198
  arteriovenous, 37
Ancylostoma duodenale, 708
  in differential diagnosis, 386-387(t)
Ancylostomiasis, 708
Anemia, 55, 178
  as complication of bronchial carcinoma, 763
Aneurysm(s), aortic, *1203, 1204*
  differential diagnosis of, 564-565(t)
  congenital, of pulmonary arteries, 573
  of ascending arch of aorta, 1201, *1202*
  of innominate artery, 1205
    differential diagnosis of, 564-565(t)
  of thoracic aorta, 1201
"Aneurysm of signs," 1201
Angiitis, hypersensitivity, 875
Angiocardiography, 125
  "levogram" phase of, 127
Angiography, 39, 123-128, *124*
  assessment of arterial deficiency emphysema with,
    1007
  in thromboembolic disease, *125,* 821
  indications for, 124
  of superior vena cava, 127
  techniques of, 123
Angiokeratoma corporis diffusum universali, 1139-
    1142
Angiomas, spider, in cirrhosis of liver, differential
    diagnosis of, 490-491(t)
Angiosarcoma, 734
Angle of Louis, 72
Anhydrase, carbonic, 56
Animal inoculation, 168
Anomaly(ies), congenital, cardiac, differential diagno-
    sis of, 504-505(t)
  of ribs, 1236
  Ebstein's, *329, 500*
  of heart and great vessels, 577
  of pulmonary vasculature, 569-577
  tracheobronchial, 13
Anthophyllite, 933
Anthrax, 599
Aorta, 38, *74*
  aneurysm of, dissecting, 1201, *1204*
    pain due to, 145
    traumatic, *1203*
  coarctation of, *1237*
  dilatation of, *1201*
  thoracic, aneurysms of, 1201
Aortic arch, 95
Aortic knob, *93*
Aortic valve, 38
Aortic vascular ring, congenital, 1205
Aortography, indications for, 127
  mediastinal lesion assessment with, *126*
  techniques of, 125
    Seldinger, *126*
Aplasia, of lung, 568-569
  thymic, hereditary, 902
Apophyses, ununited, 1235
ARD (acute respiratory disease), 675

Armillifer armillatus, 722
Arterial oxygen saturation, 54, 56
Arterial supply, systemic, to lung, 577
Arteriography, bronchial, 127
  in diagnosis of bronchial carcinoma, 756
Arterioles, precapillary, 37
Arteriosus, patent ductus (PDA), 838
  with Eisenmenger reaction, *837*
Arteriovenous anastomoses, 37
Arteritis, pulmonary, rheumatoid disease with, 888
Artery(ies), basilar, anterior, 38
  bronchial, 37
  innominate, aneurysm of, 1205
    differential diagnosis of, 564-565(t)
    buckling of, 1205
    elongation of, differential diagnosis of, 564-565(t)
  interlobar, left, 95
    right, 38, *38,* 40, *93*
  lingular, 40
  pulmonary. See *Pulmonary artery.*
  small, embolic disease to, differential diagnosis of,
    504-505(t)
  thrombosed, 816
  thrombotic, line shadows due to, 315
  "transitional," 36
Arthropod infestation, 722
Asbestos, influence on bronchogenic carcinoma,
  737
Asbestosis, 933-937, *935*
  and squamous cell carcinoma, 737
  clinical manifestations of, 936
  differential diagnosis of, 486-487(t)
  epidemiology of, 933
  pathologic characteristics of, 934
  pulmonary function studies for, 936
  relationship to neoplasia, 936
  roentgenographic manifestations of, 934
  symptoms and signs of, 936
Ascariasis, 705
  differential diagnosis of, 386-387(t)
Ascaris lumbricoides, in differential diagnosis, 386-
  387(t)
ASD (atrial septal defect), *814, 836,* 838
Aspergillosis, 664-668
  allergic, 907
  disseminated, opportunistic, *670*
  hypersensitivity, 666, *667*
  primary, 665
    differential diagnosis of, 386-387(t), 400-401(t),
      416-417(t)
  pulmonary, primary, opportunistic, *669*
  secondary, 666
    pulmonary mycetoma in, 666
  serologic studies of, 668
  with chronic debilitating disease, 668
Aspergillus fumigatus, 664-668. See also *Aspergillosis.*
  in differential diagnosis, 442-443(t)
Aspergillus niger, 664
Aspergillus species, in differential diagnosis, 386-
  387(t), 400-401(t), 410-411(t), 416-417(t), 428-429(t),
  536-537(t)
Aspiration, acute lung abscess secondary to, 960
  of metallic mercury, 831
  of solid foreign bodies, 956-958
    differential diagnosis of, 402-403(t), 418-419(t),
      514-515(t)
Aspiration pneumonia. See *Pneumonia, aspiration.*

Asthma, 969-982
  atopic, 907, 971
  bakers', 972
  bronchial, "tram-lines" in, *976*
  bronchial plugging and atelectasis in, 1058-1062
  clinical manifestations of, 977
  complications of, 981
  etiology of, 970
  extrinsic, 907, 971
  flow rates in, effect of exercise on, *974*
  incidence of, 969
  infective, 971
  intrinsic, 971
  lower respiratory tract infection in, 981
  laboratory findings in, 978
  pathogenesis of, 970
  pathologic characteristics of, 975
  pneumomediastinum with, 981
  prognosis of, 981
  pulmonary function abnormalities in, 979
  roentgenographic manifestations of, 975
  spasmodic, 236, *333*
    air-trapping in, *323*
    airway dynamics in, 977
  Tokyo-Yokohama, 973
Atelectasis, 196-239, 1062
  absence of air bronchogram in, 220
  adhesive, 197, 207, *208*
    in acute radiation pneumonitis, *208*
    postoperative, differential diagnosis of, 404-405(t)
  air-space, air-space consolidation and interstitial
    pulmonary disease, 256, *258*
  and bronchial plugging, in asthma, 1058-1062
  and consolidation, of left upper lobe, *295*
  bronchogenic carcinoma and, 742
  changes in chest wall in, 220
  cicatrization, 197, 209
    generalized, 210, *211*
    in interstitial pulmonary fibrosis, *212*
    localized, 209, *209, 210*
    with compensatory overinflation, *213, 214*
  compensatory overinflation in, 217
  compression, 197, 206, *207*
  discoid. See *Plate-like atelectasis.*
  displacement of hila in, 220
  elevation of hemidiaphragm in, 213
  lobar, 222
    combined, 230
  "mantle." See *Atelectasis, compression.*
  mediastinal displacement in, 216
  nonobstructive, 197, 203, 207. See also *Atelectasis,
    adhesive.*
  obstructive, massive pleural effusion associated with,
    353
  of lower lobes, 229, *231*
    left, *215, 233, 234*
    right, *232*
      and right middle lobe, 230, *235*
    of right middle lobe, 228, *228, 229,* 230, *298*
    of upper lobe, left, *225, 225, 226, 227, 296*
      right, 222, *222, 223, 224*
        and right middle lobe, 231, *236*
  parenchymal, 196-239
  passive, 197, 204, *205*
    with pneumothorax, *204*
  patterns of, 220
  plate-like, 301, *302, 303*

Atelectasis (*Continued*)
  plate-like, associated with pulmonary infarction, *820*
    in pulmonary embolism and infarction, 816
    line shadows due to, 301, *302, 303*
  platter. See *Atelectasis, plate-like.*
  redistribution of vascular shadows in, 220
  relaxation. See *Atelectasis, passive.*
  resorption, 197, *198*
    due to peripheral airway obstruction, *204*
  roentgenographic signs of, 211, *216*, 220
  segmental, homogeneous, *396*
    of right lower lobe, *237, 238*
  subsegmental, of left upper lobe, *239*
  total pulmonary, 221
Atresia, bronchial, congenital, 583-588
    differential diagnosis of, 440-441(t), 512-513(t)
    of lateral basal bronchus, *587*
  congenital, 326
Atrial septal defect (ASD), *814, 836, 838*
  pulmonary hypertension in, *839*
Auscultation of lungs, 150
Axillary fold, *93*
Azygography, 127
Azygos continuation, of inferior vena cava, *1200*
Azygos fissure, 61, *62, 63*
Azygos lymph node, 69
Azygos vein, *73, 78*
  dilatation of, 1197
  obstruction of, differential diagnosis of, 540-541(t)
  size of, *96*
Azygos vein enlargement, effect of pregnancy on, 78
Azygos vein shadow, *79*

Bacillus anthracis, 599-600
  in differential diagnosis, 410-411(t), 428-429(t), 548-549(t)
Bacillus proteus, 606-607
  in differential diagnosis, 426-427(t)
Bacteria, causing pleural effusion, 1146
Bacterium anitratum, 610-611
  differentiation from *Neisseria*, 611
  in differential diagnosis, 384-385(t), 428-429(t), 534-535(t)
Bacterial pulmonary infections, 170(t)
Bacteriology, in pulmonary disease, 164-174
Bacteroides species, 612
  in differential diagnosis, 384-385(t), 410-411(t), 426-427(t), 534-535(t)
Bagassosis, 915
Barium-carboxymethycellulose suspensions, 123
Barytosis, 945
Basal bronchus, anterior, *20, 28*
  lateral, *21, 29*
  medial, *20*
  posterior, *21, 29*
Basement membrane, 10
Basilar artery, anterior, 38
"Bat's wing" pattern, *880-881*
  of pulmonary edema, 857, *858, 859*
Battey bacillus, 641
Bauxitosis, differential diagnosis of, 486-487(t)
BCG (bacillus of Calmette and Guerin), 615
Bedsonia respiratory disease, 695-697

Berylliosis, 945-947
  acute, 946
    differential diagnosis of, 472-473(t)
  chronic, 946
    differential diagnosis of, 486-487(t), 550-551(t)
Beryllium disease, 945-947
Besnier-Boeck-Schaumann's disease. See *Sarcoidosis.*
Biochemical tests, 175-176
Biopsy, bronchial, 122
  bronchoscopic, 158
  lung. See *Lung biopsy.*
  lymph node, 162
    mammary, 163
    mediastinal, 163
    parasternal, 163
  needle, 161
  of scalene nodes, 138, 162
  pleural, 161
    open, 161
    procedure for, 167
  pulmonary parenchymal, 158
    indications for and methods of, 160
  transbronchial pulmonary, 159
Biopsy procedures, 158-164
Black plague. See *Pasteurella pestis.*
Blastomyces brasiliensis, in differential diagnosis, 480-481(t)
Blastomyces dermatitidis, 656-657. See also *North American blastomycosis.*
  in differential diagnosis, 386-387(t), 400-401(t), 410-411(t), 416-417(t), 428-429(t), 480-481(t), 534-535(t)
  pleural effusion due to, 1148
Blastomycosis, differential diagnosis of, 386-387(t), 400-401(t), 416-417(t)
  North American. See *North American blastomycosis.*
  South American, 673
Bleb(s), 338, *338*, 341
  apical, and pneumothorax, *372*
  definition of, 1023
  differential diagnosis of, 432-433(t)
  wall of, line shadows due to, 305
Blood, acid-base balance of, disturbances in, 56, 57(t)
  capillary, distribution of, measurement of, 183, 185
  examination of, 165
  hydrogen ion concentration of, 54
    measurement of, 185
Blood flow, and ventilation, matching of, measurement of, 184
  measurement of, 183
Blood fluke, 719
Blood gases, 54
  arterial, disturbances in, in chronic obstructive pulmonary disease, 1021
  measurement of, 185
Blood pressure, measurement of pulmonary, 183
Blood serum, biochemical test of, 176
Blood volume, measurement of, 183
Blood-gas analysis, in chronic obstructive pulmonary disease, 969
"Blue-bloater," 1008
Bochdalek, foramen of. See *Foramen of Bochdalek.*
Body plethysmograph, use of, 183
Body-section roentgenography. See *Tomography.*
Boeck's sarcoid. See *Sarcoidosis.*
Bone(s), neoplasms of, 1246
  of chest wall, 83
Bordetella pertussis. See *Hemophilus pertussis.*
Boyle's law, 180

Brachiocephalic vessels, 95
Breast shadow, 93
Breath, shortness of, 142. See also *Dyspnea.*
Breathing, "amphoric," 151
   vesicular, 151
Breathing capacity, maximal (MBC), 155, 182
Bronchial adenoma. See *Adenoma, bronchial.*
Bronchial and bronchiolar division, 8, 9(t)
Bronchial arteries, 37
Bronchial arteriography, 127
Bronchial atresia. See *Atresia, bronchial.*
Bronchial biopsy, 122
Bronchial carcinoma. See *Carcinoma, bronchial.*
Bronchial cyst(s), 1192
   congenital, 581-583
   mediastinal, 582, *585, 586*
   pulmonary, 582, *583, 584*
Bronchial dynamics, in chronic bronchitis, *994*
   in emphysema, *1014*
Bronchial fracture, differential diagnosis of, 402-403(t)
Bronchial isomerism, 13
Bronchial mucous glands, 10
Bronchial obstruction, assessment with inspiratory-expiratory roentgenography, *114*
   in Hodgkin's disease, 395
Bronchial plugging, and atelectasis, in asthma, 1058-1062
Bronchial segments, Jackson-Huber nomenclature of, 11
   lobar, 12
Bronchial tree, communication of bulla with, *343*
   left, *22-25*
   morphology of, 8
   right, frontal projection, *14-15*
      lateral projection, *16-17*
   roentgenology of, 10-15
Bronchial wall shadows. See *Tubular shadows.*
Bronchiectasis, *209,* 1039-1051
   clinical manifestations of, 1048
   cylindrical, *415,* 1044, *1045*
   cystic, 1044, *1047*
      advanced, *1049*
      differential diagnosis of, 432-433(t)
   differential diagnosis of, 418-419(t)
   incidence of, 1043
   pathogenesis of, 1043
   pathologic characteristics of, 1044
   post-tussic bronchography in assessment of, *121*
   pulmonary function studies of, 1051
   reversible, 1048, *1050*
   roentgenographic manifestations of, 1044
   saccular, 1044, *1047*
      advanced, *1049*
   secondary to sulfur dioxide inhalation, *953*
   tuberculous, 630, *634*
      with fibroproductive tuberculosis, *210*
   varicose, *234, 1046*
   with normal roentgenogram, *1254*
   yellow nails and lymphedema, syndrome of, 1051
Bronchiolar filling, use of term, 120
Bronchiole(s), 8
   respiratory 2, *2*
   terminal, 2, *2*
Bronchiolectasis, 209
Bronchiolitis, acute, 1051-1052, *1053*
   differential diagnosis of, 488-489(t)
   in adult, *1054*
   secondary to sulfur dioxide inhalation, *953*

Bronchioloalveolar carcinoma. See *Carcinoma, bronchioloalveolar.*
Bronchitis, asthmatic, 983
   chronic, 842, 982-1085, *992*
      bronchial dynamics in, *994*
      bronchographic abnormalities in, 993, *994*
      clinical and physiologic manifestations of, 1015-1023
      definition of, 982
      etiology of, 984
      incidence of, 983
      increased lung markings in, 991
      influence of air pollution in, 984
      influence of infection on, 985
      influence of smoking in, 984
      overinflation in, 991
      pathogenesis of, 984
      pathologic characteristics of, 987
      roentgenographic manifestations of, 990
      "tram-lines" in, 991
      tubular shadows in, 991
      vascular deficiency in, 991
   plastic, 1058
Bronchoconstriction, reflex local, 35
Bronchogenic carcinoma. See *Carcinoma, bronchogenic.*
Bronchogenic cysts. See *Bronchial cysts.*
Bronchogram, air. See *Air bronchogram.*
Bronchography, 118-123
   contraindications for, 119
   delayed, 121. See also *Bronchography, post-tussic.*
   in assessment of bullous disease, *1030*
   in diagnosis of bronchial carcinoma, 756
   indications for, 119
   post-tussic, 121
      bronchiectasis assessment with, *121*
   selective, 121
   techniques of, 119
      aspiration, 121
      transglottic, 120
Broncholithiasis, 645, *649*
Bronchopneumonia, *259,* 591
   acute, *299, 414*
   acute confluent, *394*
Bronchopneumonitis, recurrent, 1011
Bronchopulmonary anatomy, nomenclature of, 11, 11(t)
Bronchopulmonary disease, due to nitrogen dioxide inhalation, 950-951
   secondary to burns, 956
Bronchoscopic biopsy, 158
Bronchoscopy, 156, 158
   in bronchial carcinoma, 763
Bronchospirometry, 185
Bronchostenosis, *238*
   tuberculous, 633
Bronchovascular interstitial space, *188*
Bronchus(i), 8
   apical posterior, *26*
   basal. See *Basal bronchus.*
   epithelium of, 8
   fractures of, 1075-1076
   intermediate, definition of, 11
   lingular, *23, 25*
   lower lobe, left, 13, *23, 25*
      right, 12, *15, 17*
   main, 11
      left, *93, 95*
      right, *93, 95*

Bronchus(i) (*Continued*)
 "pig," 1066
 right middle lobe, 12, *15, 17*
 segmental. See *Segmental bronchus.*
 tracheal, 12
 upper lobe, left, 13, *23, 25, 38*
  right, 12, *15, 17, 38*
Bornholm disease, 687
Brucella species, 611
 in differential diagnosis, 398-399(t), 416-417(t), 428-429(t)
Brucellosis, 611. See also *Brucella* species.
Bubonic plague, 609-610
Budd-Chiara syndrome, 861
Bulla(e), *207, 338, 338, 341*
 arterial deficiency emphysema associated with, *1004*
 communication with bronchial tree, *343*
 definition of, 1023
 differential diagnosis of, 432-433(t), 516-517(t)
 formation of, 285
  associated with pulmonary scarring, *339*
 in arterial deficiency emphysema, 1008
 multiple, *1025*
 progressive enlargement of, *1031*
 resulting from healing of tuberculous cavity, *342*
 showing air-trapping, *1026*
 walls of, line shadows due to, *305, 307*
Bullous disease. See *Lung disease, bullous.*
Busulfan lung, 1119-1121
 differential diagnosis of, 496-497(t)
"Butterfly" pattern, of pulmonary edema, 857, *858, 859*
Byssinosis, 908

Cadmium poisoning, 954
Calcification, 276
 eggshell, 283
  of lymph nodes, *284*
 in peripheral nodules, *279, 280, 281*
 in primary tuberculosis, 620
 pleural, *367*
  and pleural thickening, *366*
   in silicatosis, *368*
  differential diagnosis of, 1164
  roentgenologic signs of, 366
 "popcorn ball," 277, *281*
 pulmonary, multiple nodular, *283*
Calcinosis, of skin, 896
"Calcispherytes," 283
Camalote, sign of, 273
Canals of Lambert, 4, 198
Cancer. See also *Carcinoma* and *Sarcoma.*
 esophagogastric, deformity of posteroinferior mediastinal line due to, *1213*
Candida albicans, 669-671. See also *Candidiasis.*
 in differential diagnosis, 386-387(t), 400-401(t), 416-417(t), 428-429(t)
Candida parakrusei, 669
Candidiasis, 668-671
 clinical manifestations of, 670
 differential diagnosis of, 386-387(t), 400-401(t)
 disseminated, opportunistic, *671*
 roentgenographic manifestations of, 670
Caplan's syndrome, 888
Carbon dioxide dissociation curve, 52, *53*
Carbon monoxide, diffusing capacity for, 183

Carbon monoxide poisoning, 1264-1266
Carbonic anhydrase, 56
Carcinoid syndrome, 730, 760
Carcinoma, alveolar-cell. See *Carcinoma, bronchiolar.*
 basal-cell, adenocystic, 724
 bronchial, anemia as complication of, 763
  arteriography in diagnosis of, 756
  biopsy methods for, 763
  bronchography in diagnosis of, 756
  bronchopulmonary manifestations of, 757
  bronchoscopy in, 763
  cavitation with, 745
  clinical manifestations of, 757
  "coin" lesion, 753
  connective-tissue manifestations of, 759
  cytology of, 764
  diagnostic procedures for, 763
  endocrine manifestations of, 760
  endoscopic examination for, 763
  excessive gonadotropin secretion in, 762
  extrapulmonary intrathoracic manifestations of, 757
  extrathoracic metastatic manifestations of, 758
  extrathoracic nonmetastatic manifestations of, 758
  fluoroscopic examination for, 756
  hematologic manifestations in, 762
  hypercalcemia with, 761
  hypernatremia associated with, 761
  hyperparathyroid-like manifestation of, 761
  inappropriate secretion of ADH in, 761
  insulin-like secretion in, 762
  lymph node involvement of, 745
  mediastinography in diagnosis of, 756
  mediastinoscopy in, 763
  metabolic manifestations of, 760
  neuromuscular manifestations of, 758
  osseous manifestations of, 759
  pleural involvement in, 753
  purpura as complication of, 763
  roentgenographic patterns of, influence of cell type on, 753
  roentgenographic techniques in diagnosis of, 756
  solitary pulmonary nodule, 753
  tomography in diagnosis of, 756
  vascular manifestations in, 762
 bronchiolar, 770-771
  differential diagnosis of, 538-539(t), 550-551(t)
  pleural effusion in, 1152
 bronchioloalveolar, *494, 772, 773.* See also *Carcinoma, bronchiolar.*
  and fibrocaseous granulomas, 276
  differential diagnosis of, 388-389(t), 444-445(t), 454-455(t), 470-471(t), 480-481(t), 496-497(t)
  widely disseminated, *774*
  widespread with mixed pattern, *775*
 bronchogenic, *118, 202, 226, 263, 268, 311, 327, 335, 396, 451,* 736-765, *767.* See also *Carcinoma, squamous cell.*
  airway obstruction due to, 742
  anaplastic, with hilar and mediastinal node metastases, *746*
  anatomic location of, 741
  atelectasis and, 742
  cavitating, *272, 425*
  classification based on cell type, 740
  differential diagnosis of, 400-401(t), 430-431(t), 444-445(t), 452-453(t), 514-515(t), 536-537(t), 550-551(t)

Carcinoma (*Continued*)
  bronchogenic, doubling-time hypothesis for, 301, 769
    epidemiology of, 736
    hilar enlargement due to, 742
    incidence of, 736
      based on cell type, 739
    influence of asbestos on, 737
    influence of cigarette smoking on, 736
    influence of industrial exposure on, 737
    influence of radioactive materials on, 737
    metastatic, *274*
    pathologic characteristics of, 739
    pleural effusion in, 1151
    primary, silicosis and, *284*
    prognosis based on cell type, 740
    relationship to pulmonary tuberculosis, 637
    roentgenographic manifestations of, 741
    roentgenographic patterns of, 741
      based on cell type, 740, 741(t)
    tuberculosis and, 739
    with cavitation, *751*
    with normal roentgenogram, *1256-1257*
    with phrenic nerve involvement and diaphragmatic paralysis, *750*
  cystic, adenoid, 724
  embryonal, *1185*
  lymphangitic spread of, *800*
  metastatic, *374*
    differential diagnosis of, 520-521(t), 538-539(t)
    pleural effusion in, 1150
  metastatic lymphangitic, differential diagnosis of, 550-551(t)
  oat cell, 740-744. See also *Carcinoma, bronchogenic.*
  of esophagus, mediastinal mass due to, *1212*
  of pancreas, with pleural effusion, differential diagnosis of, 520-521(t)
  of right upper lobe bronchus, *224*
  squamous cell, 438, 740, *743*, *754*, *796*. See also *Carcinoma, bronchogenic.*
    and asbestosis, 737
    of right main bronchus, *747*
    of trachea with mediastinal invasion, *749*
    with cavitation, *752*
    with hilar and paratracheal node metastases, *745*
    with mediastinal node metastases, *748*
  undifferentiated, 740. See also *Carcinoma, bronchogenic.*
Carcinomatosis, lymphangitic, differential diagnosis of, 480-481(t)
Cardiac anomalies, congenital, differential diagnosis of, 504-505(t)
Cardiac changes, in thromboembolic disease, 809
Cardiomegaly, pleural effusion with, *529*
Cardiophrenic angle, right, 235
Carina, angle of bifurcation of, 12
Cartilage distribution in tracheobronchial tree, 8, 9
Cat-scratch disease, 695
Cavitary disease, *422, 423, 424, 425*
  and cystic disease, 421-433
  multiplicity of lesions in, *273, 274, 275*
Cavitation, 266
  in Hodgkin's disease, *782*
  in reinfection tuberculosis, 624
  squamous cell carcinoma with, *752*
  tuberculous. *629*
    mycetoma in, *630*
  with bronchial carcinoma, 745
  with bronchogenic carcinoma, *751*

Cavity, 266, *269*
  contents of, 270
  pulmonary, tomographic assessment of, *117*
  tuberculous, bulla resulting from healing of, *342*
    containing mycetoma, *424, 630*
Cavity wall, inner lining of, 270
CCA (chimpanzee coryza agent), 685
Cells, Clara, 10
  corner, 3
  L.E. (lupus erythematosus), 867
  Reed-Sternberg, 773
  septal, 3
  type-II, 3
  Warthin-Finkelbey giant, 686
"Centimeter" branching pattern, 3, *4*
Cerebellar degeneration, subacute, 759
Cervical rib, *84*
Cervical rib syndrome, 1236
Cestoda, 712, 715
Chediak-Higashi syndrome, 905
Chemodectoma, 734, 1206
  differential diagnosis of, 444-445(t)
Chemoreceptors, 140
Chest, "flail," 1239
  funnel, 1240
  normal, 1-102
  physical examination of, 148-156
Chest disease
  roentgenographic patterns of, 377-567(t)
  roentgenologic signs of, 187-376
Chest pain, 144
Chest roentgenogram, normal, 85-99. See also *Roentgenogram, normal.*
  lateral projection, *94-95*
  posteroanterior projection, *92-93*
Chest signs, significant, 149-153
Chest wall, 82-85
  bones of, 83
  changes in, in atelectasis, 220
  diseases of, 1235-1249
  lipoma of, 1246, *1247*
  neoplasms of, 1245-1249
    primary, differential diagnosis of, 538-539(t)
  soft tissues of, 82
    neoplasms of, 1246
Chest-wall pain, 145
Cheyne-Stokes respiration, 1267
Chlorinated camphene poisoning, 955
Chondrodynia, costosternal, 1239
Chondroma, 735
  differential diagnosis of, 400-401(t), 444-445(t)
Choriocarcinoma, of uterus, 797
  primary, 1184
Choriomeningitis, lymphatic, virus of, 695
Chrysotile, 933
Chyliform effusion, 1158
Chylothorax, 1158
  traumatic, 1155
Chylous effusion, 1158
CID (cytomegalic inclusion disease), 693
  differential diagnosis of, 496-497(t)
Cigarette smoking, influence on bronchogenic carcinoma, 736
Cinebronchography, 122
Cinedensigraphy, 115
Cinefluorography, 115
Circulation, pulmonary. See *Pulmonary circulation.*
Cirrhosis, of liver, pulmonary changes in, 1265

Cirrhosis (*Continued*)
  of liver, with ascites, differential diagnosis of, 522-
    523(t)
      pleural effusion in, 1158
Clara cells, 10
Clavicle, *93*
CLE (centrilobular emphysema), 997
Clinical history, 140-148
Clostridium perfringens, 614
  in differential diagnosis, 534-535(t)
  pleural effusion due to, 1147
Clostridium welchii. See *Clostridium perfringens*.
Clubbing, 153
CMV (cytomegalovirus), 693
  differential diagnosis of, 496-497(t)
Coarctation, of aorta, *1237*
  of pulmonary artery, 573
    differential diagnosis of, 504-505(t)
Coccidioides immitis, 652-656. See also *Coccidioido-
    mycosis.*
  in differential diagnosis, 386-387(t), 400-401(t), 410-
    411(t), 416-417(t), 428-429(t), 442-443(t), 460-
    461(t), 480-481(t), 548-549(t)
Coccidioidomycoma, differential diagnosis of, 442-
    443(t)
Coccidioidomycosis, 652-656. See also *Coccidioides
    immitis.*
  benign, 653
    asymptomatic, 653
    "flu-like," 653
    lymph-node involvement in, 654
    nodular lesions in, 654
    pneumonic, 653
  differential diagnosis of, 386-387(t), 400-401(t), 416-
    417(t)
  disseminated, 654
  epidemiology of, 653
  hematology of, 654
  laboratory studies of, 654
  lymph node involvement in, *655*
  serology of, 654
Coin lesion(s), 435-447. See also entries under
    Nodule(s).
  bronchial carcinoma, 753
  Dirofilaria immitis, 711
Companion shadows of rib, 83, *84*
Compliance, 35, 197
  dynamic, measurement of, in chronic obstructive
    pulmonary disease, 968
  measurement of, 181
  static, 968
Consolidation, air-space. See *Air-space consolida-
    tion.*
  and atelectasis, of left upper lobe, *295*
  homogeneous, nonsegmental, 379-391, *380, 381,
    382, 383*
    segmental, 393-405, *394, 395, 396, 397*
  in acute alveolar pneumonia, 192
  inhomogeneous, nonsegmental, 407-411, *408, 409*
    segmental, 413-419, *414, 415*
  left upper lobe, *294*
  parenchymal, 189-195
  pulmonary, and mediastinal lymph node enlarge-
    ment, pleural effusion with, *528*
Contraceptives, oral, influence in thromboembolic
    disease, 805
Contrast media, bronchographic, 122
  water soluble, 122

Contusion, pulmonary, *1070*
  and hematoma, *1071*
  traumatic, 383
    and hematoma and pneumothorax, *1072-1073*
    laceration and hematoma, *1074*
  pulmonary parenchymal, 1069
  differential diagnosis of, 390-391(t)
"Conventional" branch, 36
Cope needle, 161
Cor pulmonale, chronic, 852
  in thromboembolic disease, 809
  renal aminoaciduria and familial retardation of
    growth, 1142-1143
Corner cells, 3
Coryza, 675
"Cotton-candy lung," *996*
Cough, 140
Coxiella burnetii, 697
Coxsackie, differential diagnosis of, 400-401(t), 410-
    411(t), 416-417(t)
Coxsackie virus respiratory infection, 687
Crepitations, 151
"Crescent sign," 713
Crocidolite, 933
Crossover phenomenon, 72
Cryptococcaceae, 673
Cryptococcosis, *449*, 657-662
  differential diagnosis of, 452-453(t)
  lymph node, *661*
  pulmonary, *660, 661*
  serologic studies of, 660
Cryptococcus neoformans, 657-662. See also *Crypto-
    coccosis.*
  in differential diagnosis, 428-429(t), 452-453(t), 480-
    481(t), 534-535(t)
  pleural effusion due to, 1148
Cultures, 167
Curschmann's spirals, 176
Cushing's syndrome, 730, 760
Cyanosis, 52, 154
Cylindroma(s), 724
  nodular metastases from, *798*
Cyst, air, pulmonary, 336, 341
  archenteric, 1210
  bronchial. See *Bronchial cysts.*
  bronchoesophageal, 1210
  bronchogenic, 1192
    differential diagnosis of, 426-427(t), 440-441(t),
      560-561(t)
  definition of, 1023
  dermoid, 1182, *1183*
  echinococcal, pulmonary, 713
  gastroenteric, 1210
    differential diagnosis of, 560-561(t)
  intradiaphragmatic, 1235
  lung, posttraumatic, 272
    traumatic, 1069-1075
    differential diagnosis of, 432-433(t)
  mesothelial, 1193
    differential diagnosis of, 560-561(t)
  neurenteric, 1210
  neurogenic, differential diagnosis of, 560-561(t)
  pleuropericardial, 1193
    in right cardiophrenic angle, *1195*
    mediastinal, anterior, *1194*
  "spring water," 287
  thoracic-duct, 1211
  toxoplasma, 703

Cystic disease, and cavitary disease, 421-433
Cystic fibrosis, of pancreas. See *Mucoviscidosis.*
Cysticercosis, 715
Cysticercus cellulosae, 716
Cytology, 176-178
Cytomegalic inclusion disease (CID), 693
  differential diagnosis of, 496-497(t)
Cytomegalovirus (CMV), 693
  differential diagnosis of, 496-497(t)
Cytomegalovirus respiratory infection, 693

Dead space, alveolar, 51
  anatomic, 51
  physiologic, 51
Dead-space gas, 30
Densitometry, roentgen, 115
Density, lung, 85, 91(t)
  alteration in, 87, *88, 89, 90*
  background, 86, 87
  effect of pneumothorax on, *371*
  local increase in, 211
  normal, 86
  subliminal, 245
  supraliminal, 245
Densography, fluoroscopic, 115
Dermatomyositis, 894-896
  differential diagnosis of, 484-485(t)
Dermoid cyst, 1182, *1183*
Desmoid tumor, 1246
Diagnosis, differential, tables of, 377-567
  roentgenologic, time factor in, 297, *300*
Dialysis, peritoneal, pleural effusion with, 1158
  differential diagnosis of, 524-525(t)
Diaphragm, 80-82
  abnormalities of, 1232
    pleural effusion with, *531*
  accessory, 1232
  contour of, 1218
    physiologic variation in, 81
  diseases of, 1217-1235
  excursion of, 1219
  hernia(s) of, 1224-1232
    traumatic, 1230, *1231*
  motion of, abnormalities of, 1219-1224
    cause of disturbance in, 1224
    restriction of, 1224
    roentgenologic assessment of, 1219
  normal, roentgenographic height of, 80
  paralysis of, 1219
    iatrogenic, *1221, 1222-1223*
  position of, abnormalities of, 1219-1224
  primary neoplasms of, 1235
  range of excursion on respiration, 81
  scalloping of, 81, *81*
Diathesis, hemorrhagic, pulmonary hemorrhage in,
    differential diagnosis of, 472-473(t)
  sarcoid, 1088
Differential diagnosis, tables of, 377-567
Diffusing capacity, for carbon monoxide, 183
  measurement of, 48
  in chronic obstructive pulmonary disease, 969
Diffusion, across alveolocapillary membrane, 47
  disturbances in, in chronic obstructive pulmonary
    disease, 1023
  intravascular, 48

Diffusion (*Continued*)
  of gas in acinar units, 47
    measurement of, 183
Diffusion defect, pathophysiology of, *49*
diGeorge's syndrome, 902
Diiodopyridone, 122
Dionosil, 123
Diplococcus pneumoniae, 592-595
  in differential diagnosis, 384-385(t), 398-399(t), 416-
    417(t), 426-427(t), 532-533(t)
  pleural effusion due to, 1147
Dirofilaria immitis, in differential diagnosis, 442-443(t)
Dirofilaria immitis "coin" lesion, 711
"Dirty chest," 991, *992,* 1008
Disappearing tumors, 1156
Discoid atelectasis. See *Plate-like atelectasis.*
Distoma pulmonale, 716. See also *Paragonimiasis.*
Diverticula, esophageal, 1211
  differential diagnosis of, 560-561(t)
  of pharynx, differential diagnosis of, 560-561(t)
  Zenker's, 1211
Diverticulosis, tracheal, 1066-1067
DL$_{CO}$ (diffusing capacity for carbon monoxide),
  183
"Double-arch sign," 713
Doubling time, 769
  for bronchogenic carcinoma, 301
Driving pressure, 43
"Drowned lung," 199, *202*
Dysautonomia, familial, 905
  differential diagnosis of, 402-403(t), 488-489(t)
Dysentery, amebic, 701
Dysgammaglobulinemias, 900
Dysostosis, cleidocranial, 1235
Dysplasia, bronchopulmonary, *1140-1141*
  pulmonary, fibrocystic, familial, 147. See also
    Hamman-Rich syndrome.
Dyspnea, 142

Eaton agent. See *Mycoplasma pneumoniae.*
Ebstein's anomaly, *329,* 500
Echinococcosis, 712
  clinical manifestations of, 715
  epidemiology of, 712
  pathologic characteristics of, 712
  roentgenographic characteristics of, 713
Echinococcus, *450*
  in differential diagnosis, 428-429(t), 442-443(t), 452-
    453(t), 536-537(t)
Echinococcus cyst, *714.* See also *Hydatid cyst.*
Echinococcus granulosus, 712. See also *Echinococco-
    sis.*
  in differential diagnosis, 428-429(t), 442-443(t), 452-
    453(t), 536-537(t)
  pleural effusion due to, 1148
ECHO (enteric cytopathic human orphan) virus, dif-
    ferential diagnosis of, 400-401(t), 410-411(t), 418-
    419(t)
  respiratory infection due to, 688
ECHOvirus pneumonia, differential diagnosis of, 548-
    549(t)
Ecthyma gangrenosa, in pseudomonas pneumonia, 601
Edema, air-space, acinar shadow with, 855
  interstitial and air-space, 257
  intra-alveolar, 199
  perivascular interstitial, *241*

Edema (*Continued*)
　pulmonary. See *Pulmonary edema.*
Effusion, chyliform, 1158
　chylous, 1158
　mediastinal, differential diagnosis of, 564-565(t)
　pleural. See *Pleural effusion.*
　pleurisy with, 1146
　pseudochylous, 1158
"Eggshell" calcification, 283
　of lymph nodes, *284*
Ehlers-Danlos syndrome, 1142
Eisenmenger reaction, 835
　with patent ductus arteriosus, *837*
"Elastic" recoil of lung and cage, 32, *32*
Electrocardiographic changes, in pulmonary thrombo-
　　embolism, 827
Electrocardiography, 178
Emboli, pulmonary, central and peripheral, without
　　cardiac enlargement, *814*
Embolic disease, to small arteries, differential diagno-
　　sis of, 504-505(t)
Embolism, fat. See *Fat embolism.*
　from oily contrast media, differential diagnosis of,
　　482-483(t)
　metallic-mercury, 831
　oil, pulmonary, iatrogenic, 830-831
　pulmonary, 804
　　and infarction, differential diagnosis of, 538-539(t)
　　　parenchymal scarring in, 816
　　　plate-like atelectasis in, 816
　　differential diagnosis of, 522-523(t)
　　line shadows in, 816
　　radioisotope scanning in, *824, 825*
　　unilateral, without infarction, *812*
　　with hemorrhage, *819*
　　without infarction, *810-811*
Embolization, peripheral, multiple, *813*
Emphysema, 332, 503, 842, 982-1085
　accuracy of roentgenologic diagnosis of, 1014
　AD. See *Emphysema, arterial deficiency.*
　alveolar-duct, 999
　arterial deficiency, 1002, *1003*
　　alterations in pulmonary vasculature and cardiac
　　　contour with, *1005*
　　assessment by angiography, *1007*
　　bullae in, *1004*, 1008
　　overinflation in, 1002
　　relationship to centrilobular emphysema, 1008
　　relationship to panlobular emphysema, 1008
　associated cardiac and vascular changes in, 999
　bronchial dynamics in, *1014*
　bronchographic abnormalities in, 1011, *1012, 1013*
　centriacinar. See *Emphysema, centrilobular.*
　centrilobular, 997
　　diagram of acinus in, *998*
　　lung architecture in, *998*
　　relationship to arterial deficiency and increased
　　　marking emphysema, 1008
　clinical and physiologic manifestations of, 1015-
　　1023
　constitutional. See *Emphysema, panlobular.*
　developing, roentgenologic demonstration of, *1009*
　diffuse, *322.* See also *Emphysema, panlobular.*
　　solitary pneumatocele associated with, *1028*
　etiology of, 1000
　focal, 940
　focal-dust (FDE), 999

Emphysema (*Continued*)
　general. See *Emphysema, panlobular.*
　idiopathic. See *Emphysema, panlobular.*
　IM. See *Emphysema, "increased marking."*
　incidence of, 1000
　"increased marking," 1008, *1010*
　　relationship to centrilobular emphysema, 1008
　　relationship to panlobular emphysema, 1008
　infantile. See *Emphysema, lobar.*
　"linear," 999
　lobar, 1033
　　congenital, 325, 1032, *1034*
　　differential diagnosis of, 516-517(t)
　　neonatal, 1032
　local, 1032-1039
　lung architecture with, *996*
　mediastinal. See also *Pneumomediastinum.*
　　pleural line in, *317*
　obstructive, chronic, differential diagnosis of, 488-
　　489(t), 506-507(t)
　　local, differential diagnosis of, 514-515(t)
　panacinar. See *Emphysema, panlobular.*
　panlobular, 995. See also *Emphysema, diffuse.*
　　relationship to arterial deficiency and increased
　　　marking emphysema, 1008
　paracicatricial, 999
　paraseptal, 999
　pathogenesis of, 1000
　primary atrophic. See *Emphysema, panlobular.*
　pulmonary, *337*
　　definition of, 993
　　pathologic characteristics of, 995
　pulmonary arterial hypertension secondary to, 1006
　roentgenographic manifestations of, 1002
　scar, 999
　senile. See *Emphysema, panlobular.*
　unilateral, *109, 511,* 1033, *1036-1037, 1038*
　　angiographic manifestations of, *1040-1041*
　　bronchographic manifestations of, *1040-1041,*
　　　1042
　　differential diagnosis of, 516-517(t)
　unilateral pulmonary, *124*
　unselective. See *Emphysema, panlobular.*
Empyema, as complication of pneumonia, 592
　loculated, *363*
Encephalomyelopathy, 759
Endocarditis, monilial, 669
Endometriosis, 735
　differential diagnosis of, 400-401(t), 444-445(t)
Endoscopic examination, 156-158
Entamoeba histolytica, 701-703. See also *Amebiasis.*
　in differential diagnosis, 386-387(t), 428-429(t), 536-
　　537(t)
　pleural effusion due to, 1148
Enteroviruses, 687
Enzymes, in pleural effusion, 176
Eosinophilia, pulmonary, tropical, 709
　pulmonary infiltration with, 869-870
　transient pulmonary shadows with, 869-870
　tropical, *710*
　　differential diagnosis of, 548-549(t)
Epithelium, of bronchi, 8
ERV (expiratory reserve volume), 179
Erythema multiforme, 680
Escherichia coli, 606
　in differential diagnosis, 398-399(t), 416-417(t), 426-
　　427(t), 534-535(t)

Esophageal disease, pain due to, 145
Esophageal hiatus, hernia through, 1211, 1224, *1226*, *1227*
   differential diagnosis of, 564-565(t)
Esophageal rupture, acute mediastinitis secondary to, *1170*
  pleural effusion due to, 1156
  pneumomediastinum due to, 1174
Esophageal-pleural stripe, 75, 77
  inferior, 76
Esophagoscopy, 158
Esophagus, *73*
  carcinoma of, mediastinal mass due to, *1212*
  diverticula of, 1211
    differential diagnosis of, 560-561(t)
  encroachment upon, in histoplasmosis, 645
  lesions of, primary, 1211
  neoplasms of, 1211
    differential diagnosis of, 562-563(t)
Ethiodol, 253
Eventration, 1220
  local, 81, 130-131
Expectoration, 140

Fabry's disease, 1139-1142
Fallot, tetralogy of. See *Tetralogy of Fallot.*
Farmer's lung, 909, *912-913*
  differential diagnosis of, 550-551(t)
Fat, in pleural fluid, 175
Fat embolism, posttraumatic, *468*
  traumatic, 828-830, *829*
    clinical manifestations of, 829
    differential diagnosis of, 470-471(t)
    roentgenographic manifestations of, 828
FDE (focal-dust emphysema), 999
Fibrin body, 735, 1162
  differential diagnosis of, 444-445(t)
Fibrocystic disease. See *Mucoviscidosis.*
Fibroma, 287, 732-733, 1188
  differential diagnosis of, 400-401(t), 444-445(t), 562-563(t)
Fibrosarcoma, 732
Fibrosis, and acute irradiation pneumonitis, 1077, *1080-1081*
  cystic, of pancreas. See *Mucoviscidosis.*
  irradiation, chronic, differential diagnosis of, 410-411(t)
  mediastinal, idiopathic, 1171
  progressive massive, *214*, 921, *927*, *928-929*
  pulmonary, 851
    diffuse idiopathic interstitial. See *Hamman-Rich syndrome.*
    diffuse interstitial, 882
      differential diagnosis of, 552-553(t)
    idiopathic interstitial, *478*
    interstitial, *477*, *479*
      cicatrization atelectasis in, *212*
      differential diagnosis of, 488-489(t)
    secondary to chronic postcapillary hypertension, differential diagnosis of, 482-483(t)
    with sarcoidosis, 1091, *1098*, *1100-1101*
Fibrothorax, 1163
  with pulmonary arterial hypertension, 842
Filaria species, in differential diagnosis, 480-481(t)
Filariasis, 709

Filariasis (*Continued*)
  Bancroftian, 709
  differential diagnosis of, 480-481(t)
Fissure(s), 59
  accessory, 61, *64*
  azygos, 61, *62*, *63*
  bulging of, 260
  horizontal, 60, *235*
  interlobar, *60*, *61*
    bulging of, *267*, *268*
    change in position of, 260
    depth of, 60
    displacement of, 211
    normal, 59
  major, 60, *237*
  minor, 60
    loculated pleural effusion in, *364*
  oblique, 60
  supernumerary, 61
Fissure line, vertical, *64*
Fistula, esophagotracheobronchial, acquired, 1067
Fixatives, gaseous, 136
  liquid, 136
Flat-worm infestation, 712-722
"Fleischner's lines," 301
Fluorodensimetry, 115
Fluoroscopic densography, 115
Fluoroscopy, 112
Foramen of Bochdalek, 80, 1217, *1218*
  hernia through, 1214, 1225
    differential diagnosis of, 566-567(t)
Foramen of Morgagni, 80, 1217, *1218*
  hernia through, 1193, *1196*, 1229
    differential diagnosis of, 566-567(t)
"Form elasticity" of lung, 345
Fossae, rhomboid, 84, 85, 1235
FRC (functional residual capacity), 33, 64, 179, 180
Friedländer's bacillus, 605
  in differential diagnosis, 532-533 (t). See also *Klebsiella-aerobacter species.*
  pleural effusion due to, 1146
Friedländer's pneumonia, differentiation from acute pneumococcal pneumonia, 605
Fungemia, 669
Fungi, causing pleural effusion, 1147
Fungus ball, intracavitary, *273*
Fusiform bacilli, 613
  in differential diagnosis, 386-387(t), 398-399(t), 416-417(t), 428-429(t)

Ganglioneuroma, 1206, *1208-1209*
  juvenile, *288-289*
  mediastinal, posterior, *1207*
Gangrene, pulmonary, in acute pneumococcal pneumonia, 595
Gas, alveolar, composition of, 30
    measurement of, 180
  blood. See *Blood gas(es).*
  dead-space, 30
  mixing efficiency of, 185
Gas exchange, alveolar-capillary, 30
Gas insufflation, contrast studies by, 128
Gastric lavage, 165
Gaucher's disease, 1142

Geotrichosis, differential diagnosis of, 386-387(t), 400-401(t), 416-417(t), 428-429(t)
Geotrichum species, in differential diagnosis, 386-387(t), 400-401(t), 416-417(t), 428-429(t)
"Ghon lesion," 277
Glands, mucous, bronchial, 10
  salivary, bronchial adenomas of, 724
Glomerulonephritis, acute, pleural effusion with, 1158
  differential diagnosis of, 522-523(t)
"Gloved-finger" shadow, 313, *314*
Glucose, in pleural fluid, 175
Goiter, intrathoracic, *1187*
Goodpasture's syndrome, 1122-1128, *1124*
  clinical manifestations of, 1125
  diagnosis and prognosis of, 1128
  differential diagnosis of, 472-473(t), 490-491(t), 496-497(t)
  pathologic characteristics of, 1123
  roentgenographic manifestations of, 1123
Granular pattern, of interstitial pulmonary disease, 248
Granular stippling pattern, of interstitial pulmonary disease, 248
Granuloma, chronic, *280*
  eosinophilic. See also *Histiocytosis-X.*
    differential diagnosis of, 390-391(t), 488-489(t), 552-553(t)
  eosinophilic xanthomatous. See *Histiocytosis-X.*
Granulomatosis, Wegener's, *275*, 873-874, 876-877, *878*
  differential diagnosis of, 430-431(t), 462-463(t)
Gravity, effect on pulmonary circulation, *44*, 45
Ground-glass pattern, of interstitial pulmonary disease, 248

Hamartoma, *281*, *437*
  differential diagnosis of, 400-401(t), 444-445(t)
  pulmonary, 730-731
Hamman-Rich disease, *248*, 253, *478*, *844*, *1107*, *1108*
Hamman-Rich syndrome, 147, 1104-1109
  clinical manifestations of, 1100
  differential diagnosis of, 488-489(t), 552-553(t)
  pathologic characteristics of, 1105
  roentgenographic manifestations of, 1106
Hamman's sign, 981
Hampton's hump, *397*, 816, *817*
Hand-Schuller-Christian disease. See *Histiocytosis-X.*
Harefield needle, 161
Heart, 76-80
  and great vessels, anomalies of, 577
  anomalies of, 577
  position of, 76
  size and contour of, 77
Heart failure, congestive, differential diagnosis of, 540-541(t)
  venous hypertension and interstitial pulmonary edema in, *848*
Hemangioendothelioma, 734
  differential diagnosis of, 444-445(t)
Hemangioma, 733, 1188
  differential diagnosis of, 444-445(t), 562-563(t)
Hemangiopericytoma, 734
  differential diagnosis of, 444-445(t)
  of right rib cage, *1248*
Hematoma, 1069-1075

Hematoma (*Continued*)
  and pulmonary contusion, *1071*
  fracture of vertebra with, differential diagnosis of, 564-565(t)
  mediastinal, differential diagnosis of, 564-565(t)
  pulmonary, differential diagnosis of, 446-447(t)
    postoperative, *1084*
    posttraumatic, *439*
  with traumatic pulmonary contusion and laceration, *1074*
  with traumatic pulmonary contusion and pneumothorax, *1072-1073*
Hematoma formation, fracture with, 1214
Hematopoiesis, extramedullary, 1214
  differential diagnosis of, 564-565(t)
Hemiazygos vein, *74*
  dilatation of, 1197
Hemidiaphragm(s), 95
  elevation of, in atelectasis, 213
  position of, 1218
  relationship between height of, 80
  "splinting" of, 1224
Hemophilus influenzae, 607-608
  in differential diagnosis, 386-387(t), 398-399(t), 416-417(t), 428-429(t), 534-535(t)
Hemophilus pertussis, 608
  in differential diagnosis, 398-399(t), 416-417(t), 428-429(t), 548-549(t)
Hemoptysis, 146
Hemorrhage, mediastinal, 1179
  spontaneous, 1180
  pulmonary, 805
    idiopathic, *190-191*, *469*, *1124*, *1126-1127*
    in hemorrhagic diathesis, differential diagnosis of, 472-473(t), 496-497(t)
  pulmonary embolism with, *819*
Hemosiderosis, pulmonary, differential diagnosis of, 472-473(t), 496-497(t)
    idiopathic, *495*, 1122-1128
      clinical manifestations of, 1125
      diagnosis and prognosis of, 1128
      differential diagnosis of, 490-491(t), 552-553(t)
      pathologic characteristics of, 1123
      roentgenographic manifestations of, 1123
    secondary to chronic venous hypertension, *850*
    secondary to chronic postcapillary hypertension, differential diagnosis of, 482-483(t)
Hemothorax, *365*, *366*
  traumatic, 1155
Hen-litter sensitivity, 918
Hepatization, 591
  gray, 593
  red, 595
Hernia(s), diaphragmatic, 1224-1232
    traumatic, 1230, *1231*
  of lung, 217, 1240, *1241*
  through esophageal hiatus, 1211, 1224, *1226*, *1227*
    differential diagnosis of, 564-565(t)
  through foramen of Bochdalek, 1214, 1225, *1228*
    differential diagnosis of, 566-567(t)
  through foramen of Morgani, 1193, *1196*, 1229
    differential diagnosis of, 566-567(t)
"Herniation," mediastinal, 217
Herpes virus respiratory infections, 689-695
Herpes zoster, pain due to, 145
Hexamethonium lung, 1121
  differential diagnosis of, 496-497(t)
Hibernomas, 733

High-kilovoltage roentgenographic technique, 105

Hilar lymph node enlargement, due to bronchogenic carcinoma, 742

histoplasmoma associated with, *647*

Hilum(a), *43*

and parenchymal lesions, communications between, 311, *311*

displacement of, in atelectasis, 220

"Hilus bifurcation sign," 297

"Hilus overlay sign," 297, *1183*

Histamine, effect of injection into pulmonary artery, 35

Histiocytes, familial lipochrome pigmentation of, 904

Histiocytosis-X, *479*, 1110-1118, *1114, 1117*

clinical manifestations of, 1118

course and prognosis of, 1118

differential diagnosis of, 488-489(t), 552-553(t)

pathologic characteristics of, 1111

roentgenographic manifestations of, 1116

Histoplasma capsulatum, 643-652. See also *Histoplasmosis.*

in differential diagnosis, 386-387(t), 398-399(t), 410-411(t), 416-417(t), 428-429(t), 442-443(t), 470-471(t), 534-535(t), 548-549(t)

pleural effusion due to, 1148

Histoplasma duboisii, 643

Histoplasmoma, *234, 262, 279, 436*, 645, *646*

associated with enlarged hilar lymph nodes, *647*

differential diagnosis of, 442-443(t)

multiple, *648*

Histoplasmosis, *239*, 643-652. See also *Histoplasma capsulatum.*

cavitary, chronic, 651

chronic, 651

differential diagnosis of. See *Histoplasma capsulatum.*

differentiation from tuberculosis, 621

disseminated, *458*, 651

acute, *652*

epidemiology of, 643

esophageal encroachment in, 645

exudative, *312*

hematology of, 651

laboratory studies of, 651

lymph node involvement in, 645

mediastinal involvement in, 645

mediastinitis secondary to, 556

nodular, diffuse, acute, 648

pericarditis in, 645

primary, 644

benign, 644, *644*

pneumonic, 644

pulmonary arterial and venous obstruction in, 645

reinfection, 651

satellite lesions in, *266*

serology of, 651

superior vena caval obstruction in, 645, *650*

Hoarseness, 142

Hodgkin's disease, *381, 528, 530, 546*, 771-784

cavitation in, *782*

clinical manifestations of, 782

differential diagnosis of, 388-389(t), 400-401(t), 418-419(t), 430-431(t), 482-483(t), 514-515(t), 550-551(t)

endobronchial involvement in, *781*

lymph node involvement in, *776*

mediastinal lymph node enlargement in, 774, *1190*

mediastinal mass in, *1191*

"nodular sclerosing," 1189

Hodgkin's disease (*Continued*)

pleuropulmonary involvement in, 775

posterior parietal lymph node involvement in, 778

pulmonary and lymph node involvement in, 779

pulmonary involvement with cavitation in, 780

retrosternal node involvement in, 777

roentgenographic manifestations of, 774

splenomegaly and bone involvement in, 783

thoracic-wall involvement in, 779

with bronchial obstruction, 395

Hodgkin's granuloma, *381, 395*

Holzknecht, space of, 76

"Honeycomb lung," 253

Honeycombing, 249

Hookworm disease, 708

Hughes-Stovin syndrome, 852-853

Humoral deficiency diseases, 899-902

Hurler's syndrome, 1245

Hyaline membrane, 208

Hyaline-membrane disease, 1135, *1136, 1137*

differential diagnosis of, 472-473(t)

Hyaline-membrane formation, lung disease characterized by, 1134-1136

Hyaloserositis, pleural, 1162

Hyaluronic acid, in pleural fluid, 175

Hydatid cyst, *450, 712, 714*. See also *Echinococcosis.*

differential diagnosis of, 428-429(t), 442-443(t), 452-453(t), 536-537(t)

Hydatid cyst disease, pleural effusion in, 1148

Hydrogen ion concentration of blood, 54

measurement of, 185

Hydronephrosis, differential diagnosis of, 522-523(t)

pleural effusion in, 1158

Hydropneumothorax, *373, 374*

encapsulated, *375*

Hydrostatic pressure, 65, *65*

Hydrothorax, and tension pneumothorax, 373

passive atelectasis with, 204

similarity to pneumothorax, *346*

tension, 375

Hygroma, 1188

differential diagnosis of, 562-563(t)

Hypercalcemia, with bronchial carcinoma, 761

Hypernatremia, associated with bronchial carcinoma, 761

Hyperplasia, lymph-node, 1192

mediastinal lymph node, differential diagnosis of, 562-563(t)

Hypersensitivity, alveolar, 908-918

diseases of, differential diagnosis of, 484-485(t), 496-497(t)

delayed, deficiency of, diseases of, 902

respiratory membrane, 908-918

tracheobronchial, 907-908

Hypersensitivity angiitis, 875

Hypertension, arterial, in mitral stenosis, *847*

postcapillary, 843-852

chronic, differential diagnosis of, 504-505(t)

hemosiderosis secondary to, differential diagnosis of, 482-483(t)

pulmonary fibrosis secondary to, differential diagnosis of, 482-483(t)

in mitral stenosis, *846*

pulmonary, 832-853

and Raynaud's phenomenon, 896

classification of, 834(t)

differential diagnosis of, 506-507(t)

high altitude, 842

Hypertension (*Continued*)
  pulmonary, in atrial septal defect, *839*
    in tetralogy of Fallot, *840*
    pain due to, 144
    pathogenesis of, 834
    pathologic characteristics of, 833
    precapillary, 835-843
    primary, *501*, *840*
      differential diagnosis of, 504-505(t)
    rheumatoid disease with, 888
    secondary to diffuse systemic sclerosis, *502*
  pulmonary arterial, fibrothorax with, *842*
    in diffuse idiopathic pulmonary fibrosis, *844*
    secondary to chronic obstructive pulmonary disease, *843*
    secondary to emphysema, 1006
    surgical resection resulting in, *842*
  pulmonary venous, interstitial pulmonary edema associated with, *849*
  venous. See also *Hypertension, postcapillary.*
    and interstitial pulmonary edema, in acute left heart failure, *848*
    chronic, pulmonary hemosiderosis secondary to, *850*
    in mitral stenosis, *847*
Hyperventilation, alveolar, 1266-1269
  clinical manifestations of, 1267
  due to extrapulmonary disorders, 1266
  etiology of, 1266
  pathogenesis of, 1266
Hypogammaglobulinemia, transient, 899
Hypogenetic lung syndrome, 569, *570*
  differential diagnosis of, 512-513(t)
Hypoplasia of lung, 568-569
Hypoventilation, alveolar, clinical manifestations of, 1261
  etiology of, 1255
  pathogenesis of, 1255
  with normal roentgenogram, 1255-1263
    idiopathic, *1259*
Hypoxemia, 46
  arterial, 55, 58
Hypoxia, 46
Hytrast, 122

IC (inspiratory capacity), 179
Immunologic deficiency syndromes, 897-905
Immunologic disease, pleural effusion in, 1153
Impaction, mucoid, 1055-1058, *1059*, *1060*, *1061*
  differential diagnosis of, 402-403(t), 442-443(t)
Industrial exposure, influence on bronchogenic carcinoma, 737
Infarct, pulmonary, *814*, *815*
  multiple, *818*
Infarction, 804
  and pulmonary embolism, differential diagnosis of, 538-539(t)
    parenchymal scarring in, 816
    plate-like atelectasis in, 816
  healed, line shadows due to, *306*
  myocardial, pain due to, 144
  pulmonary, 289, *397*, *817*
    line shadow following, *821*
    line shadows in, 816
    line shadows of pleural origin in, *818*

Infarction (*Continued*)
  pulmonary, plate-like atelectasis associated with, *820*
Infection(s), causing pleural effusion, 1146-1149
  influence in chronic bronchitis, 985
  influenza virus, 682
  pulmonary. See *Pulmonary infections.*
Influenza, differential diagnosis of, 400-401(t), 410-411(t), 416-417(t), 470-471(t)
Influenza virus infection, 682
Influenza virus pneumonia, acute, *684*
Infradiaphragmatic interruption, of inferior vena cava, *1200*
Inhalation disease, 906-965
  caused by noxious gases and soluble aerosols, 948-956
  due to inorganic dust, 918-948
    factors influencing lung reaction, 918-919
  due to organic dust, 907-918
  unrelated to dusts or fumes, 956-965
Inoculation, animal, 168
Inspiratory-expiratory roentgenography, 108
  air-trapping investigation with, 108, *109*
  bronchial obstruction assessment with, *114*
  in diagnosis of pneumothorax, 110, *110*
Insulin-like secretion, in bronchial carcinoma, 762
Interalveolar communications, *193*
Intrathoracic dynamics, roentgenologic procedures for evaluation of, 112-115
Intrathoracic lesions, change in size or position of, 286, *287*
Iodized oil, 122
IPH (idiopathic pulmonary hemosiderosis), 1122-1128.
  See also *Hemosiderosis, pulmonary, idiopathic.*
Irradiation pneumonitis. See *Pneumonitis, irradiation.*
IRV (inspiratory reserve volume), 179
Ischemia, myocardial, pain due to, 144
Isomerism, bronchial, 13

Jackson-Huber nomenclature of bronchial segments, 11

Kartagener's syndrome, 1051
Kerley "A" lines, 66, 306, *308*
Kerley "B" lines, 66, 240, *242*, *257*, 308, *309*
Kerley "C" lines, 309, *310*
Klebsiella edwardsii atlantae. See *Friedländer's bacillus.*
Klebsiella edwardsii edwardsii. See *Friedländer's bacillus.*
Klebsiella pneumonia, acute, *294*
Klebsiella pneumoniae. See *Friedländer's bacillus.*
Klebsiella-Aerobacter species, 604-606, 1146
Klebsiella-Aerobacter species, in differential diagnosis, 384-385(t), 398-399(t), 410-411(t), 416-417(t), 426-427(t), 532-533(t)
Klippel-Feil deformity, 1235
Knuckle sign, 809, *812*, *825*
Kohn, pores of, 4, *189*, *193*, 198, *199*
Kveim test, for sarcoidosis, 1103
Kymography, roentgen, 115
Kyphoscoliosis, 1243, *1244*
Kyphosis, 1243

Laceration, pulmonary, 272
  pulmonary parenchymal, 1069-1075
    differential diagnosis of, 432-433(t)
  traumatic pulmonary contusion and hematoma, 1074
Lactic dehydrogenase (LDH), 175, 176
Lambert, canals of, 4, 198
Laminagraphy. See Tomography.
Lamination, as sign of disease, 277
Landry-Guillain-Barré syndrome, 1260
Larva migrans, pulmonary, 711
Laryngoscopy, 156
Lateral decubitus roentgenographic position, 112
Lavage, gastric, 165
  tracheal, 165
LDH (lactic dehydrogenase), 175, 176
Leiomyoma, 732
  differential diagnosis of, 400-401(t), 444-445(t)
Leiomyosarcoma, 732
Letterer-Siwe's disease. See Histiocytosis-X.
Leukemia, 785-790
  chronic lymphatic, 545
  clinical manifestations of, 789
  differential diagnosis of, 482-483(t), 550-551(t), 562-563(t)
  lymph-node enlargement due to, 1188
  lymphoblastic, acute, 790
  pleural effusion in, 1149
  roentgenographic manifestations of, 789
Limiting membrane, of lung parenchyma, 10
Line shadows, 301-315
  due to healed infarction, 306
  due to healed pulmonary tuberculosis, 305
  due to parenchymal scarring, 304
  due to plate-like atelectasis, 301, 302, 303
  due to pleural thickening, 316
  due to segmental pulmonary collapse, 304
  due to thrombotic arteries, 315
  due to wall of bulla, 305, 307
  due to walls of blebs, 305
  following pulmonary infarction, 821
  in pulmonary embolism and infarction, 816
  of interstitial and bronchovascular origin, 306
  of parenchymal origin, 301
  of pleural origin, 315
    in pulmonary infarction, 818
Linguatula serrata, 722
Lingula, 27
Lingular artery, 40
Lingular bronchus, 23, 25
LIP (lymphocytic interstitial pneumonia), 736
Lipiodol, ultra-fluid, 830-831
Lipochondrodystrophy, 1245
Lipoma, 286, 733, 1186
  differential diagnosis of, 400-401(t), 444-445(t), 562-563(t)
  of chest wall, 1246, 1247
Lipomatosis, 558, 1186
  mediastinal, 1189
Listeria monocytogenes, 600
Listeriosis, 600
Lobule, 3
Loefflerella whitmore. See Pseudomonas pseudomallei.
Loeffler's syndrome, 382, 870-872, 871, 872
  differential diagnosis of, 388-389(t)
Löffler's syndrome. See Loeffler's syndrome.
Lordotic roentgenographic projection, 107
  value of, 108
Louis, angle of, 72

Lung. See also entries under Pulmonary.
  agenesis of, 568-569
  aplasia of, 568-569
  auscultation of, 150
  bullet wound of, 1083, 1085
  busulfan, 1119-1121
    differential diagnosis of, 496-497(t)
  composition of, 91(t)
  congenital cystic adenomatoid malformation of, 588
    differential diagnosis of, 410-411(t)
  "cotton-candy," 996
  development of, 58
  diagrammatic representation of, 188
  "drowned," 199, 202
  "elastic" recoil of, 32, 32
  examination of, 136
  farmers', 909, 912-913
    differential diagnosis of, 550-551(t)
  "form elasticity" of, 345
  hernia of, 217, 1240, 1241
  hexamethonium, 1121
    differential diagnosis of, 496-497(t)
  "honeycomb," 253
  in centrilobular emphysema, 998
  inflammatory pseudotumor of, 736
  inflation, postmortem, 134-136
  lymphatics of, 66
  malt-workers', 917
  mushroom-workers', 911, 914
  mycobacterial infection of, 614
  mycotic infections of, 642
  parasitic infestation of, 700
  pigeon-breeders', 915
  radiation injuries of, 1076-1085
    clinical manifestations of, 1077
    effect of dosage in, 1076
    pathologic changes resulting from, 1077
    pulmonary function aberrations in, 1077
    roentgenographic manifestations of, 1077
    time factor in, 1076
  railway-workers', 948
  rheumatoid disease of, 879-899
  sensory fibers of, 58
  "shock," 592
  smallpox-handlers', 917
    differential diagnosis of, 550-551(t)
  structure of, 2-8
  surface tension of, 34
  systemic arterial supply to, 577
  unilateral hyperlucent, 1033. See also Swyer-James syndrome.
  with emphysema, 996
Lung abscess, acute, 423
  differential diagnosis of, 452-453(t)
  secondary to aspiration pneumonia, 613, 960
  acute staphylococcal, 267, 269, 271
  due to Pseudomonas aeruginosa, 602
  tuberculous, 270
Lung biopsy, 138
  open, 159
  percutaneous, 159
Lung capacity, functional residual (FRC), 33, 64, 179, 180
  inspiratory (IC), 179
  total (TLC), 179, 180
Lung cavity. See Cavity.
Lung cyst. See Cyst.
Lung density. See Density, lung.

Lung disease. See also *Air-space disease.*
  bullous, 1023-1032
    bronchography in assessment of, *1030*
    clinical manifestations of, 1027
    differential diagnosis of, 506-507(t)
    pathologic characteristics of, 1023
    primary, 1027. See also *Emphysema, paraseptal.*
    roentgenographic manifestations of, 1024
  characterized by hyaline-membrane formation, 1134-1136
  collagen, 866-897
  connective-tissue, 866-897
  chronic, and thatched roofs, 917
  decreased roentgenographic density in, 315-341
  diffuse, 291
  diffuse interstitial, 842
  distribution of, 287
  embolic and thrombotic, 804-831
  hematologic procedures in, 178
  increased roentgenographic density in, 189-315
  infectious, 589-722
  inhalational. See *Inhalation disease.*
  "interstitial," 240
  neoplastic, 723-803
  of altered immunologic activity, 866-905
  of unknown origin, 1086-1143
  rheumatoid, *477*, 879-889, *884-885*
Lung function, 13-36
  roentgenologic methods in assessment of, 129-132
Lung herniation, *217*, 1240, *1241*
Lung infection, due to viruses, *Mycoplasma pneumonia,* and rickettsiae, 674-675
Lung parenchyma. See also entries under *Acinus(i)* and *Parenchymal.*
  diseases of, with normal roentgenogram, 1251-1253
  limiting membrane of, 10
Lung scanning, 132-134
Lung section, recording and storage of, 137
Lung syndrome, hypogenetic, 569, *570*
  differential diagnosis of, 512-513(t)
Lung tissue, resistance of, 35
  measurement of, 182
Lung torsion, 1076
  differential diagnosis of, 390-391(t)
Lung vasculature, alteration in, 327
  normal peripheral, generalized overinflation with, *333*
  reduction in, general, *328*
  local, *330*
Lung volume(s), 178, *179*
  alteration in, roentgenologic signs of, 321
  determination of, 129
  disturbances in, in chronic obstructive pulmonary disease, 1021
  in tension pneumothorax, 206
  intrapleural pressure and, 46
  maintenance of, 197
  measurement of, in chronic obstructive pulmonary disease, 968
  reserve, inspiratory (IRV), 179
Lupus erythematosus, systemic (S. L. E.), *529*, 867-869, *868*
  clinical manifestations of, 869
  differential diagnosis of, 418-419(t), 522-523(t), 540-541(t)
  laboratory findings in, 869
  pathologic characteristics of, 867

Lupus erythematosus (*Continued*)
  systemic, pleural effusion in, 1153
    pulmonary function tests for, 869
    roentgenographic manifestations of, 868
    symptoms and signs of, 869
Lupus erythematosus cell (L. E. cell), 867
Lycoperdonosis, 918
Lymph node(s), azygos, 69
  bifurcation, 69
  bronchopulmonary, 69
  carinal, 69
  eggshell calcification of, *284*
  intercostal, 69
  internal mammary, 67
  mediastinal. See *Mediastinal nodes.*
  paravertebral, 69
  prevascular, 67
  sternal, 67
  tracheobronchial, 69
Lymph node biopsy. See *Biopsy, lymph node.*
Lymph node enlargement. See also *Lymph node involvement.*
  due to lymphoma and leukemia, 1188
  hilar and mediastinal, 543-553, *544, 545*
  in infectious mononucleosis, 1192
  in sarcoidosis, 1090, *1091, 1094-1095, 1096-1097, 1098, 1100-1101*
  mediastinal, and pulmonary consolidation, pleural effusion with, *528*
  and pulmonary disease, *546*
  in Hodgkin's disease, 774, *1190*
  with pleural effusion, *547*
  metastatic, 1189
  differential diagnosis of, 562-563(t)
  non-lymphomatous, 1189
  without pulmonary abnormality, in sarcoidosis, 1090
Lymph node hyperplasia, 1192
  mediastinal, differential diagnosis of, 562-563(t)
Lymph node involvement. See also *Lymph node enlargement.*
  in bronchial carcinoma, 745
  in coccidioidomycosis, 654, *655*
  in granulomatous mediastinitis, 1190
  in histoplasmosis, 645
  in Hodgkin's disease, *776*
  in primary tuberculosis, 617
  mediastinal, in lymphosarcoma, 784
Lymphadenitis, granulomatous mediastinal, differential diagnosis of, 560-561(t)
Lymphangioma, 1188
  differential diagnosis of, 562-563(t)
Lymphatic drainage, of lungs, patterns of, 72
  of lungs and pleura, 67
Lymphatic lines, 306. See also *Septal lines.*
Lymphatic system, 66-72
Lymphatics, of lungs and pleura, 66
  of mediastinum, 66-71
Lymphedema, differential diagnosis of, 524-525(t)
  pleural effusion in, 1158
  yellow nails and bronchiectasis, 1051
Lymphocytic choriomeningitis, virus of, 695
Lymphocytic pneumonia, interstitial, 736
Lymphogranuloma venereum, 697
Lymphoid pneumonia, interstitial, 736
Lymphoma, follicular, 784
  giant, *255*
  lymph-node enlargement due to, 1188

Lymphoma (*Continued*)
  mediastinal widening in, differential diagnosis of, 562-563(t)
  pleural effusion in, 1149
    differential diagnosis of, 520-521(t), 536-537(t)
  retroperitoneal, pleural effusion in, differential diagnosis of, 520-521(t)
Lymphosarcoma, 547, 784-785
  differential diagnosis of, 388-389(t), 402-403(t), 446-447(t), 454-455(t), 460-461(t), 482-483(t), 514-515(t), 550-551(t)
  mediastinal lymph node involvement in, 784
  pleuropulmonary involvement in, 784
  pulmonary, primary, 786

MacLeod's syndrome, 331, 334, 511, 1033. See also *Swyer-James syndrome.*
  erroneous diagnosis of, 571
Macroglobulinemia, Waldenström's, 897, 898, 1122
  differential diagnosis of, 484-485(t)
Madura foot, 663
Maduromycosis, 663, 673
Magnification roentgenography, 105
Malleomyces mallei, 611
  in differential diagnosis, 426-427(t), 534-535(t)
Malleomyces pseudomallei. See *Pseudomonas pseudomallei.*
Malt-workers' lung, 917
Manubriosternal angle, 72
Manubrium, 85, 95
Maple-bark disease, 916
Mass, in anterior cardiophrenic angle, 1193
  intrathoracic, change in shape of, 287
  mediastinal. See *Mediastinal mass(es).*
  pulmonary. See *Pulmonary mass(es).*
MBC (maximal breathing capacity), 155, 182
ME (mixing efficiency), 185
Measles. See *Rubeola.*
Mediastinal configuration, 78
Mediastinal disease, 1165-1216
Mediastinal "displacement," 217
  in atelectasis, 216
Mediastinal effusion, differential diagnosis of, 564-565(t)
Mediastinal "herniation," 217
Mediastinal lesion, aortography in assessment of, 126
Mediastinal line, anterior, 75, 76
  posterior, 75, 77
Mediastinal lymph nodes. See *Mediastinal nodes.*
Mediastinal mass(es), 1179
  due to carcinoma of esophagus, 1212
  due to severe elongation of descending thoracic aorta, 1206
  in anterior compartment, 1180-1188
  in Hodgkin's disease, 1191
  in middle compartment, 1188-1205
  in posterior compartment, 1205-1216
Mediastinal nodes, anterior, 67, 68
  middle, 71
  parietal, 67, 69
    anterior, 67
    posterior, 69
  posterior, 69, 70
  visceral, 67
Mediastinal pain, 144
Mediastinal pneumography, 128
Mediastinal veins, major, dilatation of, 1197

"Mediastinal wedge," 225, 227, 228, 233
Mediastinal widening, 555-567(t), 556, 557, 558, 559
Mediastinitis, 1166-1174
  acute, 1166
    differential diagnosis of, 560-561(t)
    secondary to esophageal rupture, 1170
  chronic, 1167
  fibrous, differential diagnosis of, 560-561(t)
  granulomatous, 1167, 1172-1173
    chronic, differential diagnosis of, 560-561(t)
    lymph-node enlargement in, 1190
  sclerosing, 1171
  secondary to histoplasmosis, 556
Mediastinography, in diagnosis of bronchial carcinoma, 756
Mediastinoscopy, 157, 163
  in bronchial carcinoma, 763
Mediastinum, 72-80
  anatomic boundaries of, 73
  compartment of, 73
    anterior, 67, 73
      mass in, 1180-1188
    middle, 69, 73
      mass in, 1188-1205
    posterior, 69, 74
      mass in, 1205-1216
  left lateral aspect of, 74
  lymphatics of, 66-71
  right lateral aspect of, 73
Medical history, 147-149
Megaesophagus, 1211
  differential diagnosis of, 566-567(t)
Meigs' syndrome, differential diagnosis of, 520-521(t)
  pleural effusion in, 1157
Melioidosis, 601-604. See also *Pseudomonas pseudomallei.*
Membrana propria, 10
Membrane, basement, 10
  limiting, of lung parenchyma, 10
Mendelson's syndrome, 958, 960
Meningitis, tuberculous, 638
Meningocele, 1210
  differential diagnosis of, 560-561(t)
Meningomyelocele, 1210
"Meniscus sign," 713
Mesoazygos, 61
Mesothelial neoplasms, diffuse, 369
  local, 367
Mesothelioma, 126
  differential diagnosis of, 538-539(t)
  diffuse malignant, 370
  local, 1162
  pleural, diffuse, 1164
  local, 369
    pleural effusion in, 1152
Metastatic carcinoma. See *Carcinoma, metastatic.*
Metastatic disease, acinar shadows in, 799
Metastases. See also *Neoplasms, metastatic.*
  calcified, 278
  from trophoblastic neoplasms, differential diagnosis of, 504-505(t)
  hematogenous, 459
    differential diagnosis of, 430-431(t), 444-445(t), 452-453(t), 460-461(t), 470-471(t)
  lymphangitic, disseminated, 798
  micronodular, diffuse, 797
  nodular, from cylindroma, 798
  solitary, 265

Metazoan infestation, 705-722
Methemoglobinemia, 1264-1266
Microaerophilic streptococcus, 613
Microatelectasis. See *Atelectasis, adhesive.*
Microlithiasis, alveolar, differential diagnosis of, 472-473(t)
    pulmonary, 1131-1134, *1133*
        clinical manifestations of, 1134
        pathologic characteristics of, 1132
        roentgenographic manifestations of, 1132
Middle lobe syndrome, 1062
"Middle-lobe step," 353, *356*
"Millimeter" branching pattern, 3, *4*
Mitral stenosis, differential diagnosis of, 504-505(t)
    postcapillary hypertension in, *846*
    pulmonary ossification in, *282*
    venous and arterial hypertension in, *847*
Moniliasis, 668-671. See also *Candidiasis.*
Mononucleosis, infectious, 695, *696*
    differential diagnosis of, 548-549(t)
    lymph-node enlargement in, 1192
"Moon sign," 713
Morgagni, foramen of. See *Foramen of Morgagni.*
Mucoid impaction, 1055-1058, *1059, 1060, 1061*
    differential diagnosis of, 402-403(t), 442-443(t)
Mucorespiratory disease, 897
Mucormycosis, 671-672
Mucous glands, bronchial, 10
Mucoviscidosis, 1062-1066, *1065*
    clinical and biochemical findings in, 1064
    differential diagnosis of, 402-403(t), 488-489(t), 552-553(t)
    pathologic characteristics of, 1063
    roentgenographic manifestations of, 1063
Mueller maneuver, 97, *98,* 110
    in differentiation of lesions, 286
Mueller/Löfstedt modification, of lateral decubitus position, pleural effusion identification with, 343, *344*
Muscle slips, 81, *82*
Mushroom-workers' lung, 911, *914*
MVV (maximal voluntary ventilation), 182
Myasthenia gravis, chronic aspiration pneumonia in, *961*
Mycetoma, *273*
    in tuberculous cavity, *424, 630*
    of foot, 663
    pulmonary, in secondary aspergillosis, 666
Mycobacteria, anonymous, 640-642
    atypical, 640-642
    chromogenic, 640-642
    unclassified, 640-642
Mycobacterial infection, of lung, 614
Mycobacteriosis, anonymous, 640-642
Mycobacterium avium, 614
Mycobacterium bovis, 614
Mycobacterium fortuitum, 641
Mycobacterium kansasii, 640
Mycobacterium species, in differential diagnosis, 398-399(t), 410-411(t), 416-417(t), 426-427(t)
Mycobacterium tuberculosis, 196, 614-640
    allergy and immunity, 615
    bronchogenic spread of, *466, 631*
    epidemiology of, 614
    in differential diagnosis, 440-441(t), 480-481(t), 520-521(t), 532-533(t)
    pleural effusion due to, 1146

Mycobacterium tuberculosis (Continued)
    primary, in differential diagnosis, 384-385(t), 398-399(t), 512-513(t), 548-549(t)
    reinfection, in differential diagnosis, 384-385(t)
Mycoplasma pneumoniae, 247
    as cause of acute lower respiratory tract disease, 676
    in differential diagnosis, 400-401(t), 410-411(t), 416-417(t), 496-497(t), 548-549(t)
    lung infections due to, 674-675
    pleural effusion due to, 1149
    pneumonia due to, 678
Mycoplasma pneumoniae infections, complications of, 680
Mycosis fungoides, 784
Mycotic pulmonary infections, 172(t), 642-674
Myeloma, multiple, 790-792, *791*
    differential diagnosis of, 446-447(t), 454-455(t), 460-461(t), 538-539(t)
    pleural effusion in, 1152
Myelopathy, necrotizing, 759
Myoblastoma, differential diagnosis of, 400-401(t)
    granular cell, 734
    differential diagnosis of, 444-445(t)
Myocardial infarction, pain due to, 144
Myocardial ischemia, pain due to, 144
Myomatosis, pulmonary, 1118-1119
    differential diagnosis of, 490-491(t)
Myoneural disorders, 1260
Myopathy, carcinomatous, 759
Myxedema, differential diagnosis of, 522-523(t)
    pleural effusion in, 1158
Myxovirus respiratory infections, 681-687

Necator americanus, 708
    in differential diagnosis, 386-387(t)
Necrosis, fat, pericardial, 1193
Needle, Abrams, 161
    Cope, 161
    Harefield, 161
    Vim-Silverman, 159, 161
Needle biopsy, 161
Neisseria, differentiation from *Bacterium anitratum,* 611
Nemathelminth infestation, 705-712
Neoplasia, relationship to asbestosis, 936
Neoplasms, apical, 753
    benign, 723-736
    bone and cartilage, differential diagnosis of, 564-565(t)
    causing pleural effusion, 1149-1153
    endobronchial, differential diagnosis of, 418-419(t)
    esophageal, 1211
    differential diagnosis of, 562-563(t)
    germinal cell, 1182
    differential diagnosis of, 562-563(t)
    malignant, 736-803
    mesenchymal, 1186
    mesothelial, diffuse, 369
    local, 367
    metastatic, 792-803
        cavitation in, 801, *802*
        clinical manifestations of, 801
        cytology of, 801
        hematogenous, disseminated, 795
        lymphatic spread of, 792

Neoplasms (*Continued*)
  metastatic, pathogenesis of, 792
    pathologic characteristics of, 794
    pulmonary function tests in, 801
    roentgenographic manifestations of, 794
    solitary, 794, *795, 796*
    symptoms and signs of, 801
    vascular spread of, 792
  neurogenic, 734-735, 1205
    differential diagnosis of, 444-445(t), 562-563(t)
  of bones, 1246
  of chest wall, 1245-1249
  of esophagus, 1211
  of soft tissues of chest wall, 1246
  of thoracic spine, 1214
  osseous, 1246
  ovarian, pleural effusion in, differential diagnosis of, 520-521(t)
  pleural, differential diagnosis of, 538-539(t)
    roentgenologic signs of, 367
  primary, of chest wall, differential diagnosis of, 538-539(t)
    of diaphragm, 1235
  pulmonary, benign, differential diagnosis of, 514-515(t)
  tracheal, primary, 1192
  trophoblastic, metastases from, differential diagnosis of, 504-505(t)
Nephrotic syndrome, pleural effusion in, 1158
  differential diagnosis of, 522-523(t)
Nerve, phrenic, right, *73*
  vagus, left, *74*
    right, *73*
Nervous system, 58-59
  central, disorders of, 1255
Neurilemmomas, 734
Neuroblastoma, 1206
Neurofibromas, 734
Neurogenic tumors, differential diagnosis of, 400-401(t)
Neuropathies, peripheral, 759
Nidus, central, *279*
  as sign of disease, 277
Nipple shadow, enlarging peripheral nodule mistaken for, 768
Nitrogen dioxide inhalation, bronchopulmonary disease due to, 950-951(t)
Nocardia, differentiation from *Actinomyces israelii*, 662
Nocardia asteroides, 663
Nocardia species, 663-664. See also *Nocardiosis*.
  in differential diagnosis, 386-387(t), 400-401(t), 416-417(t), 428-429(t), 534-535(t)
  pleural effusion due to, 1147
Nocardiosis, 663-664
  differential diagnosis of, 386-387(t), 400-401(t), 416-417(t), 428-429(t), 534-535(t)
Nodular pattern, of interstitial pulmonary disease, 249, *250, 251, 475, 476*
Nodule(s), necrobiotic, 883
  rheumatoid, *886, 887*
    differential diagnosis of, 430-431(t), 446-447(t), 462-463(t)
  peripheral, calcification in, *279, 280, 281*
    enlarging, mistaken for nipple shadow, 768
  pulmonary, enlarging, *767*
    multiple, 456-463, *457, 458, 459*
    solitary, 765-770
      diagnosis of, 769

Nodule(s) (*Continued*)
  pulmonary, solitary, differentiation of benign and malignant, 766(t)
    small, 435-447, *436, 437, 438, 439*
  solitary, 772
    of carcinoid bronchial adenoma, *729*
    showing rapid growth and wide dissemination, *773*
Nonchromogens, 641
Normal lung, architecture of, *996*
North American blastomycosis, 656-657, *658*. See also *Blastomyces dermatitidis*.
  clinical manifestations of, 657
  epidemiology of, 656
  hematology of, 657
  laboratory studies of, 657
  roentgenographic manifestations of, 657
  serology of, 657

Oligemia, *200*, 808, 833
  diffuse, with generalized overinflation, *332*
    without overinflation, *329, 330, 331*
  lobar, with overinflation, *337*
    without overinflation, *336*
  pulmonary, *510, 511*
    generalized, 499-507, *500, 501, 502, 503*, 808
    lobar, 509-517
    local, 808
    segmental, 509-517
    unilateral, *335*, 509-517
Opisthorciasis, 719
Opisthorchis felineus, 719
Ornithosis, 695
Ossification, pulmonary, in mitral stenosis, *282*
Osteoarthropathy, pulmonary, 153
    hypertrophic, 759
Osteochondritis, costochondral, 1239
Osteochondroplastica, tracheobronchopathia, 1066
Osteomyelitis, 1239
OT (old tuberculin), 174, 615
Overinflation, 321
  compensatory, *218*, 325
    cicatrization atelectasis with, *213, 214*
    in atelectasis, 217
  generalized, diffuse oligemia with, *332*
    with normal peripheral lung vasculature, *333*
  in arterial deficiency emphysema, 1002
  in chronic bronchitis, 991
  lobar oligemia with, *337*
  with air-trapping, 324
  without air-trapping, 324, *327, 328*
Oxygen dissociation curve, 52, *53*
Oxygen saturation, arterial, 54, 56
Oxygen therapy, pulmonary disease resulting from, 1137-1139
Oxygen toxicity, 1137-1139, *1140-1141*

Palpation, 149
"Pancoast" tumor, 753
Pancreas, carcinoma of, pleural effusion in, differential diagnosis of, 520-521(t)
  cystic fibrosis of. See *Mucoviscidosis*.
Pancreatitis, pleural effusion in, 1157
  differential diagnosis of, 520-521(t)

Panniculitis, relapsing nodular nonsuppurative, 1142
PAP (primary atypical pneumonia), 676, 678
Papilloma, 731-732
  differential diagnosis of, 400-401(t), 460-461(t)
Paraganglioma, 734, 1206
Paragonimiasis, 716, 717, 718, 719
  differential diagnosis of, 386-387(t), 428-429(t), 460-461(t), 536-537(t)
  pleural effusion in, 1148
Paragonimus westermani, 716. See also Paragonimiasis.
  pleural effusion due to, 1148
Parainfluenza, differential diagnosis of, 400-401(t), 410-411(t), 416-417(t)
Parainfluenza virus infection, 685
Parasites, causing pleural effusion, 1148
Parasitic pulmonary infestations, 166(t), 700-701
Paraspinal line, 75, 75
  obliteration of, following vertebral fracture, 1216
Parasternal lymph node biopsy, 163
Parathion poisoning, 955
Parathyroid masses, 1186
Parenchymal atelectasis, 196-239
Parenchymal consolidation, 189-195
Parenchymal interstitial disease, 244
Parenchymal interstitial space, 188, 240
Parenchymal lesions, and hila, communications between, 311, 311
Parenchymal mass, and visceral pleura, communications between, 312
Parenchymal scarring, 304
  in pulmonary embolism and infarction, 816
  line shadows due to, 304
Pasteurella multocida, 610
Pasteurella pestis, 609-610
  in differential diagnosis, 386-387(t), 428-429(t), 532-533(t)
Pasteurella septica, 610
Pasteurella tularensis, 608-609
  in differential diagnosis, 384-385(t), 428-429(t), 532-533(t), 548-549(t)
  pleural effusion due to, 1147
Patent ductus arteriosus (PDA), 838
  with Eisenmenger reaction, 837
Pathologic examination of lung, methods of, 134-138
PDA (patent ductus arteriosus), 838
Pectoral girdle, abnormalities of, 1235-1236
Pectus carinatum, 1241
Pectus excavatum, 1240, 1242
Pentastomiasis, 722
Percussion, 149
Perfusion, alveolar, 50
  of acinar unit, 43
    measurement of, 183
  roentgenographic studies of, 132
Periarteritis nodosa, 875
Pericarditis, acute, pain due to, 144
  constrictive, differential diagnosis of, 540-541(t)
  in histoplasmosis, 645
  tuberculous, 638
"Peripheral suck," 121
Perivascular interstitial space, 240
Pertussis, 608
PEV (pulmonary extravascular fluid volume), 855
pH, 54
Phagocytic-cell deficiency, diseases of, 904-905
"Phantom tumor," 362, 1156
Pharyngitis infections, acute, 675

Pheochromocytoma, 734, 1206
Phosgene poisoning, 952
Photochromogens, 640
Phrenic nerve, right, 73
Phycomycetes, 671
  in differential diagnosis, 398-399(t), 416-417(t), 428-429(t)
Phycomycosis, 671-672
Physical examination of chest, 148-156
  method of, 149-153
Pickwickian syndrome, 1259
Picornavirus respiratory infections, 687-688
Picornaviruses, 675
P. I. E. (pulmonary infiltration with eosinophilia) syndromes, 869-870
"Pig bronchus," 1066
Pigeon-breast deformity, 1241
Pigeon-breeders' lung, 915
"Pink-puffer," 1008
Pituitary-snuff disease, 917
Planigraphy. See Tomography.
Plasmacytoma. See also Myeloma, multiple.
  differential diagnosis of, 446-447(t), 454-455(t), 460-461(t), 538-539(t)
Platyhelminth infestation, 712-722
PLE (panlobular emphysema), 995
Pleonemia, 833
  pulmonary, 836, 837
Plethysmograph, 180
  body, use of, 183
Pleura, 59-66
  lymphatics of, 66
  neoplastic involvement of, differential diagnosis of, 538-539(t)
  physiology of, 64-66
  rheumatoid disease of, 879-899
  roentgenology of, 59-64
  visceral, 59
    and parenchymal mass, communications between, 312
  "wet," 351
Pleural biopsy, 138, 161
  open, 161
  procedure for, 167
Pleural calcification, 367
  and pleural thickening, 366
    in silicatosis, 368
  differential diagnosis of, 1164
  roentgenologic signs of, 366
Pleural disease(s), 1144-1164
  rheumatoid, 879-889
  roentgenographic signs of, 341-376
  with normal roentgenogram, 1253
Pleural effusion, 165, 219, 882, 1144-1159
  bacteria causing, 1146
  cardiovascular, 1156
  diaphragmatic. See Pleural effusion, infrapulmonary.
  due to Actinomyces israelii, 1147
  due to Blastomyces dermatitidis, 1148
  due to Clostridium perfringens, 1147
  due to Cryptococcus neoformans, 1148
  due to Diplococcus pneumoniae, 1147
  due to Echinococcus granulosus, 1148
  due to Entamoeba histolytica, 1148
  due to esophageal rupture, 1156
  due to Friedländer's bacillus, 1146
  due to Histoplasma capsulatum, 1148
  due to Mycobacterium tuberculosis, 1146

Pleural effusion (*Continued*)
  due to *Mycoplasma pneumoniae*, 1149
  due to *Paragonimus westermani*, 1148
  due to *Pasteurella tularensis*, 1147
  enzymes in, 176
  fungi causing, 1147
  in acute glomerulonephritis, 1158
  in bronchiolar carcinoma, 1152
  in bronchogenic carcinoma, 1151
  in cirrhosis of liver with ascites, 1158
  in hydatid cyst disease, 1148
  in hydronephrosis, 1158
  in immunologic diseases, 1153
  in intra-abdominal malignancy, 1158
  in leukemia, 1149
  in lymphedema, 1158
  in lymphoma, 1149
  in Meigs' syndrome, 1157
  in mesothelioma, 1152
  in metastatic carcinoma, 1150
  in multiple myeloma, 1152
  in myxedema, 1158
  in nephrotic syndrome, 1158
  in pancreatitis, 1157
  in paragonimiasis, 1148
  in peritoneal dialysis, 1158
  in rheumatoid disease, 1153
  in rheumatoid pleuropulmonary disease, *519*
  in subphrenic abscess, 1157
  in systemic lupus erythematosus, 1153
  in thromboembolic disease, 818, 1154
  in tularemia, 1147
  infections causing, 1146-1149
  infrapulmonary, *357, 358-359, 360*
    associated with pneumoperitoneum, *350*
    bilateral, *361*
  large, typical arrangement of, *349*
  lateral decubitus roentgenographic position in identification of, *112*
  loculated, in minor fissure, *364*
  massive, *352*
    associated with obstructive atelectasis, *353*
  mediastinal lymph node enlargement with, *547*
  Mueller/Löfstedt modification of lateral decubitus position in identification of, 343, *344*
  neoplasms causing, 1149-1153
  parasites causing, 1148
  physical signs of, 1145
  pulmonary function studies in, 1145
  right, atypical accumulation of, *354*
  roentgenologic signs of, 345-362
  secondary to disease arising outside thorax, 1157
  subpulmonary. See *Pleural effusion, infrapulmonary.*
  supine roentgenography in assessment of, *111*
  viruses causing, 1149
  with abnormality of bony thorax, *530*
  with cardiomegaly, *529*
  with diaphragmatic abnormality, *531*
  with pulmonary consolidation and mediastinal lymph-node enlargement, *528*
  with roentgenographic evidence of disease, 527-541
  without roentgenographic evidence of disease, 518-525
Pleural fluid, atypical accumulation of, *355, 356*
  biochemical tests of, 175
  fat content of, 175
  formation and absorption of, 65, *65, 341*

Pleural fluid (*Continued*)
  free, atypical arrangement of, 351
    roentgenologic signs of, 345-362
    typical arrangement of, 345
  glucose content of, 175
  hyaluronic acid in, 175
  infrapulmonary accumulation of, *347*
  loculation of, 362
  malignant cells in, 178
  nonmalignant cells in, 176
  protein content of, 175
Pleural line, in mediastinal emphysema, *317*
Pleural masses, local, 1162
Pleural mesothelioma, local, *369*
Pleural neoplasms, differential diagnosis of, 538-539(t)
  roentgenologic signs of, 367
Pleural pain, 144
Pleural pressures, 64
Pleural thickening, *365*, 1161-1164
  and pleural calcification, *366*
    in silicatosis, *368*
  apical, *365*
  diffuse bilateral. See *Silicatosis.*
  general, 1163
  line shadows due to, *316*
  local, 1161
  roentgenologic signs of, 362
Pleurisy, with effusion, 1146
Pleuritis, 882
  and irradiation pneumonitis, *1082*
Pleuropericardial fat shadows, 78, *79*
Pleuropulmonary changes, in nonpenetrating trauma, 1069-1085
Pleuropulmonary disease, caused by external physical agents, 1068-1085
  caused by trauma, 1068-1085
  primary, 841
PMF (progressive massive fibrosis), *214*, 921, *927, 928-929*
Pneumatocele, *340*. See also *Bulla(e).*
  definition of, 1023
  solitary, associated with diffuse emphysema and air-space pneumonia, *1028*
Pneumatocele formation, in acute staphylococcal pneumonia, *285*
Pneumococcal pneumonia. See *Pneumonia, pneumococcal.*
Pneumoconiosis, aluminum, 947-948
  differential diagnosis of, 486-487(t)
  bauxite, *949*
  carbon, 942-943
  cement dust, 948
  China clay, *939*
    differential diagnosis of, 486-487(t)
  classification of, 932(t)
  coal-workers', 939-942, *941*
    clinical manifestations of, 942
    differential diagnosis of, 388-389(t), 430-431(t)
    epidemiology of, 939
    pathologic characteristics of, 940
    pulmonary function studies for, 942
    roentgenographic manifestations of, 940
    simple, differential diagnosis of, 486-487(t)
    symptoms and signs of, 942
  due to mica, 939
  due to radiopaque dusts, 945
    differential diagnosis of, 486-487(t)
  fiberglass, 948

Pneumoconiosis (*Continued*)
  graphite, 942-943
  inorganic dust, 918-948
    differential diagnosis of, 484-485(t)
  Kaolin, 939
    differential diagnosis of, 486-487(t)
  nepheline rock dust, 948
  organic dust, 907-918
    differential diagnosis of, 484-485(t)
  rare-earth, 945
  tungsten carbide, 948
Pneumocystis carinii, in differential diagnois, 480-481(t), 496-497(t)
Pneumocystis carinii infestation, 704-705
Pneumocystis carinii pneumonia, *493, 706-707*
Pneumography, mediastinal, 128
Pneumomediastinum, 1174-1179, *1176, 1177*
  and pneumothorax, *1178*
  clinical manifestations of, 1175
  differential diagnosis of, 564-565(t)
  due to esophageal rupture, 1174
  roentgenographic manifestations of, 1175
  spontaneous, *317*
  traumatic, 1174
  with asthma, 981
Pneumonia, adenoviral, 689
  air-space, 590
    acute, *194, 195, 260, 261, 355*
      due to *Pseudomonas aeruginosa, 603*
      solitary pneumatocele associated with, *1028*
  alveolar, 590
    acute, consolidation in, *192*
  aspiration, 958-964
    acute, *958, 960*
      differential diagnosis of, 470-471(t)
    acute lung abscess secondary to, 613
    chronic, *959*
      differential diagnosis of, 418-419(t)
      in myasthenia gravis, *961*
      secondary to Zenker's diverticulum, *962*
  chicken pox. See *Pneumonia, Varicella-zoster.*
  clinical diagnosis, 591
  cytomegalovirus, *694*
  due to anaerobic organisms, 611-614
  due to Gram-negative aerobic bacteria, 600-611
  due to Gram-positive aerobic bacteria, 592-600
  due to *Mycoplasma pneumoniae,* 678
  ECHOvirus, differential diagnosis of, 548-549(t)
  empyema as complication of, 592
  Friedländer's, differentiation from acute pneumo-coccal pneumonia, 605
  influenza virus, acute, *684*
  interstitial, 591
  interstitial lymphocytic, 736
    differential diagnosis of, 490-491(t)
  interstitial lymphoid, 736
  Klebsiella, acute, *294*
  lipoid, *694-695, 963, 964*
    differential diagnosis of, 402-403(t), 418-419(t), 446-447(t), 454-455(t)
  lobar, 590
  lobular, 591
  mycoplasma, *678*
    diagnosis of, laboratory procedures in, 681
  pneumococcal, *195,* 592-595. See also *Diplococcus pneumoniae.*
    acute, *380, 594*

Pneumonia (*Continued*)
  pneumococcal, acute, differentiation from Fried-länder's pneumonia, 605
    pulmonary gangrene in, 595
    clinical manifestations of, 595
    epidemiology of, 593
    pathologic characteristics of, 593
    roentgenographic manifestations of, 593
  Pneumocystis carinii, 493, 706-707
  primary atypical (PAP), *676, 678*
  pseudomonas, 600-601. See also *Pseudomonas aeruginosa.*
    ecthyma gangrenosa in, 601
  Q-fever, *697, 699*
  renal-transplantation, *700, 701*
  "scrub-typhus," 698
  staphylococcal, 595-598. See also *Staphylococcus aureus.*
    acute, complications of, 598
      pneumatocele formation in, *285*
    clinical manifestations of, 597
    development of, 597
    epidemiology of, 595
    pathologic characteristics of, 596
    roentgenographic manifestations of, 596
    staphylococcal septicemia development in, 596
  streptococcal, 598-599. See also *Streptococcus pyogenes.*
    complications of, 599
  terminal, organisms responsible for, *592*
  time factor in diagnosis of, *300*
  tuberculous, acute, *196,* 385(t), 627
  Varicella, differential diagnosis of, 548-549(t)
  Varicella-zoster, acute, *691*
    complications of, 692
    differential diagnosis of, 470-471(t)
    healed, *692*
  whooping cough, differential diagnosis of, 398-399(t)
Pneumonitis, 591
  acute, *256*
  aspiration lipid, *290*
  hydrocarbon, 952-954
    differential diagnosis of, 470-471(t)
  interstitial, desquamative, 1109-1100, *1112-1113*
    differential diagnosis of, 490-491(t)
    diffuse, 882
  irradiation, 1077, *1078*
    acute, *409*
      adhesive atelectasis in, *208*
      and fibrosis, 1077, *1080-1081*
      differential diagnosis of, 390-391(t)
    and pleuritis, *1082*
    differential diagnosis of, 410-411(t)
  manganese, 954
  obstructive, *199, 201, 226*
    carcinoma bronchial adenoma producing, *728*
    of left upper lobe, *202, 743*
    with incomplete bronchial exclusion, *744*
  radiation. See *Pneumonitis, irradiation.*
  rheumatic, 897
Pneumopericardium, diagnostic, 129
Pneumoperitoneum, diagnostic, 129, *130-131*
  infrapulmonary pleural effusion associated with, *350*
Pneumothorax, and apical blebs, *372*
  and pneumomediastinum, *1178*
  diagnostic, 128
    differentiation of lesions with, *286, 286*

Pneumothorax (*Continued*)
effect on lung density, 371
inspiratory-expiratory roentgenography in diagnosis of, 110, *110*
passive atelectasis with, 204
roentgenologic signs of, 371-376
similarity to hydrothorax, *346*
spontaneous, *205*, 1159-1161
pathogenesis of, 1159
symptoms and signs of, 1159
tension, *373*
and hydrothorax, 373
lung volume in, 206
traumatic, 1161
traumatic pulmonary contusion and hematoma, *1072-1073*
with total pulmonary collapse, 206, *206*
Poliovirus respiratory infection, 688
Polyarteritis nodosa, 875-879, *880-881*
in differential diagnosis, 388-389(t)
Polychondritis, relapsing, 1240
Polycythemia, 178
Polymyositis, 894-896
differential diagnosis of, 484-485(t)
Polyneuritis, acute, 1260
Polyserositis, familial recurring, differential diagnosis of, 524-525(t)
Polytetrafluorethylene poisoning, 955
"Popcorn ball" calcification, 277, *281*
Pores, alveolar, 4
of Kohn, 4, *189*, *193*, 198, *199*
Postmortem techniques, 137
Post-tussic bronchography, 121
PPD (purified protein derivative), 174, 615
PPLO (pleuro-pneumonia-like organisms), 676
"Precordial catch," 145
Pressure, pulmonary blood, measurement of, 183
colloid osmotic, 65, *65*
driving, 43
hydrostatic, 65, *65*
intrapleural, lung volume and, 46
intravascular, 43
of pulmonary artery, in thromboembolic disease, 822
pleural, 64
transmural vascular, 43
transpleural, 45
Pressure-volume curve, *181*
Pressure-volume relationships of lungs, *33*
Propyliodone, 122
Protein, in pleural fluid, 175
Proteinosis, alveolar, differential diagnosis of, 472-473(t)
pulmonary, 1128-1131, *1130*
Proteus species, in differential diagnosis, 384-385(t), 428-429(t)
Protozoan infestation, 701-705
Pseudocavitation, 276
"Pseudodiaphragmatic contour," 357
Pseudoforamen, 1235
Pseudolymphoma, pulmonary, primary, 735
differential diagnosis of, 388-389(t)
Pseudomonas aeruginosa, 600-601
acute air-space pneumonia due to, *603*
in differential diagnosis, 384-385(t), 398-399(t), 416-417(t), 426-427(t), 534-535(t)
lung abscess due to, *602*
Pseudomonas pseudomallei, 601-604
differentiation from *Malleomyces mallei,* 604

Pseudomonas pseudomallei (Continued)
in differential diagnosis, 384-385(t), 410-411(t), 426-427(t)
"Pseudotumor," 362
inflammatory, of lung, 736
plasma cell, 792
Psittacosis, 695
differential diagnosis of, 400-401(t), 410-411(t), 416-417(t), 548-549(t)
Pulmonary. See also entries under *Lung.*
Pulmonary abnormalities of developmental origin, 568-588
Pulmonary air cysts, 336, 341
Pulmonary arteriovenous fistula, 573, 575
clinical manifestations of, 576
differential diagnosis of, 384-385(t), 398-399(t), 440-441(t), 460-461(t)
roentgenographic manifestations of, 574
Pulmonary arteritis, rheumatoid disease with, 888
Pulmonary artery(ies), anatomic relationship to pulmonary veins, *40*, *42*
aneurysms of, congenital, 573
central, 38
changes in, in thromboembolic disease, 808
coarctation of, 573
differential diagnosis of, 504-505(t)
dilatation of, differential diagnosis of, 564-565(t)
effect of injection of histamine into, 35
left, 38, *93*
absence of, 571
anomalous origin from right pulmonary artery, 571
proximal interruption of, 571
main, 37
compression of, 841
differential diagnosis of, 504-505(t)
dilatation of, 1197, *1198*
left, *38*
right, *95*
proximal interruption of, differential diagnosis of, 512-513(t)
right, 37
absence of, 571
anomalous origin of left pulmonary artery from, 571
proximal interruption of, 571
structure of, 36, *36*
to right upper lobe, *93*
Pulmonary artery pressures, in thromboembolic disease, 822
Pulmonary artery stenosis, 573
differential diagnosis of, 504-505(t)
Pulmonary biopsy, transbronchial, 159
Pulmonary blood volume, 86, 86(t)
Pulmonary calcifications, multiple nodular, *283*
Pulmonary capillary blood, distribution of, measurement of, 185
Pulmonary cavity, tomography in assessment of, *117*
Pulmonary circulation, effect of gravity on, *44*, *45*
influences on, 45
neurogenic and chemical, 46
Pulmonary collapse, *219*
segmental, 304
line shadows due to, 304
total, with pneumothorax, 206, *206*
Pulmonary contusion. See *Contusion, pulmonary.*
Pulmonary disease, and mediastinal lymph node enlargement, 546
bacteriology in, 164-174

Pulmonary disease (*Continued*)
  diffuse, with acinar pattern, 465-473, *466, 467, 468, 469*
    with mixed acinar and reticulonodular pattern, 492-497, *493, 494, 495*
    with nodular, reticular, or reticulonodular patterns, 475-491
  diffuse interstitial, roentgenographic patterns of, 244
    modifying influences on, 254
  extrathoracic manifestations of, 153-155
  interstitial, 240-255
    air-space consolidation and air-space atelectasis, 256, *258*
    and air-space consolidation, 256, *257*
    and air-space disease, *246, 247,* 256-258
    granular pattern of, 248
    granular stippling pattern of, 248
    ground-glass pattern of, 248
    honeycomb pattern of, 253, *254,* 475, *479*
    nodular pattern of, 249, *250, 251,* 475, *476*
    reticular pattern of, 249, *252,* 475, *477, 478*
    reticulogranular pattern of, 248
    reticulonodular pattern of, 241, *245,* 253, *255,* 475
  nitrofurantoin-induced, 873
    differential diagnosis of, 484-485(t)
  obstructive, chronic, 966-1067
    assessment of airway obstruction in, 1019
    blood-gas analysis in, 969
    direct measurement of airway resistance in, 968
    disturbances in arterial blood gases in, 1021
    disturbances in diffusion in, 1023
    disturbances of lung volumes in, 1021
    expiratory flow rates in, 968
    measurement of diffusing capacity in, 969
    measurement of dynamic compliance in, 968
    measurement of lung volume in, 968
    measurement of pulmonary function in, 968
    measurement of ventilation/perfusion abnormality in, 969
    physical signs in, 1018
    pulmonary arterial hypertension secondary to, *843*
    pulmonary function studies in, 1019
    symptoms of, 1015
  of cardiac origin, 853-865
  of ferroalloy workers, 954
  organic, 1266
  resulting from oxygen therapy, 1137-1139
  roentgenologic localization of, 291
Pulmonary dysplasia, familial fibrocystic, 147. See also *Hamman-Rich syndrome.*
Pulmonary edema, *467,* 853-865
  acute, 857
    air-space consolidation in, 7
    secondary to left ventricular failure, *856*
    secondary to nitrogen dioxide inhalation, *951*
  air-space, 855
  associated with acute opium alkaloid poisoning, 864-865
  associated with renal disease, 861
  "bat's wing" pattern of, 857, *858, 859*
  "butterfly" pattern of, 857, *858, 859*
  differential diagnosis of, 470-471(t)
  in bacterial shock, 865
  "inappropriate" anatomic distribution of, 856
  interstitial, *242,* 854

Pulmonary edema (*Continued*)
  interstitial, and venous hypertension, in acute left heart failure, *848*
    associated with pulmonary venous hypertension, *849*
  differential diagnosis of, 482-483(t)
  occurring at high altitudes, 864
  neurogenic, 864
  postictal, 864
  secondary to affection of pulmonary veins, 860-861
  secondary to cardiac disease, 854-860
  secondary to hypervolemia or hypoproteinemia, 861-864
  secondary to pulmonary vein occlusion, 862-863
  secondary to pulmonary venous hypertension, 256
Pulmonary embolism. See *Embolism, pulmonary.*
Pulmonary emphysema. See *Emphysema.*
Pulmonary fibrosis. See *Fibrosis, pulmonary.*
Pulmonary function tests, 178-186
Pulmonary gangrene, in acute pneumococcal pneumonia, 595
Pulmonary hemorrhage. See *Hemorrhage, pulmonary.*
Pulmonary hypertension. See *Hypertension, pulmonary.*
Pulmonary infarction. See *Infarction, pulmonary.*
Pulmonary infections, bacterial, 170(t)
  mycotic, 172(t), 642-674
  rickettsial, 170(t)
  viral, 170(t)
Pulmonary infestations, parasitic, 166(t), 700-701
Pulmonary infiltration, with eosinophilia, 869-870
Pulmonary laceration, *272*
Pulmonary lesion, border of, 260
Pulmonary markings, 91
Pulmonary mass(es), solitary, 448-455, *449, 450, 451*
  tomography in assessment of, *118*
Pulmonary neoplasms, benign, differential diagnosis of, 514-515(t)
Pulmonary ossification, in mitral stenosis, *282*
Pulmonary osteoarthropathy, 153
  hypertrophic, 759
Pulmonary parenchymal biopsy, 158
  indications for and choice of method of, 160
Pulmonary parenchymal contusion, 1069
  differential diagnosis of, 390-391(t)
Pulmonary scarring, associated with bulla formation, *339*
Pulmonary secretions, malignant cells in, 177
  nonmalignant cells in, 176
Pulmonary sequestration. See *Sequestration, pulmonary.*
Pulmonary tuberculosis. See *Tuberculosis, pulmonary.*
Pulmonary vascular system, 36-58
  alterations in, with arterial deficiency emphysema, 1005
  anomalies of, 569-577
  diseases of, 833
  effect of change of body position on, *96*
  roentgenology of, 37-42
Pulmonary veins, 95
  anatomic relationship to pulmonary arteries, *40, 42*
  pulmonary edema secondary to affection of, 860-861
  varicosities of, 576
    differential diagnosis of, 440-441(t)
Pulmonary vein occlusion, pulmonary edema secondary to, 862-863
Pulmonary venous drainage, anomalous, 571
  partial, *572*

Pulmonary venous radicles, 37
Pulmonary ventilation, airways and, 8-36
    roentgenology of, 10-15
Pulmonic valve, 38
Purpura, as complication of bronchial carcinoma, 763

Q̇ (alveolar perfusion), 50
Q fever, differential diagnosis of, 400-401(t)
Q-fever pneumonia, 697, 699
Queensland fever. See Q-fever.

Radiation injuries, of lung. See Lung, radiation in-
    juries of.
Radicles, pulmonary venous, 37
Radicular pain, 145
Radioisotope scanning, in diagnosis of pulmonary
    embolism, 824, 825
    in thromboembolic disease, 822
Radionuclides, gaseous, 133
Railway-workers' lung, 948
Rale, 151, 152
Radiopaque dusts, pneumoconiosis due to, 486-487(t)
Ranke complex, 277, 277
    in tuberculosis, 620
Raynaud's phenomenon, 896
    and pulmonary hypertension, 896
    differential diagnosis of, 506-507(t)
Reed-Sternberg cell, 773
Reid Index, 987
Rendu-Osler-Weber's disease, 574
Reovirus respiratory infection, 688
Resection, surgical, resulting in pulmonary arterial
    hypertension, 842
Resistance, of airways, measurement of, 182
    of lung tissue, 35
        measurement of, 182
Respiration, Cheyne-Stokes, 1267
    depth of, 30
    range of diaphragmatic excursion on, 81
Respiratory bronchioles, 2, 2
Respiratory disease, acute, 675
    bedsonia, 695-697
    symptoms of, 140-147
    with normal roentgenogram, 1250-1269
Respiratory infection, adenovirus, 688-689
    Coxsackie virus, 687
    cytomegalovirus, 693
    due to rickettsia, 697-700
    due to viruses, 681-697
    myxovirus, 681-687
    picornavirus, 687-688
    poliovirus, 688
    reovirus, 688
    rhinovirus, 688
    rubeola, 686
    Varicella-zoster, 689
Respiratory muscle disorders, 1260
Respiratory syncytial virus infection, 685
    differential diagnosis of, 400-401(t), 410-411(t),
        418-419(t)
Respiratory syndromes, 675-681
Respiratory tract, upper, swabs of, 165
Respiratory tract disease, lower, acute, 676-681
Reticular pattern, of interstitial pulmonary disease,
    249, 252, 475, 477, 478

Reticulogranular pattern, of interstitial pulmonary
    disease, 248
Reticulonodular pattern, of interstitial pulmonary
    disease, 241, 245, 253, 255, 475
Reticulosis, histiocytic. See Histiocytosis-X.
Reticulum cell sarcoma. See Sarcoma, reticulum cell.
Retrocardiac space, 76
Rheumatoid disease of lungs and pleura, 879-889, 884-
    885
    differential diagnosis of, 482-483(t), 522-523(t), 540-
        541(t)
    pleural effusion in, 519, 1153
    with pulmonary arteritis and hypertension, 888
Rhinovirus, 674
Rhinovirus respiratory infection, 688
Rhomboid fossae, 84, 85, 1235
Rhonchi, 151, 152
Rib(s), abnormalities of, 1236
    accessory, anomalous, 1236
    cervical, 84
    companion shadows of, 83, 84
    congenital anomalies of, 1236
    erosion of, 1236
    first, 93
    fractures of, 1239
    inflammatory diseases of, 1239
    notching of, 1236, 1237, 1238
Rickettsia tsutsugamushi, 698
Rickettsiae, lung infection due to, 674-675, 697-700
Rickettsial pulmonary infections, 170(t)
"Right middle-lobe syndrome," 229, 230, 236, 298
Riley-Day syndrome, 905. See also Dysautonomia,
    familial.
Roentgen densitometry, 115
Roentgen kymography, 115
Roentgenogram, normal, airway diseases with, 1253-
    1255
    alveolar hypoventilation with, 1255-1263
    bronchiectasis with, 1254
    bronchogenic carcinoma with, 1256-1257
    diseases of lung parenchyma with, 1251-1253
    pleural disease with, 1253
    respiratory diseases with, 1250-1269
    with alveolar hypoventilation, 1255-1263
Roentgenographic density, decreased, in lung dis-
    eases, 315-341
    increased, in lung diseases, 189-315
Roentgenographic effect, of superimposition, 244
Roentgenographic magnification, value of, 107
Roentgenographic patterns, of chest disease, 377-567
    of diffuse interstitial pulmonary disease, 244
    of interstitial pulmonary disease, modifying in-
        fluences on, 254
Roentgenographic position, lateral decubitus, 112
    in identification of pleural effusions, 112
    oblique, 112
    supine. See Supine roentgenography.
Roentgenographic projection, lordotic, 107
    value of, 108
    routine, 104
Roentgenographic signs, dynamic, 325
    static, 324
Roentgenographic technique, 105
    air-gap, 105
    high-kilovoltage, 105
Roentgenographic underexposure, hazard of, 106
Roentgenography, body-section. See Tomography.

Roentgenography (*Continued*)
  effect of superimposition, 244
  inspiratory-expiratory. See *Inspiratory-expiratory roentgenography.*
  magnification, 105
  sectional. See *Tomography.*
  standard, 104-112
  supine, 110
    pleural effusion assessment with, *111*
Roentgenologic anatomy, 240
Roentgenologic diagnosis, time factor in, 297, *300*
Roentgenologic examination, methods of, 104-134
Roentgenologic procedures, for intrathoracic dynamics evaluation, 112-115
Roentgenology, of airways, 10-13
  of bronchial tree, 10-15
  of pleura, 59-64
  of pulmonary vascular system, 37-42
  of pulmonary ventilation, 10-15
  perception in, 99-102
Round worm infestation, 705-712
Rubeola, 686
  differential diagnosis of, 400-401(t), 410-411(t), 418-419(t), 480-481(t), 548-549(t)
Rubeola respiratory infection, 686
RV (residual volume), 64, 179, 180

Salmonella species, 607
  in differential diagnosis, 398-399(t), 416-417(t), 426-427(t), 480-481(t), 534-535(t)
Sarcoid, Boeck's. See *Sarcoidosis.*
Sarcoid diathesis, 1088
Sarcoidosis, *544*, 1087-1104
  biopsy techniques in, 1103
  clinical course and prognosis of, 1104
  clinical manifestations of, 1093
  diagnosis of, 1102
  differential diagnosis of, 404-405(t), 472-473(t), 488-489(t), 516-517(t), 552-553(t)
  disturbance in calcium metabolism in, 1102
  etiology of, 1087
  hematologic abnormalities in, 1102
  incidence of, 1087
  Kveim test for, 1103
  laboratory investigation of, 1102
  lymph-node enlargement without pulmonary abnormality in, 1090
  pathogenesis of, 1087
  pathologic characteristics of, 1089
  pulmonary fibrosis with, 1091, *1098, 1100-1101*
  pulmonary function tests in, 1099
  relationship between pulmonary tuberculosis and, 638
  roentgenographic manifestations of, 1089
  serum globulin abnormalities in, 1102
  with diffuse pulmonary disease and lymph node enlargement, 1091
  with diffuse pulmonary disease without lymph node enlargement, 1090
  with lymph node enlargement, *1091*
  with lymph node enlargement and pulmonary involvement, *1094-1095, 1096-1097*
  with lymph node enlargement, pulmonary involvement and pulmonary fibrosis, *1098, 1100-1101*

Sarcoidosis (*Continued*)
  with pulmonary involvement, 1092
Sarcoma, differential diagnosis of, 562-563(t)
  neurogenic, 734
  osteogenic, *278*
  reticulum cell, 784, *788*
    interstitial, *243*
    secondary, 787
Satellite lesions, 260
  in histoplasmosis, *266*
Scalene nodes, biopsy of, 138, 162
Scapula, *93, 95*
Schaumann body, 1089
Schistosoma haematobium, 719
Schistosoma japonicum, 719
Schistosoma mansoni, 719
Schistosoma species, in differential diagnosis, 480-481(t), 504-505(t)
Schistosomiasis, 719
  clinical manifestations of, 721
  differential diagnosis of, 480-481(t), 504-505(t)
  epidemiology of, 719
  pathologic characteristics of, 720
  roentgenographic characteristics of, 721
"Scimitar" shadow, *570*
Scimitar syndrome, 571
Sclerodactyly, 896
Scleroderma, 760, *891, 892, 893*
  clinical manifestations of, 893
  differential diagnosis of, 482-483(t)
  gastrointestinal tract involvement in, 890
  involvement of teeth in, 893
  lung involvement in, 890
  musculoskeletal system involvement in, 890
  pathologic characteristics of, 889
  pulmonary function tests in, 894
  relationship to other diseases, 894
  roentgenographic manifestations of, 889
  symptoms and signs of, 893
Sclerosis, systemic, diffuse, 889-894. See also *Scleroderma.*
    differential diagnosis of, 482-483(t)
    pulmonary hypertension secondary to, *502*
Scoliosis, 1243
Scotochromogens, 641
"Secondary lobule." See *Lobule.*
Segmental bronchi, anatomy of, *14-29*
Seldinger aortographic technique, *126*
Seminoma, 1184
Sensory fibers of lung, 58
Septal cells, 3
Septal lines, 306, 308. See also *Kerley "B" lines.*
Sequestration, bronchopulmonary, 577-581
    differential diagnosis of, 440-441(t)
    extralobar, 581
      differential diagnosis of, 440-441(t), 452-453(t)
    intralobar, 578
      clinical manifestations of, 581
      differential diagnosis of, 440-441(t), 426-427(t), 452-453(t)
      roentgenographic manifestations of, 578
  extralobar, 1235
  pulmonary, 291. See also *Sequestration, bronchopulmonary.*
  pulmonary, intralobar, *422, 579, 580*
Sequoiosis, 917
Serologic tests, 169

Serratia marcescens, 607
Serum globulin abnormalities, in sarcoidosis, 1102
SGOT (serum glutamic oxaloacetic transaminase), 176
Shadow(s), acinar. See *Acinar shadows.*
　azygos vein, 79
　breast, *93*
　bronchial wall. See *Tubular shadows.*
　companion, of rib, 83, *84*
　"gloved-finger," 313, *314*
　homogeneous, of recognizable segmental distribu-
　　tion, 393-405, *394, 395, 396, 397*
　　without recognizable segmental distribution, 379-
　　　391, *380, 381, 382, 383*
　inhomogeneous, of recognizable segmental distri-
　　bution, 413-419, *414, 415*
　　without recognizable segmental distribution, 407-
　　　411, *408, 409*
　line. See *Line shadows.*
　nipple, enlarging peripheral nodule mistaken for,
　　768
　pleuropericardial fat, 78, *79*
　pulmonary, transient, with eosinophilia, 869-870
　"scimitar," *570*
　sternomastoid muscle, 83
　tubular, 312, *313*
　　in chronic bronchitis, 991
　vascular, redistribution of, in atelectasis, 220
Shaggy heart sign, 608, *935*
Shaver's disease, 948, *949*
　differential diagnosis of, 486-487(t)
"Shock lung," 592
Shunt(s), absolute, 51
　venoarterial, extrapulmonary, 1263
　　pulmonary, 1264
　　with normal roentgenogram, 1263-1264
Sidero-silicosis, 943-945
Siderosis, 943
　differential diagnosis of, 486-487(t)
　pulmonary, *944*
"Sign of camalote," 273, 713
Silhouette sign, *215,* 228, *229,* 291, *292-296,* 298, *299,*
　349
Silicatosis, 933, 1163
　pleural thickening and pleural calcification in, *368*
Silicosis, *214,* 919-933
　"acute," *922-923*
　and primary bronchogenic carcinoma, *284*
　clinical manifestations of, 931
　differential diagnosis of, 388-389(t), 430-431(t)
　epidemiology of, 919
　pathogenesis of, 920
　pathologic characteristics of, 920
　progressing from simple to conglomerate, *924-925*
　pulmonary function tests in, 931
　relationship to pulmonary tuberculosis, 931
　roentgenographic manifestations of, 920
　simple, differential diagnosis of, 484-485(t), 550-
　　551(t)
　symptoms and signs of, 931
　uncomplicated, *251*
　with conglomeration, *927, 928-929*
　with egg-shell calcification of lymph nodes, *930*
　with predominant reticular pattern, *926*
Silo-fillers' disease, 950-951
　third phase, differential diagnosis of, 488-489(t)
Silverman needle, 159

Sisal-workers' disease, 917
Sjögren's syndrome, 896-897
　differential diagnosis of, 484-485(t)
Skin tests, 169, 174-175
S.L.E. See *Lupus erythematosus, systemic.*
Smallpox-handlers' lung, 917
　differential diagnosis of, 550-551(t)
Smears, 167
Smoking, influence in chronic bronchitis, 984
South American blastomycosis, 673
Space, of Holzknecht, 76
　retrocardiac, 76
Specimens, surgical, 137-138
"Spider" deformity, 1011
Spine, thoracic. See *Thoracic spine.*
Spirochaeta, in differential diagnosis, 386-387(t), 398-
　399(t), 416-417(t), 428-429(t)
Spirochetes, 613
Spirometry, 182
Spondylitis, ankylosing, 1245
　infectious, 1214
　suppurative, differential diagnosis of, 560-561(t)
　tuberculous, bilateral paravertebral mass associated
　　with, *1215*
Sporotrichosis, 672-673
Sporotrichum schenckii, 672-673. See also *Sporotri-
　chosis.*
　in differential diagnosis, 400-401(t), 416-417(t), 428-
　　429(t), 548-549(t)
Sprengel's deformity, 1235
"Spring water" cyst, 287
Sputum, biochemical test of, 175
　collection of, 164
Squamous cell carcinoma, 237, 272, 292, 295
Stannosis, 945
Staphylococcal septicemia, development in staphylo-
　coccal pneumonia, 596
Staphylococcus aureus, 595-598, 1147
　in differential diagnosis, 398-399(t), 416-417(t), 426-
　　427(t), 480-481(t), 512-513(t), 532-533(t)
Statidensigraphy, 115
Stenosis, mitral. See *Mitral stenosis.*
　pulmonary artery, 573
　differential diagnosis of, 504-505(t)
Sternomastoid muscle shadow, 83
Sternum, abnormalities of, 1240-1243
　body of, *95*
Stevens-Johnson syndrome, 680, 897
Stool, examination of, 165
Stratigraphy. See *Tomography.*
Streptococcus pyogenes, 598-599, 1147
　in differential diagnosis, 398-399(t), 416-417(t), 428-
　　429(t), 532-533(t)
Strongyloides stercoralis, 707. See also *Strongyloidia-
　sis.*
　in differential diagnosis, 386-387(t)
Strongyloidiasis, 707
Suberosis, 916
Subpleural interstitial space, *188*
"Suck," peripheral, 121
Sulfur dioxide inhalation, 952
　bronchiolitis and bronchiectasis secondary to,
　　953
Superimposition, roentgenographic effect of, *244*
Supine roentgenography, 110
　pleural effusion assessment with, *111*

Supra-aortic triangle, 217
Surface tension of lung, 34
Surfactant, 34, 207
Surgical resection, resulting in pulmonary arterial hypertension, 842
Surgical specimens, 137-138
Swyer-James syndrome, 88, *109, 124,* 331, *334, 511,* 1033, *1036-1037, 1038*
   differential diagnosis of, 516-517(t)
   erroneous diagnosis of, 571
Sympathetic chain, *73*
Sympathicoblastoma, 1206

Taenia solium, 715
Talcosis, *368,* 937-939, *938*
   differential diagnosis of, 486-487(t)
Tantalum, powdered, 123
Telangiectasis, 896
   hemorrhagic, hereditary, 574
Tension hydrothorax, 375
Tension pneumothorax, *373*
   and hydrothorax, 373
Teratoma, 1182
Terminal bronchiole, 2, *2*
Tetralogy of Fallot, postoperative bilateral anastomosis for, 1238
   pulmonary hypertension in, 840
Thesaurosis, 955-956, *957*
Thoracentesis, procedure for, 165
Thoracic spine, 85
   abnormalities of, 1243-1245
   curvature of, abnormalities of, 1243
   diseases of, 1214
   neoplasms of, 1214
Thoracoscopy, 157
Thorax, bony, abnormality of, pleural effusion with, *530*
Thromboembolic disease, cardiac changes in, 809
   changes in pulmonary artery in, 808
   cor pulmonale in, 809
   influence of oral contraceptives in, 805
   pleural effusions in, 818, 1154
   pulmonary, 840
   pulmonary angiography in, *125,* 821
   pulmonary artery pressures in, 822
   radioisotope scanning in, 822
Thromboembolism, pulmonary, 804-828
   anatomic distribution of, 807
   clinical manifestations of, 824
   definition of, 804
   electrocardiographic changes in, 827
   incidence of, 805
   pathogenesis of, 805
   roentgenographic manifestations of, 807
   symptoms of, 824
   with hemorrhage, 809
     differential diagnosis of, 402-403(t)
   with infarction, 809
     differential diagnosis of, 402-403(t), 430-431(t)
   without hemorrhage, 808
   without infarction, *336,* 808
     differential diagnosis of, 514-515(t)
Thrombophlebitis, migratory, 762
Thrombotic arteries, line shadows due to, 315

Thymic aplasia, hereditary, 902
Thymoma, 1180, *1181, 1182*
   differential diagnosis of, 560-561(t)
   malignant, 557
Thymus, congenital absence of, 902
Thyroid masses, 1184
Tietze's syndrome, 145, 1239
Tissues, soft, of chest wall, 82
TLC (total lung capacity), 179, 180
Toluene diisocyanate poisoning, 954
Tomographic "cut," 116
Tomography, 41, 115-118
   in diagnosis of bronchial carcinoma, 756
   indications for, 116
   pulmonary cavity assessment with, *117*
   pulmonary mass assessment with, *118*
   techniques of, 115
Tonsillitis infections, acute, 675
Torulopsis glabrata, 673-674
Toxicity, oxygen, 1137-1139, 1140-1141
   differential diagnosis of, 490-491(t)
Toxocara canis, 711
Toxocara cati, 711
Toxoplasma cysts, 703
Toxoplasma gondii, 703-704
   in differential diagnosis, 418-419(t)
Toxoplasmosis, 703-704
Trachea, 11, *93, 95*
   fractures of, 1075-1076
   squamous cell carcinoma of, *749*
"Tracheal bronchus," 14
Tracheal diverticulosis, 1066-1067
Tracheal lavage, 165
Tracheobronchial anomalies, 13
Tracheobronchial tree, *38*
   cartilage distribution in, 8, *9*
Tracheobronchomalacia, 1066-1067
Tracheobronchomegaly, 1066-1067
Tracheocele, 1066
"Tram lines," 314
   in bronchial asthma, *976*
   in chronic bronchitis, 991
Transbronchial pulmonary biopsy, 159
Transglottic bronchographic technique, 120
Trauma, closed-chest, 1069-1085
   differential diagnosis of, 522-523(t), 540-541(t)
   definition of, 1068
   nonpenetrating, pulmonary changes in, 1069-1085
   open-chest, differential diagnosis of, 540-541(t)
   penetrating, 1085
     due to surgical procedures, 1085
   pleuropulmonary disease caused by, 1068-1085
Trematoda, 719
Tremolite, 933
Trichinella spiralis, 708
Trichinosis, 708
Truncus anterior, 37, *38*
Tuberculin test, 174, 639
Tuberculoma, 633
   differential diagnosis of, 440-441(t)
   with breakdown, 635
Tuberculosis, and bronchogenic carcinoma, 739
   bacteriologic investigation of, 639
   diagnosis of, laboratory procedures in, 639
   differentiation from histoplasmosis, 621
   endobronchial, *238*
   extrapulmonary, 638

Tuberculosis (*Continued*)
  exudative, *625, 626*
    local, *624*
    with cavitation, *628*
  "fibrocaseous," 622
  fibroproductive, *627*
    with tuberculous bronchiectasis, *210*
  genitourinary, 638
  miliary, *476*, 629, *632, 633*
  primary, 291
    calcification in, 620
    lymph node involvement in, 617
  "productive," 622
  pulmonary, *117*, 290
    exudative, *408*
    healed, line shadows due to, *305*
    primary, 616-621, *618, 619*
      airway involvement of, 617
      calcification in, 620
      clinical manifestations of, 621
      lymph-node involvement in, 617
      parenchymal involvement in, 617
      pathologic characteristics of, 616
      pleural involvement in, 620
      roentgenographic manifestations of, 617
      relationship between bronchogenic carcinoma and, 637
      relationship between sarcoidosis and, 638
      relationship to silicosis, 931
    Ranke complex in, 620
    reinfection, 621-640
      anatomic distribution of, 622
      bronchogenic spread of, 627
      cavitation in, 624
      clinical course of, 637
      clinical manifestations of, 634
      pathologic characteristics of, 621
      roentgenographic manifestations of, 622
      secondary. See *Tuberculosis, reinfection.*
    terminology of, 623
Tuberculous pneumonia, acute, *196*
Tuberous sclerosis, 1118-1119, *1120*
Tubular shadows, 312, *313*
  in bronchial asthma, *976*
  in chronic bronchitis, 991
Tularemia, 608-609. See also *Pasteurella tularensis.*
  differential diagnosis of, 384-385(t), 428-429(t), 532-533(t), 548-549(t)
  pleural effusion in, 1147
  skin test for, 174
Tumor, desmoid, 1246
  disappearing, 1156
  "mixed," 724, 725
  mucoepidermoid, 725
  neurogenic, differential diagnosis of, 400-401(t)
  "Pancoast," 753
  parathyroid, differential diagnosis of, 562-563(t)
  "phantom," 362, 1156
  "postinflammatory," 792
  sulcus, pulmonary, superior, 753, *754, 755*
  thyroid, differential diagnosis of, 560-561(t)
  "vanishing," 362
  Wilms', metastatic, 795
Tumorlets, 1252
TV (tidal volume), 30, 179

Underexposure, roentgenographic, hazard of, *106*
Uniform filter effect, *219, 221*

$\dot{V}A$ (alveolar ventilation), 50
Vagus nerve, left, *74*
  right, *73*
Valsalva maneuver, 97, 98, 110
  in differentiation of lesions, 286
"Vanishing tumor," 362
Vaporized mercury poisoning, 954
$\dot{V}A/\dot{Q}$. See *Ventilation perfusion ratio.*
Varicella-zoster respiratory infection, 689
Varicella-zoster virus, differential diagnosis of, 470-471(t)
Varicosity, of pulmonary veins, 576
  differential diagnosis of, 440-441(t)
Vascular deficiency, in chronic bronchitis, 991
Vascular disease, primary, 835
  decreased flow in, 840
  increased flow in, 835
  vasoconstrictive, 841
    differential diagnosis of, 504-505(t)
  vasospastic, 841
    differential diagnosis of, 504-505(t)
Vascular pressure, transmural, 43
Vascular shadows, redistribution of, in atelectasis, 220
Vascular system, pulmonary, 36-58. See also *Pulmonary vascular system.*
Vasculature, pulmonary. See *Pulmonary vascular system.*
VC (vital capacity), 179
Vein, azygos. See *Azygos vein.*
  hemiazygos, *74*
    dilatation of, 1197
  mediastinal, major, dilatation of, 1197
  pulmonary. See *Pulmonary vein(s).*
  thrombosed, 816
Vena cava, inferior, azygos continuation of, *1200*
  infradiaphragmatic interruption of, *1200*
  superior, *73, 93*
    angiography, 127
    dilatation of, 1197, *1199*
      differential diagnosis of, 564-565(t)
    obstruction of, differential diagnosis of, 540-541(t)
    in histoplasmosis, 645, *650*
Venoarterial shunts, pulmonary, 1264
Ventilation, acinar, 30
  mechanics of, 31
    measurement of, 181
  alveolar, 50
  and blood flow, matching of, measurement of, 184
  collateral. See *Air drift, collateral.*
  roentgenographic studies of, 132
  voluntary, maximal (MVV), 182
  wasted, 51
Ventilation/perfusion abnormality, measurement of, in chronic obstructive pulmonary disease, 969
Ventilation/perfusion ratio ($\dot{V}A/\dot{Q}$), 49
  decreased, 51
  increased, 51
  inequality of, measurement of, 185
    significance of, 52
Ventricular septal defect (VSD), 838
Vertebral fracture, obliteration of paraspinal line following, *1216*
"Vesicular breathing," 151
Vim-Silverman needle, 159, 161
Vincent's angina. See *Pharyngitis infections.*
Viral pulmonary infections, 170(t)
Virus. See also under types.
  causing pleural effusion, 1149
  lung infections due to, 674-675

Virus (*Continued*)
  of lymphocytic choriomeningitis, 695
  respiratory infections due to, 681-697
Virus infection, influenza, 682
  parainfluenza, 685
  presumed, 695
Volume. See also *Lung volume* and *Pressure-volume*
  entries.
  blood, measurement of, 183
  expiratory, forced (FEV), 182
  of conducting system, 30, *31*
  of pulmonary blood, 86, 86(t)
  pulmonary extravascular fluid, 855
  reserve, 179
  residual, 64, 179, 180
  tidal, 30, 179
  tissue, pulmonary, 86, 86(t)
VSD (ventricular septal defect), 838

Waldenström's macroglobulinemia, 897, *898*, 1122
  differential diagnosis of, 484-485(t)
Warthin-Finkelbey giant cell, 686
"Waterlily" sign, 273, 713
Wegener's granulomatosis, 275, 873-874, 876-877, 878

  differential diagnosis of, 384-385(t), 532-533(t)
Westermark's sign, 87, *336*, *810*, *825*
"Wet pleura," 351
"Whispering pectoriloquy," 151
Whooping cough, 608
Whooping cough pneumonia, differential diagnosis
  of, 398-399(t). See also *Hemophilus pertussis.*
Wilms' tumor, metastatic, *795*
Wilson-Mikity syndrome, 1136-1137, *1138*
  differential diagnosis of, 490-491(t)
Wiskott-Aldrich syndrome, 902, *903*
Wuchereria bancrofti, 709

Yellow nails, with bronchiectasis and lymphedema,
  syndrome of, 1051

Zenker's diverticulum, 1211
Zinc chloride poisoning, 955
Zinc oxide fever, 955
Zonography, 116
"Zuckerguss," 735, 1162

Department of Family Medicine